# Technology

## Online Learning Center

www.mhhe.com/williams_basis_12e

The author team strongly believes in the power of the Internet to enhance accounting education. The Online Learning Center for *Financial and Managerial Accounting,* 12/e, provides students and instructors with the most complete and up-to-date collection of Web resources. Instructors can take advantage of the Internet's immediacy by downloading text updates and supplements at their own convenience.

## Online Learning  Features

For the Student

1. Learning objectives, key terms, and chapter summaries from the text.
2. Self-quiz consisting of 10 multiple-choice questions per chapter not found in the text or study guide.
3. Web tutorial consisting of 30 unique true/false and multiple-choice questions with feedback to help the student.
4. Hotlink to NetTutor™.
5. A complete set of Alternate Problems so students have another set of problems for practice.
6. Internet Exercises for each chapter.
7. Exercises tied to the Tootsie Roll annual report for each chapter.
8. Links to accounting career sites and the corporate websites of companies used in the text.

For the Instructor

1. Downloadable instructor supplements.
2. The Online Learning Center content along with the test bank, which are compatible with other course management solutions such as WebCT and Blackboard.

## PowerWeb for Accounting

Harness the assets of the Web to keep your accounting course current with PowerWeb for Accounting! This online resource provides high-quality, peer-reviewed content, including up-to-date articles from leading periodicals and journals, current news, weekly updates with assessment, interactive exercises, Web research guides, study tips, and much more! Your PowerWeb for Accounting password is located on the PowerWeb card included with new copies of this text only. Access to PowerWeb for Accounting may be purchased online from the website at http://www.dushkin.com/powerweb.

# How's Your Math?

**Do you have the math skills you need to succeed in this course?**

Why risk not succeeding in this course because you struggle with the prerequisite math skills?

Get access to a web-based, personal math tutor:

- Available 24/7, unlimited use
- Driven by artificial intelligence
- Self-paced
- An entire month's subscription **for much less** than the cost of one hour with a human tutor

ALEKS is an inexpensive, private, infinitely patient math tutor that's accessible any time, anywhere you log on.

Log On for a
**FREE** 48-hour Trial

## www.highedstudent.aleks.com

ALEKS is a registered trademark of ALEKS Corporation.

# FINANCIAL AND MANAGERIAL ACCOUNTING
## The Basis for Business Decisions

*Twelfth Edition*

# FINANCIAL AND MANAGERIAL ACCOUNTING
## The Basis for Business Decisions

*Twelfth Edition*

**Jan R. Williams**
*University of Tennessee*

**Susan F. Haka**
*Michigan State University*

**Mark S. Bettner**
*Bucknell University*

**Robert F. Meigs**
*San Diego State University*

Boston   Burr Ridge, IL   Dubuque, IA   Madison, WI   New York   San Francisco   St. Louis
Bangkok   Bogotá   Caracas   Kuala Lumpur   Lisbon   London   Madrid   Mexico City
Milan   Montreal   New Delhi   Santiago   Seoul   Singapore   Sydney   Taipei   Toronto

## *McGraw-Hill Higher Education* 🖉

*A Division of The **McGraw-Hill** Companies*

FINANCIAL AND MANAGERIAL ACCOUNTING: THE BASIS FOR BUSINESS DECISIONS
Published by McGraw-Hill/Irwin, an imprint of The McGraw-Hill Companies, Inc. 1221 Avenue of
the Americas, New York, NY, 10020. Copyright © 2002, 1999, 1996, 1993, 1990, 1987, 1984,
1981, 1972, 1967, 1962, by The McGraw-Hill Companies, Inc. All rights reserved. No part of
this publication may be reproduced or distributed in any form or by any means, or stored in a
database or retrieval system, without the prior written consent of The McGraw-Hill Companies,
Inc., including, but not limited to, in any network or other electronic storage or transmission, or
broadcast for distance learning.

Some ancillaries, including electronic and print components, may not be available to customers
outside the United States.

This book is printed on acid-free paper.

domestic      4 5 6 7 8 9 0 VNH/VNH 0 9 8 7 6 5 4 3 2

international 3 4 5 6 7 8 9 0 VNH/VNH 0 9 8 7 6 5 4 3 2

ISBN 0-07-239688-1

Vice president, Editor-in-chief:  *Robin Zwettler*
Senior sponsoring editor:  *Stewart Mattson*
Developmental editor:  *Erin Cibula*
Marketing manager:  *Ryan Blankenship*
Project manager:  *Rebecca Nordbrock*
Lead production supervisor:  *Heather D. Burbridge*
Photo research coordinator:  *David A. Tietz*
Photo researcher:  *Mary Reeg*
Lead supplement producer:  *Becky Szura*
Producer, Media technology:  *Ed Przyzycki*
Cover/Interior design:  *Artemio Ortiz Jr.*
Cover Illustration:  *Kathy Petrauskas*
Compositor:  *York Graphic Services, Inc.*
Typeface:  *10.5/12 Times Roman*
Printer:  *Von Hoffmann Press, Inc.*

**Library of Congress Cataloging-in-Publication Data**

Financial and managerial accounting: the basis for business decisions / Robert F. Meigs
. . . [et al.].--12th ed.
      p. cm.
   Rev. ed. of: Financial accounting / Robert F. Meigs. 10th ed. 2001.
   Includes index.
   ISBN 0-07-239688-1 (alk. paper)
   I. Accounting. I. Meigs, Robert F. II. Financial accounting.
HF5635 .M492 2002
   657--dc21                                                    2001030219

www.mhhe.com

*For my family—wife Elaine, daughters Jennifer and Julie, sons-in-law Todd and Dave—all of whom have supported me while working on this book, as well as throughout my professional career. —Jan R. Williams*

*To my parents, Fred and Marjorie. —Mark S. Bettner*

*For Cliff, Abi, and my mother, Fran.—Susan F. Haka*

**Jan R. Williams**   Jan R. Williams is Ernst & Young Professor of Accounting and Dean of the College of Business Administration, University of Tennessee. He received a BS degree from George Peabody College, an MBA from Baylor University, and Ph.D. from the University of Arkansas. He was formerly on the faculties of the University of Georgia and Texas Tech University. He is a CPA in Tennessee and Arkansas. Dr. Williams's primary teaching and research interest is corporate financial reporting. He is currently the author or coauthor of four books and more than 70 articles and other publications about financial reporting and accounting education.

Dr. Williams has been extensively involved in professional accounting activities with the American Accounting Association (AAA), the American Institute of CPAs (AICPA), the Tennessee Society of CPAs, and other organizations. In 1999–2000, he served as president of the AAA and in that capacity traveled throughout the world speaking on issues related to accounting education and practice. He has recently served on two task forces of the AICPA to redesign the CPA examination to meet the changing needs of the profession for the 21st century.

**Susan F. Haka**   Currently the Ernst & Young Professor of Accounting and Chair of the Department of Accounting and Information Systems at Michigan State University, Sue has received the prestigious All-University Teacher-Scholar Award and has twice received the Department's Outstanding Teaching Award. Sue also spoke twice at the American Accounting Association's New Faculty Consortium on Teaching. Sue is the editor of *Behavioral Research in Accounting,* an associate editor of the *Journal of Management Accounting Research,* and a member of the editorial boards of *The Accounting Review, Accounting Horizons,* and *Management Accounting Research.* Also active in the American Accounting Association, Sue has served as president of the Management Accounting Section and Director of the Doctoral Consortium.

**Mark S. Bettner**   Associate professor at Bucknell University, Mark Bettner has received numerous teaching and research awards. In addition to his work on the Meigs and Williams titles, he has written many ancillary materials, published in scholarly journals, and presented at numerous academic and practitioner conferences. Mark is also on the editorial advisory boards of several academic journals, including the *International Journal of Accounting and Business Society.*

# Preface

## NOTE TO STUDENTS

The primary focus of this book is discovering the meaning of accounting information—and how this information is used by decision makers. Throughout this text, we provide you with financial and managerial accounting concepts to give you an understanding of how to use accounting information to make informed decisions. We introduce you only briefly to actual accounting practices and techniques.

Today, everyone needs a basic understanding of accounting information, not just those students planning careers in business. No matter which career you choose, you will work with accounting information and use it in managing your personal financial activities. Using accounting information is simply a part of everyday life.

## OUR APPROACH

Our goals in this text are to develop your abilities to understand accounting information and to use this information in making economic decisions. To understand accounting information, you also must understand the economic activities that the information describes. In this book, we focus primarily on business activities. However, many of the accounting concepts we discuss also apply to the economic activities of individuals as well as government and nonprofit organizations.

The purpose of accounting is to provide information useful to economic decision makers. Throughout the book, we cast you in many decision-making roles. We have implemented many new elements to provide a greater understanding of how accounting information is used in decision making. Refer to our Walkthrough pages in this preface for a detailed look at the features designed to enhance your decision-making skills.

## Opening Vignette

The chapter openers feature vignettes that relate real-world companies, such as **Amazon.com** and **Nike**, to the accounting concepts covered in the chapter.

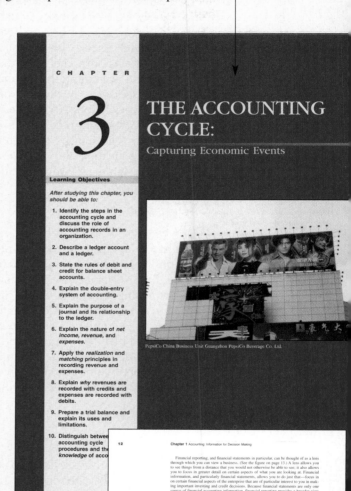

## Cash Effects

Cash Effects sections show how a transaction or method impacts the cash flow of an organization.

NEW!

## A Second Look

A Second Look box at the end of each chapter returns to the real-world company highlighted in the chapter opener. This second look allows students to relate the accounting topics they have just learned to those practiced by actual businesses.

**PepsiCo, Inc.**

Capturing the economic events of a lemonade stand is a fairly simple process. In fact, for most lemonade stands, an empty cigar box easily serves as a complete information system.

Capturing the economic events of **PepsiCo, Inc.**, however, is an entirely different matter. This giant corporation generates annual revenue in excess of $20 billion from sales of its soft drink products, its Tropicana juices, and its Frito-Lay snack foods. Employing nearly 120,000 people, and operating hundreds of manufacturing facilities and thousands of warehouses and distribution centers, **PepsiCo, Inc.**, must somehow capture complex business transactions occurring in more than 160 countries worldwide.

From lemonade stands to multinational corporations, being able to efficiently capture the effects of economic events, such as sales orders and raw material purchases, is absolutely essential for survival. Companies like **PepsiCo, Inc.**, rely upon sophisticated computer systems to capture economic activities. Some small enterprises, however, may use paper ledgers and journals to record business transactions.

• • •

Although Overnight Auto Service engaged in several business transactions in the previous chapter, we did not illustrate how these events were captured by Overnight for use by management and other interested parties. This chapter demonstrates how accounting systems record economic events related to a variety of business transactions.

## Your Turn

Your Turn boxes put students in the role of decision makers, requiring them to apply chapter concepts to situations faced by investors, creditors, and managers. Ethics icons indicate boxes that require ethical decisions.

## Case in Point

Case in Point boxes use actual business events to illustrate the relationship between accounting concepts and the real world. International icons indicate boxes that contain international information.

this framework, the FASB believes that its official *Statements* resolve accounting problems in a logical and consistent manner.

The FASB is part of the private sector of the economy—*it is not a governmental agency*. The development of accounting principles in the United States traditionally has been carried out in the private sector, although the government, acting through the SEC, exercises considerable influence.

**Securities and Exchange Commission** The Securities and Exchange Commission is a governmental agency with the *legal power* to establish accounting principles and financial reporting requirements for publicly owned corporations. In the past, the SEC has generally adopted the recommendations of the FASB, rather than develop its

its annual financial statements; in particular, management tries to make the company appear as strong as is reasonably possible. As a result, many creditors regard more frequent financial statements (for example, quarterly or even monthly) as providing important additional information beyond that in the annual financial statements. The more frequently financial statements are presented, the less able is management to window dress and make a company look financially stronger than it actually is.

Because external stakeholders, particularly creditors, carefully evaluate financial reports, the reports have a significant impact on the strategic choices of management. Suppose Overnight Auto Service was planning to raise more capital in the coming year by selling additional stock. McBryan might delay or accelerate some planned strategic decisions to strengthen the financial position and, as a result, the external financial reports of Overnight Auto Service. For example, the planned purchase of a hydraulic lift might be delayed and the choice to form a partnership with nearby Ace Towing might be accelerated. Delaying ambitious capital expenditures or expediting strategic alliances to ensure the ability to raise additional needed capital are examples of the impact that financial reporting can have on business strategy.

**America Online**

At the beginning of this chapter, we asked how you would know whether **America Online** was successful. This chapter introduced the basic financial statements allowing you to begin to answer this question.

**America Online's** income statements for 1997, 1998, and 1999, indicate that its net income (losses) were ($485 million), ($74 million), and $762 million, respectively. This means that in 1997 and 1998, the company's revenues were less than its expenses and, therefore, a net loss was reported. The 1998 loss, however, was much smaller than the 1997 loss. In 1999, revenues exceeded expenses by enough that the company reported a $762 million net income. Compared to 1997 and 1998, we would probably conclude that **America Online** was successful in 1999. Even 1998 might be considered a success when compared with 1997 because the loss was so much smaller.

Another measure of success that is sometimes cited is whether the company's operations are generating an excess of cash to be used for other purposes. **America Online's** statement of cash flows for 1997, 1998, and 1999 indicate that it had positive cash flows from operating activities (cash coming in exceeding cash being paid out) of $131 million, $437 million, and $1,099 million, respectively. This could be judged as successful in two ways. First, all three numbers are positive, indicating that in all three years the company's operations are generating cash that is available to be used for other purposes. Second, the amount of the positive cash flow is increasing each year, beginning with $131 million in 1997 and building to $1,099 million (over a billion dollars) in 1999.

At this early stage in your study of accounting, you can begin to understand how investors and creditors can use important information in the company's financial statements to learn things about a company that help them make informed decisions.

NEW!

## Management Strategy

Management Strategy boxes illustrate how accounting information is used to evaluate business strategies and to make strategic business decisions.

**FINANCIAL ANALYSIS**

Relationships among the three primary financial statements provide the opportunity to learn a great deal about a company by bringing pieces of information together in a meaningful way. In fact, some people believe that relationships in the financial statements are more important than the actual dollar figures in those statements.

For example, take another look at the balance sheet on page 51. Notice that the company has $16,600 of cash and $1,200 of accounts receivable, a total of $17,800 in what are sometimes referred to as *current* assets, denoting that they either are cash or will soon become cash. Now look at the liabilities in the balance sheet and notice that the company has notes payable of $30,000 and accounts payable of $7,000 for a total of $37,000 of liabilities. If both types of liabilities are current liabilities, meaning that they will be due in the near future and can be expected to require the use of current assets, Overnight Auto Service may have difficulty paying them because they do not have enough liquid assets to cover their liabilities. The relationship of current assets to current liabilities is called the *current ratio*. For Overnight Auto Service it is a low .48 ($17,800 divided by $37,000). This means that Overnight Auto Service has only 48 cents for every $1 of liabilities that will come due in the near future.

While the above refers exclusively to information found in the balance sheet, key information from one financial statement often is combined with information from another financial statement. For example, we may be interested in knowing the amount of cash provided by operations (cash flow statement) relative to the amount of a company's currently maturing liabilities (balance sheet). Or we might want to compare a company's net income (income statement) with the investment in assets (balance sheet) that were used to generate that income.

Many of the chapters in this text introduce you to various types of financial analysis. We build on those introductory discussions in Chapter 14, Financial Statement Analy-

NEW! ## Financial Analysis

Financial Analysis sections introduce ratios and other analytical techniques that relate to the material covered in each chapter. Chapter 14 includes comprehensive coverage of the subject of financial statement analysis. These combine to give the book a strong orientation of using accounting information for decision making.

# END-OF-CHAPTER FEATURES

- **Defined Key Terms and Self-Test Questions** review and reinforce chapter material.

- **Five Comprehensive Problems,** ranging from two to five pages in length, review and synthesize text material throughout the book.

- **Demonstration Problems** and their solutions allow students to test their knowledge of key points in the chapters.

- **Internet Assignments** at the end of chapters require students to go to a specific Internet site to answer questions.

- *Business Week* **Assignments** at the end of each chapter are assignments based on recent articles. They require students to answer questions by relating accounting concepts to current events.

- **Icons** identify exercises involving General Ledger Applications Software (GLAS), Spreadsheet Applications Template Software (SPATS), ethical issues, group activities, and international issues.

- **The Annual Report** from **Tootsie Roll Industries, Inc.,** for 1999 is used throughout the text in exercise and problem material to reveal actual business applications of text material.

# TECHNOLOGY

- **Student CD-ROM**

The Student CD-ROM is packaged with every new copy of the textbook. It includes General Ledger Applications Software (GLAS), Spreadsheet Applications Template Software (SPATS), and Tutorial Software.

 **General Ledger Applications Software (GLAS)**  The GLAS accounting program saves time and minimizes errors because it operates as an integrated system. Amounts entered in the general journal or special journals can be posted to the general ledger with a single keystroke. GLAS icons show students where this tool can be used to solve end-of-chapter problems.

 **Spreadsheet Applications Template Software (SPATS)** The SPATS software allows students to develop important spreadsheet skills by using templates to solve selected assignments identified by an icon in the end-of-chapter material.

- **Online Learning Center**

Our new website at **www.mhhe.com/business/accounting/williams_basis_12e** supports the twelfth edition with the following features:

*Tutorial Software* Provides a variety of ways to test students' knowledge of the material in the text. Students can randomly access different review methods. Explanations of right and wrong answers are provided and scores are tallied.

*Links to Professional Resources* These links send students to various sites to gather real-world data and market news.

*Quizzes* Multiple-choice online quizzes for students test their knowledge.

*Alternate Problems* Alternative versions of the end-of-chapter problems give students more practice at applying their knowledge. Solutions are provided for instructors.

***Downloadable Instructor Supplements*** Instructors can access the following supplements electronically: PowerPoint, Solutions Manual, Instructor's Manual, and SPATS solutions.

***PageOut*** PageOut is an exclusive McGraw-Hill product that allows an instructor to create a professional course website in less than an hour.

- **NetTutor™**

NEW!

NetTutor™ is an online, live tutoring service that guides students through their accounting problems step-by-step. Students also can watch as other students' questions are answered—giving them the opportunity to constantly improve their accounting skills. Students can gain access to NetTutor™ by purchasing a new textbook with the NetTutor password card. Contact your McGraw-Hill/Irwin sales representative for more information.

- **PowerWeb**

NEW!

PowerWeb is a database of online financial and managerial articles that are updated weekly. Exercises and teaching suggestions for instructors also are provided. Students can gain access to PowerWeb by purchasing a new textbook with the PowerWeb password card.

- **Interactive Financial Accounting Lab** by Ralph E. Smith and Rick Birney, both of Arizona State University (ISBN 0-07-236137-9)

**Interactive Managerial Accounting Lab** by Diane Pattison, University of San Diego; Patrick McKenzie and Rick Birney, both of Arizona State University (ISBN 0-07-236138-7)

Available in network or stand-alone versions, this innovative software allows students to solve accounting problems and receive feedback in a motivating, interactive, multimedia environment. The Administration Module and Gradebook features allow instructors to manipulate the "calendar" of assignments students are required to complete and also to track students' performance. The **Financial Accounting Lab** provides a comprehensive review of the fundamentals of the accounting cycle, while the **Managerial Accounting Lab** offers more than 15 hours of computerized exercise sets to help students learn management accounting.

- **Computerized Practice Sets**

Prepared by Leland Mansuetti and Keith Weidkamp of Sierra College, these business simulations for Windows provide a dynamic educational alternative to manual sets.

*Granite Bay Jet Ski, Level 1* (ISBN 0-07-234088-6), Instructor's Manual (ISBN 0-07-234104-1)

*Granite Bay Jet Ski, Level 2* (ISBN 0-07-234105-X), Instructor's Manual (ISBN 0-07-234106-8)

*Wheels Exquisite, Inc. Level 1* (ISBN 0-07-561243-7), Instructor's Manual (ISBN 0-07-561242-9)

- **Understanding Corporate Annual Reports: A Financial Analysis Project,** Fourth Edition, by William R. Pasewark (ISBN 0-07-238714-9) This project contains extensive instructions for obtaining and analyzing an annual report from a publicly traded corporation.

# NOTE TO INSTRUCTORS

The twelfth edition of *Financial and Managerial Accounting: The Basis for Business Decisions* features a more contemporary design, cutting-edge supplements, and fresh insights based on reviewer feedback.

We scrutinized and reworked the contents of the text for the twelfth edition. A few of our content changes include the following: the financial accounting chapters now take a corporate approach, the accounting cycle has been split into three chapters to enable faculty to cover this critical material in more manageable pieces, forms of business organization material have been integrated throughout the text, a new Chapter 24 covers performance measurement, and Tootsie Roll Industries replaces Toys "R" Us as the annual report referenced throughout the text's EOC material.

# SUMMARY OF CONTENTS AND CHANGES

## Chapter 1 Accounting: Information for Decision Making

- Accounting is introduced as a system of information for decision making.
- Both financial and managerial accounting are introduced in parallel fashion by discussing (1) users of the information, (2) their objectives with regard to the information, (3) the integrity of the information, and (4) specific characteristics of the information.

## Chapter 2 Basic Financial Statements

- Chapter 2 introduces the accounting equation and describes how a company's financial statement changes as result of a series of simple business transactions.
- The chapter ends with an illustration of a simple balance sheet, income statement, and statement of cash flows and a discussion of how these statements articulate.

*NEW!*

## Chapter 3 The Accounting Cycle: Capturing Economic Events

- This edition has added a third accounting cycle chapter to enable faculty to cover this critical material in more managable pieces.
- Chapter 3 builds on the comprehensive illustration introduced in Chapter 2.
- This chapter introduces the complete accounting cycle, from analyzing economic events to preparing financial statements (including a simple statement of cash flows).

*NEW!*

## Chapter 4 The Accounting Cycle: Accruals and Deferrals

- Chapter 4 builds on the material covered in Chapter 3 and provides thorough coverage of the adjusting entries.

*NEW!*

## Chapter 5 The Accounting Cycle: Reporting Financial Results

- Chapter 5 builds on the material covered in Chapters 3 and 4. It focuses on the relationship of the income statement, statement of retained earnings, and the balance sheet. It also describes the closing process.
- A supplemental topic, "The Worksheet," is included at the end of the chapter.

## Comprehensive Problem 1—Tony's Rentals
## Chapter 6 Accounting for Merchandising Activities

- Chapter 6 introduces students to merchandising businesses, inventories, and the cost of goods sold.
- Both perpetual and periodic inventory systems are discussed.
- Various performance measures of merchandising businesses are introduced and illustrated.

## Chapter 7 Financial Assets

- Chapter 7 addresses accounting and reporting issues related to cash and cash equivalents, short-term investments, and accounts receivable.
- Mark-to-market reporting of short-term investments is explained, and the need for estimating uncollectible accounts receivable is discussed and illustrated.

## Chapter 8 Inventories and the Cost of Goods Sold

- Chapter 8 identifies the various cost flow assumptions used by businesses in accounting for inventories.
- Both perpetual and period inventory systems are illustrated.
- FIFO versus LIFO reporting issues are illustrated (including a discussion of a LIFO reserve).

## Comprehensive Problem 2—Guitar Universe, Inc.
## Chapter 9 Plant Assets and Depreciation

- Chapter 9 focuses on accounting issues related to tangible and intangible long-term fixed assets (including the disposal of plant assets and valuation issues pertaining to certain intangible assets).
- The widespread use of straight-line depreciation is emphasized.

## Chapter 10 Liabilities

- Chapter 10 covers both current and noncurrent liabilities.
- Noncurrent liability coverage includes issues related to bonds, pensions, and other postretirement benefits.
- Chapter 10 can be used in conjunction with Appendix B, which covers the time value of money, should an instructor choose to do so.

## Chapter 11 Stockholders' Equity: Paid-in Capital

- Chapter 11 discusses various issues related to contributed capital.
- Topics include legal capital, preferred stock, treasury stock, stock splits, book value, and market value.

## Chapter 12 Income and Changes in Retained Earnings

- Chapter 12 presents net income and its components.
- Some of the specific topics covered are discontinued operations, extraordinary items, accounting changes, earnings per share, cash and stock dividends, and the statement of changes in stockholders' equity.

### Chapter 13 Statement of Cash Flows

- The statement of cash flows discussion emphasizes the broad classifications of cash flows: operating, investing, and financing.
- This chapter describes the form and content of the statement of cash flows by both the direct and the indirect method, with particular emphasis on reconciling net income to net cash provided by (or used in) operating activities.

### Chapter 14 Financial Statement Analysis

- General approaches for analyzing financial statements are introduced, as are specific ratios and other procedures for analyzing various aspects of a company's activities.
- These activities include liquidity and credit risk, profitability, quality of earnings, and capital structure.

### Comprehensive Problem 3—Tootsie Roll Industries, Inc.

### Chapter 15 Global Business and Accounting

- Chapter 15 provides students with an understanding of the issues that impact accounting in the global business environment.
- International differences in financial and management accounting procedures are discussed and related to variations in cultures, laws, economics, and technological infrastructures across countries.

### Chapter 16 Management Accounting: A Business Partner

- The three basic principles of management accounting system design are introduced and explained. A management accounting system assigns decision-making authority, provides information to support decision making, and furnishes information for performance evaluation and reward assignment.
- Demonstrates the basic manufacturing process and matching cost flows. Distinguishes period and product costs, direct and indirect costs, raw materials, work in process, and finished goods inventories.

### Chapter 17 Accounting Systems for Measuring Costs

- Chapter 17 covers manufacturing methods and related costs that result in different accounting system designs. Job order, process, and activity-based costing are introduced and demonstrated. Exhibits show how each costing method matches the cost flow with the manufacturing method.
- The impact of accounting system choices on related information for decision making is discussed as a lead-in to the next chapter. Motivations for cost allocation and choices of cost objects are introduced.

### Chapter 18 Costing and the Value Chain

- Chapter 18 focuses on how decision making across the value chain drives the type of costs created by management. The chapter also shows the need for cost information related to the value chain.
- Over the life cycle of the value chain cost procedures useful to management are introduced. These procedures include target costing, life-cycle costing, just-in-time techniques, and tracking cost of quality.

## Chapter 19 Cost-Volume-Profit Analysis

- Chapter 19 defines fixed, variable, and semivariable costs and also explains the use of contribution margin and breakeven analysis in short-run decision settings.
- An illustration depicts how the assumptions required as inputs to C-V-P can lead managers to different conclusions about a marketing decision.

## Chapter 20 Incremental Analysis

- Chapter 20 covers the definitions and importance of opportunity costs, sunk costs, incremental costs, and revenues for short-run business decisions.
- This chapter also demonstrates incremental analysis in a variety of business decision settings, including special order, where to produce, resource input mix, and pricing decisions.

## Comprehensive Problem 4—Gilster Company

## Chapter 21 Responsibility Accounting and Transfer Pricing

- Chapter 21 explains how cost, profit, and investment center structures assign decision-making authority over a firm's assets.
- The chapter also shows how top executives use accounting information to hold managers of cost, profit and investment centers responsible for their decisions.
- The impact of different transfer pricing methods on the accounting outcomes of cost, profit, and investment centers is illustrated.

## Chapter 22 Operational Budgeting

- Chapter 22 clarifies how the budgeting process (1) assigns decision-making authority, (2) requires the organization to plan and share information, and (3) is useful for evaluating and rewarding performance.
- The master budget process is demonstrated, and static and flexible budgets are contrasted.

## Chapter 23 Standard Cost Systems

- Chapter 23 explains the use of standard costing as a control mechanism; it also specifies how standards are determined as well as their motivational impact.
- Computation of overhead, materials, and labor variances is discussed, along with the use of variances for decision making.

## Chapter 24 Rewarding Business Performance

- This new chapter clarifies the role of incentive systems by presenting the methods and means that businesses use to motivate, evaluate, and reward good business decision making.
- This chapter also describes the DuPont method for analyzing the components of return on investment, residual income, and economic value added concepts. The balanced scorecard is introduced as a means for motivating, evaluating, and rewarding comprehensive business performance.

### Comprehensive Problem 5—Utease Corporation

### Chapter 25 Capital Budgeting

- Chapter 25 considers the role of capital budgeting in a firm's ability to achieve long-range goals and objectives; it also links capital and operational budgets.
- Capital budgeting procedures that account for the time value of money are illustrated, including payback, internal rate of return, and net present value.
- The following special features in the end-of-chapter material help students clarify and apply the topics introduced in the chapter.

## STUDENT-ORIENTED TEXT

Today, most careers do not center around the *preparation* of accounting information; however, every student will be a lifelong *user* of accounting information. For example, students will use accounting information to make business decisions throughout their careers.

We have worked to make this text more relevant to students' needs as well as more interesting, thereby motivating students to make the most of this learning opportunity. Evidence of this can be found in every problem and almost every exercise; now each contains an analytical element that asks students to interpret the information they are working with or to explain how they would use it in making some form of business decision.

Our approach is to involve students more directly in the learning process; that's why we challenge them to express their views. Features aimed at achieving this goal include the interactive Your Turn cases in every chapter, the analytical elements in our assignment material, and our Internet-related features.

Our Internet features encourage students to explore interesting, accounting-related websites on their own. We make this very simple by providing not only the addresses of these sites but also links to these sites through the book's website. No instructor assistance should be required.

## CONTEMPORARY TEXT

Any course is more relevant and more interesting if it is up to date. We have made this text contemporary in all respects, from coverage of real-world companies in the chapter openers to topical coverage to assignment material.

The following special features in the end-of-chapter material help students clarify and apply the topics introduced in the chapter:

## SUPPLEMENTS

### For Students

- **Study Guide** (Vol. 1 ISBN 0-07-246590-5, Vol. 2 ISBN 0-07-246584-0) For each chapter, students can measure their progress through a wealth of self-test material (with solutions) and a summary of the chapter's key points.
- **Working Papers** (Vol. 1 ISBN 0-07-246582-4, Vol. 2 ISBN 0-07-246583-2) This softcover booklet is filled with columnar paper for each Problem and Comprehensive Problem in the textbook. Throughout the working papers students encounter Checkpoints to ensure they are on the right track.

## For Instructors

- **Instructor's Manual** (Vol. 1 ISBN 0-07-246594-8, Vol. 2 ISBN 0-07-246593-X) For each chapter and appendix, you will find:

  A brief topical outline that indicates the topics to discuss in class.

  An assignment guide that provides at a glance the topical content of each Exercise, Problem, and Case.

  Comments and observations concerning the chapter content, methods of presentation, and usefulness of specific assignment material.

  Many real-world examples not found in the text, including additional *Business Week* and Internet assignments, sample assignment schedules, and suggestions for using each element of the supplemental package.

- **Solutions Manual** (Vol. 1 ISBN 0-07-246579-4, Vol. 2 ISBN 0-07-246598-0) This comprehensive manual provides solutions to all Discussion Questions, Exercises, Problems, Cases, and Comprehensive Problems.

- **Solutions Transparencies** (Vol. 1 ISBN 0-07-246580-8, Vol. 2 ISBN 0-07-246591-3) A complete set of acetates contains the solutions to all of the Exercises and Problems in the Solutions Manual.

- **Test Bank** (Vol. 1 ISBN 0-07-246588-3, Vol. 2 ISBN 0-07-246589-1) With an abundance of objective questions and short exercises, this supplement is a valuable resource for instructors who prepare their own quizzes and examinations.

- **Computerized Test Bank** (ISBN 0-07-246595-6) This computerized version of the manual test bank is available in Windows® format.

- **Ready Shows** (Vol. 1 ISBN 0-07-246852-1, Vol. 2 ISBN 0-07-246853-X) This comprehensive package is filled with multimedia aids that use PowerPoint software to illustrate chapter concepts.

- **Instructor Spreadsheet Application Template Software (SPATS)** (ISBN 0-07-246854-8) Solutions to the students' SPATS problems.

- **Case Videos (with Manual)** (ISBN 0-07-043440-9) Eight vignettes ranging from 5 to 15 minutes long cover various accounting topics as applied in real-company scenarios. A brief summary, key concepts and topics, suggested homework assignments, student handouts, small group activities, discussion questions, and teaching notes are provided for each vignette. Topical coverage includes external audits, inventory cost flows, ethics and reporting issues, cash versus accrual income, break-even analysis, capital budgeting, corporate bonds, and making investment decisions.

- **Financial Accounting Video Library** (ISBN 0-07-237616-3) and **Managerial/Cost Accounting Video Library** (ISBN 0-07-237617-1) This diverse array of videos prepared by Dallas County Community College District Telecourse can be used to stimulate classroom discussion, illustrate key concepts, or review critical material.

## WE HAVE LISTENED TO YOU

Reviewer comments for this edition and previous editions have guided us in this revision. We extend our sincere thanks for their efforts to the following people:

Elenito Ayuyao, *Los Angeles City College*
Walter Baggett, *Manhattan College*
Sharla Bailey, *Southwest Baptist University*

Jill Bale, *Doane College*

Scott Barhight, *Northampton County Area Community College*

William Barze, *St. Petersburg Junior College*

John Bayles, *Oakton Community College*

Janet Becker, *University of Pittsburgh*

Jerard Berardino, *Community College of Allegheny*

Teri Bernstein, *Santa Monica College*

Cynthia Bolt-Lee, *The Citadel*

Nancy Boyd, *Middle Tennessee State University*

Sallie Branscom, *Virginia Western Community College*

Russell Bresslauer, *Chabot College*

R. E. Bryson, *University of Alabama*

Bryan Burks, *Harding University*

Priscilla Burnaby, *Bentley College*

Loring Carlson, *Western New England College*

David Chu, *College of the Holy Cross*

Stanley Chu, *Borough Manhattan Community College*

William Cravey, *Jersey City State College*

Marcia Croteau, *University of Maryland—Baltimore County*

Brian Curtis, *Raritan Valley Community College*

Steve Czarsty, *Mary Washington College*

Larry Davis, *Southwest Virginia County College*

Victoria Doby, *Villa Julie College*

Carlton Donchess, *Bridgewater State College*

Steve Driver, *Horry-Georgetown Tech*

Pamela Druger, *Augustana College*

Anita Ellzey, *Hartford Community College*

Emmanuel Emenyonu, *Sacred Heart University*

David Erlach, *CUNY—Queens College*

Paul Everson, *Northern State University*

Brother Gerald Fitzgerald, *LaSalle University*

Ralph Fritsch, *Midwestern State University*

Mike Fujita, *Leeward Community College*

Mary Lou Gamma, *East Tennessee State University*

Don Van Gieson, *Kapiolani Community College*

Peter Gilbert, *Thomas College*

Penny Hanes, *Mercyhurst College*

Richard Hanna, *Ferris State University*

Stephen Hano, *Rockland Community College*

Sara Harris, *Arapahoe Community College*

Lyle Hicks, *Danville Area Community College*

Jeannelou Hodgens, *Florence-Darlington Technical College*

Patricia H. Holmes, *Des Moines Area Community College*

Michael Holt, *Eastern Nazarene College*

Evelyn Honaker, *Walters State Community College*

Dave Jensen, *Bucknell University*

Leo Jubb, *Essex Community College*

David Junnola, *Eastern Michigan University*
Khondkar Karim, *Monmouth University*
James Kennedy, *Texas A&M University*
Jane Kingston, *Piedmont Virginia Community College*
Ed Knudson, *Linn Benton Community College*
Raymond Krasniewski, *Ohio State University*
David Lardie, *Tunxis Community College*
Bill Lasher, *Jamestown Community College*
Suk Jun Lee, *Chapman University*
Annette M. Leps, *Goucher College*
Eric Lewis, *Union College*
Philip Little, *Western Carolina University*
J. Thomas Love, *Walters State Community College*
Dewey Martin, *Husson College*
Josie Miller, *Mercer Community College*
Merrill Moore, *Delaware Tech & Community College*
Deborah Most, *Dutchess Community College*
Haim Mozes, *Fordham University*
Frank Olive, *Nicholas College*
Bruce Oliver, *Rochester Institute of Technology*
Ginger Parker, *Creighton University*
Michael Prockton, *Finger Lakes Community College*
Gary Reynolds, *Ozark Technical College*
Renee Rigoni, *Monroe Community College*
Earl Roberts, *Delaware Tech & Community College*
Julie Rosenblatt, *Delaware Tech & Community College*
Bob Rothenberg, *SUNY—Oneonta*
Victoria Rymer, *University of Maryland*
Francis A. Sakiey, *Mercer County Community College*
Linda Schain, *Hofstra University*
Mike Schoderbek, *Rutgers University—New Brunswick*
Monica Seiler, *Queensborough Community College*
Stan Stanley, *Skagit Valley College*
Jim Stanton, *Mira Costa College*
Robert Stilson, *CUNY*
Carolyn Strickler, *Ohlone College*
Barbara Sturdevant, *SUNY*
Gene Sullivan, *Liberty University and Central Virginia Community College*
Mary Ann Swindlehurst, *Carroll Community College*
Larry Tartaglino, *Cabrillo College*
Martin Taylor, *University of Texas at Arlington*
Anne Tippett, *Tarrant County College South*
Bruce Toews, *Walla Walla College*
Cynthia Tomes, *Des Moines Area Community College*
Harold Wilson, *Middle Tennessee State University*
Steve Wilts, *Bucknell University*
Teri Yohn, *Georgetown University*

We also acknowledge the following individuals, each of whom has authored supplements to accompany the text: Charles W. Caldwell, Susan C. Galbreath, and Richard S. Rand, all of Tennessee Technological University, and Jack Terry of Comsource Associates.

Our special thanks goes to Barbara Schnathorst, The Write Solution, Inc., for assisting us with detailed reviews of our chapter and assignment material.

The assistance of Robert Zwicker of Pace University and Alice Sineath of Forsyth Technical Community College was invaluable in preparation of the manuscripts for many supplementary materials.

We appreciate the expert attention given to this project by the staff of McGraw-Hill/Irwin, especially Jeff Shelstad, Stewart Mattson, Jennifer Jackson, Erin Cibula, Jacquelyn Scruggs, Ryan Blankenship, Heather Burbridge, Rebecca Nordbrock, David Tietz, Artemio Ortiz, Becky Szura, and Ed Przyzycki.

Sincerely,

Jan R. Williams

Susan F. Haka

Mark S. Bettner

Robert F. Meigs

# Contents in Brief

# Contents

# ACCOUNTING:

Information for
Decision Making

*After studying this chapter, you should be able to:*

1. **Discuss accounting as the language of business and the role of accounting information in making economic decisions.**

2. **Discuss the significance of accounting systems in generating reliable accounting information.**

3. **Explain the importance of financial accounting information for external parties—primarily investors and creditors—in terms of the objectives and the characteristics of that information.**

4. **Explain the importance of management accounting information for internal parties—primarily management—in terms of the objectives and the characteristics of that information.**

5. **Discuss elements of the system of external and internal financial reporting that create integrity in the reported information.**

6. **Identify and discuss several professional organizations that play important roles in preparing and communicating accounting information.**

7. **Discuss the importance of personal competence, professional judgment, and ethical behavior on the part of accounting professionals.**

8. **Describe various career opportunities in accounting.***

*Supplemental Topic,* "Careers in Accounting."

© The Procter & Gamble Co., used by permission.

**Procter & Gamble (P&G)** is a large and successful company. It employs 110,000 worldwide and markets approximately 300 brands, including Folgers coffee, Tide and Cheer laundry products, Bounty towels, and Cover Girl beauty care products.

If you were interested in investing money in a company, how would you determine whether Procter & Gamble was a good company in which to invest? How could you compare P&G with other companies that may be of interest to you? If you were a manager within P&G, how would you know how well you are doing? When important decisions must be made, what information would you need to be better informed? Accounting information is intended primarily for decision making. As an investor, accounting information can help you determine where to invest your money and when to move your investment from one company to another. As a manager of a company, accounting information can help you do a better job of efficiently managing your company.

● ● ●

This chapter introduces you to two broad types of accounting information. Financial accounting information is intended primarily for investors and creditors outside the company who need information to support important decisions they make concerning the commitment of their funds. Managerial accounting information is intended primarily for internal managers so they can efficiently operate the company. Both financial and managerial information are important for the efficient operation of companies and the capital markets in which companies acquire funding.

# ACCOUNTING INFORMATION: A MEANS TO AN END

The primary purpose of accounting is to provide information that is useful for decision-making purposes. From the very start, we emphasize that accounting is *not an end*, but rather it is *a means to an end*. The final product of accounting information is the decision that is enhanced by the use of accounting information, whether that decision is made by owners, management, creditors, governmental regulatory bodies, labor unions, or the many other groups that have an interest in the financial performance of an enterprise.

Because accounting is widely used to describe all types of business activity, it is sometimes referred to as the *language of business*. Costs, prices, sales volume, profits, and return on investment are all accounting measurements. Investors, creditors, managers, and others who have a financial interest in an enterprise need a clear understanding of accounting terms and concepts if they are to understand and communicate about the enterprise. While our primary orientation in this text is the use of accounting information in business, from time to time we emphasize that accounting information is also used by governmental agencies, nonprofit organizations, and individuals in much the same manner as it is by business organizations.

**LO 1**

Discuss accounting as the language of business and the role of accounting information in making economic decisions.

## Accounting from a User's Perspective

Many people think of accounting as simply a highly technical field practiced only by professional accountants. In reality, nearly everyone uses accounting information daily. Accounting information is simply the means by which we measure and communicate economic events. Whether you manage a business, make investments, or monitor how you receive and use your money, you are working with accounting concepts and accounting information.

Our primary goal in this book is to develop your ability to understand and use accounting information in making economic decisions. To do this, you need to understand the following:

- The nature of economic activities that accounting information describes.
- The assumptions and measurement techniques involved in developing accounting information.
- The information that is most relevant for making various types of decisions.

*Accounting links decision makers with economic activities—and with the results of their decisions*

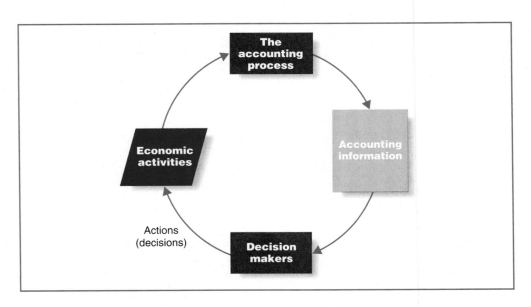

The diagram at the bottom of the previous page illustrates how economic activities flow into the accounting process, which produces accounting information, which is used by decision makers in making economic decisions and taking specific actions, which result in economic activities, and so on.

## Types of Accounting Information

Just as there are many types of economic decisions, there are also many types of accounting information. The terms *financial accounting, management accounting,* and *tax accounting often are used in describing three types of accounting information that are widely used in the business community.*

**Financial Accounting**   **Financial accounting** refers to information describing the financial resources, obligations, and activities of an economic entity (either an organization or an individual). Accountants use the term *financial position* to describe an entity's financial resources and obligations at one point in time and the term *results of operations* to describe its financial activities during the year.

In **Sony Corporation**'s 2000 financial statements to owners, financial position is presented as consisting of $64,219 million in assets (including cash, inventories, property, and equipment), with obligations against those assets of $43,300 million. This leaves $20,919 million as the owners' interest in those assets. In the same report, results of operations as measured by net income (which measures the excess of revenues over expenses) were $1,149 million for the year ending March 31, 2000.

**CASE IN POINT**

Financial accounting information is designed primarily to assist investors and creditors in deciding where to place their scarce investment resources. Such decisions are important to society, as they determine which companies and industries will receive the financial resources necessary for growth, and which will not.

Financial accounting information also is used by managers and in income tax returns. In fact, financial accounting information is used for so many different purposes that it often is called "general-purpose" accounting information.

**Management Accounting**   **Management** (or managerial) **accounting** involves the development and interpretation of accounting information intended *specifically to assist management* in running the business. Managers use this information in setting the company's overall goals, evaluating the performance of departments and individuals, deciding whether to introduce a new line of products, and in making virtually all types of managerial decisions.

A company's managers and employees constantly need such information to run and control daily business operations. For example, they need to know the amount of money in the company's bank accounts; the types, quantities, and dollar amounts of merchandise in the company's warehouse; and the amounts owed to specific creditors. Much management accounting information is financial in nature but has been organized in a manner relating directly to the decision at hand. However, management accounting information often includes evaluations of nonfinancial factors, such as political and environmental considerations, product quality, customer satisfaction, and worker productivity.

**Tax Accounting**   The preparation of income tax returns is a specialized field within accounting. To a great extent, tax returns are based on financial accounting information. However, the information often is adjusted or reorganized to conform with income tax reporting requirements.

The most challenging aspect of **tax accounting** is not the preparation of an income tax return, but *tax planning*. Tax planning means anticipating the tax effects of business transactions and structuring these transactions in a manner that will minimize the income tax burden.

**Focus of This Text**   In this textbook, we introduce the basic concepts of financial and management accounting. These discussions emphasize both the process of *financial reporting* to investors and creditors and the usefulness of financial information to an organization's management and employees. They also cover the preparation and use of accounting information that is specifically intended to support management decision-making processes.

Major income tax concepts are discussed at various points throughout the text. Comprehensive coverage of income taxes, however, is deferred to more advanced accounting courses.

Remember that the fields of financial, management, and tax accounting are *closely related*. Thus we often address financial reporting requirements and consider some of management's information needs and income tax issues within a single chapter. Our emphasis throughout this text will be on the accounting information developed in *profit-oriented business organizations*.

## ACCOUNTING SYSTEMS

**LO 2**

Discuss the significance of accounting systems in generating reliable accounting information.

An **accounting system** consists of the personnel, procedures, devices, and records used by an organization (1) to develop accounting information and (2) to communicate this information to decision makers. The design and capabilities of these systems vary greatly from one organization to the next. In very small businesses, the accounting system may consist of little more than a cash register, a checkbook, and an annual trip to an income tax preparer. In large businesses, an accounting system includes computers, highly trained personnel, and accounting reports that affect the daily operations of every department. But in every case, the basic purpose of the accounting system remains the same: *to meet the organization's needs for accounting information as efficiently as possible.*

Many factors affect the structure of the accounting system within a particular organization. Among the most important are (1) the company's *needs for accounting information* and (2) the *resources available* for operation of the system.

Viewing accounting as an information system focuses attention on the information accounting provides, the users of the information, and the support for financial decisions that is provided by the information. These relationships are depicted in the chart on the facing page. While some of the terms may not be familiar to you at this early point in your study of accounting, you will be introduced to them more completely as we proceed through this textbook and as you undertake other courses in accounting. Observe, however, that the information system produces the information presented in the middle of the diagram—cost and revenue determination, assets and liabilities, and cash flows. This information meets the needs of users of the information—investors, creditors, managers, and so on—and supports many kinds of financial decisions—performance evaluation and capital allocation, among others. These relationships are consistent with what we have already learned—namely, that accounting information is intended to be useful for decision-making purposes.

### Determining Information Needs

The types of accounting information that a company must develop vary with such factors as the size of the organization, whether it is publicly owned, and the philosophy of management. The need for some types of accounting information may be prescribed by law. For example, income tax regulations require every business to have an accounting system that can measure the company's taxable income and explain the nature and source of every item in the company's income tax return. Federal securities laws require publicly owned companies to prepare financial statements in conformity with generally accepted accounting principles. These statements must be filed with the Securities and Exchange Commission, distributed to stockholders, and made available to the public.

Other types of accounting information are required as matters of practical necessity. For example, every business needs to know the amounts receivable from each customer and the amounts owed to each creditor.

Although much accounting information clearly is essential to business operations, management still has many choices as to the types and amount of accounting information to be developed. For example, should the accounting system of a department store measure separately the sales of each department and of different types of merchandise? The answer to such questions depends on *how useful* management considers the information to be and the *cost* of developing the information.

## The Cost of Producing Accounting Information

Accounting systems should be *cost-effective*—that is, the value of the information produced should exceed the cost of producing it. Management has no choice but to produce the types of accounting reports required by law. In other cases, however, management may use *cost-effectiveness* as the criterion for deciding whether or not to produce the information.

In recent years, the development and installation of computer-based accounting systems have increased greatly the types and amount of accounting information that can be produced in a cost-effective manner.

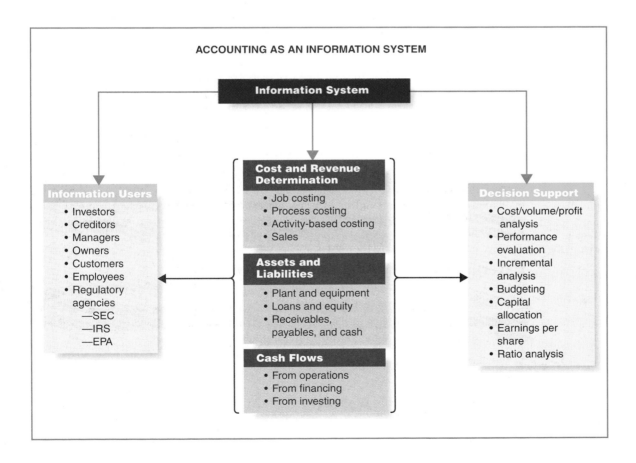

## Basic Functions of an Accounting System

In developing information about the financial position of a business and the results of its operations, every accounting system performs the following basic functions:

1. *Interpret and record* the effects of business transactions.
2. *Classify* the effects of similar transactions in a manner that permits determination of the various *totals* and *subtotals* useful to management and used in accounting reports.
3. *Summarize and communicate* the information contained in the system to decision makers.

The differences in accounting systems arise primarily in the manner and speed with which these functions are performed.

In our illustrations, we often assume the use of a simple manual accounting system. Such a system is useful in illustrating basic accounting concepts, but it is too slow and cumbersome to meet the needs of most business organizations. In a large business, transactions may occur at a rate of several hundred or several thousand per hour. To keep pace with such a rapid flow of accounting information, these companies must use accounting systems that are largely computer-based.

Some small businesses that continue to use manual accounting systems modify these systems to meet their needs as efficiently as possible.

## Who Designs and Installs Accounting Systems?

The design and installation of accounting systems is a specialized field. It involves not just accounting, but expertise in management, information systems, marketing, and—in many cases—computer programming. Thus accounting systems generally are designed and installed by a team of people with many specialized talents.

Large businesses have a staff of systems analysts, internal auditors, and other professionals who work full-time in designing and improving the accounting system. Medium-size companies often hire a CPA firm to design or update their systems. Small businesses with limited resources often purchase one of the many packaged accounting systems designed for small companies in their line of business. These packaged systems are available through office supply stores, computer stores, and software manufacturers.

## FINANCIAL ACCOUNTING INFORMATION

**LO 3**

Explain the importance of financial accounting information for external parties—primarily investors and creditors—in terms of the objectives and the characteristics of that information.

*Financial accounting* is an important subject for students who need only an introduction to the field of accounting, as well as students who will pursue accounting as a major and take many additional accounting courses. **Financial accounting** provides information about the financial resources, obligations, and activities of an enterprise that is intended for use primarily by external decision makers—investors and creditors.

## External Users of Accounting Information

What do we mean by *external users* and who are they? **External users** of accounting information are individuals and other enterprises that have a financial interest in the reporting enterprise, but they are not involved in the day-to-day operations of that enterprise. External users of financial information include the following:

- Owners
- Creditors
- Labor unions
- Governmental agencies
- Suppliers
- Customers

- Trade associations
- General public

Each of these groups of external decision makers requires unique information to be able to make decisions about the reporting enterprise. For example, customers who purchase from the enterprise need information to allow them to assess the quality of the products they buy and the faithfulness of the enterprise in fulfilling warranty obligations. Governmental agencies such as the Federal Trade Commission may have an interest in whether the enterprise meets certain governmental regulations that apply. The general public may be interested in the extent to which the reporting enterprise is socially responsible (for example, does not pollute the environment).

Providing information that meets the needs of such a large set of diverse users is difficult, if not impossible, in a single set of financial information. Therefore, external financial reporting is directed toward the information needs of two primary groups—investors and creditors. As you will soon see, investors are individuals and other enterprises that own the reporting enterprise. Creditors, on the other hand, are individuals and other enterprises that have provided credit to the reporting enterprise. For example, a commercial bank may have loaned money to the reporting enterprise, or a supplier may have permitted the reporting enterprise to purchase goods and to pay for those goods later. Our assumption is that by meeting the financial information needs of investors and creditors, we provide information that is also useful to many other users of financial information. In addition, certain external users of financial information, such as government agencies like the Federal Trade Commission, can require information that is not generally available to the public. As a result, they are not as dependent on publicly available information as are investors and creditors.

For these reasons, we sometimes refer to investors and creditors as the primary external financial information users. When you see references like these, keep in mind that we are talking about both current investors and creditors and those individuals and other enterprises that may become investors and creditors in the future.

## Objectives of External Financial Reporting

If you had invested in a company, or if you had loaned money to a company, what would be your primary financial interest in the company? You probably would be interested in two things, both of which make up the company's **cash flow prospects**. You would be interested in the return to you at some future date of the amount you had invested or loaned. We refer to this as the **return of your investment**. In addition, you would expect the company to pay you something for the use of your funds, either as an owner or a creditor. We refer to this as the **return on your investment**. Information that is useful to you in making judgments about the company's ability to provide you with what you expect in terms of the return of your funds in the future and the return on your funds while you do not have use of them is what we mean by information about *cash flow prospects*.

Assume, for example, that you loan $100,000 to a company that is owned by a friend. Your intent is not to be a long-term investor (owner), but simply to help the company financially through its difficult startup phase. Management of the company agrees to pay you interest at 12% and to repay your loan in one year. Before making this loan, you are interested in seeing information that will allow you to assess the company's ability to provide the following cash flows to you in the future:

| | |
|---|---:|
| Return on investment (that is, interest): | |
| $100,000 × 12% . . . . . . . . . . . . . . . . . . . . . . . . . . . . . . . . . . . . . . . . . . | $ 12,000 |
| Return of investment: | |
| $100,000 at maturity . . . . . . . . . . . . . . . . . . . . . . . . . . . . . . . . . . . . . | 100,000 |
| Total . . . . . . . . . . . . . . . . . . . . . . . . . . . . . . . . . . . . . . . . . . . . . . . . . . | $112,000 |

While there is always some risk in entering into a transaction of this type, before making this loan you need to feel reasonably secure that the company will be in a position to pay you these amounts.

Similarly, assume you have an opportunity to invest in a company by becoming one of a large number of owners. As an external owner, rather than an owner-manager, you will not be involved in the daily operations of the company. Before making such an investment, you want to see evidence that the company will be able to pay you a periodic return on your investment (called a *dividend* if the company is organized as a corporation) and that at some future date you can expect to sell your investment to another owner at a favorable price—in other words, that you can expect the return of your investment.

**CASE IN POINT**

One of the ways companies present information about cash flow prospects to investors and creditors is to provide a statement of cash flows. In 1999, **Intel Corporation** showed in its statement of cash flows how cash was increased from $2,038 million at the start of the year to $3,695 million at the end of the year as a result of a wide range of business activities that included its ongoing revenue and expense transactions; borrowing and repayment of debt; purchases of land, buildings, and equipment; and payments of dividends to owners.

Providing information about these cash flow prospects essentially is what financial accounting is all about. For the primary external users of financial information—investors and creditors—this information is summarized in the following table:

| Information | Investors | Creditors |
|---|---|---|
| Return *on* investment | Periodic dividends (for example, annually) | Periodic interest (for example, monthly) |
| Return *of* investment | Sale of ownership at a future date | Repayment of loan at a future date |

The accounting profession has identified certain objectives of external financial reporting to guide its efforts to refine and improve the reporting of information to external decision makers. These general objectives are displayed on the facing page and are best understood if studied from the bottom up—from general to specific.[1]

The first objective is the most general and is to provide information that is useful in making investment and credit decisions. As we indicated earlier, investors and creditors are the primary focus of external financial reporting. We believe that by meeting the information needs of investors and creditors, we provide information that is also useful to many other important financial statement users.

The second objective, which is more specific than the first, is to provide information that is useful in assessing the amount, timing, and uncertainty of future cash flows. As we discussed earlier, investors and creditors are interested in future cash flows to them, so an important objective of financial reporting is to provide information that permits that kind of analysis.

The most specific objective of external financial reporting is to provide information about the enterprise's resources, claims to those resources, and how both the resources and claims to resources change over time. An enterprise's resources are often referred to as *assets*, and the primary claims to those resources are the claims of creditors and owners.

---

[1] FASB, *Statement of Financial Accounting Concepts No. 1,* "Objectives of Financial Reporting by Business Enterprises" (Norwalk, Conn., 1978), p. 4.

## You as an Investor

You have just received a significant inheritance from a favorite uncle who included you in his will. You are considering alternative ways to invest this money to help you pay for your college education and make major purchases in the future, such as a car and a house. What are your primary considerations in choosing an investment for your newly acquired funds? What would cause you to choose to invest in one company over another?

*Our comments appear on page 36.

YOUR TURN

As we will see in Chapter 2, these objectives are met in large part by a set of financial statements. The primary financial statements are the following:

- *Statement of financial position (balance sheet).* The **balance sheet** is a position statement that shows where the company stands in financial terms at a specific date.
- *Income statement.* The **income statement** is an activity statement that shows details and results of the company's profit-related activities for a period of time (for example, a month, quarter [three months], or year).
- *Statement of cash flows.* The **statement of cash flows** is an activity statement that shows the details of the company's activities involving cash during a period of time.

**OBJECTIVES
OF FINANCIAL
REPORTING**

(Specific)

Provide information about economic resources,
claims to resources, and changes in
resources and claims.

Provide information useful in assessing amount, timing, and
uncertainty of future cash flows.

Provide information useful in making investment and credit decisions.

(General)

Financial reporting, and financial statements in particular, can be thought of as a lens through which you can view a business. (See the figure on page 13.) A lens allows you to see things from a distance that you would not otherwise be able to see; it also allows you to focus in greater detail on certain aspects of what you are looking at. Financial information, and particularly financial statements, allows you to do just that—focus in on certain financial aspects of the enterprise that are of particular interest to you in making important investing and credit decisions. Because financial statements are only one source of financial accounting information, financial reporting provides a broader view of the business than that provided by financial statements. In other words, financial reporting encompasses financial statements, but it is not limited to financial statements. Precisely how the financial statements identified earlier provide information to external users is introduced in Chapter 2 and is the major subject of several chapters thereafter.

| | |
|---|---|
| **CASH EFFECTS** | Reporting information about the cash activities of an enterprise is a particularly important aspect of providing information to both external and internal decision makers. Cash is ultimately what business activity is all about. Despite the importance of cash and information about an enterprise's cash activities, financial reporting is much more than simply displaying the increases and decreases in an enterprise's cash balance. Estimating future cash flows requires a great deal of information about things other than a company's historical record of cash transactions. Many future cash events are impounded today in things other than cash. For example, a company may have many dollars of receivables from its customers as a result of credit sales that have not yet been collected in cash. Those receivables represent expected future cash flows, even though at this moment they are not in cash form. As we develop our knowledge of financial statements, we shall see that this same conclusion can be reached for many items that appear in a company's financial statements. |

## Characteristics of Externally Reported Information

Financial information that is reported to investors, creditors, and others external to the reporting enterprise has certain qualities that must be understood for the information to have maximum usefulness. Some of these qualities are discussed in the following paragraphs.

**Financial Reporting—A Means**   As we learned in the introduction to this chapter, financial information is a means to an end, not an end in and of itself. The ultimate outcome of providing financial information is to improve the quality of decision making by external parties. Financial statements themselves are simply a means by which that end is achieved.

**Financial Reporting versus Financial Statements**   As our lens diagram on the facing page depicts, financial reporting is broader than financial statements. Stated another way, financial statements are a subset of the total information encompassed by financial reporting. Investors, creditors, and other external users of financial information learn about an enterprise in a variety of ways in addition to its formal financial statements (for example, press releases sent directly to investors and creditors, articles in *The Wall Street Journal,* and more recently open communications via the Internet). Serious investors, creditors, and other external users take advantage of many sources of information that are available to support their economic decisions about an enterprise.

**Historical in Nature**   Externally reported financial information is largely historical in nature. It looks back in time and reports the results of events and transactions that already have occurred. While historical information is very useful in assessing the future, the information itself is more about the past than it is about the future.

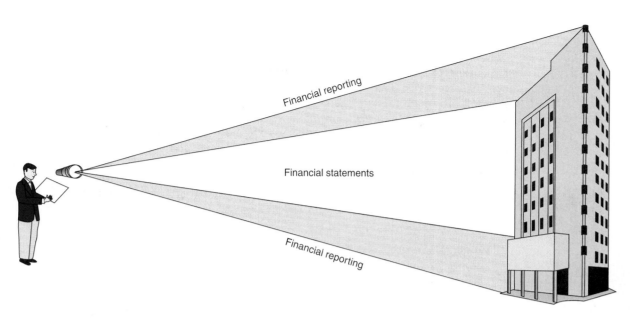

*Financial Statements: A lens to view business.*

**Inexact and Approximate Measures**  Externally reported financial information may have a look of great precision, but in fact much of it is based on estimates, judgments, and assumptions that must be made about both the past and the future. For example, assume a company purchases a piece of equipment for use in its business. To account for that asset and to incorporate the impact of it into the company's externally reported financial information, some assumptions must be made about how long it will be used by the company—how many years it will be used, how many machine-hours it will provide, and so on. The fact that a great deal of judgment underlies most accounting information is a limitation that is sometimes misunderstood.

**General-Purpose Assumption**  As we have already mentioned, we assume that by providing information that meets the needs of investors and creditors, we also meet the information needs of other external parties. We might be able to provide superior information if we treated each potential group of external users separately and prepared different information for each group. This approach is impractical, however, and we instead opt for preparing what is referred to as **general-purpose information** that we believe is useful to multiple user groups (that is, "one size fits all").

**Usefulness Enhanced via Explanation**  The accounting profession believes that the value of externally reported financial information is enhanced by including explanations from management. This information is often nonquantitative and helps to interpret the financial numbers that are presented. For this reason, financial information, including financial statements, is often accompanied by a number of notes and other explanations that help explain and interpret the numerical information.

## MANAGEMENT ACCOUNTING INFORMATION

**LO 4**

Explain the importance of management accounting information for internal parties—primarily management—in terms of the objectives and the characteristics of that information.

**Management accounting** is the preparation and use of accounting information systems to achieve the organization's objectives by supporting decision makers inside the enterprise. Internal decision makers are employed by the enterprise. These internal decision makers create and use internal accounting information not only for exclusive use inside the organization but also with the purpose of sharing some of it with external decision makers. For example, in order to meet a production schedule, a producer will design an accounting information system for suppliers detailing its production plans. The producer shares this information with its supplier companies so that they can help the producer meet its objectives. Thus, although the creator and distributor of the management accounting information is an internal decision maker, the recipient of the information is, in this case, an external decision maker. Other types of management accounting information, however, will not be available to external decision makers. Long-range plans, research and development results, capital budget details, and competitive strategies typically are closely guarded corporate secrets.

**CASE IN POINT**

**Procter & Gamble** has redefined the way it works with its retail customers, as reported in a recent annual report:

> Historically, retailers and manufacturers often approached each other as adversaries. Today, we and our customers are pioneering the use of common analytic systems, shared information resources, and mutual business goals—to better serve the one customer we both share: the consumer.

## Internal Users of Accounting Information

Every internal employee of the enterprise uses accounting information. From basic labor categories to the chief executive officer (CEO), all employees are paid, and their paychecks are generated by the accounting information system. However, the amount of use and, in particular, the involvement in the design of accounting information systems vary considerably. Examples of **internal users** of accounting information systems are as follows:

- Board of directors
- Chief executive officer (CEO)
- Chief financial officer (CFO)
- Vice presidents (information systems, human resources, treasurer, and so forth)
- Business unit managers
- Plant managers
- Store managers
- Line supervisors

Each employee has different specific goals and objectives that are designed to help the enterprise achieve its overall strategies and mission. A typical, simple organization chart is shown on the opposite page. As you can see, the information created and used by various employees will differ widely. All enterprises follow rules about the design of their accounting information systems to ensure the integrity of accounting information and to protect the enterprise's assets. There are no rules, however, about the type of internal reports or the kind of accounting information that can be generated. A snapshot look inside a firm will demonstrate the diversity of accounting information generated and used in the decision-making processes of employees.

Many enterprises use a database warehousing approach for the creation of accounting information systems. This approach, coupled with user-friendly software, allows designated employees access to information to create a variety of accounting reports, including required external financial reports. For example, detailed cost information about a production process is used by the production line supervisor to help control production costs. A process design engineer, when considering the best configuration of equipment and employees, uses the same information to reduce costs or to increase efficiency. Finally, production-related cost information appears in the external financial statements used by investors and creditors.

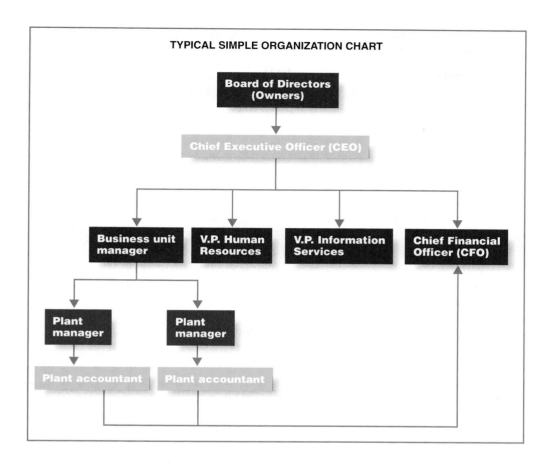

## Objectives of Management Accounting

Each enterprise has implicit and explicit goals and objectives. Many enterprises have a mission statement that describes their goals. These goals can vary widely among enterprises ranging from nonprofit organizations, where goals are aimed at serving specified constituents, to for-profit organizations, where goals are directed toward maximizing the owners' objectives. For example, the **American Cancer Society**, a nonprofit organization, has the following mission:

> The American Cancer Society is the nationwide community-based voluntary health organization dedicated to eliminating cancer as a major health problem by preventing cancer, saving lives and diminishing suffering from cancer through research, education, advocacy, and service.[2]

**Procter & Gamble**, a for-profit, global producer of consumer products, has the following purpose:

> We will provide products of superior quality and value that improve the lives of the world's consumers.[3]

**Procter & Gamble**'s annual report to shareholders provides more detail on how the company will achieve its mission. The following growth goals were identified in P&G's 1999 annual letter to its shareholders:

> Overall, we expect the Organization 2005 program to increase long-term sales growth to 6–8% and accelerate core net earnings per share growth to 13–15% in each of the next five years. We also expect to generate annual after-tax savings of $900 million by Fiscal 2004.[4]

---

[2] www.cancer.org/annReport/text_01.htm

[3] www.pg.com

[4] Procter & Gamble, 1999 Annual Report.

The constituents of these organizations receive external financial information that helps them assess the progress being made in achieving these goals and objectives. In the case of **Procter & Gamble**, quarterly and annual information is provided to shareholders. The **American Cancer Society** is required to report its activities and financial condition to regulators. Providing constituents evaluative information is only one objective of accounting systems.

Enterprises design and use their management accounting information systems to help them achieve their stated goals and missions. Multiple reports, some as part of the normal reporting process and some that are specially constructed and designed, are produced and distributed regularly. To motivate managers to achieve organizational goals, the management accounting system is also used to evaluate and reward decision-making performance. When the accounting system compares the plan or budget to the actual outcomes for a period, it creates a signal about the performance of the employee responsible for that part of the budget. In many enterprises management creates a reward system linked to performance as measured by the accounting system. For example, a manager's bonus may be based on meeting or exceeding the budget goals.

Assume, for example, that the manager of a plant has a budget to earn $500,000 in profits for the coming year. The plant manager is assigned decision-making authority over the components of the profit equation:

$$\text{Revenues} - \text{Costs} = \text{Profits}$$

That is, the plant manager oversees sales personnel that generate revenue through sales orders. The plant manager must also have decision-making authority over cost-related resources. The manager must make (or delegate) choices related to the supply of materials, the supply of labor, equipment usage, and so on. At the end of the coming year, the actual outcome for the plant will be compared to the budgeted figures, and the manager may be given a raise, a bonus, or a promotion based on the comparison.

### You as a Manager

You are a plant manager of a facility that manufactures low-cost computers intended primarily for sale to secondary schools and to individual college students. What are some of the decisions you must make and how would management accounting information help you make those decisions?

*Our comments appear on page 36.

Thus the objectives of accounting begin at the most general level with the objectives and mission of the enterprise. These general organizational goals create a need for information. The enterprise gathers historical and future information from both inside the enterprise and external sources. This information is used by the decision makers who have authority over the firm's resources and who will be evaluated and rewarded based on their decision outcomes. The diagram on the facing page presents the relationship of various management accounting objectives.

## Characteristics of Management Accounting Information

The management accounting information created and used primarily by decision makers inside the firm is intended above all for planning and control decisions. Because the goal of creating and using management accounting information differs from the reasons for producing externally reported financial information, its characteristics are different. The following paragraphs identify management accounting information characteristics.

**Importance of Timeliness** In order to plan for and control ongoing business processes, management accounting information needs to be timely. The competitive

Both the processes used to create financial accounting reports and the structure of those reports significantly impact management strategy. For example, because external financial reporting standards require companies to include pension-related obligations on their financial statements, management monitors those obligations closely. These pension-related obligations impact labor negotiations and labor-related corporate strategies.

Another example is that the processes necessary to create required external financial reports have historically determined the type of accounting information available inside of companies for internal decision making. Most plants within companies are organized as profit centers where plant-related financial statements mirror those necessary for external reporting purposes.

As you read the chapters of this book, we will remind you about how financial reporting has an impact on and is impacted by management strategies.

**MANAGEMENT STRATEGY**

environment faced by many enterprises demands immediate access to information. Enterprises are responding to this demand by creating computerized databases that link to external forecasts of industry associations, to their suppliers and buyers, and to their constituents. Time lines for development and launch of new products and services are becoming shorter and shorter, making quick access to information a priority.

In addition to needing timely information for planning purposes, enterprises are constantly monitoring and controlling ongoing activities. If a process or activity goes out of control, the enterprise can incur significant costs. For example, recalls of products can be very expensive for a company. If the company can monitor processes and prevent low-quality or defective products from reaching its customers, it can experience significant savings.

**OBJECTIVES OF
MANAGERIAL
REPORTING**

(Specific)

Provide information about decision-making
authority, for decision-making support,
and for evaluating and rewarding
decision-making performance.

Provide information useful in assessing both the past performance
and future directions of the enterprise and information
from external and internal sources.

Provide information useful to help the enterprise achieve its goals, objectives, and mission.

(General)

**CASE IN POINT**

**Sara Lee Corp.** is still feeling financial fallout from a product recall in December 1998. The Chicago-based manufacturer recalled about 15 million pounds of hot dogs and other packaged lunch meats shipped from its Zeeland, Michigan, plant after federal health officials linked the food to an outbreak of food poisoning that killed 15 people. To cover the actual costs of the recall, **Sara Lee** reported a $76 million loss in its fiscal second quarter of 1999.

**Identity of Decision Maker** Information that is produced to monitor and control processes needs to be provided to those who have decision-making authority to correct problems. Reporting scrap and rework information to line workers without providing them the responsibility for fixing the process is counterproductive. However, a self-directed work team that has been assigned decision-making responsibility over equipment and work-related activities can have a significant impact on rework and scrap if team members control the process causing the problems.

**Oriented toward the Future** Although some management accounting information, like financial accounting information, is historical in nature, the purpose in creating and generating it is to affect the future. The objective is to motivate management to make future decisions that are in the best interest of the enterprise, consistent with its goals, objectives, and mission.

**Measures of Efficiency and Effectiveness** Management accounting information measures the efficiency and effectiveness of resource usage. By comparing the enterprise's resource inputs and outputs with measures of competitors' effectiveness and efficiency, an assessment can be made of how effective management is in achieving the organization's mission. The management accounting system uses money as a common unit to achieve these types of comparisons.

**Managerial Accounting Information—A Means** As with financial information, management accounting information is a means to an end, not an end in and of itself. The ultimate objective is to design and use an accounting system that helps management achieve the goals and objectives of the enterprise.

## INTEGRITY OF ACCOUNTING INFORMATION

What enables investors and creditors to rely on financial accounting information without fear that the management of the reporting enterprise has altered the information to make the company's performance look better than it actually was? How can management be sure that internally generated information is free from bias that might favor one outcome over another? The word **integrity** refers to the following qualities: complete, unbroken, unimpaired, sound, honest, and sincere. Accounting information must have these qualities because of the significance of the information to individuals who rely on it in making important financial decisions.

The integrity of accounting information is enhanced in three primary ways. First, certain institutional features add significantly to the integrity of accounting information. These features include standards for the preparation of accounting information, an internal control structure, and audits of financial statements. Second, several professional accounting organizations play unique roles in adding to the integrity of accounting information. Finally, and perhaps most important, is the personal competence, judgment,

**LO 5**

Discuss elements of the system of external and internal financial reporting that create integrity in the reported information.

and ethical behavior of professional accountants. These three elements of the accounting profession come together to ensure that users of accounting information—investors, creditors, managers, and others—can rely on the information to be a fair representation of what it purports to represent.

## Institutional Features

**Standards for the Preparation of Accounting Information**    Accounting information that is communicated externally to investors and creditors must be prepared in accordance with standards that are understood by both the preparers and users of that information. We call these standards **generally accepted accounting principles**, often shortened to GAAP. These principles provide the general framework for determining what information is included in financial statements and how this information is to be prepared and presented. GAAP includes broad principles of measurement and presentation, as well as detailed rules that are used by professional accountants in preparing accounting information and reports.

Accounting principles are not like physical laws; they do not exist in nature waiting to be discovered. Rather, they are developed by people, in light of what we consider to be the most important objectives of financial reporting. In many ways accounting principles are similar to the rules established for an organized sport, such as baseball or basketball. For example, accounting principles, like sports rules:

- Originate from a combination of tradition, experience, and official decree.
- Require authoritative support and some means of enforcement.
- Are sometimes arbitrary.
- May change over time as shortcomings in the existing rules come to light.
- Must be clearly understood and observed by all participants in the process.

Accounting principles vary somewhat from country to country. The phrase "generally accepted accounting principles" refers to the accounting concepts in use in the United States. However, the principles in use in Canada, Great Britain, and a number of other countries are quite similar. Also, foreign companies that raise capital from American investors usually issue financial statements in conformity with generally accepted accounting principles.

Several international organizations currently are attempting to establish greater uniformity among the accounting principles in use around the world in order to facilitate business activity that increasingly is carried out in more than one country.

In the United States two organizations are particularly important in establishing generally accepted accounting principles—the Financial Accounting Standards Board (FASB) and the Securities and Exchange Commission (SEC).

**Financial Accounting Standards Board**    Today, the most authoritative source of generally accepted accounting principles is the **Financial Accounting Standards Board**. The FASB is an independent rule-making body, consisting of seven members from the accounting profession, industry, government, and accounting education. Lending support to these members are an advisory council and a large research staff.

The FASB is authorized to issue *Statements of Financial Accounting Standards* (and other authoritative accounting pronouncements), which represent official expressions of generally accepted accounting principles.

In addition to issuing authoritative *Statements,* the FASB has completed a project describing a *conceptual framework* for financial reporting. This conceptual framework sets forth the FASB's views as to the:

- Objectives of financial reporting.
- Desired characteristics of accounting information (such as relevance, reliability, and understandability).
- Elements of financial statements.

- Criteria for deciding what information to include in financial statements.
- Valuation concepts relating to financial statement amounts.

The primary purpose of the conceptual framework is to provide guidance to the FASB in developing new accounting standards. By making each new standard consistent with this framework, the FASB believes that its official *Statements* resolve accounting problems in a logical and consistent manner.

The FASB is part of the private sector of the economy—*it is not a governmental agency*. The development of accounting principles in the United States traditionally has been carried out in the private sector, although the government, acting through the SEC, exercises considerable influence.

**CASE IN POINT**

The process for establishing external financial reporting requirements varies significantly from country to country. In some countries like Germany and Japan, the government sets these reporting requirements and as a result financial reporting requirements tend to be very consistent with tax reporting requirements. Because the FASB is independent from the Internal Revenue Service (IRS) in the United States, financial reporting and tax reporting requirements are not always consistent.

**Securities and Exchange Commission** The **Securities and Exchange Commission** is a governmental agency with the *legal power* to establish accounting principles and financial reporting requirements for publicly owned corporations. In the past, the SEC has generally adopted the recommendations of the FASB, rather than develop its own set of accounting principles. Thus accounting principles continue to be developed in the private sector but are given the *force of law* when they are adopted by the SEC.

To assure widespread acceptance of new accounting standards, the FASB *needs the support* of the SEC. Therefore, the two organizations work closely together in developing new accounting standards. The SEC also reviews the financial statements of publicly owned corporations to assure compliance with its reporting requirements. In the event that a publicly owned corporation fails to comply with these requirements, the SEC may initiate legal action against the company and the responsible individuals. Thus the SEC enforces compliance with generally accepted accounting principles that are established primarily by the FASB.

**Internal Control Structure** The decisions made by management are based to a considerable extent on information developed by the accounting system. Therefore, management needs assurance that the accounting information it receives is accurate and reliable. This assurance is provided by the company's *internal control structure*.

A simple example of an internal control procedure is the use of serial numbers on checks issued. Accounting for an unbroken sequence of serial numbers provides assurance that every check issued has been recorded in the accounting records.

The **internal control structure** includes *all* measures used by an organization to guard against errors, waste, and fraud; to assure the reliability of accounting information; to promote compliance with management policies; and to evaluate the level of performance in all divisions of the company. In short, the internal control structure is intended to ensure that the entire organization *operates according to plan*.

There is a strong *interrelationship* between accounting and internal control. We have stated that the internal control structure includes measures designed to promote the reliability of accounting information. At the same time, one goal of the accounting system is to provide management with information useful in establishing internal control throughout the organization. Thus the topic of internal control goes hand in hand with the study of accounting.

**Audits of Financial Statements**   What assurance do outsiders have that the financial statements issued by management provide a complete and reliable picture of the company's financial position and operating results? In large part, this assurance is provided by an *audit* of the company's financial statements, performed by a firm of *certified public accountants (CPAs)*. These auditors are experts in the field of financial reporting and are *independent* of the company issuing the financial statements.

An **audit** is an *investigation* of a company's financial statements, designed to determine the fairness of these statements. Accountants and auditors use the term *fair* in describing financial statements that are reliable and complete, conform to generally accepted accounting principles, and are *not misleading*.

In auditing financial statements, generally accepted accounting principles are the standard by which those statements are judged. For the auditor to reach the conclusion that the financial statements are fair representations of a company's financial position, results of operations, and cash flows, the statements must comply in all important ways with generally accepted accounting principles.

The 2000 financial statements of **Sony Corporation** are accompanied by a statement issued by **PricewaterhouseCoopers LLP**, the company's auditor and one of the largest public accounting firms in the world. This statement indicates that in the auditor's opinion, the financial statements of the company are in conformity with generally accepted accounting principles and that they present fairly the financial activities of the company for 1999.

**CASE IN POINT**

## Professional Organizations

**LO 6**

Identify and discuss several professional organizations that play important roles in preparing and communicating accounting information.

Several professional accounting organizations play an active role in improving the quality of accounting information that is used by investors, creditors, management, and others. In addition to the Financial Accounting Standards Board and the Securities and Exchange Commission, discussed earlier, the American Institute of CPAs, the Institute of Management Accountants, the Institute of Internal Auditors, and the American Accounting Association are particularly important.

**American Institute of CPAs (AICPA)**   The **American Institute of CPAs** is a professional association of certified public accountants. Its mission is to provide members with the resources, information, and leadership to enable them to provide valuable services in the highest professional manner to benefit the public, employers, and clients. The AICPA participates in many aspects of the accounting profession, including the establishment of auditing standards to be followed by CPAs in the audit of financial statements. The AICPA conducts accounting research and works closely with the FASB in the establishment and interpretation of generally accepted accounting principles. In fact, prior to the establishment of the FASB, the AICPA had primary responsibility for the establishment of accounting principles.

**Institute of Management Accountants (IMA)**   The mission of the **Institute of Management Accountants** is to provide members personal and professional development opportunities through education, association with business professionals, and certification. The IMA is recognized by the financial community as a respected organization that influences the concepts and ethical practice of management accounting and financial management. The IMA sponsors a number of educational activities for its members, including national seminars and conferences, regional and local programs, self-study courses, and in-house and on-line programs. Two certification programs are available through the IMA—the Certificate in Management Accounting (CMA) and the

Certificate in Financial Management (CFM). These designations testify to the individual's competence and expertise in management accounting and financial management.

**Institute of Internal Auditors (IIA)**   With more than 70,000 members in 129 countries, the **Institute of Internal Auditors** is the primary international professional association dedicated to the promotion and development of the practice of internal auditing. It provides professional development through the Certified Internal Auditor® Program and leading-edge conferences and seminars; research through the IIA Research Foundation on trends, best practices, and other internal auditing issues; guidance through the *Standards for the Professional Practice of Internal Auditing*; and educational products on virtually all aspects of the profession. The IIA also provides audit specialty services and industry-specific auditing programs, as well as quality assurance reviews and benchmarking services.

**American Accounting Association (AAA)**   Membership in the **American Accounting Association** is made up primarily of accounting educators, although many practicing accountants are members as well. The mission of the AAA includes advancing accounting education and research, as well as influencing accounting practice. The focus of many of the AAA's activities is on improving accounting education by better preparing accounting professors and on advancing knowledge in the accounting discipline through research and publication. An important contribution of the AAA to the integrity of accounting information is its impact through accounting faculty on the many students who study accounting in college and subsequently become professional accountants.

## Competence, Judgment, and Ethical Behavior

**LO 7**

Discuss the importance of personal competence, professional judgment, and ethical behavior on the part of accounting professionals.

Preparing and presenting accounting information is not a mechanical task that can be performed entirely by a computer or even by well-trained clerical personnel. A characteristic common to all recognized professions, including medicine, law, and accounting, is the need for competent individual practitioners to solve problems using their professional judgment and applying strong ethical standards. The problems encountered in the practice of a profession are often complex, and the specific circumstances unique. In many cases, the well-being of others is directly affected by the work of a professional.

To illustrate the importance of competence, professional judgment, and ethical behavior in the preparation of financial statements, consider the following complex issues that must be addressed by the accountant:

- At what point have certain complex transactions actually taken place, thereby making it necessary to include them in financial statements that are sent to investors and creditors?
- At what point should an enterprise account for transactions that continue over a long period of time, such as a long-term contract to construct an interstate highway?
- What constitutes adequate disclosure of information that would be expected by a reasonably informed user of financial statements?
- At what point are a company's financial problems sufficient to question whether it will be able to remain in business for the foreseeable future, and when should that information be communicated to users of its financial statements?
- When have efforts by management to improve (that is, "window dress") its financial statements crossed a line that is inappropriate, making the financial statements actually misleading to investors and creditors?

Judgment always involves some risk of error. Some errors in judgment result from carelessness or inexperience on the part of the preparer of financial information or the decision maker who uses that information. Others occur simply because future events are uncertain and do not work out as expected when the information was prepared.

If the public is to have confidence in the judgment of professional accountants, these accountants first must demonstrate that they possess the characteristic of *competence*. Both the accounting profession and state governments have taken steps to assure the public of the technical competence of **certified public accountants** (CPAs). CPAs are licensed by the states, in much the same manner as states license physicians and attorneys. The licensing requirements vary somewhat from state to state, but in general, an individual must be of good character, have a college education with a major in accounting, pass a rigorous examination, and have several years of accounting experience. In addition, most states require all CPAs to spend at least 40 hours per year in continuing professional education throughout their careers.

Beginning in the year 2000, the AICPA requires its new members to have completed 150 semester hours of college work. This represents about one additional year beyond a bachelor's degree, which usually requires approximately 120–125 semester hours. Most states are changing their licensing requirements to reflect this expectation of better-educated entrants into the accounting profession.

Management accountants are not required to be licensed as CPAs. However, they voluntarily may earn a **Certificate in Management Accounting (CMA)** or a **Certificate in Internal Auditing (CIA)** as evidence of their professional competence. These certificates are issued by the IMA and the IIA, and signify competence in management accounting and internal auditing, respectively. The requirements for becoming a CMA and CIA are similar to those for becoming a CPA.

Integrity in accounting information requires honesty and a strong commitment to ethical conduct—doing the right thing. For a professional accountant, ethical behavior is just as important as competence. However, it is far more difficult to test or enforce.

Many professional organizations have codes of ethics or professional conduct that direct the activities of their members. The AICPA, for example, has a code of professional conduct that expresses the accounting profession's recognition of its responsibilities to the public, to clients, and to colleagues. The principles included in the code guide AICPA members in the performance of their professional responsibilities. This code expresses the basic tenets of ethical and professional behavior and has been codified into law in many states.

---

### You as a Professional Accountant

You are a professional accountant working for a public accounting firm and find yourself in a difficult situation. You have discovered some irregularities in the financial records of your firm's client. You are uncertain whether these irregularities are the result of carelessness on the part of the company's employees or represent intentional steps taken to cover up questionable activities. You approach your superior about this and she indicates that you should ignore it. Her response is "These things happen all of the time and usually are pretty minor. We are on a very tight time schedule to complete this engagement, so let's just keep our eyes on our goal of finishing our work by the end of the month." What would you do?

*Our comments appear on pages 36 and 37.

YOUR TURN

---

One of the principles expressed in the AICPA's code of professional conduct is the commitment of CPAs to the public interest, which is defined as the collective well-being of the community of people and institutions the profession serves. Other principles emphasize the importance of integrity, objectivity, independence, and due care in the performance of one's duties.

Expectations of ethical conduct are also important for management accountants. The code of ethics of the IMA, for example, includes the following requirements:

- *Competence.* Management accountants should be professionally competent to perform their duties of providing relevant and reliable information in accordance with relevant laws, regulations, and technical standards.
- *Confidentiality.* Management accountants should refrain from disclosing confidential information or using confidential information to their own advantage.
- *Integrity.* Management accountants should avoid conflicts of interest by refusing compromising gifts and favors, by refusing to subvert organizational objectives, by refusing to communicate biased information, and by avoiding activities that could discredit the profession.
- *Objectivity.* Management accountants should communicate information fairly and objectively and disclose all relevant information.

Users of accounting information—both external and internal—recognize that the reliability of the information is affected by the competence, professional judgment, and ethical standards of accountants. While the institutional features and professional organizations that were discussed earlier are important parts of the financial reporting system, the personal attributes of competence, professional judgment, and ethical behavior ultimately ensure the quality and reliability of accounting information.

In this text, we address the topic of ethical conduct primarily through questions, exercises, problems, and cases that emphasize the general concepts of honesty, fairness, and adequate disclosure. Most chapters include assignment material in which you are asked to make judgment calls in applying these concepts. (These assignments are identified by the scales of justice logo appearing in the margin.)

**A SECOND LOOK**

### Procter & Gamble

Let's return for a moment to **Procter & Gamble**, the company we used to introduce this chapter. P&G has many investors and creditors who have committed their funds to the company and who expect both a return on their investment and a return of their investment in the future. P&G also has extensive management personnel who have an interest in the company. Many decisions are based on the accounting information that is prepared by accountants within P&G. That information includes both financial accounting information and management accounting information.

Within P&G exist complex accounting systems that are designed to capture information about the company's many transactions. Those systems organize and communicate that information in a manner that facilitates and supports decisions by investors, creditors, managers, and others. It is particularly important that this information have integrity. That is, the information must be properly prepared, complete, and unbiased. For this to be the case, a key element is the integrity of personnel who prepare the information.

Accountants are required to have considerable education and experience to become experts in the design of accounting systems and the preparation of complex financial reports to support decision making. Many people with these qualities work for **Procter & Gamble** to support the company's need for high-quality financial information.

## SUPPLEMENTAL TOPIC

### CAREERS IN ACCOUNTING

**LO 8**

Describe various career opportunities in accounting.

Accounting—along with such fields as architecture, engineering, law, medicine, and theology—is recognized as a profession. What distinguishes a profession from other disciplines? There is no widely recognized definition of a profession, but all of these fields have several characteristics in common.

First, all professions involve a complex and evolving body of knowledge. In accounting, the complexity and the ever-changing nature of the business world, financial reporting requirements, management demands for increasingly complex information, and income tax laws certainly meet this criterion.

Second, all professions, practitioners must use their professional judgment to resolve problems and dilemmas. Throughout this text, we will point out situations requiring accountants to exercise professional judgment.

Of greatest importance, however, is the unique responsibility of professionals *to serve the public's best interest, even at the sacrifice of personal advantage.* This responsibility stems from the fact that the public has little technical knowledge in the professions, yet fair and competent performance by professionals is vital to the public's health, safety, or well-being. The practice of medicine, for example, directly affects public health, while engineering affects public safety. Accounting affects the public's well-being in many ways, because accounting information is used in the allocation of economic resources throughout society. Thus accountants have a basic social contract to avoid being associated with misleading information.

Accountants tend to specialize in specific fields, as do the members of other professions. Career opportunities in accounting may be divided into four broad areas: (1) public accounting, (2) management accounting, (3) governmental accounting, and (4) accounting education.

## Public Accounting

Certified public accountants offer a variety of accounting services to the public. These individuals may work in a CPA firm or as sole practitioners.

The work of public accountants consists primarily of auditing financial statements, income tax work, and management advisory services (management consulting).

Providing management advisory services is, perhaps, the fastest-growing area in public accounting. The advisory services extend well beyond tax planning and accounting matters; CPAs advise management on such diverse issues as international mergers, manufacturing processes, and the introduction of new products. The involvement of CPAs in the field of management consulting reflects the fact that *financial considerations enter into almost every business decision.*

A great many CPAs move from public accounting into managerial positions with their client organizations. These "alumni" from public accounting often move directly into such top management positions as controller, treasurer, chief financial officer, or chief executive officer.

## Management Accounting

In contrast to the public accountant who serves many clients, the management accountant works for one enterprise. Management accountants develop and interpret accounting information designed specifically to meet the various needs of management.

The chief accounting officer of an organization usually is called the *chief financial officer (CFO)* or *controller.* The term *controller* has been used to emphasize the fact that one basic purpose of accounting data is to aid in controlling business operations. The CFO or controller is part of the top management team, which is responsible for running the business, setting its objectives, and seeing that these objectives are met.

In addition to developing information to assist managers, management accountants are responsible for operating the company's accounting system, including the recording of transactions and the preparation of financial statements, tax returns, and other accounting reports. As the responsibilities of management accountants are so broad, many areas of specialization have developed. Among the more important are the following.

**Financial Forecasting**  A **financial forecast** (or budget) is a plan of financial operations for some *future* period. Actually, forecasting is much like financial reporting, except that the accountant is estimating future outcomes, rather than reporting past results. A forecast provides each department of a business with financial goals. Comparison of the results actually achieved with these forecast amounts is one widely used means of evaluating performance.

**Cost Accounting**    Knowing the cost of each business operation and of each manufactured product is essential to the efficient management of a business. Determining the per-unit cost of business activities and of manufactured products, and interpreting these cost data, comprise a specialized field called **cost accounting**.

**Internal Auditing**    Large organizations usually maintain a staff of *internal auditors.* **Internal auditing** is the study of the internal control structure and evaluation of efficiency of many different aspects of the company's operations. As employees, internal auditors are not independent of the organization. Therefore, they *do not* perform independent audits of the company's financial statements.

Careers in management accounting often lead to positions in top management—just as do careers in public accounting.

## Governmental Accounting

Governmental agencies use accounting information in allocating their resources and in controlling their operations. Therefore, the need for management accountants in governmental agencies is similar to that in business organizations.

**The GAO: Who Audits the Government?**    The **General Accounting Office** (GAO) audits many agencies of the federal government, as well as some private organizations doing business with the government. The GAO reports its findings directly to Congress, which, in turn, often discloses these findings to the public.

GAO investigations may be designed either to evaluate the efficiency of an entity's operations or to determine the fairness of accounting information reported to the government.

**The IRS: Audits of Income Tax Returns**    Another governmental agency that performs extensive auditing work is the **Internal Revenue Service** (IRS). The IRS handles the millions of income tax returns filed annually by individuals and business organizations and frequently performs auditing functions to verify data contained in these returns.

**The SEC: The "Watchdog" of Financial Reporting**    The SEC works closely with the FASB in establishing generally accepted accounting principles. Each year large publicly owned corporations must file audited financial statements with the SEC. If the SEC believes that a company's financial statements are deficient in any way, it conducts an investigation. If the SEC concludes that federal securities laws have been violated, it initiates legal action against the reporting entity and responsible individuals.

Many other governmental agencies, including the FBI, the Treasury Department, and the FDIC (Federal Deposit Insurance Corporation), use accountants to audit compliance with governmental regulations and to investigate suspected criminal activity. People beginning their careers in governmental accounting often move into top administrative positions.

## Accounting Education

Some accountants, including your instructor and the authors of this textbook, have chosen to pursue careers in accounting education. A position as an accounting faculty member offers opportunities for teaching, research, consulting, and an unusual degree of freedom in developing individual skills. Accounting educators contribute to the accounting profession in many ways. One, of course, lies in effective teaching; second, in publishing significant research findings; and a third, in influencing top students to pursue careers in accounting.

## What About Bookkeeping?

Some people think that the work of professional accountants consists primarily of bookkeeping. Actually, it doesn't. In fact, many professional accountants do *little or no* bookkeeping.

**Bookkeeping** is the clerical side of accounting—the recording of routine transactions and day-to-day record keeping. Today such tasks are performed primarily by computers and skilled clerical personnel, not by accountants.

Professional accountants are involved more with the *interpretation and use* of accounting information than with its actual preparation. Their work includes evaluating the efficiency of operations, resolving complex financial reporting issues, forecasting the results of future operations, auditing, tax planning, and designing efficient accounting systems. There is very little that is "routine" about the work of a professional accountant.

A person might become a proficient bookkeeper in a few weeks or months. To become a professional accountant, however, is a far greater challenge. It requires years of study, experience, and an ongoing commitment to keeping current.

We will illustrate and explain a number of bookkeeping procedures in this text, particularly in the next several chapters. But teaching bookkeeping skills is *not* our goal; the primary purpose of this text is to develop your abilities to *understand and use* accounting information in today's business world.

## Accounting as a Stepping-Stone

We have mentioned that many professional accountants leave their accounting careers for key positions in management or administration. An accounting background is invaluable in such positions, because top management works continuously with issues defined and described in accounting terms and concepts.

An especially useful stepping-stone is experience in public accounting. Public accountants have the unusual opportunity of getting an inside look at many different business organizations, which makes them particularly well suited for top management positions in other organizations.

## SUMMARY OF LEARNING OBJECTIVES

**LO 1**

**Discuss accounting as the language of business and the role of accounting information in making economic decisions.**
Accounting is the means by which information about an enterprise is communicated and, thus, is sometimes called the language of business. Many different users have need for accounting information in order to make important decisions. These users include investors, creditors, management, governmental agencies, labor unions, and others. Because the primary role of accounting information is to provide useful information for decision-making purposes, it is sometimes referred to as a means to an end, with the end being the decision that is helped by the availability of accounting information.

**LO 2**

**Discuss the significance of accounting systems in generating reliable accounting information.**
Information systems are critical to the production of quality accounting information on a timely basis and the communication of that information to decision makers. While there are different types of information systems, they all have one characteristic in common—to meet the organization's needs for accounting information as efficiently as possible.

**LO 3**

**Explain the importance of financial accounting information for external parties—primarily investors and creditors—in terms of the objectives and the characteristics of that information.**
The primary objectives of financial accounting are to provide information that is useful in making investment and credit decisions; in assessing the amount, timing, and uncertainty of future cash flows; and in learning about the enterprise's economic resources, claims to resources, and changes in claims to resources. Some of the most important characteristics of financial accounting information are it is a means to an end, it is historical in nature, it results from inexact and approximate measures of business activity, and it is based on a general-purpose assumption.

**LO 4**

**Explain the importance of management accounting information for internal parties—primarily management—in terms of the objectives and the characteristics of that information.**
Management accounting information is useful to the enterprise in achieving its goals, objectives, and mission; assessing past performance and future directions; and evaluating and reward-

ing decision-making performance. Some of the important characteristics of management accounting information are its timeliness, its relationship to decision-making authority, its future orientation, its relationship to measuring efficiency and effectiveness, and the fact that it is a means to an end.

**LO 5**

**Discuss elements of the system of external and internal financial reporting that create integrity in the reported information.**
Integrity of financial reporting is important because of the reliance that is placed on financial information by users both outside and inside the reporting organization. Important dimensions of financial reporting that work together to ensure integrity in information are institutional features (accounting principles, internal structure, and audits); professional organizations (AICPA, IMA, CIA, AAA); and the competence, judgment, and ethical behavior of individual accountants.

**LO 6**

**Identify and discuss several professional organizations that play important roles in preparing and communicating accounting information.**
The FASB and SEC are important organizations in terms of standard setting in the United States. The FASB is a private-sector organization that works closely with the SEC, which has legal authority to designate financial reporting standards for publicly held companies. Professional organizations that provide services to individual accountants in various segments of the accounting profession are the AICPA, IMA, IIA, and AAA.

**LO 7**

**Discuss the importance of personal competence, professional judgment, and ethical behavior on the part of accounting professionals.**
Personal competence and professional judgment are, perhaps, the most important factors in ensuring the integrity of financial information. Competence is demonstrated by one's education and professional certification (CPA, CMA, CIA). Professional judgment is important because accounting information is often based on inexact measurements and assumptions are required. Ethical behavior refers to the quality of accountants being motivated to "do the right thing" in applying their skills.

**LO 8**

**Describe various career opportunities in accounting.**
Accounting opens the door to many diverse career opportunities. Public accounting is the segment of the profession where professionals offer audit, tax, and consulting services to clients. Management, or managerial, accounting refers to that segment

of the accounting profession where professional accountants work for individual companies in a wide variety of capacities. Many accountants work for various governmental agencies. Some accountants choose education as a career and work to prepare students for future careers in one of the other segments of the accounting profession. While keeping detailed records (that is, bookkeeping) is a part of accounting, it is not a distinguishing characteristic of a career in accounting; in fact, many accounting careers involve little or no bookkeeping.

In this chapter we have established a framework for your study of accounting. You have learned how financial accounting provides information for external users, primarily investors and creditors, and how management accounting provides information for internal management. We have established the importance of integrity in accounting information and have learned about several things that build integrity. Looking ahead, in Chapter 2 we begin to look in greater depth at financial accounting and, more specifically, financial statements. You will be introduced to the three primary financial statements that provide information for investors and creditors. As the text progresses, you will learn more about the important information that these financial statements provide and how that information is used to make important financial decisions.

## KEY TERMS INTRODUCED OR EMPHASIZED IN CHAPTER 1

**accounting systems** (p. 6) The personnel, procedures, devices, and records used by an organization to develop accounting information and communicate that information to decision makers.

**American Accounting Association** (p. 22) A professional accounting organization consisting primarily of accounting educators that is dedicated to improving accounting education, research, and practice.

**American Institute of CPAs** (p. 21) A professional accounting organization of certified public accountants that engages in a variety of professional activities, including establishing auditing standards, conducting research, and working closely with the FASB in establishing financial reporting standards.

**audit** (p. 21) An investigation of financial statements designed to determine their fairness in relation to generally accepted accounting principles.

**balance sheet** (p. 11) A position statement that shows where the company stands in financial terms at a specific date. (Also called the statement of financial position.)

**bookkeeping** (p. 27) The clerical dimension of accounting that includes recording the routine transactions and day-to-day record keeping of an enterprise.

**cash flow prospects** (p. 9) The likelihood that an enterprise will be able to provide an investor with both a return on the investor's investment and the return of that investment.

**Certificate in Internal Auditing** (p. 23) A professional designation issued by the Institute of Internal Auditors signifying expertise in internal auditing.

**Certificate in Management Accounting** (p. 23) A professional

designation issued by the Institute of Management Accounting signifying expertise in management accounting.

**Certified Public Accountant** (p. 23) An accountant who is licensed by a state after meeting rigorous education, experience, and examination requirements.

**cost accounting** (p. 26) Determining the cost of certain business activities and interpreting cost information.

**external users** (p. 8) Individuals and other enterprises that have a financial interest in the reporting enterprise but that are not involved in the day-to-day operations of that enterprise (e.g., owners, creditors, labor unions, suppliers, customers).

**financial accounting** (p. 5) Providing information about the financial resources, obligations, and activities of an economic entity that is intended for use primarily by external decision makers—investors and creditors.

**Financial Accounting Standards Board** (p. 19) A private-sector organization that is responsible for determining generally accepted accounting principles in the United States.

**financial forecast** (p. 25) A plan of financial operations for some future period.

**General Accounting Office** (p. 26) A federal government agency that audits many other agencies of the federal government and other organizations that do business with the federal government and reports its findings to Congress.

**generally accepted accounting principles** (p. 19) Principles that provide the framework for determining what information is to be included in financial statements and how that information is to be presented.

**general-purpose information** (p. 13) Information that is intended to meet the needs of multiple users that have an interest in the financial activities of an enterprise rather than being tailored to the specific information needs of one user.

**income statement** (p. 11) An activity statement that shows details and results of the company's profit-related activities for a period of time.

**Institute of Internal Auditors** (p. 22) A professional accounting organization that is dedicated to the promotion and development of the practice of internal auditing.

**Institute of Management Accountants** (p. 21) A professional accounting organization that intends to influence the concepts and ethical practice of management accounting and financial management.

**integrity** (p. 18) The qualities complete, unbroken, unimpaired, sound, honest, and sincere.

**internal auditing** (p. 26) The study of internal control structure and evaluation of the efficiency of many different aspects of the enterprise's operations.

**internal control structure** (p. 20) Measures used by an organization to guard against errors, waste, and fraud; to assure the reliability of accounting information; to promote compliance with management policies; and to evaluate the level of performance of all divisions of the company.

**Internal Revenue Service** (p. 26) A government organization that handles millions of income tax returns filed by individuals and businesses and performs audit functions to verify the data contained in those returns.

**internal users** (p. 14) Individuals who use accounting information from within an organization (for example, board of directors, chief financial officer, plant managers, store managers).

**management accounting** (p. 5) Providing information that is intended primarily for use by internal management in decision making required to run the business.

**return of investment** (p. 9) The repayment to an investor of the amount originally invested in another enterprise.

**return on investment** (p. 9) The payment of an amount (interest, dividends) for using another's money.

**Securities and Exchange Commission** (p. 20) A governmental organization that has the legal power to establish accounting principles and financial reporting requirements for publicly held companies in the United States.

**statement of cash flows** (p. 11) An activity statement that shows the details of the company's activities involving cash during a period of time.

**statement of financial position** (p. 11) Also called the balance sheet.

**tax accounting** (p. 6) Preparation of income tax returns and anticipating the tax effects of business transactions and structuring them in such a way as to minimize the income tax burden.

## SELF-TEST QUESTIONS

*Answers to these questions appear on page 37.*

1. Which of the following does *not* describe accounting?
   a. Language of business.
   b. Is an end rather than a means to an end.
   c. Useful for decision making.
   d. Used by business, government, nonprofit organizations, and individuals.

2. To understand and use accounting information in making economic decisions, you must understand:
   a. The nature of economic activities that accounting information describes.
   b. The assumptions and measurement techniques involved in developing accounting information.
   c. Which information is relevant for a particular type of decision that is being made.
   d. All of the above.

3. Purposes of an accounting system include all of the following *except:*
   a. Interpret and record the effects of business transactions.
   b. Classify the effects of transactions to facilitate the preparation of reports.
   c. Summarize and communicate information to decision makers.
   d. Dictate the specific types of business transactions that the enterprise may engage in.

4. External users of financial accounting information include all of the following *except:*
   a. Investors.
   b. Labor unions.
   c. Line managers.
   d. General public.

5. Objectives of financial reporting to external investors and creditors include preparing information about all of the following *except:*
   a. Information used to determine which products to produce.
   b. Information about economic resources, claims to those resources, and changes in both resources and claims.
   c. Information that is useful in assessing the amount, timing, and uncertainty of future cash flows.
   d. Information that is useful in making investment and credit decisions.

6. Financial accounting information is characterized by all of the following *except:*
   a. It is historical in nature.
   b. It results from inexact and approximate measures.
   c. It is factual, so it does not require judgment to prepare.
   d. It is enhanced by management's explanation.

7. Which of the following is *not* a user of management accounting information?

   **a.** Store manager.

   **b.** Chief executive officer.

   **c.** Creditor.

   **d.** Chief financial officer.

8. Characteristics of management accounting information include all of the following *except:*

   **a.** It is audited by a CPA.

   **b.** It must be timely.

   **c.** It is oriented toward the future.

   **d.** It measures efficiency and effectiveness.

9. Which of the following are important factors in ensuring the integrity of accounting information?

   **a.** Institutional factors, such as standards for preparing information.

   **b.** Professional organizations, such as the American Institute of CPAs.

   **c.** Competence, judgment, and ethical behavior of individual accountants.

   **d.** All of the above.

10. The code of ethics of the Institute of Management Accountants includes requirements in which of the following areas?

    **a.** Competence.

    **b.** Objectivity.

    **c.** Confidentiality.

    **d.** All of the above.

## ASSIGNMENT MATERIAL

### DISCUSSION QUESTIONS

1. What do we mean when we say that accounting is a means rather than an end?

2. Accounting is sometimes described as the language of business. What is meant by this description?

3. What kinds of organizations, in addition to businesses, use accounting information?

4. What is the primary distinction between financial accounting and managerial accounting?

5. Describe the relationship among the accounting process, accounting information, decision makers, and economic activities.

6. What are some examples of nonfinancial information that is often wanted by users of accounting information?

7. What is an accounting system and what is the primary objective of such a system?

8. What do we mean when we say that an accounting system needs to be cost-effective?

9. What are the three basic functions of every accounting system?

10. Who designs and installs accounting systems?

11. Generally describe and give several examples of external users of accounting information.

12. What are the two primary external groups to which financial accounting information is directed?

13. What do we mean when we say that investors and creditors are interested in a company's cash flow prospects?

14. When you invest your savings in a company, what is the difference between the return *on* your investment and the return *of* your investment?

15. Going from general to specific, what are the three primary objectives of financial accounting information?

16. What are the three primary financial statements with which we communicate financial accounting information?

17. Do the terms *financial reporting* and *financial statements* mean the same thing? Explain.

18. Is externally reported financial information always precise and accurate?

19. What do we mean when we say that financial accounting information is "general-purpose"?

20. How does management's explanation enhance the usefulness of financial accounting information?

21. What are several examples of internal, management-prepared information that ordinarily would not be communicated externally?

22. What are some examples of internal users of accounting information?

23. What is meant by a *database warehousing approach* for the creation of useful accounting information for internal management?

24. What are the three primary ways enterprises use their management accounting information?

25. Why does management accounting information need to be timely?

26. Is management accounting information primarily historical or future oriented? How does that compare with financial accounting information?

27. How does accounting information assist management in measuring efficiency and effectiveness?

28. How is management accounting information a means to an end?

29. Why is it important for accounting information to have the quality of integrity?

30. What is meant by *generally accepted accounting principles,* and how do these principles add to the integrity of financial accounting information?

31. What is an *internal control structure,* and how does it add to the integrity of accounting information?

32. What is an *audit,* and how does it add to the integrity of accounting information?

33. What is meant by the professional designations *CPA, CMA,* and *CIA,* and how do these designations add to the integrity of accounting information?

34. What is a *code of ethics,* and how do such codes add to the integrity of accounting information?

35. What is the Financial Accounting Standards Board (FASB), and what is its role in external financial reporting?

36. What is the Securities and Exchange Commission (SEC), and what is its role in external financial reporting?

37. What is the role of the American Institute of Certified Public Accountants in the audit of financial statements?

38. What is the primary mission of the Institute of Management Accountants?

39. What is the mission of the Institute of Internal Auditors, and does the organization have primarily a U.S. or an international focus?

40. Who makes up the majority of the members of the American Accounting Association, and how has this organization affected the practice of accounting?

## EXERCISES

**EXERCISE 1.1**

You as a User of Accounting Information

**EXERCISE 1.2**

Users of Accounting Information

**LO 3, 4**

Identify several ways in which *you* currently use accounting information in your life as a student. Also identify several situations in which, while you are still a student, you might be required to supply financial information about yourself to others.

**Boeing Company** is the largest manufacturer of commercial aircraft in the United States and is a major employer in Seattle, Washington. Explain why each of the following individuals or organizations would be interested in financial information about the company.

a. **California Public Employees Retirement System**, one of the world's largest pension funds.

b. **China Airlines**, a rapidly growing airline serving the Pacific Rim.

c. Henry James, a real estate investor considering building apartments in the Seattle area.

d. **Boeing**'s management.

e. **International Aerospace Machinists**, a labor union representing many Boeing employees.

A major focus of this course is the process of financial reporting.

**a.** What is meant by the term *financial reporting*?

**b.** What are the principal accounting reports involved in the financial reporting process? In general terms, what is the purpose of these reports?

**c.** Do all business entities engage in financial reporting? Explain.

**d.** How does society benefit from the financial reporting process?

**EXERCISE 1.3**

What Is Financial Reporting?

**LO 3**

Generally accepted accounting principles play an important role in financial reporting.

**a.** What is meant by the phrase *generally accepted accounting principles?*

**b.** What are the major sources of these principles?

**c.** Is there a comprehensive list of generally accepted accounting principles? Explain.

**d.** What types of accounting reports are prepared in conformity with generally accepted accounting principles?

**EXERCISE 1.4**

Generally Accepted
Accounting Principles

**LO 6**

Describe the roles of the following organizations in establishing generally accepted accounting principles:

**a.** The FASB

**b.** The AICPA

**c.** The SEC

From which of these organizations can you most easily obtain financial information about publicly owned companies?

**EXERCISE 1.5**

Accounting Organizations

**LO 6**

You recently invested $10,000 of your savings in a security issued by a large company. The security agreement pays you 8% per year and has a maturity two years from the day you purchased it. What is the total cash flow you expect to receive from this investment, separated into the return on your investment and the return of your investment?

**EXERCISE 1.6**

Investment Return

**LO 3**

Match the terms on the left with the descriptions on the right. Each description should be used only once.

**EXERCISE 1.7**

Accounting Terminology

**LO 3, 4, 5, 7**

| **Term** | **Description** |
|---|---|
| _____ Financial accounting | a. The procedural aspect of accounting that involves keeping detailed records of business transactions, much of which is done today by computers. |
| _____ Management accounting | |
| _____ Financial reporting | |
| _____ Financial statements | b. A broad term that describes all information provided to external users, including but not limited to financial statements. |
| _____ General-purpose assumption | |
| _____ Integrity | c. An important quality of accounting information that allows investors, creditors, management, and other users to rely on the information. |
| _____ Internal control | |
| _____ Public accounting | d. The segment of the accounting profession that relates to providing audit, tax, and consulting services to clients. |
| _____ Bookkeeping | |
| | e. Procedures and processes within an organization that ensure the integrity of accounting information. |
| | f. Statement of financial position (balance sheet), income statement, statement of cash flows. |
| | g. The fact that the same information is provided to various external users, including investors and creditors. |
| | h. The area of accounting that refers to providing information to support internal management decisions. |
| | i. The area of accounting that refers to providing information to support external investment and credit decisions. |

**EXERCISE 1.8**

Accounting Organizations

Match the organizations on the left with the functions on the right. Each function should be used only once.

| Organization | Function |
|---|---|
| _____ Institute of Internal Auditors | a. Government agency responsible for financial reporting by publicly held companies. |
| _____ Securities and Exchange Commission | b. International organization dedicated to the advancement of internal auditing. |
| _____ American Institute of CPAs | c. Private-sector organization that establishes accounting standards. |
| _____ Institute of Management Accountants | d. Organization consisting primarily of accounting educators that encourages improvements in teaching and research. |
| _____ Financial Accounting Standards Board | e. Professional association of Certified Public Accountants. |
| _____ American Accounting Association | f. Organization dedicated to providing members personal and professional development opportunities in the area of management accounting. |

**EXERCISE 1.9**

Financial and Management Accounting

The major focus of accounting information is to facilitate decision making.

**a.** As an investor in a company, what would be your primary objective?

**b.** As a manager of a company, what would be your primary objective?

**c.** Is the same accounting information likely to be equally useful to you in these two different roles?

**EXERCISE 1.10**

Management Accounting Information

Management accounting information is used primarily for internal decision making by an enterprise's management.

**a.** What are the three primary purposes of management accounting information?

**b.** Which of these is the most general and which is the most specific?

**c.** Give several examples of the kinds of decisions that management accounting information supports.

**EXERCISE 1.11**

Accounting Organizations

Describe which professional organization(s) would be of greatest value to you if your position involved each of the following independent roles:

**a.** Accounting educator.

**b.** Management accountant.

**c.** Public accountant.

**EXERCISE 1.12**

Purpose of an Audit

Audits of financial statements are an important part of the accounting process to ensure integrity in financial reporting.

**a.** What is the purpose of an audit?

**b.** As an external user of accounting information, what meaning would you attach to an audit that concludes that the financial statements are fairly presented in conformity with generally accepted accounting principles?

**c.** Would your interest in investing in this same company be affected by an auditor's report that concluded the financial statements were *not* fairly presented? Why or why not?

**EXERCISE 1.13**

Audits of Financial Statements

The annual financial statements of all large, publicly owned corporations are audited.

**a.** What is an audit of financial statements?

**b.** Who performs audits?

**c.** What is the purpose of an audit?

**EXERCISE 1.14**

Ethics and Professional Judgment

Ethical conduct and professional judgment each play important roles in the accounting process.

**a.** In general terms, explain why it is important to society that people who prepare accounting information act in an ethical manner.

**b.** Identify at least three areas in which accountants must exercise *professional judgment,* rather than merely relying on written rules.

Four accounting majors, Maria Acosta, Kenzo Nakao, Helen Martin, and Anthony Mandella, recently graduated from Central University and began professional accounting careers. Acosta entered public accounting, Nakao became a managerial accountant, Martin joined a governmental agency, and Mandella (who had completed a graduate program) became an accounting faculty member.

Assume that each of the four graduates was successful in his or her chosen career. Identify the types of accounting *activities* in which each of these graduates might find themselves specializing several years after graduation.

**\*EXERCISE 1.15**

Careers in Accounting

**LO 8**

Locate the **Tootsie Roll Industries, Inc.** annual report that appears in Appendix A of this text. Briefly peruse the annual report and then respond to the following.
a. Who are the two individuals responsible for the letter to shareholders that precedes the company's financial statements?
b. What are the titles of the three financial statements that the company presents?
c. The financial statements are followed by a series of explanatory notes. What are some of the subjects covered by those notes?
d. Which firm audited the **Tootsie Roll** financial statements for 1999, and what was the general conclusion the firm reached?

**EXERCISE 1.16**

Tootsie Roll Industries, Inc.
General Information

**LO 3, 5**

Due to the introductory nature of this chapter and the conceptual nature of its contents, no items labeled **Problems** are included. In all future chapters you will find a series of Problems that generally include computations, are more complex, and generally require more time to complete than Exercises.

# CASES AND UNSTRUCTURED PROBLEMS

In the early 1980s, **Chrysler Corporation** was in severe financial difficulty and desperately needed large loans for the company to survive. What factors prevented Chrysler from simply providing potential lenders with misleading financial statements to make the company look like a risk-free investment?

**CASE 1.1**

Reliability of Financial Statements

**LO 5**

Divide into groups as instructed by your professor and discuss the following:
a. How does the description of accounting as the "language of business" relate to accounting as being useful for investors and creditors?
b. Explain how the decisions you would make might differ if you were an external investor or a member of an enterprise's management team.

**CASE 1.2**

Objectives of Financial Accounting

**LO 3**

You are employed by a business consulting firm as an information systems specialist. You have just begun an assignment with a start-up company and are discussing with the owner her need for an accounting system. How would you respond to the following questions from the owner?
a. What is the meaning of the term *accounting system?*
b. What is the purpose of an accounting system and what are its basic functions?
c. Who is responsible for designing and implementing an accounting system?

**CASE 1.3**

Accounting Systems

**LO 2**

You have recently completed your college degree with a major in accounting and have accepted a position on the accounting staff of a large corporation. In preparing for your first day on the job, your supervisor suggests that you become familiar with the basic principles included in the code of ethics of the Institute of Management Accountants. Briefly explain what you learn as you study the code and how it might affect your behavior on your new job.

**CASE 1.4**

Codes of Ethics

**LO 7**

---

\* *Supplemental Topic*, "Careers in Accounting."

# *BUSINESS WEEK* ASSIGNMENT

**CASE 1.5**

**LO 3, 4**

The role of the chief financial officer (CFO) in a company is expanding to become that of a strategist, venture capitalist, and chief communicator. In the August 2000 issue of *Business Week,* an article titled "Up from Bean Counter" by Marcia Vickers describes the CFO as a strategic partner, a visionary, someone with global ties who can fill a much broader role than just supervising transactions and keeping track of employee expense reports. He or she must be a strategist, deft communicator, dealmaker, and financier, plus be an expert in information technology and risk management.

If you were to become a CFO of a large company at some time in the future, what kinds of information would you provide for investors and creditors of your company? How would your work support that of the company's top management?

# INTERNET ASSIGNMENTS

**INTERNET 1.1**

Accessing Information on the Internet

**LO 6, 7**

The Internet is a good place to get information that is useful to you in your study of accounting. For example, you can find information about current events, professional accounting organizations, and specific companies that may support your study.

**Instructions**

**a.** Access the Rutgers University Internet site. Identify eight links to many other sites that provide information about accounting.

**www.rutgers.edu/accounting/raw**

**b.** Look under the category Accounting Resources and then Big-Five. Identify the names of the five largest public accounting firms.

**c.** Look under the category Publishers and then the sub-category of U.S. Accounting Publishers to locate the publisher of this textbook.

**d.** Find the Internet sites of the following professional accounting organizations and learn what you can about them from the information provided:

American Accounting Association

Financial Accounting Standards Board

Institute of Internal Auditors

Institute of Management Accountants

*Internet sites are time and date sensitive. It is the purpose of these exercises to have you explore the Internet. You may need to use the Yahoo! search engine* http://www.yahoo.com *(or another favorite search engine) to find a company's current web address.*

# OUR COMMENTS ON THE "YOUR TURN" CASES

**You as an Investor (p. 11)**  Your primary considerations in choosing an investment probably would include the security of your funds and the return you can expect to receive. Concerning security, you would expect to have your investment returned to you at some time in the future. Concerning return on your investment, you would expect a reasonable rate of return on the money you invested. You might have nonfinancial objectives, too. You may be interested in a particular type of company (for example, a car manufacturer, a high-tech organization), or you might be interested in a company that is located in the city where you live.

**You as a Manager (p. 16)**  Manufacturing a product like computers involves many important decisions. For example: From which suppliers should you purchase the parts you need? How should you sell or market your products? To what extent should you rely on parts and labor from countries other than your own? At what price should you sell your computers? Management accounting information is intended to provide internal decision makers information that is useful in answering these and other questions. For example, in pricing your product, what it costs to produce is an important consideration. Management accounting information may also provide insights into how reliable suppliers from other countries are compared to those that are closer to your home base.

**You as a Professional Accountant (p. 23)** This situation puts you in a very difficult position. On the one hand, you want to do the right thing and, in your opinion, that involves an in-depth study of the problem you have found. On the other hand, you are pulled in the direction of doing what your superior says to do because you may respect her position as your superior and because your responsibility is to take directions from the person with whom you are assigned to work. You might want to discuss with your superior the potential implications of the irregularities that you have found and try to convince her that some additional effort to better understand what is going on may be very important. You may want to discuss this with a peer or another person not directly involved in your engagement but whose opinion you value. You may want to talk with a person higher up in the organization than your superior, although you should be careful to avoid creating a conflict with your superior. You probably should keep a record of steps you have taken to resolve the situation and certainly keep your eyes open for a pattern of similar behavior that may be a signal to you that you need to consider a job elsewhere.

## ANSWERS TO SELF-TEST QUESTIONS

**1.** b  **2.** d  **3.** d  **4.** c  **5.** a  **6.** c  **7.** c  **8.** a  **9.** d  **10.** d

# 2

# BASIC FINANCIAL STATEMENTS

## Learning Objectives

*After studying this chapter, you should be able to:*

1. Explain the nature and general purpose of financial statements.

2. Explain certain accounting principles that are important for an understanding of financial statements and how professional judgment by accountants may affect the application of those principles.

3. Demonstrate how certain business transactions affect the elements of the accounting equation: Assets = Liabilities + Owners' Equity.

4. Explain how the statement of financial position, often referred to as the balance sheet, is an expansion of the basic accounting equation.

5. Explain how the income statement reports an enterprise's financial performance for a period of time in terms of the relationship of revenues and expenses.

6. Explain how the statement of cash flows presents the change in cash for a period of time in terms of the company's operating, investing, and financing activities.

7. Explain important relationships among the statement of financial position, income statement, and statement of cash flows, and how these statements relate to each other.

AOL screenshot copyright 2000 America Online, Inc. Used with permission.

8. Explain common forms of business ownership—sole proprietorship, partnership, and corporation—and demonstrate how they differ in terms of their presentation in the statement of financial position.

9. Discuss and illustrate the importance of nonfinancial information to supplement the information in the primary financial statements.

10. Discuss the importance of financial statements to a company and its investors and creditors and why management may take steps to improve the appearance of the company in its financial statements.

# America Online*

**America Online**'s chairman and chief executive officer, Steve Case, has observed that the interactive medium has changed our lives in remarkable ways. The interactive experience is becoming increasingly embedded in consumers' everyday routines, including communicating, shopping, keeping informed about investing, learning, and having fun. **America Online** is leading this interactive revolution with its multiple brands, including **AOL**, **Netscape**, and **CompuServe**.

**America Online** indicates in its annual report that it is financially successful. What information is used to draw this conclusion? As a potential investor in **AOL**, what information would help you assess how successful the company really is and whether you are comfortable committing your investment dollars to it?

Financial statements are important sources of information about a company. They are prepared at least annually, and many companies prepare financial statements on a quarterly (three-month) basis. These statements provide important information on the company's resources, claims on these resources, and how the resources and claims change over time. In short, they allow you to look inside the company and learn what is going on through its financial information.

• • •

In this chapter, you are introduced to the way a company keeps a record of its activities and prepares financial statements that provide useful information to interested parties. This chapter provides a framework for several chapters that follow, so think of this as an introduction to how a company communicates with interested parties about its financial activities.

---

*America Online has now merged with Time Warner to become AOL Time Warner.

# INTRODUCTION TO FINANCIAL STATEMENTS

In Chapter 1 we learned that investors and creditors are particularly interested in cash flows that they might receive. Creditors, for example, are interested in the ability of the enterprise, to which they have made loans or sold merchandise on credit, to meet its payment obligations, which may include payment of interest. Similarly, investors are interested in the market value of their stock holdings, as well as dividends that the enterprise will pay while they own the stock.

One of the primary ways investors and creditors assess the probability that an enterprise will be able to make future cash payments is to study, analyze, and understand the enterprise's financial statements. In the general sense of the word, a *statement* is simply a declaration of something believed to be true. For example, the statement "This pen is blue" is a declaration concerning the color of the pen, which the speaker believes is true. A **financial statement**, therefore, is simply a declaration of what is believed to be true communicated in terms of a monetary unit, such as the dollar. When accountants prepare financial statements, they are describing in financial terms certain attributes of the enterprise that they believe fairly represent its financial activities.

Time is an important factor in preparing and understanding an enterprise's financial statements. Statements might cover a period as short as a week or as long as a year. *Annual financial statements* of companies include information for a year. Financial statements prepared for periods of time shorter than one year (for example, for three months or one month) are referred to as *interim financial statements*. Throughout this text, we use varying lengths of time in referring to financial statements, including both annual and interim periods. As you approach a company's financial statements—either as a user or as a preparer—it is important to establish the time period those statements are intended to cover.

In this chapter, we discuss three primary financial statements:

- Statement of financial position (commonly referred to as the balance sheet).
- Income statement.
- Statement of cash flows.

In introducing these statements, we use the form of business ownership referred to as a *corporation*. The **corporation** is a unique form of organization that allows many owners to combine their resources into a business enterprise that is larger than would probably be possible based on the financial resources of a single or a small number of owners. While businesses of any size may be organized as corporations, many large businesses are corporations because of their need for the large amount of capital that the corporate form of business organization makes possible. Later in this chapter we briefly introduce two other forms of business organization—the sole proprietorship and the partnership—which may be alternatives to the corporate form for some business enterprises.

**LO 1**

Explain the nature and general purpose of financial statements.

The names of the three primary financial statements are descriptive of the information you will find in each. The **statement of financial position**, or **balance sheet**, for example, is a financial statement that describes where the enterprise stands at a specific date. It is sometimes described as a snapshot of the business in financial or dollar terms (that is, what the enterprise "looks like" at a specific date).

As businesses operate, they engage in transactions that create revenues and incur expenses that are necessary to earn those revenues. An **income statement** is an activity statement that depicts the revenues and expenses for a designated period of time. Revenues are transactions in which the enterprise is involved that already have resulted in positive cash flows or that are expected to do so in the near future, meaning that cash will come *into* the enterprise as a result of the transaction. For example, a company might sell a product for $100. This revenue transaction results in an immediate positive cash flow into the enterprise if the transaction is carried out in cash or an expected future cash

**Financial Highlights** [1]

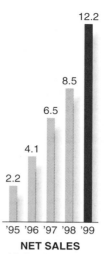

**NET SALES**
(dollars in billions)

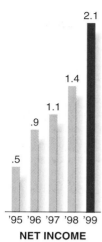

**NET INCOME**
(dollars in billions)

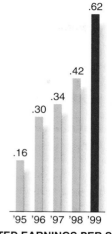

**DILUTED EARNINGS PER SHARE**
(in dollars)

*Financial highlights, such as these from a recent annual report of Cisco Systems, provide a great deal of information that is helpful in evaluating the company's performance.*

### Consolidated Statements of Operations Data[1]
(in millions, except per-share amounts)

| Years Ended | July 31, 1999 | July 25, 1998 | July 26, 1997 |
|---|---|---|---|
| Net sales | $12,154 | $8,488 | $6,452 |
| Income before provision for income taxes | $ 3,316 | $2,311 | $1,891 |
| Net income | $ 2,096[a] | $1,355[b] | $1,051[c] |
| Net income per common share (diluted)* | $ 0.62[a] | $ 0.42[b] | $ 0.34[c] |
| Shares used in per-share calculation (diluted)* | 3,398 | 3,245 | 3,128 |

[a]Net income and net income per share include purchased research and deverlopment expenses of $471 million and acquisition-related costs of $16 million. Pro forma net income and diluted net income per share, excluding these nonrecurring items net of tax, would have been $2,548 million and $0.75, respectively.
[b]Net income and net income per share include purchased research and development expenses of $594 million and realized gains on the sale of a minority stock investment of $5 million. Pro forma net income and diluted net income per share, excluding these nonrecurring items net of tax, would have been $1,885 million and $0.58, respectively.
[c]Net income and net income per share include purchased research and development expenses of $508 million and realized gains on the sale of a minority stock investment of $152 million. Pro forma net income and diluted net income per share, excluding these nonrecurring items net of tax, would have been $1,416 million and $0.45, respectively.
*Reflects the two-for-one stock split effective June 1999.

### Consolidated Balance Sheets Data[1]
(in millions)

| Years Ended | July 31, 1999 | July 25, 1998 | July 26, 1997 |
|---|---|---|---|
| Working capital | $ 1,612 | $2,033 | $2,015 |
| Total assets | $14,725 | $8,972 | $5,493 |
| Shareholders' equity | $11,678 | $7,148 | $4,325 |

[1]All results have been restated to reflect the acquisition of GeoTel Communications Corporation in a pooling-of-interests transaction.

flow if it is a credit transaction in which payment is to be received later. Expenses have the opposite effect in that they result in an immediate cash flow *out* of the enterprise (if a cash transaction) or an expected future flow of cash out of the enterprise (if a credit transaction). For example, if a company incurs a certain expense of $75 and pays it at that time, an immediate cash outflow takes place. If payment is delayed until some future date, the transaction represents an expected future cash outflow. Revenues result in **positive cash flows**—either past, present, or future—while expenses result in **negative cash flows**—either past, present, or future. *Positive* and *negative* indicate the directional impact on cash. The term *net income* (or *net loss*) is simply the difference between revenues and expenses for a designated period of time.

The **statement of cash flows** is particularly important in understanding an enterprise for purposes of investment and credit decisions. As its name implies, the statement of cash flows depicts the ways cash has changed during a designated period—the cash received from revenues and other transactions as well as the cash paid for certain expenses and other acquisitions during the period. While the interest of investors and creditors is in cash flows to themselves, rather than to the enterprise, information about cash activity of the enterprise is considered to be an important signal to investors and creditors.

## A STARTING POINT: STATEMENT OF FINANCIAL POSITION

All three financial statements contain important information, but each includes different information. For that reason, it is important to understand all three financial statements and how they relate to each other. The way they relate is sometimes referred to as **articulation**, a term we will say more about later in this chapter.

A logical starting point for understanding financial statements is the statement of financial position, also called the balance sheet. The purpose of this statement is to demonstrate where the company stands, in financial terms, at a specific point in time. As we will see later in this chapter, the other financial statements relate to the statement of financial position and show how important aspects of a company's financial position change over time. Beginning with the statement of financial position also allows us to understand certain basic accounting principles and terminologies that are important for understanding all financial statements.

Every business prepares a balance sheet at the end of the year, and many companies prepare one at the end of each month, week, or even day. It consists of a listing of the assets, the liabilities, and the owners' equity of a business. The *date* is important, as the financial position of a business may change quickly. The following statement shows the financial position of Vagabond Travel Agency at December 31, 2002.

*A balance sheet shows financial position at a specific date.*

**VAGABOND TRAVEL AGENCY**
**Balance Sheet**
**December 31, 2002**

| Assets | | Liabilities & Owners' Equity | | |
|---|---|---|---|---|
| Cash | $ 22,500 | Liabilities: | | |
| Notes Receivable | 10,000 | Notes Payable | $ 41,000 | |
| Accounts Receivable | 60,500 | Accounts Payable | 36,000 | |
| Supplies | 2,000 | Salaries Payable | 3,000 | $ 80,000 |
| Land | 100,000 | Owners' equity: | | |
| Building | 90,000 | Capital Stock | $150,000 | |
| Office Equipment | 15,000 | Retained Earnings | 70,000 | 220,000 |
| Total | $300,000 | Total | | $300,000 |

Let us briefly describe several features of this balance sheet. First, the heading communicates three things: (1) the name of the business, (2) the name of the financial statement, and (3) the date. The body of the balance sheet also consists of three distinct sections: *assets, liabilities,* and *owners' equity.*

Notice that cash is listed first among the assets, followed by notes receivable, accounts receivable, supplies, and any other assets that will *soon be converted into cash or used up in business operations.* Following these relatively "liquid" assets are the more "permanent" assets, such as land, buildings, and equipment.

Liabilities are shown before owners' equity. Each major type of liability (such as notes payable, accounts payable, and salaries payable) is listed separately, followed by a figure for total liabilities.

Owners' equity is separated into two parts—capital stock and retained earnings. Capital stock represents the amount that owners originally paid into the company to become owners. It consists of individual shares and each owner has a set number of shares. Notice in this illustration that capital stock totals $150,000. This means that the assigned value of the shares held by owners, multiplied by the number of shares, equals $150,000. For example, assuming an assigned value of $10 per share, there would be 15,000 shares ($10 × 15,000 = $150,000). Alternatively, the assigned value might be $5 per share, in which case there would be 30,000 shares ($5 × 30,000 = $150,000). The retained earning part of owners' equity is simply the accumulated earnings of previous years that remain within the enterprise. Retained earnings is considered part of the equity of the owners and serves to enhance their investment in the business.

Finally, notice that the amount of total assets ($300,000) is *equal* to the total amount of liabilities and owners' equity (also $300,000). This relationship *always exists*—in fact, the *equality of these totals* is why this financial statement is frequently called a *balance sheet.*

**The Concept of the Business Entity** Generally accepted accounting principles require that a set of financial statements describe the affairs of a specific business entity. This concept is called the *entity principle.*

A **business entity** is an economic unit that engages in identifiable business activities. For accounting purposes, the business entity is regarded as *separate from the personal activities of its owners.* For example, Vagabond is a business organization operating as a travel agency. Its owners may have personal bank accounts, homes, cars, and even other businesses. These items are not involved in the operation of the travel agency and should not appear in Vagabond's financial statements.

If the owners were to commingle their personal activities with the transactions of the business, the resulting financial statements would fail to describe clearly the financial activities of the business organization. Distinguishing business from personal activities of the owners may require judgment by the accountant.

**LO 2**

Explain certain accounting principles that are important for an understanding of financial statements and how professional judgment by accountants may affect the application of those principles.

## Assets

**Assets** are economic resources that are owned by a business and are expected to benefit future operations. In most cases, the benefit to future operations comes in the form of positive future cash flows. The positive future cash flows may come directly as the asset is converted into cash (collection of a receivable) or indirectly as the asset is used in operating the business to create other assets that result in positive future cash flows (building and land used to manufacture a product for sale). Assets may have definite physical form such as buildings, machinery, or an inventory of merchandise. On the other hand, some assets exist not in physical or tangible form, but in the form of valuable legal claims or rights; examples are amounts due from customers, investments in government bonds, and patent rights.

One of the most basic and at the same time most controversial problems in accounting is determining the dollar amount for the various assets of a business. At present, generally accepted accounting principles call for the valuation of many assets in a balance sheet at *cost,* rather than at their current value. The specific accounting principles supporting cost as the basis for asset valuation are discussed below.

**The Cost Principle**   Assets such as land, buildings, merchandise, and equipment are typical of the many economic resources that are required in producing revenue for the business. The prevailing accounting view is that such assets should be presented at their cost. When we say that an asset is shown in the balance sheet at its *historical cost,* we mean the original amount the business entity paid to acquire the asset. This amount may be different from the asset's current market value.

For example, let us assume that a business buys a tract of land for use as a building site, paying $100,000 in cash. The amount to be entered in the accounting records for the asset will be the cost of $100,000. If we assume a booming real estate market, a fair estimate of the market value of the land 10 years later might be $250,000. Although the market price or economic value of the land has risen greatly, the accounting amount as shown in the accounting records and in the balance sheet would continue unchanged at the cost of $100,000. This policy of accounting for many assets at their cost is often referred to as the **cost principle** of accounting.

Exceptions to the cost principle are found in some of the most liquid assets (i.e., assets that are expected to soon become cash). Amounts receivable from customers are generally included in the balance sheet at their *net realizable value,* which is an amount that approximates the cash that will be received when the receivable is collected. Similarly, certain investments in other enterprises are included in the balance sheet at their current market value if management's plan includes conversion into cash in the near future.

In reading a balance sheet, it is important to keep in mind that the dollar amounts listed for most assets do not indicate the prices at which the assets could be sold or the prices at which they could be replaced. A frequently misunderstood feature of a balance sheet is that it *does not* show how much the business currently is worth.

**The Going-Concern Assumption**   *Why* don't accountants change the recorded amounts of assets to correspond with changing market prices for these properties? One reason is that assets like land and buildings are being used to house the business and were acquired for *use* and not for resale; in fact, these assets usually cannot be sold without disrupting the business. The balance sheet of a business is prepared on the assumption that the business is a continuing enterprise, or a **going concern**. Consequently, the present estimated prices at which assets like land and buildings could be sold are of less importance than if these properties were intended for sale. These are frequently among the largest dollar amounts of a company's assets. Determining that an enterprise is a going concern may require judgment by the accountant.

**The Objectivity Principle**   Another reason for using cost rather than current market values in accounting for most assets is the need for a definite, factual basis for valuation. The cost of land, buildings, and many other assets purchased for cash can be rather definitely determined. Accountants use the term *objective* to describe asset valuations that are factual and can be verified by independent experts. For example, if land is shown on the

---

**YOUR TURN**

  **You as a Home Owner**

Assume you have owned your home for 10 years and need to report the value of your home to the city assessor for real estate tax assessment purposes. What information would you provide and how would you show that your information is objective?

Now, assume you are planning to sell your home. What type of information would you provide to potential buyers and how would you show that your information is objective? What ethical issues arise in these two situations that the objectivity principle helps address?

*Our comments appear on page 83.*

balance sheet at cost, any CPA who performed an audit of the business would be able to find objective evidence that the land was actually measured at the cost incurred in acquiring it. On the other hand, estimated market values for assets such as buildings and specialized machinery are not factual and objective. Market values are constantly changing, and estimates of the prices at which assets could be sold are largely a matter of judgment.

At the date an asset is acquired, the cost and market value are usually the same. With the passage of time, however, the current market value of assets is likely to differ considerably from the cost recorded in the owners' accounting records.

**The Stable-Dollar Assumption**   A limitation of measuring assets at historical cost is that the value of the monetary unit or dollar is not always stable. **Inflation** is a term used to describe the situation where the value of the monetary unit decreases, meaning that it will purchase less than it did previously. **Deflation**, on the other hand, is the opposite situation in which the value of the monetary unit increases, meaning that it will purchase more than it did previously. Typically, countries like the United States have experienced inflation rather than deflation. When inflation becomes severe, historical cost amounts for assets lose their relevance as a basis for making business decisions. For this reason, some consideration has been given to the use of balance sheets that would show assets at current appraised values or at replacement costs rather than at historical cost.

Accountants in the United States, by adhering to the cost basis of accounting, are implying that the dollar is a stable unit of measurement, as is the gallon, the acre, or the mile. The cost principle and the **stable-dollar assumption** work very well in periods of stable prices but are less satisfactory under conditions of rapid inflation. For example, if a company bought land 20 years ago for $100,000 and purchased a second similar tract of land today for $500,000, the total cost of land shown by the accounting records would be $600,000. This treatment ignores the fact that dollars spent 20 years ago had greater purchasing power than today's dollar. Thus the $600,000 total for the cost of land is a mixture of two "sizes" of dollars with different purchasing power.

After much research into this problem, the FASB required on a trial basis that large corporations annually disclose financial data adjusted for the effects of inflation. But after several years of experimentation, the FASB concluded that the costs of developing this information exceeded its usefulness. At the present time, this disclosure is optional, as judged appropriate by the accountant who prepares the financial statements.

 Many countries experience prolonged and serious inflation. Inflation can undermine the stable currency assumption. Several methods have been used in foreign countries to show the impact of inflation on a company's financial position. In the recent past, Brazilian corporate law required companies to adjust their balance sheets to current purchasing power by using indexes provided by the government. The indexes were used to devalue the local currency to provide a more objective representation of the financial condition of the company. During the 1980s and early '90s the United Kingdom asked companies to provide supplementary inflation-adjusted financial statements.

**CASE IN POINT**

## Liabilities

**Liabilities** are debts. They represent negative future cash flows for the enterprise. The person or organization to whom the debt is owed is called a **creditor**.

All businesses have liabilities; even the largest and most successful companies often purchase merchandise, supplies, and services "on account." The liabilities arising from such purchases are called *accounts payable.* Many businesses borrow money to finance expansion or the purchase of high-cost assets. When obtaining a loan, the borrower usually must sign a formal note payable. A *note payable* is a written promise to repay the amount owed by a particular date and usually calls for the payment of interest as well.

*Accounts payable,* in contrast to notes payable, involve no written promises and generally do not call for interest payments. In essence, a note payable is a *more formal* arrangement.

When a company has both notes payable and accounts payable, the two types of liabilities are listed separately in the balance sheet. Liabilities are usually listed in the order in which they are expected to be repaid.[1] Liabilities that are similar may be combined to avoid unnecessary detail in the financial statement. For example, if a company had several expenses payable at the end of the year (for example, wages, interest, taxes), it might combine these into a single line called *accrued expenses.* The word *accrued* is an accounting term communicating that the payment of certain expenses has been delayed or deferred.

Liabilities represent claims against the borrower's assets. As we shall see, the owners of a business *also* have claims to the company's assets. But in the eyes of the law, creditors' claims *take priority* over those of the owners. This means that creditors are entitled to be *paid in full,* even if such payment would exhaust the assets of the business and leave nothing for its owners.

## Owners' Equity

**Owners' equity** represents the *owners' claim* on the assets of the business. Because creditors' claims have legal priority over those of the owner, owners' equity is a *residual amount.* If you are the owner of a business, you are entitled to assets that are left after the claims of creditors have been satisfied in full. Therefore, owners' equity is always equal to *total assets minus total liabilities.* For example, using the data from the illustrated balance sheet of Vagabond Travel Agency (page 42):

| | |
|---|---:|
| Vagabond has total assets of | $300,000 |
| And total liabilities of | (80,000) |
| Therefore, the owners' equity must be | $220,000 |

Owners' equity does *not* represent a specific claim to cash or any other particular asset. Rather, it is the owners' overall financial interest in the entire company.

**Increases in Owners' Equity**    The owners' equity in a business comes from two sources:

1. *Investments of cash or other assets* by owners.
2. *Earnings* from profitable operation of the business.

**Decreases in Owners' Equity**    Decreases in owners' equity also are caused in two ways:

1. *Payments of cash or transfers of other assets* to owners.
2. *Losses* from unprofitable operation of the business.

Accounting for payments to owners and net losses are addressed in later chapters.

## The Accounting Equation

A fundamental characteristic of every statement of financial position is that the total for assets always equals the total of liabilities plus owners' equity. This agreement or balance of total assets with the total of liabilities and owners' equity is the reason for

---

[1]Short-term liabilities generally are those due within one year. Long-term liabilities are shown separately in the balance sheet, after the listing of all short-term liabilities. Long-term liabilities are addressed in Chapter 10.

calling this financial statement a *balance sheet.* But *why* do total assets equal the total of liabilities and owners' equity?

The dollar totals on the two sides of the balance sheet are always equal because these two sides are *two views of the same business.* The listing of assets shows us what things the business owns; the listing of liabilities and owners' equity tells us who supplied these resources to the business and how much each group supplied. Everything that a business owns has been supplied to it either by creditors or by the owners. Therefore, the total claims of the creditors plus the claims of the owners equal the total assets of the business.

The equality of assets on the one hand and of the claims of the creditors and the owners on the other hand is expressed in the following **accounting equation:**

LO 3
Demonstrate how certain business transactions affect the elements of the accounting equation: Assets = Liabilities + Owners' Equity.

$$\textbf{Assets} = \textbf{Liabilities} + \textbf{Owners' Equity}$$
$$\$300{,}000 = \$80{,}000 \quad + \$220{,}000$$

*The accounting equation*

The amounts listed in the equation were taken from the balance sheet illustrated on page 42. The balance sheet is simply a detailed statement of this equation. To illustrate this relationship, compare the balance sheet of Vagabond Travel Agency with the above equation.

To emphasize that the owners' equity is a *residual claim,* secondary to the claims of creditors, it is often helpful to transpose the terms of the equation, as follows:

$$\textbf{Assets} - \textbf{Liabilities} = \textbf{Owners' Equity}$$
$$\$300{,}000 - \$80{,}000 \quad = \$220{,}000$$

*Alternative form of the accounting equation*

Notice that if a business has liabilities *in excess* of its assets, the owners' equity will be a *negative* amount.

Every business transaction, no matter how simple or how complex, can be expressed in terms of its effect on the accounting equation. A thorough understanding of the equation and some practice in using it are essential to the student of accounting.

Regardless of whether a business grows or contracts, the equality between the assets and the claims against the assets is always maintained. Any increase in the amount of total assets is necessarily accompanied by an equal increase on the other side of the equation— that is, by an increase in either the liabilities or the owners' equity. Any decrease in total assets is necessarily accompanied by a corresponding decrease in liabilities or owners' equity. The continuing equality of the two sides of the balance sheet can best be illustrated by taking a new business as an example and observing the effects of various transactions.

## The Effects of Business Transactions: An Illustration

How does a statement of financial position come about? What has occurred in the past for it to exist at any point in time? The statement of financial position is a picture of the results of past business transactions that has been captured by the company's information system and organized into a concise financial description of where the company stands at a point in time. The specific items and dollar amounts are the direct results of the transactions in which the company has engaged. The balance sheets of two separate companies would almost certainly be different due to the unique nature, timing, and dollar amounts of each company's business transactions.

To illustrate how a balance sheet comes about, and later to show how the income statement and statement of cash flows relate to the balance sheet, we use an example of a small auto repair business, Overnight Auto Service.

**The Business Entity**    Assume that Michael McBryan, an experienced auto mechanic, opens his own automotive repair business, Overnight Auto Service. A distinctive feature of Overnight's operations is that all repair work is done at night. This strategy offers customers the convenience of dropping off their cars in the evening and picking them up the following morning.

Operating at night also enables Overnight to minimize its labor costs. Instead of hiring full-time employees, Overnight offers part-time work to mechanics who already have day jobs at major automobile dealerships. This eliminates the need for costly employee training programs and for such payroll fringe benefits as group health insurance and employees' pension plans, benefits usually associated with full-time employment.

**Overnight's Accounting Policies**  McBryan has taken several courses in accounting and maintains Overnight's accounting records himself. He knows that small businesses such as his are not required to prepare formal financial statements, but he prepares them anyway. He believes they will be useful to him in running the business. In addition, if Overnight is successful, McBryan plans to open more locations. He anticipates needing to raise substantial amounts of capital from investors and creditors. He believes that the financial history provided by a series of monthly financial statements will be very helpful in attracting investment capital.

**The Company's First Transaction**  McBryan officially started Overnight on January 20, 2002.  On that day he received a charter from the state to begin a small, closely held corporation whose owners consisted of himself and several family members. Capital stock issued to these investors included 8,000 shares at $10 per share. McBryan opened a bank account in the name of Overnight Auto Service, into which he deposited the $80,000 received from the issuance of the capital stock.

This transaction provided Overnight with its first asset—Cash—and also created the initial owners' equity in the business entity. A balance sheet showing the company's financial position after this initial transaction follows:

*Beginning balance sheet of a new business*

| **OVERNIGHT AUTO SERVICE**<br>**Balance Sheet**<br>**January 20, 2002** | | |
|---|---|---|
| **Assets** | **Owners' Equity** | |
| Cash . . . . . . . . . . . . . . $80,000 | Capital Stock . . . . . . . . . . . . . . . . . . $80,000 | |

Overnight's next two transactions involved the acquisition of a suitable site for its business operations.

**Purchase of an Asset for Cash**  Representing the business, McBryan negotiated with both the City of Santa Teresa and the Metropolitan Transit Authority (MTA) to purchase an abandoned bus garage. (The MTA owned the garage, but the city owned the land.)

On January 21, Overnight purchased the land from the city for *$52,000 cash.* This transaction had two immediate effects on the company's financial position: first, Overnight's cash was reduced by $52,000; and second, the company acquired a new asset—Land. The company's financial position after this transaction was as follows:

*Balance sheet totals unchanged by purchase of land for cash*

| **OVERNIGHT AUTO SERVICE**<br>**Balance Sheet**<br>**January 21, 2002** | | |
|---|---|---|
| **Assets** | **Owners' Equity** | |
| Cash . . . . . . . . . . . . . . $28,000 | Capital Stock . . . . . . . . . . . . . . . . . $80,000 | |
| Land . . . . . . . . . . . . . . 52,000 | | |
| Total . . . . . . . . . . . . . . $80,000 | Total . . . . . . . . . . . . . . . . . . . . . . $80,000 | |

**Purchase of an Asset and Financing Part of the Cost**   On January 22, Overnight purchased the old garage building from Metropolitan Transit Authority for *$36,000*. Overnight made a cash down payment of *$6,000* and issued a 90-day non-interest-bearing note payable for the *$30,000* balance owed.

As a result of this transaction, Overnight had (1) $6,000 less cash; (2) a new asset, Building, which cost $36,000; and (3) a new liability, Notes Payable, in the amount of $30,000. This transaction is reflected in the following balance sheet:

**OVERNIGHT AUTO SERVICE**
**Balance Sheet**
**January 22, 2002**

| Assets | | Liabilities & Owners' Equity | |
|---|---|---|---|
| Cash . . . . . . . . . . . . . . . | $ 22,000 | Liabilities: | |
| Land . . . . . . . . . . . . . . | 52,000 | Notes Payable . . . . . . . . . . . . . . . | $ 30,000 |
| Building . . . . . . . . . . . . | 36,000 | Owners' equity: | |
| | | Capital Stock . . . . . . . . . . . . . . . | 80,000 |
| Total . . . . . . . . . . . . . . | $110,000 | Total . . . . . . . . . . . . . . . . . . . . . | $110,000 |

*Totals increased equally by debt incurred in acquiring assets*

**Purchase of an Asset "On Account"**   On January 23, Overnight purchased tools and automotive repair equipment from Snap-On Tools Corp. The purchase price was *$13,800*, due within 60 days. After this purchase, Overnight's financial position was as follows:

**OVERNIGHT AUTO SERVICE**
**Balance Sheet**
**January 23, 2002**

| Assets | | Liabilities & Owners' Equity | |
|---|---|---|---|
| Cash . . . . . . . . . . . . . . . | $ 22,000 | Liabilities: | |
| Land . . . . . . . . . . . . . . | 52,000 | Notes Payable . . . . . . . . . . . . . . | $ 30,000 |
| Building . . . . . . . . . . . . | 36,000 | Accounts Payable . . . . . . . . . . . . | 13,800 |
| Tools and Equipment . . . | 13,800 | Total liabilities . . . . . . . . . . . . . . | $ 43,800 |
| | | Owners' equity: | |
| | | Capital Stock . . . . . . . . . . . . . . | 80,000 |
| Total . . . . . . . . . . . . . . | $123,800 | Total . . . . . . . . . . . . . . . . . . . . . | $123,800 |

*Totals increased equally by purchase of equipment on credit*

**Sale of an Asset**   After taking delivery of the new tools and equipment, Overnight found that it had purchased more than it needed. Ace Towing, a neighboring business, offered to buy the excess items. On January 24, Overnight sold some of its new tools to Ace for *$1,800,* a price equal to Overnight's cost.[2] Ace made no down payment but agreed to pay the amount due within 45 days. This transaction reduced Overnight's tools and equipment by $1,800 and created a new asset, Accounts Receivable, for that same amount. A balance sheet as of January 24 appears at the top of the following page.

---

[2] Sales of assets at prices above or below cost result in gains or losses. Such transactions are discussed in later chapters.

*No change in totals by sale of equipment at cost*

| OVERNIGHT AUTO SERVICE<br>Balance Sheet<br>January 24, 2002 | | | |
|---|---|---|---|
| **Assets** | | **Liabilities & Owners' Equity** | |
| Cash . . . . . . . . . . . . . . | $ 22,000 | Liabilities: | |
| Accounts Receivable . . . | 1,800 | Notes Payable . . . . . . . . . . . . . | $ 30,000 |
| Land . . . . . . . . . . . . . | 52,000 | Accounts Payable . . . . . . . . . . . | 13,800 |
| Building . . . . . . . . . . . | 36,000 | Total liabilities . . . . . . . . . . . . | $ 43,800 |
| Tools and Equipment . . . | 12,000 | Owners' equity: | |
| | | Capital Stock . . . . . . . . . . . . . | 80,000 |
| Total . . . . . . . . . . . . . | $123,800 | Total . . . . . . . . . . . . . . . . . . | $123,800 |

**Collection of an Account Receivable**   On January 26, Overnight received $600 from Ace Towing as partial settlement of its account receivable from Ace. This transaction caused an increase in Overnight's cash but a decrease of the same amount in accounts receivable. This transaction converts one asset into another of equal value; there is no change in the amount of total assets. After this transaction, Overnight's financial position may be summarized as follows:

*Totals unchanged by collection of a receivable*

| OVERNIGHT AUTO SERVICE<br>Balance Sheet<br>January 26, 2002 | | | |
|---|---|---|---|
| **Assets** | | **Liabilities & Owners' Equity** | |
| Cash . . . . . . . . . . . . . . | $ 22,600 | Liabilities: | |
| Accounts Receivable . . . | 1,200 | Notes Payable . . . . . . . . . . . . . | $ 30,000 |
| Land . . . . . . . . . . . . . | 52,000 | Accounts Payable . . . . . . . . . . . | 13,800 |
| Building . . . . . . . . . . . | 36,000 | Total liabilities . . . . . . . . . . . . | $ 43,800 |
| Tools and Equipment . . . | 12,000 | Owners' equity: | |
| | | Capital Stock . . . . . . . . . . . . . | 80,000 |
| Total . . . . . . . . . . . . . | $123,800 | Total . . . . . . . . . . . . . . . . . . | $123,800 |

**Payment of a Liability**   On January 27, Overnight made a partial payment of $6,800 on its account payable to Snap-On Tools. This transaction reduced Overnight's cash and accounts payable by the same amount, leaving total assets and the total of liabilities plus owners' equity in balance. Overnight's balance sheet at January 27 appears below:

*Both totals decreased by paying a liability*

| OVERNIGHT AUTO SERVICE<br>Balance Sheet<br>January 27, 2002 | | | |
|---|---|---|---|
| **Assets** | | **Liabilities & Owners' Equity** | |
| Cash . . . . . . . . . . . . . . | $ 15,800 | Liabilities: | |
| Accounts Receivable . . . | 1,200 | Notes Payable . . . . . . . . . . . . . | $ 30,000 |
| Land . . . . . . . . . . . . . | 52,000 | Accounts Payable . . . . . . . . . . . | 7,000 |
| Building . . . . . . . . . . . | 36,000 | Total liabilities . . . . . . . . . . . . | $ 37,000 |
| Tools and Equipment . . . | 12,000 | Owners' equity: | |
| | | Capital Stock . . . . . . . . . . . . . | 80,000 |
| Total . . . . . . . . . . . . . | $117,000 | Total . . . . . . . . . . . . . . . . . . | $117,000 |

**Earning of Revenue** By the last week in January, McBryan had acquired the assets Overnight needed to start operating, and he began to provide repair services for customers. Rather than recording each individual sale of repair services, he decided to accumulate them and record them at the end of the month. Sales of repair services for the last week of January were $2,200, all of which was received in cash.

Earning of revenue represents the creation of value by Overnight. It also represents an increase in the financial interest of the owners in the company. As a result, cash is increased by $2,200 and owners' equity is increased by the same amount. To distinguish owners' equity that is earned from that which was originally invested by the owners, the account *Retained Earnings* is used in the owners' equity section of the balance sheet. The following balance sheet, as of January 31, reflects the increase in assets (cash) and owners' equity (retained earnings) from the revenue earned and received in cash during the last week of January.

| OVERNIGHT AUTO SERVICE Balance Sheet January 31, 2002 | | | |
|---|---|---|---|
| **Assets** | **Liabilities & Owners' Equity** | | |
| Cash . . . . . . . . . . . . . $ 18,000 | Liabilities: | | |
| Accounts Receivable . . . 1,200 | Notes Payable . . . . . . . | $ 30,000 | |
| Land . . . . . . . . . . . . . 52,000 | Accounts Payable . . . . . | 7,000 | |
| Building . . . . . . . . . . . 36,000 | Total liabilities . . . . . . | | $ 37,000 |
| Tools and Equipment . . . 12,000 | Owners' equity: | | |
| | Capital Stock . . . . . . . . | $ 80,000 | |
| | Retained Earnings . . . . . | 2,200 | $ 82,200 |
| Total . . . . . . . . . . . . . $119,200 | Total . . . . . . . . . . . . . | | $119,200 |

*Revenues increase assets and owners' equity*

**Payment of Expenses** In order to earn the $2,200 of revenue that we have just recorded, Overnight had to pay some operating expenses, namely utilities and wages. McBryan decided to pay all operating expenses at the end of the month. For January, he owed $200 for utilities and $1,200 for wages to his employees, which he paid on January 31. Paying expenses has an opposite effect from revenues on the owners' interest in the company—their investment is reduced. Of course, paying expenses also results in a decrease of cash. The January 31 balance sheet, after the payment of utilities and wages, is as follows:

**LO 4**

Explain how the statement of financial position, often referred to as the balance sheet, is an expansion of the basic accounting equation.

| OVERNIGHT AUTO SERVICE Balance Sheet January 31, 2002 | | | |
|---|---|---|---|
| **Assets** | **Liabilities & Owners' Equity** | | |
| Cash . . . . . . . . . . . . . $ 16,600 | Liabilities: | | |
| Accounts Receivable . . . 1,200 | Notes Payable . . . . . . . | $ 30,000 | |
| Land . . . . . . . . . . . . . 52,000 | Accounts Payable . . . . . | 7,000 | |
| Building . . . . . . . . . . . 36,000 | Total liabilities . . . . . . . | | $ 37,000 |
| Tools and Equipment . . 12,000 | Owners' equity: | | |
| | Capital Stock . . . . . . . . | $ 80,000 | |
| | Retained Earnings . . . . . | 800 | 80,800 |
| Total . . . . . . . . . . . . . $117,800 | Total . . . . . . . . . . . . . | | $117,800 |

*Expenses reduce assets and owners' equity*

Notice that the expenses of $1,400 ($200 for utilities and $1,200 for wages) reduce the amount of retained earnings in the balance sheet. That balance was formerly $2,200, representing the revenues for the last week of January. It is now $800, representing the difference between the revenues for the last week of January and the $1,400 of expenses that Overnight incurred during the same period of time. From this illustration we can see that revenues enhance or increase the financial interest of owners while expenses diminish or reduce the interest of owners. In a corporation, the net effect of this activity is reflected in the balance sheet as retained earnings.

**CASE IN POINT**

The specific assets included in different companies' balance sheets vary considerably and are based primarily on the nature of each company's business. To illustrate, the 1999 balance sheet of **Federal Express** includes over $4.6 billion in property and equipment, the majority of which is flight equipment, assets critical to the company's operations. Property and equipment constitute approximately 60% of the company's total assets. **H. J. Heinz**, on the other hand, reports approximately $2.2 billion of property and equipment in its 1999 balance sheet, consisting primarily of land, buildings, and equipment. This amount represents a much smaller portion of Heinz's total assets—approximately 27%.

## Effects of These Business Transactions on the Accounting Equation

As we learned earlier, the statement of financial position, or balance sheet, is a detailed expression of the accounting equation:

$$\text{Assets} = \text{Liabilities} + \text{Owners' Equity}$$

As we have progressed through a series of business transactions, we have illustrated the effects of Overnight's January transactions on the balance sheet.

To review, Overnight's transactions during January were as follows:

**Jan. 20**   Michael McBryan started the business by depositing $80,000 received from the sale of capital stock in a company bank account.

**Jan. 21**   Purchased land for $52,000, paying cash.

**Jan. 22**   Purchased a building for $36,000, paying $6,000 in cash and issuing a note payable for the remaining $30,000.

**Jan. 23**   Purchased tools and equipment on account, $13,800.

**Jan. 24**   Sold some of the tools at a price equal to their cost, $1,800, collectible within 45 days.

**Jan. 26**   Received $600 in partial collection of the account receivable from the sale of tools.

**Jan. 27**   Paid $6,800 in partial payment of an account payable.

**Jan. 31**   Recorded $2,200 of sales revenue received in cash.

**Jan. 31**   Paid $1,400 of operating expenses in cash—$200 for utilities and $1,200 for wages.

The table on the facing page shows the effects of these transactions on the accounting equation. The effect of each transaction is shown in red. Notice that the "balances," shown in black, are the amounts appearing in Overnight's balance sheets on pages 48–51. Notice also that the accounting equation is in balance after each transaction.

| | Assets | | | | | = | Liabilities | | + | Owners' Equity | |
| | Cash | + Accounts Receivable | + Land | + Building | + Tools and Equipment | = | Notes Payable | + Accounts Payable | + | Capital Stock | Retained Earnings |
|---|---|---|---|---|---|---|---|---|---|---|---|
| Jan. 20 | $80,000 | | | | | = | | | | $80,000 | |
| Balances | $80,000 | | | | | = | | | | $80,000 | |
| Jan. 21 | −52,000 | | +$52,000 | | | = | | | | | |
| Balances | $28,000 | | $52,000 | | | = | | | | $80,000 | |
| Jan. 22 | −6,000 | | | +$36,000 | | = | +$30,000 | | | | |
| Balances | $22,000 | | $52,000 | $36,000 | | = | $30,000 | | | $80,000 | |
| Jan. 23 | | | | | +$13,800 | = | | +$13,800 | | | |
| Balances | $22,000 | | $52,000 | $36,000 | $13,800 | = | $30,000 | $13,800 | | $80,000 | |
| Jan. 24 | | +$1,800 | | | −1,800 | = | | | | | |
| Balances | $22,000 | $1,800 | $52,000 | $36,000 | $12,000 | = | $30,000 | $13,800 | | $80,000 | |
| Jan. 26 | +600 | −600 | | | | = | | | | | |
| Balances | $22,600 | $1,200 | $52,000 | $36,000 | $12,000 | = | $30,000 | $13,800 | | $80,000 | |
| Jan. 27 | −6,800 | | | | | = | | −6,800 | | | |
| Balances | $15,800 | $1,200 | $52,000 | $36,000 | $12,000 | = | $30,000 | $7,000 | | $80,000 | |
| Jan. 31 | +2,200 | | | | | = | | | | | +$2,200 |
| Jan. 31 | −1,400 | | | | | = | | | | | −1,400 |
| Balances | $16,600 | $1,200 | $52,000 | $36,000 | $12,000 | = | $30,000 | $7,000 | | $80,000 | $ 800 |

Statement of Cash Flows

Income Statement

*Multiple transactions significantly change the enterprise's financial position.*

While this table represents the impact of Overnight's transactions on the accounting equation, and thus on its financial position as shown in its balance sheet, we can now see how the other two financial statements enter the picture. Specifically, the income statement is a separate statement that shows how the statement of financial position changed as a result of its revenue and expense transactions, and the statement of cash flows shows how the company's cash increased and decreased during the period. In other words, the income statement is simply a separate financial statement that shows how retained earnings changed because of revenues and expenses during the period (far right column). The statement of cash flows is a separate financial statement that details how the company's cash changed during the period (far left column).

**YOUR TURN**

### You as a Working College Student

Assume you are out of school for the summer and decide to begin a small business to make money to help cover the cost of school next year and to have spending money this summer. You decide to establish a lawn care service. What assets would you expect to need to start and maintain your business? Assuming you are successful in getting the business started, what revenues and expenses would you expect to incur as you run your business? How would you know if you were doing well in terms of covering your costs and earning money for school next year?

*Our comments appear on page 83.

## INCOME STATEMENT

**LO 5**

Explain how the income statement reports an enterprise's financial performance for a period of time in terms of the relationship of revenues and expenses.

The income statement is a summarization of the company's revenue and expense transactions for a period of time. It is particularly important for the company's owners, creditors, and other interested parties to understand the income statement. Ultimately the company will succeed or fail based on its ability to earn revenue in excess of its expenses. Once the company's assets are acquired and business commences, revenues and expenses are important sources of cash flows for the enterprise. **Revenues** are increases in the company's assets from its profit-directed activities, and they result in positive cash flows. Similarly, **expenses** are decreases in the company's assets from its profit-directed activities, and they result in negative cash flows. *Net income* is the difference between the two. Should a company find itself in the undesirable situation of having expenses greater than revenues, we call the difference a *net loss*.

Overnight's income statement for January is relatively simple because the company did not have a large number of complex revenue and expense transactions.[3] Taking information directly from the Owners' Equity column of the previous table, we can prepare the company's income statement as follows:

---

[3] In this illustration, only revenue and expense transactions change the amount of owners' equity from the original $80,000 investment of the owner. Examples of other events and transactions that affect the amount of owners' equity, but that are *not included in net income,* are the sale of additional shares of capital stock and the payment of dividends to shareholders. These subjects are covered in later chapters.

| OVERNIGHT AUTO SERVICE |
| :---: |
| **Income Statement** |
| **For the Period January 20–31, 2002** |

| | | |
| --- | --- | --- |
| Sales Revenues . . . . . . . . . . . . . . . . . . | | $2,200 |
| Operating expenses: | | |
| Wages . . . . . . . . . . . . . . . | $1,200 | |
| Utilities . . . . . . . . . . . . . . | 200 | 1,400 |
| Net income . . . . . . . . . . . . . . . . . . . . | | $ 800 |

*An income statement displays revenues and expenses for a period of time.*

Notice that the heading for the income statement refers to a *period* of time rather than a *point* in time, as was the case with the balance sheet. The income statement reports on the financial performance of the company in terms of earning revenue and incurring expenses *over a period of time* and explains, in part, how the company's financial position changed between the beginning and ending of that period.

The relationship of net income to revenue or sales can vary considerably from company to company. For example, in the 1999 income statement of **Microsoft**, net income ($3,454 million) is reported to be almost 29% of sales. In contrast, in the 1999 income statement of **H. J. Heinz**, net income ($474 million) is only slightly more than 5% of sales. Between these two, the 1999 income statement of **Cisco Systems** reports net income ($2,096 million) at slightly more than 17% of sales.

**CASE IN POINT**

## STATEMENT OF CASH FLOWS

We already have established the importance of cash flows to investors and creditors and that the cash flows of the company are an important consideration in investors' and creditors' assessments of cash flows to them. As a result, a second set of information that is particularly important concerning how the financial position changed between two points in time (that is, the beginning and end of a month or year) is cash flow information.

We can use the entire Cash column of the analysis on page 53 to create a statement of cash flows for Overnight Auto Service. The statement classifies the various cash flows into three categories—operating, investing, and financing—and relates these categories to the beginning and ending cash balances. Cash flows from **operating activities** are the cash effects of revenue and expense transactions that are included in the income statement.[4] Cash flows from **investing activities** are the cash effects of purchasing and selling assets. Cash flows from **financing activities** are the cash effects of the owners investing in the company and creditors loaning money to the company and the repayment of either or both.

The statement of cash flows for Overnight Auto Service for the period January 20–31 is as follows:

**LO 6**

Explain how the statement of cash flows presents the change in cash for a period of time in terms of the company's operating, investing, and financing activities.

---

[4] In this illustration, net cash amounts provided by operating activities and net income are equal. This is because all revenues and all expenses are cash transactions. This will not always be the case. As we learn more about the accrual method of accounting, you will see that revenues and expenses may be recorded in a different accounting period than the one when cash is received or paid. This will cause net income and net cash from operating activities to be different amounts.

### OVERNIGHT AUTO SERVICE
### Statement of Cash Flows
### For the Period January 20–31, 2002

| | | |
|---|---:|---:|
| Cash flows from operating activities: | | |
| Cash received from revenue transactions . . . . . . . . . . . | $ 2,200 | |
| Cash paid for expenses . . . . . . . . . . . . . . . . . . . . . . . | (1,400) | |
| Net cash provided by operating activities . . . . . . . . . . . | | $ 800 |
| | | |
| Cash flows from investing activities: | | |
| Purchase of land . . . . . . . . . . . . . . . . . . . . . . . . . . . . | $(52,000) | |
| Purchase of building . . . . . . . . . . . . . . . . . . . . . . . . . | (6,000) | |
| Purchase of tools . . . . . . . . . . . . . . . . . . . . . . . . . . . | (6,800) | |
| Sale of tools . . . . . . . . . . . . . . . . . . . . . . . . . . . . . . . | 600 | |
| Net cash used by investing activities . . . . . . . . . . . . . . | | (64,200) |
| | | |
| Cash flows from financing activities: | | |
| Investment by owner . . . . . . . . . . . . . . . . . . . . . . . . . | | 80,000 |
| Increase in cash for the period . . . . . . . . . . . . . . . . . . | | $16,600 |
| Cash balance, January 20, 2002 . . . . . . . . . . . . . . . . . | | -0- |
| Cash balance, January 31, 2002 . . . . . . . . . . . . . . . . . | | $16,600 |

*A statement of cash flows shows how cash changed during the period*

Notice that the operating, investing, and financing categories include both positive and negative cash flows. (The negative cash flows are in parentheses.) Also notice that the combined total of the three categories of the statement (increase of $16,600) explains the total change from the beginning to the end of the month. On January 20, the beginning balance was zero because the company was started at that time. For February, Overnight's beginning cash balance will be $16,600, and the statement of cash flows will explain how that number either increased to a higher balance or was reduced to a lower balance as a result of its cash activities during that month. Notice also that several transactions and parts of transactions had no cash effects and, therefore, are not included in the statement of cash flows. For example, on January 22, Overnight purchased land for $36,000, only $6,000 of which was paid in cash. The remaining $30,000 is not included in the statement of cash flows because it did not affect the amount of cash. Similarly, on January 23, Overnight purchased tools and equipment for $13,800, paying no cash at that time. That transaction has no cash effect on January 23, although the cash payment of $6,800 on January 27, which is a continuation of that transaction, did affect cash and is included in the statement of cash flows. Transactions that did not affect cash are called *noncash investing and financing transactions.* In a formal statement of cash flows, these transactions are required to be noted as we explain later in this text, even though they do not affect the actual flow of cash into and out of the company.

**CASE IN POINT**

It is not unusual for a company to report an increase in cash from operating activities, but a decrease in the total amount of cash. This outcome results from decreases in cash from investing and/or financing activities. For example, in a recent year **Carnival Corporation**, which owns and operates several cruise lines, reported cash provided by operating activities of almost $1.1 billion but a decrease in total cash of almost $3 million. This was due primarily to large expenditures for property and equipment, such as cruise ships, which are presented as investing activities in the statement of cash flows.

# RELATIONSHIPS AMONG FINANCIAL STATEMENTS

As our discussion of Overnight Auto Service indicates, the statement of financial position (balance sheet), the income statement, and the statement of cash flows are all based on the same transactions, but they present different "views" of the company. They should not be thought of as alternatives to each other; rather, all are important in terms of presenting key financial information about the company.

The following diagram explains how the three financial statements relate to the period of time they cover. The horizontal line represents time (for example, a month or a year). At the beginning and ending points in time, the company prepares a statement of financial position (balance sheet) that gives a static look in financial terms of where the company stands. The other two financial statements—the income statement and the statement of cash flows—cover the intervening *period of time* between the two balance sheets and help explain important changes that occurred during the period.

**LO 7**

Explain important relationships among the statement of financial position, income statement, and statement of cash flows, and how these statements relate to each other.

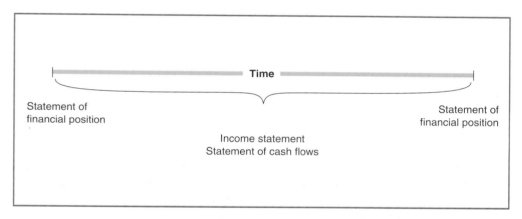

*Financial statements are closely tied to time periods*

If we understand where a company stands financially at two points in time, and if we understand the changes that occurred during the intervening period in terms of the company's profit-seeking activities (income statement) and its cash activities (statement of cash flows), we know a great deal about the company that is valuable in assessing its future cash flows—information that is useful to investors, creditors, management, and others.

Because the balance sheet, income statement, and statement of cash flows are derived from the same underlying financial information, they are said to "articulate," meaning that they relate closely to each other. The diagram on the following page indicates relationships that we have discussed in this chapter as we have introduced these three important financial statements.

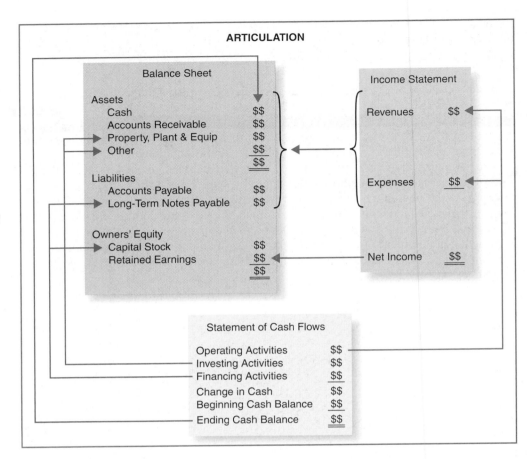

*Financial statements are based on the same underlying transactions*

The balance sheet represents an expansion of the accounting equation and explains the various categories of assets, liabilities, and owners' equity. The income statement explains changes in financial position (that is, assets and liabilities) that result from profit-generating transactions in terms of revenue and expense transactions. The resulting number, net income, represents an addition to the owners' equity in the enterprise. The statement of cash flows explains the ways cash increased and decreased during the period in terms of the enterprise's operating, investing, and financing activities. These relationships among the financial statements are called **articulation**.

**YOUR TURN**

## You as an Investor

Assume you have just inherited a relatively large sum of money and are looking for a company in which to invest. You have gotten financial statements—balance sheets, income statements, and statements of cash flows—from three different companies of interest to you. What will be your primary objective in choosing a company in which to invest your money? What key items or relationships will you look for in each financial statement that will help you decide in which company to invest?

*Our comments appear on page 83.

While these three key financial statements include important information, they do not include all possible information that might be presented about a company. For example, look again at Overnight's activities during the latter part of January. We could have prepared a separate financial statement on how liabilities changed or how the Tools and Equipment asset account changed. There is also important nonfinancial information that underlies the statement of financial position, the income statement, and the statement of cash flows that could be presented and that would benefit users of the statements. Accountants have developed methods of dealing with these other types of information, which we will learn about later in this text. At this point, we have focused our attention on the three primary financial statements that companies most often use to describe the activities that are capable of being captured in financial terms.

---

**CASH EFFECTS**

We have used the word *cash* extensively in introducing the primary financial statements. As we learned in Chapter 1, ultimately the flow of cash to investors and creditors is very important. These users of financial statements are interested in the cash activities of the enterprise in which they have invested or to which they have made loans or sold on credit. All enterprises are involved in continuous cash-to-cash cycles that vary with the nature of the underlying business. For example, Overnight Auto Service invests in a cash cycle in which it purchased land and a building necessary for its business. These assets, in turn, are used to provide services for customers that result in cash flows back into the company. Another cash cycle is much shorter in terms of time, namely the payment of wages to employees. The underlying purpose, however, is the same as the purchase of land and buildings—namely, to acquire the resources necessary to provide auto repair services that will ultimately result in positive cash flows for Overnight Auto Service. Sometimes the enterprise is able to delay a negative cash flow until it has a positive cash flow to provide the cash for payment. For example, Overnight partially purchased its building on credit, thereby allowing it to use the building to operate and generate positive cash flows, some of which will be used to repay the loan on the building. In other instances, cash payment is required before the positive cash flows from the use of the asset can take place (for example, Overnight's purchase of land for cash). In the final analysis, managing a company's cash flows is an important responsibility of management and may ultimately determine the success or failure of a business.

---

## FINANCIAL ANALYSIS

Relationships among the three primary financial statements provide the opportunity to learn a great deal about a company by bringing pieces of information together in a meaningful way. In fact, some people believe that relationships in the financial statements are more important than the actual dollar figures in those statements.

For example, take another look at the balance sheet on page 51. Notice that the company has $16,600 of cash and $1,200 of accounts receivable, a total of $17,800 in what are sometimes referred to as *current* assets, denoting that they either are cash or will soon become cash. Now look at the liabilities in the balance sheet and notice that the company has notes payable of $30,000 and accounts payable of $7,000 for a total of $37,000 of liabilities. If both types of liabilities are current liabilities, meaning that they will be due in the near future and can be expected to require the use of current assets, Overnight Auto Service may have difficulty paying them because they do not have enough liquid assets to cover their liabilities. The relationship of current assets to current liabilities is called the *current ratio.* For Overnight Auto Service it is a low .48 ($17,800 divided by $37,000). This means that Overnight Auto Service has only 48 cents for every $1 of liabilities that will come due in the near future.

While the above refers exclusively to information found in the balance sheet, key information from one financial statement often is combined with information from another financial statement. For example, we may be interested in knowing the amount of cash provided by operations (cash flow statement) relative to the amount of a company's currently maturing liabilities (balance sheet). Or we might want to compare a company's net income (income statement) with the investment in assets (balance sheet) that were used to generate that income.

Many of the chapters in this text introduce you to various types of financial analysis. We build on those introductory discussions in Chapter 14, Financial Statement Analysis, in which we provide a comprehensive treatment of how financial statements are used to inform investors and creditors.

## FORMS OF BUSINESS ORGANIZATION

**LO 8**

Explain common forms of business ownership—sole proprietorship, partnership, and corporation—and demonstrate how they differ in terms of their presentation in the statement of financial position.

In the United States, most business enterprises are organized as a *sole proprietorship,* a *partnership,* or a *corporation.* Generally accepted accounting principles can be applied to the financial statements of all three forms of organization.

### Sole Proprietorships

An unincorporated business owned by one person is called a **sole proprietorship**. Often the owner also acts as the manager. This form of business organization is common for small retail stores, farms, service businesses, and professional practices in law, medicine, and accounting. In fact, the sole proprietorship is by far the most common form of business organization in our economy.

From an accounting viewpoint, a sole proprietorship is regarded as a business entity *separate from the other affairs of its owner.* From a legal viewpoint, however, the business and its owner are not regarded as separate entities. Thus, *the owner is personally liable* for the debts of the business. If the business becomes insolvent, creditors can force the owner to sell his or her personal assets to pay the business debts. While an advantage of the sole proprietorship form of organization is its simplicity, this *unlimited liability* feature is a disadvantage to the owner.

### Partnerships

An unincorporated business owned by two or more persons voluntarily acting as partners (co-owners) is called a **partnership**. Partnerships, like sole proprietorships, are widely used for small businesses. In addition, some very large professional practices, including CPA firms, are organized as partnerships. As in the case of the sole proprietorship, the owners of a partnership are personally responsible for all debts of the business. From an accounting standpoint, a partnership is viewed as a business entity separate from the personal affairs of its owners.[5] A benefit of the partnership form over the sole proprietorship form is the ability to bring together larger amounts of capital investment from multiple owners.

### Corporations

A **corporation** is the only type of business organization recognized *under the law* as an entity separate from its owners. Therefore, the owners of a corporation are *not* personally liable for the debts of the business. These owners can lose no more than the amounts they have invested in the business—a concept known as *limited liability.* This concept is the principal reason that corporations are the most attractive form of business organization to many investors. Overnight Auto Service, the company used in our illustrations, is a corporation.

Ownership of a corporation is divided into transferable shares of capital stock, and the owners are called **stockholders** or shareholders. Stock certificates are issued by the corporation to each stockholder showing the number of shares that he or she owns. The stockholders are free to sell some or all of these shares to other investors at any time. This *transferability of ownership* adds to the attractiveness of the corporate form of organization, because investors can more easily get their money out of the business. Corporations offer an even greater opportunity than partnerships to bring together large amounts of capital from multiple owners.

There are many more sole proprietorships and partnerships than corporations, but most large businesses are organized as corporations. Thus corporations are the dominant form

---

[5] Creditors of an unincorporated business often ask to see the *personal* financial statements of the business owners, as these owners ultimately are responsible for paying the debts of the business.

of business organization in terms of the *dollar volume* of business activity. Of the three types of business, corporations are most likely to distribute financial statements to investors and other outsiders.

## Reporting Ownership Equity in the Balance Sheet

Assets and liabilities are presented in the same manner in the balance sheets of all three types of business organization. Some differences arise, however, in the presentation of the ownership equity.

**Sole Proprietorships**   A *sole proprietorship* is owned by only one person. Therefore, the owner's equity section of the balance sheet includes only one item—the equity of the owner. If Overnight Auto Service had been organized as a sole proprietorship with Michael McBryan the owner, owner's equity in the January 30 balance sheet would appear as follows:

| | |
|---|---|
| Owner's equity: | |
| Michael McBryan, Capital . . . . . . . . . . . . . . . . . . . . . . . . . . . . . . . . . . . . . . . . . | $80,800 |

*Ownership equity in a sole proprietorship . . .*

**Partnerships**   A *partnership* has two or more owners. Accountants use the term *partners' equity* instead of owners' equity and usually list separately the amount of each partner's equity in the business. If, for example, Michael McBryan had been in partnership with his sister, Rebecca McBryan, in Overnight Auto Service, and if each had contributed an equal amount of cash ($40,000) and had shared equally in the net income ($400), the partners' equity section of the balance sheet would have been presented as follows:

| | |
|---|---|
| Partners' equity: | |
| Michael McBryan, Capital . . . . . . . . . . . . . . . . . . . . . . . . . . . . . | $40,400 |
| Rebecca McBryan, Capital . . . . . . . . . . . . . . . . . . . . . . . . . . . . | 40,400 |
| Total partners' equity . . . . . . . . . . . . . . . . . . . . . . . . . . . . . | $80,800 |

*. . . in a partnership*

**Corporations**   In a business organized as a *corporation,* it is *not* customary to show separately the equity of each stockholder. In the case of large corporations, this clearly would be impossible, as these businesses may have *several million* individual stockholders (owners).

Returning to our original assumption that Overnight Auto Service is organized as a corporation, owners' equity (also referred to as **stockholders' equity** or shareholders' equity) is presented in two amounts—capital stock and retained earnings. This section of the balance sheet appears as follows:

| | |
|---|---|
| Owners' equity: | |
| Capital Stock . . . . . . . . . . . . . . . . . . . . . . . . . . . . . . . . . . | $80,000 |
| Retained Earnings . . . . . . . . . . . . . . . . . . . . . . . . . . . . . . . . | 800 |
| Total stockholders' equity . . . . . . . . . . . . . . . . . . . . . . . . . . . | $80,800 |

*. . . and in a corporation*

**Capital stock** represents the amount that the stockholders originally invested in the business in exchange for shares of the company's stock. **Retained earnings**, in contrast, represents the increase in owners' equity that has accumulated over the years as a result of profitable operations.

# THE USE OF FINANCIAL STATEMENTS BY OUTSIDERS

As we learned in Chapter 1, investors and creditors use financial statements in making *financial decisions*—that is, in selecting those companies in which they will invest resources or to which they will extend credit. For this reason, financial statements are designed primarily to meet the needs of creditors and investors. Two factors of particular concern to creditors and investors are the *solvency* and *profitability* of a business organization.

Creditors are interested in **solvency**—the ability of the business to pay its debts as they come due. Business concerns that are able to pay their debts promptly are said to be *solvent*. In contrast, a company that finds itself unable to meet its obligations as they fall due is called *insolvent*. Solvency is critical to the very survival of a business organization—a business that becomes insolvent may be forced into bankruptcy by its creditors. Once bankrupt, a business may be forced by the courts to stop its operations, sell its assets (for the purpose of paying its creditors), and end its existence.

Investors also are interested in the solvency of a business organization, but often they are even more interested in its profitability. *Profitable operations increase the value of the owners' equity* in the business. A company that continually operates unprofitably will eventually exhaust its resources and be forced out of existence. Therefore, most users of financial statements study these statements carefully for clues to the company's solvency and future profitability.

**The Short Run versus the Long Run**   In the short run, solvency and profitability may be independent of each other. A business may be operating profitably but nevertheless run out of cash and thereby become insolvent. On the other hand, a company may operate unprofitably during a given year yet have enough cash from previous periods to pay its bills and remain solvent.

Over a longer term, however, solvency and profitability go hand in hand. If a business is to survive, it must remain solvent and, in the long run, it must operate profitably.

**Evaluating Short-Term Solvency**   As discussed earlier in this chapter, one key indicator of short-term solvency is the relationship between an entity's *liquid* assets and the liabilities requiring payment *in the near future*. By studying the nature of a company's assets, and the amounts and due dates of its liabilities, users of financial statements often may anticipate whether the company is likely to have difficulty in meeting its upcoming obligations. This simple type of analysis meets the needs of many *short-term* creditors. Evaluating long-term solvency is a more difficult matter and is discussed in later chapters.

In studying financial statements, users should *always* read the accompanying notes and the auditors' report.

## The Need for Adequate Disclosure

**LO 9**

Discuss and illustrate the importance of nonfinancial information to supplement the information in the primary financial statements.

The concept of adequate **disclosure** is an important generally accepted accounting principle. Adequate disclosure means that users of financial statements are informed of any facts *necessary for the proper interpretation* of the statements. Adequate disclosure may be made either in the body of the financial statements or in *notes* accompanying the statements. It is not unusual to find a series of notes to financial statements that are longer than the statements themselves.

Among the events that may require disclosure in notes to the financial statements are occurrences after the date of the financial statements. For example, assume that Overnight Auto Service's building is destroyed by fire on February 2, and that Michael McBryan is using the financial statements to acquire additional financing for the business. Assume also that Michael has less insurance on the building than will be needed to replace it. Users of the financial statements, such as bankers who might be considering lending money to Overnight, must be informed of this important "subsequent event." This disclosure usually would be done with a note like the following:

*Note 7: Events occurring after the financial statement date*
On February 2, 2002, the building included in the January 31 statement of financial position at $36,000 was destroyed by fire. While the company has insurance on this facility, management expects to recover only approximately $30,000 of the loss.

*Notes to the statements contain vital information*

In addition to important subsequent events, many other situations may require disclosure in notes to the financial statements. Examples include lawsuits against the company, due dates of major liabilities, assets pledged as collateral to secure loans, amounts receivable from officers or other "insiders," and contractual commitments requiring large future cash outlays.

There is no comprehensive list of the items and events that may require disclosure. As a general rule, a company should disclose any financial facts that a reasonably informed person would consider *necessary to the proper interpretation* of the financial statements. Events that clearly are unimportant *do not* require disclosure.

## Management's Interest in Financial Statements

While we have emphasized the importance of financial statements to investors and creditors, the management of a business organization is vitally concerned with the financial position of the business and with its profitability and cash flows. Therefore, management is anxious to receive financial statements as frequently and as quickly as possible so that it may take action to improve areas of weak performance. Most large organizations provide managers with financial statements on at least a monthly basis. With modern technology, financial statements prepared on a weekly, daily, or even hourly basis are possible.

**LO 10**
Discuss the importance of financial statements to a company and its investors and creditors and why management may take steps to improve the appearance of the company in its financial statements.

Managers have a special interest in the *annual* financial statements, as these are the statements most widely used by decision makers outside of the organization. For example, if creditors view the annual financial statements as strong, they will be more willing to extend credit to the business than if they regard the company's financial statements as weak.

A strong statement of financial position is one that shows relatively little debt and large amounts of liquid assets relative to the liabilities due in the near future. A strong income statement is one that shows large revenues relative to the expenses required to earn the revenues. A strong statement of cash flows is one that not only shows a strong cash balance but also indicates that cash is being generated by operations. Demonstrating that these characteristics of the company are ongoing and can be seen in a series of financial statements is particularly helpful in creating confidence in the company on the part of investors and creditors. Because of the importance of the financial statements, management may take steps that are specifically intended to improve the company's financial position and financial performance. For example, cash purchases of assets may be delayed until the beginning of the next accounting period so that large amounts of cash will be included in the statement of financial position and the statement of cash flows. On the other hand, if the company is in a particularly strong cash position, liabilities due in the near future may be paid, replaced with longer-term liabilities, or even replaced by additional investments by owners to communicate that future negative cash flows will not be as great as they might otherwise appear.

These actions are sometimes called **window dressing**—measures taken by management to make the company appear as strong as possible in its financial statements. Users of financial statements should realize that, while the statements are fair representations of the financial position at the end of the period and financial performance for the period, they may not necessarily describe the typical financial situation of the business. In its annual financial statements, in particular, management tries to make the company appear as strong as is reasonably possible. As a result, many creditors regard more frequent financial statements (for example, quarterly or even monthly) as providing important additional information beyond that in the annual financial statements. The more frequently financial statements are presented, the less able is management to window dress and make a company look financially stronger than it actually is.

**MANAGEMENT STRATEGY**

Because external stakeholders, particularly creditors, carefully evaluate financial reports, the reports have a significant impact on the strategic choices of management. Suppose Overnight Auto Service was planning to raise more capital in the coming year by selling additional stock. McBryan might delay or accelerate some planned strategic decisions to strengthen the financial position and, as a result, the external financial reports of Overnight Auto Service. For example, the planned purchase of a hydraulic lift might be delayed and the choice to form a partnership with nearby Ace Towing might be accelerated. Delaying ambitious capital expenditures or expediting strategic alliances to ensure the ability to raise additional needed capital are examples of the impact that financial reporting can have on business strategy.

**A SECOND LOOK**

### America Online

At the beginning of this chapter, we asked how you would know whether **America Online** was successful. This chapter introduced the basic financial statements allowing you to begin to answer this question.

**America Online**'s income statements for 1997, 1998, and 1999, indicate that its net income (losses) were ($485 million), ($74 million), and $762 million, respectively. This means that in 1997 and 1998, the company's revenues were less than its expenses and, therefore, a net loss was reported. The 1998 loss, however, was much smaller than the 1997 loss. In 1999, revenues exceeded expenses by enough that the company reported a $762 million net income. Compared to 1997 and 1998, we would probably conclude that **America Online** was successful in 1999. Even 1998 might be considered a success when compared with 1997 because the loss was so much smaller.

Another measure of success that is sometimes cited is whether the company's operations are generating an excess of cash to be used for other purposes. **America Online**'s statement of cash flows for 1997, 1998, and 1999 indicate that it had positive cash flows from operating activities (cash coming in exceeding cash being paid out) of $131 million, $437 million, and $1,099 million, respectively. This could be judged as successful in two ways. First, all three numbers are positive, indicating that in all three years the company's operations are generating cash that is available to be used for other purposes. Second, the amount of the positive cash flow is increasing each year, beginning with $131 million in 1997 and building to $1,099 million (over a billion dollars) in 1999.

At this early stage in your study of accounting, you can begin to understand how investors and creditors can use important information in the company's financial statements to learn things about a company that help them make informed decisions.

## SUMMARY OF LEARNING OBJECTIVES

### LO 1

**Explain the nature and general purpose of financial statements.**

Financial statements are declarations of information in financial terms about an enterprise that are believed to be fair and accurate. They describe certain attributes of the enterprise that are important for decision makers, particularly investors (owners) and creditors.

### LO 2

**Explain certain accounting principles that are important for an understanding of financial statements and how professional judgment by accountants may affect the application of those principles.**

Accountants prepare financial statements by applying a set of standards or rules referred to as generally accepted accounting principles. Consistent application of these standards permits comparisons between companies and between years of a single company. Generally accepted accounting principles allow for significant latitude in how certain transactions should be accounted for, meaning that professional judgment is particularly important.

### LO 3

**Demonstrate how certain business transactions affect the elements of the accounting equation: Assets = Liabilities + Owners' Equity.**

Business transactions result in changes in the three elements of the basic accounting equation. A transaction that increases total assets must also increase total liabilities and owners' equity. Similarly, a transaction that decreases total assets must simultaneously decrease total liabilities and owners' equity. Some transactions increase one asset and reduce another. Regardless of the nature of the specific transaction, the accounting equation must stay in balance at all times.

### LO 4

**Explain how the statement of financial position, often referred to as the balance sheet, is an expansion of the basic accounting equation.**

The statement of financial position, or balance sheet, presents in great detail the elements of the basic accounting equation. Various types of assets are listed and totaled. The enterprise's liabilities are listed, totaled, and added to the owners' equity. The balancing feature of this financial statement is one of its dominant characteristics because the statement is simply an expansion of the basic accounting equation.

### LO 5

**Explain how the income statement reports an enterprise's financial performance for a period of time in terms of the relationship of revenues and expenses.**

Revenues are created as the enterprise provides goods and services for its customers. Many expenses are required to be able to provide those goods and services. The difference between the revenues and expenses is net income or net loss.

### LO 6

**Explain how the statement of cash flows presents the change in cash for a period of time in terms of the company's operating, investing, and financing activities.**

Cash is one of the most important assets, and the statement of cash flows shows in detail how the enterprise's cash balance changed between the beginning and ending of the accounting period. Operating activities relate to ongoing revenue and expense transactions. Investing activities relate to the purchase and sale of various types of assets (for example, land, buildings, and equipment). Financing activities describe where the enterprise has received its debt and equity financing. The statement of cash flows combines information about all of these activities into a concise statement of changes in cash that reconciles the beginning and ending cash balances.

### LO 7

**Explain important relationships among the statement of financial position, income statement, and statement of cash flows, and how these statements articulate.**

The three primary financial statements are based on the same underlying transactions. They are not alternatives to each other, but rather represent three different ways of looking at the financial activities of the reporting enterprise. Because they are based on the same transactions, they relate, or "articulate," very closely with each other.

### LO 8

**Explain common forms of business ownership—sole proprietorship, partnership, and corporation—and demonstrate how they differ in terms of their presentation in the statement of financial position.**

Owners' equity is one of three major elements in the basic accounting equation. Regardless of the form of organization, owners' equity represents the interest of the owners in the assets of the reporting enterprise. For a sole proprietorship, owner's equity consists only of the interest of a single owner. For a partnership, the ownership interests of all partners are added together to determine the total owners' equity of the enterprise. For a corporation, which usually has many owners, the total contribution to the enterprise represents its owners' equity. In all cases, the enterprise's net income is added to owners' equity.

**LO 9**

**Discuss and illustrate the importance of nonfinancial information to supplement the information in the primary financial statements.**

All important aspects of an enterprise's activities usually cannot be captured in financial terms. Financial statements typically are accompanied by notes that provide qualitative information that supplements and helps interpret the financial information included in the body of the financial statements.

**LO 10**

**Discuss the importance of financial statements to a company and its investors and creditors and why management may take steps to improve the appearance of the company in its financial statements.**

Financial statements are particularly important for investors and creditors in their attempts to evaluate future cash flows from the enterprise to them. Management is interested in the enterprise looking as positive as possible in its financial statements and may take certain steps to improve the overall appearance of the enterprise. A fine line, however, exists between the steps management can take and the steps that are unethical, or even illegal.

Throughout this text we emphasize how accounting information is the basis for business decisions. In this chapter you were introduced to business transactions and how they lead to three basic financial statements: statement of financial position (balance sheet), income statement, and statement of cash flows. These statements constitute some of the primary products of the accountant's work, and they provide investors, creditors, and other parties with pertinent information that is useful for decision making.

As you continue your study of financial accounting in Chapter 3, you will learn how business transactions are actually recorded, how they move through an accounting system, and how they eventually lead to the preparation of financial statements.

# KEY TERMS INTRODUCED OR EMPHASIZED IN CHAPTER 2

**accounting equation** (p. 47) Assets are equal to the sum of liabilities plus owners' equity.

**articulation** (pp. 42, 58) The close relationship that exists among the financial statements that are prepared on the basis of the same underlying transaction information.

**assets** (p. 43) Economic resources owned by an entity.

**balance sheet** (p. 40) The financial statement showing the financial position of an enterprise by summarizing its assets, liabilities, and owners' equity at a point in time. Also called the statement of financial position.

**business entity** (p. 43) An economic unit that controls resources, incurs obligations, and engages in business activities.

**capital stock** (p. 61) Transferable units of ownership in a corporation.

**corporation** (p. 40) A business organized as a separate legal entity and chartered by a state, with ownership divided into transferable shares of capital stock.

**cost principle** (p. 44) The widely used principle of accounting for assets at their original cost to the current owner.

**creditor** (p. 45) A person or organization to whom debt is owed.

**deflation** (p. 45) A decline in the general price level, resulting in an increase in the purchasing power of the monetary unit.

**disclosure** (p. 62) The accounting principle of providing with financial statements any financial and other facts that are necessary for proper interpretation of the financial statements.

**expenses** (p. 54) Past, present, or future reductions in cash required to generate revenues.

**financial statement** (p. 40) A declaration of information believed to be true communicated in monetary terms.

**financing activities** (p. 55) A major category in the statement of cash flows that reflects the results of debt and equity financing transactions.

**going-concern assumption** (p. 44) An assumption by accountants that a business will operate in the foreseeable future unless specific evidence suggests that this is not a reasonable assumption.

**income statement** (p. 40) An activity statement that subtracts from the enterprise's revenue those expenses required to generate the revenues, resulting in a net income or a net loss.

**inflation** (p. 45) An increase in the general price level, resulting in a decline in the purchasing power of the monetary unit.

**investing activities** (p. 55) A major category in the statement of cash flows that reflects the results of purchases and sales of assets, such as land, buildings, and equipment.

**liabilities** (p. 45) Debt or obligations of an entity that resulted from past transactions. They represent the claims of creditors on the enterprise's assets.

**negative cash flows** (p. 41) A payment of cash that reduces the enterprise's cash balance.

**operating activities** (p. 55) A major category in the statement of cash flows that includes the cash effects of all revenues and expenses included in the income statement.

**owners' equity** (p. 46) The excess of assets over liabilities. The amount of the owners' investment in the business, plus profits from successful operations that have been retained in the business.

**partnership** (p. 60) An unincorporated form of business organization in which two or more persons voluntarily associate for purposes of carrying out business activities.

**positive cash flows** (p. 41) Increases in cash that add to the enterprise's cash balance.

**retained earnings** (p. 61) The portion of stockholders' equity that has accumulated as a result of profitable operations.

**revenues** (p. 54) Increases in the enterprise's assets as a result of profit-oriented activities.

**sole proprietorship** (p. 60) An unincorporated business owned by a single individual.

**solvency** (p. 62) Having the financial ability to pay debts as they become due.

**stable-dollar assumption** (p. 45) An assumption by accountants that the monetary unit used in the preparation of financial statements is stable over time or changes at a sufficiently slow rate that the resulting impact on financial statements does not distort the information.

**statement of cash flows** (p. 41) An activity statement that explains the enterprise's change in cash in terms of its operating, investing, and financing activities.

**statement of financial position** (p. 40) Same as balance sheet.

**stockholders** (p. 60) Owners of capital stock in a corporation.

**stockholders' equity** (p. 61) The owners' equity of an enterprise organized as a corporation.

**window dressing** (p. 63) Measures taken by management specifically intended to make a business look as strong as possible in its balance sheet, income statement, and statement of cash flows.

## DEMONSTRATION PROBLEM

Account balances for Crystal Auto Wash at September 30, 2002, are shown below. The figure for retained earnings is not given, but it can be determined when all the available information is assembled in the form of a balance sheet.

| | | | | |
|---|---|---|---|---|
| Accounts Payable | $14,000 | Land | $68,000 |
| Accounts Receivable | 800 | Machinery & Equipment | 65,000 |
| Buildings | 52,000 | Notes Payable (due in 30 days) | 29,000 |
| Cash | 9,200 | | |
| Capital Stock | 100,000 | Salaries Payable | 3,000 |
| Retained Earnings | ? | Supplies | 400 |

### Instructions

**a.** Prepare a balance sheet at September 30, 2002.

**b.** Does this balance sheet indicate that the company is in a strong financial position? Explain briefly.

**c.** How would an income statement and a statement of cash flows allow you to better respond to part **b**?

## Solution to the Demonstration Problem

**a.**

### CRYSTAL AUTO WASH
### Balance Sheet
### September 30, 2002

| Assets | | Liabilities & Owners' Equity | |
|---|---|---|---|
| Cash | $ 9,200 | Liabilities: | |
| Accounts Receivable | 800 | Notes Payable | $ 29,000 |
| Supplies | 400 | Accounts Payable | 14,000 |
| Land | 68,000 | Salaries Payable | 3,000 |
| Building | 52,000 | Total liabilities | $ 46,000 |
| Machinery & Equipment | 65,000 | Owners' equity: | |
| | | Capital Stock | $100,000 |
| | | *Retained Earnings | 49,400 |
| Total | $195,400 | Total | $195,400 |

*Computed as $195,400 (total assets) − $46,000 (total liabilities) = $149,400 (owners' equity); $149,400 − $100,000 (capital stock) = $49,400.

**b.** The balance sheet indicates that Crystal Auto Wash is in a *weak* financial position. The only liquid assets—cash and receivables—total only $10,000, but the company has *$46,000* in debts due in the near future.

**c.** An income statement for Crystal Auto Wash would show the company's revenues and expenses for the period (month, quarter, or year) ending on the date of the balance sheet, September 30, 2002. This information would be helpful in determining whether the company was successful in selling its auto wash services at an amount that exceeds its cost of providing those services, something the company must do to remain in business and be successful. The statement of cash flows for the same period as the income statement would show where the company's cash came from and where it went in terms of its operating, investing, and financing activities. This information would be particularly helpful in assessing the strength of the company's ability to satisfy its obligations as they come due in light of the relatively weak balance sheet.

## SELF-TEST QUESTIONS

*Answers to these questions appear on page 83.*

**Note:** In order to review as many chapter concepts as possible, some self-test questions include *more than one* correct answer. In these cases, you should indicate *all* of the correct answers.

1. A set of financial statements:
   **a.** Is intended to assist users in evaluating the financial position, profitability, and future prospects of an entity.
   **b.** Is intended to assist the IRS in determining the amount of income taxes owed by a business organization.
   **c.** Includes notes disclosing information necessary for the proper interpretation of the statements.
   **d.** Is intended to assist investors and creditors in making decisions involving the allocation of economic resources.

2. Which of the following statements is *not* consistent with generally accepted accounting principles relating to asset valuation?
   **a.** Many assets are originally recorded in accounting records at their cost to the business entity.
   **b.** Subtracting total liabilities from total assets indicates what the owners' equity in the business is worth under current market conditions.
   **c.** Accountants assume that assets such as office supplies, land, and buildings will be used in business operations rather than sold at current market prices.
   **d.** Accountants prefer to base the valuation of assets upon objective, verifiable evidence rather than upon appraisals or personal opinion.

3. Arrowhead Boat Shop purchased a truck for $12,000, making a down payment of $5,000 cash and signing a $7,000 note payable due in 60 days. As a result of this transaction:
   **a.** Total assets increased by $12,000.
   **b.** Total liabilities increased by $7,000.
   **c.** From the viewpoint of a short-term creditor, this transaction makes the business more solvent.
   **d.** This transaction had no immediate effect on the owners' equity in the business.

4. A transaction caused a $10,000 *decrease* in both total assets and total liabilities. This transaction could have been:
   **a.** Purchase of a delivery truck for $10,000 cash.
   **b.** An asset with a cost of $10,000 was destroyed by fire.
   **c.** Repayment of a $10,000 bank loan.
   **d.** Collection of a $10,000 account receivable.

5. Which of the following is (are) correct about a company's balance sheet?
   **a.** It displays sources and uses of cash for the period.
   **b.** It is an expansion of the basic accounting equation: Assets = Liabilities + Owners' Equity.

**c.** It is sometimes referred to as a statement of financial position.

**d.** It is unnecessary if both an income statement and statement of cash flows are available.

6. Which of the following would you expect to find in a correctly prepared income statement?

   **a.** Cash balance at the end of the period.

   **b.** Revenues earned during the period.

   **c.** Contributions by the owner during the period.

   **d.** Expenses incurred during the period to earn revenues.

7. What information would you find in a statement of cash flows that you would not be able to get from the other two primary financial statements?

   **a.** Cash provided by or used in financing activities.

   **b.** Cash balance at the end of the period.

   **c.** Total liabilities due to creditors at the end of the period.

   **d.** Net income.

8. Which of the following statements relating to the role of professional judgment in the financial reporting process is (are) valid?

   **a.** Different accountants may evaluate similar situations differently.

   **b.** The determination of which items should be disclosed in notes to financial statements requires professional judgment.

   **c.** Once a complete list of generally accepted accounting principles is prepared, judgment need no longer enter into the financial reporting process.

   **d.** The possibility always exists that professional judgment later may prove to have been incorrect.

## ASSIGNMENT MATERIAL

### DISCUSSION QUESTIONS

1. In broad general terms, what is the purpose of accounting?

2. Why is a knowledge of accounting terms and concepts useful to persons other than professional accountants?

3. In broad terms, what is a financial statement?

4. What is the relationship between time and financial statements?

5. What is the distinction between annual and interim financial statements?

6. What is a business transaction? Give several examples of business transactions and several events that may occur that are not business transactions.

7. Explain briefly why each of the following groups might be interested in the financial statements of a business:

   **a.** Creditors

   **b.** Potential investors

   **c.** Labor unions

8. What is the primary characteristic of the form of business organization called the sole proprietorship?

9. In general terms, what are revenues and expenses? How are they related in the determination of an enterprise's net income or net loss?

10. Why is the statement of financial position, or balance sheet, a logical place to begin a discussion of financial statements?

11. What is the basic accounting equation? Briefly define the three primary elements in the equation.

12. What is meant by the cost principle, and how is that principle related to accounting for assets?

13. Why is the going-concern assumption an important consideration in understanding financial statements?

14. What is meant by the terms *inflation* and *deflation,* and how do they relate to the stable monetary unit assumption underlying financial statements?

15. Can a business transaction cause one asset to increase without affecting any other asset, liability, or owners' equity?

16. Give an example of business transactions that would:

   **a.** Cause one asset to increase and another asset to decrease, with no effect on either liabilities or owners' equity.

   **b.** Cause both total assets and liabilities to increase with no effect on owners' equity.

17. What is meant by the terms *positive cash flows* and *negative cash flows*? How do they relate to revenues and expenses?

18. What are the three categories commonly found in a statement of cash flows, and what is included in each category?

19. What is meant by the statement "The financial statements articulate"?

20. What are the major differences in the owners' equity sections of the balance sheet for a sole proprietorship, partnership, and corporation?

21. What is meant by the term *adequate disclosure,* and how do accountants fulfill this requirement in the preparation of financial statements?

22. What is meant by the term *window dressing* when referring to financial statements?

23. What are the characteristics of a strong income statement?

24. What are the characteristics of a strong statement of cash flows?

## EXERCISES

**EXERCISE 2.1**

The Nature of Assets and Liabilities

**LO 3**

Assets and liabilities are important elements of a company's financial position.

**a.** Define *assets.* Give three examples of assets other than cash that might appear in the balance sheet of (1) **American Airlines** and (2) a professional sports team, such as the **Boston Celtics**.

**b.** Define *liabilities.* Give three examples of liabilities that might appear in the balance sheet of (1) **American Airlines** and (2) a professional sports team, such as the **Boston Celtics**.

**EXERCISE 2.2**

Preparing a Balance Sheet

**LO 4**

The night manager of Majestic Limousine Service, who had no accounting background, prepared the following balance sheet for the company at February 28, 2002. The dollar amounts were taken directly from the company's accounting records and are correct. However, the balance sheet contains a number of errors in its headings, format, and the classification of assets, liabilities, and owners' equity.

**MAJESTIC LIMO**
**Manager's Report**
**8 P.M. Thursday**

| Assets | | Owners' Equity | |
|---|---|---|---|
| Capital Stock | $100,000 | Accounts Receivable | $ 78,000 |
| Retained Earnings | 62,000 | Notes Payable | 288,000 |
| Cash | 69,000 | Supplies | 14,000 |
| Building | 80,000 | Land | 70,000 |
| Automobiles | 165,000 | Accounts Payable | 26,000 |
| | $476,000 | | $476,000 |

Prepare a corrected balance sheet. Include a proper heading.

**EXERCISE 2.3**

Preparing a Balance Sheet

**LO 4**

The balance sheet items of the Perez Company as of December 31, 2002, follow in random order. You are to prepare a balance sheet for the company, using a similar sequence for assets as in the illustrated balance sheet on page 51. You must compute the amount for Retained Earnings.

| | | | |
|---|---|---|---|
| Land | $90,000 | Office Equipment | $ 10,200 |
| Accounts Payable | 43,800 | Building | 210,000 |
| Accounts Receivable | 56,700 | Capital Stock | 75,000 |
| Cash | 36,300 | Notes Payable | 213,600 |
| | | Retained Earnings | ? |

The following cases relate to the valuation of assets. Consider each case independently.

**EXERCISE 2.4**

Accounting Principles and Asset Valuation

a. World-Wide Travel Agency has office supplies costing $1,700 on hand at the balance sheet date. These supplies were purchased from a supplier that does not give cash refunds. World-Wide's management believes that the company could sell these supplies for no more than $500 if it were to advertise them for sale. However, the company expects to use these supplies and to purchase more when they are gone. In its balance sheet, the supplies were presented at $500.

b. Nofford Corporation purchased land in 1955 for $20,000. In 2002, it purchased a similar parcel of land for $300,000. In its 2002 balance sheet, the company presented these two parcels of land at a combined amount of $320,000.

c. At December 30, 2002, Lenier, Inc., purchased a computer system from a mail-order supplier for $14,000. The retail value of the system—according to the mail-order supplier—was $20,000. On January 7, however, the system was stolen during a burglary. In its December 31, 2002, balance sheet, Lenier showed this computer system at $14,000 and made no reference to its retail value or to the burglary. The December balance sheet was issued in February of 2003.

In each case, indicate the appropriate balance sheet amount of the asset under generally accepted accounting principles. If the amount assigned by the company is incorrect, briefly explain the accounting principles that have been violated. If the amount is correct, identify the accounting principles that justify this amount.

Compute the missing amounts in the following table:

**EXERCISE 2.5**

Using the Accounting Equation

| | Assets | = Liabilities + | Owners' Equity |
|---|---|---|---|
| a. | $558,000 | $342,000 | ? |
| b. | ? | 562,500 | $375,000 |
| c. | 307,500 | ? | 142,500 |

A number of business transactions carried out by Cooper Manufacturing Company are as follows:

**EXERCISE 2.6**

The Accounting Equation

a. Borrowed money from a bank.

b. Sold land for cash at a price equal to its cost.

c. Paid a liability.

d. Returned for credit some of the office equipment previously purchased on credit but not yet paid for. (Treat this the opposite of a transaction in which you purchased office equipment on credit.)

e. Sold land for cash at a price in excess of cost. (Hint: The difference between cost and sales price represents a gain that will be in the company's income statement.)

f. Purchased a computer on credit.

g. The owner invested cash in the business.

h. Purchased office equipment for cash.

i. Collected an account receivable.

Indicate the effects of each of these transactions on the total amounts of the company's assets, liabilities, and owners' equity. Organize your answer in tabular form, using the column headings shown on the next page and the code letters **I** for increase, **D** for decrease, and **NE** for no effect. The answer for transaction **a** is provided as an example:

| Transaction | Assets | = | Liabilities | + | Owners' Equity |
|:-----------:|:------:|:-:|:-----------:|:-:|:--------------:|
| (a)         | I      |   | I           |   | NE             |

**EXERCISE 2.7**

Effects of Business
Transactions

For each of the following categories, state concisely a transaction that will have the required effect on the elements of the accounting equation.

**a.** Increase an asset and increase a liability.

**b.** Decrease an asset and decrease a liability.

**c.** Increase one asset and decrease another asset.

**d.** Increase an asset and increase owners' equity.

**e.** Increase one asset, decrease another asset, and increase a liability.

**EXERCISE 2.8**

Forms of Business
Organization

Foster Software Company has assets of $850,000 and liabilities of $460,000.

**a.** Prepare the owners' equity section of Foster's balance sheet under each of the following *independent* assumptions:

    **1.** The business is organized as a sole proprietorship, owned by Johanna Schmidt.

    **2.** The business is organized as a partnership, owned by Johanna Schmidt and Mikki Yato. Schmidt's equity amounts to $240,000.

    **3.** The business is a corporation with 25 stockholders, each of whom originally invested $12,000 in exchange for shares of the company's capital stock. The remainder of the stockholders' equity has resulted from profitable operation of the business.

**b.** Assume that you are a loan officer at Security Bank. Foster has applied to your bank for a large loan to finance the development of new products. Does it matter to you whether Foster is organized as a sole proprietorship, a partnership, or a corporation? Explain.

**EXERCISE 2.9**

Factors Contributing
to Solvency

Explain whether each of the following balance sheet items increases, reduces, or has no direct effect on a company's ability to pay its obligations as they come due. Explain your reasoning.

**a.** Cash

**b.** Accounts Payable

**c.** Accounts Receivable

**d.** Capital Stock

**EXERCISE 2.10**

Professional Judgment

Professional judgment plays a major role in the practice of accounting.

**a.** In general terms, explain why judgment enters into the accounting process.

**b.** Identify at least three situations in which accountants must rely on their professional judgment, rather than on official rules.

**EXERCISE 2.11**

Statement of Cash Flows

LO 6

During the month of October 2002, Marshall Company had the following transactions:

**1.** Revenues of $10,000 were earned and received in cash.

**2.** Bank loans of $2,000 were paid off.

**3.** Equipment of $2,500 was purchased.

**4.** Expenses of $6,200 were paid.

**5.** Additional shares of capital stock were sold for $5,000.

Assuming that the cash balance at the beginning of the month was $2,700, prepare a statement of cash flows that displays operating, investing, and financing activities and that reconciles the beginning and ending cash balances.

**EXERCISE 2.12**

Income Statement

Walters, Inc., had the following transactions during the month of March 2002. Prepare an income statement based on this information, being careful to include only those items that should appear in that financial statement.

**1.** Cash received from bank loans was $10,000.

**2.** Revenues earned and received in cash were $8,500.

**3.** Dividends of $4,000 were paid to stockholders.

**4.** Expenses incurred and paid were $5,000.

An inexperienced accountant for Aaron Company prepared the following income statement for the month of August 2002:

**EXERCISE 2.13**

Income Statement

**LO 5**

| AARON COMPANY<br>August 31, 2002 | | |
| --- | --- | --- |
| Revenues: | | |
| Services provided to customers ........................... | $10,000 | |
| Investment by stockholders .............................. | 5,000 | |
| Loan from bank ........................................ | 15,000 | $30,000 |
| Expenses: | | |
| Payments to long-term creditors ......................... | $ 8,000 | |
| Expenses required to provide<br>    services to customers .............................. | 7,500 | |
| Purchase of land ...................................... | 16,000 | 31,500 |
| Net loss ............................................. | | $ 1,500 |

Prepare a revised income statement in accordance with generally accepted accounting principles.

Based on the information for Aaron Company in Exercise **2.13,** prepare a statement of cash flows in a form consistent with generally accepted accounting principles. You may assume all transactions were in cash and that the beginning cash balance was $7,200.

**EXERCISE 2.14**

Statement of Cash Flows

**LO 6**

John Banks, sole owner of Airsoft Mattress Company, has an ownership interest in the company of $50,000 at the beginning of the year 2002. During that year, he invested an additional $10,000 in the company and the company reported a net income of $25,000. Determine the balance of owners' equity that will appear in the balance sheet at the end of 2002, and explain how the amount of net income articulates with that figure in the balance sheet.

**EXERCISE 2.15**

Articulation of Financial Statements

**LO 7**

Prepare a two-column analysis that illustrates steps management might take to improve the appearance of its company's financial statements. In the left column, briefly identify three steps that might be taken. In the right column, briefly describe for each step the impact on the balance sheet, income statement, and statement of cash flows. If there is no impact on one or more of these financial statements, indicate that.

**EXERCISE 2.16**

Window Dressing Financial Statements

**LO 10**

Locate the balance sheet, income statement, and statement of cash flows of **Tootsie Roll Industries, Inc.** in Appendix A of your text. Review those statements and then respond to the following for the year ended December 31, 1999.

**a.** Did the company have a net income or net loss for the year? How much?

**b.** What were the cash balances at the beginning and end of the year? What were the most important causes of cash increases and decreases during the year? (Treat "cash equivalents" as if they were cash.)

**c.** What is the largest asset and the largest liability included in the company's balance sheet at the end of the year?

**EXERCISE 2.17**

**Tootsie Roll Industries, Inc.**
Financial Statements

**LO 4, 5, 6**

# PROBLEMS

**PROBLEM 2.1**

Preparing and Evaluating
a Balance Sheet

Listed below in random order are the items to be included in the balance sheet of Spencer Mountain Lodge at December 31, 2002:

| | | | | |
|---|---:|---|---:|---|
| Equipment | $ 29,200 | Buildings | $450,000 | |
| Land | 425,000 | Capital Stock | 125,000 | |
| Accounts Payable | 54,800 | Cash | 21,400 | |
| Accounts Receivable | 10,600 | Furnishings | 58,700 | |
| Salaries Payable | 33,500 | Snowmobiles | 15,400 | |
| Interest Payable | 12,000 | Notes Payable | 620,000 | |
| | | Retained Earnings | ? | |

## Instructions

**a.** Prepare a balance sheet at December 31, 2002. Include a proper heading and organize your balance sheet similar to the illustration on page 51. (After "Buildings," you may list the remaining assets in any order.) You will need to compute the amount to be shown for retained earnings.

**b.** Assume that no payment is due on the notes payable until 2004. Does this balance sheet indicate that the company is in a strong financial position as of December 31, 2002? Explain briefly.

**PROBLEM 2.2**

Interpreting the Effects
of Business Transactions

**LO 3**

Six transactions of Ward Moving Company, a corporation, are summarized below in equation form, with each of the six transactions identified by a letter. For each of the transactions (a) through (f) write a separate statement explaining the nature of the transaction. For example, the explanation of transaction (a) could be as follows: Purchased equipment for cash at a cost of $3,200.

| | Cash | + | Accounts Receivable | + | Land | + | Building | + | Equipment | = | Accounts Payable | + | Capital Stock |
|---|---|---|---|---|---|---|---|---|---|---|---|---|---|
| | | | | | | | | | | | **= Liabilities +** | | **Owners' Equity** |
| | | | | | | **Assets** | | | | | | | |
| Balances | $26,000 | | $39,000 | | $45,000 | | $110,000 | | $36,000 | | $42,000 | | $214,000 |
| (a) | −3,200 | | | | | | | | +3,200 | | | | |
| Balances | $22,800 | | $39,000 | | $45,000 | | $110,000 | | $39,200 | | $42,000 | | $214,000 |
| (b) | +900 | | −900 | | | | | | | | | | |
| Balances | $23,700 | | $38,100 | | $45,000 | | $110,000 | | $39,200 | | $42,000 | | $214,000 |
| (c) | −3,500 | | | | | | | | +13,500 | | +10,000 | | |
| Balances | $20,200 | | $38,100 | | $45,000 | | $110,000 | | $52,700 | | $52,000 | | $214,000 |
| (d) | −14,500 | | | | | | | | | | −14,500 | | |
| Balances | $ 5,700 | | $38,100 | | $45,000 | | $110,000 | | $52,700 | | $37,500 | | $214,000 |
| (e) | +15,000 | | | | | | | | | | | | +15,000 |
| Balances | $20,700 | | $38,100 | | $45,000 | | $110,000 | | $52,700 | | $37,500 | | $229,000 |
| (f) | | | | | | | | | +3,500 | | +3,500 | | |
| Balances | $20,700 | | $38,100 | | $45,000 | | $110,000 | | $56,200 | | $41,000 | | $229,000 |

Delta Communications was organized on December 1 of the current year and had the following account balances at December 31, listed in tabular form:

**PROBLEM 2.3**

Recording the Effects of Transactions

 LO 3

| | Assets | | | | = | Liabilities | | + | Owners' Equity |
| | Cash | + Land | + Building | + Office Equipment | = Notes Payable | + Accounts Payable | + | Capital Stock |
|---|---|---|---|---|---|---|---|---|
| Balances | $37,000 | $95,000 | $125,000 | $51,250 | $80,000 | $28,250 | | $200,000 |

Early in January, the following transactions were carried out by Delta Communications:

1. Sold capital stock to owners for $25,000.
2. Purchased land and a small office building for a total price of $90,000, of which $35,000 was the value of the land and $55,000 was the value of the building. Paid $22,500 in cash and signed a note payable for the remaining $67,500.
3. Bought several computer systems on credit for $8,500 (30-day open account).
4. Obtained a loan from Capital Bank in the amount of $20,000. Signed a note payable.
5. Paid the $28,250 account payable due as of December 31.

**Instructions**

a. List the December 31 balances of assets, liabilities, and owners' equity in tabular form shown.

b. Record the effects of each of the five transactions in the format illustrated on page 53. Show the totals for all columns after each transaction.

The items making up the balance sheet of Paulson Truck Rental at December 31 are listed below in tabular form similar to the illustration of the accounting equation on page 53.

**PROBLEM 2.4**

An Alternate Problem on Recording the Effects of Transactions

 LO 3

| | Assets | | | | = | Liabilities | | + | Owners' Equity |
| | Cash | + Accounts Receivable | + Trucks | + Office Equipment | = Notes Payable | + Accounts Payable | + | Capital Stock |
|---|---|---|---|---|---|---|---|---|
| Balances | $9,500 | $8,900 | $58,000 | $3,800 | $20,000 | $5,200 | | $55,000 |

During a short period after December 31, Paulson Truck Rental had the following transactions:

1. Bought office equipment at a cost of $2,700. Paid cash.
2. Collected $4,000 of accounts receivable.
3. Paid $3,200 of accounts payable.
4. Borrowed $10,000 from a bank. Signed a note payable for that amount.
5. Purchased two trucks for $30,500. Paid $15,000 cash and signed a note payable for the balance.
6. Sold additional stock to investors for $40,000.

**Instructions**

a. List the December 31 balances of assets, liabilities, and owners' equity in tabular form as shown above.

b. Record the effects of each of the six transactions in the tabular arrangement illustrated above. Show the totals for all columns after each transaction.

**PROBLEM 2.5**

Preparing a Balance Sheet; Effects of a Change in Assets

HERE COME THE CLOWNS! is the name of a traveling circus. The ledger accounts of the business at June 30, 2002, are listed here in alphabetical order:

| | | | |
|---|---|---|---|
| Accounts Payable | $ 26,100 | Notes Payable | $180,000 |
| Accounts Receivable | 7,450 | Notes Receivable | 9,500 |
| Animals | 189,060 | Props and Equipment | 89,580 |
| Cages | 24,630 | Retained Earnings | 27,230 |
| Capital Stock | 310,000 | Salaries Payable | 9,750 |
| Cash | ? | Tents | 63,000 |
| Costumes | 31,500 | Trucks & Wagons | 105,840 |

**Instructions**

**a.** Prepare a balance sheet by using these items and computing the amount of Cash at June 30, 2002. Organize your balance sheet similar to the one illustrated on page 51. (After "Accounts Receivable," you may list the remaining assets in any order.) Include a proper balance sheet heading.

**b.** Assume that late in the evening of June 30, after your balance sheet had been prepared, a fire destroyed one of the tents, which had cost $14,300. The tent was not insured. Explain what changes would be required in your June 30 balance sheet to reflect the loss of this asset.

**PROBLEM 2.6**

Preparing a Balance Sheet— a Second Problem

Shown below in random order is a list of balance sheet items for Smoky Mountain Farms at September 30, 2002:

| | | | |
|---|---|---|---|
| Land | $550,000 | Fences and Gates | $ 33,570 |
| Barns and Sheds | 78,300 | Irrigation System | 20,125 |
| Notes Payable | 530,000 | Cash | 16,710 |
| Accounts Receivable | 22,365 | Livestock | 120,780 |
| Citrus Trees | 76,650 | Farm Machinery | 42,970 |
| Accounts Payable | 77,095 | Retained Earnings | ? |
| Property Taxes Payable | 9,135 | Wages Payable | 5,820 |
| Capital Stock | 250,000 | | |

**Instructions**

**a.** Prepare a balance sheet by using these items and computing the amount for retained earnings. Use a sequence of assets similar to that illustrated on page 51. (After "Barns and Sheds" you may list the remaining assets in any order.) Include a proper heading for your balance sheet.

**b.** Assume that on September 30, immediately after this balance sheet was prepared, a tornado completely destroyed one of the barns. This barn had a cost of $13,700, and was not insured against this type of disaster. Explain what changes would be required in your September 30 balance sheet to reflect the loss of this barn.

**PROBLEM 2.7**

Preparing a Balance Sheet and Statement of Cash Flows; Effects of Business Transactions

The balance sheet items for The Oven Bakery (arranged in alphabetical order) were as follows at August 1, 2002. (You are to compute the missing figure for retained earnings.)

| | | | |
|---|---|---|---|
| Accounts Payable | $16,200 | Capital Stock | $80,000 |
| Accounts Receivable | 11,260 | Land | 67,000 |
| Building | 84,000 | Notes Payable | 74,900 |
| Cash | 6,940 | Salaries Payable | 8,900 |
| Equipment and Fixtures | 44,500 | Supplies | 7,000 |

During the next two days, the following transactions occurred:

**Aug. 2**  Additional capital stock was sold for $25,000. The accounts payable were paid in full. (No payment was made on the notes payable or income taxes payable.)

**Aug. 3**  Equipment was purchased at a cost of $7,200 to be paid within 10 days. Supplies were purchased for $1,250 cash from a restaurant supply center that was going out of business. These supplies would have cost $1,890 if purchased through normal channels.

## Instructions

**a.** Prepare a balance sheet at August 1, 2002.

**b.** Prepare a balance sheet at August 3, 2002, and a statement of cash flows for August 1–3. Classify the payment of accounts payable and the purchase of supplies as operating activities.

**c.** Assume the note payable does not come due for several years. Is The Oven Bakery in a stronger financial position on August 1 or on August 3? Explain briefly.

The balance sheet items of The Original Malt Shop (arranged in alphabetical order) were as follows at the close of business on September 30, 2002:

**PROBLEM 2.8**

Preparing Financial Statements; Effects of Business Transactions

 **LO 4, 5, 6**

| | | | |
|---|---|---|---|
| Accounts Payable | $ 8,500 | Land | $55,000 |
| Accounts Receivable | 1,250 | Capital Stock | 50,000 |
| Building | 45,500 | Notes Payable | ? |
| Cash | 7,400 | Retained Earnings | 4,090 |
| Furniture and Fixtures | 20,000 | Supplies | 3,440 |

The transactions occurring during the first week of October were:

**Oct. 3**  Additional capital stock was sold for $30,000. The accounts payable were paid in full. (No payment was made on the notes payable.)

**Oct. 6**  More furniture was purchased on account at a cost of $18,000, to be paid within 30 days. Supplies were purchased for $1,000 cash from a restaurant supply center that was going out of business. These supplies would have cost $1,875 if purchased under normal circumstances.

**Oct. 1–6**  Revenues of $5,500 were earned and paid in cash. Expenses required to earn the revenues of $4,000 were incurred and paid in cash.

## Instructions

**a.** Prepare a balance sheet at September 30, 2002. (You will need to compute the missing figure for Notes Payable.)

**b.** Prepare a balance sheet at October 6, 2002. Also prepare an income statement and a statement of cash flows for the period October 1–6, 2002. In your statement of cash flows, treat the purchase of supplies and the payment of accounts payable as operating activities.

**c.** Assume the note payable does not come due for several years. Is The Original Malt Shop in a stronger financial position on September 30 or on October 6? Explain briefly.

Helen Berkeley is the founder and manager of Old Town Playhouse. The business needs to obtain a bank loan to finance the production of its next play. As part of the loan application, Berkeley was asked to prepare a balance sheet for the business. She prepared the following balance sheet, which is arranged correctly but which contains several errors with respect to such concepts as the business entity and the valuation of assets, liabilities, and owner's equity.

**PROBLEM 2.9**

Preparing a Balance Sheet; Discussion of Accounting Principles

**LO 4, 8**

```
┌─────────────────────────────────────────────────────────────────────┐
│                      OLD TOWN PLAYHOUSE                                │
│                        Balance Sheet                                  │
│                     September 30, 2002                                │
├──────────────────────────────────┬────────────────────────────────────┤
```

| Assets | | Liabilities & Owner's Equity | |
|---|---|---|---|
| Cash | $ 21,900 | Liabilities: | |
| Accounts Receivable | 132,200 | Accounts Payable | $ 6,000 |
| Props and Costumes | 3,000 | Salaries Payable | 29,200 |
| Theater Building | 27,000 | Total liabilities | $35,200 |
| Lighting Equipment | 9,400 | Owner's equity: | |
| Automobile | 15,000 | Helen Berkeley, | |
| | | Capital | 50,000 |
| Total | $208,500 | Total | $85,200 |

In discussions with Berkeley and by reviewing the accounting records of Old Town Playhouse, you discover the following facts:

1. The amount of cash, $21,900, includes $15,000 in the company's bank account, $1,900 on hand in the company's safe, and $5,000 in Berkeley's personal savings account.

2. The accounts receivable, listed as $132,200, include $7,200 owed to the business by Artistic Tours. The remaining $125,000 is Berkeley's estimate of future ticket sales from September 30 through the end of the year (December 31).

3. Berkeley explains to you that the props and costumes were purchased several days ago for $18,000. The business paid $3,000 of this amount in cash and issued a note payable to Actors' Supply Co. for the remainder of the purchase price ($15,000). As this note is not due until January of next year, it was not included among the company's liabilities.

4. Old Town Playhouse rents the theater building from Kievits International at a rate of $3,000 a month. The $27,000 shown in the balance sheet represents the rent paid through September 30 of the current year. Kievits International acquired the building seven years ago at a cost of $135,000.

5. The lighting equipment was purchased on September 26 at a cost of $9,400, but the stage manager says that it isn't worth a dime.

6. The automobile is Berkeley's classic 1978 Jaguar, which she purchased two years ago for $9,000. She recently saw a similar car advertised for sale at $13,000. She does not use the car in the business, but it has a personalized license plate that reads "PLAHOUS."

7. The accounts payable include business debts of $3,900 and the $2,100 balance of Berkeley's personal Visa card.

8. Salaries payable include $25,000 offered to Mario Dane to play the lead role in a new play opening next December and $4,200 still owed to stagehands for work done through September 30.

9. When Berkeley founded Old Town Playhouse several years ago, she invested $20,000 in the business. However, Live Theatre, Inc., recently offered to buy her business for $50,000. Therefore, she listed this amount as her equity in the above balance sheet.

### Instructions

a. Prepare a corrected balance sheet for Old Town Playhouse at September 30, 2002.

b. For each of the nine numbered items above, explain your reasoning in deciding whether or not to include the items in the balance sheet and in determining the proper dollar valuation.

**PROBLEM 2.10**

Preparing a Balance Sheet; Discussion of Accounting Principles

**LO 2, 4**

Hollywood Scripts is a service-type enterprise in the entertainment field, and its manager, William Pippin, has only a limited knowledge of accounting. Pippin prepared the following balance sheet, which, although arranged satisfactorily, contains certain errors with respect to such concepts as the business entity and asset valuation. Pippin owns all of the corporation's outstanding stock.

| HOLLYWOOD SCRIPTS<br>Balance Sheet<br>November 30, 2002 | | | | |
|---|---|---|---|---|
| **Assets** | | **Liabilities & Owner's Equity** | | |
| Cash | $ 5,150 | Liabilities: | | |
| Notes Receivable | 2,700 | Notes Payable | | $ 67,000 |
| Accounts Receivable | 2,450 | Accounts Payable | | 35,805 |
| Land | 70,000 | Total liabilities | | $102,805 |
| Building | 54,320 | Owner's equity: | | |
| Office Furniture | 8,850 | Capital Stock | | 5,000 |
| Other Assets | 22,400 | Retained Earnings | | 58,065 |
| Total | $165,870 | Total | | $165,870 |

In discussion with Pippin and by inspection of the accounting records, you discover the following facts:

1. The amount of cash, $5,150, includes $3,400 in the company's bank account, $540 on hand in the company's safe, and $1,210 in Pippin's personal savings account.

2. One of the notes receivable in the amount of $500 is an IOU that Pippin received in a poker game several years ago. The IOU is signed by "B.K.," whom Pippin met at the game but has not heard from since.

3. Office furniture includes $2,900 for a Persian rug for the office purchased on November 20. The total cost of the rug was $9,400. The business paid $2,900 in cash and issued a note payable to Zoltan Carpet for the balance due ($6,500). As no payment on the note is due until January, this debt is not included in the liabilities above.

4. Also included in the amount for office furniture is a computer that cost $2,525 but is not on hand because Pippin donated it to a local charity.

5. The "Other Assets" of $22,400 represent the total amount of income taxes Pippin has paid the federal government over a period of years. Pippin believes the income tax law to be unconstitutional, and a friend who attends law school has promised to help Pippin recover the taxes paid as soon as he passes the bar exam.

6. The asset "Land" was acquired at a cost of $39,000 but was increased to a valuation of $70,000 when a friend of Pippin offered to pay that much for it if Pippin would move the building off the lot.

7. The accounts payable include business debts of $32,700 and the $3,105 balance owed on Pippin's personal MasterCard.

### Instructions

a. Prepare a corrected balance sheet at November 30, 2002.

b. For each of the seven numbered items above, use a separate numbered paragraph to explain whether the treatment followed by Pippin is in accordance with generally accepted accounting principles.

## CASES AND UNSTRUCTURED PROBLEMS

You are to prepare a balance sheet for a *hypothetical* business entity of your choosing (or specified by your instructor). Include in your balance sheet the types of assets and liabilities that you think the entity might have, and show these items at what you believe would be realistic dollar amounts. Make reasonable assumptions with regard to the company's capital stock and retained earnings.

**CASE 2.1**

Content of a Balance Sheet

LO 4

*Note:* The purpose of this assignment is to help you visualize the types of assets and liabilities relating to the operations of a specific type of business. You should complete this assignment *without* referring to an actual balance sheet for this type of business.

**CASE 2.2**

Using Financial Statements

**LO 4, 5, 6**

Obtain from the library the *annual report* of a well-known company (or a company specified by your instructor).

**Instructions**

From the balance sheet, income statement, statement of cash flows, and notes to the financial statements, answer the following:

a. What are the largest assets included in the company's balance sheet? Why would a company of this type (size and industry) have a large investment in this particular type of asset?

b. In reviewing the company's statement of cash flows:
   1. What are the primary sources and uses of cash from investing activities?
   2. Did investing activities cause the company's cash to increase or decrease?
   3. What are the primary sources and uses of cash from financing activities?
   4. Did financing activities cause the company's cash to increase or decrease?

c. In reviewing the company's income statement, did the company have a net income or a net loss for the most recent year? What percentage of total revenues was that net income or net loss?

d. Select three items in the notes accompanying the financial statements and explain briefly the importance of these items to people making decisions about investing in, or extending credit to, this company.

e. Assume that you are a lender, and this company has asked to borrow an amount of cash equal to 10% of its total assets, to be repaid in 90 days. Would you consider this company to be a good credit risk? Explain.

**CASE 2.3**

Using a Balance Sheet

**LO 4**

Sun Corporation and Terra Corporation are in the same line of business and both were recently organized, so it may be assumed that the recorded costs for assets are close to current market values. The balance sheets for the two companies are as follows at July 31, 2002:

### SUN CORPORATION
### Balance Sheet
### July 31, 2002

| Assets | | Liabilities & Owners' Equity | | |
|---|---|---|---|---|
| Cash | $ 18,000 | Liabilities: | | |
| Accounts Receivable | 26,000 | Notes Payable | | |
| Land | 37,200 | (due in 60 days) | | $12,400 |
| Building | 38,000 | Accounts Payable | | 9,600 |
| Office Equipment | 1,200 | Total liabilities | | $22,000 |
| | | Stockholders' equity: | | |
| | | Capital Stock | $60,000 | |
| | | Retained Earnings | 38,400 | 98,400 |
| Total | $120,400 | Total | | $120,400 |

| TERRA CORPORATION<br>Balance Sheet<br>July 31, 2002 | | | |
|---|---|---|---|
| **Assets** | | **Liabilities & Owners' Equity** | |
| Cash . . . . . . . . . . . . . . | $   4,800 | Liabilities: | |
| Accounts Receivable . . . | 9,600 | Notes Payable | |
| Land . . . . . . . . . . . . . . | 96,000 | (due in 60 days) . . . . . . . . . . . . . | $ 22,400 |
| Building . . . . . . . . . . . . | 60,000 | Accounts Payable . . . . . . . . . . . . . | 43,200 |
| Office Equipment . . . . . . | 12,000 | Total liabilities . . . . . . . . . . . . . . . | $ 65,600 |
| | | Stockholders' equity: | |
| | | Capital Stock . . . . . . . . $ 72,000 | |
| | | Retained Earnings . . . . . 44,800 | 116,800 |
| Total . . . . . . . . . . . . . . | $182,400 | Total . . . . . . . . . . . . . . . . . . . . . . . . | $182,400 |

## Instructions

**a.** Assume that you are a banker and that each company has applied to you for a 90-day loan of $12,000. Which would you consider to be the more favorable prospect? Explain your answer fully.

**b.** Assume that you are an investor considering purchasing all the capital stock of one or both of the companies. For which business would you be willing to pay the higher price? Do you see any indication of a financial crisis that you might face shortly after buying either company? Explain your answer fully. (For either decision, additional information would be useful, but you are to reach your decision on the basis of the information available.)

Ron Palmer is employed as a bank loan officer for Last State Bank. He is comparing two companies that have applied for loans, and he wants your help in evaluating those companies. The two companies—Purple, Inc., and Orange Company—are approximately the same size and had approximately the same cash balance at the beginning of 2001. Because the total cash flows for the three-year period are virtually the same, Ron is inclined to evaluate the two companies as equal in terms of their desirability as loan candidates.

Abbreviated information (in thousands of dollars) from Purple, Inc., and Orange Company is as follows:

**CASE 2.4**

Using Statements of Cash Flows

 **LO 6**

| | Purple, Inc. | | | Orange Company | | |
|---|---|---|---|---|---|---|
| | **2001** | **2002** | **2003** | **2001** | **2002** | **2003** |
| Cash flows from: | | | | | | |
| Operating activities | $10 | $13 | $15 | $ 8 | $3 | $(2) |
| Investing activities | (5) | (8) | (10) | (7) | (5) | 8 |
| Financing activities | 8 | (3) | 1 | 12 | 4 | -0- |
| Net from all activities | $13 | $ 2 | $ 6 | $13 | $2 | $6 |

## Instructions

**a.** Do you agree with Ron's preliminary assessment that the two companies are approximately equal in terms of their strength as loan candidates? Why or why not?

**b.** What might account for the fact that Orange Company's cash flow from financing activities is zero in 2003?

**c.** Generally, what would you advise Ron with regard to using statements of cash flows in evaluating loan candidates?

**CASE 2.5**

Ethics and Window Dressing

The date is November 18, 2002. You are the chief executive officer of Zeta Software—a publicly owned company that is currently in financial difficulty. Zeta needs large new bank loans if it is to survive.

You have been negotiating with several banks, but each has asked to see your 2002 financial statements, which will be dated December 31. These statements will, of course, be audited. You are now meeting with other corporate officers to discuss the situation, and the following suggestions have been made:

1. "We are planning to buy the WordMaster Software Co. for $8 million cash in December. The owners of WordMaster are in no hurry; if we delay this acquisition until January, we'll have $8 million more cash at year-end. That should make us look a lot more solvent."

2. "At year-end, we'll owe accounts payable of about $18 million. If we were to show this liability in our balance sheet at half that amount—say, $9 million—no one would know the difference. We could report the other $9 million as stockholders' equity and our financial position would appear much stronger."

3. "We owe Delta Programming $5 million, due in 90 days. I know some people at Delta. If we were to sign a note and pay them 12% interest, they'd let us postpone this debt for a year or more."

4. "We own land that cost us $2 million, but today is worth at least $6 million. Let's show it at $6 million in our balance sheet, and that will increase our total assets and our stockholders' equity by $4 million."

**Instructions**

Separately evaluate each of these four proposals to improve Zeta Software's financial statements. Your evaluations should consider ethical and legal issues as well as accounting issues.

## *BUSINESS WEEK* ASSIGNMENT                    BusinessWeek

**CASE 2.6**

**LO 10**

A *Business Week* (October 5, 1998) article titled "Corporate Earnings: Who Can You Trust?" by Sarah Bartlett indicates that foreign investors are flocking to the United States where they know certain bedrock principles still apply. In the United States, companies adhere to generally accepted accounting principles. Auditors scour the books to keep management honest. Regulators ensure that financial statements are properly prepared. Analysts rely on the numbers as they develop information that will make their clients money.

Why is it important that companies follow a standard set of accounting policies (called generally accepted accounting principles) in the preparation of financial statements? What features in the U.S. financial reporting system prevent management from becoming too aggressive in window dressing its financial statements?

## INTERNET ASSIGNMENTS

**INTERNET 2.1**

Gathering Financial Information

**LO 4, 5, 9**

We'd like to introduce you to EDGAR, the SEC's database of financial information about publicly owned companies. The SEC maintains EDGAR to increase the efficiency of financial reporting in the American economy and also to give the public free access to information about publicly owned companies.

**Instructions**

Access EDGAR at the following Internet address:

**www.sec.gov**

Click search Edgar archives on two consecutive screens, then type MCDONALDS CORP into the search box and press the enter key. Locate the most recent quarterly (10 Q) balance sheet.

a. What is the street address of McDonald's corporate headquarters?

b. Using the category "Financial Reports." Has the amount of the company's cash (and cash equivalents) increased or decreased since the beginning of the year?

**c.** Locate the income statement. What was the company's net income for the most recent quarter? Is this amount up or down from the preceding quarter or year?

**d.** How much cash was provided by operations during the quarter? Where did you find this information?

**e.** In Form 10Q, notes to the financial statements are called "Financial Comments." Select one of McDonald's financial comments and explain why it would be of interest to investors.

**f.** While you're in EDGAR, pick a company that interests you and learn more about it. Be prepared to tell the class which company you selected and explain what you learned.

*Internet sites are time and date sensitive. It is the purpose of these exercises to have you explore the Internet. You may need to use the Yahoo! search engine* http://www.yahoo.com *(or another favorite search engine) to find a company's current web address.*

## OUR COMMENTS ON THE "YOUR TURN" CASES

**You as a Home Owner (p. 44)**   In both situations, sales of comparable homes in the same location provide objective information about the value of your home. However, since your home has not been recently sold, the specific home value (asset value) is unknown. The ethical dilemma arises in precisely what objective information to report. For example, if 10 homes in the immediate area have sold within the last three months, which of those sales would you report? If the real estate assessor's office asked for three comparable sales, what information might be provided? Because homeowners wish to minimize their tax burden, many municipalities employ city property assessors to verify the value of real estate. Alternatively, because homeowners wish to maximize the sales price of their home they might choose different comparable home sales prices to report to a buyer than those chosen for the real estate assessor. Thus, although buyers may request comparable home sales information from the seller, they will usually undertake their own investigation to verify the value of the home.

The ethical issues are related to honest and objective (not selective) reporting. Reporting the market-driven sales prices of neighboring homes mitigates some of the ethical issues related to honest reporting.

**You as a Working College Student (p. 54)**   The assets you would need include a mower, a trimmer, one or more gas cans, and other similar items. You would also need certain other items, such as oil and gas, that are necessary for the proper functioning of your equipment. Finally, if you plan to work for people who live long distances from your location, you would need a truck or some way to transport your equipment and yourself to the work site. Revenues would consist primarily of amounts paid to you for your services. Expenses would include the cost of your equipment as well as gas, oil, and other necessities to maintain proper functioning of your equipment. You may also incur costs of repair and maintenance on your equipment. Essentially, you would know if you are doing well if you more than cover costs with the amounts you are taking in for your work. This requires detailed record keeping of your revenues and expenses.

**You as an Investor (p. 58)**   You might have several different objectives, but most people would be primarily interested in the potential for good return on their investment. For that reason, the financial strength of a company in which you invest is particularly important. In the income statement, you would be interested in whether the companies you are considering are profitable—do their revenues exceed their expenses? In the statements of financial position (balance sheets), you may be interested in the amount of their assets in comparison to their liabilities. In the statements of cash flows, you may be particularly interested in how cash is changing and the extent to which the company's operations are generating positive cash flows. Finally, you may find interesting information in notes to the financial statements and explanations by the management of each company concerning future plans and other aspects of the company that are not included in the primary financial statements.

## ANSWERS TO SELF-TEST QUESTIONS

**1.** a, c, d    **2.** b    **3.** b, d    **4.** c    **5.** b, c    **6.** b, d    **7.** a    **8.** a, b, d

CHAPTER

# 3

# THE ACCOUNTING CYCLE:

## Capturing Economic Events

## Learning Objectives

*After studying this chapter, you should be able to:*

1. Identify the steps in the accounting cycle and discuss the role of accounting records in an organization.

2. Describe a ledger account and a ledger.

3. State the rules of debit and credit for balance sheet accounts.

4. Explain the double-entry system of accounting.

5. Explain the purpose of a journal and its relationship to the ledger.

6. Explain the nature of *net income, revenue,* and *expenses.*

7. Apply the *realization* and *matching* principles in recording revenue and expenses.

8. Explain *why* revenues are recorded with credits and expenses are recorded with debits.

9. Prepare a trial balance and explain its uses and limitations.

10. Distinguish between accounting cycle procedures and the *knowledge* of accounting.

PepsiCo China Business Unit Guangzhou PepsiCo Beverage Co. Ltd.

# PepsiCo, Inc.

Capturing the economic events of a lemonade stand is a fairly simple process. In fact, for most lemonade stands, an empty cigar box easily serves as a complete information system.

Capturing the economic events of **PepsiCo, Inc.**, however, is an entirely different matter. This giant corporation generates annual revenue in excess of $20 billion from sales of its soft drink products, its Tropicana juices, and its Frito-Lay snack foods. Employing nearly 120,000 people, and operating hundreds of manufacturing facilities and thousands of warehouses and distribution centers, **PepsiCo, Inc.**, must somehow capture complex business transactions occurring in more than 160 countries worldwide.

From lemonade stands to multinational corporations, being able to efficiently capture the effects of economic events, such as sales orders and raw material purchases, is absolutely essential for survival. Companies like **PepsiCo, Inc.**, rely upon sophisticated computer systems to capture economic activities. Some small enterprises, however, may use paper ledgers and journals to record business transactions.

● ● ●

Although Overnight Auto Service engaged in several business transactions in the previous chapter, we did not illustrate how these events were captured by Overnight for use by management and other interested parties. This chapter demonstrates how accounting systems record economic events related to a variety of business transactions.

## THE ACCOUNTING CYCLE

**LO 1**

Identify the steps in the accounting cycle and discuss the role of accounting records in an organization.

In Chapter 2, we illustrated several transactions of Overnight Auto Service that occurred during the last week in January 2002. We prepared a complete set of financial statements immediately following our discussion of these transactions. For practical purposes, businesses do not prepare new financial statements after every transaction. Rather, they accumulate the effects of individual transactions in their *accounting records*. Then, at regular intervals, the data in these records are used to prepare financial statements, income tax returns, and other types of reports.

The sequence of accounting procedures used to record, classify, and summarize accounting information in financial reports at regular intervals is often termed the **accounting cycle**. The accounting cycle begins with the initial recording of business transactions and concludes with the preparation of a complete set of formal financial statements. The term *cycle* indicates that these procedures must be repeated continuously to enable the business to prepare new, up-to-date, financial statements at reasonable intervals.

The accounting cycle generally consists of eight specific steps. In this chapter, we illustrate how businesses (1) journalize (record) transactions, (2) post each journal entry to the appropriate ledger accounts, and (3) prepare a trial balance. The remaining steps of the cycle will be addressed in Chapters 4 and 5. They include (4) making end-of-period adjustments, (5) preparing an adjusted trial balance, (6) preparing financial statements, (7) journalizing and posting closing entries, and (8) preparing an after-closing trial balance.

### The Role of Accounting Records

The cyclical process of collecting financial information and maintaining accounting records does far more than facilitate the preparation of financial statements. Managers and employees of a business frequently use the information stored in the accounting records for such purposes as:

1. Establishing **accountability** for the assets and/or transactions under an individual's control.
2. Keeping track of routine business activities—such as the amounts of money in company bank accounts, amounts due from credit customers, or amounts owed to suppliers.
3. Obtaining detailed information about a particular transaction.
4. Evaluating the efficiency and performance of various departments within the organization.
5. Maintaining documentary evidence of the company's business activities. (For example, tax laws require companies to maintain accounting records supporting the amounts reported in tax returns.)

## THE LEDGER

**LO 2**

Describe a ledger account and a ledger.

An accounting system includes a separate record for each item that appears in the financial statements. For example, a separate record is kept for the asset cash, showing all increases and decreases in cash resulting from the many transactions in which cash is received or paid. A similar record is kept for every other asset, for every liability, for owners' equity, and for every revenue and expense account appearing in the income statement.

The record used to keep track of the increases and decreases in financial statement items is termed a "ledger account" or, simply, an **account**. The entire group of accounts is kept together in an accounting record called a **ledger**.

## THE USE OF ACCOUNTS

An account is a means of accumulating in one place all the information about changes in specific financial statement items, such as a particular asset or liability. For example, the Cash account provides a company's current cash balance, a record of its cash receipts, and a record of its cash disbursements.

In its simplest form, an account has only three elements: (1) a title; (2) a left side, which is called the *debit* side; and (3) a right side, which is called the *credit* side. This form of an account, illustrated below and on the following page, is called a *T account* because of its resemblance to the letter "T." In a computerized system, of course, the elements of each account are stored and formatted electronically. More complete forms of accounts will be illustrated later.

**Title of Account**

| Left or | Right or |
|---------|----------|
| Debit Side | Credit Side |

*A T account—a ledger account in its simplest form*

## DEBIT AND CREDIT ENTRIES

An amount recorded on the left, or debit, side of an account is called a **debit**, or a debit entry. Likewise, any amount entered on the right, or credit, side is called a **credit**, or a credit entry. In simple terms, debits refer to the left side of an account, and credits refer to the right side of an account.

To illustrate the recording of debits and credits in an account, let us go back to the eight cash transactions of Overnight Auto Service, described in Chapter 2. When these cash transactions are recorded in the Cash account, the receipts are listed on the debit side, and the payments are listed on the credit side. The dates of the transactions may also be listed, as shown in the following illustration:

**Cash**

| 1/20 | 80,000 | 1/21 | 52,000 |
|------|--------|------|--------|
| 1/26 | 600 | 1/22 | 6,000 |
| 1/31 | 2,200 | 1/27 | 6,800 |
| | | 1/31 | 200 |
| | | 1/31 | 1,200 |
| 1/31 Balance | 16,600 | | |

*Cash transactions entered in ledger account*

Each debit and credit entry in the Cash account represents a cash receipt or a cash payment. The amount of cash owned by the business at a given date is equal to the *balance* of the account on that date.

**Determining the Balance of a T Account**   The balance of an account is the difference between the debit and credit entries in the account. If the debit total exceeds the credit total, the account has a *debit balance*; if the credit total exceeds the debit total, the account has a *credit balance*.

In our illustrated Cash account, a dotted line has been drawn across the account following the last cash transaction recorded in January. The total cash receipts (debits) recorded in January amount to $82,800, and the total cash payments (credits) amount to $66,200. By subtracting the credit total from the debit total ($82,800 − $66,200), we determine that the Cash account has a debit balance of *$16,600* on January 31.

This debit balance is entered in the debit side of the account just below the line. In effect, the horizontal rule creates a "fresh start" in the account, with the month-end balance representing the *net result* of all the previous debit and credit entries. The Cash account now shows the amount of cash owned by the business on January 31. In a balance sheet prepared at this date, Cash in the amount of $16,600 would be listed as an asset.

### You as a Student

You probably do not use debits and credits in accounting for your personal financial activities. Does this mean that the concept of double-entry accounting does not apply to changes in your personal financial position? Explain and provide several examples.

*Our comments appear on page 131.

**YOUR TURN**

**LO 3**

State the rules of debit and credit for balance sheet accounts.

**Debit Balances in Asset Accounts**   In the preceding illustration of a Cash account, increases were recorded on the left, or debit, side of the account and decreases were recorded on the right, or credit, side. The increases were greater than the decreases and the result was a debit balance in the account.

All asset accounts *normally have debit balances.* It is hard to imagine an account for an asset such as land having a credit balance, as this would indicate that the business had disposed of more land than it had ever acquired. (For some assets, such as cash, it is possible to acquire a credit balance—but such balances are only *temporary.*)

The fact that assets are located on the *left* side of the balance sheet is a convenient means of remembering the rule that an increase in an asset is recorded on the *left* (debit) side of the account and an asset account normally has a debit *(left-hand)* balance.

*Asset accounts normally have debit balances*

**Any Asset Account**

| Debit (representing an increase) | Credit (representing a decrease) |
|---|---|

**Credit Balances in Liability and Owners' Equity Accounts**   Increases in liability and owners' equity accounts are recorded by credit entries and decreases in these accounts are recorded by debits. The relationship between entries in these accounts and their position on the balance sheet may be summed up as follows: (1) liabilities and owners' equity belong on the *right* side of the balance sheet, (2) an increase in a liability or an owners' equity account is recorded on the *right* (credit) side of the account, and (3) liability and owners' equity accounts normally have credit *(right-hand)* balances.

*Liability and owners' equity accounts normally have credit balances*

**Any Liability Account or Owners' Equity Account**

| Debit (representing a decrease) | Credit (representing an increase) |
|---|---|

**Concise Statement of the Debit and Credit Rules**   The use of debits and credits to record changes in assets, liabilities, and owners' equity may be summarized as follows:

*Debit and credit rules*

| Asset Accounts | Liability & Owners' Equity Accounts |
|---|---|
| Normally have debit balances. Thus, increases are recorded by debits and decreases are recorded by credits. | Normally have credit balances. Thus, increases are recorded by credits and decreases are recorded by debits. |

## Double-Entry Accounting — The Equality of Debits and Credits

The rules for debits and credits are designed so that *every transaction is recorded by equal dollar amounts of debits and credits.* The reason for this equality lies in the relationship of the debit and credit rules to the accounting equation:

**Assets     =  Liabilities + Owners' Equity**

**Debit Balances =          Credit Balances**

If this equation is to remain in balance, any change in the left side of the equation (assets) *must be accompanied by an equal change* in the right side (either liabilities or owners' equity). According to the debit and credit rules that we have just described, increases in the left side of the equation (assets) are recorded by *debits,* while increases in the right side (liabilities and owners' equity) are recorded by *credits.*

This system is often called **double-entry accounting.** The phrase *double-entry* refers to the need for both *debit entries* and *credit entries,* equal in dollar amount, to record every transaction. Virtually every business organization uses the double-entry system regardless of whether the company's accounting records are maintained manually or by computer. In addition, the double-entry system allows us to measure net income at the same time we record the effects of transactions on the balance sheet accounts.

**LO 4**

Explain the double-entry system of accounting.

## RECORDING TRANSACTIONS IN LEDGER ACCOUNTS: AN ILLUSTRATION

The use of debits and credits for recording transactions in accounts now will be illustrated using selected January transactions of Overnight Auto Service. At this point, we discuss only those transactions related to changes in the company's financial position and reported directly in its balance sheet. The revenue and expense transactions that took place on January 31 will be addressed later in the chapter.

Each transaction from January 20 through January 27 is analyzed first in terms of increases in assets, liabilities, and owners' equity. Second, we follow the debit and credit rules for entering these increases and decreases in specific accounts. Asset accounts will be shown on the left side of the analysis; liability and owners' equity accounts will be shown on the right side. For convenience in the following transactions, both the debit and credit entries for the transaction under discussion are shown in *red.* Entries relating to earlier transactions appear in *black.*

**Jan. 20**   Michael McBryan and family, invested $80,000 cash in exchange for capital stock.

| ANALYSIS | The asset Cash is increased by $80,000, and owners' equity (Capital Stock) is increased by the same amount. |
|---|---|
| DEBIT–CREDIT RULES | Increases in assets are recorded by debits; debit Cash $80,000.<br>Increases in owners' equity are recorded by credits; credit Capital Stock $80,000. |
| ENTRIES IN LEDGER ACCOUNTS | **Cash**<br>1/20  80,000<br><br>**Capital Stock**<br>1/20  80,000 |

*Owners invest cash in the business*

**Jan. 21**    Representing Overnight, McBryan negotiated with both the City of Santa Teresa and Metropolitan Transit Authority (MTA) to purchase an abandoned bus garage. (The city owned the land, but the MTA owned the building.) On January 21, Overnight Auto Service purchased the land from the city for $52,000 cash.

*Purchase of an asset for cash*

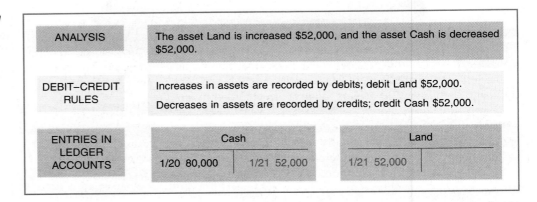

**Jan. 22**    Overnight completed the acquisition of its business location by purchasing the abandoned building from the MTA. The purchase price was $36,000; Overnight made a $6,000 cash down payment and issued a 90-day, non-interest-bearing note payable for the remaining $30,000.

*Purchase of an asset, making a small down payment*

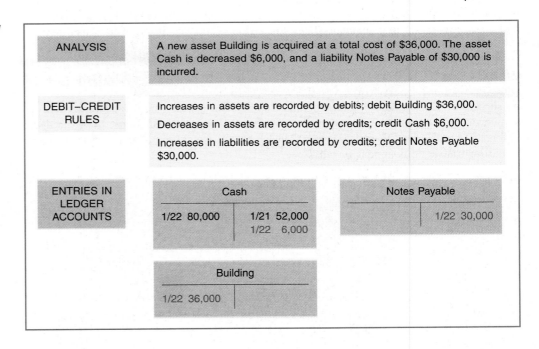

**Jan. 23**    Overnight purchased tools and equipment on account from **Snap-On Tools Corp**. The purchase price was $13,800, due in 60 days.

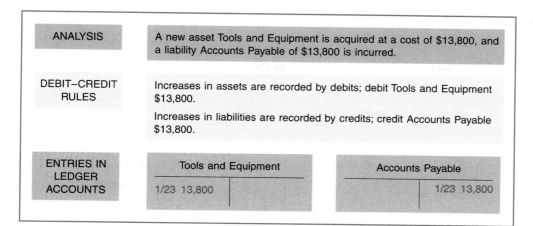

*Credit purchase of an asset*

**Jan. 24** Overnight found that it had purchased more tools than it needed. On January 24, it sold the excess tools on account to Ace Towing at a price of $1,800. The tools were sold at a price equal to their cost, so there was no gain or loss on this transaction.

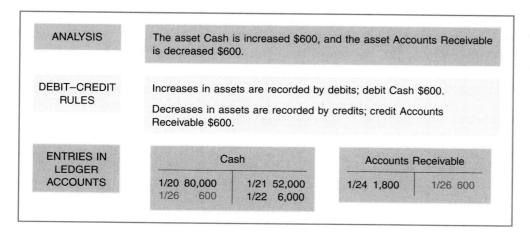

*Credit sale of an asset (with no gain or loss)*

**Jan. 26** Overnight received $600 in partial collection of the account receivable from Ace Towing.

*Collection of an account receivable*

**Jan. 27** Overnight made a $6,800 partial payment of its account payable to **Snap-On Tools Corp**.

*Payment of an account payable*

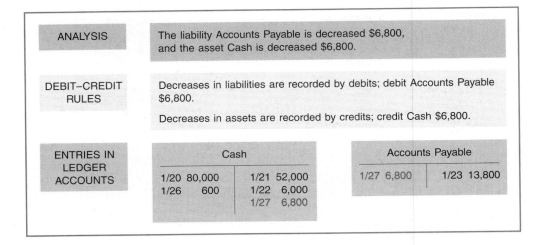

| ANALYSIS | The liability Accounts Payable is decreased $6,800, and the asset Cash is decreased $6,800. |
|---|---|
| DEBIT–CREDIT RULES | Decreases in liabilities are recorded by debits; debit Accounts Payable $6,800.<br><br>Decreases in assets are recorded by credits; credit Cash $6,800. |

ENTRIES IN LEDGER ACCOUNTS

| Cash | | | | Accounts Payable | |
|---|---|---|---|---|---|
| 1/20 80,000 | 1/21 52,000 | | | 1/27 6,800 | 1/23 13,800 |
| 1/26 600 | 1/22 6,000 | | | | |
| | 1/27 6,800 | | | | |

## THE JOURNAL

**LO 5**

Explain the purpose of a journal and its relationship to the ledger.

In the preceding discussion, we recorded Overnight Auto Service's transactions in the company's ledger accounts. We did this to stress the effects of business transactions on the individual asset, liability, and owners' equity accounts. In an actual accounting system, however, the information about each business transaction is initially recorded in an accounting record called the **journal**.

The journal is a chronological (day-by-day) record of business transactions. At convenient intervals, the debit and credit amounts recorded in the journal are transferred (posted) to the accounts in the ledger. The updated ledger accounts, in turn, serve as the basis for preparing the company's financial statements.

The simplest type of journal is called a **general journal** and is shown at the top of the following page. Note the way in which transactions are recorded in the general journal:

1. The name of the account to be debited is written first, and the dollar amount to be debited appears in the left-hand money column.

2. The name of the account credited appears below the account debited and is indented to the right. The dollar amount credited appears in the right-hand money column.

3. A brief description of each transaction appears immediately below each journal entry.

Accounting software packages automate and streamline the way in which transactions are recorded. However, recording transactions manually—without a computer—is an effective way to conceptualize the manner in which economic events are captured by accounting systems and subsequently reported in a company's financial statements.

| | GENERAL JOURNAL | | |
|---|---|---|---|
| **Date** | **Account Titles and Explanation** | **Debit** | **Credit** |
| 2002 | | | |
| Jan. 20 | Cash ........................................................ | 80,000 | |
| |     Capital Stock ......................................... | | 80,000 |
| | Owners invest cash in the business. | | |
| 21 | Land ........................................................ | 52,000 | |
| |     Cash ................................................. | | 52,000 |
| | Purchased land for business site. | | |
| 22 | Building .................................................... | 36,000 | |
| |     Cash ................................................. | | 6,000 |
| |     Notes Payable ....................................... | | 30,000 |
| | Purchased building from MTA. Paid part cash; balance payable within 90 days. | | |
| 23 | Tools and Equipment ....................................... | 13,800 | |
| |     Accounts Payable .................................... | | 13,800 |
| | Purchased tools and equipment on credit from Snap-On Tools Corp. Due in 60 days. | | |
| 24 | Accounts Receivable ....................................... | 1,800 | |
| |     Tools and Equipment ................................. | | 1,800 |
| | Sold unused tools and equipment at cost to Ace Towing. | | |
| 26 | Cash ........................................................ | 600 | |
| |     Accounts Receivable ................................. | | 600 |
| | Collected part of account receivable from Ace Towing. | | |
| 27 | Accounts Payable .......................................... | 6,800 | |
| |     Cash ................................................. | | 6,800 |
| | Made partial payment of the liability to Snap-On Tools Corp. | | |

*Journal entries of Overnight Auto Service for January 20 through January 27*

A familiarity with the general journal form of describing transactions is just as essential to the study of accounting as a familiarity with plus and minus signs is to the study of mathematics. The journal entry is a *tool* for *analyzing* and *describing* the impact of various transactions on a business entity. The ability to describe a transaction in journal entry form requires an understanding of the nature of the transaction and its effect on the financial position of the business.

## Posting Journal Entries to the Ledger Accounts (and How to "Read" a Journal Entry)

We have made the point that transactions are recorded *first* in the journal. Ledger accounts are updated *later,* through a process called **posting**. (In a computerized system, postings often occur instantaneously, rather than later.)

Posting simply means *updating the ledger accounts* for the effects of the transactions recorded in the journal. Viewed as a mechanical task, posting basically amounts to performing the steps you describe when you "read" a journal entry aloud.

Consider the first entry appearing in Overnight's general journal. If you were to read this entry aloud, you would say: "Debit Cash, $80,000; credit Capital Stock, $80,000." That's precisely what a person posting this entry should do: Debit the Cash account for $80,000, and credit the Capital Stock account for $80,000.

The posting of Overnight's first journal entry is illustrated in the following diagram:

*Posting a transaction from journal to ledger accounts*

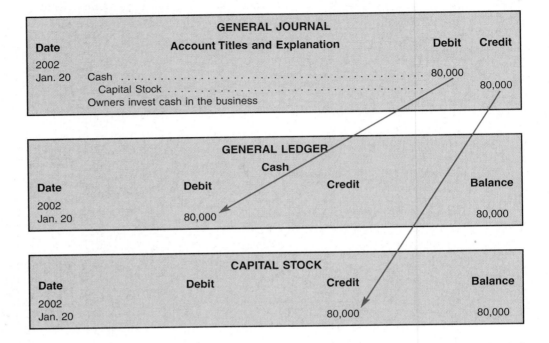

Notice that no new information is recorded during the posting process. Posting involves copying into the ledger accounts information that *already has been recorded in the journal.* In manual accounting systems, this can be a tedious and time-consuming process; but in computer-based systems, it is done instantly and automatically. In addition, computerized posting greatly reduces the risk of errors.

**Ledger Accounts after Posting**    After all the transactions through January 27 have been posted, Overnight's ledger accounts appear as shown below and on the next page. The accounts are arranged in the same order as in the balance sheet—that is, assets first, followed by liabilities and owners' equity. Each ledger account is presented in what is referred to as a *running balance* format (as opposed to simple T accounts). You will notice that the running balance format does not indicate specifically whether a particular account has a debit or credit balance. This causes no difficulty, however, because we know that asset accounts normally have debit balances, and liability and owners' equity accounts normally have credit balances.

In the ledger accounts that follow we have not yet included any of Overnight's revenue and expense transactions discussed in Chapter 2. All of the company's revenue and expense transactions took place on January 31. Before we can discuss the debit and credit rules for revenue and expense accounts, a more in-depth discussion of *net income* is warranted.

*Ledger showing transactions from January 20 through January 27*

| | | CASH | |
|---|---|---|---|
| **Date** | **Debit** | **Credit** | **Balance** |
| 2002 | | | |
| Jan. 20 | 80,000 | | 80,000 |
| 21 | | 52,000 | 28,000 |
| 22 | | 6,000 | 22,000 |
| 26 | 600 | | 22,600 |
| 27 | | 6,800 | 15,800 |

### ACCOUNTS RECEIVABLE

| Date | Debit | Credit | Balance |
|------|-------|--------|---------|
| 2002 | | | |
| Jan. 24 | 1,800 | | 1,800 |
| 26 | | 600 | 1,200 |

### LAND

| Date | Debit | Credit | Balance |
|------|-------|--------|---------|
| 2002 | | | |
| Jan. 21 | 52,000 | | 52,000 |

### BUILDING

| Date | Debit | Credit | Balance |
|------|-------|--------|---------|
| 2002 | | | |
| Jan. 22 | 36,000 | | 36,000 |

### TOOLS AND EQUIPMENT

| Date | Debit | Credit | Balance |
|------|-------|--------|---------|
| 2002 | | | |
| Jan. 23 | 13,800 | | 13,800 |
| 24 | | 1,800 | 12,000 |

### NOTES PAYABLE

| Date | Debit | Credit | Balance |
|------|-------|--------|---------|
| 2002 | | | |
| Jan. 22 | | 30,000 | 30,000 |

### ACCOUNTS PAYABLE

| Date | Debit | Credit | Balance |
|------|-------|--------|---------|
| 2002 | | | |
| Jan. 23 | | 13,800 | 13,800 |
| 27 | 6,800 | | 7,000 |

### CAPITAL STOCK

| Date | Debit | Credit | Balance |
|------|-------|--------|---------|
| 2002 | | | |
| Jan. 20 | | 80,000 | 80,000 |

## WHAT IS NET INCOME?

**LO 6**

Explain the nature of *net income, revenue,* and *expenses.*


*Net income is not an asset—it's an* increase in owners' equity

As previously noted, **net income** is *an increase in owners' equity resulting from the profitable operation of the business.* Net income does not consist of any cash or any other specific assets. Rather, net income is a *computation* of the overall effects of many business transactions on *owners' equity.* The effects of net income on the basic accounting equation are illustrated as follows:

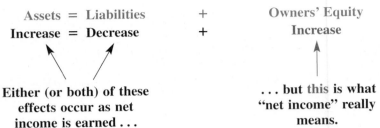

Assets = Liabilities + Owners' Equity
Increase = Decrease + Increase

Either (or both) of these effects occur as net income is earned . . .

. . . but **this** is what "net income" really means.

Our point is that net income represents an *increase in owners' equity* and has no direct relationship to the types or amounts of assets on hand. Even a business operating at a profit may run short of cash and become insolvent.

In the balance sheet, the changes in owners' equity resulting from profitable or unprofitable operations are reflected in the balance of the stockholders' equity account, *Retained Earnings.* The assets of the business organization appear in the *assets* section of the balance sheet.

### Retained Earnings

As illustrated in Chapter 1, the Retained Earnings account appears in the stockholders' equity section of the balance sheet. Earning net income causes the balance in the Retained Earnings account to increase. However, many corporations follow a policy of distributing to their stockholders some of the resources generated by profitable operations. Distributions of this nature are termed **dividends**, and they reduce both total assets and stockholders' equity. The reduction in stockholders' equity is reflected by decreasing the balance of the Retained Earnings account.

The balance in the **Retained Earnings** account represents the total net income of the corporation over the *entire lifetime* of the business, less all amounts which have been distributed to the stockholders as dividends. In short, retained earnings represent the earnings that have been *retained* by the corporation to finance growth. Some of the largest corporations have become large by consistently retaining in the business most of the resources generated by profitable operations.

**CASE IN POINT**

A recent annual report of **Campbell Soup Company** shows total stockholders' equity amounting to nearly $2 billion. Stockholders originally invested only about $71 million—less than 4% of the current equity—in exchange for capital stock. In addition to the original investment, the company has added $1.9 billion to stockholders' equity through profitable operations.

### The Income Statement: A Preview

An **income statement** is a financial statement that summarizes the profitability of a business entity for a specified period of time. In this statement, net income is determined by comparing *sales prices* of goods or services sold during the period with the *costs* incurred by the business in delivering these goods or services. The technical accounting terms for these components of net income are **revenue** and **expenses**. Therefore, accountants say that net income is equal to *revenue minus expenses*. Should expenses exceed revenue, a **net loss** results.

A sample income statement for Overnight Auto Service for the year ended December 31, 2002, is shown below. In Chapter 5, we show exactly how this income statement was developed from the company's accounting records. For now, however, the illustration will assist us in discussing some of the basic concepts involved in measuring net income.

### OVERNIGHT AUTO SERVICE
### Income Statement
### For the Year Ended December 31, 2002

**Revenue:**

| | | |
|---|---:|---:|
| Repair service revenue | | $172,000 |
| Rent revenue earned | | 3,000 |
| Total revenue | | $175,000 |

**Expenses:**

| | | |
|---|---:|---:|
| Advertising | $ 3,900 | |
| Salaries and wages | 58,750 | |
| Supplies | 7,500 | |
| Depreciation: building | 1,650 | |
| Depreciation: tools and equipment | 2,200 | |
| Utilities | 19,400 | |
| Insurance | 15,000 | |
| Interest | 30 | 108,430 |
| Income before income taxes | | 66,570 |
| Income taxes | | 26,628 |
| Net income | | $ 39,942 |

*A preview of Overnight's income statement for the year ended December 31, 2002*

**Income Must Be Related to a Specified Period of Time**   Notice that our sample income statement covers a *period of time*—namely, the year 2002. A balance sheet shows the financial position of a business at a *particular date*. An income statement, on the other hand, shows the results of business operations over a span of time. We cannot evaluate net income unless it is associated with a specific time period. For example, if an executive says, "My business earns a net income of $10,000," the profitability of the business is unclear. Does it earn $10,000 per week, per month, or per year?

The late J. Paul Getty, one of the world's first billionaires, was once interviewed by a group of business students. One of the students asked Getty to estimate the amount of his income. As the student had not specified a time period, Getty decided to have some fun with his audience and responded, "About $11,000 ... " He paused long enough to allow the group to express surprise over this seemingly low amount, and then completed his sentence, "an hour." (Incidentally, $11,000 per hour, 24 hours per day, amounts to about $100 million per year.)

**CASE IN POINT**

**Accounting Periods**   The period of time covered by an income statement is termed the company's **accounting period**. To provide the users of financial statements with timely information, net income is measured for relatively short accounting periods of equal length. This concept, called the **time period principle**, is one of the generally accepted accounting principles that guide the interpretation of financial events and the preparation of financial statements.

The length of a company's accounting period depends on how frequently managers, investors, and other interested people require information about the company's performance. Every business prepares annual income statements, and most businesses prepare quarterly and monthly income statements as well. (Quarterly statements cover a three-month period and are prepared by all large corporations for distribution to their stockholders.)

The 12-month accounting period used by an entity is called its **fiscal year**. The fiscal year used by most companies coincides with the calendar year and ends on December 31. Some businesses, however, elect to use a fiscal year that ends on some other date. It may be convenient for a business to end its fiscal year during a slack season rather than during a time of peak activity.

**CASE IN POINT**

The **Walt Disney Company** ends its fiscal year on September 30. Why? For one reason, September and October are relatively slow months at Disney's theme parks. For another, September financial statements provide timely information about the preceding summer, which is the company's busiest season.

As another example, many department stores, including **Kmart**, **Neiman-Marcus**, **Nordstrom**, and **J. C. Penney**, end their fiscal years on January 31—after the rush of the holiday season.

Let us now explore the meaning of the accounting terms *revenue* and *expenses* in more detail.

## Revenue

*Revenue is the price of goods sold and services rendered during a given accounting period.* Earning revenue causes owners' equity to increase. When a business renders services or sells merchandise to its customers, it usually receives cash or acquires an account receivable from the customer. The inflow of cash and receivables from customers increases the total assets of the company; on the other side of the accounting equation, the liabilities do not change, but owners' equity increases to match the increase in total assets. Thus revenue is the gross *increase in owners' equity* resulting from operation of the business.

Various account titles are used to describe different types of revenue. For example, a business that sells merchandise rather than services, such as **Wal-Mart** or **General Motors**, uses the term *Sales* to describe its revenue. In the professional practices of physicians, CPAs, and attorneys, revenue usually is called *Fees Earned*. A real estate office, however, might call its revenue *Commissions Earned*.

Overnight Auto Service's income statement reveals that the company records its revenue in two separate accounts: (1) *Repair Service Revenue* and (2) *Rent Revenue Earned*. A professional sports team might also have separate revenue accounts for *Ticket Sales, Concessions Revenue,* and *Revenue from Television Contracts.* Another type of revenue common to many businesses is *Interest Revenue* (or Interest Earned), stemming from the interest earned on bank deposits, notes receivable, and interest-bearing investments.

**LO 7**

Apply the *realization* and *matching* principles in recording revenue and expenses.

**The Realization Principle: When to Record Revenue**     When should revenue be recognized? In most cases, the **realization principle** indicates that revenue should be recognized *at the time goods are sold or services are rendered.* At this point, the business has essentially completed the earnings process and the sales value of the goods or services can be measured objectively. At any time prior to the sale, the ultimate value of the goods or services sold can only be estimated. After the sale, the only step that remains is to collect from the customer, usually a relatively certain event.

---

Assume that on July 25 KGPO Radio contracts with Rancho Ford to run 200 one-minute advertisements during August. KGPO runs these ads and receives full payment from Rancho Ford on September 6. In which month should KGPO recognize the advertising revenue earned from Rancho Ford—July, August, or September?

The answer is August, the month in which KGPO *rendered the services* that earned the revenue.[1] In other words, the revenue is recognized when it is *earned*, without regard to when cash payment for goods or services is received.

**CASH EFFECTS**

---

## Expenses

*Expenses are the costs of the goods and services used up in the process of earning revenue.* Examples include the cost of employees' salaries, advertising, rent, utilities, and the depreciation of buildings, automobiles, and office equipment. All these costs are necessary to attract and serve customers and thereby earn revenue. Expenses are often called the "costs of doing business," that is, the cost of the various activities necessary to carry on a business.

An expense always causes a *decrease in owners' equity.* The related changes in the accounting equation can be either (1) a decrease in assets or (2) an increase in liabilities. An expense reduces assets if payment occurs at the time that the expense is incurred. If the expense will not be paid until later, as, for example, the purchase of advertising services on account, the recording of the expense will be accompanied by an increase in liabilities.

### The Matching Principle: When to Record Expenses

A significant relationship exists between revenue and expenses. Expenses are incurred for the *purpose of producing revenue*. In measuring net income for a period, revenue should be offset by *all the expenses incurred in producing that revenue*. This concept of offsetting expenses against revenue on a basis of cause and effect is called the **matching principle**.

Timing is an important factor in matching (offsetting) revenue with the related expenses. For example, in preparing monthly income statements, it is important to offset this month's expenses against this month's revenue. We should not offset this month's expenses against last month's revenue because there is no cause and effect relationship between the two.

---

Assume that the salaries earned by sales personnel waiting on customers during July are not paid until early August. In which month should these salaries be regarded as an expense—July or August?

The answer is July, because this is the month in which the sales personnel's services *helped to produce revenue*. Just as revenue and cash receipts are not one and the same, expenses and cash payments are not identical. In fact, the cash payment of an expense may occur before, after, or in the same period that revenue is produced. In deciding when to record an expense, the critical question is "In what period does the cash expenditure help to produce revenue?" *not* "When does the cash payment occur?"

**CASH EFFECTS**

---

[1] Some readers may wonder what would happen if some of the ads were aired in August and others in September. In this case, KGPO would recognize an *appropriate portion* of the advertising revenue in August and the remainder in September. The accounting procedures for allocating revenue between accounting periods are discussed and illustrated in the next chapter.

**Expenditures Benefiting More Than One Accounting Period**  Many expenditures made by a business benefit two or more accounting periods. Fire insurance policies, for example, usually cover a period of 12 months. If a company prepares monthly income statements, a portion of the cost of such a policy should be allocated to insurance expense each month that the policy is in force. In this case, apportionment of the cost of the policy by months is an easy matter. If the 12-month policy costs $2,400, for example, the insurance expense for each month amounts to $200 ($2,400 cost ÷ 12 months).

Not all transactions can be divided so precisely by accounting periods. The purchase of a building, furniture and fixtures, machinery, a computer, or an automobile provides benefits to the business over all the years in which such an asset is used. No one can determine in advance exactly how many years of service will be received from such long-lived assets. Nevertheless, in measuring the net income of a business for a period of one year or less, accountants must *estimate* what portion of the cost of the building and other long-lived assets is applicable to the current year. Since the allocations of these costs are estimates rather than precise measurements, it follows that income statements should be regarded as useful *approximations* of net income rather than as absolutely correct measurements.

For some expenditures, such as those for advertising or employee training programs, it is not possible to estimate objectively the number of accounting periods over which revenue is likely to be produced. In such cases, generally accepted accounting principles require that the expenditure be charged *immediately to expense*. This treatment is based upon the accounting principle of **objectivity** and the concept of **conservatism**. Accountants require *objective evidence* that an expenditure will produce revenue in future periods before they will view the expenditure as creating an asset. When this objective evidence does not exist, they follow the conservative practice of recording the expenditure as an expense. *Conservatism,* in this context, means applying the accounting treatment that results in the *lowest* (most conservative) estimate of net income for the current period.

**CASE IN POINT**  Internationally, there is significant disagreement about whether some business expenditures should be immediately expensed or can be recorded as an asset. In particular, research and development costs, which must be expensed as incurred under U.S. accounting standards, can be either expensed immediately *or* recorded as an asset in Sweden and Italy.

## The Accrual Basis of Accounting

The policy of recognizing revenue in the accounting records when it is *earned* and recognizing expenses when the related goods or services are *used* is called the **accrual basis of accounting**. The purpose of accrual accounting is to measure the profitability of the *economic activities conducted* during the accounting period.

The most important concept involved in accrual accounting is the *matching principle*. Revenue is offset with all of the expenses incurred in generating that revenue, thus providing a measure of the overall profitability of the economic activity.

An alternative to the accrual basis is called *cash basis accounting*. Under cash basis accounting, revenue is recognized when cash is collected from the customer, rather than when the company sells goods or renders services. Expenses are recognized when payment is made, rather than when the related goods or services are used in business operations. The cash basis of accounting measures the amounts of cash received and paid out during the period, but it does *not* provide a good measure of the *profitability of activities* undertaken during the period.

Airlines sell many tickets weeks or even months *in advance* of scheduled flights. Yet many expenses relating to a flight—such as salaries of the flight crew and the cost of fuel used—may not be paid until *after* the flight has occurred. Recognizing these events when cash is received or paid would fail to "match" revenues and expenses in the period when flights actually occur.

**CASE IN POINT**

## Debit and Credit Rules for Revenue and Expenses

We have stressed that revenue increases owners' equity and that expenses decrease owners' equity. The debit and credit rules for recording revenue and expenses in the ledger accounts are a natural extension of the rules for recording changes in owners' equity. The rules previously stated for recording increases and decreases in owners' equity are as follows:

**LO 8**

Explain *why* revenues are recorded with credits and expenses are recorded with debits.

* *Increases* in owners' equity are recorded by *credits*.
* *Decreases* in owners' equity are recorded by *debits*.

This rule is now extended to cover revenue and expense accounts:

* *Revenue* increases owners' equity; therefore, revenue is recorded by a *credit*.
* *Expenses* decrease owners' equity; therefore, expenses are recorded by *debits*.

## DIVIDENDS

A dividend is a distribution of assets (usually cash) by a corporation to its stockholders. In some respects, dividends are similar to expenses—they reduce both the assets and the owners' equity in the business. However, *dividends are not an expense, and they are not deducted from revenue in the income statement*. The reason why dividends are not viewed as an expense is that these payments do not serve to generate revenue. Rather, they are a *distribution of profits* to the owners of the business.

Since the declaration of a dividend reduces stockholders' equity, the dividend could be recorded by debiting the Retained Earnings account. However, a clearer record is created if a separate Dividends account is debited for all amounts distributed as dividends to stockholders. The disposition of the Dividends account when financial statements are prepared will be illustrated in Chapter 5.

The debit–credit rules for revenue, expense, and dividends are summarized below:

| Owners' Equity | |
|---|---|
| Decreases recorded by Debits | Increases recorded by Credits |
| Expenses decrease owners' equity | Revenue increases owners' equity |
| Expenses are recorded by Debits | Revenue is recorded by Credits |
| Dividends reduce owner's equity | |
| Dividends are recorded by Debits | |

*Debit–credit rules related to effect on owners' equity*

**YOUR TURN**

### You as a Business Owner

You are the sole owner of a small business. The mortgage payment on your home is due, but you have very little money in your personal checking account. Therefore, you write a check for this payment from the business bank account.

Does it matter whether your business is unincorporated or organized as a corporation?

*Our comments appear on page 132.

## RECORDING REVENUE AND EXPENSE TRANSACTIONS: AN ILLUSTRATION

In Chapter 2, we introduced Overnight Auto Service, a small auto repair shop formed on January 20, 2002. Early in this chapter we journalized and posted all of Overnight's balance sheet transactions through January 27. At this point we will illustrate the manner in which Overnight's January income statement transactions were handled, and continue into February with additional transactions.

Three transactions involving revenue and expenses were recorded by Overnight on January 31, 2002. The following illustrations provide an analysis of each transaction.

**Jan. 31.** Recorded Revenue of $2,200, all of which was received in cash.

*Revenue earned and collected*

| ANALYSIS | The asset Cash is increased. |
| --- | --- |
| | Revenue has been earned. |

| DEBIT–CREDIT RULES | Increases in assets are recorded by debits; debit Cash $2,200. |
| --- | --- |
| | Revenue increases owners' equity and is recorded by a credit; credit Repair Service Revenue $2,200. |

| JOURNAL ENTRY | Jan. 31 Cash . . . . . . . . . . . . . . . . . . 2,200 |
| --- | --- |
| | Repair Service Revenue . . . . . . . . 2,200 |

**ENTRIES IN LEDGER ACCOUNTS**

| Cash | | Repair Service Revenue |
| --- | --- | --- |
| 1/27 Bal. 15,800 | | 1/31 2,200 |
| 1/31 2,200 | | |

**Jan. 31**   Paid employees' wages earned in January, $1,200.

*Incurred an expense, paying cash*

| ANALYSIS | Wages to employees are an expense.<br>The asset Cash is decreased. |
|---|---|
| DEBIT–CREDIT RULES | Expenses decrease owners' equity and are recorded by debits; debit Wages Expense $1,200.<br><br>Decreases in assets are recorded by credits; credit Cash $1,200. |
| JOURNAL ENTRY | Jan. 31        Wages Expense . . . . . . . . . . . .   1,200<br>                          Cash . . . . . . . . . . . . . . . . . . . . . . .        1,200 |

ENTRIES IN LEDGER ACCOUNTS

| Cash | | Wages Expense | |
|---|---|---|---|
| 1/27  Bal. 15,800 | 1/31  1,200 | 1/31  1,200 | |
| 1/31         2,200 | | | |

**Jan. 31**   Paid for utilities used in January, $200.

*Incurred an expense, paying cash*

| ANALYSIS | The cost of utilities is an expense.<br>The asset Cash is decreased. |
|---|---|
| DEBIT–CREDIT RULES | Expenses decrease owners' equity and are recorded by debits; debit Utilities Expense $200.<br><br>Decreases in assets are recorded by credits; credit Cash $200. |
| JOURNAL ENTRY | Jan. 31        Utilities Expense . . . . . . . . . . . . .   200<br>                          Cash . . . . . . . . . . . . . . . . . . . . . . .      200 |

ENTRIES IN LEDGER ACCOUNTS

| Cash | | Utilities Expense | |
|---|---|---|---|
| 1/27  Bal. 15,800 | 1/31  1,200 | 1/31  200 | |
| 1/31         2,200 | 1/31     200 | | |

Having analyzed and recorded all of Overnight's January transactions, next we focus upon the company's February activities. Overnight's February transactions are described, analyzed, and recorded on the following pages.

**Feb. 1**    Paid *Daily Tribune* $360 cash for newspaper advertising to be run during February.

*Incurred an expense, paying cash*

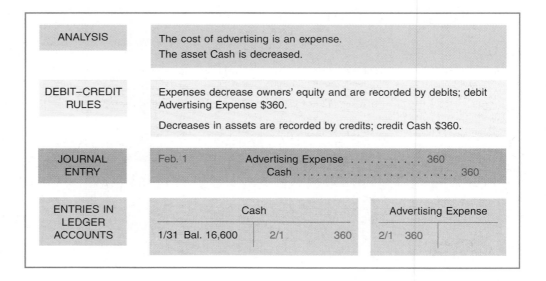

**Feb. 2**    Purchased radio advertising from KRAM to be aired in February. The cost was $470, payable within 30 days.

*Incurred an expense to be paid later*

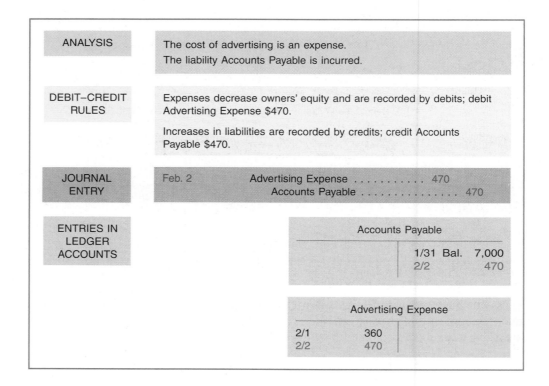

**Feb. 4** Purchased various shop supplies (such as grease, solvents, nuts, and bolts) from **NAPA Auto Parts**; cost $1,400, due in 30 days. These supplies are expected to meet Overnight's needs for *three or four months.*

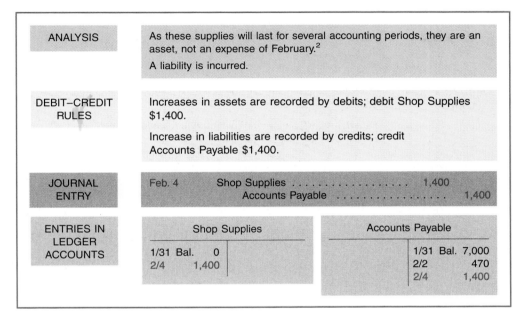

| ANALYSIS | As these supplies will last for several accounting periods, they are an asset, not an expense of February.[2] <br><br> A liability is incurred. |
|---|---|
| DEBIT–CREDIT RULES | Increases in assets are recorded by debits; debit Shop Supplies $1,400. <br><br> Increase in liabilities are recorded by credits; credit Accounts Payable $1,400. |
| JOURNAL ENTRY | Feb. 4      Shop Supplies . . . . . . . . . . . . . . . . . 1,400 <br>               Accounts Payable . . . . . . . . . . . . . . . . 1,400 |

ENTRIES IN LEDGER ACCOUNTS

| Shop Supplies | | Accounts Payable | |
|---|---|---|---|
| 1/31 Bal.   0 | | 1/31 Bal. 7,000 | |
| 2/4     1,400 | | 2/2         470 | |
| | | 2/4      1,400 | |

*When a purchase clearly benefits future accounting periods, it's an asset, not an expense*

**Feb. 15** Collected $4,980 cash for repairs made to vehicles of Airport Shuttle Service.

*Revenue earned and collected*

| ANALYSIS | The asset Cash is increased. <br><br> Revenue has been earned. |
|---|---|
| DEBIT–CREDIT RULES | Increases in assets are recorded by debits; debit Cash $4,980. <br><br> Revenue increases owners' equity and is recorded by a credit; credit Repair Service Revenue $4,980. |
| JOURNAL ENTRY | Feb. 15      Cash . . . . . . . . . . . . . . . . . . . 4,980 <br>               Repair Service Revenue . . . . . . . . . . . 4,980 |

ENTRIES IN LEDGER ACCOUNTS

| Cash | | Repair Service Revenue | |
|---|---|---|---|
| 1/31 Bal. 16,600 | 2/1       360 | | 1/31 Bal. 2,200 |
| 2/15     4,980 | | | 2/15      4,980 |

---

[2] If the supplies are expected to be used within the *current* accounting period, their cost is debited directly to the Supplies Expense account, rather than to an asset account.

Feb. 28    Billed Harbor Cab Co. $5,400 for maintenance and repair services Overnight provided in February. The agreement with Harbor Cab calls for payment to be received by March 10.

*Revenue earned but not yet collected*

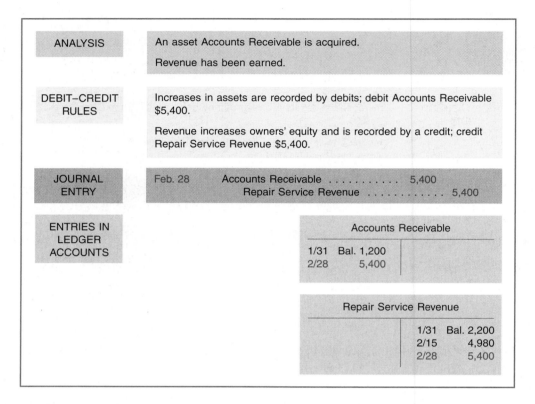

| ANALYSIS | An asset Accounts Receivable is acquired. |
| --- | --- |
| | Revenue has been earned. |
| DEBIT–CREDIT RULES | Increases in assets are recorded by debits; debit Accounts Receivable $5,400. |
| | Revenue increases owners' equity and is recorded by a credit; credit Repair Service Revenue $5,400. |

| JOURNAL ENTRY | Feb. 28    Accounts Receivable . . . . . . . . . . . 5,400 |
| --- | --- |
| |              Repair Service Revenue . . . . . . . . . . . 5,400 |

ENTRIES IN LEDGER ACCOUNTS

| Accounts Receivable | |
| --- | --- |
| 1/31   Bal. 1,200 | |
| 2/28       5,400 | |

| Repair Service Revenue | |
| --- | --- |
| | 1/31   Bal. 2,200 |
| | 2/15       4,980 |
| | 2/28       5,400 |

**YOUR TURN**

### You as Overnight Auto Service's Accountant

The owner of Harbor Cab Co. approached you at a recent chamber of commerce meeting to inform you that Harbor Cab expects a cash shortage during the month of March. Harbor Cab has asked you to extend its payment deadline from March 10 to April 10 in exchange for free cab service for a month. What would you do?

*Our comments appear on page 132.

**Feb. 28**   Paid employees' wages earned in February, $4,900.

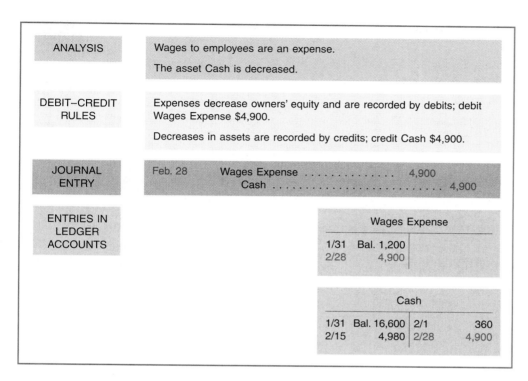

*Incurred an expense, paying cash*

**Feb. 28**   Recorded $1,600 utility bill for February. The entire amount is due March 15.

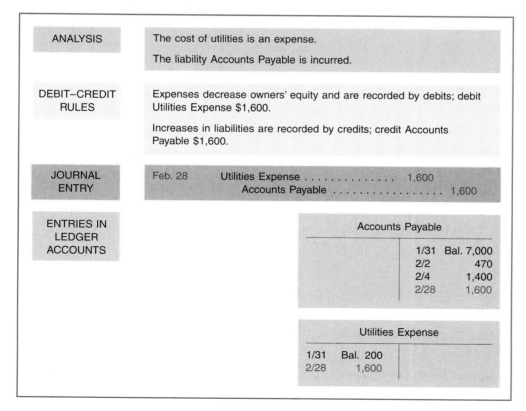

*Incurred an expense to be paid later*

**Feb. 28** Overnight Auto Services declares and pays a dividend of 40 cents per share to the owners of its 8,000 shares of capital stock—a total of $3,200.[3]

*A Dividends account signifies a reduction in owners' equity—but it's not an expense*

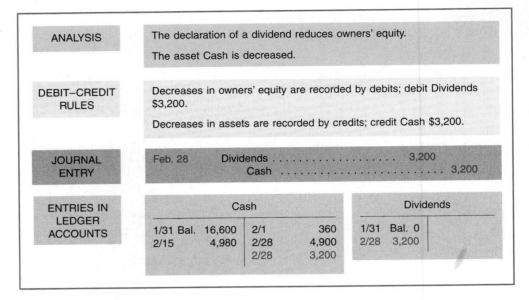

| | |
|---|---|
| **ANALYSIS** | The declaration of a dividend reduces owners' equity.<br>The asset Cash is decreased. |
| **DEBIT–CREDIT RULES** | Decreases in owners' equity are recorded by debits; debit Dividends $3,200.<br>Decreases in assets are recorded by credits; credit Cash $3,200. |
| **JOURNAL ENTRY** | Feb. 28    Dividends .................... 3,200<br>                        Cash ......................... 3,200 |

ENTRIES IN LEDGER ACCOUNTS

| Cash | | | | Dividends | | |
|---|---|---|---|---|---|---|
| 1/31 Bal. | 16,600 | 2/1 | 360 | 1/31 Bal. 0 | | |
| 2/15 | 4,980 | 2/28 | 4,900 | 2/28 3,200 | | |
| | | 2/28 | 3,200 | | | |

## The Journal

In our illustration, journal entries were shown in a very abbreviated form. The actual entries made in Overnight's journal appear on the facing page. Notice that these formal journal entries include short *explanations* of the transactions, which include such details as the terms of credit transactions and the names of customers and creditors.

---

[3] As explained earlier, dividends are not an expense. In Chapter 5, we will show how the balance in the Dividends account eventually reduces the amount of retained earnings reported in the owners' equity section of the balance sheet.

| | GENERAL JOURNAL | | |
|---|---|---|---|
| **Date** | **Account Titles and Explanation** | **Debit** | **Credit** |
| 2002 | | | |
| Jan. 31 | Cash | 2,200 | |
| |    Repair Service Revenue | | 2,200 |
| | Repair services rendered to various customers. | | |
| 31 | Wages Expense | 1,200 | |
| |    Cash | | 1,200 |
| | Paid all wages for January. | | |
| 31 | Utilities Expense | 200 | |
| |    Cash | | 200 |
| | Paid all utilities for January. | | |
| Feb. 1 | Advertising Expense | 360 | |
| |    Cash | | 360 |
| | Purchased newspaper advertising from *Daily Tribune* to run in February. | | |
| 2 | Advertising Expense | 470 | |
| |    Accounts Payable | | 470 |
| | Purchased radio advertising on account from KRAM; payment due in 30 days | | |
| 4 | Shop Supplies | 1,400 | |
| |    Accounts Payable | | 1,400 |
| | Purchased shop supplies on account from NAPA; payment due in 30 days. | | |
| 15 | Cash | 4,980 | |
| |    Repair Service Revenue | | 4,980 |
| | Repair services rendered to Airport Shuttle Service. | | |
| 28 | Accounts Receivable | 5,400 | |
| |    Repair Service Revenue | | 5,400 |
| | Billed Harbor Cab for services rendered in February. | | |
| 28 | Wages Expense | 4,900 | |
| |    Cash | | 4,900 |
| | Paid all wages for February. | | |
| 28 | Utilities Expense | 1,600 | |
| |    Accounts Payable | | 1,600 |
| | Recorded utility bill for February. | | |
| 28 | Dividends | 3,200 | |
| |    Cash | | 3,200 |
| | Paid cash dividend of 40 cents per share on 8,000 shares of capital stock owned by the McBryan family. | | |

*Journal entries contain more information than just dollar amounts*

**MANAGEMENT STRATEGY**

The accounting records of an enterprise can provide significant information about business strategies being pursued by managers. For example, Overnight Auto appears to be pursuing a business strategy of acquiring other companies as customers (e.g., Airport Shuttle Service and Harbor Cab Co.) rather than individual car owners for customers. If Overnight Auto's accounts receivable records included only receivables from individuals (e.g., Betty Brown and Joe Smith), then it would be creating a very different type of business strategy.

## FEBRUARY'S LEDGER BALANCES

After posting all of the January and February transactions, Overnight's ledger accounts appear as shown on the following page. To conserve space, we have illustrated the ledger in T account form and have carried forward each account's summary balance from January 31. For convenience, we show in *red* the *February 28 balance* of each account (debit balances appear to the left of the account; credit balances appear to the right).

The accounts in this illustration appear in *financial statement order*—that is, balance sheet accounts first (assets, liabilities, and owners' equity), followed by the income statement accounts (revenue and expenses).

# The Ledger

## Asset Accounts

### Cash

| | | | |
|---|---|---|---|
| 1/31 Bal. | 16,600 | 2/1 | 360 |
| 2/15 | 4,980 | 2/28 | 4,900 |
| | | 2/28 | 3,200 |
| Bal. $13,120 | | | |

### Accounts Receivable

| | |
|---|---|
| 1/31 | 1,200 |
| 2/28 | 5,400 |
| Bal. $6,600 | |

### Shop Supplies

| | |
|---|---|
| 1/31 Bal. | 0 |
| 2/4 | 1,400 |
| Bal. $1,400 | |

### Land

| | |
|---|---|
| 1/31 Bal. | 52,000 |
| Bal. $52,000 | |

### Building

| | |
|---|---|
| 1/31 Bal. | 36,000 |
| Bal. $36,000 | |

### Tools and Equipment

| | |
|---|---|
| 1/31 Bal. | 12,000 |
| Bal. $12,000 | |

## Liability and Owners' Equity Accounts

### Notes Payable

| | |
|---|---|
| 1/31 Bal. | 30,000 |
| | Bal. $30,000 |

### Accounts Payable

| | |
|---|---|
| 1/31 Bal. | 7,000 |
| 2/2 | 470 |
| 2/4 | 1,400 |
| 2/28 | 1,600 |
| | Bal. $10,470 |

### Capital Stock

| | |
|---|---|
| 1/31 Bal. | 80,000 |
| | Bal. $80,000 |

### Dividends

| | |
|---|---|
| 1/31 Bal. | 0 |
| 2/28 | 3,200 |
| Bal. $3,200 | |

### Repair Service Revenue

| | |
|---|---|
| 1/31 Bal. | 2,200 |
| 2/15 | 4,980 |
| 2/28 | 5,400 |
| | Bal. $12,580 |

### Advertising Expense

| | |
|---|---|
| 2/1 | 360 |
| 2/2 | 470 |
| Bal. $830 | |

### Wages Expense

| | |
|---|---|
| 1/31 Bal. | 1,200 |
| 2/28 | 4,900 |
| Bal. $6,100 | |

### Utilities Expense

| | |
|---|---|
| 1/31 Bal. | 200 |
| 2/28 | 1,600 |
| Bal. $1,800 | |

## THE TRIAL BALANCE

**LO 9**

Prepare a trial balance and explain its uses and limitations.

Since equal dollar amounts of debits and credits are entered in the accounts for every transaction recorded, the sum of all the debits in the ledger must be equal to the sum of all the credits. If the computation of account balances has been accurate, it follows that the total of the accounts with debit balances must be equal to the total of the accounts with credit balances.

Before using the account balances to prepare a balance sheet, it is desirable to *prove* that the total of accounts with debit balances is in fact equal to the total of accounts with credit balances. This proof of the equality of debit and credit balances is called a **trial balance**. A trial balance is a two-column schedule listing the names and balances of all the accounts *in the order in which they appear in the ledger*; the debit balances are listed in the left-hand column and the credit balances in the right-hand column. The totals of the two columns should agree. A trial balance taken from Overnight Auto's ledger accounts on page 111 is shown below.

*A trial balance proves the equality of debits and credits—but it also gives you a feel for how the business stands. But wait—there's more to consider.*

| OVERNIGHT AUTO SERVICE<br>Trial Balance<br>February 28, 2002 | | |
|---|---:|---:|
| Cash | $ 13,120 | |
| Accounts receivable | 6,600 | |
| Shop supplies | 1,400 | |
| Land | 52,000 | |
| Building | 36,000 | |
| Tools and equipment | 12,000 | |
| Notes payable | | $ 30,000 |
| Accounts payable | | 10,470 |
| Capital stock | | 80,000 |
| Retained earnings | | 0 |
| Dividends | 3,200 | |
| Repair service revenue | | 12,580 |
| Advertising expense | 830 | |
| Wages expense | 6,100 | |
| Utilities expense | 1,800 | |
| | $133,050 | $133,050 |

This trial balance proves the equality of the debit and credit entries in the company's accounting system. Notice that the trial balance contains both balance sheet and income statement accounts. Note also that the Retained Earnings balance is *zero*. It is zero because *no debit or credit entries were made to the Retained Earnings account in January or February.* Overnight, like most companies, updates its Retained Earnings balance only *once each year*. In Chapter 5, we show how the Retained Earnings account is updated to its proper balance at year-end on December 31.[4]

---

[4] The balance of $0 in the Retained Earnings account is a highly unusual situation. Because the company is still in its first year of operations, no entries have ever been made to update the account's balance. In any trial balance prepared after the first year of business activity, the Retained Earnings account may be expected to have a balance other than $0.

## Uses and Limitations of the Trial Balance

The trial balance provides proof that the ledger is in balance. The agreement of the debit and credit totals of the trial balance gives assurance that:

1. Equal debits and credits have been recorded for all transactions.
2. The addition of the account balances in the trial balance has been performed correctly.

Suppose that the debit and credit totals of the trial balance do not agree. This situation indicates that one or more errors have been made. Typical of such errors are (1) the posting of a debit as a credit, or vice versa; (2) arithmetic mistakes in determining account balances; (3) clerical errors in copying account balances into the trial balance; (4) listing a debit balance in the credit column of the trial balance, or vice versa; and (5) errors in addition of the trial balance.

The preparation of a trial balance does *not* prove that transactions have been correctly analyzed and recorded in the proper accounts. If, for example, a receipt of cash were erroneously recorded by debiting the Land account instead of the Cash account, the trial balance would still balance. Also, if a transaction were completely omitted from the ledger, the error would not be disclosed by the trial balance. In brief, *the trial balance proves only one aspect of the ledger, and that is the equality of debits and credits*.

## SOME CONCLUDING REMARKS

## The Accounting Cycle in Perspective

In this chapter we have (1) journalized (recorded) transactions, (2) posted each journal entry to the appropriate ledger accounts, and (3) prepared a trial balance. The steps to be covered in Chapters 4 and 5 include (4) making end-of-period adjustments, (5) preparing an adjusted trial balance, (6) preparing financial statements, (7) journalizing and posting closing entries, and (8) preparing an after-closing trial balance.

We view the accounting cycle as an efficient means of introducing basic accounting terms, concepts, processes, and reports. This is why we introduce it early in the course. As we conclude the accounting cycle in Chapters 4 and 5, please don't confuse your familiarity with this sequence of procedures with a knowledge of *accounting*. The accounting cycle is but one accounting process—and a relatively simple one at that.

**LO 10**

Distinguish between accounting cycle procedures and the *knowledge* of accounting.

Computers now free accountants to focus upon the more *analytical* aspects of their discipline. These include, for example:

• Determining the information needs of decision makers.
• Designing systems to provide the information quickly and efficiently.
• Evaluating the efficiency of operations throughout the organization.
• Assisting decision makers in interpreting accounting information.
• Auditing (confirming the reliability of accounting information).
• Forecasting the probable results of future operations.
• Tax planning.

We will emphasize such topics in later chapters of this text. But let us first repeat a very basic point from Chapter 1: The need for some familiarity with accounting concepts and processes is not limited to individuals planning careers in accounting. Today, an understanding of accounting information and of the business world go hand in hand. You cannot know much about one without understanding quite a bit about the other.

**A SECOND LOOK**

## PepsiCo, Inc.

In this chapter, we illustrated how Overnight Auto Service's accounting system captured numerous economic events. While a far more complex set of circumstances exist for **PepsiCo, Inc.**, the general accounting concepts that underlie revenue and expense recognition are pretty much the same for a multinational soft drink giant as they are for Overnight Auto Service.

In the following chapter, we examine certain adjustments to revenue and expense accounts required of most companies—both large and small—to comply with generally accepted principles of the accrual-based accounting method.

## SUMMARY OF LEARNING OBJECTIVES

### LO 1

**Identify the steps in the accounting cycle and discuss the role of accounting records in an organization.**

The accounting cycle generally consists of eight specific steps: (1) journalizing (recording) transactions, (2) posting each journal entry to the appropriate ledger accounts, (3) preparing a trial balance, (4) making end-of-period adjustments, (5) preparing an adjusted trial balance, (6) preparing financial statements, (7) journalizing and posting closing entries, and (8) preparing an after-closing trial balance.

Accounting records provide the information that is summarized in financial statements, income tax returns, and other accounting reports. In addition, these records are used by the company's management and employees for such purposes as:

- Establishing accountability for assets and transactions.
- Keeping track of routine business activities.
- Obtaining details about specific transactions.
- Evaluating the performance of units within the business.
- Maintaining a documentary record of the business's activities. (Such a record is required by tax laws and is useful for many business purposes, including audits.)

### LO 2

**Describe a ledger account and a ledger.**

A ledger account is a device for recording the increases or decreases in one financial statement item, such as a particular asset, a type of liability, or owners' equity. The general ledger is an accounting record that includes all the ledger accounts—that is, a separate account for each item included in the company's financial statements.

### LO 3

**State the rules of debit and credit for balance sheet accounts.**

Increases in assets are recorded by debits and decreases are recorded by credits. Increases in liabilities and in owners' equity are recorded by credits and decreases are recorded by debits. Notice that the debit and credit rules are related to an account's *location in the balance sheet*. If the account appears on the *left side* of the balance sheet (asset accounts), increases in the account balance are recorded by *left-side entries* (debits). If the account appears on the *right side* of the balance sheet (liability and owners' equity accounts), increases are recorded by *right-side entries* (credits).

### LO 4

**Explain the double-entry system of accounting.**

The double-entry system of accounting takes its name from the fact that every business transaction is recorded by *two types of entries*: (1) debit entries to one or more accounts and (2) credit entries to one or more accounts. In recording any transaction, the total dollar amount of the debit entries must equal the total dollar amount of the credit entries.

### LO 5

**Explain the purpose of a journal and its relationship to the ledger.**

The journal is the accounting record in which business transactions are initially recorded. The entry in the journal shows which ledger accounts have increased as a result of the transaction, and which have decreased. After the effects of the transaction have been recorded in the journal, the changes in the individual ledger accounts are then posted to the ledger.

### LO 6

**Explain the nature of *net income, revenue,* and *expenses*.**

Net income is an increase in owners' equity that results from the profitable operation of a business during an accounting period. Net income also may be defined as revenue minus expenses. Revenue is the price of goods sold and services rendered to customers during the period, and expenses are the costs of the goods and services used up in the process of earning revenue.

### LO 7

**Apply the *realization* and *matching* principles in recording revenue and expenses.**

The realization principle indicates that revenue should be recorded in the accounting records when it is *earned*—that is, when goods are sold or services are rendered to customers. The matching principle indicates that expenses should be offset against revenue on the basis of *cause and effect*. Thus, an expense should be recorded in the period in which the related good or service is consumed in the process of earning revenue.

### LO 8

**Explain *why* revenues are recorded with credits and expenses are recorded with debits.**

The debit and credit rules for recording revenue and expenses are based on the rules for recording *changes in owners' equity*. Earning revenue *increases* owners' equity; therefore, revenues are recorded with credit entries. Expenses *reduce* owners' equity and are recorded with debit entries.

### LO 9

**Prepare a trial balance and explain its uses and limitations.**

In a trial balance, separate debit and credit columns are used to list the balances of the individual ledger accounts. The two columns are then totaled to prove the equality of the debit and credit balances. This process provides assurance that (1) the total of the debits posted to the ledger was equal to the total of the credits and (2) the balances of the individual ledger accounts were correctly computed. While a trial balance proves the equality of debit and credit entries in the ledger, it does *not* detect such errors as failure to record a business transaction, improper analysis of the accounts affected by the transaction, or the posting of debit or credit entries to the wrong accounts.

**LO 10**

**Distinguish between accounting cycle procedures and the *knowledge* of accounting.**

Accounting procedures involve the steps and processes necessary to *prepare* accounting information. A knowledge of the discipline enables one to *use* accounting information in evaluating performance, forecasting operations, and making complex business decisions.

In this chapter we have illustrated the initial steps of the accounting cycle for a *service-type* business (accounting for *merchandising* activities will be discussed in Chapter 6). We have seen how businesses analyze and journalize transactions, post transactions to appropriate ledger accounts, and prepare trial balances. In Chapter 4, we will examine adjustments made for the accrual and deferral of revenue and expenses. In Chapter 5, we complete the accounting cycle by illustrating the preparation of financial statements and the year-end closing process.

# KEY TERMS INTRODUCED OR EMPHASIZED IN CHAPTER 3

**account** (p. 86) A record used to summarize all increases and decreases in a particular asset, such as cash, or any other type of asset, liability, owners' equity, revenue, or expense.

**accountability** (p. 86) The condition of being held responsible for one's actions by the existence of an independent record of those actions. Establishing accountability is a major goal of accounting records and of internal control procedures.

**accounting cycle** (p. 86) The sequence of accounting procedures used to record, classify, and summarize accounting information. The cycle begins with the initial recording of business transactions and concludes with the preparation of formal financial statements.

**accounting period** (p. 97) The span of time covered by an income statement. One year is the accounting period for much financial reporting, but financial statements are also prepared by companies for each quarter of the year and for each month.

**accrual basis of accounting** (p. 100) Calls for recording revenue in the period in which it is earned and recording expenses in the period in which they are incurred. The effect of events on the business is recognized as services are rendered or consumed rather than when cash is received or paid.

**conservatism** (p. 100) The traditional accounting practice of resolving uncertainty by choosing the solution that leads to the lower (more conservative) amount of income being recognized in the current accounting period. This concept is designed to avoid overstatement of financial strength or earnings.

**credit** (p. 87) An amount entered on the right side of a ledger account. A credit is used to record a decrease in an asset or an increase in a liability or in owners' equity.

**debit** (p. 87) An amount entered on the left side of a ledger account. A debit is used to record an increase in an asset or a decrease in a liability or in owners' equity.

**dividends** (p. 96) A distribution of resources by a corporation to its stockholders. The resource most often distributed is cash.

**double-entry accounting** (p. 89) A system of recording every business transaction with equal dollar amounts of both debit and credit entries. As a result of this system, the accounting equation always remains in balance; in addition, the system makes possible the measurement of net income and also the use of error-detecting devices such as a trial balance.

**expenses** (p. 97) The costs of the goods and services used up in the process of obtaining revenue.

**fiscal year** (p. 98) Any 12-month accounting period adopted by a business.

**general journal** (p. 92) The simplest type of journal, it has only two money columns—one for credits and one for debits. This journal may be used for all types of transactions, which are later posted to the appropriate ledger accounts.

**income statement** (p. 96) A financial statement summarizing the results of operations of a business by matching its revenue and related expenses for a particular accounting period. Shows the net income or net loss.

**journal** (p. 92) A chronological record of transactions, showing for each transaction the debits and credits to be entered in specific ledger accounts. The simplest type of journal is called a general journal.

**ledger** (p. 86) An accounting system includes a separate record for each item that appears in the financial statements. Collectively, these records are referred to as a company's ledger. Individually, these records are often referred to as ledger accounts.

**matching principle** (p. 99) The generally accepted accounting principle that determines when expenses should be recorded in the accounting records. The revenue earned during an accounting period is matched (offset) with the expenses incurred in generating this revenue.

**net income** (p. 96) An increase in owners' equity resulting from profitable operations. Also, the excess of revenue earned over the related expenses for a given period.

**net loss** (p. 97) A decrease in owners' equity resulting from unprofitable operations.

**objectivity** (p. 100) Accountants' preference for using dollar amounts that are relatively factual—as opposed to merely matters of personal opinion. Objective measurements can be verified.

**posting** (p. 93) The process of transferring information from the journal to individual accounts in the ledger.

**realization principle** (p. 98) The generally accepted accounting principle that determines when revenue should be recorded in the accounting records. Revenue is realized when services are rendered to customers or when goods sold are delivered to customers.

**retained earnings** (p. 96) That portion of stockholders' (owners') equity resulting from profits earned and retained in the business.

**revenue** (p. 97) The price of goods and services charged to customers for goods and services rendered by a business.

**time period principle** (p. 98) To provide the users of financial statements with timely information, net income is measured for relatively short accounting periods of equal length. The period of time covered by an income statement is termed the company's accounting period.

**trial balance** (p. 112) A two-column schedule listing the names and the debit or credit balances of all accounts in the ledger.

## DEMONSTRATION PROBLEM

Epler Consulting Services, Inc., opened for business on January 25, 2002. The company maintains the following ledger accounts:

| | |
|---|---|
| Cash | Capital Stock |
| Accounts Receivable | Retained Earnings |
| Office Supplies | Consulting Revenue |
| Office Equipment | Rent Expense |
| Accounts Payable | Utilities Expense |

The company engaged in the following business activity in January:

**Jan. 20**  Issued 5,000 shares of capital stock for $50,000.

**Jan. 20**  Paid $400 office rent for the remainder of January.

**Jan. 21**  Purchased office supplies for $200. The supplies will last for several months, and payment is not due until February 15.

**Jan. 22**  Purchased office equipment for $15,000 cash.

**Jan. 26**  Performed consulting services and billed clients $2,000. The entire amount will not be collected until February.

**Jan. 31**  Recorded $100 utilities expense. Payment is not due until February 20.

### Instructions

**a.** Record each of the above transactions in general journal form.

**b.** Post each entry to the appropriate ledger accounts.

**c.** Prepare a trial balance dated January 31, 2002.

**d.** Explain why the Retained Earnings account has a zero balance in the trial balance.

## Solution to the Demonstration Problem

a.

| | GENERAL JOURNAL | | |
|---|---|---|---|
| **Date** | **Account Titles and Explanation** | **Debit** | **Credit** |
| 2002 | | | |
| Jan. 20 | Cash ..................................................... | 50,000 | |
| | Capital Stock ...................................... | | 50,000 |
| | To record the issue of 5,000 shares of capital stock at $10 per share. | | |
| 20 | Rent Expense ......................................... | 400 | |
| | Cash .................................................. | | 400 |
| | To record payment of January rent expense. | | |
| 21 | Office Supplies ....................................... | 200 | |
| | Accounts Payable ................................. | | 200 |
| | To record purchase of office supplies on account. | | |
| 22 | Office Equipment ..................................... | 15,000 | |
| | Cash .................................................. | | 15,000 |
| | To record the purchase of office equipment. | | |
| 26 | Accounts Receivable ................................. | 2,000 | |
| | Consulting Revenue .............................. | | 2,000 |
| | Billed clients for consulting services rendered. | | |
| 31 | Utilities Expense ..................................... | 100 | |
| | Accounts Payable ................................. | | 100 |
| | To record January utilities expense due in February. | | |

**b.**

## The Ledger

### Asset Accounts

**Cash**

| | | | |
|---|---|---|---|
| 1/20 | 50,000 | 1/20 | 400 |
| | | 1/22 | 15,000 |
| Bal. $34,600 | | | |

**Accounts Receivable**

| | |
|---|---|
| 1/26 | 2,000 |
| Bal. $2,000 | |

**Office Supplies**

| | |
|---|---|
| 1/21 | 200 |
| Bal. $200 | |

**Office Equipment**

| | |
|---|---|
| 1/22 | 15,000 |
| Bal. $15,000 | |

### Liability and Owners' Equity Accounts

**Accounts Payable**

| | | | |
|---|---|---|---|
| | | 1/21 | 200 |
| | | 1/31 | 100 |
| | | Bal. $300 | |

**Capital Stock**

| | | | |
|---|---|---|---|
| | | 1/20 | 50,000 |
| | | Bal. $50,000 | |

**Retained Earnings**

| | |
|---|---|
| | Bal. $0 |

**Consulting Revenue**

| | | | |
|---|---|---|---|
| | | 1/26 | 2,000 |
| | | Bal. $2,000 | |

**Rent Expense**

| | |
|---|---|
| 1/20 | 400 |
| Bal. $400 | |

**Utilities Expense**

| | |
|---|---|
| 1/31 | 100 |
| Bal. $100 | |

| EPLER CONSULTING SERVICES, INC.<br>Trial Balance<br>December 31, 2002 | | |
| --- | --- | --- |
| Cash .......................................... | $34,600 | |
| Accounts receivable ................................. | 2,000 | |
| Office supplies .................................... | 200 | |
| Office equipment .................................. | 15,000 | |
| Accounts payable .................................. | | $   300 |
| Capital stock ..................................... | | 50,000 |
| Retained earnings ................................. | | 0 |
| Consulting revenue ................................ | | 2,000 |
| Rent expense ..................................... | 400 | |
| Utilities expense .................................. | 100 | |
| | $52,300 | $52,300 |

**c.** Epler's Retained Earnings account balance is zero because the company has been in business for only one week and has not yet updated the Retained Earnings account for *any* revenue or expense activities. The periodic adjustment needed to update the Retained Earnings account is discussed in Chapter 5.

## SELF-TEST QUESTIONS

*Answers to these questions appear on page 132.*

1. According to the rules of debit and credit for balance sheet accounts:
   **a.** Increases in asset, liability, and owners' equity accounts are recorded by debits.
   **b.** Decreases in asset and liability accounts are recorded by credits.
   **c.** Increases in asset and owners' equity accounts are recorded by debits.
   **d.** Decreases in liability and owners' equity accounts are recorded by debits.

2. Sunset Tours has a $3,500 account receivable from the Del Mar Rotary. On January 20, the Rotary makes a partial payment of $2,100 to Sunset Tours. The journal entry made on January 20 by Sunset Tours to record this transaction includes:
   **a.** A debit to the Cash Received account of $2,100.
   **b.** A credit to the Accounts Receivable account of $2,100.
   **c.** A debit to the Cash account of $1,400.
   **d.** A debit to the Accounts Receivable account of $1,400.

3. Indicate all of the following statements that correctly describe net income. Net income:
   **a.** Is equal to revenue minus expenses.
   **b.** Is equal to revenue minus the sum of expenses and dividends.
   **c.** Increases owners' equity.
   **d.** Is reported by a company for a specific period of time.

4. Which of the following is provided by a trial balance in which total debits equal total credits?
   **a.** Proof that no transaction was completely omitted from the ledger during the posting process.
   **b.** Proof that the correct debit or credit balance has been computed for each account.
   **c.** Proof that the ledger is in balance.
   **d.** Proof that transactions have been correctly analyzed and recorded in the proper accounts.

**5.** Which of the following explains the debit and credit rules relating to the recording of revenue and expenses?

　**a.** Expenses appear on the left side of the balance sheet and are recorded by debits; revenue appears on the right side of the balance sheet and is recorded by credits.

　**b.** Expenses appear on the left side of the income statement and are recorded by debits; revenue appears on the right side of the income statement and is recorded by credits.

　**c.** The effects of revenue and expenses on owners' equity.

　**d.** The realization principle and the matching principle.

**6.** Which of the following is *not* considered an analytical aspect of the accounting profession?

　**a.** Evaluating an organization's operational efficiency.

　**b.** Forecasting the probable results of future operations.

　**c.** Designing systems that provide information to decision makers.

　**d.** Journalizing and posting business transactions.

**7.** Indicate all correct answers. In the accounting cycle

　**a.** Transactions are posted before they are journalized.

　**b.** A trial balance is prepared after journal entries have been posted.

　**c.** The Retained Earnings account is not shown as an up-to-date figure in the trial balance.

　**d.** Journal entries are posted to appropriate ledger accounts.

**8.** Indicate all correct answers. Dividends

　**a.** Decrease owners' equity.

　**b.** Decrease net income.

　**c.** Are recorded by debiting the Dividend account.

　**d.** Are a business expense.

## ASSIGNMENT MATERIAL

## DISCUSSION QUESTIONS

**1.** Baker Construction is a small corporation owned and managed by Tom Baker. The corporation has 21 employees, few creditors, and no investor other than Tom Baker. Thus, like many small businesses, it has no obligation to issue financial statements to creditors or investors. Under these circumstances, is there any reason for this corporation to maintain accounting records?

**2.** In its simplest form, an account has only three elements or basic parts. What are these three elements?

**3.** At the beginning of the year, the Office Equipment account of Gulf Coast Airlines had a debit balance of $126,900. During the year, debit entries of $23,400 and credit entries of $38,200 were posted to the account. What was the balance of this account at the end of the year? (Indicate debit or credit balance.)

**4.** What relationship exists between the position of an account on the balance sheet and the rules for recording increases in that account?

**5.** State briefly the rules of debit and credit as applied to asset accounts and as applied to liability and owners' equity accounts.

**6.** Does the term *debit* mean increase and the term *credit* mean decrease? Explain.

**7.** What requirement is imposed by the double-entry system in the recording of any business transaction?

**8.** Explain precisely what is meant by each of the phrases listed below. Whenever appropriate, indicate whether the left or right side of an account is affected and whether an increase or decrease is indicated.

　**a.** A debit of $200 to the Cash account.

　**b.** A debit of $600 to Accounts Payable.

　**c.** A credit of $50 to Accounts Receivable.

    **d.** A debit to the Land account.

    **e.** Credit balance.

    **f.** Credit side of an account.

9. For each of the following transactions, indicate whether the account in parentheses should be debited or credited, and *give the reason* for your answer.

    **a.** Purchased land for cash. (Cash)

    **b.** Sold an old, unneeded computer on 30-day credit. (Office Equipment)

    **c.** Obtained a loan of $30,000 from a bank. (Cash)

    **d.** Purchased a copying machine on credit, promising to make payment in full within 30 days. (Accounts Payable)

    **e.** Williams Word Processing, Inc., issued 10,000 shares of capital stock. (Capital Stock)

10. Explain the effect of operating profitably on the balance sheet of a business entity.

11. Does net income represent a supply of cash that could be distributed to stockholders in the form of dividends? Explain.

12. What is the meaning of the term *revenue?* Does the receipt of cash by a business indicate that revenue has been earned? Explain.

13. What is the meaning of the term *expenses?* Does the payment of cash by a business indicate that an expense has been incurred? Explain.

14. A service enterprise performs services in the amount of $500 for a customer in May and receives payment in June. In which month is the $500 of revenue recognized? What is the journal entry to be made in May and the entry to be made in June?

15. When do accountants consider revenue to be realized? What basic question about recording revenue in accounting records is answered by the *realization principle?*

16. Late in March, Classic Auto Painters purchased paint on account, with payment due in 60 days. The company used the paint to paint customers' cars during the first three weeks of April. Late in May, the company paid the paint store from which the paint had been purchased. In which month should Classic Auto Painters recognize the cost of this paint as expense? What generally accepted accounting principle determines the answer to this question?

17. In what accounting period does the *matching principle* indicate that an expense should be recognized?

18. Explain the rules of debit and credit with respect to transactions recorded in revenue and expense accounts.

19. What are some of the limitations of a trial balance?

20. How do dividends affect owners' equity? Are they treated as a business expense? Explain.

21. How does the accrual basis of accounting differ from the cash basis of accounting? Which gives a more accurate picture of the profitability of a business? Explain.

## EXERCISES

**EXERCISE 3.1**

Accounting Terminology

**LO 1–10**

Listed below are eight technical accounting terms introduced in this chapter:

| | |
|---|---|
| Realization principle | Credit |
| Time period principle | Accounting period |
| Matching principle | Expenses |
| Net income | Accounting cycle |

Each of the following statements may (or may not) describe one of these technical terms. For each statement, indicate the term described, or answer "None" if the statement does not correctly describe any of the terms.

**a.** The span of time covered by an income statement.

**b.** The sequence of accounting procedures used to record, classify, and summarize accounting information.

**c.** The traditional accounting practice of resolving uncertainty by choosing the solution that leads to the lowest amount of income being recognized.

**d.** An increase in owners' equity resulting from profitable operations.

**e.** The generally accepted accounting principle that determines when revenue should be recorded in the accounting records.

**f.** The type of entry used to decrease an asset or increase a liability or owners' equity account.

**g.** The generally accepted accounting principle of offsetting revenue earned during an accounting period with the expenses incurred in generating that revenue.

**h.** The costs of the goods and services used up in the process of generating revenue.

Listed below in *random order* are the eight steps comprising a complete accounting cycle:

**1.** Prepare a trial balance.

**2.** Journalize and post the closing entries.

**3.** Prepare financial statements.

**4.** Post transaction data to the ledger.

**5.** Prepare an adjusted trial balance.

**6.** Make end-of-period adjustments.

**7.** Journalize transactions.

**8.** Prepare an after-closing trial balance.

**a.** List these steps in the sequence in which they would normally be performed. (A detailed understanding of these eight steps is not required until Chapters 4 and 5.)

**b.** Describe ways in which the information produced through the accounting cycle is used by a company's management and employees.

**EXERCISE 3.2**

The Accounting Cycle

**LO 1, 2, 5, 9, 10**

The purpose of this exercise is to demonstrate the *matching principle* in a familiar setting. Assume that you own a car that you drive about 15,000 miles each year.

**a.** List the various costs to you associated with owning and operating this car. Make an estimate of the total annual cost of owning and operating the car, as well as the average cost-per-mile that you drive.

**b.** Assume also that you have a part-time job. You usually do not use your car in this job, but today your employer asks you to drive 100 miles (round trip) to deliver some important documents. Your employer offers to "reimburse you for your driving expenses."

You already have a full tank of gas, so you are able to drive the whole 100 miles without stopping and you don't actually spend any money during the trip. Does this mean that you have incurred no "expenses" for which you should be reimbursed? Explain.

**EXERCISE 3.3**

The Matching Principle: You as a Driver

**LO 6, 7**

Record the following selected transactions in general journal form for Thompson Engineering, Inc. Include a brief explanation of the transaction as part of each journal entry.

| | | |
|---|---|---|
| Oct. | 1 | The company issued 5,000 additional shares of capital stock at $20 per share. |
| Oct. | 4 | The company purchased computer equipment. The equipment cost $45,000, of which $15,000 was paid in cash; a note payable was issued for the balance. |
| Oct. | 12 | Issued a check for $11,000 in full payment of a note payable to West Milton State Bank. |
| Oct. | 19 | Purchased office supplies on account for $300. Payment is not due until November 10. |
| Oct. | 25 | Collected a $12,000 account receivable from the Lewisburg School District. |
| Oct. | 30 | Declared and paid a $6,000 cash dividend to stockholders. |

**EXERCISE 3.4**

Recording Transactions in a Journal

**LO 3, 4, 5**

Transactions are *first* journalized and *then* posted to ledger accounts. In this exercise, however, your understanding of the relationship between the journal and the ledger is tested by asking you to study some ledger accounts and determine the journal entries that probably were made to produce these ledger entries. The following accounts show the first six transactions of Avenson Insurance Company. Prepare a journal entry (including a written explanation) for each transaction.

**EXERCISE 3.5**

Relationship between Journal and Ledger Accounts

**LO 2, 3, 4, 5**

| Cash | | | | Vehicles | | | |
|---|---|---|---|---|---|---|---|
| Nov. 1 | 120,000 | Nov. 8 | 33,600 | Nov. 30 | 9,400 | | |
| | | Nov. 25 | 12,000 | | | | |
| | | Nov. 30 | 1,400 | | | | |

| Land | | | | Notes Payable | | | |
|---|---|---|---|---|---|---|---|
| Nov. 8 | 70,000 | | | Nov. 25 | 12,000 | Nov. 8 | 95,000 |
| | | | | | | Nov. 30 | 8,000 |

| Building | | | | Accounts Payable | | | |
|---|---|---|---|---|---|---|---|
| Nov. 8 | 58,600 | | | Nov. 21 | 480 | Nov. 15 | 3,200 |

| Office Equipment | | | | Capital Stock | | | |
|---|---|---|---|---|---|---|---|
| Nov. 15 | 3,200 | Nov. 21 | 480 | | | Nov. 1 | 120,000 |

**EXERCISE 3.6**

Preparing a Trial Balance

**LO 9**

Using the information in the ledger accounts presented in Exercise 3–5, prepare a trial balance for Avenson Insurance Company dated November 30.

**EXERCISE 3.7**

Relationship between Net Income and Owners' Equity

**LO 6, 8**

Total assets and total liabilities of Reco Plumbing, Inc., as shown by its balance sheets at the beginning and end of the year, were as follows:

| | Beginning of Year | End of Year |
|---|---|---|
| Assets . . . . . . . . . . . . . . . . . . . . . . . . . . . . . . . . . . . . . . | $300,000 | $335,000 |
| Liabilities . . . . . . . . . . . . . . . . . . . . . . . . . . . . . . . . . | 100,000 | 110,000 |

Compute the net income or net loss from operations for the year in each of the following independent cases:

**a.** No dividends were declared or paid during the year and no additional capital stock was issued.

**b.** No dividends were declared or paid during the year, but additional capital stock was issued in the amount of $20,000.

**c.** Dividends of $10,000 were declared and paid during the year. No additional capital stock was issued.

**d.** Dividends of $15,000 were declared and paid during the year, and additional capital stock was issued in the amount of $30,000.

**e.** No dividends were declared or paid during the year, but additional capital stock was issued in the amount of $35,000.

**EXERCISE 3.8**

Effects of Transactions on the Accounting Equation

**LO 2, 3, 4, 5, 6**

Satka Fishing Expeditions, Inc., recorded the following transactions in July:

**1.** Provided an ocean fishing expedition for a credit customer; payment is due August 10.

**2.** Paid Marine Service Center for repairs to boats performed in June. (In June, Satka Fishing Expeditions, Inc., had received and properly recorded the invoice for these repairs.)

**3.** Collected the full amount due from a credit customer for a fishing expedition provided in June.

**4.** Received a bill from Baldy's Bait Shop for bait purchased and used in July. Payment is due August 3.

**5.** Purchased a new fishing boat on July 28, paying part cash and issuing a note payable for the balance. The new boat is first scheduled for use on August 5.

**6.** Declared and paid a cash dividend on July 31.

Indicate the effects that each of these transactions will have upon the following six *total amounts* in the company's financial statements for the month of July. Organize your answer in tabular form, using the column headings shown on the facing page, and use the code letters **I** for increase, **D** for decrease, and **NE** for no effect. The answer to transaction (1) is provided as an example.

| | Income Statement | | | Balance Sheet | | |
|---|---|---|---|---|---|---|
| Transaction | Revenue − | Expenses = | Net Income | Assets = | Liabilities + | Owners' Equity |
| (1) | I | NE | I | I | NE | I |

**EXERCISE 3.9**

Effects of Transactions on the Accounting Equation

**LO 2, 3, 4, 5, 6**

A number of transactions of Claypool Construction are described below in terms of accounts debited and credited:

1. Debit Wages Expense; credit Wages Payable.
2. Debit Accounts Receivable; credit Construction Revenue.
3. Debit Dividends; credit Cash.
4. Debit Office Supplies; credit Accounts Payable.
5. Debit Repairs Expense; credit Cash.
6. Debit Cash; credit Accounts Receivable.
7. Debit Tools and Equipment; credit Cash and Notes Payable.
8. Debit accounts Payable; credit Cash.

a. Indicate the effects of each transaction upon the elements of the income statement and the balance sheet. Use the code letters **I** for increase, **D** for decrease, and **NE** for no effect. Organize your answer in tabular form using the column headings shown below. The answer for transaction **1** is provided as an example.

| | Income Statement | | | Balance Sheet | | |
|---|---|---|---|---|---|---|
| Transaction | Revenue − | Expenses = | Net Income | Assets = | Liabilities + | Owners' Equity |
| (1) | NE | I | D | NE | I | D |

b. Write a one-sentence description of each transaction.

The following transactions were carried out during the month of May by M. Palmer and Company, a firm of design architects. For each of the five transactions, you are to state whether the transaction represented revenue to the firm during the month of May. Give reasons for your decision in each case.

a. M. Palmer and Company received $25,000 cash by issuing additional shares of capital stock.
b. Collected cash of $2,400 from an account receivable. The receivable originated in April from services rendered to a client.
c. Borrowed $12,800 from Century Bank to be repaid in three months.
d. Earned $83 interest on a company bank account during the month of May. No withdrawals were made from this account in May.
e. Completed plans for guest house, pool, and spa for a client. The $5,700 fee for this project was billed to the client in May, but will not be collected until June 25.

**EXERCISE 3.10**

When Is Revenue Realized?

**LO 6, 7**

During March, the activities of Evergreen Landscaping included the following transactions and events, among others. Which of these items represented expenses in March? Explain.

a. Purchased a copying machine for $2,750 cash.
b. Paid $192 for gasoline purchases for a delivery truck during March.
c. Paid $2,280 salary to an employee for time worked during March.

**EXERCISE 3.11**

When Are Expenses Incurred?

**LO 6, 7**

**d.** Paid an attorney $560 for legal services rendered in January.

**e.** Declared and paid an $1,800 dividend to shareholders.

**EXERCISE 3.12**

Preparing Journal Entries for Revenue, Expenses, and Dividends

**LO 4, 6, 7, 8**

Shown below are selected transactions of the architectural firm of Baxter, Claxter, and Stone, Inc.

**April 5** Prepared building plans for Spangler Construction Company. Sent Spangler an invoice for $900 requesting payment within 30 days. (The appropriate revenue account is entitled Drafting Fees Earned.)

**May 17** Declared a cash dividend of $5,000. The dividend will not be paid until June 25.

**May 29** Received a $2,000 bill from Bob Needham, CPA, for accounting services performed during May. Payment is due by June 10. (The appropriate expense account is entitled Professional Expenses.)

**June 4** Received full payment from Spangler Construction Company for the invoice sent on April 5.

**June 10** Paid Bob Needham, CPA, for the bill received on May 29.

**June 25** Paid the cash dividend declared on May 17.

**a.** Prepare journal entries to record the transactions in the firm's accounting records.

**b.** Identify any of the above transactions that *will not* result in a change in the company's net income.

**EXERCISE 3.13**

Annual Report; Appendix A

**LO 1, 2, 3, 7, 10**

Throughout this text we have many assignments based on the annual report of **Tootsie Roll Industries, Inc.**, in Appendix A. Refer to this annual report to respond to the following items:

**a.** Does the company's fiscal year end on December 31? How can you tell?

**b.** State the company's balance sheet in terms of A = L + E.

**d.** Did the company post more debits to the Cash account during the year than credits? How can you tell?

# PROBLEMS

**PROBLEM 3.1**

Journalizing Transactions

**LO 3, 4, 5**

Glenn Grimes is the founder and president of Heartland Construction, a real estate development venture. The business transactions during February while the company was being organized are listed below.

**Feb. 1** Grimes and several others invested $500,000 cash in the business in exchange for 25,000 shares of capital stock.

**Feb. 10** The company purchased office facilities for $300,000, of which $100,000 was applicable to the land, and $200,000 to the building. A cash payment of $60,000 was made and a note payable was issued for the balance of the purchase price.

**Feb. 16** Computer equipment was purchased from PCWorld for $12,000 cash.

**Feb. 18** Office furnishings were purchased from Hi-Way Furnishings at a cost of $9,000. A $1,000 cash payment was made at the time of purchase, and an agreement was made to pay the remaining balance in two equal installments due March 1 and April 1. Hi-Way Furnishings did not require that Heartland sign a promissory note.

**Feb. 22** Office supplies were purchased from Office World for $300 cash.

**Feb. 23** Heartland discovered that it paid too much for a computer printer purchased on February 16. The unit should have cost only $359, but Heartland was charged $395. PCWorld promised to refund the difference within seven days.

**Feb. 27** Mailed Hi-Way Furnishings the first installment due on the account payable for office furnishings purchased on February 18.

**Feb. 28** Received $36 from PCWorld in full settlement of the account receivable created on February 23.

**Instructions**

**a.** Prepare journal entries to record the above transactions. Select the appropriate account titles from the following chart of accounts:

Cash
Accounts Receivable
Office Supplies
Office Furnishings
Computer Systems

Land
Office Building
Notes Payable
Accounts Payable
Capital Stock

**b.** Indicate the effects of each transaction on the company's assets, liabilities, and owners' equity for the month of February. Organize your analysis in tabular form as shown below for the February 1 transaction:

| Transaction | Assets | = | Liabilities | + | Owners' Equity |
|---|---|---|---|---|---|
| Feb. 1 | +$500,000 (Cash) | | $0 | | +$500,000 (Capital Stock) |

Environmental Services, Inc., performs various tests on wells and septic systems. A few of the company's business transactions occurring during August are described below:

**1.** On August 1, the company billed customers $2,500 on account for services rendered. Customers are required to make full payment within 30 days.

**2.** On August 3, purchased testing supplies costing $3,800, paying $800 cash and charging the remainder on the company's 30-day account at Penn Chemicals. The testing supplies are expected to last several months.

**3.** On August 5, returned to Penn Chemicals $100 of testing supplies that were not needed. The return of these supplies reduced by $100 the amount owed to Penn Chemicals.

**4.** On August 17, the company issued an additional 2,500 shares of capital stock at $8 per share. The cash raised will be used to purchase new testing equipment in September.

**5.** On August 22, the company received $600 cash from customers it had billed on August 1.

**6.** On August 29, the company paid its outstanding account payable to Penn Chemicals.

**7.** On August 30, a cash dividend totaling $6,800 was declared and paid to the company's stockholders.

**PROBLEM 3.2**

Analyzing and Journalizing Transactions

**LO 3, 4, 5, 6, 7, 8**

**Instructions**

**a.** Prepare an analysis of each of the above transactions. Transaction **1** serves as an example of the form of analysis to be used.

   **1. (a)** The asset Accounts Receivable was increased. Increases in assets are recorded by debits. Debit Accounts Receivable, $2,500.

   **(b)** Revenue has been earned. Revenue increases owners' equity. Increases in owners' equity are recorded by credits. Credit Testing Service Revenue, $2,500.

**b.** Prepare journal entries, including explanations, for the above transactions.

**c.** How does the *realization principle* influence the manner in which the August 1 billing to customers is recorded in the accounting records?

**d.** How does the *matching principle* influence the manner in which the August 3 purchase of testing supplies is recorded in the accounting records?

Weida Surveying, Inc., provides land surveying services. During September, its transactions included the following:

| | |
|---|---|
| **Sept. 1** | Paid rent for the month of September, $4,400. |
| **Sept. 3** | Billed Fine Line Homes $5,620 for surveying services. The entire amount is due on or before September 28. (Weida uses an account entitled Surveying Revenue when billing clients.) |
| **Sept. 9** | Provided surveying services to Sunset Ridge Developments for $2,830. The entire amount was collected on this date. |
| **Sept. 14** | Placed a newspaper advertisement in the *Daily Item* to be published in the September 20 issue. The cost of the advertisement was $165. Payment is due in 30 days. |

**PROBLEM 3.3**

Analyzing and Journalizing Transactions

**LO 3, 4, 5, 6, 7, 8**

**Sept. 25**   Received a check for $5,620 from Fine Line Homes for the amount billed on September 3.

**Sept. 26**   Provided surveying services to Thompson Excavating Company for $1,890. Weida collected $400 cash, with the balance due in 30 days.

**Sept. 29**   Sent a check to the *Daily Item* in full payment of the liability incurred on September 14.

**Sept. 30**   Declared and paid a $7,600 cash dividend to the company's stockholders.

### Instructions

**a.** Analyze the effects that each of these transactions will have on the following six components of the company's financial statements for the month of September. Organize your answer in tabular form, using the column headings shown below. Use **I** for increase, **D** for decrease, and **NE** for no effect. The September 1 transaction is provided for you:

| | Income Statement | | | Balance Sheet | | |
|---|---|---|---|---|---|---|
| Transaction | Revenue | − Expenses | = Net Income | Assets | = Liabilities | + Owners' Equity |
| Sept. 1 | NE | I | D | D | NE | D |

**b.** Prepare a journal entry (including explanation) for each of the above transactions.

**c.** Three of September's transactions involve cash payments, yet only one of these transactions is recorded as an expense. Describe three situations in which a cash payment would *not* involve recognition of an expense.

**PROBLEM 3.4**

The Accounting Cycle: Journalizing, Posting, and Preparing a Trial Balance

In June 2002, Wendy Winger organized a corporation to provide aerial photography services. The company, called Aerial Views, began operations immediately. Transactions during the month of June were as follows:

**June 1**   The corporation issued 60,000 shares of capital stock to Wendy Winger in exchange for $60,000 cash.

**June 2**   Purchased a plane from Utility Aircraft for $220,000. Made a $40,000 cash down payment and issued a note payable for the remaining balance.

**June 4**   Paid Woodrow Airport $2,500 to rent office and hangar space for the month.

**June 15**   Billed customers $8,320 for aerial photographs taken during the first half of June.

**June 15**   Paid $5,880 in salaries earned by employees during the first half of June.

**June 18**   Paid Hannigan's Hangar $1,890 for maintenance and repair services on the company plane.

**June 25**   Collected $4,910 of the amounts billed to customers on June 15.

**June 30**   Billed customers $16,450 for aerial photographs taken during the second half of the month.

**June 30**   Paid $6,000 in salaries earned by employees during the second half of the month.

**June 30**   Received a $2,510 bill from Peatree Petroleum for aircraft fuel purchased in June. The entire amount is due July 10.

**June 30**   Declared a $2,000 dividend payable on July 15.

The account titles used by Aerial Views are

| | |
|---|---|
| Cash | Retained Earnings |
| Accounts Receivable | Dividends |
| Aircraft | Aerial Photography Revenue |
| Notes Payable | Maintenance Expense |
| Accounts Payable | Fuel Expense |
| Dividends Payable | Salaries Expense |
| Capital Stock | Rent Expense |

## Instructions

**a.** Analyze the effects that each of these transactions will have on the following six components of the company's financial statements for the month of June. Organize your answer in tabular form, using the column headings shown on the facing page. Use **I** for increase, **D** for decrease, and **NE** for no effect. The June 1 transaction is provided for you:

| Transaction | Income Statement | | | Balance Sheet | | |
|---|---|---|---|---|---|---|
| | Revenue | − Expenses | = Net Income | Assets | = Liabilities | + Owners' Equity |
| **June 1** | NE | NE | NE | I | NE | I |

**b.** Prepare journal entries (including explanations) for each transaction.

**c.** Post each transaction to the appropriate ledger accounts (use a running balance format as illustrated on pages 94–95).

**d.** Prepare a trial balance dated June 30, 2002.

**e.** Using figures from the trial balance prepared in part **d**, compute total assets, total liabilities, and owners' equity. Are these the figures that the company will report in its June 30 balance sheet? Explain your answer briefly.

Dr. Schekter, DVM, opened a veterinary clinic on May 1. The business transactions for May are shown below:

| | |
|---|---|
| **May 1** | Dr. Schekter invested $400,000 cash in the business in exchange for 5,000 shares of capital stock. |
| **May 4** | Land and a building were purchased for $250,000. Of this amount, $70,000 applied to the land, and $180,000 to the building. A cash payment of $100,000 was made at the time of the purchase, and a note payable was issued for the remaining balance. |
| **May 9** | Medical instruments were purchased for $130,000 cash. |
| **May 16** | Office fixtures and equipment were purchased for $50,000. Dr. Schekter paid $20,000 at the time of purchase and agreed to pay the entire remaining balance in 15 days. |
| **May 21** | Office supplies expected to last several months were purchased for $5,000 cash. |
| **May 24** | Dr. Schekter billed clients $2,200 for services rendered. Of this amount, $1,900 was received in cash, and $300 was billed on account (due in 30 days). |
| **May 27** | A $400 invoice was received for several radio advertisements aired in May. The entire amount is due on June 5. |
| **May 28** | Received a $100 payment on the $300 account receivable recorded May 24. |
| **May 31** | Paid employees $2,800 for salaries earned in May. |

A partial list of account titles used by Dr. Schekter includes:

| | |
|---|---|
| Cash | Notes Payable |
| Accounts Receivable | Accounts Payable |
| Office Supplies | Capital Stock |
| Medical Instruments | Veterinary Service Revenue  |
| Office Fixtures and Equipment | Advertising Expense |
| Land | Salary Expense  |
| Building | |

## Instructions

**a.** Analyze the effects that each of these transactions will have on the following six components of the company's financial statements for the month of May. Organize your answer in tabular form, using the column headings shown below. Use **I** for increase, **D** for decrease, and **NE** for no effect. The May 1 transaction is provided for you:

**PROBLEM 3.5**

The Accounting Cycle: Journalizing, Posting, and Preparing a Trial Balance

**LO 1–10**

| | **Income Statement** | | | **Balance Sheet** | | |
|---|---|---|---|---|---|---|
| Transaction | Revenue | − Expenses | = Net Income | Assets | = Liabilities | + Owners' Equity |
| **May 1** | NE | NE | NE | I | NE | I |

**b.** Prepare journal entries (including explanations) for each transaction.

**c.** Post each transaction to the appropriate ledger accounts (use T account format as illustrated on page 87).

**d.** Prepare a trial balance dated May 31, 2002.

**e.** Using figures from the trial balance prepared in part **d,** compute total assets, total liabilities, and owners' equity. Did May appear to be a profitable month?

# CASES AND UNSTRUCTURED PROBLEMS

**CASE 3.1**

Revenue Recognition

**LO 7, 10**

The realization principle determines when a business should recognize revenue. Listed below are three common business situations involving revenue. After each situation, we give two alternatives as to the accounting period (or periods) in which the business might recognize this revenue. Select the appropriate alternative by applying the realization principle, and explain your reasoning.

**a.** Airline ticket revenue: Most airlines sell tickets well before the scheduled date of the flight. (Period ticket sold; period of flight)

**b.** Sales on account: In June 2002, a San Diego–based furniture store had a big sale, featuring "No payments until 2003." (Period furniture sold; periods that payments are received from customers)

**c.** Magazine subscriptions revenue: Most magazine publishers sell subscriptions for future delivery of the magazine. (Period subscription sold; periods that magazines are mailed to customers)

**CASE 3.2**

Measuring Income Fairly

**LO 6, 7, 10**

Kim Morris purchased Print Shop, Inc., a printing business, from Chris Stanley. Morris made a cash down payment and agreed to make annual payments equal to 40% of the company's net income in each of the next three years. (Such "earn-outs" are a common means of financing the purchase of a small business.) Stanley was disappointed, however, when Morris reported a first year's net income far below Stanley's expectations.

The agreement between Morris and Stanley did not state precisely how "net income" was to be measured. Neither Morris nor Stanley was familiar with accounting concepts. Their agreement stated only that the net income of the corporation should be measured in a "fair and reasonable manner."

In measuring net income, Morris applied the following policies:

**1.** Revenue was recognized when cash was received from customers. Most customers paid in cash, but a few were allowed 30-day credit terms.

**2.** Expenditures for ink and paper, which are purchased weekly, were charged directly to Supplies Expense, as were the Morris family's weekly grocery and dry cleaning bills.

**3.** Morris set her annual salary at $60,000, which Stanley had agreed was reasonable. She also paid salaries of $30,000 per year to her husband and to each of her two teenage children. These family members did not work in the business on a regular basis, but they did help out when things got busy.

**4.** Income taxes expense included the amount paid by the corporation (which was computed correctly), as well as the personal income taxes paid by various members of the Morris family on the salaries they earned working for the business.

**5.** The business had state-of-the-art printing equipment valued at $150,000 at the time Morris purchased it. The first-year income statement included a $150,000 equipment expense related to these assets.

**Instructions**

**a.** Discuss the fairness and reasonableness of these income-measurement policies. (Remember, these policies do *not* have to conform to generally accepted accounting principles. But they should be *fair* and *reasonable*.)

**b.** Do you think that the net *cash flow* generated by this business (cash receipts less cash outlays) is higher or lower than the net income as measured by Morris? Explain.

## BUSINESS WEEK ASSIGNMENT

BusinessWeek

**CASE 3.3**

**LO 10**

With the rapid growth in E-commerce technology, capturing economic events and managing strategic information has never been more important to businesses. In an August 28, 2000, *Business Week* article entitled, "From Gearhead to Grand Pooh-Bah," author Andy Reinhardt describes exciting career opportunities for chief information officers (CIOs). In short, the future has never looked brighter. In companies such as **General Electric**; **Cisco Systems, Inc.**; and **Charles Schwab & Company**, CIOs report directly to the chief executive officers (CEOs). In many companies, CIOs have spearheaded initiatives that have resulted in cost reductions amounting to millions of dollars. In this fast-paced field, attaining the knowledge required to stay abreast of technology is often the key to success.

Assume that you have career aspirations of one day becoming the CIO of a successful company. If you were designing your own major, what courses would you select to best prepare for this goal? Explain briefly your reasons for selecting these courses. Would your degree plan include any courses in accounting? Explain your answer.

## INTERNET ASSIGNMENT

Visit the home page of **Johnson & Johnson Corporation** at the following Internet location:

**INTERNET 3.1**
Revenue from Various Sources

**LO 6**

### www.jnj.com

Assess the company's most recent annual report from the Investor Relations menu. From the annual report contents, select Segments of Business and Geographic Areas. How many dollars of revenue, in total, were generated by the company's worldwide operations? Of this amount, how much was generated in each of the company's four major geographic trade areas?

*Internet sites are time and date sensitive. It is the purpose of these exercises to have you explore the Internet. You may need to use the Yahoo! search engine* http://www.yahoo.com *(or other favorite search engines) to find a company's current web address.*

## OUR COMMENTS ON THE "YOUR TURN" CASES

**You as a Student (p. 88)**   The concept of double-entry accounting *does* apply to your personal financial position. The financial position of an individual may be described by the equation:

### Assets = Liabilities + Net Worth

Any change in the amount of any asset or liability causes an offsetting change *elsewhere* in the equation. Thus two or more accounts within the accounting equation must change—this is what is meant by double-entry.

For example, your spending cash results in the acquisition of another asset, in the reduction of a liability, or in the reduction of your personal net worth (the equivalent of owners' equity in a business organization). A cash receipt implies the reduction of another asset, an increase in liabilities, or an increase in net worth.

Although individuals usually do not use debits and credits to record changes in their financial positions, the concept of double-entry—that is, corresponding changes in the accounting equation—still applies.

**You as a Business Owner (p. 102)**   Indeed it does. If the business is *unincorporated,* its assets belong to you. Thus, you may withdraw these assets from the business at any time and use them for any purpose. But if the business is a corporation, these assets belong to *the corporate entity.* Even though you are the sole owner of the company, you may *not* withdraw assets from the business without *proper authorization.* Thus, your personal use of corporate assets must be viewed as compensation to you (i.e., salary), a loan, or a dividend.

*Note:* For income tax purposes, treating this expenditure as a loan probably is the best alternative. If you treat it as either salary or a dividend, you are receiving taxable income. Tax planning often plays a major role in transactions between a corporation and its owners.

 **You as Overnight Auto Service's Accountant (p. 106)**   The Institute of Management Accountants (IMA) has established a code of ethics that includes a requirement of integrity. Integrity is defined to include avoiding conflicts of interest by refusing compromising gifts and favors and by refusing to subvert organizational objectives. The offer from Harbor Cab Co. would require you to violate the integrity requirement. Free cab service for a month is a compromising gift and delaying the payment due date would subvert the organizational objectives of Overnight Auto. For more information on the IMA's code of ethics, visit their website at www.rutgers.edu/Accounting/raw/ima/imaethic.

## ANSWERS TO SELF-TEST QUESTIONS

**1.** d   **2.** b   **3.** a, c, and d   **4.** c   **5.** c   **6.** d   **7.** b, c, and d   **8.** a and c

# THE ACCOUNTING CYCLE:

## Accruals and Deferrals

### Learning Objectives

*After studying this chapter, you should be able to:*

1. Explain the purpose of adjusting entries.

2. Describe and prepare the four basic types of adjusting entries.

3. Prepare adjusting entries to convert assets to expenses.

4. Prepare adjusting entries to convert liabilities to revenue.

5. Prepare adjusting entries to accrue unpaid expenses.

6. Prepare adjusting entries to accrue uncollected revenue.

7. Explain how the principles of *realization* and *matching* relate to adjusting entries.

8. Explain the concept of *materiality.*

9. Prepare an adjusted trial balance and describe its purpose.

Creative Services of United Airlines.

When is revenue actually *earned* by a company? In many cases, revenue is earned when cash is received at the point of sale. For instance, when a taxicab driver takes someone to the airport, revenue is earned when the passenger is dropped off at the appropriate terminal and the fare is collected.

Suppose the same passenger boards a **United Airlines (UAL)** flight to London using a ticket that was purchased six months in advance. At what point should the airline recognize that ticket revenue has been earned? A recent **UAL Corporation** balance sheet provides the answer to this question.

In its balance sheet, **UAL Corporation** reports a $1.8 billion current liability account called Advance Ticket Sales. As passengers purchase tickets in advance, **UAL Corporation** credits the Advance Ticket Sales account for an amount equal to the cash it receives. It is not until passengers actually *use* their tickets that the airline reduces this liability account and records Passenger Revenue in its income statement.

● ● ●

For most companies, revenue is *not* always earned as cash is received, nor is an expense necessarily incurred as cash is disbursed. These timing differences between cash flows and the recognition of revenue and expenses are referred to as *accruals* and *deferrals*. In this chapter we will examine how accounting information must be adjusted for accruals and deferrals prior to the preparation of financial statements.

The first three steps of the accounting cycle were discussed in Chapter 3. They included (1) recording transactions, (2) posting transactions, and (3) preparing a trial balance. In this chapter, we focus solely upon the fourth step of the accounting cycle: Performing the end-of-period adjustments required to measure business income. The remaining steps of the cycle are covered in Chapter 5.

## ADJUSTING ENTRIES

There is more to the measurement of business income than merely recording simple revenue and expense transactions that affect only a single accounting period. Certain transactions affect the revenue or expenses of *two or more* accounting periods. The purpose of adjusting entries is to assign to each accounting period appropriate amounts of revenue and expense. For example, Overnight Auto Service purchased shop supplies that will be used for several months. Thus, an adjusting entry is required to record the expense associated with the shop supplies that Overnight *uses* each month.

**LO 1**

Explain the purpose of adjusting entries.

### The Need for Adjusting Entries

For purposes of measuring income and preparing financial statements, the life of a business is divided into a series of *accounting periods*. This practice enables decision makers to compare the financial statements of successive periods and to identify significant trends.

But measuring net income for a relatively short accounting period—such as a month or even a year—poses a problem because, as mentioned above, some business activities affect the revenue and expenses of *multiple accounting periods*. Therefore, **adjusting entries** are needed at the end of each accounting period to make certain that appropriate amounts of revenue and expense are reported in the company's income statement.

For example, magazine publishers often sell two- or three-year subscriptions to their publications. At the end of each accounting period, these publishers make adjusting entries recognizing the portion of their advance receipts that have been earned during the current period. Most companies also purchase insurance policies that benefit more than one period. Therefore, an adjusting entry is needed to make certain that an appropriate portion of each policy's total cost is reported in the income statement as insurance expense for the period. In short, adjusting entries are needed whenever transactions affect the revenue or expenses of more than one accounting period. These entries assign revenues to the period in which they are *earned,* and expenses to the periods in which related goods or services are *used.*

In theory, a business could make adjusting entries on a daily basis. But as a practical matter, these entries are made *only at the end of each accounting period.* For most companies, adjusting entries are made on a monthly basis.

**LO 2**

Describe and prepare the four basic types of adjusting entries.

### Types of Adjusting Entries

The number of adjustments needed at the end of each accounting period depends entirely upon the nature of the company's business activities. However, most adjusting entries fall into one of four general categories:[1]

1. *Converting assets to expenses.* A cash expenditure (or cost) that will benefit more than one accounting period usually is recorded by debiting an asset account (for example, Supplies, Unexpired Insurance, and so on) and by crediting Cash. The asset account created actually represents the *deferral* (or the postponement) of an expense. In each

---

[1] A fifth category of adjusting entries consists of adjustments related to the valuation of certain assets, such as marketable securities and accounts receivable. These valuation adjustments are explained and illustrated in Chapter 7.

future period that benefits from the use of this asset, an adjusting entry is made to allocate a portion of the asset's cost from the balance sheet to the income statement as an expense. This adjusting entry is recorded by debiting the appropriate expense account (for example, Supplies Expense or Insurance Expense) and crediting the related asset account (for example, Supplies or Unexpired Insurance).

2. *Converting liabilities to revenue.* A business may collect cash in advance for services to be rendered in future accounting periods. Transactions of this nature are usually recorded by debiting Cash and by crediting a liability account (typically called Unearned Revenue). Here, the liability account created represents the *deferral* (or the postponement) of a revenue. In the period that services are actually rendered (or that goods are sold), an adjusting entry is made to allocate a portion of the liability from the balance sheet to the income statement to recognize the revenue earned during the period. The adjusting entry is recorded by debiting the liability (Unearned Revenue) and by crediting *Revenue Earned* (or a similar account) for the value of the services.

3. *Accruing unpaid expenses.* An expense may be incurred in the current accounting period even though no cash payment will occur until a future period. These *accrued* expenses are recorded by an adjusting entry made at the end of each accounting period. The adjusting entry is recorded by debiting the appropriate expense account (for example, Interest Expense or Salary Expense) and by crediting the related liability (for example, Interest Payable or Salaries Payable).

4. *Accruing uncollected revenue.* Revenue may be earned (or *accrued*) during the current period, even though the collection of cash will not occur until a future period. Unrecorded earned revenue, for which no cash has been received, requires an adjusting entry at the end of the accounting period. The adjusting entry is recorded by debiting the appropriate asset (for example, Accounts Receivable or Interest Receivable) and by crediting the appropriate revenue account (for example, Service Revenue Earned or Interest Earned).

Each of these adjusting entry categories is illustrated in the diagram on page 138.

---

**CASH EFFECTS**

In an accrual accounting system, there are often "timing differences" between cash flows and the recognition of expenses or revenue. A company can pay cash in advance of incurring certain expenses, and it can receive cash before earning certain revenue. Likewise, it can incur certain expenses before it pays any cash, and it can earn certain revenue before it receives any cash. These timing differences, and the related adjusting entries that result from them, are summarized below:

- Adjusting entries to convert assets to expenses result from cash being paid prior to an expense being incurred.

- Adjusting entries to convert liabilities to revenue result from cash being received prior to revenue being earned.

- Adjusting entries to accrue unpaid expenses result from expenses being incurred before cash is paid.

- Adjusting entries to accrue uncollected revenue result from revenue being earned before cash is received.

---

## Characteristics of Adjusting Entries

Keep in mind two important characteristics of all adjusting entries: First, every adjusting entry *involves the recognition of either revenue or expenses.* Revenue and expenses represent changes in owners' equity. However, owners' equity cannot change by itself; *there also must be a corresponding change in either assets or liabilities.* Thus every adjusting entry affects both an income statement account (revenue or expense) and a balance sheet account (asset or liability). Rarely do adjusting entries include an entry to Cash.

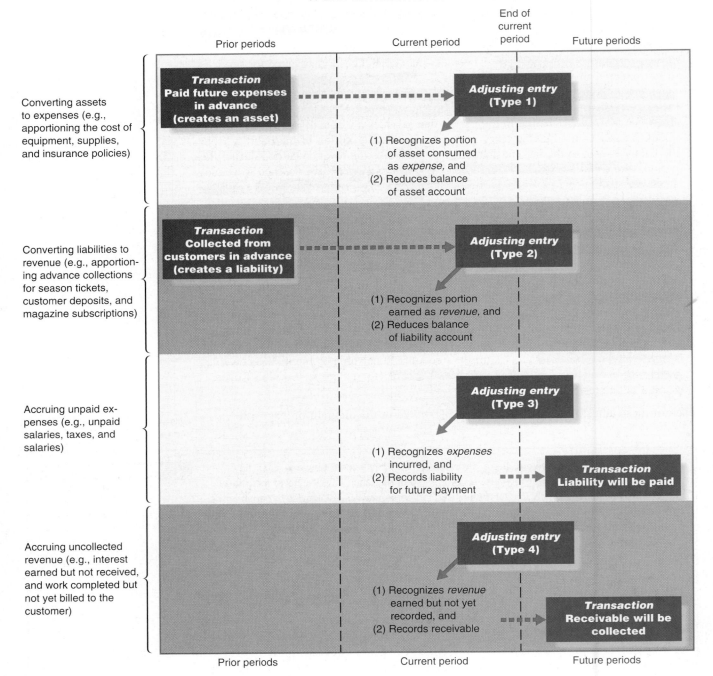

ADJUSTING ENTRIES:
A "LINK" BETWEEN ACCOUNTING PERIODS

Second, adjusting entries are based on the concepts of accrual accounting, *not upon monthly bills or month-end transactions.* No one sends Overnight Auto Service a bill saying, "Shop Supply Expense for the month is $500." Yet, Overnight must be aware of the need to record the estimated cost of shop supplies consumed if it is to measure income properly for the period. Making adjusting entries requires a greater understanding of accrual accounting concepts than does the recording of routine business transactions. In many businesses, the adjusting process is performed by the controller or by a professional accountant, rather than by the regular accounting staff.

## Year-End at Overnight Auto Service

To illustrate the various types of adjusting entries, we will again use our example involving Overnight Auto Service. Chapter 3 concluded with Overnight's trial balance dated February 28, 2002 (the end of the company's second month of operations). We will now skip ahead to *December 31, 2002*—the end of Overnight's first *year* of operations. This will enable us to illustrate the preparation of *annual* financial statements, rather than statements that cover only a single month.

Most companies make adjusting entries every *month.* We will assume that Overnight has been following this approach throughout 2002. The company's *unadjusted* trial balance dated December 31, 2002, appears below. It is referred to as an unadjusted trial balance because Overnight last made adjusting entries on *November 30;* therefore, it is still necessary to make adjusting entries for the month of December.

| OVERNIGHT AUTO SERVICE Trial Balance December 31, 2002 | | |
| --- | --- | --- |
| Cash | $ 18,592 | |
| Accounts receivable | 6,500 | |
| Shop supplies | 1,800 | |
| Unexpired insurance | 4,500 | |
| Land | 52,000 | |
| Building | 36,000 | |
| Accumulated depreciation: building | | $ 1,500 |
| Tools and equipment | 12,000 | |
| Accumulated depreciation: tools and equipment | | 2,000 |
| Notes payable | | 4,000 |
| Accounts payable | | 2,690 |
| Income taxes payable | | 1,560 |
| Unearned rent revenue | | 9,000 |
| Capital stock | | 80,000 |
| Retained earnings | | 0 |
| Dividends | 14,000 | |
| Repair service revenue | | 171,250 |
| Advertising expense | 3,900 | |
| Wages expense | 56,800 | |
| Supplies expense | 6,900 | |
| Depreciation expense: building | 1,500 | |
| Depreciation expense: tools and equipment | 2,000 | |
| Utilities expense | 19,400 | |
| Insurance expense | 13,500 | |
| Income taxes expense | 22,608 | |
| | $272,000 | $272,000 |

In the next few pages we illustrate several transactions, as well as the related adjusting entries. Both are shown in the format of general journal entries. To help distinguish between transactions and adjusting entries, transactions are printed in *blue*, and adjusting entries in *red*.

**LO 3**

Prepare adjusting entries to convert assets to expenses.

## Converting Assets to Expenses

When a business makes an expenditure that will benefit more than one accounting period, the amount usually is debited to an asset account. At the end of each period benefiting from this expenditure, an adjusting entry is made to transfer an appropriate portion of the cost from the asset account to an expense account. This adjusting entry reflects the fact that part of the asset has been used up—or become an expense—during the current accounting period.

An adjusting entry to convert an asset to an expense consists of a debit to an expense account and a credit to an asset account (or contra-asset account). Examples of these adjustments include the entries to apportion the costs of **prepaid expenses** and entries to record depreciation expense.

**Prepaid Expenses**    Payments in advance often are made for such items as insurance, rent, and office supplies. If the advance payment (or prepayment) will benefit more than just the current accounting period, the cost *represents an asset* rather than an expense. The cost of this asset will be allocated to expense in the accounting periods in which the services or the supplies are used. In summary, *prepaid expenses are assets;* they become expenses only as the goods or services are used up.

**Shop Supplies**    To illustrate, consider Overnight's accounting policies for shop supplies. As supplies are purchased, their cost is debited to the asset account Shop Supplies. It is not practical to make journal entries every few minutes as supplies are used. Instead, an estimate is made of the supplies remaining on hand at the end of each month; the supplies that are "missing" are assumed to have been used.

Prior to making adjusting entries at December 31, the balance in Overnight's Shop Supplies account is $1,800. The balance of this asset account represents shop supplies on hand on November 30. The Supplies Expense account shows a balance of $6,900, which represents the cost of supplies used through November 30. Assume that approximately $1,200 of shop supplies remain on hand at December 31. This suggests that supplies costing about $600 have been *used in December;* thus, the following *adjusting entry* is made:

*Transferring the cost of supplies used from the asset account to expense*

| | | |
|---|---|---|
| Dec. 31 | Supplies Expense . . . . . . . . . . . . . . . . . . . . . . . . . . . . . . . . . . . . . . . . . . . | 600 |
| | Shop Supplies . . . . . . . . . . . . . . . . . . . . . . . . . . . . . . . . . . . . . . . . . . . | 600 |
| | Estimate of shop supplies used in December. | |

This adjusting entry serves two purposes: (1) it charges to expense the cost of supplies used in December, and (2) it reduces the balance of the Shop Supplies account to $1,200—the amount of supplies estimated to be on hand at December 31.

**Insurance Policies**    Insurance policies also are a prepaid expense. These policies provide a service, insurance protection, over a specific period of time. As the time passes, the insurance policy *expires*—that is, it is used up in business operations.

To illustrate, assume that on March 1, Overnight purchased for $18,000 a one-year insurance policy providing comprehensive liability insurance and insurance against fire and damage to customers' vehicles while in Overnight's facilities. This expenditure (a *transaction*) was debited to an asset account, as follows:

*Purchase 12 months of insurance coverage*

| | | |
|---|---|---|
| Mar. 1 | Unexpired Insurance . . . . . . . . . . . . . . . . . . . . . . . . . . . . . . . . | 18,000 |
| | Cash . . . . . . . . . . . . . . . . . . . . . . . . . . . . . . . . . . . . . . . . . . . . . | 18,000 |
| | Purchased an insurance policy providing | |
| | coverage for the next 12 months. | |

This $18,000 expenditure provides insurance coverage for a period of one full year. Therefore, 1/12 of this cost, or $1,500, is recognized as insurance expense every month. The $13,500 insurance expense reported in Overnight's trial balance represents the portion of the insurance policy that has expired between March 1 and November 30 ($1,500/mo. × 9 months). The $4,500 amount of unexpired insurance shown in the trial balance is the remaining cost of the 12-month policy still in effect as of November 30 ($1,500/mo. × 3 months). By December 31, another full month of the policy has expired. Thus, the insurance expense for December is recorded by the following *adjusting entry* at month-end:

| | | | |
|---|---|---|---|
| Dec. 31 | Insurance Expense ................................ | 1,500 | |
| | Unexpired Insurance ............................. | | 1,500 |
| | Insurance expense for December. | | |

*Cost of insurance coverage expiring in December*

Notice the similarities between the *effects* of this adjusting entry and the one that we made previously for shop supplies. In both cases, the entries transfer to expense that portion of an asset used up during the period. This flow of costs from the balance sheet to the income statement is illustrated below:

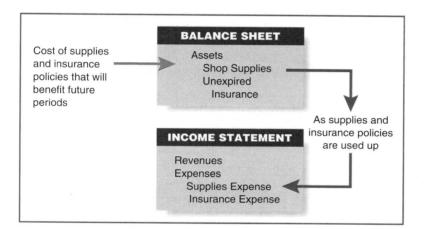

*As an asset is used up, it becomes an expense*

### You as a Car Owner

Car owners typically pay insurance premiums six months in advance. Assume that you recently paid your six-month premium of $600 on February 1 (for coverage through July 31). On March 31, you decide to switch insurance companies. You call your existing agent and ask that your policy be canceled. Are you entitled to a refund? If so, why, and how much will it be?

*Our comments appear on page 173.

**YOUR TURN**

**Recording Prepayments Directly in the Expense Accounts**   In our illustration, payments for shop supplies and for insurance covering more than one period were debited to asset accounts. However, some companies follow an alternative policy of debiting such prepayments directly to an expense account, such as Supplies Expense. At the end of the period, the adjusting entry then would be to debit Shop Supplies and credit Supplies Expense for the cost of supplies that had *not* been used.

This alternative method leads to the *same results* as does the procedure used by Overnight. Under either approach, the cost of supplies used during the current period is treated as an *expense,* and the cost of supplies still on hand is carried forward in the balance sheet as an *asset.*

In this text, we will follow Overnight's practice of recording prepayments in asset accounts and then making adjustments to transfer these costs to expense accounts as the assets expire. This approach correctly describes the *conceptual flow of costs* through the elements of financial statements. That is, a prepayment *is* an asset that later becomes an expense. The alternative approach is used widely in practice only because it is an efficient "shortcut," which standardizes the recording of transactions and may reduce the number of adjusting entries needed at the end of the period. Remember, our goal in this course is to develop your ability to understand and use accounting information, not to train you in alternative bookkeeping procedures.

The idea of shop supplies and insurance policies being used up over several months is easy to understand. But the same concept also applies to assets such as buildings and equipment. These assets are converted to expenses through the process of *depreciation.*

## The Concept of Depreciation

**Depreciable assets** are *physical objects* that retain their size and shape but that eventually wear out or become obsolete. They are not physically consumed, as are assets such as supplies, but nonetheless their economic usefulness diminishes over time. Examples of depreciable assets include buildings and all types of equipment, fixtures, furnishings—and even railroad tracks. Land, however, is *not* viewed as a depreciable asset, as it has an *unlimited* useful life.

Each period, a portion of a depreciable asset's usefulness *expires.* Therefore, a corresponding portion of its cost is recognized as *depreciation expense.*

**What Is Depreciation?** In accounting, the term **depreciation** means the *systematic allocation of the cost of a depreciable asset to expense* over the asset's useful life. This process is illustrated below:

*Depreciation: A process of allocating the cost of a depreciable asset to expense*

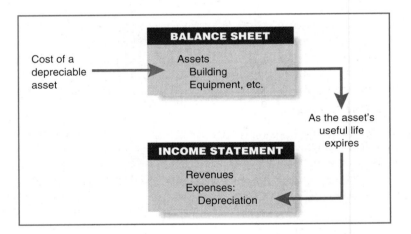

Notice the similarity of this diagram to that on the previous page.

Depreciation *is not* an attempt to record changes in the asset's market value. In the short run, the market value of some depreciable assets may even increase, but the process of depreciation continues anyway. The rationale for depreciation lies in the *matching principle.* Our goal is to offset a reasonable portion of the asset's cost against revenue in each period of the asset's **useful life**.

Depreciation expense occurs continuously over the life of the asset, but there are no daily "depreciation transactions." In effect, depreciation expense is paid in advance when the asset is originally purchased. Therefore, *adjusting entries* are needed at the end of each accounting period to transfer an appropriate amount of the asset's cost to depreciation expense.

**Depreciation Is Only an Estimate**   The appropriate amount of depreciation expense is *only an estimate*. After all, we cannot look at a building or a piece of equipment and determine precisely how much of its economic usefulness has expired during the current period.

The most widely used means of estimating periodic depreciation expense is the **straight-line method of depreciation**. Under the straight-line approach, an *equal portion* of the asset's cost is allocated to depreciation expense in every period of the asset's estimated useful life. The formula for computing depreciation expense by the straight-line method is shown below:[2]

$$\text{Depreciation expense (per period)} = \frac{\text{Cost of the asset}}{\text{Estimated useful life}}$$

The use of an *estimated useful life* is the major reason that depreciation expense is *only an estimate*. In most cases, management does not know in advance exactly how long the asset will remain in use.

How long does a building last? For purposes of computing depreciation expense, most companies estimate about 30 or 40 years. But the Empire State Building was built in 1931, and it's not likely to be torn down anytime soon. And how about Windsor Castle? While these are not typical examples, they illustrate the difficulty in estimating in advance just how long depreciable assets may remain in use.

**CASE IN POINT**

**Depreciation of Overnight's Building**   Overnight purchased its building for $36,000 on January 22. Because the building was old, its estimated remaining useful life is only 20 years. Therefore, the building's monthly depreciation expense is $150 ($36,000 cost ÷ 240 months). We will assume that Overnight did *not* record any depreciation expense in January because it operated for only a small part of the month. Thus, the building's $1,500 depreciation expense reported in Overnight's trial balance on page 139 represents 10 *full months* of depreciation recorded in 2002, from February 1 through November 30 ($150/mo. × 10 months). An additional $150 of depreciation expense is still needed on the building for December (bringing the total to be reported in the income statement for the year to $1,650).

The adjusting entry to record depreciation expense on Overnight's building for the month of December appears below:

Dec. 31   Depreciation Expense: Building  . . . . . . . . . . . . . . . . . . . . . . . . . . . . .   150  
         Accumulated Depreciation: Building  . . . . . . . . . . . . . . . . . . . . . . .   150  
        Monthly depreciation on building ($36,000 ÷ 240 mo.).

*The adjusting entry for monthly depreciation on the building*

The *Depreciation Expense: Building* account will appear in Overnight's income statement along with other expenses for the year ended December 31, 2002. The balance in the **Accumulated Depreciation: Building** account will be reported in the December 31 balance sheet as a *deduction* from the Building Account, as shown at the top of the following page:

---

[2] At this point in our discussion, we are ignoring any possible *residual value* that might be recovered upon disposal of the asset. Residual values are discussed in Chapter 9. We will assume that Overnight Auto Service depreciates its assets using the straight-line method computed without any residual values.

*How accumulated depreciation appears in the balance sheet*

| | |
|---|---:|
| Building . . . . . . . . . . . . . . . . . . . . . . . . . . . . . . . . . . . . . . . . . . . . . . . . . . . . . . | $36,000 |
| Less: Accumulated Depreciation: Building . . . . . . . . . . . . . . . . . . . . . . . . . . . . . | (1,650) |
| Book Value . . . . . . . . . . . . . . . . . . . . . . . . . . . . . . . . . . . . . . . . . . . . . . . . . . . | $34,350 |

Accumulated Depreciation: Building is an example of a **contra-asset account** because (1) it has a credit balance, and (2) it is offset against an asset account (Building) to produce the book value for the asset. Accountants often use the term **book value** (or *carrying value*) to describe the net valuation of an asset in a company's accounting records. For depreciable assets, such as buildings and equipment, book value is equal to the cost of the asset, less the related amount of accumulated depreciation. The end result of crediting the Accumulated Depreciation: Building account is much the same as if the credit had been made directly to the Building account; that is, the book value reported in the balance sheet for the building is reduced from $36,000 to $34,350.

Book value is of significance primarily for accounting purposes. It represents costs that will be offset against the revenue of future periods. It also gives users of financial statements an indication of the age of a company's depreciable assets (older assets tend to have larger amounts of accumulated depreciation associated with them than newer assets). It is important to realize that the computation of book value is based upon an asset's *historical* cost. Thus, book value is *not* intended to represent an asset's current *market value*.

**Depreciation of Tools and Equipment**    Overnight depreciates its tools and equipment over a period of five years (60 months) using the straight-line method. The December 31 trial balance shows that the company owns tools and equipment that cost $12,000. Therefore, the adjusting entry to record December's depreciation expense is:

*Monthly depreciation on tools and equipment*

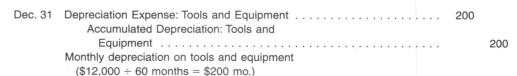

```
Dec. 31   Depreciation Expense: Tools and Equipment . . . . . . . . . . . . . . . . . . . . .   200
               Accumulated Depreciation: Tools and
                  Equipment . . . . . . . . . . . . . . . . . . . . . . . . . . . . . . . . . . . . .        200
               Monthly depreciation on tools and equipment
               ($12,000 ÷ 60 months = $200 mo.)
```

Again, we assume that Overnight did *not* record depreciation expense for tools and equipment in January because it operated for only a small part of the month. Thus, the related $2,000 depreciation expense reported in Overnight's trial balance on page 139 represents 10 *full months* of depreciation, from February 1 through November 30 ($200/mo. × 10 months). The tools and equipment still require an additional $200 of depreciation for December (bringing the total to be reported in the income statement for the year to $2,200).

What is the book value of Overnight's tools and equipment at December 31, 2002? If you said *$9,800,* you're right.[3]

---

**CASH EFFECTS**    Depreciation is a "noncash" expense. We have made the point that net income does *not* represent an inflow of cash or any other asset. Rather, it is a *computation* of the overall effect of certain business transactions on owners' equity. The computation and recognition of depreciation expense illustrate this point.

As depreciable assets "expire," owners' equity declines; but there is no corresponding cash outlay in the current period. For this reason, depreciation is called a noncash expense. Often it represents the largest difference between net income and the cash flows resulting from business operations.

---

[3] Cost, $12,000, less accumulated depreciation, which amounts to $2,200 after the December 31 adjusting entry.

## Converting Liabilities to Revenue

**LO 4**

Prepare adjusting entries to convert liabilities to revenue.

In some instances, customers may *pay in advance* for services to be rendered in later accounting periods. For example, a football team collects much of its revenue in advance through the sale of season tickets. Health clubs collect in advance by selling long-term membership contracts. Airlines sell many of their tickets well in advance of scheduled flights.

For accounting purposes, amounts collected in advance *do not represent revenue,* because these amounts have *not yet been earned.* Amounts collected from customers in advance are recorded by debiting the Cash account and crediting an *unearned revenue* account. **Unearned revenue** also may be called *deferred revenue.*

When a company collects money in advance from its customers, it has an *obligation* to render services in the future. Therefore, the balance of an unearned revenue account is considered to be a liability; *it appears in the liability section of the balance sheet, not in the income statement.* Unearned revenue differs from other liabilities because it usually will be settled by rendering services, rather than by making payment in cash. In short, it will be *worked off* rather than *paid off.* Of course, if the business is unable to render the service, it must discharge this liability by refunding money to its customers.

The largest liability in the balance sheet of **UAL Corporation (United Airlines)** is Advance Ticket Sales. This account, with a balance of more than $1.8 billion, represents unearned revenue resulting from the sale of tickets for future flights. Most of this unearned revenue will be earned as the future flights occur. Some customers, however, will change their plans and will return their tickets to **United Airlines** for a cash refund.

**CASE IN POINT**

When the company renders the services for which customers have paid in advance, it is working off its liability to these customers and is earning the revenue. At the end of the accounting period, an adjusting entry is made to transfer an appropriate amount from the unearned revenue account to a revenue account. This adjusting entry consists of a debit to a liability account (unearned revenue) and a credit to a revenue account.

To illustrate these concepts, assume that on December 1, Harbor Cab Co. agreed to rent space in Overnight's building to provide indoor storage for some of its cabs. The agreed-upon rent is $3,000 per month, and Harbor Cab paid for the first three months in advance. The journal entry to record this *transaction* on December 1 was:

| | | |
|---|---|---|
| Dec. 1 | Cash | 9,000 | |
| |     Unearned Rent Revenue | | 9,000 |
| |     Collected in advance from Harbor Cab for rental of | | |
| |       storage space for three months. | | |

Remember that Unearned Rent Revenue is a *liability* account, *not a revenue account.* Overnight will earn rental revenue *gradually* over a three-month period as it provides storage facilities for Harbor Cab. At the end of each of these three months, Overnight will make an *adjusting entry,* transferring $3,000 from the Unearned Rent Revenue account to an earned revenue account, Rent Revenue Earned, which will appear in Overnight's income statement. The first in this series of monthly transfers will be made at December 31 with the following adjusting entry:

*An "advance"—it's not revenue; it's a liability*

| | | |
|---|---|---|
| Dec. 31 | Unearned Rent Revenue | 3,000 | |
| |     Rent Revenue Earned | | 3,000 |
| |     Portion of rent received in advance from Harbor | | |
| |       Cab that was earned in December ($9,000 ÷ 3 mo.). | | |

*An adjusting entry showing that some unearned revenue has now been earned*

After this adjusting entry has been posted, the Unearned Rent Revenue account will have a $6,000 credit balance. This balance represents Overnight's obligation to render $6,000 worth of service over the next two months and will appear in the liability section of the company's balance sheet. The Rent Revenue Earned account will appear in Overnight's income statement.

The transfer of unearned revenue to earned revenue is illustrated below.

*As unearned revenue is earned, it becomes earned revenue.*

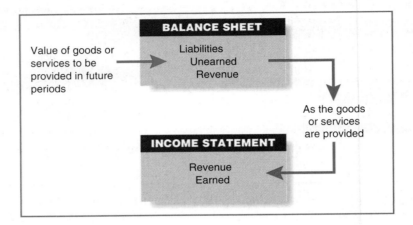

### Recording Advance Collections Directly in the Revenue Accounts

We have stressed that amounts collected from customers in advance represent liabilities, not revenue. However, some companies follow an accounting policy of crediting these advance collections directly to revenue accounts. The adjusting entry then should consist of a debit to the revenue account and a credit to the unearned revenue account for the portion of the advance payments *not yet earned*. This alternative accounting practice leads to the same results as does the method used in our illustration.

In this text, we will follow the originally described practice of crediting advance payments from customers to an unearned revenue account.

## Accruing Unpaid Expenses

**LO 5**

Prepare adjusting entries to accrue unpaid expenses.

This type of adjusting entry recognizes expenses that will be paid in *future* transactions; therefore, no cost has yet been recorded in the accounting records. Salaries of employees and interest on borrowed money are common examples of expenses that accumulate from day to day but that usually are not recorded until they are paid. These expenses are said to **accrue** over time, that is, to grow or to accumulate. At the end of the accounting period, an adjusting entry should be made to record any expenses that have accrued but that have not yet been recorded. Since these expenses will be paid at a future date, the adjusting entry consists of a debit to an expense account and a credit to a liability account. We shall now use the example of Overnight Auto Service to illustrate this type of adjusting entry.

### Accrual of Wages (or Salaries) Expense

Overnight, like many businesses, pays its employees every other Friday. This month, however, ends on a Tuesday—three days before the next scheduled payday. Thus Overnight's employees have worked for more than a week in December *for which they have not yet been paid.*

Time cards indicate that since the last payroll date, Overnight's employees have worked a total of 130 hours. Including payroll taxes, Overnight's wage expense averages about $15 per hour. Therefore, at December 31, the company owes its employees approximately

$1,950 for work performed in December.[4] The following adjusting entry should be made to record this amount both as wages expense of the current period and as a liability:

| Dec. 31 | Wages Expense | 1,950 | |
| | Wages Payable | | 1,950 |
| | To accrue wages owed to employees but unpaid as of month-end. | | |

*Wages owed as of month-end*

This adjusting entry increases Overnight's wages expense for 2002 and also creates a liability—wages payable—that will appear in the December 31 balance sheet.

On Friday, January 3, Overnight will pay its regular biweekly payroll. Let us assume that this payroll amounts to $2,397. In this case, the entry to record payment will be as shown below.[5]

| 2003 | | | |
| Jan. 3 | Wages Expense (for January) | 447 | |
| | Wages Payable (accrued in December) | 1,950 | |
| | Cash | | 2,397 |
| | Biweekly payroll, $1,950 of which had been accrued at December 31. | | |

*Payment of wages earned in two accounting periods*

**Accrual of Interest Expense**  On January 22, 2002, Overnight purchased its building, an old bus garage, from Metropolitan Transit District for $36,000. Overnight paid $6,000 cash, and issued a $30,000, 90-day note payable for the balance owed. Overnight paid the $30,000 obligation in April. There was no interest expense associated with this note payable because it was *non-interest-bearing.*

On November 30, 2002, Overnight borrowed $4,000 from American National Bank by issuing an *interest-bearing* note payable. This loan is to be repaid in three months (on February 28, 2003), along with interest computed at an annual rate of 9%. The entry made on November 30 to record this borrowing transaction appears below:

| Nov. 30 | Cash | 4,000 | |
| | Notes Payable | | 4,000 |
| | Borrowed cash from American National Bank, issuing a 9%, $4,000 note payable, due in three months. | | |

On February 28, Overnight must pay the bank $4,090. This represents the $4,000 amount borrowed, *plus $90 interest* ($4,000 × .09 × 3/12). The $90 interest charge covers a period of *three months.* Although no payment will be made until February 28, 2003, interest expense is *incurred* (or accrued) at a rate of $30 per month, as shown at the top of the following page:

---

[4] In preparing a formal payroll, wages and payroll taxes must be computed "down to the last cent." But this is not a payroll; it is an amount to be used in the company's financial statements. Therefore, a reasonable estimate will suffice. The accounting principle of *materiality* is discussed later in this chapter.

[5] In this illustration, we do not address the details associated with payroll taxes and amounts withheld. These topics are discussed in Chapter 10.

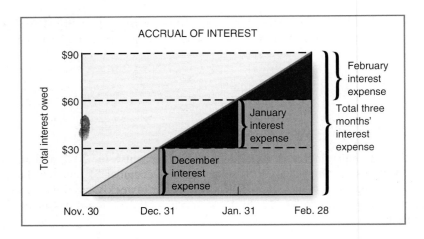

The following adjusting entry is made at December 31 to charge December operations with one month's interest expense and to record the amount of interest owed to the bank at month-end:

*Adjusting entry for interest expense incurred through Dec. 31*

| | | | |
|---|---|---|---|
| Dec. 31 | Interest Expense ......................................... | 30 | |
| | Interest Payable ...................................... | | 30 |
| | Interest expenses accrued during December on note payable ($4,000 × .09 × 1/12). | | |

The $30 interest expense that accrued in December will appear in Overnight's 2002 income statement. Both the $30 interest payable and the $4,000 note payable to American National Bank will appear as *liabilities* in the December 31, 2002, balance sheet.

Overnight will make a second adjusting entry recognizing another $30 in interest expense on January 31 of the coming year. The entry on February 28 to record the repayment of this loan, including $90 in interest charges, will be as follows:

*Payment of interest expense incurred over several months*

| | | | |
|---|---|---|---|
| 2003 | | | |
| Feb. 28 | Notes Payable ...................................... | 4,000 | |
| | Interest Payable (from December and January) ............... | 60 | |
| | Interest Expense (February only) ......................... | 30 | |
| | Cash ........................................... | | 4,090 |
| | Repaid $4,000 note payable to American National Bank, including $90 in interest charges. | | |

**LO 6**

Prepare adjusting entries to accrue uncollected revenue.

## Accruing Uncollected Revenue

A business may earn revenue during the current accounting period but not bill the customer until a future accounting period. This situation is likely to occur if additional services are being performed for the same customer, in which case the bill might not be prepared until all services are completed. Any revenue that has been *earned but not recorded* during the current accounting period should be recorded at the end of the period by means of an adjusting entry. This adjusting entry consists of a debit to an account receivable and a credit to the appropriate revenue account. The term *accrued revenue* often is used to describe revenue that has been earned during the period but that has not been recorded prior to the closing date.

To illustrate this type of adjusting entry, assume that in December, Overnight entered into an agreement to perform routine maintenance on several vans owned by Airport Shuttle Service. Overnight agreed to maintain these vans for a flat fee of $1,500 per month, payable on the fifteenth of each month.

No entry was made to record the signing of this agreement, because no services had yet been rendered. Overnight began rendering services on *December 15,* but the first monthly payment will not be received until January 15. Therefore, Overnight should make the following adjusting entry at December 31 to record the revenue *earned* from Airport Shuttle during the month:

| | | | |
|---|---|---:|---:|
| Dec. 31 | Accounts Receivable | 750 | |
| | Repair Service Revenue | | 750 |
| | To recognize revenue from services rendered on | | |
| | Airport Shuttle maintenance contract during | | |
| | December. Account is settled on the fifteenth of each month. | | |

*Adjusting entry recognizing revenue earned but not yet billed or collected*

### You as Overnight Auto's Service Department Manager

As part of your employment agreement with Overnight Auto, you earn a 5% bonus based on Overnight's profits each year. You were discussing this arrangement with friends after bowling at Jill's Lounge, when one of them asked if your bonus would not be higher if the entire month's revenue from Airport Shuttle Service ($1,500) were recognized in December rather than only 1/2 of the revenue ($750) as illustrated above. How would you respond?

*Our answer is on p. 173.

**YOUR TURN**

The collection of the first monthly fee from Airport Shuttle will occur in the next accounting period (January 15, to be exact). Of this $1,500 cash receipt, half represents collection of the receivable recorded on December 31; the other half represents revenue earned in January. Thus the entry to record the receipt of $1,500 from Airport Shuttle on January 15 will be:

| | | | |
|---|---|---:|---:|
| 2003 | | | |
| Jan. 15 | Cash | 1,500 | |
| | Accounts Receivable | | 750 |
| | Repair Service Revenue | | 750 |
| | Collected from Airport Shuttle for van maintenance, | | |
| | Dec. 15 through Jan. 15. | | |

*Entry to record collection of accrued revenue*

The net result of the December 31 adjusting entry has been to divide the revenue from maintenance of Airport Shuttle's vans between December and January in proportion to the services rendered during each month.

## Accruing Income Taxes Expense: The Final Adjusting Entry

As a corporation earns taxable income, it incurs income taxes expense, and also a liability to governmental tax authorities. This liability is paid in four installments called *estimated quarterly payments.* The first three payments normally are made on April 15, June 15, and September 15. The final installment actually is due on *December 15;* but for purposes of our illustration and assignment materials, we will assume the final payment is not due until *January 15* of the following year.[6]

---

[6] This assumption enables us to accrue income taxes in December in the same manner as in other months. Otherwise, income taxes for this month would be recorded as a mid-month transaction, rather than in an end-of-month adjusting entry. The adjusting entry for income taxes is an example of an accrued, but unpaid, expense.

In its unadjusted trial balance (page 139), Overnight shows income taxes expense of $22,608. This is the income taxes expense recognized from January 20, 2002 (the date Overnight opened for business) through November 30, 2002. Income taxes accrued through September 30 have already been paid. Thus, the $1,560 liability for income taxes payable represents only the income taxes accrued in *October* and *November.*

The amount of income taxes expense accrued for any given month is only an *estimate.* The actual amount of income taxes cannot be determined until the company prepares its annual income tax return. In our illustrations and assignment materials, we estimate income taxes expense at *40% of taxable income.* We also assume that taxable income is equal to *income before income taxes,* a subtotal often shown in an income statement. This subtotal is total revenue less all expenses *other than* income taxes.

**CASE IN POINT**

In the United States, income for income tax purposes computed using Internal Revenue Service (IRS) rules often differs from income for financial reporting purposes created in compliance with GAAP. This is because IRS rules for computing revenues and expenses are not always consistent with GAAP rules. However, in Germany and Japan, the rules for recognizing revenue and expenses for income taxes are the same as those used for financial reporting.

In 2002, Overnight earned income before income taxes of $66,570 (see the income statement illustrated on page 178 in Chapter 5). Therefore, income taxes expense *for the entire year* is estimated at $26,628 ($66,570 × 40%). Given that income taxes expense recognized through November 30 amounts to $22,608 (see the unadjusted trial balance on page 139), an additional $4,020 in income taxes expense must have accrued during *December* ($26,628 − $22,608). The adjusting entry to record this expense is shown below:

*Adjusting entry to record income taxes for December*

| | | |
|---|---|---|
| Dec. 31 Income Taxes Expense ................................. | 4,020 | |
| Income Taxes Payable ............................... | | 4,020 |
| Estimated income taxes applicable to taxable income earned during December. | | |

This entry increases the balance in the Income Taxes Expense account to the $26,628 amount required for the year ended December 31, 2002. It also increases the liability for income taxes payable to $5,580 ($1,560 + $4,020). The entry to record the payment of this liability on January 15, 2003, will be:

| | | |
|---|---|---|
| 2003 | | |
| Jan. 15 Income Taxes Payable ............................... | 5,580 | |
| Cash ........................................ | | 5,580 |
| Paid final installment on 2002 income tax liability. | | |

The above transaction is simply the payment of an outstanding liability; therefore, it is *not* considered an adjusting entry.

**Income Taxes in Unprofitable Periods** What happens to income taxes expense when *losses* are incurred? In these situations, the company recognizes a "negative amount" of income taxes expense. The adjusting entry to record income taxes at the end of an *unprofitable* accounting period consists of a *debit* to Income Taxes Payable and a *credit* to Income Taxes Expense.

First, what constitutes a material amount varies with the size of the organization. For example, a $1,000 expenditure may be material in relation to the financial statements of a small business but not to the statements of a large corporation such as **General Electric**.[8] There are no official rules as to what constitutes a material amount, but most accountants would consider amounts of less than 2% or 3% of net income to be immaterial, unless there were other factors to consider. One such other factor is the *cumulative effect* of numerous immaterial events. Each of a dozen items may be immaterial when considered by itself. When viewed together, however, the combined effect of all 12 items may be material.

Finally, materiality depends on the *nature* of the item, as well as its dollar amount. Assume, for example, that several managers systematically have been stealing money from the company that they manage. Stockholders probably would consider this fact important even if the dollar amounts were small in relation to the company's total resources.

*Note to students:* In the assignment material accompanying this textbook, you are to consider all dollar amounts to be material, unless the problem specifically raises the question of materiality.

## Effects of the Adjusting Entries

We now have discussed nine separate adjusting entries that Overnight will make at December 31. These entries appear on the next page in the format of journal entries. (Overnight also recorded many transactions throughout the month of December. The company's December transactions are not illustrated here but were accounted for in the manner described in Chapter 3.)

---

[8] This point is emphasized by the fact that General Electric rounds the dollar amounts shown in its financial statements to the nearest $1 million. This rounding of financial statement amounts is, in itself, an application of the materiality concept.

*Adjusting entries are recorded only at the end of the period.*

| | GENERAL JOURNAL | | |
|---|---|---|---|
| **Date** | **Account Titles and Explanation** | **Debit** | **Credit** |
| 2002 | | | |
| Dec. 31 | Supplies Expense | 600 | |
| |     Shop Supplies | | 600 |
| | Shop supplies used during December. | | |
| 31 | Insurance Expense | 1,500 | |
| |     Unexpired Insurance | | 1,500 |
| | Insurance expense for December. | | |
| 31 | Depreciation Expense: Building | 150 | |
| |     Accumulated Depreciation: Building | | 150 |
| | Monthly depreciation on building | | |
| |     ($36,000 ÷ 240 mo.). | | |
| 31 | Depreciation Expense: Tools and | | |
| |     Equipment | 200 | |
| |     Accumulated Depreciation: | | |
| |       Tools and Equipment | | 200 |
| | Monthly depreciation on tools and | | |
| |     equipment ($12,000 ÷ 60 mo.) | | |
| 31 | Unearned Rent Revenue | 3,000 | |
| |     Rent Revenue Earned | | 3,000 |
| | Portion of rent received in advance | | |
| |     from Harbor Cab that was earned in | | |
| |     December ($9,000 ÷ 3 mo.). | | |
| 31 | Wages Expense | 1,950 | |
| |     Wages Payable | | 1,950 |
| | To accrue wages owed to employees | | |
| |     but unpaid as of month-end. | | |
| 31 | Interest Expense | 30 | |
| |     Interest Payable | | 30 |
| | Interest expense accrued during | | |
| |     December on note payable | | |
| |     ($4,000 × .09 × 1/12). | | |
| 31 | Accounts Receivable | 750 | |
| |     Repair Service Revenue | | 750 |
| | To recognize revenue from services | | |
| |     rendered on Airport Shuttle | | |
| |     maintenance contract during | | |
| |     December. | | |
| 31 | Income Taxes Expense | 4,020 | |
| |     Income Taxes Payable | | 4,020 |
| | Estimated accrued income taxes applicable | | |
| |     to taxable income in December. | | |

After these adjustments are posted to the ledger, Overnight's ledger accounts will be up-to-date (except for the balance in the Retained Earnings account).[9] The company's **adjusted trial balance** at December 31, 2002, appears on the following page. (For emphasis, those accounts affected by the month-end adjusting entries are shown in red.)

---

[9] The balance in the Retained Earnings account will be brought up-to-date during the closing process, discussed in Chapter 5.

**LO 9**

Prepare an adjusted trial balance and describe its purpose.

**OVERNIGHT AUTO SERVICE**
**Adjusted Trial Balance**
**December 31, 2002**

| | | |
|---|---:|---:|
| Cash | $ 18,592 | |
| Accounts receivable | 7,250 | |
| Shop supplies | 1,200 | |
| Unexpired insurance | 3,000 | |
| Land | 52,000 | |
| Building | 36,000 | |
| Accumulated depreciation: building | | $ 1,650 |
| Tools and equipment | 12,000 | |
| Accumulated depreciation: tools and equipment | | 2,200 |
| Notes payable | | 4,000 |
| Accounts payable | | 2,690 |
| Wages payable | | 1,950 |
| Income taxes payable | | 5,580 |
| Interest payable | | 30 |
| Unearned rent revenue | | 6,000 |
| Capital stock | | 80,000 |
| Retained earnings (*Note:* still must be updated for transactions recorded in the accounts listed below. Closing entries serve this purpose.) | | 0 |
| Dividends | 14,000 | |
| Repair service revenue | | 172,000 |
| Rent revenue earned | | 3,000 |
| Advertising expense | 3,900 | |
| Wages expense | 58,750 | |
| Supplies expense | 7,500 | |
| Depreciation expense: building | 1,650 | |
| Depreciation expense: tools and equipment | 2,200 | |
| Utilities expense | 19,400 | |
| Insurance expense | 15,000 | |
| Interest expense | 30 | |
| Income taxes expense | 26,628 | |
| | $279,100 | $279,100 |

*Balance sheet accounts*

*Statement of retained earnings accounts*

*Income statement accounts*

Overnight's financial statements are prepared directly from the adjusted trial balance. Note the order of the accounts: all balance sheet accounts are followed by the statement of retained earnings accounts and then the income statement accounts. In Chapter 5, we illustrate exactly how these three financial statements are prepared.

## SOME CONCLUDING REMARKS

Throughout this chapter, we illustrated end-of-period adjusting entries arising from *timing differences* between cash flows and revenue or expense recognition. In short, the adjusting process helps to ensure that appropriate amounts of revenue and expense are measured and reported in a company's income statement.

Later chapters explain why accurate income measurement is of critical importance to investors and creditors in estimating the timing and amounts of a company's future cash flows. We also illustrate how understanding certain timing differences enables managers to budget and to plan for future operations.

**A SECOND LOOK**

### United Airlines (UAL)

We have examined why Advance Ticket Sales are reported in **UAL Corporation**'s balance sheet as a current liability account. We discovered that this account actually represents revenue that must be *deferred* (remain unearned) until future flight services are provided to those passengers that have made advance ticket purchases. At the end of each accounting period, **UAL** makes an adjusting entry to account for the portion of any unearned revenue that has been *earned* at the balance sheet date. It does so in much the same way as Overnight Auto Service adjusted its Unearned Revenue account on page 145.

Other accounts similar to those used by Overnight Auto Service also can be identified in **UAL**'s balance sheet as candidates for adjusting entries: Prepaid Rent, Accumulated Depreciation, and Income Taxes Payable. In Chapter 5, we continue with our illustration of Overnight Auto Service and demonstrate how adjusting entries are reflected in a company's financial statements.

## SUMMARY OF LEARNING OBJECTIVES

### LO 1

**Explain the purpose of adjusting entries.**

The purpose of adjusting entries is to allocate revenue and expenses among accounting periods in accordance with the realization and matching principles. These end-of-period entries are necessary because revenue may be earned and expenses may be incurred in periods other than the period in which related cash flows are recorded.

### LO 2

**Describe the four basic types of adjusting entries.**

The four basic types of adjusting entries are made to (1) convert assets to expenses, (2) convert liabilities to revenue, (3) accrue unpaid expenses, and (4) accrue uncollected revenue. Often a transaction affects the revenue or expenses of *two or more* accounting periods. The related cash inflow or outflow does not always coincide with the period in which these revenue or expense items are recorded. Thus, the need for adjusting entries results from *timing differences* between the receipt or disbursement of cash and the recording of revenue or expenses.

### LO 3

**Prepare adjusting entries to convert assets to expenses.**

When an expenditure is made that will benefit more than one accounting period, an asset account is debited and cash is credited. The asset account is used to *defer* (or postpone) expense recognition until a later date. At the end of each period benefiting from this expenditure, an adjusting entry is made to transfer an appropriate amount from the asset account to an *expense* account. This adjustment reflects the fact that part of the asset's cost has been *matched* against revenue in the measurement of income for the current period.

### LO 4

**Prepare adjusting entries to convert liabilities to revenue.**

Customers sometimes pay in advance for services to be rendered in later accounting periods. For accounting purposes, the cash received does *not* represent revenue until it has been *earned.* Thus, the recognition of revenue must be *deferred* until it is earned. Advance collections from customers are recorded by debiting Cash and by crediting a *liability* account for *unearned* revenue. This liability is sometimes called Customer Deposits, Advance Sales, or Deferred Revenue. As unearned revenue becomes earned, an adjusting entry is made at the end of each period to transfer an appropriate amount from the liability account to a *revenue* account. This adjustment reflects the fact that all or part of the company's obligation to its customers has been fulfilled and that revenue has been realized.

### LO 5

**Prepare adjusting entries to accrue unpaid expenses.**

Some expenses accumulate (or *accrue*) in the current period but are not *paid* until a future period. These accrued expenses are recorded as part of the adjusting process at the end of each period by debiting the appropriate expense (e.g., Salary Expense, Interest Expense, or Income Taxes Expense), and by crediting a liability account (e.g., Salaries Payable, Interest Payable, or Income Taxes Payable). In future periods, as cash is disbursed in settlement of these liabilities, the appropriate liability account is debited and Cash is credited. *Note:* Recording the accrued expense in the current period is the adjusting entry. Recording the disbursement of cash in a future period is *not* considered an adjusting entry.

### LO 6

**Prepare adjusting entries to accrue uncollected revenue.**

Some revenues are earned (or *accrued*) in the current period but are not *collected* until a future period. These revenues are normally recorded as part of the adjusting process at the end of each period by debiting an asset account called Accounts Receivable, and by crediting the appropriate revenue account. In future periods, as cash is collected in settlement of outstanding receivables, Cash is debited and Accounts Receivable is credited. *Note:* Recording the accrued revenue in the current period is the adjusting entry. Recording the receipt of cash in a future period is *not* considered an adjusting entry.

### LO 7

**Explain how the principles of *realization* and *matching* relate to adjusting entries.**

Adjusting entries are the *tools* by which accountants apply the realization and matching principles. Through these entries, revenues are recognized as they are *earned,* and expenses are recognized as resources are *used* or consumed in producing the related revenue.

### LO 8

**Explain the concept of *materiality*.**

The concept of materiality allows accountants to use estimated amounts and to ignore certain accounting principles if these actions will not have a material effect on the financial statements. A material effect is one that might reasonably be expected to influence the decisions made by the users of financial statements. Thus, accountants may account for immaterial items and events in the easiest and most convenient manner.

**LO 9**

**Prepare an adjusted trial balance and describe its purpose.**
The adjusted trial balance reports all of the balances in the general ledger *after* the end-of-period adjusting entries have been made and posted. Generally, all of a company's balance sheet accounts are listed, followed by the statement of retained earnings accounts, and finally, the income statement accounts. The amounts shown in the adjusted trial balance are carried forward directly to the financial statements. The adjusted trial balance is *not* considered one of the four general purpose financial statements introduced in Chapter 2. Rather, it is simply a *schedule* (or tool) used in preparing the financial statements.

In this chapter we have examined adjusting entries made for the accrual and deferral of expenses and revenue. In Chapter 5, we complete the remaining steps of the accounting cycle by illustrating the preparation of financial statements, the end-of-period closing process, and the after-closing trial balance.

## KEY TERMS INTRODUCED OR EMPHASIZED IN CHAPTER 4

**accrue** (p. 146) To grow or accumulate over time; for example, interest expense.

**Accumulated Depreciation** (p. 143) A contra-asset account shown as a deduction from the related asset account in the balance sheet. Depreciation taken throughout the useful life of an asset is accumulated in this account.

**adjusted trial balance** (p. 154) A schedule indicating the balances in ledger accounts *after* end-of-period adjusting entries have been posted. The amounts shown in the adjusted trial balance are carried directly into financial statements.

**adjusting entries** (p. 136) Entries made at the end of the accounting period for the purpose of recognizing revenue and expenses that are not properly measured as a result of journalizing transactions as they occur.

**book value** (p. 144) The net amount at which an asset appears in financial statements. For depreciable assets, book value represents cost minus accumulated depreciation. Also called *carrying value.*

**contra-asset account** (p. 144) An account with a credit balance that is offset against or deducted from an asset account to produce the proper balance sheet amount for the asset.

**depreciable assets** (p. 142) Physical objects with a limited life. The cost of these assets is gradually recognized as depreciation expense.

**depreciation** (p. 142) The systematic allocation of the cost of an asset to expense during the periods of its useful life.

**immaterial** (p. 152) Something of little or no consequence. Immaterial items may be accounted for in the most convenient manner, without regard to other theoretical concepts.

**matching (principle)** (p. 151) The accounting principle of offsetting revenue with the expenses incurred in producing that revenue. Requires recognition of expenses in the periods that the goods and services are used in the effort to produce revenue.

**materiality** (p. 152) The relative importance of an item or amount. Items significant enough to influence decisions are said to be *material.* Items lacking this importance are considered *immaterial.* The accounting treatment accorded to immaterial items may be guided by convenience rather than by theoretical principles.

**prepaid expenses** (p. 140) Assets representing advance payment of the expenses of future accounting periods. As time passes, adjusting entries are made to transfer the related costs from the asset account to an expense account.

**realization (principle)** (p. 151) The accounting principle that governs the timing of revenue recognition. Basically, the principle indicates that revenue should be recognized in the period in which it is earned.

**straight-line method of depreciation** (p. 143) The widely used approach of recognizing an equal amount of depreciation expense in each period of a depreciable asset's useful life.

**unearned revenue** (p. 145) An obligation to deliver goods or render services in the future, stemming from the receipt of advance payment.

**useful life** (p. 142) The period of time that a depreciable asset is expected to be useful to the business. This is the period over which the cost of the asset is allocated to depreciation expense.

## DEMONSTRATION PROBLEM

Internet Consulting Service, Inc., adjusts its accounts every month. On the facing page is the company's year-end *unadjusted* trial balance dated December 31, 2002. (Bear in mind that adjusting entries already have been made for the first eleven months of 2002, but have *not* for December.)

**INTERNET CONSULTING SERVICE, INC.**
**Unadjusted Trial Balance**
**December 31, 2002**

| | | |
|---|---:|---:|
| Cash | $ 49,100 | |
| Consulting fees receivable | 23,400 | |
| Prepaid office rent | 6,300 | |
| Prepaid dues and subscriptions | 300 | |
| Supplies | 600 | |
| Equipment | 36,000 | |
| Accumulated depreciation: equipment | | $ 10,200 |
| Notes payable | | 5,000 |
| Income taxes payable | | 12,000 |
| Unearned consulting fees | | 5,950 |
| Capital stock | | 30,000 |
| Retained earnings | | 32,700 |
| Dividends | 60,000 | |
| Consulting fees earned | | 257,180 |
| Salaries expense | 88,820 | |
| Telephone expense | 2,550 | |
| Rent expense | 22,000 | |
| Income taxes expense | 51,000 | |
| Dues and subscriptions expense | 560 | |
| Supplies expense | 1,600 | |
| Depreciation expense: equipment | 6,600 | |
| Miscellaneous expenses | 4,200 | |
| | $353,030 | $353,030 |

**Other Data**

a. On December 1, the company signed a new rental agreement and paid three months' rent in advance at a rate of $2,100 per month. This advance payment was debited to the Prepaid Office Rent account.

b. Dues and subscriptions expiring during December amounted to $50.

c. An estimate of supplies on hand was made at December 31; the estimated cost of the unused supplies was $450.

d. The useful life of the equipment has been estimated at five years (60 months) from date of acquisition.

e. Accrued interest on notes payable amounted to $100 at year-end. (Set up accounts for Interest Expense and for Interest Payable.)

f. Consulting services valued at $2,850 were rendered during December to clients who had made payment in advance.

g. It is the custom of the firm to bill clients only when consulting work is completed or, in the case of prolonged engagements, at monthly intervals. At December 31, consulting services valued at $11,000 had been rendered to clients but not yet billed. No advance payments had been received from these clients.

h. Salaries earned by employees but not paid as of December 31 amount to $1,700.

i. Income taxes expense for the year is estimated at $56,000. Of this amount, $51,000 has been recognized as expense in prior months, and $39,000 has been paid to tax authorities. The company plans to pay the $17,000 remainder of its income tax liability on January 15.

**Instructions**

**a.** Prepare the necessary adjusting journal entries on December 31, 2002.

**b.** Determine the amounts to be reported in the company's year-end adjusted trial balance for each of the following accounts:

| | |
|---|---|
| Consulting Fees Earned | Dues and Subscriptions Expense |
| Salaries Expense | Depreciation Expense: Equipment |
| Telephone Expense | Miscellaneous Expenses |
| Rent Expense | Interest Expense |
| Supplies Expense | Income Taxes Expense |

**c.** Determine the company's net income for the year ended December 31, 2002. (*Hint:* Use the amounts determined in part **b** above.)

## Solution to Demonstration Problem

**a.**

| | GENERAL JOURNAL | | |
|---|---|---|---|
| **Date** | **Account Titles and Explanation** | **Debit** | **Credit** |
| Dec. 31 2002 | | | |
| **1.** | Rent Expense . . . . . . . . . . . . . . . . . . . . . . . . . . . . . . . . . . . . . . . . . . . . . . . . . . . .<br>    Prepaid Office Rent . . . . . . . . . . . . . . . . . . . . . . . . . . . . . . . . . . . . . . . . . . .<br>Rent expense for December. | 2,100 | 2,100 |
| **2.** | Dues and Subscriptions Expense . . . . . . . . . . . . . . . . . . . . . . . . . . . . .<br>    Prepaid Dues and Subscriptions . . . . . . . . . . . . . . . . . . . . . . . . . .<br>Dues and subscriptions expense for December. | 50 | 50 |
| **3.** | Supplies Expense . . . . . . . . . . . . . . . . . . . . . . . . . . . . . . . . . . . . . . . . . . . .<br>    Supplies . . . . . . . . . . . . . . . . . . . . . . . . . . . . . . . . . . . . . . . . . . . . . . . . .<br> | 150 | 150 |
| **4.** | Depreciation Expense: Equipment . . . . . . . . . . . . . . . . . . . . . . . . . . .<br>    Accumulated Depreciation: Equipment . . . . . . . . . . . . . . . . . .<br>Depreciation expense for December ($36,000 ÷ 60 mos.). | 600 | 600 |
| **5.** | Interest Expense . . . . . . . . . . . . . . . . . . . . . . . . . . . . . . . . . . . . . . . . . . . .<br>    Interest Payable . . . . . . . . . . . . . . . . . . . . . . . . . . . . . . . . . . . . . . . . .<br>Interest accrued on notes payable in December. | 100 | 100 |
| **6.** | Unearned Consulting Fees . . . . . . . . . . . . . . . . . . . . . . . . . . . . . . . . . .<br>    Consulting Fees Earned . . . . . . . . . . . . . . . . . . . . . . . . . . . . . . . .<br>Consulting services performed for clients<br>who paid in advance. | 2,850 | 2,850 |
| **7.** | Consulting Fees Receivable . . . . . . . . . . . . . . . . . . . . . . . . . . . . . . . .<br>    Consulting Fees Earned . . . . . . . . . . . . . . . . . . . . . . . . . . . . . . . .<br>Consulting services performed in December for which<br>billings have not been made nor payments received. | 11,000 | 11,000 |
| **8.** | Salaries Expense . . . . . . . . . . . . . . . . . . . . . . . . . . . . . . . . . . . . . . . . . . .<br>    Salaries Payable . . . . . . . . . . . . . . . . . . . . . . . . . . . . . . . . . . . . . . .<br>Salaries accrued in December but not yet paid. | 1,700 | 1,700 |
| **9.** | Income Taxes Expense . . . . . . . . . . . . . . . . . . . . . . . . . . . . . . . . . . . . .<br>    Income Taxes Payable . . . . . . . . . . . . . . . . . . . . . . . . . . . . . . . . .<br>Estimated income taxes accrued on income in December. | 5,000 | 5,000 |

**b.**

| | Unadjusted Trial Balance Amount | + | Adjustment | = | Adjusted Trial Balance Amount |
|---|---|---|---|---|---|
| Consulting Fees Earned | $257,180 | | (6) $ 2,850 | | |
| | | | (7) $11,000 | | $271,030 |
| Salaries Expense | $ 88,820 | | (8) $ 1,700 | | $ 90,520 |
| Telephone Expense | $ 2,550 | | None | | $ 2,550 |
| Rent Expense | $ 22,000 | | (1) $ 2,100 | | $ 24,100 |
| Supplies Expense | $ 1,600 | | (3) $ 150 | | $ 1,750 |
| Dues and Subscriptions Expense | $ 560 | | (2) $ 50 | | $ 610 |
| Depreciation Expense: Equipment | $ 6,600 | | (4) $ 600 | | $ 7,200 |
| Miscellaneous Expenses | $ 4,200 | | None | | $ 4,200 |
| Interest Expense | None | | (5) $ 100 | | $ 100 |
| Income Taxes Expense | $ 51,000 | | (9) $ 5,000 | | $ 56,000 |

**c.** Using the figures computed in part **b**, net income for the year is computed as follows:

| | | | |
|---|---|---|---|
| Consulting Fees Earned | . . . . . . . . . . . . . . . . . . . . . . . . . . . . . . . . . . . . | | $271,030 |
| Salaries Expense | . . . . . . . . . . . . . . . . . . . . . . . . . . . . . . . | $90,520 | |
| Telephone Expense | . . . . . . . . . . . . . . . . . . . . . . . . . | 2,550 | |
| Rent Expense | . . . . . . . . . . . . . . . . . . . . . . . . . . . . . . | 24,100 | |
| Supplies Expense | . . . . . . . . . . . . . . . . . . . . . . . . . . . . | 1,750 | |
| Dues and Subscriptions Expense | . . . . . . . . . . . . . . . . . . . . . . . . . . . . . | 610 | |
| Depreciation Expense: Equipment | . . . . . . . . . . . . . . . . . . . . . . . . . . . . . . | 7,200 | |
| Miscellaneous | . . . . . . . . . . . . . . . . . . . . . . . . . . . . . . . . | 4,200 | |
| Interest Expense | . . . . . . . . . . . . . . . . . . . . . . . . . . . . . | 100 | |
| Income Taxes Expense | . . . . . . . . . . . . . . . . . . . . . . . . . . . . . | 56,000 | (187,030) |
| Net Income | . . . . . . . . . . . . . . . . . . . . . . . . . . . . . . . . . . . . | | $ 84,000 |

## SELF-TEST QUESTIONS

*The answers to these questions appear on page 173.*

1. The purpose of adjusting entries is to:
   a. Adjust the Retained Earnings account for the revenue, expense, and dividends recorded during the accounting period.
   b. Adjust daily the balances in asset, liability, revenue, and expense accounts for the effects of business transactions.
   c. Apply the realization principle and the matching principle to transactions affecting two or more accounting periods.
   d. Prepare revenue and expense accounts for recording the transactions of the next accounting period.

2. Before month-end adjustments are made, the January 31 trial balance of Rover Excursions contains revenue of $27,900 and expenses of $17,340. Adjustments are necessary for the following items:

   Portion of prepaid rent applicable to January, $2,700
   Depreciation for January, $1,440
   Portion of fees collected in advance earned in January, $3,300
   Fees earned in January, not yet billed to customers, $1,950

   Net income for January is:

   **a.** $10,560    **b.** $17,070    **c.** $7,770    **d.** Some other amount

3. The CPA firm auditing Mason Street Recording Studios found that total stockholders' equity was understated and liabilities were overstated. Which of the following errors could have been the cause?

   **a.** Making the adjustment entry for depreciation expense twice.

   **b.** Failure to record interest accrued on a note payable.

   **c.** Failure to make the adjusting entry to record revenue which had been earned but not yet billed to clients.

   **d.** Failure to record the earned portion of fees received in advance.

4. Assume Fisher Corporation usually earns taxable income, but sustains a *loss* in the current period. The entry to record income taxes expense in the current period will most likely: (Indicate all correct answers.)

   **a.** Increase the amount of that loss.

   **b.** Include a credit to the Income Taxes Expense account.

   **c.** Be an adjusting entry, rather than an entry to record a transaction completed during the period.

   **d.** Include a credit to Income Taxes Payable.

5. The concept of *materiality:* (Indicate all correct answers.)

   **a.** Requires that financial statements be accurate to the nearest dollar, but need not show cents.

   **b.** Is based upon what users of financial statements are thought to consider important.

   **c.** Permits accountants to ignore generally accepted accounting principles in certain situations.

   **d.** Permits accountants to use the easiest and most convenient means of accounting for events that are *immaterial.*

## ASSIGNMENT MATERIAL

### DISCUSSION QUESTIONS

1. What is the purpose of making adjusting entries? Your answer should relate adjusting entries to the goals of accrual accounting.

2. Do all transactions involving revenue or expenses require adjusting entries at the end of the accounting period? If not, what is the distinguishing characteristic of those transactions that do require adjusting entries?

3. Do adjusting entries affect income statement accounts, balance sheet accounts, or both? Explain.

4. Why does the recording of adjusting entries require a better understanding of the concepts of accrual accounting than does the recording of routine revenue and expense transactions occurring throughout the period?

5. Why does the purchase of a one-year insurance policy four months ago give rise to insurance expense in the current month?

6. If services have been rendered to customers during the current accounting period but no revenue has been recorded and no bill has been sent to the customers, why is an adjusting entry needed? What types of accounts should be debited and credited by this entry?

7. What is meant by the term *unearned revenue*? Where should an unearned revenue account appear in the financial statements? As the work is done, what happens to the balance of an unearned revenue account?

8. The weekly payroll for employees of Ryan Company, who work a five-day week, amounts to $20,000. All employees are paid up-to-date at the close of business each Friday. If December 31 falls on Thursday, what year-end adjusting entry is needed?

9. At year-end the adjusting entry to reduce the Unexpired Insurance account by the amount of insurance premium applicable to the current period was accidentally omitted. Which items in the income statement will be in error? Will these items be overstated or understated? Which items in the balance sheet will be in error? Will they be overstated or understated?

10. Briefly explain the concept of *materiality*. If an item is not material, how is the item treated for financial reporting purposes?

11. Assets are defined as economic resources owned by a business and expected to benefit future business operations. By this definition, the gasoline in the tank of a business automobile, unused printer cartridges, and even ballpoint pens are actually assets. Why, then, are purchases of such items routinely charged directly to expense?

## ▮ EXERCISES

Listed below are nine technical accounting terms used in this chapter:

| | | |
|---|---|---|
| Unrecorded revenue | Adjusting entries | Accrued expenses |
| Book value | Matching principle | Accumulated depreciation |
| Unearned revenue | Materiality | Prepaid expenses |

**EXERCISE 4.1**

Accounting Terminology

**LO 1–9**

Each of the following statements may (or may not) describe one of these technical terms. For each statement, indicate the accounting term described, or answer "None" if the statement does not correctly describe any of the terms.

a. The net amount at which an asset is carried in the accounting records as distinguished from its market value.

b. An accounting concept that may justify departure from other accounting principles for purposes of convenience and economy.

c. The offsetting of revenue with expenses incurred in generating that revenue.

d. Revenue earned during the current accounting period but not yet recorded or billed, which requires an adjusting entry at the end of the period.

e. Entries made at the end of the period to achieve the goals of accrual accounting by recording revenue when it is earned and by recording expenses when the related goods and services are used.

f. A type of account credited when customers pay in advance for services to be rendered in the future.

g. A balance sheet category used for reporting advance payments of such items as insurance, rent, and office supplies.

h. An expense representing the systematic allocation of an asset's cost over its useful life.

Security Service Company adjusts its accounts at the end of the month. On November 30, adjusting entries are prepared to record:

a. Depreciation expense for November.

b. Interest expense that has accrued during November.

c. Revenue earned during November that has not yet been billed to customers.

d. Salaries, payable to company employees, that have accrued since the last payday in November.

e. The portion of the company's prepaid insurance that has expired during November.

f. Earning a portion of the amount collected in advance from a customer, Harbor Restaurant.

**EXERCISE 4.2**

Effects of Adjusting Entries

**LO 1–6, 9**

Indicate the effect of each of these adjusting entries on the major elements of the company's income statement and balance sheet—that is, on revenue, expenses, net income, assets, liabilities, and owners' equity. Organize your answer in tabular form, using the column headings shown below and the symbols *I* for increase, *D* for decrease, and *NE* for no effect. The answer for adjusting entry *a* is provided as an example.

| | Income Statement | | | Balance Sheet | | |
|---|---|---|---|---|---|---|
| Adjusting Entry | Revenue − | Expenses = | Net Income | Assets = | Liabilities + | Owners' Equity |
| a | NE | I | D | D | NE | D |

**EXERCISE 4.3**

Preparing Adjusting Entries to Convert an Asset to an Expense and to Convert a Liability to Revenue

**LO 1–7**

The Golden Goals, a professional soccer team, prepare financial statements on a monthly basis. The soccer season begins in May, but in April the team engaged in the following transactions:

**a.** Paid $1,200,000 to the municipal stadium as advance rent for use of the facilities for the five-month period from May 1 through September 30. This payment was initially recorded as Prepaid Rent.

**b.** Collected $4,500,000 cash from the sale of season tickets for the team's home games. The entire amount was initially recorded as Unearned Ticket Revenue. During the month of May, the Golden Goals played several home games at which $148,800 of the season tickets sold in April were used by fans.

Prepare the two adjusting entries required on May 31.

**EXERCISE 4.4**

Preparing Adjusting Entries to Accrue Revenue and Expenses for Which No Cash Has Been Received.

**LO 1–7**

The geological consulting firm of Gilbert, Marsh, & Kester prepares adjusting entries on a monthly basis. Among the items requiring adjustment on December 31, 2002, are the following:

**1.** The company has outstanding a $50,000, 9%, 2-year note payable issued on July 1, 2001. Payment of the $50,000 note, *plus* all accrued interest for the 2-year loan period, is due in full on June 30, 2003.

**2.** The firm is providing consulting services to the Texas Oil Company at an agreed-upon rate of $1,000 per day. At December 31, 10 days of unbilled consulting services have been provided.

**a.** Prepare the two adjusting entries required on December 31 to record the accrued interest expense and the accrued consulting revenue earned.

**b.** Assume that the $50,000 note payable plus all accrued interest are paid in full on June 30, 2003. What portion of the total interest expense associated with this note will be reported in the firm's *2003* income statement?

**c.** Assume that on January 30, 2003, Gilbert, Marsh, & Kester receive $25,000 from the Texas Oil Company in full payment of the consulting services provided in December and January. What portion of this amount constitutes revenue earned in *January?*

**EXERCISE 4.5**

Get Your Tickets Early

**LO 1, 2, 4**

When **TransWorld Airlines (TWA)** sells tickets for future flights, it debits Cash and credits an account entitled Advance Ticket Sales. With respect to this Advance Ticket Sales account:

**a.** What does the balance of the account represent? Where should the account appear in **TWA**'s financial statements?

**b.** Explain the activity that normally *reduces* the balance of this account. Can you think of any *other* transaction that would reduce this account?

**EXERCISE 4.6**

Preparing Various Adjusting Entries

**LO 1–6, 9**

Sweeney & Associates, a large marketing firm, adjusts its accounts at the end of each month. The following information is available:

**1.** A bank loan had been obtained on December 1. Accrued interest on the loan at December 31 amounts to $1,200. No interest expense has yet been recorded.

**2.** Depreciation of the firm's office building is based on an estimated life of 25 years. The building was purchased in 1998 for $330,000.

**3.** Accrued, but unbilled, revenue during December amounts to $64,000.

**4.** On March 1, the firm paid $1,800 to renew a 12-month insurance policy. The entire amount was recorded as Prepaid Insurance.

**5.** The firm received $14,000 from the King Biscuit Company in advance of developing a six-month marketing campaign. The entire amount was initially recorded as Unearned Revenue. At December 31, $3,500 had actually been *earned* by the firm.

**6.** The company's policy is to pay its employees every Friday. Since December 31 fell on a Wednesday, there was an accrued liability for salaries amounting to $2,400.

**a.** Record the necessary adjusting journal entries on December 31, 2002.

**b.** By how much did Sweeney & Associates' net income increase or decrease as a result of the adjusting entries performed in part **a?** (Ignore income taxes.)

Ventura Company adjusts its accounts *monthly* and closes its accounts on December 31. On October 31, 2002, Ventura Company signed a note payable and borrowed $120,000 from a bank for a period of six months at an annual interest rate of 9%.

**EXERCISE 4.7**

Notes Payable and Interest

**LO 1, 2, 5**

**a.** How much is the total interest expense over the life of the note? How much is the monthly interest expense? (Assume equal amounts of interest expense each month.)

**b.** In the company's annual balance sheet at December 31, 2002, what is the amount of the liability to the bank?

**c.** Prepare the journal entry to record issuance of the note payable on October 31, 2002.

**d.** Prepare the adjusting entry to accrue interest on the note at December 31, 2002.

**e.** Assume the company prepared a balance sheet at March 31, 2003. State the amount of the liability to the bank at this date.

Among the ledger accounts used by Glenwood Speedway are the following: Prepaid Rent, Rent Expense, Unearned Admissions Revenue, Admissions Revenue, Prepaid Printing, Printing Expense, Concessions Receivable, and Concessions Revenue. For each of the following items, provide the journal entry (if one is needed) to record the initial transaction and provide the adjusting entry, if any, required on May 31, the end of the fiscal year.

**EXERCISE 4.8**

Relationship of Adjusting Entries to Business Transactions

**LO 1–7, 9**

**a.** On May 1, borrowed $300,000 cash from National Bank by issuing a 12% note payable due in three months.

**b.** On May 1, paid rent for six months beginning May 1 at $30,000 per month.

**c.** On May 2, sold season tickets for a total of $910,000 cash. The season includes 70 racing days: 20 in May, 25 in June, and 25 in July.

**d.** On May 4, an agreement was reached with Snack-Bars, Inc., allowing that company to sell refreshments at the track in return for 10% of the gross receipts from refreshment sales.

**e.** On May 6, schedules for the 20 racing days in May and the first 10 racing days in June were printed and paid for at a cost of $12,000.

**f.** On May 31, Snack-Bars, Inc., reported that the gross receipts from refreshment sales in May had been $165,000 and that the 10% owed to Glenwood Speedway would be remitted on June 10.

**Something to Consider** Assume that the May 1 payment of $180,000 rent was properly recorded as Prepaid Rent, but that the May 31 adjusting entry for this item was inadvertently omitted. What is the effect of this omission on Glenwood's financial statements at May 31? (Specifically consider the financial statement elements revenue, expense, net income, assets, liabilities, and owners' equity at May 31; indicate whether each would be overstated, understated, or not affected by the omission.)

The concept of materiality is a generally accepted accounting principle.

**EXERCISE 4.9**

Concept of Materiality

**LO 8**

**a.** Briefly explain the concept of materiality.

**b.** Is $2,500 a "material" dollar amount? Explain.

**c.** Describe two ways in which the concept of materiality may save accountants' time and effort in making adjusting entries.

For each of the situations described below, indicate the generally accepted accounting principle that is being *violated*. Choose from the following principles:

**EXERCISE 4.10**

Accounting Principles

**LO 1–8**

| | |
|---|---|
| Matching | Materiality |
| Cost | Realization |
| Objectivity | |

If you do not believe that the practice violates any of these principles, answer "None" and explain.

**a.** The bookkeeper of a large metropolitan auto dealership depreciates the $7.20 cost of metal wastebaskets over a period of 10 years.

**b.** A small commuter airline recognizes no depreciation expense on its aircraft because the planes are maintained in "as good as new" condition.

**c.** Palm Beach Hotel recognizes room rental revenue on the date that a reservation is received. For the winter season, many guests make reservations as much as a year in advance.

**EXERCISE 4.11**

Examining an Annual Report

**LO 1,2**

The annual report of **Tootsie Roll Industries, Inc.**, appears in Appendix A at the end of this textbook. Examine the company's consolidated balance sheet and identify specific accounts that may have required adjusting entries at the end of the year.

# PROBLEMS

**PROBLEM 4.1**

Preparing Adjusting Entries

**LO 1–7**

Florida Palms Country Club adjusts its accounts *monthly* and closes its accounts annually. Club members pay their annual dues in advance by January 4. The entire amount is initially credited to Unearned Membership Dues. At the end of each month, an appropriate portion of this amount is credited to Membership Dues Earned. Guests of the club normally pay green fees before being allowed on the course. The amounts collected are credited to Green Fee Revenue at the time of receipt. Certain guests, however, are billed for green fees at the end of the month. The following information is available as a source for preparing adjusting entries at December 31:

1. Salaries earned by golf course employees that have not yet been recorded or paid amount to $9,600.

2. The Tampa University golf team used Florida Palms for a tournament played on December 30 of the current year. At December 31, the $1,800 owed by the team for green fees had not yet been recorded or billed.

3. Membership dues earned in December, for collections received in January, amount to $106,000.

4. Depreciation of the country club's golf carts is based on an estimated life of 15 years. The carts had originally been purchased for $180,000. The straight-line method is used.
   (*Note:* The clubhouse building was constructed in 1925 and is fully depreciated.)

5. A 12-month bank loan in the amount of $45,000 had been obtained by the country club on November 1. Interest is computed at an annual rate of 8%. The entire $45,000, plus all of the interest accrued over the 12-month life of the loan, is due in full on October 31 of the upcoming year. The necessary adjusting entry was made on November 30 to record the first month of accrued interest expense. However, no adjustment has been made to record interest expense accrued in December.

6. A one-year property insurance policy had been purchased on March 1. The entire premium of $7,800 was initially recorded as Unexpired Insurance.

7. In December, Florida Palms Country Club entered into an agreement to host the annual tournament of the Florida Seniors Golf Association. The country club expects to generate green fees of $4,500 from this event.

8. Unrecorded Income Taxes Expense accrued in December amounts to $19,000. This amount will not be paid until January 15.

**Instructions**

**a.** For each of the above numbered paragraphs, prepare the necessary adjusting entry (including an explanation). If no adjusting entry is required, explain why.

**b.** Four types of adjusting entries are described on pages 136–137. Using these descriptions, identify the type of each adjusting entry prepared in part **a** above.

**c.** Although Florida Palms' clubhouse building is fully depreciated, it is in excellent physical condition. Explain how this can be.

Enchanted Forest, a large campground in South Carolina, adjusts its accounts *monthly* and closes its accounts annually on December 31. Most guests of the campground pay at the time they check out, and the amounts collected are credited to Camper Revenue. The following information is available as a source for preparing the adjusting entries at December 31:

1. Enchanted Forest invests some of its excess cash in certificates of deposit (CDs) with its local bank. Accrued interest revenue on its CDs at December 31 is $400. None of the interest has yet been received. (Debit Interest Receivable.)

2. A six-month bank loan in the amount of $12,000 had been obtained on September 1. Interest is to be computed at an annual rate of 8.5% and is payable when the loan becomes due.

3. Depreciation on buildings owned by the campground is based on a 25-year life. The original cost of the buildings was $600,000. The Accumulated Depreciation: Buildings account has a credit balance of $310,000 at December 31, prior to the adjusting entry process. The straight-line method of depreciation is used.

4. Management signed an agreement to let Boy Scout Troop 538 of Lewisburg, Pennsylvania, use the campground in June of next year. The agreement specifies that the Boy Scouts will pay a daily rate of $15 per campsite, with a clause providing a minimum total charge of $1,475.

5. Salaries earned by campground employees that have not yet been paid amount to $1,250.

6. As of December 31, Enchanted Forest has earned $2,400 of revenue from current campers who will not be billed until they check out. (Debit Camper Revenue Receivable.)

7. Several lakefront campsites are currently being leased on a long-term basis by a group of senior citizens. Six months' rent of $5,400 was collected in advance and credited to Unearned Camper Revenue on October 1 of the current year.

8. A bus to carry campers to and from town and the airport had been rented the first week of December at a daily rate of $40. At December 31, no rental payment has been made, although the campground has had use of the bus for 25 days.

9. Unrecorded Income Taxes Expense accrued in December amounts to $8,400. This amount will not be paid until January 15.

## Instructions

a. For each of the above numbered paragraphs, prepare the necessary adjusting entry (including an explanation). If no adjusting entry is required, explain why.

b. Four types of adjusting entries are described on pages 136–137. Using these descriptions, identify the type of each adjusting entry prepared in part **a** above.

c. Indicate the effects that each of the adjustments in part **a** will have on the following six *total amounts* in the campground's financial statements for the month of *December*. Organize your answer in tabular form, using the column headings shown below. Use the letters **I** for increase, **D** for decrease, and **NE** for no effect. Adjusting entry **1** is provided as an example.

| | Income Statement | | | Balance Sheet | | |
|---|---|---|---|---|---|---|
| | | | Net | | | Owners' |
| Adjustment | Revenue | − Expenses | = Income | Assets | = Liabilities | + Equity |
| 1 | I | NE | I | I | NE | I |

d. What is the amount of interest expense recognized for the *entire current year* on the $12,000 bank loan obtained September 1?

e. Compute the *book value* of the campground's buildings to be reported in the current year's December 31 balance sheet. (Refer to paragraph **3**.)

Sea Cat, Inc., operates a large catamaran that takes tourists at several island resorts on diving and sailing excursions. The company adjusts its accounts at the end of each month. Selected account balances appearing on the June 30 *adjusted* trial balance are as follows:

**PROBLEM 4.2**

Preparing and Analyzing the Effects of Adjusting Entries

**LO 1–6, 9**

**PROBLEM 4.3**

Analysis of Adjusted Data; Preparing Adjusting Entries

**LO 1–7, 9**

| | | |
|---|---:|---:|
| Prepaid Rent | $ 6,000 | |
| Unexpired Insurance | 1,400 | |
| Catamaran | 46,200 | |
| Accumulated Depreciation: Catamaran | | $9,240 |
| Unearned Passenger Revenue | | 825 |

## Other Data

**a.** The catamaran is being depreciated over a 10-year estimated useful life, with no residual value.

**b.** The unearned passenger revenue represents tickets good for future rides sold to a resort hotel for $15 per ticket on June 1. During June, 145 of the tickets were used.

**c.** Six months' rent had been prepaid on June 1.

**d.** The unexpired insurance is a 12-month fire insurance policy purchased on March 1.

## Instructions

**a.** Determine the following:

  **1.** The age of the catamaran in months.

  **2.** How many $15 tickets for future rides were sold to the resort hotel on June 1.

  **3.** The monthly rent expense.

  **4.** The original cost of the 12-month fire insurance policy

**b.** Prepare the adjusting entries that were made on June 30.

**PROBLEM 4.4**

Preparing Adjusting Entries
from a Trial Balance

**LO 1–7, 9**

The Campus Theater adjusts its accounts every *month.* Below is the company's *unadjusted* trial balance dated August 31, 2002. Additional information is provided for use in preparing the company's adjusting entries for the month of August. (Bear in mind that adjusting entries *have* already been made for the first seven months of 2002, but *not* for August.)

| CAMPUS THEATER Unadjusted Trial Balance August 31, 2002 | | |
|---|---:|---:|
| Cash | $ 20,000 | |
| Prepaid film rental | 31,200 | |
| Land | 120,000 | |
| Building | 168,000 | |
| Accumulated depreciation: building | | $ 14,000 |
| Fixtures and equipment | 36,000 | |
| Accumulated depreciation: fixtures and equipment | | 12,000 |
| Notes payable | | 180,000 |
| Accounts payable | | 4,400 |
| Unearned admissions revenue (YMCA) | | 1,000 |
| Income taxes payable | | 4,740 |
| Capital stock | | 40,000 |
| Retained earnings | | 46,610 |
| Dividends | 15,000 | |
| Admissions revenue | | 305,200 |
| Concessions revenue | | 14,350 |
| Salaries expense | 68,500 | |
| Film rental expense | 94,500 | |
| Utilities expense | 9,500 | |
| Depreciation expense: building | 4,900 | |
| Depreciation expense: fixtures and equipment | 4,200 | |
| Interest expense | 10,500 | |
| Income taxes expense | 40,000 | |
| | $622,300 | $622,300 |

## Other Data

1. Film rental expense for the month is $15,200. However, the film rental expense for several months has been paid in advance.

2. The building is being depreciated over a period of 20 years (240 months).

3. The fixtures and equipment are being depreciated over a period of 5 years (60 months).

4. On the first of each month, the theater pays the interest which accrued in the prior month on its note payable. At August 31, accrued interest payable on this note amounts to $1,500.

5. The theater allows the local YMCA to bring children attending summer camp to the movies on any weekday afternoon for a fixed fee of $500 per month. On June 28, the YMCA made a $1,500 advance payment covering the months of July, August, and September.

6. The theater receives a percentage of the revenue earned by Tastie Corporation, the concessionaire operating the snack bar. For snack bar sales in August, Tastie owes Campus Theater $2,250, payable on September 10. No entry has yet been made to record this revenue. (Credit Concessions Revenue.)

7. Salaries earned by employees, but not recorded or paid as of August 31, amount to $1,700. No entry has yet been made to record this liability and expense.

8. Income taxes expense for August is estimated at $4,200. This amount will be paid in the September 15 installment payment.

9. Utilities expense is recorded as monthly bills are received. No adjusting entries for utilities expense are made at month-end.

## Instructions

a. For each of the numbered paragraphs, prepare the necessary adjusting entry (including an explanation).

b. Refer to the balances shown in the *unadjusted* trial balance at August 31. How many *months* of expense are included in each of the following account balances? (Remember, Campus Theater adjusts its accounts *monthly*. Thus, the accounts shown were last adjusted on 7/31/02.)

   1. Utilities Expense
   2. Depreciation Expense
   3. Accumulated Depreciation: Building

c. Assume the theater has been operating profitably all year. Although the August 31 trial balance shows substantial income taxes *expense,* income taxes *payable* is a much smaller amount. This relationship is quite normal throughout much of the year. Explain.

Ken Hensley Enterprises, Inc., is a small recording studio in St. Louis. Rock bands use the studio to mix high-quality demo recordings distributed to talent agents. New clients are required to pay in advance for studio services. Bands with established credit are billed for studio services at the end of each month. Adjusting entries are performed on a *monthly* basis. An *unadjusted* trial balance dated December 31, 2002, follows. (Bear in mind that adjusting entries already have been made for the first eleven months of 2002, but *not* for December.)

**PROBLEM 4.5**

Preparing Adjusting Entries, Financial Statements, and Closing Entries from a Trial Balance

**LO 1–7, 9**

**KEN HENSLEY ENTERPRISES, INC.**
**Unadjusted Trial Balance**
**December 31, 2002**

| | | |
|---|---:|---:|
| Cash | $ 44,850 | |
| Accounts receivable | 81,400 | |
| Studio supplies | 7,600 | |
| Unexpired insurance | 500 | |
| Prepaid studio rent | 4,000 | |
| Recording equipment | 90,000 | |
| Accumulated depreciation: recording equipment | | $ 52,500 |
| Notes payable | | 16,000 |
| Interest payable | | 840 |
| Income taxes payable | | 3,200 |
| Unearned studio revenue | | 9,600 |
| Capital stock | | 80,000 |
| Retained earnings | | 38,000 |
| Studio revenue earned | | 107,000 |
| Salaries expense | 18,000 | |
| Supplies expense | 1,200 | |
| Insurance expense | 1,000 | |
| Depreciation expense: recording equipment | 16,500 | |
| Studio rent expense | 21,000 | |
| Interest expense | 840 | |
| Utilities expense | 2,350 | |
| Income taxes expense | 17,900 | |
| | $307,140 | $307,140 |

**Other Data**

1. Records show that $4,400 in studio revenue had not yet been billed or recorded as of December 31.
2. Studio supplies on hand at December 31 amount to $6,900.
3. On August 1, 2002, the studio purchased a six-month insurance policy for $1,500. The entire premium was initially debited to Unexpired Insurance.
4. The studio is located in a rented building. On November 1, 2002, the studio paid $6,000 rent in advance for November, December, and January. The entire amount was debited to Prepaid Studio Rent.
5. The useful life of the studio's recording equipment is estimated to be five years (or 60 months). The straight-line method of depreciation is used.
6. On May 1, 2002, the studio borrowed $16,000 by signing a 12-month, 9% note payable to First Federal Bank of St. Louis. The entire $16,000 plus 12 months' interest is due in full on April 30, 2003.
7. Records show that $3,600 of cash receipts originally recorded as Unearned Studio Revenue had been earned as of December 31.
8. Salaries earned by recording technicians that remain unpaid at December 31 amount to $540.
9. The studio's accountant estimates that income taxes expense for the *entire year* ended December 31, 2002, is $19,600. (Note that $17,900 of this amount has already been recorded.)

**Instructions**

a. For each of the above numbered paragraphs, prepare the necessary adjusting entry (including an explanation). If no adjusting entry is required, explain why.

**b.** Using figures from the company's unadjusted trial balance in conjunction with the adjusting entries made in part **a**, compute net income for the year ended December 31, 2002.

**c.** Was the studio's monthly rent for the last 2 months of 2002 more or less than during the first 10 months of the year? Explain your answer.

Koyne Corporation recently hired Jane McDonald as its new bookkeeper. McDonald was not very experienced and made six recording errors during the last accounting period. The nature of each error is described in the following table.

**PROBLEM 4.6**

Understanding the Effects of Various Errors

**LO 1–7, 9**

**Instructions**

Indicate the effect of the following errors on each of the financial statement elements described in the column headings in the table. Use the following symbols: **O** = overstated, **U** = understated, and **NE** = no effect.

| Error | Total Revenue | Total Expenses | Net Income | Total Assets | Total Liabilities | Owners' Equity |
|---|---|---|---|---|---|---|
| **a.** Recorded a dividend as an expense reported in the income statement. | | | | | | |
| **b.** Recorded the payment of an account payable as a debit to accounts payable and a credit to an expense account. | | | | | | |
| **c.** Failed to record depreciation expense. | | | | | | |
| **d.** Recorded the sale of capital stock as a debit to cash and a credit to retained earnings. | | | | | | |
| **e.** Recorded the receipt of a customer deposit as a debit to cash and a credit to fees earned. | | | | | | |
| **f.** Failed to record expired portion of an insurance policy. | | | | | | |
| **g.** Failed to record accrued interest earned on an outstanding note receivable. | | | | | | |

## CASES AND UNSTRUCTURED PROBLEMS

Property Management Professionals provides building management services to owners of office buildings and shopping centers. The company closes its accounts at the *end of the calendar year*. The manner in which the company has recorded several transactions occurring during 2002 is described as follows:

**CASE 4.1**

Should This Be Adjusted?

**LO 1–7**

**a.** On September 1, received advance payment from a shopping center for property management services to be performed over the three-month period beginning September 1. The entire amount received was credited directly to a *revenue* account.

**b.** On December 1, received advance payment from the same customer described in part **a** for services to be rendered over the three-month period beginning December 1. This time, the entire amount received was credited to an *unearned* revenue account.

**c.** Rendered management services for many customers in December. Normal procedure is to record revenue on the date the customer is billed, which is early in the month after the services have been rendered.

Indicate the effect of the following errors on each of the financial statement elements described in the column headings in the table. Use the following symbols: **O** = overstated, **U** = understated, and **NE** = no effect.

Property Management Professionals provides building management services to owners of office buildings and shopping centers. The company closes its accounts at the *end of the calendar year.* The manner in which the company has recorded several transactions occurring during 2002 is described as follows:

**a.** On September 1, received advance payment from a shopping center for property management services to be performed over the three-month period beginning September 1. The entire amount received was credited directly to a *revenue* account.

**b.** On December 1, received advance payment from the same customer described in part **a** for services to be rendered over the three-month period beginning December 1. This time, the entire amount received was credited to an *unearned* revenue account.

**CASE 4.2**

The Concept of Materiality

**LO 8**

**c.** Rendered management services for many customers in December. Normal procedure is to record revenue on the date the customer is billed, which is early in the month after the services have been rendered.

**d.** On December 15, made full payment for a one-year insurance policy that goes into effect on January 2, 2003. The cost of the policy was debited to Unexpired Insurance.

**e.** Numerous purchases of equipment were debited to asset accounts, rather than to expense accounts.

**f.** Payroll expense is recorded when employees are paid. Payday for the last two weeks of December falls on January 2, 2003.

**Instructions**

# BUSINESS WEEK ASSIGNMENT      BusinessWeek

**CASE 4.3**

**LO 1, 2, 4**

For each item above, explain whether an adjusting entry is needed at *December 31, 2002,* and state the reasons for your answer. If you recommend an adjusting entry, explain the effects this entry would have on assets, liabilities, owners' equity, revenue, and expense in the 2002 financial statements.

The concept of materiality is one of the most basic generally accepted accounting principles.

**a.** Answer the following questions:

     **1.** Why is the materiality of a transaction or an event a matter of professional judgment?

     **2.** What criteria should accountants consider in determining whether a transaction or an event is material?

     **3.** Does the concept of materiality mean that financial statements are not precise, down to the

# INTERNET ASSIGNMENT

**INTERNET 4.1**

Identifying Accounts Requiring Adjusting Entries

**LO 1–6**

     last dollar? Does this concept make financial statements less useful to most users?

**b.** **Avis Rent-a-Car** purchases a large number of cars each year for its rental fleet. The cost of any individual automobile is immaterial to **Avis**, which is a very large corporation. Would it be acceptable for **Avis** to charge the purchase of automobiles for its rental fleet directly to expense, rather than to an asset account? Explain.

Most of the major airlines have expanded their frequent-flier programs to include "partnering" arrangements with other businesses. In a March 6, 2000, *Business Week* article entitled, "You've Got Miles!" author Wendy Zellner reports that companies, including **America Online (AOL)** and **Safeway, Inc.**, now offer their customers travel miles with certain airlines. These companies pay the airlines in advance for travel miles redeemed by their customers in the future. Until recently, it was a common practice among several major carriers to record these advances as *revenue* at

## OUR COMMENTS ON THE "YOUR TURN" CASES

**You as a Car Owner (p. 141)** Yes, in most cases you will receive a full refund equal to the unexpired portion of your policy. You are entitled to a refund because you will not consume four full months of coverage that remain on your policy at the time of cancellation. Thus you should receive a check for $400 (or $100 per month for April, May, June, and July).

**You as Overnight Auto's Service Department Manager (p. 149)** It is true that by accruing an entire month's revenue from Airport Shuttle Services, Overnight's reported income for December would have increased by $750 (the difference between recognizing the entire month's revenue of $1,500 and the $750 already recorded). However, to record revenue for services not yet performed is in conflict with generally accepted accounting principles (GAAP). Furthermore, the practice of overstating revenue to increase one's bonus is also unethical.

The timing of revenue recognition is a complex issue faced by business managers, auditors, tax authorities, and the financial reporting enforcement arm of the SEC. A case in point is the recent news that **McKesson HBOC** had reported more than $44 million in revenues that had not, in fact, been realized. As this information became public, **McKesson**'s shareholders filed lawsuits and the company's stock price dropped by nearly 50%.

## ANSWERS TO SELF-TEST QUESTIONS

**1.** c.      **2.** d $11,670 ($27,900 − $17,340 − $2,700 − $1,440 + $3,300 + $1,950)      **3.** d

**4.** b, c      **5.** b, c, d

# CHAPTER

# 5

# THE ACCOUNTING CYCLE:

## Reporting Financial Results

## Learning Objectives

*After studying this chapter, you should be able to:*

1. Prepare an income statement, a statement of retained earnings, and a balance sheet.

2. Explain how the income statement and the statement of retained earnings relate to the balance sheet.

3. Explain the concept of *adequate disclosure.*

4. Explain the purposes of *closing entries;* prepare these entries.

5. Prepare an after-closing trial balance.

6. Use financial statement information to evaluate profitability and solvency.

7. Explain how *interim* financial statements are prepared in a business that closes its accounts only at year-end.

8. Prepare a worksheet and explain its usefulness.*

© Spender Grant/PhotoEdit

*Supplemental Topic, "The Worksheet."

# Huffy Corporation

Every kid knows that falling off of a bicycle can really hurt! **Huffy Corporation**, a major bicycle manufacturer with executive offices in Miamisburg, Ohio, knows falling profits and the declining market share of its bicycles can really hurt, too.

In response to massive operating losses and increased foreign competition, **Huffy Corporation** announced recently its decision to discontinue domestic manufacturing operations. While the company still imports bicycles assembled in Mexico, Taiwan, and China, all of its U.S. manufacturing facilities have been closed.

Investors actually viewed favorably **Huffy**'s intention to downsize operations. In the months following the announcement to close its domestic plants, the company's stock price increased significantly. In short, investors may have anticipated that the decision to rely solely on offshore manufacturing will improve **Huffy**'s solvency and future profit performance.

● ● ●

In this chapter, we examine how companies prepare general purpose financial statements used by investors, creditors, and managers. In addition, we discuss how certain events, such as the closing of **Huffy Corporation**'s domestic manufacturing facilities, are disclosed in the notes that accompany financial statements. We also illustrate several methods of evaluating solvency and profitability using financial statement information.

In Chapter 3, we introduced the first of the eight steps in the accounting cycle by illustrating how Overnight Auto Service (1) captured (journalized) economic events, (2) posted these transactions to its general ledger, and (3) prepared an *unadjusted* trial balance from its general ledger account balances. We continued our illustration of the accounting cycle in Chapter 4 by (4) performing the adjusting entries made by Overnight and (5) presenting the company's *adjusted* trial balance at year-end.

In this chapter, we complete the accounting cycle by (6) preparing Overnight's financial statements, (7) performing year-end closing entries, and (8) presenting the company's *after-closing* trial balance.

## PREPARING FINANCIAL STATEMENTS

**LO 1**

Prepare an income statement, a statement of retained earnings, and a balance sheet.

Publicly owned companies—those with shares listed on a stock exchange—have obligations to release annual and quarterly information to their stockholders and to the public. These companies don't simply prepare financial statements—they publish *annual reports.*

An annual report *includes* comparative financial statements for several years and a wealth of other information about the company's financial position, business operations, and future prospects. (For illustrative purposes, the 1999 annual report of **Tootsie Roll Industries, Inc.,** appears in Appendix A.) Before an annual report is issued, the financial statements must be *audited* by a firm of Certified Public Accountants (CPAs). Publicly owned companies must file their audited financial statements and detailed supporting schedules with the Securities and Exchange Commission (SEC).

The activities surrounding the preparation of an annual report become very intense as the new year approaches. Once the fiscal year has ended, it often takes several *months* before the annual report is available for distribution. Thus, many accountants refer to the months of December through March as the "busy season."[1] We cannot adequately discuss all of the activities associated with the preparation of an annual report in a single chapter. Thus, here we focus on the *preparation of financial statements.*

**CASE IN POINT**

**Coca-Cola** does business in more than 195 countries—and in all 50 of the United States. Shortly after its December 31 year-end, the company must file more than 200 separate income tax returns, each measuring the taxable income earned in a different geographic region. Many of these returns run several hundred pages in length, and each must be prepared according to local tax regulations. (Even within the United States, income tax regulations vary from one state to the next.)

The adjusted trial balance prepared in Chapter 4 is reprinted at the top of the following page. The income statement, statement of retained earnings, and balance sheet can be prepared *directly from the amounts shown in this adjusted trial balance.* For illustrative purposes, we have made marginal notes indicating which accounts appear in which financial statements. Overnight's financial statements for the year ended December 31, 2002, are illustrated on page 178.

---

[1] Some companies elect to end their fiscal year during a seasonal low point in business activity. However, most companies *do* end their fiscal year on December 31.

## OVERNIGHT AUTO SERVICE
### Adjusted Trial Balance
### December 31, 2002

| | | |
|---|---:|---:|
| Cash | $ 18,592 | |
| Accounts receivable | 7,250 | |
| Shop supplies | 1,200 | |
| Unexpired insurance | 3,000 | |
| Land | 52,000 | |
| Building | 36,000 | |
| Accumulated depreciation: building | | $ 1,650 |
| Tools and equipment | 12,000 | |
| Accumulated depreciation: tools and equipment | | 2,200 |
| Notes payable | | 4,000 |
| Accounts payable | | 2,690 |
| Wages payable | | 1,950 |
| Income taxes payable | | 5,580 |
| Interest payable | | 30 |
| Unearned rent revenue | | 6,000 |
| Capital stock | | 80,000 |
| Retained earnings (*Note:* still must be updated for transactions recorded in the accounts listed below. Closing entries serve this purpose.) | | 0 |
| Dividends | 14,000 | |
| Repair service revenue | | 172,000 |
| Rent revenue earned | | 3,000 |
| Advertising expense | 3,900 | |
| Wages expense | 58,750 | |
| Supplies expense | 7,500 | |
| Depreciation expense: building | 1,650 | |
| Depreciation expense: tools and equipment | 2,200 | |
| Utilities expense | 19,400 | |
| Insurance expense | 15,000 | |
| Interest expense | 30 | |
| Income taxes expense | 26,628 | |
| | $279,100 | $279,100 |

*Balance sheet accounts* (Cash through Capital stock)

*Statement of retained earnings accounts* (Retained earnings and Dividends)

*Income statement accounts* (Repair service revenue through Income taxes expense)

The income statement is prepared first because it determines the amount of net income to be reported in the statement of retained earnings. The statement of retained earnings is prepared second because it determines the amount of retained earnings to be reported in the balance sheet. Note that we have not included Overnight's statement of cash flows with the other three reports. For an in-depth discussion of the statement of cash flows, see Chapter 13.

Amounts are taken directly from the adjusted trial balance

## OVERNIGHT AUTO SERVICE
### Income Statement
### For the Year Ended December 31, 2002

| | | |
|---|---:|---:|
| **Revenue:** | | |
| Repair service revenue | | $172,000 |
| Rent revenue earned | | 3,000 |
| Total revenue | | $175,000 |
| **Expenses:** | | |
| Advertising | $ 3,900 | |
| Wages expense | 58,750 | |
| Supplies expense | 7,500 | |
| Depreciation: building | 1,650 | |
| Depreciation: tools and equipment | 2,200 | |
| Utilities expense | 19,400 | |
| Insurance | 15,000 | |
| Interest | 30 | 108,430 |
| Income before income taxes | | $ 66,570 |
| Income taxes | | 26,628 |
| Net income | | $ 39,942 > |

Net income also appears in the statement of retained earnings

## OVERNIGHT AUTO SERVICE
### Statement of Retained Earnings
### For the Year Ended December 31, 2002

| | | |
|---|---:|---:|
| Retained earnings, Jan. 20, 2002 | | $ 0 |
| Add: Net income | | 39,942 ◄ |
| Subtotal | | $39,942 |
| Less: Dividends | | 14,000 |
| Retained earnings, Dec. 31, 2002 | | $25,942 > |

The ending balance in the Retained Earnings account also appears in the balance sheet

## OVERNIGHT AUTO SERVICE
### Balance Sheet
### December 31, 2002

| Assets | | |
|---|---:|---:|
| Cash | | $ 18,592 |
| Accounts receivable | | 7,250 |
| Shop supplies | | 1,200 |
| Unexpired insurance | | 3,000 |
| Land | | 52,000 |
| Building | $36,000 | |
| Less: Accumulated depreciation | 1,650 | 34,350 |
| Tools and equipment | $12,000 | |
| Less: Accumulated depreciation | 2,200 | 9,800 |
| Total assets | | $126,192 |

| Liabilities & Stockholders' Equity | | |
|---|---:|---:|
| **Liabilities:** | | |
| Notes payable | | $ 4,000 |
| Accounts payable | | 2,690 |
| Wages payable | | 1,950 |
| Income taxes payable | | 5,580 |
| Interest payable | | 30 |
| Unearned rent revenue | | 6,000 |
| Total liabilities | | $ 20,250 |
| **Stockholders' equity:** | | |
| Capital stock | | 80,000 |
| Retained earnings | | 25,942 ◄ |
| Total stockholders' equity | | $105,942 |
| Total liabilities and stockholders' equity | | $126,192 |

# The Income Statement

Alternative titles for the income statement include *earnings statement, statement of operations,* and *profit and loss statement.* However, *income* statement is the most popular term for this important financial statement. The income statement is used to summarize the *operating* results of a business by matching the revenue earned during a given period of time with the expenses incurred in generating that revenue.

The revenue and expenses shown in Overnight's income statement are taken directly from the company's adjusted trial balance. Overnight's 2002 income statement shows that revenue exceeded expenses for the year, thus producing a net income of $39,942. Bear in mind, however, that this measurement of net income is not absolutely accurate or precise due to the *assumptions and estimates* in the accounting process.

An income statement has certain limitations. For instance, the amounts shown for depreciation expense are based upon estimates of the useful lives of the company's building and equipment. Also, the income statement includes only those events that have been evidenced by actual business transactions. Perhaps during the year Overnight's advertising has caught the attention of many potential customers. A good "customer base" is certainly an important step toward profitable operations; however, the development of a customer base is not reflected in the income statement because its value cannot be measured *objectively* until actual transactions take place. Despite these limitations, the income statement is of vital importance to the users of a company's financial statements.

**LO 2**

Explain how the income statement and the statement of retained earnings relate to the balance sheet.

# The Statement of Retained Earnings

*Retained Earnings* is that portion of stockholders' (owners') equity created by earning net income and retaining the related resources in the business. The resources retained from being profitable may include, but are certainly not limited to, *cash.* The statement of retained earnings summarizes the increases and decreases in retained earnings resulting from business operations during the period. Increases in retained earnings result from earning net income; decreases result from net losses and from the declaration of dividends.

The format of this financial statement is based upon the following relationships:

$$\text{Retained Earnings at the beginning of the period} + \text{Net Income} - \text{Dividends} = \text{Retained Earnings at the end of the period}$$

*Statement of retained earnings*

The amount of retained earnings at the *beginning* of the period is shown at the top of the statement. Next, the net income for the period is added (or net loss subtracted), and any dividends declared during the period are deducted. This short computation determines the amount of retained earnings at the *end* of the accounting period. The ending retained earnings ($25,942 in our example) appears at the bottom of the statement and also in the company's year-end balance sheet.

Our illustration of the statement of retained earnings for Overnight is unusual in that retained earnings at the date of the company's formation (January 20, 2002) is *$0.* This occurred only because 2002 was the *first year* of Overnight's business operations. The ending retained earnings ($25,942) becomes the beginning retained earnings for the following year.

**A Word about Dividends**   In Chapter 3, the declaration and payment of a cash dividend were treated as a single event recorded by one journal entry. A small corporation with only a few stockholders may choose to declare and pay a dividend on the same day. In large corporations, an interval of a month or more will separate the date of declaration from the later date of payment. A liability account, Dividends Payable, comes into existence when the dividend is declared, and is discharged when the dividend is paid. Because Overnight reports no dividends payable in its adjusted trial balance, we may assume that it declared and had paid the entire $14,000 at December 31, 2002.[2]

Finally, it is important to realize that dividends paid to stockholders are *not* reported in the income statement as an expense. In short, dividends represent a decision by a corporation to distribute a portion of its income to stockholders. Thus, the amount of the dividend is not included in the computation of income.

## The Balance Sheet

The balance sheet lists the amounts of the company's assets, liabilities, and owners' equity at the *end* of the accounting period. The balances of Overnight's asset and liability accounts are taken directly from the adjusted trial balance on page 177. The amount of retained earnings at the end of the period, $25,942, was determined in the *statement of retained earnings.*

Balance sheets can be presented with asset accounts appearing on the left and liabilities and owners' equity accounts appearing on the right. They may also be presented in *report form,* with liabilities and owners' equity listed *below* (rather than to the right of) the asset section. It is also common for corporations to refer to owners' equity as *stockholders'* equity.

## RELATIONSHIP AMONG THE FINANCIAL STATEMENTS

A set of financial statements becomes easier to understand if we recognize that the income statement, statement of retained earnings, and balance sheet all are *related to one another.* These relationships are emphasized by the arrows in the right-hand margin of our illustration on page 178.

The balance sheet prepared at the end of the preceding period and the one prepared at the end of the current period both include the amount of retained earnings at the respective balance sheet dates. The statement of retained earnings summarizes the factors (net income and dividends) that have caused the amount of retained earnings to change between these two balance sheet dates. The income statement explains in greater detail the change in retained earnings resulting from profitable (or unprofitable) operation of the business. Thus, the income statement and the retained earnings statement provide informative links between successive balance sheets.

**LO 3**

Explain the concept of *adequate disclosure.*

## Drafting the Notes that Accompany Financial Statements

To the users of financial statements, **adequate disclosure** is perhaps the most important accounting principle. This principle simply means that financial statements should be accompanied by any information necessary for the statements to be *interpreted properly.*

Most disclosures appear within the several pages of **notes** that accompany the financial statements. Drafting these notes can be one of the most challenging tasks confronting accountants at the end of the period. The content of these notes often cannot be drawn directly from the accounting records. Rather, drafting these notes requires an *in-depth understanding* of the company and its operations, of accounting principles, and of how decision makers interpret and use accounting information.

---

[2] Details related to the declaration and payment of dividends are discussed in Chapter 12.

Two items always disclosed in the notes to financial statements are the accounting methods in use and the due dates of major liabilities. Thus Overnight's 2002 financial statements should include the notes shown below:

**Note 1: Depreciation policies**
Depreciation expense in the financial statements is computed by the straight-line method. Estimated useful lives are 20 years for the building and 5 years for tools and equipment.

**Note 2: Maturity dates of liabilities**
The Company's notes payable consist of a single obligation that matures on February 28 of the coming year. The maturity value of this note, including interest charges, will amount to $4,090.

---

Note 2 above, maturity dates of liabilities, should be of particular importance to American National Bank. Specifically, bankers will want to know if Overnight will have enough cash to pay this $4,090 liability in just two months. The company's balance sheet reports cash of $18,592. However, it also reports additional liabilities coming due, other than the note payable, in excess of $10,000. Furthermore, the company has an $18,000 insurance policy to renew on March 1. Even though Overnight's income statement reports net income of $39,942, the company's balance sheet doesn't report enough liquid assets to satisfy all of its upcoming obligations.

**CASH EFFECTS**

---

## What Types of Information Must Be Disclosed?

There is no comprehensive list of all information that should be disclosed in financial statements. The adequacy of disclosure is based on a combination of official rules, tradition, and accountants' professional judgment.

As a general rule, a company should disclose any facts that an intelligent person would consider necessary for the statements to be *interpreted properly*. In addition to accounting methods in use and the due dates of major liabilities, businesses may need to disclose such matters as the following:

- Lawsuits pending against the business
- Scheduled plant closings
- Governmental investigations into the safety of the company's products or the legality of its pricing policies
- Significant events occurring *after* the balance sheet date but before the financial statements are actually issued
- Specific customers that account for a large portion of the company's business
- Unusual transactions or conflicts of interest between the company and its key officers

Let us stress again that *there is no comprehensive list of items that must be disclosed.* Throughout this course, we will identify and discuss many items that may require disclosure in financial statements.

In some cases, companies must even disclose information that could have a *damaging effect* on the business. For example, a manufacturer may need to disclose that it is being sued by customers who have been injured by its products. The fact that a disclosure might prove embarrassing—or even damaging to the business—is *not* a valid reason for not disclosing the information. The concept of adequate disclosure demands a *good faith effort* by management to keep the users of financial statements informed about the company's operations.

Companies are *not* required to disclose information that is immaterial or that does not have a direct *financial* impact on the business. For example, a company is not required by generally accepted accounting principles to disclose the resignation, firing, or death of a key executive. Of course, companies often *do* disclose such nonfinancial events on a voluntary basis.

Disclosures that accompany financial statements should be limited to *facts* and *reasonable estimates*. They should not include *optimistic speculation* that cannot be substantiated.

For a look at the types of disclosure made by publicly owned corporations, see the **Toot-sie Roll Industries, Inc.,** annual report, which appears in Appendix A.

**YOUR TURN**

### You as Overnight Auto's Independent Auditor

Assume that Overnight Auto Service is being sued by a former employee injured while on the job. The person claims that Overnight had been negligent in providing a safe work environment. If the plaintiff prevails, Overnight may have to pay damages well in excess of what is covered by its insurance policies. As Overnight's independent auditor, you have asked that the company disclose information about this lawsuit in the notes that accompany the financial statements. Overnight's management disagrees with your suggestion because in its opinion, the likelihood of the plaintiff prevailing is extremely remote. How should you respond?

*Our answer is on p. 214.

## CLOSING THE TEMPORARY EQUITY ACCOUNTS

**LO 4**

Explain the purpose of *closing entries;* prepare these entries.

As previously stated, revenue increases retained earnings, and expenses and dividends decrease retained earnings. If the only financial statement that we needed were a balance sheet, these changes in retained earnings could be recorded directly in the Retained Earnings account. However, owners, managers, investors, and others need to know amounts of specific revenues and expenses, and the amount of net income earned in the period. Therefore, we maintain *separate ledger accounts* to measure each type of revenue and expense, and the dividends distributed.

These revenue, expense, and dividends accounts are called *temporary,* or *nominal,* accounts, because they accumulate the transactions of *only one accounting period.* At the end of this accounting period, the changes in retained earnings accumulated in these temporary accounts are transferred into the Retained Earnings account. This process serves two purposes. First, it *updates the balance of the Retained Earnings account* for changes in retained earnings occurring during the accounting period. Second, it *returns the balances of the temporary accounts to zero,* so that they are ready for measuring the revenue, expenses, and dividends of the next accounting period.

The Retained Earnings account and other balance sheet accounts are called *permanent,* or *real,* accounts, because their balances continue to exist beyond the current accounting period. The process of transferring the balances of the temporary accounts into the Retained Earnings account is called *closing* the accounts. The journal entries made for the purpose of closing the temporary accounts are called **closing entries.**

Revenue and expense accounts are closed at the end of each accounting period by *transferring their balances* to a summary account called **Income Summary.** When the credit balances of the revenue accounts and the debit balances of the expense accounts have been transferred into one summary account, the balance of the Income Summary account will be the *net income* or *net loss* for the period. If revenue (credit balances) exceeds expenses (debit balances), the Income Summary account will have a credit balance representing net income. Conversely, if expenses exceed revenue, the Income Summary account will have a debit balance representing net loss. This is consistent with the rule that increases in owners' equity are recorded by credits and decreases are recorded by debits.

While adjusting entries are usually made on a monthly basis, it is common practice to close accounts only *once each year.* Thus, we will demonstrate the closing of the temporary accounts of Overnight Auto Service at December 31, 2002, the end of its first year of operations.

On the following pages, Overnight's temporary accounts are illustrated in T account form. We have eliminated the detail of every transaction posted to each account throughout the year. Therefore, each account shows only its December 31, 2002, balance as reported in the adjusted trial balance on page 177.

## Closing Entries for Revenue Accounts

Revenue accounts have credit balances. Therefore, closing a revenue account means transferring its credit balance to the Income Summary account. This transfer is accomplished by a journal entry debiting the revenue account in an amount equal to its credit balance, with an offsetting credit to the Income Summary account. The debit portion of this closing entry returns the balance of the revenue account to zero; the credit portion transfers the former balance of the revenue account into the Income Summary account.

Overnight uses two revenue accounts: (1) Repair Service Revenue, which had a credit balance of $172,000 at December 31, 2002, and (2) Rent Revenue Earned, which had a credit balance of $3,000 at December 31, 2002. Two separate journal entries could be made to close these accounts, but the use of one *compound journal entry* is an easier, time-saving method of closing more than one account. A compound journal entry is an entry that includes debits or credits to more than one account. The compound closing entry for Overnight's revenue accounts is as follows:

| GENERAL JOURNAL | | | |
|---|---|---|---|
| Date | Account Titles and Explanation | Debit | Credit |
| 2002 | | | |
| Dec. 31 | Repair Service Revenue . . . . . . . . . . . . . . . . . . . . . . . . . . | 172,000 | |
| | Rent Revenue Earned . . . . . . . . . . . . . . . . . . . . . . . . . . | 3,000 | |
| | Income Summary . . . . . . . . . . . . . . . . . . . . . . . . . | | 175,000 |
| | To close the Repair Service Revenue and Rent Revenue Earned accounts. | | |

After this closing entry has been posted, the two revenue accounts each have *zero* balances, whereas Income Summary has a credit balance of $175,000, as illustrated below:

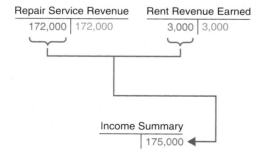

## Closing Entries for Expense Accounts

Expense accounts have debit balances. Closing an expense account means transferring its debit balance to the Income Summary account. The journal entry to close an expense, therefore, consists of a credit to the expense account in an amount equal to its debit balance, with an offsetting debit to the Income Summary account.

There are nine expense accounts in Overnight's ledger (see the adjusted trial balance on page 177). Again, a compound journal entry is used to close each of these accounts. The required closing entry is shown below:

| | GENERAL JOURNAL | | |
|---|---|---|---|
| **Date** | **Account Titles and Explanation** | **Debit** | **Credit** |
| 2002 | | | |
| Dec. 31 | Income Summary ........................................ | 135,058 | |
| |     Advertising Expense ............................... | | 3,900 |
| |     Wages Expense ................................... | | 58,750 |
| |     Supplies Expense ................................. | | 7,500 |
| |     Depreciation Expense: Building ..................... | | 1,650 |
| |     Depreciation Expense: Tools | | |
| |       and Equipment ................................ | | 2,200 |
| |     Utilities Expense ................................. | | 19,400 |
| |     Insurance Expense ............................... | | 15,000 |
| |     Interest Expense ................................. | | 30 |
| |     Income Taxes Expense ............................ | | 26,628 |
| |     To close the expense accounts. | | |

After this closing entry has been posted, the Income Summary account has a credit balance of *$39,942* ($175,000 credit posted − $135,058 debit posted), and the nine expense accounts each have zero balances as shown below. This $39,942 credit balance equals the net income reported in Overnight's income statement. Had the company's income statement reported a *net loss* for the year, the Income Summary account would have a *debit balance* equal to the amount of the loss reported.

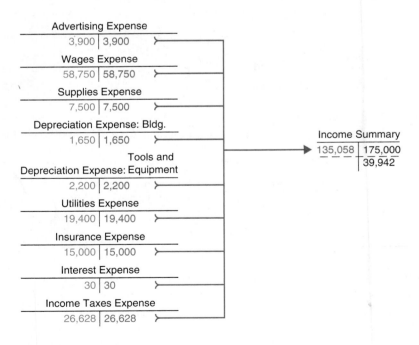

## Closing the Income Summary Account

The nine expense accounts have now been closed, and the total amount of $135,058 formerly contained in these accounts appears in the debit column of the Income Summary account. The revenue of $175,000 earned during 2002 appears in the credit column of the Income Summary account. Since the credit entry representing revenue of $175,000 is larger than the debit entry representing total expenses of $135,058, the Income Summary has a credit balance of $39,942.

The net income of $39,942 earned during the year causes an increase in Overnight's owners' equity. Thus, the $39,942 credit balance of the Income Summary account is transferred to the Retained Earnings account by the following closing entry:

| GENERAL JOURNAL | | | |
|---|---|---|---|
| **Date** | **Account Titles and Explanation** | **Debit** | **Credit** |
| 2002 | | | |
| Dec. 31 | Income Summary .................................. | 39,942 | |
| | Retained Earnings ......................... | | 39,942 |
| | Transferring net income earned in 2002 to the Retained Earnings account. | | |

After this closing entry has been posted, the Income Summary account has a zero balance, and the net income for the year ended December 31, 2002, appears as an increase (or credit entry) in the Retained Earnings account as shown below:

| Income Summary | | Retained Earnings |
|---|---|---|
| $135,058 (Expenses) | $175,000 (Revenue) | 1/20 bal. 0 |
| $39,942 | $39,942 (Income) | 12/31 $39,942 (Income) |

Income is transferred to Retained Earnings
as Income Summary is closed.

## Closing the Dividends Account

As explained earlier in the chapter, dividends paid to stockholders are *not* considered an expense of the business and, therefore, are *not* taken into account in determining net income for the period. Since dividends are not an expense, the Dividends account is *not* closed to the Income Summary account. Instead, it is closed directly to the Retained Earnings account, as shown by the following entry:

| GENERAL JOURNAL | | | |
|---|---|---|---|
| **Date** | **Account Titles and Explanation** | **Debit** | **Credit** |
| 2002 | | | |
| Dec. 31 | Retained Earnings ................................ | 14,000 | |
| | Dividends ................................. | | 14,000 |
| | To transfer dividends declared in 2002 to the Retained Earnings account. | | |

After this closing entry has been posted, the Dividends account will have a zero balance, and the Retained Earnings account will have an ending credit balance of $25,942, as shown below:

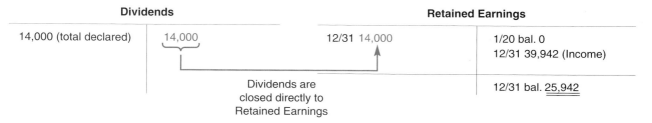

| Dividends | | | Retained Earnings |
|---|---|---|---|
| 14,000 (total declared) | 14,000 | 12/31 14,000 | 1/20 bal. 0 |
| | | | 12/31 39,942 (Income) |
| | Dividends are closed directly to Retained Earnings | | 12/31 bal. 25,942 |

**YOUR TURN**

**You as a Software Developer**

Assume that you are the developer of business software applications. How might you design an accounting software package that would enable a business to perform its year-end closing process *without* having to make all of the general journal entries illustrated on pages 183–185?

*Our answer is on p. 214.

## SUMMARY OF THE CLOSING PROCESS

Let us now summarize the process of closing the accounts.

1. Close the various *revenue* accounts by transferring their balances into the Income Summary account.
2. Close the various *expense* accounts by transferring their balances into the Income Summary account.
3. Close the *Income Summary* account by transferring its balance into the Retained Earnings account.
4. Close the *Dividends* account by transferring its balance into the Retained Earnings account.

The closing of the accounts may be illustrated graphically by use of T accounts as follows:

*Flowchart of the closing process*

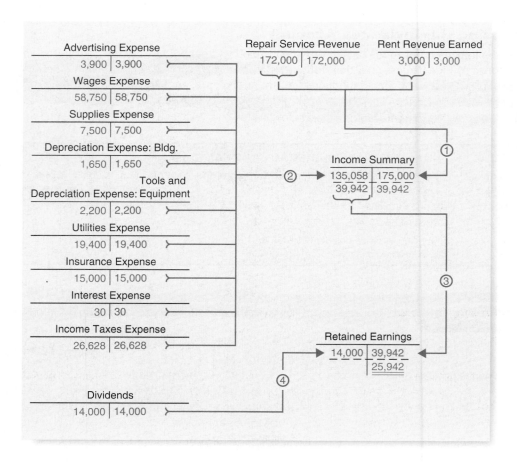

## AFTER-CLOSING TRIAL BALANCE

After the revenue and expense accounts have been closed, it is desirable to prepare an **after-closing trial balance** that consists solely of balance sheet accounts. There is always the possibility that an error in posting the closing entries may have upset the equality of debits and credits in the ledger. The after-closing trial balance, or *post-closing trial balance* as it is often called, is prepared from the ledger. It gives assurance that the accounts are in balance and ready for recording transactions in the new accounting period. The after-closing trial balance of Overnight Auto Service follows:

**LO 5**

Prepare an after-closing trial balance.

**OVERNIGHT AUTO SERVICE**
**After-Closing Trial Balance**
**December 31, 2002**

| | | |
|---|---:|---:|
| Cash | $ 18,592 | |
| Accounts receivable | 7,250 | |
| Shop supplies | 1,200 | |
| Unexpired insurance | 3,000 | |
| Land | 52,000 | |
| Building | 36,000 | |
| Accumulated depreciation: building | | $ 1,650 |
| Tools and equipment | 12,000 | |
| Accumulated depreciation: tools and equipment | | 2,200 |
| Notes payable | | 4,000 |
| Accounts payable | | 2,690 |
| Wages payable | | 1,950 |
| Income taxes payable | | 5,580 |
| Interest payable | | 30 |
| Unearned rent revenue | | 6,000 |
| Capital stock | | 80,000 |
| Retained earnings, Dec. 31 | | 25,942 |
| | $130,042 | $130,042 |

*The balances in the temporary equity accounts have been closed into the Retained Earnings account*

In comparison with the adjusted trial balance (page 177), an after-closing trial balance contains only *balance sheet* accounts. Also, the Retained Earnings account no longer has a zero balance. Through the closing of the revenue, expense, and dividends accounts, the Retained Earnings account has been brought up-to-date.

## A Last Look at Overnight: Was 2002 a Good Year?

Let us now consider the financial results of Overnight's first fiscal year.

**LO 6**

Use financial statement information to evaluate profitability and solvency.

**Evaluating Profitability**  In 2002, Overnight earned a net income of nearly *$40,000.* Thus, net income for the first year of operations amounts to 50% of the stockholders' $80,000 investment. This is a very impressive rate of return for the first year of operations. Of course, Overnight's stockholders (members of the McBryan family) have taken a certain amount of risk by investing their financial resources in this business. Does a 50% *return on investment* adequately compensate the stockholders for their risk? Stated differently, could they invest their $80,000 in a less risky venture and still generate a 50% rate of return? Probably not.

But in evaluating profitability, the real question is not how the business *did,* but how it *is likely to do in the future.* To generate a substantial return on investment in the first year of operations indicates good profit potential. Overnight's rental contract with Harbor Cab Company is also promising. In 2002, only $3,000 in revenue was earned by renting storage space to the company for its cabs (December's rent). In 2003, Overnight will earn 12 full months of rent revenue from Harbor Cab ($33,000 more than it earned in 2002). In addition, if Harbor Cab stores its cabs in Overnight's garage, Overnight becomes the likely candidate to perform any necessary maintenance and repairs.

**MANAGEMENT STRATEGY**

One of the primary uses of accounting information is to direct management's attention to problems and opportunities. The Harbor Cab Co. rental agreement presents a strategic business opportunity to Overnight Auto—to obtain the right to service cabs stored in Overnight's facility.

Overnight's management should also direct its attention to the expense section of the income statement. The expense amounts for insurance and utilities may be excessive and offer a potential for significant cost savings. Before renewing its insurance policies, Overnight should obtain competitive quotes from several insurance companies. Perhaps comparable insurance is available for substantially less than $18,000 per year. To reduce utility expense management should consider:

- Is the lighting system efficient?
- Is the heating system efficient and is the building adequately insulated?
- Are employees using company phones for personal calls?

At first glance these items may seem small and unimportant. But if Overnight could save just 10% on its insurance and utility bills, it would have increased net income in 2002 by more than $300 per month.

**Evaluating Solvency**   *Solvency* refers to a company's ability to meet its cash obligations as they become due. Solvency, at least in the short term, may be independent of profitability. And in the short term, Overnight appears to have *potential* cash flow problems. In the very near future, Overnight must make cash expenditures for the following items:

*Items requiring cash payment in near future*

| | |
|---|---:|
| Note and interest payable | $ 4,090 |
| Accounts payable | 2,690 |
| Wages payable | 1,950 |
| Income taxes payable | 5,580 |
| Insurance policy renewal | 18,000 |
| Total expenditures coming due | $32,310 |

These outlays exceed the company's liquid assets (cash and accounts receivable) reported in its December 31, 2002, balance sheet.

**CASH EFFECTS**   The liquid assets reported in Overnight's balance sheet represent cash and accounts receivable at a *point in time* (December 31, 2002). Thus, while these liquid assets are currently insufficient to cover the cash expenditures coming due, this may not be the case for long. Based on its past performance, Overnight is likely to generate revenue in excess of $40,000 during the next several months. If a substantial amount of this revenue is received in cash, and expenses are kept under control, the company may actually become more solvent than it appears to be now.

## FINANCIAL ANALYSIS

Other commonly used measures of Overnight's *profitability* include:

| Measure | Computation | Overnight's Performance |
|---|---|---|
| Net Income Percentage | $\dfrac{\text{Net Income}}{\text{Total Revenue}}$ | $\dfrac{\$~39{,}942}{\$175{,}000} = \underline{\underline{22.8\%}}$ |

*Significance:* An indicator of management's ability to control costs.

| Measure | Computation | Overnight's Performance |
|---|---|---|
| Return on Equity | $\dfrac{\text{Net Income}}{\text{Average Stockholders' Equity}}$ | $\dfrac{\$39{,}942}{\$52{,}971} = \underline{\underline{75.4\%}}$ |

*Significance:* A measure of income generated per average dollar of stockholders' equity.

*Average stockholders' equity of $52,971 is simply the average of Overnight's beginning stockholders' equity of $80,000, and its ending stockholders' equity of $105,942.

Other commonly used measures of Overnight's *solvency* include:

| Measure | Computation | Overnight's Performance |
|---|---|---|
| Working Capital | Current Assets − Current Liabilities | $\$30{,}042 - \$20{,}250 = \underline{\underline{\$9{,}792}}$ |

*Significance:* A measure of short-term debt paying ability expressed in dollars.

| Measure | Computation | Overnight's Performance |
|---|---|---|
| Current Ratio | $\dfrac{\text{Current Assets}}{\text{Current Liabilities}}$ | $\dfrac{\$30{,}042}{\$20{,}250} = \underline{\underline{1.48{:}1}}$ |

*Significance:* A measure of short-term debt paying ability expressed in dollars.

*Current assets are those assets expected to leave the balance sheet in the near future, several of which are very liquid. For Overnight, current assets include Cash, Accounts Receivable, Shop Supplies, and Unexpired Insurance. Current liabilities are those liabilities expected to leave the balance sheet in the near future, most of which must be settled in cash. All of Overnight's liabilities are considered current liabilities.

## Preparing Financial Statements Covering Different Periods of Time

**LO 7**

Explain how interim financial statements are prepared in a business that closes its accounts only at year-end.

Many businesses prepare financial statements every quarter, as well as at year-end. In addition, they may prepare financial statements covering other time periods, such as one month or the year-to-date.

When a business closes its accounts only at year-end, the revenue, expense, and dividends accounts have balances representing the activities of the *year-to-date.* Thus, at *June 30,* these account balances represent the activities recorded over the past six months. Year-to-date financial statements can be prepared directly from an adjusted trial balance. But how might this business prepare **interim financial statements** covering only the month of June? Or the quarter (three months) ended June 30?

The answer is by doing a little *subtraction.* As an example, assume that the adjusted balance in Overnight's Repair Service Revenue account at the ends of the following months was as shown below:

| | |
|---|---|
| March 31 (end of the first quarter) | $38,000 |
| May 31 | 67,000 |
| June 30 | 80,000 |

*Revenue amounts are for the year-to-date*

At each date, the account balance represents the revenue earned since January 1. Thus the March 31 balance represents three months' revenue; the May 31 balance, five months' revenue; and the June 30 balance, the revenue earned over a period of six months.

To prepare an income statement for the *six months* ended June 30, we simply use the June 30 balance in the revenue account—*$80,000.* But to prepare an income statement for the *month* ended June 30, we would have to subtract from the June 30 balance of this account its balance as of May 31. The remainder, *$13,000,* represents the amount of revenue recorded in the account during June ($80,000 − $67,000 = $13,000).

To prepare an income statement for the *quarter* ended June 30, we would subtract from the June 30 balance in this revenue account its balance as of March 31. Thus the revenue earned during the second quarter (April 1 through June 30) amounts to *$42,000* ($80,000 − $38,000 = $42,000).

This process of subtracting prior balances from the current balance is repeated for each revenue and expense account, as well as for the dividends account.

This sounds like a bigger job than it really is. There are only about 10 or 15 accounts involved, and in a computerized system, the entire process is done automatically. Even in a manual system, a person using a calculator can complete this process in a few minutes.

Computations like these are not required for the balance sheet accounts. A balance sheet always is based on the account balances *at the balance sheet date.* Therefore, a June 30 balance sheet looks exactly the same *regardless* of the time period covered by the other financial statements.

## FINAL COMMENTS

We have now completed the *entire accounting cycle*—from the initial recording of transactions in Chapter 3, through an after-closing trial balance in this chapter. The steps comprising this cycle are listed below, and are also illustrated in the form of a flow chart diagram on page 191.

1. *Journalize (record) transactions.* Enter all transactions in the journal, thus creating a chronological record of events.
2. *Post to ledger accounts.* Post debits and credits from the journal to the proper ledger accounts, thus creating a record classified by accounts.
3. *Prepare a trial balance.* Prove the equality of debits and credits in the ledger.
4. *Make end-of-period adjustments.* Make adjusting entries in the general journal and post to ledger accounts.
5. *Prepare an adjusted trial balance.* Prove again the equality of debits and credits in the ledger. (*Note:* These are the amounts used in the preparation of financial statements.)
6. *Prepare financial statements and appropriate disclosures.* An income statement shows the results of operation for the period. A statement of retained earnings shows changes in retained earnings during the period. A balance sheet shows the financial position of the business at the end of the period. Financial statements should be accompanied by *notes* disclosing facts necessary for the proper interpretation of those statements.
7. *Journalize and post the closing entries.* The closing entries "zero" the revenue, expense, and dividends accounts, making them ready for recording the events of the next accounting period. These entries also bring the balance in the Retained Earnings account up-to-date.
8. *Prepare an after-closing trial balance.* This step ensures that the ledger remains in balance after posting of the closing entries.

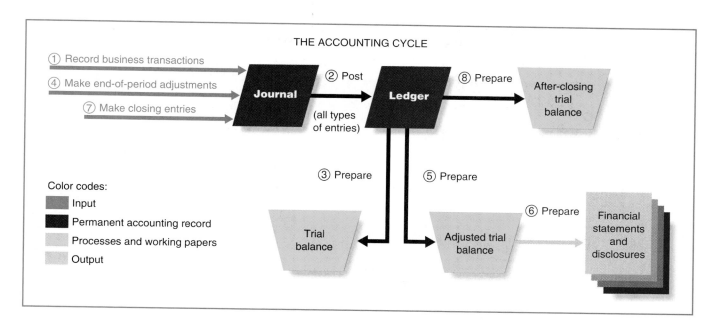

## Huffy Corporation

The closure of domestic production facilities was a major event in the life of **Huffy Corporation**. Management made significant disclosures pertaining to this decision in the notes that accompany the company's financial statements. A small portion of management's disclosure appears below:

> During the fourth quarter of 1999, the Company closed its remaining domestic bicycle manufacturing facilities in Farmington, Missouri, and Southaven, Mississippi, and reorganized its bicycle operations. During the first quarter of 2000, the Company increased imports from a global network of sourcing partners to offset this loss of production capacity. Closing the plants eliminated the costs required to operate the facilities and completed Huffy Bicycle Company's transformation from a single brand manufacturer and marketer of bicycles, to a multi-brand design, marketing, and distribution company.

> The financial ramifications of the plant closures were reported in Huffy's income statement as severance pay, shut-down costs, and other items related to reorganization activities. In Chapter 12, we learn more about how these nonrecurring events are reported as components of net income.

**A SECOND LOOK**

## SUPPLEMENTAL TOPIC

### THE WORKSHEET

A **worksheet** illustrates in one place the relationships among the unadjusted trial balance, proposed adjusting entries, and the financial statements. A worksheet is prepared at the end of the period, but *before* the adjusting entries are formally recorded in the accounting records. It is not a formal step in the accounting cycle. Rather, it is a tool used by accountants to work out the details of the proposed end-of-period adjustments. It also provides them with a preview of how the financial statements will look.

A worksheet for Overnight Auto Service at December 31, 2002, is illustrated on the following page.

**LO 8**

Prepare a worksheet and explain its uses.

## OVERNIGHT AUTO SERVICE
### Worksheet
### For the Year Ended December 31, 2002

| | Trial Balance | | Adjustments* | | Adjusted Trial Balance | | Income Statement | | Balance Sheet | |
|---|---|---|---|---|---|---|---|---|---|---|
| | Dr | Cr | Dr | Cr | Dr | Cr | Dr | Cr | Dr | Cr |
| **Balance sheet accounts:** | | | | | | | | | | |
| Cash | 18,592 | | | | 18,592 | | | | 18,592 | |
| Accounts Receivable | 6,500 | | (h) 750 | | 7,250 | | | | 7,250 | |
| Shop Supplies | 1,800 | | | (a) 600 | 1,200 | | | | 1,200 | |
| Unexpired Insurance | 4,500 | | | (b) 1,500 | 3,000 | | | | 3,000 | |
| Land | 52,000 | | | | 52,000 | | | | 52,000 | |
| Building | 36,000 | | | | 36,000 | | | | 36,000 | |
| Accumulated Depreciation: Building | | 1,500 | | (c) 150 | | 1,650 | | | | 1,650 |
| Tools and Equipment | 12,000 | | | | 12,000 | | | | 12,000 | |
| Accumulated Depreciation: Tools and Equipment | | 2,000 | | (d) 200 | | 2,200 | | | | 2,200 |
| Notes Payable | | 4,000 | | | | 4,000 | | | | 4,000 |
| Accounts Payable | | 2,690 | | | | 2,690 | | | | 2,690 |
| Income Taxes Payable | | 1,560 | | (i) 4,020 | | 5,580 | | | | 5,580 |
| Unearned Rent Revenue | | 9,000 | (e) 3,000 | | | 6,000 | | | | 6,000 |
| Capital Stock | | 80,000 | | | | 80,000 | | | | 80,000 |
| Retained Earnings | | 0 | | | | 0 | | | | 0 |
| Dividends | 14,000 | | | | 14,000 | | | | 14,000 | |
| Wages Payable | | | | (f) 1,950 | | 1,950 | | | | 1,950 |
| Interest Payable | | | | (g) 30 | | 30 | | | | 30 |
| **Income statement accounts:** | | | | | | | | | | |
| Repair Service Revenue | | 171,250 | | (h) 750 | | 172,000 | | 172,000 | | |
| Advertising Expense | 3,900 | | | | 3,900 | | 3,900 | | | |
| Wages Expense | 56,800 | | (f) 1,950 | | 58,750 | | 58,750 | | | |
| Supplies Expense | 6,900 | | (a) 600 | | 7,500 | | 7,500 | | | |
| Depreciation Expense: Building | 1,500 | | (c) 150 | | 1,650 | | 1,650 | | | |
| Depreciation Expense: Tools and Equipment | 2,000 | | (d) 200 | | 2,200 | | 2,200 | | | |
| Utilities Expense | 19,400 | | | | 19,400 | | 19,400 | | | |
| Insurance Expense | 13,500 | | (b) 1,500 | | 15,000 | | 15,000 | | | |
| Income Taxes Expense | 22,608 | | (i) 4,020 | | 26,628 | | 26,628 | | | |
| Rent Revenue Earned | | | | (e) 3,000 | | 3,000 | | 3,000 | | |
| Interest Expense | | | (g) 30 | | 30 | | 30 | | | |
| | 272,000 | 272,000 | 12,200 | 12,200 | 279,100 | 279,100 | 135,058 | 175,000 | 144,042 | 104,100 |
| Net income | | | | | | | 39,942 | | | 39,942 |
| **Totals** | | | | | | | 175,000 | 175,000 | 144,042 | 144,042 |

*Adjustments:
(a) Shop supplies used in December.
(b) Portion of insurance cost expiring in December.
(c) Depreciation on building for December.
(d) Depreciation of tools and equipment for December.
(e) Earned one-third of rent revenue collected in advance from Harbor Cab.
(f) Unpaid wages owed to employees at December 31.
(g) Interest payable accrued during December.
(h) Repair service revenue earned in December but not yet billed.
(i) Income taxes expense for December.

## Isn't This Really a "Spreadsheet"?

Yes. The term *worksheet* is a holdover from the days when these schedules were prepared manually on large sheets of columnar paper. Today, most worksheets are prepared on a computer using spreadsheet software, such as *Lotus 1-2-3*™ or *Excel*™, or with **general ledger software** such as *Peachtree*™ or *Dac-Easy*™.

Since the worksheet is simply a tool used by accountants, it often isn't printed out in hard copy—it may exist only on a computer screen. But the concept remains the same; the worksheet displays *in one place* the unadjusted account balances, proposed adjusting entries, and financial statements as they will appear if the proposed adjustments are made.

## How Is a Worksheet Used?

A worksheet serves several purposes. It allows accountants to *see the effects* of adjusting entries without actually entering these adjustments in the accounting records. This makes it relatively easy for them to correct errors or make changes in estimated amounts. It also enables accountants and management to preview the financial statements before the final drafts are developed. Once the worksheet is complete, it serves as the source for recording adjusting and closing entries in the accounting records and for preparing financial statements.

Another important use of the worksheet is in the preparation of *interim financial statements*. Interim statements are financial statements developed at various points *during* the fiscal year. Most companies close their accounts only once each year. Yet they often need to develop quarterly or monthly financial statements. Through the use of a worksheet, they can develop these interim statements *without* having to formally adjust and close their accounts.

## The Mechanics: How It's Done

Whether done manually or on a computer, the preparation of a worksheet involves five basic steps. We begin by describing these steps as if the worksheet were being prepared manually. Afterward, we explain how virtually all of the mechanical steps can be performed automatically by a computer.

1. *Enter the ledger account balances in the Trial Balance columns.* The worksheet begins with an unadjusted trial balance—that is, a listing of the ledger account balances at the end of the period *prior* to making any adjusting entries. In our illustration, the unadjusted trial balance appears in *blue*.

    Notice our inclusion of the captions "Balance sheet accounts" and "Income statement accounts." These captions are optional, but they help clarify the relationships between the ledger accounts and the financial statements. (*Hint:* A few lines should be left blank immediately below the last balance sheet account. It is often necessary to add a few more accounts during the adjusting process. Additional income statement accounts may also be necessary.)

2. *Enter the adjustments in the Adjustments columns.* The next step is the most important: Enter the appropriate end-of-period adjustments in the Adjustments columns. In our illustration, these adjustments appear in *red*.

    Notice that each adjustment includes both debit and credit entries, which are linked together by the small key letters appearing to the left of the dollar amount. Thus, adjusting entry *a* consists of a $600 debit to Supplies Expense and a $600 credit to Shop Supplies. Because the individual adjusting entries include equal debit and credit amounts, the totals of the debit and credit Adjustment columns should be equal.

    Sometimes the adjustments require adding accounts to the original trial balance. (The four ledger account titles printed in *red* were added during the adjusting process.)

3. *Prepare an adjusted trial balance.* Next, an adjusted trial balance is prepared. The balances in the original trial balance (*blue*) are adjusted for the debit or credit amounts in the Adjustments columns (*red*). This process of horizontal addition or subtraction is called *cross-footing.* The adjusted trial balance is totaled to determine that the accounts remain in balance.

   At this point, the worksheet is almost complete. We have emphasized that financial statements are prepared *directly from the adjusted trial balance.* Thus we have only to arrange these accounts into the format of financial statements. For this reason, we show the adjusted trial balance amounts in *blue*—both in the Adjusted Trial Balance columns and when these amounts are *extended* (carried forward) into the financial statement columns.

4. *Extend the adjusted trial balance amounts into the appropriate financial statement columns.* The balance sheet accounts—assets, liabilities, and owners' equity—are extended into the Balance Sheet columns; income statement amounts, into the Income Statement columns. (The "Balance Sheet" and "Income Statement" captions in the original trial balance should simplify this procedure. Notice each amount is extended to only one column. Also, the account retains the same debit or credit balance as shown in the adjusted trial balance.)

5. *Total the financial statement columns; determine and record net income or net loss.* The final step in preparing the worksheet consists of totaling the Income Statement and Balance Sheet columns and then bringing each set of columns into balance. These tasks are performed on the bottom three lines of the worksheet. In our illustration, the amounts involved in this final step are shown in *black.*

When the Income Statement and Balance Sheet columns are first totaled, the debit and credit columns will not agree. But each set of columns should be out-of-balance by the *same amount*—and that amount should be the amount of net income or net loss for the period.

Let us briefly explain *why* both sets of columns initially are out-of-balance by this amount. First consider the Income Statement columns. The Credit column contains the revenue accounts, and the Debit column, the expense accounts. The difference, therefore, represents the net income (net loss) for the period.

Now consider the Balance Sheet columns. All of the balance sheet amounts are shown at up-to-date amounts *except* for the Retained Earnings account, which still contains the balance from the *beginning* of the period. To bring the Retained Earnings account up-to-date, we must add net income and subtract any dividends. The dividends already appear in the Balance Sheet Debit column. So what's the only thing missing? The net income (or net loss) for the period.

To bring both sets of columns into balance, we enter the net income (or net loss) on the next line. The same amount will appear in both the Income Statement columns and the Balance Sheet columns. But in one set of columns it appears as a debit, and in the other, it appears as a credit.[3] After this amount is entered, each set of columns should balance.

**Computers Do the Pencil-Pushing** When a worksheet is prepared by computer, accountants perform only *one* of the steps listed above—*entering the adjustments.* The computer automatically lists the ledger accounts in the form of a trial balance. After the accountant has entered the adjustments, it automatically computes the adjusted account balances and completes the worksheet. (Once the adjusted balances are determined, completing the worksheet involves nothing more than putting these amounts in the appropriate column and determining the column totals.)

---

[3] To bring the Income Statement columns into balance, net *income* is entered in the *Debit column.* This is because the Credit column (revenue) exceeds the Debit column (expenses). But in the balance sheet, net income is an element of owners' equity, which is represented by a credit. In event of a net *loss,* this situation reverses.

## What-If: A Special Application of Worksheet Software

We have discussed a relatively simple application of the worksheet concept—illustrating the effects of proposed *adjusting entries* on account balances. But the same concept can be applied to proposed *future transactions*. The effects of the proposed transactions simply are entered in the "Adjustments" columns. Thus, without disrupting the accounting records, accountants can prepare schedules showing how the company's financial statements might be affected by such events as a merger with another company, a 15% increase in sales volume, or the closure of a plant.

There is a tendency to view worksheets as mechanical and old-fashioned. This is not at all the case. Today, the mechanical aspects are handled entirely by computer. The real purpose of a worksheet is to show quickly and efficiently how specific events or transactions will affect the financial statements. This isn't bookkeeping—it's *planning*.

# END-OF-CHAPTER REVIEW

## SUMMARY OF LEARNING OBJECTIVES

### LO 1

**Prepare an income statement, a statement of retained earnings, and a balance sheet.**

The financial statements are prepared directly from the adjusted trial balance. The income statement is prepared by reporting all revenue earned during the period, less all expenses incurred in generating the related revenue. The statement of retained earnings reconciles the *beginning* Retained Earnings account balance with its *ending* balance. The retained earnings statement reports any increase to Retained Earnings resulting from net income earned for the period, as well as any decreases to Retained Earnings resulting from dividends declared or a net loss incurred for the period. The balance sheet reveals the company's financial position by reporting its economic resources (assets), and the claims against those resources (liabilities and owners' equity).

### LO 2

**Explain how the income statement and the statement of retained earnings relate to the balance sheet.**

An income statement shows the revenue and expenses of a business for a specified accounting period. In the statement of retained earnings, the net income figure from the income statement is added to the beginning Retained Earnings balance, while dividends declared during the period are subtracted, in arriving at the ending Retained Earnings balance. The ending Retained Earnings balance is then reported in the balance sheet as a component of owners' equity.

### LO 3

**Explain the concept of *adequate disclosure*.**

Adequate disclosure is a generally accepted accounting principle, meaning that financial statements should include any information that an informed user needs to interpret the statements properly. The appropriate disclosures usually are contained in several pages of notes that accompany the statements.

### LO 4

**Explain the purposes of *closing entries*; prepare these entries.**

Closing entries serve two basic purposes. The first is to return the balances of the temporary owners' equity accounts (revenue, expenses, and dividend accounts) to zero so that these accounts may be used to measure the activities of the next reporting period. The second purpose of closing entries is to update the balance of the Retained Earnings account. Four closing entries generally are needed: (1) close the revenue accounts to the Income Summary account, (2) close the expense accounts to the Income Summary account, (3) close the balance of the Income Summary account to the Retained Earnings account, and (4) close the Dividends account to the Retained Earnings account.

### LO 5

**Prepare an after-closing trial balance.**

After the revenue and expense accounts have been closed, it is desirable to prepare an after-closing trial balance consisting solely of balance sheet accounts. The after-closing trial balance, or post-closing trial balance, gives assurance that the accounts of the general ledger are in balance and ready for recording transactions for the new accounting period.

### LO 6

**Use financial statement information to evaluate profitability and solvency.**

Profitability is an increase in stockholders' equity resulting from revenue exceeding expenses, whereas solvency refers to a company's ability to meet its cash obligations as they come due. Solvency, at least in the short term, may be *independent* of profitability. Financial statements are useful tools for evaluating both profitability and solvency. Used separately, or in combination, the income statement and balance sheet help interested parties to measure a company's current financial performance, and to forecast its profit and cash flow potential. On page 189, we illustrated several measures of profitability and solvency computed using financial statement information. Throughout the remainder of this text we introduce and discuss many additional measures.

### LO 7

**Explain how *interim* financial statements are prepared in a business that closes its accounts only at year-end.**

When a business closes its accounts only at year-end, the revenue, expense, and dividend accounts have balances representing the activities of the year-to-date. To prepare an income statement for any period shorter than the year-to-date, we subtract from the current balance in the revenue or expense account the balance in the account as of the beginning of the desired period. This process of subtracting prior balances from the current balance is repeated for each revenue and expense account and for the dividend account. No computations of this type are required for the balance sheet accounts, as a balance sheet is based on the account balances at the balance sheet date.

### LO 8

**Prepare a worksheet and explain its usefulness.***

A worksheet is a "testing ground" on which the ledger accounts are adjusted, balanced, and arranged in the format of financial

---

*Supplemental Topic, "The Worksheet."*

statements. A worksheet consists of a trial balance, the end-of-period adjusting entries, an adjusted trial balance, and columns showing the ledger accounts arranged as an income statement and as a balance sheet. The completed worksheet is used as the basis for preparing financial statements and for recording adjusting and closing entries in the formal accounting records.

In Chapter 5 we have completed our study of the accounting cycle for a service-type business. We have also completed our continued illustrated example of Overnight Auto Service. In Chapter 6 we will extend these concepts by focusing on some additional steps needed to account for inventories of goods sold by wholesale or retail merchandising businesses.

## KEY TERMS INTRODUCED OR EMPHASIZED IN CHAPTER 5

**adequate disclosure** (p. 180) The generally accepted accounting principle of providing with financial statements any information that users need to interpret those statements properly.

**after-closing trial balance** (p. 187) A trial balance prepared after all closing entries have been made. Consists only of accounts for assets, liabilities, and owners' equity.

**closing entries** (p. 182) Journal entries made at the end of the period for the purpose of closing temporary accounts (revenue, expense, and dividend accounts) and transferring balances to the Retained Earnings account.

**general ledger software** (p. 193) Computer software used for recording transactions, maintaining journals and ledgers, and preparing financial statements. Also includes spreadsheet capabilities for showing the effects of proposed adjusting entries or transactions on the financial statements without actually recording these entries in the accounting records.

**Income Summary** (p. 182) The summary account in the ledger to which revenue and expense accounts are closed at the end of the period. The balance (credit balance for a net income, debit balance for a net loss) is transferred to the Retained Earnings account.

**interim financial statements** (p. 189) Financial statements prepared for periods of less than one year (includes monthly and quarterly statements).

**notes (accompanying financial statements)** (p. 180) Supplemental disclosures that accompany financial statements. These notes provide users with various types of information considered necessary for the proper interpretation of the statements.

**worksheet** (p. 191) A multicolumn schedule showing the relationships among the current account balances (a trial balance), proposed or actual adjusting entries or transactions, and the financial statements that would result if these adjusting entries or transactions were recorded. Used both at the end of the accounting period as an aid to preparing financial statements and for planning purposes.

# DEMONSTRATION PROBLEM

Jan's Dance Studio, Inc., performs adjusting entries every month, but closes its accounts only at year-end. The studio's year-end *adjusted trial balance* dated December 31, 2002, appears below. (Bear in mind, the balance shown for Retained Earnings was last updated on December 31, *2001*).

### JAN'S DANCE STUDIO, INC.
### Adjusted Trial Balance
### December 31, 2002

| | | |
|---|---:|---:|
| Cash | $171,100 | |
| Accounts receivable | 9,400 | |
| Prepaid studio rent | 3,000 | |
| Unexpired insurance | 7,200 | |
| Supplies | 500 | |
| Equipment | 18,000 | |
| Accumulated depreciation: equipment | | $ 7,200 |
| Notes payable | | 10,000 |
| Accounts payable | | 3,200 |
| Salaries payable | | 4,000 |
| Income taxes payable | | 6,000 |
| Unearned studio revenue | | 8,800 |
| Capital stock | | 100,000 |
| Retained earnings | | 40,000 |
| Dividends | 6,000 | |
| Studio revenue earned | | 165,000 |
| Salary expense | 85,000 | |
| Supply expense | 3,900 | |
| Rent expense | 12,000 | |
| Insurance expense | 1,900 | |
| Advertising expense | 500 | |
| Depreciation expense: equipment | 1,800 | |
| Interest expense | 900 | |
| Income taxes expense | 23,000 | |
| | $344,200 | $344,200 |

### Instructions

**a.** Prepare an income statement and statement of retained earnings for the year ended December 31, 2002. Also prepare the studio's balance sheet dated December 31, 2002.

**b.** Prepare the necessary closing entries at December 31, 2002.

**c.** Prepare an after-closing trial balance dated December 31, 2002.

## Solution to Demonstration Problem

a.

| JAN'S DANCE STUDIO, INC. Income Statement For the Year Ended December 31, 2002 | | |
|---|---:|---:|
| **Revenue:** | | |
| Studio revenue earned | | $165,000 |
| **Expenses:** | | |
| Salary expense | $85,000 | |
| Supply expense | 3,900 | |
| Rent expense | 12,000 | |
| Insurance expense | 1,900 | |
| Advertising expense | 500 | |
| Depreciation expense: equipment | 1,800 | |
| Interest expense | 900 | 106,000 |
| Income before income taxes | | $ 59,000 |
| Income taxes expense | | 23,000 |
| Net income | | $ 36,000 |

| JAN'S DANCE STUDIO, INC. Statement of Retained Earnings For the Year Ended December 31, 2002 | |
|---|---:|
| Retained earnings, January 1, 2002 | $40,000 |
| Add: Net income earned in 2002 | 36,000 |
| Subtotal | $76,000 |
| Less: Dividends declared in 2002 | 6,000 |
| Retained earnings, December 31, 2002 | $70,000 |

## JAN'S DANCE STUDIO, INC.
### Balance Sheet
### December 31, 2002

### Assets

| | | |
|---|---:|---:|
| Cash | | $171,100 |
| Accounts receivable | | 9,400 |
| Prepaid studio rent | | 3,000 |
| Unexpired insurance | | 7,200 |
| Supplies | | 500 |
| Equipment | $18,000 | |
| Less: Accumulated depreciation: equipment | 7,200 | 10,800 |
| Total assets | | $202,000 |

### Liabilities & Stockholders' Equity

**Liabilities:**

| | | |
|---|---:|---:|
| Notes payable | | $ 10,000 |
| Accounts payable | | 3,200 |
| Salaries payable | | 4,000 |
| Income taxes payable | | 6,000 |
| Unearned studio revenue | | 8,800 |
| Total liabilities | | $ 32,000 |

**Stockholders' equity:**

| | | |
|---|---:|---:|
| Capital stock | | $100,000 |
| Retained earnings | | 70,000 |
| Total stockholders' equity | | $170,000 |
| Total liabilities and stockholders' equity | | $202,000 |

## GENERAL JOURNAL

| Date | Account Titles and Explanation | Debit | Credit |
|---|---|---:|---:|
| Dec. 31 2002 | | | |
| **1.** | Studio Revenue Earned | 165,000 | |
| |     Income Summary | | 165,000 |
| | To close Studio Revenue Earned. | | |
| **2.** | Income Summary | 129,000 | |
| |     Salary Expense | | 85,000 |
| |     Supply Expense | | 3,900 |
| |     Rent Expense | | 12,000 |
| |     Insurance Expense | | 1,900 |
| |     Advertising Expense | | 500 |
| |     Depreciation Expense: Equipment | | 1,800 |
| |     Interest Expense | | 900 |
| |     Income Taxes Expense | | 23,000 |
| | To close all expense accounts. | | |
| **3.** | Income Summary | 36,000 | |
| |     Retained Earnings | | 36,000 |
| | To transfer net income earned in 2002 to the Retained Earnings account ($165,000 − $129,000 = $36,000). | | |
| **4.** | Retained Earnings | 6,000 | |
| |     Dividends | | 6,000 |
| | To transfer dividends declared in 2002 to the Retained Earnings account. | | |

| JAN'S DANCE STUDIO, INC. After-Closing Trial Balance December 31, 2002 | | |
|---|---|---|
| Cash | $171,100 | |
| Accounts receivable | 9,400 | |
| Prepaid studio rent | 3,000 | |
| Unexpired insurance | 7,200 | |
| Supplies | 500 | |
| Equipment | 18,000 | |
| Accumulated depreciation: equipment | | $ 7,200 |
| Notes payable | | 10,000 |
| Accounts payable | | 3,200 |
| Salaries payable | | 4,000 |
| Income taxes payable | | 6,000 |
| Unearned studio revenue | | 8,800 |
| Capital stock | | 100,000 |
| Retained earnings, December 31 | | 70,000 |
| | $209,200 | $209,200 |

## SELF-TEST QUESTIONS

*The answers to these questions appear on page 214.*

1. For a publicly owned company, indicate which of the following accounting activities are likely to occur at or shortly after year-end. (More than one answer may be correct.)
   a. Preparing of income tax returns.
   b. Adjusting and closing the accounts.
   c. Drafting disclosures that accompany the financial statements.
   d. An audit of the financial statements by a firm of CPAs.

2. Which of the following financial statements is generally prepared first?
   a. Income statement.
   b. Balance sheet.
   c. Statement of retained earnings.
   d. Statement of cash flows.

3. Which of the following accounts would *never* be reported in the income statement as an expense?
   a. Depreciation expense
   b. Income taxes expense.
   c. Interest expense.
   d. Dividends expense.

4. Which of the following accounts would *never* appear in the after-closing trial balance? (More than one answer may be correct.)
   a. Unearned revenue.
   b. Dividends
   c. Accumulated depreciation.
   d. Income taxes expense.

5. Which of the following journal entries is required to close the Income Summary account of a profitable company?

    **a.** Debit Income Summary, credit Retained Earnings.

    **b.** Credit Income Summary, debit Retained Earnings.

    **c.** Debit Income Summary, credit Capital Stock.

    **d.** Credit Income Summary, debit Capital Stock.

**6.** Indicate those items for which generally accepted accounting principles *require* disclosure in notes accompanying the financial statements. (More than one answer may be correct.)

    **a.** A large lawsuit was filed against the company two days *after* the balance sheet date.

    **b.** The depreciation method in use, given that several different methods are acceptable under generally accepted accounting principles.

    **c.** Whether small but long-lived items—such as electric pencil sharpeners and handheld calculators—are charged to asset accounts or to expense accounts.

    **d.** As of year-end, the chief executive officer had been hospitalized because of chest pains.

**7.** Ski West adjusts its accounts at the end of each month, but closes them only at the end of the calendar year (December 31). The ending balances in the Equipment Rental Revenue account and the Cash account in February and March appear below.

| | Feb. 28 | Mar. 31 |
|---|---|---|
| Cash | $14,200 | $26,500 |
| Equipment rental revenue | 12,100 | 18,400 |

Ski West prepares financial statements showing separately the operating results of each month. In the financial statements prepared for the *month* ended March 31, Equipment Rental Revenue and Cash should appear as follows:

    **a.** Equipment Rental Revenue, $18,400; Cash, $26,500

    **b.** Equipment Rental Revenue, $18,400; Cash, $12,300

    **c.** Equipment Rental Revenue, $6,300; Cash, $26,500

    **d.** Equipment Rental Revenue, $6,300; Cash, $12,300

**8.** Which of the following accounts is *not* closed to the Income Summary account at the end of the accounting period? (More than one answer may be correct.)

    **a.** Rent Expense.

    **b.** Accumulated Depreciation.

    **c.** Unearned Revenue.

    **d.** Supplies Expense.

## ASSIGNMENT MATERIAL

## DISCUSSION QUESTIONS

    **1.** Explain briefly the items generally included in a company's annual report. (You may use the annual report appearing in Appendix A to support your answer.)

    **2.** Discuss several limitations of the income statement.

    **3.** Some people think that a company's retained earnings represent *cash* reserved for the payment of dividends. Are they correct? Explain.

    **4.** Are dividends paid to stockholders ever reported in the income statement as an expense? Explain.

    **5.** Discuss the relationship among the income statement, the statement of retained earnings, and the balance sheet.

    **6.** Identify several items that may require disclosure in the notes that accompany financial statements.

    **7.** What type of accounts are referred to as *temporary* or *nominal* accounts? What is meant by these terms?

    **8.** What type of accounts are referred to as *permanent* or *real* accounts? What is meant by these terms?

9. Explain *why* the Dividends account is closed directly to the Retained Earnings account.

10. Which accounts appear in a company's after-closing trial balance? What is the purpose of an after-closing trial balance?

11. Can a company be both profitable *and* insolvent? Explain.

12. What are interim financial statements? Do accounts that appear in a company's interim balance sheet require any special computations to be reported correctly? Explain.

13. Explain the accounting principle of *adequate disclosure.*

14. Briefly describe the content of the *notes* that accompany financial statements.

15. How does depreciation expense differ from other operating expenses?

16. Explain the need for closing entries and describe the process by which temporary owners' equity accounts are closed at year-end.

*17. Explain several purposes that may be served by preparing a worksheet (or using computer software that achieves the goals of a worksheet).

## EXERCISES

Listed below are nine technical terms used in this chapter:

| | | |
|---|---|---|
| Solvency | Nominal accounts | Real accounts |
| Adequate disclosure | After-closing trial balance | Closing entries |
| Income summary | Interim financial statements | Dividends |

**EXERCISE 5.1**

Accounting Terminology

**LO 1–7**

Each of the following statements may (or may not) describe one of these technical terms. For each statement, indicate the accounting term described, or answer "None" if the statement does not describe any of the items.

a. The accounting principle intended to assist users in *interpreting* financial statements.

b. A term used to describe a company's ability to pay its obligations as they come due.

c. A term used in reference to accounts that are closed at year-end.

d. A term used in reference to accounts that are not closed at year-end.

e. A document prepared to assist management in detecting whether any errors occurred in posting the closing entries.

f. A policy decision by a corporation to distribute a portion of its income to stockholders.

g. The process by which the Retained Earnings account is updated at year-end.

h. Entries made during the accounting period to correct errors in the original recording of complex transactions.

Tutors for Rent, Inc., performs adjusting entries every month, but closes its accounts *only at year-end.* The company's year-end *adjusted trial balance* dated December 31, 2002, was:

**EXERCISE 5.2**

Financial Statement Preparation

**LO 1, 2, 6**

---

*Supplemental Topic,* "The Worksheet."

**TUTORS FOR RENT, INC.**
**Adjusted Trial Balance**
**December 31, 2002**

| | | |
|---|---:|---:|
| Cash | $ 91,100 | |
| Accounts receivable | 4,500 | |
| Supplies | 300 | |
| Equipment | 12,000 | |
| Accumulated depreciation: equipment | | $ 5,000 |
| Accounts payable | | 1,500 |
| Income taxes payable | | 3,500 |
| Capital stock | | 25,000 |
| Retained earnings | | 45,000 |
| Dividends | 2,000 | |
| Tutoring revenue earned | | 96,000 |
| Salary expense | 52,000 | |
| Supply expense | 1,200 | |
| Advertising expense | 300 | |
| Depreciation expense: equipment | 1,000 | |
| Income taxes expense | 11,600 | |
| | $176,000 | $176,000 |

**a.** Prepare an income statement and statement of retained earnings for the year ended December 31, 2002. Also prepare the company's balance sheet dated December 31, 2002.

**b.** Does the company appear to be solvent? Defend your answer.

**c.** Has the company been profitable in the past? Explain.

**EXERCISE 5.3**

Financial Statement Preparation

**LO 1, 2, 6**

Wilderness Guide Services, Inc., performs adjusting entries every month, but closes its accounts *only at year-end.* The company's year-end *adjusted trial balance* dated December 31, 2002, follows:

**WILDERNESS GUIDE SERVICES, INC.**
**Adjusted Trial Balance**
**December 31, 2002**

| | | |
|---|---:|---:|
| Cash | $ 12,200 | |
| Accounts receivable | 31,000 | |
| Camping supplies | 7,900 | |
| Unexpired insurance policies | 2,400 | |
| Equipment | 70,000 | |
| Accumulated depreciation: equipment | | $ 60,000 |
| Notes payable (due 4/1/03) | | 18,000 |
| Accounts payable | | 9,500 |
| Capital stock | | 25,000 |
| Retained earnings | | 15,000 |
| Dividends | 1,000 | |
| Guide revenue earned | | 102,000 |
| Salary expense | 87,500 | |
| Camping supply expense | 1,200 | |
| Insurance expense | 9,600 | |
| Depreciation expense: equipment | 5,000 | |
| Interest expense | 1,700 | |
| | $229,500 | $229,500 |

**a.** Prepare an income statement and statement of retained earnings for the year ended December 31, 2002. Also prepare the company's balance sheet dated December 31, 2002. (Hint: Unprofitable companies have no income taxes expense.)

**b.** Does the company appear to be solvent? Defend your answer.

**c.** Has the company been profitable in the past? Explain.

Refer to the adjusted trial balance of Tutors for Rent, Inc., illustrated in Exercise 5.2 to respond to the following items:

**a.** Prepare all necessary closing entries at December 31, 2002.

**b.** Prepare an after-closing trial balance dated December 31, 2002.

**c.** Compare the Retained Earnings balance reported in the after-closing trial balance prepared in part **b** to the balance reported in the adjusted trial balance. Explain *why* the two balances are different. (Include in your explanation why the balance reported in the after-closing trial balance has increased or decreased subsequent to the closing process.)

**EXERCISE 5.4**

Preparing Closing Entries and an After-Closing Trial Balance

**LO 2, 4, 5**

Refer to the adjusted trial balance of Wilderness Guide Services, Inc., illustrated in Exercise 5.3 to respond to the following items:

**a.** Prepare all necessary closing entries at December 31, 2002.

**b.** Prepare an after-closing trial balance dated December 31, 2002.

**c.** Compare the Retained Earnings balance reported in the after-closing trial balance prepared in part **b** to the balance reported in the adjusted trial balance. Explain *why* the two balances are different. (Include in your explanation why the balance reported in the after-closing trial balance has increased or decreased subsequent to the closing process.)

**EXERCISE 5.5**

Preparing Closing Entries and an After-Closing Trial Balance

**LO 2, 4, 5**

Gerdes Psychological Services, Inc., closes its temporary owners' equity accounts once each year on December 31. The company recently issued the following income statement as part of its annual report:

**EXERCISE 5.6**

Preparing Closing Entries

**LO 2, 4**

| GERDES PSYCHOLOGICAL SERVICES, INC. Income Statement For the Year Ended December 31, 2002 | | |
|---|---:|---:|
| **Revenue:** | | |
| Counseling revenue | | $225,000 |
| **Expenses:** | | |
| Advertising expense | $ 1,800 | |
| Salaries expense | 94,000 | |
| Office supplies expense | 1,200 | |
| Utilities expense | 850 | |
| Malpractice insurance expense | 6,000 | |
| Office rent expense | 24,000 | |
| Continuing education expense | 2,650 | |
| Depreciation expense: fixtures | 4,500 | |
| Miscellaneous expense | 6,000 | |
| Income taxes expense | 29,400 | 170,400 |
| Net income | | $ 54,600 |

The firm's statement of retained earnings indicates that a $6,000 cash dividend was declared and paid during 2002.

**a.** Prepare the necessary closing entries on December 31, 2002.

**b.** If the firm's Retained Earnings account had a $92,000 balance on January 1, 2002, at what amount should Retained Earnings be reported in the firm's balance sheet dated December 31, 2002?

**EXERCISE 5.7**

Distinction between the
Adjusting and the Closing
Process

**LO 2, 4**

When Torretti Company began business on August 1, it purchased a one-year fire insurance policy and debited the entire cost of $7,200 to Unexpired Insurance. Torretti *adjusts* its accounts at the end of each month and *closes* its books at the end of the year.

**a.** Give the *adjusting entry* required at December 31 with respect to this insurance policy.

**b.** Give the *closing entry* required at December 31 with respect to insurance expense. Assume that this policy is the only insurance policy Torretti had during the year.

**c.** Compare the dollar amount appearing in the December 31 adjusting entry (part **a**) with that in the closing entry (part **b**). Are the dollar amounts the same? Why or why not? Explain.

**EXERCISE 5.8**

Interim Results

**LO 1, 2, 7**

Ski Powder Resort ends its fiscal year on April 30. The business adjusts its accounts monthly, but *closes them only at year-end* (April 30). The resort's busy season is from December 1 through March 31.

Adrian Pride, the resort's chief financial officer, keeps a close watch on Lift Ticket Revenue and Cash. The balances of these accounts at the ends of each of the last five months are as follows:

|  | Lift Ticket Revenue | Cash |
|---|---|---|
| November 30 | $ 30,000 | $ 9,000 |
| December 31 | 200,000 | 59,000 |
| January 31 | 640,000 | 94,000 |
| February 28 | 850,000 | 116,000 |
| March 31 | 990,000 | 138,000 |

Mr. Pride prepares income statements and balance sheets for the resort. Indicate what amounts will be shown in these statements for (1) Lift Ticket Revenue and (2) Cash, assuming they are prepared for:

**a.** The *month* ended February 28.

**b.** The entire "busy season to date"—that is, December 1 through March 31.

**c.** In terms of Lift Ticket Revenue and increases in Cash, which has been the resort's best month? (Indicate the dollar amounts.)

**EXERCISE 5.9**

Understanding the Effects of
Errors on the Financial
Statements

**LO 2, 3**

Indicate the effect of the following errors on each of the financial statement elements described in the column headings in the table below. Use the following symbols: **O** = overstated, **U** = understated, and **NE** = no effect.

| Error | Net Income | Total Assets | Total Liabilities | Retained Earnings |
|---|---|---|---|---|
| **a.** Recorded a dividend as an *expense* in the income statement |  |  |  |  |
| **b.** Recorded unearned revenue as *earned* revenue in the income statement. |  |  |  |  |
| **c.** Failed to record accrued wages payable at the end of the accounting period. |  |  |  |  |
| **d.** Recorded a declared but unpaid dividend by debiting Dividends and crediting Cash. |  |  |  |  |
| **e.** Failed to disclose a pending lawsuit in the notes accompanying the financial statements. |  |  |  |  |

**EXERCISE 5.10**

Examining an Annual Report

**LO 3, 6**

The annual report of **Tootsie Roll Industries, Inc.,** appears in Appendix A at the end of this textbook.

**a.** Review the notes accompanying the company's consolidated financial statements. Identify the 11 major topic headings.

**b.** Does the company use straight-line depreciation? How can you tell?

**c.** What portion of the company's total revenue came from a single major customer in each of the three years reported?

**d.** Using information from the consolidated financial statements, evaluate briefly the company's profitability and solvency.

## PROBLEMS

Party Wagon, Inc., provides musical entertainment at weddings, dances, and various other functions. The company performs adjusting entries *monthly*, but prepares closing entries *annually* on December 31. The company recently hired Jack Armstrong as its new accountant. Jack's first assignment was to prepare an income statement, a statement of retained earnings, and a balance sheet using an *adjusted* trial balance given to him by his predecessor, dated December 31, 2002.

From the adjusted trial balance, Jack prepared the following set of financial statements:

**PROBLEM 5.1**

Correcting Classification Errors

**LO 1, 2, 4, 6**

---

**PARTY WAGON, INC.**
**Income Statement**
**For the Year Ended December 31, 2002**

**Revenue:**

| | | |
|---|---:|---:|
| Party revenue earned | | $130,000 |
| Unearned party revenue | | 1,800 |
| Accounts receivable | | 9,000 |
| Total revenue | | $140,800 |

**Expenses:**

| | | |
|---|---:|---:|
| Insurance expense | $ 1,800 | |
| Office rent expense | 12,000 | |
| Supplies expense | 1,200 | |
| Dividends | 1,000 | |
| Salary expense | 75,000 | |
| Accumulated depreciation; van | 16,000 | |
| Accumulated depreciation; equipment and music | 14,000 | |
| Repair & maintenance expense | 2,000 | |
| Travel expense | 6,000 | |
| Miscellaneous expense | 3,600 | |
| Interest expense | 4,400 | 137,000 |
| Income before income taxes | | $ 3,800 |
| Income taxes payable | | 400 |
| Net income | | $ 3,400 |

*(Handwritten annotations: "liability", "asset" pointing to Unearned party revenue and Accounts receivable; "under assets" pointing to Dividends, Accumulated depreciation entries)*

---

**PARTY WAGON, INC.**
**Statement of Retained Earnings**
**For the Year Ended December 31, 2002**

| | |
|---|---:|
| Retained earnings (per adjusted trial balance) | $15,000 |
| Add: Income | 3,400 |
| Less: Income taxes expense | 2,000 |
| Retained earnings (12/31/02) | $16,400 |

*(Handwritten annotation: "Dividends" written over "Income taxes expense")*

*(handwritten margin notes: "depreciation expense", "assets", "Int. Payable →", arrows pointing to entries)*

## PARTY WAGON, INC.
## Balance Sheet
## December 31, 2002

### Assets

| | | |
|---|---:|---:|
| Cash | | $15,000 |
| Supplies | | 500 |
| Van | $40,000 | |
| Less: Depreciation expense: van | 8,000 | 32,000 |
| Equipment and music | $35,000 | |
| Less: Depreciation expense: music & equipment | 7,000 | 28,000 |
| Total assets | | $75,500 |

### Liabilities & Stockholders' Equity

**Liabilities:**

| | |
|---|---:|
| Accounts payable | $ 7,000 |
| Notes payable | 39,000 |
| Salaries payable | 1,600 |
| Prepaid rent | 2,000 |
| Unexpired insurance | 4,500 |
| Total liabilities | $54,100 |

**Stockholders' Equity:**

| | |
|---|---:|
| Capital stock | 5,000 |
| Retained earnings | 16,400 |
| Total stockholders' equity | $21,400 |
| Total liabilities and stockholders' equity | $75,500 |

### Instructions

**a.** Prepare a corrected set of financial statements dated December 31, 2002. (You may assume that all of the figures in the company's adjusted trial balance were reported correctly except for Interest Payable of $200, which was mistakenly omitted in the financial statements prepared by Jack.)

**b.** Prepare the necessary year-end closing entries.

**c.** Using the financial statement prepared in part **a**, briefly evaluate the company's profitability and solvency.

**PROBLEM 5.2**

Preparing Financial Statements and Closing Entries of a Profitable Company

**LO 1, 2, 4, 5, 6**

Lawn Pride, Inc., provides lawn mowing services to both commercial and residential customers. The company performs adjusting entries on a *monthly* basis, whereas closing entries are prepared *annually* at December 31. An *adjusted* trial balance dated December 31, 2002, follows.

### Instructions

**a.** Prepare an income statement and statement of retained earnings for the year ended December 31, 2002. Also prepare the company's balance sheet dated December 31, 2002.

**b.** Prepare the necessary year-end closing entries.

**c.** Prepare an after-closing trial balance.

**d.** Using the financial statement prepared in part **a**, briefly evaluate the company's profitability and solvency.

| LAWN PRIDE, INC. Adjusted Trial Balance December 31, 2002 | | |
|---|---|---|
| | **Debits** | **Credits** |
| Cash | $ 58,525 | |
| Accounts receivable | 4,800 | |
| Unexpired insurance | 8,000 | |
| Prepaid rent | 3,000 | |
| Supplies | 1,075 | |
| Trucks | 150,000 | |
| Accumulated depreciation: trucks | | $120,000 |
| Mowing equipment | 20,000 | |
| Accumulated depreciation: mowing equipment | | 12,000 |
| Accounts payable | | 1,500 |
| Notes payable | | 50,000 |
| Salaries payable | | 900 |
| Interest payable | | 150 |
| Income taxes payable | | 1,050 |
| Unearned mowing revenue | | 900 |
| Capital stock | | 20,000 |
| Retained earnings | | 30,000 |
| Dividends | 5,000 | |
| Mowing revenue earned | | 170,000 |
| Insurance expense | 2,400 | |
| Office rent expense | 36,000 | |
| Supplies expense | 5,200 | |
| Salary expense | 60,000 | |
| Depreciation expense: trucks | 30,000 | |
| Depreciation expense: mowing equipment | 4,000 | |
| Repair and maintenance expense | 3,000 | |
| Fuel expense | 1,500 | |
| Miscellaneous expense | 5,000 | |
| Interest expense | 3,000 | |
| Income taxes expense | 6,000 | |
| | $406,500 | $406,500 |

Mystic Masters, Inc., provides fortunetelling services over the Internet. In recent years the company has experienced severe financial difficulty. Its accountant prepares adjusting entries on a *monthly* basis, and closing entries on an *annual* basis, at December 31. An *adjusted* trial balance dated December 31, 2002, follows.

**PROBLEM 5.3**

Preparing Financial Statements and Closing Entries of an Unprofitable Company

### Instructions

**a.** Prepare an income statement and statement of retained earnings for the year ended December 31, 2002. Also prepare the company's balance sheet dated December 31, 2002. (*Hint*: The company incurred no income taxes expense in 2002.)

**b.** Prepare the necessary year-end closing entries.

**c.** Prepare an after-closing trial balance.

**d.** Using the financial statement prepared in part **a**, briefly evaluate the company's performance.

**e.** Identify information that the company is apt to disclose in the notes that accompany the financial statements prepared in part **a**.

| MYSTIC MASTERS, INC.<br>Adjusted Trial Balance<br>December 31, 2002 | | |
|---|---|---|
| | **Debits** | **Credits** |
| Cash | $ 960 | |
| Accounts receivable | 300 | |
| Unexpired insurance | 2,000 | |
| Prepaid rent | 1,500 | |
| Supplies | 200 | |
| Furniture and fixtures | 8,400 | |
| Accumulated depreciation: furniture and fixtures | | $ 5,200 |
| Accounts payable | | 6,500 |
| Notes payable | | 24,000 |
| Salaries payable | | 1,700 |
| Interest payable | | 360 |
| Unearned client revenue | | 200 |
| Capital stock | | 4,000 |
| Retained earnings | | 2,600 |
| Client revenue earned | | 52,000 |
| Insurance expense | 6,000 | |
| Office rent expense | 9,000 | |
| Supplies expense | 440 | |
| Salary expense | 48,000 | |
| Depreciation expense: furniture and fixtures | 1,400 | |
| Office and telephone expense | 3,000 | |
| Internet service expense | 4,900 | |
| Legal expense | 1,500 | |
| Interest expense | 4,000 | |
| Miscellaneous expense | 5,000 | |
| | $96,600 | $96,600 |

**PROBLEM 5.4**

Interim Financial Statements

**LO 1, 2, 7**

Guardian Insurance Agency adjusts its accounts monthly but closes them only at the end of the calendar year. Below are the adjusted balances of the revenue and expense accounts at September 30 of the current year and at the ends of two earlier months:

| | **Sept. 30** | **Aug. 31** | **June 30** |
|---|---|---|---|
| Commissions Earned | $144,000 | $128,000 | $90,000 |
| Advertising Expense | 28,000 | 23,000 | 15,000 |
| Salaries Expense | 36,000 | 32,000 | 24,000 |
| Rent Expense | 22,500 | 20,000 | 15,000 |
| Depreciation Expense | 2,700 | 2,400 | 1,800 |

**Instructions**

**a.** Prepare a three-column income statement, showing net income for three separate time periods, all of which end on September 30. Use the format illustrated below. Show supporting computations for the amounts of revenue reported in the first two columns.

| GUARDIAN INSURANCE AGENCY<br>Income Statement<br>For the Following Time Periods in 2002 | | | |
|---|---|---|---|
| | Month<br>Ended<br>Sept. 30 | Quarter<br>Ended<br>Sept. 30 | 9 Months<br>Ended<br>Sept. 30 |
| Revenue: | | | |
| Commissions Earned | $ | $ | $ |
| Expenses: | | | |

**b.** Briefly explain how you determined the dollar amounts for each of the three time periods. Would you apply the same process to the balances in Guardian's balance sheet accounts? Explain.

**c.** Assume that Guardian adjusts *and closes* its accounts at the end of *each month*. Briefly explain how you then would determine the revenue and expenses that would appear in each of the three columns of the income statement prepared in part **a**.

Brushstroke Art Studio, Inc., provides quality instruction to aspiring artists. The business adjusts its accounts *monthly,* but performs closing entries *annually* on December 31. This is the studio's *unadjusted* trial balance dated December 31, 2002.

**PROBLEM 5.5**

Short Comprehensive Problem Including Both Adjusting and Closing Entries

**LO 1–4, 6**

| BRUSHSTROKE ART STUDIO<br>Unadjusted Trial Balance<br>December 31, 2002 | Debits | Credits |
|---|---|---|
| Cash | $ 22,380 | |
| Client fees receivable | 71,250 | |
| Supplies | 6,000 | |
| Prepaid studio rent | 2,500 | |
| Studio equipment | 96,000 | |
| Accumulated depreciation: studio equipment | | $ 52,000 |
| Accounts payable | | 6,420 |
| Note payable | | 24,000 |
| Interest payable | | 480 |
| Unearned client fees | | 8,000 |
| Income taxes payable | | 5,000 |
| Capital stock | | 50,000 |
| Retained earnings | | 20,000 |
| Client fees earned | | 82,310 |
| Supply expense | 4,000 | |
| Salary expense | 17,250 | |
| Interest expense | 480 | |
| Studio rent expense | 11,250 | |
| Utilities expense | 3,300 | |
| Depreciation expense: studio equipment | 8,800 | |
| Income taxes expense | 5,000 | |
| | $248,210 | $248,210 |

### Other Data

1. Supplies on hand at December 31, 2002, total $1,000.
2. The studio pays rent quarterly (every 3 months). The last payment was made November 1, 2002. The next payment will be made early in February 2003.
3. Studio equipment is being depreciated over 120 months (10 years).
4. On October 1, 2002, the studio borrowed $24,000 by signing a 12-month, 12%, note payable. The entire amount, plus interest, is due on September 30, 2003.
5. At December 31, 2002, $3,000 of previously unearned client fees had been *earned.*
6. Accrued, but *unrecorded* and uncollected client fees earned total $690 at December 31, 2002.
7. Accrued, but *unrecorded* and unpaid salary expense totals $750 at December 31, 2002.
8. Accrued income taxes payable for the *entire year* ending December 31, 2002, *total* $7,000. The full amount is due early in 2003.

### Instructions

a. Prepare the necessary adjusting journal entries on December 31, 2002. Prepare also an *adjusted trial balance* dated December 31, 2002.

b. From the adjusted trial balance prepared in part **a**, prepare an income statement and statement of retained earnings for the year ended December 31, 2002. Also prepare the company's balance sheet dated December 31, 2002.

c. Prepare the necessary year-end closing entries.

d. Prepare an after-closing trial balance.

e. Has the studio's monthly office rent remained the same throughout the year? If not, has it gone up or down? Explain.

**\*PROBLEM 5.6**

Short Comprehensive Problem Including Adjusting Entries, Closing Entries, and Worksheet Preparation

Refer to the demonstration problem in Chapter 4 (pages 158–161). Prepare a 10-column worksheet for Internet Consulting Service, Inc., dated December 31, 2002. At the bottom of your worksheet, prepare a brief explanation keyed to each adjusting entry.

**\*PROBLEM 5.7**

Short Comprehensive Problem Including Adjusting Entries, Closing Entries, and Worksheet Preparation

Refer to Problem 4.4 on pages 168–169. Prepare a 10-column worksheet for Campus Theater dated August 31, 2002. At the bottom of your worksheet, prepare a brief explanation keyed to each adjusting entry.

## CASES AND UNSTRUCTURED PROBLEMS

**CASE 5.1**

Working for the Competition

This problem focuses on the following question: *Is it ethical for a CPA (or CPA firm) to provide similar services to companies that compete directly with one another?* These services may include assistance in the preparation of financial statements, income tax services, consulting engagements, and audit work.

### Instructions

a. *Before* doing any research, discuss this question as a group. Identify potential arguments on *each side* of the issue.

b. Arrange an interview with a practicing (or retired) public accountant. Learn the accounting profession's position on this issue, and discuss the various arguments developed in part **a**.

---

*\*Supplemental Topic*, "The Worksheet."

c. Develop your group's position on this issue and be prepared to explain it in class. Explain why you have chosen to overlook the conflicting arguments developed in part **a**. (If your group is not in agreement, dissenting members may draft a dissenting opinion.)

Listed below are five items that may—or may not—require disclosure in the notes that accompany financial statements.

**CASE 5.2**
Adequate Disclosure
**LO 3**

a. Mandella Construction Co. uses the percentage-of-completion method to recognize revenue on long-term construction contracts. This is one of two acceptable methods of accounting for such projects. Over the life of the project, both methods produce the same overall results; but the annual results may differ substantially.

b. One of the most popular artists at Spectacular Comics is leaving the company and going to work for a competitor.

c. Shortly after the balance sheet date, but before the financial statements are issued, one of Coast Foods' two processing plants was damaged by a tornado. The plant will be out of service for at least three months.

d. The management of Soft Systems believes that the company has developed systems software that will make Windows® virtually obsolete. If they are correct, the company's profits could increase by 10-fold or more.

e. College Property Management (CPM) withheld a $500 security deposit from students who, in violation of their lease, kept a dog in their apartment. The students have sued CPM for this amount in small claims court.

### Instructions

For each case, explain what, if any, disclosure is required under generally accepted accounting principles. Explain your reasoning.

## BUSINESS WEEK ASSIGNMENT

Not long ago, **Ford Motor Company** was involved in what may prove to be the worst business crisis in automotive history: The Firestone tire recall. In an August 28, 2000, *Business Week* article entitled, "How Will Firestone and Ford Steer Through This Blowout?" authors Joann Muller and Nicole St. Pierre reported that 60% of the 6.5 million tires targeted for recall were found on Ford's popular Explorer and Mercury Mountaineer. The financial impact of this crisis is difficult, if not impossible, to estimate. However, Ford spokesman Michael Vaughn was quoted in the article as saying, "The ramifications of this are immense."

**CASE 5.3**
**LO 3**

Discuss how you think Ford should have disclosed information about the Firestone tire recall in its annual report. Does the company have an ethical obligation to address this issue? Examine the notes that accompany Ford's most recent financial statements. Did the company follow your suggestions?

## INTERNET ASSIGNMENT

Visit the home page of the **Ford Motor Company** at:

**www.ford.com**

**INTERNET 5.1**
Annual Report Disclosures
**LO 3**

From Ford's home page, access the company's most recent annual report. Locate the notes to the financial statements and identify the kinds of information disclosed in these footnotes.

*Internet sites are time and date sensitive. It is the purpose of these exercises to have you explore the Internet. You may need to use the Yahoo! search engine* http://www.yahoo.com *(or other favorite search engine) to find a company's current web address.*

## OUR COMMENTS ON THE "YOUR TURN" CASES

**You as an Independent Auditor (p. 182)** Pending lawsuits are usually disclosed in the notes to the financial statements only if there is *reasonable certainty* that the defendant will incur a significant loss. Thus, Overnight need *not* disclose its pending lawsuit if the risk of it sustaining a material loss is *remote.* This is certainly an issue requiring the *professional judgments* of the company's management, accountants, legal counsel, and its auditors. Coverage of financial uncertainties such as pending lawsuits is addressed in Chapter 10 of this textbook.

**You as a Business Software Developer (p. 186)** Most accounting software packages do *not* require that the general journal entries illustrated on pages 183–185 be recorded. Before using the software for the first time, the business designates which account numbers in its chart of accounts correspond to *revenues, expenses, and dividends,* and which account numbers correspond to balance sheet items. At the end of the accounting period, a menu item is selected to initiate the closing process. The software then identifies the *temporary accounts* and closes them *automatically* by following the logic presented in the flowchart on page 186.

## ANSWERS TO SELF-TEST QUESTIONS

**1.** a, b, c, d    **2.** a.    **3.** d    **4.** b, d    **5.** a    **6.** a, b    **7.** c    **8.** b, c

## Tony's Rentals

### A COMPREHENSIVE ACCOUNTING CYCLE PROBLEM

On September 1, 2002, Anthony and Christine Ferrara formed a corporation called Tony's Rentals, Inc., for the purpose of operating an equipment rental yard. The new corporation was able to begin operations immediately by purchasing the assets and taking over the location of Rent-It, an equipment rental company that was going out of business. Tony's Rentals, Inc., uses the following accounts and their corresponding account numbers:

| | | | |
|---|---|---|---|
| Cash | 1 | Income Taxes Payable | 29 |
| Accounts Receivable | 4 | Capital Stock | 30 |
| Prepaid Rent | 6 | Retained Earnings | 35 |
| Unexpired Insurance | 7 | Dividends | 38 |
| Office Supplies | 8 | Income Summary | 40 |
| Rental Equipment | 10 | Rental Fees Earned | 50 |
| Accumulated Depreciation: | | Salaries Expense | 60 |
| Rental Equipment | 12 | Maintenance Expense | 61 |
| Notes Payable | 20 | Utilities Expense | 62 |
| Accounts Payable | 22 | Rent Expense | 63 |
| Interest Payable | 25 | Office Supplies Expense | 64 |
| Salaries Payable | 26 | Depreciation Expense | 65 |
| Dividends Payable | 27 | Interest Expense | 66 |
| Unearned Rental Fees | 28 | Income Taxes Expense | 67 |

The corporation closes its accounts and prepares financial statements at the end of each month. During September, the corporation entered into the following transactions:

**Sept. 1**  Issued to Anthony and Christine Ferrara 20,000 shares of capital stock in exchange for a total of $80,000 cash.

**Sept. 1**  Purchased for $180,000 all of the equipment formerly owned by Rent-It. Paid $70,000 cash and issued a one-year note payable for $110,000, plus interest at the annual rate of 9%.

**Sept. 1**  Paid $9,000 to Shapiro Realty as three months' advance rent on the rental yard and office formerly occupied by Rent-It.

**Sept. 4**  Purchased office supplies on account from Modern Office Co., $1,630. Payment due in 30 days. (These supplies are expected to last for several months; debit the Office Supplies asset account.)

**Sept. 8**  Received $10,000 cash as advance payment on equipment rental from McBryan Construction Company. (Credit Unearned Rental Fees.)

**Sept. 12**  Paid salaries for the first two weeks in September, $3,600.

**Sept. 15**  Excluding the McBryan advance, equipment rental fees earned during the first 15 days of September amounted to $8,100, of which $6,800 was received in cash.

**Sept. 17**  Purchased on account from Earth Movers, Inc., $340 in parts needed to repair a rental tractor. (Debit an expense account.) Payment is due in 10 days.

**Sept. 23**  Collected $210 of the accounts receivable recorded on September 15.

**Sept. 25**  Rented a backhoe to Mission Landscaping at a price of $100 per day, to be paid when the backhoe is returned. Mission Landscaping expects to keep the backhoe for about two or three weeks.

**Sept. 26**  Paid biweekly salaries, $3,600.

**Sept. 27**  Paid the account payable to Earth Movers, Inc., $340.

**Sept. 28**  Declared a dividend of 10 cents per share, payable on October 15.

**Sept. 29**     Tony's Rentals was named, along with Mission Landscaping and Collier Construction, as a co-defendant in a $25,000 lawsuit filed on behalf of Kevin Davenport. Mission Landscaping had left the rented backhoe in a fenced construction site owned by Collier Construction. After working hours on September 26, Davenport had climbed the fence to play on parked construction equipment. While playing on the backhoe, he fell and broke his arm. The extent of the company's legal and financial responsibility for this accident, if any, cannot be determined at this time. (*Note:* This event does not require a journal entry at this time, but may require disclosure in notes accompanying the statements.)

**Sept. 29**     Purchased a 12-month public-liability insurance policy for $2,700. This policy protects the company against liability for injuries and property damage caused by its equipment. However, the policy goes into effect on October 1, and affords no coverage for the injuries sustained by Kevin Davenport on September 26.

**Sept. 30**     Received a bill from Universal Utilities for the month of September, $270. Payment is due in 30 days.

**Sept. 30**     Equipment rental fees earned during the second half of September and received in cash amounted to $8,450.

## Data for Adjusting Entries

**a.** The advance payment of rent on September 1 covered a period of three months.

**b.** Interest accrued on the note payable to Rent-It amounted to $825 at September 30.

**c.** The rental equipment is being depreciated by the straight-line method over a period of 10 years.

**d.** Office supplies on hand at September 30 are estimated at $1,100.

**e.** During September, the company earned $4,840 of the rental fees paid in advance by McBryan Construction Co. on September 8.

**f.** As of September 30, Tony's Rentals has earned five days' rent on the backhoe rented to Mission Landscaping on September 25.

**g.** Salaries earned by employees since the last payroll date (September 26) amounted to $900 at month-end.

**h.** It is estimated that Tony's Rentals is subject to a combined federal and state income tax rate of 40% of income before income taxes (total revenue minus all expenses *other than* income taxes). These taxes will be payable on December 15.

## Instructions

**a.** Journalize the above transactions.

**b.** Post to ledger accounts.

**c.** Prepare a 10-column worksheet for the month ended September 30, 2002.

**d.** Prepare an income statement and a statement of retained earnings for the month of September, and a balance sheet (in report form) as of September 30.

**e.** Prepare required disclosures to accompany the September 30 financial statements of Tony's Rentals, Inc. Your solution should include a separate note addressing each of the following areas: (1) depreciation policy, (2) maturity dates of major liabilities, and (3) potential liability due to pending litigation.

**f.** Prepare adjusting and closing entries and post to ledger accounts.

**g.** Prepare an after-closing trial balance as of September 30.

**h.** During September, this company's cash balance has fallen from $80,000 to less than $20,000. Does it appear headed for insolvency in the near future? Explain your reasoning.

**i.** Would it be ethical for Christine Ferrara to maintain the accounting records for this company, or must they be maintained by someone who is *independent* of the organization?

# ACCOUNTING FOR MERCHANDISING ACTIVITIES

## Learning Objectives

*After studying this chapter, you should be able to:*

1. Describe the *operating cycle* of a merchandising company.

2. Define *subsidiary ledgers* and explain their usefulness.

3. Account for purchases and sales of merchandise in a *perpetual* inventory system.

4. Explain how a *periodic* inventory system operates.

5. Discuss the factors to be considered in selecting an inventory system.

6. Define *special journals* and explain their usefulness.

7. Account for additional merchandising transactions related to purchases and sales.

8. Measure the performance of a merchandising business.

Mall of America

The Internet provides a convenient and efficient approach to retail shopping. Using a mouse and a modem to purchase a set of golf clubs, however, isn't a terribly *fun* or exciting experience. More and more, this missing fun factor is what traditional shopping malls are offering to win back a growing number of Internet shoppers.

Take, for instance, the unbelievable retailing experience found at the **Mall of America** in Bloomington, Minnesota. In addition to the mall's 400 retail stores, the 5 million square foot structure is home to Underwater World (a gigantic underground aquarium) and Camp Snoopy (a massive indoor amusement park). Those in the market for a set of golf clubs can even try out various brands using a virtual simulator in one the mall's sporting goods stores. You can't do that on the Internet!

These attractions, and more, lure over 40 million shoppers to the Mall of America each year. The Mall's patrons generate over $540 in annual sales per *square foot*. The **Simon Property Group** of Indianapolis, the Mall of America's principal investor, owns hundreds of other mall properties throughout the United States, many of which feature creative ways to bring *fun* back into the shopping experience. More than 2.5 billion shoppers visit these malls annually.

● ● ●

In this chapter we examine accounting issues related to merchandising businesses, such as the retail stores in a shopping mall. In addition to discussing the unique features of a merchandising company's financial statements, we illustrate ways to use financial information to evaluate the performance of these enterprises.

The preceding chapters focused on organizations that rendered *services* to their customers. We now shift our attention to merchandising organizations. These companies earn most of their revenue by selling *merchandise* to customers. Many of the **Mall of America**'s 400 stores are good examples of merchandising companies. For these businesses, managing **inventory** (goods that are purchased for the purpose of resale to customers) is of utmost importance. The opening story illustrates how high sales volume is essential to the mall's success. For any large shopping mall to be successful, all of its stores must be able to acquire and sell inventory quickly.

In most merchandising companies, inventory is a relatively liquid asset—that is, it usually is sold within a few days or weeks. For this reason, inventory appears near the top of the balance sheet, immediately below accounts receivable.

## MERCHANDISING COMPANIES

### The Operating Cycle of a Merchandising Company

**LO 1**

Describe the *operating cycle* of a merchandising company.

The series of transactions through which a business generates its revenue and its cash receipts from customers is called the **operating cycle**. The operating cycle of a merchandising company consists of the following basic transactions: (1) purchases of merchandise; (2) sales of the merchandise, often on account; and (3) collection of the accounts receivable from customers. As the word *cycle* suggests, this sequence of transactions repeats continuously. Some of the cash collected from the customers is used to purchase more merchandise, and the cycle begins anew. This continuous sequence of merchandising transactions is illustrated below.

*The operating cycle repeats continuously*

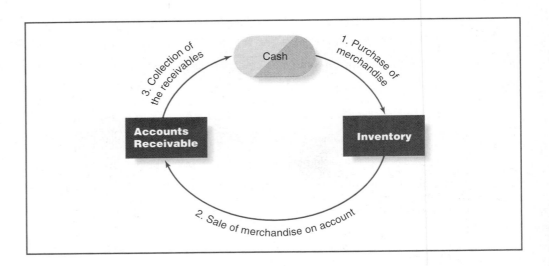

**Comparing Merchandising Activities with Manufacturing Activities** Most merchandising companies purchase their inventories from other business organizations in a *ready-to-sell* condition. Companies that manufacture their inventories, such as **General Motors**, **IBM**, and **Boeing Aircraft**, are called *manufacturers*, rather than merchandisers. The operating cycle of a manufacturing company is longer and more complex than that of a merchandising company, because the first transaction—purchasing merchandise—is replaced by the many activities involved in manufacturing the merchandise.

Our examples and illustrations in this chapter are limited to companies that purchase their inventory in a ready-to-sell condition. The basic concepts, however, also apply to manufacturers.

**Retailers and Wholesalers**   Merchandising companies include both retailers and wholesalers. A *retailer* is a business that sells merchandise directly to the public. Retailers may be large or small; they vary in size from giant department store chains, such as **Sears, Roebuck & Co.** and **Wal-Mart**, to small neighborhood businesses, such as gas stations and convenience stores. In fact, more businesses engage in retail sales than in any other type of business activity.

The other major type of merchandising company is the *wholesaler.* Wholesalers buy large quantities of merchandise from several different manufacturers and then resell this merchandise to many different retailers. As wholesalers do not sell directly to the public, even the largest wholesalers are not well known to most consumers. Nonetheless, wholesaling is a major type of merchandising activity.

The Internet has allowed wholesalers to become more visible to the global business community. A case in point is **KG Instruments® International**, a business that specializes in the development and distribution of fine stringed instruments and their accessories. The trading office and showroom are located at Campsie, New South Wales, Australia. The company welcomes business from importers, wholesalers, and dealers.

**CASE IN POINT**

The concepts discussed in the remainder of this chapter apply equally to retailers and to wholesalers.

## Income Statement of a Merchandising Company

Selling merchandise introduces a new and major cost of doing business: the *cost* to the merchandising company of the goods that it resells to its customers. This cost is termed the **cost of goods sold**. In essence, the cost of goods sold is an *expense;* however, this item is of such importance to a merchandising company that it is shown separately from other expenses in the income statement.

A highly condensed income statement for a merchandising business appears below. In comparison with the income statement of a service-type business, the new features of this statement are the inclusion of *cost of goods sold* and a subtotal called *gross profit.*

| COMPUTER BARN | |
| :--- | ---: |
| Condensed Income Statement | |
| For the Year Ended December 31, 2002 | |
| Revenue from sales | $900,000 |
| Less: Cost of goods sold | 540,000 |
| Gross profit | $360,000 |
| Less: Expenses | 270,000 |
| Net income | $ 90,000 |

*Condensed income statement for a merchandising company*

Revenue from sales represents the *sales price* of merchandise sold to customers during the period. The cost of goods sold, on the other hand, represents the *cost* incurred by the merchandising company for purchasing these goods from the company's suppliers. The difference between revenue from sales and the cost of goods sold is called **gross profit** (or gross margin).

Gross profit is a useful means of measuring the profitability of sales transactions, but it does *not* represent the overall profitability of the business. A merchandising company has many expenses other than the cost of goods sold. Examples include salaries, rent, advertising, and depreciation. The company earns a net income only if its gross profit exceeds the sum of its other expenses.

## What Accounting Information Does a Merchandising Company Need?

Before we illustrate how a merchandising company accounts for the transactions in its operating cycle, let us consider the basic types of information that the company's accounting system should develop. The company needs accounting information that will (1) meet its financial reporting requirements, (2) serve the needs of company personnel in conducting daily business operations, and (3) meet any special reporting requirements, such as information required by income tax authorities.

To meet its financial reporting requirements, a merchandising company must measure and record its revenue from sales transactions, as well as the cost of goods sold. (Other types of revenue and expenses must also be recorded, but this is done in the same manner as in a service-type business.) In addition, the accounting system must provide a complete record of the company's assets and liabilities.

The information appearing in financial statements is very condensed. For example, the amount shown as accounts receivable in a balance sheet represents the *total* accounts receivable at the balance sheet date. Managers and other employees need much more detailed accounting information than that provided in financial statements. In billing customers, for example, managers need to know the amount receivable from each credit customer. In addition, the accounting system must provide the dates and amounts of all charges and payments affecting each customer's account.

In most respects, the information needed for income tax purposes parallels that used in the financial statements. Differences between income tax rules and financial reporting requirements will be discussed in later chapters.

Let us now see how the accounting system of a merchandising company meets the company's needs for financial information.

## General Ledger Accounts

Up to now, we have been posting transactions only in *general ledger* accounts. These general ledger accounts are used to prepare financial statements and other accounting reports that *summarize* the financial position of a business and the results of its operations.

Although general ledger accounts provide a useful *overview* of a company's financial activities, they do not provide much of the *detailed information* needed by managers and other company employees in daily business operations. This detailed information is found in accounting records called *subsidiary ledgers*.

## Subsidiary Ledger Accounts

**LO 2**

Define *subsidiary ledgers* and explain their usefulness.

A **subsidiary ledger** contains a separate account for each of the *items* included in the balance of a general ledger account. For example, an *accounts receivable subsidiary ledger* contains a separate account for *each credit customer*. If the company has 500 credit customers, there are 500 accounts in the accounts receivable subsidiary ledger. The balances of these 500 subsidiary ledger accounts add up to the balance in the general ledger account.

An accounts receivable subsidiary ledger provides the information used in billing credit customers and in reviewing their creditworthiness. The account includes information on the dates and amounts of past charges and payments, the current balance owed, and the customer's billing address. In fact, each account provides a *complete history* of the credit transactions between the company and the individual customer.

When you call the phone company, electric company, or other businesses to inquire about your bill, they always ask you for your account number. This is the number assigned to your account in their accounts receivable subsidiary ledger. The company representative then views your account on a computer screen and is able to discuss the details of your past transactions.

CASE IN POINT

Most businesses maintain a number of different subsidiary ledgers, each providing detailed information about a different general ledger account. A general ledger account that summarizes the content of a subsidiary ledger is called a **controlling account** (or control account).

For convenience, the word *subsidiary* can be omitted in describing a specific subsidiary ledger. Thus the accounts receivable subsidiary ledger might simply be called the *accounts receivable ledger* (or *customer ledger*).

**Subsidiary Ledgers Needed for Merchandising Transactions**   In addition to a subsidiary ledger for accounts receivable, every merchandising company also maintains an *accounts payable subsidiary ledger,* showing the amount owed to each creditor. Many merchandising companies also maintain an *inventory subsidiary ledger,* with a separate account for each type of merchandise that the company sells. Thus the inventory ledger of a large department store contains thousands of accounts. Each of these accounts shows, for *one type of product,* the quantities, unit costs, and total costs of all units purchased, sold, and currently in inventory.

The diagram on page 224 shows the relationship between several subsidiary ledgers and the related controlling accounts in the general ledger.

**Other Types of Subsidiary Ledgers**   In this chapter we discuss the subsidiary ledgers for inventory, accounts payable, and accounts receivable. However, subsidiary ledgers also are maintained for many other general ledger accounts. The schedule below lists some of the general ledger accounts usually supported by a subsidiary ledger.

| Controlling Account in the General Ledger | Unit of Organization within the Subsidiary Ledger |
| --- | --- |
| Cash | Each bank account |
| Notes Receivable | Each note receivable |
| Accounts Receivable | Each credit customer |
| Inventory | Each type of product offered for sale |
| Plant Assets | Each asset (or group of similar assets) |
| Notes Payable | Each note payable |
| Accounts Payable | Each creditor |
| Capital Stock (only in a business organized as a corporation) | Each stockholder (this ledger shows each stockholder's name, address, and the number of shares owned) |
| Sales (or any revenue account) | Each department, branch location, or product line |
| Cost of Goods Sold | Same organization as the sales ledger |
| Many expense accounts | Each department incurring these types of expense |
| Payroll Expenses (including payroll taxes) | Each employee |

Subsidiary ledgers are intended to meet the information needs of the company's *managers and employees.* These accounting records are *not* used in the preparation of financial statements, nor are they usually made available to persons outside of the business organization.

**Subsidiary Ledgers in Computer-Based Systems**   At first, it may seem that maintaining subsidiary ledgers with hundreds or thousands of separate accounts would involve a great deal of work. However, business organizations big enough to require large subsidiary ledgers use computer-based accounting systems. In a computer-based accounting system, subsidiary ledger accounts and general ledger control accounts are posted *automatically* as transactions are recorded. In addition, the computer automatically reconciles the subsidiary ledgers with the controlling accounts. Thus no significant effort is required of accounting personnel to maintain subsidiary ledgers in a computer-based system.

*General ledger accounts supported by a subsidiary ledger*

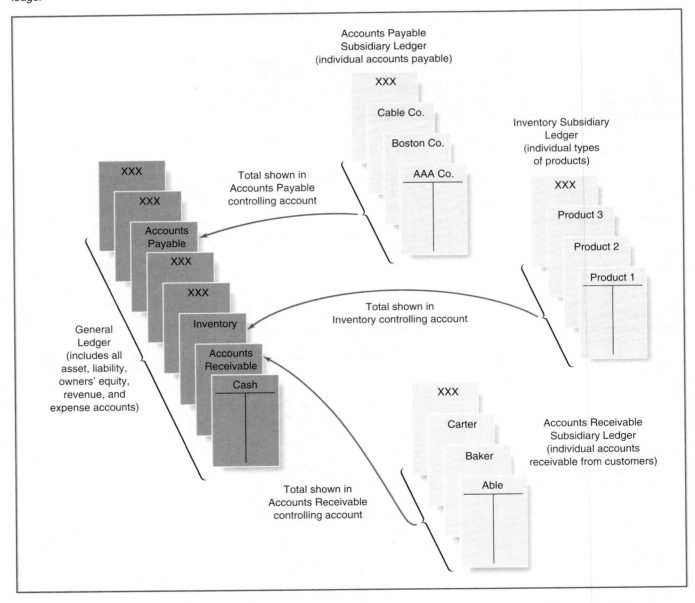

## You as a Credit Manager

Assume you are the credit manager for Wilson, Inc., a small manufacturer of toys. You have just received a request from Dave's Toy Store asking that the store's credit limit be increased from $30,000 to $50,000. Dave has been a customer of Wilson for the past five years.

Describe the information that you can obtain from the accounts receivable ledger that will assist you in making the decision about whether to increase Dave's credit limit. What *other information* would assist you in making this decision?

*Our comments appear on page 258.

**YOUR TURN**

## Two Approaches Used in Accounting for Merchandising Transactions

Either of two approaches may be used in accounting for merchandising transactions: (1) a *perpetual inventory system* or (2) a *periodic inventory system*. In the past, both systems were in widespread use. Today, however, most large businesses (and many smaller ones) use computers to assist in maintaining perpetual systems. Periodic systems are used primarily in small businesses with manual accounting systems.

## PERPETUAL INVENTORY SYSTEMS

In a **perpetual inventory system**, merchandising transactions are recorded *as they occur.* The system draws its name from the fact that the accounting records are kept perpetually up-to-date. Purchases of merchandise are recorded by debiting an asset account entitled Inventory. When merchandise is sold, two entries are necessary: one to recognize the *revenue earned* and the second to recognize the related *cost of goods sold.*[1] This second entry also reduces the balance of the Inventory account to reflect the sale of some of the company's inventory.

A perpetual inventory system uses an *inventory subsidiary ledger.* This ledger provides company personnel with up-to-date information about each type of product that the company buys and sells, including the per-unit cost and the number of units purchased, sold, and currently on hand.

To illustrate the perpetual inventory system, we follow specific items of merchandise through the operating cycle of Computer Barn, a retail store. The transactions comprising this illustration are as follows:

**LO 3**

Account for purchases and sales of merchandise in a *perpetual* inventory system.

**Sept. 1** Purchased 10 Regent CX-21 computer monitors on account from Okawa Wholesale Co. The monitors cost $600 each, for a total of $6,000; payment is due in 30 days.

**Sept. 7** Sold two monitors on account to RJ Travel Agency at a retail sales price of $1,000 each, for a total of $2,000. Payment is due in 30 days.

**Oct. 1** Paid the $6,000 account payable to Okawa Wholesale Co.

**Oct. 7** Collected the $2,000 account receivable from RJ Travel Agency.

In addition to a general ledger, Computer Barn maintains separate subsidiary ledgers for accounts receivable, inventory, and accounts payable.

---

[1] In some perpetual systems, only the number of *units* sold is recorded at the time of sale, and the dollar costs are entered at a later date—perhaps monthly. Such variations in perpetual systems are discussed in Chapter 8.

**Purchases of Merchandise**    Purchases of inventory are recorded at cost. Thus Computer Barn records its purchase of the 10 computer monitors on September 1 as follows:

*Purchase of merchandise: the start of the cycle*

| | | |
|---|---:|---:|
| Inventory | 6,000 | |
|     Accounts Payable (Okawa Wholesale Co.) | | 6,000 |
| Purchased 10 Regent CX-21 computer monitors for $600 each; payment due in 30 days. | | |

    The data contained in this entry are posted to the general ledger *and to the subsidiary ledgers*. First, the entry is posted to the Inventory and Accounts Payable controlling accounts in the general ledger. The debit to Inventory also is posted to the Regent CX-21 Monitors account in the inventory subsidiary ledger.[2] The quantity of monitors purchased (10) and the per-unit cost ($600) also are recorded in this subsidiary ledger account. (This subsidiary ledger account is illustrated on the following page.) The credit to Accounts Payable also is posted to the account for Okawa Wholesale Co. in Computer Barn's accounts payable subsidiary ledger.

**Sales of Merchandise**    The revenue earned in a sales transaction is equal to the *sales price* of the merchandise and is credited to a revenue account entitled Sales. Except in rare circumstances, sales revenue is considered realized when the merchandise is *delivered to the customer,* even if the sale is made on account. Therefore, Computer Barn will recognize the revenue from the sale to RJ Travel Agency on September 7, as follows:

*Entries to record a sale . . .*

| | | |
|---|---:|---:|
| Accounts Receivable (RJ Travel Agency) | 2,000 | |
|     Sales | | 2,000 |
| Sold two Regent CX-21 monitors for $1,000 each; payment due in 30 days. | | |

    The *matching principle* requires that revenue be matched (offset) with all of the costs and expenses incurred in producing that revenue. Therefore, a *second journal entry* is required at the date of sale to record the cost of goods sold.

*and the related cost of goods sold*

| | | |
|---|---:|---:|
| Cost of Goods Sold | 1,200 | |
|     Inventory | | 1,200 |
| To transfer the cost of two Regent CX-21 monitors ($600 each) from Inventory to the Cost of Goods Sold account. | | |

Notice that this second entry is based on the *cost* of the merchandise to Computer Barn, not on its retail sales price. The per-unit cost of the Regent monitors ($600) was determined from the inventory subsidiary ledger (see page 227).

    Both of the journal entries relating to this sales transaction are posted to Computer Barn's general ledger. In addition, the $2,000 debit to Accounts Receivable (first entry) is posted to the account for RJ Travel Agency in the accounts receivable ledger. The credit to Inventory (second entry) also is posted to the Regent CX-21 Monitors account in the inventory subsidiary ledger.

**Payment of Accounts Payable to Suppliers**    The payment to Okawa Wholesale Co. on October 1 is recorded as follows:

*Payment of an account payable*

| | | |
|---|---:|---:|
| Accounts Payable (Okawa Wholesale Co.) | 6,000 | |
|     Cash | | 6,000 |
| Paid account payable. | | |

---

[2] In journal entries, it is common practice to indicate specific suppliers and customers using a parenthetical note following the account title Accounts Payable or Accounts Receivable. Similar notations usually are *not* used with the Inventory account, because *many different types of products* may be purchased or sold in a single transaction. The detailed product information used in posting to the inventory ledger is found in the *invoice* (bill) that the seller sends to the buyer.

Both portions of this entry are posted to the general ledger. In addition, payment of the account payable is entered in the Okawa Wholesale Co. account in the Computer Barn's accounts payable subsidiary ledger.

**Collection of Accounts Receivable from Customers**   On October 7, collection of the account receivable from RJ Travel Agency is recorded as follows:

| | | |
|---|---|---|
| Cash ............................................................ | 2,000 | |
|     Accounts Receivable (RJ Travel Agency) .......................... | | 2,000 |
| Collected an account receivable from a credit customer. | | |

*Collection of an account receivable*

Both portions of this entry are posted to the general ledger; the credit to Accounts Receivable also is posted to the RJ Travel Agency account in the accounts receivable ledger.

Collection of the cash from RJ Travel Agency completes Computer Barn's operating cycle with respect to these two units of merchandise.

**The Inventory Subsidiary Ledger**   An inventory subsidiary ledger includes a separate account for each type of product in the company's inventory. Computer Barn's subsidiary inventory record for Regent monitors is illustrated below.

*Inventory subsidary ledger account*

Inventory

| Item Regent CX-21 | | | | Primary supplier Okawa Wholesale Co. | | | | | |
|---|---|---|---|---|---|---|---|---|---|
| Description Computer monitor | | | | Secondary supplier Forbes Importers, Inc. | | | | | |
| Location Storeroom 2 | | | | Inventory level: Min 2 Max 10 | | | | | |

| | Purchased | | | Sold | | | Balance | | |
|---|---|---|---|---|---|---|---|---|---|
| Date | Units | Unit Cost | Total | Units | Unit Cost | Cost of Goods Sold | Units | Unit Cost | Total |
| Sept 1 | 10 | $600 | $6,000 | | | | 10 | $600 | $6,000 |
| 7 | | | | 2 | $600 | $1,200 | 8 | $600 | $4,800 |

When Regent CX-21 monitors are purchased, the quantity, unit cost, and total cost are entered in this subsidiary ledger account. When any of these monitors are sold, the number of units, unit cost, and total cost of the units sold also are recorded in this subsidiary ledger account. After each purchase or sales transaction, the Balance columns are updated to show the quantity, unit cost, and total cost of the monitors still on hand.[3]

An inventory ledger provides useful information to a variety of company personnel. A few examples of the company personnel who utilize this information on a daily basis are the following:

- *Sales managers* use the inventory ledger to see at a glance which products are selling quickly and which are not.

---

[3] In our illustration, all of the Regent monitors were purchased on the same date and have the same unit cost. Often a company's inventory of a given product includes units acquired at several *different* per-unit costs. This situation is addressed in Chapter 8.

- *Accounting personnel* use these records to determine the unit costs of merchandise sold.
- *Sales personnel* use this subsidiary ledger to determine the quantities of specific products currently on hand and the physical location of this merchandise.
- *Employees responsible for ordering merchandise* refer to the inventory ledger to determine when specific products should be reordered, the quantities to order, and the names of major suppliers.

## Taking a Physical Inventory

The basic characteristic of the perpetual inventory system is that the Inventory account is *continuously updated* for all purchases and sales of merchandise. When a *physical inventory* is taken, management uses the inventory ledger to determine on a product-by-product basis whether inventory on hand corresponds to the amount indicated in the inventory subsidiary ledger. Over time normal inventory shrinkage may cause some discrepancies between the quantities of merchandise shown in the inventory records and the quantities actually on hand. **Inventory shrinkage** refers to unrecorded decreases in inventory resulting from such factors as breakage, spoilage, employee theft, and shoplifting.

In order to ensure the accuracy of their perpetual inventory records, most businesses take a *complete physical count* of the merchandise on hand at least once a year. This procedure is called **taking a physical inventory**, and it usually is performed near year-end.

Once the quantity of merchandise on hand has been determined by a physical count, the per-unit costs in the inventory ledger accounts are used to determine the total cost of the inventory. The Inventory controlling account and the accounts in the inventory subsidiary ledger then are *adjusted* to the quantities and dollar amounts indicated by the physical inventory.

To illustrate, assume that at year-end the Inventory controlling account and inventory subsidiary ledger of Computer Barn both show an inventory with a cost of $72,200. A physical count, however, reveals that some of the merchandise listed in the accounting records is missing; the items actually on hand have a total cost of $70,000. Computer Barn would make the following adjusting entry to correct its Inventory controlling account:

*Adjusting for inventory shrinkage*

| | | |
|---|---|---|
| Cost of Goods Sold . . . . . . . . . . . . . . . . . . . . . . . . . . . . . . . . . . . . . . . . . . . . . | 2,200 | |
|     Inventory . . . . . . . . . . . . . . . . . . . . . . . . . . . . . . . . . . . . . . . . . . . . . | | 2,200 |

To adjust the perpetual inventory records to reflect the results of the year-end physical count.

Computer Barn also will adjust the appropriate accounts in its inventory subsidiary ledger to reflect the quantities indicated by the physical count.

Reasonable amounts of inventory shrinkage are viewed as a normal cost of doing business and simply are debited to the Cost of Goods Sold account, as illustrated above.[4]

## Closing Entries in a Perpetual Inventory System

As explained and illustrated in the previous chapters, revenue and expense accounts are *closed* at the end of each accounting period. A merchandising business with a perpetual inventory system makes closing entries that parallel those of a service-type business. The Sales account is a revenue account and is closed into the Income Summary account along with other revenue accounts. The Cost of Goods Sold account is closed into the Income Summary account in the same manner as the other expense accounts.

---

[4] If a large inventory shortage is caused by an event such as a fire or theft, the cost of the missing or damaged merchandise may be debited to a special loss account, such as Fire Loss. In the income statement, a loss is deducted from revenue in the same manner as an expense.

**You as the Audit Senior on the Audit of Computer Barn**

The auditors of large, publicly traded merchandising companies are required to investigate the balances of inventory accounts. In order to evaluate the reasonableness of these account balances, auditors use physical observation of the inventory as part of the evaluation process. Assume you are the Audit Senior on the audit of Computer Barn. You have arrived at one of Computer Barn's stores to observe a sample of the inventory on hand. The store manager tells you that it is too dangerous for you to access the storage room to observe the physical inventory because merchandise is being unloaded. What should you do?

*Our comments appear on page 258.

YOUR TURN

## PERIODIC INVENTORY SYSTEMS

A **periodic inventory system** is an *alternative* to a perpetual inventory system. In a periodic inventory system, no effort is made to keep up-to-date records of either the inventory or the cost of goods sold. Instead, these amounts are determined only periodically—usually at the end of each year.

### Operation of a Periodic Inventory System

A traditional periodic inventory system operates as follows. When merchandise is purchased, its cost is debited to an account entitled *Purchases,* rather than to the Inventory account. When merchandise is sold, an entry is made to recognize the sales revenue, but *no entry* is made to record the cost of goods sold or to reduce the balance of the Inventory account. As the inventory records are not updated as transactions occur, there is no inventory subsidiary ledger.

**LO 4**
Explain how a *periodic* inventory system operates.

The foundation of the periodic inventory system is the taking of a *complete physical inventory* at year-end. This physical count determines the amount of inventory appearing in the balance sheet. The cost of goods sold for the entire year then is determined by a short computation.

**Data for an Illustration**  To illustrate, assume that Special Occasions, a party supply store, has a periodic inventory system. At December 31, 2002, the following information is available:

1. The inventory on hand at the end of *2001* cost $14,000.
2. During *2002,* purchases of merchandise for resale to customers totaled $130,000.
3. Inventory on hand at the end of *2002* cost $12,000.

The inventories at the end of 2001 and at the end of 2002 were determined by taking a complete physical inventory at (or very near) each year-end. (Because the Inventory account was not updated as transactions occurred during 2002, it still shows a balance of $14,000—the inventory on hand at the *beginning* of the year.)

The $130,000 cost of merchandise purchased during 2002 was recorded in the Purchases account.

**Recording Purchases of Merchandise**  Special Occasions made many purchases of merchandise during 2002. The entry to record the first of these purchases is as follows:

```
Jan. 6   Purchases  . . . . . . . . . . . . . . . . . . . . . . . . . . . . . . . . . . . . . . . 2,000
                 Accounts Payable (Paper Products Co.)  . . . . . . . . . . . . . . . . . . .        2,000
             Purchased inventory on account; payment due in 30 days.
```

This entry was posted to the Purchases and Accounts Payable accounts in the general ledger. The credit portion also was posted to the account for Paper Products Co. in Special Occasions' accounts payable subsidiary ledger. The debit to Purchases was *not* "double-posted," as there is *no inventory subsidiary ledger* in a periodic system.

**Computing the Cost of Goods Sold**  The year-end inventory is determined by taking a complete physical count of the merchandise on hand. Once the ending inventory is known, the cost of goods sold for the entire year can be determined by a short computation. This computation is shown below, using the numbered information items for Special Occasions presented on page 229:

*Computation of the cost of goods sold*

| | |
|---|---:|
| Inventory (beginning of the year) (1) . . . . . . . . . . . . . . . . . . . . . . . . . . . . . . . . . . . | $ 14,000 |
| Add: Purchases (2) . . . . . . . . . . . . . . . . . . . . . . . . . . . . . . . . . . . . . . . . . . . | 130,000 |
| Cost of goods available for sale . . . . . . . . . . . . . . . . . . . . . . . . . . . . . . . . . . . | $144,000 |
| Less: Inventory (end of the year) (3) . . . . . . . . . . . . . . . . . . . . . . . . . . . . . . . . | 12,000 |
| Cost of goods sold . . . . . . . . . . . . . . . . . . . . . . . . . . . . . . . . . . . . . . . . . . | $132,000 |

**Recording Inventory and the Cost of Goods Sold**  Special Occasions has now determined its inventory at the end of 2002 and its cost of goods sold for the year. But neither of these amounts has yet been recorded in the company's accounting records.

In a periodic system, the ending inventory and the cost of goods sold are recorded during the company's year-end *closing procedures*. (The term *closing procedures* refers to the end-of-period adjusting and closing entries.)

## Closing Process in a Periodic Inventory System

There are several different ways of recording the ending inventory and cost of goods sold in a periodic system, but they all produce the same results. One approach is to *create* a Cost of Goods Sold account with the proper balance as part of the closing process. Once this account has been created, the company can complete its closing procedures in the same manner as if a perpetual inventory system had been in use.

**Creating a Cost of Goods Sold Account**  A Cost of Goods Sold account is created with two special closing entries. The first entry creates the new account by bringing together the costs contributing toward the cost of goods sold. The second entry adjusts the Cost of Goods Sold account to its proper balance and records the ending inventory in the Inventory account.

The costs contributing to the cost of goods sold include (1) beginning inventory and (2) purchases made during the year. These costs are brought together by closing both the Inventory account (which contains its beginning-of-the-year balance) and the Purchases account into a new account entitled Cost of Goods Sold. This year-end closing entry is:

*Creating a Cost of Goods Sold account . . .*

```
Dec. 31   Cost of Goods Sold  . . . . . . . . . . . . . . . . . . . . . . . . . . . . . . . .  144,000
                 Inventory (beginning balance)  . . . . . . . . . . . . . . . . . . . . . . .           14,000
                 Purchases  . . . . . . . . . . . . . . . . . . . . . . . . . . . . . . . . . . . . .           130,000
             To close the temporary accounts contributing to the cost of
             goods sold for the year.
```

Special Occasions' Cost of Goods Sold account now includes the cost of all goods *available for sale* during the year. Of course, not all of these goods were sold; the physical inventory taken at the end of 2002 shows that merchandise costing $12,000 is still on hand. Therefore, a second closing entry is made transferring the cost of merchandise still on hand *out* of the Cost of Goods Sold account and *into* the Inventory account. For Special Occasions, this second closing entry is:

| | | | |
|---|---|---|---|
| Dec. 31 | Inventory (year-end balance) | 12,000 | |
| | Cost of Goods Sold | | 12,000 |
| | To reduce the balance of the Cost of Goods Sold account by the cost of merchandise still on hand at year-end. | | |

*and adjusting its balance*

With these two entries, Special Occasions has created a Cost of Goods Sold account with a balance of $132,000 ($144,000 − $12,000) and has brought its Inventory account up-to-date.

**Completing the Closing Process**   Special Occasions may now complete its closing process in the same manner as a company using a perpetual inventory system. The company will make the usual four closing entries, closing the (1) revenue accounts, (2) expense accounts (including Cost of Goods Sold), (3) Income Summary account, and (4) Dividends account.

## Comparison of Perpetual and Periodic Inventory Systems

The table on the following page provides a comparison of the way in which various events are recorded in perpetual and periodic systems. Perpetual systems are used when management needs information throughout the year about inventory levels and gross profit. Periodic systems are used when the primary goals are to develop annual data and to minimize record-keeping requirements. A single business may use *different inventory systems* to account for *different types of merchandise.*

**Who Uses Perpetual Systems?**   When management or employees *need up-to-date information about inventory levels,* there is no substitute for a perpetual inventory system. Almost all manufacturing companies use perpetual systems. These businesses need current information to coordinate their inventories of raw materials with their production schedules. Most large merchandising companies—and many small ones—also use perpetual systems.

In the days when all accounting records were maintained by hand, businesses that sold many types of low-cost products had no choice but to use periodic inventory systems. A **Wal-Mart** store, for example, may sell several thousand items *per hour.* Imagine the difficulty of keeping a perpetual inventory system up-to-date if the records were maintained by hand. But with today's *point-of-sale terminals* and *bar-coded merchandise,* many high-volume retailers now use perpetual inventory systems. In fact, Wal-Mart has been a leader in developing perpetual inventory systems among retailers.

Perpetual inventory systems are not limited to businesses with point-of-sale terminals. Many small businesses with manual accounting systems also use perpetual inventory systems. However, these businesses may update their inventory records on a weekly or a monthly basis, rather than at the time of each sales transaction.

Whether accounting records are maintained manually or by computer, most businesses use perpetual inventory systems in accounting for products with a *high per-unit cost.* Examples include automobiles, heavy machinery, electronic equipment, home appliances, and jewelry. Management has a greater interest in keeping track of inventory when the merchandise is expensive. Also, sales volume usually is low enough that a perpetual system can be used, even if accounting records are maintained by hand.

## A Summary of the Journal Entries Made in Perpetual and Periodic Inventory Systems

| Event | Perpetual System | Periodic System |
|---|---|---|
| *Acquiring merchandise inventory* | Inventory ........................ xxx<br>   Accounts Payable (or Cash) ............ xxx<br>To record the purchase of merchandise inventory. | Purchases ........................ xxx<br>   Accounts Payable (or cash) ............ xxx<br>To record the purchase of merchandise inventory. |
| *Sale of merchandise inventory* | Accounts Receivable (or Cash) ....... xxx<br>   Sales ........................ xxx<br>To record the sale of merchandise inventory.<br><br>Cost of Goods Sold ............... xxx<br>   Inventory ........................ xxx<br>To update Cost of Goods Sold and Inventory accounts. | Accounts Receivable (or Cash) ....... xxx<br>   Sales ........................ xxx<br>To record the sale of merchandise inventory.<br><br>No entry at the time of sale is made in a periodic system to update the Cost of Goods Sold and Inventory accounts. |
| *Settlement of Accounts Payable to suppliers* | Accounts Payable ............... xxx<br>   Cash ........................ xxx<br>To record payment of merchandise inventory purchased on account. | Accounts Payable ............... xxx<br>   Cash ........................ xxx<br>To record payment of merchandise inventory purchased on account. |
| *Collections from credit customers* | Cash ........................ xxx<br>   Accounts Receivable ............ xxx<br>To record cash collections from credit customers. | Cash ........................ xxx<br>   Accounts Receivable ............ xxx<br>To record cash collections from credit customers. |
| *Creating year-end balances for Cost of Goods Sold and Inventory accounts* | No entry necessary. Cost of Goods Sold and Inventory accounts *should* both reflect year-end balances in a perpetual system. If a year-end physical count reveals *less* inventory on hand than reported in the Inventory account, the following entry is needed to record inventory shrinkage:<br><br>Cost of Goods Sold ............... xxx<br>   Inventory (shrinkage amount) ......... xxx<br>To reduce year-end inventory balance for shrinkage. | Cost of Goods Sold ............... xxx<br>Inventory (beginning balance)<br>   Purchases ........................ xxx<br>To close the Purchases and Inventory balances to the Cost of Goods Sold account.<br><br>Inventory (ending balance) ......... xxx<br>   Cost of Goods Sold ............... xxx<br>To create the year-end balance in the Inventory account. |

*Note:* In a periodic inventory system, the Cost of Goods Sold account is both debited and credited to create its year-end balance.

**Who Uses Periodic Systems?**   Periodic systems are used when the need for current information about inventories and sales *does not justify the cost* of maintaining a perpetual system. In a small retail store, for example, the owner may be so familiar with the inventory that formal perpetual inventory records are unnecessary. Most businesses— large and small—use periodic systems for inventories that are *immaterial* in dollar amount, or when management has little interest in the quantities on hand. As stated previously, businesses that sell many low-cost items and have manual accounting systems sometimes have no choice but to use the periodic method.

**Dale's Market** is a small grocery store in San Diego, California. Sales are recorded on a mechanical cash register at the checkout stand. The daily register tapes show only the sales prices of the items sold. Even if Dale were willing to spend all night updating his inventory records, he has no place to start. His accounting system does not indicate the types or costs of products sold during the day.

**CASE IN POINT**

## Selecting an Inventory System

**LO 5**

Discuss the factors to be considered in selecting an inventory system.

Accountants—and business managers—often must select an inventory system appropriate for a particular situation. Some of the factors usually considered in these decisions are listed below:

| Factors Suggesting a Perpetual Inventory System | Factors Suggesting a Periodic Inventory System |
| --- | --- |
| Large company with professional management. | Small company, run by owner. |
| Management and employees wanting information about items in inventory and the quantities of specific products that are selling. | Accounting records of inventories and specific product sales not needed in daily operations; such information developed primarily for use in annual income tax returns. |
| Items in inventory with a high per-unit cost. | Inventory with many different kinds of low-cost items. |
| Low volume of sales transactions or a computerized accounting system (for example, point-of-sale terminals). | High volume of sales transactions and a manual accounting system. |
|  | Lack of full-time accounting personnel. |
| Merchandise stored at multiple locations or in warehouses separate from the sales sites. | All merchandise stored at the sales site (for example, in the store). |

**The Trend in Today's Business World**   Advances in technology are quickly extending the use of perpetual inventory systems to more businesses and more types of inventory. This trend is certain to continue. Throughout this textbook, you may assume that a *perpetual inventory system* is in use unless we specifically state otherwise.

**YOUR TURN**

### You as a Buyer for a Retail Business

Assume you are in charge of purchasing merchandise for Acme Hardware Stores. You are currently making a decision about the purchase of barbecue grills for sale during the upcoming summer season. You must decide how many of each brand and type of grill to order. Describe the types of accounting information that would be useful in making this decision and where this information might be found.

*Our comments appear on page 258.

## MODIFYING AN ACCOUNTING SYSTEM

**LO 6**

Define *special journals* and explain their usefulness.

Throughout this textbook we illustrate the effects of many transactions using the format of a two-column *general journal*. This format is ideal for textbook illustrations, as it allows us to concisely show the effects of *any type* of business transactions.

But while general journal entries are useful for our purposes, they are not the most efficient way for a business to record routine transactions. A supermarket, for example, may sell 10,000 to 15,000 items *per hour*. Clearly, it would not be practical to make a general journal entry to record each of these sales transactions. Therefore, most businesses use *special journals,* rather than a general journal, to record *routine transactions that occur frequently.*

### Special Journals Provide Speed and Efficiency

A **special journal** is an accounting record or device designed to record *a specific type of routine transaction quickly and efficiently.*

Some special journals are maintained by hand. An example is the *check register* in your personal checkbook. If properly maintained, this special journal provides an efficient record of all cash disbursements made by check.

But many special journals are highly automated. Consider the **point-of-sale (POS) terminals** that you see in supermarkets and large retail stores. These devices record sales transactions and the related cost of goods sold as quickly as the bar-coded merchandise can be passed over the scanner.

Relative to the general journal, the special journals offer the following advantages:

- Transactions are recorded faster and more efficiently.
- Many special journals may be in operation at one time, further increasing the company's ability to handle a large volume of transactions.
- Automation may reduce the risk of errors.
- Employees maintaining special journals generally do not need expertise in accounting.
- The recording of transactions may be an automatic side effect of other basic business activities, such as collecting cash from customers.

Most businesses use separate special journals to record repetitive transactions such as sales of merchandise, cash receipts, cash payments, purchases of merchandise on account, and payrolls. There are no rules for the design or content of special journals. Rather, they are tailored to suit the needs, activities, and resources of the particular business organization.

Let us stress that the *accounting principles* used in special journals are the *same* as those used for transactions recorded in a general journal. The differences lie in the *recording techniques,* not in the information that is recorded.

Remember also that special journals are *highly specialized* in terms of the transactions they can record. Thus every business still needs a general journal to record transactions that do not fit into any of its special journals, including, for example, adjusting entries, closing entries, and unusual events such as a loss sustained from a fire.

## TRANSACTIONS RELATING TO PURCHASES

In addition to the basic transactions illustrated and explained in this chapter, merchandising companies must account for a variety of additional transactions relating to purchases of merchandise. Examples include discounts offered for prompt payment, merchandise returns, and transportation costs. In our discussion of these transactions, we continue to assume the use of a *perpetual* inventory system.

**LO 7**

Account for additional merchandising transactions related to purchases and sales.

### Credit Terms and Cash Discounts

Manufacturers and wholesalers normally sell their products to merchandisers *on account*. The credit terms are stated in the seller's bill, or *invoice*. One common example of credit terms is "net 30 days," or "n/30," meaning full payment is due in 30 days. Another common form of credit terms is "10 eom," meaning payment is due 10 days after the end of the month in which the purchase occurred.

Manufacturers and wholesalers usually allow their customers 30 or 60 days in which to pay for credit purchases. Frequently, however, sellers offer their customers a small discount to encourage earlier payment.

Perhaps the most common credit terms offered by manufacturers and wholesalers are *2/10, n/30*. This expression is read "2, 10, net 30," and means that full payment is due in 30 days, but that the buyer may take a *2% discount* if payment is made within 10 days. The period during which the discount is available is termed the *discount period*. Because the discount provides an incentive for the customer to make an early cash payment, it is called a *cash discount*. Buyers, however, often refer to these discounts as *purchase discounts*, while sellers frequently call them *sales discounts*.

Most well-managed companies have a policy of taking advantage of all cash discounts available on purchases of merchandise.[5] These companies initially record purchases of merchandise at the *net cost*—that is, the invoice price *minus* any available discount. After all, this is the amount that the company expects to pay.

To illustrate, assume that on November 3 Computer Barn purchases 100 spreadsheet programs from PC Products. The cost of these programs is $100 each, for a total of $10,000. However, PC Products offers credit terms of 2/10, n/30. If Computer Barn pays for this purchase within the discount period, it will have to pay only *$9,800*, or 98% of the full invoice price. Therefore, Computer Barn will record this purchase as follows:

| | | |
|---|---|---|
| Inventory . . . . . . . . . . . . . . . . . . . . . . . . . . . . . . . . . . . . . . . . . . . . . . . . . . . . . . | 9,800 | |
|     Accounts Payable (PC Products) . . . . . . . . . . . . . . . . . . . . . . . . . . . . . . | | 9,800 |
| To record purchase of 100 spreadsheet programs at net cost | | |
|   ($100 × 98% × 100 units). | | |

*Purchase recorded at net cost*

If the invoice is paid within the discount period, Computer Barn simply records payment of a $9,800 account payable.

---

[5] The terms 2/10, n/30 offer the buyer a 2% discount for sending payment 20 days before it is otherwise due. Saving 2% over only 20 days is equivalent to earning an annual rate of return of more than 36% (2% × 365/20 = 36.5%). Thus taking cash discounts represents an excellent investment opportunity. Most companies take advantage of all cash discounts, even if they must borrow the necessary cash from a bank to make payment within the discount period.

Through oversight or carelessness, Computer Barn might fail to make payment within the discount period. In this event, Computer Barn must pay PC Products the entire invoice price of *$10,000*, rather than the recorded liability of $9,800. The journal entry to record payment *after the discount period*—on, say, December 3—is:

*Recording the loss of a cash discount*

| | | |
|---|---|---|
| Accounts Payable (PC Products) . . . . . . . . . . . . . . . . . . . . . . . . . . . . . . . . . . . | 9,800 | |
| Purchase Discounts Lost . . . . . . . . . . . . . . . . . . . . . . . . . . . . . . . | 200 | |
|    Cash . . . . . . . . . . . . . . . . . . . . . . . . . . . . . . . . . . . . . . | | 10,000 |

To record payment of invoice after expiration of discount period.

Notice that the $200 paid above the $9,800 recorded amount is debited to an account entitled Purchase Discounts Lost. Purchase Discounts Lost is an *expense account*. The only benefit to Computer Barn from this $200 expenditure was a *20-day delay* in paying an account payable. Thus the lost purchase discount is basically a *finance charge*, similar to interest expense. In an income statement, finance charges usually are classified as nonoperating expenses.

The fact that purchase discounts *not taken* are recorded in a separate expense account is the primary reason why a company should record purchases of merchandise at *net cost*. The use of a Purchase Discounts Lost account immediately brings to management's attention any failure to take advantage of the cash discounts offered by suppliers.

**Recording Purchases at Gross Invoice Price**  As an alternative to recording purchases at net cost, some companies record merchandise purchases at the gross (total) invoice price. If payment is made within the discount period, these companies must record the amount of the purchase discount *taken*.

To illustrate, assume that Computer Barn followed a policy of recording purchases at gross invoice price. The entry on November 3 to record the purchase from PC Products would have been:

*Purchases recorded at gross price*

| | | |
|---|---|---|
| Inventory . . . . . . . . . . . . . . . . . . . . . . . . . . . . . . . . . . . . . . . . . . . . . . . . | 10,000 | |
|    Accounts Payable (PC Products) . . . . . . . . . . . . . . . . . . . . . . . . . . . . | | 10,000 |

To record purchase of 100 spreadsheet programs at gross invoice price ($100 × 100 units).

If payment is made within the discount period, Computer Barn will discharge this $10,000 account payable by paying only $9,800. The entry will be:

*Buyer records discounts taken*

| | | |
|---|---|---|
| Accounts Payable (PC Products) . . . . . . . . . . . . . . . . . . . . . . . . . . . . . . . . | 10,000 | |
|    Cash . . . . . . . . . . . . . . . . . . . . . . . . . . . . . . . . . . . . . . . . . | | 9,800 |
|    Purchase Discounts Taken . . . . . . . . . . . . . . . . . . . . . . . . . . . . . . | | 200 |

Paid a $10,000 invoice within the discount period; taking a 2% purchase discount.

*Purchase Discounts Taken* is treated as a reduction in the cost of goods sold.

Both the net cost and gross price methods are widely used and produce substantially the same results in financial statements.[6]

**MANAGEMENT STRATEGY**

A shortcoming of the gross price method as compared to the net cost method for valuing inventory is that it does not direct management's attention to discounts lost. Instead these discounts are buried in the costs assigned to inventory. Management can use financial reporting policies to motivate the purchasing staff to take advantage of purchase discounts when possible. By recording inventory with the net cost method, management can highlight the success of their purchasing efforts to obtain the lowest possible costs for purchased inventory. Because of the advantage of the net cost method, it is the approach recommended by the authors of this textbook.

---

[6] The net cost method values the ending inventory at net cost, whereas the gross cost method shows this inventory at gross invoice price. This difference, however, is usually *immaterial*.

## Returns of Unsatisfactory Merchandise

On occasion, a buyer may find the purchased merchandise unsatisfactory and want to return it to the seller for a refund. Most sellers permit such returns.

To illustrate, assume that on November 9 Computer Barn returns to PC Products five of the spreadsheet programs purchased on November 3, because these programs were not properly labeled. As Computer Barn has not yet paid for this merchandise, the return will reduce the amount that Computer Barn owes PC Products. The gross invoice price of the returned merchandise was $500 ($100 per program). Assume that Computer Barn records purchases at *net cost*. Therefore, these spreadsheet programs are carried in Computer Barn's inventory subsidiary ledger at a per-unit cost of *$98*, or $490 for the five programs being returned. The entry to record this purchase return is:

| | | |
|---|---|---|
| Accounts Payable (PC Products) ........................................ | 490 | |
|     Inventory ................................................................ | | 490 |
| Returned five mislabeled spreadsheet programs to supplier. Net | | |
|   cost of the returned items, $490 ($100 × 98% × 5 units). | | |

*Return is based on recorded acquisition cost*

The reduction in inventory must also be recorded in the subsidiary ledger accounts.

## Transportation Costs on Purchases

The purchaser sometimes may pay the costs of having the purchased merchandise delivered to its premises. Transportation costs relating to the *acquisition* of inventory, or any other asset, are *not expenses* of the current period; rather, these charges are *part of the cost of the asset* being acquired.[7] If the purchaser is able to associate transportation costs with specific products, these costs should be debited directly to the Inventory account as part of the cost of the merchandise.

Often, many different products arrive in a single shipment. In such cases, it may be impractical for the purchaser to determine the amount of the total transportation cost applicable to each product. For this reason, many companies follow the convenient policy of debiting all transportation costs on inbound shipments of merchandise to an account entitled *Transportation-in*. The dollar amount of transportation-in usually is too small to show separately in the financial statements. Therefore, it is often simply added to the amount reported in the income statement as cost of goods sold.

This treatment of transportation costs is not entirely consistent with the *matching principle*. Some of the transportation costs apply to merchandise still in inventory rather than to goods sold during the current period. We have mentioned, however, that transportation costs are relatively small in dollar amount. The accounting principle of *materiality,* therefore, usually justifies accounting for these costs in the most convenient manner.

## TRANSACTIONS RELATING TO SALES

Credit terms and merchandise returns also affect the amount of sales revenue earned by the seller. To the extent that credit customers take advantage of cash discounts or return merchandise for a refund, the seller's revenue is reduced. Thus revenue shown in the income statement of a merchandising concern is often called *net sales*.

The term **net sales** means total sales revenue *minus* sales returns and allowances and *minus* sales discounts. The following partial income statement illustrates this relationship:

---

[7] The cost of an asset includes all reasonable and necessary costs of getting the asset to an appropriate location and putting it into usable condition.

*What are net sales?*

| COMPUTER BARN<br>Partial Income Statement<br>For the Year Ended December 31, 2002 | | | |
|---|---|---|---|
| **Revenue:** | | | |
| Sales | | | $912,000 |
| Less: Sales returns and allowances | | $8,000 | |
| Sales discounts | | 4,000 | 12,000 |
| Net sales | | | $900,000 |

The details of this computation seldom are shown in an actual income statement. The normal practice is to begin the income statement with the amount of net sales.

## Sales Returns and Allowances

Most merchandising companies allow customers to obtain a refund by returning any merchandise considered to be unsatisfactory. If the merchandise has only minor defects, customers sometimes agree to keep the merchandise if an *allowance* (reduction) is made in the sales price.

Under the perpetual inventory system, two entries are needed to record the sale of merchandise: one to recognize the revenue earned and the other to transfer the cost of the merchandise from the Inventory account to Cost of Goods Sold. If some of the merchandise is returned, both of these entries are partially reversed.

First, let us consider the effects on revenue of granting either a refund or an allowance. Both refunds and allowances have the effect of nullifying previously recorded sales and reducing the amount of revenue earned by the business. The journal entry to reduce sales revenue as the result of a sales return (or allowance) is shown below:

*A sales return reverses recorded revenue . . .*

| | | |
|---|---|---|
| Sales Returns and Allowances | 200 | |
|     Accounts Receivable (or Cash) | | 200 |
| Customer returned merchandise purchased on account for | | |
|   $200. Allowed customer full credit for returned merchandise. | | |

Sales Returns and Allowances is a **contra-revenue account**—that is, it is deducted from gross sales revenue as a step in determining net sales.

Why use a separate Sales Returns and Allowances account rather than merely debiting the Sales account? The answer is that using a separate contra-revenue account enables management to see both the total amount of sales *and* the amount of sales returns. The relationship between these amounts gives management an indication of *customer satisfaction* with the merchandise.

If merchandise is returned by the customer, a second entry is made to remove the cost of this merchandise from the Cost of Goods Sold account and restore it to the inventory records. This entry is:

*and the recorded cost of goods sold*

| | | |
|---|---|---|
| Inventory | 160 | |
|     Cost of Goods Sold | | 160 |
| To restore in the Inventory account the cost of merchandise returned by a customer. | | |

Notice that this entry is based on the *cost* of the returned merchandise to the seller, *not on its sales price*. (This entry is not necessary when a sales *allowance* is granted to a customer who keeps the merchandise.)

Special accounts are maintained in the inventory subsidiary ledger for returned merchandise. Often this merchandise will be returned to the supplier or sold to a damaged-goods liquidator rather than being offered again for sale to the company's regular customers.[8]

## Sales Discounts

We have explained that sellers frequently offer cash discounts, such as 2/10, n/30, to encourage customers to make early payments for purchases on account.

Sellers and buyers account for cash discounts quite differently. To the seller, the cost associated with cash discounts is not the discounts *lost* when payments are delayed, but rather the discounts *taken* by customers who do pay within the discount period. Therefore, sellers design their accounting systems to measure the sales discounts *taken* by their customers. To achieve this goal, the seller records the sale and the related account receivable at the *gross* (full) invoice price.

To illustrate, assume that Computer Barn sells merchandise to Susan Hall for $1,000, offering terms of 2/10, n/30. The sales revenue is recorded at the full invoice price, as follows:

| | | |
|---|---|---|
| Accounts Receivable (Susan Hall) | 1,000 | |
| Sales | | 1,000 |
| Sold merchandise on account. Invoice price, $1,000; terms, 2/10, n/30. | | |

*Sales are recorded at the gross sales price*

If Hall makes payment after the discount period has expired, Computer Barn records the receipt of $1,000 cash in full payment of this account receivable. If Hall pays *within* the discount period, however, she will pay only *$980* to settle her account. In this case, Computer Barn will record the receipt of Hall's payment as follows:

| | | |
|---|---|---|
| Cash | 980 | |
| Sales Discounts | 20 | |
| Accounts Receivable (Susan Hall) | | 1,000 |
| Collected a $1,000 account receivable from a customer who took a 2% discount for early payment. | | |

*Seller records discounts taken by customers*

Sales Discounts is another contra-revenue account. In computing net sales, sales discounts are deducted from gross sales along with any sales returns and allowances. (If the customer has returned part of the merchandise, a discount may be taken only on the gross amount owed *after* the return.)

Contra-revenue accounts have much in common with expense accounts; both are deducted from gross revenue in determining net income, and both have debit balances. Thus contra-revenue accounts (Sales Returns and Allowances and Sales Discounts) are closed to the Income Summary account *in the same manner as expense accounts*.

## Delivery Expenses

If the seller incurs any costs in delivering merchandise to the customer, these costs are debited to an expense account entitled Delivery Expense. In an income statement, delivery expense is classified as a regular operating expense, not as part of the cost of goods sold.

---

[8] An inventory of returned merchandise should not be valued in the accounting records at a cost that exceeds its *net realizable value*. The possible need to write down the carrying value of inventory is discussed in Chapter 8.

## Accounting for Sales Taxes

Sales taxes are levied by many states and cities on retail sales.[9] Sales taxes actually are imposed on the consumer, not on the seller. However, the seller must collect the tax, file tax returns at times specified by law, and remit to governmental agencies the taxes collected.

For cash sales, sales tax is collected from the customer at the time of the sales transaction. For credit sales, the sales tax is included in the amount charged to the customer's account. The liability to the governmental unit for sales taxes may be recorded at the time the sale is made, as shown in the following journal entry:

*Sales tax recorded at time of sale*

| | | |
|---|---|---|
| Cash (or Accounts Receivable) | 1,070 | |
| Sales Tax Payable | | 70 |
| Sales | | 1,000 |
| To record sales of $1,000, subject to 7% sales tax. | | |

This approach requires a separate credit entry to the Sales Tax Payable account for each sale. At first glance, this may seem to require an excessive amount of bookkeeping. However, today's point-of-sale terminals automatically record the sales tax liability at the time of each sale.

## EVALUATING THE PERFORMANCE OF A MERCHANDISING COMPANY

**LO 8**

Measure the performance of a merchandising business.

In evaluating the performance of a merchandising business, managers and investors look at more than just net income. Two key measures of past performance and future prospects are trends in the company's *net sales* and *gross profit*.

## Net Sales

Most investors and business managers consider the *trend* in net sales to be a key indicator of both past performance and future prospects. Increasing sales suggest the probability of larger profits in future periods. Declining sales, on the other hand, may provide advance warning of financial difficulties.

## FINANCIAL ANALYSIS

As a measure of performance, the trend in net sales has some limitations, especially when the company is adding new stores. For these companies, an increase in overall net sales in comparison to the prior year may have resulted solely from sales at the new stores. Sales at existing stores may even be declining. Business managers and investors often focus on measures that adjust for changes in the number of stores from period to period, and on measures of space utilization. These measures include:

1. **Comparable store sales.** Net sales at established stores, excluding new stores opened during the period. Indicates whether customer demand is rising or falling at established locations. (Also called *same-store sales.*)
2. **Sales per square foot of selling space.** A measure of how effectively the company is using its physical facilities (such as floor space or, in supermarkets, shelf space).

---

[9] Sales taxes are applicable only when merchandise is sold to the *final consumer;* thus no sales taxes are normally levied when manufacturers or wholesalers sell merchandise to retailers.

## Gross Profit Margins

Increasing net sales is *not enough* to ensure increasing profitability. Some products are more profitable than others. In evaluating the profitability of sales transactions, managers and investors keep a close eye on the company's **gross profit margin** (also called *gross profit rate*).

Gross profit margin is the dollar amount of gross profit, expressed as a *percentage* of net sales revenue. Gross profit margins can be computed for the business as a whole, for specific sales departments, and for individual products.

To illustrate the computation of gross profit margin, assume that Computer Barn has two separate sales departments. One of these departments sells computer hardware, and the other sells software. The sales, cost of goods sold, and gross profit of these departments in 2002 are as follows:

|  | Hardware Department | Software Department | The Entire Company |
|---|---|---|---|
| Net sales | $400,000 | $500,000 | $900,000 |
| Cost of goods sold | 300,000 | 240,000 | 540,000 |
| Gross profit | $100,000 | $260,000 | $360,000 |

Assume that two products sold in the Software Department: Report Writer (a word processing program) and Dragon Slayer (a computer game). *Per-unit* information about these products follows:

|  | Report Writer | Dragon Slayer |
|---|---|---|
| Sales price | $100 | $50 |
| Cost of goods sold | 65 | 20 |
| Gross profit | $ 35 | $30 |

**The Overall Gross Profit Margin**   The average gross profit margin (gross profit rate) earned by Computer Barn in 2002 is 40% (gross profit, $360,000, divided by net sales, $900,000 = 40%). But each sales department may have a gross profit margin that differs from that of the business viewed as a whole.

**Departmental Profit Margins**   Departmental profit margins are computed using *departmental* gross profit and net sales information, as follows:

| | |
|---|---|
| Hardware Department ($100,000 ÷ $400,000) | 25% |
| Software Department ($260,000 ÷ $500,000) | 52% |

**Profit Margins for Individual Products**   Finally, profit margins can be computed for specific products using *per-unit* amounts:

| | |
|---|---|
| Report Writer ($35 ÷ $100) | 35% |
| Dragon Slayer ($30 ÷ $50) | 60% |

Notice that Dragon Slayer has a higher profit margin, even though Report Writer is the more expensive product. This higher profit margin means that *at a given dollar of sales volume* (say, $10,000 in sales) Dragon Slayer is the more profitable product.

**Using Information about Profit Margins** Investors usually compute companies' overall gross profit rates from one period to the next. High—or increasing—margins generally indicate popular products and successful marketing strategies. A substandard or declining profit margin, on the other hand, often indicates weak customer demand or intense price competition.[10]

---

**CASH EFFECTS** Increasing gross margins do not always result in increased cash flows from operations. In fact, a company with increasing gross margins may actually have *negative* operating cash flows if it is experiencing (1) difficulty in collecting outstanding accounts receivable, (2) a buildup of unsold inventory, or (3) rapidly increasing selling and administrative expenses.

---

Management uses information about departments and products for many purposes. These include setting prices, deciding which products to carry and to advertise, and evaluating the performance of departmental managers. By concentrating sales efforts on the products and departments with the *highest margins,* management usually can increase the company's overall gross profit rate.

**A Closing Comment** Remember that only a perpetual inventory system provides management with current information about departmental gross profit and profit margins. This is the primary reason most large companies use perpetual systems.

**A SECOND LOOK**

**Mall of America**

Many of the Mall of America's 400 retail stores are excellent examples of merchandising companies. Throughout this chapter, we have discussed issues related to how these businesses manage inventory. Retail merchants, like those found at the Mall of America, understand the importance of selling inventory quickly and collecting outstanding receivables on a timely basis. On page 220, we illustrate the cyclical nature of inventory and receivables management in terms of a company's operating cycle.

In Chapter 7, we discuss how merchandising companies actually *measure* how efficiently their receivables are being converted into cash. In Chapter 8, we discuss ways in which these companies measure how quickly their inventory is being sold.

---

[10] We discuss the interpretation of gross profit in greater depth in Chapter 14.

## SUMMARY OF LEARNING OBJECTIVES

### LO 1

**Describe the *operating cycle* of a merchandising company.**
The operating cycle is the repeating sequence of transactions by which a company generates revenue and cash receipts from customers. In a merchandising company, the operating cycle consists of the following transactions: (1) purchases of merchandise, (2) sale of the merchandise—often on account, and (3) collection of accounts receivable from customers.

### LO 2

**Define *subsidiary ledgers* and explain their usefulness.**
Subsidiary ledgers provide a detailed record of the individual items comprising the balance of a general ledger controlling account. With respect to merchandising transactions, subsidiary ledgers are needed to keep track of the amounts receivable from individual customers, the amounts owed to specific suppliers, and the quantities of specific products in inventory.

### LO 3

**Account for purchases and sales of merchandise in a *perpetual* inventory system.**
In a perpetual inventory system, purchases of merchandise are recorded by debiting the asset Inventory account. Two entries are required to record each sale: one to recognize sales revenue and the second to record the cost of goods sold. This second entry consists of a debit to Cost of Goods Sold and a credit to Inventory.

### LO 4

**Explain how a *periodic* inventory system operates.**
In a periodic system, up-to-date records are *not* maintained for inventory or the cost of goods sold. Thus less record keeping is required than in a perpetual system.

The beginning and ending inventories are determined by taking a complete physical count at each year-end. Purchases are recorded in a Purchases account, and no entries are made to record the cost of individual sales transactions. Instead, the cost of goods sold is determined at year-end by a computation such as the following (dollar amounts are provided only for purposes of example):

| | |
|---|---:|
| Beginning inventory | $ 30,000 |
| Add: Purchases | 180,000 |
| Cost of goods available for sale | $210,000 |
| Less: Ending inventory | 40,000 |
| Cost of goods sold | $170,000 |

The amounts of inventory and the cost of goods sold are recorded in the accounting records during the year-end closing procedures.

### LO 5

**Discuss the factors to be considered in selecting an inventory system.**
In general terms, a perpetual system should be used when (1) management and employees need timely information about inventory levels and product sales, and (2) the company has the resources to develop this information at a reasonable cost. A periodic system should be used when the usefulness of current information about inventories does not justify the cost of maintaining a perpetual system.

Perpetual systems are most widely used in large companies with computerized accounting systems and in businesses that sell high-cost merchandise. Periodic systems are most often used in small businesses with manual accounting systems and that sell many types of low-cost merchandise.

### LO 6

**Define *special journals* and explain their usefulness.**
Special journals are accounting records or devices designed to record a specific type of transaction in a highly efficient manner. Because a special journal is used only to record a specific type of transaction, the journal may be located at the transaction site and maintained by employees other than accounting personnel. Thus special journals reduce the time, effort, and cost of recording routine business transactions.

### LO 7

**Account for additional merchandising transactions related to purchases and sales.**
Buyers should record purchases at the net cost and record any cash discounts lost in an expense account. Sellers record sales at the gross sales price and record in a contra-revenue account all cash discounts taken by customers.

The buyer records a purchase return by crediting the Inventory account for the net cost of the returned merchandise. In recording a sales return, the seller makes two entries: one to record Sales Returns and Allowances (a contra-revenue account) for the amount of the refund and the other to transfer the cost of the returned merchandise from the Cost of Goods Sold account back into the Inventory account.

Buyers record transportation charges on purchased merchandise either as part of the cost of the merchandise or directly as part of the cost of goods sold. Sellers view the cost of delivering merchandise to customers as an operating expense.

Sales taxes are collected by retailers from their customers and paid to state and city governments. Thus collecting sales taxes increases the retailer's assets and liabilities. Paying the sales tax to the government is payment of the liability, not an expense.

**LO 8**

**Measure the Performance of a Merchandising Business.**
There are numerous measures used to evaluate the performance of merchandising businesses. In this chapter, we introduced three of these measures: (1) comparable store sales, which helps determine whether customer demand is rising or falling at established locations, (2) sales per square foot of selling space, which is a measure of how effectively a merchandising business is using its facilities to generate revenue, and (3) gross profit percentages, which help users of financial statements gain insight about a company's pricing policies and the demand for its products.

You now have seen how both service-type businesses and merchandising companies measure and report the results of their operations. Many of the illustrations, examples, and assignments throughout the remainder of this textbook will involve merchandising companies.

## KEY TERMS INTRODUCED OR EMPHASIZED IN CHAPTER 6

**comparable store sales** (p. 240) A comparison of sales figures at established stores with existing "track records." (Also called *same-store sales*.)

**contra-revenue account** (p. 238) A debit balance account that is offset against revenue in the income statement. Examples include Sales Discounts and Sales Returns and Allowances.

**controlling account** (p. 223) A general ledger account that summarizes the content of a specific subsidiary ledger.

**cost of goods sold** (p. 221) The cost to a merchandising company of the goods it has sold to its customers during the period.

**gross profit** (p. 221) Net sales revenue minus the cost of goods sold.

**gross profit margin** (p. 241) Gross profit expressed as a percentage of net sales. Also called *gross profit rate*.

**inventory** (p. 220) Merchandise intended for resale to customers.

**inventory shrinkage** (p. 228) The loss of merchandise through such causes as shoplifting, breakage, and spoilage.

**net sales** (p. 237) Gross sales revenue less sales returns and allowances and sales discounts. The most widely used measure of dollar sales volume; usually the first figure shown in an income statement.

**operating cycle** (p. 220) The repeating sequence of transactions by which a business generates its revenue and cash receipts from customers.

**periodic inventory system** (p. 229) An alternative to the perpetual inventory system. It eliminates the need for recording the cost of goods sold as sales occur. However, the amounts of inventory and the cost of goods sold are not known until a complete physical inventory is taken at year-end.

**perpetual inventory system** (p. 225) A system of accounting for merchandising transactions in which the Inventory and Cost of Goods Sold accounts are kept perpetually up-to-date.

**point-of-sale (POS) terminals** (p. 234) Electronic cash registers used for computer-based processing of sales transactions. The POS terminal identifies each item of merchandise from its bar code and then automatically records the sale and updates the computer-based inventory records. These terminals permit the use of perpetual inventory systems in many businesses that sell a high volume of low-cost merchandise.

**sales per square foot of selling space** (p. 240) A measure of efficient use of available space.

**special journal** (p. 234) An accounting record or device designed for recording large numbers of a particular type of transaction quickly and efficiently. A business may use many different kinds of special journals.

**subsidiary ledger** (p. 222) A ledger containing separate accounts for each of the items making up the balance of a controlling account in the general ledger. The total of the account balances in a subsidiary ledger are equal to the balance in the general ledger controlling account.

**taking a physical inventory** (p. 228) The procedure of counting all merchandise on hand and determining its cost.

## ■ DEMONSTRATION PROBLEM

STAR-TRACK sells satellite tracking systems for receiving television broadcasts from communications satellites in space. At December 31, 2001, the company's inventory amounted to $44,000. During the first week in January 2002, STAR-TRACK made only one purchase and one sale. These transactions were as follows:

Jan. 3  Sold a tracking system to Mystery Mountain Resort for $20,000 cash. The system consisted of seven different devices, which had a total cost to STAR-TRACK of $11,200.

Jan. 7  Purchased two Model 400 and four Model 800 satellite dishes from Yamaha Corp. The total cost of this purchase amounted to $10,000; terms 2/10, n/30.

STAR-TRACK records purchases of merchandise at net cost. The company has full-time accounting personnel and uses a manual accounting system.

## Instructions

**a.** Briefly describe the operating cycle of a merchandising company.

**b.** Prepare journal entries to record these transactions, assuming that STAR-TRACK uses a perpetual inventory system.

**c.** Explain what information in part **b** should be posted to subsidiary ledger accounts.

**d.** Compute the balance in the Inventory controlling account at January 7.

**e.** Prepare journal entries to record the two transactions, assuming that STAR-TRACK uses a *periodic* inventory system.

**f.** Compute the cost of goods sold for the first week of January, assuming use of the periodic system. As the amount of ending inventory, use your answer to part **d.**

**g.** Which type of inventory system do you think STAR-TRACK should use? Explain your reasoning.

**h.** Determine the gross profit margin on the January 3 sales transaction.

## Solution to the Demonstration Problem

**a.** The operating cycle of a merchandising company consists of purchasing merchandise, selling that merchandise to customers (often on account), and collecting the sales proceeds from these customers. In the process, the business converts cash into inventory, the inventory into accounts receivable, and the accounts receivable into cash.

**b.** Journal entries assuming use of a *perpetual* inventory system:

| GENERAL JOURNAL | | | |
|---|---|---|---|
| **Date** | **Account Titles and Explanation** | **Debit** | **Credit** |
| 2002 | | | |
| Jan. 3 | Cash ............................................. | 20,000 | |
| | Sales ....................................... | | 20,000 |
| | Sold tracking system to Mystery Mountain Resort. | | |
| 3 | Cost of Goods Sold ............................. | 11,200 | |
| | Inventory .................................. | | 11,200 |
| | To record cost of merchandise sold. | | |
| 7 | Inventory ...................................... | 9,800 | |
| | Accounts Payable (Yamaha Corp.) ........... | | 9,800 |
| | Purchased merchandise. Terms, 2/10, n/30; net cost, $9,800 ($10,000, less 2%). | | |

**c.** The debits and credits to the Inventory account should be posted to the appropriate accounts in the inventory subsidiary ledger. The information posted would be the costs and quantities of the types of merchandise purchased or sold. The account payable to Yamaha also should be posted to the Yamaha account in STAR-TRACK's accounts payable ledger. No postings are required to the accounts receivable ledger, as this was a cash sale. If STAR-TRACK maintains more than one bank account, however, the debit to cash should be posted to the proper account in the cash subsidiary ledger.

**d.** $42,600 ($44,000 beginning balance, less $11,200, plus $9,800).

**e.** Journal entries assuming use of a *periodic* inventory system:

| GENERAL JOURNAL | | |
|---|---|---|
| 2002 | | |
| Jan. 3 Cash . . . . . . . . . . . . . . . . . . . . . . . . . . . . . . . . . . . . . . . . . . . . . . . . . . . | 20,000 | |
| Sales . . . . . . . . . . . . . . . . . . . . . . . . . . . . . . . . . . . . . . . . . . . . . | | 20,000 |
| Sold tracking system to Mystery Mountain Resort. | | |
| 7 Purchases . . . . . . . . . . . . . . . . . . . . . . . . . . . . . . . . . . . . . . . . . . . . | 9,800 | |
| Accounts Payable (Yamaha Corp.) . . . . . . . . . . . . . . . . . . . . . | | 9,800 |
| Purchased merchandise. Terms, 2/10, n/30; net cost, $9,800 ($10,000, less 2%). | | |

**f.** Computation of the cost of goods sold:

| | |
|---|---|
| Inventory, January 1 . . . . . . . . . . . . . . . . . . . . . . . . . . . . . . . . . . . . . . . . . . . . . . . . | $44,000 |
| Add: Purchases . . . . . . . . . . . . . . . . . . . . . . . . . . . . . . . . . . . . . . . . . . . . . . . . . . | 9,800 |
| Cost of goods available for sale . . . . . . . . . . . . . . . . . . . . . . . . . . . . . . . . . . . . . | $53,800 |
| Less: Inventory, January 7 (per part **d**) . . . . . . . . . . . . . . . . . . . . . . . . . . . . . . | 42,600 |
| Cost of goods sold . . . . . . . . . . . . . . . . . . . . . . . . . . . . . . . . . . . . . . . . . . . . . . . . | $11,200 |

**g.** STAR-TRACK should use a *perpetual* inventory system. The items in its inventory have a high per-unit cost. Therefore, management will want to know the costs of the individual products included in specific sales transactions and will want to keep track of the items in stock. Although the company has a manual accounting system, its volume of sales transactions is low enough that maintaining a perpetual inventory record will not be difficult.

**h.** Gross profit = Sales revenue − Cost of goods sold
= $20,000 − $11,200
= $8,800

Gross profit margin = Gross profit ÷ Sales revenue
= $8,800 ÷ $20,000
= 44%

## ◼ SELF-TEST QUESTIONS

*Answers to these questions appear on page 258.*

1. Mark and Amanda Carter own an appliance store and a restaurant. The appliance store sells merchandise on a 12-month installment plan; the restaurant sells only for cash. Which of the following statements are true? (More than one answer may be correct.)

   **a.** The appliance store has a longer operating cycle than the restaurant.

   **b.** The appliance store probably uses a perpetual inventory system, whereas the restaurant probably uses a periodic system.

   **c.** Both businesses require subsidiary ledgers for accounts receivable and inventory.

   **d.** Both businesses probably have subsidiary ledgers for accounts payable.

2. Which of the following types of information are found in subsidiary ledgers, but *not* in the general ledger? (More than one answer may be correct.)

   **a.** Total cost of goods sold for the period.

   **b.** The quantity of a particular product sold during the period.

**c.** The dollar amount owed to a particular creditor.

**d.** The portion of total current assets that consists of cash.

3. Marietta Corporation uses a *perpetual* inventory system. The company sells merchandise costing $3,000 at a sales price of $4,300. In recording this transaction, Marietta will make all of the following entries *except:*

**a.** Credit Sales, $4,300.

**b.** Credit Inventory, $4,300.

**c.** Debit Cost of Goods Sold, $3,000.

**d.** Credit one or more accounts in the inventory subsidiary ledger for amounts totaling $3,000.

4. Fashion House uses a *perpetual* inventory system. At the beginning of the year, inventory amounted to $50,000. During the year, the company purchased merchandise for $230,000, and sold merchandise costing $245,000. A physical inventory taken at year-end indicated shrinkage losses of $4,000. *Prior* to recording these shrinkage losses, the year-end balance in the company's Inventory account was:

**a.** $31,000.  **b.** $35,000.  **c.** $50,000.  **d.** Some other amount.

5. Best Hardware uses a *periodic* inventory system. Its inventory was $38,000 at the beginning of the year and $40,000 at the end. During the year, Best made purchases of merchandise totaling $107,000. Identify all of the correct answers:

**a.** To use this system, Best must take a complete physical inventory twice each year.

**b.** Prior to making adjusting and closing entries at year-end, the balance in Best's Inventory account is $38,000.

**c.** The cost of goods sold for the year is $109,000.

**d.** As sales transactions occur, Best makes no entries to update its inventory records or record the cost of goods sold.

6. The two basic approaches to accounting for inventory and the cost of goods sold are the *perpetual* inventory system and the *periodic* inventory system. Indicate which of the following statements are correct. (More than one answer may be correct.)

**a.** Most large merchandising companies and manufacturing businesses use periodic inventory systems.

**b.** As a practical matter, a grocery store or a large department store could not maintain a perpetual inventory system without the use of point-of-sale terminals.

**c.** In a periodic inventory system the cost of goods sold is not determined until a complete physical inventory is taken.

**d.** In a perpetual inventory system, the Cost of Goods Sold account is debited promptly for the cost of merchandise sold.

7. Big Brother, a retail store, purchased 100 television sets from Krueger Electronics on account at a cost of $200 each. Krueger offers credit terms of 2/10, n/30. Big Brother uses a perpetual inventory system and records purchases at *net cost*. Big Brother determines that 10 of these television sets are defective and returns them to Krueger for full credit. In recording this return, Big Brother will:

**a.** Debit Sales Returns and Allowances.

**b.** Debit Accounts Payable, $1,960.

**c.** Debit Cost of Goods Sold, $1,960.

**d.** Credit Inventory, $2,000.

8. Two of the lawnmowers sold by Garden Products Co. are the LawnMaster and the Mark 5. LawnMasters sell for $250 apiece, which results in a 35% profit margin. Each Mark 5 costs Garden Products $300 and sells for $400. Indicate all correct answers.

**a.** The dollar amount of gross profit is greater on the sale of a Mark 5 than a LawnMaster.

**b.** The profit margin is higher on Mark 5s than on LawnMasters.

**c.** Garden profits more by selling one Mark 5 than by selling one LawnMaster.

**d.** Garden profits more by selling $2,000 worth of Mark 5s than $2,000 worth of LawnMasters.

## ASSIGNMENT MATERIAL

### DISCUSSION QUESTIONS

1. Describe the operating cycle of a merchandising company.

2. Compare and contrast the merchandising activities of a wholesaler and a retailer.

3. The income statement of a merchandising company includes a major type of cost that does not appear in the income statement of a service-type business. Identify this cost and explain what it represents.

4. During the current year, Green Bay Company earned a gross profit of $350,000, whereas New England Company earned a gross profit of only $280,000. Both companies had net sales of $900,000. Does this mean that Green Bay is more profitable than New England? Explain.

5. Thornhill Company's income statement shows gross profit of $432,000, cost of goods sold of $638,000, and other expenses totaling $390,000. Compute the amounts of (a) revenue from sales (net sales) and (b) net income.

6. Explain the need for subsidiary ledgers in accounting for merchandising activities.

7. All Night Auto Parts, Inc., maintains subsidiary ledgers for accounts receivable, inventory, and accounts payable. Explain in detail what information from the following journal entry should be posted and to which subsidiary and general ledger accounts:

| | | |
|---|---:|---:|
| Inventory . . . . . . . . . . . . . . . . . . . . . . . . . . . . . . . . . . . . . . . . . . . . . . . . . . . | 420 | |
|     Accounts Payable (Boss Automotive) . . . . . . . . . . . . . . . . . . . . . . . . . . . | | 420 |
| Purchased 12 Boss LoadMaster II shock absorbers. Cost, | | |
|    $35 per unit. | | |

8. What is meant by the phrase "reconciling a subsidiary ledger"? In general terms, what is the purpose of this procedure?

9. Define the term *inventory shrinkage*. How is the amount of inventory shrinkage determined in a business using a perpetual inventory system, and how is this shrinkage recorded in the accounting records?

10. Briefly contrast the accounting procedures in *perpetual* and *periodic* inventory systems.

11. Miracle Home Cleanser uses a *periodic* inventory system. During the current year the company purchased merchandise with a cost of $55,000. State the cost of goods sold for the year under each of the following alternative assumptions:

  **a.** No beginning inventory; ending inventory $3,500.

  **b.** Beginning inventory $10,000; no ending inventory.

  **c.** Beginning inventory $2,000; ending inventory $7,200.

  **d.** Beginning inventory $8,000; ending inventory $1,400.

12. Evaluate the following statement: "Without electronic point-of-sale terminals, it simply would not be possible to use perpetual inventory systems in businesses that sell large quantities of many different products."

13. Explain the distinguishing characteristics of (a) a general journal and (b) a special journal.

14. How does a balance arise in the Purchase Discounts Lost account? Why does management pay careful attention to the balance (if any) in this account?

15. European Imports pays substantial freight charges to obtain inbound shipments of purchased merchandise. Should these freight charges be debited to the company's Delivery Expense account? Explain.

16. Outback Sporting Goods purchases merchandise on terms of 4/10, n/60. The company has a line of credit that enables it to borrow money as needed from Northern Bank at an annual interest rate of 13%. Should Outback pay its suppliers within the 10-day discount period if it must draw on its line of credit (borrow from Northern Bank) to make these early payments? Explain.

17. TireCo is a retail store in a state that imposes a 6% sales tax. Would you expect to find sales tax expense and sales tax payable in TireCo's financial statements? Explain.

18. A seller generally records sales at the full invoice price, but the buyer often records purchases at *net cost*. Explain the logic of the buyer and seller recording the transaction at different amounts.

19. Western Stores, a chain of hardware stores, had an increase in net sales of 8% for this year in relation to the prior year. Does this mean that the company's marketing strategies, such as advertising, pricing, and product mix, are succeeding?

20. Define the term *gross profit margin*. Explain several ways in which management might improve a company's overall profit margin.

## EXERCISES

Assume that you have been given the responsibility of ordering T-shirts to be sold at a series of 10 summer rock concerts that will be sponsored by your student organization. The T-shirts, which will be specifically designed for each concert, will come in two styles, short and long sleeve. You must decide on the optimal number of T-shirts to order for each concert. The following information about last year's activities is all that is available to help you make your decisions:

1. Last year, the short sleeve and long sleeve T-shirts were sold on the night of the concert at $15 and $20, respectively. On the following day, any unsold T-shirts were put on sale on campus at a reduced price of $7.50. Any shirts not sold on that day were donated to a local orphanage.

2. For each concert, you have (a) the total cost of the shirts for that concert, (b) the amount of cash receipts from the combined sales on the night of the concert and on the next day, and (c) the total attendance figures.
   a. Describe the *additional information* about last year's shirt sales that would be useful in making your ordering decisions.
   b. Explain how you would make the ordering decisions for this year, assuming that you had *both* the information described above and the additional information identified in part **a.**
   c. Describe the types of information from this year's shirt sales that you would record and pass on to the person performing this task next year.

**EXERCISE 6.1**

Determining the Information Needs for Ordering Merchandise

**LO 3**

Shown below are selected transactions of Kiger's, a retail store that uses a perpetual inventory system.

a. Purchased merchandise on account.

b. Recognized the revenue from a sale of merchandise on account. (Ignore the related cost of goods sold.)

c. Recognized the cost of goods sold relating to the sale in transaction **b.**

d. Collected in cash the account receivable from the customer in transaction **b.**

e. Following the taking of a physical inventory at year-end, made an adjusting entry to record a normal amount of inventory shrinkage.

Indicate the effects of each of these transactions on the elements of the company's financial statements shown below. Organize your answer in tabular form, using the column headings shown below. (Notice that the cost of goods sold is shown separately from all other expenses.) Use the code letters **I** for increase, **D** for decrease, and **NE** for no effect.

**EXERCISE 6.2**

Effects of Basic Merchandising Transactions

**LO 1**

| | Income Statement | | | | Balance Sheet | | |
|---|---|---|---|---|---|---|---|
| Transaction | Net Sales − | Cost of Goods Sold − | All Other Expenses = | Net Income | Assets = | Liabilities + | Owners' Equity |
| a | ___ | ___ | ___ | ___ | ___ | ___ | ___ |

Listed below are eight typical merchandising transactions of Everyday Auto Parts, a retail auto supply store.

a. Purchased merchandise from Acme Wholesale on account.

b. Paid an account payable to a supplier.

**EXERCISE 6.3**

Subsidiary Ledgers

**LO 2, 7**

c. Sold merchandise for cash.

d. Sold merchandise on account.

e. Collected an account receivable from a customer.

f. Returned merchandise to a supplier, receiving credit against the amount owed.

g. Gave a cash refund to a customer who returned merchandise.

h. Reduced the account receivable from a credit customer who returned merchandise.

Among the accounting records of Everyday Auto Parts are subsidiary ledgers for inventory, accounts receivable, and accounts payable. For each of the eight transactions, you are to indicate any subsidiary ledger (or ledgers) to which the transaction would be posted. Use the following codes:

Inv = Inventory subsidiary ledger

AR = Accounts receivable subsidiary ledger

AP = Accounts payable subsidiary ledger

Also indicate whether each posting causes the balance in the subsidiary ledger account to *increase* or *decrease*. Organize your answer in tabular form as illustrated below. The answer for transaction **a** is provided as an example.

| Transaction | Subsidiary Ledger | Effect on Subsidiary Account Balance |
|:---:|:---:|:---:|
| a | Inv | Increase |
|   | AP | Increase |

**EXERCISE 6.4**

Perpetual Inventory System

 LO 3

Roland Industries uses a perpetual inventory system. On January 1 the Inventory account had a balance of $1.2 million. During the first few days of January the following transactions occurred:

**Jan. 2**   Purchased merchandise on credit from McNamer Supply for $106,000.

**Jan. 3**   Sold merchandise for cash, $98,000. The cost of this merchandise was $75,000.

a. Prepare entries in general journal form to record the above transactions.

b. What was the balance of the Inventory account at the close of business January 3?

**EXERCISE 6.5**

Evaluating Performance

 LO 7

Shown below are selected statistics from the recent annual reports of two well-known retailers.

| | Sears, Roebuck & Co. | Broadway Stores, Inc. |
|:---|:---:|:---:|
| Percentage increase (decrease) in net sales | 7.2% | (0.3)% |
| Percentage increase in comparable store net sales | 4.7% | 3.1% |

a. Explain the meaning and significance of each of the two measures.

b. Evaluate the performance of the two companies based on the two measures.

**EXERCISE 6.6**

Taking a Physical Inventory

 LO 3

Frisbee Hardware uses a perpetual inventory system. At year-end, the Inventory account has a balance of $250,000, but a physical count shows that the merchandise on hand has a cost of only $246,000.

a. Explain the probable reason(s) for this discrepancy.

b. Prepare the journal entry required in this situation.

c. Indicate all the accounting records to which your journal entry in part **b** should be posted.

**EXERCISE 6.7**

Periodic Inventory Systems

 LO 4

Boston Bait Shop uses a periodic inventory system. At December 31, Year 1, the accounting records include the following information:

| | |
|:---|---:|
| Inventory (as of December 31, Year 1) | $ 2,800 |
| Net sales | 79,600 |
| Purchases | 30,200 |

A complete physical inventory taken at December 31, Year 2, indicates merchandise costing $3,000 remains in stock.

**a.** How were the amounts of beginning and ending inventory determined?

**b.** Compute the amount of the cost of goods sold in Year 2.

**c.** Prepare two closing entries at December 31, Year 2: the first to create a Cost of Goods Sold account with the appropriate balance and the second to bring the Inventory account up-to-date.

**d.** Prepare a partial income statement showing the shop's gross profit for the year.

**e.** Describe why a company such as Boston Bait Shop would use a periodic inventory system rather than a perpetual inventory system.

This exercise stresses the relationships between the information recorded in a periodic inventory system and the basic elements of an income statement. Each of the five lines represents a separate set of information. You are to fill in the missing amounts. A net loss in the right-hand column is to be indicated by placing brackets around the amount, as for example, in line **e** <15,000>.

**EXERCISE 6.8**

Relationships within Periodic Inventory Systems

**LO 4**

| | Net Sales | Beginning Inventory | Net Purchases | Cost of Ending Inventory | Goods Sold | Gross Profit | Expenses | Net Income or (Loss) |
|---|---|---|---|---|---|---|---|---|
| a. | 240,000 | 76,000 | 104,000 | 35,200 | ? | 95,200 | 72,000 | ? |
| b. | 480,000 | 72,000 | 272,000 | ? | 264,000 | ? | ? | 20,000 |
| c. | 630,000 | 207,000 | ? | 166,500 | 441,000 | 189,000 | 148,500 | ? |
| d. | 810,000 | ? | 450,000 | 135,000 | ? | 234,000 | 270,000 | ? |
| e. | ? | 156,000 | ? | 153,000 | 396,000 | 135,000 | ? | <15,000> |

Select a specific merchandising business in your area. Briefly describe the nature of the business, and indicate whether you think a perpetual or a periodic inventory system is more appropriate. *Explain your reasoning and be prepared to discuss your answer in class.* (Notice that you are not asked to determine the type of inventory system actually in use.)

**EXERCISE 6.9**

Selecting an Appropriate Inventory System

**LO 5**

Golf World sold merchandise to Mulligans for $10,000, offering terms of 1/15, n/30. Mulligans paid for the merchandise within the discount period. Both companies use perpetual inventory systems.

**a.** Prepare journal entries in the accounting records of Golf World to account for this sale and the subsequent collection. Assume the original cost of the merchandise to Golf World had been $6,500.

**b.** Prepare journal entries in the accounting records of Mulligans to account for the purchase and subsequent payment. Mulligans records purchases of merchandise at *net cost*.

**c.** Assume that because of a change in personnel, Mulligans failed to pay for this merchandise within the discount period. Prepare the journal entry in the accounting records of Mulligans to record payment *after* the discount period.

**EXERCISE 6.10**

Cash Discounts

**LO 7**

Shown below is selected information from recent annual reports of three well-known retailers. (Dollar amounts are stated in millions.)

**EXERCISE 6.11**

Gross Profit Margins

**LO 8**

| | Kmart | Nordstrom | Toys "R" Us |
|---|---|---|---|
| Net sales . . . . . . . . . . . . . . . . . . . . . . . . . . . . . . . | $31,437 | $ ? | $9,232 |
| Cost of goods sold . . . . . . . . . . . . . . . . . . . . . . . . | $24,390 | 3,082 | ? |
| Gross profit . . . . . . . . . . . . . . . . . . . . . . . . . . . . | ? | 1,371 | ? |
| Gross profit rate . . . . . . . . . . . . . . . . . . . . . . . . . | ?% | ?% | 30.6% |

a. Fill in the missing amounts and percentages. (Round dollar amounts to the nearest million, and percentages to the nearest tenth of 1 percent.)

b. Based on these data, comment on the relative sales volume and gross profit margins of **Kmart** and **Toys "R" Us**. Are these data consistent with your knowledge (or impression) of these two retailers?

**EXERCISE 6.12**

Comparison of Inventory Systems

**LO 3, 4, 5**

Sky Probe sells state-of-the-art telescopes to individuals and organizations interested in studying the solar system. At December 31 last year, the company's inventory amounted to $250,000. During the first week of January this year, the company made only one purchase and one sale. These transactions were as follows:

**Jan. 2**   Sold one telescope costing $90,000 to Central State University for cash, $117,000.

**Jan. 5**   Purchased merchandise on account from Lunar Optics, $50,000. Terms, net 30 days.

a. Prepare journal entries to record these transactions assuming that Sky Probe uses the perpetual inventory system. Use separate entries to record the sales revenue and the cost of goods sold for the sale on January 2.

b. Compute the balance of the Inventory account on January 7.

c. Prepare journal entries to record the two transactions, assuming that Sky Probe uses the periodic inventory system.

d. Compute the cost of goods sold for the first week of January assuming use of a periodic inventory system. Use your answer to part **b** as the ending inventory.

e. Which inventory system do you believe that a company such as Sky Probe would probably use? Explain your reasoning.

**EXERCISE 6.13**

The Periodic Inventory System

**LO 4, 5**

Mountain Mabel's is a small general store located just outside of Yellowstone National Park. The store uses a periodic inventory system. Every January 1, Mabel and her husband close the store and take a complete physical inventory while watching the Rose Parade on television. Last year, the inventory amounted to $6,240; this year it totaled $4,560. During the current year, the business recorded sales of $150,000 and purchases of $74,400.

**Instructions**

a. Compute the cost of goods sold for the current year.

b. Explain why a small business such as this might use the periodic inventory system.

c. Explain some of the *disadvantages* of the periodic system to a larger business, such as a **Sears** store.

**EXERCISE 6.14**

Using an Annual Report

**LO 8**

The annual report of **Tootsie Roll Industries, Inc.**, appears in Appendix A at the end of this textbook. Use this report to complete the following requirements:

a. Calculate the gross profit percentage of **Tootsie Roll Industries** for each of the years shown in the company's income statements.

b. Evaluate the company's trend in sales and gross profit to date.

c. Does management seem optimistic about future trends in sales and gross profit? Explain.

## PROBLEMS

**PROBLEM 6.1**

Evaluating Profitability

**LO 1, 3, 8**

Claypool Hardware is the only hardware store in a remote area of northern Minnesota. Some of Claypool's transactions during the current year are as follows:

**Nov. 5**   Sold lumber on account to Bemidji Construction, $13,390. The inventory subsidiary ledger shows the cost of this merchandise was $9,105.

**Nov. 9**   Purchased tools on account from Owatonna Tool Company, $3,800.

**Dec. 5**   Collected in cash the $13,390 account receivable from Bemidji Construction.

**Dec. 9**   Paid the $3,800 owed to Owatonna Tool Company.

**Dec. 31** Claypool's personnel counted the inventory on hand and determined its cost to be $182,080. The accounting records, however, indicate inventory of $183,790 and a cost of goods sold of $695,222. The physical count of the inventory was observed by the company's auditors and is considered correct.

## Instructions

**a.** Prepare journal entries to record these transactions and events in the accounting records of Claypool Hardware. (The company uses a perpetual inventory system.)

**b.** Prepare a partial income statement showing the company's gross profit for the year. (Net sales for the year amount to $1,024,900.)

**c.** Claypool purchases merchandise inventory at the same wholesale prices as other hardware stores. Due to its remote mountain location, however, the company must pay between $18,000 and $20,000 per year in extra transportation charges to receive delivery of merchandise. (These additional charges are included in the amount shown as cost of goods sold.)

Assume that an index of key business ratios in your library shows hardware stores of Claypool's approximate size (in total assets) average net sales of $1 million per year and a gross profit rate of 25%.

Is Claypool able to pass its extra transportation costs on to its customers? Does the business appear to suffer or benefit financially from its remote location? Explain your reasoning and support your conclusions with specific accounting data comparing the operations of Claypool Hardware with the industry averages.

Office Solutions sells fax machines, copiers, and other types of office equipment. On May 10, the company purchased for the first time a new plain-paper fax machine manufactured by Mitsui Corporation. Transactions relating to this product during May and June were as follows:

**PROBLEM 6.2**

Perpetual Inventory System and an Inventory Subsidiary Ledger

LO 1, 2, 3

**May 10** Purchased five P-500 fax machines on account from Mitsui Corporation, at a cost of $300 each. Payment due in 30 days.

**May 23** Sold four P-500 fax machines on account to Foster & Cole, stockbrokers; sales price, $500 per machine. Payment due in 30 days.

**May 24** Purchased an additional seven P-500 fax machines on account from Mitsui. Cost, $300 per machine; payment due in 30 days.

**June 9** Paid $1,500 cash to Mitsui Corporation for the fax machines purchased on May 10.

**June 19** Sold two P-500 fax machines to Tri-State Realty for cash. Sales price, $525 per machine.

**June 22** Collected $2,000 from Foster & Cole in full settlement of the credit sale on May 23.

## Instructions

**a.** Prepare journal entries to record these transactions in the accounting records of Office Solutions. (The company uses a perpetual inventory system.)

**b.** Post the appropriate information from these journal entries to an inventory subsidiary ledger account like the one illustrated on page 227.)

**c.** How many Mitsui P-500 fax machines were in inventory on May 31? From what accounting record did you obtain the answer to this question?

**d.** Describe the types of information contained in any inventory subsidiary ledger account and explain how this information may be useful to various company personnel in conducting daily business operations.

Shown below is information from the financial reports of Knauss Supermarkets for the past few years.

**PROBLEM 6.3**

Trend Analysis

LO 8

| | 2002 | 2001 | 2000 |
|---|---|---|---|
| Net sales (in millions) | $5,495 | $5,184 | $4,800 |
| Number of stores | 448 | 445 | 430 |
| Square feet of selling space (in millions) | 11.9 | 11.1 | 10.0 |
| Average net sales of comparable stores (in millions) | $10.8 | $11.0 | $11.4 |

### Instructions

**a.** Calculate the following statistics for Knauss Supermarkets:

1. The percentage change in net sales from 2000 to 2001 and 2001 to 2002. *Hint*: The percentage change is computed by dividing the dollar amount of the change between years by the amount of the base year. For example, the percentage change in net sales from 2000 to 2001 is computed by dividing the difference between 2001 and 2000 net sales by the amount of 2000 net sales, or ($5,184 − $4,800) ÷ $4,800 = 8% increase.

2. The percentage change in net sales per square foot of selling space from 2000 to 2001 and 2001 to 2002.

3. The percentage change in comparable store sales from 2000 to 2001 and 2001 to 2002.

**b.** Evaluate the sales performance of Knauss Supermarkets.

**PROBLEM 6.4**

Comparison of Net Cost and Gross Price Methods

**LO 3, 7**

Lamprino Appliance uses a perpetual inventory system. The following are three recent merchandising transactions:

**June 10**  Purchased 10 televisions from Mitsu Industries on account. Invoice price, $300 per unit, for a total of $3,000. The terms of purchase were 2/10, n/30.

**June 15**  Sold one of these televisions for $450 cash.

**June 20**  Paid the account payable to Mitsu Industries within the discount period.

### Instructions

**a.** Prepare journal entries to record these transactions assuming that Lamprino records purchases of merchandise at:

1. Net cost

2. Gross invoice price

**b.** Assume that Lamprino did *not* pay Mitsu Industries within the discount period but instead paid the full invoice price on July 10. Prepare journal entries to record this payment assuming that the original liability had been recorded at:

1. Net cost

2. Gross invoice price

**c.** Assume that you are evaluating the efficiency of Lamprino's bill-paying procedures. Which accounting method—net cost or gross invoice price—provides you with the most *useful* information? Explain.

**PROBLEM 6.5**

Merchandising Transactions

**LO 3, 7**

The following is a series of related transactions between Siogo Shoes, a shoe wholesaler, and Sole Mates, a chain of retail shoe stores:

**Feb. 9**  Siogo Shoes sold Sole Mates 100 pairs of hiking boots on account, terms 1/10, n/30. The cost of these boots to Siogo Shoes was $60 per pair, and the sales price was $100 per pair.

**Feb. 12**  United Express charged $80 for delivering this merchandise to Sole Mates. These charges were split evenly between the buyer and seller, and were paid immediately in cash.

**Feb. 13**  Sole Mates returned 10 pairs of boots to Siogo Shoes because they were the wrong size. Siogo Shoes allowed Sole Mates full credit for this return.

**Feb. 19**  Sole Mates paid the remaining balance due to Siogo Shoes within the discount period.

Both companies use a perpetual inventory system.

### Instructions

**a.** Record this series of transactions in the general journal of Siogo Shoes. (The company records sales at gross sales price.)

**b.** Record this series of transactions in the general journal of Sole Mates. (The company records purchases of merchandise at *net cost* and uses a Transportation-in account to record transportation charges on inbound shipments.)

**c.** Sole Mates does not always have enough cash on hand to pay for purchases within the discount period. However, it has a line of credit with its bank, which enables Sole Mates to easily borrow money for short periods of time at an annual interest rate of 11%. (The bank charges interest only for the number of days until Sole Mates repays the loan.) As a matter of general policy, should Sole Mates take advantage of 1/10, n/30 cash discounts even if it must borrow the money to do so at an annual rate of 11%? Explain fully—and illustrate any supporting computations.

CPI sells computer peripherals. At December 31, 2001, CPI's inventory amounted to $500,000. During the first week in January 2002, the company made only one purchase and one sale. These transactions were as follows:

**PROBLEM 6.6**

A Comprehensive Problem

**LO 1–8**

**Jan. 2**  Purchased 20 modems and 80 printers from Sharp. The total cost of these machines was $25,000, terms 3/10, n/60.

**Jan. 6**  Sold 30 different types of products on account to Pace Corporation. The total sales price was $10,000, terms 5/10, n/90. The total cost of these 30 units to CPI was $6,100 (net of the purchase discount).

CPI has a full-time accountant and a computer-based accounting system. It records sales at the gross sales price and purchases at net cost and maintains subsidiary ledgers for accounts receivable, inventory, and accounts payable.

### Instructions

**a.** Briefly describe the operating cycle of a merchandising company. Identify the assets and liabilities directly affected by this cycle.

**b.** Prepare journal entries to record these transactions, assuming that CPI uses a *perpetual* inventory system.

**c.** Explain the information in part **b** that should be posted to subsidiary ledger accounts.

**d.** Compute the balance in the Inventory controlling account at the close of business on January 6.

**e.** Prepare journal entries to record the two transactions, assuming that CPI uses a *periodic* inventory system.

**f.** Compute the cost of goods sold for the first week of January assuming use of the periodic system. (Use your answer to part **d** as the ending inventory.)

**g.** Which type of inventory system do you think CPI most likely would use? Explain your reasoning.

**h.** Compute the gross profit margin on the January 6 sales transaction.

## CASES AND UNSTRUCTURED PROBLEMS

In each of the following situations, indicate whether you would expect the business to use a periodic inventory system or a perpetual inventory system. Explain the reasons for your answer.

**CASE 6.1**

Selecting an Inventory System

**LO 5**

**a.** The Frontier Shop is a small retail store that sells boots and Western clothing. The store is operated by the owner, who works full-time in the business, and by one part-time salesclerk. Sales transactions are recorded on an antique cash register. The business uses a manual accounting system, which is maintained by ACE Bookkeeping Service. At the end of each month, an employee of ACE visits The Frontier Shop to update its accounting records, prepare sales tax returns, and perform other necessary accounting services.

**b.** Allister's Corner is an art gallery in the Soho district of New York. All accounting records are maintained manually by the owner, who works in the store on a full-time basis. The store sells three or four paintings each week, at sales prices ranging from about $5,000 to $50,000 per painting.

**c.** A publicly owned corporation publishes about 200 titles of college-level textbooks. The books are sold to college bookstores throughout the country. Books are distributed to these bookstores from four central warehouses, located in California, Texas, Ohio, and Virginia.

**d.** Toys-4-You operates a national chain of 86 retail toy stores. The company has a state-of-the-art computerized accounting system. All sales transactions are recorded on electronic point-of-sale terminals. These terminals are tied into a central computer system that provides the national headquarters with information about the profitability of each store on a weekly basis.

**e.** Mr. Jingles is an independently owned and operated ice cream truck.

**f.** TransComm is a small company that sells very large quantities of a single product. The product is a low-cost, 3.5-inch, double-sided, double-density floppy computer disc, manufactured by a large Japanese company. Sales are made only in large quantities, primarily to chains of computer stores and large discount stores. This year, the average sales transaction amounted to $14,206 of merchandise. All accounting records are maintained by a full-time employee using commercial accounting software and a personal computer.

## CASE 6.2

A Cost-Benefit Analysis

**LO 4, 8**

Village Hardware is a retail store selling hardware, small appliances, and sporting goods. The business follows a policy of selling all merchandise at exactly twice the amount of its cost to the store and uses a *periodic* inventory system.

At year-end, the following information is taken from the accounting records:

| | |
|---|---:|
| Net sales ................................................... | $580,000 |
| Inventory, January 1 ........................................ | 58,000 |
| Purchases ................................................. | 297,500 |

A physical count indicates merchandise costing $49,300 is on hand at December 31.

### Instructions

**a.** Prepare a partial income statement showing computation of the gross profit for the year.

**b.** On seeing your income statement, the owner of the store makes the following comment: "Inventory shrinkage losses are really costing me. If it weren't for shrinkage losses, the store's gross profit would be 50% of net sales. I'm going to hire a security guard and put an end to shoplifting once and for all."

Determine the amount of loss from inventory shrinkage stated (1) at cost and (2) at retail sales value. (*Hint*: Without any shrinkage losses, the cost of goods sold and the amount of gross profit would each amount to 50% of net sales.)

**c.** Assume that Village Hardware could virtually eliminate shoplifting by hiring a security guard at a cost of $1,800 per month. Would this strategy be profitable? Explain your reasoning.

## CASE 6.3

Out of Balance

**LO 2**

Marcus Dean works in the accounts payable department of Artistic Furniture, a large retail furniture store. At month-end, Dean's supervisor assigned him the task of reconciling the accounts payable subsidiary ledger with the controlling account.

Dean found that the balance of the controlling account was $4,500 higher than the sum of the subsidiary ledger accounts. He traced this error to a transaction occurring early in the month. Artistic had purchased $9,400 in merchandise on account from Appalachian Woods, a regular supplier. The transaction had been recorded correctly in Artistic's journal and posted correctly to the Inventory and Accounts Payable accounts in the general ledger. The $9,400 credit to Accounts Payable, however, had erroneously been posted as *$4,900* to the Appalachian Woods account in Artistic's accounts payable subsidiary ledger.

Artistic uses its subsidiary ledger as the basis for making payment to its suppliers. In the middle of the month, Artistic had sent a check to Appalachian in the amount of $4,900. This $4,900 payment was recorded and posted correctly to both the general and subsidiary ledger accounts. Thus, at the end of the month, the subsidiary ledger account for Appalachian Woods had a zero balance.

Dean learned that Appalachian had failed to detect Artistic's error. The month-end statement from Appalachian simply said, "Account paid in full." Therefore, Dean proposed the following "correcting entry" to bring Artistic's controlling account into balance with the subsidiary ledger and the supplier's month-end statement:

| | | |
|---|---:|---:|
| Accounts Payable .......................................... | 4,500 | |
|    Miscellaneous Revenue ................................... | | 4,500 |
| To reduce Accounts Payable controlling account for unpaid | | |
|   amount that was not rebilled by the supplier. | | |

This entry is to be posted to the general ledger accounts, but not to the accounts payable subsidiary ledger.

## Instructions

**a.** Will the proposed correcting entry bring the Accounts Payable controlling account into agreement with the accounts in the subsidiary ledger?

**b.** Identify and discuss any ethical considerations that you see in this situation, and suggest an appropriate course of action.

Identify one local business that uses a perpetual inventory system and another that uses a periodic system. Interview an individual in each organization who is familiar with the inventory system and the recording of sales transactions. (Interviews are to be planned and conducted in accordance with the instructions in the Preface of this textbook.)

**CASE 6.4**

Group Assignment with Business Community Involvement

**LO 3, 4, 5, 6**

## Instructions

Separately for each business organization:

**a.** Describe the procedures used in accounting for sales transactions, keeping track of inventory levels, and determining the cost of goods sold.

**b.** Explain the reasons offered by the person interviewed as to *why* the business uses this type of system.

**c.** Indicate whether your group considers the system in use appropriate under the circumstances. If not, recommend specific changes. *Explain your reasoning.*

## *BUSINESS WEEK* ASSIGNMENT

BusinessWeek

In the world of retailing, ups and downs are the norm. A chain of stores that is booming in one year may experience stagnant sales growth the next. In a September 18, 2000, *Business Week* article entitled, "An Early Case of Holiday Blues," authors Wendy Zellner, Robert Berner, Julie Forster, and Louise Lee identify various winners and losers in the volatile retail sector.

The authors report that **Gap, Inc.**, a once shining retail star in the clothing sector, had just posted a 14% decline in same-store sales. In the consumer electronics sector, however, the authors speculate that **Best Buy Co.** is likely to experience a 3% to 5% growth in same-store sales.

Explain what is meant by the article's reference to *same-store sales*.

**CASE 6.5**

**LO 8**

## INTERNET ASSIGNMENT

You can find a large amount of information on the Internet to evaluate the performance of companies. Many companies provide links to this information on their home pages.

Access the home page of **Gap, Inc.**, at the following Internet location:

### www.gap.com

Click on "Financial Information" under the category "Company" to view a listing of the information that is available about the company.

**INTERNET 6.1**

Exploring the Gap via the Company's Home Page

**LO 8**

## Instructions

**a.** Click on one of the "Monthly Sales Reports" and evaluate the company's sales performance for the month and year-to-date.

**b.** Under the category "SEC filings," click on "Gap's page" to get to the SEC's EDGAR database of financial information about publicly owned companies. Select the Gap's most recent 10-Q, which is a required quarterly filing that includes quarterly financial statements. Use the financial statements and "Management's Discussion and Analysis of Operations" to answer the following questions:

**1.** Did sales increase or decrease in the current quarter in relation to the same quarter in the preceding year?

**2.** Did inventory increase or decrease in the current quarter in relation to the same quarter in the preceding year?

3. How many new stores did the company open this quarter? How many did it close?

4. What was the amount of sales per average square foot of selling space in this quarter? Was this an improvement over the same quarter for the preceding year?

*Internet sites are time and date sensitive. It is the purpose of these exercises to have you explore the Internet. You may need to use the Yahoo! search engine* http://www.yahoo.com *(or other favorite search engine) to find a company's current web address.*

## OUR COMMENTS ON THE "YOUR TURN" CASES

**You as a Credit Manager (p. 225)**   The accounts receivable subsidiary ledger provides a historical record of sales to Dave's Toy Store. You, as the credit manager, can readily see how much Dave has purchased from your company for the last week, month, year, or any longer period of time. The ledger also provides you with information about Dave's payment history. You can determine definitely whether Dave's Toy Store has paid its bills from your company on a timely basis. Other information that would be useful for your decision would be recent financial statements of Dave's Toy Stores, and current credit reports from agencies such as Dun & Bradstreet.

**You as an Audit Senior (p. 229)**   An issue of key importance in auditing inventory is that *the auditor be present* when the physical inventory count is made. A major fraud discovered at **McKesson & Robbins** Company in 1938 motivated the accounting profession to change audit procedures to include the physical observation of inventory. Prior to that time, auditors avoided responsibility for determining either the physical existence or the accuracy of the count of inventory. In 1937 **McKesson & Robbins** reported assets of $87 million of which approximately $10 million of inventory was subsequently determined to be nonexistent.

You should contact the store manager's supervisor and explain that the agreed-upon physical inventory procedures are not being followed by the store manager. It is the supervisor's responsibility to inform the store manager to allow you access to the physical inventory.

**You as a Buyer for a Retail Business (p. 234)**   If Acme maintains perpetual inventory records, these records would provide a host of information that would be useful to your purchasing decision. From the perpetual inventory records, you can determine the number, brand, and type of grills currently on hand and the number of each sold in prior summer seasons. This information will be very useful in estimating the merchandise needs for the current season.

If Acme does not have perpetual inventory records, you would be forced to make your decision without this information about inventory on hand and prior sales, or to spend a significant amount of time developing the information.

## ANSWERS TO SELF-TEST QUESTIONS

**1.** a, b, d     **2.** b, c     **3.** b     **4.** b     **5.** b, d     **6.** b, c, d     **7.** b     **8.** a, c

# CHAPTER 7

# FINANCIAL ASSETS

## Learning Objectives

*After studying this chapter, you should be able to:*

1. Define financial assets and explain their valuation in the balance sheet.

2. Describe the objectives of cash management.

3. Explain means of achieving internal control over cash transactions.

4. Prepare a bank reconciliation and explain its purpose.

5. Account for uncollectible receivables using the allowance and direct write-off methods.

6. Evaluate the liquidity of various financial assets.

7. Explain how transactions discussed in this chapter affect net income and cash flows.

*8. Account for transactions involving marketable securities.

†9. Explain, compute, and account for the accrual of interest revenue.

Xerox Corporation

---

*Supplemental Topic A, "Accounting for Marketable Securities."

†Supplemental Topic B, "Notes Receivable and Interest Revenue."

**Xerox** is a very large company that provides solutions for managing both paper and online documents. Today, documents are key to knowledge sharing; according to **Xerox**, managing documents is the most critical issue managers face.

You might think that **Xerox** would have most of its money tied up in plant assets. In fact, the company shows approximately $2.5 billion in plant assets on its 1999 balance sheet. That same financial statement shows a total of more than $28 billion in assets, many of which are financial assets. These include various forms of receivables (i.e., amounts customers owe to **Xerox**) and investments. These soft assets make up a much greater portion of **Xerox**'s total assets than the bricks-and-mortar-type assets such as land, buildings, and equipment.

● ● ●

Financial assets represent various claims to not only cash but also securities that may be converted to cash, if needed. The ability of a company to meet its maturing obligations (i.e., its liquidity) is extremely important, and financial assets are critical to a company's debt-paying ability. In this chapter, we learn about financial assets and how various types of financial assets contribute to a company's liquidity.

## How Much Cash Should a Business Have?

Most businesspeople would say, "As little as necessary."

In a well-managed company, daily cash receipts are deposited promptly in the bank. Often, a principal source of these daily receipts is the collection of accounts receivable. If the daily receipts exceed routine cash outlays, the company can meet its obligations while maintaining relatively low balances in its bank accounts.

Cash that will not be needed in the immediate future often is invested in highly liquid, short-term securities. These investments are more productive than cash because they earn revenue in the forms of interest and dividends. If the business should need more cash than it has in its bank accounts, it can easily convert some of its investments back into cash.

The term **financial assets** describes not just cash, but also those assets easily and directly *convertible into known amounts of cash.* These assets include cash, short-term investments (also called **marketable securities**), and receivables. We address these three types of financial assets in a single chapter because they are so closely related. All of these assets represent *forms of money;* financial resources flow quickly among these asset categories.

In summary, businesses "store" money in three basic forms: cash, short-term investments, and receivables. The flow of cash among these types of financial assets is summarized in the illustration at the bottom of this page.

## The Valuation of Financial Assets

In the balance sheet, financial assets are shown at their *current values,* meaning the amounts of cash that these assets represent. Interestingly, current value is measured differently for each type of financial asset.

The current value of cash is simply its face amount. But the current value of marketable securities may change daily, based on fluctuations in stock prices, interest rates, and other factors. Therefore, short-term investments appear in the balance sheet at their current *market values.* (Notice that the valuation of these investments represents an exception to the cost principle.)

Accounts receivable, like cash, have stated face amounts. But large companies usually do not expect to collect every dollar of their accounts receivable. Some customers simply will be unable to make full payment. Therefore, receivables appear in the balance sheet at the estimated *collectible* amount—called **net realizable value.**

**LO 1**

Define financial assets and explain their valuation in the balance sheet.

*Money flows among the financial assets.*

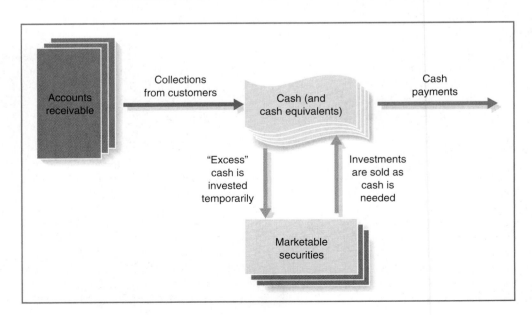

These three methods of determining the current value of financial assets are summarized below:

| Type of Financial Asset | Basis for Valuation in the Balance Sheet |
|---|---|
| Cash (and cash equivalents) | Face amount |
| Short-term investments (marketable securities) | Current market value |
| Receivables | Net realizable value |

# CASH

Accountants define *cash* as money on deposit in banks and any items that banks will accept for deposit. These items include not only coins and paper money, but also checks, money orders, and travelers' checks. Banks also accept drafts signed by customers using bank credit cards, such as Visa and MasterCard. Thus sales to customers using bank cards are considered *cash sales,* not credit sales, to the enterprise that makes the sale.

Most companies maintain several bank accounts as well as keep a small amount of cash on hand. Therefore, the Cash account in the general ledger is often a *controlling account.* A cash subsidiary ledger includes separate accounts corresponding to each bank account and each supply of cash on hand within the organization.

## Reporting Cash in the Balance Sheet

Cash is listed first in the balance sheet because it is the most liquid of all assets. For purposes of balance sheet presentation, the balance in the Cash controlling account is combined with that of the controlling account for **cash equivalents**.

**Cash Equivalents** Some short-term investments are so liquid that they are termed *cash equivalents*. Examples include money market funds, U.S. Treasury bills, and high-grade commercial paper (very short-term notes payable that are issued by large, creditworthy corporations). These assets are considered so similar to cash that they are combined with the amount of cash in the balance sheet. Therefore, the first asset listed in the balance sheet often is called Cash and Cash Equivalents.

To qualify as a cash equivalent, an investment must be very safe, have a very stable market value, and mature within 90 days of the date of acquisition. Investments in even the highest quality stocks and bonds of large corporations are *not* viewed as meeting these criteria. Short-term investments that do not qualify as cash equivalents are listed in the balance sheet as Marketable Securities.

**Restricted Cash** Some bank accounts are restricted as to their use, so they are not available to meet the normal operating needs of the company. For example, a bank account may contain cash specifically earmarked for the repayment of a noncurrent liability, such as a bond payable. Restricted cash should be presented in the balance sheet as part of the section entitled "Investments and Funds."

As a condition for granting a loan, banks often require the borrower to maintain a **compensating balance** (minimum average balance) on deposit in a non-interest-bearing checking account. This agreement does not actually prevent the borrower from using the cash, but it does mean the company must quickly replenish this bank account. Compensating balances are included in the amount of cash listed in the balance sheet, but these balances should be disclosed in the notes accompanying the financial statements.

**Lines of Credit**   Many businesses arrange **lines of credit** with their banks. A line of credit means that the bank has agreed *in advance* to lend the company any amount of money up to a specified limit. The company can borrow this money at any time simply by drawing checks on a special bank account. A liability to the bank arises as soon as any money is borrowed—that is, as soon as a portion of the credit line is used.

The *unused* portion of a line of credit is neither an asset nor a liability; it represents only the *ability* to borrow money quickly and easily. Although an unused line of credit does not appear as an asset or a liability in the balance sheet, it increases the company's solvency. Thus unused lines of credit usually are *disclosed* in notes accompanying the financial statements.

**CASE IN POINT**

A recent annual report of **J.C. Penney**, the giant retailer, included the following note to the financial statements:

Confirmed lines of credit available to **J.C. Penney** amounted to $1.2 billion. None was in use at [the balance sheet date].

## The Statement of Cash Flows

A balance sheet shows the cash owned at the end of the accounting period. As we learned in Chapter 2, cash *transactions* of the accounting period are summarized in the statement of cash flows.

In both the balance sheet and the statement of cash flows, the term *cash* includes cash equivalents. Transfers of money between bank accounts and cash equivalents do *not* appear in a statement of cash flows, because these transactions do not change the amount of cash owned. However, any *interest* received from owning cash equivalents is included in the statement of cash flows as cash receipts from operating activities.

## Cash Management

**LO 2**

Describe the objectives of cash management.

The term **cash management** refers to planning, controlling, and accounting for cash transactions and cash balances. Because cash moves so readily between bank accounts and other financial assets, cash management really means the management of *all financial resources.* Efficient management of these resources is essential to the success—even to the survival—of every business organization. The basic objectives of cash management are as follows:

- *Provide accurate accounting for cash receipts, cash disbursements, and cash balances.* Many of the total transactions of a business involve the receipt or disbursement of cash. Also, cash transactions affect every classification within the financial statements— assets, liabilities, owners' equity, revenue, and expenses. If financial statements are to be reliable, it is *absolutely essential* that cash transactions be recorded correctly.

- *Prevent or minimize losses from theft or fraud.* Cash is more susceptible to theft than any other asset and, therefore, requires physical protection.

- *Anticipate the need for borrowing and assure the availability of adequate amounts of cash for conducting business operations.* Every business organization must have sufficient cash to meet its financial obligations as they come due. Otherwise, its creditors may force the business into bankruptcy.

- *Prevent unnecessarily large amounts of cash from sitting idle in bank accounts that produce no revenue.* Well-managed companies frequently review their bank balances for the purpose of transferring any excess cash into cash equivalents or other investments that generate revenue.

**Using Excess Cash Balances Efficiently**   Cash equivalents are safe, liquid investments, but they generate only a modest rate of return. These investments are useful for investing *temporary* surpluses of cash, which soon will be needed for other purposes. If a business has large amounts of cash that can be invested on a long-term basis, however, it should expect to earn a higher rate of return than is available from cash equivalents. Cash that is available for long-term investment may be used to finance growth and expansion of the business, or to repay debt. If the cash is not needed for business purposes, it may be distributed to the company's stockholders.

### You as a Financial Advisor

Assume that you were hired by Whitlock Corporation to help manage its financial assets. The company historically has kept an average cash balance of $5 million in a corporate checking account. Whitlock's chief financial officer is very conservative and risk averse. On numerous occasions he has openly refused to "play the stock market" with company funds.

As a financial advisor, propose several low-risk investment alternatives for the company's $5 million cash surplus.

*Our comments appear on page 312.

**YOUR TURN**

## Internal Control over Cash

Internal control over cash is sometimes regarded merely as a means of preventing fraud and theft. A good system of internal control, however, will also aid in achieving the other objectives of efficient cash management, including accurate accounting for cash transactions, anticipating the need for borrowing, and the maintenance of adequate but not excessive cash balances.

The major steps in achieving internal control over cash transactions and cash balances include the following:

**LO 3**

Explain means of achieving internal control over cash transactions.

- Separate the function of handling cash from the maintenance of accounting records. Employees who handle cash *should not have access to the accounting records,* and accounting personnel should not have access to cash.

- For each department within the organization, prepare a *cash budget* (or forecast) of planned cash receipts, cash payments, and cash balances, scheduled month-by-month for the coming year.

- Prepare a *control listing* of cash receipts at the time and place the money is received. For cash sales, this listing may be a cash register tape, created by ringing up each sale on a cash register. For checks received through the mail, a control listing of incoming checks should be prepared by the employee assigned to open the mail.

- Require that all cash receipts be *deposited daily* in the bank.

- Make all payments *by check*. The only exception should be for small payments to be made in cash from a *petty cash fund.* (Petty cash funds are discussed later in this chapter.)

- Require that the validity and amount of every expenditure be verified *before* a check is issued in payment. Separate the function of approving expenditures from the function of signing checks.

- Promptly reconcile bank statements with the accounting records.

A company may supplement its system of internal control by obtaining a fidelity bond from an insurance company. Under a fidelity bond, the insurance company agrees to reimburse an employer for *proven* losses resulting from fraud or embezzlement by bonded employees.

**Cash Over and Short**   In handling over-the-counter cash receipts, a few errors in making change inevitably will occur. These errors may cause a cash shortage or overage at the end of the day when the cash is counted and compared with the reading on the cash register.

For example, assume that total cash sales recorded on the point-of-sale terminals during the day amount to $4,500.00. However, the cash receipts in the register drawers total only $4,487.30. The following entry would be made to adjust the accounting records for this $12.70 shortage in the cash receipts:

| | | |
|---|---|---|
| Cash Over and Short . . . . . . . . . . . . . . . . . . . . . . . . . . . . . . . . . . . . . . . . . . . . | 12.70 | |
|    Cash . . . . . . . . . . . . . . . . . . . . . . . . . . . . . . . . . . . . . . . . . . . . . . . . | | 12.70 |

To record a $12.70 shortage in cash receipts for the day
  ($4,500.00 − $4,487.30).

The account entitled Cash Over and Short is debited with shortages and credited with overages. If the account has a debit balance, it appears in the income statement as a miscellaneous expense; if it has a credit balance, it is shown as a miscellaneous revenue.

## Cash Disbursements

To achieve adequate internal control over cash disbursements, all payments—except those from petty cash—should be *made by check.* The use of checks automatically provides a written record of each cash payment. In addition, adequate internal control requires that every transaction requiring a cash payment be *verified, approved,* and *recorded* before a check is issued. Responsibility for approving cash disbursements should be *clearly separated* from the responsibility for signing checks.

**The Voucher System**   One widely used method of establishing internal control over cash disbursements is a voucher system. In a typical **voucher system,** the accounting department is responsible for approving cash payments and for recording the transactions. In approving an expenditure, the accounting department will examine such supporting documents as the supplier's invoice, the purchase order, and the receiving report. Once payment has been approved, the accounting department signs a **voucher** authorizing payment and records the transaction in the accounting records. (Other names for a "voucher" include *invoice approval form* and *check authorization.*)

The voucher and supporting documents then are sent to the treasurer or other official in the finance department. This official reviews the voucher and supporting documents before issuing a check. When the check is signed, the voucher and supporting documents are perforated or stamped "PAID" to eliminate any possibility of their being presented later in support of another check.

Notice that neither the personnel in the accounting department nor the personnel in the finance department are in a position to make unapproved cash disbursements. Accounting personnel who approve and record disbursements are not authorized to sign checks. Finance department personnel, who issue and sign checks, are not authorized to issue a check unless they have first received an authorization voucher from the accounting department.

## Bank Statements

Each month the bank provides the depositor with a statement of the depositor's account, accompanied by the checks paid and charged to the account during the month.[1] As illustrated below, a bank statement shows the balance on deposit at the beginning of the month, the deposits, the checks paid, any other additions and subtractions during the

---

[1] Large businesses may receive bank statements on a weekly basis.

month, and the new balance at the end of the month. (To keep the illustration short, we have shown a limited number of deposits rather than one for each business day in the month.)

*A bank statement provides an independent record of cash transactions*

---

**Western National Bank**
**100 Olympic Boulevard**
**Los Angeles, California**

**Customer Account No. 501390**
**Parkview Company**
**109 Parkview Road**
**Los Angeles, California**

**Bank Statement**
**For the Month Ended July 31, 2002**

| Date | Deposits and Credits | Checks and Debits | | Balance |
|---|---|---|---|---|
| June 30 | | | | 5,029.30 |
| July 1 | 300.00 | | | 5,329.30 |
| July 2 | 1,250.00 | 1,100.00 | | 5,479.30 |
| July 3 | | 415.20 | 10.00 | 5,054.10 |
| July 8 | 993.60 | | | 6,047.70 |
| July 10 | | 96.00 | 400.00 | 5,551.70 |
| July 12 | 1,023.77 | 1,376.57 | | 5,198.90 |
| July 15 | | 425.00 | | 4,773.90 |
| July 18 | 1,300.00 | 2,095.75 | | 3,978.15 |
| July 22 | 500.00 CM | 85.00 | 5.00 DM | 4,388.15 |
| July 24 | 1,083.25 | 1,145.27 | | 4,326.13 |
| July 30 | 711.55 | 50.25 NSF | | 4,987.43 |
| July 31 | 24.74 INT | 12.00 SC | | 5,000.17 |

Explanation of Symbols

| | | | | |
|---|---|---|---|---|
| CM | Credit Memoranda | INT | Interest on average balance | |
| DM | Debit Memoranda | NSF | Not Sufficient Funds | |
| E | Error correction | SC | Service Charge | |

Summary of activity:

| | |
|---|---|
| Previous statement balance, June 30, 2002 . . . . . . . . . . . . . . . . . . . . . . . . . . . . . . | $5,029.30 |
| Deposits and credit memoranda (9 items) . . . . . . . . . . . . . . . . . . . . . . . . . . . . . . | 7,186.91 |
| Checks and debit memoranda (13 items) . . . . . . . . . . . . . . . . . . . . . . . . . . . . . . | (7,216.04) |
| Current statement balance, July 31, 2002 . . . . . . . . . . . . . . . . . . . . . . . . . . . . . . | $5,000.17 |

---

## Reconciling the Bank Statement

A **bank reconciliation** is a schedule *explaining any differences* between the balance shown in the bank statement and the balance shown in the depositor's accounting records. Remember that both the bank and the depositor are maintaining independent records of the deposits, the checks, and the current balance of the bank account. Each month, the depositor should prepare a bank reconciliation to verify that these independent sets of records are in agreement. This reconciliation may disclose internal control failures, such as unauthorized cash disbursements or failures to deposit cash receipts, as well as errors in either the bank statement or the depositor's accounting records. In addition, the reconciliation identifies certain transactions that must be recorded in the depositor's accounting records and helps to determine the actual amount of cash on deposit.

For strong internal control, the employee who reconciles the bank statement should not have any other responsibilities for physically handling cash.

**LO 4**

Prepare a bank reconciliation and explain its purpose.

**Normal Differences between Bank Records and Accounting Records**  The balance shown in a monthly bank statement seldom equals the balance appearing in the depositor's accounting records. Certain transactions recorded by the depositor may not have been recorded by the bank. The most common examples are:

- *Outstanding checks.* Checks issued and recorded by the company but not yet presented to the bank for payment.

- *Deposits in transit.* Cash receipts recorded by the depositor that reached the bank too late to be included in the bank statement for the current month.

In addition, certain transactions appearing in the bank statement may not have been recorded by the depositor. For example:

- *Service charges.* Banks often charge a fee for handling small accounts. The amount of this charge usually depends on both the average balance of the account and the number of checks paid during the month.

- *Charges for depositing NSF checks.* **NSF** stands for "Not Sufficient Funds." When checks are deposited in an account, the bank generally gives the depositor immediate credit. On occasion, one of these checks may prove to be uncollectible, because the maker of the check does not have sufficient funds in his or her account. In such cases, the bank will reduce the depositor's account by the amount of this uncollectible item and return the check to the depositor marked "NSF." The depositor should view an NSF check as an account receivable from the maker of the check, not as cash.

- *Credits for interest earned.* The checking accounts of *unincorporated* businesses often earn interest. At month-end, this interest is credited to the depositor's account and reported in the bank statement. (Current law prohibits interest on corporate checking accounts.)

- *Miscellaneous bank charges and credits.* Banks charge for services—such as printing checks, handling collections of notes receivable, and processing NSF checks. The bank *deducts* these charges from the depositor's account and notifies the depositor by including a debit memorandum in the monthly bank statement. If the bank collects a note receivable on behalf of the depositor, it credits the depositor's account and issues a credit memorandum.[2]

In a bank reconciliation, the balances shown in the bank statement and in the accounting records both are *adjusted for any unrecorded transactions.* Additional adjustment may be required to correct any errors discovered in the bank statement or in the accounting records.

**Steps in Preparing a Bank Reconciliation**  The specific steps in preparing a bank reconciliation are as follows:

1. Compare deposits listed in the bank statement with the deposits shown in the accounting records. Any deposits not yet recorded by the bank are deposits in transit and should be added to the balance shown in the bank statement.

2. Arrange paid checks in sequence by serial numbers and compare each check with the corresponding entry in the accounting records. Any checks issued but not yet paid by the bank should be listed as outstanding checks to be deducted from the balance reported in the bank statement.

3. Add to the balance per the depositor's accounting records any credit memoranda issued by the bank that have not been recorded by the depositor.

---

[2] Banks view each depositor's account as a *liability.* Debit memoranda are issued for transactions that reduce this liability, such as bank service charges. Credit memoranda are issued to recognize an increase in this liability, as results, for example, from interest earned by the depositor.

4. Deduct from the balance per the depositor's records any debit memoranda issued by the bank that have not been recorded by the depositor.

5. Make appropriate adjustments to correct any errors in either the bank statement or the depositor's accounting records.

6. Determine that the adjusted balance of the bank statement is equal to the adjusted balance in the depositor's records.

7. Prepare journal entries to record any items in the bank reconciliation listed as adjustments to the balance per the depositor's records.

**Illustration of a Bank Reconciliation**   The July bank statement sent by the bank to Parkview Company was illustrated on page 267. This statement shows a balance of cash on deposit at July 31 of *$5,000.17*. Assume that on July 31, Parkview's ledger shows a bank balance of *$4,262.83*. The employee preparing the bank reconciliation has identified the following reconciling items:

1. A deposit of $410.90 made after banking hours on July 31 does not appear in the bank statement.

2. Four checks issued in July have not yet been paid by the bank. These checks are:

| Check No. | Date | Amount |
|---|---|---|
| 801 | July 15 | $100.00 |
| 888 | July 24 | 10.25 |
| 890 | July 27 | 402.50 |
| 891 | July 30 | 205.00 |

3. Two credit memoranda were included in the bank statement:

| Date | Amount | Explanation |
|---|---|---|
| July 22 | $500.00 | Proceeds from collection of a non-interest-bearing note receivable from J. David. The bank's collection department collected this note for Parkview Company. |
| July 31 | 24.74 | Interest earned on average account balance during July. |

4. Three debit memoranda accompanied the bank statement:

| Date | Amount | Explanation |
|---|---|---|
| July 22 | $ 5.00 | Fee charged by bank for handling collection of note receivable. |
| July 30 | 50.25 | Check from customer J. B. Ball deposited by Parkview Company charged back as NSF. |
| July 31 | 12.00 | Service charge by bank for the month of July. |

5. Check no. 875 was issued July 20 in the amount of $85 but was erroneously recorded in the cash payments journal as $58. The check, in payment of telephone expense, was paid by the bank and correctly listed at $85 in the bank statement. In Parkview's ledger, the Cash account is *overstated* by $27 because of this error ($85 − $58 = $27).

The July 31 bank reconciliation for Parkview Company is shown on page 270. (The numbered arrows coincide both with the steps in preparing a bank reconciliation listed on pages 268–269 and with the reconciling items just listed.)

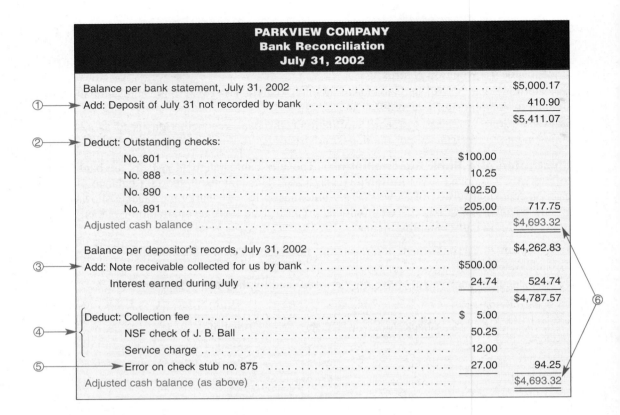

① Add: Deposit of July 31 not recorded by bank

② Deduct: Outstanding checks:

③ Add: Note receivable collected for us by bank

④ Deduct: Collection fee / NSF check of J. B. Ball / Service charge

⑤ Error on check stub no. 875

⑥

**PARKVIEW COMPANY**
**Bank Reconciliation**
**July 31, 2002**

| | | |
|---|---:|---:|
| Balance per bank statement, July 31, 2002 | | $5,000.17 |
| Add: Deposit of July 31 not recorded by bank | | 410.90 |
| | | $5,411.07 |
| Deduct: Outstanding checks: | | |
| No. 801 | $100.00 | |
| No. 888 | 10.25 | |
| No. 890 | 402.50 | |
| No. 891 | 205.00 | 717.75 |
| Adjusted cash balance | | $4,693.32 |
| Balance per depositor's records, July 31, 2002 | | $4,262.83 |
| Add: Note receivable collected for us by bank | $500.00 | |
| Interest earned during July | 24.74 | 524.74 |
| | | $4,787.57 |
| Deduct: Collection fee | $  5.00 | |
| NSF check of J. B. Ball | 50.25 | |
| Service charge | 12.00 | |
| Error on check stub no. 875 | 27.00 | 94.25 |
| Adjusted cash balance (as above) | | $4,693.32 |

**Updating the Accounting Records** The last step in reconciling a bank statement is to update the depositor's accounting records for any unrecorded cash transactions brought to light. In the bank reconciliation, every adjustment to the *balance per depositor's records* is a cash receipt or a cash payment that has not been recorded in the depositor's accounts. Therefore, *each of these items should be recorded*.

In this illustration and in our assignment material, we follow a policy of making one journal entry to record the unrecorded cash receipts and another to record the unrecorded cash reductions. (Acceptable alternatives would be to make separate journal entries for each item or to make one compound entry for all items.) Based on our recording policy, the entries to update the accounting records of Parkview Company are:

*Per bank credit memoranda . . .*

| | | |
|---|---:|---:|
| Cash | 524.74 | |
| Notes Receivable | | 500.00 |
| Interest Revenue | | 24.74 |

To record collection of note receivable from J. David collected by bank and interest earned on bank account in July.

*per bank debit memoranda (and correction of an error)*

| | | |
|---|---:|---:|
| Bank Service Charges | 17.00 | |
| Accounts Receivable (J. B. Ball) | 50.25 | |
| Telephone Expense | 27.00 | |
| Cash | | 94.25 |

To record bank charges (service charge, $12; collection fee, $5); to reclassify NSF check from customer J. B. Ball as an account receivable; and to correct understatement of cash payment for telephone expense.

## Petty Cash Funds

We have emphasized the importance of making all significant cash disbursements by check. However, every business finds it convenient to have a small amount of cash on hand with which to make some minor expenditures. Examples of these expenditures include such things as small purchases of office supplies, taxi fares, and doughnuts for an office meeting.

To create a petty cash fund, a check is drawn payable to "Petty Cash" for a round amount, such as $200, which will cover these small expenditures for a period of two or three weeks. This check is cashed and the money is kept on hand in a petty cash box. One employee is designated as the *custodian* of the fund.

The custodian makes all payments from this fund and obtains a receipt or prepares a "petty cash voucher" explaining the nature and amount of each expenditure. At the end of the period (or when the fund runs low), a check is drawn payable to Petty Cash reimbursing the fund for the expenditures made during the period. The issuance of this check is recorded by debiting the appropriate expense accounts and crediting Cash. As a practical matter, because of the small amount of petty cash expenditures, the entire debit portion of this entry often is charged to the Miscellaneous Expense account.

## The Cash Budget as a Control Device

Many businesses prepare detailed *cash budgets* that include forecasts of the monthly cash receipts and expenditures of each department within the organization. Management (or the internal auditors) will investigate any cash flows that differ significantly from the budgeted amounts. Thus each department manager is held accountable for the monthly cash transactions occurring within his or her department.

## SHORT-TERM INVESTMENTS

Companies with large amounts of liquid resources often hold most of these resources in the form of marketable securities rather than cash.

The first and most liquid asset listed in a recent balance sheet of **Microsoft Corporation** was "Cash and short-term investments . . . $8.94 billion." But who wants nearly $9 billion sitting in a corporate checking account and not earning any interest? Certainly not **Microsoft**. A footnote indicates that less than 10% of this asset was held in the form of cash. More than 90% was invested in short-term interest-bearing securities. If we assume **Microsoft** earns interest on these investments at an annual rate of, say, 5%, that's nearly $450 million in interest revenue per year.

**CASE IN POINT**

Marketable securities consist primarily of investments in bonds and in the capital stocks of publicly owned corporations. These marketable securities are traded (bought and sold) daily on organized securities exchanges, such as the New York Stock Exchange, the Tokyo Stock Exchange, and Mexico's Bolsa. A basic characteristic of all marketable securities is that they are *readily marketable*—meaning that they can be purchased or sold quickly and easily *at quoted market prices.*

Investments in marketable securities earn a return for the investor in the form of interest, dividends, and—if all goes well—an increase in market value. Meanwhile, these investments are *almost as liquid as cash itself.* They can be sold immediately over the telephone, simply by placing a "sell order" with a brokerage firm such as **Merrill Lynch** or **Salomon Smith Barney**, or on the Internet, by using an online brokerage firm such as **DLJ Direct**.

Because of their liquidity, investments in marketable securities usually are listed immediately after cash in the balance sheet.

## Mark-to-Market: A Principle of Asset Valuation

Accounting principles are not carved in stone. Rather, they evolve and change as the accounting profession seeks to increase the usefulness of accounting information. A 1993 change in the way companies account for short-term investments provides an excellent case in point.

Short-term investments once appeared in the balance sheet at the lower of their cost or current market value. This valuation method reflected the *cost principle,* tempered by *conservatism.* But in 1993, the FASB changed the rules. Short-term investments in marketable securities now appear in the balance sheet at their *current market value* as of the balance sheet date.[3]

Marketable securities are classified as one of three types: (1) available-for-sale securities, (2) trading securities, or (3) held-to-maturity securities. These classifications are based, in large part, on management's *intent* regarding the length of time the securities will be held. Most corporations classify their marketable securities as *available for sale.* In view of this fact, the remainder of our discussion focuses exclusively on this particular classification.

To achieve the objective of presenting marketable securities classified as available for sale at current market value, the balance sheet valuation of these investments is *adjusted to market value* at the balance sheet date. Hence, this valuation principle often is called **mark-to-market**. When the value of marketable securities is adjusted to current market value, an offsetting entry is made to an account entitled **Unrealized Holding Gain (or Loss) on Investments**. This account appears as a special stockholders' equity account in the balance sheet.

The following table summarizes the intent and the corresponding treatment of unrealized holding gains and losses of available-for-sale investments.

| Classification | Management's Intent | Treatment of Unrealized Holding Gains and Losses |
|---|---|---|
| Available-for-sale securities | Held for short-term resale (often 6 to 18 months) | Reported in stockholders' equity section of the balance sheet |

To illustrate, assume that Foster Corporation classifies all of its short-term investments as available for sale. The company currently owns marketable securities that had cost *$200,000,* but now have a market value of *$230,000.* A condensed balance sheet appears below.

| **FOSTER CORPORATION** **Balance Sheet** **December 31, 2002** | | | |
|---|---|---|---|
| **Assets** | | **Liabilities & Stockholders' Equity** | |
| **Current assets:** | | **Liabilities:** | |
| Cash | $ 50,000 | (Detail not shown) | $350,000 |
| Marketable securities (cost, | | **Stockholders' equity:** | |
| $200,000; market value, | | Capital stock | 100,000 |
| $230,000) | 230,000 | Retained earnings | 420,000 |
| Accounts receivable | 300,000 | Unrealized holding | |
| Total current assets | $580,000 | Gain on investments | 30,000 |
| Other assets: | | Total Stockholders' Equity | $550,000 |
| (Detail not shown) | 320,000 | | |
| Total | $900,000 | Total | $900,000 |

[3] FASB, *Statement of Financial Accounting Standards No. 115,* "Accounting for Certain Investments in Debt and Equity Securities" (Norwalk, Conn., 1993).

Although the $200,000 cost of the marketable securities is *disclosed* in the balance sheet, the basis for the amount in the money columns is *$230,000*—the securities' *current market value.*

The difference between cost and current market value also appears as an *element of stockholders' equity*, labeled Unrealized Holding Gain (or Loss) on Investments. When the market value of the investments is *above* cost, as in the case just presented, this special equity account represents a holding *gain*. But if the market value is below cost, the equity account represents a holding *loss* and is shown as a *reduction* in total stockholders' equity.

Unrealized holding gains and losses are *not* subject to income taxes. Income taxes are levied on gains and losses only when the investments are sold. Nonetheless, unrealized gains and losses are shown in the balance sheet net of the expected *future* income tax effects. These expected future tax effects are included in the company's tax liability rather than in the amount shown as unrealized holding gain or loss. Such "deferred tax adjustments" are beyond the scope of our introductory discussion and are addressed in later accounting courses. In the discussions and assignment materials of this chapter, holding gains and losses simply represent the difference between the cost and the current market value of the securities owned.

Accounting for marketable securities, including the mark-to-market adjustments, is discussed further in *Supplemental Topic A* at the end of this chapter.

**Our Assessment of Mark-to-Market**   The authors of this text commend the FASB on this change in accounting principles. Reporting short-term investments at market value substantially enhances the usefulness of the balance sheet in evaluating the solvency of a business.

Mark-to-market is not always used internationally for valuing short-term investments. Germany and Japan continue to use the lower of cost or market valuation techniques because their accounting standards setters (Ministry of Finance for Japan and the German government) believe the techniques are more conservative.

**CASE IN POINT**

## ACCOUNTS RECEIVABLE

One of the key factors underlying the growth of the American economy is the trend toward selling goods and services on credit. Accounts receivable comprise the largest financial asset of many merchandising companies.

Accounts receivable are relatively liquid assets, usually converting into cash within a period of 30 to 60 days. Therefore, accounts receivable from customers usually appear in the balance sheet immediately after cash and short-term investments in marketable securities.

Sometimes companies sell merchandise on longer-term installment plans, requiring 12, 24, or even 48 months to collect the entire amount receivable from the customer. By definition, the normal period of time required to collect accounts receivable is part of a company's *operating cycle*. Therefore, accounts receivable arising from normal sales transactions usually are classified as current assets, even if the credit terms extend beyond one year.[4]

---

[4] The period used to define current assets is one year or the company's operating cycle, whichever is longer. The *operating cycle* is the period of time needed to convert cash into inventory, the inventory into accounts receivable, and the accounts receivable back into cash. We discuss the classification of certain assets as current assets in greater depth in Chapter 14.

**MANAGEMENT STRATEGY**

In a statement of cash flows, the cash receipts from collecting receivables are included in the subtotal, net cash flow from operating activities. Collections of accounts receivable often represent a company's largest and most consistent source of cash receipts. Thus monitoring the collection of receivables is an important part of efficient cash management.

**Dell Computer Corp.** learned that managing to squeeze time out of every step in its operating cycle between taking an order and collecting the cash can pay off. **Dell** converts the average sale to cash in less than 24 hours through the use of Internet ordering, credit cards, and electronic payment. By contrast, competitors, such as **Compaq** and **Gateway** take 35 days and 16.4 days, respectively.

A company's ability to generate the cash needed for routine business operations often depends on the amount, collectibility, and maturity dates of its receivables. Users of financial reports can judge a company's ability to collect receivables by looking at the cash flow statement.

---

**LO 5**

Account for uncollectible receivables using the allowance and direct write-off methods.

## Uncollectible Accounts

We have stated that accounts receivable are shown in the balance sheet at the estimated collectible amount—called *net realizable value.* No business wants to sell merchandise on account to customers who will be unable to pay. Many companies maintain their own credit departments that investigate the creditworthiness of each prospective customer. Nonetheless, if a company makes credit sales to hundreds—perhaps thousands—of customers, some accounts inevitably will turn out to be uncollectible.

A limited amount of uncollectible accounts is not only expected—it is evidence of a sound credit policy. If the credit department is overly cautious, the business may lose many sales opportunities by rejecting customers who should have been considered acceptable credit risks.

**Reflecting Uncollectible Accounts in the Financial Statements**    An account receivable that has been determined to be uncollectible is no longer an asset. The loss of this asset represents an *expense,* termed Uncollectible Accounts Expense.

In measuring business income, one of the most fundamental principles of accounting is that revenue should be *matched* with (offset by) the expenses incurred in generating that revenue. Uncollectible accounts expense is *caused by selling goods* on credit to customers who fail to pay their bills. Therefore, this expense is incurred in the time period in which the *related sales* are made, even though specific accounts receivable may not be determined to be uncollectible until a later accounting period. Thus an account receivable that originates from a credit sale in January and is determined to be uncollectible in August represents an expense in *January.* Accurately estimating the amount of uncollectible receivables requires significant judgment on the part of accountants.

To illustrate, assume that World Famous Toy Co. begins business on January 1, 2002, and makes most of its sales on account. At January 31, accounts receivable amount to $250,000. On this date, the credit manager reviews the accounts receivable and estimates that approximately $10,000 of these accounts will prove to be uncollectible. The following adjusting entry should be made at January 31:

*Provision for uncollectible accounts*

| | | |
|---|---|---|
| Uncollectible Accounts Expense . . . . . . . . . . . . . . . . . . . . . . . . . . . . . . . . | 10,000 | |
|     Allowance for Doubtful Accounts . . . . . . . . . . . . . . . . . . . . . . . . . . . . . | | 10,000 |

To record the portion of total accounts receivable estimated to be uncollectible.

The Uncollectible Accounts Expense account created by the debit part of this entry is closed into the Income Summary account in the same manner as any other expense account. The Allowance for Doubtful Accounts that was credited in the above journal entry appears in the balance sheet as a deduction from the face amount of the accounts receivable. It reduces the accounts receivable to their *net realizable value* in the balance sheet, as shown by the following illustration:

**WORLD FAMOUS TOY CO.**
**Partial Balance Sheet**
**January 31, 2002**

| Current assets: | | |
|---|---|---|
| Cash and cash equivalents | | $ 75,000 |
| Marketable securities | | 25,000 |
| Accounts receivable | $250,000 | |
| Less: Allowance for doubtful accounts | 10,000 | 240,000 |
| Inventory | | 300,000 |
| Total current assets | | $640,000 |

*How much is the estimated net realizable value of the accounts receivable?*

## The Allowance for Doubtful Accounts

There is no way of telling in advance *which* accounts receivable will prove to be uncollectible. It is therefore not possible to credit the accounts of specific customers for our estimate of probable uncollectible accounts. Neither should we credit the Accounts Receivable controlling account in the general ledger. If the Accounts Receivable controlling account were to be credited with the estimated amount of doubtful accounts, this controlling account would no longer be in balance with the total of the numerous customers' accounts in the subsidiary ledger. A practical alternative, therefore, is to credit a separate account called **Allowance for Doubtful Accounts** with the amount estimated to be uncollectible.

The Allowance for Doubtful Accounts often is described as a *contra-asset* account or a *valuation* account. Both of these terms indicate that the Allowance for Doubtful Accounts has a credit balance, which is offset against the asset Accounts Receivable to produce a more useful and reliable measure of a company's liquidity.

**Estimating the Amount of Uncollectible Accounts**   Before financial statements are prepared at the end of the accounting period, an estimate of the expected amount of uncollectible accounts receivable should be made. This estimate is based on past experience and modified in accordance with current business conditions. Losses from uncollectible receivables tend to be greater during periods of recession than in periods of growth and prosperity. Because the allowance for doubtful accounts is an estimate and not a precise calculation, *professional judgment* plays a considerable part in determining the size of this valuation account.

**Monthly Adjustments of the Allowance Account**   In the adjusting entry made by World Famous Toy Co. at January 31, the amount of the adjustment ($10,000) was equal to the estimated amount of uncollectible accounts. This is true only because January was the first month of operations and this was the company's first estimate of its uncollectible accounts. In future months, the amount of the adjusting entry will depend on two factors: (1) the *estimate* of uncollectible accounts and (2) the *current balance* in the Allowance for Doubtful Accounts. Before we illustrate the adjusting entry for a future month, let us see why the balance in the allowance account may change during the accounting period.

## Writing Off an Uncollectible Account Receivable

Whenever an account receivable from a specific customer is determined to be uncollectible, it no longer qualifies as an asset and should be written off. To *write off* an account receivable is to reduce the balance of the customer's account to zero. The journal entry to accomplish this consists of a credit to the Accounts Receivable control-ling account in the general ledger (and to the customer's account in the subsidiary ledger) and an offsetting debit to the Allowance for Doubtful Accounts.

To illustrate, assume that early in February, World Famous Toy Co. learns that Discount Stores has gone out of business and that the $4,000 account receivable from this customer is now worthless. The entry to write off this uncollectible account receivable is:

*Writing off a receivable "against the allowance"*

| | | |
|---|---|---|
| Allowance for Doubtful Accounts . . . . . . . . . . . . . . . . . . . . . . . . . . . . . . . . . . . . . . | 4,000 | |
|     Accounts Receivable (Discount Stores) . . . . . . . . . . . . . . . . . . . . . . . . . . . | | 4,000 |

To write off the receivable from Discount Stores as uncollectible.

The important thing to note in this entry is that the debit is made to the Allowance for Doubtful Accounts and *not* to the Uncollectible Accounts Expense account. The estimated expense of credit losses is charged to the Uncollectible Accounts Expense account at the end of each accounting period. When a specific account receivable is later determined to be worthless and is written off, this action does not represent an additional expense but merely confirms our previous estimate of the expense. If the Uncollectible Accounts Expense account were first charged with *estimated* credit losses and then later charged with *proven* credit losses, we would be double-counting the actual uncollectible accounts expense.

Notice also that the entry to write off an uncollectible account receivable reduces both the asset account and the contra-asset account by the same amount. Thus writing off an uncollectible account *does not change* the net realizable value of accounts receivable in the balance sheet. The following illustration shows the net realizable value of World Famous Toy Co.'s accounts receivable before and after the write-off of the account receivable from Discount Stores:

*What happens to net realizable value?*

| Before the Write-off | | After the Write-off | |
|---|---|---|---|
| Accounts Receivable . . . . . . . . . | $250,000 | Accounts Receivable . . . . . . . . . | $246,000 |
| Less: Allowance for Doubtful | | Less: Allowance for Doubtful | |
|     Accounts . . . . . . . . . . . . . . | 10,000 |     Accounts . . . . . . . . . . . . . . | 6,000 |
| Net Realizable Value . . . . . . . . . | $240,000 | Net Realizable Value . . . . . . . . . | $240,000 |

Let us repeat the point that underlies the allowance approach. Credit losses are recognized as an expense in the period in which the *sale occurs,* not the period in which the account is determined to be uncollectible. The reasoning for this position is based on the *matching principle.*

**Write-offs Seldom Agree with Previous Estimates**    The total amount of accounts receivable actually written off will seldom, if ever, be exactly equal to the estimated amount previously credited to the Allowance for Doubtful Accounts.

If the amounts written off as uncollectible turn out to be less than the estimated amount, the Allowance for Doubtful Accounts will continue to show a credit balance. If the amounts written off as uncollectible are greater than the estimated amount, the Allowance for Doubtful Accounts will acquire a *temporary debit balance,* which will be eliminated by the adjustment at the end of the period.

## Recovery of an Account Receivable Previously Written Off

Occasionally a receivable that has been written off as worthless will later be collected in full or in part. Such collections are often referred to as *recoveries* of bad debts. Collection of an account receivable previously written off is evidence that the write-off was an error; the receivable should therefore be reinstated as an asset.

Let us assume, for example, that a past-due account receivable in the amount of $200 from J. B. Barker was written off on February 16 by the following entry:

| | | |
|---|---|---|
| Allowance for Doubtful Accounts . . . . . . . . . . . . . . . . . . . . . . . . . . . . . . . . . . | 200 | |
|    Accounts Receivable (J. B. Barker) . . . . . . . . . . . . . . . . . . . . . . . . . . . . . . | | 200 |
| To write off the receivable from J. B. Barker as uncollectible. | | |

*Barker account considered uncollectible*

On February 27, the customer, J. B. Barker, pays the account in full. The entry to restore Barker's account will be:

| | | |
|---|---|---|
| Accounts Receivable (J. B. Barker) . . . . . . . . . . . . . . . . . . . . . . . . . . . . . . . . | 200 | |
|    Allowance for Doubtful Accounts . . . . . . . . . . . . . . . . . . . . . . . . . . . . . . | | 200 |
| To reinstate as an asset an account receivable previously written off. | | |

*Barker account reinstated*

Notice that this entry is *exactly the opposite* of the entry made when the account was written off as uncollectible. A separate entry will be made in the cash receipts journal to record the collection from Barker:

| | | |
|---|---|---|
| Cash . . . . . . . . . . . . . . . . . . . . . . . . . . . . . . . . . . . . . . . . . . . . . . . . . . . . . | 200 | |
|    Accounts Receivable (J. B. Barker) . . . . . . . . . . . . . . . . . . . . . . . . . . . . . . | | 200 |
| To record the collection of receivable from J. B. Barker. | | |

## Monthly Estimates of Credit Losses

At the end of each month, management should again estimate the probable amount of uncollectible accounts and adjust the Allowance for Doubtful Accounts to this new estimate.

To illustrate, assume that at the end of February the credit manager of World Famous Toy Co. analyzes the accounts receivable and estimates that approximately *$11,000* of these accounts will prove uncollectible. Currently, the Allowance for Doubtful Accounts has a credit balance of only *$6,000,* determined as follows:

| | | |
|---|---|---|
| Balance at January 31 (credit) . . . . . . . . . . . . . . . . . . . . . . . . . . . . . . . . . . . . | | $10,000 |
| Less: Write-offs of accounts considered worthless: | | |
|    Discount Stores . . . . . . . . . . . . . . . . . . . . . . . . . . . . . . . . . . . . . . . | $4,000 | |
|    J. B. Barker . . . . . . . . . . . . . . . . . . . . . . . . . . . . . . . . . . . . . . . . . . | 200 | 4,200 |
| Subtotal . . . . . . . . . . . . . . . . . . . . . . . . . . . . . . . . . . . . . . . . . . . . . . . . . . | | $ 5,800 |
| Add: Recoveries of accounts previously written off: J. B. Barker . . . . . . . . . . . . | | 200 |
| Balance at end of February (prior to adjusting entry) . . . . . . . . . . . . . . . . . . | | $ 6,000 |

*Current balance in the allowance account*

To increase the balance in the allowance account to $11,000 at February 28, the month-end adjusting entry must add $5,000 to the allowance. The entry will be:

| | | |
|---|---|---|
| Uncollectible Accounts Expense . . . . . . . . . . . . . . . . . . . . . . . . . . . | 5,000 | |
|    Allowance for Doubtful Accounts . . . . . . . . . . . . . . . . . . . . . . . . | | 5,000 |
| To increase the Allowance for Doubtful Accounts to $11,000, | | |
|   computed as follows: | | |
|    Required allowance at Feb. 28 . . . . . . . . . . . . . . . . . . . . . . . . | $11,000 | |
|    Credit balance prior to adjustment . . . . . . . . . . . . . . . . . . . . . | 6,000 | |
|    Required adjustment . . . . . . . . . . . . . . . . . . . . . . . . . . . . . . . | $ 5,000 | |

*Increasing the allowance for doubtful accounts*

**Estimating Credit Losses—The Balance Sheet Approach**   The most widely used method of estimating the probable amount of uncollectible accounts is based on **aging the accounts receivable**. This method is sometimes called the *balance sheet* approach because the method emphasizes the proper balance sheet valuation of accounts receivable.

"Aging" accounts receivable means classifying each receivable according to its age. An aging schedule for the accounts receivable of Valley Ranch Supply follows:

| | Total | Not Yet Due | 1–30 Days Past Due | 31–60 Days Past Due | 61–90 Days Past Due | Over 90 Days Past Due |
|---|---|---|---|---|---|---|
| **VALLEY RANCH SUPPLY** Analysis of Accounts Receivable by Age December 31, 2002 | | | | | | |
| Animal Care Center | $ 9,000 | $ 9,000 | | | | |
| Butterfield, John D. | 2,400 | | | $ 2,400 | | |
| Citrus Groves, Inc. | 4,000 | 3,000 | $ 1,000 | | | |
| Dairy Fresh Farms | 1,600 | | | | $ 600 | $1,000 |
| Eastlake Stables | 13,000 | 7,000 | 6,000 | | | |
| (Other customers) | 70,000 | 32,000 | 22,000 | 9,600 | 2,400 | 4,000 |
| Totals | $100,000 | $51,000 | $29,000 | $12,000 | $3,000 | $5,000 |

An aging schedule is useful to management in reviewing the status of individual accounts receivable and in evaluating the overall effectiveness of credit and collection policies. In addition, the schedule is used as the basis for estimating the amount of uncollectible accounts.

The longer an account is past due, the greater the likelihood that it will not be collected in full. Based on past experience, the credit manager estimates the percentage of credit losses likely to occur in each age group of accounts receivable. This percentage, when applied to the total dollar amount in the age group, gives the estimated uncollectible portion for that group. By adding together the estimated uncollectible portions for all age groups, the *required balance* in the Allowance for Doubtful Accounts is determined. The following schedule lists the group totals from the aging schedule and shows how the estimated total amount of uncollectible accounts is computed:

| | Age Group Total | | Percentage Considered Uncollectible* | | Estimated Uncollectible Accounts |
|---|---|---|---|---|---|
| **VALLEY RANCH SUPPLY** Estimated Uncollectible Accounts Receivable December 31, 2002 | | | | | |
| Not yet due ................. | $ 51,000 | × | 1% | = | $ 510 |
| 1–30 days past due ............ | 29,000 | × | 3% | = | 870 |
| 31–60 days past due ........... | 12,000 | × | 10% | = | 1,200 |
| 61–90 days past due ........... | 3,000 | × | 20% | = | 600 |
| Over 90 days past due .......... | 5,000 | × | 50% | = | 2,500 |
| Totals ..................... | $100,000 | | | | $5,680 |

*These percentages are estimated each month by the credit manager, based on recent experience and current economic conditions.

At December 31, Valley Ranch Supply has total accounts receivable of $100,000, of which $5,680 are estimated to be uncollectible. Thus an adjusting entry is needed to increase the Allowance for Doubtful Accounts from its present level to $5,680. If the allowance account currently has a credit balance of, say, $4,000, the month-end adjusting entry should be in the amount of $1,680.[5]

**An Alternative Approach to Estimating Credit Losses**   The procedures just discussed describe the *balance sheet* approach to estimating and recording credit losses. This approach is based on an aging schedule, and the Allowance for Doubtful Accounts is *adjusted to a required balance.* An alternative method, called the *income statement* approach, focuses on estimating the uncollectible accounts *expense* for the period. Based on past experience, the uncollectible accounts expense is estimated at some percentage of net credit sales. The adjusting entry is made in the *full amount of the estimated expense,* without regard for the current balance in the Allowance for Doubtful Accounts.

To illustrate, assume that a company's past experience indicates that about 2% of its credit sales will prove to be uncollectible. If credit sales for September amount to $150,000, the month-end adjusting entry to record uncollectible accounts expense is:

| | | | |
|---|---|---|---|
| Uncollectible Accounts Expense | 3,000 | | *The income statement* |
|    Allowance for Doubtful Accounts | | 3,000 | *approach* |
| To record uncollectible accounts expense, estimated at 2% of | | | |
|   credit sales ($150,000 × 2% = $3,000). | | | |

This approach is fast and simple—no aging schedule is required and no consideration is given to the existing balance in the Allowance for Doubtful Accounts. The aging of accounts receivable, however, provides a more reliable estimate of uncollectible accounts because of the consideration given to the age and collectibility of specific accounts receivable at the balance sheet date.

In past years, many small companies used the income statement approach in preparing monthly financial statements but used the balance sheet method in annual financial statements. Today, however, most businesses have computer software that quickly and easily prepares monthly aging schedules of accounts receivable. Thus most businesses today use the *balance sheet approach* in their monthly as well as annual financial statements.

**Conservatism in the Valuation of Accounts Receivable**   We previously have made reference to the accounting concept of **conservatism**. In accounting, conservatism means resolving uncertainty in a manner that minimizes the risk of overstating the company's current financial position. With respect to the valuation of accounts receivable, conservatism suggests that the allowance for doubtful accounts should be *at least adequate.* That is, it is better to err on the side of the allowance being a little too large, rather than a little too small.

Notice that conservatism in the valuation of assets also leads to a conservative measurement of net income in the current period. The larger the valuation allowance, the larger the current charge to uncollectible accounts expense.

---

[5] If accounts receivable written off during the period *exceed* the Allowance for Doubtful Accounts at the last adjustment date, the allowance account temporarily acquires a *debit balance.* This situation seldom occurs if the allowance is adjusted each month but often occurs if adjusting entries are made only at year-end.

If Valley Ranch Supply makes only an annual adjustment for uncollectible accounts, the allowance account might have a debit balance of, say, $10,000. In this case, the year-end adjusting entry should be for *$15,680* in order to bring the allowance to the required credit balance of $5,680.

Regardless of how often adjusting entries are made, the balance in the allowance account of Valley Ranch Supply should be *$5,680 at year-end.* Uncollectible accounts expense will be the same for the year, regardless of whether adjusting entries are made annually or monthly. The only difference is in whether this expense is recognized in one annual adjusting entry or in 12 monthly adjusting entries, each for a smaller amount.

## Direct Write-off Method

Some companies do not use any valuation allowance for accounts receivable. Instead of making end-of-period adjusting entries to record uncollectible accounts expense on the basis of estimates, these companies recognize no uncollectible accounts expense until specific receivables are determined to be worthless. This method makes no attempt to match revenue with the expense of uncollectible accounts.

When a particular customer's account is determined to be uncollectible, it is written off directly to Uncollectible Accounts Expense, as follows:

Uncollectible Accounts Expense . . . . . . . . . . . . . . . . . . . . . . . . . . . . . . . . . . . . . . 250
    Accounts Receivable (Bell Products) . . . . . . . . . . . . . . . . . . . . . . . . . . . . . . . 250
To write off the receivable from Bell Products as uncollectible.

When the **direct write-off method** is used, the accounts receivable will be listed in the balance sheet at their gross amount, and *no valuation allowance* will be used. The receivables, therefore, are not stated at estimated net realizable value.

The allowance method is preferable to the direct write-off method because the allowance method does a better job of matching revenues and expenses. In some situations, however, use of the direct write-off method is acceptable. If a company makes most of its sales for cash, the amount of its accounts receivable will be small in relation to other assets. The expense from uncollectible accounts should also be small. Consequently, the direct write-off method is acceptable because its use does not have a *material* effect on the reported net income. Another situation in which the direct write-off method works satisfactorily is in a company that sells all or most of its output to a few large companies that are financially strong. In this setting there may be no basis for making advance estimates of any credit losses.

## Income Tax Regulations and Financial Reporting

In previous chapters we made the point that companies often use different accounting methods in preparing their income tax returns and their financial statements. The accounting treatments accorded to uncollectible accounts receivable provide an excellent example of this concept.

Current income tax regulations *require* taxpayers to use the direct write-off method in determining the uncollectible accounts expense used in computing *taxable income.* From the standpoint of accounting theory, the allowance method is better because it enables expenses to be *matched* with the related revenue and thus provides a more logical measurement of net income. Therefore, most companies use the allowance method in their financial statements.[6]

## Internal Controls for Receivables

One of the most important principles of internal control is that employees who have custody of cash or other negotiable assets must not maintain accounting records. In a small business, one employee often is responsible for handling cash receipts, maintaining accounts receivable records, issuing credit memoranda, and writing off uncollectible accounts. Such a combination of duties is an invitation to fraud. The employee in this situation is able to remove the cash collected from a customer without making any record of the collection. The next step is to dispose of the balance in the customer's account. This can be done by issuing a credit memo indicating that the customer has returned merchandise, or by writing off the customer's account as uncollectible. Thus the em-

---

[6] An annual survey of accounting practices of 600 publicly owned corporations consistently shows more than 500 of these companies using the allowance method in their financial statements. All of these companies, however, use the direct write-off method in their income tax returns.

ployee has the cash, the customer's account shows a zero balance due, and the books are in balance.

In summary, employees who maintain the accounts receivable subsidiary ledger should *not have access* to cash receipts. The employees who maintain accounts receivable or handle cash receipts should *not* have authority to issue credit memoranda or to authorize the write-off of receivables as uncollectible. These are classic examples of incompatible duties.

## Management of Accounts Receivable

Management has two conflicting objectives with respect to the accounts receivable. On the one hand, management wants to generate as much sales revenue as possible. Offering customers lengthy credit terms, with little or no interest, has proven to be an effective means of generating sales revenue.

Every business, however, would rather sell for cash than on account. Unless receivables earn interest, which usually is not the case, they are nonproductive assets that produce no revenue as they await collection. Therefore, another objective of cash management is to minimize the amount of money tied up in the form of accounts receivable.

Several tools are available to a management that must offer credit terms to its customers yet wants to minimize the company's investment in accounts receivable. We have already discussed offering credit customers cash discounts (such as 2/10, n/30) to encourage early payment. Other tools include *factoring* accounts receivable and selling to customers who use national credit cards.

## Factoring Accounts Receivable

The term **factoring** describes transactions in which a business either sells its accounts receivable to a financial institution (often called a *factor*) or borrows money by pledging its accounts receivable as collateral (security) for a loan. In either case, the business obtains cash immediately instead of having to wait until the receivables can be collected.

Factoring accounts receivable is a practice limited primarily to small business organizations that do not have well-established credit. Large and solvent organizations usually are able to borrow money using unsecured lines of credit, so they need not factor their accounts receivable.

### You as an Accounts Receivable Manager

One of your accounts receivable customers discovered that you plan to factor your accounts receivable to the John Doe Collection Agency. That customer has called you to ask about the legality and ethics of factoring accounts receivable. He complains that he entered into a contract to pay your company and not a collection agency. He says he did not give you permission to sell his receivable and that selling the receivables to another organization eliminates his obligation to pay the receivable. How would you respond to the customer?

*Our comments appear on p. 312.

YOUR TURN

## Credit Card Sales

Many retailing businesses minimize their investment in receivables by encouraging customers to use credit cards such as American Express, Visa, and MasterCard. A customer who makes a purchase using one of these cards signs a multiple-copy form, which includes a *credit card draft*. A credit card draft is similar to a check that is drawn on the funds of the credit card company rather than on the personal bank account of the customer. The credit card company promptly pays a discounted amount of cash to the merchant to redeem these drafts. At the end of each month, the credit card company bills the credit card holder for all the drafts it has redeemed during the month. If the credit card holder fails to pay the amount owed, the credit card company sustains the loss.

By making sales through credit card companies, merchants receive cash more quickly from credit sales and avoid uncollectible accounts expense. Also, the merchant avoids the expenses of investigating customers' credit, maintaining an accounts receivable subsidiary ledger, and making collections from customers.

**Bank Credit Cards**     Some widely used credit cards (such as Visa and MasterCard) are issued by banks. When the credit card company is a bank, the retailing business may deposit the signed credit card drafts directly in its bank account. Because banks accept these credit card drafts for immediate deposit, sales to customers using bank credit cards are recorded as *cash sales.*

In exchange for handling the credit card drafts, the bank makes a monthly service charge that usually runs between $1^1/4\%$ and $3^1/2\%$ of the amount of the drafts. This monthly service charge is deducted from the merchant's bank account and appears with other bank service charges in the merchant's monthly bank statement.

**Other Credit Cards**     When customers use nonbank credit cards (such as American Express and Carte Blanche), the retailing business cannot deposit the credit card drafts directly in its bank account. Instead of debiting Cash, the merchant records an account receivable from the credit card company. Periodically, the credit card drafts are mailed (or transmitted electronically) to the credit card company, which then sends a check to the merchant. Credit card companies, however, do not redeem the drafts at the full sales price. The agreement between the credit card company and the merchant usually allows the credit card company to take a discount of between $3^1/2\%$ and 5% when redeeming the drafts.

To illustrate, assume that Bradshaw Camera Shop sells a camera for $200 to a customer who uses a Quick Charge credit card. The entry would be:

*This receivable is from the credit card company*

| | | |
|---|---:|---:|
| Accounts Receivable (Quick Charge Co.) | 200 | |
|    Sales | | 200 |
| To record sale to customer using Quick Charge credit card. | | |

At the end of the week, Bradshaw Camera Shop mails credit card drafts totaling $1,200 to Quick Charge Company, which redeems the drafts after deducting a 5% discount. When payment is received by Bradshaw, the entry is:

| | | |
|---|---:|---:|
| Cash | 1,140 | |
| Credit Card Discount Expense | 60 | |
|    Accounts Receivable (Quick Charge Co.) | | 1,200 |
| To record collection of account receivable from Quick Charge Co., less 5% discount. | | |

The expense account, Credit Card Discount Expense, is included among the selling expenses in the income statement of Bradshaw Camera Shop.

## ▌ FINANCIAL ANALYSIS

Collecting accounts receivable *on time* is important; it spells the success or failure of a company's credit and collection policies. A past-due receivable is a candidate for write-off as a credit loss. To help us judge how good a job a company is doing in granting credit and collecting its receivables, we compute the ratio of net sales to average receivables. This **accounts receivable turnover rate** tells us how many times the company's average investment in receivables was converted into cash during the year. The ratio is computed by dividing annual net sales by average accounts receivable.[7]

**LO 6**

Evaluate the liquidity of various financial assets.

---

[7] From a conceptual point of view, net *credit* sales should be used in computing the accounts receivable turnover rate. It is common practice, however, to use the net sales figure, as the portion of net sales made on account usually is not disclosed in financial statements.

For example, recent financial statements of **3M (Minnesota Mining and Manufacturing Company)** show net sales of $9.4 billion. Receivables were $1.6 billion at the beginning of the year and $1.4 billion at the end of the year. Adding these two amounts and dividing the total by 2 gives us average receivables of $1.5 billion. Now we divide the year's net sales by the average receivables ($9.4 ÷ $1.5 = 6.3); the result indicates an accounts receivable turnover rate of *6.3 times* per year for 3M. The higher the turnover rate, the more liquid the company's receivables.

Another step that will help us judge the liquidity of a company's accounts receivable is to convert the accounts receivable turnover rate to the *number of days* (on average) required for the company to collect its accounts receivable. This is a simple calculation: divide the number of days in the year by the turnover rate. Continuing our **3M** example, divide 365 days by the turnover rate of 6.3 (365 ÷ 6.3 = 57.9 days). This calculation tells us that on average, **3M** waited approximately *58 days* to collect a sale on credit.

The data just described for computing the accounts receivable turnover rate and the average number of days to collect accounts receivable can be concisely stated as shown in the following equations:

**Accounts Receivable Turnover**

$$\frac{\text{Net Sales}}{\text{Average Accounts Receivable}} = \frac{\$9.4}{(\$1.6 + \$1.4) \div 2} = \frac{\$9.4}{\$1.5} = 6.3 \text{ times}$$

**Average Number of Days to Collect Accounts Receivable**

$$\frac{\text{Days in Year}}{\text{Accounts Receivable Turnover}} = \frac{365}{6.3} = 58 \text{ days}$$

Management closely monitors these ratios in evaluating the company's policies for extending credit to customers and the effectiveness of its collection procedures. Short-term creditors, such as factors, banks, and merchandise suppliers, also use these ratios to evaluate a company's ability to generate the cash necessary to pay its short-term liabilities.

In the annual audit of a company by a CPA firm, the independent auditors will verify receivables by communicating directly with the people who owe the money. This *confirmation* process is designed to provide evidence that the customers and other debtors actually exist and that they acknowledge their indebtedness. The CPA firm also may verify the credit rating of major debtors.

---

## You as a Credit Manager

Assume that you were hired by Regis Department Stores in 1999 to develop and implement a new credit policy. At the time of your hire, the average collection period for an outstanding receivable was in excess of 90 days (far greater than the industry average). Thus the primary purpose of the new policy was to better screen credit applicants in an attempt to improve the quality of the company's accounts receivable.

**YOUR TURN**

Shown below are sales and accounts receivable data for the past four years (in thousands):

|  | 2002 | 2001 | 2000 | 1999 |
|---|---|---|---|---|
| Sales ............................... | $17,000 | $14,580 | $9,600 | $9,000 |
| Average Accounts Receivable ....................... | $ 1,700 | $ 1,620 | $1,600 | $1,800 |

Based on the above data, was the credit policy you developed successful? Explain.

*Our comments appear on page 312.

## Concentrations of Credit Risk

Assume that a business operates a single retail store in a town in which the major employer is a steel mill. What would happen to the collectibility of the store's accounts receivable if the steel mill were to close, leaving most of the store's customers unemployed? This situation illustrates what accountants call a *concentration of credit risk*, because many of the store's credit customers can be affected *in a similar manner* by certain changes in economic conditions. Concentrations of credit risk occur if a significant portion of a company's receivables are due from a few major customers or from customers operating in the same industry or geographic region.

The FASB requires companies to disclose all significant concentrations of credit risk in the notes accompanying their financial statements. The basic purpose of these disclosures is to assist users of the financial statements in evaluating the extent of the company's vulnerability to credit losses stemming from changes in specific economic conditions.

## Notes Receivable and Interest Charges

**LO 7**

Explain how transactions discussed in this chapter affect net income and cash flows.

Accounts receivable usually do not bear interest. When interest will be charged, creditors usually require the debtor to sign a formal promissory note. Accounting for notes receivable and interest charges is discussed in *Supplemental Topic B* at the end of this chapter.

---

**CASH EFFECTS**     Early in this chapter, we summarized the valuation of financial assets in the balance sheet (page 263). The following table summarizes the reporting of transactions involving these assets in the *income statement* and any cash effects to be presented in the *statement of cash flows*. Note that most of these transactions have no cash flow effects.

| Transactions | Presentation in the: | |
| --- | --- | --- |
| | **Income Statement** | **Statement of Cash Flows** |
| Cash sales | Included in net sales | Cash receipts from operating activities |
| Investments in cash equivalents | No effect | Omitted—does not change cash total |
| Conversion of cash equivalents back into cash | No effect | Omitted—does not change cash total |
| Interest received from cash equivalents | *Nonoperating revenue | Cash receipts from operating activities |
| Investments in marketable securities | No effect | Cash used in investing activities |
| Conversion of marketable securities into cash | Nonoperating item (only the amount of gain or loss) | Cash receipts from investing activities (total proceeds) |
| *Interest and dividends from investments | *Nonoperating revenue (recognized *as received*) | Cash receipts from operating activities |
| *Year-end mark-to-market adjustment of available-for-sale marketable securities | No effect | Omitted—not a cash transaction |
| Sales on account | Included in net sales | Omitted—not a cash transaction |
| Collections of accounts receivable | No effect | Cash receipts from operating activities |
| Addition to an allowance for doubtful accounts | Operating expense | Omitted—not a cash transaction |
| Write-off of an uncollectible account against the allowance | No effect | Omitted—not a cash transaction |
| Write-off of an account using the direct write-off method | Operating expense | Omitted—not a cash transaction |
| †Interest revenue on notes receivable | Nonoperating revenue (recognized *as earned*) | Cash receipts from operating activities (recognized *as received*) |

*Topic is covered in *Supplemental Topic A.*

†Topic is covered in *Supplemental Topic B.*

## Xerox

Financial assets are particularly important because they provide a company's liquidity. In other words, they are the assets to retire the company's liabilities as they come due.

The asset section of **Xerox**'s 1999 balance sheet (dollars in millions) appears as follows:

**A SECOND LOOK**

| Assets | |
|---|---|
| Cash | $ 126 |
| Accounts receivable, net | 2,622 |
| Finance receivables, net | 5,115 |
| Inventories | 2,961 |
| Deferred taxes and other current assets | 1,161 |
| Total Current Assets | 11,985 |
| Finance receivables due after one year, net | 8,203 |
| Land, buildings and equipment, net | 2,456 |
| Investments in affiliates, at equity | 1,615 |
| Goodwill, net | 1,724 |
| Other assets | 1,701 |
| Investment in discontinued operations | 1,130 |
| Total Assets | $28,814 |

These financial assets include:

| | |
|---|---|
| Cash | $ 126 |
| Accounts receivable | 2,622 |
| Finance receivables, net | 5,115 |
| Finance receivables due after one year | 8,203 |
| Investments in affiliates | 1,615 |

These assets total $17,681 million—over $17.5 billion—and more than 60% of the company's total assets. To say that Xerox has a significant investment in financial assets is an understatement. All of the receivables are amounts due from customers for sales transactions. The investment amount represents stock purchases that Xerox has made in affiliate companies. Cash, of course, is the most liquid asset and is the balance available for the immediate payment of obligations.

## SUPPLEMENTAL TOPIC A

## ACCOUNTING FOR MARKETABLE SECURITIES

There are four basic accountable events relating to investments in marketable securities: (1) purchase of the investments, (2) receipt of dividend revenue and interest revenue, (3) sales of securities owned, and (4) end-of-period mark-to-market adjustment.

**LO 8**

Account for transactions involving marketable securities.

## Purchases of Marketable Securities

Investments in marketable securities originally are recorded at cost, which includes any brokerage commissions.[1] To illustrate, assume that MedCo purchases as a short-term investment 4,000 shares of the capital stock of **AT&T**. The purchase price is *$50 per share,* plus a brokerage commission of *$800.* The entry to record the purchase of these shares is:

---

[1] In purchasing some types of interest-bearing securities, the investors also must purchase any accrued interest. The amount of accrued interest should be debited to a separate account, entitled Accrued Interest Receivable. Accounting for accrued interest is explained in *Supplemental Topic B,* beginning on page 288.

| | | |
|---|---|---|
| Marketable Securities (AT&T capital stock) . . . . . . . . . . . . . . . . . . . . . . . | 200,800 | |
|     Cash . . . . . . . . . . . . . . . . . . . . . . . . . . . . . . . . . . . . . . . . . . . . . . . | | 200,800 |

Purchased 4,000 shares of AT&T capital stock. Total cost,
$200,800 ($50 × 4,000 shares + $800); cost per share,
$50.20 ($200,800 ÷ 4,000 shares).

Marketable Securities is a controlling account, representing the balance sheet value of *all* of MedCo's short-term investments. MedCo—like most investors—also maintains a *marketable securities subsidiary ledger,* with a separate account for each security owned. (Notice the computation in the explanation of our journal entry of the $50.20 *cost per share.* This amount will be used in computing any gains or losses when MedCo sells some of these investment shares.)

## Recognition of Investment Revenue

Most investors recognize interest and dividend revenue *as it is received.* Thus the entries involve a debit to Cash and a credit to either Interest Revenue or Dividend Revenue.

To illustrate, assume that MedCo receives an $0.80 per share dividend on its 4,000 shares of AT&T. The entry to record this cash receipt is:

| | | |
|---|---|---|
| Cash . . . . . . . . . . . . . . . . . . . . . . . . . . . . . . . . . . . . . . . . . . . . . . . . . | 3,200 | |
|     Dividend Revenue . . . . . . . . . . . . . . . . . . . . . . . . . . . . . . . . . . . . . | | 3,200 |

Received a quarterly cash dividend of 80 cents per share on
4,000 shares of AT&T capital stock.

The policy of recognizing revenue as it is received eliminates the need for adjusting entries to accrue any investment revenue receivable at year-end.[2]

## Sales of Investments

When an investment is sold, a gain or a loss often results. A sales price in excess of cost produces a **gain,** whereas a sales price below cost results in a **loss**.

**Sale at a Price Resulting in a Gain**  To illustrate, assume that MedCo sells 1,000 shares of its AT&T stock for $55 per share, less a brokerage commission of $200. The entry would be:

| | | |
|---|---|---|
| Cash . . . . . . . . . . . . . . . . . . . . . . . . . . . . . . . . . . . . . . . . | 54,800 | |
|     Marketable Securities (AT&T capital stock) . . . . . . . . . . . . . . . | | 50,200 |
|     Gain on Sale of Investments . . . . . . . . . . . . . . . . . . . . . . . . | | 4,600 |

Sold 1,000 shares of AT&T capital stock at a gain:

| | |
|---|---|
| Sales price ($55 × 1,000 shares − $200) . . . . . . . . . . . . . . . . | $54,800 |
| Cost ($50.20 per share × 1,000 shares) . . . . . . . . . . . . . . . . . | 50,200 |
| Gain on sale . . . . . . . . . . . . . . . . . . . . . . . . . . . . . . . . . . . . | $ 4,600 |

This transaction results in a gain because MedCo sold the shares at a price above cost. The gain—representing the profit on the sale—increases MedCo's net income for the period. At the end of the period, the credit balances in any gain accounts are closed into the Income Summary account, along with the credit balances of the revenue accounts.

---

[2] Dividend revenue does not accrue from day to day, but interest revenue does. There is nothing wrong with accruing interest revenue receivable at the end of each accounting period, but this usually is unnecessary. Accountants seldom make adjusting entries for immaterial amounts. In most cases, recognizing interest revenue as it is *received* produces essentially the same annual results as recording this revenue as it accrues. Thus the convenient practice of recognizing interest revenue as it is received often is justified by the principle of *materiality.*

**Sale at a Price Resulting in a Loss** Assume that several months later, MedCo sells another 1,000 shares of its AT&T stock, this time at a price *below* cost. The sales price is $48 per share, again less a brokerage commission of $200. The entry would be:

| | | |
|---|---:|---:|
| Cash . . . . . . . . . . . . . . . . . . . . . . . . . . . . . . . . . . . . . . . . . . . . . . | 47,800 | |
| Loss on Sale of Investments . . . . . . . . . . . . . . . . . . . . . . . . . . . | 2,400 | |
|     Marketable Securities (AT&T capital stock) . . . . . . . . . . . . . . | | 50,200 |
| Sold 1,000 shares of AT&T capital stock at a loss: | | |
|   Sales price ($48 × 1,000 shares − $200) . . . . . . . . . . . . . . . | $47,800 | |
|   Cost ($50.20 per share × 1,000 shares) . . . . . . . . . . . . . . . | 50,200 | |
|   Loss on sale . . . . . . . . . . . . . . . . . . . . . . . . . . . . . . . . . . . . | $ (2,400) | |

This loss decreases MedCo's net income for the period. At the end of the period, the debit balances in any loss accounts are closed into the Income Summary account, along with the debit balances of expense accounts.

## Adjusting Marketable Securities to Market Value

At the end of each accounting period, the balance in the Marketable Securities account is adjusted to its *current market value*. Hence, this adjustment is described by the phrase "mark-to-market." Mark-to-market is an interesting concept because it represents a *departure from the cost principle*. At present, marketable securities are the only assets likely to appear in the balance sheet at an amount *above cost*.

The mark-to-market adjustment is easy to make and involves only two accounts: (1) the Marketable Securities controlling account and (2) a special owners' equity account, entitled Unrealized Holding Gain (or Loss) on Investments. The adjustment to the Marketable Securities account may be either a debit or a credit—whichever is necessary to adjust the account's balance to current market value.[3] (The market values of securities owned can be determined easily from the morning newspaper—remember, marketable securities trade daily at *quoted market prices*.)

When we change the valuation of an asset, there is a corresponding change in either total liabilities or total owners' equity. In the case of the mark-to-market adjustment, the corresponding change is recorded in the owners' equity account, Unrealized Holding Gain (or Loss) on Investments.

**The Mark-to-Market Adjustment: An Illustration** Assume that prior to making any adjusting entry, MedCo's Marketable Securities account has a balance of *$250,000* at year-end. If the current market value of the securities owned is, say, *$265,000*, MedCo will make the following adjustment at year-end:

| | | |
|---|---:|---:|
| Marketable Securities . . . . . . . . . . . . . . . . . . . . . . . . . . . . . . . . . . . . | 15,000 | |
|     Unrealized Holding Gain (or Loss) on Investments . . . . . . . . . . . . . . . . | | 15,000 |
| To adjust the balance sheet valuation of marketable securities to | | |
|   their current market value of $265,000. | | |

But if the market value of the securities were only *$240,000*—$10,000 *less* than the balance in the Marketable Securities account—the adjusting entry would be:

| | | |
|---|---:|---:|
| Unrealized Holding Gain (or Loss) on Investments . . . . . . . . . . . . . . . . . . . | 10,000 | |
|     Marketable Securities . . . . . . . . . . . . . . . . . . . . . . . . . . . . . . . . . . . . | | 10,000 |
| To adjust the balance sheet valuation of marketable securities owned | | |
|   to a market value of $240,000. | | |

---

[3] The adjustment to the Marketable Securities account does *not* change the carrying value of individual securities. This adjustment is based on the total value of *all* securities owned. Thus mark-to-market adjustments *do not affect* the amounts of realized gains or losses recognized when specific securities are sold. Realized gains and losses are determined by comparing the *cost* of the securities sold with the proceeds from the sale.

Notice that the Unrealized Holding Gain (or Loss) account may have either a debit or credit balance. A debit balance represents an unrealized holding *loss,* meaning that the current market value of the securities owned is *below* the investor's cost. A credit balance represents an unrealized holding *gain,* indicating that market value of the securities *exceeds* the investor's cost.

**Mark-to-Market Affects Only the Balance Sheet**     In Chapter 4 we made the point that adjusting entries usually affect both the balance sheet and the income statement. The mark-to-market adjustment of marketable securities is an exception to this rule—it affects *only the balance sheet.*[4]

The gains and losses recorded in the mark-to-market adjusting entries are *unrealized*—that is, they have not been finalized through sales of the securities. These unrealized gains and losses are *not* included in the investor's income statement. Rather, the Unrealized Holding Gain (or Loss) account appears in the *stockholders' equity section of the balance sheet.*

Because the Unrealized Holding Gain (or Loss) account does not enter into the determination of net income, it is not closed at the end of the accounting period. Instead, its balance is adjusted from one period to the next. At any balance sheet date, the Unrealized Holding Gain (or Loss) account represents the *difference between* the cost of the marketable securities owned and their current market value.

## Reporting Investment Transactions in the Financial Statements

In a multiple-step income statement, interest revenue, dividend revenue, and gains and losses from sales of investments usually appear as *nonoperating items,* after the determination of income from operations.

In a statement of *cash flows,* receipts of dividends and interest are classified as *operating activities.* Purchases and sales of marketable securities classified as available for sale are presented as *investing activities,* regardless of whether sales transactions result in a gain or a loss. (In the statement of cash flows, the *total sales proceeds* are listed as cash receipts from investing activities, regardless of whether the investment is sold at a gain or at a loss.)

**Mark-to-Market and Income Taxes**     In income tax returns, the gains and losses on sales of investments are called *capital gains* and *capital losses.* Capital gains and losses are included in income tax returns only when the securities are *sold.* Thus mark-to-market adjustments *do not* enter into the computation of taxable income.

## SUPPLEMENTAL TOPIC B

## NOTES RECEIVABLE AND INTEREST REVENUE

A promissory note is an unconditional promise in writing to pay on demand or at a future date a definite sum of money.

The person who signs the note and thereby promises to pay is called the *maker* of the note. The person to whom payment is to be made is called the *payee* of the note. In the illustration below, Pacific Rim Corp. is the maker of the note and First National Bank is the payee.

---

[4] This exception applies only to those short-term investments classified as available for sale. It does not apply to short-term investments, classified as trading securities. Held-to-maturity securities and trading securities are addressed in more advanced accounting courses.

| $100,000 | Los Angeles, California | July 10, 2002 |
|----------|------------------------|---------------|

*Simplified form of promissory note.*

One year    **AFTER DATE**    Pacific Rim Corp.    **PROMISES TO PAY**

**TO THE ORDER OF**      First National Bank

---One hundred thousand and no/100---    **DOLLARS**

**PLUS INTEREST COMPUTED AT THE RATE OF**    12% per annum

**SIGNED**    *G. L. Smith*

**TITLE**    **Treasurer**

From the viewpoint of the maker, Pacific Rim, the illustrated note is a liability and is recorded by crediting the Notes Payable account. However, from the viewpoint of the payee, First National Bank, this same note is an asset and is recorded by debiting the Notes Receivable account. The maker of a note expects to pay cash at the *maturity date* (or due date); the payee expects to receive cash at that date.

## Nature of Interest

Interest is a charge made for the use of money. A borrower incurs interest expense. A lender earns interest revenue. When you encounter notes payable in a company's financial statements, you know that the company is borrowing and you should expect to find interest expense. When you encounter notes receivable, you should expect interest revenue.

**LO 9**

Explain, compute, and account for the accrual of interest revenue.

**Computing Interest**    A formula used in computing interest is as follows:

### Interest = Principal × Rate of Interest × Time

(This formula is often expressed as $I = P \times R \times T$.)

Interest rates usually are stated on an *annual basis*. For example, the total interest charge on a $100,000, one-year, 12% note receivable is computed as follows:

### $P \times R \times T = \$100,000 \times .12 \times 1 = \$12,000$

If the term of the note were only *four months* instead of one year, the total interest revenue earned in the life of the note would be $4,000, computed as follows:

### $P \times R \times T = \$100,000 \times .12 \times {}^{4}/_{12} = \$4,000$

In making interest computations, it is convenient to assume that each month has *30* days. Thus a year has *360* days and each month represents $^{1}/_{12}$ of the year. As these assumptions greatly simplify the computation of interest and assist students in focusing on the underlying concepts, we will use them in our illustrations and assignment material.[1]

If the term of a note is expressed in days, the exact number of days in each month must be considered in determining the maturity date of the note. The day on which a note is dated is not counted, but the date on which it matures is. Thus a two-day note dated today matures the day *after* tomorrow.

To illustrate these concepts, assume that a 60-day, 12% note for $100,000 is drawn on June 10. The *total* interest charge on this note will be $2,000, computed as follows:

### $P \times R \times T = \$100,000 \times .12 \times {}^{60}/_{360} = \$2,000$

---

[1] Prior to the widespread use of computers, these assumptions were widely used in the business community. Today, however, most financial institutions compute interest using a 365-day year and the actual number of days in each month. The differences between these assumptions usually are *not material* in dollar amount.

The $102,000 **maturity value** of the note ($100,000 principal, plus $2,000 interest) will be payable on *August 9*. The **maturity date** is determined as follows:

| | |
|---|---:|
| Days remaining in June (30 − 10) . . . . . . . . . . . . . . . . . . . . . . . . . . . . . . . . . . . . . . . . . . | 20 |
| Days in July . . . . . . . . . . . . . . . . . . . . . . . . . . . . . . . . . . . . . . . . . . . . . . . . . . . . . . . . . . | 31 |
|   Subtotal . . . . . . . . . . . . . . . . . . . . . . . . . . . . . . . . . . . . . . . . . . . . . . . . . . . . . . . . . | 51 |
| Days in August needed to complete the term of the note (including maturity date) . . . . . . . . . | 9 |
| Specified term of note (in days) . . . . . . . . . . . . . . . . . . . . . . . . . . . . . . . . . . . . . . . . . . . . . | 60 |

## Accounting for Notes Receivable

In most fields of business, notes receivable are seldom encountered; in some fields they occur frequently and may constitute an important part of total assets. In banks and financial institutions, for example, notes receivable often represent the company's largest asset category and generate most of the company's revenue. Some retailers that sell on installment plans, such as **Sears, Roebuck & Co.**, also own large amounts of notes receivable from customers.

All notes receivable are usually posted to a single account in the general ledger. A subsidiary ledger is not essential because the notes themselves, when filed by due dates, are the equivalent of a subsidiary ledger and provide any necessary information as to maturity, interest rates, collateral pledged, and other details. The amount debited to Notes Receivable is always the *face amount* of the note, regardless of whether the note bears interest. When an interest-bearing note is collected, the amount of cash received may be larger than the face amount of the note. The interest collected is credited to an Interest Revenue account, and only the face amount of the note is credited to the Notes Receivable account.

**Illustrative Entries**   Assume that on December 1 a 90-day, 12% note receivable is acquired from a customer, Marvin White, in settlement of an existing account receivable of $30,000. The entry for acquisition of the note is as follows:

*Note received to replace account receivable*

| | | |
|---|---:|---:|
| Notes Receivable . . . . . . . . . . . . . . . . . . . . . . . . . . . . . . . . . . . . . . . . . . . . . . . | 30,000 | |
|     Accounts Receivable (Marvin White) . . . . . . . . . . . . . . . . . . . . . . . . . . . | | 30,000 |
| Accepted 90-day, 12% note in settlement of account receivable. | | |

At December 31, the end of the company's fiscal year, the interest earned to date on notes receivable should be accrued by an adjusting entry as follows:

*Adjusting entry for interest revenue earned in December*

| | | |
|---|---:|---:|
| Interest Receivable . . . . . . . . . . . . . . . . . . . . . . . . . . . . . . . . . . . . . . . . . . . . . . | 300 | |
|     Interest Revenue . . . . . . . . . . . . . . . . . . . . . . . . . . . . . . . . . . . . . . . . . . . . . | | 300 |
| To accrue interest for the month of December on Marvin White | | |
|   note ($30,000 × 12% × $^{1}/_{12}$ = $300). | | |

To simplify this illustration, we will assume our company makes adjusting entries *only at year-end*. Therefore, no entries are made to recognize the interest revenue accruing during January and February.

On March 1 (90 days after the date of the note) the note matures. The entry to record collection of the note will be:

*Collection of principal and interest*

| | | |
|---|---:|---:|
| Cash . . . . . . . . . . . . . . . . . . . . . . . . . . . . . . . . . . . . . . . . . . . . . . . . . . . . . . . . . | 30,900 | |
|     Notes Receivable . . . . . . . . . . . . . . . . . . . . . . . . . . . . . . . . . . . . . . . . . . . . | | 30,000 |
|     Interest Receivable . . . . . . . . . . . . . . . . . . . . . . . . . . . . . . . . . . . . . . . . . . | | 300 |
|     Interest Revenue . . . . . . . . . . . . . . . . . . . . . . . . . . . . . . . . . . . . . . . . . . . . | | 600 |
| Collected 90-day, 12% note from Marvin White ($30,000 × 12% × $^{3}/_{12}$ = | | |
|   $900 interest, of which $600 was earned in current year). | | |

The preceding three entries show that interest is being earned throughout the term of the note and that the interest should be apportioned between years on a time basis. The revenue of each year will then include the interest actually earned in that year.

**If the Maker of a Note Defaults**  A note receivable that cannot be collected at maturity is said to have been **defaulted** by the maker. Immediately after the default of a note, an entry should be made by the holder to transfer the amount due from the Notes Receivable account to an account receivable from the debtor.

To illustrate, assume that on March 1, our customer, Marvin White, had defaulted on the note used in the preceding example. In this case, the entry on March 1 would have been:

| | | |
|---|---|---|
| Accounts Receivable (Marvin White) | 30,900 | |
| Notes Receivable | | 30,000 |
| Interest Receivable | | 300 |
| Interest Revenue | | 600 |
| To record default by Marvin White on 90-day, 12% note. | | |

Notice that the interest earned on the note is recorded through the maturity date and is included in the account receivable from the maker. The interest receivable on a defaulted note is just as valid a claim against the maker as is the principal amount of the note.

If the account receivable from White cannot be collected, it ultimately will be written off against the Allowance for Doubtful Accounts. Therefore, the balance in the Allowance for Doubtful Accounts should provide for estimated uncollectible *notes* receivable as well as uncollectible *accounts* receivable.

For many companies, the provision for doubtful accounts is small and does not have a material effect on net income for the period. Notes receivable, however, are the largest and most important asset for nearly every bank. Interest on these notes is a bank's largest and most important type of revenue. Thus the collectibility of notes owned by a bank is a key factor in determining the success or failure of that bank.

**Citicorp**, the nation's largest bank, recently added a staggering $3 billion to its allowance for doubtful loans to developing countries. The related expense caused **Citicorp** to report one of the largest net losses for a single quarter (three-month period) in the history of American business. **Citicorp** is not alone in having problems with uncollectible loans. In recent years, uncollectible loans have been the largest expense in the income statements of many American banks and savings and loan associations.

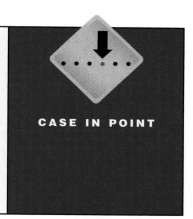

**CASE IN POINT**

**Discounting Notes Receivable**  In past years some companies sold their notes receivable to banks in order to obtain cash prior to the maturity dates of these notes. As the banks purchased these notes at a "discount" from their maturity values, this practice became known as *discounting* notes receivable.

Discounting notes receivable is not a widespread practice today because most banks no longer purchase notes receivable from their customers. Interestingly, the practice of discounting notes receivable is most widespread among banks themselves. Many banks sell large packages of their notes receivable (loans) to agencies of the federal government or to other financial institutions. From a conceptual point of view, discounting notes receivable is essentially the same as selling accounts receivable to a factor.

## The Decision of Whether to Accrue Interest

The concept of interest accruing from day to day applies not only to notes receivable but to all interest-bearing investments (such as cash equivalents and bonds) and to interest-bearing debt. But in our discussions of cash equivalents and marketable securities, we stated that investors generally recognize interest revenue as it is received. In accounting for notes receivable, why did we accrue the interest earned, instead of recognizing revenue as cash was received?

The answer lies in the concept of *materiality*. Interest does, in fact, accrue from day to day. But the interest revenue earned from cash equivalents and investments in marketable securities usually represents only a small part of the investor's total revenue. In short, it usually is *not material* in relation to other financial statement amounts. Thus the principle of materiality often justifies investors' accounting for this revenue in the most convenient manner.

Most notes receivable, however, are owned by *financial institutions*. For these businesses, interest revenue *is* material. In fact, it generally is the company's primary source of revenue. In these circumstances, greater care must be taken to assign interest revenue to the period in which it actually is *earned*.

## SUMMARY OF LEARNING OBJECTIVES

### LO 1

**Define financial assets and explain their valuation in the balance sheet.**

Financial assets are cash and other assets that convert directly into *known amounts* of cash. The three basic categories are cash, marketable securities, and receivables. In the balance sheet, financial assets are listed at their *current value*. For cash, this means the face amount; for marketable securities, current market value; and for receivables, net realizable value.

### LO 2

**Describe the objectives of cash management.**

The objectives of cash management are accurate accounting for cash transactions, the prevention of losses through theft or fraud, and maintaining adequate—but not excessive—cash balances.

### LO 3

**Explain means of achieving internal control over cash transactions.**

The major steps in achieving internal control over cash transactions are as follows: (1) separate cash handling from the accounting function, (2) prepare departmental cash budgets, (3) prepare a control listing of all cash received through the mail and from over-the-counter cash sales, (4) deposit all cash receipts in the bank daily, (5) make all payments by check, (6) verify every expenditure before issuing a check in payment, and (7) promptly reconcile bank statements.

### LO 4

**Prepare a bank reconciliation and explain its purpose.**

The cash balance shown on the month-end bank statement usually will differ from the amount of cash shown in the depositor's ledger. The difference is caused by items that have been recorded by either the depositor or the bank, but not recorded by both. Examples are outstanding checks and deposits in transit. The bank reconciliation adjusts the cash balance per the books and the cash balance per the bank statement for any unrecorded items and thus produces the correct amount of cash to be included in the balance sheet at the end of the month.

The purpose of a bank reconciliation is to achieve the control inherent in the maintenance of two independent records of cash transactions: one record maintained by the depositor and the other by the bank. When these two records are reconciled (brought into agreement), we gain assurance of a correct accounting for cash transactions.

### LO 5

**Account for uncollectible receivables using the allowance and direct write-off methods.**

Under the allowance method, the portion of each period's credit sales expected to prove uncollectible is *estimated.* This estimated amount is recorded by a debit to Uncollectible Accounts Expense and a credit to the contra-asset account Allowance for Doubtful Accounts. When specific accounts are determined to be uncollectible, they are written off by debiting Allowance for Doubtful Accounts and crediting Accounts Receivable.

Under the direct write-off method, uncollectible accounts are charged to expense in the period that they are determined to be worthless.

The allowance method is theoretically preferable because it is based on the matching principle. However, only the direct write-off method must be used in income tax returns.

### LO 6

**Evaluate the liquidity of various financial assets.**

The most liquid financial asset is cash, followed by cash equivalents, marketable securities, and receivables. The liquidity of receivables varies depending on their collectibility and maturity dates.

The allowance for doubtful accounts should provide for those receivables that may prove to be uncollectible. However, users of financial statements may also want to evaluate the concentrations-of-credit-risk disclosure and, perhaps, the credit ratings of major debtors. The accounts receivable turnover rate provides insight as to how quickly receivables are collected.

### LO 7

**Explain how transactions discussed in this chapter affect net income and cash flows.**

These effects are summarized in the table on page 284.

### *LO 8

**Account for transactions involving marketable securities.**

When securities are purchased, they are recorded at cost. Interest and dividends generally are recognized as revenue when they are received. When securities are sold, the cost is compared to the sales price, and the difference is recorded as a gain or a loss. At the end of each accounting period, the balance of the controlling account is adjusted to reflect the *current market value* of the securities owned.

*Supplemental Topic A,* "Accounting for Marketable Securities."

**†LO 9**

**Explain, compute, and account for the accrual of interest revenue.**

Interest is a contractual amount that accumulates (accrues) day by day. The amount of interest accruing over a time period may be computed by the formula *Principal × Rate × Time.*

Whether interest revenue is recognized as it *accrues* or as it *is received* depends on the *materiality* of the amounts involved.

This is the first of three chapters in which we explore the issues involved in accounting for assets. The central theme in these chapters is the valuation of assets.

The valuation of assets affects not only the balance sheet but also the measurement of net income. With respect to cash, there is little question as to the appropriate valuation. The savings and loan crisis in the late 1980s, however, showed that the valuation of notes receivable requires professional judgment and can be a measurement of critical importance.

In the next two chapters, we explore the valuation of inventories and of plant assets. For each of these assets, you will see that several *alternative* valuation methods are acceptable. These different methods, however, may produce *significantly different results.* An understanding of these alternative accounting methods is essential to the proper use and interpretation of financial statements and in the preparation of income tax returns.

# KEY TERMS INTRODUCED OR EMPHASIZED IN CHAPTER 7

**accounts receivable turnover rate** (p. 282) A ratio used to measure the liquidity of accounts receivable and the reasonableness of the accounts receivable balance. Computed by dividing net sales by average receivables.

**aging the accounts receivable** (p. 277) The process of classifying accounts receivable by age groups such as current, 1–30 days past due, 31–60 days past due, etc. A step in estimating the uncollectible portion of the accounts receivable.

**Allowance for Doubtful Accounts** (p. 275) A valuation account or contra-account relating to accounts receivable and showing the portion of the receivables estimated to be uncollectible.

**bank reconciliation** (p. 267) An analysis that explains the difference between the balance of cash shown in the bank statement and the balance of cash shown in the depositor's records.

**cash equivalents** (p. 263) Very short-term investments that are so liquid that they are considered equivalent to cash. Examples include money market funds, U.S. Treasury bills, certificates of deposit, and commercial paper. These investments must mature within 90 days of acquisition.

**cash management** (p. 264) Planning, controlling, and accounting for cash transactions and cash balances.

**compensating balance** (p. 263) A minimum average balance that a bank may require a borrower to leave on deposit in a non-interest-bearing account.

---
†*Supplemental Topic B,* "Notes Receivable and Interest Revenue."

**conservatism** (p. 279) A traditional practice of resolving uncertainties by choosing an asset valuation at the lower end of the range of reasonableness. Also refers to the policy of postponing recognition of revenue to a later date when a range of reasonable choice exists. Designed to avoid overstatement of financial strength and earnings.

**default** (p. 291) Failure to pay interest or principal of a promissory note at the due date.

**direct write-off method** (p. 280) A method of accounting for uncollectible receivables in which no expense is recognized until individual accounts are determined to be worthless. At that point the account receivable is written off, with an offsetting debit to uncollectible accounts expense. Fails to match revenue and related expenses.

**factoring** (p. 281) Transactions in which a business either sells its accounts receivable to a financial institution (often called a *factor*) or borrows money by pledging its accounts receivable as collateral.

**financial assets** (p. 262) Cash and assets convertible directly into known amounts of cash (such as marketable securities and receivables).

**gain** (p. 286) An increase in owners' equity resulting from a transaction other than earning revenue or investment by the owners. The most common example is the sale of an asset at a price above book value.

**line of credit** (p. 264) A prearranged borrowing agreement in which a bank stands ready to advance the borrower without delay any amount up to a specified credit limit. Once used, a line of credit becomes a liability. The unused portion of the line represents the ability to borrow cash without delay.

**loss** (p. 286) A decrease in owners' equity resulting from any transaction other than an expense or a distribution to the owners. The most common example is sale of an asset at a price below book value.

**marketable securities** (p. 262) Highly liquid investments, primarily in stocks and bonds, that can be sold at quoted market prices in organized securities exchanges.

**mark-to-market** (p. 272) The balance sheet valuation standard applied to investments in marketable securities. Involves adjusting the controlling account for securities owned to its total market value at each balance sheet date. (Represents an exception to the cost principle.)

**maturity date** (p. 290) The date on which a note becomes due and payable.

**maturity value** (p. 290) The value of a note at its maturity date, consisting of principal plus interest.

**net realizable value** (p. 262) The balance sheet valuation standard applied to receivables. Equal to the gross amount of accounts and notes receivable, less an estimate of the portion that may prove to be uncollectible.

**NSF check** (p. 268) A customer's check that was deposited but returned because of a lack of funds (Not Sufficient Funds) in the account on which the check was drawn.

**Unrealized Holding Gain (or Loss) on Investments** (p. 272) A special owners' equity account representing the difference between the cost of investments owned and their market value at the balance sheet date. In short, gains or losses on these investments that have not been "realized" through sale of the securities.

**voucher** (p. 266) A written authorization used to approve a transaction for recording and payment.

**voucher system** (p. 266) An accounting system designed to provide strong internal control over cash disbursements. Requires that every transaction that will result in a cash payment be verified, approved, and recorded before a check is prepared.

## DEMONSTRATION PROBLEM

Shown below are selected transactions of Gulf Corp. during the month of December.

**Dec. 5**  Sold 2,000 shares of **AT&T** capital stock at $53 per share, less a brokerage commission of $200. These marketable securities had been acquired nine months earlier at a total cost of $112,000.

**Dec. 8**  An account receivable from S. Willis in the amount of $700 is determined to be uncollectible and is written off against the Allowance for Doubtful Accounts.

**Dec. 15**  Unexpectedly received $200 from F. Hill in full payment of her account. The $200 account receivable from Hill previously had been written off as uncollectible.

**Dec. 20**  Sold 1,000 shares of **IBM** capital stock at a price of $60 per share, less a brokerage commission of $150. These investment shares had been acquired at a total cost of $52,000.

**Dec. 31**  Replenished the petty cash fund. Petty cash vouchers indicated office supplies expense, $44; miscellaneous expense, $32.

**Dec. 31**  The month-end bank reconciliation includes the following items: outstanding checks, $12,320; deposit in transit, $3,150; check from customer T. Jones returned "NSF," $358; bank service charges, $10; bank collected $20,000 in maturing U.S. Treasury bills (a cash equivalent) on the company's behalf. (These Treasury bills had cost $19,670, so the amount collected includes $330 interest revenue.)

### Data for Adjusting Entries

**1.** An aging of accounts receivable indicates probable uncollectible accounts totaling $9,000. Prior to the month-end adjustment, the Allowance for Doubtful Accounts had a credit balance of $5,210.

**2.** Prior to any year-end adjustment, the balance in the Marketable Securities account was $213,800. At year-end, marketable securities owned had a cost of $198,000 and a market value of $210,000.

### Instructions

**a.** Prepare entries in general journal entry form for the December transactions. In adjusting the accounting records from the bank reconciliation, make one entry to record any increases in the Cash account and a separate entry to record any decreases.

**b.** Prepare the month-end adjustments indicated by the two numbered paragraphs.

**c.** What is the adjusted balance in the Unrealized Gain (or Loss) on Investments account at December 31? Where in the financial statements does this account appear?

## Solution to the Demonstration Problem

**a.**

| | GENERAL JOURNAL | | |
|---|---|---|---|
| Dec. 5 | Cash | 105,800 | |
| | Loss on Sale of Investments | 6,200 | |
| |     Marketable Securities | | 112,000 |
| | Sold 2,000 shares of AT&T capital stock at a price below cost. | | |
| 8 | Allowance for Doubtful Accounts | 700 | |
| |     Accounts Receivable (S. Willis) | | 700 |
| | To write off receivable from S. Willis as uncollectible. | | |
| 15 | Accounts Receivable (F. Hill) | 200 | |
| |     Allowance for Doubtful Accounts | | 200 |
| | To reinstate account receivable previously written off as uncollectible. | | |
| 15 | Cash | 200 | |
| |     Accounts Receivable (F. Hill) | | 200 |
| | To record collection of account receivable. | | |
| 20 | Cash | 59,850 | |
| |     Marketable Securities | | 52,000 |
| |     Gain on Sale of Investments | | 7,850 |
| | Sold 1,000 shares of IBM at a price above cost. | | |
| 31 | Office Supplies Expense | 44 | |
| | Miscellaneous Expense | 32 | |
| |     Cash | | 76 |
| | To replenish petty cash fund. | | |
| 31 | Cash | 20,000 | |
| |     Cash Equivalents | | 19,670 |
| |     Interest Revenue | | 330 |
| | To record collection of maturing T-bills by bank. | | |
| 31 | Accounts Receivable (T. Jones) | 358 | |
| | Bank Service Charges | 10 | |
| |     Cash | | 368 |
| | To record bank service charge and to reclassify NSF check from T. Jones as an account receivable. | | |
| **b.** | **Adjusting Entries** | | |
| Dec. 31 | Uncollectible Accounts Expense | 3,790 | |
| |     Allowance for Doubtful Accounts | | 3,790 |
| | To increase Allowance for Doubtful Accounts to $9,000 ($9,000 − $5,210 = $3,790). | | |
| 31 | Unrealized Gain (or Loss) on Investments | 3,800 | |
| |     Marketable Securities | | 3,800 |
| | To reduce the balance in the Marketable Securities account to a market value of $210,000. | | |

**c.** The Unrealized Gain (or Loss) on Investments account has a *$12,000 credit balance,* representing the unrealized gain on securities owned as of December 31. (The unrealized gain is equal to the $210,000 market value of these securities, less their $198,000 cost.) The account appears in the stockholders' equity section of Gulf Corp.'s balance sheet.

# SELF-TEST QUESTIONS

*Answers to these questions appear on page 313.*

1. In general terms, financial assets appear in the balance sheet at:
   a. Face value.
   b. Current cash value.
   c. Cost.
   d. Estimated future sales value.

2. Which of the following practices contributes to efficient cash management?
   a. Never borrow money—maintain a cash balance sufficient to make all necessary payments.
   b. Record all cash receipts and cash payments at the end of the month when reconciling the bank statements.
   c. Prepare monthly forecasts of planned cash receipts, payments, and anticipated cash balances up to a year in advance.
   d. Pay each bill as soon as the invoice arrives.

3. Each of the following measures strengthens internal control over cash receipts *except:*
   a. The use of a voucher system.
   b. Preparation of a daily listing of all checks received through the mail.
   c. The deposit of cash receipts in the bank on a daily basis.
   d. The use of cash registers.

## Use the following data for questions 4 and 5

Quinn Company's bank statement at January 31 shows a balance of $13,360, while the ledger account for Cash in Quinn's ledger shows a balance of $12,890 at the same date. The only reconciling items are the following:

- Deposit in transit, $890.
- Bank service charge, $24.
- NSF check from customer Greg Denton in the amount of $426.
- Error in recording check No. 389 for rent: check was written in the amount of $1,320, but was recorded improperly in the accounting records as $1,230.
- Outstanding checks, $?????

4. What is the total amount of outstanding checks at January 31?
   a. $1,048.   b. $868.   c. $1,900.   d. $1,720.

5. Assuming a single journal entry is made to adjust Quinn Company's accounting records at January 31, the journal entry includes:
   a. A debit to Rent Expense for $90.
   b. A credit to Accounts Receivable, G. Denton, for $426.
   c. A credit to Cash for $450.
   d. A credit to Cash for $1,720.

6. Which of the following best describes the application of generally accepted accounting principles to the valuation of accounts receivable?
   a. Realization principle—Accounts receivable are shown at their net realizable value in the balance sheet.
   b. Matching principle—The loss due to an uncollectible account is recognized in the period in which the sale is made, not in the period in which the account receivable is determined to be worthless.
   c. Cost principle—Accounts receivable are shown at the initial cost of the merchandise to customers, less the cost the seller must pay to cover uncollectible accounts.
   d. Principle of conservatism—Accountants favor using the lowest reasonable estimate for the amount of uncollectible accounts.

7. On January 1, Dillon Company had a $3,100 credit balance in the Allowance for Doubtful Accounts. During the year, sales totaled $780,000 and $6,900 of accounts receivable were written off as uncollectible. A December 31 aging of accounts receivable indicated the amount probably uncollectible to be $5,300. (No recoveries of accounts previously written off were made during the year.) Dillon's financial statements for the current year should include:

     **a.** Uncollectible accounts expense of $9,100.

     **b.** Uncollectible accounts expense of $5,300.

     **c.** Allowance for Doubtful Accounts with a credit balance of $1,500.

     **d.** Allowance for Doubtful Accounts with a credit balance of $8,400.

8. Under the *direct write-off* method of accounting for uncollectible accounts:

     **a.** The current year uncollectible accounts expense is less than the expense would be under the allowance approach.

     **b.** The relationship between the current period net sales and current period uncollectible accounts expense illustrates the matching principle.

     **c.** The Allowance for Doubtful Accounts is debited when specific accounts receivable are determined to be worthless.

     **d.** Accounts receivable are not stated in the balance sheet at net realizable value, but at the balance of the Accounts Receivable controlling account.

9. Which of the following actions is *least* likely to increase a company's accounts receivable turnover?

     **a.** Encouraging customers to use bank credit cards, such as Visa and MasterCard, rather than other national credit cards, such as American Express and Diners' Club.

     **b.** Offer customers larger cash discounts for making early payments.

     **c.** Reduce the interest rate charged to credit customers.

     **d.** Sell accounts receivable to a factor.

*10. Puget Sound Co. sold marketable securities costing $80,000 for $92,000 cash. In the company's income statement and statement of cash flows, respectively, this will appear as:

     **a.** A $12,000 gain and a $92,000 cash receipt.

     **b.** A $92,000 gain and an $8,000 cash receipt.

     **c.** A $12,000 gain and an $80,000 cash receipt.

     **d.** A $92,000 sale and a $92,000 cash receipt.

†11. On October 1, *2001,* Coast Financial loaned Barr Corporation $300,000, receiving in exchange a nine-month, 12% note receivable. Coast ends its fiscal year on December 31 and makes adjusting entries to accrue interest earned on all notes receivable. The interest earned on the note receivable from Barr Corporation during *2002* will amount to:

     **a.** $9,000.      **b.** $18,000.      **c.** $27,000.      **d.** $36,000.

## ASSIGNMENT MATERIAL

## DISCUSSION QUESTIONS

1. Briefly describe the flow of cash among receivables, cash, and marketable securities.

2. Different categories of financial assets are valued differently in the balance sheet. These different valuation methods have one common goal. Explain.

3. What are *cash equivalents?* Provide two examples. Why are these items often combined with cash for the purpose of balance sheet presentation?

4. What are lines of credit? From the viewpoint of a short-term creditor, why do lines of credit increase a company's solvency? How are the unused portions of these lines presented in financial statements?

---

*Supplemental Topic A,* "Accounting for Marketable Securities."

†*Supplemental Topic B,* "Notes Receivable and Interest Revenue."

5. Does the expression "efficient management of cash" mean anything more than procedures to prevent losses from fraud or theft? Explain.

6. Why are cash balances in *excess* of those needed to finance business operations viewed as relatively nonproductive assets? Suggest several ways in which these excess cash balances may be utilized effectively.

7. List several principles to be observed by a business in establishing strong internal control over cash receipts.

8. What is the basic control feature in a *voucher system?*

9. List two items often encountered in reconciling a bank statement that may cause cash per the bank statement to be *larger* than the balance of cash shown in the depositor's accounting records.

10. Describe the nature and usefulness of a *cash budget.*

11. Why are investments in marketable securities shown separately from cash equivalents in the balance sheet?

12. Why must an investor who owns numerous marketable securities maintain a marketable securities subsidiary ledger?

13. Explain the valuation procedure termed *mark-to-market* for short-term investments classified as available-for-sale securities.

14. What does the account Unrealized Holding Gain (or Loss) on Investment represent? How is this account presented in the financial statements for short-term investments classified as available-for-sale securities?

15. Explain the relationship between the *matching principle* and the need to estimate uncollectible accounts receivable.

16. In making the annual adjusting entry for uncollectible accounts, a company may utilize a *balance sheet approach* to make the estimate, or it may use an *income statement approach.* Explain these two alternative approaches.

17. What is the direct write-off method of handling credit losses as opposed to the allowance method? What is its principal shortcoming?

18. Must companies use the same method of accounting for uncollectible accounts receivable in their financial statements and in their income tax returns? Explain.

19. What are the advantages to a retailer of making credit sales only to customers who use nationally recognized credit cards?

20. Alta Mine Company, a restaurant that had always made cash sales only, adopted a new policy of honoring several nationally known credit cards. Sales did not increase, but many of Alta Mine's regular customers began charging dinner bills on the credit cards. Has the new policy been beneficial to Alta Mine Company? Explain.

21. How is the accounts receivable turnover rate computed? Why is this rate significant to short-term creditors?

22. How does an annual audit by a CPA firm provide assurance that a company's accounts receivable and notes receivable are fairly presented in the company's financial statements?

23. Explain how each of the following is presented in (1) a multiple-step income statement and (2) a statement of cash flows.

   a. Sale of marketable securities at a loss.

   b. Adjusting entry to create (or increase) the allowance for doubtful accounts.

   c. Entry to write off an uncollectible account against the allowance.

   d. Adjusting entry to increase the balance in the Marketable Securities account to a higher market value (assume these investments are classified as available-for-sale securities).

*24. The market values of some marketable securities may change from day to day. How do these changes in market value affect the investor's *taxable income?*

†25. Determine the maturity date and maturity value of each of the following notes. (Assume a 360-day year in computing interest and maturity values, but count actual days to the maturity dates.)

   a. A $10,000, 9%, one-year note dated July 1, 2001.

   b. A $20,000, 8%, 90-day note dated March 11.

---

*Supplemental Topic A, "Accounting for Marketable Securities."

†Supplemental Topic B, "Notes Receivable and Interest Revenue."

# EXERCISES

**EXERCISE 7.1**

You as a Student

**LO 4**

Assume that the following information relates to your most recent bank statement dated September 30:

| | |
|---|---|
| Balance per bank statement at September 30 . . . . . . . . . . . . . . . . . . . . . . . . . . . . . . . . . . . | $3,400 |

Checks written that had not cleared the bank as of September 30:

| | | |
|---|---|---|
| #203 | University tuition . . . . . . . . . . . . . . . . . . . . . . . . . . . . . . . . . . . . . . . . . . | $1,500 |
| #205 | University bookstore . . . . . . . . . . . . . . . . . . . . . . . . . . . . . . . . . . . . . . . | 350 |
| #208 | Rocco's pizza . . . . . . . . . . . . . . . . . . . . . . . . . . . . . . . . . . . . . . . . . . . . | 25 |
| #210 | Stereo purchase . . . . . . . . . . . . . . . . . . . . . . . . . . . . . . . . . . . . . . . . . . | 425 |
| #211 | October apartment rent . . . . . . . . . . . . . . . . . . . . . . . . . . . . . . . . . . . . | 500 |

Interest amounting to $4 was credited to your account by the bank in September. The bank's service charge for the month was $5. In addition to your bank statement, you received a letter from your parents informing you that they had made a $2,400 electronic funds transfer directly into your account on October 2. After reading your parents' letter, you looked in your checkbook and discovered its balance was $601. Adding your parents' deposit brought that total to $3,001.

Prepare a bank reconciliation to determine your correct checking account balance. Explain why neither your bank statement nor your checkbook shows this amount.

**EXERCISE 7.2**

Financial Assets

**LO 1, 2**

The following financial assets appeared in the balance sheet of Fantasy Comics:

| **Current assets** | |
|---|---|
| Cash . . . . . . . . . . . . . . . . . . . . . . . . . . . . . . . . . . . . . . . . . . . . . . . . . . . . . . . . . . . . . . . . . . . . . | $325,000 |
| Marketable Securities . . . . . . . . . . . . . . . . . . . . . . . . . . . . . . . . . . . . . . . . . . . . . . . . . . . . | 912,500 |
| Accounts Receivable . . . . . . . . . . . . . . . . . . . . . . . . . . . . . . . . . . . . . . . . . . . . . . . . . . . . . | 700,000 |

**a.** Define *financial assets.*

**b.** A different approach is used in determining the balance sheet value for each category of financial assets, although these three approaches all serve a common goal. Explain.

**c.** Why do companies hold much of their financial assets in the form of marketable securities and receivables instead of cash?

**d.** Define the following items and explain how they would be presented in Fantasy Comics' financial statements.

    **1.** Cash equivalents.

    **2.** A large compensating balance in the company's checking account.

    **3.** Unused lines of credit.

**EXERCISE 7.3**

Grandmother's Secret

**LO 2, 3**

The former bookkeeper of **White Electric Supply** is serving time in prison for embezzling nearly $416,000 in less than five years. She describes herself as "an ordinary mother of three kids and a proud grandmother of four." Like so many other "ordinary" employees, she started out by taking only small amounts. By the time she was caught, she was stealing lump sums of $5,000 and $10,000.

Her method was crude and simple. She would write a check for the correct amount payable to a supplier for, say, $15,000. However, she would record in the company's check register an amount significantly greater, say, $20,000. She would then write a check payable to herself for the $5,000 difference. In the check register, next to the number of each check she had deposited in her personal bank account, she would write the word "void," making it appear as though the check had been destroyed. This process went undetected for nearly five years.

**a.** What controls must have been lacking at **White Electric Supply** to enable the bookkeeper to steal nearly $416,000 before being caught?

**b.** What the bookkeeper did was definitely unethical. But *what if* one of her grandchildren had been ill and needed an expensive operation? If this had been the case, would it have been ethical for her to take company funds to pay for the operation if she intended to pay the company back in full? Defend your answer.

D. J. Fletcher, a trusted employee of Bluestem Products, found himself in personal financial difficulties and decided to "borrow" $3,000 from the company and to conceal his theft.

As a first step, Fletcher removed $3,000 in currency from the cash register. This amount represented the bulk of the cash received in over-the-counter sales during the three business days since the last bank deposit. Fletcher then removed a $3,000 check from the day's incoming mail; this check had been mailed in by a customer, Michael Adams, in full payment of his account. Fletcher made no journal entry to record the $3,000 collection from Adams, but deposited the check in Bluestem Products' bank account in place of the $3,000 over-the-counter cash receipts he had stolen.

In order to keep Adams from protesting when his month-end statement reached him, Fletcher made a journal entry debiting Sales Returns and Allowances and crediting Accounts Receivable—Michael Adams. Fletcher posted this entry to the two general ledger accounts affected and to Adams's account in the subsidiary ledger for accounts receivable.

**a.** Did these actions by Fletcher cause the general ledger to be out of balance or the subsidiary ledger to disagree with the controlling account? Explain.

**b.** Assume that Bluestem Products prepares financial statements at the end of the month without discovering the theft. Would any items in the balance sheet or the income statement be in error? Explain.

**c.** Several weaknesses in internal control apparently exist in Bluestem Products. Indicate three specific changes needed to strengthen internal control over cash receipts.

**EXERCISE 7.4**

Embezzlement Issues

**LO 2, 3**

Shown below is the information needed to prepare a bank reconciliation for Warren Electric at December 31:

**1.** At December 31, cash per the bank statement was $15,200; cash per the company's records was $17,500.

**2.** Two debit memoranda accompanied the bank statement: service charges for December of $25, and a $775 check drawn by Jane Jones marked "NSF."

**3.** Cash receipts of $10,000 on December 31 were not deposited until January 4.

**4.** The following checks had been issued in December but were not included among the paid checks returned by the bank: no. 620 for $1,000, no. 630 for $3,000, and no. 641 for $4,500.

**a.** Prepare a bank reconciliation at December 31.

**b.** Prepare the necessary journal entry or entries to update the accounting records.

**c.** Assume that the company normally is *not* required to pay a bank service charge if it maintains a minimum average daily balance of $1,000 throughout the month. If the company's average daily balance for December had been $8,000, why did it have to pay a $25 service charge?

**EXERCISE 7.5**

Bank Reconciliation

**LO 4**

The following footnote appeared in a recent financial statement of **Westinghouse Electric**:

The Corporation considers all investment securities with a maturity of three months or less when acquired to be cash equivalents. All cash and temporary investments are placed with high-credit-quality financial institutions, and the amount of credit exposure to any one financial institution is limited. At December 31, cash and cash equivalents include restricted funds of $42 million.

**a.** Are the company's cash equivalents debt or equity securities? How do you know?

**b.** Explain what is meant by the statement that "the credit exposure to any one financial institution is limited."

**c.** Explain what is meant by the term *restricted funds* used in the footnote.

**EXERCISE 7.6**

Cash and Cash Equivalents

**LO 1, 2**

**EXERCISE 7.7**

Interest Rate Shopping

Well-managed companies frequently transfer excess cash into revenue-generating cash equivalents, such as bank money market accounts. These accounts differ with respect to the minimum balances they require and the interest rates that they pay. Shown below, for example, is recent information about money market accounts offered by several large banks:

| Bank | Minimum Balance | Annual Percentage Rate |
|------|-----------------|------------------------|
| First Federal | $ 2,500 | 3.50% |
| Chase Manhattan | 25,000 | 5.55 |
| Republic Bank | 5,000 | 5.02 |
| Bank of America | 25,000 | 3.20 |
| Citibank | 25,000 | 5.11 |

Contact several banks in your area that offer money market accounts. Be certain to find out (1) the minimum balances they require, (2) their respective interest rates, (3) whether they are insured against losses, and (4) the type of securities in which each money market account is invested, such as commercial paper, U.S. Treasury bills, etc.

If you were a manager with $500,000 of excess cash to invest for 90 days or less, to which of these money market accounts would you transfer funds? Defend your answer.

**EXERCISE 7.8**

The Nature of Marketable Securities

Many companies hold much of their total financial assets in the form of marketable securities.

**a.** Define *marketable securities*. Why are these securities considered to be financial assets?

**b.** What is the basic advantage of keeping financial assets in the form of marketable securities instead of in cash?

**c.** Explain how investments in marketable securities are valued in the investor's balance sheet.

**d.** Discuss whether the valuation of marketable securities represents a departure from (1) the cost principle and (2) the objectivity principle.

**e.** Do you think that mark-to-market benefits the *users* of financial statements? Explain.

**EXERCISE 7.9**

Reporting Uncollectable Accounts

The credit manager of Montour Fuel has gathered the following information about the company's accounts receivable and credit losses during the current year:

| | | |
|---|---|---|
| Net credit sales for the year ............................................ | | $8,000,000 |
| Accounts receivable at year-end ........................................ | | 1,750,000 |
| Uncollectible accounts receivable: | | |
| Actually written off during the year ........................... | $96,000 | |
| Estimated portion of year-end receivables expected to prove uncollectible (per aging schedule) ........................ | 84,000 | 180,000 |

Prepare one journal entry summarizing the recognition of uncollectible accounts expense for the entire year under each of the following independent assumptions:

**a.** Uncollectible accounts expense is estimated at an amount equal to 2.5% of net credit sales.

**b.** Uncollectible accounts expense is recognized by adjusting the balance in the Allowance for Doubtful Accounts to the amount indicated in the year-end aging schedule. The balance in the allowance account at the *beginning* of the current year was $25,000. (Consider the effect of the write-offs during the year on the balance in the Allowance for Doubtful Accounts.)

**c.** The company uses the direct write-off method of accounting for uncollectible accounts.

**d.** Which of the three methods gives investors and creditors the most accurate assessment of a company's liquidity? Defend your answer.

The following information was taken from recent annual reports of **Huffy Corporation** and **Ohio Power Company** (Huffy is a manufacturer of bicycles and Ohio Power Company is a public utility; dollar amounts are stated in thousands):

**EXERCISE 7.10**

Industry Characteristics and Collection Performance

**LO 6**

|  | Huffy | OPC |
|---|---|---|
| Net sales .......................................... | $708,000 | $2,106,000 |
| Average accounts receivable ............................... | $103,000 | $ 208,000 |

**a.** Compute for each company the accounts receivable turnover rate for the year.

**b.** Compute for each company the number of days (on average) required to collect an outstanding receivable (round answer to the nearest whole day).

**c.** Explain why the figures computed for **Huffy** in parts **a** and **b** are so different from those computed for **Ohio Power Company**.

Six events pertaining to financial assets are described as follows:

**a.** Invested idle cash in marketable securities and classified them as available for sale.

**b.** Collected an account receivable.

**c.** Sold marketable securities at a loss (proceeds from the sale were equal to the market value reflected in the last balance sheet).

**d.** Determined a particular account receivable to be uncollectible and wrote it off against the allowance for doubtful accounts.

**e.** Received interest earned on an investment in marketable securities (company policy is to recognize interest as revenue *when received*).

**f.** Made a mark-to-market adjustment increasing the balance in the Marketable Securities account to reflect a rise in the market value of securities owned.

Indicate the effects of each transaction or adjusting entry upon the financial measurements in the four column headings listed below. Use the code letters **I** for increase, **D** for decrease, and **NE** for no effect.

**EXERCISE 7.11**

Analyzing the Effects of Transactions

**LO 1, 7**

| Transaction | Total Assets | Net Income | Net Cash Flow from Operating Activities | Net Cash Flow (from Any Source) |
|---|---|---|---|---|
| a |  |  |  |  |

**St. Jude Medical, Inc.,** is a publicly owned corporation engaged in the manufacture of heart valves and other medical products. In recent years, the company has accumulated large amounts of cash and cash equivalents as a result of profitable operations. A recent annual report showed cash and cash equivalents amounting to more than 50% of the company's total assets. During the period that these large holdings of cash and cash equivalents have accumulated, the company has paid no cash dividends.

**EXERCISE 7.12**

Cash Management

**LO 2**

Some financial analysts thought St. Jude was holding too much cash.

**a.** Why would anyone think that a company was holding "too much cash"?

**b.** What can a corporation do to efficiently utilize cash balances in excess of the amounts needed for current operations?

**c.** Evaluate St. Jude's policies of accumulating liquid resources instead of paying dividends from the perspectives of:

**1.** The company's creditors.

**2.** The company's stockholders.

Explain how each of the following items is reported in a complete set of financial statements, including the accompanying notes. (In one or more cases, the item may not appear in the financial statements.) The answer to the first item is provided as an example.

**EXERCISE 7.13**

Reporting Financial Assets

 **LO 1**

a. Cash equivalents.

b. Cash in a special fund being accumulated as legally required for the purpose of retiring a specific long-term liability.

c. Compensating balances.

d. The amount by which the current market value of securities classified as available for sale exceeds their cost.

e. The allowance for doubtful accounts receivable.

f. The accounts receivable turnover rate.

g. Realized gains and losses on investments sold during the period.

h. Proceeds from converting cash equivalents into cash.

i. Proceeds from converting investments in marketable securities into cash.

**Example:**   **a.** Cash equivalents normally are *not* shown separately in financial statements. Rather, they are combined with other types of cash and reported under the caption "Cash and Cash Equivalents." A note to the statements often shows the breakdown of this asset category.

---

**EXERCISE 7.14**

Analyzing Accounts Receivable

**LO 1, 5, 6**

Shown below are the net sales and the average amounts of accounts receivable of two beverage companies in a recent year:

| | (Dollars in Millions) | |
| --- | ---: | ---: |
| | Average Accounts Receivable | Net Sales |
| **Adolph Coors Company** ........................... | $147 | $ 1,764 |
| **Anheuser-Busch Companies, Inc.** ................... | 652 | 11,394 |

a. For each of these companies, compute:

    1. The number of times that the average balance of accounts receivable turned over during this fiscal year. (Round to the nearest tenth.)

    2. The number of days (on average) that each company must wait to collect its accounts receivable. (Round to the nearest day.)

b. Based on your computations in part **a**, which company's accounts receivable appear to be the more liquid asset? Explain briefly.

---

**\*EXERCISE 7.15**

Mark-to-Market

**LO 1, 7, 8**

**Weis Markets** accumulates large amounts of excess cash throughout the year. It typically invests these funds in marketable securities until they are needed. The company's most recent financial statements revealed a $14 million unrealized gain on short-term investments. Footnotes to the financial statements disclosed that **Weis** classifies its short-term investments as available-for-sale securities.

a. Explain the meaning of the company's unrealized gain on short-term investments.

b. How does the unrealized gain impact the company's financial statements?

c. Is the unrealized loss included in the computation of the company's taxable income? Explain.

d. Evaluate the mark-to-market concept from the perspective of the company's creditors.

---

**\*EXERCISE 7.16**

Accounting for Marketable Securities

**LO 1, 7, 8**

McGoun Industries pays income taxes on capital gains at a rate of 30%. At December 31, *2001*, the company owns marketable securities that cost $90,000, but have a current market value of $260,000.

a. How will users of McGoun's financial statements be made aware of this substantial increase in the market value of the company's investments?

b. As of December 31, 2001, what income taxes has McGoun paid on the increase in value of these investments? Explain.

---

\**Supplemental Topic A,* "Accounting for Marketable Securities."

**c.** Prepare a journal entry at January 4, 2002, to record the cash sale of these investments at $260,000.

**d.** What effect will the sale recorded in part **c** have on McGoun's tax obligation for 2002?

On September 1, Health Wise International acquired a 12%, nine-month note receivable from Herbal Innovations, a credit customer, in settlement of a $22,000 account receivable. Prepare journal entries to record the following:

**a.** The receipt of the note on September 1 in settlement of the account receivable.

**b.** The adjustment to record accrued interest revenue on December 31.

**c.** The collection of the principal and interest on May 31.

†**EXERCISE 7.17**

Notes and Interest

**LO 9**

The annual report of **Tootsie Roll Industries, Inc.,** appears in Appendix A at the end of this textbook. Use this report to answer the following questions:

**a.** What is the total dollar value of the company's financial assets for the most current year reported?

**b.** Does the company report any investments in marketable securities? If so, how does it report unrealized gains and losses?

**c.** What is the company's allowance for uncollectible accounts for the most current year reported?

**d.** On average, for how many days do the company's accounts receivable remain outstanding before collection?

**EXERCISE 7.18**

Using the Annual Report of Tootsie Roll Industries, Inc.

**LO 1, 6**

## PROBLEMS

The cash transactions and cash balances of Banner, Inc., for July were as follows:

**1.** The ledger account for Cash showed a balance at July 31 of $125,568.

**2.** The July bank statement showed a closing balance of $114,828.

**3.** The cash received on July 31 amounted to $16,000. It was left at the bank in the night depository chute after banking hours on July 31 and therefore was not recorded by the bank on the July statement.

**4.** Also included with the July bank statement was a debit memorandum from the bank for $50 representing service charges for July.

**5.** A credit memorandum enclosed with the July bank statement indicated that a non-interest-bearing note receivable for $4,000 from Rene Manes, left with the bank for collection, had been collected and the proceeds credited to the account of Banner, Inc.

**6.** Comparison of the paid checks returned by the bank with the entries in the accounting records revealed that check no. 821 for $519, issued July 15 in payment for office equipment, had been erroneously entered in Banner's records as $915.

**7.** Examination of the paid checks also revealed that three checks, all issued in July, had not yet been paid by the bank: no. 811 for $314; no. 814 for $625; no. 823 for $175.

**8.** Included with the July bank statement was a $200 check drawn by Howard Williams, a customer of Banner, Inc. This check was marked "NSF." It had been included in the deposit of July 27 but had been charged back against the company's account on July 31.

**PROBLEM 7.1**

Bank Reconciliation

**LO 1, 4**

### Instructions

**a.** Prepare a bank reconciliation for Banner, Inc., at July 31.

**b.** Prepare journal entries (in general journal form) to adjust the accounts at July 31. Assume that the accounts have not been closed.

**c.** State the amount of cash that should be included in the balance sheet at July 31.

**d.** Explain why the balance per the company's bank statement is often larger than the balance shown in its accounting records.

---

†*Supplemental Topic B,* "Notes Receivable and Interest Revenue."

**PROBLEM 7.2**

Protecting Cash

**LO 2, 3, 4**

Osage Farm Supply had poor internal control over its cash transactions. Facts about the company's cash position at November 30 are described below.

The accounting records showed a cash balance of $35,400, which included a deposit in transit of $1,245. The balance indicated in the bank statement was $20,600. Included in the bank statement were the following debit and credit memoranda:

| Debit Memoranda: | |
|---|---|
| Check from customer G. Davis, deposited by Osage Farm Supply, but charged back as NSF | $ 130 |
| Bank service charges for November | 15 |
| **Credit Memorandum:** | |
| Proceeds from collection of a note receivable from Regal Farms, which Osage Farm Supply had left with the bank's collection department | $6,255 |

Outstanding checks as of November 30 were as follows:

| Check No. | Amount |
|---|---|
| 8231 | $ 400 |
| 8263 | 524 |
| 8288 | 176 |
| 8294 | 5,000 |

Bev Escola, the company's cashier, has been taking portions of the company's cash receipts for several months. Each month, Escola prepares the company's bank reconciliation in a manner that conceals her thefts. Her bank reconciliation for November is illustrated as follows:

| | | |
|---|---|---|
| Balance per bank statement, Nov. 30 | | $20,600 |
| Add: Deposits in transit | $2,145 | |
|     Collection of note from Regal Farms | 6,255 | 8,400 |
| Subtotal | | $30,000 |
| Less: Outstanding checks: | | |
|     No. 8231 | $400 | |
|     8263 | 524 | |
|     8288 | 176 | 1,000 |
| Adjusted cash balance per bank statement | | $29,000 |
| Balance per accounting records, Nov. 30 | | $35,400 |
| Add: Credit memorandum from bank | | 6,255 |
| Subtotal | | $29,145 |
| Less: Debit memoranda from bank: | | |
|     NSF check of G. Davis | $ 15 | |
|     Bank service charges | 130 | 145 |
| Adjusted cash balance per accounting records | | $29,000 |

**Instructions**

a. Determine the amount of the cash shortage that has been concealed by Escola in her bank reconciliation. (As a format, we suggest that you prepare the bank reconciliation correctly. The amount of the shortage then will be the difference between the adjusted balances per the bank statement and per the accounting records. You can then list this unrecorded cash shortage as the final adjustment necessary to complete your reconciliation.)

**b.** Carefully review Escola's bank reconciliation and explain in detail how she concealed the amount of the shortage. Include a listing of the dollar amounts that were concealed in various ways. This listing should total the amount of the shortage determined in part **a.**

**c.** Suggest some specific internal control measures that appear to be necessary for Osage Farm Supply.

Super Star, a Hollywood Publicity firm, uses the balance sheet approach to estimate uncollectible accounts expense. At year-end an aging of the accounts receivable produced the following classification:

**PROBLEM 7.3**

Aging Accounts Receivable; Write-offs

| | |
|---|---|
| Not yet due | $500,000 |
| 1–30 days past due | 210,000 |
| 31–60 days past due | 80,000 |
| 61–90 days past due | 15,000 |
| Over 90 days past due | 30,000 |
| Total | $835,000 |

On the basis of past experience, the company estimated the percentages probably uncollectible for the above five age groups to be as follows: Group 1, 1%; Group 2, 3%; Group 3, 10%; Group 4, 20%; and Group 5, 50%.

The Allowance for Doubtful Accounts before adjustment at December 31 showed a credit balance of $11,800.

### Instructions

**a.** Compute the estimated amount of uncollectible accounts based on the above classification by age groups.

**b.** Prepare the adjusting entry needed to bring the Allowance for Doubtful Accounts to the proper amount.

**c.** Assume that on January 10 of the following year, Super Star learned that an account receivable that had originated on September 1 in the amount of $8,250 was worthless because of the bankruptcy of the client, April Showers. Prepare the journal entry required on January 10 to write off this account.

**d.** The firm is considering the adoption of a policy whereby clients whose outstanding accounts become more than 60 days past due will be required to sign an interest-bearing note for the full amount of their outstanding balance. What advantages would such a policy offer?

Wilcox Mills is a manufacturer that makes all sales on 30-day credit terms. Annual sales are approximately $30 million. At the end of 2001, accounts receivable were presented in the company's balance sheet as follows:

**PROBLEM 7.4**

Accounting for Uncollectible Accounts

| | |
|---|---|
| Accounts Receivable from Clients | $3,100,000 |
| Less: Allowance for Doubtful Accounts | 80,000 |

During 2002, $165,000 of specific accounts receivable were written off as uncollectible. Of these accounts written off, receivables totaling $15,000 were subsequently collected. At the end of 2002, an aging of accounts receivable indicated a need for an $90,000 allowance to cover possible failure to collect the accounts currently outstanding.

Wilcox Mills makes adjusting entries in its accounting records *only at year-end.* Monthly and quarterly financial statements are prepared from worksheets, without any adjusting or closing entries actually being entered in the accounting records. (In short, you may assume the company adjusts its accounts only at year-end.)

## Instructions

**a.** Prepare the following general journal entries:

   **1.** One entry to summarize all accounts written off against the allowance for doubtful accounts during 2002.

   **2.** Entries to record the $15,000 in accounts receivable that were subsequently collected.

   **3.** The adjusting entry required at December 31, 2002, to increase the allowance for doubtful accounts to $90,000.

**b.** Notice that the allowance for doubtful accounts was only $80,000 at the end of 2001, but uncollectible accounts during 2002 totaled $150,000 ($165,000 less the $15,000 reinstated). Do these relationships appear reasonable, or was the allowance for doubtful accounts greatly understated at the end of 2001? Explain.

**\*PROBLEM 7.5**

Accounting for Marketable
Securities

**LO 1, 8**

At December 31, 2001, Weston Manufacturing Co. owned the following investments in the capital stock of publicly owned companies (all classified as available-for-sale securities):

|  | Cost | Current Market Value |
|---|---|---|
| Wolfe Computer, Inc. (5,000 shares: cost, $50 per share; market value, $65) .......................... | $250,000 | $325,000 |
| Quality Foods (4,000 shares: cost, $80 per share; market value, $75) ............................... | 320,000 | 300,000 |
| Totals ...................................................... | $570,000 | $625,000 |

In *2002*, Weston engaged in the following two transactions:

**Apr. 10**  Sold 1,000 shares of its investment in Wolfe Computer at a price of $66 per share, less a brokerage commission of $200.

**Aug. 7**  Sold 2,000 shares of its Quality Foods stock at a price of $72 per share, less a brokerage commission of $300.

At December 31, 2002, the market values of these stocks were: Wolfe Computer, $62 per share; Quality Foods, $70.

## Instructions

**a.** Illustrate the presentation of marketable securities and the unrealized holding gain or loss in Weston's balance sheet at December 31, *2001*. Include a caption indicating the section of the balance sheet in which each of these accounts appears.

**b.** Prepare journal entries to record the transactions on April 10 and August 7.

**c.** Prior to making a mark-to-market adjustment at the end of 2002, determine the unadjusted balance in the Marketable Securities controlling account and the Unrealized Holding Gain (or Loss) on Investments. (Assume that no unrealized gains or losses have been recognized since last year.)

**d.** Prepare a schedule showing the cost and market values of securities owned at the end of 2002. (Use the same format as the schedule illustrated above.)

**e.** Prepare the "mark-to-market" adjusting entry required at December 31, 2002.

**f.** Illustrate the presentation of the marketable securities and unrealized holding gain (or loss) in the balance sheet at December 31, *2002*. (Follow the same format as in part **a.**)

**g.** Illustrate the presentation of the net *realized* gains (or losses) in the 2002 income statement. Assume a multiple-step income statement and show the caption identifying the section in which this amount would appear.

**h.** Explain how both the realized and unrealized gains and losses will affect the company's 2002 income tax return.

---

*\*Supplemental Topic A,* "Accounting for Marketable Securities."

Eastern Supply sells a variety of merchandise to retail stores on open account, but it insists that any customer who fails to pay an invoice when due must replace it with an interest-bearing note. The company adjusts and closes its accounts at December 31. Among the transactions relating to notes receivable were the following:

†**PROBLEM 7.6**

Notes Receivable

**LO 9**

**Sept. 1** Received from a customer (Party Plus) a nine-month, 10% note for $75,000 in settlement of an account receivable due today.

**June 1** Collected in full the nine-month, 10% note receivable from Party Plus, including interest.

**Instructions**

**a.** Prepare journal entries (in general journal form) to record: (1) the receipt of the note on September 1; (2) the adjustment for interest on December 31; and (3) collection of principal and interest on June 1. (To better illustrate the allocation of interest revenue between accounting periods, we will assume Eastern Supply makes adjusting entries *only at year-end*.)

**b.** Assume that instead of paying the note on June 1, the customer (Party Plus) had defaulted. Give the journal entry by Eastern Supply to record the default. Assume that Party Plus has sufficient resources that the note eventually will be collected.

**c.** Explain why the company insists that any customer who fails to pay an invoice when due must replace it with an interest-bearing note.

## CASES AND UNSTRUCTURED PROBLEMS

Most banks offer a variety of cash management options to individuals and small businesses. These include, for example, T-bills, money market funds, daily "sweeps" of checking accounts, and CDs.

**CASE 7.1**

Cash Management

**LO 2**

**Instructions**

**a.** Arrange an interview with a representative of a local bank. Inquire as to the options the bank provides for temporarily investing cash balances not needed in the near future. Gain an understanding of the various cash management options available to individuals and to small businesses, including the expected yields.

**b.** Briefly explain each of the options discussed in this interview, along with the expected yields (if determinable). Identify the option you consider best suited to:

**1.** An individual whose checking account often has as much as $10,000 that will not be needed within the next 30 days.

**2.** A small business that has about $400,000 in liquid resources that will not be needed for the next nine months.

Explain the reasons for your choices and be prepared to explain these reasons in class.

Affections manufactures candy and sells only to retailers. It is not a publicly owned company and its financial statements are not audited. But the company frequently must borrow money. Its creditors insist that the company provide them with unaudited financial statements at the end of each quarter.

**CASE 7.2**

"Improving" the Balance Sheet

**LO 1, 2, 4, 5, 6, 8**

In October, management met to discuss the fiscal year ending next December 31. Due to a sluggish economy, Affections was having difficulty collecting its accounts receivable, and its cash position was unusually low. Management knew that if the December 31 balance sheet did not look good, the company would have difficulty borrowing the money it would need to boost production for Valentine's Day.

Thus the purpose of the meeting was to explore ways in which Affections might improve its December 31 balance sheet. Some of the ideas discussed are as follows:

**1.** Offer customers purchasing Christmas candy a 10% discount if they make payment within 30 days.

---

†*Supplemental Topic B,* "Notes Receivable and Interest Revenue."

2. Allow a 30-day grace period on all accounts receivable overdue at the end of the year. As these accounts will no longer be overdue, the company will not need an allowance for overdue accounts.

3. For purposes of balance sheet presentation, combine all forms of cash, including cash equivalents, compensating balances, and unused lines of credit.

4. Require officers who have borrowed money from the company to repay the amounts owed at December 31. This would convert into cash the "notes receivable from officers," which now appear in the balance sheet as noncurrent assets. The loans could be renewed immediately after year-end.

5. Present investments in marketable securities at their market value, rather than at cost.

6. Treat inventory as a financial asset and show it at current sales value. As Affections is not a publicly owned company, it is not legally required to prepare its financial statements in conformity with generally accepted accounting principles.

7. On December 31, draw a large check against one of the company's bank accounts and deposit it in another of the company's accounts in a different bank. The check won't clear the first bank until after year-end. This will substantially increase the amount of cash in bank accounts at year-end.

### Instructions

a. Separately evaluate each of these proposals. Consider ethical issues as well as accounting issues.

b. Do you consider it ethical for management to hold this meeting in the first place? That is, should management plan in advance how to improve financial statements that will be distributed to creditors and investors?

**CASE 7.3**

Accounting Principles

**LO 1, 5, 9**

In each of the situations described below, indicate the accounting principles or concepts, if any, that have been violated and explain briefly the nature of the violation. If you believe the practice is *in accord* with generally accepted accounting principles, state this as your position and defend it.

a. A small business in which credit sales fluctuate greatly from year to year uses the direct write-off method both for income tax purposes and in its financial statements.

b. A manufacturing company charges all of its petty cash expenditures to Miscellaneous Expense, rather than to the various expense accounts that reflect the nature of each expenditure.

c. Computer Systems often sells merchandise in exchange for interest-bearing notes receivable, maturing in 6, 12, or 24 months. The company records these sales transactions by debiting Notes Receivable for the maturity value of the notes, crediting Sales for the sales price of the merchandise, and crediting Interest Revenue for the balance of the maturity value of the note. The cost of goods sold also is recorded.

d. A company has $400,000 in unrestricted cash, $1 million in a bank account specifically earmarked for the construction of a new factory, and $2 million in cash equivalents. In the balance sheet, these amounts are combined and shown as "Cash and cash equivalents . . . $3.4 million."

**CASE 7.4**

If Things Get Any Better, We'll Be Broke

**LO 6, 7**

Rock, Inc., sells stereo equipment. Traditionally, the company's sales have been in the following categories: cash sales, 25%; customers using national credit cards, 35%; sales on account (due in 30 days), 40%. With these policies, the company earned a modest profit, and monthly cash receipts exceeded monthly cash payments by a comfortable margin. Uncollectible accounts expense was approximately 1% of net sales. (The company uses the direct write-off method in accounting for uncollectible accounts receivable.)

Two months ago, the company initiated a new credit policy, which it calls "Double Zero." Customers may purchase merchandise on account, with no down payment and no interest charges. The accounts are collected in 12 monthly installments of equal amounts.

The plan has proven quite popular with customers, and monthly sales have increased dramatically. Despite the increase in sales, however, Rock is experiencing cash flow problems—it hasn't been generating enough cash to pay its suppliers, most of which require payment within 30 days.

The company's bookkeeper has prepared the following analysis of monthly operating results:

| Sales | Before Double Zero | Last Month |
|---|---|---|
| Cash | $12,500 | $ 5,000 |
| National credit card | 17,500 | 10,000 |
| 30-day accounts | 20,000 | –0– |
| Double Zero accounts | –0– | 75,000 |
| Total monthly sales | $50,000 | $ 90,000 |
| Cost of goods sold and expenses | 40,000 | 65,000 |
| Net income | $10,000 | $ 25,000 |
| **Cash receipts** | | |
| Cash sales | $12,500 | $ 5,000 |
| National credit card companies | 17,500 | 10,000 |
| 30-day accounts | 19,500 | –0– |
| Double Zero accounts | –0– | 11,250 |
| Total monthly cash receipts | $49,500 | $ 26,250 |
| Accounts written off as uncollectible | $ 500 | $ –0– |
| Accounts receivable at month-end | $20,000 | $135,000 |

The bookkeeper offers the following assessment: "Double Zero is killing us. Since we started that plan, our accounts receivable have increased nearly sevenfold, and they're still growing. We can't afford to carry such a large nonproductive asset on our books. Our cash receipts are down to nearly half of what they used to be. If we don't go back to more cash sales and receivables that can be collected more quickly, we'll become insolvent."

Maxwell "Rock" Swartz, founder and chief executive officer, shouts back: "Why do you say that our accounts receivable are nonproductive? They're the most productive asset we have! Since we started Double Zero, our sales have nearly doubled, our profits have more than doubled, and our bad debt expense has dropped to nothing!"

**Instructions**

**a.** Is it logical that the Double Zero plan is causing sales and profits to increase while also causing a decline in cash receipts? Explain.

**b.** Why has the uncollectible accounts expense dropped to zero? What would you expect to happen to the company's uncollectible accounts expense in the future—say, next year? Why?

**c.** Do you think that the reduction in monthly cash receipts is permanent or temporary? Explain.

**d.** In what sense are the company's accounts receivable a "nonproductive" asset?

**e.** Suggest several ways that Rock may be able to generate the cash it needs to pay its bills without terminating the Double Zero plan.

**f.** Would you recommend that the company continue offering Double Zero financing, or should it return to the use of 30-day accounts? Explain the reasons for your answer, and identify any unresolved factors that might cause you to change this opinion in the future.

## BUSINESS WEEK ASSIGNMENT

BusinessWeek

**CASE 7.5**

**LO 1, 6**

In the September 18, 2000, issue of *Business Week*, an article by Pallavi Gogoi titled "An eBay of Deadbeats," stated that the Internet can be used to sell virtually everything from fine art to used wedding dresses. So, why not sell off problem receivables, credit card bills, auto loans, and home mortgages? The article reported that sites offering problem receivables are attracting major companies, such as **Sprint Corp.**, which recently put $145 million of unpaid telephone bills up for sale on DebtAuction.com.

Why would **Sprint** try to sell its uncollected receivables? Why would a buyer be interested in purchasing such assets?

## INTERNET ASSIGNMENT

**INTERNET 7.1**

Returns on Idle Cash

**LO 1, 2, 6**

Prudent cash management is an important function in any business. Large amounts of excess cash sitting idle in non-interest-bearing checking accounts can cost a company thousands—even millions—of dollars annually in forgone revenue. Thus, many businesses invest large amounts of idle cash in two-month, six-month, and one-year Treasury bills. The United States Treasury sells Treasury bills to investors and pays them interest for 3, 6, or 12 months.

Visit the **Bloomberg** home page at the following address:

### www.Bloomberg.com

Search the Bloomberg site for information on Treasury bills.

### Instructions
**a.** Prepare a table showing the interest rate yields on three-month, six-month, and one-year Treasury bills.
**b.** Make a recommendation to management concerning the seemingly conflicting objectives of (1) having cash available immediately to meet obligations and (2) earning a return on idle cash.

*Internet sites are time and date sensitive. It is the purpose of these exercises to have you explore the Internet. You may need to use the Yahoo! search engine* http://www.yahoo.com *(or other favorite search engine) to find a company's current web address.*

## OUR COMMENTS ON THE "YOUR TURN" CASES

**You as a Financial Advisor (p. 265)** Alternative uses for the company's cash surplus may include investments in (1) certificates of deposit—CDs—with staggered maturity dates, (2) short-term notes issued by the U.S. Treasury Department, or (3) money market accounts. If these alternatives are deemed unacceptable, management may wish to distribute a cash dividend to the company's shareholders. As a financial advisor, you should alert management to the fact that the $5 million checking account balance may not be as safe as it thinks. Should the bank run into financial problems, the FDIC would insure only a fraction of the $5 million total.

**You as an Accounts Receivable Manager (p. 281)** Factoring accounts receivable is neither illegal nor unethical. Your customer has a contract to pay whoever owns the receivable. Article 9 of the Uniform Commercial Code* provides the legal requirements for the sale of accounts receivable to a third party. The ethics of the situation may depend on what customers were promised when they made purchases on account. At a minimum, a letter should be sent to all customers explaining that the receivables have been sold and will now be collected by a collection agency. Many customers do not like their accounts receivable to be sold to a third party. Thus using factoring as a short-term solution to a cash flow problem may cause long-term problems with lost customers and ultimately lost revenues.

**You as a Credit Manager (p. 283)** Shown below are accounts receivable turnover rates and average-days-outstanding figures for the past four years.

**Note:** Days outstanding were computed by dividing 365 days by the turnover rate.

---
*See **www.law.cornell.edu/ucc/ucc.table.html** for more details about the Uniform Commercial Code.

| | **2002** | **2001** | **2000** | **1999** |
|---|---|---|---|---|
| Sales ................................. | $17,000 | $14,580 | $9,600 | $9,000 |
| Divided by | | | | |
|   Average accounts receivable ................. | 1,700 | 1,620 | 1,600 | 1,800 |
| Turnover rate ............................. | 10 times | 9 times | 6 times | 5 times |
| Days outstanding ......................... | 37 days | 41 days | 61 days | 73 days |

Based on these data, it appears that the new credit policy was successful in two ways. First, over the four-year period, it resulted in the doubling of the company's accounts receivable turnover rate (and thereby reduced its average collection period from 73 days to 37 days). Furthermore, the new policy successfully improved the quality of accounts receivable without adversely affecting sales growth.

## ANSWERS TO SELF-TEST QUESTIONS

**1.** b    **2.** c    **3.** a    **4.** c    **5.** a    **6.** b    **7.** a    **8.** d    **9.** c    **10.** a
**11.** b ($300,000 $\times$ 12% $\times$ $^6/_{12}$)

# CHAPTER 8

# INVENTORIES AND THE COST OF GOODS SOLD

## Learning Objectives

*After studying this chapter, you should be able to:*

1. In a perpetual inventory system, determine the cost of goods sold using (a) specific identification, (b) average cost, (c) FIFO, and (d) LIFO. Discuss the advantages and shortcomings of each method.

2. Explain the need for taking a physical inventory.

3. Record shrinkage losses and other year-end adjustments to inventory.

4. In a periodic inventory system, determine the ending inventory and the cost of goods sold using (a) specific identification, (b) average cost, (c) FIFO, and (d) LIFO.

5. Explain the effects on the income statement of errors in inventory valuation.

6. Estimate the cost of goods sold and ending inventory by the gross profit method and by the retail method.

7. Compute the inventory turnover rate and explain its uses.

*8. Define a "LIFO reserve" and explain its implications to users of financial statements.

---

*Supplemental Topic, "LIFO Reserves."

Courtesy Walgreens

Having the right merchandise available at the right time and in the right place is critically important to all companies that sell products. These businesses include many stores where everyone shops regularly, such as drugstores and department stores.

Consider a chain such as **Walgreens**—one of the nation's fastest growing retailers whose strategy is to become the most convenient and technologically advanced health care retailer. When you shop at **Walgreens**, you expect merchandise to be available and ready to purchase. Whenever your expectations are not met, you most probably find another place to shop.

• • •

Accounting for merchandise inventory presents one of the greatest challenges for merchandising companies. These companies must maintain not only a record of inventory items for sale but also the prices at which these items are purchased and sold, both of which change over time. This adds a significant complication to accounting for inventory and the expense included in the income statement when inventory is sold to customers. You learn how to account for inventory and its cost in this chapter.

### Inventory Defined

In a merchandising company, inventory consists of all goods owned and held for sale to customers. Inventory is expected to be converted into cash within the company's *operating cycle*.[1] In the balance sheet, inventory is listed immediately after accounts receivable, because it is just one step farther removed from conversion into cash than customer receivables.

## THE FLOW OF INVENTORY COSTS

Inventory is a nonfinancial asset and usually is shown in the balance sheet at its cost.[2] As items are sold from this inventory, their costs are removed from the balance sheet and transferred into the cost of goods sold, which is offset against sales revenue in the income statement. This flow of costs is illustrated in the following diagram:

*Flow of costs through financial statements*

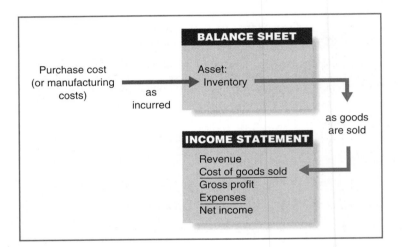

In a perpetual inventory system, entries in the accounting records parallel this flow of costs. When merchandise is purchased, its cost (net of allowable cash discounts) is added to the asset account Inventory. As the merchandise is sold, its cost is removed from the Inventory account and transferred to the Cost of Goods Sold account.

The valuation of inventory and of the cost of goods sold is of critical importance to managers and to external users of financial statements. In many cases, inventory is a company's largest asset, and the cost of goods sold is its largest expense. These two accounts have a significant effect on the financial statement subtotals and ratios used in evaluating the solvency and profitability of the business.

Several different methods of pricing inventory and of measuring the cost of goods sold are acceptable under generally accepted accounting principles. These different methods may produce significantly different results, both in a company's financial statements

---

[1] As explained in Chapter 6, the *operating cycle* of a merchandising business is the period of time required to convert cash into inventory, inventory into accounts receivable, and accounts receivable into cash. Assets expected to be converted into cash within one year or the operating cycle, whichever is longer, are regarded as current assets.

[2] Some companies deal in inventories that can be sold in a worldwide market at quoted market prices. Examples include mutual funds, stock brokerages, and companies that deal in commodities such as agricultural crops or precious metals. Often these companies value their inventories at market price rather than at cost. Our discussions in this chapter are directed to the far more common situation in which inventories are valued at cost.

and in its income tax returns. Therefore, managers and investors should understand the effects of the different inventory valuation methods.

## Which Unit Did We Sell?

Purchases of merchandise are recorded in the same manner under all of the inventory valuation methods. The differences in these methods lie in determining *which costs* should be removed from the Inventory account when merchandise is sold.

We illustrated the basic entries relating to purchases and sales of merchandise in Chapter 6. In that introductory discussion, however, we made a simplifying assumption: All of the units in inventory had been acquired at the same unit cost. In practice, a company often has in its inventory identical units of a given product that were acquired at *different costs*. Acquisition costs may vary because the units were purchased at different dates, from different suppliers, or in different quantities.

When identical units of inventory have different unit costs, a question arises as to *which of these costs* should be used in recording sales transactions.

## Data for an Illustration

To illustrate the alternative methods of measuring the cost of goods sold, assume that Mead Electric Company sells electrical equipment and supplies. Included in the company's inventory are five Elco AC-40 generators. These generators are identical; however, two were purchased on January 5 at a per-unit cost of *$1,000,* and the other three were purchased a month later, shortly after Elco had announced a price increase, at a per-unit cost of *$1,200.* These purchases are reflected in Mead's inventory subsidiary ledger as follows:

**Item** Elco AC-40   **Primary supplier** Elco Manufacturing
**Description** Portable generator   **Secondary supplier** Vegas Wholesale Co.
**Location** Daily St. warehouse   **Inventory level: Min:** 2   **Max:** 5

| | Purchased | | | Sold | | | Balance | | |
| | | Unit | | | Unit | Cost of Goods | | Unit | |
| Date | Units | Cost | Total | Units | Cost | Sold | Units | Cost | Total |
|---|---|---|---|---|---|---|---|---|---|
| Jan. 5 | 2 | $1,000 | $2,000 | | | | 2 | $1,000 | $2,000 |
| Feb. 5 | 3 | 1,200 | 3,600 | | | | ⎰2 | 1,000 ⎱ | |
| | | | | | | | ⎱3 | 1,200 ⎰ | 5,600 |
| | | | | | | | | | |
| | | | | | | | | | |

*Inventory subsidiary ledger record*

Notice that on February 5, the Balance columns contain two "layers" of unit cost information, representing the units purchased at the two different unit costs. A new **cost layer** is created whenever units are acquired at a different per-unit cost. (As all units comprising a cost layer are sold, the layer is eliminated from the inventory. Therefore, a business is unlikely to have more than three or four cost layers in its inventory at any given time.)

Now assume that on March 1, Mead sells one of these Elco generators to Boulder Construction Company for $1,800 cash. What cost should be removed from the Inventory account and recognized as the cost of goods sold—$1,000 or $1,200?

In answering such questions, accountants may use an approach called **specific identification**, or they may adopt a cost **flow assumption**. Either of these approaches is acceptable. Once an approach has been selected, however, it should be *applied consistently* in accounting for all sales of this particular type of merchandise.

## Specific Identification

**LO 1**

In a perpetual inventory system, determine the cost of goods sold using (a) specific identification, (b) average cost, (c) FIFO, and (d) LIFO. Discuss the advantages and shortcomings of each method.

The specific identification method can be used only when the actual costs of individual units of merchandise can be determined from the accounting records. For example, each of the generators in Mead's inventory may have an identification number, and these numbers may appear on the purchase invoices. With this identification number, Mead's accounting department can determine whether the generator sold to Boulder Construction cost $1,000 or $1,200. The *actual cost* of this particular unit then is used in recording the cost of goods sold.

## Cost Flow Assumptions

If the items in inventory are *homogeneous* in nature (identical, except for insignificant differences), it is *not necessary* for the seller to use the specific identification method. Rather, the seller may follow the more convenient practice of using a *cost flow assumption*. Using a cost flow assumption, often referred to as simply a **flow assumption**, is particularly common where the company has a large number of virtually identical inventory items.

When a flow assumption is in use, the seller simply makes an *assumption* as to the sequence in which units are withdrawn from inventory. For example, the seller might assume that the oldest merchandise always is sold first or that the most recently purchased items are the first to be sold.

Three flow assumptions are in widespread use:

1. *Average cost.* This assumption values all merchandise—units sold and units remaining in inventory—at the *average* per-unit cost. (In effect, the average-cost method assumes that units are withdrawn from the inventory in random order.)
2. *First-in, first-out (FIFO).* As the name implies, FIFO involves the assumption that goods sold are the *first* units that were purchased—that is, the *oldest* goods on hand. Thus the remaining inventory is comprised of the most recent purchases.
3. *Last-in, first-out (LIFO).* Under LIFO, the units sold are assumed to be those *most recently* acquired. The remaining inventory, therefore, is assumed to consist of the earliest purchases.

The cost flow assumption selected by a company *need not* correspond to the actual physical movement of the company's merchandise. When the units of merchandise are identical (or nearly identical), it *does not matter* which units are delivered to the customer in a particular sales transaction. Therefore, in measuring the income of a business that sells units of identical merchandise, accountants consider the flow of *costs* to be more important than the physical flow of the merchandise.

The use of a flow assumption *eliminates the need for separately identifying each unit sold and looking up its actual cost.* Experience has shown that these flow assumptions provide useful and reliable measurements of the cost of goods sold, as long as they are applied consistently to all sales of the particular type of merchandise.

## Average-Cost Method

When the **average-cost method** is in use, the *average cost* of all units in inventory is computed after every purchase. This average cost is computed by dividing the total cost of goods available for sale by the number of units in inventory. Because the average cost may change following each purchase, this method also is called *moving average.*

As of January 5, Mead had only two Elco generators in its inventory, each acquired at a purchase cost of $1,000. Therefore, the average cost is $1,000 per unit. After the purchase on February 5, Mead had five Elco generators in inventory, acquired at a total cost of $5,600 (2 units @ $1,000, plus 3 units @ $1,200 = $5,600). Therefore, the *average* per-unit cost now is *$1,120* ($5,600 ÷ 5 units = $1,120).

On March 1, two entries are made to record the sale of one of these generators to Boulder Construction Company. The first recognizes the revenue from this sale, and the second recognizes the cost of the goods sold. These entries follow, with the cost of goods sold measured by the average-cost method:

| | | |
|---|---|---|
| Cash . . . . . . . . . . . . . . . . . . . . . . . . . . . . . . . . . . . . . . . . . . . . . . . . . . . . | 1,800 | |
| Sales . . . . . . . . . . . . . . . . . . . . . . . . . . . . . . . . . . . . . . . . . . . . . . . . | | 1,800 |
| To record the sale of one Elco AC-40 generator. | | |

| | | |
|---|---|---|
| Cost of Goods Sold . . . . . . . . . . . . . . . . . . . . . . . . . . . . . . . . . . . . . . . . | 1,120 | |
| Inventory . . . . . . . . . . . . . . . . . . . . . . . . . . . . . . . . . . . . . . . . . . . . . . | | 1,120 |
| To record the cost of one Elco AC-40 generator sold to Boulder Construction Co. Cost determined by the average-cost method. | | |

(The entry to recognize the $1,800 in sales revenue is the same, regardless of the inventory method in use. Therefore, we will not repeat this entry in our illustrations of the other cost flow assumptions.)

When the average-cost method is in use, the inventory subsidiary ledger is modified slightly from the format illustrated on page 317. Following the sale on March 1, Mead's subsidiary ledger card for Elco generators will appear as follows, modified to show the average unit cost:

| | Purchased | | | Sold | | | Balance | | |
|---|---|---|---|---|---|---|---|---|---|
| Date | Units | Unit Cost | Total | Units | Unit Cost | Cost of Goods Sold | Units | Unit Cost | Total |
| Jan. 5 | 2 | $1,000 | $2,000 | | | | 2 | $1,000* | $2,000 |
| Feb. 5 | 3 | 1,200 | 3,600 | | | | 5 | 1,120** | 5,600 |
| Mar. 1 | | | | 1 | $1,120 | $1,120 | 4 | 1,120 | 4,480 |
| | | | | | | | | | |
| | | | | | | | | | |

*$2,000 total cost ÷ 2 units = $1,000.
**$5,600 total cost ÷ 5 units = $1,120.

*Inventory subsidiary record— average-cost basis*

Notice that the Unit Cost column for purchases still shows actual unit costs—$1,000 and $1,200. The Unit Cost columns relating to sales and to the remaining inventory, however, show the *average unit cost* ($5,600 total ÷ 5 units = $1,120). As all units are valued at this same average cost, the inventory has only one cost layer.

Under the average-cost assumption, all items in inventory are assigned the *same* per-unit cost (the average cost). Hence, it does not matter which units are sold; the cost of goods sold always is based on the current average unit cost. When one generator is sold on March 1, the cost of goods sold is $1,120; if three generators had been sold on this date, the cost of goods sold would have been $3,360 (3 units × $1,120 per unit).

## First-In, First-Out Method

The **first-in, first-out method**, often called *FIFO*, is based on the assumption that the *first merchandise purchased is the first merchandise sold.* Thus the accountant for Mead Electric would assume that the generator sold on March 1 was one of those purchased on *January 5*. The entry to record the cost of goods sold would be:

```
Cost of Goods Sold ........................................  1,000
     Inventory ............................................         1,000
To record the cost of one Elco AC-40 generator sold to Boulder
  Construction Co. Cost determined by the FIFO flow assumption.
```

Following this sale, Mead's inventory ledger would appear as follows:

*Inventory subsidiary record—FIFO basis*

| Date | Purchased | | | Sold | | | Balance | | |
|---|---|---|---|---|---|---|---|---|---|
| | Units | Unit Cost | Total | Units | Unit Cost | Cost of Goods Sold | Units | Unit Cost | Total |
| Jan. 5 | 2 | $1,000 | $2,000 | | | | 2 | $1,000 | $2,000 |
| Feb. 5 | 3 | 1,200 | 3,600 | | | | ⎰2 | 1,000 | |
| | | | | | | | ⎱3 | 1,200 | 5,600 |
| Mar. 1 | | | | 1 | $1,000 | $1,000 | ⎰1 | 1,000 | |
| | | | | | | | ⎱3 | 1,200 | 4,600 |

Notice that FIFO uses actual purchase costs, rather than an average cost. Thus, if merchandise has been purchased at several different costs, the inventory will include several different cost layers. The cost of goods sold for a given sales transaction also may involve several different cost layers. To illustrate, assume that Mead had sold *four* generators to Boulder Construction, instead of only one. Under the FIFO flow assumption, Mead would assume that it first sold the two generators purchased on January 5 and then two of those purchased on February 5. Thus the total cost of goods sold ($4,400) would include items at *two different unit costs*, as follows:

```
2 generators from Jan. 5 purchase @ $1,000 ......................  $2,000
2 generators from Feb. 5 purchase @ $1,200 ......................  $2,400
Total cost of goods sold (4 units) ..............................  $4,400
```

As the cost of goods sold always is recorded at the oldest available purchase costs, the units remaining in inventory are valued at the more recent acquisition costs.

## Last-In, First-Out Method

The **last-in, first-out method**, commonly known as *LIFO*, is among the most widely used methods of determining the cost of goods sold and valuing inventory. As the name suggests, the *most recently* purchased merchandise (the last in) is assumed to be sold first. If Mead were using the LIFO method, it would assume that the generator sold on March 1 was one of those acquired on *February 5*, the most recent purchase date. Thus, the cost transferred from inventory to the cost of goods sold would be *$1,200*.

The journal entry to record the cost of goods sold is illustrated below, along with the inventory subsidiary ledger record after this entry has been posted.

```
Cost of Goods Sold ........................................  1,200
     Inventory ............................................         1,200
To record the cost of one Elco AC-40 generator sold to Boulder
  Construction Co. Cost determined by the LIFO flow assumption.
```

| | Purchased | | | Sold | | | Balance | | |
|---|---|---|---|---|---|---|---|---|---|
| Date | Units | Unit Cost | Total | Units | Unit Cost | Cost of Goods Sold | Units | Unit Cost | Total |
| Jan. 5 | 2 | $1,000 | $2,000 | | | | 2 | $1,000 | $2,000 |
| Feb. 5 | 3 | 1,200 | 3,600 | | | | {2 | 1,000} | |
| | | | | | | | {3 | 1,200} | 5,600 |
| Mar. 1 | | | | 1 | $1,200 | $1,200 | {2 | 1,000} | |
| | | | | | | | {2 | 1,200} | 4,400 |
| | | | | | | | | | |

*Inventory subsidiary record—LIFO basis*

Like FIFO, the LIFO method uses actual purchase costs, rather than an average cost. Thus the inventory may have several different cost layers. If a sale includes more units than are included in the most recent cost layer, some of the goods sold are assumed to come from the next most recent layer. For example, if Mead had sold four generators (instead of one) on March 1, the cost of goods sold determined under the LIFO assumption would be $4,600, as follows:

| | |
|---|---|
| 3 generators from Feb. 5 purchase @ $1,200 .................................... | $3,600 |
| 1 generator from Jan. 5 purchase @ $1,000 ............................. | $1,000 |
| Total cost of goods sold (4 units) ...................................... | $4,600 |

As LIFO transfers the most recent purchase costs to the cost of goods sold, the goods remaining in inventory are valued at the oldest acquisition costs.

## Evaluation of the Methods

All three of the cost flow assumptions just described are acceptable for use in financial statements and in income tax returns. As we have explained, it is not necessary that the physical flow of merchandise correspond to the cost flow assumption. Different flow assumptions may be used for different types of inventory or for inventories in different geographical locations.

The only requirement for using a flow assumption is that the units to which the assumption is applied should be *homogeneous* in nature—that is, virtually identical to one another. If each unit is unique, the specific identification method is needed in order to achieve a proper matching of sales revenue with the cost of goods sold.

Each inventory valuation method has certain advantages and shortcomings. In the final analysis, the selection of inventory valuation methods is a managerial decision. However, the method (or methods) used in financial statements always should be disclosed in notes accompanying the statements.

**Specific Identification** The specific identification method is best suited to inventories of high-priced, low-volume items. This is the only method that exactly parallels the physical flow of the merchandise. If each item in the inventory is unique, as in the case of valuable paintings, custom jewelry, and most real estate, specific identification is clearly the logical choice.

The specific identification method has an intuitive appeal, because it assigns actual purchase costs to the specific units of merchandise sold or in inventory. However, when the units in inventory are identical (or nearly identical), the specific identification method may produce *misleading results* by implying differences in value that—under current market conditions—do not exist.

As an example, assume that a coal dealer has purchased 100 tons of coal at a cost of $60 per ton. A short time later, the company purchases another 100 tons of the *same grade* of coal—but this time, the cost is $80 per ton. The two purchases are in separate piles; thus it would be possible for the company to use the specific identification method in accounting for sales.

Assume now that the company has an opportunity to sell 10 tons of coal at a retail price of $120 per ton. Does it really matter from which pile this coal is removed? The answer is *no;* the coal is a homogeneous product. Under current market conditions, the coal in each pile is equally valuable. To imply that it is more profitable to sell coal from one pile rather than the other is an argument of questionable logic.

Let us try to make this point in a more personal way: Would you be willing to shovel the more recently purchased coal out of the way so that the customer can get its truck back to the lower-cost coal pile?

**Average Cost**   Identical items will have the same accounting values only under the average-cost method. Assume, for example, that a hardware store sells a given size nail for 65 cents per pound. The hardware store buys the nails in 100-pound quantities at different times at prices ranging from 40 to 50 cents per pound. Several hundred pounds of nails are always on hand, stored in a large bin. The average-cost method properly recognizes that when a customer buys a pound of nails it is not necessary to know exactly which nails the customer selected from the bin in order to measure the cost of goods sold. Therefore, the average-cost method avoids the shortcomings of the specific identification method. It is not necessary to keep track of the specific items sold and of those still in inventory. Also, it is not possible to manipulate income merely by selecting the specific items to be delivered to customers.

A shortcoming of the average-cost method is that changes in current replacement costs of inventory are concealed because these costs are averaged with older costs. Thus neither the valuation of ending inventory nor the cost of goods sold will quickly reflect changes in the current replacement cost of merchandise.

**First-In, First-Out**   The distinguishing characteristic of the FIFO method is that the oldest purchase costs are transferred to the cost of goods sold, while the most recent costs remain in inventory.

Over the past 50 years, we have lived in an inflationary economy, which means that most prices tend to rise over time. When purchase costs are rising, the FIFO method assigns *lower* (older) costs to the cost of goods sold and the higher (more recent) costs to the goods remaining in inventory.

By assigning lower costs to the cost of goods sold, FIFO usually causes a business to report somewhat *higher profits* than would be reported under the other inventory valuation methods. Some companies favor the FIFO method for financial reporting purposes, because their goal is to report the highest net income possible. For income tax purposes, however, reporting more income than necessary results in paying more income taxes than necessary.

Some accountants and decision makers believe that FIFO tends to *overstate* a company's profitability. Revenue is based on current market conditions. By offsetting this revenue with a cost of goods sold based on older (and lower) prices, gross profits may be overstated consistently.

A conceptual advantage of the FIFO method is that in the balance sheet inventory is valued at recent purchase costs. Therefore, this asset appears in the balance sheet at an amount closely approximating its current replacement cost.

**Last-In, First-Out**   The LIFO method is one of the most interesting and controversial flow assumptions. The basic assumption in the LIFO method is that the most recently purchased units are sold first and that the older units remain in inventory. This assumption is *not* in accord with the physical flow of merchandise in most businesses. Yet there are strong logical arguments in support of the LIFO method, in addition to income tax considerations.

For the purpose of measuring income, most accountants consider the *flow of costs* more important than the physical flow of merchandise. Supporters of the LIFO method contend that the measurement of income should be based on *current market conditions.* Therefore, current sales revenue should be offset by the *current* cost of the merchandise sold. By the LIFO method, the costs assigned to the cost of goods sold are relatively current because they reflect the most recent purchases. By the FIFO method, on the other hand, the cost of goods sold is based on older costs.

Income tax considerations, however, provide the principal reason for the popularity of the LIFO method. Remember that the LIFO method assigns the most recent inventory purchase costs to the cost of goods sold. In the common situation of rising prices, these most recent costs are also the highest costs. By reporting a higher cost of goods sold than results from other inventory valuation methods, the LIFO method usually results in *lower taxable income.* In short, if inventory costs are rising, a company can reduce the amount of its income tax obligation by using the LIFO method in its income tax return.

It may seem reasonable that a company would use the LIFO method in its tax return to reduce taxable income and use the FIFO method in its financial statements to increase the amount of net income reported to investors and creditors. However, income tax regulations allow a corporation to use LIFO in its income tax return *only* if the company also uses LIFO in its financial statements. Thus income tax considerations often provide the overriding reason for selecting the LIFO method.

There is one significant shortcoming to the LIFO method. The valuation of the asset inventory is based on the company's oldest inventory acquisition costs. After the company has been in business for many years, these oldest costs may greatly understate the current replacement cost of the inventory. Thus, when an inventory is valued by the LIFO method, the company also should disclose the current replacement cost of the inventory in a note to the financial statements.

During periods of rising inventory replacement costs, the LIFO method results in the lowest valuation of inventory and measurement of net income. Therefore, LIFO is regarded as the most *conservative* of the inventory pricing methods. FIFO, on the other hand, is the least conservative method.[3]

## Do Inventory Methods Really Affect Performance?

Except for their effects on income taxes, the answer to this question is *no.*

During a period of rising prices, a company might *report* higher profits by using FIFO instead of LIFO. But the company would not really *be* any more profitable. An inventory valuation method affects only the *allocation of costs* between the Inventory account and the Cost of Goods Sold account. It has *no effect* on the total costs actually *incurred* in purchasing or manufacturing inventory. Except for income taxes, differences in the profitability reported under different inventory methods exist "only on paper."

The inventory method in use *does* affect the amount of income taxes owed. To the extent that an inventory method reduces these taxes, it *does* increase profitability.

---

The cash payments relating to inventory occur when suppliers are *paid.* In a statement of cash flows, these outlays are included among the cash payments for operating activities. For merchandising and manufacturing businesses, these payments often represent the largest use of cash. It is important to note that inventory valuation methods have *no effect* on the cash paid to purchase or manufacture inventory. They do, however, affect cash payments for income taxes.     **CASH EFFECTS**

---

[3] During a prolonged period of *declining* inventory replacement costs, this situation reverses: FIFO becomes the most conservative method, and LIFO the least conservative.

The table below summarizes characteristics of the basic inventory valuation methods.

| Inventory Valuation Methods: A Summary | | | |
|---|---|---|---|
| | Costs Allocated to: | | |
| **Valuation Method** | **Cost of Goods Sold** | **Inventory** | **Comments** |
| Specific identification | Actual costs of the units sold | Actual cost of units remaining | • Parallels physical flow<br>• Logical method when units are unique<br>• May be misleading when the units are identical |
| Flow assumptions (acceptable only for an inventory of *homogeneous units*): | | | |
| Average cost | Number of units sold times the *average unit cost* | Number of units on hand times the *average unit cost* | • Assigns all units the same *average unit cost*<br>• Current costs are averaged in with older costs |
| First-in, first-out (FIFO) | Costs of *earliest purchases* on hand at the time of the sale (first-in, first-out) | Cost of *most recently* purchased units | • Cost of goods sold is based on older costs<br>• Inventory valued at most recent costs<br>• May overstate income during periods of rising prices; may increase income taxes due |
| Last-in, first-out (LIFO) | Cost of *most recently purchased* units (last-in, first-out) | Costs of *earliest* purchases (assumed *still* to be in inventory) | • Cost of goods sold shown at most recent prices<br>• Inventory shown at old (and perhaps out of date) costs<br>• Most conservative method during periods of rising prices; often results in lower income taxes |

### The Principle of Consistency

The principle of **consistency** is one of the basic concepts underlying reliable financial statements. This principle means that once a company has adopted a particular accounting method, it should *follow that method consistently,* rather than switch methods from one year to the next. Thus, once a company has adopted a particular inventory flow assumption (or the specific identification method), it should continue to apply that assumption to all sales of that type of merchandise.

The principle of consistency does *not* prohibit a company from *ever* changing its accounting methods. If a change is made, however, the reasons for the change must be explained, and the effects of the change on the company's net income must be fully disclosed.[4]

### Just-in-Time (JIT) Inventory Systems

In recent years, much attention has been paid to the **just-in-time (JIT) inventory system** in manufacturing operations. The phrase "just-in-time" usually means that purchases of raw materials and component parts arrive just in time for use in the manufacturing process—often within a few hours of the time they are scheduled for use. A second

---

[4] Disclosure of the effects of such "accounting changes" is discussed in Chapter 11. A change in the method of pricing inventory for tax purposes requires the approval of the Internal Revenue Service.

application of the just-in-time concept is completing the manufacturing process just in time to ship the finished goods to customers.

One advantage of a just-in-time system lies in reducing the amount of money tied up in inventories of raw materials and finished goods. Also, the manufacturing company does not need to maintain large inventory storage facilities. A disadvantage of a just-in-time system is that a delay in the arrival of essential materials may bring manufacturing operations to a halt. Therefore, just-in-time scheduling of incoming materials is feasible only when the suppliers and the transportation systems are highly reliable.

Even when the suppliers are other divisions of the same company, the use of just-in-time systems can be fraught with difficulties. **General Motors** is a case in point because recently a strike by unionized autoworkers at one plant shut down operations across multiple GM plants.

**MANAGEMENT STRATEGY**

Although a just-in-time system reduces the size of a company's inventories, it does not eliminate them entirely. A recent annual report of **Dell Computer Corporation**, for example, shows inventories in excess of *$273 million* (**Dell** reports its inventories by the FIFO method).

**Dell Computer Corporation** generates millions in revenue each day by selling computers on the Internet. The company has long been a model of just-in-time manufacturing. **Dell** doesn't start ordering components or assembling computers until an order has been booked. Most of its suppliers keep components warehoused just minutes from **Dell**'s factories. The JIT philosophy applies to suppliers, assemblers, and distributors. A customer order placed Monday morning can be on a delivery truck by Tuesday evening.

**CASE IN POINT**

The concept of minimizing inventories applies more to manufacturing operations than to retailers. Ideally, manufacturers have buyers "lined up" for their merchandise even before the goods are produced. Many retailers, in contrast, want to offer their customers a large selection of in-stock merchandise—which means a big inventory.

The just-in-time concept actually involves much more than minimizing the size of inventories. It has been described as the philosophy of constantly working to increase efficiency throughout the organization. One basic goal of an accounting system is to provide management with useful information about the efficiency—or inefficiency—of operations.

## TAKING A PHYSICAL INVENTORY

In Chapter 6 we explained the need for businesses to make a complete physical count of the merchandise on hand at least once a year. The primary reason for this procedure of "taking inventory" is to adjust the perpetual inventory records for unrecorded **shrinkage losses**, such as theft, spoilage, or breakage.

The **physical inventory** usually is taken at (or near) the end of the company's fiscal year.[5] Often a business selects a fiscal year ending in a season of low activity. For example, many large retailers use a fiscal year that starts February 1 and ends January 31.

**LO 2**

Explain the need for taking a physical inventory.

[5] The reason for taking a physical inventory near year-end is to ensure that any shrinkage losses are reflected in the annual financial statements. The stronger the company's system of internal control over inventories, the farther away this procedure may be moved from the balance sheet date. Obviously, no one wants to spend New Year's Eve counting inventory.

## Recording Shrinkage Losses

**LO 3**

Record shrinkage losses and other year-end adjustments to inventory.

In most cases, the year-end physical count of the inventory reveals some shortages or damaged merchandise. The costs of missing or damaged units are removed from the inventory records using the same flow assumption as is used in recording the costs of goods sold.

To illustrate, assume that a company's inventory subsidiary ledger shows the following 158 units of a particular product in inventory at year-end:

| | |
|---|---:|
| 8 units purchased Nov. 2 @ $100 . . . . . . . . . . . . . . . . . . . . . . . . . . . . . . . . . . . . . . . . . . . . . | $ 800 |
| 150 units purchased Dec. 10 @ $115 . . . . . . . . . . . . . . . . . . . . . . . . . . . . . . . . . . . . . . . | 17,250 |
| Total (158 units) . . . . . . . . . . . . . . . . . . . . . . . . . . . . . . . . . . . . . . . . . . . . . . . . . . . . . . . | $18,050 |

A year-end physical count, however, discloses that only *148* of these units actually are on hand. Based on this physical count, the company should adjust its inventory records to reflect the loss of 10 units.

The inventory flow assumption in use affects the measurement of shrinkage losses in the same way it affects the cost of goods sold. If the company uses *FIFO,* for example, the missing units will be valued at the oldest purchase costs shown in the inventory records. Thus 8 of the missing units will be assumed to have cost $100 per unit and the other 2, $115 per unit. Under FIFO, the shrinkage loss amounts to *$1,030* (8 units @ $100 + 2 units @ $115). But if this company uses *LIFO,* the missing units all will be assumed to have come from the most recent purchase (on December 10). Therefore, the shrinkage loss amounts to *$1,150* (10 units @ $115).

If shrinkage losses are small, the costs removed from inventory may be charged (debited) directly to the Cost of Goods Sold account. If these losses are *material* in amount, the offsetting debit should be entered in a special loss account, such as Inventory Shrinkage Losses. In the income statement, a loss account is deducted from revenue in the same manner as an expense account.

## LCM and Other Write-Downs of Inventory

In addition to shrinkage losses, the value of inventory may decline because the merchandise has become obsolete or is unsalable for other reasons. If inventory has become obsolete or is otherwise unsalable, its carrying value in the accounting records should be *written down* to zero (or to its "scrap value," if any). A **write-down** of inventory reduces both the carrying amount of the inventory in the balance sheet and the net income of the current period. The reduction in income is handled in the same manner as a shrinkage loss. If the write-down is relatively small, the loss is debited directly to the Cost of Goods Sold account. If the write-down is *material in amount,* however, it is charged to a special loss account, perhaps entitled Loss from Write-Down of Inventory.

**CASE IN POINT** Determining the materiality of an inventory write-down is a matter of professional judgment. For example, **Egghead.Com.Inc.,** a leading on-line seller of hardware and software peripherals, generally charges the entire cost of obsolete inventory directly to the Cost of Goods Sold account, thereby reducing its gross profit. In a recent income statement, **Egghead.Com.Inc.,** reported gross profit at 12.3% of sales. This figure, however, included a $6.2 million inventory write-down. Had the write-down been charged to a separate account for inventory losses, gross profit as a percentage of sales would have been 15.7%. Given the magnitude of this write-down, some might argue that it should have been treated separately.

**The Lower-of-Cost-or-Market (LCM) Rule**  An asset is an economic resource. It may be argued that no economic resource is worth more than it would cost to *replace* that resource in the open market. For this reason, accountants traditionally have valued inventory in the balance sheet at the lower of its (1) cost or (2) market value. In this context, "market value" means *current replacement cost*. Thus the inventory is valued at the lower of its historical cost or its current replacement cost.

The **lower-of-cost-or-market** rule may be applied in conjunction with any flow assumption as well as with the specific identification method. If the current replacement cost of the ending inventory is substantially *below* the cost shown in the accounting records, the inventory is written down to this replacement cost. The offsetting debit is charged to either the Cost of Goods Sold account or the Loss from Write-Down of Inventory account, depending on the materiality of the dollar amount.

In their financial statements, most companies state that inventory is valued at the lower-of-cost-or-market. In our inflationary economy, however, the lower of these two amounts usually is cost, especially for companies using LIFO.[6]

## The Year-End Cutoff of Transactions

Making a proper *cutoff* of transactions is an essential step in the preparation of reliable financial statements. A proper cutoff simply means that the transactions occurring near year-end are *recorded in the right accounting period.*

One aspect of a proper cutoff is determining that all purchases of merchandise through the end of the period are recorded in the inventory records and included in the physical count of merchandise on hand at year-end. Of equal importance is determining that the cost of all merchandise sold through the end of the period has been removed from the inventory accounts and charged to the Cost of Goods Sold. This merchandise should *not* be included in the year-end physical count.

If some sales transactions have not been recorded as of year-end, the quantities of merchandise shown in the inventory records will exceed the quantities actually on hand. When the results of the physical count are compared with the inventory records, these unrecorded sales easily could be mistaken for inventory shortages.

Making a proper cutoff may be difficult if sales transactions are occurring while the merchandise is being counted. For this reason, many businesses count their physical inventory during nonbusiness hours, even if they must shut down their sales operations for a day.

**Matching Revenue and the Cost of Goods Sold**  Accountants must determine that both the sales revenue and the cost of goods sold relating to sales transactions occurring near year-end are recorded in the *same* accounting period. Otherwise, the revenues and expenses from these transactions will not be properly matched in the company's income statements.

**Goods in Transit**  A sale should be recorded *when title to the merchandise passes to the buyer.* In making a year-end cutoff of transactions, questions may arise when goods are in transit between the seller and the buyer as to which company owns the merchandise. The answer to such questions lies in the terms of shipment. If these terms are **F.O.B.** (free on board) **shipping point**, title passes at the point of shipment and the goods are the property of the buyer while in transit. If the terms of the shipment are **F.O.B. destination**, title does not pass until the shipment reaches its destination and the goods belong to the seller while in transit.

---

[6] A notable exception is the petroleum industry, in which the replacement cost of inventory can fluctuate very quickly and in either direction. Large oil companies occasionally report LCM adjustments of several hundred million dollars in a single year.

Many companies ignore these distinctions, because goods in transit usually arrive within a day or two. In such cases, the amount of merchandise in transit usually is *not material* in dollar amount, and the company may follow the *most convenient* accounting procedures. It usually is most convenient to record all purchases when the inbound shipments arrive and all sales when the merchandise is shipped to the customer.

In some industries, however, goods in transit may be very material. Oil companies, for example, often have millions of dollars of inventory in transit in pipelines and supertankers. In these situations, the company must consider the terms of each shipment in recording its purchases and sales.

**YOUR TURN**

### You as a Shipping Department Manager

In organizing your shipping orders for the month of December, you have received a note from the plant controller asking you to instruct your bookkeeper to file some paperwork for shipping orders currently scheduled for shipment in early January, as if they were shipped in late December. What should you do?

*Our comments appear on p. 356.

## Periodic Inventory Systems

In our preceding discussions, we have emphasized the perpetual inventory system—that is, inventory records that are kept continuously up-to-date. Virtually all large business organizations use perpetual inventory systems.

**LO 4**

In a periodic inventory system, determine the ending inventory and the cost of goods sold using (a) specific identification, (b) average cost, (c) FIFO, and (d) LIFO.

Some small businesses, however, use *periodic* inventory systems. In a periodic inventory system, the cost of merchandise purchased during the year is debited to a *Purchases* account, rather than to the Inventory account. When merchandise is sold to a customer, an entry is made recognizing the sales revenue, but no entry is made to reduce the inventory account or to recognize the cost of goods sold.

The inventory on hand and the cost of goods sold for the year are not determined until year-end. At the end of the year, all goods on hand are counted and priced at cost. The cost assigned to this ending inventory is then used to compute the cost of goods sold, as shown below. (The dollar amounts are assumed for the purpose of completing the illustration.)

| | |
|---|---:|
| Inventory at the beginning of the year | $10,000 |
| Add: Purchases during the year | 80,000 |
| Cost of goods available for sale during the year | $90,000 |
| Less: Inventory at the end of the year | 7,000 |
| Cost of goods sold | $83,000 |

The only item in this computation that is kept continuously up-to-date in the accounting records is the Purchases account. The amounts of inventory at the beginning and end of the year are determined by annual physical observation.

Determining the cost of the year-end inventory involves two distinct steps: counting the merchandise and pricing the inventory—that is, determining the cost of the units on hand. Together, these procedures determine the proper valuation of inventory and the cost of goods sold.

**Applying Flow Assumptions in a Periodic System**   In our discussion of perpetual inventory systems, we have emphasized the costs that are transferred from inventory *to the cost of goods sold.* In a periodic system, the emphasis shifts to determining the costs that should be assigned *to inventory* at the end of the period.

To illustrate, assume that The Kitchen Counter, a retail store, uses a periodic inventory system. The year-end physical inventory indicates that 12 units of a particular model food processor are on hand. Purchases of these food processors during the year are as follows:

| | Number of Units | Cost per Unit | Total Cost |
|---|---|---|---|
| Beginning inventory . . . . . . . . . . . . . . . . . . . . . . . . . . . . . . . . | 10 | $ 80 | $ 800 |
| First purchase (Mar. 1) . . . . . . . . . . . . . . . . . . . . . . . . . | 5 | 90 | 450 |
| Second purchase (July 1) . . . . . . . . . . . . . . . . . . . . . . . . | 5 | 100 | 500 |
| Third purchase (Oct. 1) . . . . . . . . . . . . . . . . . . . . . . . . . | 5 | 120 | 600 |
| Fourth purchase (Dec. 1) . . . . . . . . . . . . . . . . . . . . . . . . | 5 | 130 | 650 |
| Available for sale . . . . . . . . . . . . . . . . . . . . . . . . . . . | 30 | | $3,000 |
| Units in ending inventory . . . . . . . . . . . . . . . . . . . . . . . . | 12 | | |
| Units sold . . . . . . . . . . . . . . . . . . . . . . . . . . . . . . . . | 18 | | |

This schedule shows that 30 food processors were available for sale in the course of the year, of which 12 are still on hand. Thus 18 of these food processors apparently were sold.[7] We will now use these data to determine the cost of the year-end inventory and the cost of goods sold using the specific identification method and the average-cost, FIFO, and LIFO flow assumptions.

**Specific Identification**  If specific identification is used, the company must identify the 12 food processors on hand at year-end and determine their actual costs from purchase invoices. Assume that these 12 units have an actual total cost of $1,240. The cost of goods sold then is determined by subtracting this ending inventory from the cost of goods available for sale:

| | |
|---|---|
| Cost of goods available for sale . . . . . . . . . . . . . . . . . . . . . . . . . . . . . . . . . . . . . | $3,000 |
| Less: Ending inventory (specific identification) . . . . . . . . . . . . . . . . . . . . . . . . . . . . . | 1,240 |
| Cost of goods sold  . . . . . . . . . . . . . . . . . . . . . . . . . . . . . . . . . . . . . . . . . . . . | $1,760 |

**Average Cost**  The average cost is determined by dividing the total cost of goods available for sale during the year by the total number of units available for sale. Thus the average per-unit cost is *$100* ($3,000 ÷ 30 units). Under the average-cost method, the ending inventory would be priced at $1,200 (12 units × $100 per unit), and the cost of goods sold would be *$1,800* ($3,000 cost of goods available for sale, less $1,200 in costs assigned to the ending inventory).

**FIFO**  Under the FIFO flow assumption, the oldest units are assumed to be the first sold. The ending inventory, therefore, is assumed to consist of the *most recently* acquired goods. (Remember, we are now talking about the goods *remaining in inventory,* not the goods sold.) Thus the inventory of 12 food processors would be valued at the following costs:

---

[7] The periodic inventory method does not distinguish between merchandise sold and shrinkage losses. Shrinkage losses are included automatically in the cost of goods sold.

| | |
|---|---:|
| 5 units from the Dec. 1 purchase @ $130 ........................................ | $ 650 |
| 5 units from the Oct. 1 purchase @ $120 ........................................ | 600 |
| 2 units from the July 1 purchase @ $100 ........................................ | 200 |
| Ending inventory, 12 units at FIFO cost ........................................ | $1,450 |

The cost of goods sold would be *$1,550* ($3,000 − $1,450).

Notice that the FIFO method results in an inventory valued at relatively recent purchase costs. The cost of goods sold, however, is based on the older acquisition costs.

**LIFO**    Under LIFO, the last units purchased are considered to be the first goods sold. Therefore, the ending inventory is assumed to contain the *earliest* purchases. The 12 food processors in inventory would be priced as follows:

| | |
|---|---:|
| 10 units from the beginning inventory @ $80 ........................................ | $800 |
| 2 units from the Mar. 1 purchase @ $90 ........................................ | 180 |
| Ending inventory, 12 units at LIFO cost ........................................ | $980 |

The cost of goods sold under the LIFO method is *$2,020* ($3,000 − $980).

Notice that the cost of goods sold under LIFO is *higher* than that determined by the FIFO method ($2,020 under LIFO, as compared with $1,550 under FIFO). LIFO always results in a higher cost of goods sold when purchase costs are rising. Thus LIFO tends to minimize reported net income and income taxes during periods of rising prices in both perpetual and periodic systems.

Notice also that the LIFO method may result in an ending inventory that is priced *well below* its current replacement cost. In this illustration, ending inventory is determined at $80 and $90 per unit, but the most recent purchase price is $130 per unit.

**CASE IN POINT**

Although FIFO techniques are allowed for financial reporting in nearly all countries, LIFO is more controversial. The International Accounting Standards Committee's conceptual framework does not embrace LIFO because it leads to outdated numbers in the balance sheet. Australia, New Zealand, and Sweden are countries that do not permit the use of LIFO inventory valuation techniques for financial reporting purposes.

**Receiving the Maximum Tax Benefit from the LIFO Method**    Many companies that use LIFO in a perpetual inventory system *restate* their year-end inventory at the costs indicated by the *periodic* LIFO costing procedures illustrated above. This restatement is accomplished by either debiting or crediting the Inventory account and making an offsetting entry to the Cost of Goods Sold account.

Often, restating ending inventory using periodic costing procedures results in older (and lower) unit costs than those shown in the periodic inventory records. By assigning less cost to the ending inventory, it follows that more of these costs will be assigned to the cost of goods sold. A higher cost of goods sold, in turn, means less taxable income.

Let us briefly explain why applying LIFO at year-end may result in a lower valuation of inventory than does applying LIFO on a perpetual basis. Consider the last purchase in our example. This purchase of five food processors was made on December 31, at the relatively high unit cost of $130. Assuming these units were not sold prior to year-end, they would be included in the year-end inventory in perpetual inventory records, even if these records were maintained on a LIFO basis. When the ending inventory is priced using "periodic LIFO," however, this last-minute purchase is *not* included in inventory, but rather is transferred to the income statement as part of cost of goods sold.

Both the LIFO and average-cost methods produce different valuations of inventory under perpetual and periodic costing procedures. Only companies using LIFO, however, usually adjust their perpetual records to indicate the unit costs determined by periodic costing procedures. When FIFO is in use, the perpetual and periodic costing procedures result in exactly the same valuation of inventory.

**Pricing the Year-End Inventory by Computer**   If purchase records are maintained by computer, as is now the case for most companies, the value of the ending inventory can be computed automatically using any of the flow assumptions that have been discussed. Only the number of units must be entered at year-end. A computer also can apply the specific identification method, but the system requires an identification number for each unit in the ending inventory. This is one reason why the specific identification method usually is not used for inventories consisting of a large number of low-cost items.

## Importance of an Accurate Valuation of Inventory

The most important liquid assets in the balance sheets of most companies are cash, accounts receivable, and inventory. Of these assets, inventory often is the largest. It also is the only one of these assets for which alternative valuation methods are considered acceptable.

Because of the relatively large size of inventory, and many different products may be stored in different locations, an error in inventory valuation may not be readily apparent. Even a small error in the valuation of inventory may have a material effect on net income. Therefore, care must be taken in counting and pricing the inventory at year-end.

An error in the valuation of inventory will affect several balance sheet measurements, including assets and total owners' equity. It also will affect key figures in the *income statement*, including the cost of goods sold, gross profit, and net income. And remember that the ending inventory of one year is the beginning inventory of the next. Thus an error in inventory valuation will *carry over* into the financial statements of the following year.

**Effects of an Error in Valuing Ending Inventory**   To illustrate, assume that some items of merchandise in a company's inventory are overlooked during the year-end physical count. As a result of this error, the ending inventory will be *understated.* The costs of the uncounted merchandise erroneously will be transferred out of the Inventory account and included in the cost of goods sold. This overstatement of the cost of goods sold, in turn, results in an understatement of gross profit and net income.[8]

**Inventory Errors Affect Two Years**   An error in the valuation of ending inventory affects not only the financial statements of the current year but also the income statement for the *following* year.

Assume that the ending inventory in 2001 is *understated* by $10,000. As we have described above, the cost of goods sold in 2001 is also overstated by this amount, and both gross profit and net income are *understated.*

The ending inventory in 2001, however, becomes the *beginning inventory* in 2002. An understatement of the beginning inventory results in an understatement of the cost of goods sold and, therefore, an *overstatement* of gross profit and net income in 2002.

Notice that the original error has exactly the *opposite effects* on the net incomes of the two successive years. Net income was *understated* by the amount of the error in 2001 and *overstated* by the same amount in 2002. For this reason, inventory errors are said to be "counterbalancing" or "self-correcting" over a two-year period.

**LO 5**

Explain the effects on the income statement of errors in inventory valuation.

---

[8] If income tax effects are ignored, the amount of the error is exactly the same in inventory, gross profit, and net income. If tax effects are considered, the amount of the error may be lessened in the net income figure.

The fact that offsetting errors occur in the financial statements of two successive years does not lessen the consequences of errors in inventory valuation. Rather, it *exaggerates* the misleading effects of the error on *trends* in the company's performance from one year to the next.

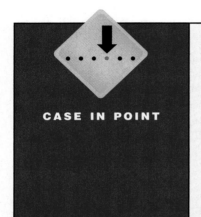

**CASE IN POINT**

Some small businesses purposely have understated ending inventory in their income tax returns as an easy—though fraudulent—means of understating taxable income. In the following year, however, the effect of this error will reverse, and taxable income will be overstated. To avoid paying income taxes on this overstated income, the business may again understate its ending inventory, this time by an even greater amount. If this type of fraud continues for very long, the inventory becomes so understated that the situation becomes obvious.

When the Internal Revenue Service audits the income tax return of a small business, the IRS agents invariably try to determine whether inventory has been understated. If such an understatement exists, they will try to determine the taxpayer's intent. If the understatement has been allowed to reverse itself in the following year, the auditors probably will view the incident as an honest mistake. If they find a consistent pattern of understated inventories, however, they may prosecute the taxpayer for income tax evasion—a criminal offense.

**Effects of Errors in Inventory Valuation: A Summary**  The following table summarizes the effects of an error in the valuation of ending inventory over two successive years. In this table we indicate the effects of the error on various financial statement measurements using the code letters **U** (understated), **O** (overstated), and **NE** (no effect). The effects of errors in the valuation of inventory are the same regardless of whether the company uses a perpetual or a periodic inventory system. The NE for owners' equity at year-end in the Following Year column results from the offsetting of the first-year error in the second year.

| **Original Error: Ending Inventory Understated** | Year of the Error | Following Year |
| --- | --- | --- |
| Beginning inventory | NE | U |
| Cost of goods available for sale | NE | U |
| Ending inventory | U | NE |
| Cost of goods sold | O | U |
| Gross profit | U | O |
| Net income | U | O |
| Owners' equity at year-end | U | NE |

| **Original Error: Ending Inventory Overstated** | Year of the Error | Following Year |
| --- | --- | --- |
| Beginning inventory | NE | O |
| Cost of goods available for sale | NE | O |
| Ending inventory | O | NE |
| Cost of goods sold | U | O |
| Gross profit | O | U |
| Net income | O | U |
| Owners' equity at year-end | O | NE |

## Techniques for Estimating the Cost of Goods Sold and the Ending Inventory

Taking a physical inventory every month would be very expensive and time-consuming. Therefore, if a business using a periodic inventory system prepares monthly or quarterly financial statements, it usually *estimates* the amounts of its inventory and cost of goods sold. One approach to making these estimates is called the gross profit method; another—used primarily by retail stores—is the retail method.

## The Gross Profit Method

The **gross profit method** is a quick and simple technique for estimating the cost of goods sold and the amount of inventory on hand. In using this method, it is assumed that the rate of gross profit earned in the preceding year (or several years) will remain the same for the current year. When we know the rate of gross profit, we can divide the dollar amount of net sales into two elements: (1) the gross profit and (2) the cost of goods sold. We view net sales as 100%. If the gross profit rate, for example, is 40% of net sales, the cost of goods sold must be 60%. In other words, the cost of goods sold percentage (or **cost ratio**) is determined by deducting the gross profit rate from 100%.

**LO 6**

Estimate the cost of goods sold and the ending inventory by the gross profit method and by the retail method.

When the gross profit rate is known, the ending inventory can be estimated by the following procedures:

1. Determine the *cost of goods available for sale* from the general ledger records of beginning inventory and net purchases.
2. Estimate the *cost of goods sold* by multiplying the net sales by the cost ratio.
3. Deduct the estimated *cost of goods sold* from the *cost of goods available for sale* to find the estimated ending inventory.

To illustrate, assume that Metro Hardware has a beginning inventory of $50,000 on January 1. During the month of January, net purchases amount to $20,000 and net sales total $30,000. Assume that the company's normal gross profit rate is 40% of net sales; it follows that the cost ratio is *60%*. Using these facts, the inventory on January 31 may be estimated as follows:

| | | | |
|---|---|---|---|
| Goods available for sale: | | | |
|   Beginning inventory, Jan. 1 . . . . . . . . . . . . . . . . . . . . . . . . . . . . . . . . . | | $50,000 | |
|   Purchases . . . . . . . . . . . . . . . . . . . . . . . . . . . . . . . . . . . . . . . . . . . . . | | 20,000 | |
|     Cost of goods available for sale . . . . . . . . . . . . . . . . . . . . . . . . . . . . . | | $70,000 | *Step 1 . . .* |
| Deduct: Estimated cost of goods sold: | | | |
|   Net sales . . . . . . . . . . . . . . . . . . . . . . . . . . . . . . . . . . . . . . . . . | $30,000 | | |
|   Cost ratio (100% − 40%) . . . . . . . . . . . . . . . . . . . . . . . . . . . . . . | 60% | | |
|     Estimated cost of goods sold ($30,000 × 60%) . . . . . . . . . . . . . . . | | 18,000 | *Step 2 . . .* |
| Estimated ending inventory, Jan. 31 . . . . . . . . . . . . . . . . . . . . . . . . . . . | | $52,000 | *Step 3 . . .* |

The gross profit method of estimating inventory has several uses apart from the preparation of monthly financial statements. For example, if an inventory is destroyed by fire, the company must estimate the amount of the inventory on hand at the date of the fire to file an insurance claim. The most convenient way to determine this inventory amount may be the gross profit method.

The gross profit method is also used at year-end after the taking of a physical inventory to confirm the overall reasonableness of the amount determined by the counting and pricing process. The gross profit method is not, however, a satisfactory substitute for periodically taking an actual physical inventory.

## The Retail Method

The **retail method** of estimating inventory and the cost of goods sold is similar to the gross profit method. The basic difference is that the retail method is based on the cost ratio of the *current period,* rather than that of the prior year.

To determine the cost ratio of the current period, the business must keep track of both the cost of all goods available for sale during the period and the *retail sales prices* assigned to these goods. To illustrate, assume that during June the cost of goods available for sale in Tennis Gallery totaled $45,000. The store had offered this merchandise for sale to its customers at retail prices totaling $100,000. The cost ratio in June was *45%* ($45,000 ÷ $100,000). This cost ratio is used to estimate the monthly cost of goods sold and the month-end inventory by the same procedures as are applied under the gross profit method.

Many retail stores also use their current cost ratio as a quick method of pricing the inventory counted at year-end. In a retail store, the retail sales price is clearly marked on the merchandise. Therefore, employees quickly can determine the retail price of the ending inventory. This retail price is then reduced to a close approximation of cost simply by multiplying by the cost ratio.

Assume, for example, that the annual physical inventory at Tennis Gallery indicates the merchandise on hand at year-end has a retail sales price of $120,000. If the cost ratio for the year has been 44%, the cost of this inventory is approximately $52,800 ($120,000 × 44%). This version of the retail method approximates valuation of the inventory at average cost. A variation of this method approximates a LIFO valuation of the ending inventory.

## "Textbook" Inventory Systems Can Be Modified . . . and They Often Are

In this chapter we have described the basic characteristics of the most common inventory systems. In practice, businesses often modify these systems to suit their particular needs. Some businesses also use *different inventory systems for different purposes.*

We described one modification in Chapter 6—a company that maintains very little inventory may simply charge (debit) all purchases directly to the cost of goods sold. Another common modification is to maintain perpetual inventory records showing only the *quantities* of merchandise bought and sold, with no dollar amounts. Such systems require less record keeping than a full-blown perpetual system, and they still provide management with useful information about sales and inventories. To generate the dollar amounts needed in financial statements and tax returns, these companies might use the gross profit method, the retail method, or a periodic inventory system.

**CASE IN POINT**

**Apple Computer** maintains a perpetual inventory system. The daily entries reflect only the *quantities* of units produced and sold—not the dollar costs. Dollar amounts are computed and recorded in the inventory records at the end of the month. In transferring costs from inventory accounts to the cost of goods sold, Apple uses a FIFO flow assumption. But the inventory cost layers don't represent units purchased at different prices—they represent units manufactured in different months.

**Sears** and **Wal-Mart** maintain perpetual inventory records showing both quantities and dollar amounts. But the dollar amounts are recorded at *retail prices.* When cost data are needed, these companies apply cost ratios to the retail amounts.

**Fleming Cos.** is the world's largest food wholesaler. To assist management in monitoring sales, profit margins, and inventory, **Fleming** maintains a perpetual inventory system. In its interim financial statements, however, it uses the *gross profit method.* Why? Some of **Fleming**'s inventories are subject to significant spoilage losses. The gross profit method automatically provides for normal amounts of shrinkage. Adjusting the perpetual records to reflect these losses would require a complete physical inventory.

Businesses such as restaurants often update their inventory records by physically counting products on a daily or weekly basis. In effect, they use frequent periodic counts as the basis for maintaining a perpetual inventory system.

In summary, real-world inventory systems often differ from the illustrations in a textbook. But the underlying principles remain much the same.

## FINANCIAL ANALYSIS

Inventory often is the largest of a company's current assets. But how liquid is this asset? How quickly will it be converted into cash? As a step toward answering these questions, short-term creditors often compute the **inventory turnover rate**.

**LO 7**

Compute the inventory turnover rate and explain its uses.

### Inventory Turnover Rate

The inventory turnover rate is equal to the cost of goods sold divided by the average amount of inventory (beginning inventory plus ending inventory, divided by 2). This ratio indicates how many *times* in the course of a year the company is able to sell the amount of its average inventory. The higher this rate, the more quickly the company sells its inventory.

To illustrate, a recent annual report of **J.C. Penney** shows a cost of goods sold of $21,859 million and average inventory of $6,097 million. The inventory turnover rate for Penney's, therefore, is *3.59* ($21,859 ÷ $6,097). We may compute the number of *days* required for the company to sell its inventory by dividing 365 days by the turnover rate. Thus J.C. Penney requires *102 days* to turn over (sell) the amount of its average inventory (365 days ÷ 3.59).

Users of financial statements find the inventory turnover rate useful in evaluating the liquidity of the company's inventory. In addition, managers and independent auditors use this computation to help identify inventory that is not selling well and that may have become obsolete. A declining turnover rate indicates that merchandise is not selling as quickly as it used to. Comparing a company's inventory turnover with that of competitors is particularly useful in evaluating how effective a company is at managing its inventory, often one of its largest assets.

---

Most businesses sell merchandise on account. Therefore, the sale of inventory often does not provide an immediate source of cash. To determine how quickly inventory is converted into cash, the number of days required to *sell the inventory* must be combined with the number of days required to *collect the accounts receivable.*

The number of days required to collect accounts receivable depends on a company's *accounts receivable turnover rate.* This figure is computed by dividing net sales by the average accounts receivable. The number of days required to collect these receivables then is determined by dividing 365 days by the turnover rate. Data for the J.C. Penney annual report indicate that the company needed *49 days* (on average) to collect its accounts receivable.

**CASH EFFECTS**

---

**Length of the Operating Cycle**  The *operating cycle* of a merchandising company is the average time period between the purchase of merchandise and the conversion of this merchandise back into cash. In other words, the merchandise acquired as inventory gradually is converted into accounts receivable by sale of the goods on account, and these receivables are converted into cash through the process of collection.

The operating cycle of J.C. Penney was approximately *151 days,* computed by adding the average 102 days required to sell its inventory and the 49 days required to collect its accounts receivable from customers. From the viewpoint of short-term creditors, the shorter the operating cycle, the higher the quality of the company's liquid assets because they will be converted into cash quicker.

**You as a Banker**

Assume that you are a commercial loan officer at a large bank. One of your clients recently submitted an application for a $300,000 five-year loan. You have worked with this business before on numerous occasions and have periodically been forced to deal with late and missed payments attributed to cash flow problems. Thus you are surprised to see in the business plan accompanying the application that management expects to reduce the company's operating cycle from 190 days to 90 days. A note to the business plan indicates that the reduction in the operating cycle will result from (1) a tighter credit policy and (2) the implementation of a just-in-time inventory system.

As a banker, are you comfortable that these changes are related to the company's operating cycle?

*Our comments appear on page 356.

## Accounting Methods Can Affect Analytical Ratios

The accounting methods selected by a company may affect the ratios and financial statement subtotals used in evaluating the company's financial position and the results of its operations. To illustrate, let us consider the effects of inventory valuation methods on inventory turnover rates.

Assume that during a period of rising prices Alpha Company uses LIFO, whereas Beta Company uses FIFO. In all other respects, the two companies *are identical;* they have the same size inventories, and they purchase and sell the same quantities of merchandise at the same prices and on the same dates. Thus each company *physically* turns over its inventory at *exactly the same rate.*

Because Alpha uses the LIFO method, however, its inventory is valued at older (and lower) costs than is the inventory of Beta Company. Also, Alpha's cost of goods sold includes more recent (and higher) costs than does Beta's. When these amounts are used in computing the inventory turnover rate (cost of goods sold divided by average inventory), Alpha *appears* to have the higher turnover rate.

We already have stated that the inventories of these two companies are turning over at exactly the same rate. Therefore, the differences in the turnover rates computed from the companies' financial statements are caused *solely by the different accounting methods used in the valuation of the companies' inventories.*

Inventory turnover is not the only ratio that will be affected. Alpha will report less gross profit and lower net income than Beta.

Users of financial statements must understand the typical effects of different accounting methods. Also, a financial analyst should be able to restate on a *comparable basis* the financial statements of companies that use different accounting methods. Notes accompanying the financial statements sometimes provide the information necessary for comparing the operating results of companies using LIFO with those of companies using the FIFO method.

**Oshkosh B'Gosh, Inc.** (a publicly owned maker of children's clothing) uses LIFO. A note accompanying the financial statements reads in part:

Although the LIFO method results in a better matching of costs and revenue, information relating to the first-in, first-out (FIFO) method may be useful in comparing operating results to those companies not on LIFO. Had earnings been reported on a FIFO basis the results would have been: . . .

In the remainder of the note, the company discloses the ending inventory, cost of goods sold, and net income that would have resulted from use of the FIFO method.

**Walgreens**

At the beginning of this chapter, we discussed how important having the right inventory available to meets the needs of customers is for a retail company such as **Walgreens**. The company's 1999 balance sheet includes more than $2,462 million in inventories, essentially goods available on the shelves of the many **Walgreens** stores.

How important is the inventory asset in **Walgreens** balance sheet? Total assets are approximately $5,907 million. This means that the inventory asset makes up almost 42% of **Walgreens'** assets. Inventory is also the largest by far of the company's most liquid assets. Inventory makes up almost 75% of the company's liquid assets, which consist of cash, accounts receivable, inventories, and other current assets.

**Walgreens'** inventory turnover (i.e., cost of sales divided by inventory) was 5.27 and 5.49 in 1999 and 1998, respectively. This means that inventory turned over between five and six times per year, and the average number of days inventory is retained before it is sold is in the range of 65 to 70 days. To effectively evaluate these numbers, one would need information for more years, as well as information about competing companies.

A SECOND LOOK

## SUPPLEMENTAL TOPIC

### LIFO RESERVES

We have stated that a significant shortcoming in the LIFO method is that the asset inventory is valued at the company's oldest inventory acquisition costs. After a period of years, these outdated costs may significantly understate the current replacement cost of the inventory. The difference between the LIFO cost of an inventory and its current replacement cost often is called a **LIFO reserve**.[1]

**LO 8**

Define a LIFO reserve and explain its implications to users of financial statements.

In a recent balance sheet, **Ford Motor Company** reported inventories of approximately $5.7 billion valued by the LIFO method. A note accompanying the balance sheet, however, explained that the current replacement cost of these inventories exceeded $6.9 billion. Therefore, **Ford** had a LIFO reserve of more than $1.2 billion.

CASE IN POINT

### The Significance of a LIFO Reserve

Users of financial statements should understand the implications of a large LIFO reserve.

**Comparing LIFO and FIFO Inventories**   A LIFO reserve indicates that the company's inventory is *undervalued* in terms of its current replacement cost and the valuation that would have resulted from use of the FIFO method. Thus the inventories of companies using LIFO are not directly comparable to those of companies using FIFO. Fortunately, this problem is solved in the notes to the financial statements: Companies using LIFO disclose the current replacement cost (or FIFO cost) of their inventories.

**Liquidation of a LIFO Reserve**   The existence of a LIFO reserve may cause a company's profits to rise dramatically if inventory falls to an abnormally low level at

---

[1] The phrase "LIFO reserve" is used by accountants, investors, and business managers in conversation and many types of financial literature. The FASB, however, discourages use of the word "reserve" in formal financial statements, as this word has several different meanings. Therefore, in financial statements a LIFO reserve is more appropriately described as "the difference between the LIFO cost and current (replacement) cost of inventory."

year-end. As the company reduces its inventories, the costs transferred to the cost of goods sold come from older—and lower—cost layers. The inclusion of these old and low costs in the cost of goods sold can cause the company's gross profit rate to soar. This situation is often referred to as a **"liquidation" of a LIFO reserve**.

---

**CASH EFFECTS**    The inclusion of outdated figures in the cost of goods sold resulting from the liquidation of the LIFO reserve can cause taxable income to soar. Unfortunately, when taxable income soars, cash expenditures made for income taxes soar as well. When this happens, the amount of cash available (after taxes) may fall short of what is needed to replenish depleted levels of inventory.

---

Many factors may cause the liquidation of a LIFO reserve. For example, the company may be unable to make the purchases necessary to replenish its inventory because of shortages or strikes. Often a company discontinues a particular product line and sells its entire inventory of this merchandise. Also, management deliberately may delay making normal year-end purchases to liquidate a portion of the company's LIFO reserve.

Users of financial statements should recognize that the abnormal profits that result from the liquidation of a LIFO reserve *do not* represent an improvement in financial performance. Rather, these profits are a one-time occurrence, resulting from old and relatively low unit costs temporarily being used in measuring the cost of goods sold. Users of financial statements easily can determine whether a company's reported earnings are affected by the liquidation of a LIFO reserve. This liquidation occurs whenever a company using LIFO ends its fiscal year with its inventory at a substantially lower level than at the beginning of the year. If material in dollar amount, the financial impact of this liquidation should be disclosed in notes accompanying the financial statements.

**Assessing the Income Tax Benefits of Using LIFO**    A LIFO reserve represents the amount by which a company has reduced its taxable income over the years through use of the LIFO method. Referring to our Case in Point, (page 337), **Ford Motor Company** has reduced its taxable income (over a long span of years) by more than $1.2 billion. If we assume that **Ford** pays income taxes at a rate of, say, 33%, using LIFO has saved the company about $400 million in income taxes.

---

**YOUR TURN**

### You as a Business Owner

Assume that you have been using the LIFO inventory method in your building supply business for the past 10 years. Each year, your accountant brings to your attention the significant tax savings that have resulted from your decision to use LIFO instead of FIFO.

During December, a major supplier was unable to make deliveries due to a strike by the truck drivers' union. As a consequence, inventory levels at year-end were nearly depleted. You have just received a call from your accountant informing you that taxable income for the year ended December 31 was unexpectedly high, and that the estimated tax payments made throughout the year fell far short of the company's actual tax liability.

The news from your accountant made you angry and confused, as you were certain that LIFO always results in the lowest possible taxable income during periods of rising prices. While the past year was inflationary, income taxes were much higher than expected. What happened?

*Our comments appear on page 356.

## SUMMARY OF LEARNING OBJECTIVES

### LO 1

**In a perpetual inventory system, determine the cost of goods sold using (a) specific identification, (b) average cost, (c) FIFO, and (d) LIFO. Discuss the advantages and shortcomings of each method.**

By the *specific identification method,* the actual costs of the specific units sold are transferred from inventory to the cost of goods sold. (Debit Cost of Goods Sold; credit Inventory.) This method achieves the proper matching of sales revenue and cost of goods sold when the individual units in the inventory are unique. However, the method becomes cumbersome and may produce misleading results if the inventory consists of homogeneous items.

The remaining three methods are flow assumptions, which should be applied only to an inventory of homogeneous items.

By the *average-cost method,* the average cost of all units in the inventory is computed and used in recording the cost of goods sold. This is the only method in which all units are assigned the same (average) per-unit cost.

*FIFO* (first-in, first-out) is the assumption that the first units purchased are the first units sold. Thus inventory is assumed to consist of the most recently purchased units. FIFO assigns current costs to inventory but older (and often lower) costs to the cost of goods sold.

*LIFO* (last-in, first-out) is the assumption that the most recently acquired goods are sold first. This method matches sales revenue with relatively current costs. In a period of inflation, LIFO usually results in lower reported profits and lower income taxes than the other methods. However, the oldest purchase costs are assigned to inventory, which may result in inventory becoming grossly understated in terms of current replacement costs.

### LO 2

**Explain the need for taking a physical inventory.**

In a perpetual inventory system, a physical inventory is taken to adjust the inventory records for shrinkage losses. In a periodic inventory system, the physical inventory is the basis for determining the cost of the ending inventory and for computing cost of goods sold.

### LO 3

**Record shrinkage losses and other year-end adjustments to inventory.**

Shrinkage losses are recorded by removing from the Inventory account the cost of the missing or damaged units. The offsetting debit may be to Cost of Goods Sold, if the shrinkage is normal in amount, or to a special loss account. If inventory is found to be obsolete and unlikely to be sold, it is written down to zero (or its scrap value, if any). If inventory is valued at the lower-of-cost-or-market, it is written down to its current replacement cost, if at year-end this amount is substantially below the cost shown in the inventory records.

### LO 4

**In a periodic inventory system, determine the ending inventory and the cost of goods sold using (a) specific identification, (b) average cost, (c) FIFO, and (d) LIFO.**

The cost of goods sold is determined by combining the beginning inventory with the purchases during the period and subtracting the cost of the ending inventory. Thus the cost assigned to ending inventory also determines the cost of goods sold.

By the specific identification method, the ending inventory is determined by the specific costs associated with the units on hand. By the average-cost method, the ending inventory is determined by multiplying the number of units on hand by the average cost of the units available for sale during the year. By FIFO, the units in inventory are priced using the unit costs from the most recent cost layers. By the LIFO method, inventory is priced using the unit costs in the oldest cost layers.

### LO 5

**Explain the effects on the income statement of errors in inventory valuation.**

In the current year, an error in the costs assigned to ending inventory will cause an opposite error in the cost of goods sold and, therefore, a repetition of the original error in the amount of gross profit. For example, understating ending inventory results in an overstatement of the cost of goods sold and an understatement of gross profit.

The error has exactly the opposite effects on the cost of goods sold and the gross profit of the following year, because the error is now in the cost assigned to *beginning* inventory.

### LO 6

**Estimate the cost of goods sold and ending inventory by the gross profit method and by the retail method.**

Both the gross profit and retail methods use a cost ratio to estimate the cost of goods sold and ending inventory. The cost of goods sold is estimated by multiplying net sales by this cost ratio; ending inventory then is estimated by subtracting this cost of goods sold from the cost of goods available for sale.

In the gross profit method, the cost ratio is 100% minus the company's historical gross profit rate. In the retail method, the cost ratio is the percentage of cost to the retail prices of merchandise available for sale.

**LO 7**

**Compute the inventory turnover rate and explain its uses.**
The inventory turnover rate is equal to the cost of goods divided by the average inventory. Users of financial statements find the inventory turnover rate useful in evaluating the liquidity of the company's inventory. In addition, managers and independent auditors use this computation to help identify inventory that is not selling well and that may have become obsolete.

**\*LO 8**

**Define a "LIFO reserve" and explain its implications to users of financial statements.**
A LIFO reserve is the amount by which the current replacement cost of inventory exceeds the LIFO cost shown in the accounting records.

If a company has a large LIFO reserve, neither its inventory nor its cost of goods sold are comparable to those of a company using FIFO. Also, a LIFO reserve may cause earnings to increase dramatically if inventory falls below normal levels. Notes accompanying the financial statements provide the statement users with information useful in evaluating the implications of a LIFO reserve.

In this chapter we have learned that different inventory valuation methods can have significant effects on net income as reported in financial statements and on income tax returns as well. In the following chapter, we will see that a similar situation exists with respect to the alternative methods used in depreciating plant and equipment.

## KEY TERMS INTRODUCED OR EMPHASIZED IN CHAPTER 8

**average-cost method** (p. 318) A method of valuing all units in inventory at the same average per-unit cost, which is recomputed after every purchase.

**consistency (in inventory valuation)** (p. 324) An accounting principle that calls for the use of the same method of inventory pricing from year to year, with full disclosure of the effects of any change in method. Intended to make financial statements comparable.

**cost layer** (p. 317) Units of merchandise acquired at the same unit cost. An inventory comprised of several cost layers is characteristic of all inventory valuation methods except *average cost*.

**cost ratio** (p. 333) The cost of merchandise expressed as a percentage of its retail selling price. Used in inventory estimating techniques, such as the gross profit method and the retail method.

**first-in, first-out (FIFO) method** (p. 319) A method of computing the cost of inventory and the cost of goods sold based on the assumption that the first merchandise acquired is the first merchandise sold and that the ending inventory consists of the most recently acquired goods.

**flow assumption** (p. 317) Assumption as to the sequence in which units are removed from inventory for the purpose of sale.

Is not required to parallel the physical movement of merchandise if the units are homogeneous.

**F.O.B. destination** (p. 327) A term meaning the seller bears the cost of shipping goods to the buyer's location. Title to the goods remains with the seller while the goods are in transit.

**F.O.B. shipping point** (p. 327) The buyer of goods bears the cost of transportation from the seller's location to the buyer's location. Title to the goods passes at the point of shipment, and the goods are the property of the buyer while in transit.

**gross profit method** (p. 333) A method of estimating the cost of the ending inventory based on the assumption that the rate of gross profit remains approximately the same from year to year.

**inventory turnover rate** (p. 335) The cost of goods sold divided by the average amount of inventory. Indicates how many times the average inventory is sold during the course of the year.

**just-in-time (JIT) inventory system** (p. 324) A technique designed to minimize a company's investment in inventory. In a manufacturing company, this means receiving purchases of raw materials just in time for use in the manufacturing process and completing the manufacture of finished goods just in time to fill sales orders. Just-in-time also may be described as the philosophy of constantly striving to become more efficient by purchasing and storing less inventory.

**last-in, first-out (LIFO) method** (p. 320) A method of computing the cost of goods sold by use of the prices paid for the most recently acquired units. Ending inventory is valued on the basis of prices paid for the units first acquired.

**LIFO reserve** (p. 337) The difference between the current replacement cost of a company's inventory and the LIFO cost shown in the accounting records. The fact that a LIFO reserve can become very large is the principal shortcoming of the LIFO method.

**liquidation of a LIFO reserve** (p. 338) Selling merchandise from a LIFO inventory to the point at which old and relatively low costs are transferred from inventory into the cost of goods sold. Tends to inflate reported profits.

**lower-of-cost-or-market (LCM)** (p. 327) A method of inventory pricing in which goods are valued at original cost or replacement cost (market), whichever is lower.

**physical inventory** (p. 325) A systematic count of all goods on hand, followed by the application of unit prices to the quantities counted and development of a dollar valuation of the ending inventory.

**retail method** (p. 334) A method of estimating the cost of goods sold and ending inventory. Similar to the gross profit method, except that the cost ratio is based on current cost-to-retail price relationships rather than on those of the prior year.

**shrinkage losses** (p. 325) Losses of inventory resulting from theft, spoilage, or breakage.

**specific identification** (p. 317) Recording as the cost of goods sold the actual costs of the specific units sold. Necessary if each unit in inventory is unique, but not if the inventory consists of homogeneous products.

**write-down (of an asset)** (p. 326) A reduction in the carrying amount of an asset because it has become obsolete or its usefulness has otherwise been impaired. Involves a credit to the appropriate asset account, with an offsetting debit to a loss account.

---

\* *Supplemental Topic,* "LIFO Reserves."

## DEMONSTRATION PROBLEM

The Audiophile sells high-performance stereo equipment. Massachusetts Acoustic recently introduced the Carnegie-440, a state-of-the-art speaker system. During the current year, The Audiophile purchased nine of these speaker systems at the following dates and acquisition costs:

| Date | Units Purchased | Unit Cost | Total Cost |
|------|----------------|-----------|-----------|
| Oct. 1 ........................................ | 2 | $3,000 | $ 6,000 |
| Nov. 17 ....................................... | 3 | 3,200 | 9,600 |
| Dec. 1 ........................................ | 4 | 3,250 | 13,000 |
| Available for sale during the year ................... | 9 | | $28,600 |

On *November 21,* The Audiophile sold four of these speaker systems to the Boston Symphony. The other five Carnegie-440s remained in inventory at December 31.

### Instructions

Assume that The Audiophile uses a *perpetual inventory system.* Compute (1) the cost of goods sold relating to the sale of Carnegie-440 speakers to the Boston Symphony and (2) the ending inventory of these speakers at December 31, using each of the following flow assumptions:

**a.** Average cost

**b.** First-in, first-out (FIFO)

**c.** Last-in, first-out (LIFO)

Show the number of units and the unit costs of the cost layers comprising the cost of goods sold and the ending inventory.

### Solution to the Demonstration Problem

**a. 1.** Cost of goods sold (at average cost):

Average unit cost at Nov. 21 [($6,000 + $9,600) ÷ 5 units] .......... $ 3,120

Cost of goods sold (4 units × $3,120 per unit) ................... $12,480

   **2.** Inventory at Dec. 31 (at average cost):

Units remaining after sale of Nov. 21 (1 unit @ $3,120) ........... $ 3,120

Units purchased on Dec. 1 (4 units @ $3,250) ................. 13,000

Total cost of 5 units in inventory .......................... $16,120

Average unit cost at Dec. 31 .............................. $ 3,224

Inventory at Dec. 31 (5 units × $3,224 per unit) ................. $16,120

**b. 1.** Cost of goods sold (FIFO basis):

(2 units @ $3,000 + 2 units @ $3,200) ..................... $12,400

   **2.** Inventory at Dec. 31 (4 units @ $3,250 + 1 unit @ $3,200) .......... $16,200

**c. 1.** Cost of goods sold (LIFO basis):

(3 units @ $3,200 + 1 unit @ $3,000) ...................... $12,600

   **2.** Inventory at Dec. 31 (4 units @ $3,250 + 1 unit @ $3,000) .......... $16,000

## SELF-TEST QUESTIONS

*Answers to these questions appear on page 356.*

**1.** The primary purpose for using an inventory flow *assumption* is to:

   **a.** Parallel the physical flow of units of merchandise.

   **b.** Offset against revenue an appropriate cost of goods sold.

    **c.** Minimize income taxes.

    **d.** Maximize the reported amount of net income.

2. Ace Auto Supply uses a perpetual inventory record. On March 10, the company sells two Shelby four-barrel carburetors. Immediately prior to this sale, the perpetual inventory records indicate three of these carburetors on hand, as follows:

| Date | Quantity Purchased | Unit Cost | Units on Hand | Total Cost |
|------|--------------------|-----------|---------------|------------|
| Feb. 4 | 1 | $220 | 1 | $220 |
| Mar. 2 | 2 | 235 | 3 | 690 |

With respect to the sale on March 10: (More than one of the following answers may be correct.)

    **a.** If the average-cost method is used, the cost of goods sold is $460.

    **b.** If these carburetors have identification numbers, Ace must use the specific identification method to determine the cost of goods sold.

    **c.** If the company uses LIFO, the cost of goods sold will be $15 higher than if it were using FIFO.

    **d.** If the company uses LIFO, the carburetor *remaining* in inventory after the sales will be assumed to have cost $220.

3. T-Shirt City uses a *periodic* inventory system. During the first year of operations, the company made four purchases of a particular product. Each purchase was for 500 units and the prices paid were $9 per unit in the first purchase, $10 per unit in the second purchase, $12 per unit in the third purchase, and $13 per unit in the fourth purchase. At year-end, 650 of these units remained unsold. Compute the cost of goods sold under the FIFO method and LIFO method, respectively.

    **a.** $13,700 (FIFO) and $16,000 (LIFO).

    **b.** $8,300 (FIFO) and $6,000 (LIFO).

    **c.** $16,000 (FIFO) and $13,700 (LIFO).

    **d.** $6,000 (FIFO) and $8,300 (LIFO).

4. Trent Department Store uses a perpetual inventory system but adjusts its inventory records at year-end to reflect the results of a complete physical inventory. In the physical inventory taken at the ends of 2001 and 2002, Trent's employees failed to count the merchandise in the store's window displays. The cost of this merchandise amounted to $13,000 at the end of 2001 and $19,000 at the end of 2002. As a result of these errors, the cost of goods sold for 2002 will be:

    **a.** Understated by $19,000.

    **b.** Overstated by $6,000.

    **c.** Understated by $6,000.

    **d.** None of the above.

5. In July 2002, the accountant for LBJ Imports is in the process of preparing financial statements for the quarter ended June 30, 2002. The physical inventory, however, was last taken on June 5 and the accountant must establish the approximate cost at June 30 from the following data:

| | |
|---|---|
| Physical inventory, June 5, 2002 | $900,000 |
| Transactions for the period June 5–June 30: | |
|     Sales | 700,000 |
|     Purchases | 400,000 |

The gross profit on sales has consistently averaged 40% of sales. Using the gross profit method, compute the approximate inventory cost at June 30, 2002.

    **a.** $420,000.    **b.** $880,000.    **c.** $480,000.    **d.** $1,360,000.

6. Allied Products maintains a large inventory. The company has used the LIFO inventory method for many years, during which the purchase costs of its products have risen substantially. (More than one of the following answers may be correct.)

   **a.** Allied would have reported a *higher* net income in past years if it had been using the average-cost method.

   **b.** Allied's financial statements imply a *lower* inventory turnover rate than they would if the company were using FIFO.

   **c.** If Allied were to let its inventory fall far below normal levels, the company's gross profit rate would *decline.*

   **d.** Allied would have paid more income taxes in past years if it had been using the FIFO method.

## ASSIGNMENT MATERIAL

## DISCUSSION QUESTIONS

1. Is the cost of merchandise acquired during the period classified as an asset or an expense? Explain.

2. Briefly describe the advantages of using a cost flow assumption, rather than the specific identification method, to value an inventory.

3. Under what circumstances do generally accepted accounting principles permit the use of an inventory cost flow assumption? Must a flow assumption closely parallel the physical movement of the company's merchandise?

4. Assume that a company has in its inventory units of a particular product that were purchased at several different per-unit costs. When some of these units are sold, explain how the cost of goods sold is measured under each of the following cost flow assumptions in a perpetual inventory system:

   **a.** Average cost

   **b.** FIFO

   **c.** LIFO

5. A large art gallery has in inventory more than 100 paintings. No two are alike. The least expensive is priced at more than $1,000 and the higher-priced items carry prices of $100,000 or more. Which of the four methods of inventory valuation discussed in this chapter would you consider to be most appropriate for this business? Give reasons for your answer.

6. During a period of steadily increasing purchase costs, which inventory flow assumption results in the highest reported profits? The lowest taxable income? The valuation of inventory that is closest to current replacement cost? Briefly explain your answers.

7. Assume that during the first year of Hatton Corporation's operation, there were numerous purchases of identical items of merchandise. However, there was no change during the year in the prices paid for this merchandise. Under these special circumstances, how would the financial statements be affected by the choice between the FIFO and LIFO methods of inventory valuation?

8. Apex Corporation operates in two locations: New York and Oregon. The LIFO method is used in accounting for inventories at the New York facility and the specific identification method for inventories at the Oregon location. Does this concurrent use of two inventory methods indicate that Apex is violating the accounting principle of consistency? Explain.

9. What are the characteristics of a *just-in-time* inventory system? Briefly explain some advantages and risks of this type of system.

10. Why do companies that use perpetual inventory systems also take an annual *physical inventory?* When is this physical inventory usually taken? Why?

11. Under what circumstances might a company write down its inventory to carrying value below cost?

12. What is meant by the year-end *cutoff* of transactions? If merchandise in transit at year-end is material in dollar amount, what determines whether these goods should be included in the inventory of the buyer or the seller? Explain.

13. Briefly explain the operation of a *periodic* inventory system. Include an explanation of how the cost of goods sold is determined.

14. Assume that a *periodic* inventory system is in use. Explain which per-unit acquisition costs are assigned to the year-end inventory under each of the following inventory costing procedures:

    a. The average-cost method
    b. FIFO
    c. LIFO

15. Why do companies using LIFO in a perpetual inventory system often restate their ending inventory at the per-unit costs that result from applying *periodic* LIFO costing procedures?

16. Explain why errors in the valuation of inventory at the end of the year are sometimes called "counterbalancing" or "self-correcting."

17. Briefly explain the *gross profit method* of estimating inventories. In what types of situations is this technique likely to be useful?

18. Estimate the ending inventory by the gross profit method, given the following data: beginning inventory, $40,000; net purchases, $100,000; net sales, $112,000; average gross profit rate, 25% of net sales.

19. A store using the *retail inventory method* takes its physical inventory by applying current retail prices as marked on the merchandise to the quantities counted. Does this procedure mean that the inventory will appear in the financial statements at retail selling price? Explain.

20. How is the *inventory turnover rate* computed? Why is this measurement of interest to short-term creditors?

21. Baxter Corporation has been using FIFO during a period of rising costs. Explain whether you would expect each of the following measurements to be higher or lower if the company had been using LIFO.

    a. Net income
    b. Inventory turnover rate
    c. Income taxes expense

22. In anticipation of *declining* inventory replacement costs, the management of Computer Products Co. elects to use the *FIFO* inventory method rather than LIFO. Explain how this decision should affect the company's future:

    a. Rate of gross profit.
    b. Net cash flow from operating activities.

23. Notes to the financial statements of two well-known clothing manufacturers follow:

    **J. P. Stevens & Co., Inc.**
       Inventories: The inventories are stated at the lower of cost, determined principally by the LIFO method, or market.

    **Bobbie Brooks, Incorporated**
       Inventories: Inventories are stated at the lower of cost (first-in, first-out method) or market value assuming a period of rising prices.

    a. Which company is using the more conservative method of pricing its inventories? Explain.
    b. Based on the inventory methods in use in their financial statements, which company is in the better position to minimize the amount of income taxes that it must pay? Explain.
    c. Could either company increase its cash collections from customers or reduce its cash payments to suppliers of merchandise by switching from FIFO to LIFO, or from LIFO to FIFO? Explain.

*24. What is a *LIFO reserve?* What is likely to happen to the gross profit rate of a company with a large LIFO reserve if it sells most of its inventory?

---

* *Supplemental Topic,* "LIFO Reserves."

## EXERCISES

Listed below are nine technical accounting terms introduced in this chapter.

| | | |
|---|---|---|
| Retail method | FIFO method | Average-cost method |
| Gross profit method | LIFO method | Lower-of-cost-or-market |
| Flow assumption | *LIFO reserve | Specific identification |

**\*EXERCISE 8.1**

Accounting Terminology

**LO 1–8**

Each of the following statements may (or may not) describe one of these technical terms. For each statement, indicate the term described, or answer "None" if the statement does not correctly describe any of the terms.

**a.** A pattern of transferring unit costs from the Inventory account to the cost of goods sold that may (or may not) parallel the physical flow of merchandise.

**b.** The excess of the current replacement cost of any inventory of merchandise over the cost of the inventory determined by the LIFO assumption.

**c.** The only flow assumption in which all units of merchandise are assigned the same per-unit cost.

**d.** The method used to record the cost of goods sold when each unit in the inventory is unique.

**e.** The most conservative of the flow assumptions during a period of sustained inflation.

**f.** The flow assumption that provides the most current valuation of inventory in the balance sheet.

**g.** A technique for estimating the cost of goods sold and the ending inventory that is based on the relationship between cost and sales price during the *current* accounting period.

On May 10, Dayton Computing sold 90 Millennium laptop computers to Apex Publishers. At the date of this sale, Dayton's perpetual inventory records included the following cost layers for the Millennium laptops:

**EXERCISE 8.2**

Cost Flow Assumptions

**LO 1**

| Purchase Date | Quantity | Unit Cost | Total Cost |
|---|---|---|---|
| Apr. 9 . . . . . . . . . . . . . . . . . . . . . . . . . . . . . . . . . . | 70 | $1,200 | $ 84,000 |
| May 1 . . . . . . . . . . . . . . . . . . . . . . . . . . . . . . . . . . | 30 | 1,250 | 37,500 |
| Total on hand . . . . . . . . . . . . . . . . . . . . . . . . . . | 100 | | $121,500 |

Prepare journal entries to record the cost of the 90 Millennium laptops sold on May 10, assuming that Dayton Computing uses the:

**a.** Specific identification method (62 of the units sold were purchased on April 9, and the remaining units were purchased on May 1).

**b.** Average-cost method.

**c.** FIFO method.

**d.** LIFO method.

**e.** Discuss briefly the financial reporting differences that may arise from choosing the FIFO method over the LIFO method.

The Warm-Up Shop sells heating oil, coal, and kerosene fuel to residential customers. Heating oil is kept in large storage tanks that supply the company's fleet of delivery trucks. Coal is kept in huge bins that are loaded and emptied from the top by giant scooping machines. Kerosene is sold "off the shelf" in five-gallon containers at the company's retail outlet. Separate inventory records are maintained for each fuel type.

**EXERCISE 8.3**

Physical Flow versus Cost Flow

**LO 1**

**a.** Which of the cost flow assumptions (average-cost, FIFO, or LIFO) best describes the *physical flow* of:

**1.** The heating oil inventory? Explain.

---

\* *Supplemental Topic,* "LIFO Reserves."

2. The coal inventory? Explain.

3. The kerosene inventory? Explain.

b. Which of these cost flow assumptions is likely to result in the *lowest* income tax liability for the company? Explain.

c. Explain why management keeps separate inventory records for its heating oil, coal, and kerosene inventories.

**EXERCISE 8.4**

Effects of Different Flow Assumptions

 **LO 1**

Walkers, a chain of retail stores, uses FIFO. The following are selected data from the company's most recent financial statements (dollar amounts are in thousands):

| | |
|---|---:|
| Cost of goods sold . . . . . . . . . . . . . . . . . . . . . . . . . . . . . . . . . . . . . . . . . . | $60,000 |
| Income before income taxes . . . . . . . . . . . . . . . . . . . . . . . . . . . . . . . . . . . | 15,000 |
| Income taxes expense (and payments) . . . . . . . . . . . . . . . . . . . . . . . . . . . | 6,000 |
| Net income . . . . . . . . . . . . . . . . . . . . . . . . . . . . . . . . . . . . . . . . . . . . . . . . | 9,000 |
| Net cash provided by operating activities . . . . . . . . . . . . . . . . . . . . . . . . . | 10,000 |

A note to the financial statements disclosed that had Walkers been using *LIFO,* the cost of goods sold would have been $64,000.

(The company's income taxes expense amounts to 40% of income before taxes; assume income taxes are paid in cash in the same year they are recognized as expense.)

a. Explain how LIFO can result in a higher cost of goods sold. Would you expect the LIFO method to result in the company's inventory being shown at a greater amount?

b. Assuming that Walkers had been using *LIFO,* compute the following amounts for the current year. Show supporting computations, with dollar amounts in thousands.

1. Income before income taxes

2. Income taxes expense (which are equal to cash payments)

3. Net income

4. Net cash provided by operating activities

**EXERCISE 8.5**

Transfer of Title

 **LO 2**

Jensen Tire had two large shipments in transit at December 31. One was a $125,000 inbound shipment of merchandise (shipped December 28, F.O.B. shipping point), which arrived at Jensen's receiving dock on January 2. The other shipment was an $95,000 outbound shipment of merchandise to a customer, which was shipped and billed by Jensen on December 30 (terms F.O.B. shipping point) and reached the customer on January 3.

In taking a physical inventory on December 31, Jensen counted all goods on hand and priced the inventory on the basis of average cost. The total amount was $600,000. No goods in transit were included in this figure.

What amount should appear as inventory on the company's balance sheet at December 31? Explain. If you indicate an amount other than $600,000, state which asset or liability other than inventory also would be changed in amount.

**EXERCISE 8.6**

Inventory Write-Downs

 **LO 3**

Late in the year, Software City began carrying WordCrafter, a new word processing software program. At December 31, Software City's perpetual inventory records included the following cost layers in its inventory of WordCrafter programs:

| Purchase Date | Quantity | Unit Cost | Total Cost |
|---|---:|---:|---:|
| Nov. 14 . . . . . . . . . . . . . . . . . . . . . . . . . . . . . . . . . | 8 | $400 | $3,200 |
| Dec. 12 . . . . . . . . . . . . . . . . . . . . . . . . . . . . . . . . . | 20 | 310 | 6,200 |
| Total available for sale at Dec. 31 . . . . . . . . . . . . . | 28 | | $9,400 |

a. At December 31, Software City takes a physical inventory and finds that all 28 units of Word-Crafter are on hand. However, the current replacement cost (wholesale price) of this product is only $250 per unit. Prepare the entries to record:

1. This write-down of the inventory to the lower-of-cost-or-market at December 31.

2. The cash sale of 15 WordCrafter programs on January 9, at a retail price of $350 each. Assume that Software City uses the FIFO flow assumption. (Company policy is to charge LCM adjustments of less than $2,000 to Cost of Goods Sold and larger amounts to a separate loss account.)

**b.** Now assume that the current replacement cost of the WordCrafter programs is $405 each. A physical inventory finds only 25 of these programs on hand at December 31. (For this part, return to the original information and ignore what you did in part **a**.)

1. Prepare the journal entry to record the shrinkage loss assuming that Software City uses the FIFO flow assumption.

2. Prepare the journal entry to record the shrinkage loss assuming that Software City uses the LIFO flow assumption.

3. Which cost flow assumption (FIFO or LIFO) results in the lowest net income for the period? Would using this assumption really mean that the company's operations are less efficient? Explain.

Pemberton Products uses a *periodic* inventory system. The company's records show the beginning inventory of PH4 oil filters on January 1, and the purchases of this item during the current year to be as follows:

**EXERCISE 8.7**

Costing Inventory in a Periodic System

 **LO 4**

| | | | |
|---|---|---|---|
| Jan. 1 | Beginning inventory | 9 units @ $3.00 | $ 27.00 |
| Feb. 23 | Purchase | 12 units @ $3.50 | 42.00 |
| Apr. 20 | Purchase | 30 units @ $3.80 | 114.00 |
| May 4 | Purchase | 40 units @ $4.00 | 160.00 |
| Nov. 30 | Purchase | 19 units @ $5.00 | 95.00 |
| | Totals | 110 units | $438.00 |

A physical count indicates 20 units in inventory at year-end.

Determine the cost of the ending inventory, based on each of the following methods of inventory valuation. (Remember to use *periodic* inventory costing procedures.)

**a.** Average cost

**b.** FIFO

**c.** LIFO

**d.** Which of the above methods (if any) results in the same ending inventory valuation under *both* periodic and perpetual costing procedures? Explain.

Boswell Electric prepared the following condensed income statements for two successive years:

**EXERCISE 8.8**

Effects of Errors in Inventory Valuation

 **LO 5**

| | 2002 | 2001 |
|---|---|---|
| Sales | $2,000,000 | $1,500,000 |
| Cost of goods sold | 1,250,000 | 900,000 |
| Gross profit on sales | $ 750,000 | $ 600,000 |
| Operating expenses | 400,000 | 350,000 |
| Net income | $ 350,000 | $ 250,000 |

At the end of 2001 (right-hand column above), the inventory was understated by $40,000, but the error was not discovered until after the accounts had been closed and financial statements prepared at the end of 2002. The balance sheets for the two years showed owner's equity of $500,000 at the end of 2001 and $580,000 at the end of 2002. (Boswell is organized as a sole proprietorship and does not incur income taxes expense.)

**a.** Compute the corrected net income figures for 2001 and 2002.

**b.** Compute the gross profit amounts and the gross profit percentages for each year based on corrected data.

**c.** What correction, if any, should be made in the amounts of the company's owner's equity at the end of 2001 and at the end of 2002?

---

**EXERCISE 8.9**

Estimating Inventory by the Gross Profit Method

**LO 6**

When Laura Rapp arrived at her store on the morning of January 29, she found empty shelves and display racks; thieves had broken in during the night and stolen the entire inventory. Rapp's accounting records showed that she had inventory costing $50,000 on January 1. From January 1 to January 29, she had made net sales of $70,000, and net purchases of $80,000. The gross profit during the past several years had consistently averaged 45% of net sales. Rapp wishes to file an insurance claim for the theft loss.

**a.** Using the gross profit method, estimate the cost of Rapp's inventory at the time of the theft.

**b.** Does Rapp use the periodic inventory method or does she account for inventory using the perpetual method? Defend your answer.

---

**EXERCISE 8.10**

Estimating Inventory by the Retail Method

**LO 6**

Phillips Supply uses a periodic inventory system but needs to determine the approximate amount of inventory at the end of each month without taking a physical inventory. Phillips has provided the following inventory data:

|  | Cost Price | Retail Selling Price |
| --- | --- | --- |
| Inventory of merchandise, June 30 . . . . . . . . . . . . . . . . . . . . . . . . . . | $300,000 | $500,000 |
| Purchases during July . . . . . . . . . . . . . . . . . . . . . . . . . . . . . . . . . . | 222,000 | 400,000 |
| Goods available for sale during July . . . . . . . . . . . . . . . . . . . . . . . . | $522,000 | $900,000 |
| Net sales during July . . . . . . . . . . . . . . . . . . . . . . . . . . . . . . . . . . . |  | $600,000 |

**a.** Estimate the cost of goods sold and the cost of the July 31 ending inventory using the retail method of evaluation.

**b.** Was the cost of Phillips inventory, as a percentage of retail selling prices, higher or lower in July than it was in June? Explain.

---

**EXERCISE 8.11**

Evaluating Cost Flow Assumptions

**LO 1, 7**

A note to the recent financial statements of **The Quaker Oats Company** includes the following information:

> Inventories: Inventories are valued at the lower-of-cost-or-market, using various cost methods. The percentage of year-end inventories valued using each of the methods is as follows:
>
> June 30 (fiscal year-end)
>
> Average cost . . . . . . . . . . . . . . . . . . . . . . . . . . . . . . . . . . . . . . . . . . . . . . . . . . . . . . . . . . 54%
>
> Last-in, first-out (LIFO) . . . . . . . . . . . . . . . . . . . . . . . . . . . . . . . . . . . . . . . . . . . . . . . . . . 29%
>
> First-in, first-out (FIFO) . . . . . . . . . . . . . . . . . . . . . . . . . . . . . . . . . . . . . . . . . . . . . . . . . . . 17%

**Instructions**

**a.** Does the company's use of three different inventory methods violate the accounting principle of consistency?

**b.** Assuming that the replacement cost of inventories has been steadily rising, would the company's reported net income be higher or lower if all inventories were valued by the FIFO method?

**c.** Assuming that replacement costs are steadily rising, which cost flow assumption (FIFO or LIFO) would result in the computation of the highest inventory turnover rate? Would the use of this method to account for inventories really mean that the company could sell physical quantities of inventory more quickly? Explain.

SnowWorld, a successful manufacturer of ski apparel, has been using LIFO during a period of rising prices.

a. Indicate whether each of the following financial measurements would have been *higher, lower,* or *unaffected* had the company been using FIFO. Explain the reasoning behind your answers.

1. Gross profit rate
2. Reported net income
3. Current ratio (assume greater than 1 to 1)
4. Inventory turnover rate
5. Accounts receivable turnover rate
6. Cash payments to merchandise suppliers
7. Net cash flow from operating activities (assume positive)

b. Provide *your own* assessment of whether using LIFO has made SnowWorld more or less (1) solvent and (2) "well-off." Explain fully.

**EXERCISE 8.12**

FIFO versus LIFO: A Challenging Analysis

**LO 1, 7**

A recent annual report of **Gateway, Inc.**, shows cost of goods sold, $5,922, inventory at the beginning of the year, $249, and inventory at the end of the year, $168. (These dollar amounts are in millions.)

a. Compute the inventory turnover rate for the year (round to the nearest tenth).

b. Using the assumption of 365 days in a year, compute the number of days required for the company to sell the amount of its average inventory (round to the nearest day).

c. Assume that an average of 30 days is required for **Gateway** to collect its accounts receivable. What is the length of **Gateway**'s *operating cycle?*

**EXERCISE 8.13**

Inventory Turnover Rate

**LO 7**

A recent balance sheet of **Kmart** contains the following information about inventories (dollar amounts are in thousands):

**\*EXERCISE 8.14**

Cost Flows, Cash Flows, and LIFO Reserves

**LO 8**

| Inventories: | | |
|---|---|---|
| At replacement cost | . . . . . . . . . . . . . . . . . . . . . . . . . . . . . . . . . . | $6,500,000 |
| Less LIFO reserve | . . . . . . . . . . . . . . . . . . . . . . . . . . . . . . . . | 100,000 |
| LIFO | . . . . . . . . . . . . . . . . . . . . . . . . . . . . . . . . . . . . . | $6,400,000 |

The income statement indicates that the company pays income taxes equal to approximately 35% of income before taxes.

a. Assume that if **Kmart** had used *FIFO,* inventory would appear at the amount shown as replacement cost. Over the life of the company, determine the *cumulative amounts* by which the use of LIFO has *reduced* the following financial statement amounts. (Include a brief explanation of each answer.)

1. Taxable income
2. Income taxes expense
3. Net income

b. Would **Kmart**'s net income over the years have been higher or lower had the company been using *FIFO?* How about the net cash flows provided by operating activities? Explain fully.

c. Assume that in the coming year, **Kmart** liquidates some of its LIFO reserve. What effect would you expect this action to have on the company's *gross profit rate?* Explain.

The annual report of **Tootsie Roll Industries, Inc.** appears in Appendix A at the end of this textbook. Using figures from the income statement and balance sheet, answer the following questions:

a. What was the company's inventory turnover rate for the most recent year reported?

b. Using your answer from part **a**, what was the average number of days that merchandise remained in inventory before it was sold?

**EXERCISE 8.15**

Using an Annual Report

**LO 7**

---

\* *Supplemental Topic,* "LIFO Reserves."

c. Is the company's operating cycle influenced significantly by its accounts receivable turnover rate? Explain.

## PROBLEMS

**PROBLEM 8.1**

Four Methods of Inventory Valuation

On January 15, 2002, BassTrack sold 1,000 Ace-5 fishing reels to Angler's Warehouse. Immediately prior to this sale, BassTrack's perpetual inventory records for Ace-5 reels included the following cost layers:

| Purchase Date | Quantity | Unit Cost | Total Cost |
|---|---|---|---|
| Dec. 12, 2001 ........................... | 600 | $29 | $17,400 |
| Jan. 9, 2002 ........................... | 900 | 32 | 28,800 |
| Total on hand ........................... | 1,500 | | $46,200 |

### Instructions

*Note:* We present this problem in the normal sequence of the accounting cycle—that is, journal entries before ledger entries. However, you may find it helpful to work part **b** first.

a. Prepare a separate journal entry to record the cost of goods sold relating to the January 15 sale of 1,000 Ace-5 reels, assuming that BassTrack uses:

1. Specific identification (500 of the units sold were purchased on December 12, and the remaining 500 were purchased on January 9).
2. Average cost.
3. FIFO.
4. LIFO.

b. Complete a subsidiary ledger record for Ace-5 reels using each of the four inventory valuation methods listed above. Your inventory records should show both purchases of this product, the sale on January 15, and the balance on hand at December 12, January 9, and January 15. Use the formats for inventory subsidiary records illustrated on pages 319–321 of this chapter.

c. Refer to the cost of goods sold figures computed in part **a**. For financial reporting purposes, can the company use the valuation method that resulted in the *lowest* cost of goods sold if, for tax purposes, it used the method that resulted in the *highest* cost of goods sold? Explain.

*Problems 8.2 and 8.3 are based on the following data:*

Speed World Cycles sells high-performance motorcycles and Motocross racers. One of Speed World's most popular models is the Kazomma 900 dirt bike. During the current year, Speed World purchased eight of these cycles at the following costs:

| Purchase Date | Units Purchased | Unit Cost | Total Cost |
|---|---|---|---|
| July 1 ........................... | 2 | $4,950 | $ 9,900 |
| July 22 ........................... | 3 | 5,000 | 15,000 |
| Aug. 3 ........................... | 3 | 5,100 | 15,300 |
| | 8 | | $40,200 |

On *July 28*, Speed World sold four Kazomma 900 dirt bikes to the Vince Wilson racing team. The remaining four bikes remained in inventory at September 30, the end of Speed World's fiscal year.

Assume that Speed World uses a *perpetual inventory system*. (See the data given following Problem 8.1.)

### Instructions

**a.** Compute (a) the cost of goods sold relating to the sale on July 28 and (b) the ending inventory of Kazomma 900 dirt bikes at September 30, using the following cost flow assumptions:

   **1.** Average cost

   **2.** FIFO

   **3.** LIFO

Show the number of units and the unit costs of each layer comprising the cost of goods sold and ending inventory.

**b.** Using the cost figures computed in part **a**, answer the following questions:

   **1.** Which of the three cost flow assumptions will result in Speed World Cycles reporting the *highest net income* for the current year? Would this always be the case? Explain.

   **2.** Which of the three cost flow assumptions will *minimize the income taxes owed* by Speed World Cycles for the year. Would you expect this usually to be the case? Explain.

   **3.** May Speed World Cycles use the cost flow assumption that results in the highest net income for the current year in its financial statements, but use the cost flow assumption that minimizes taxable income for the current year in its income tax return? Explain.

**PROBLEM 8.2**

Alternative Cost Flow
Assumptions in a Perpetual
System

**LO 1**

Assume that Speed World uses a *periodic inventory system*. (See the data given following Problem 8.1.)

### Instructions

**a.** Compute (a) the cost of goods sold relating to the sale on July 28 and (b) the ending inventory of Kazomma 900 dirt bikes at September 30, using the following cost flow assumptions:

   **1.** Average cost

   **2.** FIFO

   **3.** LIFO

Show the number of units and unit costs in each cost layer of the *ending inventory*. You may determine the cost of goods sold by deducting ending inventory from the cost of goods available for sale.

**b.** If Speed World Cycles uses the LIFO cost flow assumption for financial reporting purposes, can it use the FIFO method for income tax purposes? Explain.

**PROBLEM 8.3**

Alternative Cost Flow
Assumptions in a Periodic
System

**LO 4**

Mario's Nursery uses a perpetual inventory system. At December 31, the perpetual inventory records indicate the following quantities of a particular blue spruce tree:

**PROBLEM 8.4**

Year-End Adjustments;
Shrinkage Losses and LCM

**LO 1, 2, 3**

| | Quantity | Unit Cost | Total Cost |
|---|---|---|---|
| First purchase (oldest) | 130 | $25.00 | $ 3,250 |
| Second purchase | 120 | 28.50 | 3,420 |
| Third purchase | 100 | 39.00 | 3,900 |
| Total | 350 | | $10,570 |

A year-end physical inventory, however, shows only 310 of these trees on hand.

In its financial statements, Mario's values its inventories at the lower-of-cost-or-market. At year-end, the per-unit replacement cost of this tree is $40. (Use $3,500 as the "level of materiality" in deciding whether to debit losses to Cost of Goods Sold or to a separate loss account.)

### Instructions

Prepare the journal entries required to adjust the inventory records at year-end, assuming that:

**a.** Mario's uses:

   **1.** Average cost.

   **2.** Last-in, first-out.

b. Mario's uses the first-in, first-out method. However, the replacement cost of the trees at year-end is $20 apiece, rather than the $40 stated originally. [Make separate journal entries to record (1) the shrinkage losses and (2) the restatement of the inventory at a market value lower than cost. Record the shrinkage losses first.]

c. Assume that the company had been experiencing monthly inventory shrinkage of 30 to 60 trees for several months. In response, management placed several hidden security cameras throughout the premises. Within days, an employee was caught on film loading potted trees into his pickup truck. The employee's attorney asked that the case be dropped because the company had "unethically used a hidden camera to entrap his client." Do you agree with the attorney? Defend your answer.

**PROBLEM 8.5**

Periodic Inventory Costing Procedures

**LO 4**

Mach IV Audio uses a periodic inventory system. One of the store's most popular products is a minidisc car stereo system. The inventory quantities, purchases, and sales of this product for the most recent year are as follows:

| | Number of Units | Cost per Unit | Total Cost |
|---|---|---|---|
| Inventory, Jan. 1 | 10 | $299 | $ 2,990 |
| First purchase (May 12) | 15 | 306 | 4,590 |
| Second purchase (July 9) | 20 | 308 | 6,160 |
| Third purchase (Oct. 4) | 8 | 315 | 2,520 |
| Fourth purchase (Dec. 18) | 19 | 320 | 6,080 |
| Goods available for sale | 72 | | $22,340 |
| Units sold during the year | 51 | | |
| Inventory, Dec. 31 | 21 | | |

**Instructions**

a. Using *periodic* costing procedures, compute the cost of the December 31 inventory and the cost of goods sold for the minidisc systems during the year under each of the following cost flow assumptions:

1. First-in, first-out
2. Last-in, first-out
3. Average cost (Round to nearest dollar, except unit cost.)

b. Which of the three inventory pricing methods provides the most realistic balance sheet valuation of inventory in light of the current replacement cost of the minidisc units? Does this same method also produce the most realistic measure of income in light of the costs being incurred by Mach IV Audio to replace the minidisc systems when they are sold? Explain.

**PROBLEM 8.6**

Effects of Inventory Errors on Earnings

**LO 5**

The owners of Hexagon Health Foods are offering the business for sale. The income statements of the business for the three years of its existence are summarized below.

| | 2002 | 2001 | 2000 |
|---|---|---|---|
| Net sales | $875,000 | $840,000 | $820,000 |
| Cost of goods sold | 481,250 | 487,200 | 480,000 |
| Gross profit on sales | $393,750 | $352,800 | $340,000 |
| Gross profit percentage | 45% | 42% | 41% |

In negotiations with prospective buyers of the business, the owners of Hexagon are calling attention to the rising trends of the gross profit and of the gross profit percentage as very favorable elements.

Assume that you are retained by a prospective purchaser of the business to make an investigation of the fairness and reliability of the enterprise's accounting records and financial statements. You find everything in order except for the following: (1) An arithmetic error in the computation of inventory at the end of 2000 had caused a $40,000 understatement in that inventory, and (2) a duplication of figures in the computation of inventory at the end of 2002 had caused an overstatement of $81,750 in that inventory. The company uses the periodic inventory system and these errors had not been brought to light prior to your investigation.

### Instructions

**a.** Prepare a revised three-year schedule similar to the one illustrated on page 352.

**b.** Comment on the trend of gross profit and gross profit percentage before and after the revision.

Between The Ears is a popular Internet music store (*www.BTE.com*). During the current year, the company's cost of goods available for sale amounted to $462,000. The retail sales value of this merchandise amounted to $840,000. Sales for the year were $744,000.

**PROBLEM 8.7**

Retail Method

**LO 2, 3, 6**

### Instructions

**a.** Using the retail method, estimate (1) the cost of goods sold during the year and (2) the inventory at the end of the year.

**b.** At year-end, BTE.com takes a physical inventory. The general manager walks through the warehouse counting each type of product and reading its retail price into a tape recorder. From the recorded information, another employee prepares a schedule listing the entire ending inventory at retail sales prices. The schedule prepared for the current year reports ending inventory at $84,480 at retail sales prices.

   **1.** Use the cost ratio computed in part **a** to reduce the inventory counted by the general manager from its retail value to an estimate of its costs.

   **2.** Determine the estimated shrinkage losses (measured at cost) incurred by BTE.com during the year.

   **3.** Compute BTE.com's gross profit for the year. (Include inventory shrinkage losses in the cost of goods sold.)

**c.** What controls might BTE.com implement to reduce inventory shrinkage?

## CASES AND UNSTRUCTURED PROBLEMS

Our Little Secret is a small manufacturer of swimsuits and other beach apparel. The company is closely held and has no external reporting obligations, other than payroll reports and income tax returns. The company's accounting system is grossly inadequate. Accounting records are maintained by clerical employees with little knowledge of accounting and with many other job responsibilities. Management has decided that the company must hire a competent controller, who can establish and oversee an adequate accounting system.

Amy Lee, CPA, has applied for this position. During a recent interview, Dean Frost, the company's director of personnel, said, "Amy, the job is yours. But you should know that we have a big inventory problem here.

"For some time now, it appears that we have been understating our ending inventory in income tax returns. No one knows when this all got started, or who was responsible. We never even counted our inventory until a few months ago. But the problem is pretty big. In our latest tax return—that's for 2002—we listed inventory at only about half its actual cost. That's an understatement of, maybe, $400,000.

"We don't know what to do. We sure don't want a big scandal—tax evasion, and all that. Maybe the best thing is continue understating inventory by the same amount as we did in 2002. That way, taxable income will be correctly stated in future years. Anyway, this is just something I thought you should know about."

**CASE 8.1**

It's Not Right, but at Least It's Consistent

**LO 5**

### Instructions

**a.** Briefly identify the ethical issues raised for Lee by Frost's disclosure.

**b.** From Lee's perspective, evaluate the possible solution proposed by Frost.

**c.** Identify and discuss the alternative ethical courses of action that are open to Lee.

**CASE 8.2**

Dealing with the Bank

Avery Frozen Foods owes the bank $50,000 on a line of credit. Terms of the agreement specify that Avery must maintain a minimum current ratio of 1.2 to 1, or the entire outstanding balance becomes immediately due in full. To date, the company has complied with the minimum requirement. However, management has just learned that a failed warehouse freezer has ruined thousands of dollars of frozen foods inventory. If the company records this loss, its current ratio will drop to approximately 0.8 to 1.

Whether any or all of this loss may be covered by insurance currently is in dispute and will not be known for at least 90 days—perhaps much longer. There are several reasons why the insurance company may have no liability.

In trying to decide how to deal with the bank, management is considering the following options: (1) postpone recording the inventory loss until the dispute with the insurance company is resolved, (2) increase the current ratio to 1.2 to 1 by making a large purchase of inventory on account, (3) explain to the bank what has happened, and request that it be flexible until things get back to normal.

### Instructions

**a.** Given that the company hopes for at least partial reimbursement from the insurance company, is it really unethical for management to postpone recording the inventory loss in the financial statements it submits to the bank?

**b.** Is it possible to increase the company's current ratio from 0.8 to 1 to 1.2 to 1 by purchasing more inventory on account? Explain.

**c.** What approach do you think the company should follow in dealing with the bank?

**CASE 8.3**

What If They'd Used FIFO?

**Wal-Mart** uses LIFO. Recent financial statements included the following data (dollars in billions):

| | |
|---|---:|
| Average inventory (throughout the year) | $ 16.786 |
| Current assets (at year-end) | 21.132 |
| Current liabilities (at year-end) | 16.762 |
| Net sales | 137.634 |
| Cost of goods sold | 108.725 |
| Gross profit | 28.909 |

A note accompanying these statements indicated that had the company used the *FIFO* inventory method:

**1.** Average inventory would have been $17.197 billion ($411 million *higher* than the LIFO amount).

**2.** Ending inventory would have been valued at a cost of $17.549 billion ($473 million *higher* than the LIFO cost).

**3.** The cost of goods sold would have been $108.6 billion ($125 million *lower* than that reported in the company's income statement).

### Instructions

**a.** Using the data contained in the company's financial statements (based on the LIFO method), compute the following analytical measurements. (Round to the nearest tenth.) Be prepared to discuss these measurements in class.

    **1.** Inventory turnover rate

    **2.** Current ratio

    **3.** Gross profit rate

**b.** *Recompute* the three ratios required in part **a** in a manner that will be *directly comparable* to those of a company using the FIFO method in its financial statements. (Round to the nearest tenth.)

**c.** Notice that the cost of goods sold is *lower* under FIFO than LIFO. What circumstances must the company have encountered to cause this situation? (Were replacement costs, on average, rising or falling?)

**d.** Do you think that **Wal-Mart**'s accounts receivable turnover rate increases significantly the number of days in the company's operating cycle? Explain. (See Chapter 6 for a discussion of a company's operating cycle.)

Jackson Specialties has been in business for 52 years. The company maintains a perpetual inventory system, uses a LIFO flow assumption, and ends its fiscal year at December 31. At year-end, the cost of goods sold and inventory are adjusted to reflect periodic LIFO costing procedures.

A railroad strike has delayed the arrival of purchases ordered during the past several months of 2002, and Jackson Specialties has not been able to replenish its inventories as merchandise is sold. At December 22, one product appears in the company's perpetual inventory records at the following unit costs:

**\*CASE 8.4**

LIFO Liquidation

**LO 8**

| Purchase Date | Quantity | Unit Cost | Total Cost |
|---|---|---|---|
| Nov. 14, 1954 ............................. | 3,000 | $6 | $18,000 |
| Apr. 12, 1955 ............................. | 2,000 | 8 | 16,000 |
| Available for sale at Dec. 22, 2002 .............. | 5,000 | | $34,000 |

Jackson Specialties has another 8,000 units of this product on order at the current wholesale cost of $30 per unit. Because of the railroad strike, however, these units have not yet arrived (the terms of purchase are F.O.B. destination). Jackson Specialties also has an order from a customer who wants to purchase 4,000 units of this product at the retail sales price of $47 per unit. Jackson Specialties intends to make this sale on December 30, regardless of whether the 8,000 units on order arrive by this date. (The 4,000-unit sale will be shipped by truck, F.O.B. shipping point.)

**Instructions**

**a.** Are the units in inventory really almost 50 years old? Explain.

**b.** Prepare a schedule showing the sales revenue, cost of goods sold, and gross profit that will result from this sale on December 30, assuming that the 8,000 units currently on order (1) arrive before year-end and (2) do not arrive until some time in the following year. (In each computation, show the number of units comprising the cost of goods sold and their related per-unit costs.)

**c.** Comment on these results.

**d.** Might management be wise to delay this sale by a few days? Explain.

---

## BUSINESS WEEK ASSIGNMENT
BusinessWeek

Managers at **Herman Miller Inc.** are justifiably proud of their furniture plant in Holland, Michigan, according to "Reinventing Herman Miller," an article in the April 3, 2000, issue of *Business Week* by David Rocks. While the physical facilities are appealing, the article reports that best of all is the plant's performance. A sign near the front door indicates that there has not been a late shipment in 70 days, something that is rare in the furniture industry. Emphasizing Miller's efficiency is the name of its newest division, called SQA, which stands for "simple, quick, affordable." Having inventory at the right place, at the right time, and in the right quantities is an important part of successful business activities.

As a consumer, what do you look for when you go into a department store, a clothing store, or a drugstore? What makes you want to come back to a store? What makes you want to go to a competing store next time? How can a store manager handle inventory to keep your business? How does a manager know if a store is selling its merchandise fast enough?

**CASE 8.4**

**LO 7**

---

\* *Supplemental Topic A,* "LIFO Reserves."

## INTERNET ASSIGNMENT

**INTERNET 8.1**

Inventory Turnover

**LO 7**

A company's inventory turnover rate is one measure of its potential to convert inventory into cash. But what is considered a "good" inventory turnover rate? The answer to that question depends on a variety of industry and company characteristics.

Access the EDGAR database at the following Internet address:

**www.sec.gov/**

Locate the most recent 10-K reports of **McDonald's**, and the **Ford Motor Company**. Compute the inventory turnover rates of each company. Does the higher turnover rate of **McDonald's** mean that the company manages its inventory more efficiently than **Ford**? Explain.

*Internet sites are time and date sensitive. It is the purpose of these exercises to have you explore the Internet. You may need to use the Yahoo! search engine* http://www.yahoo.com *(or other favorite search engine) to find a company's current web address.*

## OUR COMMENTS ON THE "YOUR TURN" CASES

**You as a Shipping Department Manager (p. 328)** The request from the plant controller presents an ethical dilemma. It is inappropriate to mark the shipments as being shipped when in fact they are awaiting shipment until January. It is also unethical for the plant controller to ask you to alter your records.

To resolve this issue, the first step is to consider whether the company has a code of conduct or other personnel codes that provide guidance about how potential conflicts between supervisors and employees can be resolved. If your company has no policies or the conflict is not resolved by company policies, then consider that The International Federation of Accountants provides guidance about how to resolve ethical conflicts in Section 2 of its Code of Ethics for Professional Accountants.* It recommends: (1) Review the conflict problem with the immediate superior. If it appears the superior is involved in the conflict problem, raise the issue with the next higher level of management. (2) Seek counseling and advice on a confidential basis with an independent advisor or the applicable professional accountancy body. (3) If the ethical conflict still exists after fully exhausting all levels of internal review, as a last resort on significant matters (e.g., fraud) resign and submit an information memo to the appropriate representative of the organization.

**You as a Banker (p. 336)** Over time, a tighter credit policy is likely to improve the quality of the company's credit accounts and should decrease the average time that its accounts receivable remain outstanding. Tighter credit policies may, however, reduce the company's overall level of sales. The adoption of a just-in-time inventory system will increase inventory turnover and will have the potential to greatly reduce the length of time that cash remains tied up in inventory. In short, if the changes suggested by management are successful, they should result in a reduced operating cycle. Whether they will reduce the cycle by 100 days remains to be seen, however. It is the banker's professional responsibility to view these projections with cautious optimism.

**You as a Business Owner (p. 338)** The LIFO method normally does result in a lower taxable income during periods of rising prices, as long as the old, low-cost inventory layers are not depleted. In our example, the truck drivers' strike forced the business to sell almost all of its inventory—including the old, low-cost layers. When these items were sold, their relatively low and outdated acquisition costs were matched against the revenues of the current period. As a consequence, the unusually high gross profit on these sales drove taxable income up unexpectedly. This risk associated with the LIFO method is sometimes referred to as the *liquidation of the LIFO reserve.*

## ANSWERS TO SELF-TEST QUESTIONS

**1.** b   **2.** a, c, d   **3.** a   **4.** b   **5.** b   **6.** a, d

---

* For more information visit www.ifac.org.

# Guitar Universe, Inc.

Guitar Universe, Inc., is a popular source of musical instruments for professional and amateur musicians. The company's accountants make necessary adjusting entries *monthly,* and make all closing entries *annually.* Guitar Universe is growing rapidly and prides itself on having no long-term liabilities.

The company has provided the following *trial balance* dated *December 31, 2002:*

| GUITAR UNIVERSE, INC.<br>Trial Balance<br>December 31, 2002 | | |
|---|---:|---:|
| Cash | $ 45,000 | |
| Marketable securities | 25,000 | |
| Accounts receivable | 125,000 | |
| Allowance for doubtful accounts | | $ 5,000 |
| Merchandise inventory | 250,000 | |
| Office supplies | 1,200 | |
| Prepaid insurance | 6,600 | |
| Building and fixtures | 1,791,000 | |
| Accumulated depreciation | | 800,000 |
| Land | 64,800 | |
| Accounts payable | | 70,000 |
| Unearned customer deposits | | 8,000 |
| Income taxes payable | | 75,000 |
| Capital stock | | 1,000,000 |
| Retained earnings | | 240,200 |
| Unrealized holding gain on investments | | 6,000 |
| Sales | | 1,600,000 |
| Cost of goods sold | 958,000 | |
| Bank service charges | 200 | |
| Uncollectible accounts expense | 9,000 | |
| Salary and wages expense | 395,000 | |
| Office supply expense | 400 | |
| Insurance expense | 6,400 | |
| Utilities expense | 3,600 | |
| Depreciation expense | 48,000 | |
| Income taxes expense | 75,000 | |
| | $3,804,200 | $3,804,200 |

Other information pertaining to Guitar Universe's trial balance is shown below:

1. The company's most recent bank statement reports a balance of $46,975. Included with the bank statement was a $2,500 check from Iggy Bates, a professional musician, charged back to Guitar Universe as NSF. The bank's monthly service charge was $25. Three checks written by Guitar Universe to suppliers of merchandise inventory had not yet cleared the bank for payment as of the statement date. These checks included: No. 507, $4,000; No. 511, $9,000; and No. 521, $8,000. Deposits made by Guitar Universe of $16,500 had reached the bank too late for inclusion in the current statement. The company prepares a bank reconciliation at the end of each month.

2. Guitar Universe has a portfolio of marketable securities. The initial investment in the portfolio was $19,000. As of December 31, the market value of these securities was $27,500. Management classifies all short-term investments as "available for sale."

3. During December, $6,400 of accounts receivable were written off as uncollectible. A recent aging of the company's accounts receivable helped management to conclude that an allowance for doubtful accounts of $8,500 was needed at December 31, 2002.

4. The company uses a perpetual inventory system. A year-end physical count revealed that several guitars reported in the inventory records were missing. The cost of the missing units amounted to $1,350. This amount is not considered significant relative to the total cost of inventory on hand.

5. At December 31, approximately $900 in office supplies remained on hand.

6. The company pays for its insurance policies 12 months in advance. Its most recent payment was made on November 1, 2002. The cost of this policy was slightly higher than the cost of coverage for the previous 12 months.

7. Depreciation expense related to the company's building and fixtures is $5,000 for the month ending December 31, 2002.

8. Although Guitar Universe carries an extensive inventory, it is not uncommon for musicians to order custom guitars made to their exact specifications. Manufacturers do not allow any sales returns of custom-made guitars. Thus, all customers must pay in advance for these special orders. The entire sales amount is collected at the time a custom order is placed, and is credited to an account entitled, "Unearned Customer Deposits." As of December 31, $4,800 of these deposits remained unearned. Assume that the cost of goods sold and the reduction in inventory associated with all custom orders is recorded when the custom merchandise is delivered to customers. Thus, the adjusting entry requires only a decrease to unearned customer deposits and an increase to sales.

9. Accrued income taxes payable for the *entire year ending* December 31, 2002, total $81,000. No income tax payments are due until early in 2002.

## Instructions

a. Prepare a bank reconciliation and make the necessary journal entry to update the accounting records of Guitar Universe as of December 31, 2002.

b. Prepare the necessary adjusting entry to update the company's marketable securities portfolio to its mark-to-market value.

c. Prepare the adjusting entry at December 31, 2002, to report the company's accounts receivable at their net realizable value.

d. Prepare the entry to account for the guitars missing from the company's inventory at the end of the year.

e. Prepare the adjusting entry to account for the office supplies used during December.

f. Prepare the adjusting entry to account for the expiration of the company's insurance policies during December.

g. Prepare the adjusting entry to account for the depreciation of the company's building and fixtures during December.

h. Prepare the adjusting entry to report the portion of unearned customer deposits that were earned during December.

i. Prepare they adjusting entry to account for income taxes expense that accrued during December.

j. Based upon the adjustments made to the accounting records in parts **a** through **i** above, prepare the company's adjusted trial balance at December 31, 2002.

k. Using the adjusted trial balance prepared in part **j** above, prepare an *annual* income statement, statement of retained earnings, and a balance sheet dated December 31, 2002.

l. Using the financial statements prepared in part **k** above, approximately how many days does an account receivable remain outstanding before it is collected? You may assume that the company's ending accounts receivable balance on December 31 is a close approximation of its average accounts receivable balance throughout the year.

**m.** Using the financial statements prepared in part **k**, approximately how many days does an item of merchandise remain in stock before it is sold? You may assume that the company's ending merchandise inventory balance on December 31 is a close approximation of its average merchandise inventory balance throughout the year.

**n.** Using the financial statements prepared in part **k**, approximately how many days does it take to convert the company's inventory into cash? Stated differently, what is the length of the company's operating cycle?

**o.** Comment briefly upon the company's financial condition from the perspective of a short-term creditor.

# 9

# PLANT AND INTANGIBLE ASSETS

## Learning Objectives

*After studying this chapter, you should be able to:*

1. Determine the cost of plant assets.

2. Distinguish between capital expenditures and revenue expenditures.

3. Compute depreciation by the straight-line and declining-balance methods.

4. Account for disposals of plant assets.

5. Explain the nature of intangible assets, including goodwill.

6. Account for the depletion of natural resources.

7. Explain the cash effects of transactions involving plant assets.

*8. Account for depreciation using methods other than straight-line or declining-balance.

---

* *Supplemental Topic,* "Other Depreciation Methods."

AMAZON.COM

Here's something of an accounting riddle . . . What is it that can't be felt, seen, smelled, or tasted, but is worth millions —sometimes billions—of dollars to a company? The answer? Goodwill.

Consider **Amazon.com**, the world's most widely recognized online retailer. The largest noncurrent asset in a recent **Amazon** balance sheet, reported at $535 million, is goodwill. So what is goodwill? In simple terms, goodwill arises when one company purchases another company for an amount in excess of the fair value of the assets it acquires. The *premium* paid for these businesses is reported in the balance sheet of the purchasing company as goodwill.

**Amazon** recently purchased several companies, including **Exchange.com**, **Accept.com**, **LiveBid.com**, and others. The goodwill figure reported in Amazon's balance sheet indicates that the amount **Amazon** paid for these companies was significantly more than the fair value of the tangible assets it actually received. **Amazon** was willing to pay this excess amount because it expected the companies to generate superior earnings performance in the future. Each year, a portion of **Amazon**'s goodwill figure is reported as amortization expense in the company's income statement. In other words, a portion of the total goodwill is *matched* to the revenue earned in each period. When **Amazon** initially purchased these other companies, it had recorded nearly $750 million in total goodwill. Over time, it has already charged $215 million of this amount to the income statement as amortization expense. The $535 million remaining in **Amazon**'s balance sheet is that portion of the $750 million to be matched against future revenue.

● ● ●

In this chapter we discuss the nature of goodwill and other intangible assets. In addition, we will examine accounting issues related to a company's investment in tangible assets such as plant, equipment, and natural resources.

## Plant Assets as a "Stream of Future Services"

**Plant assets** are similar to long-term prepaid expenses. Ownership of a delivery truck, for example, may provide about 100,000 miles of transportation. The cost of the truck is entered in an asset account, which in essence represents the *advance purchase* of these transportation services. Similarly, a building represents the advance purchase of many years of housing services. As the years go by, these services are utilized by the business, and the cost of the plant asset gradually is transferred to depreciation expense.

## Major Categories of Plant Assets

Plant and equipment items are often classified into the following groups:

1. **Tangible plant assets.** The term *tangible* denotes physical substance, as exemplified by land, a building, or a machine. This category may be subdivided into two distinct classifications:
   a. **Plant property subject to depreciation.** Included are plant assets of limited useful life such as buildings and office equipment.
   b. **Land.** The only plant asset not subject to depreciation is land, which has an un- limited term of existence.
2. **Intangible assets.** The term *intangible assets* is used to describe assets that are used in the operation of the business but have no physical substance and are noncurrent. Examples include patents, copyrights, trademarks, franchises, and goodwill. Current assets such as accounts receivable or prepaid rent are not included in the intangible classification, even though they also are lacking in physical substance.
3. **Natural resources.** A site acquired for the purpose of extracting or removing some valuable resource such as oil, minerals, or timber is classified as a *natural resource*, not as land. This type of plant asset is gradually converted into *inventory* as the nat- ural resource is extracted from the site.

## Accountable Events in the Lives of Plant Assets

For all categories of plant assets, there are three basic *accountable events:* (1) acquisi- tion, (2) allocation of the acquisition cost to expense over the asset's useful life (depre- ciation), and (3) sale or disposal.

## ACQUISITIONS OF PLANT ASSETS

**LO 1**

Determine the cost of plant assets.

The cost of a plant asset includes all expenditures that are *reasonable* and *necessary* for getting the asset to the desired location and *ready for use.* Thus many incidental costs may be included in the cost assigned to a plant asset. These include, for example, sales taxes on the purchase price, delivery costs, and installation costs.

But only reasonable and necessary costs should be included. Assume, for example, that a machine is dropped and damaged while it is being unloaded. The cost of repair- ing this damage should be recognized as an expense of the current period, *not* added to the cost of the machine. Although it is necessary to repair the machine, it was not nec- essary to drop it—and that's what brought about the need for the repairs.

Companies often purchase plant assets on an installment plan or by issuing a note payable. Interest charges after the asset is ready for use are recorded as interest expense, not as part of the cost of the asset. But if a company constructs a plant asset for its own use, the interest charges *during the construction period* are viewed as part of the asset's cost.[1]

---

[1] *FASB Statement No. 34,* "Capitalization of Interest Costs" (Norwalk, Conn.: 1979).

## Determining Cost: An Example

The concept of including in the cost of a plant asset all of the incidental charges necessary to put the asset in use is illustrated by the following example. A factory in Minneapolis orders a machine from a San Francisco tool manufacturer at a list price of $10,000. Payment will be made in 48 monthly installments of $250, which include $2,000 in interest charges. Sales taxes of $600 must be paid, as well as freight charges of $1,250. Installation and other set-up costs amount to $400. The cost of this machine to be debited to the Machinery account is computed as follows:

| | |
|---|---|
| List price* | $10,000 |
| Sales taxes | 600 |
| Transportation charges | 1,250 |
| Cost of installation and set-up | 400 |
| Total | $12,250 |

*The $2,000 in interest charges on the installment purchase will be recognized as interest expense over the next 48 months. (Accounting for installment notes payable is discussed in the next chapter.)

*All reasonable and necessary costs are capitalized*

## Some Special Considerations

**Land** When land is purchased, various incidental costs are generally incurred in addition to the purchase price. These additional costs may include commissions to real estate brokers, escrow fees, legal fees for examining and insuring the title, delinquent taxes paid by the purchaser, and fees for surveying, draining, clearing, and grading the property. All these expenditures become part of the cost of the land.

Sometimes land purchased as a building site has on it an old building that is not suitable for the buyer's use. In this case, the only useful asset being acquired is the land. Therefore, the entire purchase price is charged to the Land account, along with the costs of tearing down and removing the unusable building.

**Land Improvements** Improvements to real estate such as driveways, fences, parking lots, landscaping, and sprinkler systems have a limited life and are therefore subject to depreciation. For this reason, they should be recorded in a separate account entitled Land Improvements.

**Buildings** Old buildings are sometimes purchased with the intention of repairing them prior to placing them in use. Repairs made under these circumstances are charged to the Buildings account. After the building has been placed in use, ordinary repairs are considered to be maintenance expense when incurred.

**Equipment** When equipment is purchased, all of the sales taxes, delivery costs, and costs of getting the equipment in good running order are treated as part of the cost of the asset. Once the equipment has been placed in operation, maintenance costs (including interest, insurance, and property taxes) are treated as expenses of the current period.

**Allocation of a Lump-Sum Purchase** Several different types of plant assets may be purchased at one time. Separate controlling accounts are maintained for each type of plant asset, such as land, buildings, and equipment.[2]

When land and buildings (and perhaps other assets) are purchased for a lump sum, the purchase price must be *allocated* among the types of assets acquired. An appraisal may be needed for this purpose. Assume, for example, that Holiday Workout purchases

[2] Each controlling account is supported by a subsidiary ledger providing information about the cost, annual depreciation, and book value of each asset (or group of similar assets).

a complete fitness center from Golden Health Spas. Holiday purchases the entire facility at a bargain price of $800,000. The allocation of this cost on the basis of an appraisal is illustrated as follows:

*Total cost is allocated in proportion to appraised values*

| | Value per Appraisal | Percentage of Total Appraised Value | Allocation of $800,000 Cost |
|---|---|---|---|
| Land | $ 250,000 | 25% | $200,000 |
| Land improvements | 50,000 | 5 | 40,000 |
| Building | 300,000 | 30 | 240,000 |
| Equipment | 400,000 | 40 | 320,000 |
| Total | $1,000,000 | 100% | $800,000 |

Assuming that Holiday purchased this facility for cash, the journal entry to record this acquisition would be:

*The journal entry allocating the total costt*

| | | |
|---|---|---|
| Land | 200,000 | |
| Land Improvements | 40,000 | |
| Building | 240,000 | |
| Equipment | 320,000 | |
| Cash | | 800,000 |

To record purchase of fitness center from Golden Health Spas for cash.

**YOUR TURN**

**You as the New Facility Manager for Holiday Workout**

Assume you have been hired as manager of the new Golden Health Spas facility that was recently purchased by Holiday Workout. One of your responsibilities as manager is to show that the facility is profitable. In fact, your contract specifies a bonus if the profits are at least 10% above the budgeted amount each year. In a recent conversation with the appraiser, it becomes clear to you that the items classified as land in the appraisal were really building improvements. No one at Holiday Workout is aware of this misclassification. As a result, the appraised value for the building asset account should be $350,000 instead of $300,000. When budgeted profits for the Golden Health Spas facility are computed each year, a charge for depreciation on the building is deducted from the profits. What impact does the improper appraisal have on your ability to achieve the bonus? What should you do?

*Our comments appear on p. 400.

**LO 2**

Distinguish between capital expenditures and revenue expenditures.

## Capital Expenditures and Revenue Expenditures

Expenditures for the purchase or expansion of plant assets are called **capital expenditures** and are recorded in asset accounts. Accountants often use the verb **capitalize** to mean charging an expenditure to an asset account rather than to an expense account. Expenditures for ordinary repairs, maintenance, fuel, and other items necessary to the ownership and use of plant and equipment are called **revenue expenditures** and are recorded by debiting expense accounts. The charge to an expense account is based on the assumption that the benefits from the expenditure will be used up in the current period, and therefore the cost should be deducted from the revenue of the period in determining the net income. Charging an expenditure directly to an expense account is often called "expensing" the item.

A business may purchase many small items that will benefit several accounting periods but that have a relatively low cost. Examples of such items include auto batteries, wastebaskets, and pencil sharpeners. Such items are theoretically capital expenditures, but if they are recorded as assets in the accounting records it will be necessary to compute and record the related depreciation expense in future periods. We have previously mentioned the idea that the extra work involved in developing more precise accounting information should be weighed against the benefits that result. Thus, for reasons of convenience and economy, expenditures that are *not material* in dollar amount are treated in the accounting records as expenses of the current period.

In brief, any material expenditure that will benefit several accounting periods is considered a *capital expenditure*. Any expenditure that will benefit only the current period or that is not material in amount is treated as a *revenue expenditure*.

Many companies develop formal policy statements defining capital and revenue expenditures as a guide toward consistent accounting practice from year to year. These policy statements often set a minimum dollar amount (such as $500) for expenditures that are to be capitalized.

## DEPRECIATION

We first introduced the concept of depreciation in Chapter 4. We will now expand that discussion to address such topics as residual values and alternative depreciation methods.

### Allocating the Cost of Plant and Equipment over the Years of Use

Tangible plant assets, with the exception of land, are of use to a company for only a limited number of years. **Depreciation**, as the term is used in accounting, is the *allocation of the cost of a tangible plant asset to expense in the periods in which services are received from the asset.* In short, the basic purpose of depreciation is to apply the *matching principle*—that is, to offset the revenue of an accounting period with the costs of the goods and services being consumed in the effort to generate that revenue.

Earlier in this chapter, we described a delivery truck as a stream of transportation services to be received over the years that the truck is owned and used. The cost of the truck initially is debited to an asset account, because the purchase of these transportation services will benefit many future accounting periods. As these services are received, however, the cost of the truck gradually is removed from the balance sheet and allocated to expense, through the process of depreciation.

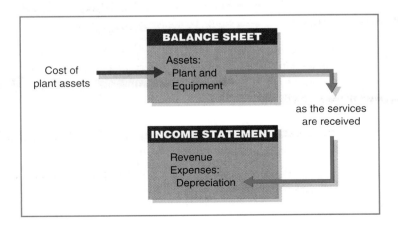

*Depreciation: a process of allocating the cost of an asset to expense*

The journal entry to record depreciation expense consists of a debit to Depreciation Expense and a credit to Accumulated Depreciation. The credit portion of the entry removes from the balance sheet that portion of the asset's cost estimated to have been used up during the current period. The debit portion of the entry allocates this expired cost to expense.

Separate Depreciation Expense and Accumulated Depreciation accounts are maintained for different types of depreciable assets, such as factory buildings, delivery equipment, and office equipment. These separate accounts help accountants to measure separately the costs of different business activities, such as manufacturing, sales, and administration.

**Depreciation Is Not a Process of Valuation** Depreciation is a process of *cost allocation,* not a process of asset valuation. Accounting records do not attempt to show the current market values of plant assets. The market value of a building, for example, may increase during some accounting periods within the building's useful life. The recognition of depreciation expense continues, however, without regard to such temporary increases in market value. Accountants recognize that the building will render useful services only for a limited number of years and that the full cost of the building should be *systematically allocated to expense* during these years.

**CASH EFFECTS** Depreciation differs from most other expenses in that it does not depend on cash payments at or near the time the expense is recorded. For this reason, depreciation often is called a "noncash" expense. Bear in mind, however, that large cash payments usually are required at the time depreciable assets are purchased.

**Book Value** Plant assets are shown in the balance sheet at their book values (or *carrying values*). The **book value** of a plant asset is its *cost minus the related accumulated depreciation.* Accumulated depreciation is a contra-asset account, representing that portion of the asset's cost that has *already* been allocated to expense. Thus book value represents the portion of the asset's cost that remains to be allocated to expense in future periods.

## Causes of Depreciation

The need to systematically allocate plant asset costs over multiple accounting periods arises from two major causes: (1) deterioration and (2) obsolescence.

**Physical Deterioration** Physical deterioration of a plant asset results from use, as well as from exposure to sun, wind, and other climatic factors. When a plant asset has been carefully maintained, it is not uncommon for the owner to claim that the asset is as "good as new." Such statements are not literally true. Although a good repair policy may greatly lengthen the useful life of a machine, every machine eventually reaches the point at which it must be discarded. In brief, the making of repairs does not eliminate the need for recognition of depreciation.

**Obsolescence** The term *obsolescence* means the process of becoming out of date or obsolete. An airplane, for example, may become obsolete even though it is in excellent physical condition; it becomes obsolete because better planes of superior design and performance have become available.

Chrysler Corporation recently opened the Jefferson North Assembly Plant in the heart of Detroit. Did Chrysler build this plant because existing facilities had become physically deteriorated beyond use? The answer is no. While existing facilities could still be used to produce automobiles, their production methods had become obsolete.

The Jefferson North Assembly Plant employs some of the most innovative technologies in the automotive industry. As a result, Chrysler can produce vehicles of higher quality, at a lower cost, and with less pollution than ever before.

**CASE IN POINT**

## Methods of Computing Depreciation

In Chapter 4, we computed depreciation only by the **straight-line depreciation** method. Companies actually may use any of several depreciation methods. Generally accepted accounting principles require only that a depreciation method result in a *rational and systematic* allocation of cost over the asset's useful life. The straight-line method is by far the most commonly used depreciation method for financial reporting purposes.

**LO 3**
Compute depreciation by the straight-line and declining-balance methods.

The straight-line method allocates an *equal portion* of depreciation expense to each period of the asset's useful life. Most of the other depreciation methods are various forms of accelerated depreciation. The term **accelerated depreciation** means that larger amounts of depreciation are recognized in the early years of the asset's life, and smaller amounts are recognized in the later years. Over the entire life of the asset, however, both the straight-line method and accelerated methods recognize the same *total* amount of depreciation.

The differences between the straight-line methods and accelerated methods are illustrated in the following graphs:

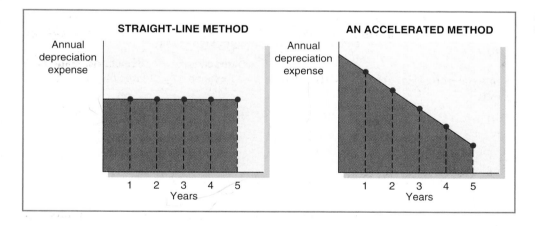

*Both methods recognize the same total depreciation*

There is only one straight-line method. But there are several accelerated methods, each producing slightly different results. Different depreciation methods may be used for different assets. Of course, the depreciation methods in use should be disclosed in notes accompanying the financial statements.

In this chapter, we illustrate and explain straight-line depreciation and one variation of the most widely used accelerated method, which is called *fixed-percentage-of-declining-balance.* Other depreciation methods are discussed briefly in the *Supplemental Topic* at the end of the chapter.

**Data for Our Illustrations**   Our illustrations of depreciation methods are based on the following data: On January 2, S&G Wholesale Grocery acquires a new delivery truck. The data and estimates needed for the computation of the annual depreciation expense are:

| | |
|---|---:|
| Cost . . . . . . . . . . . . . . . . . . . . . . . . . . . . . . . . . . . . . . . . . . . . . . . . . . . . . . . . . . . . . . . . . . . . . . . . | $17,000 |
| Estimated residual value . . . . . . . . . . . . . . . . . . . . . . . . . . . . . . . . . . . . . . . . . . . . . . . . . | $ 2,000 |
| Estimated useful life . . . . . . . . . . . . . . . . . . . . . . . . . . . . . . . . . . . . . . . . . . . . . . . . . . . . . | 5 years |

## The Straight-Line Method

Under the straight-line method, an *equal portion* of the asset's cost is recognized as depreciation expense in each period of the asset's useful life. Annual depreciation expense is computed by deducting the estimated **residual value** (or **salvage value**) from the cost of the asset and dividing the remaining *depreciable cost* by the years of estimated useful life. Using the data in our example, the annual straight-line depreciation is computed as follows:

$$\frac{\text{Cost} - \text{Residual Value}}{\text{Years of Useful Life}} = \frac{\$17,000 - \$2,000}{5 \text{ years}} = \$3,000 \text{ per year}$$

This same depreciation computation is shown in tabular form as follows:

*Computing depreciation by the straight-line method*

| | |
|---|---:|
| Cost of the depreciable asset . . . . . . . . . . . . . . . . . . . . . . . . . . . . . . . . . . . . . . . . . . . . . | $17,000 |
| Less: Estimated residual value (amount to be realized by sale of asset when it is retired from use) . . . . . . . . . . . . . . . . . . . . . . . . . . . . . . . . . . . . . . . . | 2,000 |
| Total amount to be depreciated (depreciable cost) . . . . . . . . . . . . . . . . . . . . . . . | $15,000 |
| Estimated useful life . . . . . . . . . . . . . . . . . . . . . . . . . . . . . . . . . . . . . . . . . . . . . . . . . . . . | 5 years |
| Depreciation expense each year ($15,000 ÷ 5) . . . . . . . . . . . . . . . . . . . . . . . . . | $ 3,000 |

The following schedule summarizes the effects of straight-line depreciation over the entire life of the asset:

**Depreciation Schedule: Straight-Line Method**

*Constant annual depreciation expense*

| Year | Computation | Depreciation Expense | Accumulated Depreciation | Book Value |
|---|---|---:|---:|---:|
| | | | | $17,000 |
| First . . . . . . . . . . . . . . . . . . . | $15,000 × 1/5 | $ 3,000 | $ 3,000 | 14,000 |
| Second . . . . . . . . . . . . . . . . . | $15,000 × 1/5 | 3,000 | 6,000 | 11,000 |
| Third . . . . . . . . . . . . . . . . . . . | $15,000 × 1/5 | 3,000 | 9,000 | 8,000 |
| Fourth . . . . . . . . . . . . . . . . . . | $15,000 × 1/5 | 3,000 | 12,000 | 5,000 |
| Fifth . . . . . . . . . . . . . . . . . . . . | $15,000 × 1/5 | 3,000 | 15,000 | 2,000 |
| Total . . . . . . . . . . . . . . . . . | | $15,000 | | |

(We present several depreciation schedules in this chapter. In each schedule we highlight in red those features that we want to emphasize.)

Notice that the depreciation expense over the life of the truck totals *$15,000*—the cost of the truck *minus the estimated residual value.* The residual value is *not* part of the cost "used up" in business operations. Instead, the residual value is expected to be recovered in cash upon disposal of the asset.

In practice, residual values are ignored if they are not expected to be *material* in amount. Traditionally, buildings, office equipment, furniture, fixtures, and special-purpose equipment seldom are considered to have significant residual values. Assets such as vehicles, aircraft, and construction equipment, in contrast, often do have residual values that are material in amount.

It often is convenient to state the portion of an asset's depreciable cost that will be written off during the year as a percentage, called the *depreciation rate*. When straight-line depreciation is in use, the depreciation rate is simply *1* divided by the *life* (in years) of the asset. The delivery truck in our example has an estimated life of 5 years, so the depreciation expense each year is $\frac{1}{5}$, or *20%*, of the depreciable amount. Similarly, an asset with a 10-year life has a depreciation rate of $\frac{1}{10}$, or *10%;* and an asset with an 8-year life, a depreciation rate of $\frac{1}{8}$, or *12½%*.

---

### You as a Business Owner

Assume you are the owner of a trucking company that has just invested $150,000 in a new truck. Working with your accountant, you are in the process of estimating its useful life and residual value. Your estimates will be used to compute straight-line depreciation expense for financial reporting purposes.

What factors should you take into consideration in developing these estimates? Discuss briefly how these factors will influence the amount of depreciation expense reported by your company each year.

*Our comments appear on page 400.

**YOUR TURN**

---

**Depreciation for Fractional Periods**   When an asset is acquired in the middle of an accounting period, it is not necessary to compute depreciation expense to the nearest day or week. In fact, such a computation would give a misleading impression of great precision. Since depreciation is based on an estimated useful life of many years, the depreciation applicable to any one year is *only an approximation.*

One widely used method of computing depreciation for part of a year is to round the calculation to the nearest whole month. In our example, S&G acquired the delivery truck on January 2. Therefore, we computed a full year's depreciation for the year of acquisition. Assume, however, that the truck had been acquired later in the year, say, on *October 1*. Thus the truck would have been in use for only 3 months (or $\frac{3}{12}$) of the first year. In this case, depreciation expense for the first year would be limited to only *$750*, or $\frac{3}{12}$ of a full year's depreciation ($3,000 $\times$ $\frac{3}{12}$ = $750).

An even more widely used approach, called the **half-year convention**, is to record six months' depreciation on all assets acquired during the year. This approach is based on the assumption that the actual purchase dates will average out to approximately midyear. The half-year convention is widely used for assets such as office equipment, automobiles, and machinery.

Assume that S&G Wholesale Grocery uses straight-line depreciation with the half-year convention. Depreciation on the $17,000 delivery truck with the 5-year life is summarized as follows:

| Year | Computation | Depreciation Expense | Accumulated Depreciation | Book Value |
|------|-------------|----------------------|--------------------------|------------|
| **Depreciation Schedule** Straight-Line Method with Half-Year Convention | | | | |
| | | | | $17,000 |
| First | $15,000 × $\frac{1}{5}$ × $\frac{1}{2}$ | $ 1,500 | $ 1,500 | 15,500 |
| Second | $15,000 × $\frac{1}{5}$ | 3,000 | 4,500 | 12,500 |
| Third | $15,000 × $\frac{1}{5}$ | 3,000 | 7,500 | 9,500 |
| Fourth | $15,000 × $\frac{1}{5}$ | 3,000 | 10,500 | 6,500 |
| Fifth | $15,000 × $\frac{1}{5}$ | 3,000 | 13,500 | 3,500 |
| Sixth | $15,000 × $\frac{1}{5}$ × $\frac{1}{2}$ | 1,500 | 15,000 | 2,000 |
| Total | | $15,000 | | |

*Straight-line with the half-year convention*

When the half-year convention is in use, we ignore the date on which the asset was actually purchased. We simply recognize *one-half year's depreciation* in both the first year and last year of the depreciation schedule. Notice that our depreciation schedule now includes depreciation expense in 6 years, instead of 5. Taking only a partial year's depreciation in the first year always extends the depreciation program into one additional year.

The half-year convention enables us to treat similar assets acquired at different dates during the year as a single group. For example, assume that an insurance company purchases hundreds of desktop computers throughout the current year at a total cost of $600,000. The company depreciates these computers by the straight-line method, assuming a 5-year life and no residual value. Using the half-year convention, the depreciation expense on all of the computers purchased during the year may be computed as follows: $600,000 ÷ 5 years × $^{6}/_{12}$ = $60,000. If we did not use the half-year convention, depreciation would have to be computed separately for computers purchased in different months.

## The Declining-Balance Method

By far the most widely used accelerated depreciation method is called **fixed-percentage-of-declining-balance depreciation**. However, the method is used primarily in *income tax returns,* rather than financial statements.[3]

Under the declining-balance method, an accelerated *depreciation rate* is computed as a specified percentage of the straight-line depreciation rate. Annual depreciation expense then is computed by applying this accelerated depreciation rate to the undepreciated cost (current book value) of the asset. This computation may be summarized as follows:

$$\frac{\text{Depreciation}}{\text{Expense}} = \frac{\text{Remaining}}{\text{Book Value}} \times \frac{\text{Accelerated}}{\text{Depreciation Rate}}$$

The accelerated depreciation rate *remains constant* throughout the life of the asset. Hence, the rate represents the "fixed-percentage" described in the name of this depreciation method. The book value (cost minus accumulated depreciation) *decreases every year* and represents the "declining-balance."

Thus far, we have described the accelerated depreciation rate as a "specified percentage" of the straight-line rate. Most often, this specified percentage is 200%, meaning that the accelerated rate is exactly twice the straight-line rate. As a result, the declining-balance method of depreciation often is called *double-declining-balance* (or 200%-declining-balance). Tax rules, however, often specify a *lower* percentage, such as 150% of the straight-line rate. This version of the declining-balance method may be described as "150%-declining-balance."[4]

**Double-Declining-Balance**     To illustrate the double-declining-balance method, consider our example of the $17,000 delivery truck. The estimated useful life is 5 years; therefore, the straight-line depreciation rate is 20% (1 ÷ 5 years). Doubling this straight-line rate indicates an accelerated depreciation rate of 40%. Each year, we will recognize as depreciation expense 40% of the truck's current book value, as follows:

---

[3] In 1986, Congress adopted an accelerated method of depreciation called the *Modified Accelerated Cost Recovery System* (or MACRS). Companies may use straight-line depreciation for federal income tax purposes, but most prefer to use MACRS because of its favorable income tax consequences. MACRS is the *only* accelerated depreciation method that may be used in federal income tax returns.

[4] The higher the specified percentage of the straight-line rate, the more accelerated this depreciation becomes. Experience and tradition have established 200% of the straight-line rate as the maximum level. For federal income tax purposes, MACRS (see footnote 3 above) is based upon a 200%-declining-balance for some assets, and a 150%-declining-balance method for others. The 150%-declining-balance slows down the rates at which taxpayers may depreciate specific types of assets in their income tax returns.

| Depreciation Schedule: 200% Declining-Balance Method | | | | |
|---|---|---|---|---|
| Year | Computation | Depreciation Expense | Accumulated Depreciation | Book Value |
| | | | | $17,000 |
| First . . . . . . . . . . . . . . | $17,000 × 40% | $ 6,800 | $ 6,800 | 10,200 |
| Second . . . . . . . . . . . . | $10,200 × 40% | 4,080 | 10,880 | 6,120 |
| Third . . . . . . . . . . . . . | $ 6,120 × 40% | 2,448 | 13,328 | 3,672 |
| Fourth . . . . . . . . . . . . . | $ 3,672 × 40% | 1,469 | 14,797 | 2,203 |
| Fifth . . . . . . . . . . . . . . | $ 2,203 − $2,000 | 203 | 15,000 | 2,000 |
| Total . . . . . . . . . . . . | | $15,000 | | |

*Declining-balance at twice the straight-line rate*

Notice that the estimated residual value of the delivery truck *does not* enter into the computation of depreciation expense until the very end. This is because the declining-balance method provides an *"automatic"* residual value. As long as each year's depreciation expense is equal to only a portion of the undepreciated cost of the asset, the asset *will never be entirely written off.* However, if the asset has a significant residual value, depreciation should *stop at this point.* Since our delivery truck has an estimated residual value of *$2,000,* the depreciation expense for the fifth year should be *limited to $203,* rather than the $881 indicated by taking 40% of the remaining book value. By limiting the last year's depreciation expense in this manner, the book value of the truck at the end of the fifth year will be equal to its $2,000 estimated residual value.

In the schedule illustrated above, we computed a full year's depreciation in the first year because the asset was acquired on January 2. But if the half-year convention were in use, depreciation in the first year would be *reduced by half,* to $3,400. The depreciation in the second year would be ($17,000 − $3,400) × 40%, or *$5,440.*

**150%-Declining-Balance**   Now assume that we wanted to depreciate this truck using 150% of the straight-line rate. In this case, the depreciation rate will be 30%, instead of 40% (a 20% straight-line rate × 150% = 30%). The depreciation schedule appears as follows:

| Depreciation Schedule: 150% Declining-Balance Method | | | | |
|---|---|---|---|---|
| Year | Computation | Depreciation Expense | Accumulated Depreciation | Book Value |
| | | | | $17,000 |
| First . . . . . . . . . | $17,000 × 30% | $ 5,100 | $ 5,100 | 11,900 |
| Second . . . . . . . | $11,900 × 30% | 3,570 | 8,670 | 8,330 |
| Third . . . . . . . . . | $8,330 × 30% | 2,499 | 11,169 | 5,831 |
| Fourth . . . . . . . . | ($5,831 − $2,000) ÷ 2 | 1,916* | 13,085 | 3,915 |
| Fifth . . . . . . . . . | $3,915 − $2,000 | 1,915* | 15,000 | 2,000 |
| Total | | $15,000 | | |

*Switched to the straight-line method for Years 4 and 5.

*Declining-balance at 150% of the straight-line rate*

Notice that we switched to straight-line depreciation in the last 2 years. The undepreciated cost of the truck at the end of Year 3 was *$5,831.* To depreciate the truck to an estimated residual value of $2,000 at the end of Year 5, $3,831 in depreciation expense must be recognized over the next 2 years. At this point, *larger depreciation charges* can be recognized if we simply allocate this $3,831 by the straight-line method, rather than continuing to compute 30% of the remaining book value. (In our table, we round the allocation of this amount to the nearest dollar.)

Allocating the remaining book value over the remaining life by the straight-line method does *not* represent a change in depreciation methods. Rather, a switch to straight-line when this will result in larger depreciation is *part of the declining-balance method.* This is the way in which we arrive at the desired residual value.

## Which Depreciation Methods Do Most Businesses Use?

Many businesses use the straight-line method of depreciation in their financial statements and accelerated methods in their income tax returns. The reasons for these choices are easy to understand.

Accelerated depreciation methods result in higher charges to depreciation expense early in the asset's life and, therefore, lower reported net income than straight-line depreciation. Most publicly owned companies want to appear as profitable as possible— certainly as profitable as their competitors. Therefore, the overwhelming majority of publicly owned companies use straight-line depreciation in their financial statements.

For income tax purposes, it's a different story. Management usually wants to report the *lowest* possible taxable income in the company's income tax returns. Accelerated depreciation methods can substantially reduce both taxable income and tax payments for a period of years.[5]

Accounting principles and income tax laws both permit companies to use *different depreciation methods* in their financial statements and their income tax returns. Therefore, many companies use straight-line depreciation in their financial statements and accelerated methods (variations of the declining-balance method) in their income tax returns.

**The Differences in Depreciation Methods: Are They "Real"?**   Using the straight-line depreciation method will cause a company to *report* higher profits than would be reported if an accelerated method were in use. But *is* the company better off than if it had used an accelerated method? The answer is *no!* Depreciation—no matter how it is computed—*is only an estimate.* The amount of this estimate has *no effect* on the actual financial strength of the business. Thus a business that uses an accelerated depreciation method in its financial statements is simply measuring its net income *more conservatively* than a business that uses straight-line.

---

**CASH EFFECTS**   The benefits of using an accelerated method for income tax purposes are real because the amount of depreciation claimed affects the amount of taxes owed. Lower income taxes translate directly into increased cash availability.

---

In the preceding chapter, we made the point that if a company wants to use LIFO in its income tax return, it *must* use LIFO in its financial statements. *No such requirement exists for depreciation methods.* A company may use an accelerated method in its income tax returns and the straight-line method in its financial statements—and most companies do.

---

[5] For a *growing* business, the use of accelerated depreciation in income tax returns may reduce taxable income *every* year. This is because a growing business may always have more assets in the early years of their recovery periods than in the later years.

YOUR TURN

## You as a Business Consultant

Assume you are a consultant to a promising new service company. The company is owned privately by a pool of 100 investors. However, its goal is to "go public" after just five years of operations. The company's current investment in buildings and office equipment is expected to be adequate until its stock is traded publicly.

Management has recently given you a business plan to review. In it, you note that an accelerated method of depreciation was used in making all income projections. Using this information, you have recomputed depreciation expense under the straight-line method. A comparison of your depreciation expense figures for the next five years with those of management is shown below (based on average useful life of 20 years):

| | Annual Depreciation Expense (in 000's) | |
| --- | --- | --- |
| | Accelerated | Straight-line |
| Year 1 | $2,000 | $1,000 |
| Year 2 | 1,800 | 1,000 |
| Year 3 | 1,620 | 1,000 |
| Year 4 | 1,450 | 1,000 |
| Year 5 | 1,305 | 1,000 |

Explain to management why the company should consider using straight-line depreciation for financial reporting purposes instead of the accelerated method.

*Our comments appear on pages 400–401.

## Financial Statement Disclosures

A company should *disclose* in notes to its financial statements the methods used to depreciate plant assets. Readers of the statements should recognize that accelerated depreciation methods transfer the costs of plant assets to expense more quickly than the straight-line method. Thus accelerated methods result in more *conservative* (lower) balance sheet valuations of plant assets and measurements of net income.

**Estimates of Useful Life and Residual Value** Estimating the useful lives and residual values of plant assets is the *responsibility of management.* These estimates usually are based on the company's past experience with similar assets, but they also reflect the company's current circumstances and management's future plans. Thus the estimated lives of similar assets may vary from one company to another.

The estimated lives of plant assets affect the amount of net income reported each period. The longer the estimated useful life, the smaller the amount of cost transferred each period to depreciation expense and the larger the amount of reported net income. Bear in mind, however, that all large corporations are *audited* annually by a firm of independent public accountants. One of the responsibilities of these auditors is to determine that management's estimates of the useful lives of plant assets are reasonable under the circumstances.

Automobiles typically are depreciated over relatively short estimated lives—say, from 3 to 5 years. Most other types of equipment are depreciated over a period of from 5 to 15 years. Buildings are depreciated over much longer lives—perhaps 30 to 50 years for a new building and 15 years or more for a building acquired used.

**The Principle of Consistency** The *consistent* application of accounting methods is a generally accepted accounting principle. With respect to depreciation methods, this principle means that a company should *not change* from year to year the method used in computing the depreciation expense for a given plant asset. However, management *may* use different methods in computing depreciation for different assets. Also, as we have stressed repeatedly, a company may—and often *must*—use different depreciation methods in its financial statements and income tax returns.

**Revision of Estimated Useful Lives**   What should be done if, after a few years of using a plant asset, management decides that the asset actually is going to last for a considerably longer or shorter period than was originally estimated? When this situation arises, a *revised estimate* of useful life should be made and the periodic depreciation expense decreased or increased accordingly.

The procedure for correcting the depreciation schedule is to spread the remaining undepreciated cost of the asset *over the years of remaining useful life.* This correction affects only the amount of depreciation expense that will be recorded in the current and future periods. The financial statements of past periods are *not* revised to reflect changes in the estimated useful lives of depreciable assets.

To illustrate, assume that a company acquires a $10,000 asset estimated to have a 5-year useful life and no residual value. Under the straight-line method, the annual depreciation expense is $2,000. At the end of the third year, accumulated depreciation amounts to $6,000, and the asset has an undepreciated cost (or book value) of $4,000.

At the beginning of the fourth year, it is decided that the asset will last for 5 *more* years. The revised estimate of useful life is, therefore, a total of 8 years. The depreciation expense to be recognized for the fourth year and for each of the remaining years is $800, computed as follows:

| | |
|---|---:|
| Undepreciated cost at end of third year ($10,000 − $6,000) . . . . . . . . . . . . . . . . . . . . | $4,000 |
| Revised estimate of remaining years of useful life . . . . . . . . . . . . . . . . . . . . . . . . . . . | 5 years |
| Revised amount of annual depreciation expense ($4,000 ÷ 5) . . . . . . . . . . . . . . . . . . | $ 800 |

## The Impairment of Plant Assets

On occasion, it may become apparent that a company cannot reasonably expect to recover the cost of certain plant assets, either through use or through sale. For example, a computer manufacturer may have paid a very high price to acquire specialized production equipment. If new technology soon renders the equipment obsolete, however, it may become apparent that it is worth far less than its cost.

If the cost of an asset cannot be recovered through future use or sale, the asset should be *written down* to its net realizable value. The offsetting debit is to a loss account. These write-offs generally do *not* enter into the determination of taxable income.

**CASE IN POINT**

Several years ago, **Chrysler Corporation** made a strategic commitment to focus on its core automotive manufacturing business. Thus the company sold its **Thrifty Rent-A-Car** subsidiary. Realizing it could not possibly recover the cost of this subsidiary, **Chrysler** recorded a $100 million charge against income to write down **Thrifty**'s assets to their net realizable values.

## DISPOSAL OF PLANT AND EQUIPMENT

**LO 4**

Account for disposals of plant assets.

When depreciable assets are disposed of at any date other than the end of the year, an entry should be made to record depreciation for the *fraction of the year* ending with the date of disposal. If the half-year convention is in use, six months' depreciation should be recorded on all assets disposed of during the year. In the following illustrations of the disposal of items of plant and equipment, it is assumed that any necessary entries for fractional-period depreciation already have been recorded.

As units of plant and equipment wear out or become obsolete, they must be scrapped, sold, or traded in on new equipment. Upon the disposal or retirement of a depreciable asset, the cost of the property is removed from the asset account, and the accumulated depreciation is removed from the related contra-asset account. Assume, for example, that office equipment purchased 10 years ago at a cost of $20,000 has been fully depreciated and is no longer useful. The entry to record the scrapping of the worthless equipment is as follows:

| | | |
|---|---|---|
| Accumulated Depreciation: Office Equipment . . . . . . . . . . . . . . . . . . . . . . | 20,000 | |
|     Office Equipment . . . . . . . . . . . . . . . . . . . . . . . . . . . . . . . . . . . . . . . | | 20,000 |

*Scrapping a fully depreciated asset*

To remove from the accounts the cost and the accumulated depreciation on fully depreciated office equipment now being scrapped. No salvage value.

Once an asset has been fully depreciated, no more depreciation should be recorded on it, even though the property may be in good condition and is still in use. The objective of depreciation is to spread the *cost* of an asset over the periods of its usefulness; in no case can depreciation expense be greater than the amount paid for the asset. When a fully depreciated asset remains in use beyond the original estimate of useful life, the asset account and the Accumulated Depreciation account should remain in the accounting records without further entries until the asset is retired.

## Gains and Losses on Disposals of Plant and Equipment

Since the residual values and useful lives of plant assets are only estimates, it is not uncommon for plant assets to be sold at prices that differ from their book value at the date of disposal. When plant assets are sold, any gain or loss on the disposal is computed by comparing the *book value with the amount received from the sale.* A sales price in excess of the book value produces a gain; a sales price below the book value produces a loss. These gains or losses, if material in amount, should be shown separately in the income statement following the computation of income from operations.

Asset dispositions occur frequently in many businesses, and the gains and losses that result often are material in amount. For instance, recent financial statements of **U.S. Steel** and **Dow Chemical** reported gains on asset dispositions of $40 million and $24 million, respectively. The income statements of **Consolidated Freightlines** and **Ford Motor Company**, on the other hand, reported losses on asset dispositions of $4 million and $235 million, respectively.

**CASE IN POINT**

**Disposal at a Price above Book Value**   Assume that a machine costing $10,000 has a book value of $2,000 at the time it is sold for $3,000 cash. The journal entry to record this disposal is as follows:

| | | |
|---|---|---|
| Cash . . . . . . . . . . . . . . . . . . . . . . . . . . . . . . . . . . . . . . . . . . . . . . . . . . | 3,000 | |
| Accumulated Depreciation: Machinery . . . . . . . . . . . . . . . . . . . . . . . . . . | 8,000 | |
|     Machinery . . . . . . . . . . . . . . . . . . . . . . . . . . . . . . . . . . . . . . . . . . | | 10,000 |
|     Gain on Disposal of Plant Assets . . . . . . . . . . . . . . . . . . . . . . . . . . | | 1,000 |

*Gain on disposal of plant asset*

To record sale of machinery at a price above book value.

**Disposal at a Price below Book Value**   Now assume instead that the same machine is sold for $500. The journal entry in this case would be as follows:

*Loss on disposal of plant asset*

| | | |
|---|---:|---:|
| Cash | 500 | |
| Accumulated Depreciation: Machinery | 8,000 | |
| Loss on Disposal of Plant Assets | 1,500 | |
|     Machinery | | 10,000 |

To record sale of machinery at a price below book value.

The disposal of a depreciable asset at a price *equal to* book value would result in neither a gain nor a loss. The entry for such a transaction would consist of a debit to Cash for the amount received, a debit to Accumulated Depreciation for the balance accumulated, and a credit to the asset account for the original cost.

### Trading in Used Assets for New Ones

Certain types of depreciable assets, such as automobiles and trucks, sometimes are traded in for new assets of the same kind. In most instances, a trade-in is viewed as both a *sale* of the old asset and a purchase of a new one.

To illustrate, assume that Rancho Landscape has an old pickup truck that originally cost $10,000 but that now has a book value (and tax basis) of $2,000. Rancho trades in this old truck for a new one with a fair market value of $15,000. The truck dealership grants Rancho a trade-in allowance of $3,500 for the old truck, and Rancho pays the remaining $11,500 cost of the new truck in cash. Rancho Landscape should record this transaction as follows:

*Entry to record a typical trade-in*

| | | |
|---|---:|---:|
| Vehicles (new truck) | 15,000 | |
| Accumulated Depreciation: Trucks (old truck) | 8,000 | |
|     Vehicles (old truck) | | 10,000 |
|     Gain on Disposal of Plant Assets | | 1,500 |
|     Cash | | 11,500 |

Traded in old truck for a new one costing $15,000. Received $3,500
  trade-in allowance on the old truck, which had a book value of $2,000.

Notice that Rancho views the $3,500 trade-in allowance granted by the truck dealership as the *sales price* of the old truck. Thus Rancho recognizes a *$1,500 gain* on the disposal (trade-in) of this asset ($3,500 trade-in allowance − $2,000 book value = $1,500 gain).

For financial reporting purposes, gains and losses on routine trade-ins are recorded in the accounting records whenever the transaction also involves the payment of a significant amount of cash (or the creation of debt).[6] Income tax rules do *not* permit recognition of gains or losses on exchanges of assets that are used for similar purposes. Thus the $1,500 gain recorded in our example is not regarded as taxable income.[7]

## INTANGIBLE ASSETS

### Characteristics

**LO 5**

Explain the nature of intangible assets, including goodwill.

As the word *intangible* suggests, assets in this classification have no physical substance. Common examples are goodwill, patents, and trademarks. Intangible assets are classified in the balance sheet as a subgroup of plant assets. However, not all assets that lack

---

[6] The FASB Emerging Issues Task Force takes the position that when 25% or more of the transaction value is comprised of cash or monetary obligations, the transaction should be viewed as *monetary*, rather than nonmonetary. Thus gains on most routine trade-ins should be *recognized in full*, rather than "deferred" as they are for income tax purposes. See *EITF Abstract Nos. 84-29, 86-29, and 87-29.*

[7] Had the trade-in allowance been less than book value, the resulting loss would *not be deductible* in the determination of taxable income.

physical substance are regarded as intangible assets. An account receivable, for example, has no physical attributes but is classified as a current asset and is not regarded as an intangible. In brief, *intangible assets are assets that are used in the operation of the business but that have no physical substance and are noncurrent.*

The basis of valuation for intangible assets is cost. In some companies, however, certain intangible assets such as trademarks may be of great importance but may have been acquired without incurring any significant cost. These intangible assets appear in the balance sheet at their *cost,* regardless of their value to the company. Intangible assets are listed only if significant costs are incurred in their acquisition or development. If these costs are *insignificant,* they are treated as revenue expenditures (ordinary expenses).

## Operating Expenses versus Intangible Assets

For an expenditure to qualify as an intangible asset, there must be reasonable evidence of future benefits. Many expenditures offer some prospects of yielding benefits in subsequent years, but the existence and life span of these benefits are so uncertain that most companies treat these expenditures as operating expenses. Examples are the expenditures for intensive advertising campaigns to introduce new products and the expense of training employees to work with new types of machinery or office equipment. There is little doubt that some benefits from these outlays continue beyond the current period, but because of the uncertain duration of the benefits, it is almost universal practice to treat expenditures of this nature as an expense of the current period.

## Amortization

The term **amortization** describes the systematic write-off to expense of the cost of an intangible asset over its useful life. The usual accounting entry for amortization consists of a debit to Amortization Expense and a credit to the intangible asset account. There is no theoretical objection to crediting an accumulated amortization account rather than the intangible asset account, but this method is seldom encountered in practice.

Although it is difficult to estimate the useful life of an intangible such as a trademark, it is highly probable that such an asset will not contribute to future earnings on a permanent basis. The cost of the intangible asset should, therefore, be deducted from revenue during the years in which it may be expected to aid in producing revenue. Under the current rules of the Financial Accounting Standards Board, the maximum period for amortization of an intangible asset is *40 years.*[8] The straight-line method normally is used for amortizing intangible assets.

## Goodwill

Business executives used the term **goodwill** in a variety of ways before it became part of accounting terminology. One of the most common meanings of goodwill in a nonaccounting sense concerns the benefits derived from a favorable reputation among customers. To accountants, however, goodwill has a very specific meaning not necessarily limited to customer relations. It means the *present value of future earnings in excess of the normal return on net identifiable assets.* Above-average earnings may arise not only from favorable customer relations but also from such factors as superior management, manufacturing efficiency, and weak competition.

The **present value** of future cash flows is the amount that a knowledgeable investor would pay today for the right to receive those future cash flows. (The present value concept is discussed further in later chapters and in Appendix B.)

---

[8] *APB Opinion No. 17,* "Intangible Assets," AICPA (New York: 1970), par. 29.

The phrase *normal return on net identifiable assets* also requires explanation. *Net assets* means the owners' equity in a business, or assets minus liabilities. Goodwill, however, is not an *identifiable* asset. The existence of goodwill is implied by the ability of a business to earn an above-average return; however, the cause and precise dollar value of goodwill are largely matters of personal opinion. Therefore, **net identifiable assets** mean all assets *except goodwill,* minus liabilities.

A *normal return* on net identifiable assets is the rate of return that investors demand in a particular industry to justify their buying a business at the fair market value of its net identifiable assets. A business has goodwill when investors will pay a *higher* price because the business earns *more* than the normal rate of return.

Assume that two similar restaurants are offered for sale and that the normal return on the fair market value of the net identifiable assets of restaurants of this type is 15% a year. The relative earning power of the two restaurants during the past five years is as follows:

*Which business is worth more?*

| | Mandarin Coast | Golden Dragon |
|---|---|---|
| Fair market value of net identifiable assets . . . . . . . . . . . . . . . . . . . . | $1,000,000 | $1,000,000 |
| Normal rate of return on net assets . . . . . . . . . . . . . . . . . . . . . . . . | 15% | 15% |
| Normal earnings, computed as 15% of net identifiable assets . . . . . . | 150,000 | 150,000 |
| Average actual net income for past five years . . . . . . . . . . . . . . . . | $ 150,000 | $ 200,000 |
| Earnings in excess of normal . . . . . . . . . . . . . . . . . . . . . . . . . . . . | $     –0– | $   50,000 |

An investor presumably would be willing to pay $1,000,000 to buy Mandarin Coast, because this restaurant earns the normal 15% return that justifies the fair market value of its net identifiable assets. Although Golden Dragon has the same amount of net identifiable assets, an investor probably would be willing to pay *more* for Golden Dragon than for Mandarin Coast, because Golden Dragon has a long record of superior earnings. The *extra amount* that a buyer would pay to purchase Golden Dragon represents the value of this business's *goodwill.*

**CASE IN POINT**

Accounting for goodwill has significant variation around the world. Some countries (for example, Denmark, Switzerland, and Germany) allow goodwill to be charged directly to equity with no requirement for amortization. Other countries (e.g., Japan or South Korea) severely limit the time period for amortizing goodwill to five years. Finally, accounting requirements in some countries (e.g., France or China) make no mention of goodwill.

**Estimating Goodwill**    How much will an investor pay for goodwill? Above-average earnings in past years are of significance to prospective purchasers only if they believe that these earnings *will continue* after they acquire the business. Investors' appraisals of goodwill, therefore, will vary with their estimates of the *future earning power* of the business. Very few businesses, however, are able to maintain above-average earnings for more than a few years. Consequently, the purchaser of a business will usually limit any amount paid for goodwill to not more than four or five times the amount by which annual earnings exceed normal earnings.

Arriving at a fair value for the goodwill of an ongoing business is a difficult and subjective process. Any estimate of goodwill is in large part a matter of personal opinion. The following are two methods that a prospective purchaser might use in estimating a value for goodwill:

1. *Value the business as a whole, and then subtract the current market value of the net identifiable assets.* The value of a business often is expressed by the *price-earnings ratio* (p/e ratio) of the company's stock. A p/e ratio shows the current relationship between the market price of a company's stock and the company's earnings.

Assume that highly successful restaurants in this area currently sell at about 6½ times annual earnings.[9] This p/e ratio suggests that Golden Dragon is worth about $1,300,000 ($200,000 average net income × 6½). As the net identifiable assets have a market value of $1,000,000, this implies the existence of *$300,000* in goodwill.

2. *Capitalize the amount by which earnings exceed normal amounts.* "Capitalizing" an earnings stream means dividing those earnings by the investor's required rate of return. The result is the maximum amount that the investor could pay for the excess earnings to achieve the required rate of return on the investment. To illustrate, assume that the prospective buyer decides to capitalize the $50,000 annual excess earnings of Golden Dragon at a rate of 25%. This approach results in a *$200,000* estimate ($50,000 ÷ .25 = $200,000) for the value of goodwill. (Note that $50,000 per year represents a 25% return on a $200,000 investment.)

A weakness in the capitalization method is that *no provision is made for the recovery of the investment.* If the prospective buyer is to earn a 25% return on the $200,000 investment in goodwill, either the excess earnings must continue *forever* (an unlikely assumption) or the buyer must be able to recover the $200,000 investment at a later date by selling the business at a price above the fair market value of net identifiable assets.

Notice that our two approaches resulted in very different estimates of Golden Dragon's goodwill—$300,000 and $200,000. Such differences occur often in practice. The value of goodwill depends on *future performance.* Therefore, there is *no* "surefire way" of determining its real value. At best, the value of a company's goodwill is only an educated guess.

Notice that the two approaches to valuing Golden Dragon's goodwill are dependent on numbers reported in external financial reports. Earnings is a key component in both computations; however, both approaches also use current market information. The first begins by valuing the business as a whole with a price/earnings multiple and then deducts the current fair market value of the business's assets. The second approach capitalizes the amount by which reported earnings exceed normal earnings, where normal earnings are based on current market conditions.

When considering the purchase or sale of existing businesses, most managers use a variety of methods to value those businesses; to a certain extent these methods are based on numbers from external financial reports.

**MANAGEMENT STRATEGY**

**Recording Goodwill in the Accounts** Because of the difficulties in objectively estimating the value of goodwill, this asset is recorded only when it is *purchased.* Goodwill is purchased when one company buys another. The purchaser records the identifiable assets it has purchased at their fair market values and then debits any additional amount paid to an asset account entitled Goodwill.

Generally accepted accounting principles have historically required that goodwill be amortized over a period *not exceeding* 40 years. However, the concept of *conservatism* suggests that goodwill should be amortized over a much shorter period under most

---

[9] Investments in small businesses involve more risk and less liquidity than investments in publicly owned companies. For these reasons, the p/e ratios of small businesses tend to be substantially lower than those of publicly owned corporations.

circumstances. The FASB is currently examining the maximum time period over which goodwill may be amortized.[10]

**But Most Goodwill Never Gets Recorded!**    Many businesses never purchase goodwill but *generate it internally* by developing good customer relations, superior management, or other factors that result in above-average earnings. Because there is no objective way of determining the value of goodwill unless the business is sold, internally generated goodwill is *not recorded* in the accounting records. Thus goodwill may be an important asset of a successful business but *may not even appear* in the company's balance sheet.

The absence of internally generated goodwill is, perhaps, the principal reason why a balance sheet does not indicate a company's current market value.

**Goodwill or Bad Judgment?**    Some companies have paid huge amounts for goodwill, only to discover that the businesses they have purchased do *not* continue to earn above-normal rates of return. In these cases, the goodwill is not an asset with future economic value. Rather, it indicates that the company paid too high a price to acquire the other business. If it becomes apparent that purchased goodwill does *not* have real economic value, it should be written off immediately.

In summary, the best evidence of a company's goodwill is not the amount listed in the balance sheet. Rather, it is a long and ongoing track record of *above-average earnings.*

## Patents

A patent is an exclusive right granted by the federal government for manufacture, use, and sale of a particular product. The purpose of this exclusive grant is to encourage the invention of new products and processes. When a company acquires a patent by purchase from the inventor or other holder, the purchase price should be recorded by debiting the intangible asset account Patents.

Patents are granted for 17 years, and the period of amortization should not exceed that period. However, if the patent is likely to lose its usefulness in less than 17 years, amortization should be based on the shorter estimated useful life. Assume that a patent is purchased from the inventor at a cost of $100,000 after 5 years of the legal life have expired. The remaining *legal* life is, therefore, 12 years. But if the estimated *useful* life is only 4 years, amortization should be based on this shorter period. The entry to record the annual amortization expense would be:

*Entry for amortization of patent*

| | | |
|---|---|---|
| Amortization Expense: Patents . . . . . . . . . . . . . . . . . . . . . . . . . . . . . . . . . . . . | 25,000 | |
|     Patents . . . . . . . . . . . . . . . . . . . . . . . . . . . . . . . . . . . . . . . . . . . . . . . | | 25,000 |

To amortize cost of patent on a straight-line basis over an estimated life
of 4 years.

## Trademarks and Trade Names

Coca-Cola's famous name, usually printed in a distinctive typeface, is a classic example of a trademark known around the world. A trademark is a name, symbol, or design that identifies a product or group of products. A permanent exclusive right to the use of a trademark, brand name, or commercial symbol may be obtained by registering it with the federal government.

The costs of developing a trademark or brand name often consist of advertising campaigns, which should be treated as expenses when incurred. If a trademark or brand name

---

[10] In addition to determining the maximum time period over which goodwill may be amortized, the FASB is examining alternative ways to present amortization expense associated with goodwill in the financial statements.

is *purchased,* however, the cost may be substantial. Such cost should be capitalized and amortized to expense over a period of not more than 40 years. If the use of the trademark is discontinued or its contribution to earnings becomes doubtful, any unamortized cost should be written off immediately.

## Franchises

A franchise is a right granted by a company or a governmental unit to conduct a certain type of business in a specific geographical area. An example of a franchise is the right to operate a McDonald's restaurant in a specific neighborhood. The cost of franchises varies greatly and often is quite substantial. When the cost of a franchise is small, it may be charged immediately to expense or amortized over a short period such as 5 years. When the cost is material, amortization should be based on the life of the franchise (if limited); the amortization period, however, may not exceed 40 years.

## Copyrights

A copyright is an exclusive right granted by the federal government to protect the production and sale of literary or artistic materials for the life of the creator plus 50 years. The cost of obtaining a copyright in some cases is minor and therefore is chargeable to expense when paid. Only when a copyright is *purchased* will the expenditure be *material enough* to warrant its being capitalized and spread over the useful life. The revenue from copyrights is usually limited to only a few years, and the purchase cost should, of course, be amortized over the years in which the revenue is expected.

## Other Intangibles and Deferred Charges

Among the other intangibles found in the published balance sheets of large corporations are moving costs, plant rearrangement costs, formulas, processes, name lists, and film rights. Some companies group items of this type under the title of Deferred Charges, meaning expenditures that will provide benefits beyond the current year and that will be written off to expense over their useful economic lives. It is also common practice to combine these items under the heading of Other Assets, which is listed at the bottom of the balance sheet.

## Research and Development (R&D) Costs

The spending of billions of dollars each year on research and development of new products is a striking characteristic of U.S. industry. The annual research and development expenditures of some companies often exceed $1 billion and account for a substantial percentage of their total costs and expenses.

In the past, some companies treated all research and development costs as expenses in the year incurred; other companies in the same industry recorded these costs as intangible assets to be amortized over future years. This diversity of practice prevented financial statements of different companies from being comparable.

The lack of uniformity in accounting for R&D was ended when the Financial Accounting Standards Board ruled that all research and development expenditures should be charged to expense *when incurred.*[11] This action by the FASB had the beneficial effect of reducing the number of alternative accounting practices and helping to make financial statements of different companies more comparable.

---

[11] FASB, Statement No. 2, "Accounting for Research and Development Costs" (Norwalk, Conn.: 1974), par. 12.

## FINANCIAL ANALYSIS

The success of many businesses frequently depends on research and development activities (R&D). To better understand a company's commitment to funding R&D, users of financial statements often examine trends in a company's R&D expenditures as a percentage of total operating expenses:

### R&D % = R&D Costs ÷ Total Operating Expenses

R&D expenditures as a percentage of total operating costs are naturally higher in some industries than in others. To illustrate this point, recent R&D figures of well-known companies from four industries are shown below:

|  | R&D Costs (in millions) | ÷ | Total Operating Expenses (in millions) | = | R&D% |
|---|---|---|---|---|---|
| **Chemical Products** | | | | | |
| DuPont . . . . . . . . . . . . . . . . . . . . . . . . . . . | $1,617 | | $26,950 | | 6.0% |
| Dow Chemical . . . . . . . . . . . . . . . . . . . . . | 807 | | 17,055 | | 4.7 |
| **Computer Hardware** | | | | | |
| Sun Microsystems . . . . . . . . . . . . . . . . . . | 1,263 | | 10,205 | | 12.4 |
| Silicon Graphics . . . . . . . . . . . . . . . . . . . . | 301 | | 2,692 | | 11.2 |
| **Pharmaceuticals** | | | | | |
| Eli Lilly & Co. . . . . . . . . . . . . . . . . . . . . . . | 1,784 | | 6,758 | | 26.4 |
| Pfizer . . . . . . . . . . . . . . . . . . . . . . . . . . . . | 2,279 | | 10,950 | | 20.8 |
| **Computer Software** | | | | | |
| Netscape . . . . . . . . . . . . . . . . . . . . . . . . | 123 | | 396 | | 31.1 |
| Microsoft . . . . . . . . . . . . . . . . . . . . . . . . . | 3,775 | | 12,019 | | 31.4 |

## NATURAL RESOURCES

### Accounting for Natural Resources

**LO 6**

Account for the depletion of natural resources.

Mining properties, oil and gas reserves, and tracts of standing timber are leading examples of natural resources. The distinguishing characteristic of these assets is that they are physically removed from their natural environment and are converted into inventory. Theoretically, a coal mine might be regarded as an underground inventory of coal; however, such an inventory is certainly not a current asset. In the balance sheet, mining property and other natural resources are classified as property, plant, and equipment. Once the coal is removed from the ground, however, this coal *does* represent inventory.

We have explained that plant assets such as buildings and equipment depreciate because of physical deterioration or obsolescence. A mine or an oil reserve does not depreciate for these reasons, but it is gradually *depleted* as the natural resource is removed from the ground. Once all of the coal has been removed from a coal mine, for example, the mine is "fully depleted" and will be abandoned or sold for its residual value.

To illustrate the **depletion** of a natural resource, assume that Rainbow Minerals pays $45 million to acquire the Red Valley Mine, which is believed to contain 10 million tons of coal. The residual value of the mine after all of the coal is removed is estimated to be $5 million. The depletion that will occur over the life of the mine is the original cost minus the residual value, or $40 million. This depletion will occur at the rate of *$4 per* *ton* ($40 million ÷ 10 million tons) as the coal is removed from the mine. If we assume that 2 million tons are mined during the first year of operations, the entry to record the depletion of the mine would be as follows:

| | | |
|---|---|---|
| Inventory ........................................ | 8,000,000 | |
|     Accumulated Depletion: Red Valley Mine ................... | | 8,000,000 |
| To record depletion of the Red Valley Mine for the year; | | |
|   2,000,000 tons mined @ $4 per ton. | | |

*Recording depletion*

Once removed from the mine, coal becomes merchandise available for sale. Therefore, the estimated cost of this coal is debited to the Inventory account. As the coal is sold, this cost is transferred from the Inventory account to the Cost of Goods Sold account.

Accumulated Depletion is a *contra-asset account* similar to the Accumulated Depreciation account; it represents the portion of the mine that has been used up (depleted) to date. In Rainbow Mineral's balance sheet, the Red Valley Mine now appears as follows:

| | | |
|---|---|---|
| Property, Plant, & Equipment: | | |
|   Mining properties: Red Valley Mine ..................... | $45,000,000 | |
|   Less: Accumulated depletion ......................... | 8,000,000 | $37,000,000 |

*The mine gradually is turned into inventory*

**Depreciation of Buildings and Equipment Closely Related to Natural Resources**   Buildings and equipment installed at a mine or drilling site may be useful only at that particular location. Consequently, such assets should be depreciated over their normal useful lives or over the life of the natural resource, *whichever is shorter.* Often depreciation on such assets is computed using the units-of-output method, which is discussed in the *Supplemental Topic* at the end of this chapter.

## Depreciation, Amortization, and Depletion—A Common Goal

The processes of depreciation, amortization, and depletion discussed in this chapter all have a common goal. That goal is to *allocate the acquisition cost of a long-lived asset to expense over the years in which the asset contributes to revenue.* By allocating the acquisition cost of long-lived assets over the years that benefit from the use of these assets, we stress again the importance of the *matching principle.* The determination of income requires the matching of revenue with the expenses incurred to produce that revenue.

## PLANT TRANSACTIONS AND THE STATEMENT OF CASH FLOWS

The cash effects of plant and equipment transactions are *very different* from the effects reported in the income statement. Cash payments for plant assets occur when those assets are *purchased*—or, more precisely, when payment is made. Cash receipts often occur when assets are sold. (These receipts are equal to the *total proceeds* received from the sale, not just the amount of any gain.) Cash flows relating to acquisitions and disposals of plant assets appear in the statement of cash flows, classified as *investing activities.*

**LO 7**

Explain the cash effects of transactions involving plant assets.

---

**CASH EFFECTS** Depreciation and amortization expense both *reduce net income,* but they have *no effect on cash flows.* As a result, both tend to make net income *less* than the net cash flows from operating activities. Likewise, the write-down of impaired assets is another example of a **noncash charge or expense** against income having no immediate effect on cash flows.

In some circumstances, the purchase or sale of a plant asset does not result in an immediate cash payment or cash receipt. For example, a company may finance the purchase of plant assets by issuing a note payable, or it may sell plant assets in exchange for a note receivable.

---

**Noncash Investing Activities** Not all purchases and sales of plant assets result in cash payments or cash receipts during the current accounting period. For example, a company may finance the purchase of plant assets by issuing notes payable, or it may sell plant assets in exchange for notes receivable. The noncash aspects of investing and financing activities are summarized in a special schedule that accompanies a statement of cash flows. This schedule will be illustrated and explained in Chapter 13.

**A SECOND LOOK**

**Amazon.com**

**Amazon.com**'s balance sheet reports goodwill amounting to hundreds of millions of dollars. As discussed in this chapter, goodwill represents the potential for *superior earnings* in future reporting periods. Does **Amazon.com** really have superior earnings potential?

Comparative income statements reveal that **Amazon.com** has *never* operated profitably. In fact, a recent income statement reports a *net loss* of nearly *$720 billion.* Poor earnings performance has many people concerned about **Amazon.com**'s future viability, given that it is over $2 billion in debt. If current trends continue, will the company be able to settle its outstanding obligations?

To better grasp the answer to this question, we examine various measures of a company's debt paying ability in Chapter 10.

---

## SUPPLEMENTAL TOPIC

**LO 8**

Account for depreciation using methods other than straight-line or declining-balance.

### OTHER DEPRECIATION METHODS

Most companies that prepare financial statements in conformity with generally accepted accounting principles use the straight-line method of depreciation. However, any rational and systematic method is acceptable, as long as costs are allocated to expense in a reasonable manner. Several such methods are discussed here.

### The Units-of-Output Method

Under the **units-of-output** method, depreciation is based on some measure of output *other than* the passage of time. When depreciation is based on units of output, more depreciation is recognized in the periods in which the assets are most heavily used.

To illustrate this method, consider S&G's delivery truck, which cost $17,000 and has an estimated salvage value of $2,000. Assume that S&G plans to retire this truck after it has been driven 100,000 miles. The depreciation rate *per mile of operation* amounts to *15 cents,* computed as follows:

$$\frac{\text{Cost} - \text{Residual Value}}{\text{Estimated Units of Output (Miles)}} = \frac{\text{Cost per}}{\text{Unit of Output (Mile)}}$$

$$\frac{\$17,000 - \$2,000}{100,000 \text{ miles}} = \$0.15 \text{ Depreciation per Mile}$$

At the end of each year, the amount of depreciation to be recorded would be determined by multiplying the 15-cent rate by the number of miles the truck had been driven during the year. After the truck has gone 100,000 miles, it is fully depreciated, and the depreciation process is stopped.

This method provides an excellent matching of expense with revenue. However, the method should be used only when the total units of output can be estimated with reasonable accuracy. Also, this method is used only for assets such as vehicles and certain types of machinery. Assets such as buildings, computers, and furniture do not have well-defined "units of output."

In many cases, units-of-output is an *accelerated method*. Often assets are used more extensively in the earlier years of their useful lives than in the later years.

## MACRS

Most businesses use a depreciation method called **MACRS** (Modified Accelerated Cost Recovery System) in their federal income tax returns. Some small businesses also use this method in their financial statements, so they do not have to compute depreciation in several different ways. MACRS is based on the declining-balance method, but should be considered for use in financial statements only if the *designated "recovery periods"* and the *assumption of no salvage value* are reasonable. For publicly traded companies, the use of MACRS in financial statements is usually not considered to be in conformity with generally accepted accounting principles.

### Sum-of-the-Years' Digits

**Sum-of-the-years' digits**, or **SYD**, is a form of accelerated depreciation. It generally produces results that lie between the double-declining-balance and 150%-declining-balance methods.

SYD is something of a "traditional" topic in accounting textbooks. But it is the most complex of the accelerated methods—especially when partial years are involved. And SYD is rarely used in today's business world. As shown in the table on page 386, only 11 of the 600 corporations surveyed—less than 2%—make any use of this method. Because of its complexity, it is even less frequently used in small businesses. SYD is seldom used for income tax purposes, because tax laws usually define allowable depreciation rates in terms of the declining-balance method. For these reasons, we will defer coverage of the mechanics of this method to later accounting courses.

## Decelerated Depreciation Methods

Depreciation methods do exist that recognize *less* depreciation expense in the early years of an asset's useful life and *more in the later years*. Such methods may achieve a reasonable matching of depreciation expense and revenue when the plant asset is expected to become *increasingly productive* over time. Utility companies, for example, may use these methods for new power plants that will be more fully utilized as the population of the area increases.

These depreciation methods are rarely used; thus we will again defer coverage to later accounting courses.

## Depreciation Methods in Use: A Survey

Every year, the American Institute of Certified Public Accountants conducts a survey of 600 publicly owned companies to determine the accounting methods most widely used in financial statements.

The various depreciation methods in use during a recent year are summarized below:

*Straight-line is clearly the method most widely used in financial statements*

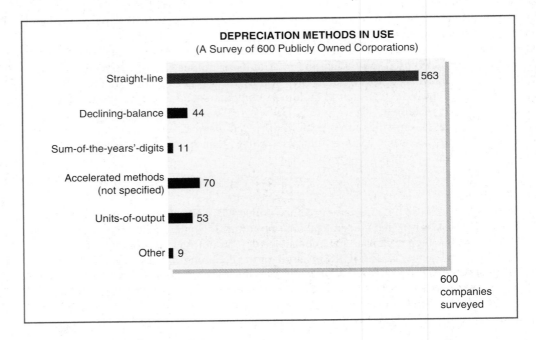

Notice that the number of methods in use exceeds 600. This is because some companies use different depreciation methods for different types of assets.

Bear in mind this survey indicates only the depreciation methods used in financial statements. In income tax returns, most companies use accelerated depreciation methods such as MACRS.

## SUMMARY OF LEARNING OBJECTIVES

### LO 1

**Determine the cost of plant assets.**

Plant assets are long-lived assets acquired for use in the business and not for resale to customers. The matching principle requires that we include in the plant and equipment accounts those costs that will provide services over a period of years. During these years, the use of the plant assets contributes to the earning of revenues. The cost of a plant asset includes all expenditures reasonable and necessary in acquiring the asset and placing it in a position and condition for use in the operations of the business.

### LO 2

**Distinguish between capital expenditures and revenue expenditures.**

Capital expenditures include any material expenditure that will benefit several accounting periods. Therefore, these expenditures are charged to asset accounts (capitalized) and are recognized as expense in future periods.

Revenue expenditures are charged directly to expense accounts because either (1) there is no objective evidence of future benefits or (2) the amounts are immaterial.

### LO 3

**Compute depreciation by the straight-line and declining-balance methods.**

Straight-line depreciation assigns an equal portion of an asset's cost to expense in each period of the asset's life. Declining-balance is an accelerated method. Each year, a fixed (and relatively high) depreciation rate is applied to the remaining book value of the asset. There are several variations of declining-balance depreciation.

### LO 4

**Account for disposals of plant assets.**

When plant assets are disposed of, depreciation should be recorded to the date of disposal. The cost is then removed from the asset account and the total recorded depreciation is removed from the accumulated depreciation account. The sale of a plant asset at a price above or below book value results in a gain or loss to be reported in the income statement.

Because different depreciation methods are used for income tax purposes, the gain or loss reported in income tax returns may differ from that shown in the income statement. The gain or loss shown in the financial statement is recorded in the company's general ledger accounts.

### LO 5

**Explain the nature of intangible assets, including goodwill.**

Intangible assets are assets owned by the business that have no physical substance, are noncurrent, and are used in business operations. Examples include trademarks and patents.

Among the most interesting intangible assets is goodwill. Goodwill is the present value of future earnings in excess of a normal return on net identifiable assets. It stems from such factors as a good reputation, loyal customers, and superior management. Any business that earns significantly more than a normal rate of return actually has goodwill. But goodwill is recorded in the accounts only if it is *purchased* by acquiring another business at a price higher than the fair market value of its net identifiable assets.

All intangible assets, including goodwill, should be amortized to expense over their useful economic lives. This period may not exceed 40 years but usually is much shorter.

### LO 6

**Account for the depletion of natural resources.**

Natural resources (or wasting assets) include mines, oil fields, and standing timber. Their cost is converted into inventory as the resource is mined, pumped, or cut. This allocation of the cost of a natural resource to inventories is called depletion. The depletion rate per unit extracted equals the cost of the resource (less residual value) divided by the estimated number of units it contains.

### LO 7

**Explain the cash effects of transactions involving plant assets.**

Depreciation is a noncash expense; cash expenditures for the acquisition of plant assets are independent of the amount of depreciation for the period. Cash payments to acquire plant assets (and cash receipts from disposals) appear in the statement of cash flows, classified as investing activities.

Write-downs of plant assets also are noncash charges, which do not involve cash payments.

### *LO 8

**Account for depreciation using methods other than straight-line or declining-balance.**

Most companies that prepare financial statements in conformity with generally accepted accounting principles use the straight-line method of depreciation (see survey results on page 386). Other accepted methods include the units-of-output method, sum-of-the-years' digits, and in rare circumstances, decelerated depreciation methods.

---

* *Supplemental Topic,* "Other Depreciation Methods."

This chapter completes our discussion of the valuation of the major types of business assets. To review, we have seen that cash is reported in the financial statements at face value, marketable securities at market value, accounts receivable at their net realizable value, inventories at the lower-of-cost-or-market, and plant assets at cost less accumulated depreciation. Two ideas that are consistently reflected in each of these valuation bases are the matching principle and the concept of conservatism. In the next chapter, we will turn our attention to the measurement of liabilities.

## KEY TERMS INTRODUCED OR EMPHASIZED IN CHAPTER 9

**accelerated depreciation** (p. 367)  Methods of depreciation that call for recognition of relatively large amounts of depreciation in the early years of an asset's useful life and relatively small amounts in the later years.

**amortization** (p. 377)  The systematic write-off to expense of the cost of an intangible asset over the periods of its economic usefulness.

**book value** (p. 366)  The cost of a plant asset minus the total recorded depreciation, as shown by the Accumulated Depreciation account. The remaining undepreciated cost is also known as *carrying value.*

**capital expenditures** (p. 364)  Costs incurred to acquire a long-lived asset. Expenditures that will benefit several accounting periods.

**capitalize** (p. 364)  A verb with two different meanings in accounting. The first is to debit an expenditure to an asset account, rather than directly to expense. The second is to estimate the value of an investment by dividing the annual return by the investor's required rate of return.

**depletion** (p. 382)  Allocating the cost of a natural resource to the units removed as the resource is mined, pumped, cut, or otherwise consumed.

**depreciation** (p. 365)  The systematic allocation of the cost of an asset to expense over the years of its estimated useful life.

**fixed-percentage-of-declining-balance depreciation** (p. 370)  An accelerated method of depreciation in which the rate is a multiple of the straight-line rate and is applied each year to the undepreciated cost of the asset. The most commonly used rate is double the straight-line rate.

**goodwill** (p. 377)  The present value of expected future earnings of a business in excess of the earnings normally realized in the industry. Recorded when a business entity is purchased at a price in excess of the fair value of its net identifiable assets (excluding goodwill) less liabilities.

**half-year convention** (p. 369)  The practice of taking six months' depreciation in the year of acquisition and in the year of disposition, rather than computing depreciation for partial periods to the nearest month. This method is widely used and is acceptable for both income tax reporting and financial reports, as long as it is applied to all assets of a particular type acquired during the year. The half-year convention generally is not used for buildings.

**intangible assets** (p. 362)  Those assets that are used in the operation of a business but that have no physical substance and are noncurrent.

**MACRS** (p. 385)  The Modified Accelerated Cost Recovery System. The accelerated depreciation method permitted in federal income tax returns for assets acquired after December 31, 1986. Depreciation is based on prescribed recovery periods and depreciation rates.

**natural resources** (p. 362)  Mines, oil fields, standing timber, and similar assets that are physically consumed and converted into inventory.

**net identifiable assets** (p. 378)  Total of all assets, except goodwill, minus liabilities.

**noncash charge or expense** (p. 384)  A charge against earnings—either an expense or a loss—that does not require a cash expenditure at or near the time of recognition. Thus, the charge reduces net income, but does not affect cash flows (except, perhaps, for income tax payments). Examples are depreciation and the write-off of asset values because an asset has become impaired.

**plant assets** (p. 362)  Long-lived assets that are acquired for use in business operations rather than for resale to customers.

**present value** (p. 377)  The amount that a knowledgeable investor would pay today for the right to receive future cash flows. The present value is always less than the sum of the future cash flows because the investor requires a return on the investment.

**residual (salvage) value** (p. 368)  The portion of an asset's cost expected to be recovered through sale or trade-in of the asset at the end of its useful life.

**revenue expenditures** (p. 364)  Expenditures that will benefit only the current accounting period.

**straight-line depreciation** (p. 367)  A method of depreciation that allocates the cost of an asset (minus any residual value) equally to each year of its useful life.

**sum-of-the-years' digits (SYD) depreciation** (p. 385)  A long-established but seldom-used method of accelerated depreciation. Usually produces results that lie in between 200%- and 150%-declining-balance.

**tangible plant assets** (p. 362)  Plant assets that have physical substance but that are not natural resources. Include land, buildings, and all types of equipment.

**units-of-output** (p. 384)  A depreciation method in which cost (minus residual value) is divided by the estimated units of lifetime output. The unit depreciation cost is multiplied by the actual units of output each year to compute the annual depreciation expense.

## DEMONSTRATION PROBLEM

On April 1, 2001, Argo Industries purchased new equipment at a cost of $325,000. The useful life of this equipment was estimated at 5 years, with a residual value of $25,000.

### Instructions

Compute the annual depreciation expense for each year until this equipment becomes fully depreciated under each depreciation method listed below. Because you will record depreciation for only a fraction of a year in 2001, depreciation will extend through 2006 for both methods. Show supporting computations.

**a.** Straight-line, with depreciation for fractional years rounded to the nearest whole month.

**b.** 200%-declining-balance, with the half-year convention. Limit depreciation in 2006 to an amount that reduces the undepreciated cost to the estimated residual value.

**c.** Assume that the equipment is sold at the end of December 2003, for $175,000 cash. Record the necessary gain or loss resulting from the sale under the straight-line method.

## Solution to the Demonstration Problem

| | Expense under Each Method of Depreciation | |
|---|---|---|
| | a | b |
| **Year** | **Straight-Line** | **200%-Declining-Balance** |
| 2001 | $ 45,000 | $ 65,000 |
| 2002 | 60,000 | 104,000 |
| 2003 | 60,000 | 62,400 |
| 2004 | 60,000 | 37,440 |
| 2005 | 60,000 | 22,464 |
| 2006 | 15,000 | 8,696 |
| Totals | $300,000 | $300,000 |

**c.** Entry to record sale of equipment in 2003:

| | | |
|---|---|---|
| Cash | 175,000 | |
| Accumulated Depreciation: Equipment | 165,000 | |
| Equipment | | 325,000 |
| Gain on Sale of Equipment | | 15,000 |

Supporting computations:

**a.** 2001: ($325,000 − $25,000) × $\frac{1}{5}$ × $\frac{9}{12}$ = $45,000

    2002–2005: $300,000 × $\frac{1}{5}$ = $60,000

    2006: $300,000 × $\frac{1}{5}$ × $\frac{3}{12}$ = $15,000

**b.**

| | Undepreciated Cost | Rate | Depreciation Expense |
|---|---|---|---|
| 2001 | $325,000 | × 40% × $\frac{1}{2}$ = | $ 65,000 |
| 2002 | 260,000 | × 40% = | 104,000 |
| 2003 | 156,000 | × 40% = | 62,400 |
| 2004 | 93,600 | × 40% = | 37,440 |
| 2005 | 56,160 | × 40% = | 22,464 |
| 2006 | 33,696 | − $25,000 = | 8,696 |

**c.** Accumulated depreciation at the end of 2003:

| | |
|---|---:|
| Depreciation expense, 2001 . . . . . . . . . . . . . . . . . . . . . | $ 45,000 |
| Depreciation expense, 2002 . . . . . . . . . . . . . . . . . . . | 60,000 |
| Depreciation expense, 2003 . . . . . . . . . . . . . . . . . . | 60,000 |
| Accumulated depreciation at the end of 2003 . . . . . . . | $165,000 |
| | |
| Original cost of equipment in 2001 . . . . . . . . . . . . . . | $325,000 |
| Less: Accumulated depreciation at the end of 2003 . . . | (165,000) |
| Book value of equipment at time of disposal . . . . . . . . | $160,000 |
| | |
| Cash proceeds from sale . . . . . . . . . . . . . . . . . . . . . | $175,000 |
| Less: Book value of equipment at time of disposal . . . . | (160,000) |
| Gain on sale of disposal . . . . . . . . . . . . . . . . . . . . . | $ 15,000 |

## SELF-TEST QUESTIONS

*Answers to these questions appear on page 401.*

1. In which of the following situations should the named company *not* record any depreciation expense on the asset described?

   **a.** Commuter Airline is required by law to maintain its aircraft in "as good as new" condition.

   **b.** Metro Advertising owns an office building that has been increasing in value each year since it was purchased.

   **c.** Computer Sales Company has in inventory a new type of computer, designed "never to become obsolete."

   **d.** None of the above answers is correct—in each case, the named company should record depreciation on the asset described.

2. Which of the following statements is (are) correct?

   **a.** Accumulated depreciation represents a cash fund being accumulated for the replacement of plant assets.

   **b.** The cost of a machine includes the cost of repairing damage to the machine during the installation process.

   **c.** A company may use different depreciation methods in its financial statements and its income tax return.

   **d.** The use of an accelerated depreciation method causes an asset to wear out more quickly than does use of the straight-line method.

3. On April 1, 2001, Sanders Construction paid $10,000 for equipment with an estimated useful life of 10 years and a residual value of $2,000. The company uses the double-declining-balance method of depreciation and applies the half-year convention to fractional periods. In 2002, the amount of depreciation expense to be recognized on this equipment is:

   **a.** $1,600.    **b.** $1,440.    **c.** $1,280.    **d.** Some other amount.

4. Evergreen Mfg. is a rapidly growing company that acquires more equipment every year. Evergreen uses straight-line depreciation in its financial statements and an accelerated method in its tax returns. Identify all correct statements:

   **a.** Using straight-line depreciation in the financial statements instead of an accelerated method increases Evergreen's reported net income.

   **b.** Using straight-line depreciation in the financial statements instead of an accelerated method increases Evergreen's annual net cash flow.

   **c.** Using an accelerated method instead of straight-line in income tax returns increases Evergreen's net cash flow.

   **d.** As long as Evergreen keeps growing, it will report more depreciation in its income tax returns *each year* than it does in its financial statements.

5. Delta Company sold a plant asset that originally cost $50,000 for $22,000 cash. If Delta correctly reports a $5,000 gain on this sale, the *accumulated depreciation* on the asset at the date of sale must have been:

   **a.** $33,000.    **b.** $28,000.    **c.** $23,000.    **d.** Some other amount.

6. In which of the following situations would Burton Industries include goodwill in its balance sheet?

   **a.** The fair market value of Burton's net identifiable assets amounts to $2,000,000. Normal earnings for this industry are 15% of net identifiable assets. Burton's net income for the past five years has averaged $390,000.

   **b.** Burton spent $800,000 during the current year for research and development for a new product that promises to generate substantial revenue for at least 10 years.

   **c.** Burton acquired Baxter Electronics at a price in excess of the fair market value of Baxter's net identifiable assets.

   **d.** A buyer wishing to purchase Burton's entire operation has offered a price in excess of the fair market value of Burton's net identifiable assets.

## ASSIGNMENT MATERIAL

## DISCUSSION QUESTIONS

1. **Coca-Cola**'s distinctive trademark is more valuable to the company than its bottling plants. But the company's bottling plants are listed in the balance sheet, and the famous trademark isn't. Explain.

2. Identify the basic "accountable events" in the life of a depreciable plant asset. Which of these events directly affect the net income of the current period? Which directly affect cash flows (other than income tax payments)?

3. Which of the following characteristics would prevent an item from being included in the classification of plant and equipment? (a) Intangible, (b) limited life, (c) unlimited life, (d) held for sale in the regular course of business, (e) not capable of rendering benefits to the business in the future.

4. The following expenditures were incurred in connection with a large new machine acquired by a metals manufacturing company. Identify those that should be included in the cost of the asset. (a) Freight charges, (b) sales tax on the machine, (c) payment to a passing motorist whose car was damaged by the equipment used in unloading the machine, (d) wages of employees for time spent in installing and testing the machine before it was placed in service, (e) wages of employees assigned to lubricate and make minor adjustments to the machine one year after it was placed in service.

5. What is the distinction between a *capital expenditure* and a *revenue expenditure*?

6. If a capital expenditure is erroneously treated as a revenue expenditure, will the net income of the current year be overstated or understated? Will this error have any effect on the net income reported in future years? Explain.

7. Shoppers' Market purchased for $220,000 a site on which it planned to build a new store. The site consisted of three acres of land and included an old house and two barns. County property tax records showed the following appraised values for this property: land, $160,000; buildings, $40,000. Indicate what Shoppers' should do with this $220,000 cost in its financial statements, and explain your reasoning.

8. Which of the following statements best describes the nature of depreciation?

   **a.** Regular reduction of asset value to correspond to the decline in market value as the asset ages.

   **b.** A process of correlating the book value of an asset with its gradual decline in physical efficiency.

   **c.** Allocation of cost in a manner that will ensure that plant and equipment items are not carried on the balance sheet at amounts in excess of net realizable value.

   **d.** Allocation of the cost of a plant asset to the periods in which benefits are received.

9. Should depreciation continue to be recorded on a building when ample evidence exists that the current market value is greater than original cost and that the rising trend of market values is continuing? Explain.

10. Explain what is meant by an *accelerated* depreciation method. Are accelerated methods more widely used in financial statements or in income tax returns? Explain.

11. One accelerated depreciation method is called *fixed-percentage-of-declining-balance.* Explain what is meant by the terms "fixed-percentage" and "declining-balance." For what purpose is this method most widely used?

12. An accountant for a large corporation said the company computes depreciation on its plant assets by using several different methods. But a note to the company's financial statements says all depreciation is computed by the straight-line method. Explain.

13. Criticize the following quotation: "We shall have no difficulty in paying for new plant assets needed during the coming year because our estimated outlays for new equipment amount to only $80,000, and we have more than twice that amount in our accumulated depreciation account at present."

14. Explain two approaches to computing depreciation for a fractional period in the year in which an asset is purchased. (Neither of your approaches should require the computation of depreciation to the nearest day or week.)

15. **a.** Does the accounting principle of consistency require a company to use the same method of depreciation for all of its plant assets?

     **b.** Is it acceptable for a corporation to use different depreciation methods in its financial statements and its income tax returns?

16. After 4 years of using a machine acquired at a cost of $15,000, Ohio Construction Company determined that the original estimated life of 10 years had been too short and that a total useful life of 12 years was a more reasonable estimate. Explain briefly the method that should be used to revise the depreciation program, assuming that straight-line depreciation has been used. Assume that the revision is made after recording depreciation and closing the accounts at the end of 4 years of use.

17. Define *intangible assets.* Would an account receivable arising from a sale of merchandise under terms of 2/10, n/30 qualify as an intangible asset under your definition?

18. Over what period of time should the cost of various types of intangible assets be amortized by regular charges against revenue? (Your answer should be in the form of a principle or guideline rather than a specific number of years.) What method of amortization is generally used?

19. Under what circumstances should *goodwill* be recorded in the accounts?

20. In reviewing the financial statements of Digital Products Company with a view to investing in the company's stock, you notice that net tangible assets total $1 million, that goodwill is listed at $400,000, and that average earnings for the past five years have been $50,000 a year. How would these relationships influence your thinking about the company?

21. Mineral King recognizes $20 depletion for each ton of ore mined. During the current year the company mined 600,000 tons but sold only 500,000 tons, as it was attempting to build up inventories in anticipation of a possible strike by employees. How much depletion should be deducted from revenue of the current year?

22. Explain the meaning of an *impairment* of an asset. Provide several examples. What accounting event should occur when an asset has become substantially impaired?

23. Several years ago March Metals purchased for $120,000 a well-known trademark for padlocks and other security products. After using the trademark for three years, March Metals discontinued it altogether when the company withdrew from the lock business and concentrated on the manufacture of aircraft parts. Amortization of the trademark at the rate of $3,000 a year is being continued on the basis of a 40-year life, which the owner of March Metals says is required by accounting standards. Do you agree? Explain.

# EXERCISES

Assume that you recently applied for a student loan to go to graduate school. As part of the application process, your bank requested a list of your assets. Aside from an extensive CD collection, your only other asset is a pickup truck. You purchased the truck six years ago for $15,000. Its current fair market value is approximately $5,000.

a. What factors caused your pickup truck to depreciate $10,000 in value?

b. Assume that the bank is willing to lend you money for graduate school. Even with the loan, however, you still need to raise an additional $5,000. Do you think that the bank will lend you $5,000 more for graduate school if you agree to use your truck as collateral? Explain.

c. Assume that the truck has been used solely in a delivery service business that you operated while in college. Would your balance sheet necessarily show $10,000 in accumulated depreciation related to the truck? Explain.

**EXERCISE 9.1**

You as a Student

**LO 2, 3**

Identify the following expenditures as capital expenditures or revenue expenditures:

a. Immediately after acquiring a new delivery truck, paid $225 to have the name of the store and other advertising material painted on the vehicle.

b. Painted delivery truck at a cost of $250 after 2 years of use.

c. Purchased new battery at a cost of $40 for 2-year-old delivery truck.

d. Installed an escalator at a cost of $12,500 in a three-story building that had been used for some years without elevators or escalators.

e. Purchased a pencil sharpener at a cost of $8.50.

f. Original life of the delivery truck had been estimated at 4 years and straight-line depreciation of 25% yearly had been recognized. After 3 years' use, however, it was decided to recondition the truck thoroughly, including adding a new engine.

**EXERCISE 9.2**

Distinguishing Capital Expenditures from Revenue Expenditures

**LO 1, 2**

On August 3, Sajay Construction purchased special-purpose equipment at a cost of $1,000,000. The useful life of the equipment was estimated to be 8 years, with a residual value of $50,000.

a. Compute the depreciation expense to be recognized each calendar year for financial reporting purposes under the straight-line depreciation method (half-year convention).

b. Compute the depreciation expense to be recognized each calendar year for financial reporting purposes under the 200% declining-balance method (half-year convention).

c. Which of these two depreciation methods (straight-line or double-declining-balance) results in the highest net income for financial reporting purposes during the first two years of the equipment's use? Explain.

**EXERCISE 9.3**

Depreciation for Fractional Years

**LO 3**

On January 2, 2001, Jansing Corporation acquired a new machine with an estimated useful life of 5 years. The cost of the equipment was $40,000 with a residual value of $5,000.

a. Prepare a complete depreciation table under the three depreciation methods listed below. Use a format similar to the illustrations on pages 369 and 371. In each case, assume that a full year of depreciation was taken in 2001.

1. Straight-line.

2. 200% declining-balance.

3. 150% declining-balance.

b. Comment on significant differences or similarities that you observe among the patterns of depreciation expense recognized under each of these methods.

**EXERCISE 9.4**

Depreciation Methods

**LO 3**

A recent annual report of **H. J. Heinz Company** includes the following note:

**Depreciation:** For financial reporting purposes, depreciation is provided on the straight-line method over the estimated useful lives of the assets. Accelerated depreciation methods generally are used for income tax purposes.

a. Is the company violating the accounting principle of consistency by using different depreciation methods in its financial statements than in its income tax returns? Explain.

**EXERCISE 9.5**

Evaluation of Disclosures in Annual Reports

**LO 3**

**b.** *Why* do you think that the company uses accelerated depreciation methods in its income tax returns?

**c.** Would the use of accelerated depreciation in the financial statements be more conservative or less conservative than the current practice of using the straight-line method? Explain.

**EXERCISE 9.6**

Revision of Depreciation Estimates

 **LO 3**

Strong Industries uses straight-line depreciation on all of its depreciable assets. The company records annual depreciation expense at the end of each calendar year. On January 11, 2001, the company purchased a machine costing $90,000. The machine's useful life was estimated to be 12 years with a residual value of $18,000. Depreciation for partial years is recorded to the nearest full month.

In 2005, after almost 5 years of experience with the machine, management decided to revise its estimated life from 12 years to 20 years. No change was made in the estimated residual value. The revised estimate of the useful life was decided *prior* to recording annual depreciation expense for the year ended December 31, 2005.

**a.** Prepare journal entries in chronological order for the above events, beginning with the purchase of the machinery on January 11, 2001. Show separately the recording of depreciation expense in 2001 through 2005.

**b.** What factors may have caused the company to revise its estimate of the machine's useful life?

**EXERCISE 9.7**

Accounting for Trade-ins

 **LO 4**

Bedford Bus Service traded in a used bus for a new one. The original cost of the old bus was $52,000. Accumulated depreciation at the time of the trade-in amounted to $34,000. The new bus costs $65,000 but Bedford was given a trade-in allowance of $12,000.

**a.** What amount of cash must Bedford pay to acquire the new bus?

**b.** Compute the gain or loss on the disposal for financial reporting purposes.

**c.** Explain how the gain or loss would be reported in the company's income statement.

**EXERCISE 9.8**

Estimating Goodwill

 **LO 5**

During the past several years the annual net income of Goldtone Appliance Company has averaged $540,000. At the present time the company is being offered for sale. Its accounting records show the book value of net assets (total assets minus all liabilities) to be $2,800,000. The fair market value of Goldtone's net identifiable assets, however, is $3,000,000.

An investor negotiating to buy the company offers to pay an amount equal to the fair market value for the net identifiable assets and to assume all liabilities. In addition, the investor is willing to pay for goodwill an amount equal to net earnings in excess of 15% on the fair market value of net identifiable assets, capitalized at a rate of 25%.

On the basis of this agreement, what price should the investor offer for Goldtone Appliance?

**EXERCISE 9.9**

The Write-Down of Impaired Assets

 **LO 4, 7**

For several years, a number of **Food Lion, Inc.**, grocery stores have become unprofitable. The company closed, and continues to close, many of these locations. It is apparent that the company will not be able to recover the cost of the assets associated with the closed stores. Thus, the current value of these impaired assets must be written down (see the Case in Point on page 374).

A recent **Food Lion** income statement reports a $9.5 million charge against income pertaining to the write-down of impaired assets.

**a.** Explain why **Food Lion** must write down the current carrying value of its unprofitable stores.

**b.** Explain why the recent $9.5 million charge to write down these impaired assets is considered a noncash expense.

**EXERCISE 9.10**

Ethics: "Let the Buyer Beware"

 **LO 1, 5**

Bill Gladstone has owned and operated Gladstone's Service Station for over 30 years. The business, which is currently the town's only service station, has always been extremely profitable. Gladstone recently decided that he wanted to sell the business and retire. His asking price exceeds the fair market value of its net identifiable assets by nearly $50,000. Gladstone attributes this premium to the above-normal returns that the service station has always generated.

Gladstone recently found out about two issues that could have a profound effect upon the future of the business: (1) A well-known service station franchise will be built across the street from his station in approximately 18 months, and (2) one of his underground fuel tanks *may* have developed a very slow leak.

**a.** How might these issues affect the $50,000 in goodwill that Gladstone included in his selling price?

**b.** Assume that Gladstone is *not* disclosing this information to potential buyers. Does he have an ethical obligation to do so? Defend your answer.

Salter Mining Company purchased the Northern Tier Mine for $21 million cash. The mine was estimated to contain 2.5 million tons of ore and to have a residual value of $1 million.

During the first year of mining operations at the Northern Tier Mine, 50,000 tons of ore were mined, of which 40,000 tons were sold.

**a.** Prepare a journal entry to record depletion during the year.

**b.** Show how the Northern Tier Mine, and its accumulated depletion, would appear in Salter Mining Company's balance sheet after the first year of operations.

**c.** Will the entire amount of depletion computed in part **a** be deducted from revenue in the determination of income for the year? Explain.

**d.** Indicate how the journal entry in part **a** affects the company's current ratio (its current assets divided by its current liabilities). Do you believe that the activities summarized in this entry do, in fact, make the company any more or less liquid? Explain.

**EXERCISE 9.11**

Depletion of Natural Resources

**LO 6**

Locate an annual report in your library (or some other source) that includes a large gain or loss on the disposal of fixed assets. Report to the class the amount of the gain or loss and where in the company's income statement it is reported. Describe how the gain or loss is reported in the company's statement of cash flows. Summarize any discussion in the footnotes concerning the cause of the disposal.

**EXERCISE 9.12**

Researching a Real Company

**LO 5, 7**

During the current year, Airport Auto Rentals purchased 60 new automobiles at a cost of $13,000 per car. The cars will be sold to a wholesaler at an estimated $4,000 each as soon as they have been driven 50,000 miles. Airport Auto Rentals computes depreciation expense on its automobiles by the units-of-output method, based on mileage.

**a.** Compute the amount of depreciation to be recognized for each mile that a rental automobile is driven.

**b.** Assuming that the 60 rental cars are driven a total of 1,650,000 miles during the current year, compute the total amount of depreciation expense that Airport Auto Rentals should recognize on this fleet of cars for the year.

**c.** In this particular situation, do you believe the units-of-output depreciation method achieves a better matching of expenses with revenue than would the straight-line method? Explain.

**\*EXERCISE 9.13**

Units-of-Output Method

**LO 8**

The annual report of **Tootsie Roll Industries, Inc.**, appears in Appendix A at the end of this textbook. Use this annual report to answer the following questions:

**a.** What method of computing depreciation expense does the company use for financial reporting purposes?

**b.** What method of computing depreciation expense does the company use for federal income tax purposes?

**c.** The company's income statement reports amortization of intangible assets. What types of intangible assets would you guess require amortization?

**EXERCISE 9.14**

Using an Annual Report to Determine Depreciation Methods Used

**LO 1, 3**

## PROBLEMS

Prescott College recently purchased new computing equipment for its library. The following information refers to the purchase and installation of this equipment:

**1.** The list price of the equipment was $275,000; however, Prescott College qualified for an "education discount" of $25,000. It paid $50,000 cash for the equipment, and issued a 3-month, 9% note payable for the remaining balance. The note, plus accrued interest charges of $4,500, was paid promptly at the maturity date.

**2.** In addition to the amounts described in 1, Prescott paid sales taxes of $15,000 at the date of purchase.

**PROBLEM 9.1**

Determining the Cost of Plant Assets

**LO 1, 2, 3**

---

\* *Supplemental Topic,* "Other Depreciation Methods."

3. Freight charges for delivery of the equipment totaled $1,000.

4. Installation and training costs related to the equipment amounted to $5,000.

5. During installation, one of the computer terminals was accidentally damaged by a library employee. It cost the college $500 to repair this damage.

6. As soon as the computers were installed, the college paid $4,000 to print admissions brochures featuring the library's new, state-of-the-art computing facilities.

## Instructions

a. In one sentence, make a general statement summarizing the nature of expenditures that qualify for inclusion in the cost of plant assets such as computing equipment.

b. For each of the six numbered paragraphs, indicate which items should be included by Prescott College in the total cost debited to its Computing Equipment account. Also briefly indicate the proper accounting treatment of those items that *are not* included in the cost of the equipment.

c. Compute the total cost debited to the college's Computing Equipment account.

d. Prepare a journal entry at the end of the current year to record depreciation on the computing equipment. Prescott College will depreciate this equipment by the straight-line method (half-year convention) over an estimated useful life of 5 years. Assume a zero residual value.

---

**PROBLEM 9.2**

Comparison of Straight-Line and Accelerated Methods

 **LO 3, 4**

Miller & Hiller, Inc., purchased a new machine on September 1, 2001, at a cost of $108,000. The machine's estimated useful life at the time of the purchase was 5 years, and its residual value was $8,000.

## Instructions

a. Prepare a complete depreciation schedule, beginning with calendar year 2001, under each of the methods listed below (assume that the half-year convention is used):

1. Straight-line.
2. 200% declining-balance.
3. 150% declining-balance.

b. Which of the three methods computed in part **a** is most common for financial reporting purposes? Explain.

c. Assume that Miller & Hiller sell the machine on December 31, 2004, for $30,000 cash. Compute the resulting gain or loss from this sale under each of the depreciation methods used in part **a**. Does the gain or loss reported in the company's income statement have any direct cash effects? Explain.

---

**PROBLEM 9.3**

Issues Involving Alternative Depreciation Methods

**LO 1–4**

Cole's Hardware purchased new shelving for its store on April 1, 2001. The shelving is expected to have a 20-year life and no residual value. The following expenditures were associated with the purchase:

| | |
|---|---:|
| Cost of the shelving . . . . . . . . . . . . . . . . . . . . . . . . . . . . . . . . . . . . . . . . . . . . . . . . . . . . . . . . | $12,000 |
| Freight charges . . . . . . . . . . . . . . . . . . . . . . . . . . . . . . . . . . . . . . . . . . . . . . . . . . . . . . . | 520 |
| Sales taxes . . . . . . . . . . . . . . . . . . . . . . . . . . . . . . . . . . . . . . . . . . . . . . . . . . . . . . . . . . . | 780 |
| Installation of shelving . . . . . . . . . . . . . . . . . . . . . . . . . . . . . . . . . . . . . . . . . . . . . . . . . | 2,700 |
| Cost to repair shelf damaged during installation . . . . . . . . . . . . . . . . . . . . . . . . . . . | 400 |

## Instructions

a. Compute depreciation expense for the years 2001 through 2004 under each depreciation method listed below:

1. Straight-line, with fractional years rounded to the nearest whole month.
2. 200% declining-balance, using the half-year convention.
3. 150% declining-balance, using the half-year convention.

b. Cole's Hardware has two conflicting objectives. Management wants to report the highest possible earnings in its financial statements, yet it also wants to minimize its taxable income reported to the IRS. Explain how both of these objectives can be met.

c. Which of the depreciation methods applied in part **a** resulted in the lowest reported book value at the end of 2004? Is book value an estimate of an asset's fair market value? Explain.

d. Assume that Cole's Hardware sold the old shelving that was being replaced. The old shelving had originally cost $9,000. Its book value at the time of the sale was $400. Record the sale of the old shelving under the following conditions:

   1. The shelving was sold for $1,000 cash.
   2. The shelving was sold for $300 cash.

During the current year, Escola Developers disposed of plant assets in the following transactions:

**Feb. 10**  Office equipment costing $26,000 was given to a scrap dealer at no charge. At the date of disposal, accumulated depreciation on the office equipment amounted to $25,800.

**Apr. 1**  Escola sold land and a building to Claypool Associates for $900,000, receiving $100,000 cash and a 5-year, 9% note receivable for the remaining balance. Escola's records showed the following amounts: Land, $50,000; Building, $550,000; Accumulated Depreciation: Building (at the date of disposal), $250,000.

**Aug. 15**  Escola traded in an old truck for a new one. The old truck had cost $26,000, and its accumulated depreciation amounted to $18,000. The list price of the new truck was $39,000, but Escola received a $10,000 trade-in allowance for the old truck and paid only $29,000 in cash. Escola includes trucks in its Vehicles account.

**Oct. 1**  Escola traded in its old computer system as part of the purchase of a new system. The old system had cost $15,000, and its accumulated depreciation amounted to $11,000. The new computer's list price was $8,000. Escola accepted a trade-in allowance of $500 for the old computer system, paying $2,500 down in cash, and issuing a 1-year, 8% note payable for the $5,000 balance owed.

**PROBLEM 9.4**

Disposal of Plant Assets

## Instructions

a. Prepare journal entries to record each of the disposal transactions. Assume that depreciation expense on each asset has been recorded up to the date of disposal. Thus, you need not update the accumulated depreciation figures stated in the problem.

b. Will the gains and losses recorded in part **a** above affect the *gross profit* reported in Escola's income statement? Explain.

c. Explain how the financial reporting of gains and losses on plant assets differs from the financial reporting of *unrealized* gains and losses on marketable securities discussed in Chapter 7.

During the current year, King Carpet Corporation incurred the following expenditures which should be recorded either as operating expenses or as intangible assets:

a. Expenditures were made for the training of new employees. The average employee remains with the company for five years, but is trained for a new position every two years.

b. King purchased a controlling interest in a vinyl flooring company. The expenditure resulted in the recording of a significant amount of goodwill. King expects to earn above average returns on this investment for no more than 15 years.

c. King incurred large amounts of research and development costs in developing a dirt-resistant carpet fiber. The company expects that the fiber will be patented and that sales of the resulting products will contribute to revenue for at least 20 years. The legal life of the patent, however, will be only 17 years.

d. King made an expenditure to acquire the patent on a popular carpet cleaner. The patent had a remaining legal life of 14 years, but King expects to produce and sell the product for only 6 more years.

e. King spent a large amount to sponsor the televising of the Olympic Games. King's intent was to make television viewers more aware of the company's name and its product lines.

**PROBLEM 9.5**

Accounting for Intangible Assets under GAAP

## Instructions

Explain whether each of the above expenditures should be recorded as an operating expense or an intangible asset. If you view the expenditure as an intangible asset, indicate the number of years over which the asset should be amortized. Explain your reasoning.

**PROBLEM 9.6**

Accounting for Goodwill

Kivi Service Stations is considering expanding its operations to include the greater Dubuque area. Rather than build new service stations in the Dubuque area, management plans to acquire existing service stations and convert them into Kivi outlets.

Kivi is evaluating two similar acquisition opportunities. Information relating to each of these service stations is presented below:

| | Phil's Garage | Gas N' Go |
| --- | --- | --- |
| Estimated normal rate of return on net assets | 20% | 20% |
| Fair market value of net identifiable assets | $950,000 | $980,000 |
| Actual average net income for past five years | 250,000 | 260,000 |

### Instructions

**a.** Compute an estimated fair value for any goodwill associated with Kivi purchasing Phil's Garage. Base your computation upon an assumption that successful service stations typically sell at about 9.25 times their annual earnings (i.e., are expected to have p/e ratios of approximately 9.25:1).

**b.** Compute an estimated fair value for any goodwill associated with Kivi purchasing Gas N' Go. Base your computation upon an assumption that Kivi's management wants to capitalize excess earnings at 25%.

**c.** Many of Kivi's existing service stations are extremely profitable. If Kivi acquires Phil's Garage or Gas N' Go, should it also record the goodwill associated with its existing locations? Explain.

## CASES AND UNSTRUCTURED PROBLEMS

**CASE 9.1**

Are Useful Lives "Flexible"?

Robert Lynch is the controller of Print Technologies, a publicly owned company. The company is experiencing financial difficulties and is aggressively looking for ways to cut costs.

Suzanne Bedell, the CEO, instructs Lynch to lengthen from 5 to 10 years the useful life used in computing depreciation on certain special-purpose machinery. Bedell believes that this change represents a substantial cost savings, as it will reduce the depreciation expense on these assets by nearly one-half.

*Note:* The proposed change affects only the depreciation expense recognized in financial statements. Depreciation deductions in income tax returns will not be affected.

### Instructions

**a.** Discuss the extent to which Bedell's idea will, in fact, achieve a cost savings. Consider the effects on both net income and cash flows.

**b.** Who is responsible for estimating the useful lives of plant assets?

**c.** Discuss any ethical issues that Lynch should consider with respect to Bedell's instructions.

**CASE 9.2**

Departures from GAAP—Are They Ethical?

Martin Cole owns Delta Construction Co. The company maintains accounting records for the purposes of exercising control over its construction activities and meeting its reporting obligations regarding payrolls and income tax returns. As it has no other financial reporting obligations, Delta does not prepare formal financial statements.

The company owns land and several other assets with current market values well in excess of their historical costs. Cole directs the company's accountant, Maureen O'Shaughnessey, to prepare a balance sheet in which assets are shown at estimated market values. Cole says this type of balance sheet will give him a better understanding of where the business stands. He also thinks it will be useful in obtaining bank loans, as loan applications always ask for the estimated market values of real estate owned.

## Instructions

**a.** Would the financial statements requested by Cole be in conformity with generally accepted accounting principles?

**b.** Is Delta Construction under any legal or ethical obligation to prepare financial statements that *do* conform to generally accepted accounting principles?

**c.** Discuss any ethical issues that O'Shaughnessey should consider with respect to Cole's request.

The following is a note accompanying a recent financial statement of **International Paper Company**:

> ### Plant, Properties, and Equipment
> Plant, properties, and equipment are stated at cost less accumulated depreciation.
>
> For financial reporting purposes, the company uses the units-of-production method of depreciating its major pulp and paper mills and certain wood products facilities, and the straight-line method for other plants and equipment.
>
> Annual straight-line depreciation rates for financial reporting purposes are as follows: buildings 2½% to 8%; machinery and equipment 5% to 33%; woods equipment 10% to 16%. For tax purposes, depreciation is computed utilizing accelerated methods.

**\*CASE 9.3**

Depreciation Policies in Annual Reports

**LO 3, 8**

## Instructions

**a.** Are the depreciation methods used in the company's financial statements determined by current income tax laws? If not, who is responsible for selecting these methods? Explain.

**b.** Does the company violate the consistency principle by using different depreciation methods for its paper mills and wood products facilities than it uses for its other plant and equipment? If not, what does the principle of consistency mean? Explain.

**c.** What is the estimated useful life of the machinery and equipment being depreciated with a straight-line depreciation rate of:

**1.** 5%.

**2.** 33% (round to the nearest year).

Who determines the useful lives over which specific assets are to be depreciated?

**d.** Why do you think the company uses accelerated depreciation methods for income tax purposes, rather than using the straight-line method?

## BUSINESS WEEK ASSIGNMENT

BusinessWeek

It is not uncommon for companies to patent ideas that never materialize as sellable goods or services. In an April 3, 2000, *Business Week* article entitled, "For Sale: Great Ideas, Barely Used," author Pamela L. Moore reports that only about 3% of all patents granted are ever brought to market. The article introduces readers to **Yet2.com**, a new business venture that specializes in using the Internet to find buyers willing to invest in unused patents. **Polaroid Corporation**, for example, is planning to list as many as 900 of its 1,500 unused patents on **Yet2.com**'s site. **Rockwell International** intends to list a portion of its 5,000 unused patents as well. Other companies expressing interest include **DuPont**, **3M**, **Boeing**, **Dow**, **Ford**, **Polaroid**, **Siemens**, **Toyota**, and **Toshiba**.

**CASE 9.4**

**LO 1, 2, 5**

## Instructions

Assume that your company has 50 unused patents in which it has invested approximately $50,000. You have decided to list these patents with **Yet2.com** and have set a *minimum* selling price of $250,000. Should these patents be reported in your balance sheet at $250,000 until they are sold? Defend your answer.

---

\* *Supplemental Topic,* "Other Depreciation Methods."

## INTERNET ASSIGNMENT

**INTERNET 9.1**

R&D in the Pharmaceutical Industry

**LO 2**

The pharmaceutical industry spends billions of dollars each year on research and development. Rather than capitalize these R&D expenditures as intangible assets, companies are required to charge them to expense in the year incurred.

Perform a keyword search of Pharmaceutical Companies using the following search engine:

**www.yahoo.com**

Your search will result in a list of companies that research and develop pharmaceutical products. Select five of these companies and obtain their 10-K reports (using EDGAR) at the following Internet address:

**www.sec.gov**

**Instructions**

**a.** For each of the companies you selected, determine:

1. Total R&D expense for the most current year.
2. Total R&D expense as a percentage of total operating costs and expenses.
3. Total R&D expense as a percentage of net sales.
4. The percentage by which operating income would have increased had the entire R&D expenditure been recorded as an intangible asset instead of being charged to expense.

**b.** Using information from the 10-K reports, summarize briefly the kinds of drugs being researched and developed by each of these companies. To a potential investor, which company appears to be the most innovative and promising? Explain.

*Internet sites are time and date sensitive. It is the purpose of these exercises to have you explore the Internet. You may need to use the Yahoo! search engine* http://www.yahoo.com *(or other favorite search engine) to find a company's current web address.*

## OUR COMMENTS ON THE "YOUR TURN" CASES

**As the New Facility Manager for Holiday Workout (p. 364)**    Your ability to earn profits 10% over the budgeted amount will be impacted by the amount of the charge for depreciation on the building. The amount of depreciation each year will depend on the dollar amount recorded for the building asset. Thus, if you ask the bookkeeper to correct the building account, it may make it more difficult to achieve your bonus.

However, it is your ethical responsibility to inform Holiday Workout's management about the error in the appraisal. Management will respect your integrity. Your reputation for honesty and ethical behavior will be enhanced.

**As a Business Owner (p. 369)**    Many factors may influence the useful life and residual value of a truck. These factors may include (1) the miles the truck will be driven each year, (2) the amount of maintenance it receives, (3) road conditions, (4) the climate in which it is driven, and (5) new technologies that make new trucks more fuel efficient and/or powerful.

To the extent that the company can prevent excessive physical deterioration and obsolescence from occurring, estimates of the truck's useful life and residual value will increase. A prolonged life and high residual value will reduce depreciation expense reported by the company each year. If, on the other hand, the truck is expected to undergo excessive abuse or become obsolete, estimates of its useful life and residual value will decrease. This, in turn, will increase the amount of depreciation expense reported by the company each year.

**As a Business Consultant (p. 373)**    As shown, using the accelerated method requires higher charges to depreciation expense and, therefore, results in a lower reported net income than the straight-line method. Of course, the manner in which depreciation is computed has no *real effect* on a company's profitability or financial position. However, because this business intends to go public within five years, management may want the company to appear as profitable as generally accepted accounting principles will allow.

## ANSWERS TO SELF-TEST QUESTIONS

**1.** c (Depreciation is not recorded on inventory.) [$10,000 − ($10,000 × 20% × ½)]   **2.** c   **3.** d $1,800, computed 20%   **4.** a, c, d   **5.** a [Cost, $50,000, less book value, $17,000 (sales price, less gain)]   **6.** c

# 10

# LIABILITIES

© Image Bank

## Learning Objectives

*After studying this chapter, you should be able to:*

1. Define *liabilities* and distinguish between current and long-term liabilities.

2. Account for notes payable and interest expense.

3. Describe the costs relating to payrolls.

4. Prepare an amortization table allocating payments between interest and principal.

5. Describe corporate bonds and explain the tax advantage of debt financing.

6. Explain the concept of present value.

7. Account for postretirement costs.

8. Describe and account for deferred income taxes.

9. Evaluate the safety of creditors' claims.

*10. Define *loss contingencies* and explain their presentation in financial statements.

†11. Account for bonds issued at a discount or premium.

---

\* *Supplemental Topic A,* "Estimated Liabilities, Loss Contingencies, and Commitments."

† *Supplemental Topic B,* "Bonds Issued at a Discount or a Premium."

Buying items on credit has never been easier. Each day, large retailers and credit card companies seem to encourage consumers to go deeper and deeper into debt. Add to credit card debt other long-term obligations—such as home mortgages and automobile loans—and it's no wonder that payments on total household debt consume nearly 98% of total disposable income in the United States.

Large corporations also have jumped on the bandwagon in recent years by issuing more debt than ever to finance expansion and acquisitions. The tremendous debt service costs associated with corporate borrowing can siphon away a significant portion of a company's operating cash flows.

Consider, for example, **E. I. duPont de Nemours & Co.** In a recent balance sheet, **DuPont** reports total liabilities of $27 billion in comparison to total stockholders' equity of only $13 billion. The company's disproportionate reliance on debt financing burdens the company with billions of dollars in debt service costs annually. Notes accompanying **DuPont**'s recent financial statements reveal management's intent to reduce current debt levels to improve the company's overall financial flexibility. Other major corporations are likely to do the same.

● ● ●

Creditors and investors evaluate carefully the liabilities appearing in financial reports. Thoroughly understanding short-term versus long-term debt is important for managers choosing how to finance their businesses. This chapter provides a basic understanding of concepts related to liabilities as well as describing how liabilities are recorded and later presented in the financial statements. In addition, the impact of debt on various financial ratios is illustrated.

# The Nature of Liabilities

**LO 1**

Define *liabilities* and distinguish between current and long-term liabilities.

Liabilities may be defined as *debts or obligations arising from past transactions or events* that require settlement at a future date. All liabilities have certain characteristics in common; however, the specific terms of different liabilities, and the rights of the creditors, vary greatly.

**Distinction between Debt and Equity**   Businesses have two basic sources of financing: liabilities and owners' equity. Liabilities differ from owners' equity in several respects. The feature that most clearly distinguishes the claims of creditors from owners' equity is that all liabilities eventually *mature*—that is, they come due. Owners' equity does not mature. The date on which a liability comes due is called the **maturity date**.[1]

Although all liabilities mature, their maturity dates vary. Some liabilities are so short in term that they are paid before the financial statements are prepared. Long-term liabilities, in contrast, may not mature for many years. The maturity dates of key liabilities may be a critical factor in the solvency of a business.

The providers of borrowed capital are *creditors* of the business, not owners. As creditors, they have financial claims against the business but usually do *not* have the right to control business operations. The traditional roles of owners, managers, and creditors may be modified, however, in an *indenture contract*. Creditors sometimes insist on being granted some control over business operations as a condition of making a loan, particularly if the business is in poor financial condition. Indenture contracts may impose such restrictions as limits on management salaries and on dividends, and may require the creditor's approval for additional borrowing or for large capital expenditures.

The claims of creditors have *legal priority* over the claims of owners. If a business ceases operations and liquidates, creditors must be *paid in full* before any distributions are made to the owners. The relative security of creditors' claims, however, can vary among the creditors. Sometimes the borrower pledges title to specific assets as **collateral** for a loan. If the borrower defaults on a secured loan, the creditor may foreclose on the pledged assets. Assets that have been pledged as security for loans should be identified in notes accompanying the borrower's financial statements.

Liabilities that are not secured by specific assets are termed *general credit obligations*. The priorities of general credit obligations vary with the nature of the liability and the terms of indenture contracts.

**Many Liabilities Bear Interest**   Many long-term liabilities, and some short-term ones, require the borrower to pay interest. Only interest accrued *as of the balance sheet date* appears as a liability in the borrower's balance sheet. The borrower's obligation to pay interest in *future* periods sometimes is disclosed in the notes to the financial statements, but it is not shown as an existing liability.

**Estimated Liabilities**   Most liabilities are for a definite dollar amount, clearly stated by contract. Examples include notes payable, accounts payable, and accrued expenses, such as interest payable and salaries payable. In some cases, however, the dollar amount of a liability must be *estimated* at the balance sheet date.

**Estimated liabilities** have two basic characteristics: The liability is *known to exist,* and the precise dollar amount cannot be determined until a later date. For instance, the automobiles sold by most automakers are accompanied by a warranty obligating the automaker to replace defective parts for a period of several years. As each car is sold, the automaker *incurs a liability* to perform any work that may be required under the warranty. The dollar amount of this liability, however, can only be estimated.

---

[1] Some liabilities are *due on demand,* which means that the liability is payable upon the creditor's request. From a bank's point of view, customers' checking accounts are "demand liabilities." Liabilities due on demand may come due at any time and are classified as current liabilities.

## CURRENT LIABILITIES

Current liabilities are obligations that must be paid within one year or within the operating cycle, whichever is longer. Another requirement for classification as a current liability is the expectation that the debt will be paid from current assets (or through the rendering of services). Liabilities that do not meet these conditions are classified as long-term liabilities.

The time period used in defining current liabilities parallels that used in defining current assets. The amount of *working capital* (current assets less current liabilities) and the *current ratio* (current assets divided by current liabilities) are valuable indicators of a company's ability to pay its debts in the near future.

Among the most common examples of current liabilities are accounts payable, short-term notes payable, the current portion of long-term debt, accrued liabilities (such as interest payable, income taxes payable, and payroll liabilities), and unearned revenue.

### Accounts Payable

Accounts payable often are subdivided into the categories of *trade* accounts payable and *other* accounts payable. Trade accounts payable are short-term obligations to suppliers for purchases of merchandise. Other accounts payable include liabilities for any goods and services other than merchandise.

Technically, the date at which a trade account payable comes into existence depends on whether goods are purchased F.O.B. shipping point or F.O.B. destination. Under F.O.B. shipping point, a liability arises and title to the goods transfers when the merchandise is *shipped* by the supplier. Under F.O.B. destination, a liability does not arise and title of ownership does not transfer until the goods are actually *received* by the buyer. However, unless *material* amounts of merchandise are purchased on terms F.O.B. shipping point, most companies follow the convenient practice of recording trade accounts payable when merchandise is received.

### Notes Payable

Notes payable are issued whenever bank loans are obtained. Other transactions that may give rise to notes payable include the purchase of real estate or costly equipment, the purchase of merchandise, and the substitution of a note for a past-due account payable.

Notes payable usually require the borrower to pay an interest charge. Normally, the interest rate is stated separately from the **principal amount** of the note.[2]

To illustrate, assume that on November 1, Porter Company borrows $10,000 from its bank for a period of six months at an annual interest rate of 12%. Six months later on May 1, Porter Company will have to pay the bank the principal amount of $10,000, plus $600 interest ($10,000 $\times$ .12 $\times$ $^6\!/_{12}$). As evidence of this loan, the bank will require Porter Company to issue a note payable similar to the following illustration.

The journal entry in Porter Company's accounting records for this November 1 borrowing is:

| | | |
|---|---|---|
| Cash . . . . . . . . . . . . . . . . . . . . . . . . . . . . . . . . . . . . . . . . . . . . . . | 10,000 | |
|    Notes Payable . . . . . . . . . . . . . . . . . . . . . . . . . . . . . . . . . . . . . . | | 10,000 |
| Borrowed $10,000 for 6 months at 12% interest per year. | | |

*Face amount of note*

Notice that no liability is recorded for the interest charges when the note is issued. At the date that money is borrowed, the borrower has a liability *only for the principal amount*

**LO 2**
Account for notes payable and interest expense.

---

[2] An alternative form of note is one in which the interest charges are included in the face amount. This form of note is seldom used today, largely because of the disclosure requirements under "truth-in-lending" laws.

*Note payable written for the principal amount with the interest rate stated separately*

| | |
|---|---|
| Miami, Florida | November 1, 20___ |
| Six months **AFTER THIS DATE** | Porter Company |
| **PROMISES TO PAY TO SECURITY NATIONAL BANK THE SUM OF $** | $10,000 |
| **WITH INTEREST AT THE RATE OF** 12% | **PER ANNUM.** |
| **SIGNED** | *John Caldwell* |
| **TITLE** | Treasurer |

*of the loan;* the liability for interest accrues day by day over the life of the loan. At December 31, two months' interest expense has accrued, and the following year-end adjusting entry is made:

*A liability for interest accrues day by day*

| | | |
|---|---|---|
| Interest Expense . . . . . . . . . . . . . . . . . . . . . . . . . . . . . . . . . . . . . . . . . . . . . . . . | 200 | |
| Interest Payable . . . . . . . . . . . . . . . . . . . . . . . . . . . . . . . . . . . . . . . . . . . . . . | | 200 |

To record interest expense incurred through year-end on 12%,
6-month note dated Nov. 1 ($10,000 × 12% × $^2/_{12}$ = $200).

For simplicity, we will assume that Porter Company makes adjusting entries *only at year-end*. Thus the entry on May 1 to record payment of the note will be:

*Payment of principal and interest*

| | | |
|---|---|---|
| Notes Payable . . . . . . . . . . . . . . . . . . . . . . . . . . . . . . . . . . . . . . . . . . . . . . . | 10,000 | |
| Interest Payable . . . . . . . . . . . . . . . . . . . . . . . . . . . . . . . . . . . . . . . . . . . . . . | 200 | |
| Interest Expense . . . . . . . . . . . . . . . . . . . . . . . . . . . . . . . . . . . . . . . . . . . . . . | 400 | |
| Cash . . . . . . . . . . . . . . . . . . . . . . . . . . . . . . . . . . . . . . . . . . . . . . . . . . . . | | 10,600 |

To record payment of 12%, 6-month note on maturity
date and to recognize interest expense incurred since
Jan. 1 ($10,000 × 12% × $^4/_{12}$ = $400).

If Porter Company paid this note *prior* to May 1, interest charges usually would be computed only through the date of early payment.[3]

## The Current Portion of Long-Term Debt

Some long-term debts, such as mortgage loans, are payable in a series of monthly or quarterly installments. In these cases, the *principal* amount due within one year (or the operating cycle) is regarded as a current liability, and the remainder of the obligation is classified as a long-term liability.

As the maturity date of a long-term liability approaches, the obligation eventually becomes due within the current period. Long-term liabilities that become payable within the coming year are *reclassified* in the balance sheet as current liabilities.[4] Changing the

---

[3] Computing interest charges only through the date of payment is the normal business practice. However, some notes are written in a manner requiring the borrower to pay interest for the full term of the note even if payment is made early. Borrowers should look carefully at these terms.

[4] Exceptions are made to this rule if the liability will be *refinanced* (that is, extended or renewed) on a long-term basis or if a special *sinking fund* has been accumulated for the purpose of repaying this obligation. In these cases, the debt remains classified as a long-term liability, even though it will mature within the current period.

classification of a liability does not require a journal entry; the obligation is simply shown in a different section of the balance sheet.

## Accrued Liabilities

**Accrued liabilities** arise from the recognition of expenses for which payment will be made in a future period. Thus accrued liabilities also are called *accrued expenses*. Examples of accrued liabilities include interest payable, income taxes payable, and a number of liabilities relating to payrolls. As accrued liabilities stem from the recording of expenses, the *matching* principle governs the timing of their recognition.

All companies incur accrued liabilities. In most cases, however, these liabilities are paid at frequent intervals. Therefore, they usually do not accumulate to large amounts. In a balance sheet, accrued liabilities frequently are included in the amount shown as accounts payable.

## Payroll Liabilities

The preparation of a payroll is a specialized accounting function beyond the scope of this text. But we believe that every business student should have some understanding of the various costs associated with payrolls. Every employer must compute, record, and pay a number of costs in addition to the wages and salaries owed to employees. In fact, one might say that the total wages and salaries expense (or gross pay) represents only the starting point of payroll computations.

To illustrate, assume that a manufacturing company employs 50 highly skilled factory employees. If monthly wages for this workforce average $100,000, the costs incurred by this employer in a typical monthly payroll might be as follows:

**LO 3**

Describe the costs relating to payrolls.

| | |
|---|---:|
| Gross pay (wages expense) | $100,000 |
| Social Security and Medicare taxes | 7,650 |
| Federal and state unemployment taxes | 6,200 |
| Workers' compensation insurance premiums | 4,000 |
| Group health insurance premiums | 10,500 |
| Contributions to employee pension plan and other postretirement costs | 5,000 |
| Total factory payroll costs for January | $133,350 |

*Notice the costs in addition to employees' wages*

The amounts shown in red are **payroll taxes** and insurance premiums required by law. Costs shown in green currently are not required by law but often are included in the total compensation package provided to employees.

In our example, total payroll-related costs exceed wages expense *by more than 30%*. This relationship will vary from one employer to another, but our illustration is typical of many payrolls.

**Payroll Taxes and Mandated Costs**  All employers must pay Social Security and Medicare taxes on the wages or salary paid to each employee. These taxes currently amount to 7.65% of the employee's earnings.[5] Federal unemployment taxes apply only to the *first $7,000* earned by each employee during the year (state unemployment taxes may vary). Thus these taxes tend to drop off dramatically as the year progresses.

---

[5] Social Security and Medicare taxes of the *same amount* are also levied on the employees and are withheld from their paychecks. Thus total Social Security and Medicare taxes amount to more than 15% of gross wages and salaries. There is a limit on the portion of an employee's earnings subject to Social Security taxes. However, this limit, now nearly $80,000 (and increasing annually), exceeds most employees' annual earnings. There is no cap on employee wages or salaries subject to Medicare taxes.

**Workers' compensation** is a state-mandated program that provides insurance to employees against job-related injury. The premiums vary greatly by state and by occupational classification. In some high-risk industries (e.g., roofers), workers' compensation premiums may exceed 50% of the employees' wages.

**Other Payroll-Related Costs**   Many employers pay some or all of the costs of health insurance for their employees as well as make contributions to employee pension plans. Annual health insurance premiums usually cost between $1,800 and $3,600 per employee (including family members). Contributions to employees' pension plans, if any, vary greatly among employers.

**Amounts Withheld from Employees' Pay**   Our illustration specifies only those taxes levied on the employer. Employees, too, incur taxes on their earnings. These include federal and state income taxes and the employees' shares of Social Security and Medicare taxes. Employers must withhold these amounts from the employees' pay and forward them directly to the appropriate tax authorities. (The net amount of cash actually paid to employees—that is, total wages and salaries expense less the amounts withheld—often is called the employees' *take-home pay*.)

Amounts withheld from employees' pay do *not* represent taxes on the employer. These amounts are simply portions of the original wages and salaries expense that must be sent directly to tax authorities, rather than paid to the employees. With respect to these taxes, the employer is required by law to act as the tax *collector*. In the employer's balance sheet, these withholdings represent current liabilities until they are deposited with the proper tax authorities.

## Unearned Revenue

A liability for unearned revenue arises when a customer pays in advance. Upon receipt of an advance payment from a customer, the company debits Cash and credits a liability account such as Unearned Revenue or Customers' Deposits. As the services are rendered to the customer, an entry is made debiting the liability account and crediting a revenue account. Notice that the liability for unearned revenue normally is satisfied by rendering services to the creditor, rather than by making cash payments.

Unearned revenue ordinarily is classified as a current liability because activities involved in earning revenue are part of the business's normal operating cycle.

**YOUR TURN**

### You as a Public Accountant for Small Businesses

Assume you are a sole proprietor of Balance & Income, CPAs. One of your clients is Pawn Shop, Inc., for which you undertake normal accounting duties, including preparing monthly statements, completing required tax returns, and recording monthly revenues and expenses. However, Pawn Shop cashes its own checks and pays its own bills from its own bank accounts. Mr. Swidle, the manager of Pawn Shop, asks you if you would be willing to keep a check received from a customer as a down payment for merchandise to be delivered in the future until the transaction is complete. Mr. Swidle explains that he does not want to cash the check now because he is unsure how long it will be before Pawn Shop obtains the desired merchandise. How should you respond to Mr. Swidle?

*Our comments appear on page 450.

## LONG-TERM LIABILITIES

Long-term obligations usually arise from major expenditures, such as acquisitions of plant assets, the purchase of another company, or refinancing an existing long-term obligation that is about to mature. Thus transactions involving long-term liabilities are relatively few in number but often involve large dollar amounts. In contrast, current liabilities usually arise from routine operating transactions.

Many businesses regard long-term liabilities as an alternative to owners' equity as a source of permanent financing. Although long-term liabilities eventually mature, they often are *refinanced*—that is, the maturing obligation simply is replaced with a new long-term liability.

## Maturing Obligations Intended to Be Refinanced

One special type of long-term liability is an obligation that will mature in the current period but that is expected to be refinanced on a long-term basis. For example, a company may have a bank loan that comes due each year but is routinely extended for the following year. Both the company and the bank may intend for this arrangement to continue on a long-term basis.

If management has both the *intent* and the *ability* to refinance soon-to-mature obligations on a long-term basis, these obligations are classified as long-term liabilities. In this situation, the accountant looks to the *economic substance* of the situation rather than to its legal form.

When the economic substance of a transaction differs from its legal form or its outward appearance, financial statements should reflect the *economic substance*. Accountants summarize this concept with the phrase *"Substance takes precedence over form."* Today's business world is characterized by transactions of ever-increasing complexity. Recognizing those situations in which the substance of a transaction differs from its form is one of the greatest challenges confronting the accounting profession.

## Installment Notes Payable

Purchases of real estate and certain types of equipment often are financed by the issuance of long-term notes that call for a series of installment payments. These payments (often called **debt service**) may be due monthly, quarterly, semiannually, or at any other interval. If these installments continue until the debt is completely repaid, the loan is said to be "fully amortizing." Often, however, installment notes contain a due date at which the remaining unpaid balance is to be repaid in a single "balloon" payment.

Some installment notes call for installment payments equal to the periodic interest charges (an "interest only" note). Under these terms, the principal amount of the loan is payable at a specified maturity date. More often, however, the installment payments are *greater* than the amount of interest accruing during the period. Thus only a portion of each installment payment represents interest expense, and the remainder of the payment reduces the principal amount of the liability. As the amount owed is reduced by each payment, the portion of each successive payment representing interest expense will *decrease,* and the portion going toward repayment of principal will *increase.*

**Allocating Installment Payments between Interest and Principal**  In accounting for an installment note, the accountant must determine the portion of each payment that represents interest expense and the portion that reduces the principal amount of the liability. This distinction is made in advance by preparing an **amortization table**.

> **LO 4**
> Prepare an amortization table allocating payments between interest and principal.

To illustrate, assume that on October 15, Year 1, King's Inn purchases furnishings at a total cost of $16,398. In payment, the company issues an installment note payable for this amount, plus interest at 12% per annum (or 1% per month). This note will be paid in 18 monthly installments of $1,000 each, beginning on November 15. An amortization table for this installment note payable is shown on the following page (amounts of interest expense are *rounded to the nearest dollar*).

**Preparing an Amortization Table**  Let us explore the content of this table. First, notice that the payments are made on a *monthly* basis. Therefore, the amounts of the payments (column A), interest expense (column B), and reduction in the unpaid balance (column C) are all *monthly amounts.*

The interest rate used in the table is of special importance; this rate must coincide with the period of time *between payment dates*—in this case, one month. Thus, if payments are made monthly, column B must be based on the *monthly* rate of interest. If payments were made quarterly, this column would use the quarterly rate of interest.

An amortization table begins with the original amount of the liability ($16,398) listed at the top of the Unpaid Balance column. The amounts of the monthly payments, shown in column A, are specified by the installment contract. The monthly interest expense, shown in column B, is computed for each month by applying the monthly interest rate to the unpaid balance at the *beginning of that month*. The portion of each payment that reduces the amount of the liability (column C) is simply the remainder of the payment (column A minus column B). Finally, the unpaid balance of the liability (column D) is reduced each month by the amount indicated in column C.

### AMORTIZATION TABLE
### (12% Note Payable for $16,398; Payable in 18 Monthly Installments of $1,000)

| Interest Period | Payment Date | (A) Monthly Payment | (B) Interest Expense (1% of the Last Unpaid Balance) | (C) Reduction in Unpaid Balance (A) − (B) | (D) Unpaid Balance |
|---|---|---|---|---|---|
| Issue date | Oct. 15, Year 1 | — | — | — | $16,398 |
| 1 | Nov. 15 | $1,000 | $164 | $836 | 15,562 |
| 2 | Dec. 15 | 1,000 | 156 | 844 | 14,718 |
| 3 | Jan. 15, Year 2 | 1,000 | 147 | 853 | 13,865 |
| 4 | Feb. 15 | 1,000 | 139 | 861 | 13,004 |
| 5 | Mar. 15 | 1,000 | 130 | 870 | 12,134 |
| 6 | Apr. 15 | 1,000 | 121 | 879 | 11,255 |
| 7 | May 15 | 1,000 | 113 | 887 | 10,368 |
| 8 | June 15 | 1,000 | 104 | 896 | 9,472 |
| 9 | July 15 | 1,000 | 95 | 905 | 8,567 |
| 10 | Aug. 15 | 1,000 | 86 | 914 | 7,653 |
| 11 | Sept. 15 | 1,000 | 77 | 923 | 6,730 |
| 12 | Oct. 15 | 1,000 | 67 | 933 | 5,797 |
| 13 | Nov. 15 | 1,000 | 58 | 942 | 4,855 |
| 14 | Dec. 15 | 1,000 | 49 | 951 | 3,904 |
| 15 | Jan. 15, Year 3 | 1,000 | 39 | 961 | 2,943 |
| 16 | Feb. 15 | 1,000 | 29 | 971 | 1,972 |
| 17 | Mar. 15 | 1,000 | 20 | 980 | 992 |
| 18 | Apr. 15 | 1,000 | 8* | 992 | −0− |

*In the last period, interest expense is equal to the amount of the final payment minus the remaining unpaid balance. This compensates for the cumulative effect of rounding interest amounts to the nearest dollar.

**CASH EFFECTS**    Note that the total monthly cash payment (column A) does not change from period to period. What does change, however, is the portion of the cash payment allocated to interest expense each month (column B) versus the amount by which the outstanding loan balance is reduced (column C).

Rather than continuing to make monthly payments, King's Inn could settle this liability at any time by paying the amount currently shown as the unpaid balance.

Notice that the amount of interest expense listed in column B *changes every month.* In our illustration, the interest expense is *decreasing* each month, because the unpaid balance is continually decreasing.[6]

Preparing each horizontal line in an amortization table involves making the same computations, based on a new unpaid balance. Thus an amortization table of any length can be easily and quickly prepared by computer. (Most "money management" software includes a program for preparing amortization tables.) Only three items of data need to be entered into the computer: (1) the original amount of the liability, (2) the amount of periodic payments, and (3) the interest rate (per payment period).

**Using an Amortization Table**   Once an amortization table has been prepared, the entries to record each payment are taken directly from the amounts shown in the table. For example, the entry to record the first monthly payment (November 15, Year 1) is:

| | | |
|---|---|---|
| Interest Expense . . . . . . . . . . . . . . . . . . . . . . . . . . . . . . . . . . . . . . . . . . . | 164 | |
| Installment Note Payable . . . . . . . . . . . . . . . . . . . . . . . . . . . . . . . . . . . | 836 | |
| Cash . . . . . . . . . . . . . . . . . . . . . . . . . . . . . . . . . . . . . . . . . . . . | | 1,000 |
| Made Nov. payment on installment note payable. | | |

*Payment is allocated between interest and principal*

Similarly, the entry to record the *second* payment, made on *December 15, Year 1,* is:

| | | |
|---|---|---|
| Interest Expense . . . . . . . . . . . . . . . . . . . . . . . . . . . . . . . . . . . . . . . . . . . | 156 | |
| Installment Note Payable . . . . . . . . . . . . . . . . . . . . . . . . . . . . . . . . . . . | 844 | |
| Cash . . . . . . . . . . . . . . . . . . . . . . . . . . . . . . . . . . . . . . . . . . . . | | 1,000 |
| Made Dec. payment on installment note payable. | | |

*Notice that interest expense is less in December*

At December 31, Year 1, King's Inn should make an adjusting entry to record one-half month's accrued interest on this liability. The amount of this adjusting entry is based on the unpaid balance shown in the amortization table as of the last payment (December 15). This entry is:

| | | |
|---|---|---|
| Interest Expense . . . . . . . . . . . . . . . . . . . . . . . . . . . . . . . . . . . . . . . . . . . | 74 | |
| Interest Payable . . . . . . . . . . . . . . . . . . . . . . . . . . . . . . . . . . . . . . . . . . . | | 74 |
| Adjusting entry to record interest expense on installment note | | |
| for the last half of Dec.: $14,718 $\times$ 1% $\times$ $\frac{1}{2}$ = $74. | | |

*Year-end adjusting entry*

**The Current Portion of Long-Term Debt**   Notice that as of December 31, Year 1, the unpaid balance of this note is $14,718. As of December 31, *Year 2,* however, the unpaid balance will be only $3,904. Thus the principal amount of this note will be reduced by *$10,814* during Year 2 ($14,718 − $3,904 = $10,814). In the balance sheet prepared at December 31, Year 1, the $10,814 portion of this debt that is scheduled for repayment within the *next 12 months* should be classified as a *current liability.* The remaining $3,904 should be classified as a long-term liability.

## SPECIAL TYPES OF LIABILITIES

The types of liabilities discussed up to this point are encountered in all types of business organizations—large and small. We will now address some special types of liabilities that are found primarily in the financial statements of large, publicly owned corporations.

---

[6] If the monthly payments were *less* than the amount of the monthly interest expense, the unpaid balance of the note would *increase* each month. This, in turn, would cause the interest expense to increase each month. This pattern, termed *negative amortization,* occurs temporarily in some "adjustable-rate" home mortgages.

**LO 5**

Describe corporate bonds and explain the tax advantage of debt financing.

## Bonds Payable

Financially sound corporations may arrange limited amounts of long-term financing by issuing notes payable to banks or to insurance companies. But to finance a large project, such as developing an oil field or purchasing a controlling interest in the capital stock of another company, a corporation may need more capital than any single lender can supply. When a corporation needs to raise large amounts of long-term capital—perhaps 50, 100, or 500 million dollars (or more)—it generally sells additional shares of capital stock or issues **bonds payable**.

## What Are Bonds?

The issuance of bonds payable is a technique for splitting a very large loan into many transferable units, called bonds. Each bond represents a *long-term, interest-bearing note payable,* usually in the face amount (or par value) of $1,000 or some multiple of $1,000. The bonds are sold to the investing public, enabling many different investors (bond-holders) to participate in the loan.

Bonds usually are very long-term notes, maturing in perhaps 30 or 40 years. The bonds are transferable, however, so individual bondholders may sell their bonds to other investors at any time. Most bonds call for semiannual interest payments to the bond-holders, with interest computed at a specified *contract rate* throughout the life of the bond. Thus investors often describe bonds as "fixed income" investments.

An example of a corporate bond issue is the 8½% bonds of **Pacific Bell** (a Pacific Telesis company, known as **PacBell**), due August 15, 2031. Interest on these bonds is payable semiannually on February 15 and August 15. With this bond issue, **PacBell** borrowed $225 million by issuing 225,000 bonds of $1,000 each.

**PacBell** did not actually print and issue 225,000 separate notes payable. Each bond-holder is issued a single *bond certificate* indicating the number of bonds purchased. Each certificate is in the face amount of $25,000 and, therefore, represents ownership of 25 bonds. Investors such as mutual funds, banks, and insurance companies often buy thousands of bonds at one time.

**The Issuance of Bonds Payable**   When bonds are issued, the corporation usually utilizes the services of an investment banking firm, called an **underwriter**. The underwriter guarantees the issuing corporation a specific price for the entire bond issue and makes a profit by selling the bonds to the investing public at a higher price. The corporation records the issuance of the bonds at the net amount received from the underwriter. The use of an underwriter assures the corporation that the entire bond issue will be sold without delay and that the entire amount of the proceeds will be available at a specific date.

**Transferability of Bonds**   Corporate bonds, like capital stocks, are traded daily on organized securities exchanges, such as the *New York Bond Exchange*. The holders of a 25-year bond issue need not wait 25 years to convert their investments into cash. By placing a telephone call to a broker, an investor may sell bonds within a matter of minutes at the going market price. This quality of *liquidity* is one of the most attractive features of an investment in corporate bonds.

**Quoted Market Prices**   Bond prices are quoted as a *percentage* of their face value or *maturity* value, which is usually $1,000. The maturity value is the amount the issuing company must pay to redeem the bond at the date it matures (becomes due). A $1,000 bond quoted at *102* would therefore have a market price of $1,020 (102% of $1,000). Bond prices are quoted at the nearest one-eighth of a percentage point. The following line from the financial page of a daily newspaper summarizes the previous day's trading in bonds of **Sears, Roebuck & Company**:

*What is the market value of this bond?*

| Bonds | Sales | High | Low | Close | Net Change |
|-------|-------|------|-----|-------|------------|
| Sears R 7⅞'07 | 245 | 97½ | 95½ | 97 | +1 |

This line of condensed information indicates that 245 of Sears' 7⅞%, $1,000 bonds maturing in 2007 were traded during the day. The highest price is reported as 97½, or $975 for a bond of $1,000 face value. The lowest price was 95½, or $955 for a $1,000 bond. The closing price (last sale of the day) was 97, or $970. This was one point above the closing price of the previous day, an increase of $10 in the price of a $1,000 bond.

**Types of Bonds** Bonds secured by the pledge of specific assets are called *mortgage bonds.* An unsecured bond is called a *debenture bond;* its value rests on the general credit of the corporation. A debenture bond issued by a very large and strong corporation may have a higher investment rating than a secured bond issued by a corporation in less satisfactory financial condition.

Bond interest is paid semiannually by mailing to each bondholder a check for six months' interest on the bonds he or she owns.[7] Many bonds are *callable,* which means that the corporation has the right to redeem the bonds *in advance* of the maturity date by paying a specified *call price.* To compensate bondholders for being forced to give up their investments, the call price usually is somewhat higher than the face value of the bonds.

Traditionally, bonds have appealed to conservative investors, interested primarily in a reliable income stream from their investments. To make a bond issue more attractive to these investors, some corporations create a bond **sinking fund**, designated for repaying the bonds at maturity. At regular intervals, the corporation deposits cash into this sinking fund. A bond sinking fund is not classified as a current asset, because it is not available for the payment of current liabilities. Such funds are shown in the balance sheet under the caption "Long-Term Investments," which appears just below the current asset section.

As an additional attraction to investors, corporations sometimes include a conversion privilege in the bond indenture. A **convertible bond** is one that may be exchanged at the option of the bondholder for a specified number of shares of capital stock. Thus the market value of a convertible bond tends to fluctuate with the market value of an equivalent number of shares of capital stock.

**Junk Bonds** In recent years, some corporations have issued securities that have come to be known as **junk bonds**. This term describes a bond issue that involves a substantially greater risk of default than normal. A company issuing junk bonds usually has so much long-term debt that its ability to meet interest and principal repayment obligations has become questionable. To compensate bondholders for this unusual level of risk, junk bonds promise a substantially higher rate of interest than do "investment quality" bonds.

---

The risk associated with junk bonds can make them a real gamble for investors in more ways than one. Donald Trump sold $1.2 billion in junk bonds, secured primarily by the Trump Taj Mahal and the Trump Plaza—the largest casino junk bond issue in history. The risk did not scare away high-rolling investors, however, who eagerly placed bets on the chance of receiving an 11.25% contract rate of interest.

**CASE IN POINT**

---

## Tax Advantage of Bond Financing

A principal advantage of raising money by issuing bonds instead of stock is that interest payments are *deductible* in determining income subject to corporate income taxes.

---

[7] In recent years, corporations have issued only *registered* bonds, for which interest is paid by mailing a check to the registered owners of the bonds. In past decades, some companies issued *coupon bonds* or *bearer bonds,* which had a series of redeemable coupons attached. At each interest date, the bondholder had to "clip" the coupon and present it to a bank to collect the interest. These bonds posed a considerable hazard to investors— if the investor lost the coupon, or forgot about an interest date, he or she received no interest. In many states, issuing coupon bonds now is illegal.

Dividends paid to stockholders, however, are *not deductible* in computing taxable income.

To illustrate, assume that a corporation pays income taxes at a rate of *30%* on its taxable income. If this corporation issues $10 million of 10% bonds payable, it will incur interest expense of $1 million per year. This interest expense, however, will reduce taxable income by $1 million, thus reducing the corporation's annual income taxes by $300,000. As a result, the *after-tax* cost of borrowing the $10 million is only *$700,000*, as follows:

| | |
|---|---:|
| Interest expense ($10,000,000 × 10%) . . . . . . . . . . . . . . . . . . . . . . . . . . . . . . . . . | $1,000,000 |
| Less: Income tax savings ($1,000,000 deduction × 30%) . . . . . . . . . . . . . . . . . | 300,000 |
| After-tax cost of borrowing . . . . . . . . . . . . . . . . . . . . . . . . . . . . . . . . . . . . . . . . . | $ 700,000 |

A shortcut approach to computing the after-tax cost of borrowing is simply multiplying the interest expense by *1 minus the company's tax rate*, as follows: $1,000,000 × (1 − .30) = $700,000.

## Accounting for Bonds Payable

Accounting for bonds payable closely parallels accounting for notes payable. The accountable events for a bond issue usually are (1) issuance of the bonds, (2) semiannual interest payments, (3) accrual of interest payable at the end of each accounting period,[8] and (4) retirement of the bonds at maturity.

To illustrate these events, assume that on March 1, 2002, Wells Corporation issues $1 million of 12%, 20-year bonds payable.[9] These bonds are dated March 1, 2002, and interest is computed from this date. Interest on the bonds is payable semiannually, each September 1 and March 1. If all of the bonds are sold at par value (face amount), the issuance of the bonds on March 1 will be recorded by the following entry:

*Entry at the issuance date*

| | | |
|---|---:|---:|
| Cash . . . . . . . . . . . . . . . . . . . . . . . . . . . . . . . . . . . . . . . . . . . . . . . . . | 1,000,000 | |
|     Bonds Payable . . . . . . . . . . . . . . . . . . . . . . . . . . . . . . . . . . . . . . | | 1,000,000 |
| Issued 12% 20-year bonds payable at a price of 100. | | |

Every September 1 during the term of the bond issue, Wells Corporation must pay $60,000 to the bondholders ($1,000,000 × .12 × ¹/₂ = $60,000). This semiannual interest payment will be recorded as shown below:

*Entry to record semiannual interest payments*

| | | |
|---|---:|---:|
| Bond Interest Expense . . . . . . . . . . . . . . . . . . . . . . . . . . . . . . . . . . . . | 60,000 | |
|     Cash . . . . . . . . . . . . . . . . . . . . . . . . . . . . . . . . . . . . . . . . . . . . . . . | | 60,000 |
| Semiannual payment of bond interest. | | |

Every December 31, Wells Corporation must make an adjusting entry to record the four months' interest that has accrued since September 1:

*Adjusting entry at year-end—if necessary*

| | | |
|---|---:|---:|
| Bond Interest Expense . . . . . . . . . . . . . . . . . . . . . . . . . . . . . . . . . . . . | 40,000 | |
|     Bond Interest Payable . . . . . . . . . . . . . . . . . . . . . . . . . . . . . . . . . . | | 40,000 |
| To accrue bond interest payable for four months ended Dec. 31 ($1,000,000 × .12 × ⁴/₁₂ = $40,000). | | |

---

[8] To simplify our illustrations, we assume in all of our examples and assignment material that adjusting entries for accrued bond interest payable are made *only at year-end*. In practice, these adjustments usually are made on a monthly basis.

[9] The amount of $1 million is used only for purposes of illustration. As explained earlier, actual bond issues are for many millions of dollars.

The accrued liability for bond interest payable will be paid within a few months and, therefore, is classified as a current liability.

Two months later, on March 1, a semiannual interest payment is made to bondholders. This transaction represents payment of the four months' interest accrued at December 31, and of two months' interest that has accrued since year-end. Thus the entry to record the semiannual interest payments every March 1 will be:

| | | |
|---|---|---|
| Bond Interest Expense .......................................... | 20,000 | |
| Bond Interest Payable ........................................... | 40,000 | |
|    Cash ...................................................... | | 60,000 |

To record semiannual interest payment to bondholders, and to recognize two months' interest expense accrued since year-end ($1,000,000 × .12 × $2/12$ = $20,000).

*Interest payment following the year-end adjusting entry*

When the bonds mature 20 years later on March 1, 2022, two entries are required: one to record the regular semiannual interest payment and a second to record the retirement of the bonds. The entry to record the retirement of the bond issue is:

| | | |
|---|---|---|
| Bonds Payable ................................................. | 1,000,000 | |
|    Cash ...................................................... | | 1,000,000 |

Paid face amount of bonds at maturity.

*Redeeming the bonds at the maturity date*

**Bonds Issued between Interest Dates**  The semiannual interest dates (such as January 1 and July 1, or April 1 and October 1) are printed on the bond certificates. However, bonds are often issued between the specified interest dates. The *investor* is then required to pay the interest accrued to the date of issuance *in addition* to the stated price of the bond. This practice enables the corporation to pay a full six months' interest on all bonds outstanding at the semiannual interest payment date. The accrued interest collected from investors who purchase bonds between interest payment dates is thus returned to them on the next interest payment date.

To illustrate, let us modify our illustration to assume that Wells Corporation issues $1 million of 12% bonds at a price of 100 on *May 1*—two months *after* the date printed on the bonds. The amount received from the bond purchasers now will include two months' accrued interest, as follows:

| | | |
|---|---|---|
| Cash ........................................................ | 1,020,000 | |
|    Bonds Payable ............................................ | | 1,000,000 |
|    Bond Interest Payable .................................... | | 20,000 |

Issued $1,000,000 face value of 12%, 20-year bonds at 100 plus accrued interest for two months ($1,000,000 × 12% × $2/12$ = $20,000).

*Bonds issued between interest dates*

Four months later on the regular semiannual interest payment date, a full six months' interest ($60 per $1,000 bond) will be paid to all bondholders, *regardless of when they purchased their bonds.* The entry for the semiannual interest payment is illustrated below:

| | | |
|---|---|---|
| Bond Interest Payable ........................................... | 20,000 | |
| Bond Interest Expense .......................................... | 40,000 | |
|    Cash ...................................................... | | 60,000 |

Paid semiannual interest on $1,000,000 face value of 12% bonds.

*Notice only part of the interest payment is charged to expense*

Now consider these interest transactions from the standpoint of the *investors.* They paid for two months' accrued interest at the time of purchasing the bonds and then received checks for six months' interest after holding the bonds for only four months. They have, therefore, been reimbursed properly for the use of their money for four months.

When bonds are subsequently sold by one investor to another, they sell at the quoted market price *plus accrued interest* since the last interest payment date. This practice enables the issuing corporation to pay all the interest for an interest period to the investor owning the bond at the interest date. Otherwise, the corporation would have to make partial payments to every investor who bought or sold the bond during the interest period.

The amount that investors will pay for bonds is the *present value* of the principal and interest payments they will receive. Before going further in our discussion of bonds payable, it will be helpful to review the concepts of present value and effective interest rate.

## The Concept of Present Value

**LO 6**

Explain the concept of present value.

The concept of present value is based on the time value of money—the idea that receiving money today is preferable to receiving money at some later date. Assume, for example, that a bond will have a maturity value of $1,000 five years from today but will pay no interest in the meantime. Investors would not pay $1,000 for this bond today, because they would receive no return on their investment over the next five years. There are prices less than $1,000, however, at which investors would buy the bond. For example, if the bond could be purchased for $600, the investor could expect a return (interest) of $400 from the investment over the five-year period.

The **present value** of a future cash receipt is the amount that a knowledgeable investor will pay *today* for the right to receive that future payment. The exact amount of the present value depends on (1) the amount of the future payment, (2) the length of time until the payment will be received, and (3) the rate of return required by the investor. However, the present value will always be *less* than the future amount. This is because money received today can be invested to earn interest and grow to a larger amount in the future.

The rate of interest that will cause a given present value to grow to a given future amount is called the *discount rate* or *effective rate*. The effective interest rate required by investors at any given time is regarded as the going *market rate* of interest. (The procedures for computing the present value of a future amount are illustrated in Appendix B at the end of this textbook. The concept of present value is very useful in managing your personal financial affairs. We suggest that you read Appendix B—even if it has not been assigned.)

**The Present Value Concept and Bond Prices**   The price at which bonds sell is the present value to investors of the future principal and interest payments. If the bonds sell at par, the market rate is equal to the *contract interest rate* (or nominal rate) printed on the bonds. The *higher* the effective interest rate that investors require, the *less* they will pay for bonds with a given contract rate of interest. For example, if investors insist on a 10% return, they will pay less than $1,000 for a 9%, $1,000 bond. Thus, if investors require an effective interest rate *greater* than the contract rate of interest, the bonds will sell at a *discount* (a price less than their face value). On the other hand, if market conditions support an effective interest rate of *less* than the contract rate, the bonds will sell at a *premium* (a price above their face value).

A corporation wishing to borrow money by issuing bonds must pay the going market rate of interest. Since market rates of interest fluctuate constantly, it must be expected that the contract rate of interest may vary somewhat from the market rate at the date the bonds are issued. Thus bonds may be issued at a slight discount or premium. (The issuance of bonds at a discount or premium is discussed in *Supplemental Topic B* at the end of this chapter.)

## Bond Prices after Issuance

As stated earlier, many corporate bonds are traded daily on organized securities exchanges at quoted market prices. After bonds are issued, their market prices vary *inversely* with changes in market interest rates. As interest rates rise, investors will be willing to pay less money to own a bond that pays a given contract rate of interest. Conversely, as interest rates decline, the market prices of bonds rise.

**CASE IN POINT**

**IBM** sold to underwriters $500 million of 9³/₈%, 25-year debenture bonds. The underwriters planned to sell the bonds to the public at a price of 99⁵/₈. Just as the bonds were offered for sale, however, a change in Federal Reserve credit policy started an upward surge in interest rates. The underwriters encountered great difficulty selling the bonds. Within one week, the market price of the bonds had fallen to 94¹/₂. The underwriters dumped their unsold inventory at this price and sustained one of the largest underwriting losses in Wall Street history.

During the months that followed, interest rates soared to record levels. Within five months, the price of the bonds had fallen to 76³/₈. Thus nearly one-fourth of the market value of these bonds evaporated in less than half a year. At this time, the financial strength of **IBM** was never in question; this dramatic loss in market value was caused entirely by rising interest rates.

Changes in the current level of interest rates are not the only factors influencing the market prices of bonds. The length of time remaining until the bonds mature is another major force. As a bond nears its maturity date, its market price normally moves closer and closer to the maturity value. This trend is dependable because the bonds are redeemed at par value on the maturity date.

**Volatility of Short-Term and Long-Term Bond Prices**   When interest rates fluctuate, the market prices of long-term bonds are affected to a far greater extent than are the market prices of bonds due to mature in the near future. To illustrate, assume that market interest rates suddenly soar from 9% to 12%. A 9% bond scheduled to mature in a few days will still have a market value of approximately $1,000—the amount to be collected in a few days from the issuing corporation. However, the market price of a 9% bond maturing in 10 years will drop significantly. Investors who must accept these below market interest payments for many years will buy the bonds only at a discounted price.

In summary, fluctuations in interest rates have a far greater effect on the market prices of long-term bonds than on the prices of short-term bonds.

Remember that after bonds have been issued, they belong to the bondholder, *not to the issuing corporation.* Therefore, changes in the market price of bonds subsequent to their issuance *do not* affect the amounts shown in the financial statements of the issuing corporation, and these changes are not recorded in the company's accounting records.

**YOUR TURN**

**You as a Financial Advisor**

Assume that you are the financial advisor for a recently retired couple. Your clients want to invest their savings in such a way as to receive a stable stream of cash flow every year throughout their retirement. They have expressed their concerns to you regarding the volatility of long-term bond prices when interest rates fluctuate.

If your clients invest their savings in a variety of long-term bonds and hold these bonds until maturity, will interest rate fluctuations affect their annual cash flow during their retirement years?

*Our comments appear on page 450.

## Early Retirement of Bonds Payable

Bonds are sometimes retired before the maturity date. The principal reason for retiring bonds early is to relieve the issuing corporation of the obligation to make future interest payments. If interest rates decline to the point that a corporation can borrow at an interest rate below that being paid on a particular bond issue, the corporation may benefit from retiring those bonds and issuing new bonds at a lower interest rate.

Most bond issues contain a call provision, permitting the corporation to redeem the bonds by paying a specified price, usually a few points above par. Even without a call provision, the corporation may retire its bonds before maturity by purchasing them in the open market. If the bonds can be purchased by the issuing corporation at less than their carrying value, a *gain* is realized on the retirement of the debt. If the bonds are reacquired by the issuing corporation at a price in excess of their carrying value, a *loss* must be recognized.[10]

For example, assume that Briggs Corporation has outstanding a 13%, $10 million bond issue, callable on any interest date at a price of 104. Assume also that the bonds were issued at par and will not mature for nine years. Recently, however, market interest rates have declined to less than 10%, and the market price of Briggs's bonds has increased to 106.[11]

Regardless of the market price, Briggs can call these bonds at 104. If the company exercises this call provision for 10% of the bonds ($1,000,000 face value), the entry will be:

*Bonds called at a price above carrying value*

| | |
|---|---:|
| Bonds Payable .......................................... 1,000,000 | |
| Loss on Early Retirement of Bonds ......................... 40,000 | |
|      Cash ................................................ | 1,040,000 |

To record the call of $1 million in bonds payable at a call price of 104.

Notice that Briggs *called* these bonds, rather than repurchasing them at market prices. Therefore, Briggs is able to retire these bonds at their call price of 104. (Had the market price of the bonds been *below* 104, Briggs might have been able to retire the bonds at less cost by purchasing them in the open market.)

## Lease Payment Obligations

A company may purchase the assets needed in its business operations or, as an alternative, it may lease them. A *lease* is a contract in which the lessor gives the lessee the right to use an asset for a specified period of time in exchange for periodic rental payments. The **lessor** is the owner of the property; the **lessee** is a tenant or renter. Examples of assets frequently acquired by lease include automobiles, building space, computers, and equipment.

## Operating Leases

When the lessor gives the lessee the right to use leased property for a limited period of time but retains the usual risks and rewards of ownership, the contract is known as an **operating lease**. An example of an operating lease is a contract leasing office space in an office building. If the building increases in value, the *lessor* can receive the benefits of this increase by either selling the building or increasing the rental rate once the lease term has expired. Likewise, if the building declines in value, it is the lessor who bears the loss.

In accounting for an operating lease, the lessor views the monthly lease payments received as rental revenue, and the lessee regards these payments as rental expense. No asset or liability (other than a short-term liability for accrued rent payable) relating to the lease appears in the lessee's balance sheet. Thus operating leases are sometimes termed **off-balance-sheet financing**.

## Capital Leases

Some lease contracts are intended to provide financing to the lessee for the eventual purchase of the property or to provide the lessee with use of the property over most of its useful life. These lease contracts are called **capital leases** (or financing leases). In

---

[10] The FASB has ruled that the gains and losses from early retirements of debt be classified in a special section of the income statement and identified as *extraordinary items*. The presentation of extraordinary items is explained and illustrated in Chapter 12.

[11] Falling interest rates cause bond prices to rise. On the other hand, falling interest rates also provide the issuing company with an incentive to call the bonds and, perhaps, replace them with bonds bearing a lower rate of interest. For this reason, call prices often serve as an approximate "ceiling" on market prices.

contrast to an operating lease, a capital lease transfers most of the risks and rewards of ownership from the lessor to the *lessee*. Assume, for example, that City Realty leases a new automobile for a period of three years. Also assume that at the end of the lease, title to the automobile transfers to City Realty at no additional cost. Clearly, City Realty is not merely renting the use of the automobile; rather, it is using the lease agreement as a means of *financing the purchase* of the car.

From an accounting viewpoint, capital leases are regarded as *essentially equivalent to a sale* of the property by the lessor to the lessee, even though title to the leased property has not been transferred. Thus a capital lease should be recorded by the *lessor as a sale* of property and by the *lessee as a purchase*. In such lease agreements, an appropriate interest charge usually is added to the regular sales price of the property in determining the amount of the lease payments.

Some companies use capital lease agreements as a means of financing the sale of their products to customers. In accounting for merchandise "sold" through a capital lease, the lessor debits *Lease Payments Receivable* and credits *Sales* for an amount equal to the *present value* of the future lease payments. In most cases, the present value of these future payments is equal to the regular sales price of the merchandise. In addition, the lessor transfers the cost of the leased merchandise from the Inventory account to the Cost of Goods Sold account. When lease payments are received, the lessor recognizes an appropriate portion of the payment as representing interest revenue and the remainder as a reduction in Lease Payments Receivable.

When equipment is acquired through a capital lease, the lessee *debits an asset account,* Leased Equipment, and *credits a liability account,* Lease Payment Obligation, for the present value of the future lease payments. Lease payments made by the lessee are allocated between Interest Expense and a reduction in the liability Lease Payment Obligation. The portion of the lease payment obligation that will be repaid within the next year is classified as a current liability, and the remainder is classified as long-term.

*No rent expense is recorded by the lessee in a capital lease.* The asset account Leased Equipment is usually depreciated by the lessee over the life of the equipment rather than the term of the lease. Accounting for capital leases is illustrated in Appendix B at the end of this textbook.

**Distinguishing between Capital Leases and Operating Leases**  The FASB has taken the position that the risks and returns of ownership transfer to the lessee under any of the following circumstances:

- The lease transfers ownership of the property to the lessee at the end of the lease term.
- The lease contains a bargain purchase option.
- The lease term is equal to 75% or more of the estimated economic life of the leased property.
- The present value of the minimum lease payments amounts to 90% or more of the fair value of the lease property.

Thus, if a lease contains any of these provisions, it is viewed as a capital lease. Otherwise, it is accounted for as an operating lease.

 External financial reporting requirements for leases vary significantly around the world. In many countries, external reporting requirements do not distinguish between operating leases and capital leases. Reporting requirements in China, Switzerland, Italy, and India do not recognize capitalization of lease agreements. Thus, for companies reporting in those countries, all leases are treated as operating leases.

**CASE IN POINT**

## Liabilities for Pensions and Other Postretirement Benefits

Many employers agree to pay their employees a pension; that is, monthly cash payments for life, beginning at retirement. Pensions are not an expense of the years in which cash payments are made to retired workers. Employees earn the right to receive the pension *while they are working for their employer.* Therefore, the employer's cost of future pension payments *accrues* over the years that each employee is on the payroll.

The amounts of the retirement benefits that will be paid to today's workers after they retire are not known with certainty. Among other things, these amounts depend on how long retired employees live. Therefore, the employer's obligation for future pension payments arising during the current year *can only be estimated.*

Employers do not usually pay retirement pensions directly to retired employees. Most employers meet their pension obligations by making periodic deposits in a **pension fund** (or pension plan) throughout the years of each worker's employment.

A pension fund is *not an asset* of the employer. Rather, it is an *independent entity* managed by a trustee (usually a bank or an insurance company). As the employer makes deposits in the pension fund, the trustee invests the money in securities such as stocks and bonds. Over time, the pension fund earns investment income and normally accumulates to a balance far in excess of the employer's deposits. The *pension fund*—not the employer—disburses monthly pension benefits to retired workers.

If the employer meets *all* of its estimated pension obligations by promptly depositing cash in a pension fund, the pension fund is said to be *fully funded.* If a pension plan is fully funded, *no liability* for pension payments appears in the employer's balance sheet. The employer's obligation is discharged in the *current period* through the payments made to the pension fund. The employer records each payment to this fund by debiting Pension Expense and crediting Cash.

Most pension plans are fully funded; therefore, most corporations do *not* report any pension liability. However, an employer must credit a liability account, Unfunded Pension Liability, for any portion of its periodic pension expense that has not been paid to the pension fund.

**Determining Pension Expense** From a conceptual point of view, the pension expense of a given period is the *present value* of the future pension rights granted to employees as a result of their services during the period. The computation of annual pension expense is complex and involves many assumptions. The amount of this expense is computed not by accountants, but rather by an **actuary**. The factors considered by the actuary are as follows:

- Average age, retirement age, and life expectancy of employees
- Employee turnover rates
- Compensation levels and estimated rate of pay increases
- Expected rate of return to be earned on pension fund assets

As a step in determining the pension expense for the year, the actuary estimates the employer's total pension liability as of year-end. The estimates are updated annually, and estimating errors in prior years are adjusted in the current year.

For example, assume that the actuarial firm of Gibson & Holt computes a pension expense for Cramer Cable Company of $400,000 for 2002. This amount represents the present value of pension rights granted to Cramer's employees for the work they performed during the year. To fully fund this obligation, Cramer transfers $400,000 to National Trust Co., the trustee of the company's pension plan.

An entry summarizing Cramer's fully funded pension expense for 2002 is as follows:

| | | |
|---|---|---|
| Pension Expense | 400,000 | |
|    Cash | | 400,000 |
| Pension expense for the year as determined by actuarial firm of | | |
|    Gibson & Holt; fully funded by payments to National Trust Co. | | |

**Postretirement Benefits Other Than Pensions**   In addition to pension plans, many companies have promised their employees other types of **postretirement benefits**, such as continuing health insurance. In most respects, these nonpension postretirement benefits are accounted for in the same manner as are pension benefits. Most companies, however, do not fully fund their obligations for nonpension postretirement benefits. Thus recognition of the annual expense often includes a credit to an unfunded liability for part of the cost.

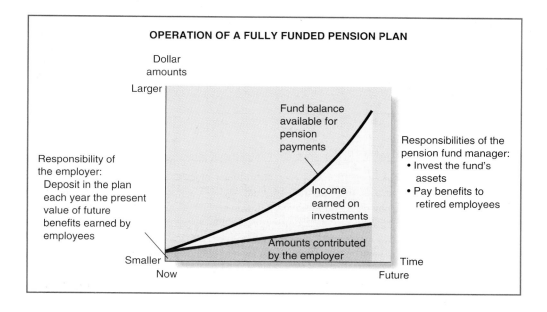

**OPERATION OF A FULLY FUNDED PENSION PLAN**

Continuing with our illustration of Cramer Cable Company, assume that Gibson & Holt computes for the company a $250,000 nonpension postretirement benefits expense for 2002. Unlike its pension expense, however, Cramer does *not* fully fund its nonpension obligations.

For 2002, only $140,000 of the total amount was paid in cash. The entry to summarize this expense for the year is:

| | | |
|---|---|---|
| Nonpension Postretirement Benefits Expense | 250,000 | |
|    Cash | | 140,000 |
|    Unfunded Liability for Nonpension Postretirement Benefits | | 110,000 |
| To record nonpension postretirement benefits expense per report of | | |
|    Gibson & Holt, actuaries; expense funded to the extent of $140,000. | | |

Any portion of the unfunded liability that the company intends to fund during the next year is classified as a *current liability*; the remainder is classified as a *long-term liability*.

**Unfunded Postretirement Costs Are Noncash Expenses**   Postretirement costs are recognized as expense as workers earn the right to receive these benefits. If these costs are fully funded, the company makes cash payments within the current period equal to this expense. But if these benefits are *not* funded, the cash payments are not made until after the employees retire. Thus an unfunded retirement plan involves a long lag between the recognition of expense and the related cash payments.

Unfunded retirement benefits often are called a noncash expense. That is, the expense is charged against current earnings, but there are no corresponding cash payments in the period. In the journal entry above, notice that expense exceeds the cash outlays by $110,000 ($250,000 − $140,000 = $110,000). This corresponds to the growth in the unfunded liability.

**Unfunded Liabilities for Postretirement Costs: Can They Really Be Paid?** Many of America's largest and best-known corporations have obligations for unfunded postretirement benefits that can only be described as enormous. For many companies, this liability is equal to, or *greater than,* the total amount of stockholders' equity.

**CASE IN POINT**

**General Motors** reports an unfunded liability for postretirement costs of more than *$34 billion*. That compares with total stockholders' equity of a little more than $16 billion. One might say that **GM**'s employees have a far greater "financial stake" in the company's long-term prospects than do its stockholders.

**MANAGEMENT STRATEGY**

Until recently, companies were not required to show their unfunded liability for postretirement costs in their balance sheets. Instead, they charged benefit payments for retired workers directly to expense. This pay-as-you-go treatment, however, fails to achieve the *matching principle.* It is the cost of benefits paid to *today's* workers that is helping the company produce revenue, not the cost of benefits paid to workers who have already retired.

A few years ago, the FASB changed the rules for measuring and reporting postretirement costs. Companies now must estimate the present value of the retirement benefits earned each year by their employees. This estimated amount is recognized as expense and any unfunded portion is recorded as a liability. This change in how postretirement benefits are reported has had a significant impact on the strategic management of those benefits. As a result of the associated balance sheet liability and income statement expense, a company carefully negotiates with employees and their representatives (unions) about these postretirement benefits.

Now that the liabilities for postretirement benefits are included in the financial statements, many investors are stunned by their size. They wonder—with just cause—whether **General Motors** and other large corporations can really pay liabilities this large. Interesting question.

Let us suggest some things to consider in evaluating a company's ability to pay its unfunded liability for postretirement costs. First, remember that this liability represents only the *present value* of the estimated future payments. The future payments are expected to be *substantially more* than the amount shown in the balance sheet. Next, this liability may *continue to grow,* especially if the company has more employees today than in the past. On the other hand, this liability does *not* have to be paid all at once. It will be paid over a *great many years*—the life span of today's workforce.

In evaluating a company's ability to meet its postretirement obligations, we suggest looking to the *statement of cash flows,* rather than the balance sheet or income statement. In the statement of cash flows, payments of postretirement costs are classified as operating activities. Thus, if a company has a steadily increasing net cash flow from operating activities, it is more likely to be able to handle these costs—at least *at present.* But if the net cash flow from operating activities starts to decline, the company may have no choice but to reduce the benefits it provides to retired employees. Often these benefits are *not* contractual and can be reduced at management's discretion.

**CASH EFFECTS**

## Deferred Income Taxes

We have seen in earlier chapters that differences sometimes exist between the way certain revenues or expenses are recognized in financial statements and the way these same items are reported in income tax returns. For example, most companies use the straight-line method of depreciation in their financial reports but use an accelerated method in their income tax returns.

**LO 8**

Describe and account for deferred income taxes.

Another example is installment sales. When a company sells merchandise on an installment plan, it usually recognizes the sales revenue immediately for financial reporting purposes. But in its income tax returns, the company may use the *installment method,* which *postpones* recognition of this sales revenue until payments are received from the customer.

Because of such differences between accounting principles and tax rules, income reported in the income statement of one year may appear in the income tax return of a *different* year. Most differences result in *postponing* (deferring) the recognition of income for tax purposes. The recognition of income in income tax returns may be postponed by those tax rules allowing the taxpayer to either (1) accelerate the recognition of expenses (such as accelerated depreciation methods) or (2) delay the recognition of revenue (such as the installment method).

In summary, income appearing in the income statement today may not be subject to income taxes until future years. However, the *matching principle* requires that the income shown in an income statement be offset by all related income taxes expense, regardless of when these taxes will be paid. Thus the entry to record a corporation's income taxes expense might appear as follows:

| | | | |
|---|---|---|---|
| Income Taxes Expense | 1,000,000 | | *Payment of some taxes* |
|     Income Taxes Payable | | 800,000 | *expense often can be deferred* |
|     Deferred Income Taxes | | 200,000 | |
| To record corporate income taxes applicable to the income of the current year. | | | |

Income Taxes Payable is a current liability representing the portion of the income taxes expense that must be paid when the company files its income tax return for the current year. The portion of income taxes expense that is deferred to future tax returns is credited to a liability account entitled **Deferred Income Taxes**.[12]

**Deferred Income Taxes in Financial Statements** Whether deferred income taxes are classified as current or long-term liabilities depends on the classification of the assets and liabilities that *caused* the tax deferrals. For example, installment receivables are classified as current assets. Therefore, if the methods used in accounting for installment receivables result in deferred taxes, the deferred taxes are classified as a current

---

[12] Some timing differences, such as those associated with postretirement costs, may require that companies report deferred income taxes as an *asset account* instead of a liability. In this chapter, we limit our examples to the more common situations in which deferred income taxes are classified as liabilities.

liability. Depreciable assets, however, are not current assets. Therefore, if deferred taxes result from the use of accelerated depreciation methods in income tax returns, the deferred tax liability is classified as long-term.

The amount of income taxes deferred during the current period is recognized as expense but does *not* require an immediate cash outlay. To the extent that a company is able to defer income taxes, its net cash flow from operating activities will *exceed* its net income. Bear in mind, however, that deferred income taxes are tax obligations that have been *postponed* to future periods. The company has *not eliminated* its obligation to pay these taxes.

Growing businesses often are able to defer part of their income taxes expense every year. Of course, some of the income taxes deferred in prior years constantly are coming due. Nonetheless, the liability for deferred taxes usually continues to grow as the company grows—just as does the overall liability for accounts payable. Deferring income taxes, when possible within the limits of tax law, is a logical part of a company's cash management.

Accounting for deferred taxes involves a number of complex issues that will be addressed in more advanced accounting courses.

**CASE IN POINT**

 In some countries, financial reporting requirements are consistent with tax reporting requirements. As a result, deferred income taxes do not typically appear on the financial statements of companies in Germany, Japan, and Switzerland where tax and financial reporting requirements are consistent.

### Liabilities and Cash Flows

How the payment of liabilities is classified in a statement of cash flows depends on the type of transaction creating that liability. If the liability stems from the *recognition of an expense* or the purchase of inventory, payment is viewed as an *operating activity.* Thus payments of trade accounts payable, accrued expenses, pension obligations, and income taxes are all classified as operating activities. Most interest payments also are classified as operating activities.[13] If a liability is incurred for the purpose of borrowing cash or financing the purchase of a plant asset, repayment of the principal amount is classified as a *financing activity.*

**CASH EFFECTS** Bear in mind that some expenses entering into the determination of net income *do not require immediate cash payments.* Examples discussed in this chapter include deferred income taxes and unfunded postretirement costs. The recognition of such noncash expenses reduces net income to an amount *less than* the net cash flows resulting from operating activities during the period.

**Liabilities and Financial Statement Disclosures** A company should disclose the *maturity dates* of its major liabilities. These disclosures assist users of the financial statements in evaluating the company's ability to meet obligations maturing in the near future.

The FASB also requires companies to disclose the *current value* of most long-term liabilities.[14] This information helps users of the statements evaluate the likelihood of the company's attempting to retire these liabilities *prior* to the scheduled maturity dates.

---

[13] As explained in Chapter 9, interest incurred while a plant asset is *under construction* is "capitalized" as part of the cost of that asset. Interest payments that are capitalized are classified as investing activities rather than operating activities.

[14] *Current value* means either market value (as in the case of bonds payable) or the *present value* of the expected future payments (as with unfunded postretirement obligations). The current value disclosure requirement does *not* apply to a company's obligation for deferred income taxes.

## EVALUATING THE SAFETY OF CREDITORS' CLAIMS

Creditors, of course, want to be sure that their claims are safe—that is, that they will be paid on time. Actually, *everyone* associated with a business—management, owners, employees—should be concerned with the company's ability to pay its debts. If a business becomes *insolvent* (unable to pay its obligations), it may be forced into **bankruptcy**.[15]

Not only does management want the business to remain solvent, it wants the company to maintain a high *credit rating* with agencies such as Dun & Bradstreet and Standard & Poor's. A high credit rating helps a company borrow money more easily and at lower interest rates.

In evaluating debt-paying ability, short-term creditors and long-term creditors look at different relationships. Short-term creditors are interested in the company's *immediate* solvency. Long-term creditors, in contrast, are interested in the company's ability to meet its interest obligations over a *period of years,* as well as its ability to repay or refinance large obligations as they come due.

In previous chapters we introduced several measures of short-term solvency and long-term credit risk. These measures are summarized in the table on page 427—along with the *interest coverage ratio,* which is discussed below.

**Interest Coverage Ratio**   Creditors, investors, and managers all feel more comfortable when a company has enough income to cover its interest payments by a wide margin. One widely used measure of the relationship between earnings and interest expense is the **interest coverage ratio**.

The interest coverage ratio is computed by dividing *operating income* by the annual interest expense. From a creditor's point of view, the higher this ratio, the better. In past years, most companies with good credit ratings had interest coverage ratios of, perhaps, 4 to 1 or more. With the spree of junk bond financing in the 1980s, many large corporations let their interest coverage ratios decline below 2 to 1. In most cases, their credit ratings dropped accordingly.

**YOUR TURN**

### You as a Loan Officer

Assume that you are a loan officer for First Federal National Bank. A local business wishes to obtain a five-year loan in the amount of $150,000 to purchase a new piece of equipment. All of the company's solvency ratios look promising except for its interest coverage ratio, which is 3 to 1.

The company's CEO contends that this ratio is acceptable, considering that the company's $375,000 in operating income for the year included depreciation expense of $200,000 and a nonpension postretirement benefits expense of $50,000 (all of which was unfunded). Interest expense was, of course, $125,000 ($375,000 ÷ $125,000 = 3 times coverage).

What point was the CEO trying to make? Do you agree?

*Our comments appear on page 451.

**Less Formal Means of Determining Creditworthiness**   Not all decisions to extend credit involve formal analysis of the borrower's financial statements. Most suppliers of goods or services, for example, will sell on account to almost any long-established business—unless they know the customer to be in severe financial difficulty. If the

---

[15] Bankruptcy is a legal status under which the company's fate is determined largely by the U.S. Bankruptcy Court. Sometimes the company is reorganized and allowed to continue its operations. In other cases, the business is closed and its assets are sold. Often managers and other employees lose their jobs. In almost all bankruptcies, the company's creditors and owners incur legal costs and sustain financial losses.

customer is not a well-established business, these suppliers may investigate the customer's credit history by contacting a credit-rating agency.

In lending to small businesses organized as corporations, lenders may require key stockholders to *personally guarantee* repayment of the loan.

## How Much Debt Should a Business Have?

All businesses incur some debts as a result of normal business operations. These include, for example, accounts payable and accrued liabilities. But many businesses aggressively use long-term debt, such as mortgages and bonds payable, to finance growth and expansion. Is this wise? Does it benefit the stockholders? The answer hinges on another question: *Can the borrowed funds be invested to earn a return higher than the rate of interest paid to creditors?*

Using borrowed money to finance business operations is called applying **leverage**. Extensive use of leverage—that is, a great deal of debt—sometimes benefits a business dramatically. But if things don't work out, it can "wipe out" the borrower.

If borrowed money can be invested to earn a rate of return *higher* than the interest rates paid to the lenders, net income and the return on stockholders' equity will *increase*.[16] For example, if you borrow money at an interest rate of 9% and invest it to earn 15%, you will benefit from "the spread."

But leverage is a double-edged sword—the effects may be favorable *or unfavorable*. If the rate of return earned on the borrowed money falls *below* the rate of interest being paid, the use of borrowed money *reduces* net income and the return on equity. Companies with large amounts of debt sometimes become victims of their own debt-service requirements.

The effects of leverage may be summarized as follows:

| Relationship of Return on Assets to Interest Rate on Borrowed Funds | Effect on Net Income and Return on Equity |
|---|---|
| Return on Assets > Interest Rates Being Paid | Increase |
| Return on Assets < Interest Rates Being Paid | Decrease |

Bear in mind that over time, both the return on assets and the interest rates that the company must pay may *change*.

The more leverage a company applies, the greater the effects on net income and the return on equity. Using more leverage simply means having more debt. Therefore, the *debt ratio* is a basic measure of the amount of leverage being applied.

## FINANCIAL ANALYSIS

The following table provides a summary of common measures used by creditors and investors to evaluate a company's *short-term and long-term debt-paying ability:*

---

[16] The rate of return earned on invested capital usually is viewed as the overall *return on assets*—that is, operating income divided by average total assets. *Return on equity* is net income expressed as a percentage of average stockholders' equity. Both of these return on investment measures are discussed in Chapter 14.

**Measures of Debt-Paying Ability**

| Short-Term | Long-Term |
|---|---|
| **Quick ratio**—Most liquid assets divided by current liabilities; a stringent measure of solvency. | **Debt ratio**—Total liabilities divided by total assets. Measures percentage of capital structure financed by creditors. |
| **Current ratio**—Current assets divided by current liabilities; the most common measure of solvency, but less stringent than the quick ratio. | **Interest coverage ratio**—Operating income divided by interest expense. Shows how many times the company earns its annual interest obligations. |
| **Working capital**—Current assets less current liabilities; the "uncommitted" liquid resources. | **Trend in net cash flows from operating activities**—Indicates trend in cash-generating ability. Determined from comparative statements of cash flow. |
| **Turnover rates**—Measures of how quickly receivables are collected or inventory is sold. (Computed separately for receivables and inventory.) | **Trend in net income**—Less related to debt-paying ability than cash flow, but still an excellent measure of long-term financial health. |
| **Operating cycle**—The period of time required to convert inventory into cash. | |
| **Net cash flows from operating activities**—Measures a company's ability to generate cash. (Shown in the statement of cash flows.) | |
| **Lines of credit**—Indicates ready access to additional cash should the need arise. | |

## DuPont

As noted at the start of this chapter, **E. I. du Pont de Nemours & Co.**'s disproportionate reliance upon debt financing burdens the company with billions of dollars in debt service costs annually. Where can investors and creditors look to ascertain exactly how much a company pays each year in debt service costs? A recent statement of cash flows reports that **DuPont** spent $3.5 billion during the year to service its short-term debt, and $8.86 billion to service its long-term borrowings (for a total in excess of $12 billion). These figures are staggering, given that the company's cash flows from continuing operations for the year amount to only $4.84 billion.

Principal repayments of debt obligations are reported in the statement of cash flows as *financing* activities. Other financing activities reported in **DuPont**'s recent statement of cash flows include cash outflows in excess of $2 billion related to treasury stock acquisitions and dividend payments to the company's preferred and common stockholders. Treasury stock acquisitions and dividends on preferred and common stock are discussed in Chapters 11 and 12.

**A SECOND LOOK**

## SUPPLEMENTAL TOPIC A

# ESTIMATED LIABILITIES, LOSS CONTINGENCIES, AND COMMITMENTS

## Estimated Liabilities

The term *estimated liabilities* refers to *liabilities that appear in financial statements at estimated dollar amounts.* Let us again consider the example of the automaker's liability to honor its new car warranties. A manufacturer's liability for warranty work is recorded by an entry debiting Warranty Expense and crediting Liability for Warranty Claims. The *matching principle* requires that the expense of performing warranty work be recognized in the period in which the products are *sold,* in order to offset this expense against the related sales revenue. As the warranty may extend several years into the future, the dollar amount of this liability (and expense) must be estimated. Because of the uncertainty regarding when warranty work will be performed, accountants traditionally have classified the liability for warranty claims as a current liability.

By definition, estimated liabilities involve some degree of uncertainty. However, (1) the liabilities are known to exist, and (2) the uncertainty as to dollar amount is *not so great* as to prevent the company from making a reasonable estimate and recording the liability.

## Loss Contingencies

**Loss contingencies** are similar to estimated liabilities but may involve much more uncertainty. A loss contingency is a *possible loss* (or expense), stemming from *past events,* that is expected to be resolved in the future.

Central to the definition of a loss contingency is the element of *uncertainty*—uncertainty as to the amount of loss and, in some cases, uncertainty as to *whether or not any loss actually has been incurred.* A common example of a loss contingency is a lawsuit pending against a company. The lawsuit is based on past events, but until the suit is resolved, uncertainty exists as to the amount (if any) of the company's liability.

Loss contingencies differ from estimated liabilities in two ways. First, a loss contingency may involve a *greater degree of uncertainty.* Often the uncertainty extends to whether any loss or expense actually has been incurred. In contrast, the loss or expense relating to an estimated liability is *known to exist.*

Second, the concept of a loss contingency extends not only to possible liabilities, but also to possible *impairments of assets.* Assume, for example, that a bank has made large loans to a foreign country now experiencing political instability. Uncertainty exists as to the amount of loss, if any, associated with this loan. From the bank's point of view, this loan is an asset that may be impaired, not a liability.

**Loss Contingencies in Financial Statements** The manner in which loss contingencies are presented in financial statements depends on the *degree of uncertainty involved.*

Loss contingencies are *recorded* in the accounting records only when both of the following criteria are met: (1) It is *probable* that a loss has been incurred, and (2) the amount of loss can be *reasonably estimated.* An example of a loss contingency that usually meets these criteria and is recorded in the accounts is the obligation a company has for product warranties and defects.

When these criteria are *not* met, loss contingencies are *disclosed* in notes to the financial statements if there is a *reasonable possibility* that a material loss has been incurred. Pending lawsuits, for example, usually are disclosed in notes accompanying the financial statements, but the loss, if any, is not recorded in the accounting records until the lawsuit is settled. Companies need *not* disclose loss contingencies if the risk of a material loss having occurred is considered *remote.*

Notice the *judgmental nature* of the criteria used in accounting for loss contingencies. These criteria involve assessments as to whether the risk of material loss is "probable," "reasonably possible," or "remote." Thus the *professional judgments* of the company's management, accountants, legal counsel, and auditors are the deciding factors in accounting for loss contingencies.

When loss contingencies are disclosed in notes to the financial statements, the note should describe the nature of the contingency and, if possible, provide an estimate of the amount of possible loss. If a reasonable estimate of the amount of possible loss cannot be made, the disclosure should include the range of possible loss or a statement that an estimate cannot be made. The following note is typical of the disclosure of the loss contingency arising from pending litigation:

**LO 10**

Define *loss contingencies* and explain their presentation in financial statements.

### Note 8: Contingencies
In October of 2002, the Company was named as defendant in a $408 million patent infringement lawsuit. The Company denies all charges and is preparing its defense against them. It is not possible at this time to determine the ultimate legal or financial responsibility that may arise as a result of this litigation.

Sometimes a *portion* of a loss contingency qualifies for immediate recognition, whereas the remainder only meets the criteria for disclosure. Assume, for example, that a company is required by the Superfund Act to clean up an environmental hazard over a 10-year period. The company cannot predict the total cost of the project but considers it probable that it will lose at least $1 million. The company should recognize a $1 million expected loss and record it as a liability. In addition, it should disclose in the notes to the financial statements that the actual cost ultimately may exceed the recorded amount.

*Note disclosure of a loss contingency*

**DuPont** accrues a liability for environmental remediation activities when it is probable that a liability has been incurred and reasonable estimates of the liability can be made. Much of this accrual relates to the Superfund Act, which mandates that the company clean up its waste sites over the next two decades.

Remediation activities tend to occur over relatively long periods of time and vary substantially in cost from site to site. The company's assessment of remediation costs is a continuous process that takes into account the relevant factors affecting each specific site. **DuPont** has accrued over $600 million related to future environmental clean-up activities. Although the company cannot estimate with precision the actual amount it will eventually incur, it apparently believes that costs of at least $600 million appear probable.

**CASE IN POINT**

Notice that loss contingencies relate only to possible losses from *past events*. For **DuPont**, these past events were related to the improper disposal of hazardous wastes. The risk that losses may result from *future* events is *not* a loss contingency. The risk of future losses generally is *not* disclosed in financial statements for several reasons.[1] For one, any disclosure of future losses would be sheer speculation. For another, no one can foresee all of the events that might give rise to future losses.

## Commitments

Contracts for future transactions are called **commitments**. They are not liabilities, but, if material, they are disclosed in notes to the financial statements. For example, a professional baseball club may issue a three-year contract to a player at an annual salary of, say, $5 million. This is a commitment to pay for services to be rendered in the future. There is no obligation to make payment until the services are received. As liabilities stem only from *past transactions*, this commitment has not yet created a liability.

Other examples of commitments include a corporation's long-term employment contract with a key officer, a contract for construction of a new plant, and a contract to buy or sell inventory at future dates. The common quality of all these commitments is an intent to enter into transactions *in the future*. Commitments that are material in amount should be disclosed in notes to the financial statements.

---

[1] The risk of future losses *is* disclosed if this risk stems from *existing contracts*, such as a written guarantee of another company's indebtedness (called a loan guarantee, or an accommodation endorsement).

## SUPPLEMENTAL TOPIC B

### BONDS ISSUED AT A DISCOUNT OR A PREMIUM

Underwriters normally sell corporate bonds to investors either at par or at a price very close to par. Therefore, the underwriter usually purchases these bonds from the issuing corporation at a discount—that is, at a price below par. The discount generally is quite small—perhaps 1% or 2% of the face amount of the bonds.

When bonds are issued, the borrower records a liability equal to the *amount received*. If the bonds are issued at a small discount—which is the normal case—this liability is slightly smaller than the face value of the bond issue. At the maturity date, of course, the issuing corporation must redeem the bonds at full face value. Thus, over the term of the bond issue, the borrower's liability gradually *increases* from the original issue price to the maturity value.

**Bond Discount: Part of the Cost of Borrowing**   When bonds are issued at a discount, the borrower must repay more than the amount originally borrowed. Thus any discount in the issuance price becomes an additional cost of the overall borrowing transaction.

In terms of cash outlays, the additional cost represented by the discount is not paid until the bonds mature. But the *matching principle* may require the borrower to recognize this cost gradually over the life of bond issue.[1] After all, the borrower does benefit from the use of the borrowed funds throughout this entire period.

**LO 11**

Account for bonds issued at a discount or premium.

### Accounting for Bond Discount: An Illustration

To illustrate, assume that on January 1, 2002, SCUBA TECH sells $1 million of 9%, 40-year bonds to an underwriter at a price of *98* ($980 for each bond). On January 1, 2002, it receives $980,000 cash from the underwriter and records a liability of this amount. But when these bonds mature in 40 years, SCUBA TECH will owe its bondholders $1,000,000. Thus the company's liability to bondholders will *increase by $20,000* over the life of the bond issue. The gradual "growth" in this liability is illustrated below:

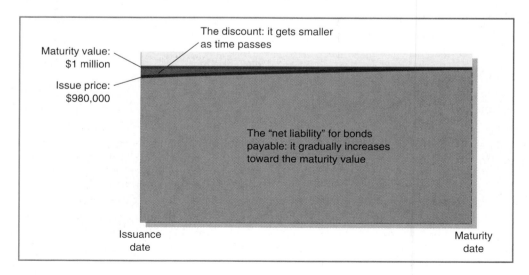

Notice that the long-term liability is increasing very *gradually*—at an average rate of $500 per year ($20,000 increase ÷ 40-year life of the bond issue).

When bonds are issued, the amount of any discount is debited to an account entitled *Discount on Bonds Payable*. Thus SCUBA TECH will record the issuance of these bonds as follows:

---

[1] If the amount of the discount is immaterial, it may be charged directly to expense as a matter of convenience.

```
Cash . . . . . . . . . . . . . . . . . . . . . . . . . . . . . . . . . . . . . . . . . . . . . . . . .    980,000
Discount on Bonds Payable  . . . . . . . . . . . . . . . . . . . . . . . . . . . . .     20,000
      Bonds Payable  . . . . . . . . . . . . . . . . . . . . . . . . . . . . . . . . . . . .                1,000,000
Issued $1,000,000 face value 40-year bonds to an underwriter
   at a price of 98.
```

SCUBA TECH's liability at the date of issuance will appear as follows:

| Long-term liabilities: | | |
|---|---|---|
| Bonds Payable . . . . . . . . . . . . . . . . . . . . . . . . . . . . . . . . . . . . . . | $1,000,000 | |
| Less: Discount on Bonds Payable . . . . . . . . . . . . . . . . . . . . . . . . | 20,000 | $980,000 |

*The net liability for bonds payable*

The debit balance account Discount on Bonds Payable is a *contra-liability account.* In the balance sheet, it is shown as a *reduction* in the amount of the long-term liability. Thus the net liability originally is equal to the *amount borrowed.*

**Amortization of the Discount**   Over the 40-year life of the bond issue, adjusting entries are made to gradually transfer the balance in the Discount account into interest expense. Thus the balance in the Discount account gradually declines, and the carrying value of the bonds—face value *less* the unamortized discount—rises toward the bonds' maturity value.

Assuming the bonds pay interest annually on December 31 each year, SCUBA TECH will make the following *adjusting entry* to amortize the bond discount:

```
Interest Expense . . . . . . . . . . . . . . . . . . . . . . . . . . . . . . . . . . . . . .    500
      Discount on Bonds Payable  . . . . . . . . . . . . . . . . . . . . . . . . . . . .              500
Recognized one year's amortization of discount on 40-year bonds
   payable ($20,000 original discount × 1/40).
```

Notice that amortization of the discount *increases* SCUBA TECH's annual interest expense. It does not, however, require any immediate cash outlay. The interest expense represented by the discount will not be paid until the bonds mature. As the discount is amortized, the carrying amount of the bonds (face or maturity value less the discount) increases.

## Accounting for Bond Premium

If bonds are issued at a *premium* (a price above par), the borrower would again record the liability at the amount borrowed. The amount in excess of par value would be credited to a special account entitled Premium on Bonds Payable. In the balance sheet, bond premium is *added* to the face value of the bonds to determine the net liability. As this premium is amortized, the carrying value of the liability gradually *declines* toward the maturity value.

Amortization of bond premium is recorded by debiting Premium on Bonds Payable and *crediting* Interest Expense. Therefore, amortization of a premium *reduces* the annual interest expense to an amount *less* than the annual cash payments made to bondholders.

## Bond Discount and Premium in Perspective

From a conceptual point of view, investors might pay a premium price to purchase bonds that pay an *above-market* rate of interest. If the bonds pay a *below-market* rate, investors will buy them only at a discount.

But these concepts seldom come into play when bonds are issued. Most bonds are issued *at* the market rate of interest. Corporate bonds *almost never* are issued at a premium. Bonds often are issued at a small discount, but this discount represents only the underwriter's profit margin, not investors' response to a below-market interest rate.[2] The annual effects of amortizing bond discount or premium are diluted further because these amounts are amortized over the entire life of the bond issue—usually 20 years or more.

In summary, bond discounts and premiums *seldom have a material effect* on a company's annual interest expense or its financial position.[3] For this reason, we defer further discussion of this topic to more advanced accounting courses.

---

[2] Professor Bill Schwartz of Virginia Commonwealth University conducted a study of 685 bond issues in a given year. *None* of these bonds was issued at a premium, and *over* 95% were issued either at par or at a discount of less than 2% of face value.

[3] Some companies issue *zero-coupon* bonds, which pay *no* interest but are issued at huge discounts. In these situations, amortization of the discount *is* material and may comprise much of the company's total interest expense. Zero-coupon bonds are a specialized form of financing that will be discussed in later accounting courses and courses in corporate finance.

## SUMMARY OF LEARNING OBJECTIVES

**LO 1**

**Define *liabilities* and distinguish between current and long-term liabilities.**

Liabilities are debts arising from past transactions or events and that require payment (or the rendering of services) at some future date. Current liabilities are those maturing within one year or the company's operating cycle (whichever is longer) and that are expected to be paid from current assets. Liabilities classified as long-term include obligations maturing more than one year in the future and shorter-term obligations that will be refinanced or paid from noncurrent assets.

**LO 2**

**Account for notes payable and interest expense.**

Initially, a liability is recorded only for the principal amount of a note—that is, the amount owed *before* including any interest charges. Interest expense accrues over time. Any accrued interest expense is recognized at the end of an accounting period by an adjusting entry that records both the expense and a short-term liability for accrued interest payable.

**LO 3**

**Describe the costs relating to payrolls.**

The basic cost of payrolls is, of course, the salaries and wages earned by employees. However, all employers also incur costs for various payroll taxes, such as the employer's share of Social Security and Medicare, workers' compensation premiums, and unemployment insurance. Many employers also incur costs for various employee benefits, such as health insurance and postretirement benefits. (These additional payroll related costs often amount to 30% to 40% of the basic wages and salaries expense.)

**LO 4**

**Prepare an amortization table allocating payments between interest and principal.**

An amortization table includes four money columns, showing (1) the amount of each payment, (2) the portion of the payment representing interest expense, (3) the portion of the payment that reduces the principal amount of the loan, and (4) the remaining unpaid balance (or principal amount). The table begins with the original amount of the loan listed in the unpaid balance column. A separate line then is completed showing the allocation of each payment between interest and principal reduction and indicating the new unpaid balance subsequent to the payment.

**LO 5**

**Describe corporate bonds and explain the tax advantage of debt financing.**

Corporate bonds are transferable long-term notes payable. Each bond usually has a face value of $1,000 (or a multiple of $1,000), calls for interest payments at a contractual rate, and has a stated maturity date. By issuing thousands of bonds to the investing public at one time, the corporation divides a very large and long-term loan into many transferable units.

The principal advantage of issuing bonds instead of capital stock is that interest payments to bondholders are deductible in determining taxable income, whereas dividend payments to stockholders are not.

**LO 6**

**Explain the concept of present value.**

The basic concept of present value is that an amount of money that will not be paid or received until some future date is equivalent to a smaller amount of money today. This is because the smaller amount available today could be invested to earn interest and thereby accumulate over time to the larger future amount. The amount today considered equivalent to the future amount is termed the present value of that future amount.

The concept of present value is used in the valuation of all long-term liabilities except deferred taxes. It also determines the current values of financial instruments and is widely used in investment decisions. Readers who are not familiar with this concept are encouraged to now read Appendix B at the end of this textbook.

**LO 7**

**Account for postretirement costs.**

The annual expense for postretirement costs is the present value of the future benefits earned by employees as a result of their services during the current year. This amount is estimated by an actuary. To the extent that the employer funds this expense each year—that is, contributes cash to a pension plan—no liability arises. However, the employer must report a liability for any unfunded postretirement obligations. (Pension plans usually are fully funded, meaning that the employer reports no liability for pension payments. But other postretirement benefits, such as health insurance for retired workers, normally are not fully funded.)

**LO 8**

**Describe and account for deferred income taxes.**

Differences sometimes exist between when certain revenue or expense items are recognized in financial statements and when these items are reported in tax returns. Most of these differences result in postponing (deferring) the recognition of income for tax purposes. That portion of the income taxes expense that is deferred to future tax returns is credited to a liability account entitled Deferred Income Taxes.

## LO 9

**Evaluate the safety of creditors' claims.**

Short-term creditors may evaluate the safety of their claims using such measures of solvency as the current ratio, quick ratio, the available lines of credit, and the debtor's credit rating. Long-term creditors look more to signs of stability and long-term financial health, including the debt ratio, interest coverage ratio, and the trends in net income and net cash flow from operating activities.

## *LO 10

**Define *loss contingencies* and explain their presentation in financial statements.**

A loss contingency is a possible loss (or expense) stemming from past events that will be resolved as to existence and amount by some future event. Loss contingencies are accrued (recorded) if (1) it is probable that a loss has been incurred and (2) the amount of loss can be estimated reasonably. Even if these conditions are not met, loss contingencies should be disclosed if it is reasonably possible that a material loss has been incurred.

## †LO 11

**Account for bonds issued at a discount or premium.**

When bonds are issued at a discount, the borrower must repay more than the amount originally borrowed. Thus any discount in the issuance price represents additional cost in the overall borrowing transaction. The matching principle requires that the borrower recognize this cost gradually over the life of the bond issue as interest expense.

If bonds are issued at a premium, the borrower will repay an amount less than the amount originally borrowed. Thus the premium serves to reduce the overall cost of the borrowing transaction. Again, the matching principle requires that this reduction in interest expense be recognized gradually over the life of the bond issue.

Businesses have two basic means of financing their assets and business operations: with liabilities or with owners' equity. In the next two chapters, we turn our attention to the owners' equity in various types of business organizations.

## KEY TERMS INTRODUCED OR EMPHASIZED IN CHAPTER 10

**accrued liabilities** (p. 407) The liability to pay an expense that has accrued during the period. Also called *accrued expenses.*

---

* *Supplemental Topic A,* "Estimated Liabilities, Loss Contingencies, and Commitments."
† *Supplemental Topic B,* "Bonds Issued at a Discount or a Premium."

**actuary** (p. 420) A statistician who performs computations involving assumptions as to human life spans. One function is computing companies' liabilities for pensions and postretirement benefits.

**amortization table** (p. 409) A schedule that indicates how installment payments are allocated between interest expense and repayments of principal.

**bankruptcy** (p. 425) A legal status in which the financial affairs of an insolvent business (or individual) are managed, in large part, by the U.S. Bankruptcy Court.

**bonds payable** (p. 412) Long-term debt securities that subdivide a very large and long-term corporate debt into transferable increments of $1,000 or multiples thereof.

**capital lease** (p. 418) A lease contract that finances the eventual purchase by the lessee of leased property. The lessor accounts for a capital lease as a sale of property; the lessee records an asset and a liability equal to the present value of the future lease payments. Also called a *financing lease.*

**collateral** (p. 404) Assets that have been pledged to secure specific liabilities. Creditors with secured claims can foreclose on (seize title to) these assets if the borrower defaults.

**commitments** (p. 429) Agreements to carry out future transactions. Not a liability because the transaction has not yet been performed, but may be disclosed in notes to the financial statements.

**convertible bond** (p. 413) A bond that may be exchanged (at the bondholder's option) for a specified number of shares of the company's capital stock.

**debt service** (p. 409) The combined cash outlays required for repayment of principal amounts borrowed and for payments of interest expense during the period.

**deferred income taxes** (p. 423) A liability account to pay income taxes that have been postponed to a future year's income tax return. In some cases, this account can also be an asset account representing income taxes to be saved in a future year's income tax return.

**estimated liabilities** (p. 404) Liabilities known to exist, but that must be recorded in the accounting records at estimated dollar amounts.

**interest coverage ratio** (p. 425) Operating income divided by interest expense. Indicates the number of times that the company was able to earn the amount of its interest charges.

**junk bonds** (p. 413) Bonds payable that involve a greater than normal risk of default and, therefore, must pay higher than normal rates of interest in order to be attractive to investors.

**lessee** (p. 418) The tenant, user, or renter of leased property.

**lessor** (p. 418) The owner of property leased to a lessee.

**leverage** (p. 426) The use of borrowed money to finance business operations.

**loss contingencies** (p. 428) Situations involving uncertainty as to whether a loss has occurred. The uncertainty will be resolved by a future event. An example of a loss contingency is the possible loss relating to a lawsuit pending against a company. Although loss contingencies are sometimes recorded in the accounts, they are more frequently disclosed only in notes to the financial statements.

**maturity date** (p. 404) The date on which a liability becomes due.

**off-balance-sheet financing** (p. 418) An arrangement in which the use of resources is financed without the obligation for future payments appearing as a liability in the balance sheet. An operating lease is a common example of off-balance-sheet financing.

**operating lease** (p. 418) A lease contract which is in essence a rental agreement. The lessee has the use of the leased property, but the lessor retains the usual risks and rewards of ownership. The periodic lease payments are accounted for as rent expense by the lessee and as rental revenue by the lessor.

**payroll taxes** (p. 407) Taxes levied on an employer based on the amount of wages and salaries being paid to employees during the period. Include the employers' share of Social Security and Medicare taxes, unemployment taxes, and (though not called a "tax") workers' compensation premiums.

**pension fund** (p. 420) A fund managed by an independent trustee into which an employer company makes periodic payments. The fund is used to make pension payments to retired employees.

**postretirement benefits** (p. 421) Benefits that will be paid to retired workers. The present value of the future benefits earned by workers during the current period is an expense of the period. If not fully funded, this expense results in a liability for unfunded postretirement benefits. (For many companies, these liabilities have become very large.)

**present value (of a future amount)** (p. 416) The amount of money that an informed investor would pay today for the right to receive the future amount, based on a specific rate of return required by the investor.

**principal amount** (p. 405) The unpaid balance of an obligation, exclusive of any interest charges for the current period.

**sinking fund** (p. 413) Cash set aside by a corporation at regular intervals (usually with a trustee) for the purpose of repaying a bond issue at its maturity date.

**underwriter** (p. 412) An investment banking firm that handles the sale of a corporation's stocks or bonds to the public.

**workers' compensation** (p. 408) A state-mandated insurance program insuring workers against job-related injuries. Premiums are charged to employers as a percentage of the employees' wages and salaries. The amounts vary by state and by the employees' occupations but, in some cases, can be very substantial.

## DEMONSTRATION PROBLEM

Listed below are selected items from the financial statements of G & H Pump Mfg. Co. for the year ended December 31, 2002.

| | |
|---|---:|
| Deferred income taxes | $ 140,000 |
| Note payable to Porterville Bank | 99,000 |
| Income taxes payable | 63,000 |
| Loss contingency relating to lawsuit | 200,000 |
| Accounts payable and accrued expenses | 163,230 |
| Mortgage note payable | 240,864 |
| Bonds payable | 2,200,000 |
| Unamortized premium on bonds payable | 1,406 |
| Accrued bond interest payable | 110,000 |
| Pension expense | 61,400 |
| Unfunded liability for nonpension postretirement benefits | 807,000 |
| Unearned revenue | 25,300 |

### Other Information

1. $26,000 of the deferred taxes arose from assets or liabilities classified as current.
2. The note payable owed to Porterville Bank is due in 30 days. G & H has arranged with this bank to renew the note for an additional two years.
3. G & H has been sued for $200,000 by someone claiming the company's pumps are excessively noisy. It is reasonably possible, but not probable, that a loss has been sustained.
4. The mortgage note is payable at $8,000 per month over the next three years. During the next 12 months, the principal amount of this note will be reduced to $169,994.
5. The bonds payable mature in seven months. A sinking fund has been accumulated to repay the full maturity of this bond issue.

**6.** The company's pension plan is fully funded. During *2003,* the company intends to fund $100,000 of its unfunded liability for *nonpension* postretirement benefits.

## Instructions

**a.** Using this information, prepare the current liabilities and long-term liabilities sections of a classified balance sheet at December 31, 2002.

**b.** Explain briefly how the information in each of the six numbered paragraphs affected your presentation of the company's liabilities.

## Solution to the Demonstration Problem

**a.**

**G & H PUMP MFG. CO.**
**Partial Balance Sheet**
**December 31, 2002**

| Liabilities: | | |
|---|---:|---:|
| **Current liabilities:** | | |
| Accounts payable and accrued expenses | | $ 163,230 |
| Income taxes payable | | 63,000 |
| Accrued bond Interest payable | | 110,000 |
| Unearned revenue | | 25,300 |
| Current portions of long-term debt: | | |
| Deferred income taxes | $ 26,000 | |
| Mortgage note payable | 70,870 | |
| Unfunded liability for nonpension postretirement benefits | 100,000 | 196,870 |
| Total current liabilities | | $ 558,400 |
| **Long-term liabilities:** | | |
| Note payable to Porterville Bank | | $ 99,000 |
| Deferred income taxes | | 114,000 |
| Mortgage note payable | | 169,994 |
| Bonds payable | $2,200,000 | |
| Add: Premium on bonds payable | 1,406 | 2,201,406 |
| Unfunded liability for nonpension postretirement benefits | | 707,000 |
| Total long-term liabilities | | $3,291,400 |
| Total liabilities | | $3,849,800 |

**b. 1.** The $26,000 in deferred income taxes arising from current items is classified as a current liability, and the remaining $114,000 ($140,000 − $26,000) as long-term.

**2.** Although the note payable to Porterville Bank is due in 30 days, it is classified as a long-term liability as it will be refinanced on a long-term basis.

**3.** The pending lawsuit is a loss contingency requiring disclosure, but it is not listed in the liability section of the balance sheet.

**4.** The $70,870 of the mortgage note that will be repaid within the next 12 months ($240,864 − $169,994) is a current liability; the remaining balance, due after December 31, 2003, is long-term debt.

**5.** Although the bonds payable mature in seven months, they will be repaid from a sinking fund, rather than from current assets. Therefore, these bonds retain their long-term classification.

**6.** As the pension fund is fully funded, the employer has no pension liability. The portion of the unfunded nonpension postretirement benefits that will be funded next year is a current liability, and the remainder is classified as long-term.

## SELF-TEST QUESTIONS

*Answers to these questions appear on page 451.*

1. Which of the following is characteristic of liabilities rather than of equity? (More than one answer may be correct.)
   a. The obligation matures.
   b. Interest paid to the provider of the capital is deductible in the determination of taxable income.
   c. The capital providers' claims are *residual* in the event of liquidation of the business.
   d. The capital providers normally have the right to exercise control over business operations.

2. On October 1, Dalton Corp. borrows $100,000 from National Bank, signing a six-month note payable for that amount, plus interest to be computed at a rate of 9% per annum. Indicate all correct answers.
   a. Dalton's liability at October 1 is only $100,000.
   b. The maturity value of this note is $104,500.
   c. At December 31, Dalton will have a liability for accrued interest payable in the amount of $4,500.
   d. Dalton's total liability for this loan at November 30 is $101,500.

3. Identify all correct statements concerning payrolls and related payroll costs.
   a. Both employers and employees pay Social Security and Medicare taxes.
   b. Workers' compensation premiums are withheld from employees' wages.
   c. An employer's total payroll costs usually exceed total wages expense by about 7¹/2%.
   d. Under current law, employers are required to pay Social Security taxes on employees' earnings, but they are not required to pay for health insurance.

4. Identify the types of information that can readily be determined from an amortization table for an installment loan. (More than one answer may be correct.)
   a. Interest expense on this liability for the current year.
   b. The present value of the future payments under current market conditions.
   c. The unpaid balance remaining after each payment.
   d. The portion of the unpaid balance that is a current liability.

5. Which of the following statements is (are) correct? (More than one statement may be correct.)
   a. A bond issue is a technique for subdividing a very large loan into many small, transferable units.
   b. Bond interest payments are contractual obligations, whereas the board of directors determines whether or not dividends will be paid.
   c. As interest rates rise, the market prices of bonds fall; as interest rates fall, bond prices tend to rise.
   d. Bond interest payments are deductible in determining income subject to income taxes, whereas dividends paid to stockholders are not deductible.

6. Identify all statements that are *consistent* with the concept of present value. (More than one answer may be correct.)
   a. The present value of a future amount always is *less* than that future amount.
   b. An amount of money available today is considered *more* valuable than the *same sum* that will not become available until a future date.
   c. The amount of an unfunded liability for postretirement benefits is substantially *less* than the actual amounts expected to be paid to retired workers.
   d. The liability for an installment note payable is recorded at only the *principal* amount, rather than the sum of the scheduled future payments.

7. Silverado maintains a fully funded pension plan. During 2002, $1 million was paid to retired workers, and workers currently employed by the company earned a portion of the right to receive pension payments expected to total $6 million *over their lifetimes.* Silverado's pension *expense* for 2002 amounts to:

    **a.** $1 million.

    **b.** $6 million.

    **c.** $7 million.

    **d.** Some other amount.

**8.** Deferred income taxes result from:

    **a.** The fact that bond interest is deductible in the computation of taxable income.

    **b.** Depositing income taxes due in future years in a special fund managed by an independent trustee.

    **c.** Differences between when certain revenue and expense items are recognized in financial statements and in income tax returns.

    **d.** The inability of a bankrupt company to pay its income tax liability on schedule.

**9.** Identify those trends that are *unfavorable* from the viewpoint of a bondholder. (More than one answer may be correct.)

    **a.** Market interest rates are steadily rising.

    **b.** The issuing company's interest coverage ratio is steadily rising.

    **c.** The issuing company's net cash flow from operating activities is steadily declining.

    **d.** The issuing company's debt ratio is steadily declining.

**\*10.** A basic difference between *loss contingencies* and "real" liabilities is:

    **a.** Liabilities stem from past transactions; loss contingencies stem from future events.

    **b.** Liabilities always are recorded in the accounting records, whereas loss contingencies never are.

    **c.** The extent of uncertainty involved.

    **d.** Liabilities can be large in amount, whereas loss contingencies are immaterial.

**\*11.** Which of the following situations require recording a liability in 2002? (More than one answer may be correct.)

    **a.** In 2002, a company manufactures and sells stereo equipment that carries a three-year warranty.

    **b.** In 2002, a theater group receives payments in advance from season ticket holders for productions to be performed in 2003.

    **c.** A company is a defendant in a legal action. At the end of 2002, the company's attorney feels it is possible the company will lose and that the amount of the loss might be material.

    **d.** During 2002, a Midwest agricultural cooperative is concerned about the risk of loss if inclement weather destroys the crops.

## ASSIGNMENT MATERIAL

### DISCUSSION QUESTIONS

**1.** Define *liabilities*. Identify several characteristics that distinguish liabilities from owners' equity.

**2.** Explain the relative priority of the claims of owners and of creditors to the assets of a business. Do all creditors have equal priority? Explain.

**3.** Define *current liabilities* and *long-term liabilities*. Under what circumstances might a 10-year bond issue be classified as a current liability? Under what circumstances might a note payable maturing 30 days after the balance sheet date be classified as a long-term liability?

**4.** Jonas Company issues a 90-day, 12% note payable to replace an account payable to Smith Supply Company in the amount of $8,000. Draft the journal entries (in general journal form) to record the issuance of the note payable and the payment of the note at the maturity date.

**5.** Explain why an employer's "total cost" of a payroll may exceed by a substantial amount the total wages and salaries earned by employees.

---

\* *Supplemental Topic A,* "Estimated Liabilities, Loss Contingencies, and Commitments."

6. What are workers' compensation premiums? Who pays them? Who pays Social Security and Medicare taxes?

7. Ace Garage has an unpaid mortgage loan of $63,210, payable at $1,200 per month. An amortization table indicates that $527 of the current monthly payment represents interest expense. What will be the amount of this mortgage obligation immediately *after* Ace makes this current payment?

8. A friend of yours has just purchased a house and has taken out a $50,000, 11% mortgage, payable at $476.17 per month. After making the first monthly payment, he received a receipt from the bank stating that only $17.84 of the $476.17 had been applied to reducing the principal amount of the loan. Your friend computes that at the rate of $17.84 per month, it will take over 233 years to pay off the $50,000 mortgage. Do you agree with your friend's analysis? Explain.

9. Briefly explain the income tax advantage of raising capital by issuing bonds rather than by selling capital stock.

10. Tampa Boat Company pays federal income taxes at a rate of 30% on taxable income. Compute the company's annual *after-tax* cost of borrowing on a 10%, $5 million bond issue. Express this after-tax cost as a percentage of the borrowed $5 million.

11. Why is the *present value* of a future amount always *less* than the future amount?

12. Why do bond prices vary inversely with interest rates?

13. Some bonds now being bought and sold by investors on organized securities exchanges were issued when interest rates were much higher than they are today. Would you expect these bonds to be trading at prices above or below their face values? Explain.

14. *The Wall Street Journal* recently quoted a market price of *102* for an issue of 8% **Nabisco** bonds. What would be the market price for $25,000 face value of these bonds (ignoring accrued interest)? Is the market rate of interest for bonds of this quality higher or lower than 8%? Explain.

15. The 6% bonds of Central Gas & Electric are selling at a market price of 72, whereas the 6% bonds of Interstate Power are selling at a price of 97. Does this mean that Interstate Power has a better credit rating than Central Gas & Electric? Explain. (Assume current long-term interest rates are in the 11 to 13% range.)

16. Explain how the lessee accounts for an operating lease and a capital lease. Why is an operating lease sometimes called *off-balance-sheet financing?*

17. Ortega Industries has a fully funded pension plan. Each year, pension expense runs in excess of $10 million. At the present time, employees are entitled to receive pension benefits with a present value of $125 million. Explain what liability, if any, Ortega Industries should include in its balance sheet as a result of this pension plan.

18. Why do large corporations often show no liability for pensions owed to retired employees, but huge liabilities for "nonpension postretirement benefits"?

19. When are the costs of postretirement benefits recognized as expense? When are the related cash payments made?

20. What is meant by the term *deferred income taxes?* How is this item presented in financial statements?

21. A $200 million bond issue of NDP Corp. (a solvent company) recently matured. The entire maturity value was paid from a bond sinking fund. What effect did this transaction have on the company's current ratio? On its debt ratio? Explain.

22. As a result of issuing 20-year bonds payable, Low-Cal Foods now has an interest coverage ratio of .75 to 1. Should this ratio be of greater concern to short-term creditors or to stockholders? Explain.

23. There is an old business saying that "You shouldn't *be* in business if your company doesn't earn higher than bank rates." This means that if a company is to succeed, its return on assets should be *significantly higher* than its cost of borrowing. Why is this so important?

*24. Define *estimated liabilities* and provide two examples. Are estimated liabilities recorded in accounting records?

---

* *Supplemental Topic A,* "Estimated Liabilities, Loss Contingencies, and Commitments."

**\*25.** What is the meaning of the term *loss contingency*? Give several examples. How are loss contingencies presented in financial statements? Explain.

**\*26.** What is the meaning of the term *commitment*? Give several examples. How are commitments usually presented in financial statements? Explain.

**†27.** Does issuing bonds at a discount increase or decrease the issuing company's cost of borrowing? Explain.

# EXERCISES

**EXERCISE 10.1**

You as a Student

**LO 4**

Assume that you will have a 10-year, $10,000 loan to repay to your parents when you graduate from college next month. The loan, plus 8% annual interest on the unpaid balance, is to be repaid in 10 annual installments of $1,490 each, beginning one year after you graduate. You have accepted a well-paying job and are considering an early settlement of the entire unpaid balance in just three years (immediately after making the third annual payment of $1,490).

Prepare an amortization schedule showing how much money you will need to save to pay your parents the entire unpaid balance of your loan three years after your graduation. (Round amounts to the nearest dollar.)

**EXERCISE 10.2**

Effects of Transactions on the Accounting Equation

**LO 1–4**

Listed below are eight events or transactions of GemStar Corporation.

**a.** Made an adjusting entry to record interest on a short-term note payable.

**b.** Made a monthly installment payment of a fully amortizing, six-month, interest-bearing installment note payable.

**c.** Recorded a regular biweekly payroll, including the amounts withheld from employees, the issuance of paychecks, and payroll taxes on the employer.

**d.** Came within 12 months of the maturity date of a note payable originally issued for a period of 18 months.

**e.** Made an adjusting entry to accrue interest payable on a long-term bond issue.

**f.** Leased equipment, signing a long-term capital lease.

**g.** Recognized pension expense for the year and made the annual payment to a fully funded pension plan.

**h.** Made an adjusting entry to record income taxes expense, part of which will be deferred to future income tax returns (assume deferred taxes are a long-term liability).

Indicate the effects of each of these transactions on the following financial statement categories. Organize your answer in tabular form, using the illustrated column headings. Use the following code letters to indicate the effects of each transaction on the accounting element listed in the column heading: **I** for increase, **D** for decrease, and **NE** for no effect.

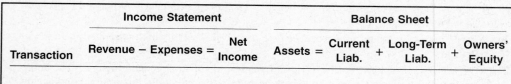

| | Income Statement | | | Balance Sheet | | | |
|---|---|---|---|---|---|---|---|
| Transaction | Revenue − Expenses = | | Net Income | Assets = | Current Liab. + | Long-Term Liab. + | Owners' Equity |

**EXERCISE 10.3**

Effects of Transactions on Various Financial Measurements

**LO 1, 4, 5, 7**

Eight events relating to liabilities follow:

**a.** Paid the liability for interest payable accrued at the end of the last accounting period.

**b.** Made the current monthly payment on a 12-month installment note payable, including interest and a partial repayment of principal.

**c.** Recorded a five-year capital lease payment obligation.

**d.** Made a monthly payment of the lease payment obligation described in **c.** (Ignore any effects on the long-term portion of this obligation.)

---

\* *Supplemental Topic A,* "Estimated Liabilities, Loss Contingencies, and Commitments."

† *Supplemental Topic B,* "Bonds Issued at a Discount or a Premium."

e. Recorded the cost of *fully funded* postretirement benefits earned by employees (assume payment is made immediately). ← not a liability? just an expense

f. Recorded the cost of *unfunded* postretirement benefits earned by employees (a portion of these unfunded benefits is due next year).

g. Recorded income taxes expense for the period, part of which is deferred. (The deferred taxes are classified as a long-term liability.)

h. Made the year-end adjusting entry to amortize a small discount on bonds payable.

Indicate the effects of each transaction or adjusting entry on the financial measurements in the five column headings listed below. Use the code letters **I** for increase, **D** for decrease, and **NE** for no effect.

| Transaction | Current Liabilities | Long-Term Liabilities | Net Income | Net Cash Flow from Operating Activities | Net Cash Flow (from All) Sources |
|---|---|---|---|---|---|
| a | | | | | |

Using the following information, prepare a listing of Chernin Corporation's (a) current liabilities and (b) long-term liabilities. If you do not list a particular item as a liability, explain your reasoning.

| | |
|---|---|
| Capital lease payment obligation (of which $10,000 will be repaid within the next 12 months) | $ 80,000 |
| Interest expense that will arise from existing liabilities over the next 12 months | 125,000 |
| Lawsuit pending against the company claiming $500,000 in damages. Legal counsel can make no reasonable estimate of the company's potential liability at this time. | 500,000 |
| 20-year bond issue that matures in 2 years. (The entire amount will be repaid from a bond sinking fund.) | 900,000 |
| Accrued interest payable on the 20-year bond issue as of the balance sheet date | 36,000 |
| Three-year commitment to John Higgins as chief financial officer at a salary of $250,000 per year | 750,000 |
| Note payable due in 90 days, but that will be extended for an additional 18 months | 75,000 |
| Cash deposits from customers for goods and services to be delivered over the next 9 months | 300,000 |

Magnum Plus, Inc., is a manufacturer of hunting supplies. The following is a summary of the company's annual payroll-related costs:

| | | |
|---|---|---|
| Wages and salaries expense (of which $2,200,000 was withheld from employees' pay and forwarded directly to tax authorities) | | $7,200,000 |
| Payroll taxes | | 580,000 |
| Workers' compensation premiums | | 250,000 |
| Group health insurance premiums | | 725,000 |
| Contributions to employees' pension plan (fully funded) | | 450,000 |
| Other postretirement benefits (e.g., medical benefits): | | |
| Funded | $125,000 | |
| Unfunded | 225,000 | 350,000 |

---

\* *Supplemental Topic A,* "Estimated Liabilities, Loss Contingencies, and Commitments."

a. Compute Magnum's total payroll-related costs for the year.

b. Compute the net amount of cash actually paid to employees (their take-home pay).

c. Express total payroll-related costs as a percentage of (1) total wages and salaries expense, and (2) employees' take-home pay. (Round computations to the nearest 1%.)

d. Discuss briefly how the costs of postretirement benefits may have been determined. Which amounts related to postretirement benefits result in a liability? Will the costs associated with future postretirement items be more, less, or the same as the postretirement liability reported currently in the company's balance sheet? Explain.

**EXERCISE 10.6**

Use of an Amortization Table

Glen Pool Club, Inc., has a $150,000 mortgage liability. The mortgage is payable in monthly installments of $1,543, which include interest computed at an annual rate of 12% (1% monthly).

a. Prepare a partial amortization table showing the original balance of this loan, and the allocation of the first two monthly payments between interest expense and the reduction in the mortgage's unpaid balance. (Round to the nearest dollar.)

b. Prepare the journal entry to record the second monthly payment.

c. Will monthly interest increase, decrease, or stay the same over the life of the loan? Explain your answer.

**EXERCISE 10.7**

After-Tax Cost of Borrowing

Mississippi Rail, Inc., issued $50 million of 10% bonds payable at face (par) value. The company pays income taxes at an average rate of 40% of its taxable income.

Compute the company's annual after-tax cost of borrowing on this bond issue, stated as (a) a total dollar amount and (b) a percentage of the amount borrowed.

**EXERCISE 10.8**

Bond Interest on Bonds Issued at Par

**LO 5**

On March 31, 2002, Gardner Corporation received authorization to issue $50,000 of 9%, 30-year debenture bonds. The bonds pay interest on March 31 and September 30. The entire issue was dated March 31, 2002, but the bonds were not issued until April 30, 2002. They were issued at par.

a. Prepare the journal entry at April 30, 2002, to record the sale of the bonds.

b. Prepare the journal entry at September 30, 2002, to record the semiannual bond interest payment.

c. Prepare the adjusting entry at December 31, 2002, to record bond interest expense accrued since September 30, 2002. (Assume that no monthly adjusting entries to accrue interest expense had been made prior to December 31, 2002.)

d. Explain why the issuing corporation charged its bond investors for interest accrued in April 2002, prior to the issuance date (see part **b** above).

**†EXERCISE 10.9**

Bond Price Volatility

**LO 5, 11**

Select a bond issue from the financial pages of a daily newspaper such as *The Wall Street Journal*. Track the activity of the bond issue over a three-day period.

a. What volume of bonds was traded each day?

b. What was the closing price of the bonds at the end of each day?

c. What factors may have influenced the daily changes in price of these bonds?

**†EXERCISE 10.10**

Basic Entries for a Bond Issue: Issuance, Interest Payments, and Retirement

**LO 5, 11**

Mellilo Corporation issued $5 million of 20-year, 9.5% bonds on July 1, 2002, at 98. Interest is due on June 30 and December 31 of each year, and all of the bonds in the issue mature on June 30, 2023. Mellilo's fiscal year ends on December 31. The company uses the straight-line method to amortize bond discounts. Prepare the following journal entries:

a. July 1, 2002, to record the issuance of the bonds.

b. December 31, 2002, to pay interest and amortize the bond discount (make two separate entries).

c. June 30, 2023, to pay interest, amortize the bond discount, and retire the bonds at maturity (make three separate entries).

d. Briefly explain the effect of amortizing the bond discount upon (1) annual net income and (2) annual net cash flow from operating activities. (Ignore possible income tax effects.)

---

† *Supplemental Topic B,* "Bonds Issued at a Discount or a Premium."

On July 1, Pine Region Dairy leased equipment from Farm America for a period of three years. The lease calls for monthly payments of $2,500 payable in advance on the first day of each month, beginning July 1.

Prepare the journal entry needed to record this lease in the accounting records of Pine Region Dairy on July 1 under each of the following independent assumptions:

**a.** The lease represents a simple rental arrangement.

**b.** At the end of three years, title to this equipment will be transferred to Pine Region Dairy at no additional cost. The present value of the 36 monthly lease payments is $76,000, of which $2,500 is paid in cash on July 1. None of the initial $2,500 is allocated to interest expense.

**c.** Why is situation **a,** the operating lease, sometimes called off-balance-sheet financing?

**d.** Would it be acceptable for a company to account for a capital lease as an operating lease to report rent expense rather than a long-term liability?

**EXERCISE 10.11**

Accounting for Leases

**LO 6**

At the end of the current year, Western Electric received the following information from its actuarial firm:

| | |
|---|---|
| Pension expense . . . . . . . . . . . . . . . . . . . . . . . . . . . . . . . . . . . . . . . . . . . . . . . . . | $2,500,000 |
| Nonpension postretirement benefits expense . . . . . . . . . . . . . . . . . . . . . . . . . . . . . | 750,000 |

The pension plan is fully funded. Western Electric has funded only $50,000 of the nonpension postretirement benefits this year.

**a.** Prepare the journal entry to summarize pension expense for the entire year.

**b.** Prepare the journal entry to summarize the nonpension postretirement benefits expense for the entire year.

**c.** If the company becomes insolvent in future years, what prospects, if any, do today's employees have of receiving the pension benefits that they have earned to date?

**d.** Does the company have an ethical responsibility to fully fund its nonpension postretirement benefits?

**EXERCISE 10.12**

Pension Plans

**LO 6, 7**

The following journal entry summarizes for the current year the income taxes expense of Wilson's Software Warehouse:

| | | |
|---|---|---|
| Income Taxes Expense . . . . . . . . . . . . . . . . . . . . . . . . . . . . . . . . . . . . . . | 1,500,000 | |
| Cash . . . . . . . . . . . . . . . . . . . . . . . . . . . . . . . . . . . . . . . . . . . . . . . . . . | | 960,000 |
| Income Taxes Payable . . . . . . . . . . . . . . . . . . . . . . . . . . . . . . . . . . . . | | 340,000 |
| Deferred Income Taxes . . . . . . . . . . . . . . . . . . . . . . . . . . . . . . . . . . . | | 200,000 |
| To record income taxes expense for the current year. | | |

**EXERCISE 10.13**

Deferred Income Taxes

**LO 8**

Of the deferred income taxes, only $30,000 is classified as a current liability.

**a.** Define deferred income taxes payable.

**b.** What is the amount of income taxes that the company has paid or expects to pay in conjunction with its income tax return for the current year?

**c.** Illustrate the allocation of the liabilities shown in the above journal entry between the classifications of current liabilities and long-term liabilities.

## EXERCISE 10.14

Safety of Creditors' Investments

Shown below are data from recent reports of two publicly owned toy makers. Dollar amounts are stated in thousands.

|  | Tyco Toys, Inc. | Hasbro, Inc. |
|---|---|---|
| Total assets . . . . . . . . . . . . . . . . . . . . . . . . . . . . . . . . . . . | $615,132 | $2,616,388 |
| Total liabilities . . . . . . . . . . . . . . . . . . . . . . . . . . . . . . . . | 349,792 | 1,090,776 |
| Interest expense . . . . . . . . . . . . . . . . . . . . . . . . . . . . . . | 28,026 | 37,588 |
| Operating income . . . . . . . . . . . . . . . . . . . . . . . . . . . . | 13,028 | 304,672 |

**a.** Compute for each company (1) the debt ratio and (2) the interest coverage ratio. (Round the debt ratio to the nearest percent and the interest coverage ratio to two decimal places.)

**b.** In your opinion, which of these companies would a long-term creditor probably view as the safer investment? Explain.

## EXERCISE 10.15

Examining **Tootsie Roll Industries**' Capital Structure

LO 9

To answer the following questions use the annual report for **Tootsie Roll Industries, Inc.,** in Appendix A at the end of the textbook:

**a.** Compute the company's current ratio and quick ratio for the most recent year reported. Do these ratios provide support that **Tootsie Roll** is able to repay its current liabilities as they come due? Explain.

**b.** Compute the company's debt ratio. Does **Tootsie Roll** appear to have excessive debt? Explain.

**c.** Examine the company's statement of cash flows. Does **Tootsie Roll**'s cash flow from operating activities appear adequate to cover its current liabilities as they come due? Explain.

# PROBLEMS

## *PROBLEM 10.1

Effects of Transactions on Financial Statements

LO 1, 2, 3, 4, 7, 10

Fifteen transactions or events affecting Computer Specialists, Inc., are as follows:

**a.** Made a year-end adjusting entry to accrue interest on a note payable that has the interest rate stated separately from the principal amount.

**b.** A liability classified for several years as long-term becomes due within the next 12 months.

**c.** Recorded the regular biweekly payroll, including payroll taxes, amounts withheld from employees, and the issuance of paychecks.

**d.** Earned an amount previously recorded as unearned revenue.

**e.** Made arrangements to extend a bank loan due in 60 days for another 18 months.

**f.** Made a monthly payment on a fully amortizing installment note payable. (Assume this note is classified as a current liability.)

**g.** Called bonds payable due in seven years at a price above the carrying value of the liability in the accounting records.

**h.** Made a monthly payment on an operating lease.

**i.** Made a monthly payment on a capital lease. (Assume only eight months remain in the lease term.)

**j.** Recorded pension expense on a fully funded pension plan.

**k.** Recorded nonpension postretirement expense; the liability is unfunded, but 20% of the amount of expense will be funded within 12 months.

**l.** Recorded income taxes expense for the year, including a considerable amount of deferred taxes (assume deferred taxes are long-term liabilities).

***m.** Recorded an estimated liability for warranty claims.

***n.** Entered into a two-year commitment to buy all hard drives from a particular supplier at a price 10% below market.

***o.** Received notice that a lawsuit has been filed against the company for $7 million. The amount of the company's liability, if any, cannot be reasonably estimated at this time.

_* Supplemental Topic A, "Estimated Liabilities, Loss Contingencies, and Commitments."_

## Instructions

Indicate the effects of each of these transactions upon the following elements of the company's financial statements. Organize your answer in tabular form, using the column headings shown below. Use the following code letters to indicate the effects of each transaction on the accounting element listed in the column heading: **I** for increase, **D** for decrease, and **NE** for no effect.

| | Income Statement | | | Balance Sheet | | | | | |
|---|---|---|---|---|---|---|---|---|---|
| Transaction | Revenue | – Expense | = Net Income | Assets | = Current Liab. | + Long-Term Liab. | + Owners' Equity | | |
| a. | | | | | | | | | |

The following are selected items from the accounting records of Seattle Chocolates for the year ended December 31, 2002:

**\*PROBLEM 10.2**

Balance Sheet Presentation of Liabilities

**LO 1, 2, 4, 10**

| | |
|---|---|
| Note payable to Northwest Bank | $500,000 |
| Income taxes payable | 40,000 |
| Accrued expenses and payroll taxes | 60,000 |
| Mortgage note payable | 750,000 |
| Accrued interest on mortgage note payable | 5,000 |
| Trade accounts payable | 250,000 |
| Unearned revenue | 15,000 |
| Potential liability in pending lawsuit | 100,000 |

## Other Information

**1.** The note payable to Northwest Bank is due in 60 days. Arrangements have been made to renew this note for an additional 12 months.

**2.** The mortgage requires payments of $6,000 per month. An amortization table shows that its balance will be paid down to $739,000 by December 31, 2003.

**3.** Accrued interest on the mortgage note payable is paid monthly. The next payment is due near the end of the first week in January 2003.

**4.** Seattle Chocolates has been sued for $100,000 in a contract dispute. It is not possible at this time, however, to make a reasonable estimate of the possible loss, if any, that the company may have sustained.

## Instructions

**a.** Using the information provided, prepare the current and long-term liability sections of the company's balance sheet dated December 31, 2002. (Within each classification, items may be listed in any order.)

**b.** Explain briefly how the information in each of the four numbered paragraphs above influenced your presentation of the company's liabilities.

During the fiscal year ended December 31, Swanson Corporation engaged in the following transactions involving notes payable:

**PROBLEM 10.3**

Notes Payable: Accruing Interest

**LO 2**

| | |
|---|---|
| **Aug. 6** | Borrowed $12,000 from Maple Grove Bank, signing a 45-day, 12% note payable. |
| **Sept. 16** | Purchased office equipment from Seawald Equipment. The invoice amount was $18,000, and Seawald agreed to accept, as full payment, a 10%, three-month note for the invoice amount. |
| **Sept. 20** | Paid Maple Grove Bank the note plus accrued interest. |

\* *Supplemental Topic A,* "Estimated Liabilities, Loss Contingencies, and Commitments."

**Nov. 1**   Borrowed $250,000 from Mike Swanson, a major corporate stockholder. The corporation issued Swanson a $250,000, 15%, 90-day note payable.

**Dec. 1**   Purchased merchandise inventory in the amount of $5,000 from Gathman Corporation. Gathman accepted a 90-day, 14% note as full settlement of the purchase. Swanson Corporation uses a perpetual inventory system.

**Dec. 16**   The $18,000 note payable to Seawald Equipment matured today. Swanson paid the accrued interest on this note and issued a new 30-day, 16% note payable in the amount of $18,000 to replace the note that matured.

### Instructions

**a.** Prepare journal entries (in general journal form) to record the above transactions. Use a 360-day year in making the interest calculations.

**b.** Prepare the adjusting entry needed at December 31, prior to closing the accounts. Use one entry for all three notes (round to the nearest dollar.)

**c.** Provide a possible explanation why the new 30-day note payable to Seawald Equipment pays 16% interest instead of the 10% rate charged on the September 16 note.

**PROBLEM 10.4**

Preparation and Use of an Amortization Table

**LO 4**

On September 1, 2002, Quick Lube signed a 30-year, $1,080,000 mortgage note payable to Mifflinburg Bank and Trust in conjunction with the purchase of a building and land. The mortgage note calls for interest at an annual rate of 12% (1% per month). The note is fully amortizing over a period of 360 months.

The bank sent Quick Lube an amortization table showing the allocation of monthly payments between interest and principal over the life of the loan. A small part of this amortization table is illustrated below. (For convenience, amounts have been rounded to the nearest dollar.)

| Amortization Table (12%, 30-Year Mortgage Note Payable for $1,080,000; Payable in 360 Monthly Installments of $11,110) | | | | | |
|---|---|---|---|---|---|
| Interest Period | Payment Date | Monthly Payment | Interest Expense | Principal Reduction | Unpaid Balance |
| Issue date | Sept. 1, 2002 | — | — | — | $1,080,000 |
| 1 | Oct. 1 | $11,110 | $10,800 | $310 | 1,079,690 |
| 2 | Nov. 1 | 11,110 | 10,797 | 313 | 1,079,377 |

### Instructions

**a.** Explain whether the amounts of interest expense and the reductions in the unpaid principal are likely to change in any predictable pattern from month to month.

**b.** Prepare journal entries to record the first two monthly payments on this mortgage.

**c.** Complete this amortization table for two more monthly installments—those due on December 1, 2002, and January 1, 2003. (Round amounts to the nearest dollar.)

**d.** Will any amounts relating to this 30-year mortgage be classified as current liabilities in Quick Lube's December 31, 2002, balance sheet? Explain, but you need not compute any additional dollar amounts.

**PROBLEM 10.5**

Bond Interest (Bonds Issued at Par)

**LO 5**

Blue Mountain Power Company obtained authorization to issue 20-year bonds with a face value of $10 million. The bonds are dated May 1, 2002, and have a contract rate of interest of 10%. They pay interest on November 1 and May 1. The bonds were issued on August 1, 2002, at 100 plus three months' accrued interest.

### Instructions

Prepare the necessary journal entries in general journal form on:

**a.** August 1, 2002, to record the issuance of the bonds.

**b.** November 1, 2002, to record the first semiannual interest payment on the bond issue.

**c.** December 31, 2002, to record interest expense accrued through year-end. (Round to the nearest dollar.)

**d.** May 1, 2003, to record the second semiannual interest payment. (Round to the nearest dollar.)

**e.** What was the prevailing market rate of interest on the date that the bonds were issued? Explain.

On September 1, 2002, Park Rapids Lumber Company issued $80 million in 20-year, 10% debenture bonds. Interest is payable semiannually on March 1 and September 1. Bond discounts and premiums are amortized by the straight-line method at each interest payment date and at year-end. The company's fiscal year ends at December 31.

†PROBLEM 10.6

Amortization of a Bond Discount and Premium

**LO 11**

### Instructions

**a.** Make the necessary adjusting entries at December 31, 2002, and the journal entry to record the payment of bond interest on March 1, 2003, under each of the following assumptions:

 **1.** The bonds were issued at 98. (Round to the nearest dollar.)

 **2.** The bonds were issued at 101. (Round to the nearest dollar.)

**b.** Compute the net bond liability at December 31, 2003, under assumptions **1** and **2** above. (Round to the nearest dollar.)

**c.** Under which of the above assumptions, **1** or **2**, would the investor's effective rate of interest be higher? Explain.

The following items were taken from the accounting records of Minnesota Satellite Telephone Corporation (MinnSat) for the year ended December 31, 2002 (dollar amounts are in thousands):

**PROBLEM 10.7**

Reporting Liabilities in a Balance Sheet

**LO 1, 5, 7, 8**

| | |
|---|---:|
| Accounts payable | $ 65,600 |
| Accrued expenses payable (other than interest) | 11,347 |
| 6³/4% Bonds payable, due Feb. 1, 2003 | 100,000 |
| 8¹/2% Bonds payable, due June 1, 2003 | 250,000 |
| Unamortized bond discount (8¹/2% bonds of '03) | 260 |
| 11% Bonds payable, due June 1, 2012 | 300,000 |
| Unamortized bond premium (11% bonds of '12) | 1,700 |
| Accrued interest payable | 7,333 |
| Bond interest expense | 61,000 |
| Other interest expense | 17,000 |
| Notes payable (short-term) | 110,000 |
| Lease payment obligations—capital leases | 23,600 |
| Pension obligation | 410,000 |
| Unfunded obligations for postretirement benefits other than pensions | 72,000 |
| Deferred income taxes | 130,000 |
| Income taxes expense | 66,900 |
| Income taxes payable | 17,300 |
| Operating income | 280,800 |
| Net income | 134,700 |
| Total assets | 2,093,500 |

### Other Information

**1.** The 6³/4% bonds due in February 2003 will be refinanced in January 2003 through the issuance of $150,000 in 9%, 20-year general debentures.

**2.** The 8¹/2% bonds due June 1, 2003, will be repaid entirely from a bond sinking fund.

**3.** MinnSat is committed to total lease payments of $14,400 in 2003. Of this amount, $7,479 is applicable to operating leases, and $6,921 to capital leases. Payments on capital leases will be applied as follows: $2,300 to interest expense and $4,621 to reduction in the capitalized lease payment obligation.

**4.** MinnSat's pension plan is fully funded with an independent trustee.

---

† *Supplemental Topic B,* "Bonds Issued at a Discount or a Premium."

5. The obligation for postretirement benefits other than pensions consists of a commitment to maintain health insurance for retired workers. During 2003, MinnSat will fund $18,000 of this obligation.

6. The $17,300 in income taxes payable relates to income taxes levied in 2002 and must be paid on or before March 15, 2003. No portion of the deferred tax liability is regarded as a current liability.

### Instructions

a. Using this information, prepare the current liabilities and long-term liabilities sections of a classified balance sheet as of December 31, 2002. (Within each classification, items may be listed in any order.)

b. Explain briefly how the information in each of the six numbered paragraphs affected your presentation of the company's liabilities.

c. Compute as of December 31, 2002, the company's (1) debt ratio and (2) interest coverage ratio.

d. Based solely on information stated in this problem, indicate whether this company appears to be an outstanding, medium, or poor long-term credit risk. State specific reasons for your conclusion.

# CASES AND UNSTRUCTURED PROBLEMS

**\*CASE 10.1**

The Nature of Liabilities

**LO 1, 3, 10**

Listed below are eight publicly owned corporations and a liability that regularly appears in each corporation's balance sheet:

a. **Wells Fargo & Company** (banking): Deposits: interest bearing

b. **The New York Times Company:** Unexpired subscriptions

c. **The Hollywood Park Companies** (horse racing): Outstanding mutuel tickets

d. **American Greetings** (greeting cards and gift wrap products manufacturer): Sales returns

e. **Wausau Paper Mills Company:** Current maturities of long-term debt

f. **Club Med., Inc.** (resorts): Amounts received for future vacations

g. **Apple Computer, Inc.:** Accrued marketing and distribution

h. **General Motors Corporation:** Postretirement costs other than pensions

### Instructions

Briefly explain what you believe to be the nature of each of these liabilities, including how the liability arose and the manner in which it is likely to be discharged.

**\*CASE 10.2**

Liabilities: Recognition and Disclosure

**LO 1, 7, 10**

The events described below occurred at Redford Grain Corporation on *December 31,* the last day of the company's fiscal year.

a. The company was named as defendant in a $30 million lawsuit. Redford's legal counsel stated that the lawsuit was without merit and that Redford would defend itself vigorously in court. However, the legal counsel also stated that it was impossible at this time to predict the outcome of the litigation or the liability, if any, that might ultimately be determined.

b. Signed a note payable to obtain a bank loan. The note was in the principal amount of $300,000, to mature in nine months, plus interest of $22,500 (computed at 10% per year).

c. Recorded income taxes expense for the year at an estimated amount of $220,000, which included $30,000 in deferred taxes resulting from the use of accelerated depreciation methods in income tax returns. The actual amount of tax expense will not be known until March, when the company files its income tax return for the year ended December 31.

d. The general ledger included an account entitled Income Taxes Withheld with a balance at December 31 of $16,500.

e. Recognized $2,700,000 in pension expense for the year. The pension plan is fully funded.

---

\* *Supplemental Topic A,* "Estimated Liabilities, Loss Contingencies, and Commitments."

**f.** Recognized $650,000 in postretirement expense *other* than pensions. Of this amount $270,000 was paid this year and $300,000 will be funded next year.

**g.** Signed a contract with another grain dealer calling for the purchase by Redford of 50,000 bushels of wheat per month for six months at a price of $4 per bushel, a price slightly below market value.

**h.** Signed a contract with a labor union on specifying annual increases in wage rates of 5% for the next three years. The increase in labor costs for the first year of the agreement was estimated to be $1,200,000.

### Instructions

For each of the above eight events, you are to state the dollar amount (if any) that would appear in the current liability section of Redford Grain Corporation's balance sheet at December 31. For any event that does not affect current liabilities, you are to indicate whether it should appear in the financial statements and the proper location and amount.

**Occidental Petroleum** has two bond issues outstanding with the following characteristics:

**CASE 10.3**

Factors Affecting Bond Prices

| Issue | Interest Rate | Maturity | Current Price |
|-------|---------------|----------|---------------|
| A | 10⅛% | 2001 | 112 |
| B | 10⅛% | 2009 | 118 |

### Instructions

Answer the following questions regarding these bond issues:

**a.** Which issue, A or B, has the higher effective rate of interest? How can you tell?

**b.** Assume that the bonds of both issues have face values of $1,000 each. How much total interest does each bond from *issue A* provide investors in *12 months?* How much total interest does each bond from *issue B* provide investors in *12 months?*

**c.** Note that both issues are by the same company, have the same contract rate of interest, and have identical credit ratings. In view of these facts, explain the current price difference of each issue.

Discuss each of the following situations, indicating whether the situation is a loss contingency that should be recorded or disclosed in the financial statements of Aztec Airlines. If the situation is not a loss contingency, explain how (if at all) it should be reported in the company's financial statements. (Assume that all dollar amounts are material.)

**\*CASE 10.4**

Loss Contingencies

**LO 10**

**a.** Aztec estimates that $700,000 of its accounts receivable will prove to be uncollectible.

**b.** The company's president is in poor health and has previously suffered two heart attacks.

**c.** As with any airline, Aztec faces the risk that a future airplane crash could cause considerable loss.

**d.** Aztec is being sued for $10 million for failing to adequately provide for passengers whose reservations were cancelled as a result of the airline overbooking certain flights. This suit will not be resolved for a year or more.

## BUSINESS WEEK ASSIGNMENT

BusinessWeek

In a June 1, 2000, *Business Week* article entitled, "You Should Be Worried Sick About Health Insurance," author Ellen Hoffman notes the number of large companies that no longer offer health insurance benefits to retired employees has accelerated in recent years. The decision to discontinue health insurance benefits to retirees is often based upon rising health care costs and their impact on the financial statements. Since 1993, companies have been required to report as a

**CASE 10.5**

**LO 7**

---

*\* Supplemental Topic A,* "Estimated Liabilities, Loss Contingencies, and Commitments."

long-term liability the unfunded portion of retirement benefits related to health care. As health care costs rise, the rate at which this unfunded benefit accrues increases as well.

**Instructions**

Discuss the ethical implications of a company's decision to discontinue health insurance benefits as part of its retirement package. Your discussion should take into consideration a company's obligation to its current retirees, its current employees, and to its stockholders.

## INTERNET ASSIGNMENT

**INTERNET 10.1**

Credit Ratings on Bonds

**LO 9**

The Internet provides a wealth of information concerning long-term liabilities, bond rating agencies, and credit markets. Visit the home page of **Bonds-Online** at the following Internet address:

**www.bonds-online.com**

**Instructions**

a. From the home page menu, locate Corporate Bonds and select Corporate Bond Search. In the Ranges section, select Aaa/AAA as both the minimum and maximum rating (this is the highest credit rating a company can receive). Leave all other items in the Ranges section blank. Select "no" for both items in the Apply Constraints section. In the Industry Group section, select only Industrials. Leave all fields in other sections blank. Select "Find Bonds." Identify several of the companies listed and the current yields of their bonds.

b. Perform a second search by selecting B/B as both the minimum and maximum rating (this is a relatively low credit rating). Again, select "no" for both items in the Apply Constraints section and select only Industrials in the Industry Group section. Leave all fields in other sections blank. Identify several of the companies listed and the current yields of their bonds.

c. Compare the yields of the bonds from the search conducted in part **a** to those from the search conducted in part **b**. Which search produced the highest yields? Explain why.

*Internet sites are time and date sensitive. It is the purpose of these exercises to have you explore the Internet. You may need to use the Yahoo! search engine* http://www.yahoo.com *(or other favorite search engine) to look for a company's current web address.*

## OUR COMMENTS ON THE "YOUR TURN" CASES

**As a Public Accountant for Small Businesses (p. 408)** Mr. Swidle needs to explain more carefully about the specific nature of the merchandise and when the merchandise will be delivered. You should question why Mr. Swidle does not want to put the check in Pawn Shop's bank account and have you record the Cash and associated Customer Deposit journal entry. The code of professional conduct requires that a professional accountant in public practice should not hold clients' monies if there is reason to believe that they were obtained from, or are to be used for, any illegal activities. You must satisfy yourself that there are good reasons for your firm to keep the money rather than recording the appropriate journal entry in Pawn Shop's records.

**As a Financial Advisor (p. 417)** The interest payments generated by a bond remain constant, regardless of fluctuations in market interest rates that occur over the bond's life. Thus, if bond issuers consistently fulfill their responsibility to make timely interest payments, the couple's annual cash flow from their investment will remain relatively stable throughout their retirement.

Fluctuations in market interest rates could adversely affect the couple should they decide to sell any of their bonds *before* the bonds mature. If interest rates are relatively high at the time the bonds are sold, their selling price may be substantially less than their redemption value at maturity.

**As a Loan Officer (p. 425)**   The point that the CEO was trying to make is that $250,000 of the company's total expenses for the year were noncash expenses. As such, these expenses reduced operating income without reducing cash flow from operations. While impossible to determine from the limited information provided, the company's ability to service its debt *may be* better than the low interest coverage ratio suggests.

It is interesting to note that some credit analysts *add back* significant noncash expenses to income from operations when computing the interest coverage ratio. In this case, the addition of these two noncash items would increase the company's interest coverage ratio to 5 to 1 [($375,000 + $200,000 + $50,000) ÷ 125,000 = 5 times coverage].

## ANSWERS TO SELF-TEST QUESTIONS

**1.** a, b     **2.** a, b, d     **3.** a, d     **4.** a, c, d     **5.** a, b, c, d     **6.** a, b, c, d     **7.** d     **8.** c

**9.** a, c     **\*10.** c     **\*11.** a, b

---

\* *Supplemental Topic A,* "Estimated Liabilities, Loss Contingencies, and Commitments."

# STOCKHOLDERS' EQUITY: PAID-IN CAPITAL

## Learning Objectives

*After studying this chapter, you should be able to:*

1. Discuss the advantages and disadvantages of organizing a business as a corporation.

2. Distinguish between publicly owned and closely held corporations.

3. Describe the rights of stockholders and the roles of corporate directors and officers.

4. Account for paid-in capital and prepare the equity section of a corporate balance sheet.

5. Contrast the features of common stock with those of preferred stock.

6. Discuss the factors affecting the market price of preferred stock and common stock.

7. Explain the significance of par value, book value, and market value of capital stock.

8. Explain the purpose and effects of a stock split.

9. Account for treasury stock transactions.

© David Burnett/Contact Press Images/Picture Quest

It is certainly not unusual for companies to invest large amounts of excess cash in the marketable securities of other companies. These investments often earn returns in the form of interest, dividends, and capital appreciation. While it is common for businesses to purchase shares of *other* companies, would a company ever purchase *its own* shares on the open market? Absolutely.

Each year, for example, **Microsoft Corporation** spends billions of dollars to purchase shares of its own stock on the open market. These purchases often are referred to as treasury stock transactions. Many of these shares purchased by **Microsoft** are reissued to company employees in compliance with formal stock option and stock purchase plans. **Microsoft** is not unique in this regard. In fact, it is difficult to find a major corporation that does *not* engage in treasury stock transactions on a regular basis.

● ● ●

In this chapter we explore numerous issues related to stockholders' equity. In addition to treasury stock transactions, we will discuss common stock, preferred stock, stock splits, and other related topics. We will also discuss why businesses incorporate and describe the factors that influence the price of their shares on the open market.

## CORPORATIONS

The corporate form is the organization of choice for many businesses—large and small. The owners of a corporation are called **stockholders**. In many small corporations, there are only one or two stockholders. But in large corporations, such as **IBM** and **AT&T**, there are literally millions of stockholders.

A **corporation** is the only form of business organization recognized under the law as a *legal entity,* with rights and responsibilities *separate from those of its owners.* The assets of a corporation belong to the corporation *itself,* not to the stockholders. The corporation is responsible for its own debts and must pay income taxes on its earnings. As a separate legal entity, a corporation has status in court; it may enter into contracts, and it may sue and be sued as if it were a person. The major advantages and disadvantages of this form of business organization are summarized on page 455.

What types of businesses choose the corporate form of organization? The answer, basically, is *all kinds.* When we think of corporations, we often think of large, well-known companies such as **ExxonMobil**, **General Motors**, and **Procter & Gamble**. Indeed, almost all large businesses are organized as corporations. Limited shareholder liability, transferability of ownership, professional management, and continuity of existence make the corporation the best form of organization for pooling the resources of a great many equity investors. Not all corporations, however, are large and publicly owned. Many small businesses are organized as corporations.

**CASE IN POINT**

Many locally owned stores, gas stations, and restaurants are organized as corporations and have a small number of stockholders—sometimes two or three members of the same family. Large, publicly held corporations, on the other hand, have many stockholders. For example, recent annual reports of **Dow Chemical** and **Aluminum Company of America (ALCOA)** indicate that they have approximately 97,200 and 95,800 stockholders, respectively.

### Why Businesses Incorporate

Businesses incorporate for many reasons, but the two of greatest importance are (1) limited shareholder liability and (2) transferability of ownership.

We have previously discussed the concept of **limited personal liability**. This simply means that shareholders have no *personal* liability for the debts of the corporation. Thus, if the corporation becomes insolvent, the most that a stockholder usually can lose is the amount of his or her equity investment. In this era of multimillion-dollar lawsuits, limited personal liability appeals to the owners of large and small businesses alike.

Another special feature of the corporation is the *transferability of ownership*—the idea that ownership is represented by transferable shares of **capital stock**. For a small, family-owned business, this provides a convenient means of gradually transferring ownership and control of the business from one generation to the next. For a large company, it makes ownership of the business a *highly liquid investment,* which can be purchased and sold in organized securities exchanges.[1] This liquidity is essential to a large corporation's ability to raise equity capital from thousands—perhaps millions—of individual investors.

There are many other reasons why specific businesses may be organized as corporations—we cannot possibly discuss them all. For example, some states allow an individ-

---

[1] These securities exchanges include, among others, the New York Stock Exchange, the National Association of Securities Dealers' Automated Quotations (Nasdaq), the Tokyo Stock Exchange, and Mexico's Bolsa. Collectively, stock exchanges often are described simply as *the stock market.*

| Advantages of the Corporate Form | Disadvantages of the Corporate Form |
|---|---|
| 1. *Stockholders are not personally liable for the debts of a corporation.* Thus the most that a stockholder can lose by investing in a corporation is the amount of his or her investment. This concept is called *limited personal liability* and often is cited as the greatest advantage of the corporate form of organization. | 1. *Heavy taxation.* Corporate earnings are subject to **double taxation.** First, the corporation must pay *corporate income taxes* on its earnings. Second, stockholders must pay *personal income taxes* on any portion of these earnings that they receive as *dividends.* Together, these two levels of taxation may consume from 60% to 70% of a corporation's pretax earnings. |
| 2. *Transferability of ownership.* Ownership of a corporation is evidenced by *transferable shares of stock,* which may be sold by one investor to another. Investment in these shares has the advantage of *liquidity,* because investors easily may convert their corporate ownership into cash by selling their shares. | 2. *Greater regulation.* Corporations are affected by state and federal laws to a far greater extent than are unincorporated businesses. For example, the owners' ability to *remove business assets* from a corporation is restricted by law. A corporation must obtain authorization from government agencies to issue capital stock. Also, federal laws require publicly owned corporations to make extensive public disclosure of their financial activities. |
| 3. *Professional management.* The stockholders own a corporation, but they do not manage it on a daily basis. To administer the affairs of the corporation, the stockholders elect a *board of directors.* The directors, in turn, hire professional managers to run the business. An individual stockholder has *no right* to participate in management *unless he or she has been hired by the directors as a corporate manager.* | 3. *Cost of formation.* An *unincorporated business* can be formed at little or no cost. Forming a corporation, however, normally requires the services of an attorney. |
| 4. *Continuity of existence.* Changes in the names and identities of stockholders do not directly affect the corporation. Therefore, the corporation may continue its operations *without disruption,* despite the retirement or death of individual stockholders. This characteristic is essential in the undertaking of most large-scale business ventures. | 4. *Separation of ownership and management.* The separation of ownership and management is an advantage in many cases, but may be a disadvantage in others. If stockholders do not approve of the manner in which management runs the business, they may find it difficult to take the united action necessary to remove that management group. |

**LO 1**

Discuss the advantages and disadvantages of organizing a business as a corporation.

ual or a corporation to own *only one liquor license.* A business that needs to serve liquor at several different sites, such as a chain of hotels or restaurants, must organize *each location* as a separate corporation.

## You as a Loan Officer

GOTCHA! is a small business that manufactures board games. It is one of the many business ventures of Gayle Woods, who is very wealthy and one of your bank's most valued customers. She has done business with your bank for more than 20 years, and the balance in her personal checking account normally exceeds $500,000. GOTCHA! is organized as a corporation, and Woods is the only stockholder.

GOTCHA! has applied for a $200,000 line of credit, which it intends to use to purchase copyrights to additional board games. Although the company is profitable, its most recent balance sheet shows total assets of only $52,000, including $47,000 in copyrights. The corporation has just under $3,000 in liabilities and over $49,000 in stockholders' equity.

Do you consider GOTCHA! a good credit risk? Would you make the loan? Under what conditions?

**YOUR TURN**

*Our comments appear on page 490.

## Publicly Owned Corporations

**LO 2**

Distinguish between publicly owned and closely held corporations.

The capital stock of most large corporations can be bought and sold (traded) through organized securities exchanges. As these shares are available for purchase by the general public, these large corporations are said to be **publicly owned**.

Far more people have a financial interest in the shares of publicly owned companies than one might expect. If you purchase the stock of such a corporation, you become a stockholder with a *direct* ownership interest—that is, *you* are a stockholder. But mutual funds and pension funds invest heavily in the stocks of many publicly owned corporations. Thus, if you invest in a mutual fund or you are covered by a pension plan, you probably have an *indirect* financial interest in the stocks of many publicly owned corporations.

> **CASE IN POINT**
>
> The stockholders in **General Motors** include more than one million men and women, as well as many pension funds, mutual investment funds, labor unions, universities, and other organizations. Almost every person covered by an employee pension plan has an indirect ownership interest in **GM**.

Corporations whose shares are *not* traded on any organized stock exchanges are said to be **closely held**. Because there is no organized market for buying and selling their shares, these corporations usually have relatively few stockholders. Often, a closely held corporation is owned by one individual or by the members of one family.

**Publicly Owned Corporations Face Different Rules**   Government seeks to protect the interests of the public. Therefore, publicly owned corporations are subject to far more regulation than those that are closely held. For example, publicly owned corporations are *required by law* to:

- Prepare and issue quarterly and annual financial statements in conformity with generally accepted accounting principles. (These statements are **public information**.)
- Have their annual financial statements audited by an independent firm of Certified Public Accountants.
- Comply with federal securities laws, which include both criminal penalties and civil liability for deliberately or carelessly distributing misleading information to the public.
- Submit much of their financial information to the Securities and Exchange Commission for review.

Closely held corporations normally are exempt from these requirements. But our discussions will focus primarily on the accounting and reporting issues confronting *publicly owned companies*. After all, these are the companies whose financial statements you are most likely to see—and the companies in which you are likely to invest.

## FORMATION OF A CORPORATION

In the United States, a corporation is brought into existence under the laws of a particular state. The state in which the corporation is formed is called the **state of incorporation**.

The state of incorporation is not necessarily where the corporation does business. Rather, a state often is selected because of the leniency of its laws regulating corporate activities. Indeed, many corporations conduct most—sometimes all—of their business activities *outside* the state in which they are incorporated.

The first step in forming a corporation is to obtain a *corporate charter* from the state of incorporation. To obtain this charter, the organizers of the corporation submit an application called the *articles of incorporation*. Once the charter is obtained, the stockholders in the new corporation hold a meeting to elect a *board of directors* and to pass *bylaws* that will govern the corporation's activities. The directors in turn hold a meeting at which the top corporate officers and managers are appointed.

**Organization Costs**   Forming a corporation is more costly than starting a sole proprietorship. The costs may include, for example, attorneys' fees, incorporation fees paid to the state, and other outlays necessary to bring the corporation into existence. Conceptually, organization costs are an *intangible asset* that will benefit the corporation over its entire life. As a practical matter, however, most corporations expense those costs immediately, even though they are usually spread over a five-year period for income tax purposes.

Thus you will seldom see organization costs in the balance sheet of a publicly owned corporation. They have long since been recognized as an expense.

**Rights of Stockholders**   A corporation is owned collectively by its stockholders. Each stockholder's ownership interest is determined by the number of *shares* that he or she owns.

Assume that a corporation issues 10,000 shares of capital stock. If you own 1,000 of these shares, you own *10%* of the corporation. If you acquire another 500 shares from another stockholder, you will own *15%*.

Each stockholder, or the stockholder's brokerage firm, receives from the corporation a **stock certificate** indicating the number of shares he or she owns.

The ownership of capital stock in a corporation usually carries the following basic rights:

**LO 3**

Explain the rights of stockholders and the roles of corporate directors and officers.

1. *To vote for directors and on certain other key issues*. A stockholder has one vote for each share owned. The issues on which stockholders may vote are specified in the corporation's bylaws.

   Any stockholder—or group of stockholders—that owns *more than 50%* of the capital stock has the power to elect the board of directors and to set basic corporate policies. Therefore, these stockholders control the corporation. Beyond their voting rights, stockholders have *no managerial authority* unless they have been appointed by the board to a management role.

2. *To participate in any dividends declared by the board of directors*. Stockholders in a corporation *may not* make withdrawals of company assets, as may the owners of unincorporated businesses. However, the directors may elect to distribute some or all of the earnings of a profitable corporation to its stockholders in the form of cash *dividends*.

   Dividends can be distributed only after they have been formally *declared* (authorized) by the board of directors. Dividends are paid to all shareholders in proportion to the number of shares owned.

3. *To share in the distribution of assets if the corporation is liquidated*. When a corporation ends its existence, the creditors must first be paid in full. Any remaining assets are divided among the shareholders—again, in proportion to the number of shares owned.

*Stockholders' meetings* usually are held once each year. At these meetings, stockholders may ask questions of management and vote on certain issues. In large corporations, these meetings usually are attended by relatively few people—often less than 1% of the company's stockholders. Prior to these meetings, however, the management group requests that stockholders who do not plan to attend send in *proxy statements,* granting management the voting rights associated with their shares.

Through this proxy system, management usually can secure the voting rights from enough shares to ensure its control of the corporation. In a publicly owned corporation, dissatisfied stockholders seldom are able to muster the voting power to overrule management. Therefore, dissatisfied stockholders normally sell their shares and invest in a company more to their liking.

**Functions of the Board of Directors** The primary functions of the **board of directors** are to set corporate policies and to protect the interests of the stockholders. Specific duties of the directors include hiring corporate officers and setting these officers' salaries, declaring dividends, and reviewing the findings of both internal auditors and independent auditors.

A closely held corporation might have only one active director—who is also the principal stockholder. But publicly owned corporations have larger boards—usually a dozen people or more.

The board of a large corporation always includes several members of top management. In recent years, increasing importance has been attached to the inclusion of "outside" directors. The term *outside directors* refers to individuals who are *not* officers of the corporation and, therefore, bring an *independent perspective* to the board.

**CASE IN POINT**

A recent annual report of **General Mills** includes a report from the *audit committee* of the company's board of directors. The first paragraph of this report describes the committee's responsibilities:

The Audit Committee of the Board of Directors is composed of six outside directors. Its primary function is to oversee the Company's system of internal controls, financial reporting practices and audits to ensure their quality, integrity and objectivity are sufficient to protect stockholders' assets.

**Functions of the Corporate Officers** The top management of a corporation is appointed (hired) by the board of directors. These individuals are called the *corporate officers,* or, more simply, "top management." Individual stockholders *do not* have the right to transact corporate business *unless they have been properly appointed to a managerial post.*

The top level of management usually includes a chief executive officer (CEO) or president, a chief financial officer (CFO) or controller, a treasurer, and a secretary. In addition, a vice-president usually oversees each functional area, such as sales, personnel, and production.

The responsibilities of the CFO (controller), treasurer, and secretary are most directly related to the accounting phase of business operation. The CFO is responsible for the maintenance of adequate internal control and for the preparation of accounting records and financial statements. Such specialized activities as budgeting, tax planning, and preparation of tax returns are usually placed under the CFO's jurisdiction. The *treasurer* has custody of the company's funds and is generally responsible for planning and controlling the company's cash position. The treasurer's department also has responsibility for relations with the company's financial institutions and major creditors.

The *secretary* represents the corporation in many contractual and legal matters and maintains minutes of the meetings of directors and stockholders. Other responsibilities of the secretary are to coordinate the preparation of the annual report and to manage the investor relations department. In small corporations, one officer frequently acts as both secretary and treasurer.

The organization chart on the next page indicates lines of authority extending from stockholders to the directors to the CEO and other officers.

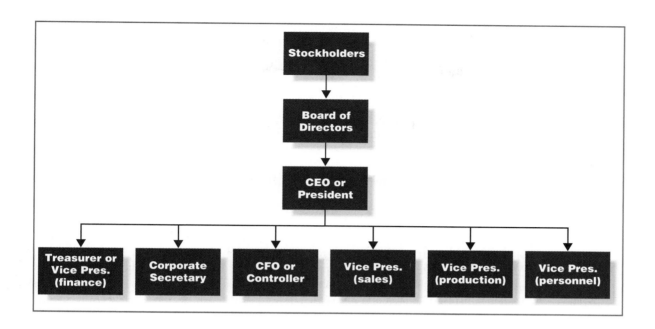

### You as a Chief Financial Officer (CFO)

Assume you have been the CFO for BlendMaster's Gourmet Coffee for the past five years. As part of your compensation each year, you have been awarded 2,000 shares of BlendMaster's stock. You have just learned that BlendMaster's union workers are planning a major strike within the next two weeks. You know that this strike will significantly increase costs for the year and that reported net income will suffer. Because reported net income will be below the expectations of market analysts, you know that when the news of the union strike becomes public, the market price of BlendMaster's shares will drop. Your daughter is attending an expensive private college and you use the proceeds from the sale of the BlendMaster's stock to pay for her college. A tuition payment is due in three months. What should you do?

*Our comments appear on p. 490.

**YOUR TURN**

## Stockholder Records in a Corporation

A large corporation with shares listed on the New York Stock Exchange usually has millions of shares outstanding and hundreds of thousands of stockholders. Each day many stockholders sell their shares; the buyers of these shares become new members of the company's family of stockholders.

A corporation must have an up-to-date record of the names and addresses of this constantly changing group of stockholders so that it can send dividend checks, financial statements, and voting forms to the right people.

There are numerous stock exchanges around the world. There are 8 exchanges in the United States and 35 exchanges in the European Union. The most heavily traded European exchanges are in London, Frankfurt, and Paris. Other stock exchanges are more thinly traded such as the *Bolsa Mexicana de Valores*. Each of these exchanges may have different requirements associated with the financial reports that are distributed to shareholders.

**CASE IN POINT**

**Stockholders Subsidiary Ledger**   When there are numerous stockholders, it is not practical to include a separate account for each stockholder in the general ledger. Instead, a single controlling account entitled Capital Stock appears in the general ledger, and a **stockholders subsidiary ledger** is maintained. This ledger contains an account for each individual stockholder. Entries in the stockholders subsidiary ledger are made in *number of shares,* rather than in dollars. Thus each stockholder's account shows the number of shares owned and the dates of acquisitions and sales. This record enables the corporation to send each stockholder a single dividend check, even though the stockholder may have acquired shares on different dates.

A corporation that has more than one type of capital stock will maintain a separate set of stockholders subsidiary records for each issue.

**Stock Transfer Agent and Stock Registrar**   Large, publicly owned corporations use an independent **stock transfer agent** and a **stock registrar** to maintain their stockholder records and to establish strong internal control over the issuance of stock certificates. These transfer agents and registrars are usually large banks or trust companies. When stock certificates are transferred from one owner to another, the old certificates are sent to the transfer agent, who cancels them, makes the necessary entries in the stockholders subsidiary ledger, and prepares a new certificate for the new owner of the shares. This new certificate then must be registered with the stock registrar before it represents valid and transferable ownership of stock in the corporation.

Small, closely held corporations generally do not use the services of independent registrars and transfer agents. In these companies, the stockholder records usually are maintained by a corporate officer. To prevent the accidental or fraudulent issuance of an excessive number of stock certificates, the corporation should require that each certificate be signed by at least two designated corporate officers.

## PAID-IN CAPITAL OF A CORPORATION

**LO 4**

Account for paid-in capital and prepare the equity section of a corporate balance sheet.

Stockholders' equity of a corporation is normally increased in one of two ways: (1) from contributions by investors in exchange for capital stock—called **paid-in capital** or **contributed capital**—and (2) from the retention of profits earned by the corporation over time—called **retained earnings**. As previously noted, our focus in this chapter is primarily on issues related to paid-in capital. In Chapter 12, we shift our attention to issues concerning retained earnings.

### Authorization and Issuance of Capital Stock

The articles of incorporation specify the number of shares that a corporation has been authorized to issue by the state of incorporation. Issues of capital stock that will be sold to the general public must be approved by the federal Securities and Exchange Commission, as well as by state officials.

Corporations normally obtain authorization for more shares than they initially plan to issue. This way, if more capital is needed later, the corporation already has the authorization to issue additional shares.

Shares that have been *issued* and are in the hands of stockholders are called the *outstanding* shares. At any time, these outstanding shares represent 100% of the stockholders' investment in the corporation.

When a large amount of stock is to be issued, most corporations use the services of an investment banking firm, frequently referred to as an **underwriter**. The underwriter guarantees the issuing corporation a specific price for the stock and makes a profit by selling the shares to the investing public at a slightly higher price. The corporation records the issuance of the stock at the net amount received from the underwriter. The use of an underwriter assures the corporation that the entire stock issue will be sold without delay and that the entire amount of funds to be raised will be available on a specific date.

The price that a corporation will seek for a new issue of stock is based on such factors as (1) expected future earnings and dividends, (2) the financial strength of the company, and (3) the current state of the investment markets. If the corporation asks for too much, however, it simply will not find an underwriter or other buyers willing to purchase the shares.

**State Laws Affect the Balance Sheet Presentation of Stockholders' Equity**
The number of ledger accounts that a corporation must use in the stockholders' equity section of its balance sheet is determined largely by state laws. We have seen that corporations use separate stockholders' equity accounts to represent (1) contributed capital, or paid-in capital; and (2) earned capital, or retained earnings. Up to this point we have assumed that all paid-in capital is presented in a single account entitled Capital Stock. But this often is not the case.

Some corporations issue several *different types* (or classes) of capital stock. In these situations, a separate account is used to indicate each type of stock outstanding. A legal concept called *par value* also affects the balance sheet presentation of paid-in capital.

**Par Value**   **Par value (or stated value)** represents the **legal capital** per share—the amount below which stockholders' equity cannot be reduced, except by losses from business operations (or by special legal action). The directors cannot declare a dividend that would cause total stockholders' equity to fall below the par value of the outstanding shares. Par value, therefore, may be regarded as a minimum cushion of equity capital existing for the protection of creditors.

Because of the legal restrictions associated with par value, state laws require corporations to show separately in the stockholders' equity section of the balance sheet the par value of shares issued. This special balance sheet presentation has led some people to believe that par value has some special significance. In many corporations, however, the par value of the shares issued is a small portion of total stockholders' equity.

A corporation may set the par value of its stock at $1 per share, $5 per share, or any other amount that it chooses. Most large corporations set the par value of their common stocks at nominal amounts, such as 1 cent per share or $1 per share. The par value of the stock is *no indication of its market value;* the par value merely indicates the amount per share to be entered in the Capital Stock account. The stocks of **Ford** and **AT&T** have par values of $1; **Compaq Computer**'s stock has a par value of 1 cent, and **Microsoft**'s stock has a par value of one-tenth of a cent. The market value of each of these securities is far above its par value. Microsoft's stock, for example, has recently traded at a market value in excess of $100 per share, or more than *100,000 times* its par value.

**Issuance of Par Value Stock**   Authorization of a stock issue does not bring an asset into existence, nor does it give the corporation any capital. The obtaining of authorization from the state for a stock issue merely affords a legal opportunity to obtain assets through the sale of stock. Additional capital is created for the company only when that stock is sold to stockholders.

When par value stock is *issued,* the Capital Stock account is credited with the par value of the shares issued, regardless of whether the issuance price is more or less than par. Assuming that 50,000 shares of $2 par value stock have been authorized and that 10,000 of these authorized shares are sold at a price of $2 each, Cash would be debited and Capital Stock would be credited for $20,000. When stock is sold for more than par value, the Capital Stock account is credited with the par value of the shares issued, and a separate account, **Additional Paid-in Capital**, is credited for the excess of selling price over par. If, for example, our 10,000 shares were issued at a price of $10 per share, the entry would be:

*Stockholders' investment in excess of par value*

| | | |
|---|---|---|
| Cash | 100,000 | |
| Capital Stock | | 20,000 |
| Additional Paid-in Capital | | 80,000 |
| Issued 10,000 shares of $2 par value stock at a price of $10 a share. | | |

The additional paid-in capital does not represent a profit to the corporation. It is part of the *invested capital* and it will be added to the capital stock in the balance sheet to show the total paid-in capital. The stockholders' equity section of the balance sheet is illustrated below. (The $150,000 in retained earnings is assumed in order to have a complete illustration.)

*Corporation's capital classified by source*

**Stockholders' equity:**

| | |
|---|---|
| Capital stock, $2 par value; authorized, 50,000 shares; issued and outstanding, 10,000 shares | $ 20,000 |
| Additional paid-in capital | 80,000 |
| Total paid-in capital | $100,000 |
| Retained earnings | 150,000 |
| Total stockholders' equity | $250,000 |

If stock is issued by a corporation for *less* than par, the account Discount on Capital Stock should be debited for the difference between the issuance price and the par value. A discount on capital stock reduces, rather than increases, the amount of stockholders' equity in the balance sheet. The issuance of stock at a discount is seldom encountered; it is illegal in many states.

**No-Par Stock** Some states allow corporations to issue stock without designating a par or stated value. When this "no-par" stock is issued, the *entire issue price* is credited to the Capital Stock account and is viewed as legal capital not subject to withdrawal.

## Common Stocks and Preferred Stocks

The account title Capital Stock is widely used when a corporation has issued only *one type* of stock. In order to appeal to as many investors as possible, however, some corporations issue several types (or classes) of capital stock, each providing investors with different rights and opportunities.

The basic type of capital stock issued by every corporation often is called **common stock**. Common stock possesses the traditional rights of ownership—voting rights, participation in dividends, and a residual claim to assets in the event of liquidation. When the rights of stockholders are modified, the term **preferred stock** is normally used to describe the resulting type of capital stock. A few corporations issue two or more classes of preferred stock, with each class having distinctive features designed to appeal to a particular type of investor. In summary, we may say that *every* corporation has common stock and that some corporations also have one or more types of preferred stock.

The following stockholders' equity section illustrates the balance sheet presentation for a corporation having both preferred and common stock. As before, a retained earnings amount is assumed so we can provide a complete example.

**LO 5**

Contrast the features of common stock with those of preferred stock.

| Stockholders' equity: | |
| --- | --- |
| 9% cumulative preferred stock, $100 par value, authorized 100,000 shares, issued 50,000 shares | $ 5,000,000 |
| Common stock, $5 par value, authorized 3 million shares, issued 2 million shares | 10,000,000 |
| Additional paid-in capital: | |
| Preferred stock | 200,000 |
| Common stock | 20,000,000 |
| Total paid-in capital | $35,200,000 |
| Retained earnings | 13,500,000 |
| Total stockholders' equity | $48,700,000 |

*Balance sheet presentation of common stock and of preferred stock*

## Characteristics of Preferred Stock

Most preferred stocks have the following distinctive features:

1. Preferred as to dividends.
2. Cumulative dividend rights.
3. Preferred as to assets in event of the liquidation of the company.
4. Callable at the option of the corporation.
5. No voting power.

Another very important but less common feature of some preferred stocks is a clause permitting the *conversion* of preferred stock into common at the option of the holder. Preferred stocks vary widely with respect to the special rights and privileges granted. Careful study of the terms of the individual preferred stock contract is a necessary step in the evaluation of any preferred stock.

**Stock Preferred as to Dividends** Corporations often make periodic cash payments, called **dividends,** to stockholders.[2] Dividends normally represent a distribution of accumulated profit and therefore cannot exceed the amount of a corporation's retained earnings.

Preferred stock is said to have dividend preference because preferred stock investors are entitled to receive a specified amount each year before any dividend is paid to common stock investors. The specified dividend may be stated as a dollar amount, such as $5 per share. Some preferred stocks, however, state the specified dividend as a *percentage of par value.* For example, a share of preferred stock with a par value of $100 and a dividend preference of 9% must provide a $9 dividend each year to each share of preferred stock before any dividends can be paid on the common shares. (Preferred stocks often have par values substantially higher than common stocks. This is largely a matter of tradition and has little significance.)

**Consolidated Edison** has two issues of preferred stock that are publicly traded on the New York Stock Exchange. The first issue is a $5 preferred stock that pays annual dividends of $5 per share and has no par value. The other issue is a 4.65% preferred with a $100 par value that pays annual dividends of $4.65 per share.

Dividends on both of these issues of preferred stock must be paid in full before **Consolidated Edison** pays any dividend on its common stock.

CASE IN POINT

---

[2] In Chapter 12, we will discuss specific accounting issues related to cash dividends and other forms of distributions to stockholders. For the purposes of this chapter, dividends may be viewed simply as the distribution to stockholders of accumulated profits that reduce both cash and retained earnings.

The holders of preferred stock have no guarantee that they will always receive the indicated dividend. A corporation is obligated to pay dividends to stockholders only when the board of directors declares a dividend. Dividends must be paid on preferred stock before anything is paid to the common stockholders, but if the corporation is not prospering, it may decide not to pay any dividends at all. For a corporation to pay dividends, profits must be earned and cash must be available. Despite this limitation, preferred stocks generally offer investors *more assurance* of regular dividend payments than do common stocks.

**Cumulative Preferred Stock**    The dividend preference carried by most preferred stocks is a *cumulative* one. If all or any part of the regular dividend on the preferred stock is omitted in a given year, the amount omitted is said to be *in arrears* and must be paid in a subsequent year before any dividend can be paid on the common stock.

Assume that a corporation was organized January 1, 2000, with 10,000 shares of $8 cumulative preferred stock and 50,000 shares of common stock. Dividends paid in 2000 were at the rate of $8 per share of preferred stock and $2 per share of common. In 2001, earnings declined sharply and the only dividend paid was $2 per share on the preferred stock. No dividends were paid in 2002. What is the status of the preferred stock at December 31, 2002?

Dividends are *in arrears* in the amount of *$14* per share ($6 omitted during 2001 and $8 omitted in 2002). On the entire issue of 10,000 shares of preferred stock, the dividends in arrears amount to *$140,000* ($14 × 10,000 shares). This amount must be paid to preferred stockholders before any future dividends can be paid to common stockholders.

Dividends in arrears are not listed among the liabilities of a corporation, because no liability exists until a dividend is declared by the board of directors. Nevertheless, the amount of any dividends in arrears on preferred stock is an important factor to investors and should always be *disclosed*. This disclosure is usually made by a note accompanying the balance sheet such as the following:

*Footnote disclosure of dividends in arrears.*

**Note 6: Dividends in arrears**

As of December 31, 2002, dividends on the $8 cumulative preferred stock were in arrears to the extent of $14 per share and amounted in total to $140,000.

In 2003, we shall assume that the company earned large profits, has available cash, and wished to pay dividends on both the preferred and common stocks. Before paying a dividend on the common, the corporation must pay the $140,000 in arrears on the cumulative preferred stock *plus* the regular $8 per share applicable to the current year. The preferred stockholders would, therefore, receive a total of $220,000 in dividends in 2003 ($22 per share); the board of directors would then be free to declare dividends on the common stock.

For a *noncumulative* preferred stock, any unpaid or omitted dividend is lost forever. However, few preferred stocks are noncumulative.

**Stock Preferred as to Assets**    Most preferred stocks carry a preference as to assets in the event of liquidation of the corporation. If the business is terminated, the preferred stock is entitled to payment in full of its par value or a higher stated liquidation value before any payment is made on the common stock. This priority also includes any dividends in arrears.

**Callable Preferred Stock**    Many preferred stocks include a *call provision*. This provision grants the issuing corporation the right to repurchase the stock from the stockholders at a stipulated *call price*. The call price is usually higher than the par value of the stock. For example, $100 par value preferred stock may be callable at $105 or $110 per share. In addition to paying the call price, a corporation that redeems its preferred stock must pay any dividends in arrears. A call provision gives a corporation flexibility in adjusting its capital structure.

**Convertible Preferred Stock**   In order to add to the attractiveness of preferred stock as an investment, corporations sometimes offer a *conversion privilege* that entitles the preferred stockholders to exchange their shares for common stock at a stipulated ratio. If the corporation prospers, its common stock will probably rise in market value, and dividends on the common stock will probably increase. The investor who buys a convertible preferred stock rather than common stock has greater assurance of regular dividends. In addition, through the conversion privilege, the investor is assured of an opportunity to share in any substantial increase in value of the company's common stock.

As an example, assume that Remington Corporation issued a 9%, $100 par, convertible preferred stock on January 1, at a price of $100 per share. Each share was convertible into four shares of the company's $10 par value common stock at any time. The common stock had a market price of $20 per share on January 1 and an annual dividend of $1 per share was being paid. During the next few years, Remington Corporation's earnings increased, the dividend on the common stock was raised to an annual rate of $3, and the market price of the common stock rose to $40 per share. At this point the preferred stock would have a market value of *at least $160,* since it could be converted at any time into four shares of common stock with a market value of $40 each. In other words, the market value of a convertible preferred stock will tend to move in accordance with the price of the common.

When the dividend rate is increased on the common stock, some holders of the preferred stock may convert their holdings into common stock in order to obtain a higher cash return on their investments. If the holder of 100 shares of the preferred stock presented these shares for conversion, Remington Corporation would make the following journal entry:

| | | |
|---|---|---|
| 9% Convertible Preferred Stock .................................... | 10,000 | |
|    Common Stock ................................................ | | 4,000 |
|    Additional Paid-in Capital: Common Stock ...................... | | 6,000 |
| To record the conversion of 100 shares of preferred stock, | | |
|   par $100, into 400 shares of $10 par value common stock. | | |

*Conversion of preferred stock into common*

Note that the issue price recorded for the 400 shares of common stock is based on the *carrying value of the preferred stock* in the accounting records, not on market prices at the date of conversion. (If the preferred stock originally had been issued at a price greater than par value, its carrying value would include a proportionate share of the related additional paid-in capital, as well as the par value.)

**Other Features of Preferred Stock**   Occasionally you may encounter preferred stock with some very unusual characteristics. For example, there are "participating preferreds," allowing preferred stockholders to receive dividends that are greater than the stated dollar amount or percentage. There also are "super preferreds," granting enormous voting rights—perhaps the controlling interest—to the preferred stockholders. And there are "redeemable preferreds," allowing preferred shareholders to sell their shares back to the corporation at an agreed-upon price. We will leave further discussion of such unusual features of preferred stock to more advanced courses in accounting and corporate finance.

## Stock Issued for Assets Other Than Cash

Corporations generally sell their capital stock for cash and use the cash to buy the various types of assets needed in the business. Sometimes, however, a corporation may issue shares of its capital stock in a direct exchange for land, buildings, or other assets. Stock may also be issued in payment for services rendered by attorneys and promoters in the formation of the corporation.

When a corporation issues capital stock in exchange for services or for assets other than cash, the transaction should be recorded at the current *market value* of the goods or services received. For some types of assets such as land or buildings, the services of a firm of professional appraisers may be useful in establishing current market value.

Often, the best evidence as to the market value of these goods or services is the *market value of the shares* issued in exchange. For example, assume that a company issues 10,000 shares of its $1 par value common stock in exchange for land. Competent appraisers may have differing opinions as to the market value of the land. But let us assume that the company's stock is currently selling on a stock exchange for $90 per share. It is logical to say that the cost of the land to the company is $900,000, the market value of the shares issued in exchange.

In summary, these transactions should be recorded at the current market value of either (1) the assets received or (2) the shares issued in exchange—*whichever can be determined more objectively.*

Once the valuation has been decided, the entry to record the issuance of the stock in exchange for the land is as follows:

*Notice the use of current market values*

| | | |
|---|---:|---:|
| Land .......................................................... | 900,000 | |
|     Common Stock ......................................... | | 10,000 |
|     Additional Paid-in Capital: Common Stock .................. | | 890,000 |

To record the issuance of 10,000 shares of $1 par value common stock in exchange for land. Current market value of stock ($90 per share) used as basis for valuing the land.

## Subscriptions to Capital Stock

Small, newly formed corporations sometimes offer investors an opportunity to "subscribe" to shares of the company's capital stock. Under a subscription plan, the investors agree to purchase specified numbers of shares at a stated price *at a future date,* often by making a series of installment payments. The stock is issued after the entire subscription price has been collected.

Selling stock through subscriptions is similar to selling merchandise on a layaway plan. One reason for this procedure is to attract small investors. Another reason is to appeal to investors who prefer not to invest cash until the corporation is ready to start business operations. Accounting for subscriptions to capital stock is explained and illustrated in more advanced accounting courses.

## Donated Capital

On occasion, a corporation may receive assets as a gift. To increase local employment, for example, some cities have given corporations the land on which to build factories. When a corporation receives such a gift, both total assets and total stockholders' equity increase by the market value of the assets received. *No profit is recognized when a gift is received;* the increase in stockholders' equity is regarded as *paid-in capital.* The receipt of a gift is recorded by debiting the appropriate asset accounts and crediting an account entitled **Donated Capital.**

The Donated Capital account appears in the stockholders' equity section of the balance sheet, along with any Additional Paid-in Capital accounts. In addition, the *notes* accompanying the financial statements normally explain the nature of the donation.

**CASE IN POINT**

The annual report of **Lands' End, Inc.**, includes the following note that describes the $8.4 million of donated capital on the company's balance sheet:

Donated capital: In 1988 and 1989, a corporation owned by the principal shareholder of the company contributed $7.0 million and $1.4 million in cash, respectively, to the company in order to fund the cost of constructing an activity center in Dodgeville for use by company employees. These transactions were recorded as donated capital.

# Book Value per Share of Common Stock

Because the equity of each stockholder in a corporation is determined by the number of shares he or she owns, an accounting measurement of interest to many stockholders is book value per share of common stock. **Book value per share** is equal to the net assets represented by one share of stock. The term *net assets* means total assets minus total liabilities; in other words, net assets are equal to *total stockholders' equity*. Thus, in a corporation that has issued common stock only, the book value per share is computed by dividing total stockholders' equity by the number of shares outstanding (or subscribed).

For example, assume that a corporation has 4,000 shares of common stock outstanding and the stockholders' equity section of the balance sheet is as follows:

| | |
|---|---:|
| **Stockholders' equity:** | |
| Common stock, $1 par value (4,000 shares outstanding) | $ 4,000 |
| Additional paid-in capital | 40,000 |
| Retained earnings | 76,000 |
| Total stockholders' equity | $120,000 |

The book value per share is *$30;* it is computed by dividing the stockholders' equity of $120,000 by the 4,000 shares of outstanding stock. In computing book value, we are concerned not with the number of authorized shares but with the outstanding shares, because the total of the outstanding shares represents 100% of the stockholders' equity.

**Book Value When a Company Has Both Preferred and Common Stock**   Book value is usually computed only for common stock. If a company has both preferred and common stock outstanding, the computation of book value per share of common stock requires two steps. First, the redemption value or *call price* of the entire preferred stock issue and any *dividends in arrears* are deducted from total stockholders' equity. Second, the remaining amount of stockholders' equity is divided by the number of common shares outstanding to determine book value per common share. This procedure reflects the fact that the common stockholders are the *residual owners* of the corporate entity.

*How much is book value per share?*

To illustrate the computation of book value per share when callable preferred stock is outstanding, assume that the stockholders' equity of Video Company at December 31 is as follows:

*Two classes of stock*

| | |
|---|---:|
| **Stockholders' equity:** | |
| 8% preferred stock, $100 par value, callable at $110, 10,000 shares authorized and outstanding | $1,000,000 |
| Common stock, $10 stated value, authorized 100,000 shares, issued and outstanding 50,000 shares | 500,000 |
| Additional paid-in capital: Common stock | 750,000 |
| Total paid-in capital | $2,250,000 |
| Retained earnings | 130,000 |
| Total stockholders' equity | $2,380,000 |

Because of a weak cash position, Video Company has paid no dividends during the current year. As of December 31, dividends in arrears on the cumulative preferred stock total *$80,000.*

All the equity belongs to the common stockholders, except the $1.1 million call price ($110 × 10,000 shares) applicable to the preferred stock and the $80,000 of dividends in arrears on preferred stock. The calculation of book value per share of common stock is as follows:

| | | |
|---|---:|---:|
| Total stockholders' equity . . . . . . . . . . . . . . . . . . . . . . . . . . . . . . . . . . | | $2,380,000 |
| Less: Equity of preferred stockholders: | | |
|    Call price of preferred stock . . . . . . . . . . . . . . . . . . . . . . . . . . . . | $1,100,000 | |
|    Dividends in arrears . . . . . . . . . . . . . . . . . . . . . . . . . . . . . . . . . | 80,000 | 1,180,000 |
| Equity of common stockholders . . . . . . . . . . . . . . . . . . . . . . . . . . . . . | | $1,200,000 |
| Number of common shares outstanding . . . . . . . . . . . . . . . . . . . . . | | 50,000 |
| Book value per share of common stock ($1,200,000 ÷ 50,000 shares) . . . . . . . . . . | | $24 |

---

**CASH EFFECTS**     In a statement of cash flows, transactions with the stockholders of a corporation are classified as *financing activities.* Thus the issuance of capital stock for cash represents a *receipt* from financing activities. Distributions of cash to stockholders—including the payment of cash dividends—represent a cash *outlay,* which is also classified under financing activities.

Transactions with owners do not always have an immediate effect on cash flows. Consider an exchange of the corporation's capital stock for a noncash asset, such as land. Cash is not increased or decreased by this event. These types of noncash transactions are described in a special schedule that accompanies the statement of cash flows.

## MARKET VALUE

After shares of stock have been issued, they may be sold by one investor to another. The price at which these shares change hands represents the *current market price* of the stock. This market price may differ substantially from such amounts as par value, the original issue price, and the current book value. Which is the most relevant amount? That depends on your point of view.

After shares are issued, they belong to the stockholder, not to the issuing corporation. Thus changes in the market price of these shares affect the financial position of the stockholder, but not that of the issuing company. This concept explains why the issuing company and stockholders apply very different accounting principles to the same outstanding shares.

**Accounting by the Issuer**     From the viewpoint of the issuing company, outstanding stock represents an amount invested in the company by its owners at a particular date. While the market value of the stockholders' investment may change, the amount of resources that they originally invested does not.

Thus the company issuing stock records the issue price—that is, the proceeds received from issuing the stock—in its paid-in capital accounts. The balances in these accounts remain unchanged unless (1) more shares are issued or (2) outstanding shares are permanently retired (for example, perferred stock is called or stock is purchased on the open market and then retired).

**Accounting by the Investor**     From the investor's point of view, shares owned in a publicly owned company are an asset, usually termed Marketable Securities.

To the investor, the current market value of securities owned is far more relevant than the original issue price—or than the securities' par values or book values. The market value indicates what the securities are worth today. Changes in market value directly affect the investor's solvency, financial position, and net worth. For these reasons, investors show investments in marketable securities at current market value in their balance sheets.

CASE IN POINT

In a single day, the market price of **IBM**'s capital stock dropped over $31 per share, falling from $135 to $103.25. Of course, this was not a typical day. The date, October 19, 1987, will long be remembered as "Black Monday." On this day, stock prices around the word suffered the greatest one-day decline in history.

Stocks listed on the New York Stock Exchange lost about 20% of their value in less than six hours. Given that the annual dividends on these stocks averaged about 2% of their market value, this one-day market loss was approximately equal to the loss by investors of all dividend revenue for about 10 years.

How did this disastrous decline in **IBM**'s stock price affect the balance sheet of **IBM**? Actually, it didn't. **IBM**'s stock isn't owned by **IBM**—it is owned by the company's stockholders.

Because market prices are of such importance to investors, we will briefly discuss the factors that most affect the market prices of preferred and common stocks.

## Market Price of Preferred Stock

Investors buy preferred stocks primarily to receive the dividends that these shares pay. Thus dividend rate is one important factor in determining the market price of a preferred stock. Another important factor is *risk*. In the long run, a company must be profitable enough to pay dividends. If there is a distinct possibility that the company will *not* operate profitably and pay dividends, the price of its preferred stock will decline.

LO 6

Discuss the factors affecting the market price of preferred stock and common stock.

A third factor greatly affecting the value of preferred stocks is the level of *interest rates*. What happens to the market price of an 8% preferred stock, originally issued at a par value of $100, if government policies and other factors cause long-term interest rates to rise to, say, 15% or 16%? If investments offering a return of 16% with the same level of risk are readily available, investors will no longer pay $100 for a share of preferred stock that provides a dividend of only $8 per year. Thus the market price of the preferred stock will fall to about half of its original issue price, or about $50 per share. At this market price, the stock offers a 16% return (called the **dividend yield**) to an investor purchasing the stock.

However, if the prevailing long-term interest rates should again decline to the 8% range, the market price of an 8% preferred stock should rise to approximately par value. In summary, the market price of preferred stock *varies inversely with interest rates.* As interest rates rise, preferred stock prices decline; as interest rates fall, preferred stock prices rise.

CASE IN POINT

The preceding point is illustrated by the performance of **Philadelphia Electric**'s 9¹/₂%, $100 par value, preferred stock as interest rates have fluctuated over *four nonconsecutive years:*

|  | Long-Term Interest Rates* | Stock Price |
|---|---|---|
| Year 1 ........................................ | 15¹/₄% | $60 |
| Year 2 ........................................ | 13¹/₂ | 68 |
| Year 3 ........................................ | 9¹/₄ | 99 |
| Year 4 ........................................ | 7¹/₄ | 106 |

*The long-term interest rates cited in this example are the market yields of federally insured 30-year, fixed-rate mortgages over a selected 13-year period.

## Market Price of Common Stock

Prevailing interest rates also affect the market price of common stock. However, dividends paid to common stockholders are not fixed in amount. Both the amount of the dividend and the market price of the stock may increase dramatically if the corporation is successful. Alternatively, if the company is unsuccessful, the common stockholders may not even recover their original investment. Therefore, the most important factors in the market price of common stock are *investors' expectations* as to the future profitability of the business and the *risk* that this level of profitability may not be achieved.

Bear in mind that after shares have been issued they belong to the stockholders, not to the issuing corporation. Therefore, changes in the market price of the shares do not affect the financial statements of the corporation, and these changes are not recorded in the corporation's accounting records. The paid-in capital shown in a corporate balance sheet represents the amount received when the stock was issued, not the current market value of shares.

**YOUR TURN**

### You as an Investor

Assume that you are considering making a short-term investment in one of two stocks, a common stock or a preferred stock. You expect that the return on the two investments will be similar, and they have similar amounts of risk. In addition, you believe that interest rates will be increasing significantly in the next six months. Make a decision as to which stock is the better investment and support your choice.

*Our comments appear on page 490.

## Book Value and Market Price

To some extent, *book value* is used in evaluating the reasonableness of the market price of a stock. However, it must be used with great caution; the fact that a stock is selling at less than book value does not necessarily indicate a bargain.

**LO 7**

Explain the significance of par value, book value, and market value of capital stock.

Book value is a historical concept, representing the amounts invested by stockholders plus the amounts earned and retained by the corporation. If a stock is selling at a price well *above* book value, investors believe that management has created a business worth substantially more than the historical cost of the resources entrusted to its care. This, in essence, is the sign of a successful corporation. If the excess of market price over book value becomes very great, however, investors should consider whether the company's prospects really justify a market price so much above the underlying book value of the company's resources.

On the other hand, if the market price of a stock is *less than* book value, investors believe that the company's resources are worth less than their cost while under the control of current management. Thus the relationship between book value and market price is one measure of investors' *confidence in a company's management.*

**CASE IN POINT**

Shortly after the introduction of its Windows software, the common stock of **Microsoft Corp.** rose to a market value of more than $100 per share, although its book value per share was only about $6.50. Investors believed that **Microsoft**'s products—and its management—made the business worth far more than the historical amounts of capital that had been invested.

In contrast, the common stock of **Tucson Electric Power** at one point sold at a market price of $5 per share, although its book value was more than $20 per share. This utility company had invested heavily in plant assets intended to generate more electrical power. Unfortunately, demand for this power did not develop, and the company found itself unable to sell its additional output. These new facilities produced very little revenue but increased operating expenses substantially. Although these new facilities had a high book value, investors did not consider them to be worth the amounts that management had invested.

## Stock Splits

**LO 8**
Explain the purpose and the effects of a stock split.

Over time, the market price of a corporation's common stock may appreciate in value so much that it becomes too expensive for many investors. When this happens, a corporation may *split* its stock by increasing the number of its common shares outstanding. The purpose of a **stock split** is to reduce substantially the market price of the company's common stock, with the intent of making it more affordable to investors.

For example, assume that Pelican Corporation has outstanding 1 million shares of $10 par value common stock. The market price is currently $90 per share. To make the stock more affordable, the corporation decides to increase the number of outstanding shares from 1 million to 2 million. This action is called a *2-for-1 stock split*. A stockholder who owned 100 shares of the stock before the split will own 200 shares after the split. Since the number of outstanding shares has been doubled without any change in total assets or total stockholders' equity, the market price of the stock should drop immediately from $90 to approximately $45 per share. In splitting its stock, a corporation is required to reduce the par value per share in proportion to the size of the split. As this was a 2-for-1 split, the company must reduce the par value of the stock from $10 to $5 per share. Had it been a 4-for-1 split, the par value would have been reduced from $10 to $2.50 per share.

*A stock split does not change the balance of any accounts in the balance sheet;* consequently, the transaction may be recorded merely by a *memorandum entry*. For Pelican Corporation, this memorandum entry might read as follows:

**Sept. 30**   Memorandum: Issued additional 1 million shares of common stock in a 2-for-1 stock split. Par value reduced from $10 per share to $5 per share.

*Memorandum entry to record a stock split*

The description of common stock also is changed in the balance sheet to reflect the lower par value and the greater number of shares outstanding.

Stock may be split in any desired ratio. Among the more common ratios are 2-for-1, 3-for-2, and 3-for-1. The determining factor is the number of shares needed to bring the price of the stock into the desired trading range. For example, assume that a $5 par value stock is selling at a price of $150 per share and that management wants to reduce the price to approximately $30 per share. This objective may be accomplished with a *5-for-1* stock split ($150 ÷ 5 = $30). Par value *after* the 5-for-1 stock split is $1 per share ($5 par value × ¹/₅).

## Treasury Stock

**LO 9**
Account for treasury stock transactions.

**Treasury stock** may be defined as shares of a corporation's own capital stock that have been issued and later *reacquired by the issuing company* but that have not been canceled or permanently retired. Treasury shares may be held indefinitely or may be issued again at any time. Shares of capital stock held in the treasury are not entitled to receive dividends, to vote, or to share in assets upon dissolution of the company. In the computation of earnings per share, shares held in the treasury are not regarded as outstanding shares.

Corporations frequently reacquire shares of their own capital stock by purchase in the open market. Paying out cash to reacquire shares reduces the assets of the corporation and reduces the stockholders' equity by the same amount. One reason for such purchases is to have stock available to reissue to officers and employees under stock option or bonus plans. Other reasons may include a desire to increase the reported earnings per share or to support the current market price of the stock.

**MANAGEMENT STRATEGY**

## Recording Purchases of Treasury Stock

Purchases of treasury stock are usually recorded by debiting the Treasury Stock account with the cost of the stock. For example, if Torrey Corporation reacquires 1,500 shares of its own $5 par stock at a price of $100 per share, the entry is as follows:

| | | |
|---|---|---|
| Treasury Stock . . . . . . . . . . . . . . . . . . . . . . . . . . . . . . . . . . . . . . . . . . . | 150,000 | |
| Cash . . . . . . . . . . . . . . . . . . . . . . . . . . . . . . . . . . . . . . . . . . . . . . | | 150,000 |
| Purchased 1,500 shares of $5 par treasury stock at $100 per share. | | |

Note that the Treasury Stock account is debited for the *cost* of the shares purchased, not their par value.

**Treasury Stock Is Not an Asset** When treasury stock is purchased, the corporation is eliminating part of its stockholders' equity by a payment to one or more stockholders. The purchase of treasury stock should be regarded as a *reduction of stockholders' equity,* not as the acquisition of an asset. For this reason, the Treasury Stock account should appear in the balance sheet as a deduction in the stockholders' equity section.[3]

The presentation of treasury stock in Torrey Corporation's balance sheet appears as follows, based on assumed numbers except for treasury stock:

| | |
|---|---|
| **Stockholders' equity:** | |
| Common stock, $5 par value, authorized 250,000 shares, issued 100,000 shares (of which 1,500 are held in treasury) . . . . . . . . . . . . . . . . . . . . . . . . . . . . . . | $   500,000 |
| Additional paid-in capital: Common stock . . . . . . . . . . . . . . . . . . . . . . . . . | 900,000 |
| Total paid-in capital . . . . . . . . . . . . . . . . . . . . . . . . . . . . . . . . . | $1,400,000 |
| Retained earnings . . . . . . . . . . . . . . . . . . . . . . . . . . . . . . . . . . . | 600,000 |
| Subtotal . . . . . . . . . . . . . . . . . . . . . . . . . . . . . . . . . . . . . . . . | $2,000,000 |
| Less: Treasury stock (1,500 shares of common, at $100 cost) . . . . . . . . . . . . . | 150,000 |
| Total stockholders' equity . . . . . . . . . . . . . . . . . . . . . . . . . . . . . | $1,850,000 |

## Reissuance of Treasury Stock

When treasury shares are reissued, the Treasury Stock account is credited for the cost of the shares reissued and Additional Paid-in Capital from Treasury Stock Transactions is debited or credited for any *difference* between cost and the reissue price. To illustrate, assume that 1,000 of the treasury shares acquired by Torrey Corporation at a cost of $100 per share are now reissued at a price of $115 per share. The entry to record the reissuance of these shares at a price above cost would be:

*Treasury stock reissued at a price above cost*

| | | |
|---|---|---|
| Cash . . . . . . . . . . . . . . . . . . . . . . . . . . . . . . . . . . . . . . . . . . . . . . | 115,000 | |
| Treasury Stock . . . . . . . . . . . . . . . . . . . . . . . . . . . . . . . . . . . . | | 100,000 |
| Additional Paid-in Capital: Treasury Stock Transactions . . . . . . . . . . . | | 15,000 |
| Sold 1,000 shares of treasury stock, which cost $100,000, at a price of $115 per share. | | |

The $15,000 of additional paid-in capital resulting from the reissuance of Torrey's treasury stock will be reported in the stockholders' equity section of the company's

---

[3] Despite a lack of theoretical support, a few corporations do classify treasury stock as an asset on the grounds that the shares could be sold for cash just as readily as shares owned in another corporation. The same argument could be made for treating unissued shares as assets. Treasury shares are basically the same as unissued shares, and an unissued share of stock is definitely not an asset.

balance sheet. It appears immediately after additional paid-in capital from common stock, as illustrated below:

| Stockholders' equity: | |
|---|---:|
| Common stock, $5 par value, authorized 250,000 shares, issued 100,000 shares (of which 500 are held in treasury) | $ 500,000 |
| Additional paid-in capital: | |
| Common stock | 900,000 |
| Treasury stock | 15,000 |
| Total paid-in capital | $1,415,000 |
| Retained earnings | 600,000 |
| Subtotal | $2,015,000 |
| Less: Treasury stock (500 shares of common, at $100 cost) | 50,000 |
| Total stockholders' equity | $1,965,000 |

If treasury stock is reissued at a price below cost, additional paid-in capital from previous treasury stock transactions is reduced (debited) by the excess of cost over the reissue price. To illustrate, assume that Torrey Corporation reissues its remaining 500 shares of treasury stock (cost $100 per share) at a price of $90 per share. The entry would be:

| | | |
|---|---:|---:|
| Cash | 45,000 | |
| Additional Paid-in Capital: Treasury Stock Transactions | 5,000 | |
| Treasury Stock | | 50,000 |
| Sold 500 shares of treasury stock, which cost $50,000, at a price of $90 each. | | |

*Reissued at a price below cost*

If there is no additional paid-in capital from previous treasury stock transactions, the excess of the cost of the treasury shares over the reissue price may be recorded as a debit to the Additional Paid-in Capital: Common Stock account.

**No Profit or Loss on Treasury Stock Transactions**   Notice that *no gain or loss is recognized on treasury stock transactions,* even when the shares are reissued at a price above or below cost. A corporation earns profits by selling goods and services to outsiders, not by issuing or reissuing shares of its own capital stock. When treasury shares are reissued at a price above cost, the corporation receives from the new stockholder an amount of paid-in capital that is larger than the reduction in stockholders' equity that occurred when the corporation acquired the treasury shares. Conversely, if treasury shares are reissued at a price below cost, the corporation ends up with less paid-in capital as a result of the purchase and reissuance of the shares. Thus any changes in stockholders' equity resulting from treasury stock transactions are regarded as changes in *paid-in capital* and are *not* included in the measurement of net income.

**Restriction of Retained Earnings for Treasury Stock Owned**   Purchases of treasury stock, like cash dividends, are distributions of assets to the stockholders in the corporation. Many states have a legal requirement that distributions to stockholders (including purchases of treasury stock) cannot exceed the balance in the Retained Earnings account. Therefore, retained earnings usually are restricted by an amount equal to the *cost* of any shares held in the treasury.

## Stock Buyback Programs

In past years, most treasury stock transactions involved relatively small dollar amounts. Hence, the topic was not of much importance to investors or other users of financial statements. Late in 1987, however, many corporations initiated large buyback programs, in which they repurchased large amounts of their own common stock.[4] As a result of these programs, treasury stock has become a material item in the balance sheets of many corporations.

**CASE IN POINT**

Shown below is the cost of the treasury stock listed in the balance sheets of several publicly owned corporations at the end of a recent year.

| | Treasury Stock | |
|---|---|---|
| Company | At Cost (in thousands) | As a % of Other Elements of Stockholders' Equity* |
| Coca-Cola ............................... | $ 5,201,194 | 57 |
| ExxonMobil ............................ | 16,887,000 | 33 |
| Lotus ................................ | 287,655 | 41 |
| King World ........................... | 162,054 | 32 |

*To place these holdings in perspective, we have shown the cost of the treasury stock as a percentage of total stockholders' equity before *deducting the cost of the repurchased shares.*

*To place these holdings in perspective, we have shown the cost of the treasury stock as a percentage of total stockholders' equity before *deducting the cost of the repurchased shares.*

These large buyback programs serve several purposes. First, by creating demand for the company's stock in the marketplace, these programs tend to increase the market value of the shares. Also, reducing the number of shares outstanding usually increases earnings per share. When stock prices are low, some companies find that they can increase earnings per share by a greater amount through repurchasing shares than through expanding business operations.

**CASH EFFECTS**

As noted previously, transactions between the corporation and its stockholders are classified in the statement of cash flows as *financing activities.* Accordingly, the purchase and reissuance of treasury stock result in cash flows from financing activities. When treasury stock is purchased, a financing cash *outflow* is reported in the statement of cash flows. When treasury stock is reissued, the amount of cash received is reported as a financing cash *inflow* in the statement of cash flows.

Because treasury stock transactions do not give rise to gains or losses, they have no effect on the corporation's net income. Any difference between the purchase price of the treasury stock and the cash received when it is reissued is reported as an increase or decrease in the corporation's paid-in capital.

---

[4] On October 19, 1987, a date known as *Black Monday,* stocks around the world suffered a record one-day decline. Within hours of the market's close on Black Monday, many large corporations announced their intention to enter the market and spend hundreds of millions of dollars repurchasing their own shares. In the opinion of the authors, these announcements helped stabilize the investment markets and avoided a possible stock market collapse.

# FINANCIAL ANALYSIS

The following information was taken from a recent annual report of **Microsoft Corporation** (in millions):

| | |
|---|---:|
| Net income . . . . . . . . . . . . . . . . . . . . . . . . . . . . . . . . . . . . . . . . . . . . . | $ 9,421 |
| Preferred stock dividends . . . . . . . . . . . . . . . . . . . . . . . . . . . . . . . . | 13 |
| Average number of common shares outstanding . . . . . . . . . . . . . . . | 5,196 |
| Average common stockholders' equity . . . . . . . . . . . . . . . . . . . . . . . | 18,520 |
| Average total stockholders' equity . . . . . . . . . . . . . . . . . . . . . . . . . . | 34,903 |

These frequently used measures of profitability can be derived from the above figures:

| Profitability Measure | Computation | Significance |
|---|---|---|
| Earnings per share | $\dfrac{\text{Net income} - \text{Preferred Dividends}}{\text{Average Number of Common Shares Outstanding}}$ | Net income applicable to each share of common stock |
| Return on common stockholders' equity | $\dfrac{\text{Net Income} - \text{Preferred Dividends}}{\text{Average Common Stockholders' Equity}}$ | The rate of return earned on the common stockholders' equity appropriate when company has both common and preferred stock |
| Return on equity | $\dfrac{\text{Net Income}}{\text{Average Total Equity}}$ | The rate of return earned on the stockholders' equity in the business |

Using the figures provided, **Microsoft**'s three profitability measures would be:

Earnings per share:    ($9,421 − $13) ÷ 5,196 shares = $1.81

Return on common
stockholders' equity:    ($9,421 − $13) ÷ $18,520 = 51%

Return on equity:    $9,421 ÷ $34,903 = 27%

## Microsoft Corporation

Throughout this chapter we have explored numerous issues related to stockholders' equity, including treasury stock transactions, the issuance of common stock, characteristics of preferred stock, and preferred stock dividends. A recent annual report issued by **Microsoft** reveals activities involving several of these issues. For instance, during the year **Microsoft** (1) issued $2.25 billion of common stock, (2) spent $4.9 billion on treasury stock purchases, (3) declared a $13 million preferred stock dividend, and (4) converted $980 of its convertible preferred stock into common stock.

In Chapter 12, we introduce the statement of stockholders' equity. This commonly issued financial statement summarizes all transactions during the year that contributed to the change in total stockholders' equity reported in the balance sheet.

**A SECOND LOOK**

# END-OF-CHAPTER REVIEW

## SUMMARY OF LEARNING OBJECTIVES

**LO 1**

**Discuss the advantages and disadvantages of organizing a business as a corporation.**

The primary advantages are no personal liability of stockholders for the debts of the business, the transferability of ownership shares, continuity of existence, ability to hire professional management, and the relative ease of accumulating large amounts of capital. The primary disadvantages are double taxation of earnings and greater governmental regulation.

**LO 2**

**Distinguish between publicly owned and closely held corporations.**

The stock of publicly owned corporations is available for purchase by the general public, usually on an organized stock exchange. Stock in a closely held corporation, in contrast, is not available to the public.

Publicly owned corporations tend to be so large that individual stockholders seldom control the corporation; in essence, most stockholders in publicly owned companies are investors, rather than owners in the traditional sense. Closely held corporations usually are quite small, and one or two stockholders often do exercise control. Publicly owned corporations are subject to more government regulation than are closely held companies, and they must disclose to the public much information about their business operations.

**LO 3**

**Explain the rights of stockholders and the roles of corporate directors and officers.**

Stockholders in a corporation normally have the right to elect the board of directors, to share in dividends declared by the directors, and to share in the distribution of assets if the corporation is liquidated.

The directors formulate company policies, review the actions of the corporate officers, and protect the interests of the company's stockholders. Corporate officers are professional managers appointed by the board of directors to manage the business on a daily basis.

**LO 4**

**Account for paid-in capital and prepare the equity section of a corporate balance sheet.**

When capital stock is issued, appropriate asset accounts are debited for cash or the market value of the goods or services received in exchange for the stock. A capital stock account (which indicates the type of stock issued) is credited for the par value of the issued shares. Any excess of the market value received over the par value of the issued shares is credited to an Additional Paid-in Capital account.

The equity section of a corporate balance sheet shows for each class of capital stock outstanding (1) the total par value (legal capital) and (2) any additional paid-in capital. Together, these amounts represent the corporation's total paid-in capital. In addition, the equity section shows separately any earned capital—that is, retained earnings.

**LO 5**

**Contrast the features of common stock with those of preferred stock.**

Common stock represents the residual ownership of a corporation. These shares have voting rights and cannot be called. Also, the common stock dividend is not fixed in dollar amount—thus it may increase or decrease based on the company's performance.

Preferred stock has preference over common stock with respect to dividends and to distributions in the event of liquidation. This preference means that preferred stockholders must be paid in full before any payments are made to holders of common stock. The dividends on preferred stock usually are fixed in amount. In addition, the stock may be callable at the option of the issuing corporation and often has no voting rights. Preferred stocks sometimes have special features, such as being convertible into shares of common stock.

**LO 6**

**Discuss the factors affecting the market price of preferred stock and common stock.**

The market price of preferred stock varies inversely with interest rates. As interest rates rise, preferred stock prices decline; as interest rates fall, preferred stock prices rise. If a company's ability to continue the preferred dividend is in doubt, the solvency of the company also affects preferred stock prices.

Interest rates also affect the market price of common stock. However, common stock dividends are not fixed in amount. Both the amount of the dividend and the market value of the stock may fluctuate, based on the prosperity of the company. Therefore, the principal factor in the market price of common stock is investors' expectations as to the future profitability of the company.

**LO 7**

**Explain the significance of par value, book value, and market value of capital stock.**

Par value has the least significance. It is a legal concept, representing the amount by which stockholders' equity cannot be reduced except by losses. Intended as a buffer for the protection of creditors, it usually is so low as to be of little significance.

Book value per share is the net assets per share of common stock. This value is based on amounts invested by stockholders, plus retained earnings. It often provides insight into the reasonableness of market price.

To investors, market price is the most relevant of the three values. This is the price at which they can buy or sell the stock today. Changes in market price directly affect the financial position of the stockholder, but not of the issuing company. Therefore, market values do not appear in the equity section of the issuing company's balance sheet—but they are readily available in the daily newspaper and on the Internet.

## LO 8

**Explain the purpose and the effects of a stock split.**

When the market price of a corporation's common stock appreciates in value significantly, it may become too expensive for many investors. When this happens, the corporation may split its stock by increasing the number of its common shares outstanding. The purpose of a stock split is to reduce the market price of the company's common stock, with the intent of making it more affordable to investors. A stock split does not change the balance of any ledger account; consequently, the transaction is recorded merely by a memorandum entry.

## LO 9

**Account for treasury stock transactions.**

Purchases of treasury stock are recorded by debiting a contra-equity account entitled Treasury Stock. No profit or loss is recorded when the treasury shares are reissued at a price above or below cost. Rather, any difference between the reissuance price and the cost of the shares is debited or credited to a paid-in capital account. While treasury stock transactions may affect cash flow, they have no effect on the net income of the corporation.

We will continue our discussion of stockholders' equity issues in Chapter 12. Specifically, we will address those events that affect retained earnings, including stock dividends and special income-related issues.

## KEY TERMS INTRODUCED OR EMPHASIZED IN CHAPTER 11

**Additional Paid-in Capital** (p. 461) An account showing the amounts invested in a corporation by stockholders in excess of par value or stated value. In short, this account shows paid-in capital in excess of legal capital.

**board of directors** (p. 458) Persons elected by common stockholders to direct the affairs of a corporation.

**book value per share** (p. 467) The stockholders' equity represented by each share of common stock, computed by dividing common stockholders' equity by the number of common shares outstanding.

**capital stock** (p. 454) Transferable units of ownership in a corporation. A broad term that can refer to common stock, preferred stock, or both.

**closely held corporation** (p. 456) A corporation owned by a small group of stockholders. Not publicly owned.

**common stock** (p. 462) A type of capital stock that possesses the basic rights of ownership, including the right to vote. Represents the residual element of ownership in a corporation.

**contributed capital** (p. 460) The stockholders' equity that results from capital contributions by investors in exchange for shares of common or preferred stock. Also referred to as paid-in capital.

**corporation** (p. 454) A business organized as a legal entity separate from its owners. Chartered by the state with ownership divided into shares of transferable stock. Stockholders are not liable for debts of the corporation.

**dividends** (p. 463) Distribution of assets (usually cash) by a corporation to its stockholders. Normally viewed as a distribution of profits, dividends cannot exceed the amount of retained earnings. Must be formally declared by the board of directors and distributed on a per-share basis. *Note:* Stockholders *cannot* simply withdraw assets from a corporation at will.

**dividend yield** (p. 469) The annual dividend paid to a share of stock, expressed as a percentage of the stock's market value. Indicates the rate of return represented by the dividend.

**donated capital** (p. 466) An account showing capital given to a corporation for which no payment has been made and for which no capital stock has been issued in exchange. Shown in the balance sheet as an element of paid-in capital.

**double taxation** (p. 455) The fact that corporate income is taxed to the corporation when earned and then again taxed to the stockholders when distributed as dividends.

**legal capital** (p. 461) Equal to the par value or stated value of capital stock issued. This amount represents a permanent commitment of capital by the owners of a corporation and cannot be removed without special legal action. Of course, it may be eroded by losses.

**limited personal liability** (p. 454) The concept that the owners of a corporation are not personally liable for the debts of the business. Thus stockholders' potential financial losses are limited to the amount of their equity investment.

**paid-in capital** (p. 460) The amounts invested in a corporation by its stockholders (also includes donated capital).

**par value (or stated value)** (p. 461) The legal capital of a corporation. Represents the minimum amount per share invested in the corporation by its owners and cannot be withdrawn except by special legal action.

**preferred stock** (p. 462) A class of capital stock usually having preferences as to dividends and in the distribution of assets in event of liquidation.

**public information** (p. 456) Information that, by law, must be made available to the general public. Includes the quarterly and annual financial statements—and other financial information—about publicly owned corporations.

**publicly owned corporation** (p. 456) Any corporation whose shares are offered for sale to the general public.

**retained earnings** (p. 460) The element of owners' equity in a corporation that has accumulated through profitable business operations. Net income increases retained earnings; net losses and dividends reduce retained earnings.

**state of incorporation** (p. 456) The state in which the corporation is legally formed. This may or may not be the state in which the corporation conducts most or any of its business.

**stock certificate** (p. 457) A document issued by a corporation (or its transfer agent) as evidence of the ownership of the number of shares stated on the certificate.

**stockholders** (p. 454) The owners of a corporation. The name reflects the fact that their ownership is evidenced by transferable shares of capital stock.

**stockholders subsidiary ledger** (p. 460) A record showing the number of shares owned by each stockholder.

**stock registrar** (p. 460) An independent fiscal agent, such as a bank, retained by a corporation to provide assurance against overissuance of stock certificates.

**stock split** (p. 471) An increase in the number of shares outstanding with a corresponding decrease in par value per share. The additional shares are distributed proportionately to all common shareholders. The purpose of a stock split is to reduce market price per share and encourage wider public ownership of the company's stock. A 2-for-1 stock split will give each stockholder twice as many shares as previously owned.

**stock transfer agent** (p. 460) A bank or trust company retained by a corporation to maintain its records of capital stock ownership and make transfers from one investor to another.

**treasury stock** (p. 471) Shares of a corporation's stock that have been issued and then reacquired, but not canceled.

**underwriter** (p. 460) An investment banking firm that handles the sale of a corporation's stock to the public.

# DEMONSTRATION PROBLEM

The stockholders' equity section of Rockhurst Corporation's balance sheet appears as follows:

| Stockholders' equity: | | |
|---|---:|---:|
| 6% preferred stock, $100 par value, callable at | | |
| $102 per share, 200,000 shares authorized . . . . . . . . . . . . . . . . . . . . . . . . . . . | | $12,000,000 |
| Common stock, $5 par value, 5,000,000 shares authorized . . . . . . . . . . . . . . . . . | | 14,000,000 |
| Additional paid-in capital: | | |
| Preferred stock . . . . . . . . . . . . . . . . . . . . . . . . . . . . . . . . . . | $  360,000 | |
| Common stock . . . . . . . . . . . . . . . . . . . . . . . . . . . . . . . . . . . | 30,800,000 | 31,160,000 |
| Retained earnings . . . . . . . . . . . . . . . . . . . . . . . . . . . . . . . . . . . . . . . . . . . | | 2,680,000 |
| Total stockholders' equity . . . . . . . . . . . . . . . . . . . . . . . . . . . . . . . . . . . | | $59,840,000 |

## Instructions

On the basis of this information, answer the following questions and show any necessary supporting computations:

**a.** How many shares of preferred stock have been issued?

**b.** What is the total annual dividend requirement on the outstanding preferred stock?

**c.** How many shares of common stock have been issued?

**d.** What was the average price per share received by the corporation for its common stock?

**e.** What is the total amount of legal capital?

**f.** What is the total paid-in capital?

**g.** What is the book value per share of common stock? (Assume no dividends in arrears.)

## Solution to the Demonstration Problem

**a.** <u>120,000</u> shares ($12,000,000 total par value, divided by $100 par value per share)

**b.** <u>$720,000</u> (120,000 shares outstanding × $6 per share)

**c.** <u>2,800,000</u> shares ($14,000,000 total par value, divided by $5 par value per share)

**d.**

| Par value of common shares issued and subscribed . . . . . . . . . . . . . . . . . . . . . | $14,000,000 |
|---|---:|
| Additional paid-in capital on common shares . . . . . . . . . . . . . . . . . . . . . . . . . | 30,800,000 |
| Total issue price of common shares . . . . . . . . . . . . . . . . . . . . . . . . . . . . . . . . | $44,800,000 |
| Number of common shares issued (part **c**) . . . . . . . . . . . . . . . . . . . . . . . . . | 2,800,000 |
| Average issue price per share ($44,800,000 ÷ 2,800,000 shares) . . . . . . . . . . . . | $16 |

**e.** $26,000,000 ($12,000,000 preferred, $14,000,000 common)

**f.** $57,160,000 ($26,000,000 legal capital, plus $31,160,000 additional paid-in capital)

**g.**

| | |
|---|---:|
| Total stockholders' equity . . . . . . . . . . . . . . . . . . . . . . . . . . . . . . . . . . . . . . | $59,840,000 |
| Less: Claims of preferred stockholders (120,000 shares × $102 call price) . . . . . . . . . . . . . . . . . . . . . . . . . . . . . . . . . . . . . . . . . | 12,240,000 |
| Equity of common stockholders . . . . . . . . . . . . . . . . . . . . . . . . . . . . . . . . | $47,600,000 |
| Number of common shares outstanding (part **c**) . . . . . . . . . . . . . . . . . . . . . | 2,800,000 |
| Book value per share ($47,600,000 ÷ 2,800,000 shares) . . . . . . . . . . . . . . . . . . | $17 |

# SELF-TEST QUESTIONS

*Answers to these questions appear on page 490.*

1. When a business is organized as a corporation, which of the following is true?

   **a.** Stockholders are liable for the debts of the business in proportion to their percentage ownership of capital stock.

   **b.** Stockholders do *not* have to pay personal income taxes on dividends received, because the corporation is subject to income taxes on its earnings.

   **c.** Fluctuations in the market value of outstanding shares of capital stock do *not* affect the amount of stockholders' equity shown in the balance sheet.

   **d.** Each stockholder has the right to bind the corporation to contracts and to make other managerial decisions.

2. Great Plains Corporation was organized with authorization to issue 100,000 shares of $1 par value common stock. Forty thousand shares were issued to Tom Morgan, the company's founder, at a price of $5 per share. No other shares have yet been issued. Which of the following statements is true?

   **a.** Morgan owns *40%* of the stockholders' equity of the corporation.

   **b.** The corporation should recognize a $160,000 gain on the issuance of these shares.

   **c.** If the balance sheet includes retained earnings of $50,000, total *paid-in* capital amounts to $250,000.

   **d.** In the balance sheet, the Additional Paid-in Capital account will have a $160,000 balance, regardless of the profits earned or losses incurred since the corporation was organized.

3. Which of the following is *not* a characteristic of the *common stock* of a large, publicly owned corporation?

   **a.** The shares may be transferred from one investor to another without disrupting the continuity of business operations.

   **b.** Voting rights in the election of the board of directors.

   **c.** A cumulative right to receive dividends.

   **d.** After issuance, the market value of the stock is unrelated to its par value.

4. Tri-State Electric is a profitable utility company that has increased its dividend to *common* stockholders every year for 42 consecutive years. Which of the following is *least* likely to affect the market price of the company's *preferred* stock by a significant amount?

   **a.** A decrease in long-term interest rates.

   **b.** An increase in long-term interest rates.

   **c.** The board of directors announces its intention to increase common stock dividends in the current year.

   **d.** Whether or not the preferred stock carries a conversion privilege.

**5.** The following information is taken from the balance sheet and related disclosures of Blue Oyster Corporation:

| | |
|---|---:|
| Total paid-in capital . . . . . . . . . . . . . . . . . . . . . . . . . . . . . . . . . . . . . . . . . . . . . | $5,400,000 |
| Outstanding shares: | |
| Common stock, $5 par value . . . . . . . . . . . . . . . . . . . . . . . . . . . . . . . . . . . . | 100,000 shares |
| 6% preferred stock, $100 par value, callable at $108 per share . . . . . . . . . . . . . . . . . . . . . . . . . . . . . . . . . . . . . . . . . . . . . . | 10,000 shares |
| Preferred dividends in arrears . . . . . . . . . . . . . . . . . . . . . . . . . . . . . . . . . . | 2 years |
| Total stockholders' equity . . . . . . . . . . . . . . . . . . . . . . . . . . . . . . . . . . . . . . | $4,700,000 |

Which of the following statements is(are) true? (For this question, more than one answer may be correct.)

**a.** The preferred dividends in arrears amount to $120,000 and should appear as a liability in the corporate balance sheet.

**b.** The book value per share of common stock is $35.

**c.** The stockholders' equity section of the balance sheet should indicate a deficit of $700,000.

**d.** The company has paid no dividend on its *common* stock during the past two years.

**6.** On December 10, 2001, Totem Corporation reacquired 2,000 shares of its own $5 par stock at a price of $60 per share. In 2002, 500 of the treasury shares are reissued at a price of $70 per share. Which of the following statements is correct?

**a.** The treasury stock purchased is recorded at cost and is shown in Totem's December 31, 2001, balance sheet as an asset.

**b.** The two treasury stock transactions result in an overall reduction in Totem's stockholders' equity of $85,000.

**c.** Totem recognizes a gain of $10 per share on the reissuance of the 500 treasury shares in 2002.

**d.** Totem's stockholders' equity was increased by $110,000 when the treasury stock was acquired.

# ASSIGNMENT MATERIAL

## DISCUSSION QUESTIONS

**1.** Why are large corporations often said to be *publicly owned?*

**2.** Distinguish between corporations and sole proprietorships in terms of the following characteristics:

**a.** Owners' liability for debts of the business.

**b.** Transferability of ownership interest.

**c.** Continuity of existence.

**d.** Federal taxation on income.

**3.** What are the basic rights of the owner of a share of corporate stock? In what way are these basic rights commonly modified with respect to the owner of a share of preferred stock?

**4.** Explain the meaning of the term *double taxation* as it applies to corporate profits.

**5.** Distinguish between *paid-in capital* and *retained earnings* of a corporation. Why is such a distinction useful?

**6.** Explain the significance of *par value*. Does par value indicate the reasonable market price for a share of stock? Explain.

**7.** Describe the usual nature of the following features as they apply to a share of preferred stock: (a) cumulative, (b) convertible, and (c) callable.

8. Why is noncumulative preferred stock often considered an unattractive form of investment?

9. When stock is issued by a corporation in exchange for assets other than cash, accountants face the problem of determining the dollar amount at which to record the transaction. Discuss the factors to be considered and explain their significance.

10. State the classification (asset, liability, stockholders' equity, revenue, or expense) of each of the following accounts:

   a. Cash (received from the issuance of capital stock)

   b. Organization Costs

   c. Preferred Stock

   d. Retained Earnings

   e. Donated Capital

   f. Additional Paid-in Capital

   g. Income Taxes Payable

11. A professional baseball team received as a gift from the city the land on which to build a stadium. What effect, if any, will the receipt of this gift have on the baseball team's balance sheet and income statement? Explain.

12. Explain the following terms:

   a. Stock transfer agent

   b. Stockholders subsidiary ledger

   c. Underwriter

   d. Stock registrar

13. What does *book value per share* of common stock represent? Does it represent the amount common stockholders would receive in the event of liquidation of the corporation? Explain briefly.

14. How is book value per share of common stock computed when a company has both preferred and common stock outstanding?

15. What would be the effect, if any, on book value per share of common stock as a result of each of the following independent events: (a) a corporation obtains a bank loan; (b) a dividend is declared (to be paid in the next accounting period)?

16. In the great stock market crash of October 19, 1987, the market price of **IBM**'s capital stock fell by over $31 per share. Explain the effects, if any, of this decline in share price on **IBM**'s balance sheet.

17. Assume that you asked your stockbroker to purchase 100 shares of **ExxonMobil Corporation** stock. How would this transaction affect the financial statements of **ExxonMobil**? Explain.

18. What is the purpose of a *stock split?*

19. What is *treasury stock?* Why do corporations purchase their own shares? Is treasury stock an asset? How should it be reported in the balance sheet?

20. In many states, the corporation law requires that retained earnings be restricted for dividend purposes to the extent of the cost of treasury shares. What is the reason for this legal rule?

## EXERCISES

Assume that you have recently obtained your scuba instructor's certification and have decided to start a scuba diving school.

**EXERCISE 11.1**

Form of Organization

**LO 1, 2, 3**

a. Describe the advantages and disadvantages of organizing your scuba diving school as a:

   1. Sole proprietorship

   2. Corporation

b. State your opinion about which form of organization would be best and explain the basis for your opinion.

**EXERCISE 11.2**

Accounting Terminology

**LO 1–9**

Listed below are 12 technical accounting terms discussed in this chapter:

| | | |
|---|---|---|
| Par value | Board of directors | Double taxation |
| Book value | Paid-in capital | Dividends in arrears |
| Market value | Preferred stock | Closely held corporation |
| Retained earnings | Common stock | Publicly owned corporation |

Each of the following statements may (or may not) describe one of these technical terms. For each statement, indicate the term described, or answer "None" if the statement does not correctly describe any of the terms.

**a.** A major *disadvantage* of the corporate form of organization.

**b.** From investors' point of view, the most important value associated with capital stock.

**c.** Cash available for distribution to the stockholders.

**d.** The class of capital stock that normally has the most voting power.

**e.** A distribution of assets that may be made in future years to the holders of common stock.

**f.** The group of stockholders that controls more than 50% of a corporation's voting shares.

**g.** A corporation whose shares are traded on an organized stock exchange.

**h.** Equity arising either from investments by owners or from the donation of assets to a corporation.

**i.** The element of stockholders' equity that is increased by net income.

**j.** Total assets divided by the number of common shares outstanding.

**k.** The class of stock whose market price normally rises as interest rates increase.

**EXERCISE 11.3**

Stockholders' Equity Section of a Balance Sheet

**LO 4, 5**

When Enviro Systems, Inc., was formed, the company was authorized to issue 5,000 shares of $100 par value, 8% cumulative preferred stock, and 100,000 shares of $2 stated value common stock. The preferred stock is callable at $106.

Half of the preferred stock was issued at a price of $103 per share, and 70,000 shares of the common stock were sold for $13 per share. At the end of the current year, Enviro Systems, Inc., has retained earnings of $297,000.

**a.** Prepare the stockholders' equity section of the company's balance sheet at the end of the current year.

**b.** Assume Enviro Systems' common stock is trading at $22 per share and its preferred stock is trading at $105 per share at the end of the current year. Would the stockholders' equity section prepared in part **a** be affected by this additional information?

**EXERCISE 11.4**

Dividends: Preferred and Common

**LO 4, 5**

A portion of the stockholders' equity section from the balance sheet of Palermo Corporation appears as follows:

| Stockholders' equity: | |
|---|---|
| Preferred stock, 9% cumulative, $50 par, 40,000 shares authorized and issued | $2,000,000 |
| Preferred stock, 12% noncumulative, $100 par, 8,000 shares authorized and issued | 800,000 |
| Common stock, $5 par, 400,000 shares authorized and issued | 2,000,000 |
| Total paid-in capital | $4,800,000 |

Assume that all the stock was issued on January 1 and that no dividends were paid during the first two years of operations. During the third year, Palermo Corporation paid total cash dividends of $736,000.

**a.** Compute the amount of cash dividends paid during the third year to each of the three classes of stock.

**b.** Compute the dividends paid *per share* during the third year for each of the three classes of stock.

**c.** What was the average issue price of each type of preferred stock?

The year-end balance sheet of Maui Corporation includes the following stockholders' equity section (with certain details omitted):

| Stockholders' equity: | |
|---|---|
| Capital stock: | |
| 7% cumulative preferred stock, $100 par value, callable at $105 .......................................... | $ 15,000,000 |
| Common stock, $5 par value, 5,000,000 shares authorized, 4,000,000 shares issued ............................... | 20,000,000 |
| Additional paid-in capital: | |
| Preferred stock ........................................... | 300,000 |
| Common stock ........................................... | 44,000,000 |
| Retained earnings ........................................... | 64,450,000 |
| Total stockholders' equity ........................................... | $143,750,000 |

From this information, compute answers to the following questions:

**a.** How many shares of preferred stock have been issued?

**b.** What is the total amount of the annual dividends paid to preferred stockholders?

**c.** What was the average issuance price per share of common stock?

**d.** What is the amount of legal capital and the amount of total paid-in capital?

**e.** What is the book value per share of common stock?

**f.** Is it possible to determine the fair market value per share of common stock from the stockholders' equity section above? Explain.

Hudson Creek Development Co. issued 20,000 shares of its $2 par value common stock in exchange for 300 acres of land. The land recently had been appraised at $450,000.

**a.** Record this transaction under each of the following assumptions:

**1.** Hudson is a closely held corporation. None of its shares have changed hands in several years.

**2.** Hudson is a publicly owned corporation. Its stock currently is trading at $21.50 per share.

**b.** For each of your two journal entries, explain the reasoning behind the value that you assigned to the *land*.

Five events pertaining to Lowlands Manufacturing Co. are described below.

**a.** Issued common stock for cash.

**b.** Issued common stock for equipment.

**c.** The market value of the corporation's stock increased.

**d.** Declared and paid a cash dividend to stockholders.

**e.** Received a building site as a donation from the city.

Indicate the immediate effects of the events on the financial measurements in the four columnar headings listed below. Use the code letters **I** for increase, **D** for decrease, and **NE** for no effect.

| Event | Current Assets | Stockholders' Equity | Net Income | Net Cash Flow (from Any Source) |
|---|---|---|---|---|
| a | | | | |

**EXERCISE 11.8**

Computing Book Value

**LO 4, 5, 6, 7**

The following information is necessary to compute the net assets (stockholders' equity) and book value per share of common stock for Ringside Corporation:

| | |
|---|---|
| 8% cumulative preferred stock, $100 par (callable at $110) . . . . . . . . . . . . . . . . . . . | $200,000 |
| Common stock, $5 par, authorized 100,000 shares, issued 60,000 shares . . . . . . . . . | 300,000 |
| Additional paid-in capital . . . . . . . . . . . . . . . . . . . . . . . . . . . . . . . . . . . . . . . . . . | 452,800 |
| Deficit . . . . . . . . . . . . . . . . . . . . . . . . . . . . . . . . . . . . . . . . . . . . . . . . . . . . . . . | 146,800 |
| Dividends in arrears on preferred stock, 1 full year . . . . . . . . . . . . . . . . . . . . . . . | 16,000 |

**a.** Compute the amount of net assets (stockholders' equity).

**b.** Compute the book value per share of common stock.

**c.** Is book value per share (answer to part **b**) the amount common stockholders should expect to receive if Ringside Corporation were to cease operations and liquidate? Explain.

**EXERCISE 11.9**

Recording Treasury Stock Transactions

**LO 9**

Cachet, Inc., engaged in the following transactions involving treasury stock:

**Feb. 10** Purchased for cash 14,500 shares of treasury stock at a price of $30 per share.
**June 4** Reissued 6,000 shares of treasury stock at a price of $33 per share.
**Dec. 22** Reissued 4,000 shares of treasury stock at a price of $28 per share.

**a.** Prepare general journal entries to record these transactions.

**b.** Compute the amount of retained earnings that should be restricted because of the treasury stock still owned at December 31.

**c.** Does a restriction on retained earnings affect the dollar amount of retained earnings reported in the balance sheet? Explain briefly.

**EXERCISE 11.10**

Effects of a Stock Split

**LO 8**

The common stock of Newton Corporation was trading at $45 per share on October 15, 2001. A year later, on October 15, 2002, it was trading at $100 per share. On this date, Newton's board of directors decided to split the company's common stock.

**a.** If the company decides on a 2-for-1 split, at what price would you expect the stock to trade immediately after the split goes into effect?

**b.** If the company decides on a 4-for-1 split, at what price would you expect the stock to trade immediately after the split goes into effect?

**c.** Why do you suppose Newton's board of directors decided to split the company's stock?

**EXERCISE 11.11**

Treasury Stock Presentation

**LO 9**

Vanari Company was experiencing financial difficulty late in the current year. The company's income was sluggish, and the market price of its common stock was tumbling. On December 21, the company began to buy back shares of its own stock in an attempt to boost its market price per share and to improve its earnings per share.

**a.** Is it unethical for a company to purchase shares of its own stock to improve measures of financial performance? Defend your answer.

**b.** Assume that the company classified the shares of treasury stock as short-term investments in the current asset section of its balance sheet. Is this appropriate? Explain.

**EXERCISE 11.12**

Tootsie Roll Industries

**LO 4, 7**

The annual report of **Tootsie Roll Industries, Inc.,** appears in Appendix A of this text. This report contains information describing the details of the company's stockholders' equity.

**a.** What are the par values of the company's two classes of common stock?

**b.** For the most current year shown, how many shares of each class of common stock are authorized? What is the meaning of authorized shares?

**c.** What is the total stockholders' equity amount for **Tootsie Roll** for the most recent year reported? Does this figure mean that the total outstanding stock is actually worth this amount? Explain your answer.

# PROBLEMS

Early in 1999, Sinclair Press was organized with authorization to issue 100,000 shares of $100 par value preferred stock and 500,000 shares of $1 par value common stock. Ten thousand shares of the preferred stock were issued at par, and 170,000 shares of common stock were sold for $15 per share. The preferred stock pays an 8% cumulative dividend and is callable at $105.

During the first four years of operations (1999 through 2002), the corporation earned a total of $1,025,000 and paid dividends of 75 cents per share in each year on its outstanding common stock.

**PROBLEM 11.1**

Stockholders' Equity in a Balance Sheet

**LO 4, 5, 6**

**Instructions**

**a.** Prepare the stockholders' equity section of the balance sheet at December 31, 2002. Include a supporting schedule showing your computation of the amount of retained earnings reported. (Hint: Income increases retained earnings, whereas dividends decrease retained earnings.)

**b.** Are there any dividends in arrears on the company's preferred stock at December 31, 2002? Explain your answer.

**c.** Assume that interest rates increase steadily from 1999 through 2002. Would you expect the market price of the company's preferred stock to be higher or lower than its call price of $105 at December 21, 2002?

Banner Publications was organized early in 1997 with authorization to issue 20,000 shares of $100 par value preferred stock and 1 million shares of $1 par value common stock. All of the preferred stock was issued at par, and 300,000 shares of common stock were sold for $20 per share. The preferred stock pays a 10% cumulative dividend and is callable at $105.

During the first five years of operations (1997 through 2001) the corporation earned a total of $4,460,000 and paid dividends of $1 per share each year on the common stock. In 2002, however, the corporation reported a net loss of $1,600,000 and paid no dividends.

**PROBLEM 11.2**

Stockholders' Equity Section

**LO 4, 5, 6**

**Instructions**

**a.** Prepare the stockholders' equity section of the balance sheet at December 31, 2002. Include a supporting schedule showing your computation of retained earnings at the balance sheet date. (Hint: Income increases retained earnings, whereas dividends and net losses decrease retained earnings.)

**b.** Draft a note to accompany the financial statements disclosing any dividends in arrears at the end of 2002.

**c.** Do the dividends in arrears appear as a liability of the corporation as of the end of 2002? Explain.

Maria Martinez organized Manhattan Transport Company in January 1999. The corporation immediately issued at $8 per share one-half of its 200,000 authorized shares of $2 par value common stock. On January 2, *2000,* the corporation sold at par value the entire 5,000 authorized shares of 8%, $100 par value, cumulative preferred stock. On January 2, *2001,* the company again needed money and issued 5,000 shares of an authorized 10,000 shares of no-par, cumulative preferred stock for a total of $512,000. The no-par shares have a stated dividend of $9 per share.

The company declared no dividends in 1999 and 2000. At the end of 2000, its retained earnings were $170,000. During 2001 and 2002 combined, the company earned a total of $890,000. Dividends of 50 cents per share in 2001 and $1.60 per share in 2002 were paid on the common stock.

**PROBLEM 11.3**

Stockholders' Equity in a Balance Sheet

**LO 4, 5, 6**

**Instructions**

**a.** Prepare the stockholders' equity section of the balance sheet at December 31, 2002. Include a supporting schedule showing your computation of retained earnings at the balance sheet date. (Hint: Income increases retained earnings, whereas dividends decrease retained earnings.)

**b.** Assume that on January 2, 2000, the corporation could have borrowed $500,000 at 8% interest on a long-term basis instead of issuing the 5,000 shares of the $100 par value cumulative preferred stock. Identify two reasons a corporation may choose to issue cumulative preferred stock rather than finance operations with long-term debt.

**PROBLEM 11.4**

Stockholders' Equity: A Short Comprehensive Problem

LO 4, 5

Early in the year Roger Gordon and several friends organized a corporation called Mobile Communications, Inc. The corporation was authorized to issue 50,000 shares of $100 par value, 10% cumulative preferred stock and 400,000 shares of $2 par value common stock. The following transactions (among others) occurred during the year:

**Jan. 6**   Issued for cash 20,000 shares of common stock at $14 per share. The shares were issued to Gordon and 10 other investors.

**Jan. 7**   Issued an additional 500 shares of common stock to Gordon in exchange for his services in organizing the corporation. The stockholders agreed that these services were worth $7,000.

**Jan. 12**  Issued 2,500 shares of preferred stock for cash of $250,000.

**June 4**   Acquired land as a building site in exchange for 15,000 shares of common stock. In view of the appraised value of the land and the progress of the company, the directors agreed that the common stock was to be valued for purposes of this transaction at $15 per share.

**Nov. 15**  The first annual dividend of $10 per share was declared on the preferred stock to be paid December 20.

**Dec. 20**  Paid the cash dividend declared on November 15.

**Dec. 31**  After the revenue and expenses were closed into the Income Summary account, that account indicated a net income of $106,500.

**Instructions**

**a.** Prepare journal entries in general journal form to record the above transactions. Include entries at December 31 to close the Income Summary account and the Dividends account.

**b.** Prepare the stockholders' equity section of the Mobile Communications, Inc., balance sheet at December 31.

**PROBLEM 11.5**

Analysis of an Equity Section of a Balance Sheet

LO 4, 5

The year-end balance sheet of DeskTop Products includes the following stockholders' equity section (with certain details omitted):

| Stockholders' equity: | |
|---|---:|
| 7¹/₂% cumulative preferred stock, $100 par value, callable at $105, 100,000 shares authorized | $ 2,400,000 |
| Common stock, $2 par value, 900,000 shares authorized | 900,000 |
| Additional paid-in capital: Common stock | 8,325,000 |
| Donated capital | 720,000 |
| Retained earnings | 2,595,000 |
| Total stockholders' equity | $14,940,000 |

**Instructions**

From this information, compute answers to the following questions:

**a.** How many shares of preferred stock have been issued?

**b.** What is the total amount of the annual dividends paid to preferred stockholders?

**c.** How many shares of common stock are outstanding?

**d.** What was the average issuance price per share of common stock?

**e.** What is the amount of legal capital?

**f.** What is the total amount of paid-in capital?

**g.** What is the book value per share of common stock? (There are no dividends in arrears.)

**h.** Assume that retained earnings at the beginning of the year amounted to $717,500 and that net income for the year was $3,970,000. What was the dividend declared during the year on *each share* of common stock? (Hint: Net income increases retained earnings, whereas dividends decrease retained earnings.)

**Quanex Corporation** is a publicly owned company. The following information is excerpted from a recent balance sheet. Dollar amounts (except for per share amounts) are stated in thousands.

PROBLEM 11.6

Analysis of an Equity Section—More Comprehensive

**LO 1–7**

| Stockholders' equity: | |
| --- | --- |
| Convertible $17.20 preferred stock, no par value, 1,000,000 shares authorized; 345,000 shares issued and outstanding; $250 per share liquidation preference (call price) | $ 86,250 |
| Common stock, par value $0.50; 25,000,000 shares authorized | 6,819 |
| Additional paid-in capital | 87,260 |
| Retained earnings | 57,263 |
| Total stockholders' equity | $237,592 |

**Instructions**

From this information, answer the following questions:

**a.** How many shares of common stock have been issued?

**b.** What is the total amount of the annual dividends paid to preferred stockholders?

**c.** What is the total amount of paid-in capital?

**d.** What is the book value per share of common stock?

**e.** Briefly explain the advantages and disadvantages to **Quanex** of being publicly owned rather than operating as a closely held corporation.

**f.** What is meant by the term *convertible* used in the caption of the preferred stock? Is there any more information that investors need to know to evaluate this conversion feature?

**g.** Assume that the preferred stock currently is selling at *$248* per share. Does this provide a higher or lower dividend yield than an 8%, $50 par value preferred with a market price of $57 per share? Show computations (round to the nearest tenth of 1%). Explain why one preferred stock might yield less than another.

Compuwiz Corporation is the producer of popular business software. Recently, an investment service published the following per-share amounts relating to the company's only class of stock:

PROBLEM 11.7

Par, Book, and Market Values

**LO 4, 7**

| | |
| --- | --- |
| Par value | $ 0.001 |
| Book value (estimated) | 6.50 |
| Market value | 73.00 |

**Instructions**

**a.** Without reference to dollar amounts, explain the nature and significance of *par value, book value,* and *market value.*

**b.** Comment on the *relationships,* if any, among the per-share amounts shown for the company. What do these amounts imply about Compuwiz and its operations? Comment on what these amounts imply about the security of *creditors'* claims against the company.

Early in 2000, Bell Corporation was formed with authorization to issue 50,000 shares of $1 par value common stock. All shares were issued at a price of $8 per share. The corporation reported net income of $82,000 in 2000, $25,000 in 2001, and $70,000 in 2002. No dividends were declared in any of these three years.

In 2001, the company purchased $35,000 of its own shares in the open market. In 2002, it reissued all of its treasury stock for $40,000.

PROBLEM 11.8

Reporting Stockholder's Equity with Treasury Stock

**LO 4, 5, 7, 9**

### Instructions

**a.** Prepare the stockholders' equity section of the balance sheet at December 31, 2002. Include a supporting schedule showing your computation of retained earnings at the balance sheet date. (Hint: Income increases retained earnings.)

**b.** As of December 31, compute the company's book value per share of common stock.

**c.** Explain how the treasury stock transactions in 2001 and 2002 were reported in the company's statement of cash flows.

**PROBLEM 11.9**

Reporting Stockholders' Equity with Treasury Stock and Stock Splits

**LO 4, 5, 7, 8, 9**

Early in 1998, Parker Industries was formed with authorization to issue 200,000 shares of $10 par value common stock and 30,000 shares of $100 par value cumulative preferred stock. During 1998, all the preferred stock was issued at par, and 120,000 shares of common stock were sold for $16 per share. The preferred stock is entitled to a dividend equal to 10% of its par value before any dividends are paid on the common stock.

During its first five years of business (1998 through 2002), the company earned income totaling $3,200,000 and paid dividends of 50 cents per share each year on the common stock outstanding.

On January 2, 2000, the company purchased 20,000 shares of its own common stock in the open market for $400,000. On January 2, 2002, it reissued 10,000 shares of this treasury stock for $250,000. The remaining 10,000 were still held in treasury at December 31, 2002.

### Instructions

**a.** Prepare the stockholders' equity section of the balance sheet at December 31, 2002. Include supporting schedules showing (1) your computation of any paid-in capital on treasury stock and (2) retained earnings at the balance sheet date. (Hint: Income increases retained earnings, whereas dividends reduce retained earnings. Dividends are not paid on shares of stock held in treasury.)

**b.** As of December 31, compute the company's book value per share of common stock. (Hint: Book value per share is computed only on the shares of stock outstanding.)

**c.** At December 31, 2002, shares of the company's common stock were trading at $30. Explain what would have happened to the market price per share had the company split its stock 2-for-1 at this date. Also explain what would have happened to the par value of the common stock and to the number of common shares outstanding.

## CASES AND UNSTRUCTURED PROBLEMS

**CASE 11.1**

Factors Affecting the Market Prices of Preferred and Common Stocks

**LO 5, 7**

ADM Labs is a publicly owned company with several issues of capital stock outstanding. Over the past decade, the company has consistently earned modest profits and has increased its common stock dividend annually by 5 or 10 cents per share. Recently the company introduced several new products that you believe will cause future sales and profits to increase dramatically. You also expect a gradual increase in long-term interest rates from their present level of about 11% to, perhaps, 12% to $12\frac{1}{2}$%.

### Instructions

Based on these forecasts, explain whether you would expect to see the market prices of the following issues of ADM capital stock increase or decrease. Explain your reasoning in each answer.

**a.** 10%, $100 par value, preferred stock (currently selling at $90 per share).

**b.** $5 par value common stock (currently paying an annual dividend of $2.50 and selling at $40 per share).

**c.** 7%, $100 par value, convertible preferred stock (currently selling at $125 per share).

**CASE 11.2**

Factors Affecting the Market Prices of Common Stocks

**LO 7**

Each of the following situations describes a recent event that affected the stock market price of a particular company.

**a.** The price of a common share of **McDonnell Douglas, Inc.**, increased by $5\frac{1}{8}$ dollars per share in the several days after it was announced that Saudia Airlines would order $6 billion of commercial airliners from **Boeing** and **McDonnell Douglas**.

**b. Citicorp**'s common stock price fell $3^5/_8$ per share shortly after the Federal Reserve Board increased the discount rate by $^1/_4\%$. The discount rate is the rate charged to banks for short-term loans they need to meet their reserve requirements.

**c.** The price of a common share of **Ventitex, Inc.**, a manufacturer of medical devices, fell $10^1/_4$ (27.7%) after it was announced that representatives of the Federal Drug Administration paid a visit to the company.

## Instructions
For each of the independent situations described, explain the likely underlying rationale for the change in market price of the stock.

Interview the owners of two local small businesses. One business should be organized as a corporation and the other as either a sole proprietorship or a partnership. Inquire as to:

- *Why* this form of entity was selected.
- Have there been any unforeseen complications with this form of entity?
- Is the form of entity likely to be changed in the foreseeable future? And if so, why?

**CASE 11.3**

Selecting a Form of Business Organization

**LO 1, 2, 3**

---

# BUSINESS WEEK ASSIGNMENT

BusinessWeek

In a November 6, 2000, *Business Week* article entitled, "When Is a Stock Like a Bond," author Eric Uhlfelder highlights some of the features that make preferred stocks similar to bonds, yet more attractive. For instance, many preferred stocks currently have dividend yields of 9% and 10% compared to 6% and 7% rates of bonds issued by comparable companies. The article also points out, however, that the hybrid nature of preferred stocks often makes them difficult to understand for anyone without extensive knowledge of fixed income investments.

**CASE 11.4**

**LO 5**

## Instructions
Compare and contrast the similarities and differences between preferred stocks and long-term fixed income investments, such as bonds.

---

# INTERNET ASSIGNMENT

Visit the home page of **Staples, Inc.**, at the following Internet address:

**www.staples.com**

Locate the company's most current balance sheet by selecting Corporate Information.

**INTERNET 11.1**

Credit Ratings on Bonds

**LO 4, 5, 7, 9**

## Instructions
Answer the following questions:

**a.** Does the company report preferred stock in its balance sheet? If so, how many shares are currently outstanding?

**b.** What classifications of common stock does the company report in its balance sheet? What is the par value of each?

**c.** Does the company report any treasury stock? If so, what percentage of total stockholders' equity does it represent?

*Internet sites are time and date sensitive. It is the purpose of these exercises to have you explore the Internet. You may need to use the Yahoo! search engine http://www.yahoo.com (or other favorite search engine) to find a company's current web address.*

# OUR COMMENTS ON THE "YOUR TURN" CASES

**As a Loan Officer (p. 455)**     GOTCHA! does *not* appear to be a good credit risk for a $200,000 loan. The company has few liquid assets that can be used to repay a loan. Also, the proposed loan is very large in relation to the small corporation's assets and owners' equity. Because GOTCHA! is organized as a corporation, Woods is not personally responsible for the company's debts—unless she agrees to be.

Most loan officers would want to find a way to make this loan. They certainly would not want to refuse a 20-year customer of the bank a loan that amounts to less than half of the normal balance she maintains in her checking account. But they would ask that Woods *personally guarantee* the loan, rather than depend solely on GOTCHA! for repayment. (Woods will not be offended by this requirement; in situations such as this, it is standard business practice.)

**As a Chief Financial Officer (CFO) (p. 459)**     Do not consider selling the stock before the information about the strike becomes public. The Securities Exchange Act of 1934 precludes trading referred to as "insider trading." Specifically, insider trading occurs when a member of the board of directors, an employee of the corporation, or a major stockholder has inside information. Inside information is generally defined as any knowledge that would have a significant effect on share prices if it were to become publicly known. If the director or employee executes trades to take advantage of this private information, it is referred to as insider trading. Insider trading is considered unethical and is prohibited by law in the United States. However, in some countries, insider trading is an accepted business practice (for more information, visit www.sec.gov).

**As an Investor (p. 470)**     While rising interest rates are not favorable for the market price on any type of stock, the market value of preferred stock is likely to be affected more so than common stock. If interest rates increase, the value of the preferred stock will fall. Because you are investing for the short term, you probably should invest in the common stock rather than the preferred stock.

# ANSWERS TO SELF-TEST QUESTIONS

**1.** c     **2.** d     **3.** c     **4.** c     **5.** b, c, d     **6.** b

# INCOME AND CHANGES IN RETAINED EARNINGS

## Learning Objectives

*After studying this chapter, you should be able to:*

1. Describe how discontinued operations, extraordinary items, and accounting changes are presented in the income statement.

2. Compute earnings per share.

3. Distinguish between basic and diluted earnings per share.

4. Account for cash dividends and stock dividends, and explain the effects of these transactions on a company's financial statements.

5. Describe and prepare a statement of retained earnings.

6. Define *prior period adjustments,* and explain how they are presented in financial statements.

7. Define *comprehensive income,* and explain how it differs from net income.

8. Describe and prepare a statement of stockholders' equity.

The Home Depot

# Home Depot, Inc.

A company's net income is a very important factor in evaluating its financial success or failure. Consider **Home Depot, Inc.**, for example. **Home Depot** was founded in 1978 and has rapidly become the world's largest home improvement retailer and the world's third-largest retailer overall.

One of the remarkable attributes of this very successful company is the rate of growth from year to year of its primary income statement figures—sales and net income. From 1997 to 1998, for example, **Home Depot**'s sales increased more than 25% from $24,156 million to $30,219 million. This trend continued between 1998 and 1999 when sales grew over 27% from $30,219 million to $38,434 million. Net income followed a similar pattern: From 1997 to 1998, **Home Depot**'s net income increased more than 39% from $1,160 million to $1,614 million. From 1998 to 1999, **Home Depot**'s net income increased from $1,614 million to $2,320 million, an increase of almost 44%. Such growth represents very large increases in key measures of performance.

● ● ●

For investors seeking companies in which to place their funds, a pattern of increases in key performance figures such as sales and net income would be very attractive. In this chapter, we look more closely at the income statement and learn about the useful information available in that financial statement for making important investment and credit decisions. In addition to learning more about how an income statement is prepared, you will learn about earnings per share, dividends, and other key factors that indicate the financial success of a company.

## REPORTING THE RESULTS OF OPERATIONS

The most important aspect of corporate financial reporting, in the view of many investors, is periodic income. Both the market price of common stock and the amount of cash dividends per share depend on the current and future earnings of the corporation.

### Developing Predictive Information

Revenues are measures of the value of products and services that have been sold to customers. Revenue represents the increases in the company's assets that result from its profit-directed activities. Generally, revenues increase cash either at the time they are included in the income statement or at an earlier or later date. Expenses, on the other hand, are measures of the cost of producing and providing the products and services that are sold to customers. They represent decreases in the company's assets that result from its profit-directed activities. Expenses decrease cash at the time they are incurred, or at an earlier or later date. An income statement presents a company's revenues and expenses for a stated period of time, such as a quarter or year.

As this brief description of revenues and expenses indicates, the income statement provides important information for investors and creditors as they attempt to make estimates of future cash flows. Because of the importance of income reporting in making assessments about the future, events and transactions that are irregular—in that they do not recur often or are different from the company's normal, ongoing operations—require careful attention in the preparation of an income statement. Investors, creditors, and other financial statement users have a need, as well as a right, to know those aspects of a company's income that can reasonably be expected to repeat in the future and those that should not be expected to occur on a regular basis.

For information about financial performance to be of maximum usefulness to investors, creditors, and other financial statement users, the results of items that are unusual and not likely to recur should be presented separately from the results of the company's normal, recurring activities. Income from normal, recurring activities should provide more useful information for predicting future earnings than income that mixes the results of normal, recurring activities with the results of unusual and nonrecurring activities.

The need to separate types of revenue and expense transactions into two major categories—normal, recurring and unusual, nonrecurring—has resulted in a multiple-section income statement that is often encountered in business today and that we discuss in the following section. Three categories of unusual, nonrecurring events that require special treatment are (1) the results of *discontinued operations,* (2) the impact of *extraordinary items,* and (3) the effects of *changes in accounting principles.* One of the challenges that has faced the accounting profession is to define these terms with sufficient clarity that users of financial statements can reliably compare the information provided by different companies.

### Reporting Irregular Items: An Illustration

To illustrate the presentation of irregular items in an income statement, assume that Ross Corporation operates both a small chain of retail stores and two motels. Near the end of the current year, the company sells both motels to a national hotel chain. In addition, Ross Corporation reports two "extraordinary items" and changes the method it uses in computing depreciation expense. An income statement illustrating the correct format for reporting these events appears on the following page.

| ROSS CORPORATION<br>Income Statement<br>For the Year Ended December 31, 2002 | | |
| --- | --- | --- |
| Net sales . . . . . . . . . . . . . . . . . . . . . . . . . . . . . . . . | | $8,000,000 |
| **Cost and expenses:** | | |
| Cost of goods sold . . . . . . . . . . . . . . . . . . . . . . . . . . | $4,500,000 | |
| Selling expenses . . . . . . . . . . . . . . . . . . . . . . . . . . . . | 1,500,000 | |
| General and administrative expenses . . . . . . . . . . . . . . . | 920,000 | |
| Loss on settlement of lawsuit . . . . . . . . . . . . . . . . . . . . | 80,000 | |
| Income taxes (on continuing operations) . . . . . . . . . . . . . | 300,000 | 7,300,000 |
| Income from continuing operations . . . . . . . . . . . . . . . . . | | $ 700,000 |
| **Discontinued operations:** | | |
| Operating loss on motels (net of $90,000<br>income tax benefit) . . . . . . . . . . . . . . . . . . . . . . . . . | $ (210,000) | |
| Gain on sale of motels (net of $195,000<br>income taxes) . . . . . . . . . . . . . . . . . . . . . . . . . . . . | 455,000 | 245,000 |
| Income before extraordinary items and<br>cumulative effect of accounting change . . . . . . . . . . . . . | | $ 945,000 |
| **Extraordinary items:** | | |
| Gain on condemnation of land by<br>State Highway Department (net of $45,000<br>income taxes) . . . . . . . . . . . . . . . . . . . . . . . . . . . . | $ 105,000 | |
| Loss from earthquake damage to<br>Los Angeles store (net of $75,000 income<br>tax benefit) . . . . . . . . . . . . . . . . . . . . . . . . . . . . . . | (175,000) | (70,000) |
| **Cumulative effect of change in<br>accounting principle:** | | |
| Effect on prior years' income of change<br>in method of computing depreciation<br>(net of $60,000 income taxes) . . . . . . . . . . . . . . . . . . . | | 140,000 |
| Net income . . . . . . . . . . . . . . . . . . . . . . . . . . . . . . . . | | $1,015,000 |

*Notice the order in which the "special items" are reported*

*Note:* This income statement is designed to illustrate the presentation of various irregular items. Rarely, if ever, will all these types of events appear in the income statement of one company within a single year.

## Continuing Operations

The first section of the income statement contains only the results of *continuing business activities*—that is, the retail stores. Notice that the income taxes expense shown in this section ($300,000) relates *only to continuing operations*. The income taxes relating to the irregular items are shown separately in the income statement as adjustments to the amounts of these items.

**Income from Continuing Operations**    The subtotal *income from continuing operations* measures the profitability of the ongoing operations. This subtotal should be helpful in making predictions of the company's future earnings. For example, if we predict no significant change in the profitability of its retail stores, we would expect Ross Corporation to earn a net income of approximately $700,000 next year.

## Discontinued Operations

If management enters into a formal plan to sell or discontinue a **segment of the business**, the results of that segment's operations are shown separately in the income statement. This enables users of the financial statements to better evaluate the performance of the company's ongoing (continuing) operations.

**LO 1**

Describe how discontinued operations, extraordinary items, and accounting changes are presented in the income statement.

Two items are included in the **discontinued operations** section of the income statement: (1) the income or loss from *operating* the segment prior to its disposal and (2) the gain or loss on *disposal* of the segment. Notice also that the income taxes relating to the discontinued operations are *shown separately* from the income taxes expense relating to continuing business operations.

**Discontinued Operations Must Be a Segment of the Business** To qualify for separate presentation in the income statement, the discontinued operations must represent an *entire segment* of the business. A segment of a business is a separate line of business activity or an operation that services a distinct category of customers.

For example, **Pizza Hut** once was a segment of **PepsiCo**. From time to time, PepsiCo closed individual Pizza Hut stores. Such store closures did *not* qualify as discontinued operations, because PepsiCo remained in the pizza parlor business. But when PepsiCo disposed of the entire Pizza Hut chain, these restaurant activities were shown in PepsiCo's income statement as discontinued operations.

**Discontinued Operations Are Not Really Unusual** In recent years, a characteristic of the American economy has been the restructuring of many large corporations. As part of this restructuring, corporations often sell one or more segments of the business. Thus the presence of discontinued operations is not uncommon in the income statements of large corporations.

During 1998, the **Dixie Group, Inc.**, discontinued its textile operations, which consisted of its knit fabric and apparel and the specialty yarns businesses. These operations had generally been unprofitable (approximately $16.9 million operating loss in 1996, $2.8 million operating profit in 1997, and $1.9 million operating loss in 1998). The discontinued operations resulted in a loss on disposal in the 1998 income statement. **Dixie Group**'s income from continuing operations for 1998 was $9,108,000; the loss from discontinued operations (both operations and disposal transactions) of $30,110,000, resulting in a final net loss for 1998 of $21,002,000.

## Extraordinary Items

The second category of irregular events requiring disclosure in a separate section of the income statement is extraordinary items. An **extraordinary item** is a gain or loss that is (1) *unusual in nature* and (2) *not expected to recur in the foreseeable future*. By definition, extraordinary items are rare and do not appear often in the same company's income statements. An example of an extraordinary item is the loss of a company's plant due to an earthquake.

When a gain or loss qualifies as an extraordinary item, it appears after the section on discontinued operations (if any), following the subtotal *income before extraordinary items*. Because the extraordinary item is so unusual, this subtotal is considered necessary to show investors what the net income *would have been* if the extraordinary gain or loss *had not occurred*. Extraordinary items are shown net of any related income tax effects.

**Other Unusual Gains and Losses** Some transactions are not typical of normal operations but also do not meet the criteria for separate presentation as extraordinary items.

Extraordinary items are defined more loosely by Swedish companies than is allowed under the U.S. GAAP and may include such items as gains or losses on the sale of fixed assets, costs associated with plant closures, and foreign currency exchange gains or losses. In the Mexican GAAP, there are no specific definitions of extraordinary items. In practice, however, operations and gains or losses on fixed asset sales that are different from normal activities are considered extraordinary items.

Among such events are losses incurred because of strikes and the gains or losses resulting from sales of plant assets. Such items, if material, should be individually listed as items of revenue or expense, rather than being combined with other items in broad categories such as sales revenue or general and administrative expenses.

In the income statement of Ross Corporation (page 495), the $80,000 loss resulting from the settlement of a lawsuit was listed separately in the income statement but was *not* shown as an extraordinary item. This loss was important enough to bring to the attention of readers of the income statement by presenting it as a separate item, but was not considered so unusual or infrequent enough to be any extraordinary item.

**Distinguishing between the Unusual and the Extraordinary** In the past, some corporate managements had a tendency to classify many *losses* as extraordinary, while classifying most *gains* as a part of normal, recurring operations. This resulted in reporting higher income before extraordinary items, but the final net income figure was not affected. To counter this potentially misleading practice, the accounting profession now defines extraordinary items very carefully and intends for them to be quite rare.

A key question is whether the event is *likely to happen again,* considering the company's environment. A farm located along the banks of the Mississippi River may, from time to time, incur flood damage. Even if these floods are, say, 10 years apart, the resulting losses would *not* be considered extraordinary. Such losses *are* expected to happen again in the foreseeable future.

Now consider a business located in San Francisco that sustains damage from an earthquake. Earthquakes do recur in this region, but the likelihood of one particular business sustaining material damage in multiple incidents is remote. Therefore, material damage caused by earthquakes generally *is* considered extraordinary. The same reasoning applies to tornadoes and lightning—such events are not expected to strike twice in the same place.

There is no comprehensive list of extraordinary items. Thus the classification of a specific event is a matter of *judgment*. The following table is intended to provide you with general guidance on how these judgments are made.

| Event | Analysis |
|---|---|
| Losses from a natural disaster that affects the company at *infrequent* intervals. | Not extraordinary—likely to happen again. |
| Losses from a natural disaster *not* likely to affect the company again. | Extraordinary—not expected to happen again. |
| Gains or losses from seizures of assets by a government—either through expropriation or condemnation. | Specifically called extraordinary by the FASB. For a multinational company, such losses may happen again. But for political reasons, it is better to assume that they won't. |
| *Material* loss from theft. | Extraordinary. Small theft losses, like shoplifting, are routine. But *material* theft losses are not. |
| Losses from inventories that have become obsolete. | Not extraordinary—a normal business risk. |
| Losses from an inventory made unsalable by a *newly enacted law.* | The FASB specifically identifies as extraordinary the immediate financial impact of newly enacted laws or regulations. |
| Receipt by a company of a large gift. | Does not appear in the income statement. Assets received as a gift are accounted for as *donated capital* (see Chapter 11). |
| Losses incurred from *acts of terrorism,* such as the bombing of the World Trade Center in New York. | Extraordinary—not likely to affect the same business twice. (The judgmental element of financial reporting involves *social responsibility.* Most accountants would be reluctant to dignify acts of terrorism as being anything other than isolated events.) |

**CASE IN POINT**

The most common type of extraordinary item is a gain or loss a company sustains when it repays its own debt. For example, **Sears, Roebuck & Company**'s 1999 annual report includes an extraordinary loss of $24 million in its 1998 income statement, presented for comparative purposes. This gain resulted from the early retirement of debt that was due in 2000 at a loss of $37 million, reducing income taxes by $13 million, for a net loss of $24 million. This extraordinary loss caused the company's 1998 net income to decline from the net income before extraordinary items of $1,072 million to $1,048 million.

**Restructuring Charges**  One important type of unusual loss relates to restructuring of operations. As indicated previously, restructuring of operations has become a common aspect of the American economy. In fact, the 1990s were sometimes called the decade of corporate downsizing. As companies struggle to meet the competitive challenges of a global economy, they incur significant costs to close plants, reduce workforces, and consolidate operating facilities.

**Restructuring charges** consist of items such as losses on write-downs or sales of plant assets, severance pay for terminated workers, and expenses related to the relocation of operations and remaining personnel. In determining operating income they are presented in the company's income statement as a single item like the loss incurred in the settlement of a lawsuit in the Ross Corporation income statement on page 495. If the restructuring involves discontinuing a segment of the business, the expenses related to that aspect of the restructuring are presented as discontinued operations.

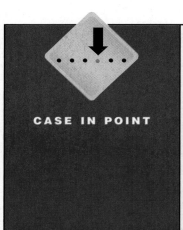

**CASE IN POINT**

**Black & Decker Corporation** recently reported the following information (in millions):

| | |
|---|---|
| Sales | $4,914.4 |
| Cost of goods sold | 3,156.6 |
| Selling, general, and administrative expenses | 1,309.6 |
| Restructuring costs | 91.3 |
| Operating income | $ 356.9 |

A financial statement note explains that a major component of the $91.3 million restructuring costs was the elimination of approximately 1,500 positions and, as a result, an accrual of $74.6 million for the severance of employees. Further explanation indicates that the company plans to outsource certain products that are currently manufactured by the company and, as a result, is closing several small manufacturing facilities. This resulted in an additional $6.6 million write-down to fair value of land and building being included in the restructuring charge, as were other write-downs of equipment made obsolete or redundant due to decisions to close certain facilities.

## Changes in Accounting Principles

The accounting principle of *consistency* refers to the fact that a business generally should continue to use the same accounting principles and methods from one period to the next. However, this principle does not mean that a business can *never* make a change in its accounting methods. A change may be made if the need for the change can be justified and the effects of the change are *properly disclosed* in the financial statements.

**The Cumulative Effect of an Accounting Change**  In reporting most changes in accounting principle, the *cumulative effect* of the change on the income of *prior* years is shown in the income statement of the year in which the change is made. To compute this one-time "catch-up adjustment," we recompute the income of prior years *as if the new accounting method had always been in use.* The difference between this recomputed net income and the net income actually reported in those periods is the cumulative effect of the accounting change.

To illustrate, assume that Ross Corporation has been using the double-declining-balance method of depreciation but decides in the current year to change to the straight-line method. The company determines that if the straight-line method had always been in use, the total net income of prior years would have been $140,000 higher than was actually reported. This $140,000 is the *cumulative effect* of the change in accounting principle and is shown as a separate item in the current year's income statement (following discontinued operations and extraordinary items, if any). Depreciation expense in the current and future years' income statements is computed by the straight-line method, just as if this method had always been in use.

**Changes in Principle versus Changes in Estimate**   A change in accounting principle refers to a change in the *method* used to compute financial statement amounts, rather than a change in the underlying estimates. For example, a switch from straight-line to another method of computing depreciation is regarded as a change in accounting principle. However, a change in the estimated useful life used in computing depreciation expense is a *change in estimate.* This distinction is an important one. When we change an accounting *principle* (method), the cumulative effect of the change on the income of prior years usually is reported as a one-time adjustment to income in the year of the change. Changes in *estimate,* however, affect only the current year and future years; no effort is made to recompute the income of prior years.

---

YOUR TURN

### You as an Investor

One of the most important determinants of a company's stock price is expected future earnings. Assume that you are considering investing in Unison Corporation and are evaluating the company's profitability in the current year. The net income of the corporation, which amounted to $3,000,000, includes the following items:

| | |
|---|---|
| Loss on a discontinued segment of the business (net of income tax benefit) | $750,000 |
| Extraordinary loss (net of income tax benefit) | 300,000 |
| Cumulative effect of change in accounting principle (increase in net income, net of related income taxes) | 500,000 |

Adjust net income to develop a number that represents a good starting point for predicting the future net income of Unison Corporation. Explain the reason for each of the adjustments. Explain how this adjusted number may help you predict future earnings for the company.

*Our comments appear on page 531.

---

## Earnings per Share (EPS)

One of the most widely used accounting statistics is **earnings per share** of common stock. Investors who buy or sell stock in a corporation need to know the annual earnings per share. Stock market prices are quoted on a per-share basis. If you are considering investing in a company's stock at a price of $100 per share, you need to know the earnings per share and the annual dividend per share to decide whether this price is reasonable. In other words, how much earning power and how much dividend income would you be getting for each share you buy?

LO 2

Compute earnings per share.

**Computing Earnings per Share**   To compute earnings per share, the common stockholders' share of the company's net income is divided by the average number of common shares outstanding. The concept of earnings per share applies only to *common stock;* preferred stockholders have no claim to earnings beyond the stipulated preferred stock dividends.

Computing earnings per share is easiest when the corporation has issued only common stock, and the number of outstanding shares has not changed during the year. In this case, earnings per share is equal to net income divided by the number of shares outstanding.

**What Happens If More Shares Are Issued?**   In many companies, the number of shares of stock outstanding changes one or more times during the year. If additional shares are sold during the year, or if shares of common stock are retired (repurchased from the shareholders), the computation of earnings per share is based on the *weighted-average* number of shares outstanding.[1]

The weighted-average number of shares for the year is determined by multiplying the number of shares outstanding by the fraction of the year that number of shares outstanding remained unchanged. For example, assume that 100,000 shares of common stock were outstanding during the first nine months of 2002 and 140,000 shares during the last three months. The increase in shares outstanding resulted from the sale of 40,000 shares for cash. The weighted-average number of shares outstanding during 2002 is *110,000,* determined as follows:

| | |
|---|---:|
| 100,000 shares $\times$ $^9/_{12}$ of a year . . . . . . . . . . . . . . . . . . . . . . . . . . . . . . . . . . . . . . . | 75,000 |
| 140,000 shares $\times$ $^3/_{12}$ of a year . . . . . . . . . . . . . . . . . . . . . . . . . . . . . . . . . . . . . . . | 35,000 |
| Weighted-average number of common shares outstanding . . . . . . . . . . . . . . . . . . . . . | 110,000 |

This procedure gives more meaningful earnings per share data than if the total number of shares outstanding at the end of the year were used in the calculations. The numerator in the earnings per share calculation is net income, which was earned over the entire accounting period (a year in this example). By using the weighted-average number of shares, we recognize that the cash received from the sale of the 40,000 additional shares was available to generate earnings only during the last three months of the year. Although the weighted-average number of shares outstanding is used in earnings per share computations, this figure does not appear in the stockholders' equity section of the balance sheet. A balance sheet prepared at year-end reports the *actual* number of shares outstanding at that date, regardless of when these shares were issued.

**Preferred Dividends and Earnings per Share**   When a company has preferred stock outstanding, the preferred stockholders participate in net income only to the extent of the preferred stock dividends. To determine the earnings *applicable to the common stock,* we first deduct from net income the amount of current year preferred dividends. The annual dividend on *cumulative* preferred stock is *always* deducted, even if not declared by the board of directors for the current year. Noncumulative preferred dividends are deducted only if declared.

To illustrate, let us assume that Tanner Corporation has 200,000 shares of common stock and 10,000 shares of $6 cumulative preferred stock outstanding throughout the

---

[1] When the number of shares outstanding changes as a result of a stock split or a stock dividend (discussed later in this chapter), the computation of the weighted-average number of shares outstanding should be adjusted *retroactively* rather than weighted for the period the new shares were outstanding. This makes earnings per share data for prior years consistent in terms of the current capital structure.

year. Net income for the year totals $560,000. Earnings per share of common stock would be computed as follows:

| | |
|---|---:|
| Net income .................................................................. | $560,000 |
| Less: Dividends on preferred stock (10,000 shares × $6) ..................... | 60,000 |
| Earnings applicable to common stock ....................................... | $500,000 |
| Weighted-average number of common shares outstanding .................... | 200,000 |
| Earnings per share of common stock ($500,000 ÷ 200,000 shares) ............. | $2.50 |

Even when there are preferred dividends in arrears, only the *current year's* cumulative preferred stock dividend is deducted in the earnings per share computation. Dividends in arrears from previous years have already been deducted in the prior years' earnings per share computations.

**Presentation of Earnings per Share in the Income Statement**   All publicly owned corporations are *required* to present earnings per share figures in their income statements.[2] If an income statement includes subtotals for income from continuing operations, or for income before extraordinary items, per-share figures are shown for these amounts as well as for net income. These additional per-share amounts are computed by substituting the amount of the appropriate subtotal for the net income figure in the preceding calculation.

To illustrate all of the potential per-share computations, we will expand our Tanner Corporation example to include income from continuing operations and income before extraordinary items. We should point out, however, that all of these figures seldom appear in the same income statement. Very few companies have discontinued operations, an extraordinary item, and an accounting change to report in the same year. The condensed income statement shown on the following page is intended to illustrate the proper format for presenting earnings per share figures and to provide a review of the calculations.

**Interpreting the Different per-Share Amounts**   To informed users of financial statements, each of these figures has a different significance. Earnings per share from continuing operations represents the results of continuing and ordinary business activity. This figure is the most useful one for predicting future operating results. *Net earnings* per share, on the other hand, shows the overall operating results of the current year, including any discontinued operations or extraordinary items.

## FINANCIAL ANALYSIS

The relationship between earnings per share and stock price is expressed by the **price-earnings (p/e) ratio**. This ratio is simply the current stock price divided by the earnings per share for the year (last four quarters). (A p/e ratio is *not* computed if the company has sustained a net *loss* for this period.) P/e ratios are of such interest to investors that they are published daily in the financial pages of major newspapers. Price-earnings ratios and other measures useful for evaluating financial performance are covered in Chapter 14.

Stock prices actually reflect investors' expectations of *future* earnings. The p/e ratio, however, is based on the earnings over the *past* year. Thus, if investors expect earnings to *increase* substantially from current levels, the p/e ratio will be quite high—perhaps

---

[2] The FASB has exempted closely held corporations (those not publicly owned) from the requirement of computing and reporting earnings per share.

20, 30, or even more. But if investors expect earnings to *decline* from current levels, the p/e ratio will be quite low, say, 8 or less. A mature company with very stable earnings usually sells between 10 and 12 times earnings. Thus the p/e ratio reflects *investors' expectations* of the company's future prospects.[3]

Unfortunately, the term *earnings per share* often is used without qualification in referring to various types of per-share data. When using per-share information, it is important to know exactly *which* per-share statistic is being presented. For example, the price-earnings ratios (market price divided by earnings per share) for common stocks listed on major stock exchanges are reported daily in *The Wall Street Journal* and many other newspapers. Which earnings per share figures are used in computing these ratios? If a company reports an extraordinary gain or loss, the price-earnings ratio is computed using the per-share *earnings before the extraordinary item.* Otherwise, the ratio is based on *net earnings*.

## Basic and Diluted Earnings per Share

**LO 3**

Distinguish between basic and diluted earnings per share.

Let us assume that a company has an outstanding issue of preferred stock that is convertible into shares of common stock at a rate of two shares of common stock for each share of preferred stock. The conversion of this preferred stock would increase the number of common shares outstanding and might *dilute* (reduce) earnings per share. Any common stockholder interested in the trend of earnings per share needs to know what effect the conversion of the preferred stock would have on earnings per share of common stock. Keep in mind that the decision to convert the preferred shares into common shares is made by the stockholders, not the corporation.

*Earnings per share figures are required in the income statements of publicly owned companies*

| TANNER CORPORATION<br>Condensed Income Statement<br>For the Year Ended December 31, 2002 | | |
|---|---|---|
| Net sales | | $9,000,000 |
| Costs and expenses (including taxes on continuing operations) | | 8,310,000 |
| Income from continuing operations | | $ 690,000 |
| Loss from discontinued operations (net of income tax benefits) | | (90,000) |
| Income before extraordinary items and cumulative effect of accounting change | | $ 600,000 |
| Extraordinary loss (net of income tax benefit) | $(120,000) | |
| Cumulative effect of accounting change (net of related income taxes) | 80,000 | (40,000) |
| Net income | | $ 560,000 |
| **Earnings per share of common stock:** | | |
| Earnings from continuing operations | | $3.15[a] |
| Loss from discontinued operations | | (.45) |
| Earnings before extraordinary items and cumulative effect of accounting change | | $2.70[b] |
| Extraordinary loss | | (.60) |
| Cumulative effect of accounting change | | .40 |
| Net earnings | | $2.50[c] |

[a]($690,000 − $60,000 preferred dividends) ÷ 200,000 shares
[b]($600,000 − $60,000) ÷ 200,000 shares
[c]($560,000 − $60,000) ÷ 200,000 shares

---

[3] A word of caution—if current earnings are *very low,* the p/e ratio tends to be quite high *regardless* of whether future earnings are expected to rise or fall. In such situations, the p/e ratio is not a meaningful measurement.

To inform investors of the potential dilution that might occur, two figures are presented for each income number from the income statement. The first figure, called **basic earnings per share**, is based on the weighted-average number of common shares *actually outstanding* during the year. This figure excludes the potential dilution represented by the convertible preferred stock. The second figure, called **diluted earnings per share**, incorporates the *impact that conversion* of the preferred stock would have on basic earnings per share.

Basic earnings per share are computed in the same manner as illustrated in our preceding example of Tanner Corporation. Diluted earnings per share, on the other hand, are computed on the assumption that all the preferred stock *had been converted into common stock at the beginning of the current year.*[4] (The mechanics of computing diluted earnings per share are covered in more advanced accounting courses.)

Diluted earnings per share represent a *hypothetical case* and are often referred to as *pro forma calculations,* meaning that they incorporate events and transactions that have not yet occurred. Diluted earnings per share are computed even though the preferred stock actually was *not* converted during the year. The purpose of showing diluted earnings per share is to alert common stockholders to what *could* have happened. When the difference between basic and diluted earnings per share is significant, investors should recognize the *risk* that future earnings per share may be reduced by conversions of other securities into additional shares of common stock.

When a company reports both basic and diluted earnings per share, the price-earnings ratio shown in newspapers is based on the *basic figure.*

Management's choice among the available types of stock to issue—that is, common stock, preferred stock, or another type of hybrid stock—is influenced by the firm's strategies, goals, and the type of investors that own the stock. In particular, the choice of redeemable preferred stock may be influenced by the tax code. Because financial reporting requirements differ from IRS requirements, companies sometimes create certain attributes of preferred stock that can be treated as debt for tax purposes but may appear as equity for financial reporting purposes.

**MANAGEMENT STRATEGY**

## OTHER TRANSACTIONS AFFECTING RETAINED EARNINGS

### Cash Dividends

Investors buy stock in a corporation in the hope of getting their original investment back as well as a reasonable return on that investment. The return on a stock investment is a combination of two forms: (1) the increase in value of the stock (stock appreciation) and (2) **cash dividends**.

**LO 4**

Account for cash dividends and stock dividends, and explain the effects of these transactions on a company's financial statement.

Many profitable corporations do not pay dividends. Generally, these corporations are in an early stage of development and must conserve cash for the purchase of plant and equipment or for other needs of the company. These so-called growth companies cannot obtain sufficient financing at reasonable interest rates to finance their operations, so they must rely on their earnings. Often only after a significant number of years of profitable operations does the board of directors decide that paying cash dividends is appropriate.

---

[4] If the preferred stock had been issued during the current year, we would assume that it was converted into common stock on the date it was issued.

The preceding discussion suggests three requirements for the payment of a cash dividend. These are:

1. *Retained earnings.* Since dividends represent a distribution of earnings to stockholders, the theoretical maximum for dividends is the total undistributed net income of the company, represented by the credit balance of the Retained Earnings account. As a practical matter, many corporations limit dividends to amounts significantly less than annual net income, in the belief that a major portion of the net income must be retained in the business if the company is to grow and to keep pace with its competitors.

2. *An adequate cash position.* The fact that the company reports large earnings does not necessarily mean that it has a large amount of cash on hand. Cash generated from earnings may have been invested in new plant and equipment, or in paying off debts, or in acquiring a larger inventory. There is no necessary relationship between the balance in the Retained Earnings account and the balance in the Cash account. The traditional expression of "paying dividends out of retained earnings" is misleading. Cash dividends can be paid only out of cash.

3. *Dividend action by the board of directors.* Even though a company's net income is substantial and its cash position seemingly satisfactory, dividends are not paid automatically. A formal action by the board of directors is necessary to declare a dividend.

**YOUR TURN**

### You as a Board Member

Assume that you are a member of the board of directors of Petstuff, Inc., a chain of pet supply stores. The corporation has been in existence for about eight years and has grown significantly in terms of number of stores, sales, and net income.

At a recent stockholders' meeting, several stockholders complained that the board of directors were unethically refusing to declare and distribute cash dividends. They noted that the corporation had been retaining a large amount of earnings and that these earnings should be distributed to the stockholders. How would you respond to the concerns of these stockholders?

*Our comments appear on page 531.

## Dividend Dates

Four significant dates are involved in the distribution of a dividend. These are:

1. *Date of declaration.* On the day on which the dividend is declared by the board of directors, a liability to make the payment comes into existence.

2. *Ex-dividend date.* The **ex-dividend date** is significant for investors in companies whose stocks trade on stock exchanges. To permit the compilation of the list of stockholders as of the record date, it is customary for the stock to go *ex-dividend* three business days before the date of record (see following discussion). A person who buys the stock before the ex-dividend date is entitled to receive the dividend that has already been declared; conversely, a stockholder who sells shares before the ex-dividend date does not receive the dividend. A stock is said to be selling ex-dividend on the day that it *loses* the right to receive the latest declared dividend.

3. *Date of record.* The **date of record** follows the date of declaration, usually by two or three weeks, and is always stated in the dividend declaration. To be eligible to receive the dividend, a person must be listed in the corporation's records as the owner of the stock on this date.

4. *Date of payment.* The declaration of a dividend always includes announcement of the date of payment as well as the date of record. Usually the date of payment comes two to four weeks after the date of record.

Journal entries are required only on the dates of declaration and of payment, as these are the only transactions affecting the corporation declaring the dividend. These entries are illustrated below:

| | | | |
|---|---|---|---|
| Dec. 15 | Dividends . . . . . . . . . . . . . . . . . . . . . . . . . . . . . . . . . . . . . . . . . . | 100,000 | | *Entries made on declaration* |
| | Dividends Payable . . . . . . . . . . . . . . . . . . . . . . . . . . . . . . | | 100,000 | *date and . . .* |
| | To record declaration of a cash dividend of $1 per share on the 100,000 shares of common stock outstanding. Payable Jan. 25 to stockholders of record on Jan. 10. | | | |

| | | | |
|---|---|---|---|
| Jan. 25 | Dividends Payable . . . . . . . . . . . . . . . . . . . . . . . . . . . . . . . | 100,000 | | *on payment date* |
| | Cash . . . . . . . . . . . . . . . . . . . . . . . . . . . . . . . . . . . . . . . . . | | 100,000 | |
| | To record payment of $1 per share dividend declared Dec. 15 to stockholders of record on Jan. 10. | | | |

Notice that no entries are made on either the ex-dividend date or the date of record. These dates are of importance only in determining *to whom* the dividend checks should be sent. From the stockholders' point of view, it is the *ex-dividend date* that determines who receives the dividend. The date of record is of significance primarily to the stock transfer agent and the stock registrar.

Just when is the ex-dividend date in our example? It falls three *business days* before the date of record. Weekends and holidays are not counted as "business days." Thus, if January 10 is a Friday, the ex-dividend date is *January 7*. But if January 10 falls on a Monday, the ex-dividend date would be *January 5*. In this case, investors would need to purchase their shares on or before *January 4* if they are to receive this dividend.

At the end of the accounting period, a closing entry is required to transfer the debit balance of the Dividends account into the Retained Earnings account. (Some companies follow the alternative practice of debiting Retained Earnings when the dividend is declared instead of using a Dividends account. Under either method, the balance of the Retained Earnings account ultimately is reduced by all dividends declared during the period.)

Most dividends are paid in cash, but occasionally a dividend declaration calls for payment in assets *other than* cash. A large distillery once paid a dividend consisting of a bottle of whiskey for each share of stock. (This must have posed quite a storage problem to an investor owning several thousand shares.) When a corporation goes out of existence (particularly a small corporation with only a few stockholders), it may choose to distribute noncash assets to its owners rather than first converting these assets into cash.

## Liquidating Dividends

A *liquidating dividend* occurs when a corporation pays a dividend that *exceeds the balance in the Retained Earnings account*. Thus the dividend returns to stockholders all or part of their paid-in capital investment. Liquidating dividends usually are paid only when a corporation is going out of existence or is making a permanent reduction in the size of its operations. Normally dividends are paid as a result of profitable operations; stockholders may assume that a dividend represents a distribution of profits unless they are notified by the corporation that the dividend is a return of invested capital.

## Stock Dividends

**Stock dividend** is a term used to describe a distribution of *additional shares of stock* to a company's stockholders in proportion to their present holdings. In brief, the dividend is payable in *additional shares of stock* rather than in cash. Most stock dividends consist of additional shares of common stock distributed to holders of common stock, and our discussion will be limited to this type of stock dividend.

An important distinction must be drawn between a cash dividend and a stock dividend. A *cash dividend* is a distribution of cash by a corporation to its stockholders. Thus a cash dividend reduces both assets and stockholders' equity. In a *stock dividend,* however, *no assets are distributed.* Thus a stock dividend causes *no change* in assets or in total stockholders' equity. Each stockholder receives additional shares, but his or her percentage ownership in the corporation is *no larger than before.*

To illustrate this point, assume that a corporation with 2,000 shares of stock is owned equally by James Davis and Susan Miller, each owning 1,000 shares of stock. The corporation declares a stock dividend of 10% and distributes 200 additional shares (10% of 2,000 shares), with 100 shares going to each of the two stockholders. Davis and Miller now hold 1,100 shares apiece, but each *still owns one-half of the business.* Furthermore, the corporation has not changed in size; its assets and liabilities and its total stockholders' equity are exactly the same as before the dividend.

Now let us consider the logical effect of this stock dividend on the *market price* of the company's stock. Assume that before the stock dividend, the outstanding 2,000 shares in our example had a market price of $110 per share. This price indicates a total market value for the corporation of $220,000 (2,000 shares $\times$ $110 per share). As the stock dividend does not change total assets or total stockholders' equity, the total market value of the corporation *should remain $220,000* after the stock dividend. As 2,200 shares are now outstanding, the market price of each share *should fall* to $100 ($220,000 $\div$ 2,200 shares). In short, the market value of the stock *should fall in proportion* to the number of new shares issued. Whether the market price per share *will* fall in proportion to a small increase in number of outstanding shares is another matter. (In fact, market price may *rise* after the declaration of a stock dividend. Puzzling, but true.)

**Entries to Record a Stock Dividend**   In accounting for relatively *small* stock dividends (say, less than 20%), the *market value* of the new shares is transferred from the Retained Earnings account to the paid-in capital accounts. This process sometimes is called *capitalizing* retained earnings. The overall effect is the same as if the dividend had been paid in cash, and the stockholders had immediately reinvested the cash in the business in exchange for additional shares of stock. Of course, no cash actually changes hands—the new shares of stock are sent directly to the stockholders.

To illustrate, assume that on June 1, Aspen Corporation has outstanding 100,000 shares of $5 par value common stock with a market value of $25 per share. On this date, the company declares a 10% stock dividend, distributable on July 15 to stockholders of record on June 20. The entry at June 1 to record the *declaration* of this dividend is:

| | | |
|---|---|---|
| *Stock dividend declared; note use of market price of stock* | Retained Earnings ........................................ | 250,000 | |
| | Stock Dividend to Be Distributed ............................ | | 50,000 |
| | Additional Paid-in Capital: Stock Dividends .................... | | 200,000 |
| | Declared a 10% stock dividend consisting of 10,000 shares (100,000 shares $\times$ 10%) of $5 par value common stock, market price $25 per share. Distributable July 15 to stockholders of record on June 20. | | |

The Stock Dividend to Be Distributed account is *not a liability* because there is no obligation to distribute cash or any other asset. If a balance sheet is prepared between the date of declaration of a stock dividend and the date of distribution of the shares, this account, as well as Additional Paid-in Capital: Stock Dividends, should be presented in the stockholders' equity section of the balance sheet.

Notice that the Retained Earnings account was reduced by the *market value* of the shares to be issued (10,000 shares $\times$ $25 per share = $250,000). Notice also that *no change* occurs in the total amount of stockholders' equity. The amount removed from the Retained Earnings account was simply transferred into two other stockholders' equity accounts.

On July 15, the entry to record the *distribution* of the dividend shares is:

| | | |
|---|---|---|
| Stock Dividend to Be Distributed . . . . . . . . . . . . . . . . . . . . . . . . . . . . . . . . . | 50,000 | |
|    Common Stock . . . . . . . . . . . . . . . . . . . . . . . . . . . . . . . . . . . . . . . . . . . . | | 50,000 |

Distributed 10,000 share stock dividend declared June 1.

*Stock dividend distributed*

**Reasons for Stock Dividends** Although stock dividends cause *no change* in total assets, liabilities, or stockholders' equity, they are popular both with management and with stockholders. Management often finds stock dividends appealing because they allow management to distribute something of perceived value to stockholders while conserving cash, which may be needed for other purposes like expanding facilities and introducing new product lines.

Stockholders like stock dividends because they receive more shares, often the stock price does *not* fall proportionately, and the dividend is not subject to income taxes (until the shares received are sold). Also, *large* stock dividends tend to keep the stock price down in a trading range that appeals to most investors.

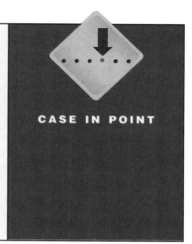

An investor who purchased 100 shares of **Home Depot, Inc.**, early in 1985 would have paid about $1,700. By 2000, 15 years later, that stock was worth about $273,000!

Does this mean that each share increased in value from $17 to more than $2,730? No—in fact, this probably couldn't happen. Investors like to buy stock in lots of 100 shares. At $2,730 per share, who could afford 100 shares? Certainly not the average "small investor."

**Home Depot**'s board of directors *wanted* to attract small investors. These investors help create more demand for the company's stock—and in many cases, they also become loyal customers.

So as the price of **Home Depot**'s stock rose, the board declared numerous stock splits and stock dividends. By 2000, an investor who had purchased 100 shares in 1985 owned over *3,900* shares without ever having had to purchase additional shares. Each share had a market value of up to $70. But, most important, each of these shares was trading at a price affordable to the average investor.

**CASE IN POINT**

**Distinction between Stock Splits and Large Stock Dividends** What is the difference between a 2-for-1 stock split (discussed in Chapter 11) and a 100% stock dividend? There is very little difference; both will double the number of outstanding shares without changing total stockholders' equity, and both should reduce the market price of the stock approximately in half. The stock dividend, however, will not result in a change in the par value of the stock and will be recorded by a transfer from the Retained Earnings account to the contributed capital accounts. For large stock dividends (that is, over 25% of the outstanding stock), the transfer is usually limited to the par or stated value of the stock, rather than the market value, as illustrated earlier. This transfer is made for the sole purpose of maintaining a balance in the stock account that reflects the number of shares that have been issued. A 2-for-1 stock split will reduce the par value per share by one-half, but it will not change the dollar balance of any account.

After an increase in the number of shares as a result of a stock split or stock dividend, earnings per share are computed in terms of the increased number of shares. In presenting 5- or 10-year summaries, the earnings per share for earlier years are *retroactively restated* to reflect the increased number of shares currently outstanding and thus make the year-to-year trend of earnings per share a more valid comparison.

## Statement of Retained Earnings

The term *retained earnings* refers to the portion of stockholders' equity derived from profitable operations. Retained earnings is increased by earning net income and is reduced by incurring net losses and by the declaration of dividends.

 **LO 5**

Describe and prepare a statement of retained earnings.

In addition to a balance sheet, an income statement, and a statement of cash flows, some companies present a **statement of retained earnings**, as illustrated below.

| SALT LAKE CORPORATION<br>Statement of Retained Earnings<br>For the Year Ended December 31, 2002 | | |
|---|---:|---:|
| Retained earnings, Dec. 31, 2001 . . . . . . . . . . . . . . . . . . . . . . | | $ 750,000 |
| Net income for 2002 . . . . . . . . . . . . . . . . . . . . . . . . . . . . | | 280,000 |
|   Subtotal . . . . . . . . . . . . . . . . . . . . . . . . . . . . . . . . . | | $1,030,000 |
| Less dividends: | | |
|     Cash dividends on preferred stock ($5 per share) . . . . . . . . | $ 17,500 | |
|     Cash dividends on common stock ($2 per share) . . . . . . . . . | 55,300 | |
|     10% stock dividend . . . . . . . . . . . . . . . . . . . . . . . . . . . | 140,000 | 212,800 |
| Retained earnings, Dec. 31, 2002 . . . . . . . . . . . . . . . . . . . . . | | $ 817,200 |

Notice that the 2002 net income is added to the beginning balance of retained earnings. Earlier in this text when we studied the accounting cycle, we learned that as part of the end-of-period process of closing the books and preparing financial statements, the revenue and expense accounts are brought to a zero balance, and the net amount of these items (either net income or net loss) is added to or subtracted from owners' equity. For a corporation, net income or loss is added to or subtracted from retained earnings. The addition of net income in the statement of retained earnings is a reflection of this closing process. Notice, also, in the statement of retained earnings that the balance is reduced by the amounts of cash dividends declared during the year, as well as the amount of the stock dividend that was declared. These dividend adjustments to retained earnings are made based on their declaration, even though cash may not have been paid yet (cash dividends) or the stock may not have been issued yet (stock dividend).

## Prior Period Adjustments

**LO 6**

Define *prior period adjustments,* and explain how they are presented in financial statements.

On occasion, a company may discover that a *material error* was made in the measurement of net income in a prior year. Because net income is closed into the Retained Earnings account, an error in reported net income will cause an error in the amount of retained earnings shown in all subsequent balance sheets. When such errors are discovered, they should be corrected. The correction, called a **prior period adjustment**, is shown in the *statement of retained earnings* as an adjustment to the balance of retained earnings at the beginning of the current year. The amount of the adjustment is shown net of any related income tax effects.

To illustrate, assume that late in 2002 Salt Lake Corporation discovers that it failed to record depreciation on certain assets in 2001. After considering the income tax effects of this error, the company finds that the net income reported in 2001 was overstated by $35,000. Thus the current balance of the Retained Earnings account ($600,000 at December 31, 2001) also is *overstated by $35,000*. The statement of retained earnings in *2002* must include a *correction* of the retained earnings at the beginning of the year. (See the illustration on the following page.)

Prior period adjustments rarely appear in the financial statements of large, publicly owned corporations. The financial statements of these corporations are audited annually by Certified Public Accountants and are not likely to contain material errors that subsequently will require correction by prior period adjustments. Such adjustments are much more likely to appear in the financial statements of closely held corporations that are not audited on an annual basis.

**SALT LAKE CORPORATION**
**Statement of Retained Earnings**
**For the Year Ended December 31, 2002**

| | | |
|---|---:|---:|
| Retained earnings, Dec. 31, 2001 | | |
|   As originally reported .................................... | | $750,000 |
|   Less: Prior period adjustment for error in recording 2001 | | |
|     depreciation expense (net of $15,000 income taxes) ......... | | 35,000 |
|   As restated ........................................... | | $715,000 |
| Net income for 2002 ...................................... | | 280,000 |
|   Subtotal ............................................. | | $995,000 |
| Less dividends: | | |
|     Cash dividends on preferred stock ($5 per share) .......... | $ 17,500 | |
|     Cash dividends on common stock ($2 per share) .......... | 55,300 | |
|     10% stock dividend ................................. | 140,000 | 212,800 |
| Retained earnings, Dec. 31, 2002 ......................... | | $782,200 |

*Notice the adjustment to beginning retained earnings*

**Restrictions of Retained Earnings** Some portion of retained earnings may be restricted because of various contractual agreements. A restriction of retained earnings prevents a company from declaring a dividend that would cause retained earnings to fall below a designated level. Most companies disclose restrictions of retained earnings in notes accompanying the financial statements. For example, a company with total retained earnings of $10 million might include the following note in its financial statements:

**Note 7: Restriction of retained earnings**

As of December 31, 2002, certain long-term debt agreements prohibited the declaration of cash dividends that would reduce the amount of retained earnings below $5,200,000. Retained earnings in excess of this restriction total $4,800,000.

*Note disclosure of restrictions placed on retained earnings*

## Comprehensive Income

The Financial Accounting Standards Board (FASB) has identified certain changes in financial position that should be recorded but should not enter into the determination of net income. One way to describe these events is that they are *recognized* (that is, recorded and become a part of the financial statements) but not *realized* (that is, not a part of the determination of the company's net income). We have studied one of these items earlier in this text—the change in market value of available-for-sale debt and equity investments.

Recall from Chapter 7 the way changes in value for various types of investments are recorded. Those investments identified as available for sale are revalued to their current market value at the end of each accounting period. These changes in value are accumulated and reported in a separate stockholders' equity account. The change in value does *not* enter into the determination of net income as it would had investments been sold. The change in market value of available-for-sale investments adds to the amount of stockholders' equity if the value has gone up; it subtracts from the amount of stockholders' equity if the value has gone down. This adjustment is described as an element of *other comprehensive income.*

**Comprehensive income** is a term that identifies the total of net income plus or minus the elements of other comprehensive income. Comprehensive income may be displayed to users of financial statements in any of the following ways:

- *As a second income statement.* One income statement displays the components of net income and the other displays the components of comprehensive income, one element of which is net income.

**LO 7**

Define *comprehensive income,* and explain how it differs from net income.

- *As a single income statement* that includes both the components of net income and the components of other comprehensive income.
- *As an element in the changes in stockholders' equity* displayed as a column in the statement of stockholders' equity (discussed later in this chapter).

In addition to the presentation of each year's changes in the elements of other comprehensive income, the accumulated amount of these changes is an element in the stockholders' equity section of the balance sheet. The components of comprehensive income are presented net of income tax, much like an extraordinary item.

**Tootsie Roll Industries, Inc.**, whose financial statements are included in Appendix A of this text, follows the two income statement approach in presenting both net income and comprehensive income. The final figure in the first 1999 income statement (stated in thousands) is $71,310 and is called net earnings. This item then becomes the starting point for the second income statement that ends with $72,893 and is called comprehensive earnings. The net effect of the two elements of other comprehensive income causes that amount to be slightly higher than net earnings.

---

**CASH EFFECTS**

Transactions between the corporation and its owners that increase or decrease cash are presented in the statement of cash flows as financing activities. Examples are the sale and repurchase of stock and the payment of cash dividends.

Stock dividends and stock splits, on the other hand, are important transactions that affect the company's stockholders' equity, but they do *not* affect the company's cash. Accordingly, they are not included in the statement of cash flows as financing activities. These transactions represent changes *within* the company's stockholders' equity, but they do not affect the total amount of stockholders' equity, nor do they affect the company's cash balances.

---

## Statement of Stockholders' Equity

**LO 8**

Describe and prepare a statement of stockholders' equity.

Many corporations expand their statement of retained earnings to show the changes during the year in *all* of the stockholders' equity accounts. This expanded statement, called a **statement of stockholders' equity**, is illustrated (at the top of the following page) for Salt Lake Corporation.

The top line of the statement includes the beginning balance of each major category of stockholders' equity. Notice that the fourth column, Retained Earnings, is identical to the statement of retained earnings for Salt Lake Corporation that was presented on page 509. All events and transactions that affect retained earnings are the same as those presented in that illustration (prior period adjustment, distribution of stock dividend, net income, and declaration of cash dividends on both preferred and common stock). We have added several other stock transactions to illustrate the full range of information you will typically find in a statement of stockholders' equity:

- Issuance of common stock for $260,000 (resulting in an increase in both common stock and additional paid-in capital).
- Conversion of shares of preferred stock into common stock at $100,000, resulting in a decrease in 5% convertible preferred stock and an increase in common stock and additional paid-in capital.
- Purchase of $47,000 of treasury stock, increasing the amount of treasury stock and decreasing the total of stockholders' equity (as discussed in Chapter 11).

## Stockholders' Equity Section of the Balance Sheet

The stockholders' equity section of Salt Lake Corporation's balance sheet for the year ended December 31, 2002, is shown on the next page. Note that these figures are taken directly from the last line of the statement of stockholders' equity as illustrated on the next page.

| | 5% Convertible Preferred Stock ($100 par value) | Common Stock ($10 par value) | Additional Paid-in Capital | Retained Earnings | Treasury Stock | Total Stockholders' Equity |
|---|---|---|---|---|---|---|
| **SALT LAKE CORPORATION** Statement of Stockholders' Equity For the Year Ended December 31, 2002 | | | | | | |
| Balances, Dec. 31, 2001 | $400,000 | $200,000 | $300,000 | $750,000 | $ –0– | $1,650,000 |
| Prior period adjustment (net of $15,000 taxes) | | | | (35,000) | | (35,000) |
| Issued 5,000 common shares @ $52 | | 50,000 | 210,000 | | | 260,000 |
| Conversion of 1,000 preferred into 3,000 common shares | (100,000) | 30,000 | 70,000 | | | |
| Distributed 10% stock dividend (2,800 shares at $50; market price) | | 28,000 | 112,000 | (140,000) | | |
| Purchased 1,000 shares of common stock held in treasury at $47 a share | | | | | (47,000) | (47,000) |
| Net income | | | | 280,000 | | 280,000 |
| Cash dividends: | | | | | | |
| Preferred ($5 a share) | | | | (17,500) | | (17,500) |
| Common ($2 a share) | | | | (55,300) | | (55,300) |
| Balances, Dec. 31, 2002 | $300,000 | $308,000 | $692,000 | $782,200 | $(47,000) | $2,035,200 |

Note: The numbers that are not bracketed represent positive stockholders' equity amounts. The bracketed numbers represent negative stockholders' equity amounts.

You should be able to explain the nature and origin of each account and disclosure printed in red as a result of having studied this chapter.

The published financial statements of leading corporations indicate that there is no one standard arrangement for the various items making up the stockholders' equity section. Variations occur in the selection of titles, in the sequence of items, and in the extent of detailed classification. Many companies, in an effort to avoid excessive detail in the balance sheet, will combine several related ledger accounts into a single balance sheet item.

| **Stockholders' Equity** | | |
|---|---|---|
| **Capital stock:** | | |
| 5% convertible preferred, $100 par value, 3,000 shares authorized and issued | | $ 300,000 |
| Common stock, $10 par value, 100,000 shares authorized, issued 30,800 (of which 1,000 are held in treasury) | | 308,000 |
| **Additional paid-in capital:** | | |
| From issuance of common stock | $580,000 | |
| From stock dividends | 112,000 | 692,000 |
| Total paid-in capital | | $1,300,000 |
| Retained earnings | | 782,200 |
| Subtotal | | $2,082,200 |
| Less: Treasury stock (1,000 shares at $47 per share) | | 47,000 |
| Total stockholders' equity | | $2,035,200 |

## Home Depot

Now that we have studied the income statement and other changes in retained earnings, let's take a closer look at the **Home Depot, Inc.** annual report for the year ended January 30, 2000. The income statement reveals no irregular items, such as segment disposals, extraordinary items, or changes in accounting principle. This means that for purposes of projecting future profitability, the company's net income figure is more reliable than it would otherwise be. As we would expect, basic earnings per share exceeds diluted earnings per share: $1.03 versus $1.00 for 2001, $.73 versus $.71 for 2000, and $.53 versus $.52 for 1999. This means that there is some risk of reduction in EPS should convertible securities actually be converted to common stock.

**Home Depot** presents a detailed statement of stockholders' equity and comprehensive income in its annual report. This statement discloses the impact of events such as stock purchased for compensation plans, cash dividends to stockholders, and the conversion of certain securities into common stock. Elements of other comprehensive income are presented as part of this financial statement, as opposed to the separate income statement or two income statement approaches described in the text.

As part of management's analysis and interpretation, **Home Depot** presents some interesting information about sales. For example, they disclose the number of sales transactions (797,229,000 in 1999—a 19.9% increase over 1998), and average sale of $47.87 in 1999—a 6.3% increase over 1998), and average weekly sales per operating store ($876,000 in 1999—a 3.8% increase over 1998), and an average sales per square foot of store space ($422.53 in 1999—a 3.1% increase over 1998). This type of detailed information, while not required by generally accepted accounting principles, is very helpful to the serious analyst in better understanding the company's profitability and prospects for the future.

## SUMMARY OF LEARNING OBJECTIVES

### LO 1

**Describe how discontinued operations, extraordinary items, and accounting changes are presented in the income statement.**

Each of these irregular items is shown in a separate section of the income statement, following income or loss from ordinary and continuing operations. Each special item is shown net of any related income tax effects.

### LO 2

**Compute earnings per share.**

Earnings per share are computed by dividing the income applicable to the common stock by the weighted-average number of common shares outstanding. If the income statement includes subtotals for income from continuing operations, or for income before extraordinary items, per-share figures are shown for these amounts, as well as for net income.

### LO 3

**Distinguish between basic and diluted earnings per share.**

Diluted earnings per share are computed for companies that have outstanding securities convertible into shares of common stock. In such situations, the computation of basic earnings per share is based on the number of common shares actually outstanding during the year. The computation of diluted earnings per share, however, is based on the potential number of common shares outstanding if the various securities were converted into common shares. The purpose of showing diluted earnings is to alert investors to the extent to which conversions of securities could reduce basic earnings per share.

### LO 4

**Account for cash dividends and stock dividends, and explain the effects of these transactions on a company's financial statements.**

Cash dividends reduce retained earnings at the time the company's board of directors declares the dividends. At that time, the dividends become a liability for the company. Stock dividends generally are recorded by transferring the market value of the additional shares to be issued from retained earnings to the appropriate paid-in capital accounts. Stock dividends increase the number of shares outstanding but do not change total stockholders' equity, nor do they change the relative amount of the company owned by each individual stockholder.

### LO 5

**Describe and prepare a statement of retained earnings.**

A statement of retained earnings shows the changes in the balance of the Retained Earnings account during the period. In its simplest form, this financial statement shows the beginning balance of retained earnings, adds the net income for the period, subtracts any dividends declared, and thus computes the ending balance of retained earnings.

### LO 6

**Define *prior period adjustments,* and explain how they are presented in financial statements.**

A prior period adjustment corrects errors in the amount of net income reported in a *prior* year. Because the income of the prior year has already been closed into retained earnings, the error is corrected by increasing or decreasing the Retained Earnings account. Prior period adjustments appear in the statement of retained earnings as adjustments to beginning retained earnings. They are *not* reported in the income statement for the current period.

### LO 7

**Define *comprehensive income,* and explain how it differs from net income.**

Net income is a component of comprehensive income. Comprehensive income is broad and includes the effect of certain transactions that are recognized in the financial statements but that are not included in net income because they have not yet been realized. An example is the change in market value of available-for-sale investments. Net income is presented in the income statement. Comprehensive income may be presented in a combined statement with net income, in a separate statement of comprehensive income, or as a part of the statement of stockholders' equity.

### LO 8

**Describe and prepare a statement of stockholders' equity.**

This expanded version of the statement of retained earnings explains the changes during the year in each stockholders' equity account. It is not a required financial statement but is often prepared instead of a statement of retained earnings. The statement lists the beginning balance in each stockholders' equity account, explains the nature and the amount of each change, and computes the ending balance in each equity account.

In the next chapter, we turn our attention to the statement of cash flows. We introduced this statement in Chapter 2 and since then have explained the cash effects of many transactions. Now we will see how a cash flow statement is prepared from accounting records maintained on the accrual basis.

## KEY TERMS INTRODUCED OR EMPHASIZED IN CHAPTER 12

**basic earnings per share** (p. 503) Net income applicable to the common stock divided by weighted-average number of common shares outstanding during the year.

**cash dividend** (p. 503) A distribution of cash by a corporation to its stockholders.

**comprehensive income** (p. 509) Net income plus or minus certain changes in financial position that are recorded as direct adjustments to stockholders' equity (for example, changes in the value of available-for-sale investments) rather than as elements in the determination of net income.

**date of record** (p. 504) The date on which a person must be listed as a shareholder to be eligible to receive a dividend. Follows the date of declaration of a dividend by two or three weeks.

**diluted earnings per share** (p. 503) Earnings per share computed under the assumption that all convertible securities had been converted into additional common shares at the beginning of the current year. The purpose of this pro forma computation is to alert common stockholders to the risk that future earnings per share might be reduced by the conversion of other securities into common stock.

**discontinued operations** (p. 496) The net operating results (revenue and expenses) of a segment of a company that has been or is being sold, as well as the gain or loss on disposal.

**earnings per share** (p. 499) Net income applicable to the common stock divided by the weighted-average number of common shares outstanding during the year.

**ex-dividend date** (p. 504) A date three days prior to the date of record specified in a dividend declaration. A person buying a stock prior to the ex-dividend date also acquires the right to receive the dividend. The three-day interval permits the compilation of a list of stockholders as of the date of record.

**extraordinary items** (p. 496) Transactions and events that are unusual in nature and occur infrequently—for example, most large earthquake losses. Such items are shown separately in the income statement after the determination of income before extraordinary items.

**price-earnings (p/e) ratio** (p. 501) Market price of a share of common stock divided by annual earnings per share.

**prior period adjustment** (p. 508) A correction of a material error in the earnings reported in the financial statements of a prior year. Prior period adjustments are recorded directly in the Retained Earnings account and are not included in the income statement of the current period.

**restructuring charges** (p. 498) Costs related to reorganizing and downsizing the company to make the company more efficient. These costs are presented in the income statement as a single line item in determining operating income.

**segment of a business** (p. 495) Those elements of a business that represent a separate and distinct line of business activity or that service a distinct category of customers.

**statement of retained earnings** (p. 508) A financial statement explaining the change during the year in the amount of retained earnings. May be expanded into a statement of stockholders' equity.

**statement of stockholders' equity** (p. 510) An expanded version of a statement of retained earnings. Summarizes the changes during the year in all stockholders' equity accounts. Not a required financial statement, but widely used as a substitute for the statement of retained earnings.

**stock dividend** (p. 505) A distribution of additional shares to common stockholders in proportion to their holdings.

## DEMONSTRATION PROBLEM

The stockholders' equity of Franklin Corporation at December 31, 2002, is shown below.

| Stockholders' equity: | |
|---|---:|
| Common stock, $10 par, 100,000 shares authorized, 40,000 shares issued | $ 400,000 |
| Additional paid-in capital: Common stock | 200,000 |
| Total paid-in capital | $ 600,000 |
| Retained earnings | 1,500,000 |
| Total stockholders' equity | $2,100,000 |

Transactions affecting stockholders' equity during 2002 are as follows:

**Mar. 31**  A 5-for-4 stock split proposed by the board of directors was approved by vote of the stockholders. The 10,000 new shares were distributed to stockholders.

**Apr. 1**  The company purchased 2,000 shares of its common stock on the open market at $37 per share.

**July 1**  The company reissued 1,000 shares of treasury stock at $48 per share.

**July 1**   Issued for cash 20,000 shares of previously unissued $8 par value common stock at a price of $47 per share.

**Dec. 1**   A cash dividend of $1 per share was declared, payable on December 30, to stockholders of record at December 14.

**Dec. 22**   A 10% stock dividend was declared; the dividend shares are to be distributed on January 15 of the following year. The market price of the stock on December 22 was $48 per share.

The net income for the year ended December 31, 2002, amounted to $177,000, after an extraordinary loss of $47,400 (net of related income tax benefits).

## Instructions

**a.** Prepare journal entries (in general journal form) to record the transactions affecting stockholders' equity that took place during the year.

**b.** Prepare the lower section of the income statement for 2002, beginning with *income before extraordinary items* and showing the extraordinary loss and the net income. Also illustrate the presentation of earnings per share in the income statement, assuming that earnings per share are determined on the basis of the *weighted-average* number of shares outstanding during the year.

**c.** Prepare a statement of retained earnings for the year ending December 31, 2002.

## Solution to the Demonstration Problem

**a.**

| GENERAL JOURNAL | | | Page 1 | |
|---|---|---|---|---|
| **Date** | | **Account Titles and Explanations** | **Debit** | **Credit** |
| Mar. | 31 | Memorandum: A 5-for-4 stock split increased the number of shares of common stock outstanding from 40,000 to 50,000 and reduced the par value from $10 to $8 per share. The 10,000 new shares were distributed. | | |
| Apr. | 1 | Treasury Stock ................................ | 74,000 | |
| | |     Cash .................................... | | 74,000 |
| | | Acquired 2,000 shares of treasury stock at $37. | | |
| July | 1 | Cash ........................................ | 48,000 | |
| | |     Treasury Stock ........................... | | 37,000 |
| | |     Additional Paid-in Capital: Treasury | | |
| | |       Stock Transactions ..................... | | 11,000 |
| | | Sold 1,000 shares of treasury stock at $48 per share. | | |
| | 1 | Cash ........................................ | 940,000 | |
| | |     Common Stock, $8 par ..................... | | 160,000 |
| | |     Additional Paid-in Capital: Common Stock ... | | 780,000 |
| | | Issued 20,000 shares. | | |
| Dec. | 1 | Dividends ................................... | 69,000 | |
| | |     Dividends Payable ........................ | | 69,000 |
| | | To record declaration of cash dividend of $1 per share on 69,000 shares of common stock outstanding (1,000 shares in treasury are not entitled to receive dividends). | | |
| | | **Note:** Entry to record the payment of the cash dividend is not shown here because the action does not affect the stockholders' equity. | | |

| GENERAL JOURNAL (continued) | | | | Page 1 |
|---|---|---|---|---|
| **Date** | | **Account Titles and Explanations** | **Debit** | **Credit** |
| Dec. | 22 | Retained Earnings . . . . . . . . . . . . . . . . . . . . . . . . . . . . . . . . . . . | 331,200 | |
| | |     Stock Dividends to Be Distributed . . . . . . . . . . . . . . . . . | | 55,200 |
| | |     Additional Paid-in Capital: Stock Dividends . . . . . . . . . . . | | 276,000 |
| | | To record declaration of 10% stock dividend | | |
| | |    consisting of 6,900 shares of $8 par value common | | |
| | |    stock to be distributed on Jan. 15 of next year. | | |
| Dec. | 31 | Income Summary . . . . . . . . . . . . . . . . . . . . . . . . . . . . . . . . . . | 177,000 | |
| | |     Retained Earnings . . . . . . . . . . . . . . . . . . . . . . . . . . . . . . . | | 177,000 |
| | | To close Income Summary account. | | |
| Dec. | 31 | Retained Earnings . . . . . . . . . . . . . . . . . . . . . . . . . . . . . . . . | 69,000 | |
| | |     Dividends . . . . . . . . . . . . . . . . . . . . . . . . . . . . . . . . . . . . . . . | | 69,000 |
| | | To close Dividends account. | | |

**b.**

## FRANKLIN CORPORATION
### Partial Income Statement
### For the Year Ended December 31, 2002

| | |
|---|---|
| Income before extraordinary items . . . . . . . . . . . . . . . . . . . . . . . . . . . . . . . . . | $224,400 |
| Extraordinary loss (net of income tax benefits) . . . . . . . . . . . . . . . . . . . . . . . . | (47,400) |
| Net income . . . . . . . . . . . . . . . . . . . . . . . . . . . . . . . . . . . . . . . . . . . . . . . . . | $177,000 |
| Earnings per share:* | |
|   Income before extraordinary items . . . . . . . . . . . . . . . . . . . . . . . . . . . . . . | $3.60 |
|   Extraordinary loss . . . . . . . . . . . . . . . . . . . . . . . . . . . . . . . . . . . . . . . . . | (0.60) |
|   Net income . . . . . . . . . . . . . . . . . . . . . . . . . . . . . . . . . . . . . . . . . . . . . . | $3.00 |

*The 59,000 weighted-average number of shares of common stock outstanding during 2002 determined as follows:

| | |
|---|---|
| Jan. 1–Mar. 31: (40,000 + 10,000 shares issued pursuant to a 5-for-4 split) $\times$ $\frac{1}{4}$ of year . . . . . . . . . . . . | 12,500 |
| Apr. 1–June 30: (50,000 − 2,000 shares of treasury stock) $\times$ $\frac{1}{4}$ of year . . . . . . . . . . . . . . . . . . . . . | 12,000 |
| July 1–Dec. 31: (50,000 + 20,000 shares of new stock − 1,000 shares of treasury stock) $\times$ $\frac{1}{2}$ of year . . | 34,500 |
| Weighted-average number of shares outstanding . . . . . . . . . . . . . . . . . . . . . . . . . . . . . . . . . . . . . . . | 59,000 |

**c.**

## FRANKLIN CORPORATION
### Statement of Retained Earnings
### For the Year Ended December 31, 2002

| | | |
|---|---|---|
| Retained earnings, Dec. 31, 2001 . . . . . . . . . . . . . . . . . . . . . . . . . . . | | $1,500,000 |
| Net income for 2002 . . . . . . . . . . . . . . . . . . . . . . . . . . . . . . . . . . . | | 177,000 |
|   Subtotal . . . . . . . . . . . . . . . . . . . . . . . . . . . . . . . . . . . . . . . . . | | $1,677,000 |
| Less: Cash dividends ($1 per share) . . . . . . . . . . . . . . . . . . . . . . . | $ 69,000 | |
|   10% stock dividend . . . . . . . . . . . . . . . . . . . . . . . . . . . . . . . . . | 331,200 | 400,200 |
| Retained earnings, Dec. 31, 2002 . . . . . . . . . . . . . . . . . . . . . . . . . | | $1,276,800 |

## SELF-TEST QUESTIONS

*Answers to these questions appear on page 531.*

1. The primary purpose of showing special types of events separately in the income statement is to:

   a. Increase earnings per share.

   b. Assist users of the income statement in evaluating the profitability of normal, ongoing operations.

   c. Minimize the income taxes paid on the results of ongoing operations.

   d. Prevent unusual losses from recurring.

2. Which of the following situations would *not* be presented in a separate section of the current year's income statement of Lower Corporation? During the current year:

   a. Lower's St. Louis headquarters are destroyed by a tornado.

   b. Lower sells its entire juvenile furniture operations and concentrates on its remaining children's clothing segment.

   c. Lower's accountant discovers that the entire price paid several years ago to purchase company offices in Texas had been charged to a Land account; consequently, no depreciation has ever been taken on these buildings.

   d. Lower changes from the straight-line method of depreciation to the double-declining-balance method.

3. When a corporation has outstanding both common and preferred stock:

   a. Basic and diluted earnings per share are reported only if the preferred stock is cumulative.

   b. Earnings per share are reported for each type of stock outstanding.

   c. Earnings per share are computed without regard to the amount of dividends declared on common stock.

   d. Earnings per share are computed without regard to the amount of the annual preferred dividends.

4. Which of the following is (are) *not* true about a stock dividend?

   a. Total stockholders' equity does not change when a stock dividend is declared but does change when it is distributed.

   b. Between the time a stock dividend is declared and when it is distributed, the company's commitment is presented in the balance sheet as a current liability.

   c. Stock dividends do not change the relative portion of the company owned by individual stockholders.

   d. Stock dividends have no impact on the amount of the company's assets.

5. The statement of retained earnings:

   a. Need not be prepared if a separate statement of stockholders' equity accompanies the financial statements.

   b. Indicates the amount of cash available for the payment of dividends.

   c. Includes prior period adjustments and cash dividends, but not stock dividends.

   d. Shows revenue, expenses, and dividends for the accounting period.

## ASSIGNMENT MATERIAL

## DISCUSSION QUESTIONS

1. What is the purpose of arranging an income statement to show subtotals for *income from continuing operations* and *income before extraordinary items?*

2. Pappa Joe's owns 30 pizza parlors and a minor league baseball team. During the current year, the company sold three of its pizza parlors and closed another when the lease on the building expired. Should any of these events be classified as discontinued operations in the company's income statement? Explain.

3. Define *extraordinary items*. Give three examples of losses that qualify as extraordinary items and three examples of losses that would *not* be classified as extraordinary.

4. In an effort to make the company more competitive, Rytech, Inc., incurred significant expenses related to a reduction in the number of employees, consolidation of offices and facilities, and disposition of assets that are no longer productive. Explain how these costs should be presented in the financial statements of the company, and describe how an investor should view these costs in predicting future earnings of the company.

5. Both the *cumulative effect of a change in accounting principle* and a *prior period adjustment* relate to the income of past accounting periods. Distinguish between these two items and explain how each is shown in the financial statements.

6. In the current year, Maddox Products decided to switch from an accelerated method of depreciation to the straight-line method. Will the cumulative effect of this change in accounting principle increase or decrease the amount of net income reported in the current year? Explain.

7. *Earnings per share* and *book value per share* are statistics that relate to common stock. When both preferred and common stock are outstanding, explain the computation involved in determining the following:
   a. Earnings allocable to the common stockholders.
   b. Aggregate book value allocable to the common stockholders.

8. Assume a corporation has only common stock outstanding. Is the number of common shares used in the computation of earnings per share *always* the same as the number of common shares used in computing book value per share for this corporation? Is the number of common shares used in computing these two statistics *ever* the same? Explain.

9. Explain how each of the following is computed:
   a. Price-earnings ratio.
   b. Basic earnings per share.
   c. Diluted earnings per share.

10. Throughout the year, Gold Seal Company had 2 million shares of common stock and 150,000 shares of convertible preferred stock outstanding. Each share of preferred is convertible into four shares of common. What number of shares should be used in the computation of (a) basic earnings per share and (b) diluted earnings per share?

11. A financial analyst notes that Wampler Corporation's earnings per share have been rising steadily for the past five years. The analyst expects the company's net income to continue to increase at the same rate as in the past. In forecasting future basic earnings per share, what special risk should the analyst consider if Wampler's basic earnings are significantly larger than its diluted earnings?

12. Explain the significance of the following dates relating to cash dividends: date of declaration, date of record, date of payment, ex-dividend date.

13. What is the purpose of a *stock dividend?*

14. Distinguish between a *stock split* and a *stock dividend*. Is there any reason for the difference in accounting treatment of these two events?

15. What are *prior period adjustments?* How are they presented in financial statements?

16. Identify three items that may appear in a statement of retained earnings as changes in the amount of retained earnings.

17. If a company's total stockholders' equity is unchanged by the distribution of a stock dividend, how is it possible for a stockholder who received shares in the distribution of the dividend to benefit?

18. What is a liquidating dividend, and how does it relate to a regular (nonliquidating) dividend?

19. In discussing stock dividends and stock splits in an investments class you are taking, one of the students says, "Stock splits and stock dividends are exactly the same—both are distributions of a company's stock to existing owners without payment to the company." Do you agree? Why or why not?

20. A *statement of stockholders' equity* sometimes is described as an "expanded" statement of retained earnings. Why?

# EXERCISES

Assume that when you were in high school you saved $1,000 to invest for your college education. You purchased 200 shares of Willis Incorporated, a small but profitable company. Over the three years that you have owned the stock, the corporation's board of directors took the following actions:

1. Declared a 2-for-1 stock split.
2. Declared a 20% stock dividend.
3. Declared a 3-for-1 stock split.

The current price of the stock is $10 per share.

a. Calculate the current number of shares and the market value of your investment.

b. Explain the likely reason the board of directors of the company has not declared a cash dividend.

c. State your opinion as to whether or not you would have been better off if the board of directors had declared a cash dividend instead of the stock dividend and stock splits.

**EXERCISE 12.1**

Stock Dividends and Stock Splits

**LO 4**

The following are 10 technical accounting terms introduced or emphasized in Chapters 11 and 12:

| | | |
|---|---|---|
| P/e ratio | Treasury stock | Discontinued operations |
| Stock dividend | Extraordinary item | Prior period adjustment |
| Basic earnings per share | Stock subscriptions | Diluted earnings per share |
| Comprehensive income | | |

Each of the following statements may (or may not) describe one of these technical terms. For each statement, indicate the term described, or answer "None" if the statement does not correctly describe any of the terms.

a. A gain or loss that is unusual in nature and not expected to recur in the foreseeable future.

b. The asset represented by shares of capital stock that have not yet been issued or subscribed.

c. A distribution of additional shares of stock that reduces retained earnings but causes no change in total stockholders' equity.

d. An agreement to purchase shares of stock at a specified price in the future.

e. An adjustment to the beginning balance of retained earnings to correct an error previously made in the measurement of net income.

f. A statistic expressing a relationship between the current market value of a share of common stock and the underlying earnings per share.

g. A separate section sometimes included in an income statement as a way to help investors evaluate the profitability of ongoing business activities.

h. A pro forma figure indicating what earnings per share would have been if all securities convertible into common stock had been converted at the beginning of the current year.

i. A broadly defined measure of financial performance that includes, but is not limited to, net income.

**EXERCISE 12.2**

Accounting Terminology

**LO 1, 2, 3, 4, 6, 7**

During the current year, SunSports, Inc., operated two business segments: a chain of surf and dive shops and a small chain of tennis shops. The tennis shops were not profitable and were sold near year-end to another corporation. SunSports' operations for the current year are summarized below. The first two captions, "Net sales" and "Costs and expenses," relate only to the company's continuing operations.

**EXERCISE 12.3**

Discontinued Operations

**LO 1, 2**

| | |
|---|---|
| Net sales ........................................... | $10,800,000 |
| Costs and expenses (including applicable income taxes) ................... | 8,600,000 |
| Operating loss from tennis shops (net of income tax benefit) ................ | 192,000 |
| Loss on sale of tennis shops (net of income tax benefit) ................... | 348,000 |

The company had 175,000 shares of a single class of capital stock outstanding throughout the year.

a. Prepare a condensed income statement for the year. At the bottom of the statement, show any appropriate earnings per share figures. (A condensed income statement is illustrated on page 502.)

b. Which earnings per share figure in part **a** do you consider most useful in predicting future operating results for SunSports, Inc.? Why?

---

**EXERCISE 12.4**

Reporting an Extraordinary Item

 **LO 1, 2**

For the year ended December 31, Global Exports had net sales of $9,000,000, costs and other expenses (including income taxes) of $6,200,000, and an extraordinary gain (net of income tax) of $685,000.

a. Prepare a condensed income statement (including earnings per share), assuming that 900,000 shares of common stock were outstanding throughout the year. (A condensed income statement is illustrated on page 502.)

b. Which earnings per share figure is used in computing the price-earnings ratio for Global Exports reported in financial publications such as *The Wall Street Journal*? Explain briefly.

---

**EXERCISE 12.5**

Computing Earnings per Share: Effect of Preferred Stock

**LO 2**

The net income of Tiny Tot Furniture, Inc., amounted to $1,850,000 for the current year.

a. Compute the amount of earnings per share assuming that the shares of capital stock outstanding throughout the year consisted of:

1. 400,000 shares of $1 par value common stock and no preferred stock.
2. 100,000 shares of 8%, $100 par value preferred stock and 300,000 shares of $5 par value common stock. The preferred stock has a call price of $105 per share.

b. Is the earnings per share figure computed in part **a(2)** considered to be basic or diluted? Explain.

---

**EXERCISE 12.6**

Restating Earnings per Share after a Stock Dividend

**LO 2, 4**

The 2002 annual report of Software City, Inc., included the following comparative summary of earnings per share over the last three years:

|  | 2002 | 2001 | 2000 |
|---|---|---|---|
| Earnings per share . . . . . . . . . . . . . . . . . . . . . . . . . . . . . . . | $3.15 | $2.41 | $1.64 |

In 2003, Software City, Inc., declared and distributed a 100% stock dividend. Following this stock dividend, the company reported earnings per share of $1.88 for 2003.

a. Prepare a three-year schedule similar to the one above, but compare earnings per share during the years 2003, 2002, and 2001. (Hint: All per-share amounts in your schedule should be based on the number of shares outstanding *after* the stock dividend.)

b. In preparing your schedule, which figure (or figures) did you have to restate? Why? Explain the logic behind your computation.

---

**EXERCISE 12.7**

Cash Dividends, Stock Dividends, and Stock Splits

 **LO 4**

Universal Cable Corporation has 1,000,000 shares of $1 par value capital stock outstanding on January 1. The following equity transactions occurred during the current year:

**Apr. 30**    Distributed additional shares of capital stock in a 2-for-1 stock split. Market price of stock was $35 per share.

**June 1**    Declared a cash dividend of 60 cents per share.

**July 1**    Paid the 60-cent cash dividend to stockholders.

**Aug. 1**    Declared a 5% stock dividend. Market price of stock was $19 per share.

**Sept. 10**    Issued shares resulting from the 5% stock dividend declared on August 1.

**Dec. 15**    Declared a 50% stock dividend. Market price of stock was $23 per share.

a. Prepare journal entries to record the above transactions.

b. Compute the number of shares of capital stock outstanding at year-end.

c. What is the par value per share of Universal Cable stock at the end of the year?

d. Determine the effect of each of the following on *total* stockholders' equity: stock split, declaration and payment of a cash dividend, declaration and distribution of a small stock dividend, declaration and distribution of a large stock dividend. (Your answers should be either *increase, decrease,* or *no effect.*)

Wansley Corporation has a total of 80,000 shares of common stock outstanding and no preferred stock. Total stockholders' equity at the end of the current year amounts to $5 million and the market value of the stock is $66 per share. At year-end, the company declares a 10% stock dividend—one share for each 10 shares held. If all parties concerned clearly recognize the nature of the stock dividend, what should you expect the market price per share of the common stock to be on the ex-dividend date?

**EXERCISE 12.8**

Effect of Stock Dividends on Stock Price

**LO 4**

Five events pertaining to Lowlands Manufacturing Co. are described below.

a. Declared and paid a cash dividend.

b. Issued a 10% stock dividend.

c. Issued a 2-for-1 stock split.

d. Purchased treasury stock.

e. Reissued the treasury stock at a price greater than the purchase price.

Indicate the immediate effects of the events on the financial measurements in the four columnar headings listed below. Use the code letters **I** for increase, **D** for decrease, and **NE** for no effect.

**EXERCISE 12.9**

Reporting the Effects of Transactions

**LO 8**

| Event | Current Assets | Stockholders' Equity | Net Income | Net Cash Flow (from Any Source) |
|-------|----------------|----------------------|------------|---------------------------------|
|       |                |                      |            |                                 |

Explain the immediate effects, if any, of each of the following transactions on a company's earnings per share:

a. Split the common stock 4-for-1.

b. Realized a gain from the sale of a discontinued operation.

c. Switched from an accelerated method of depreciation to the straight-line method, resulting in a reduction in the Accumulated Depreciation account.

d. Declared and paid a cash dividend on common stock.

e. Declared and distributed a stock dividend on common stock.

f. Acquired several thousand shares of treasury stock.

**EXERCISE 12.10**

Effects of Various Transactions on Earnings per Share

**LO 2, 4**

You have now learned about the following financial statements issued by corporations: balance sheet, income statement, statement of retained earnings, statement of stockholders' equity, and statement of cash flows. Listed below are various items frequently of interest to a corporation's owners, potential investors, and creditors, among others. You are to specify which of the above corporate financial statements, if any, reports the desired information. If the listed item is not reported in any formal financial statement issued by a corporation, indicate an appropriate source for the desired information.

a. Number of shares of stock outstanding as of year-end.

b. Total dollar amount of cash dividends declared during the current year.

c. Market value per share at balance sheet date.

d. Cumulative dollar effect of an accounting error made in a previous year.

e. Cumulative dollar effect of switching from one generally accepted accounting principle to another acceptable accounting method during the current year.

f. Detailed disclosure of why the number of shares of stock outstanding at the end of the current year is greater than the number outstanding at the end of the prior year.

g. Earnings per share of common stock.

h. Book value per share.

i. Price-earnings (p/e) ratio.

j. The total amount the corporation paid to buy back shares of its own stock, which it now holds.

**EXERCISE 12.11**

Where to Find Financial Information

**LO 1, 5, 8**

**EXERCISE 12.12**

Comprehensive Income

**LO 7**

Lane, Inc., had revenues of $450,000 and expenses (other than income taxes) of $250,000 for the current year. The company is subject to a 35% income tax rate. In addition, available-for-sale investments, which were purchased for $17,500 early in the year, had a market value at the end of the year of $19,200.

**a.** Determine the amount of Lane's net income for the year.

**b.** Determine the amount of Lane's comprehensive income for the year.

**c.** How would your answers to parts **a** and **b** differ if the market value of Lane's investments at the end of the year had been $14,200?

**EXERCISE 12.13**

Analysis of Stock Information

**LO 1, 8**

Use the annual report of **Tootsie Roll Industries, Inc.**, in Appendix A of this text to answer these questions:

**a.** Study the income statements of **Tootsie Roll**. Do they include any nonrecurring items that might affect your use of the statements in predicting the future performance of the company?

**b.** Study the stock information included in Note 4 and respond to the following:

   **1.** What is the primary difference between the two classes of common stock that the company has in its capital structure?

   **2.** Has the company been active in issuing stock dividends and/or stock splits and, if so, what has been the impact of these distributions on the number of outstanding shares?

**c.** Looking at the balance sheets for 1998 and 1999:

   **1.** What is the total amount of paid-in capital for each year?

   **2.** For 1999, why is the amount of common stock only $22,815 thousand while the total stockholders' equity is much higher at $430,646 thousand?

## ▮ PROBLEMS

**PROBLEM 12.1**

Reporting Unusual Events; Using Predictive Subtotals

**LO 1, 2**

Atlantic Airlines operated both an airline and several motels located near airports. During the year just ended, all motel operations were discontinued and the following operating results were reported:

| | |
|---|---:|
| **Continuing operations (airline):** | |
|   Net sales . . . . . . . . . . . . . . . . . . . . . . . . . . . . . . . . . . . . . . . . . . | $51,120,000 |
|   Costs and expenses (including income taxes on continuing operations) . . . . . . . | 43,320,000 |
| **Other data:** | |
|   Operating income from motels (net of income taxes) . . . . . . . . . . . . . . . . . . . | 864,000 |
|   Gain on sale of motels (net of income taxes) . . . . . . . . . . . . . . . . . . . . . . . | 4,956,000 |
|   Extraordinary loss (net of income tax benefit) . . . . . . . . . . . . . . . . . . . . . . . | 3,360,000 |

The extraordinary loss resulted from the destruction of an airliner by terrorists.

Atlantic Airlines had 1,000,000 shares of capital stock outstanding throughout the year.

**Instructions**

**a.** Prepare a condensed income statement, including proper presentation of the discontinued motel operations and the extraordinary loss. Include all appropriate earnings per share figures.

**b.** Assume that you expect the profitability of Atlantic's airlines operations to *decline by 6%* next year, and the profitability of the motels to decline by 10%. What is your estimate of the company's net earnings per share next year?

**PROBLEM 12.2**

Format of an Income Statement and a Statement of Retained Earnings

**LO 1, 2, 5, 6**

Shown below (and the top of the following page) are data relating to the operations of Ashton Software, Inc., during 2002.

| | |
|---|---:|
| **Continuing operations:** | |
|   Net sales . . . . . . . . . . . . . . . . . . . . . . . . . . . . . . . . . . . . . . . . . . . . . | $19,850,000 |
|   Costs and expenses (including applicable income taxes) . . . . . . . . . . . . . . . . . | 16,900,000 |

**Other data:**

| | |
|---|---|
| Operating income during 2002 on segment of the business discontinued near year-end (net of income taxes) | 140,000 |
| Loss on disposal of discontinued segment (net of income tax benefit) | 550,000 |
| Extraordinary loss (net of income tax benefit) | 900,000 |
| Cumulative effect of change in accounting principle (increase in net income, net of related income taxes) | 100,000 |
| Prior period adjustment (increase in 2001 depreciation expense, net of income tax benefit) | 350,000 |
| Cash dividends declared | 950,000 |

**Instructions**

**a.** Prepare a condensed income statement for 2002, including earnings per share statistics. Ashton Software, Inc., had 200,000 shares of $1 par value common stock and 80,000 shares of $6.25, $100 par value preferred stock outstanding throughout the year.

**b.** Prepare a statement of retained earnings for the year ended December 31, 2002. As originally reported, retained earnings at December 31, 2001, amounted to $7,285,000.

**c.** Compute the amount of cash dividend *per share of common stock* declared by the board of directors for 2002. Assume no dividends in arrears on the preferred stock.

**d.** Assume that 2003 earnings per share is a single figure and amounts to $8.00. Assume also that there are no changes in outstanding common or preferred stock in 2003. Do you consider the $8.00 earnings per share figure in 2003 to be a favorable or unfavorable statistic in comparison with 2002 performance? Explain.

The income statement below was prepared by a new and inexperienced employee in the accounting department of Aspen, Inc., a business organized as a corporation.

**PROBLEM 12.3**

Reporting Unusual Events: A Comprehensive Problem

**LO 1, 2, 5, 6**

**ASPEN, INC.**
**Income Statement**
**For the Year Ended December 31, 2002**

| | | |
|---|---|---|
| Net sales | | $10,800,000 |
| Gain on sale of treasury stock | | 62,000 |
| Excess of issuance price over par value of capital stock | | 510,000 |
| Prior period adjustment (net of income taxes) | | 60,000 |
| Extraordinary gain (net of income taxes) | | 36,000 |
| Total revenue | | $11,468,000 |
| **Less:** | | |
| Cost of goods sold | $6,000,000 | |
| Selling expenses | 1,104,000 | |
| General and administrative expenses | 1,896,000 | |
| Loss from settlement of litigation | 24,000 | |
| Income taxes on continuing operations | 720,000 | |
| Operating loss on discontinued operations (net of income tax benefit) | 252,000 | |
| Loss on disposal of discontinued operations (net of income tax benefit) | 420,000 | |
| Cumulative effect of change in accounting principle (net of income tax benefit) | 84,000 | |
| Dividends declared on capital stock | 350,000 | |
| Total costs and expenses | | 10,850,000 |
| Net income | | $    618,000 |

### Instructions

**a.** Prepare a corrected income statement for the year ended December 31, 2002, using the format illustrated on page 502. Include at the bottom of your income statement all appropriate earnings-per-share figures. Assume that throughout the year the company had outstanding a weighted average of 200,000 shares of a single class of capital stock.

**b.** Prepare a statement of retained earnings for 2002. (As originally reported, retained earnings at December 31, 2001, amounted to $1,550,000.)

**c.** What does the $62,000 "gain on sale of treasury stock" represent? How would you report this item in Aspen's financial statements at December 31, 2002?

**PROBLEM 12.4**

Effects of Stock Dividends, Stock Splits, and Treasury Stock Transactions

**LO 4**

At the beginning of the year, Foreign Adventures, Inc., has total stockholders' equity of $840,000 and 40,000 outstanding shares of a single class of capital stock. During the year, the corporation completes the following transactions affecting its stockholders' equity accounts:

**Jan. 10** A 5% stock dividend is declared and distributed. (Market price, $20 per share.)

**Mar. 15** The corporation acquires 2,000 shares of its own capital stock at a cost of $21.00 per share.

**May 30** All 2,000 shares of the treasury stock are reissued at a price of $31.50 per share.

**July 31** The capital stock is split 2-for-1.

**Dec. 15** The board of directors declares a cash dividend of $1.10 per share, payable on January 15.

**Dec. 31** Net income of $357,000 (equal to $4.25 per share) is reported for the year ended December 31.

### Instructions

Compute the amount of total stockholders' equity, the number of shares of capital stock outstanding, and the book value per share following each successive transaction. Organize your solution as a three-column schedule with these separate column headings: (1) Total Stockholders' Equity, (2) Number of Shares Outstanding, and (3) Book Value per Share.

**PROBLEM 12.5**

Preparing a Statement of Stockholders' Equity

**LO 4, 8**

The following is a summary of the transactions affecting the stockholders' equity of Marble Oasis Corporation during the current year:

| | |
|---|---:|
| Prior period adjustment (net of income tax benefit) | $ (80,000) |
| Issuance of common stock: 10,000 shares of $10 par value capital stock at $34 per share | 340,000 |
| Declaration and distribution of 5% stock dividend (6,000 shares, market price $36 per share) | (216,000) |
| Purchased 1,000 shares of treasury stock at $35 | (35,000) |
| Reissued 500 shares of treasury stock at a price of $36 per share | 18,000 |
| Net income | 820,000 |
| Cash dividends declared ($1 per share) | (142,700) |

Parentheses ( ) indicate a reduction in stockholders' equity.

### Instructions

**a.** Prepare a statement of stockholders' equity for the year. Use the column headings and beginning balances shown below. (Notice that all additional paid-in capital accounts are combined into a single column.)

| | Capital Stock ($10 par value) | Additional Paid-in Capital | Retained Earnings | Treasury Stock | Total Stockholders' Equity |
|---|---|---|---|---|---|
| Balances, Jan. 1 | $1,100,000 | $1,800,000 | $900,000 | $ –0– | $3,800,000 |

**b.** What was the overall effect on total stockholders' equity of the 5% stock dividend of 6,000 shares? What was the overall effect on total stockholders' equity of the cash dividend declared? Do these two events have the same impact on stockholders' equity? Why or why not?

At the beginning of 2002, OverNight Letter showed the following amounts in the stockholders' equity section of its balance sheet:

**PROBLEM 12.6**

Recording Stock Dividends and Treasury Stock Transactions

**LO 4**

| Stockholders' equity: | |
|---|---:|
| Capital stock, $1 par value, 500,000 shares authorized, 382,000 issued | $ 382,000 |
| Additional paid-in capital: Capital stock | 4,202,000 |
| Total paid-in capital | $4,584,000 |
| Retained earnings | 2,704,600 |
| Total stockholders' equity | $7,288,600 |

The transactions relating to stockholders' equity during the year are as follows:

**Jan. 3**     Declared a dividend of $1 per share to stockholders of record on January 31, payable on February 15.

**Feb. 15**     Paid the cash dividend declared on January 3.

**Apr. 12**     The corporation purchased 6,000 shares of its own capital stock at a price of $40 per share.

**May 9**     Reissued 4,000 shares of the treasury stock at a price of $44 per share.

**June 1**     Declared a 5% stock dividend to stockholders of record at June 15, to be distributed on June 30. The market price of the stock at June 1 was $42 per share. (The 2,000 shares remaining in the treasury do not participate in the stock dividend.)

**June 30**     Distributed the stock dividend declared on June 1.

**Aug. 4**     Reissued 600 of the 2,000 remaining shares of treasury stock at a price of $37 per share.

**Dec. 31**     The Income Summary account, showing net income for the year of $1,928,000, was closed into the Retained Earnings account.

**Dec. 31**     The $382,000 balance in the Dividends account was closed into the Retained Earnings account.

**Instructions**

**a.** Prepare in general journal form the entries to record the above transactions.

**b.** Prepare the stockholders' equity section of the balance sheet at December 31, 2002. Use the format illustrated on page 511. Include a supporting schedule showing your computation of retained earnings at that date.

**c.** Compute the maximum cash dividend per share that legally could be declared at December 31, 2002, without impairing the paid-in capital of OverNight Letter. (Hint: The availability of retained earnings for dividends is restricted by the cost of treasury stock owned.)

Rapid Process, Inc., manufactures a variety of computer peripherals, such as tape drives and printers. Listed below are five events that occurred during the current year.

**PROBLEM 12.7**

Effects of Transactions

**LO 8**

**1.** Declared a $1.00 per share cash dividend.

**2.** Paid the cash dividend.

**3.** Purchased 1,000 shares of treasury stock for $20.00 per share.

**4.** Reissued 500 shares of the treasury stock at a price of $18.00 per share.

**5.** Declared a 15 percent stock dividend.

**Instructions**

**a.** Indicate the effects of each of these events on the financial measurements in the four columnar headings listed on the next page. Use the following code letters: **I** for increase, **D** for decrease, and **NE** for no effect.

| Event | Current Assets | Stockholders' Equity | Net Income | Net Cash Flow (from Any Source) |
|---|---|---|---|---|
| | | | | |

**b.** For each event, *explain* the reasoning behind your answers. Be prepared to explain this reasoning in class.

**PROBLEM 12.8**

Preparing the Stockholders' Equity Section: A Challenging Case

 **LO 4**

The Mandella family decided early in 2001 to incorporate their family-owned vineyards under the name Mandella Corporation. The corporation was authorized to issue 500,000 shares of a single class of $10 par value capital stock. Presented below is the information necessary to prepare the stockholders' equity section of the company's balance sheet at the end of 2001 and at the end of 2002.

**2001.** In January the corporation issued to members of the Mandella family 150,000 shares of capital stock in exchange for cash and other assets used in the operation of the vineyards. The fair market value of these assets indicated an issue price of $30 per share. In December, Joe Mandella died, and the corporation purchased 10,000 shares of its own capital stock from his estate at $34 per share. Because of the large cash outlay to acquire this treasury stock, the directors decided not to declare cash dividends in 2001 and instead declared a 10% stock dividend to be distributed in January of 2002. The stock price at the declaration date was $35 per share. (The treasury shares do not participate in the stock dividend.) Net income for 2001 was $940,000.

**2002.** In January the corporation distributed the stock dividend declared in 2001, and in February, the 10,000 treasury shares were sold to Maria Mandella at $39 per share. In June, the capital stock was split 2-for-1. (Approval was obtained to increase the authorized number of shares to 1 million.) On December 15, the directors declared a cash dividend of $2 per share, payable in January of 2003. Net income for 2002 was $1,080,000.

**Instructions**

Using the format illustrated on page 511, prepare the stockholders' equity section of the balance sheet at:

**a.** December 31, 2001.

**b.** December 31, 2002.

Show any necessary computations in supporting schedules.

**PROBLEM 12.9**

Format of an Income Statement; EPS

 **LO 1, 2**

The following information is excerpted from the financial statements in a recent annual report of Falcon Manufacturing Corporation. (Dollar figures and shares of stock are in thousands.)

| | |
|---|---|
| Extraordinary loss on extinguishment of debt . . . . . . . . . . . . . . . . . . . . . . . . . . . . . | $ (8,490) |
| Loss from continuing operations . . . . . . . . . . . . . . . . . . . . . . . . . . . . . . . . . . . . . . . | $(16,026) |
| Cumulative effect of change in accounting for income taxes . . . . . . . . . . . . . . . . . . | $(28,197) |
| Income from discontinued operations . . . . . . . . . . . . . . . . . . . . . . . . . . . . . . . . . . | $ 6,215 |
| Preferred stock dividend requirements . . . . . . . . . . . . . . . . . . . . . . . . . . . . . . . . . . | $ (2,778) |
| Weighted-average number of shares of common stock outstanding . . . . . . . . . . . . . | 39,739 |

**Instructions**

**a.** Rearrange the items to present in good form the last portion of the income statement for Falcon Manufacturing Corporation, beginning with "Loss from continuing operations."

**b.** Calculate the amount of *net loss* per share for the period. (Do *not* calculate per-share amounts for subtotals, such as income from continuing operations, or loss before extraordinary items, etc. You are required to compute only a single earnings per share amount.)

## CASES AND UNSTRUCTURED PROBLEMS

The following events were reported in the financial statements of large, publicly owned corporations:

**a. Atlantic Richfield Company (ARCO)** sold or abandoned the entire noncoal minerals segment of its operations. In the year of disposal, this segment had an operating loss. **ARCO** also incurred a loss of $514 million on disposal of its noncoal minerals segment of the business.

**b. American Airlines** increased the estimated useful life used in computing depreciation on its aircraft. If the new estimated life had always been in use, the net income reported in prior years would have been substantially higher.

**c. Union Carbide Corp.** sustained a large loss as a result of the explosion of a chemical plant.

**d. AT&T** changed the method used to depreciate certain assets. Had the new method always been in use, the net income of prior years would have been $175 million lower than was actually reported.

**e. Georgia Pacific Corporation** realized a $10 million gain as a result of condemnation proceedings in which a governmental agency purchased assets from the company in a "forced sale."

### Instructions
Indicate whether each event should be classified as a discontinued operation, an extraordinary item, or the cumulative effect of an accounting change or included among the revenue and expenses of normal and recurring business operations. Briefly explain your reasons for each answer.

**CASE 12.1**

What's This?

**LO 1**

Memphis Publishing, Inc. (MPI), publishes two newspapers and, until recently, owned a professional baseball team. The baseball team had been losing money for several years and was sold at the end of 2002 to a group of investors who plan to move it to a larger city. Also in 2002, MPI suffered an extraordinary loss when its Raytown printing plant was damaged by a tornado. The damage has since been repaired. A condensed income statement follows:

**CASE 12.2**

Is There Life without Baseball?

**LO 1**

| MEMPHIS PUBLISHING, INC. Income Statement For the Year Ended December 31, 2002 | | |
|---|---:|---:|
| Net revenue | | $41,000,000 |
| Costs and expenses | | 36,500,000 |
| Income from continuing operations | | $ 4,500,000 |
| Discontinued operations: | | |
|    Operating loss on baseball team | $(1,300,000) | |
|    Gain on sale of baseball team | 4,700,000 | 3,400,000 |
| Income before extraordinary items | | $ 7,900,000 |
| Extraordinary loss: | | |
|    Tornado damage to Raytown printing plant | | (600,000) |
| Net income | | $ 7,300,000 |

### Instructions
On the basis of this information, answer the following questions. Show any necessary computations and explain your reasoning.

**a.** What would MPI's net income have been for 2002 if it *had not* sold the baseball team?

**b.** Assume that for 2003 you expect a 7% increase in the profitability of MPI's newspaper business but had projected a $2,000,000 operating loss for the baseball team if MPI had continued to operate the team in 2003. What amount would you forecast as MPI's 2003 net income *if the company had continued to own and operate the baseball team?*

**c.** Given your assumptions in part **b,** but given that MPI *did* sell the baseball team in 2002, what would you forecast as the company's estimated net income for 2003?

**d.** Assume that the expenses of operating the baseball team in 2002 amounted to $32,200,000, net of any related income tax effects. What was the team's *net revenue* for the year?

**CASE 12.3**

Using Earnings per Share
Statistics

For many years New York Studios has produced television shows and operated several FM radio stations. Late in the current year, the radio stations were sold to Times Publishing, Inc. Also during the current year, New York Studios sustained an extraordinary loss when one of its camera trucks caused an accident in an international grand prix auto race. Throughout the current year, the company had 3 million shares of common stock and a large quantity of convertible preferred stock outstanding. Earnings per share reported for the current year were as follows:

| | Basic | Diluted |
|---|---|---|
| Earnings from continuing operations . . . . . . . . . . . . . . . . . . . . . . . . . . . . . . . . . . | $8.20 | $6.80 |
| Earnings before extraordinary items . . . . . . . . . . . . . . . . . . . . . . . . . . . . . . . . . . | $6.90 | $5.50 |
| Net earnings . . . . . . . . . . . . . . . . . . . . . . . . . . . . . . . . . . . . . . . . . . . . . . . . . . . . | $3.60 | $2.20 |

**Instructions**

**a.** Briefly explain why New York Studios reports diluted earnings per share amounts as well as basic earnings per share. What is the purpose of showing investors the diluted figures?

**b.** What was the total dollar amount of the extraordinary loss sustained by New York Studios during the current year?

**c.** Assume that the price-earnings ratio shown in the morning newspaper for New York Studios' common stock indicates that the stock is selling at a price equal to 10 times the reported earnings per share. What is the approximate market price of the stock?

**d.** Assume that you expect both the revenue and expenses involved in producing television shows to increase by 10% during the coming year. What would you forecast as the company's basic earnings per share for the coming year under each of the following independent assumptions? (Show your computations and explain your reasoning.)

   **1.** *None* of the convertible preferred stock is converted into common stock during the coming year.

   **2.** *All* of the convertible preferred stock is converted into common stock at the beginning of the coming year.

**CASE 12.4**

Interpreting a Statement of
Stockholders' Equity

The following information is excerpted from the Statement of Common Stockholders' Equity included in a recent annual report of **Quaker Oats Company and Subsidiaries**. (Dollar figures are in millions.)

| | Common Stock | | Additional Paid-in Capital | Retained Earnings | Treasury Stock | |
|---|---|---|---|---|---|---|
| | Shares | Amount | | | Shares | Amount |
| Balances, beginning of year | 83,989,396 | $420.0 | $19.5 | $ 998.4 | 4,593,664 | $(132.9) |
| Net income | | | | 203.0 | | |
| Cash dividends declared on common stock | | | | (95.2) | | |
| Common stock issued for stock option plans | | | (1.4) | | (601,383) | 16.7 |
| Repurchases of common stock | | | | | 1,229,700 | (68.6) |
| Balances, year-end | 83,989,396 | $420.0 | $18.1 | $1,106.2 | 5,221,981 | $(184.8) |

## Instructions

Use the information presented on the previous page to answer the following questions.

a. How many shares of common stock are outstanding at the *beginning* of the year? At the *end* of the year?

b. What was the total common stock dividend declared during the presented year? **Quaker**'s annual report disclosed that the common stock dividend during that year was $1.20 per share (30 cents per quarter). Approximately how many shares of common stock were entitled to the $1.20 per share dividend during the year? Is this answer compatible with your answers to part **a**?

c. The statement presented indicates that common stock was both issued and repurchased during the year, yet the number of common shares shown and the common stock amount (first and second columns) did not change from beginning to end of the year. Explain.

d. What was the average price per share **Quaker** paid to acquire the treasury shares held at the *beginning* of the year?

e. Was the aggregate issue price of the 601,383 treasury shares issued during the year for stock option plans higher or lower than the cost **Quaker** paid to acquire those treasury shares? (Hint: Analyze the impact on Additional Paid-in Capital.)

f. What was the average purchase price per share paid by **Quaker** to acquire treasury shares *during the current year?*

g. In its annual report, **Quaker** disclosed that the (weighted) average number of common shares outstanding during the year was 79,307,000. In part **a** above, you determined the number of common shares outstanding as of the end of the year. Which figure is used in computing *earnings per share?* Which is used in computing *book value per share?*

Elliot-Cole is a publicly owned international corporation, with operations in over 90 countries. Net income has been growing at approximately 15% per year, and the stock consistently trades at about 20 times earnings.

To attract and retain key management leadership, the company has developed a compensation plan in which managers receive earnings in the form of bonuses as well as opportunities to purchase shares of the company's stock at a reduced price. In general, the higher the company's net income each year, the greater the benefit to management in terms of their personal compensation.

During the current year, political unrest and economic upheaval threatened Elliot-Cole's business operations in three foreign countries. At year-end, the company's auditors insisted that management write off the company's assets in these countries, stating that these assets were "severely impaired." Said one corporate official, "We can't argue with that. Each of these countries is a real trouble spot. We might be pulling out of these places at any time, and any assets probably would just be left behind."

Management agreed that the carrying value of Elliot-Cole's assets in these three countries should be reduced to "scrap value"—which was nothing. These write-downs amounted to approximately 18% of the company's income *prior* to recognition of these losses. (These write-offs are for financial reporting purposes only; they have *no effect* on the company's income tax obligations.)

At the meeting with the auditors, one of Elliot-Cole's officers states, "There's no doubt we should write these assets off. But of course, this is an extraordinary loss. A loss of this size can't be considered a routine matter."

### CASE 12.5

Classification of Unusual Items—and the Potential Financial Impact

**LO 1, 2, 8**

## Instructions

a. Explain the logic behind writing down the book values of assets that are still in operation.

b. Evaluate the officer's statement concerning the classification of these losses. Do you agree that they should be classified as an extraordinary item? Explain.

c. Explain the effect that the classification of these losses—that is, as ordinary or extraordinary—will have in the current period on Elliot-Cole's:

1. Net income.

2. Income before extraordinary items.

3. Income from continuing operations.

4. Net cash flow from operating activities.

d. Explain how the classification of these losses will affect the p/e ratio reported in newspapers such as *The Wall Street Journal.*

**e.** Does management appear to have any self-interest in the classification of these losses? Explain.

**f.** Explain how (if at all) these write-offs are likely to affect the earnings of *future* periods.

**g.** What "ethical dilemma" confronts management in this case?

## BUSINESS WEEK ASSIGNMENT

BusinessWeek

**CASE 12.6**

**LO 1, 3**

Following is an excerpt from "What the Earnings Reports Don't Tell You," a *Business Week* article by Susan Scherreik published October 16, 2000:

> The curtain is rising on the third-quarter-earnings drama, and the setting is ominous: slower economic growth, higher oil prices, and a weak and stumbling euro. U.S. corporations will be hard pressed to deliver crowd pleasing profits in this scenario, and so now more than ever companies are likely to resort to various accounting games—all perfectly legal—to puff up their profits and win over the audience.
>
> Over the past few years, investment managers and accounting professionals have complained increasingly about the ploys that companies sometimes use to boost their profits: making selective disclosures in earnings releases, paying expenses with stock options, or bolstering the bottom line by taking investment profits when operating profits fall short. "We'll see companies playing the same games as before, only more so," predicts Fred Hickey, editor of The *High-Tech Strategist,* a newsletter in Nashua, N.H.

### Instructions

As an investor in this situation, how would you analyze companies in which you already have investments, as well as companies in which you may be interested in investing? What steps can you take to make sure you have a solid understanding of a company's profitability and prospects for the future?

## INTERNET ASSIGNMENT

**INTERNET 12.1**

Comparing Price-Earnings
Ratios

The normal price-earnings ratio of a company varies depending on expected future earnings of the company and the general price level of the stock market. On average, mature companies have lower price-earnings ratios, usually less than 20, than do emerging companies, which may be over 100. This is because of the steep growth in earnings that is characteristic of an emerging company.

### Instructions

**a.** Visit *Fortune* magazine's Internet site and select a Fortune 500 corporation. The site's address is

**www.fortune.com**

**b.** Visit NASDAQ's home page at

**www.nasdaq.com**

Click on quotes at the top of the screen, then click flash quotes for NASDAQ 100 and select a small corporation.

**c.** Get Detailed Quotes for the companies from PCQUOTE's Internet site at

**www.pcquote.com**

Indicate the current price of each corporation's stock, including its high and low price for the day. (If either of the companies has a net loss for the most recent period, go back and replace it with a profitable company.)

**d.** Compare the price-earnings ratios (as shown on the Detailed Quote screen) of the two companies. Speculate as to why one company has a higher price-earnings ratio than the other.

*Internet sites are time and date sensitive. It is the purpose of these exercises to have you explore the Internet. You may need to use the Yahoo! search engine* http://www.yahoo.com *(or other favorite search engine) to find a company's current web address.*

## OUR COMMENTS ON THE "YOUR TURN" CASES

**As an Investor (p. 499)**   The best starting point for estimating future net income would be income from *continuing operations*. Working backwards from net income, it is calculated as $3,550,000 ($3,000,000 + $750,000 + $300,000 − $500,000). Discontinued operations, extraordinary items, and accounting changes generally would not be expected to be experienced in future years and, therefore, should be eliminated in predicting future amounts.

**As a Board Member (p. 504)**   Just because the corporation has earnings does not mean that there is cash available for dividends. The earnings may be invested in new stores, inventories, or any other type of asset. Because the corporation is small and growing, most likely it needs all the capital it can get. Profitable operations are one of the most important sources of financing for a small business.

It is not unethical to retain earnings in the business. In fact, it might be unethical and illegal to distribute cash dividends if there is significant debt outstanding to creditors. In general, creditors must be satisfied prior to distributing excessive dividends. Many long-term debt agreements prevent distribution of dividends if the result of the distribution is that retained earnings fall below a prespecified level.

To appease the stockholders, the board of directors might consider declaring a stock dividend or a stock split. This would provide the stockholders with additional shares of stock while retaining the company's liquid assets.

## ANSWERS TO SELF-TEST QUESTIONS

**1.** b    **2.** c    **3.** c    **4.** a, b    **5.** a

CHAPTER

# 13

# STATEMENT OF CASH FLOWS

## Learning Objectives

*After studying this chapter, you should be able to:*

1. Explain the purposes and uses of a statement of cash flows.

2. Describe how cash transactions are classified within a statement of cash flows.

3. Compute the major cash flows relating to operating activities.

4. Explain why net income differs from net cash flows from operating activities.

5. Distinguish between the direct and indirect methods of reporting operating cash flows.

6. Compute the cash flows relating to investing and financing activities.

7. Discuss the likely effects of various business strategies on cash flows.

*8. Compute net cash flows from operating activities using the *indirect* method.

†9. Explain how a worksheet may be helpful in preparing a statement of cash flows.

* *Supplemental Topic A,* "The Indirect Method."

† *Supplemental Topic B,* "A Worksheet for Preparing a Statement of Cash Flows."

Harrah's Entertainment, Inc.

# Harrah's Entertainment, Inc.

**Harrah's Entertainment, Inc.**, is best known for its casinos. In the company's 1999 annual report, however, **Harrah's** states that the company's people are its most important asset. The company attributes much of its success to the leadership provided by its employees and management.

Cash flow is an important aspect of any business, but particularly one like **Harrah's** whose primary line of business is entertaining people. Early in this text we introduced the idea that investors and creditors are interested in cash flow information. They want to know that they will receive a reasonable return on the money they have committed, as an investor or creditor, to a company. In addition to a return on their money, they also want the assurance that they will get their investment back at some future time. We refer to these future cash flows as cash flow prospects because they are cash flows that we expect in the future.

● ● ●

Historical cash flow information about a company is helpful to investors and creditors in judging future cash flows from the company to themselves. For that reason, one of the three primary financial statements is the statement of cash flows. We introduced this statement in Chapter 2, and in Chapter 13 we go into considerably more depth to help you understand how a company prepares its statement of cash flows. During 1999, **Harrah's Entertainment**'s cash increased $74,586 thousand, from $158,995 thousand to $233,581 thousand. This includes significant amounts of cash coming in and moving out of the business. For presentation purposes, **Harrah's** classified these cash flows in three categories—operating activities, investing activities, and financing activities. In this chapter, we focus on what is included in each of these categories and how they can help you better understand the financial activities of companies like **Harrah's Entertainment**.

## STATEMENT OF CASH FLOWS

### Purposes of the Statement

**LO 1**

Explain the purposes and uses of a statement of cash flows.

The basic purpose of a statement of cash flows is to provide information about the *cash receipts* and *cash payments* of a business entity during the accounting period. (The term **cash flows** includes both cash receipts and cash payments.) In addition, the statement is intended to provide information about the *investing* and *financing* activities of the company during the period. A statement of cash flows assists investors, creditors, and others in assessing such factors as:

- The company's ability to generate positive cash flows in future periods.
- The company's ability to meet its obligations and to pay dividends.
- The company's need for external financing.
- Reasons for differences between the amount of net income and the related net cash flows from operating activities.
- Both the cash and noncash aspects of the company's investment and financing transactions for the period.
- Causes of the change in the amount of cash and cash equivalents between the beginning and the end of the accounting period.

Stated simply, a statement of cash flows helps users of financial statements evaluate a company's ability to have sufficient cash—both on a short-run and on a long-run basis. For this reason, the statement of cash flows is useful to virtually everyone interested in the company's financial health: short- and long-term creditors, investors, management—and both current and prospective competitors.

**CASE IN POINT**

The governments of Germany, Denmark, Switzerland, and Japan do not require that companies provide their statement of cash flows to investors. Although the French government does not require the statement of cash flows, it does recommend that companies provide a statement of cash flows to their investors. Instead, many governments require a statement called "changes in financial position." Changes in financial position is a statement that describes how an entity's financial resources and obligations have changed from one point in time to another.

### Example of a Statement of Cash Flows

An example of a statement of cash flows appears on the following page. Cash outflows are shown in parentheses.[1]

### Classification of Cash Flows

**LO 2**

Describe how cash transactions are classified within a statement of cash flows.

The cash flows shown in the statement are grouped into three major categories: (1) **operating activities**, (2) **investing activities**, and (3) **financing activities**.[2] We will now look briefly at the way cash flows are classified among these three categories.

**Operating Activities**    The operating activities section shows the *cash effects* of revenue and expense transactions. Stated another way, the operating activities section of the statement of cash flows includes the cash effects of those transactions reported in the income statement. To illustrate this concept, consider the effects of credit sales. Credit

---

[1] In this illustration, net cash flows from operating activities are determined by the *direct method.* An alternative approach, called the *indirect method,* is illustrated later in this chapter.

[2] A fourth classification, "effects of changes in exchange rates on cash," is used in the cash flow statements of companies with foreign currency holdings. This classification, as well as other complexities, are discussed in more advanced accounting courses.

## ALLISON CORPORATION
## Statement of Cash Flows
## For the Year Ended December 31, 2002

**Cash flows from operating activities:**

| | | |
|---|---|---|
| Cash received from customers | $ 870,000 | |
| Interest and dividends received | 10,000 | |
|   Cash provided by operating activities | | $ 880,000 |
| Cash paid to suppliers and employees | $(764,000) | |
| Interest paid | (28,000) | |
| Income taxes paid | (38,000) | |
|   Cash disbursed for operating activities | | (830,000) |
| Net cash flows from operating activities | | $ 50,000 |

**Cash flows from investing activities:**

| | | |
|---|---|---|
| Purchases of marketable securities | $ (65,000) | |
| Proceeds from sales of marketable securities | 40,000 | |
| Loans made to borrowers | (17,000) | |
| Collections on loans | 12,000 | |
| Purchases of plant assets | (160,000) | |
| Proceeds from sales of plant assets | 75,000 | |
| Net cash flows from investing activities | | (115,000) |

**Cash flows from financing activities:**

| | | |
|---|---|---|
| Proceeds from short-term borrowing | $ 45,000 | |
| Payments to settle short-term debts | (55,000) | |
| Proceeds from issuing bonds payable | 100,000 | |
| Proceeds from issuing capital stock | 50,000 | |
| Dividends paid | (40,000) | |
| Net cash flows from financing activities | | 100,000 |

| | | |
|---|---|---|
| **Net increase (decrease) in cash** | | $ 35,000 |
| Cash and cash equivalents, Jan. 1 | | 20,000 |
| Cash and cash equivalents, Dec. 31 | | $ 55,000 |

sales are reported in the income statement in the period when the sales occur. But the cash effects occur later—when the receivables are collected in cash. If these events occur in different accounting periods, the income statement and the operating activities section of the statement of cash flows will differ. Similar differences may exist between the recognition of an expense and the related cash payment. Consider, for example, the expense of postretirement benefits earned by employees during the current period. If this expense is not funded with a trustee, the cash payments may not occur for many years— after today's employees have retired.

Cash flows from operating activities include:

| **Cash Receipts** | **Cash Payments** |
|---|---|
| Collections from customers for sales of goods and services | Payments to suppliers of merchandise and services, including payments to employees |
| Interest and dividends received | Payments of interest |
| Other receipts from operations; for example, proceeds from settlement of litigation | Payments of income taxes |
| | Other expenditures relating to operations; for example, payments in settlement of litigation |

Notice that receipts and payments of *interest* are classified as operating activities, not as investing or financing activities.

**Investing Activities**     Cash flows relating to investing activities present the cash effects of transactions involving plant assets, intangible assets, and investments. They include:

| Cash Receipts | Cash Payments |
|---|---|
| Cash proceeds from selling investments and plant assets | Payments to acquire investments and plant assets |
| Cash proceeds from collecting principal amounts on loans | Amounts advanced to borrowers |

**Financing Activities**     Cash flows classified as financing activities include the following items that result from debt and equity financing transactions:

| Cash Receipts | Cash Payments |
|---|---|
| Proceeds from both short-term and long-term borrowing | Repayment of amounts borrowed (excluding interest payments) |
| Cash received from owners (for example, from issuing stock) | Payments to owners, such as cash dividends |

Repayment of amounts borrowed refers to repayment of *loans,* not to payments made on accounts payable or accrued liabilities. Payments of accounts payable and of accrued liabilities are considered payments to suppliers of merchandise and services and are classified as cash outflows from operating activities. Also, remember that all interest payments are classified as operating activities.

**Why Are Receipts and Payments of Interest Classified as Operating Activities?**     One might argue that interest and dividend receipts are related to investing activities, and that interest payments are related to financing activities. The FASB considered this point of view but decided instead to classify interest and dividend receipts and interest payments as operating activities. The FASB wanted net cash flows from operating activities to reflect the cash effects of the revenue and expense transactions entering into the determination of net income. Because dividend and interest revenue and interest expense enter into the determination of net income, the FASB decided to classify the related cash flows as operating activities. Payments of dividends, however, *do not* enter into the determination of net income. Therefore, dividend payments are classified as financing activities.

**Cash and Cash Equivalents**     For purposes of preparing a statement of cash flows, the FASB has defined cash as including *both cash and cash equivalents.* **Cash equivalents** are short-term, highly liquid investments, such as money market funds, commercial paper, and Treasury bills. Transfers of money between a company's bank accounts and these cash equivalents are *not viewed as cash receipts or cash payments.* Money is considered cash regardless of whether it is held in currency, in a bank account, or in the form of cash equivalents. Interest received from owning cash equivalents is included in cash receipts from operating activities.

Cash equivalents are limited to short-term, highly liquid investments such as those specified above. Marketable securities, such as investments in the stocks and bonds of other companies, *do not qualify as cash equivalents.* Therefore, purchases and sales of marketable securities *do* result in cash flows that are reported in the statement of cash flows as investing activities.

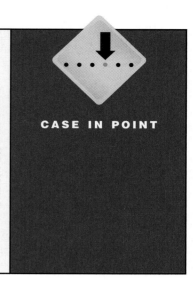

**H. J. Heinz Company**'s 1999 financial statements include the following cash flow information (in thousands of dollars):

|  | 1999 | 1998 | 1997 |
|---|---|---|---|
| Operating activities | $ 910,136 | $ 1,065,744 | $ 874,998 |
| Investing activities | (390,529) | 27,162 | (386,313) |
| Financing activities | (515,490) | $(1,146,601) | (429,760) |

Management's discussion and analysis explains in great detail how the company's strong operating cash flows are used to support an aggressive program of acquiring needed plant assets and other companies. The negative cash flows from financing activities generally reflect the use of cash for payment of dividends to stockholders and the purchase of treasury stock.

**CASE IN POINT**

### Critical Importance of Cash Flows from Operating Activities

In the long run, a company must have a strategy that generates positive net cash flows from its operating activities if it is to survive. A business with negative cash flows from operations will not be able to raise cash from other sources indefinitely. In fact, the ability of a business to raise cash through financing activities is highly dependent on its ability to generate cash from its normal business operations. Creditors and stockholders are reluctant to invest in a company that does not generate enough cash from operating activities to ensure prompt payment of maturing liabilities, interest, and dividends.

Similarly, companies cannot expect to survive indefinitely on cash provided by investing activities. At some point, plant assets, investments, and other assets available for sale will be depleted.

**MANAGEMENT STRATEGY**

## The Approach to Preparing a Statement of Cash Flows

The items listed in an income statement and a balance sheet represent the balances of specific general ledger accounts. Notice, however, that the captions used in the statement of cash flows *do not* correspond to specific ledger accounts. A statement of cash flows summarizes *cash transactions* during the accounting period. The general ledger, however, is maintained on the **accrual basis** of accounting, not the cash basis. Thus an amount such as "Cash received from customers . . . $870,000" does not appear as the balance in a specific ledger account, but it is derived from one or more such accounts.

In a small business, it may be practical to prepare a statement of cash flows directly from the special journals for cash receipts and cash payments. For most businesses, however, it is easier to prepare the statement of cash flows by examining the income statement and the *changes* during the period in all of the balance sheet accounts *except for* Cash. This approach is based on the double-entry system of accounting; any transaction affecting cash must also affect some other asset, liability, or owners' equity account.[3] The change in these *other accounts* determines the nature of the cash transaction.

---

[3] Revenue, expenses, and dividends represent changes in owners' equity and, therefore, may be regarded as owners' equity accounts.

To illustrate this approach, assume that the Marketable Securities controlling account of Allison Corporation shows the following activity during the year:

| | |
|---|---:|
| Balance, Jan. 1, 2002 . . . . . . . . . . . . . . . . . . . . . . . . . . . . . . . . . . . . . . . . . . . . | $64,000 |
| Increases during the year . . . . . . . . . . . . . . . . . . . . . . . . . . . . . . . . . . . . . . . . | 65,000 |
| Decreases during the year . . . . . . . . . . . . . . . . . . . . . . . . . . . . . . . . . . . . . . . . | (44,000) |
| Balance, Dec. 31, 2002 . . . . . . . . . . . . . . . . . . . . . . . . . . . . . . . . . . . . . . . . . . . | $85,000 |

Also assume that the company's income statement for the year includes a *$4,000 loss* on sales of marketable securities.

Increases in the Marketable Securities account represent the cost of securities *purchased* during the year. These debit entries provide the basis for the item *"Purchases of marketable securities . . . $(65,000)"* appearing in the investing activities section of the statement of cash flows (page 535). Thus increases in the asset marketable securities correspond to an outflow of cash.

Decreases of $44,000 represent the *cost* of securities sold during the year. Remember, however, that the income statement shows that these securities were sold at a *loss of $4,000*. The cash proceeds from these sales, which also appear in the statement of cash flows, may be computed as follows:

| | |
|---|---:|
| Cost of marketable securities sold . . . . . . . . . . . . . . . . . . . . . . . . . . . . . . . . . . . | $44,000 |
| Less: Loss on sales of marketable securities . . . . . . . . . . . . . . . . . . . . . . . . . . . | 4,000 |
| Proceeds from sales of marketable securities . . . . . . . . . . . . . . . . . . . . . . . . . . . | $40,000 |

By looking at the changes occurring in the Marketable Securities account and the related income statement account, we were able to determine two items appearing in the company's statement of cash flows. We could have assembled the same information from the company's cash journals, but we would have had to review the journals for the entire year and then add together the cash flows of numerous individual transactions. In summary, it usually is more efficient to prepare a statement of cash flows by analyzing the *changes in noncash accounts* in the balance sheet than by locating and combining numerous entries in the company's journals.

## PREPARING A STATEMENT OF CASH FLOWS: AN ILLUSTRATION

Earlier in this chapter we illustrated the statement of cash flows of Allison Corporation. We will now show how this statement was developed from the company's accrual-basis accounting records.

Basically, a statement of cash flows can be prepared from the information contained in an income statement and *comparative* balance sheets at the beginning and end of the period. It is also necessary, however, to have some detailed information about the *changes* occurring during the period in certain balance sheet accounts. Shown on the next two pages are Allison's income statement and comparative balance sheets for the current year, along with additional information about the changes in account balances.

**Additional Information**    An analysis of changes in the balance sheet accounts of Allison Corporation provides the following information about the company's activities in the current year. To assist in the preparation of a statement of cash flows, we have classified this information into the categories of operating activities, investing activities, and financing activities.

## Operating Activities

1. Accounts receivable increased by $30,000 during the year.
2. Dividend revenue is recognized on the cash basis, but interest revenue is recognized on the accrual basis. Accrued interest receivable decreased by $1,000 during the year.
3. Inventory increased by $10,000 and accounts payable increased by $15,000 during the year.
4. During the year, short-term prepaid expenses increased by $3,000 and accrued expenses payable (other than for interest or income taxes) decreased by $6,000. Depreciation for the year amounted to $40,000.
5. The accrued liability for interest payable increased by $7,000 during the year.
6. The accrued liability for income taxes payable decreased by $2,000 during the year.

## Investing Activities

7. Analysis of the Marketable Securities account shows debit entries of $65,000, representing the cost of securities purchased, and credit entries of $44,000, representing the cost of securities sold. (No marketable securities are classified as cash equivalents.)

| ALLISON CORPORATION Income Statement For the Year Ended December 31, 2002 | | |
|---|---:|---:|
| **Revenue and gains:** | | |
| Net sales . . . . . . . . . . . . . . . . . . . . . . . . . . . . . . . . . . . . . . . . . . . . . . . . . . . | | $900,000 |
| Dividend revenue . . . . . . . . . . . . . . . . . . . . . . . . . . . . . . . . . . . . . . . | | 3,000 |
| Interest revenue . . . . . . . . . . . . . . . . . . . . . . . . . . . . . . . . . . . . . | | 6,000 |
| Gain on sales of plant assets . . . . . . . . . . . . . . . . . . . . . . . . . . . . | | 31,000 |
| Total revenue and gains . . . . . . . . . . . . . . . . . . . . . . . . . . . . . . . . . . . | | $940,000 |
| **Costs, expenses, and losses:** | | |
| Cost of goods sold . . . . . . . . . . . . . . . . . . . . . . . . . . . . . . . | $500,000 | |
| Operating expenses (including depreciation of $40,000) . . . . . . . . . | 300,000 | |
| Interest expense . . . . . . . . . . . . . . . . . . . . . . . . . . . . . . . . . | 35,000 | |
| Income taxes expense . . . . . . . . . . . . . . . . . . . . . . . . . . . . . . | 36,000 | |
| Loss on sales of marketable securities . . . . . . . . . . . . . . . . . . | 4,000 | |
| Total costs, expenses, and losses . . . . . . . . . . . . . . . . . . . . . | | 875,000 |
| Net income . . . . . . . . . . . . . . . . . . . . . . . . . . . . . . . . . . . . . . . . . . | | $ 65,000 |

8. Analysis of the Notes Receivable account shows $17,000 in debit entries, representing cash loaned to borrowers by Allison Corporation during the year, and $12,000 in credit entries, representing collections of notes receivable. (Collections of interest were recorded in the Interest Revenue account and are considered cash flows from operating activities.)

|  | 2002 | 2001 |
|---|---|---|
| **ALLISON CORPORATION** |  |  |
| **Comparative Balance Sheets** |  |  |
| **December 31, 2002 and 2001** |  |  |
| **Assets** |  |  |
| **Current assets:** |  |  |
| Cash and Cash Equivalents | $ 55,000 | $ 20,000 |
| Marketable Securities | 85,000 | 64,000 |
| Notes Receivable | 17,000 | 12,000 |
| Accounts Receivable | 110,000 | 80,000 |
| Accrued Interest Receivable | 2,000 | 3,000 |
| Inventory | 100,000 | 90,000 |
| Prepaid Expenses | 4,000 | 1,000 |
| Total current assets | $373,000 | $270,000 |
| **Plant and Equipment (net of accumulated depreciation)** | 616,000 | 500,000 |
| Total assets | $989,000 | $770,000 |
| **Liabilities & Stockholders' Equity** |  |  |
| **Current liabilities:** |  |  |
| Notes Payable (short-term) | $ 45,000 | $ 55,000 |
| Accounts Payable | 76,000 | 61,000 |
| Interest Payable | 22,000 | 15,000 |
| Income Taxes Payable | 8,000 | 10,000 |
| Other Accrued Expenses Payable | 3,000 | 9,000 |
| Total current liabilities | $154,000 | $150,000 |
| **Long-term liabilities:** |  |  |
| Notes Payable (long-term) | 40,000 | –0– |
| Bonds Payable | 400,000 | 300,000 |
| Total liabilities | $594,000 | $450,000 |
| **Stockholders' equity:** |  |  |
| Capital Stock | $ 60,000 | $ 50,000 |
| Additional Paid-in Capital | 140,000 | 100,000 |
| Retained Earnings | 195,000 | 170,000 |
| Total stockholders' equity | $395,000 | $320,000 |
| Total liabilities & stockholders' equity | $989,000 | $770,000 |

9. Allison's plant asset accounts increased by $116,000 during the year. An analysis of the underlying transactions indicates the following:

|  | Effect on Plant Asset Accounts |
|---|---|
| Purchased $200,000 in plant assets, paying $160,000 cash and issuing a long-term note payable for the $40,000 balance | $200,000 |
| Sold for $75,000 cash plant assets with a book value of $44,000 | (44,000) |
| Recorded depreciation expense for the period | (40,000) |
| Net change in plant asset controlling accounts | $116,000 |

## Financing Activities

10. During the year, Allison Corporation borrowed $45,000 cash by issuing short-term notes payable to banks. Also, the company repaid $55,000 in principal amounts due on these loans and other notes payable. (Interest payments are classified as operating activities.)

11. The company issued bonds payable for $100,000 cash.

12. The company issued for cash 1,000 shares of $10 par value capital stock at a price of $50 per share.

13. Cash dividends declared and paid to stockholders amounted to $40,000 during the year.

## Cash and Cash Equivalents

14. Cash and cash equivalents as shown in Allison Corporation's balance sheets amounted to $20,000 at the beginning of the year and $55,000 at year-end—a net increase of $35,000.

Using this information, we will now illustrate the steps in preparing Allison Corporation's statement of cash flows and a supporting schedule disclosing the noncash investing and financing activities. In our discussion, we will often refer to these items of additional information by citing the paragraph numbers shown in the list just described.

The distinction between accrual-basis measurements and cash flows is of fundamental importance in understanding financial statements and other accounting reports. To assist in making this distinction, we use two colors in our illustrated computations. We show in **blue** the accrual-based data from Allison Corporation's income statement and the preceding numbered paragraphs. The cash flows that we compute from these data are shown in red.

## Cash Flows from Operating Activities

As shown in our statement of cash flows on page 535, the net cash flows from operating activities are determined by combining certain cash inflows and subtracting certain cash outflows. The inflows are cash received from customers, and interest and dividends received; the outflows are cash paid to suppliers and employees, interest paid, and income taxes paid.

In computing each of these cash flows, our starting point is an income statement amount, such as net sales, cost of goods sold, or interest expense. As you study each computation, be sure that you *understand why* the income statement amount must be increased or decreased to determine the related cash flows. You will find that an understanding of these computations will do more than show you how to compute cash flows; it will also strengthen your understanding of the income statement and the balance sheet.

**Cash Received from Customers** To the extent that sales are made for cash, there is no difference between the amount of cash received from customers and the amount recorded as sales revenue. Differences arise, however, when sales are made on account. If accounts receivable have increased during the year, credit sales have exceeded collections of accounts receivable. Therefore, we must *deduct the increase* in accounts receivable over the year from net sales to determine the amount of cash received during the year. If accounts receivable have decreased over the year, collections of these accounts exceeded credit sales. Therefore, we must *add the decrease* in accounts receivable to net sales to determine the amount of cash received during the year. The relationship between cash received from customers and net sales is summarized below:

**LO 3**

Compute the major cash flows relating to operating activities.

$$\text{Cash Received from Customers} = \text{Net Sales} \begin{cases} + \text{ Decrease in Accounts Receivable} \\ \quad\quad\quad\quad\text{or} \\ - \text{ Increase in Accounts Receivable} \end{cases}$$

The increase or decrease in accounts receivable is determined simply by comparing the year-end balance in the account to its balance at the beginning of the year.

In our Allison Corporation example, paragraph **1** of the additional information tells us that accounts receivable have *increased* by $30,000 during the year. The income statement shows net sales for the year of $900,000. Therefore, the amount of cash received from customers is computed as follows:

| | |
|---|---|
| Net sales (accrual basis) | $900,000 |
| Less: Increase in accounts receivable | 30,000 |
| Cash received from customers | $870,000 |

**Interest and Dividends Received** Our next objective is to determine the amounts of cash received during the year from dividends and interest on the company's investments. As explained in paragraph **2** of the additional information, dividend revenue is recorded on the cash basis. Therefore, the $3,000 shown in the income statement also represents the amount of cash received as dividends.

Interest revenue, on the other hand, is recognized on the accrual basis. We have already shown how to convert one type of revenue, net sales, from the accrual basis to the cash basis. We may use the same approach to convert interest revenue from the accrual basis to the **cash basis**. Our formula for converting net sales to the cash basis may be modified to convert interest revenue to the cash basis as follows:

$$\frac{\text{Interest}}{\text{Received}} = \frac{\text{Interest}}{\text{Revenue}} \begin{cases} + \text{ Decrease in Interest Receivable} \\ \text{or} \\ - \text{ Increase in Interest Receivable} \end{cases}$$

The income statement for Allison Corporation shows interest revenue of $6,000, and paragraph **2** states that the amount of accrued interest receivable has *decreased* by $1,000 during the year. Thus the amount of cash received as interest may be computed as follows:

| | |
|---|---|
| Interest revenue (accrual basis) | $6,000 |
| Add: Decrease in accrued interest receivable | 1,000 |
| Interest received (cash basis) | $7,000 |

The amounts of interest and dividends received in cash are combined for presentation in the statement of cash flows:

| | |
|---|---|
| Interest received (cash basis) | $ 7,000 |
| Dividends received (cash basis) | 3,000 |
| Interest and dividends received | $10,000 |

## Cash Payments for Merchandise and for Expenses

The next item in the statement of cash flows, "Cash paid to suppliers and employees," includes all cash payments for purchases of merchandise and for operating expenses (excluding interest and income taxes). Payments of interest and income taxes are listed as separate items in the statement. The amounts of cash paid for purchases of merchandise and for operating expenses are computed separately.

**Cash Paid for Purchases of Merchandise**   An accrual basis income statement reflects the *cost of goods sold* during the year, regardless of whether the merchandise was acquired or paid for in that period. The statement of cash flows, on the other hand, reports the *cash paid* for merchandise during the year, even if the merchandise was acquired in a previous period or remains unsold at year-end. The relationship between cash payments for merchandise and the cost of goods sold depends on the changes during the period in *two* related balance sheet accounts: inventory and accounts payable to suppliers of merchandise. This relationship may be stated as follows:

$$
\begin{array}{c}
\text{Cash Payments} \\
\text{for Purchases}
\end{array} =
\begin{array}{c}
\text{Cost of} \\
\text{Goods Sold}
\end{array}
\left\{
\begin{array}{c}
\textbf{+ Increase in} \\
\textbf{Inventory} \\
\textbf{or} \\
\textbf{- Decrease in} \\
\textbf{Inventory}
\end{array}
\right\}
\text{ and }
\left\{
\begin{array}{c}
\textbf{+ Decrease in} \\
\textbf{Accounts Payable} \\
\textbf{or} \\
\textbf{- Increase in} \\
\textbf{Accounts Payable}
\end{array}
\right\}
$$

*why cost of goods sold?*

Using information from the Allison Corporation income statement and paragraph **3** the cash payments for purchases may be computed as follows:

| | |
|---|---:|
| Cost of goods sold | $500,000 |
| Add: Increase in inventory | 10,000 |
| Net purchases (accrual basis) | $510,000 |
| Less: Increase in accounts payable to suppliers | 15,000 |
| Cash payments for purchases of merchandise | $495,000 |

Here is the logic behind this computation: If a company is increasing its inventory, it is *buying more merchandise than it sells* during the period. However, if the company is increasing its account payable to merchandise creditors, it is *not paying cash* for all of these purchases.

**Cash Payments for Expenses**   Expenses, as shown in the income statement, represent the cost of goods and services used up during the period. However, the amounts shown as expenses may differ from the cash payments made during the period. Consider, for example, depreciation expense. Recording depreciation expense *requires no cash payment,* but it does increase total expenses measured on the accrual basis. Thus, in converting accrual-basis expenses to the cash basis, we must deduct depreciation expense and any other noncash expenses from our accrual-basis operating expenses. Other noncash expenses—expenses not requiring cash outlays—include amortization of intangible assets, any unfunded portion of postretirement benefits expense, and amortization of bond discount.

A second type of difference arises from short-term *timing differences* between the recognition of expenses and the actual cash payments. Expenses are recorded in accounting records when the related goods or services are used. However, the cash payments for these expenses might occur (1) in an earlier period, (2) in the same period, or (3) in a later period. Let us briefly consider each case.

1. If payment is made in advance, the payment creates an asset, termed a prepaid expense, or, in our formula, a "prepayment." Thus, to the extent that prepaid expenses increase over the year, cash payments *exceed* the amount recognized as expense.

2. If payment is made in the same period, the cash payment is equal to the amount of expense.

3. If payment is made in a later period, the payment reduces a liability for an accrued expense payable. Thus, to the extent that accrued expenses payable decrease over the year, cash payments exceed the amount recognized as expense.

The relationship between cash payments and accrual-basis expenses is summarized below:

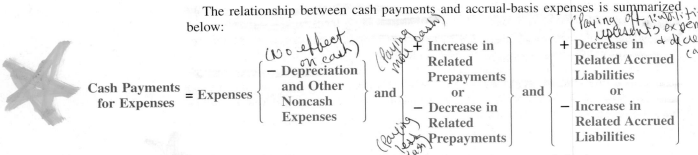

*Handwritten annotations: "(No effect on cash)", "(Paying more cash)", "(Paying less cash)", "(Paying off liabilities represents expense & decreases cash)"*

$$\text{Cash Payments for Expenses} = \text{Expenses} \begin{Bmatrix} - \text{Depreciation and Other Noncash Expenses} \end{Bmatrix} \text{and} \begin{Bmatrix} + \text{Increase in Related Prepayments} \\ \text{or} \\ - \text{Decrease in Related Prepayments} \end{Bmatrix} \text{and} \begin{Bmatrix} + \text{Decrease in Related Accrued Liabilities} \\ \text{or} \\ - \text{Increase in Related Accrued Liabilities} \end{Bmatrix}$$

In a statement of cash flows, cash payments for interest and for income taxes are shown separately from cash payments for operating expenses. Using information from Allison Corporation's income statement and from paragraph **4**, we may compute the company's cash payments for operating expenses as follows:

| | | |
|---|---|---|
| Operating expenses (including depreciation) | | $300,000 |
| Less: Noncash expenses (depreciation) | | 40,000 |
| Subtotal | | $260,000 |
| Add: Increase in short-term prepayments | $3,000 | |
| Decrease in accrued liabilities | 6,000 | 9,000 |
| Cash payments for operating expenses | | $269,000 |

**Cash Paid to Suppliers and Employees** The caption used in our cash flow statement, "Cash paid to suppliers and employees," includes cash payments for both purchases of merchandise and for operating expenses. This cash outflow may now be computed by combining the two previous calculations:

| | |
|---|---|
| Cash payments for purchases of merchandise | $495,000 |
| Cash payments for operating expenses | 269,000 |
| Cash payments to suppliers and employees | $764,000 |

**Cash Payments for Interest and Taxes** Interest expense and income taxes expense may be converted to cash payments with the same formula we used to convert operating expenses. Allison Corporation's income statement shows interest expense of $35,000, and paragraph **5** states that the liability for interest payable increased by $7,000 during the year. The fact that the liability for unpaid interest *increased* over the year means that *not all of the interest expense shown in the income statement was paid in cash* in the current year. To determine the amount of interest actually paid, we must *subtract* from total interest expense the portion that has been financed through an increase in the liability for interest payable. The computation is as follows:

| | |
|---|---|
| Interest expense | $35,000 |
| Less: Increase in related accrued liability | 7,000 |
| Interest paid | $28,000 |

Similar reasoning is used to determine the amount of income taxes paid by Allison Corporation during the year. The accrual-based income taxes expense reported in the income statement amounts to $36,000. However, paragraph **6** states that the company has

*Handwritten margin note: "Interest paid = Interest expense {+ Decrease in Int. Payable / Increase in Int. Payable}"*

reduced its liability for income taxes payable by $2,000 over the year. Incurring income taxes expense increases the tax liability; making cash payments to tax authorities reduces it. Thus, if the liability *decreased* over the year, cash payments to tax authorities *must have been greater* than the income taxes expense for the current year. The amount of the cash payments is determined as follows:

| | |
|---|---:|
| Income taxes expense | $36,000 |
| Add: Decrease in related accrued liability | 2,000 |
| Income taxes paid | $38,000 |

**A Quick Review** We have now shown the computation of each cash flow relating to Allison Corporation's operating activities. Previously we illustrated a complete statement of cash flows for the company. For your convenience, we will again show the operating activities section of that statement, illustrating the information developed in the preceding paragraphs.

| Cash flows from operating activities: | | |
|---|---:|---:|
| Cash received from customers | $ 870,000 | |
| Interest and dividends received | 10,000 | |
| Cash provided by operating activities | | $ 880,000 |
| Cash paid to suppliers and employees | $(764,000) | |
| Interest paid | (28,000) | |
| Income taxes paid | (38,000) | |
| Cash disbursed for operating activities | | (830,000) |
| Net cash flows from operating activities | | $ 50,000 |

## Differences between Net Income and Net Cash Flows from Operating Activities

Allison Corporation reported net income of *$65,000,* but net cash flows from operating activities of only *$50,000.* What caused this $15,000 difference?

The answer, in short, is many things. First, *depreciation expense* reduces net income but does not affect net cash flows. Next, all the adjustments that we made to net sales, cost of goods sold, and expenses represented short-term *timing differences* between net income and the underlying net cash flows from operating activities. Finally, *nonoperating gains and losses* may cause differences between net income and net cash flows from operations.

Nonoperating gains and losses may result from sales of plant assets, marketable securities, and other investments, and from the retirement of long-term debt. These gains and losses affect the cash flows relating to investing or financing activities, not the cash flows from operating activities.

**LO 4**

Explain why net income differs from net cash flows from operating activities.

In 1999 **Procter & Gamble Company (P&G)** reported a $3,763 million net income, yet it had $5,544 million in cash provided by operating activities in its statement of cash flows. This significant difference ($1,781 million) was caused primarily by depreciation and amortization, and to a lesser extent by a growth in accounts payable and other liabilities.

During 1999, **P&G** also purchased $2,828 million in capital assets (investing activities), and paid $1,626 million in dividends and $2,533 to purchase treasury stock (financing activities).

**CASE IN POINT**

## Reporting Operating Cash Flows: The Direct and Indirect Methods

**LO 5**

Distinguish between the direct and indirect methods of reporting operating cash flows.

In our illustration, we use the **direct method** of computing and reporting the net cash flows from operating activities. The direct method shows the *specific cash inflows and outflows* comprising the operating activities of the business. The FASB has expressed its preference for the direct method, but it also allows companies to use an alternative, called the **indirect method**.

Computation of net cash flows from operating activities by the indirect method looks quite different from the direct method computation. However, both methods result in the *same net cash flows* from operating activities. Under the indirect method, the computation begins with accrual-based net income (as shown in the income statement) and then shows the various adjustments necessary to *reconcile net income with net cash flows from operating activities.* The general format of this computation is summarized as follows:

> Net income
> Add:  • Expenses that do not require cash outlays in the period (such as depreciation expense)
>    • Operating cash inflows not recorded as revenue in the period
>    • Nonoperating losses deducted in the determination of net income
> Less:  • Revenues that do not result in cash inflows in the period
>    • Operating cash outflows not recorded as expense in the period
>    • Nonoperating gains included in the determination of net income
> Net cash flows from operating activities

The preceding summary describes the differences between net income and net cash flows from operating activities in broad, general terms. In an actual statement of cash flows, a dozen or more specific items may appear in this reconciliation. (*Supplementary Schedule A,* on page 551, illustrates the application of the indirect method to the operating activities of Allison Corporation.)

In this chapter we emphasize the *direct* method, as we consider it to be the more informative and more readily understood approach, and it is the method recommended by the FASB. Most of our assignment material is based on the direct method. Further coverage of the indirect method is provided in *Supplemental Topic A* at the end of the chapter.

## Cash Flows from Investing Activities

**LO 6**

Compute the cash flows relating to investing and financing activities.

Paragraphs **7** through **9** in the additional information for our Allison Corporation example provide most of the information necessary to determine the cash flows from investing activities. In the following discussion, we illustrate the presentation of these cash flows and explain the sources of the information contained in the numbered paragraphs.

Much information about investing activities can be obtained simply by looking at the changes in the related asset accounts during the year. Debit entries in these accounts represent purchases of the assets, or cash outlays. Credit entries represent sales of the assets, or cash receipts. However, credit entries in asset accounts represent only the *cost* (or *book value*) of the assets sold. To determine the cash proceeds from these sales transactions, we must adjust the amount of the credit entries for any gains or losses recognized on the sales.

**Purchases and Sales of Securities** To illustrate, consider paragraph **7**, which summarizes the debit and credit entries to the Marketable Securities account. As explained earlier in this chapter, the $65,000 in debit entries represents purchases of marketable securities. The $44,000 in credit entries represents the *cost* of marketable securities sold during the period. However, the income statement shows that these securities were sold at a *$4,000 loss*. Thus the cash proceeds from these sales amounted to only *$40,000* ($44,000 cost, minus $4,000 loss on sale). In the statement of cash flows, these investing activities are summarized as follows:

| | |
|---|---|
| Purchases of marketable securities | $(65,000) |
| Proceeds from sales of marketable securities | 40,000 |

**Loans Made and Collected**  Paragraph **8** provides all the information necessary to summarize the cash flows from making and collecting loans:

| | |
|---|---|
| Loans made to borrowers | $(17,000) |
| Collections on loans | 12,000 |

This information comes directly from the Notes Receivable account. Debit entries in the account represent new loans made during the year; credit entries indicate collections of the *principal* amount on outstanding notes (loans). (Interest received is credited to the Interest Revenue account and is included among the cash receipts from operating activities.)

**Cash Paid to Acquire Plant Assets**  Paragraph **9** states that Allison Corporation purchased plant assets during the year for $200,000, paying $160,000 in cash and issuing a long-term note payable for the $40,000 balance. Notice that *only the $160,000 cash payment* appears in the statement of cash flows. However, one objective of this financial statement is to show all of the company's *investing and financing activities* during the year. Therefore, the *noncash aspects* of these transactions are shown in a supplementary schedule, as follows:

| Supplementary Schedule of Noncash Investing and Financing Activities | |
|---|---|
| Purchases of plant assets | $200,000 |
| Less: Portion financed through issuance of long-term debt | 40,000 |
| Cash paid to acquire plant assets | $160,000 |

This supplementary schedule accompanies the statement of cash flows.

**Proceeds from Sales of Plant Assets**  Assume that an analysis of the plant asset accounts shows net credit entries totaling $44,000 in the year. ("Net credit entries" means all credit entries, net of related debits to accumulated depreciation when assets were sold.) These net credit entries represent the *book value* of plant assets sold during the year. However, the income statement shows that these assets were sold at a *gain of $31,000*. Therefore, the *cash proceeds* from sales of plant assets amounted to $75,000, as follows:

| | |
|---|---|
| Book value of plant assets sold | $44,000 |
| Add: Gain on sales of plant assets | 31,000 |
| Proceeds from sales of plant assets | $75,000 |

The amount credited to the Accumulated Depreciation account during the year is not a cash flow and is not included in the statement of cash flows.

**A Quick Review**    We have now shown the computation of each cash flow related to Allison Corporation's investing activities. Earlier we illustrated a complete statement of cash flows for the company. For your convenience, we show the investing activities section of that statement, illustrating the information developed in the preceding paragraphs.

| Cash flows from investing activities: | | |
|---|---:|---:|
| Purchases of marketable securities | $ (65,000) | |
| Proceeds from sales of marketable securities | 40,000 | |
| Loans made to borrowers | (17,000) | |
| Collections on loans | 12,000 | |
| Purchases of plant assets | (160,000) | |
| Proceeds from sales of plant assets | 75,000 | |
| Net cash flows from investing activities | | (115,000) |

## Cash Flows from Financing Activities

Cash flows from financing activities are determined by analyzing the debit and credit changes recorded during the period in the related liability and stockholders' equity accounts. Cash flows from financing activities are more easily determined than those relating to investing activities, because financing activities seldom involve gains or losses.[4] Thus the debit or credit changes in the balance sheet accounts usually are equal to the amounts of the related cash flows.

Credit changes in such accounts as Notes Payable and the accounts for long-term debt and paid-in capital usually indicate cash receipts; debit changes indicate cash payments.

**Short-Term Borrowing Transactions**    To illustrate, consider paragraph **10**, which provides the information supporting the following cash flows:

| | |
|---|---:|
| Proceeds from short-term borrowing | $45,000 |
| Payments to settle short-term debts | (55,000) |

Notice that both the proceeds from short-term borrowing of $45,000 (a positive cash flow) and the payments to settle short-term debts of $55,000 (a negative cash flow) are presented in the statement of cash flows. Presenting both directions of the changes in cash, rather than combining the two and presenting a net amount of $10,000 ($55,000 − $45,000), is an important feature of the statement of cash flows. Presenting both positive and negative cash flows is referred to as presenting *gross* cash flows rather than presenting *net* cash flows.

Is it possible to determine the proceeds of short-term borrowing transactions throughout the year without carefully reviewing each cash receipt? The answer is yes—the proceeds from short-term borrowing are equal to the *sum of the credit entries* in the short-term *Notes Payable* account. Payments to settle short-term debts are equal to the *sum of the debit entries* in this account.

**Proceeds from Issuing Bonds Payable and Capital Stock**    Paragraph **11** states that Allison Corporation received cash of $100,000 by issuing bonds payable. This amount was determined by summing the credit entries in the Bonds Payable account. The Bonds Payable account included no debit entries during the year; thus no bonds were retired.

---

[4] An early retirement of debt is an example of a financing transaction that may result in a gain or a loss.

Paragraph **12** states that during the year Allison Corporation issued capital stock for $50,000. The proceeds from issuing stock are equal to the sum of the credit entries made in the Capital Stock and Additional Paid-in Capital accounts ($10,000 + $40,000).

**Cash Dividends Paid to Stockholders**  Paragraph **13** states that Allison Corporation declared and paid cash dividends of $40,000 during the year. If dividends are both declared and paid during the same year, the cash payments are equal to the related debit entries in the Retained Earnings account.

If the balance sheet includes a liability for dividends payable, the amounts debited to Retained Earnings represent dividends *declared* during the period, which may differ from the amount of dividends *paid*. To determine cash dividends paid, we must adjust the amount of dividends declared by adding any decrease (or subtracting any increase) in the Dividends Payable account over the period.

*[handwritten margin notes: Cash dividends paid to stockholders; Dividends declared { + decrease in dividends payable − increase in dividends payable ]*

**A Quick Review**  We have now shown the computation of each cash flow related to Allison Corporation's investing activities. Earlier we illustrated a complete statement of cash flows for the company. For your convenience, we show the financing activities section of that statement, illustrating the information developed in the preceding paragraphs.

| Cash flows from financing activities: | | |
|---|---:|---:|
| Proceeds from short-term borrowing | $ 45,000 | |
| Payments to settle short-term debts | (55,000) | |
| Proceeds from issuing bonds payable | 100,000 | |
| Proceeds from issuing capital stock | 50,000 | |
| Dividends paid | (40,000) | |
| Net cash flows from financing activities | | 100,000 |

## Relationship between the Statement of Cash Flows and the Balance Sheet

The first asset appearing in the balance sheet is Cash and Cash Equivalents. The statement of cash flows explains in some detail the change in this asset from one balance sheet date to the next. The last three lines in the statement of cash flows illustrate this relationship, as shown in our Allison Corporation example:

| Net increase (decrease) in cash and cash equivalents | $35,000 |
|---|---:|
| Cash and cash equivalents, beginning of year | 20,000 |
| Cash and cash equivalents, end of year | $55,000 |

This is often referred to as a reconciliation of the beginning and ending cash balances.

**Litton Industries, Inc.**'s 1997 statement of cash flows indicated a very significant decline in cash—from approximately $77 million at the beginning of the year to slightly over $4 million at the end of the year. Does this indicate that the company had financial troubles? Not necessarily. The company reported strong cash provided by operating activities (approximately $223 million in 1997 compared to approximately $70 million in 1996). The primary explanation for the significant decline in cash was that the company repaid approximately $127 million in debt during 1997, while in 1996 it increased its debt and equity financing by over $630 million. This decline in external financing during 1997, plus aggressive purchases of plant assets, resulted in the decline in cash during that year. Further evidence of the company's financial strength is that cash increased to more than $16 million by the end of 1998 and to over $30 million by the end of 1999.

**CASE IN POINT**

## The Statement of Cash Flows: A Second Look

We have now completed our explanation of Allison Corporation's statement of cash flows. We have analyzed each type of cash flow by reconciling amounts included in the other two financial statements—the income statement and the balance sheet—to determine the amounts of individual operating, investing, and financing cash flows. In computing cash flows from operating activities, we used the direct method in which major categories of both positive and negative cash flows were determined and presented.

In a second illustration on the following page we use the indirect method to determine the amount of operating cash flows. Rather than adjusting each individual operating cash flow category for changes in balance sheet accounts, these same adjustments are made to net income. In this second illustration, we also illustrate two *supplementary schedules* that often accompany the statement of cash flows.

*Supplementary Schedule A* illustrates the determination of net cash flows from operating activities by the *indirect method*. The purpose of this schedule is to explain the differences between the reported net income and the net cash flows from operating activities. This supplementary schedule also is required of companies that use the direct method of reporting operating cash flows. The indirect method is covered in greater depth in Supplemental Topic A of this chapter.

*Supplementary Schedule B* discloses any noncash aspects of the company's investing and financing activities. This type of supplementary schedule is required whenever some aspects of the company's investing and financing activities do not coincide with cash flows occurring within the current period, but still have important impacts on the company's financial position. This disclosure is required when either the direct or the indirect method is used to determine operating cash flows.

## ▌ FINANCIAL ANALYSIS

The users of a statement of cash flows usually are particularly interested in the *net cash flows from operating activities.* Is the amount large enough to provide for necessary replacements of plant assets and maturing liabilities? And if so, is there enough left for the current dividend to look secure—or even be increased?

Consider two competitors in the import craft supplies business, Gonzalez, Inc., and Alvarez Company. These companies have approximately the same size assets, liabilities, and sales. Selected information from their most recent statements of cash flows follows:

| | Beginning Cash Balance | Net Cash Flow from (in thousands) | | | Ending Cash Balance |
|---|---|---|---|---|---|
| | | Operating Activities | Investing Activities | Financing Activities | |
| Gonzalez | $150 | $600 | $(500) | $400 | $650 |
| Alvarez | 150 | 50 | 500 | (50) | 650 |

Which company is in the stronger cash flow position? Although both have the same beginning and ending cash balances ($150,000 and $650,000, respectively), Gonzalez is in the stronger position because of its strong operating cash flows of $600,000. Gonzalez has been able to invest $500,000 in operating assets, while financing only $400,000 and still have a $650,000 ending cash balance. Alvarez, on the other hand, has generated only a small amount of cash from operations ($50,000) and has sold assets to generate cash ($500,000) to support its ending cash balance. Also, Alvarez has not been able to finance its assets acquisitions and even has had to reduce its financing, possibly due to its weak operating cash flows.

## ALLISON CORPORATION
## Statement of Cash Flows
## For the Year Ended December 31, 2002

**Cash flows from operating activities:**

| | |
|---|---:|
| Net cash provided by operating activities (see Supplementary Schedule A) | $ 50,000 |

**Cash flows from investing activities:**

| | | |
|---|---:|---:|
| Purchases of marketable securities | $ (65,000) | |
| Proceeds from sales of marketable securities | 40,000 | |
| Loans made to borrowers | (17,000) | |
| Collections on loans | 12,000 | |
| Cash paid to acquire plant assets (see Supplementary Schedule B) | (160,000) | |
| Proceeds from sales of plant assets | 75,000 | |
| Net cash used in investing activities | | (115,000) |

**Cash flows from financing activities:**

| | | |
|---|---:|---:|
| Proceeds from short-term borrowing | $ 45,000 | |
| Payments to settle short-term debts | (55,000) | |
| Proceeds from issuing bonds payable | 100,000 | |
| Proceeds from issuing capital stock | 50,000 | |
| Dividends paid | (40,000) | |
| Net cash provided by financing activities | | 100,000 |
| Net increase (decrease) in cash | | $ 35,000 |
| Cash and cash equivalents, Jan. 1 | | 20,000 |
| Cash and cash equivalents, Dec. 31 | | $ 55,000 |

*Notice this supplementary schedule illustrates the indirect method of determining cash flows from operations*

### Supplementary Schedule A: Net Cash Provided by Operating Activities

| | | |
|---|---:|---:|
| Net income | | $ 65,000 |
| Add: Depreciation expense | | 40,000 |
| Decrease in accrued interest receivable | | 1,000 |
| Increase in accounts payable | | 15,000 |
| Increase in accrued liabilities | | 7,000 |
| Nonoperating loss on sales of marketable securities | | 4,000 |
| Subtotal | | $ 132,000 |
| Less: Increase in accounts receivable | $ 30,000 | |
| Increase in inventory | 10,000 | |
| Increase in prepaid expenses | 3,000 | |
| Decrease in accrued liabilities | 8,000 | |
| Nonoperating gain on sales of plant assets | 31,000 | 82,000 |
| Net cash provided by operating activities | | $ 50,000 |

### Supplementary Schedule B: Noncash Investing and Financing Activities

| | |
|---|---:|
| Purchases of plant assets | $ 200,000 |
| Less: Portion financed through issuance of long-term debt | 40,000 |
| Cash paid to acquire plant assets | $ 160,000 |

Assume further that each company has current liabilities at the end of the year totaling $500,000. While both are in an equally good cash position with regard to paying these liabilities, Gonzalez followed a much more positive path to get in this position than did Alvarez. Whether Alvarez will be able to sustain its cash position over time, and therefore be able to meet its recurring obligations in the future, is questionable.

Even more important than net cash flows from operating activities in any one year is the *trend* in cash flows over a period of years—and the *consistency* of that trend from year to year. From everyone's perspective, the best results are net cash flows from operating activities that increase each year by a substantial—but also predictable—percentage.[5]

**Free Cash Flow**   Many analysts put a company's cash flows into perspective by computing an amount called **free cash flow**. Free cash flow is intended to represent the cash flow available to management for discretionary purposes, *after* the company has met all of its basic obligations relating to business operations.

The term *free cash flow* is widely cited within the business community. Different analysts compute this measure in different ways because there is no widespread agreement as to the basic obligations relating to business operations. For example, are all expenditures for plant assets "basic obligations," or only those expenditures made to maintain the current level of productive capacity?

One common method of computing free cash flow is to deduct from the net cash flows from operating activities any net cash used for investments in plant assets and any dividends paid. This computation is shown below, using information from the Allison Corporation statement of cash flows shown earlier.

*What's left for discretionary purposes?*

| | | |
|---|---:|---:|
| Net cash flows from operating activities | | $ 50,000 |
| Less: Net cash used for acquiring plant assets | | |
| ($160,000 − $75,000 proceeds) | $85,000 | |
| Dividends paid | 40,000 | 125,000 |
| Free cash flow | | $(75,000) |

This computation suggests that Allison Corporation *did not* generate enough cash from operations to meet its basic obligations. Thus management had to raise cash from other sources. But, of course, an analyst always should look behind the numbers. For example, was Allison's purchase of plant assets during the year a basic obligation, or did it represent a discretionary expansion of the business?

As we have stated throughout this text, no single ratio or financial measurement ever tells the whole story.

## Annotated Statement of Cash Flows: ABM Industries Incorporated

A recent statement of cash flows of **ABM Industries Incorporated** appears on the following page. We have added notations that highlight some of the concepts emphasized in this chapter.

---

[5] Percentage change is the dollar amount of change from one year to the next, expressed as a percentage of (divided by) the amount from the *earlier* of the two years. For example, if net cash provided by operating activities was $100,000 in the first year and $120,000 in the second year, the percentage increase is 20%, computed as follows: ($120,000 − $100,000) ÷ $100,000.

## ABM INDUSTRIES INCORPORATED
## Consolidated Statement of Cash Flows
## Year Ended October 31, 1998

| (In thousands of dollars) | 1998 | |
|---|---|---|
| Cash flows from operating activities: | | |
| Cash received from customers | $1,463,918 | |
| Other operating cash receipts | 1,331 | |
| Interest received | 682 | ← ABM uses the direct method and operations is a net source of cash |
| Cash paid to suppliers and employees | (1,406,600) | |
| Interest paid | (3,334) | |
| Income taxes paid | (23,936) | |
| Net cash provided by operating activities | 32,061 | |
| Cash flows from investing activities: | | |
| Additions to property, plant, and equipment | (11,715) | |
| Proceeds from sale of assets | 497 | |
| Increase (decrease) in investments and long-term receivables | 495 | |
| Intangible assets acquired | (10,010) | |
| Net cash used in investing activities | (20,733) | ← Notice investing was a net use of cash . . . |
| Cash flows from financing activities: | | |
| Common stock issued, including tax benefit | 15,151 | |
| Dividends paid | (10,708) | |
| Increase (decrease) in bank overdraft | (10,500) | |
| Increase (decrease) in notes payable | (528) | |
| Long-term borrowings | 93,204 | |
| Repayments of long-term borrowings | (97,886) | |
| Net cash provided by financing activities | (11,267) | ← financing also was a net use of cash |
| Net (decrease) increase in cash and cash equivalents | 61 | |
| Cash and cash equivalents beginning of year | 1,783 | |
| Cash and cash equivalents end of year | $ 1,844 | ← Ties into balance sheet |
| Reconciliation of net income to net cash provided by operating activities: | | |
| Net income | $ 33,930 | |
| Adjustments: | | |
| Depreciation and amortization | 19,593 | |
| Impairment of long-lived assets | — | |
| Provision for bad debts | 2,821 | |
| Gain on sale of assets | (202) | |
| Increase (decrease) in deferred income taxes | (4,521) | |
| Increase in accounts receivable | (28,907) | |
| Decrease (increase) in inventories | (1,768) | |
| Increase in prepaid expenses and other current assets | (2,440) | ← Supplementary schedule uses the indirect method |
| Decrease (increase) in other assets | 454 | |
| (Increase) decrease in income taxes payable | 4,163 | |
| Increase in retirement plans accrual | 2,561 | |
| Increase (decrease) in insurance claims liability | (778) | |
| Increase in trade accounts payable and other accrued liabilities | 7,155 | |
| Total adjustments to net income | (1,869) | |
| Net cash provided by operating activities | $ 32,061 | |
| Supplemental data: | | |
| Non-cash investing activities: | | |
| Common stock issued for net assets of business acquired | $ 1,348 | |

## MANAGING CASH FLOWS

Management can do much to influence the cash flows of a particular period. In fact, it has a responsibility to manage cash flows. No business can afford to run out of cash and default on its obligations. Even being a few days late in meeting payrolls, or paying suppliers or creditors, can severely damage important business relationships. Thus one of management's most basic responsibilities is to ensure that the business has enough cash to meet its obligations as they come due.

### Budgeting: The Primary Cash Management Tool

The primary tool used by management to anticipate and shape future cash flows is a *cash budget*. A **cash budget** is a *forecast* of future cash receipts and payments. This budget is *not* a financial statement and is not widely distributed to people outside of the organization. To managers, however, it is among the most useful of all accounting reports.

In many ways, a cash budget is similar to a statement of cash flows. However, the budget shows the results *expected in future periods,* rather than those achieved in the past. Also, the cash budget is more *detailed,* usually showing expected cash flows month-by-month and separately for every department within the organization.

Cash budgets serve many purposes. Among the most important are:

- Encouraging managers to plan and coordinate the activities of their departments in advance.
- Providing managers with advance notice of the resources at their disposal and the results they are expected to achieve.
- Providing targets useful in evaluating departmental performance.
- Providing advance warnings of potential cash shortages.

**YOUR TURN**

### You as a Student

How is predicting future cash flows—receipts and outlays—useful in your daily life? Forecast your cash outlays in the coming month for: (1) housing, (2) food, and (3) other. Where will the cash come from to finance these outlays?

*Our comments appear on page 588.

### What Priority Should Managers Give to Increasing Net Cash Flows?

Creditors and investors look to a company's cash flows to protect their investment and provide future returns. Trends in key cash flows (such as from operations and free cash flow) affect a company's credit rating, stock price, and access to additional investment capital. For these reasons, management is under constant pressure to improve the key measures of cash flow. Unfortunately, the pressure to report higher cash flows in the current period may *conflict* with managers' long-run responsibilities.

**LO 7**

Discuss the likely effects of various business strategies on cash flows.

**Short-Term Results versus Long-Term Growth**     Often, short-term operating results can be improved at the expense of long-term growth. For example, reducing expenditures for developing new products will increase earnings and net cash flows in the current period. But over time, this strategy may lessen the company's competitiveness and long-term profitability.

In contrast, the strategies most likely to promote long-term growth may *reduce* earnings and cash flows in the near term—often by large amounts.

**Merck**, the world's largest pharmaceutical company, spends as much as *$1.3 billion* each year in its efforts to develop new products. And even after **Merck** makes a "breakthrough" discovery, it takes years of testing before a new product is brought to market.

Most expenditures for research and development (R&D) are paid in cash and charged immediately to expense. Thus, in any given year, **Merck**'s R&D costs *reduce* both earnings and cash flow by more than $1 billion (before taxes). Yet **Merck**'s ongoing commitment to R&D has been a key factor in the company's success.

**MANAGEMENT STRATEGY**

**One-Time Boosts to Cash Flows**   Some strategies can increase the net cash flows of the current period, but *without having much effect* on future cash flows. Such strategies include collecting receivables more quickly and reducing the size of inventory.

Assume, for example, that a company offers 60-day terms to its credit customers. Thus credit sales made in January are collected in March, and credit sales made in February are collected in April. Notice that in each month, the company is collecting about *one month's* amount of credit sales.

Now assume that on March 1, the company changes its policies to allow only *30-day* credit terms. In April, the company will collect *two months* of credit sales—those made in February (under the former 60-day terms) *and* those made in March (under the new 30-day terms).

This significantly increases the cash received from customers for the month of April. But it does not signal higher cash flows for the months ahead. In May, the company will collect only those credit sales made in April. Thus it quickly returns to the pattern of collecting about *one month's* credit sales in the current month. Shortening the collection period provided only a one-time boost in cash receipts.

A similar one-time boost may be achieved by reducing the size of inventory. This reduces the need for purchasing merchandise, *but only while inventory levels are falling.* Once the company stabilizes the size of its inventory at the new and lower level, its monthly purchases must return to approximately the quantity of goods sold during the period.

## Some Strategies for Permanent Improvements in Cash Flow

Several strategies may improve cash flows in *both* the short and long term. These are *deferring income taxes, peak pricing,* and developing an *effective product mix.*

**Deferring Income Taxes**   *Deferring* income taxes means using accounting methods for income tax purposes that legally postpone the payment of income taxes. An example is using an *accelerated depreciation method* for income tax purposes.

Deferring taxes may benefit a growing business *every year*. Thus it is an effective and popular cash management strategy.[6]

**Peak Pricing**   Some businesses have more customers than they can handle—at least at certain times of the day or year. Examples of such businesses include popular restaurants, resort hotels, telephone companies, and providers of electricity.

**Peak pricing** is a strategy of using sales prices both to increase revenue and to ration goods and services when total demand exceeds supply (or capacity). A higher price is charged during the peak periods of customer demand, and a lower price during off-

---

[6] The Modified Accelerated Cost Recovery System (MACRS) is an accelerated method widely used for income tax purposes. Deferred income taxes were discussed further in Chapter 10. The reason a growing business can benefit from deferred taxes *every year* is that each year it defers a *greater amount* than comes due from the past.

peak periods. Peak pricing has two related goals. First, it *increases the seller's revenue* during the periods of greatest demand. Second, it *shifts* some of the demand to off-peak periods, when the business is better able to service additional customers.

**MANAGEMENT STRATEGY**

**Beach House** is a popular seafood restaurant in Cardiff-by-the-Sea. A lobster dinner regularly costs $16.95. But from *4:30 to 6:00 P.M.*, it's only *$9.95*. Why? Because prior to 6:00 P.M. Beach House has lots of empty tables. Later, the restaurant becomes so crowded that it often has to turn customers away.

In many situations, peak pricing benefits the business *and the public*. Off-peak prices generally are *lower* than if peak pricing were not employed. Thus peak pricing may make goods and services available to customers who otherwise could not afford them. Also, peak pricing may prevent systems, such as cellular telephones, from becoming so overloaded that they simply cannot function.

It is important to recognize, however, that peak pricing is *not always appropriate*. For example, we would not expect hospitals or physicians to raise their prices during epidemics or natural disasters. The alternative to peak pricing is a single price all the time. In a single-price situation, demand in excess of capacity normally is handled on the basis of first-come, first-served.

**YOUR TURN**

### You as a Marketing Manager

Assume you are the marketing manager for **Toys "R" Us** (the international chain). In the 1996 Christmas season, a doll called Tickle-Me-Elmo had a suggested retail price of $29.95. The doll became overwhelmingly popular and was in short supply. Customers who bought the doll were able to resell it for *hundreds of dollars* just by running a classified ad in the newspaper.

Much news coverage was given to the phenomenal prices these dolls commanded. **Toys "R" Us** easily could have sold Tickle-Me-Elmo's for $100 or more.

Would you have raised Elmo's price during this temporary period of excess demand? Explain your reasoning.

*Our comments appear on page 589.

**Develop an Effective Product Mix**    Another tool for increasing revenue and cash receipts is the mix of products offered for sale. The dual purposes of an effective **product mix** are to (1) increase total sales and (2) increase gross margins (that is, the excess of the selling price over the cost of the product).

Some products complement one another, meaning the customer who buys one product often may purchase the other. Common examples of **complementary products** include french fries at a hamburger stand, snacks at a movie theater, and a car wash connected to a gas station.

Some complementary products are *essential* to satisfying the customer. (Would you be happy at a sports stadium that didn't sell food?) Others increase sales by *attracting customers* who also purchase other types of merchandise.

Some complementary products appear to be only incidental to the company's main product lines. But, in reality, these incidental items may *be* the company's most important products.

**Remco Business Products, Inc.**, sells a variety of office products, including copy machines. Like most businesses that sell major appliances, it also sells long-term service contracts to provide maintenance and repairs at a fixed annual fee. These service contracts actually are **Remco**'s most profitable product. In fact, if you purchase a service contract, you won't need to buy a copier. **Remco** will lend you one for the life of the service contract at no additional charge.

**CASE IN POINT**

## Concluding Comments . . .

Managers and investors alike must look beyond changes in earnings and cash flows from one period to the next. Consider the factors that *cause* these changes and how they may affect future operations.

There is more to financial statement analysis than looking at current numbers and short-term trends. The informed decision maker must *understand the company's business activities* and *anticipate the long-term effects* of its business strategies.

Whether you are an investor, a manager, or a taxpayer, you need to understand the difference between cash flows and the accrual basis of accounting. Accrual-based information is used in determining the profitability and the financial position of a business—especially a business of considerable financial strength. But in evaluating such factors as solvency, the prospects for short-term survival, and the ability of a business to seize investment opportunities, cash flows may be more relevant than accrual-based measurements.

**CASH EFFECTS**

## Harrah's Entertainment, Inc.

As we began Chapter 13, we took a quick look at **Harrah's Entertainment, Inc.**, observing that the company's cash increased by $74,586,000 during 1999. Now that we have learned more about the three primary sources of cash flows, we can better understand how **Harrah's** cash increased so much during 1999.

Following is a summary of the major categories of cash flows for **Harrah's Entertainment, Inc.**, for 1999, 1998, and 1997 (dollars in thousands):

**A SECOND LOOK**

|  | 1999 | 1998 | 1997 |
|---|---|---|---|
| Beginning cash balance | $158,995 | $116,443 | $105,594 |
| Net cash from: |  |  |  |
| Operating activities | 514,406 | 300,371 | 255,102 |
| Investing activities | (184,364) | (763,238) | (220,953) |
| Financing activities | (255,456) | 505,419 | (23,300) |
| Ending cash balance | $233,581 | $158,995 | $116,443 |

What conclusions can you draw about **Harrah's** cash flows during this three-year period? The following items are important in assessing the company's cash position:

- Cash has consistently risen over the three-year period from $105,594 thousand in 1997 to $233,581 thousand in 1999.

- Operating activities have provided strong cash flows each year, amounting to much more than both beginning and ending cash balances each year.

- The company has consistently invested in assets over the three-year period, with cash flows from investing activities being a large negative number (i.e., cash is being paid out) each year.

- The company's use of financing for asset acquisitions has varied from year to year, providing a great deal of cash in 1998, but using cash in 1997 and 1999 when debt was retired.

## SUPPLEMENTAL TOPIC A

### THE INDIRECT METHOD

**LO 8**

Compute net cash flows from operating activities using the *indirect* method.

In a statement of cash flows, the net cash flows from operating activities may be determined by either the *direct method* or the *indirect method*. We previously illustrated both methods using data in our Allison Corporation example, but placed primary emphasis on the direct method. For your convenience, these illustrations are repeated. (Accrual-based data appear in **blue**; cash flows are shown in **red**.)

|  |  |  |
|---|---:|---:|
| **Direct Method** | | |
| Cash flows from operating activities: | | |
| Cash received from customers . . . . . . . . . . . . . . . . . . . . . . . . . . . . . | $ 870,000 | |
| Interest and dividends received . . . . . . . . . . . . . . . . . . . . . . . . . . . | 10,000 | |
| Cash provided by operating activities . . . . . . . . . . . . . . . . . . . . . . | | $880,000 |
| Cash paid to suppliers and employees . . . . . . . . . . . . . . . . . . . . . | $(764,000) | |
| Interest paid . . . . . . . . . . . . . . . . . . . . . . . . . . . . . . . . . . . | (28,000) | |
| Income taxes paid . . . . . . . . . . . . . . . . . . . . . . . . . . . . . . . . | (38,000) | |
| Cash disbursed for operating activities . . . . . . . . . . . . . . . . . . . . . | | (830,000) |
| Net cash provided by operating activities . . . . . . . . . . . . . . . . . . . . . | | $ 50,000 |
| **Indirect Method** | | |
| Net income . . . . . . . . . . . . . . . . . . . . . . . . . . . . . . . . . . . . . . | | $ 65,000 |
| Add: Depreciation expense . . . . . . . . . . . . . . . . . . . . . . . . . . . . . . | | 40,000 |
| Decrease in accrued interest receivable . . . . . . . . . . . . . . . . . . . . | | 1,000 |
| Increase in accounts payable . . . . . . . . . . . . . . . . . . . . . . . . . . . | | 15,000 |
| Increase in accrued interest liabilities . . . . . . . . . . . . . . . . . . . . . | | 7,000 |
| Nonoperating loss on sales of marketable securities . . . . . . . . . . . . | | 4,000 |
| Subtotal . . . . . . . . . . . . . . . . . . . . . . . . . . . . . . . . . . . . . . . . | | $132,000 |
| Less: Increase in accounts receivable . . . . . . . . . . . . . . . . . . . . . . | $30,000 | |
| Increase in inventory . . . . . . . . . . . . . . . . . . . . . . . . . . . . | 10,000 | |
| Increase in prepaid expenses . . . . . . . . . . . . . . . . . . . . . . . . | 3,000 | |
| Decrease in accrued operating expenses payable . . . . . . . . . . . . . | 6,000 | |
| Decrease in accrued income taxes payable . . . . . . . . . . . . . . . . . | 2,000 | |
| Nonoperating gain on sales of plant assets . . . . . . . . . . . . . . . . . | 31,000 | 82,000 |
| Net cash provided by operating activities . . . . . . . . . . . . . . . . . . . . | | $ 50,000 |

### Comparison of the Direct and Indirect Methods

The two methods of computing net cash flows from operating activities are more similar than they appear at first glance. Both methods are based on the same accounting information and both result in the *same net cash flow*. Also, the computations underlying both methods are quite similar. Both methods convert accrual-based income statement amounts into cash flows by adjusting for changes in related balance sheet accounts.

To illustrate the similarity in the computations, look briefly at the formulas for computing the cash inflows and outflows shown under the direct method (pages 541–544). Each formula begins with an income statement amount and then adds or subtracts the change during the period in related balance sheet accounts. Now look at our illustration of the indirect method. Notice that this computation also focuses on the net changes during the period in balance sheet accounts.

The difference between the two methods lies only in approach. However, the two approaches provide readers of the statement of cash flows with different types of information. The direct method informs these readers of the nature and dollar amounts of the *specific cash inflows and outflows* comprising the operating activities of the business. The indirect method, in contrast, *explains why* the net cash flows from operating activities differ from another measurement of performance—net income.

## Differences between Net Income and Net Cash Flows from Operating Activities

As previously stated, net cash flows from operating activities differ from net income for three major reasons. (***Note:*** In the following discussions we assume that both net income and net cash flows are positive amounts.)

1. *Noncash expenses.* Some expenses, such as depreciation expense, reduce net income but do not require any cash outlay during the current period.
2. *Timing differences.* Revenues and expenses are measured using the concepts of accrual accounting. Net cash flows, on the other hand, reflect the effects of cash transactions. Revenues and expenses may be recognized in a different accounting period from the related cash flows.
3. *Nonoperating gains and losses.* By definition, net cash flows from operating activities show only the effects of those cash transactions classified as operating activities. Net income, on the other hand, may include gains and losses relating to investing and financing activities.

## Reconciling Net Income with Net Cash Flows

To further develop your understanding of the indirect method, we now discuss two common adjustments required to reconcile net income with net cash flows from operating activities. The nature and dollar amounts of these adjustments are determined by an accountant using a worksheet or a computer program; they are *not* entered in the company's accounting records.

1. *Adjustments for Noncash Expenses*

   Depreciation is an example of a noncash expense—that is, depreciation expense reduces net income but does not require any cash outlay during the period. (The cash outflow related to depreciation resulted when the asset was purchased—before any depreciation was ever recognized.) Depreciation causes expenses on the accrual basis to exceed cash payments, and net income for the period is less than net cash flows. To reconcile net income with net cash flows, we add back to net income the amount of depreciation and any other noncash expenses. (Other noncash expenses included unfunded pension expense, amortization of intangible assets, depletion of natural resources, and amortization of bond discount.)

2. *Adjusting for Timing Differences*

   Timing differences between elements of net income and net cash flows arise whenever revenue or expenses are recognized by debiting or crediting an account *other than* cash. Changes over the period in the balances of these asset and liability accounts represent differences between the amount of revenue or expenses recognized in the income statement and the net cash flows from operating activities. The balance sheet accounts that give rise to these timing differences include Accounts Receivable, Inventories, Prepaid Expenses, Accounts Payable, and Accrued Expenses Payable. Let us look at the effects of changes in each type of account.

**Changes in Accounts Receivable** Receivables increase as revenue is earned and decrease as cash is collected from customers. A net increase in Accounts Receivable over the period indicates that the revenue from credit sales exceeds collections from customers. In other words, part of the revenue recognized increased receivables rather than cash. In our reconciliation of these two amounts, the net increase in Accounts Receivable is *deducted* from net income to determine cash provided by revenue transactions.

On the other hand, a net decrease in Accounts Receivable indicates cash receipts in excess of revenue from credit sales and is added to the amount of net income.

**YOUR TURN**

### You as an Accounts Receivable Manager

Your job is to manage the accounts receivable department for a national home improvement retail chain. Each store in the chain prepares separate financial statements that are evaluated by corporate headquarters and are consolidated to prepare the year-end financial statements sent to investors. The company has a standard policy for customers of 2/10, net/30. That is, customers get a 2% discount if they pay in 10 days, but must pay the full amount within 30 days of the sale. The manager of one of the largest stores in the Northeast has complained that almost all of his store's customers take advantage of the discount. At most stores in the Southwest, however, almost none of the customers take advantage of the discount. The northeastern store manager asked you to make an exception to the standard policy for his store. This manager has requested the discount be dropped to help improve the store's cash flow statement. Will dropping the discount improve the store's cash flows? Would it be ethical for you to drop the standard policy for this store?

*Our comments appear on page 589.

**Changes in Inventory** The balance in the Inventory account increases as merchandise is purchased and decreases as goods are sold. A net increase in the Inventory account during the period indicates that purchases exceed the cost of goods sold. To reconcile net income with net cash flows, we deduct from net income the amount of these additional purchases (the net increase in the balance of the Inventory account).

A net decrease in the balance of the Inventory account over the period indicates that the cost of goods sold (reported in the income statement) exceeds purchases made during the period. In other words, some of the inventory sold this period was purchased in an earlier period. To the extent that the cost of goods sold consists of a decrease in inventory, cash payment is not required in the current period. Therefore, we add to net income the amount of a net decrease in Inventory.

**Changes in Prepaid Expenses** Prepaid Expenses appear in the balance sheet as assets. Increases in these assets result from cash payments, and decreases result from expiring amounts being recognized as expenses of the period. A net *increase* over the period in the amount of Prepaid Expenses indicates that cash payments made for these items exceeded the amounts recognized as expense. In determining net cash flows from operating activities, we deduct from net income the net increase in a company's Prepaid Expenses.

A net *decrease* in Prepaid Expenses indicates that cash outlays during the period were less than the amounts deducted as expense in the computation of net income. A net decrease in Prepaid Expenses is added back to net income.

**Changes in Accounts Payable** Accounts Payable are increased by purchases on account and are reduced by cash payments to suppliers. A net increase in Accounts Payable indicates that the accrual-based figure for purchases, which is included in the cost of goods sold, is greater than the cash payments made to suppliers. Therefore, in converting net income to cash flows, we add back the amount of merchandise purchases financed by a net increase in Accounts Payable.

A net decrease in Accounts Payable indicates that cash payments to suppliers exceed the purchases made during the period. Thus a net decrease in Accounts Payable is subtracted from net income in the computation of net cash flows.

**Changes in Accrued Expenses Payable**   The liability for Accrued Expenses Payable increases with the recognition of expenses that will be paid in the future and decreases as cash payments are made. A net increase in Accrued Expenses Payable indicates that expenses in the period exceed the related cash payments. Thus net income is less than net cash flows, and the increase in the Accrued Expenses Payable account should be added to net income.

A net decrease in Accrued Expenses Payable indicates that cash payments exceed the related amounts of expense. This decrease, therefore, is subtracted from net income.

The liability Deferred Income Taxes may be viewed as a long-term accrued expense payable. However, in the reconciliation of net income with net cash flows from operating activities, the change in the liability Deferred Income Taxes is shown separately from the net change in other accrued expenses payable. A net increase in this liability is added to net income; a net decrease is subtracted.

**A Helpful Hint Based on Debits and Credits**   In our preceding discussion, we explained *why* increases and decreases in a number of asset and liability accounts represent differences between the net income and net cash flows for the period. We do not expect you to memorize the effects of all of these changes. Rather, we recommend that you identify the types of transactions that cause a given account balance to increase or decrease and then *evaluate the effects* of these transactions on net income and net cash flows. This type of analysis will enhance your understanding of the relationships between accrual accounting and cash transactions.

However, let us offer you a quick hint. Double-entry accounting provides a simple rule that will let you check your analysis. For those asset and liability accounts that explain timing differences between net income and net cash flows, *a net credit change in the account's balance is always added to net income; a net debit change is always subtracted.* (For practice, test this rule on the adjustments in the summary of the indirect method appearing below. It applies to every adjustment that describes an increase or decrease in a balance sheet account.)

3. *Adjusting for Nonoperating Gains and Losses*
   Nonoperating gains and losses include gains and losses from sales of investments, plant assets, and discontinued operations (which relate to investing activities); and gains and losses on early retirement of debt (which relate to financing activities).

   In a statement of cash flows, cash flows are classified as operating activities, investing activities, or financing activities. Nonoperating gains and losses, by definition, do not affect *operating activities*. However, these gains and losses do enter into the determination of net income. Therefore, in converting net income to net cash flows from operating activities, we *add back any nonoperating losses* and *deduct any nonoperating gains* included in net income. The full cash effect of the transaction is then presented as an investing activity (for example, sale of a building) or as a financing activity (for example, retirement of debt) in the statement of cash flows.

## The Indirect Method: A Summary

The adjustments to net income explained in our preceding discussion are summarized as follows:

| | |
|---|---|
| Net income | |
| **Add:** | Depreciation |
| | Decrease in accounts receivable |
| | Decrease in inventories |
| | Decrease in prepaid expenses |
| | Increase in accounts payable |
| | Increase in accrued expenses payable |
| | Increase in deferred income taxes payable |
| | Nonoperating losses deducted in computing net income |
| **Deduct:** | Increase in accounts receivable |
| | Increase in inventories |
| | Increase in prepaid expenses |
| | Decrease in accounts payable |
| | Decrease in accrued expenses payable |
| | Decrease in deferred income taxes payable |
| | Nonoperating gains added in computing net income |
| Net cash provided by (used in) operating activities | |

## Indirect Method May Be Required in a Supplementary Schedule

The FASB recommends use of the *direct method* in presenting net cash flows from operating activities. The majority of companies, however, elect to use the indirect method. One reason is that the FASB requires companies opting for the direct method to meet an additional reporting requirement.

Companies using the direct method are required to provide a *supplementary schedule* illustrating the computation of net cash flows from operating activities by the indirect method. However, no supplementary computations are required of companies that present the indirect method computations in their cash flow statements because this same information is already presented in the body of the statement under the indirect method. In the opinion of these authors, this reporting requirement undermines the FASB's efforts to encourage use of the direct method.

## SUPPLEMENTAL TOPIC B

### A WORKSHEET FOR PREPARING A STATEMENT OF CASH FLOWS

**LO 9**

Explain how a worksheet may be helpful in preparing a statement of cash flows.

A statement of cash flows is developed by *systematically analyzing changes in the noncash balance sheet accounts*. This process can be formalized and documented through the preparation of a specially designed worksheet. The worksheet also provides the accountant with visual assurance that the changes in balance sheet accounts have been fully explained.

### Data for an Illustration

We will illustrate the worksheet approach using the 2002 financial data of Auto Supply Co.[1] Shown below are the balances in Auto's balance sheet accounts at the beginning and end of 2002. (Please notice in this illustration that the account balances at the end

---

[1] Our example involving Allison Corporation was quite comprehensive. Therefore, a worksheet for Allison Corporation would be too long and detailed for use as an introductory illustration of a worksheet for the statement of cash flows.

of the current year appear in the *right-hand* column. This format also is used in the work-sheet.)

| AUTO SUPPLY CO. Comparative Balance Sheets | | |
|---|---|---|
| | **December 31,** | |
| | **2001** | **2002** |
| **Assets** | | |
| Cash | $ 50,000 | $ 45,000 |
| Marketable Securities | 40,000 | 25,000 |
| Accounts Receivable | 320,000 | 330,000 |
| Inventory | 240,000 | 235,000 |
| Plant and Equipment (net of accumulated depreciation) | 600,000 | 640,000 |
| Totals | $1,250,000 | $1,275,000 |
| **Liabilities & Stockholders' Equity** | | |
| Accounts Payable | $ 150,000 | $ 160,000 |
| Accrued Expenses Payable | 60,000 | 45,000 |
| Mortgage Note Payable (long-term) | –0– | 70,000 |
| Bonds Payable (due in 2015) | 500,000 | 350,000 |
| Capital Stock (no par value) | 160,000 | 160,000 |
| Retained Earnings | 380,000 | 490,000 |
| Totals | $1,250,000 | $1,275,000 |

*Changes in the noncash accounts are the key to identifying cash flows*

**Additional Information**  The following information also is used in the preparation of the worksheet. (Accrual-based measurements appear in **blue**; cash flows, in **red**.)

1. Net income for the year amounted to *$250,000*. Cash dividends of *$140,000* were declared and paid.
2. Auto's only noncash expense was depreciation, which totaled *$60,000*.
3. Marketable securities costing *$15,000* were sold for *$35,000* cash, resulting in a *$20,000* nonoperating gain.
4. The company purchased plant assets for *$100,000*, making a *$30,000* cash down payment and issuing a *$70,000* mortgage note payable for the balance of the purchase price.

## The Worksheet

Auto Supply Co. reports cash flows from operating activities by the *indirect method.*[2] A worksheet for preparing a statement of cash flows appears on the following page.

To set up the worksheet, the company's balance sheet accounts are listed in the top portion of the worksheet, with the beginning balances in the first column and the year-end balances in the last (right-hand) column. (For purposes of illustration, we have shown these accounts and account balances in **black**.)

The two middle columns are used to (1) explain the changes in each balance sheet account over the year and (2) indicate how each change affected cash.

---

[2] If the worksheet utilizes the direct method, numerous subclassifications are required within the operating activities section. Such worksheets are illustrated in more advanced accounting courses.

**Entries in the Two Middle Columns** The entries in the *top portion of the worksheet* summarize the transactions recorded in the account over the year. (Because these entries summarize transactions recorded on the **accrual basis,** they are shown in **blue**.)

For each summary entry in the top portion of the worksheet, we make an offsetting entry (in the opposite column) in the *bottom portion* of the worksheet indicating the *cash effects* of the transactions. These cash effects are classified as operating, investing, or financing activities and are explained with a descriptive caption. (Entries representing the *cash effects* of transactions and the related descriptive captions appear in **red**.)

Entries in the two middle columns may be made in any sequence, but we recommend the following approach:

1. Explain the changes in the Retained Earnings account.
2. Account for depreciation expense (and any other noncash expenses).
3. Account for timing differences between net income and cash flows from operating activities.
4. Explain any remaining changes in balance sheet accounts *other than Cash*. (Hint: Changes in asset accounts represent investing activities; changes in liability and equity accounts represent financing activities.)
5. Compute and record the net increase or decrease in cash.

Using this approach, the entries in our illustrated worksheet are explained next.

## Entry

*Step 1: Explain the changes in retained earnings*

1. Auto's net income explains a $250,000 *credit* to the Retained Earnings account. In the bottom portion of the working paper, an offsetting entry is made in the *Sources* column and is classified as an operating activity.[3]

2. Cash dividends of $140,000 caused a *debit* to the Retained Earnings account during 2002. The offsetting entry falls into the *Uses* column; payments of dividends are classified as a financing activity.

With these first two entries, we have explained how Auto's Retained Earnings account increased during 2002 from $380,000 to $490,000.

*Step 2: Account for noncash expenses*

3. Auto's only noncash expense was depreciation. In the top portion of the worksheet, depreciation explains a $60,000 credit (decrease) in Plant and Equipment (which includes the Accumulated Depreciation accounts). The offsetting entry in the bottom of the worksheet is placed in the Sources column. We have explained that depreciation is not really a source of cash, but that it *is* added back to net income as a step in computing the cash flows from operating activities.

*Step 3: Account for timing differences*

4–7. Fluctuations in current assets and current liabilities create *timing differences* between net income and the net cash flows from operating activities. In the top portion of the worksheet, entries (4) through (7) summarize the changes in these current asset and current liability accounts. In the bottom portion, they show how these changes affect the computation of cash flows from operating activities.

*Step 4: Explain any remaining changes in noncash accounts*

8. In 2002, Auto sold marketable securities with a cost of $15,000 for $35,000 cash, resulting in a $20,000 nonoperating gain. In the top portion of the worksheet, the entry explains the $15,000 credit change in the Marketable Securities account. In the bottom portion, it reports cash proceeds of $35,000. The difference? The $20,000 nonoperating gain, which is *removed from the Operating Activities section* of the worksheet and included instead within the amount reported as "Proceeds from sales of marketable securities in the investing activities category."

---

[3] When the *indirect method* is used, net income serves as the *starting point* for computing net cash flows from operating activities.

## AUTO SUPPLY CO
## Worksheet for a Statement of Cash Flows
## For the Year Ended December 31, 2002

| Balance sheet effects: | Effects of Transactions | | | |
|---|---|---|---|---|
| | Beginning Balance | Debit Changes | Credit Changes | Ending Balance |
| **Assets** | | | | |
| Cash and Cash Equivalents . . . . . . . | 50,000 | | (x)    5,000 | 45,000 |
| Marketable Securities . . . . . . . . . . . | 40,000 | | (8)  15,000 | 25,000 |
| Accounts Receivable . . . . . . . . . . . . | 320,000 | (4)   10,000 | | 330,000 |
| Inventory . . . . . . . . . . . . . . . . . . . . | 240,000 | | (5)    5,000 | 235,000 |
| Plant and Equipment (net of accumulated depreciation). . . . . | 600,000 | (9) 100,000 | (3)  60,000 | 640,000 |
| Totals . . . . . . . . . . . . . . . . . . . . | 1,250,000 | | | 1,275,000 |
| **Liabilities & Stockholders' Equity** | | | | |
| Accounts Payable . . . . . . . . . . . . . . | 150,000 | | (6)  10,000 | 160,000 |
| Accrued Expenses Payable . . . . . . . | 60,000 | (7)   15,000 | | 45,000 |
| Mortgage Note Payable . . . . . . . . . . | –0– | | (9)  70,000 | 70,000 |
| Bonds Payable . . . . . . . . . . . . . . . . | 500,000 | (10) 150,000 | | 350,000 |
| Capital Stock . . . . . . . . . . . . . . . . . | 160,000 | | | 160,000 |
| Retained Earnings . . . . . . . . . . . . . | 380,000 | (2) 140,000 | (1) 250,000 | 490,000 |
| Totals . . . . . . . . . . . . . . . . . . . . | 1,250,000 | 415,000 | 415,000 | 1,275,000 |

| Cash effects: | Sources | Uses | |
|---|---|---|---|
| **Operating activities:** | | | |
| Net income . . . . . . . . . . . . . . . . . . . . . . | (1) 250,000 | | |
| Depreciation expense . . . . . . . . . . . . . . . | (3)   60,000 | | |
| Increase in accounts receivable . . . . . . . . . | | (4)   10,000 | |
| Decrease in inventory . . . . . . . . . . . . . . . . | (5)     5,000 | | |
| Increase in accounts payable . . . . . . . . . . . | (6)   10,000 | | |
| Decrease in accrued expenses payable . . . . . . . . . . . . . . . . . . . . . . | | (7)   15,000 | |
| Gain on sales of marketable securities . . . . . . . . . . . . . . . . . . . . . . . | | (8)   20,000 | |
| **Investing activities:** | | | |
| Proceeds from sales of marketable securities . . . . . . . . . . . . . . . . | (8)   35,000 | | |
| Cash paid to acquire plant assets . . . . . . . . . . . . . . . . . . . . . . . . . | | (9)   30,000 | |
| **Financing activities:** | | | |
| Dividends paid . . . . . . . . . . . . . . . . . . . . . | | (2) 140,000 | |
| Payments to retire bonds payable . . . . . . . . | | (10) 150,000 | |
| Subtotals . . . . . . . . . . . . . . . . . . . . . . . . | 360,000 | 365,000 | |
| Net decrease in cash . . . . . . . . . . . . . . . . . | (x)     5,000 | | |
| Totals . . . . . . . . . . . . . . . . . . . . . . . . . . | 365,000 | 365,000 | |

*Up here we summarize the changes in each noncash account*

*Down here we identify and classify the related cash effects of these changes*

Cash provided by operations— $280,000

Cash provided by investing activities— $5,000

Cash used in financing activities— $290,000

9. Auto purchased $100,000 in plant assets, paying $30,000 cash and issuing a $70,000 note payable. These events explain a $100,000 debit in Plant and Equipment and the $70,000 credit change in Mortgage Note Payable; they involved a cash outlay of $30,000, which is classified as an investing activity. (The $70,000 financed by issuance of a note payable is a *noncash* investing and financing activity.)

10. The $150,000 debit change in Auto's Bonds Payable account indicates that this amount of the liability has been repaid—that is, $150,000 in bonds has been retired. This is included in the financing activities category.

At this point, we should check to determine that our entries in the two middle columns *fully explain* the differences between the beginning and ending balance of each noncash balance sheet account. If the top portion of the worksheet explains the changes in every noncash account, the bottom section should include all of the cash flows for the year.

*Step 5: Compute and record the net change in cash*

(x) We now total the Sources (cash increases) and Uses (cash decreases) columns in the bottom portion of the worksheet. The difference between these column subtotals represents the *net increase or decrease* in cash. In our example, the Sources column totals $360,000, while the Uses column totals $365,000, indicating a *$5,000 decrease* in cash over the period. Notice that this is exactly the amount by which Cash decreased during 2002: $50,000 − $45,000 = $5,000. Our last entry, labeled *(x)*, explains the credit change in the Cash account at the top of the worksheet and brings the bottom of the worksheet into balance.

A formal statement of cash flows, reporting the cash flows from operating activities by the indirect method, can be prepared directly from the bottom portion of this worksheet. (Amounts appearing in accrual-based accounting records are shown in **blue**; cash flows appear in **red**.)

## AUTO SUPPLY CO.
### Statement of Cash Flows
### For the Year Ended December 31, 2002

**Cash flows from operating activities:**

| | | |
|---|---:|---:|
| Net income | | $250,000 |
| Add: Depreciation expense | | 60,000 |
| Decrease in inventory | | 5,000 |
| Increase in accounts payable | | 10,000 |
| Subtotal | | $325,000 |
| Less: Increase in accounts receivable | $ 10,000 | |
| Decrease in accrued expenses payable | 15,000 | |
| Gain on sales of marketable securities | 20,000 | 45,000 |
| Net cash provided by operating activities | | $280,000 |

**Cash flows from investing activities:**

| | | |
|---|---:|---:|
| Proceeds from sales of marketable securities | $ 35,000 | |
| Cash paid to acquire plant assets (see supplementary schedule below) | (30,000) | |
| Net cash provided by investing activities | | 5,000 |

**Cash flows from financing activities:**

| | | |
|---|---:|---:|
| Dividends paid | $(140,000) | |
| Payments to retire bonds payable | (150,000) | |
| Net cash used in financing activities | | (290,000) |
| Net decrease in cash | | $ (5,000) |
| Cash and cash equivalents, Dec. 31, 2001 | | 50,000 |
| Cash and cash equivalents, Dec. 31, 2002 | | $ 45,000 |

### Supplementary Schedule: Noncash Investing and Financing Activities

| | |
|---|---:|
| Purchases of plant assets | $100,000 |
| Less: Portion financed through issuance of long-term debt | 70,000 |
| Cash paid to acquire plant assets | $ 30,000 |

*Compare the content of this statement with the worksheet on page 565*

# END-OF-CHAPTER REVIEW

## SUMMARY OF LEARNING OBJECTIVES

### LO 1

**Explain the purposes and uses of a statement of cash flows.**
The primary purpose of a statement of cash flows is to provide information about the cash receipts and cash payments of the entity, and how they relate to the entity's operating, investing, and financing activities. Readers of financial statements use this information to assess the solvency of a business and to evaluate its ability to generate positive cash flows in future periods, pay dividends, and finance growth.

### LO 2

**Describe how cash transactions are classified within a statement of cash flows.**
Cash flows are classified as (1) operating activities, (2) investing activities, or (3) financing activities. Receipts and payments of interest are classified as operating activities.

### LO 3

**Compute the major cash flows relating to operating activities.**
The major operating cash flows are (1) cash received from customers, (2) cash paid to suppliers and employees, (3) interest and dividends received, (4) interest paid, and (5) income taxes paid. These cash flows are computed by converting the income statement amounts for revenue, cost of goods sold, and expenses from the accrual basis to the cash basis. This is done by adjusting the income statement amounts for changes occurring over the period in related balance sheet accounts.

### LO 4

**Explain why net income differs from net cash flows from operating activities.**
Net income differs from net operating cash flows for several reasons. One reason is noncash expenses, such as depreciation and the amortization of intangible assets. These expenses, which require no cash outlays when they are recognized, reduce net income but do not require cash payments. Another reason is the many timing differences existing between the recognition of revenue and expense and the occurrence of the underlying cash flows. Finally, nonoperating gains and losses enter into the determination of net income, but the related cash flows are classified as investing or financing activities, not operating activities.

### LO 5

**Distinguish between the direct and indirect methods of reporting operating cash flows.**
The direct and indirect methods are alternative formats for reporting net cash flows from operating activities. The *direct* method shows the specific cash inflows and outflows comprising the operating activities of the business. Under the *indirect* method, the computation begins with accrual-based net income and then makes adjustments necessary to arrive at net cash flows from operating activities. Both methods result in the same dollar amount of net cash flows from operating activities.

### LO 6

**Compute the cash flows relating to investing and financing activities.**
Cash flows from investing and financing activities are determined by examining the entries in the related asset and liability accounts, along with any related gains or losses shown in the income statement. Debit entries in asset accounts represent purchases of assets (an investing activity). Credit entries in asset accounts represent the cost of assets sold. The amount of these credit entries must be adjusted by any gains or losses recognized on these sales transactions.

Debit entries to liability accounts represent repayment of debt, while credit entries represent borrowing. Both types of transactions are classified as financing activities. Other financing activities include the issuance of stock (indicated by credits to the paid-in capital accounts) and payment of dividends (indicated by a debit change in the Retained Earnings account).

### LO 7

**Discuss the likely effects of various business strategies on cash flows.**
It is difficult to predict the *extent* to which a business strategy will affect cash flows. However, an informed decision maker should understand the *direction* in which a strategy is likely to affect cash flows—both in the short term and over a longer term.

### *LO 8

**Compute net cash flows from operating activities using the *indirect* method.**
The indirect method uses net income (as reported in the income statement) as the starting point in the computation of net cash flows from operating activities. Adjustments to net income necessary to arrive at net cash flows from operating activities are described in three categories: noncash expenses, timing differences, and nonoperating gains and losses. Adjustments reconcile net income (accrual basis) to net cash flows from operating activities. Specific adjustments from each category are illustrated in the summary analysis of the indirect method on page 562.

---

\* *Supplemental Topic A,* "The Indirect Method."

**†LO 9**

**Explain how a worksheet may be helpful in preparing a statement of cash flows.**

A worksheet can be used to analyze the changes in balance sheet accounts other than Cash and, thereby, determine the related cash flows. In the top portion of the worksheet, entries are made summarizing the changes in each noncash account. In the bottom half, offsetting entries are made to represent the cash effects of the transactions summarized in the top portion. The entries in the bottom half of the worksheet are classified into the same categories as in a statement of cash flows—operating, investing, and financing. The statement of cash flows then is prepared from the data in the bottom portion of the worksheet.

In this chapter we have discussed the importance of the statement of cash flows in terms of providing information for investors and creditors. We have seen how we convert accrual accounting information to cash-based information and arrange that information so that investors and creditors can better understand the cash effects of a company's operating, investing, and financing activities. In the next chapter we take a broader look at financial statement analysis, including how information from the cash flow statement is combined with information from the other financial statements, to better understand a company's financial activities.

## KEY TERMS INTRODUCED OR EMPHASIZED IN CHAPTER 13

**accrual basis** (p. 537)  A method of summarizing operating results in terms of revenue earned and expenses incurred, rather than cash receipts or cash payments.

**cash basis** (p. 542)  The practice of summarizing operating results in terms of cash receipts and cash payments, rather than revenue earned or expenses incurred.

**cash budget** (p. 552)  A detailed forecast of expected future cash receipts, usually organized department by department and month by month for the coming year.

**cash equivalents** (p. 536)  Highly liquid short-term investments, such as Treasury bills, money market funds, and commercial paper. For purposes of preparing a statement of cash flows, money held in cash equivalents is considered the same as cash. Thus transfers between a bank account and cash equivalents are not considered receipts or disbursements of cash.

**cash flows** (p. 534)  A term describing both cash receipts (inflows) and cash payments (outflows).

**complementary products** (p. 555)  Products that "fit together"—that tie in with a company's other products. As a result, customers attracted to one product may also purchase others.

**direct method** (p. 546)  A method of reporting net cash flows from operating activities by listing specific types of cash inflows and outflows. This is the method recommended by the FASB, but the indirect method is an acceptable alternative.

**financing activities** (p. 536)  Transactions such as borrowing, repaying borrowed amounts, raising equity capital, or making distributions to owners. The cash effects of these transactions are reported in the financing activities section of the statement of cash flows. Noncash aspects of these transactions are disclosed in a supplementary schedule.

**free cash flow** (p. 552)  The portion of the annual net cash flows from operating activities that remains available for discretionary purposes after the basic obligations of the business have been met. Can be computed in several different ways.

**indirect method** (p. 546)  A way of reporting net cash flows from operating activities that reconciles this figure with the amount of net income shown in the income statement. An alternative to the direct method.

**investing activities** (p. 536)  Transactions involving acquisitions or sales of investments or plant assets. The cash aspects of these transactions are shown in the investing activities section of the statement of cash flows. Noncash aspects of these transactions are disclosed in a supplementary schedule to this financial statement.

**operating activities** (p. 534)  Transactions entering into the determination of net income, with the exception of gains and losses relating to financing or investing activities. The category includes such transactions as selling goods or services, earning investment income, and incurring costs and expenses. The cash effects of these transactions are reflected in the operating activities section of the statement of cash flows.

**peak pricing** (p. 555)  The strategy of charging a higher price during periods of high demand, and a lower price during periods of slack demand. Intended to both maximize revenue and shift excess demand to periods in which it can be more easily accommodated.

**product mix** (p. 555)  The variety and relative quantities of goods and services that a company offers for sale.

## ▍ DEMONSTRATION PROBLEM

You are the chief accountant for Modern Consumer Products, Inc. Your assistant has prepared an income statement for the current year and has developed the following additional information by analyzing changes in the company's balance sheet accounts.

---

† *Supplemental Topic B*, "A Worksheet for Preparing a Statement of Cash Flows."

---

**MODERN CONSUMER PRODUCTS, INC.**
**Income Statement**
**For the Year Ended December 31, 2002**

**Revenue:**

| | |
|---|---|
| Net sales .................................................... | $9,500,000 |
| Interest income ........................................... | 320,000 |
| Gain on sales of marketable securities ....................... | 70,000 |
| Total revenue and gains .................................. | $9,890,000 |

**Costs and expenses:**

| | | |
|---|---|---|
| Cost of goods sold ............................. | $4,860,000 | |
| Operating expenses (including depreciation of $700,000) ................................. | 3,740,000 | |
| Interest expense ............................... | 270,000 | |
| Income taxes .................................. | 300,000 | |
| Loss on sales of plant assets ..................... | 90,000 | |
| Total costs, expenses, and losses ............................. | | 9,260,000 |
| Net income ...................................................... | | $ 630,000 |

Changes in the company's balance sheet accounts over the year are summarized as follows:

1. Accounts Receivable decreased by $85,000.
2. Accrued Interest Receivable increased by $15,000.
3. Inventory decreased by $280,000, and Accounts Payable to suppliers of merchandise decreased by $240,000.
4. Short-term prepayments of operating expenses decreased by $18,000, and accrued liabilities for operating expenses increased by $35,000.
5. The liability for Accrued Interest Payable decreased by $16,000 during the year.
6. The liability for Accrued Income Taxes Payable increased by $25,000 during the year.
7. The following schedule summarizes the total debit and credit entries during the year in other balance sheet accounts:

| | Debit Entries | Credit Entries |
|---|---|---|
| Marketable Securities ...................................... | $ 120,000 | $ 210,000 |
| Notes Receivable (cash loans made to others) ................ | 250,000 | 190,000 |
| Plant Assets (see paragraph **8**) ........................... | 3,800,000 | 360,000 |
| Notes Payable (short-term borrowing) ....................... | 620,000 | 740,000 |
| Bonds Payable ............................................. | | 1,100,000 |
| Capital Stock .............................................. | | 50,000 |
| Additional Paid-in Capital (from issuance of stock) ............. | | 840,000 |
| Retained Earnings (see paragraph **9** below) .................. | 320,000 | 630,000 |

8. The $360,000 in credit entries to the plant asset accounts is net of any debits to accumulated depreciation when plant assets were retired. Thus the $360,000 in credit entries represents the *book value* of all plant assets sold or retired during the year.
9. The $320,000 debit to retained earnings represents dividends declared and paid during the year. The $630,000 credit entry represents the net income for the year.
10. All investing and financing activities were cash transactions.
11. Cash and cash equivalents amounted to $448,000 at the beginning of the year and to $330,000 at year-end.

## Instructions

You are to prepare a statement of cash flows for the current year, following the format illustrated on page 535. Cash flows from operating activities are to be determined by the *direct method*. Place brackets around dollar amounts representing cash outlays. Show separately your computations of the following amounts:

**a.** Cash received from customers

**b.** Interest received

**c.** Cash paid to suppliers and employees

**d.** Interest paid

**e.** Income taxes paid

**f.** Proceeds from sales of marketable securities

**g.** Proceeds from sales of plant assets

**h.** Proceeds from issuing capital stock

## Solution to the Demonstration Problem

### MODERN CONSUMER PRODUCTS, INC.
### Statement of Cash Flows
### For the Year Ended December 31, 2002

| | | |
|---|---:|---:|
| **Cash flows from operating activities:** | | |
| Cash received from customers (a) | $ 9,585,000 | |
| Interest received (b) | 305,000 | |
| Cash provided by operating activities | | $9,890,000 |
| Cash paid to suppliers and employees (c) | $(7,807,000) | |
| Interest paid (d) | (286,000) | |
| Income taxes paid (e) | (275,000) | |
| Cash disbursed for operating activities | | (8,368,000) |
| Net cash provided by operating activities | | $1,522,000 |
| **Cash flows from investing activities:** | | |
| Purchases of marketable securities | $ (120,000) | |
| Proceeds from sales of marketable securities (f) | 280,000 | |
| Loans made to borrowers | (250,000) | |
| Collections on loans | 190,000 | |
| Cash paid to acquire plant assets | (3,800,000) | |
| Proceeds from sales of plant assets (g) | 270,000 | |
| Net cash used in investing activities | | (3,430,000) |
| **Cash flows from financing activities:** | | |
| Proceeds from short-term borrowing | $ 740,000 | |
| Payments to settle short-term debts | (620,000) | |
| Proceeds from issuing bonds payable | 1,100,000 | |
| Proceeds from issuing capital stock (h) | 890,000 | |
| Dividends paid | (320,000) | |
| Net cash provided by financing activities | | 1,790,000 |
| Net increase (decrease) in cash | | $ (118,000) |
| Cash and cash equivalents, Jan. 1 | | 448,000 |
| Cash and cash equivalents, Dec. 31 | | $ 330,000 |

**Supporting computations:**

a. Cash received from customers:

| | |
|---|---:|
| Net sales .......................................... | $9,500,000 |
| Add: Decrease in accounts receivable ........................... | 85,000 |
| Cash received from customers ................................. | $9,585,000 |

b. Interest received:

| | |
|---|---:|
| Interest income ..................................... | $ 320,000 |
| Less: Increase in accrued interest receivable ..................... | 15,000 |
| Interest received ....................................... | $ 305,000 |

c. Cash paid to suppliers and employees:

Cash paid for purchases of merchandise:

| | | |
|---|---:|---:|
| Cost of goods sold ................................. | | $4,860,000 |
| Less: Decrease in inventory .......................... | | 280,000 |
| Net purchases ................................. | | $4,580,000 |
| Add: Decrease in accounts payable to suppliers ................... | | 240,000 |
| Cash paid for purchases of merchandise ....................... | | $4,820,000 |

Cash paid for operating expenses:

| | | |
|---|---:|---:|
| Operating expenses ...................................... | | $3,740,000 |
| Less: Depreciation (a "noncash" expense) ............... | $700,000 | |
| Decrease in prepayments ...................... | 18,000 | |
| Increase in accrued liabilities for operating expenses ........................... | 35,000 | 753,000 |
| Cash paid for operating expenses ........................... | | $2,987,000 |
| Cash paid to suppliers and employees ($4,820,000 + $2,987,000) ............................. | | $7,807,000 |

d. Interest paid:

| | |
|---|---:|
| Interest expense ....................................... | $ 270,000 |
| Add: Decrease in accrued interest payable ...................... | 16,000 |
| Interest paid ......................................... | $ 286,000 |

e. Income taxes paid:

| | |
|---|---:|
| Income taxes expense ................................... | $ 300,000 |
| Less: Increase in accrued income taxes payable ................... | 25,000 |
| Income taxes paid ..................................... | $ 275,000 |

f. Proceeds from sales of marketable securities:

| | |
|---|---:|
| Cost of marketable securities sold (credit entries to the Marketable Securities account) ........................ | $ 210,000 |
| Add: Gain reported on sales of marketable securities ............... | 70,000 |
| Proceeds from sales of marketable securities ................... | $ 280,000 |

g. Proceeds from sales of plant assets:

| | |
|---|---:|
| Book value of plant assets sold (paragraph **8**) ..................... | $ 360,000 |
| Less: Loss reported on sales of plant assets ...................... | 90,000 |
| Proceeds from sales of plant assets ......................... | $ 270,000 |

h. Proceeds from issuing capital stock:

| | |
|---|---:|
| Amounts credited to the Capital Stock account ................... | $ 50,000 |
| Add: Amounts credited to Additional Paid-in Capital account ........... | 840,000 |
| Proceeds from issuing capital stock ......................... | $ 890,000 |

# SELF-TEST QUESTIONS

*Answers to these questions appear on page 589.*

1. The statement of cash flows is designed to assist users in assessing each of the following, *except:*
   a. The ability of a company to remain solvent.
   b. The company's profitability.
   c. The major sources of cash receipts during the period.
   d. The reasons why net cash flows from operating activities differ from net income.

2. Which of the following is *not* included in the statement of cash flows, or in a supplementary schedule accompanying the statement of cash flows?
   a. Disclosure of the amount of cash invested in money market funds during the accounting period.
   b. A reconciliation of net income to net cash flows from operating activities.
   c. Disclosure of investing or financing activities that did not involve cash.
   d. The amount of cash and cash equivalents owned by the business at the end of the accounting period.

3. Cash flows are grouped in the statement of cash flows into the following major categories:
   a. Operating activities, investing activities, and financing activities.
   b. Cash receipts, cash disbursements, and noncash activities.
   c. Direct cash flows and indirect cash flows.
   d. Operating activities, investing activities, and collecting activities.

4. The following is a list of various cash payments and cash receipts:

| | |
|---|---|
| Cash paid to suppliers and employees | $400,000 |
| Dividends paid | 18,000 |
| Interest paid | 12,000 |
| Purchases of plant assets | 45,000 |
| Interest and dividends received | 17,000 |
| Payments to settle short-term debt | 29,000 |
| Income taxes paid | 23,000 |
| Cash received from customers | 601,000 |

   Based only on the above items, net cash flows from operating activities are:
   a. $138,000.   b. $91,000.   c. $183,000.   d. $120,000.

5. During the current year, two transactions were recorded in the Land account of Nolan Industries. One involved a debit of $320,000 to the Land account; the second was a $210,000 credit to the Land account. Nolan Industries' income statement for the year reported a loss on sale of land in the amount of $25,000. All transactions involving the Land account were cash transactions. These transactions would be shown in the statement of cash flows as:
   a. $320,000 cash provided by investing activities, and $210,000 cash disbursed for investing activities.
   b. $210,000 cash provided by investing activities, and $320,000 cash disbursed for investing activities.
   c. $235,000 cash provided by investing activities, and $320,000 cash disbursed for investing activities.
   d. $185,000 cash provided by investing activities, and $320,000 cash disbursed for investing activities.

6. Which of the following business strategies is *most likely* to increase the net cash flows of a software developer in the short run but *reduce* them over a longer term?
   a. Develop software that is more costly to create but easier to update and improve.
   b. Lower the price of existing versions of products as customer demand begins to fall.

    **c.** Purchase the building in which the business operates (assume the company currently rents this location).

    **d.** Reduce expenditures for the purpose of developing new products.

## ASSIGNMENT MATERIAL

### DISCUSSION QUESTIONS

1. Briefly state the purposes of a statement of cash flows.

2. Does a statement of cash flows or an income statement best measure the profitability of a financially sound business? Explain.

3. Two supplementary schedules frequently accompany a statement of cash flows. Briefly explain the content of these schedules.

4. Give two examples of cash receipts and two examples of cash payments that fit into each of the following classifications:

    **a.** Operating activities

    **b.** Investing activities

    **c.** Financing activities

5. Why are payments and receipts of interest classified as operating activities rather than as financing or investing activities?

6. Define *cash equivalents* and list three examples.

7. During the current year, Foster Corporation transferred $300,000 from its bank account into a money market fund. Will this transaction appear in a statement of cash flows? If so, in which section? Explain.

8. In the long run, is it more important for a business to have positive cash flows from its operating activities, investing activities, or financing activities? Why?

9. Of the three types of business activities summarized in a statement of cash flows, which type is *least* likely to show positive net cash flows in a successful, growing business? Explain your reasoning.

10. The items and amounts listed in a balance sheet and an income statement correspond to specific accounts in a company's ledger. Is the same true about the items and amounts in a statement of cash flows? Explain.

11. Wilshire, Inc., had net sales for the year of $840,000. Accounts receivable increased from $90,000 at the beginning of the year to $162,000 at year-end. Compute the amount of cash collected during the year from customers.

12. Describe the types of cash payments summarized by the caption "Cash paid to suppliers and employees."

13. Identify three factors that may cause net income to differ from net cash flows from operating activities.

14. Briefly explain the difference between the *direct* and *indirect methods* of computing net cash flows from operating activities. Which method results in higher net cash flows?

15. Are cash payments of accounts payable viewed as operating activities or financing activities? Referring to the statement of cash flows illustrated on page 535, state the caption that includes amounts paid on accounts payable.

16. Discount Club acquired land by issuing $500,000 of capital stock. No cash changed hands in this transaction. Will the transaction be disclosed in the company's statement of cash flows? Explain.

17. The only transaction recorded in the plant asset accounts of Rogers Corporation in the current year was a $150,000 credit to the Land account. Assuming that this credit resulted from a cash transaction, does this entry indicate a cash receipt or a cash payment? Should this $150,000 appear in the statement of cash flows, or is some adjustment necessary?

18. During the current year, the following credit entries were posted to the paid-in capital accounts of Moser Shipyards:

| Capital Stock ........................................................ | $10,000,000 |
|---|---|
| Additional Paid-in Capital ............................................ | 98,500,000 |

Explain the type of cash transaction that probably caused these credit changes, and illustrate the presentation of this transaction in a statement of cash flows.

19. At the beginning of the current year, Frieds Corporation had dividends payable of $1,500,000. During the current year, the company declared cash dividends of $3,800,000, of which $900,000 appeared as a liability at year-end. Determine the amount of cash dividends *paid* during this year.

20. Define the term *free cash flow*. Explain the significance of this measurement to (1) short-term creditors, (2) long-term creditors, (3) stockholders, and (4) management.

21. Describe a *cash budget* and explain its usefulness to management.

22. Explain the concept of *peak pricing* and provide an example from your own experience.

23. From management's perspective, identify some of the characteristics of an effective product mix.

24. Explain why speeding up the collection of accounts receivable provides only a one-time increase in cash receipts.

## EXERCISES

The statement of cash flows for Auto Supply Co. appears on page 567. Assume that with respect to routine business operations, this was a *typical year*. Use this cash flow statement to evaluate the company's ability to maintain the current level of dividend payments over the foreseeable future. Explain your reasoning.

**EXERCISE 13.1**

Using a Statement of Cash Flows

**LO 1, 2**

**ABM Industries, Incorporated**'s 1998 statement of cash flows appears on page 553. Study the statement and respond to the following questions:

**a.** What was the company's free cash flow in 1998?

**b.** What were the major sources and uses of cash from financing activities during 1998? Did the net effect of financing activities result in an increase or a decrease in cash during the year?

**c.** What happened to the total amount of cash and cash equivalents during the year? Assuming 1998 was a typical year for **ABM Industries**, is the company in a position to continue its dividend payments in the future? Explain.

**d.** Look at the reconciliation of net income to net cash provided by operating activities and explain the following:

1. Gain on the sale of assets.

2. Increase in accounts receivable.

3. Increase in retirement plans accrual.

**EXERCISE 13.2**

Using a Statement of Cash Flows

**LO 1, 2, 4**

An analysis of the Marketable Securities controlling account of Presley Products, Inc., shows the following entries during the year:

**EXERCISE 13.3**

Computing Cash Flows

**LO 6**

| Balance, Jan. 1 ........................................................ | $ 290,000 |
|---|---|
| Debit entries ......................................................... | 125,000 |
| Credit entries ......................................................... | (140,000) |
| Balance, Dec. 31 ..................................................... | $ 275,000 |

In addition, the company's income statement includes a $35,000 loss on sales of marketable securities. None of the company's marketable securities is considered a cash equivalent.

Compute the amounts that should appear in the statement of cash flows as:

**a.** Purchases of marketable securities.

**b.** Proceeds from sales of marketable securities.

**EXERCISE 13.4**

Comparing Net Sales and Cash Receipts

**LO 3, 4**

During the current year, Frisky, Inc., made cash sales of $270,000 and credit sales of $460,000. During the year, accounts receivable decreased by $32,000.

**a.** Compute for the current year the amounts of:

1. Net sales reported as revenue in the income statement.

2. Cash received from collecting accounts receivable.

3. Cash received from customers.

**b.** Write a brief statement explaining *why* cash received from customers differs from the amount of net sales.

**EXERCISE 13.5**

Computing Cash Paid for Purchases of Merchandise

**LO 3**

The general ledger of Techpro provides the following information relating to purchases of merchandise:

|  | End of Year | Beginning of Year |
|---|---|---|
| Inventory | $820,000 | $780,000 |
| Accounts payable to merchandise suppliers | 430,000 | 500,000 |

The company's cost of goods sold during the year was $3,550,000. Compute the amount of cash payments made during the year to suppliers of merchandise.

**EXERCISE 13.6**

Reporting Lending Activities and Interest Revenue

**LO 3, 6**

During the current year, Dakota Savings and Loan Association made new loans of $14 million. In addition, the company collected $36 million from borrowers, of which $30 million was interest revenue. Explain how these cash flows will appear in the company's statement of cash flows, indicating the classification and the dollar amount of each cash flow.

**EXERCISE 13.7**

Format of a Statement of Cash Flows

**LO 2**

The accounting staff of Alabama Outfitters, Inc., has assembled the following information for the year ended December 31, 2002:

| | |
|---|---|
| Cash and cash equivalents, Jan. 1 | $ 27,400 |
| Cash and cash equivalents, Dec. 31 | 66,400 |
| Cash paid to acquire plant assets | 21,000 |
| Proceeds from short-term borrowing | 10,000 |
| Loans made to borrowers | 5,000 |
| Collections on loans (excluding interest) | 4,000 |
| Interest and dividends received | 27,000 |
| Cash received from customers | 795,000 |
| Proceeds from sales of plant assets | 9,000 |
| Dividends paid | 55,000 |
| Cash paid to suppliers and employees | 635,000 |
| Interest paid | 19,000 |
| Income taxes paid | 71,000 |

Using this information, prepare a statement of cash flows. Include a proper heading for the financial statement, and classify the given information into the categories of operating activities, investing activities, and financing activities. Determine net cash flows from operating activities by the direct method. Place brackets around the dollar amounts of all cash disbursements.

Indicate how you would expect the following strategies to affect the company's net cash flows from *operating activities* (1) in the near future and (2) in later periods (after the strategy's long-term effects have "taken hold"). *Fully explain your reasoning.*

**a.** A successful pharmaceutical company substantially reduces its expenditures for research and development.

**b.** A restaurant that previously sold only for cash adopts a policy of accepting bank credit cards, such as Visa and MasterCard.

**c.** A manufacturing company reduces by 50% the size of its inventories of raw materials (assume no change in inventory storage costs).

**d.** Through tax planning, a rapidly growing real estate developer is able to defer significant amounts of income taxes.

**e.** A rapidly growing software company announces that it will stop paying cash dividends for the foreseeable future and will instead distribute stock dividends.

**EXERCISE 13.8**

Effects of Business Strategies

**LO 7**

An analysis of the annual financial statements of Waller Recycle Corporation reveals the following:

**a.** The company had a $5 million extraordinary loss from the early retirement of bonds payable.

**b.** Depreciation for the year amounted to $8 million.

**c.** During the year, $2 million in cash was transferred from the company's checking account into a money market fund.

**d.** Accounts receivable from customers increased by $4 million over the year.

**e.** Cash received from customers during the year amounted to $167 million.

**f.** Prepaid expenses decreased by $1 million over the year.

**g.** Dividends declared during the year, $7 million; dividends paid during the year, $6 million.

**h.** Accounts payable (to suppliers of merchandise) increased by $2.5 million during the year.

**i.** The liability for accrued income taxes payable amounted to $5 million at the beginning of the year and $3 million at year-end.

In the computation of net cash flows from operating activities by the *indirect method,* explain whether each of the above items should be *added to net income, deducted from net income,* or *omitted from the computation.* Briefly explain your reasons for each answer.

***EXERCISE 13.9**

An Analysis of Possible Reconciling Items

**LO 4, 8**

The following data are taken from the income statement and balance sheet of Miller Machinery, Inc.:

***EXERCISE 13.10**

Computation of Net Cash Flows from Operating Activities—Indirect Method

**LO 8**

|  | Dec. 31 2002 | Jan. 1 2002 |
|---|---|---|
| **Income statement:** | | |
| Net Income | $427,000 | |
| Depreciation Expense | 125,000 | |
| Amortization of Intangible Assets | 40,000 | |
| Gain on Sale of Plant Assets | 90,000 | |
| Loss on Sale of Investments | 35,000 | |
| **Balance sheet:** | | |
| Accounts Receivable | $335,000 | $380,000 |
| Inventory | 503,000 | 575,000 |
| Prepaid Expenses | 22,000 | 10,000 |
| Accounts Payable (to merchandise suppliers) | 379,000 | 410,000 |
| Accrued Expenses Payable | 180,000 | 155,000 |

---

* *Supplemental Topic A,* "The Indirect Method."

Using this information, prepare a partial statement of cash flows for the year ended December 31, 2002, showing the computation of net cash flows from operating activities by the *indirect* method.

**EXERCISE 13.11**

**Tootsie Roll Industries**: Using a Statement of Cash Flows

**LO 1, 2, 6**

Statements of cash flows for **Tootsie Roll Industries, Inc.** appear in Appendix A.

**a.** Focus on the statement of cash flows for the year ended December 31, 1998, and respond to the following:

   **1.** Describe the major reasons why the company's cash and cash equivalents increased by $20,311,000 during the year.

   **2.** Assuming that the company had not purchased shares of its own stock during 1998, calculate the amount of:

   —Cash flows for the year from financing activities.

   —Cash and cash equivalents at the end of the year.

   **3.** Calculate the amount of the company's free cash flow.

   **4.** From a cash flow perspective do you believe the company's performance was better in the year ended December 31, 1998, than in the prior year? Justify your answer.

**b.** Comparing 1999 and 1998, what were the primary changes in cash flows that occurred? Is the company's cash position stronger or weaker at the end of 1999 than 1998?

# PROBLEMS

**PROBLEM 13.1**

Classifying Cash Flows

**LO 2**

Among the transactions of Alvarez Communications were the following:

   **a.** Made payments on accounts payable to merchandise suppliers.

   **b.** Paid the principal amount of a note payable to First Bank.

   **c.** Paid interest charges relating to a note payable to First Bank.

   **d.** Issued bonds payable for cash; management plans to use this cash in the near future to expand manufacturing and warehouse capabilities.

   **e.** Paid salaries to employees in the finance department.

   **f.** Collected an account receivable from a customer.

   **g.** Transferred cash from the general bank account into a money market fund.

   **h.** Used the cash received in **d,** above, to purchase land and a building suitable for a manufacturing facility.

   **i.** Made a year-end adjusting entry to recognize depreciation expense.

   **j.** At year-end, purchased for cash an insurance policy covering the next 12 months.

   **k.** Paid the quarterly dividend on preferred stock.

   **l.** Paid the semiannual interest on bonds payable.

   **m.** Received a quarterly dividend from an investment in the preferred stock of another corporation.

   **n.** Sold for cash an investment in the preferred stock of another corporation.

   **o.** Received cash upon the maturity of an investment in cash equivalents. (Ignore interest.)

**Instructions**

Most of the preceding transactions should be included among the activities summarized in a statement of cash flows. For each transaction that should be included in this statement, indicate whether the transaction should be classified as an operating activity, an investing activity, or a financing activity. If the transaction *should not be included* in the current year's statement of cash flows, briefly explain why not. (Assume that net cash flows from operating activities are determined by the *direct method*.)

**PROBLEM 13.2**

Format of a Statement of Cash Flows

**LO 2, 3, 6**

The accounting staff of Reizenstein Company has assembled the following information for the year ended December 31, 2002:

| | | |
|---|---|---|
| Cash sales ............................................... | $ 800,000 | O |
| Credit sales ............................................. | ~~2,500,000~~ | I |
| Collections on accounts receivable ......................... | 2,200,000 | O |
| Cash transferred from the money market fund to the general bank account ......................................... | ~~250,000~~ | |
| Interest and dividends received .......................... | 100,000 | O |
| Purchases (all on account) ............................... | ~~1,800,000~~ | |
| Payments on accounts payable to merchandise suppliers .................. | 1,500,000 | O |
| Cash payments for operating expenses ...................... | 1,050,000 | O |
| Interest paid ............................................ | 180,000 | O |
| Income taxes paid ...................................... | 95,000 | O |
| Loans made to borrowers ................................ | 500,000 | I |
| Collections on loans (excluding receipts of interest) ...................... | 260,000 | I |
| Cash paid to acquire plant assets .......................... | 3,100,000 | I |
| Book value of plant assets sold ........................... | 660,000 | I |
| Loss on sales of plant assets ............................. | 80,000 | $580 cash |
| Proceeds from issuing bonds payable ....................... | 2,500,000 | F |
| Dividends paid ......................................... | 120,000 | F |
| Cash and cash equivalents, Jan. 1 ......................... | 517,000 | B |

## Instructions

Prepare a statement of cash flows in the format illustrated on page 535. Place brackets around amounts representing cash outflows. Use the *direct method* of reporting cash flows from operating activities.

Some of the items above will be listed in your statement without change. However, you will have to combine certain given information to compute the amounts of (1) collections from customers, (2) cash paid to suppliers and employees, and (3) proceeds from sales of plant assets. (Hint: Not every item listed above is used in preparing a statement of cash flows.)

An analysis of the income statement and the balance sheet accounts of Fellini Fashions at December 31, 2002, provides the following information:

**PROBLEM 13.3**

Reporting Investing Activities

**LO 6**

| | |
|---|---|
| **Income statement items:** | |
| Gain on Sale of Marketable Securities ............................... | $ 42,000 |
| Loss on Sales of Plant Assets ..................................... | 33,000 |
| **Analysis of balance sheet accounts:** | |
| **Marketable Securities account:** | |
| Debit entries ..................................... | $ 75,000 |
| Credit entries ..................................... | 90,000 |
| **Notes Receivable account:** | |
| Debit entries ..................................... | 210,000 |
| Credit entries ..................................... | 162,000 |
| **Plant and Equipment accounts:** | |
| Debit entries to plant asset accounts ...................... | 196,000 |
| Credit entries to plant asset accounts ..................... | 120,000 |
| Debit entries to accumulated depreciation accounts ...................... | 75,000 |

## Additional Information

1. Except as noted in **4,** payments and proceeds relating to investing transactions were made in cash.
2. The marketable securities are not cash equivalents.

3. All notes receivable relate to cash loans made to borrowers, not to receivables from customers.

4. Purchases of new equipment during the year ($196,000) were financed by paying $70,000 in cash and issuing a long-term note payable for $126,000.

5. Debits to the accumulated depreciation accounts are made whenever depreciable plant assets are retired. Thus the book value of plant assets retired during the year was $45,000 ($120,000 − $75,000).

### Instructions

**a.** Prepare the investing activities section of a statement of cash flows. Show supporting computations for the amounts of (1) proceeds from sales of marketable securities and (2) proceeds from sales of plant assets. Place brackets around numbers representing cash outflows.

**b.** Prepare the supporting schedule that should accompany the statement of cash flows in order to disclose the noncash aspects of the company's investing and financing activities.

**c.** Assume that Fellini Fashions' management expects approximately the same amount of cash to be used for investing activities next year. In general terms, explain how the company might generate cash for this purpose.

**PROBLEM 13.4**

Reporting Investing Activities

 **LO 6**

An analysis of the income statement and the balance sheet accounts of Xavier Imports at December 31, 2002, provides the following information:

| | |
|---|---:|
| **Income statement items:** | |
| Gain on Sales of Plant Assets . . . . . . . . . . . . . . . . . . . . . . . . . . . . . . . . . . . . . . . . | $ 12,000 |
| Loss on Sales of Marketable Securities . . . . . . . . . . . . . . . . . . . . . . . . . . . . . . . . | 16,000 |
| **Analysis of balance sheet accounts:** | |
| **Marketable Securities account:** | |
| Debit entries . . . . . . . . . . . . . . . . . . . . . . . . . . . . . . . . . . . . . . . . . . . . . . . . . . | $ 78,000 |
| Credit entries . . . . . . . . . . . . . . . . . . . . . . . . . . . . . . . . . . . . . . . . . . . . . . . . . | 62,000 |
| **Notes Receivable account:** | |
| Debit entries . . . . . . . . . . . . . . . . . . . . . . . . . . . . . . . . . . . . . . . . . . . . . . . . . . | 55,000 |
| Credit entries . . . . . . . . . . . . . . . . . . . . . . . . . . . . . . . . . . . . . . . . . . . . . . . . . | 60,000 |
| **Plant and Equipment accounts:** | |
| Debit entries to plant asset accounts . . . . . . . . . . . . . . . . . . . . . . . . . . . . . . . . | 150,000 |
| Credit entries to plant asset accounts . . . . . . . . . . . . . . . . . . . . . . . . . . . . . . . . | 140,000 |
| Debit entries to accumulated depreciation accounts . . . . . . . . . . . . . . . . . . . . . | 100,000 |

### Additional Information

1. Except as noted in **4** below, payments and proceeds relating to investing transactions were made in cash.

2. The marketable securities are not cash equivalents.

3. All notes receivable relate to cash loans made to borrowers, not to receivables from customers.

4. Purchases of new equipment during the year ($150,000) were financed by paying $70,000 in cash and issuing a long-term note payable for $80,000.

5. Debits to the accumulated depreciation accounts are made whenever depreciable plant assets are sold or retired. Thus the book value of plant assets sold or retired during the year was $40,000 ($140,000 − $100,000).

### Instructions

**a.** Prepare the investing activities section of a statement of cash flows. Show supporting computations for the amounts of (1) proceeds from sales of marketable securities and (2) proceeds from sales of plant assets. Place brackets around amounts representing cash outflows.

**b.** Prepare the supplementary schedule that should accompany the statement of cash flows in order to disclose the noncash aspects of the company's investing and financing activities.

**c.** Does management have *more* control or *less* control over the timing and amount of cash outlays for investing activities than for operating activities? Explain.

The following income statement and selected balance sheet account data are available for Juarez Interiors, Inc., at December 31, 2002:

**PROBLEM 13.5**

Reporting Operating Cash Flows by the Direct Method

**LO 3**

### JUAREZ INTERIORS, INC.
### Income Statement
### For the Year Ended December 31, 2002

**Revenue:**

| | | |
|---|---|---|
| Net sales | | $2,850,000 |
| Dividend income | | 104,000 |
| Interest income | | 70,000 |
| Gain on sales of marketable securities | | 4,000 |
| Total revenue and gains | | $3,028,000 |
| **Costs and expenses:** | | |
| Cost of goods sold | $1,550,000 | |
| Operating expenses | 980,000 | |
| Interest expense | 185,000 | |
| Income taxes | 110,000 | |
| Total costs and expenses | | 2,825,000 |
| Net income | | $ 203,000 |

| Selected account balances: | End of Year | Beginning of Year |
|---|---|---|
| Accounts receivable | $ 650,000 | $ 720,000 |
| Accrued interest receivable | 9,000 | 6,000 |
| Inventories | 800,000 | 765,000 |
| Short-term prepayments | 20,000 | 15,000 |
| Accounts payable (merchandise suppliers) | 570,000 | 562,000 |
| Accrued operating expenses payable | 65,000 | 94,000 |
| Accrued interest payable | 21,000 | 12,000 |
| Accrued income taxes payable | 22,000 | 35,000 |

### Additional Information

1. Dividend revenue is recognized on the cash basis. All other income statement amounts are recognized on the accrual basis.
2. Operating expenses include depreciation expense of $115,000.

### Instructions

a. Prepare a partial statement of cash flows, including only the *operating activities* section of the statement and using the *direct method*. Place brackets around numbers representing cash payments. Show supporting computations for the following:
   1. Cash received from customers
   2. Interest and dividends received
   3. Cash paid to suppliers and employees
   4. Interest paid
   5. Income taxes paid
b. Management of Juarez Interiors, Inc., is exploring ways to increase the cash flows from operations. One way that cash flows could be increased is through more aggressive collection of receivables. Assuming that management has already taken all the steps possible to increase revenues and reduce expenses, describe two other ways that cash flows from operations could be increased.

**\*PROBLEM 13.6**

Reporting Operating Cash
Flows by the Indirect Method

**LO 4, 8**

**PROBLEM 13.7**

Preparing a Statement of Cash
Flows: A Comprehensive
Problem without a Worksheet

**LO 2, 3, 4, 6, 7**

Using the information presented in Problem **13.5**, prepare a partial statement of cash flows for the current year, showing the computation of net cash flows from operating activities by the *indirect method*. Explain why the decline in accounts receivable over the year was *added* to net income in computing the cash flows from operating activities.

You are the controller for Millennium Technologies. Your staff has prepared an income statement for the current year and has developed the following additional information by analyzing changes in the company's balance sheet accounts.

| MILLENNIUM TECHNOLOGIES Income Statement For the Year Ended December 31, 2002 | | |
|---|---:|---:|
| **Revenue:** | | |
| Net sales | | $3,200,000 |
| Interest revenue | | 40,000 |
| Gain on sales of marketable securities | | 34,000 |
| Total revenue and gains | | $3,274,000 |
| **Costs and expenses:** | | |
| Cost of goods sold | $1,620,000 | |
| Operating expenses (including depreciation of $150,000) | 1,240,000 | |
| Interest expense | 42,000 | |
| Income taxes | 100,000 | |
| Loss on sales of plant assets | 12,000 | |
| Total costs, expenses, and losses | | 3,014,000 |
| Net income | | $ 260,000 |

## Additional Information

1. Accounts receivable increased by $60,000.
2. Accrued interest receivable decreased by $2,000.
3. Inventory decreased by $60,000, and accounts payable to suppliers of merchandise decreased by $16,000.
4. Short-term prepayments of operating expenses increased by $6,000, and accrued liabilities for operating expenses decreased by $8,000.
5. The liability for accrued interest payable increased by $4,000 during the year.
6. The liability for accrued income taxes payable decreased by $14,000 during the year.
7. The following schedule summarizes the total debit and credit entries during the year in other balance sheet accounts:

| | Debit Entries | Credit Entries |
|---|---:|---:|
| Marketable Securities | $ 60,000 | $ 38,000 |
| Notes Receivable (cash loans made to borrowers) | 44,000 | 28,000 |
| Plant Assets (see paragraph **8**) | 500,000 | 36,000 |
| Notes Payable (short-term borrowing) | 92,000 | 82,000 |
| Capital Stock | | 20,000 |
| Additional Paid-in Capital—Capital Stock | | 160,000 |
| Retained Earnings (see paragraph **9**) | 120,000 | 260,000 |

---

\* *Supplemental Topic A,* "The Indirect Method."

8. The $36,000 in credit entries to the Plant Assets account is net of any debits to Accumulated Depreciation when plant assets were retired. Thus the $36,000 in credit entries represents the book value of all plant assets sold or retired during the year.

9. The $120,000 debit to retained earnings represents dividends declared and paid during the year. The $260,000 credit entry represents the net income shown in the income statement.

10. All investing and financing activities were cash transactions.

11. Cash and cash equivalents amounted to $244,000 at the beginning of the year and to $164,000 at year-end.

## Instructions

a. Prepare a statement of cash flows for the current year. Use the *direct method* of reporting cash flows from operating activities. Place brackets around dollar amounts representing cash outflows. Show separately your computations of the following amounts:

   1. Cash received from customers.
   2. Interest received.
   3. Cash paid to suppliers and employees.
   4. Interest paid.
   5. Income taxes paid.
   6. Proceeds from sales of marketable securities.
   7. Proceeds from sales of plant assets.
   8. Proceeds from issuing capital stock.

b. Explain the *primary reason* why:

   1. The amount of cash provided by operating activities was substantially greater than the company's net income.
   2. There was a net decrease in cash over the year, despite the substantial amount of cash provided by operating activities.

c. Millenium's controller thinks that through more efficient cash management, the company could have held the increase in accounts receivable for the year to $10,000, without affecting net income. Explain how holding down the growth in receivables affects cash. Compute the effect that limiting the growth in receivables to $10,000 would have had on the company's net increase or decrease in cash (and cash equivalents) for the year.

SPACENET 2010 was founded in 2001 to apply a new technology for efficiently transmitting closed-circuit (cable) television signals without the need for an in-ground cable. The company earned a profit of $115,000 in 2001, its first year of operations, even though it was serving only a small test market. In 2002, the company began dramatically expanding its customer base. Management expects both sales and net income to more than triple in each of the next five years.

   Comparative balance sheets at the ends of 2001 and 2002, the company's first two years of operations, appear on the next page. (Notice that the balances at the end of the current year appear in the right-hand column.)

**†PROBLEM 13.8**

Prepare and Analyze a Statement of Cash Flows with a Worksheet

**LO 1–9**

## Additional Information

The following information regarding the company's operations in 2002 is available in either the company's income statement or its accounting records:

1. Net income for the year was $440,000. The company has never paid a dividend.

2. Depreciation for the year amounted to $147,000.

3. During the year the company purchased plant assets costing $2,200,000, for which it paid $1,850,000 in cash and financed $350,000 by issuing a long-term note payable. (Much of the cash used in these purchases was provided by short-term borrowing, as described below.)

4. In 2002, SPACENET 2010 borrowed $1,450,000 against a $5 million line of credit with a local bank. In its balance sheet, the resulting obligations are reported as notes payable (short-term).

5. Additional shares of capital stock (no par value) were issued to investors for $500,000 cash.

---

† *Supplemental Topic B*, "A Worksheet for Preparing a Statement of Cash Flows."

| SPACENET 2010 Comparative Balance Sheets | | |
|---|---|---|
| | December 31, 2001 | 2002 |
| **Assets** | | |
| Cash and cash equivalents ............................ | $ 80,000 | $ 37,000 |
| Accounts receivable ................................. | 100,000 | 850,000 |
| Plant and equipment (net of accumulated depreciation) ..................................... | 600,000 | 2,653,000 |
| Totals .......................................... | $780,000 | $3,540,000 |
| | | |
| **Liabilities & Stockholders' Equity** | | |
| Notes payable (short-term) ........................... | $ –0– | $1,450,000 |
| Accounts payable .................................. | 30,000 | 63,000 |
| Accrued expenses payable ........................... | 45,000 | 32,000 |
| Notes payable (long-term) ........................... | 390,000 | 740,000 |
| Capital stock (no par value) .......................... | 200,000 | 700,000 |
| Retained earnings ................................. | 115,000 | 555,000 |
| Totals .......................................... | $780,000 | $3,540,000 |

## Instructions

**a.** Prepare a worksheet for a statement of cash flows, following the general format illustrated on page 565. (*Note:* If this problem is completed as a group assignment, each member of the group should be prepared to explain in class all entries in the worksheet, as well as the group's conclusions in parts **c** and **d.**)

**b.** Prepare a formal statement of cash flows for 2002, including a supplementary schedule of non-cash investing and financing activities. (Follow the format illustrated on page 567. Cash provided by operating activities is to be presented by the *indirect method.*)

**c.** Briefly explain how operating activities can be a net *use* of cash when the company is operating so profitably.

**d.** Because of the expected rapid growth, management forecasts that operating activities will be an even greater use of cash in the year 2003 than in 2002. If this forecast is correct, does SPACENET 2010 appear to be heading toward insolvency? Explain.

**\*PROBLEM 13.9**

Prepare and Analyze a Statement of Cash Flows; Involves Preparation of a Worksheet

**LO 1–9**

Wonder Tool, Inc., sells a single product (a combination screwdriver, plier, hammer, and crescent wrench) exclusively through television advertising. The comparative income statements and balance sheets are for the past two years.

## Additional Information

The following information regarding the company's operations in 2002 is available from the company's accounting records:

**1.** Early in the year the company declared and paid a $4,000 cash dividend.

**2.** During the year marketable securities costing $15,000 were sold for $14,000 cash, resulting in a $1,000 nonoperating loss.

**3.** The company purchased plant assets for $20,000, paying $2,000 in cash and issuing a note payable for the $18,000 balance.

**4.** During the year the company repaid a $10,000 note payable, but incurred an additional $18,000 in long-term debt as described in **3,** above.

**5.** The owners invested $15,000 cash in the business as a condition of the new loans described in paragraph **4,** above.

---

\* *Supplemental Topic A,* "The Indirect Method," and *Supplemental Topic B,* "A Worksheet for Preparing a Statement of Cash Flows."

## WONDER TOOL, INC.
### Comparative Income Statement
### For the Years Ended December 31, 2001 and 2002

|  | 2001 | 2002 |
|---|---|---|
| Sales | $500,000 | $350,000 |
| Less: cost of goods sold | 200,000 | 140,000 |
| Gross profit on sales | $300,000 | $210,000 |
| Less: operating expenses (including depreciation of $34,000 in 2001 and $35,000 in 2002) | 260,000 | 243,000 |
| Loss on sale of marketable securities | –0– | 1,000 |
| Net income (loss) | $ 40,000 | ($ 34,000) |

## WONDER TOOL, INC.
### Comparative Balance Sheets

|  | December 31, 2001 | December 31, 2002 |
|---|---|---|
| **Assets** |  |  |
| Cash and cash equivalents | $ 10,000 | $ 60,000 |
| Marketable securities | 20,000 | 5,000 |
| Accounts receivable | 40,000 | 23,000 |
| Inventory | 120,000 | 122,000 |
| Plant and equipment (net of accumulated depreciation) | 300,000 | 285,000 |
| Totals | $490,000 | $495,000 |
| **Liabilities & Stockholders' Equity** |  |  |
| Accounts payable | $ 50,000 | $ 73,000 |
| Accrued expenses payable | 17,000 | 14,000 |
| Note payable | 245,000 | 253,000 |
| Capital stock (no par value) | 120,000 | 135,000 |
| Retained earnings | 58,000 | 20,000 |
| Totals | $490,000 | $495,000 |

## Instructions

**a.** Prepare a worksheet for a statement of cash flows, following the general format illustrated on page 565. (*Note:* If this problem is completed as a group assignment, each member of the group should be prepared to explain in class all entries in the worksheet, as well as the group's conclusions in parts **c, d,** and **e.**)

**b.** Prepare a formal statement of cash flows for 2002, including a supplementary schedule of non-cash investing and financing activities. (Use the format illustrated on page 567. Cash provided by operating activities is to be presented by the *indirect method.*)

**c.** Explain how Wonder Tool, Inc., achieved positive cash flows from operating activities, despite incurring a net loss for the year.

**d.** Does the company's financial position appear to be improving or deteriorating? Explain.

**e.** Does Wonder Tool, Inc., appear to be a company whose operations are growing or contracting? Explain.

**f.** Assume that management *agrees* with your conclusions in parts **c, d,** and **e.** What decisions should be made and what actions (if any) should be taken? Explain.

## CASES AND UNSTRUCTURED PROBLEMS

**CASE 13.1**

Another Look at Allison
Corporation

 **LO 1**

This case is based on the statement of cash flows for Allison Corporation, illustrated on page 535. Use this statement to evaluate the company's ability to continue paying the current level of dividends—$40,000 per year. The following information also is available:

1. The net cash flows from operating activities shown in the statement are relatively normal for Allison Corporation. Net cash flows from operating activities have not varied by more than a few thousand dollars in any of the past three years.

2. The net outflow for investing activities was unusually high, because the company modernized its production facilities during the year. The normal investing cash outflow is about $45,000 per year, the amount required to replace existing plant assets as they are retired. Over the long run, marketable securities transactions and lending transactions have a very small impact on Allison's net cash flows from investing activities.

3. The net cash flows from financing activities were unusually large in the current year because of the issuance of bonds payable and capital stock. These securities were issued to finance the modernization of the production facilities. In a typical year, financing activities include only short-term borrowing transactions and payments of dividends.

### Instructions

a. Based solely on the company's past performance, do you believe that the $40,000 annual dividend payments are secure? That is, does the company appear able to pay this amount in dividends every year without straining its cash position? Do you think it more likely that Allison Corporation will increase or decrease the amount of dividends that it pays? Explain fully.

b. Should any of the unusual events appearing in the statement of cash flows for the current year affect your analysis of the company's ability to pay future dividends? Explain.

**CASE 13.2**

Cash Budgeting for You as a
Student

**LO 1, 7**

Individuals generally do not prepare statements of cash flows concerning their personal activities. But they do engage in cash budgeting—if not on paper, then at least in their heads.

Assume, for example, it is December 29—a Monday. In two days your rent for January, $200, will be due. You now have $140 in the bank; every Friday you receive a paycheck for $100. You probably see the problem. And it probably doesn't look too serious; you can find a way to deal with it. That's what *budgeting* is all about.

Let's take this example a step further. In addition to the facts given above, your weekly cash payments include meals, $30; entertainment, $20; and gasoline, $10.

### Instructions

a. Using the following cash budget, compute your cash balance at the end of weeks 2, 3, and 4.

|  | Week | | | |
| --- | --- | --- | --- | --- |
|  | 1 | 2 | 3 | 4 |
| Beginning cash balance | $ 140 | $(20) | $  ? | $  ? |
| Expected cash receipts | 100 | 100 | 100 | 100 |
| Less: Expected cash outlays: | | | | |
| Monthly rent | (200) | | | |
| Meals | (30) | | | |
| Entertainment | (20) | | | |
| Gasoline | (10) | | | |
| Ending cash balance | $ (20) | $  ? | $  ? | $  ? |

b. Evaluate your financial situation.

It is late summer and National Motors, an auto manufacturer, is facing a financial crisis. A large issue of bonds payable will mature next March, and the company must issue stock or new bonds to raise the money to retire this debt. Unfortunately, profits and cash flows have been declining over recent years. Management fears that if cash flows and profits do not improve in the current year, the company will not be able to raise the capital needed to replace the maturing bonds. Therefore, members of management have made the following proposals to improve the cash flows and profitability that will be reported in the financial statements dated this coming December 31.

**CASE 13.3**

Lookin' Good?

**LO 1, 4, 7**

1. Switch from the LIFO method to the FIFO method of valuing inventories. Management estimates that the FIFO method will result in a lower cost of goods sold but in higher income taxes for the current year. However, the additional income taxes will not actually be paid until early next year.

2. Switch from the 150%-declining-balance method of depreciation to the straight-line method and lengthen the useful lives over which assets are depreciated. (These changes would be made only for financial reporting purposes, not for income tax purposes.)

3. Pressure dealers to increase their inventories—in short, to buy more cars. (The dealerships are independently owned; thus dealers are the customers to whom National Motors sells automobiles.) Management estimates that this strategy could increase sales for the current year by 5%. However, any additional sales in the current year would be almost entirely offset by fewer sales in the following year.

4. Require dealers to pay for purchases more quickly. Currently, dealers must pay for purchases of autos within 60 days. Management is considering reducing this period to 30 days.

5. Pass up cash discounts offered for prompt payment (that is, 2/10, n/30), and do not pay any bills until the final due date.

6. Borrow at current short-term interest rates (about 10%) and use the proceeds to pay off long-term debt bearing an interest rate of 13%.

7. Substitute stock dividends for the cash dividends currently paid on capital stock.

**Instructions**

a. Prepare a schedule with four columns. The first column is to be headed "Proposals" and is to contain the paragraph numbers of the seven proposals listed above. The next three columns are to be headed with the following financial statement captions: (1) "Net Income," (2) "Net Cash Flows from Operating Activities," and (3) "Cash."

For each of the seven proposals in the left column, indicate whether you expect the proposal to "Increase," "Decrease," or have "No Effect" in the current year on each of the financial statement captions listed in the next three columns. (*Note:* Only a few months remain in the current year. Therefore, you are to determine the *short-term* effects of these proposals.)

b. For each of the seven proposals, write a short paragraph explaining the reasoning behind your answers to part **a.**

"Peak pricing is unfair. It makes goods and services available only to the wealthy and prices the average person out of the market."

**CASE 13.4**

Peak Pricing

**LO 7**

**Instructions**

a. Comment on the extent to which you agree or disagree with the preceding statement.

b. What is the alternative to peak pricing?

c. Explain how peak pricing might be applied by:
   1. A hotel in Palm Springs, California. (Palm Springs is a winter resort in southern California with wonderful golf facilities. In the summer months, however, temperatures are well over 100 degrees and the tourist business slows dramatically.)
   2. Movie theaters.

d. Both in general terms and using specific examples, describe the conditions (if any) under which you might regard peak pricing as *unethical*.

## BUSINESS WEEK ASSIGNMENT

BusinessWeek

**CASE 13.5**

**LO 1, 7**

A September 19, 2000, *Business Week* article by Gene Marcial entitled "'Very Undervalued' PSINet Could Soon Have Suitors Calling," describes the situation PSINet finds itself in as uneasy. Following are excerpts from this article:

> In the market's current state of edginess, the Street takes no prisoners in cases where companies warn that they won't meet analysts' expectations. Shares of such companies get punished swiftly. So when PSINet (PSIX), a provider of Internet access and related products to large companies, lowered its second-half revenue and cash-flow forecasts on Friday, September 15, its stock quickly tumbled. It landed at 11³/4 a share, down from 15 earlier that same day. The stock has continued to slip and is currently at 9 as analysts cut their estimates and lowered price targets. The stock traded as high as 60 in early March.
>
> But in Wall Street's quirky logic, some pros now deem the stock as an opportunistic buy. The reason: They believe PSINet will be in play as a takeover target.

### Instructions

If you were an investor holding 1,000 shares in PSINet, how would you react to the decline in value described in the previous quotation? Would you hold your shares or sell them? Why do you think PSINet is considered a takeover target?

## INTERNET ASSIGNMENT

**INTERNET 13.1**

Comparing Cash Flow Information from Two Companies

**LO 2, 3, 6**

In the long run, a company must generate positive net cash flows from operating activities to survive. A business that has negative cash flows from operations will not be able to raise cash indefinitely from other sources and will eventually cease existing. Many creditors and stockholders are reluctant to invest in companies that do not generate positive cash flows from operations. However, some investors will invest in companies with negative cash flows from operations due to an optimistic future outlook for the company. Thus, investors have invested millions of dollars into Internet companies that have negative cash flows from operations.

### Instructions

a. Visit **Coca-Cola**'s Internet site (**www.coke.com**) and select Investor Relations. Under Financial Information, select the most recent Annual Report. In the Annual Report, view the Consolidated Statements of Cash Flows.

b. Visit **Amazon.com**'s Internet site (**www.amazon.com**) and select About Amazon.com. Then select Investor Relations and click SEC Filings. Select the most recent 10-K filing and view the Cash Flow Statement.

c. Compare the Net Cash Provided by Operating Activities for each company. Which company has higher Net Cash Provided by Operating Activities? Speculate why one company has much higher Net Cash Provided by Operating Activities than the other company.

d. What type of company may have Negative Net Cash Provided by Operating Activities?

e. What type of company may have large Positive Net Cash Provided by Operating Activities?

*Internet sites are time and date sensitive. It is the purpose of these exercises to have you explore the Internet. You may need to use the Yahoo! search engine* http://www.yahoo.com *(or other favorite search engine) to find a company's current web address.*

## OUR COMMENTS ON THE "YOUR TURN" CASES

**As a Student (p. 553)** Predicting future cash flows can help you plan and manage your financial affairs, begin saving for major cash outlays, and avoid financial crises.

Forecasting your own cash flows for the coming month will vary with your lifestyle and the time of year. For example, your housing costs may be based on rent or on the costs of home ownership. Don't forget utilities.

Your projected food costs will depend on what and where you eat. Other expenditures include such things as clothing, entertainment, transportation (including auto insurance and car repairs), and school expenses.

Where will the cash come from? Good question. Do *you* know?

**As a Marketing Manager (p. 556)**   We would advise you *not* to raise Elmo's price (and **Toys "R" Us** didn't). The additional revenue that **Toys "R" Us** might receive from raising the price of a single product is probably immaterial. On the other hand, raising the price of a popular and highly publicized toy right before Christmas might lead to charges of price gouging and other bad publicity.

In fact, an alternative to consider would be to cut Elmo's price, not raise it. You might publicize the reduced sales price and promise to continue it for at least a month after Christmas. In the long term, the chance to enhance customer relations is far more important than a short-term increase in revenue.

**As an Accounts Receivable Manager (p. 560)**   The actual cash flows from sales are reduced for those customers who take advantage of the discount allowed in the standard policy. Thus, on average, the cash flows from sales of comparable merchandise will be lower for the store in the Northeast, where customers have traditionally taken the discount, than for stores in the Southwest, where customers have decided not to use the available discount. However, eliminating the discount for the northeastern store may cause customers to purchase products elsewhere and significantly reduce cash flows from sales. In addition, it will most certainly delay the receipt of cash because customers will delay cash payment from 10 to 30 days. If corporate management compares the cash flow statements of stores without recognizing the differences in customer attitudes toward the discount, the manager of the northeastern store may be at a disadvantage.

It would be unethical to make an exception to the corporate customer discount policy as requested by the manager of the northeastern store. Corporate policies of this nature are determined by top headquarters management such as the president, vice-president of marketing, and/or the CEO. The individuals in the organization who are responsible for determining those policies must approve exceptions or changes to standard policies.

## ANSWERS TO SELF-TEST QUESTIONS

**1.** b    **2.** a    **3.** a    **4.** c    **5.** d    **6.** d

# FINANCIAL STATEMENT ANALYSIS

## Learning Objectives

*After studying this chapter, you should be able to:*

1. Explain the uses of dollar and percentage changes, trend percentages, component percentages, and ratios.

2. Discuss the quality of a company's earnings, assets, and working capital.

3. Explain the nature and purpose of classifications in financial statements.

4. Prepare a classified balance sheet and compute widely used measures of liquidity and credit risk.

5. Prepare a multiple-step and a single-step income statement and compute widely used measures of profitability.

6. Put a company's net income into perspective by relating it to sales, assets, and stockholders' equity.

7. Compute the ratios widely used in financial statement analysis and explain the significance of each.

8. Analyze financial statements from the viewpoints of common stockholders, creditors, and others.

Courtesy Johnson & Johnson

# Johnson & Johnson

**Johnson & Johnson** has $27.5 billion in sales and is the world's most comprehensive and broadly based manufacturer of health care products and related services. Other measures of **Johnson & Johnson**'s size include the facts that it employs 97,800 people, has 190 operating companies in 51 countries throughout the world, and sells products in more than 175 countries.

How does one get a handle on the financial performance of a huge company such as **Johnson & Johnson**? Financial statements, including the balance sheet, income statement, and statement of cash flows, provide a wealth of information that is helpful in performing this significant task. Financial statement analysis involves taking key items from these financial statements and gleaning as much useful information as possible from them. For example, we might compare the amount of **Johnson & Johnson**'s most liquid assets ($13,200 million in 1999) with its obligations that will come due soon ($7,454 million in 1999) and determine that the ratio is approximately 1.77. This means that the company has $1.77 of cash and assets near cash for every $1.00 in currently maturing liabilities.

● ● ●

We might determine that the company's 1999 net income ($4,167 million) represented a return in excess of 14% on the total assets used to generate that income ($29,163 million). Is a 1.77 ratio of cash and other liquid assets to currently maturing liabilities good or bad? Is a return on assets of 14% satisfactory or unsatisfactory? These are difficult questions to answer. To make these judgments we would need more information than we have at this point. For example, we would like to know the trend in these financial measures for **Johnson & Johnson** for several years. We would also like to know information about other companies with similar operating characteristics (i.e., in the same industry). We will study all of this and more in this chapter as we look at the interesting and challenging subject of financial statement analysis.

Financial measures are used often to evaluate corporate performance. As a result, the Securities and Exchange Commission, the Financial Accounting Standards Board, the financial press, and the accounting profession are committed to high-quality financial reporting. Throughout this text, we have emphasized the importance of integrity in financial reporting as a means of protecting the interests of investors and creditors. This chapter explores in-depth financial statement analysis, building on the introductory sections of this important subject in preceding chapters.

Our discussion of financial statement analysis is divided into three sections. First, we consider general tools of analysis that emphasize comparing information about enterprises with relevant benchmarks. Second, we consider measures of liquidity and credit risk, followed by a consideration of profitability. Third, we present and discuss a comprehensive illustration in which we analyze a company's financial statements from the perspective of three important users of information—common stockholders, long-term creditors, and short-term creditors. Throughout this chapter, we draw on information that was covered in earlier chapters and we use new information that is presented here for the first time.

## Financial Statements Are Designed for Analysis

In today's global economy, investment capital is always on the move. Through organized capital markets such as the New York Stock Exchange, investors each day shift billions of investment dollars among different companies, industries, and nations. Capital flows to those areas in which investors expect to earn the greatest returns with the least risk. How do investors forecast risk and potential returns? One of the most important ways is by analyzing accounting information for a specific company in the context of its unique industry setting.

The goal of accounting information is to provide economic decision makers with useful information. The financial statements generated through the accounting process are designed to assist users in identifying key relationships and trends. The financial statements of most publicly owned companies are classified and are presented in comparative form. Often, the word *consolidated* appears in the headings of the statements. Users of financial statements should have a clear understanding of these terms.

Most business organizations prepare **classified financial statements**, meaning that items with certain characteristics are placed together in a group, or classification. The purpose of these classifications is to *develop useful subtotals* that will assist users of the statements in their analyses. These classifications and subtotals are standardized throughout most of American business, a practice that assists decision makers in comparing the financial statements of different companies. An example of a classified financial statement is a balance sheet that separates assets and liabilities into current and noncurrent categories.

In **comparative financial statements**, the financial statement amounts *for several time periods* appear side by side in vertical columns. This assists investors in identifying and evaluating significant changes and trends.

Most large corporations own other companies through which they conduct some of their business activities. A corporation that owns other businesses is the **parent company**, and the owned companies are called **subsidiaries**. For example, **PepsiCo.**, which makes Pepsi Cola, also owns and operates **Tropicana** and **Frito-Lay**. In essence, these subsidiaries are part of the organization generally known as PepsiCo. **Consolidated financial statements** present the financial position and operating results of the parent company and its subsidiaries *as if they were a single business organization.*

**For Example . . .**   At this point, take a brief look at the financial statements of **Tootsie Roll Industries, Inc.**, which appear in Appendix A at the end of the text. These financial statements illustrate all of the concepts discussed; they are classified and presented in comparative form, and they describe a consolidated business entity. These financial statements also have been *audited* by **PricewaterhouseCoopers LLP**, an international public accounting firm.

# ▨ TOOLS OF ANALYSIS

Significant changes in financial data are easier to see when financial statement amounts for two or more years are placed side by side in adjacent columns. Such a statement is called a *comparative financial statement*. The amounts for the most recent year are usually placed in the left-hand money column, closest to the words that describe the item. The balance sheet, income statement, and statement of cash flows are often prepared in the form of comparative statements. A highly condensed comparative income statement covering three years is shown below.

| BENSON CORPORATION<br>Comparative Income Statement<br>For the Years Ended December 31, 2002, 2001, 2000<br>(in thousands of dollars) | | | |
|---|---|---|---|
| | **2002** | **2001** | **2000** |
| Net sales . . . . . . . . . . . . . . . . . . . . . . . . . . . . . . . . . . . . . . . . . . . | $600 | $500 | $400 |
| Cost of goods sold . . . . . . . . . . . . . . . . . . . . . . . . . . . . . . . . . . | 370 | 300 | 235 |
| Gross profit . . . . . . . . . . . . . . . . . . . . . . . . . . . . . . . . . . . . . . . . | $230 | $200 | $165 |
| Expenses . . . . . . . . . . . . . . . . . . . . . . . . . . . . . . . . . . . . . . . . . . | 194 | 160 | 115 |
| Net income . . . . . . . . . . . . . . . . . . . . . . . . . . . . . . . . . . . . . . . . | $ 36 | $ 40 | $ 50 |

*Condensed three-year income statement*

Comparative statements place important financial information in a context that is useful for gaining better understanding. For example, knowing that Benson Corporation had sales of $600,000 in 2002 after years in which sales were $500,000 (2001) and $400,000 (2000) is helpful in understanding Benson's sales trend.

Few figures in a financial statement are highly significant in and of themselves. It is their relationship to other quantities or the amount and direction of change that is important. Analysis is largely a matter of establishing significant relationships and identifying changes and trends. Four widely used analytical techniques are (1) dollar and percentage changes, (2) trend percentages, (3) component percentages, and (4) ratios.

## Dollar and Percentage Changes

The dollar amount of change from year to year is significant, and expressing the change in percentage terms adds perspective. For example, if sales this year have increased by $100,000, the fact that this is an increase of 10% over last year's sales of $1 million puts it in a different perspective than if it represented a 1% increase over sales of $10 million for the prior year.

The dollar amount of any change is the difference between the amount for a *comparison* year and the amount for a *base* year. The percentage change is computed by dividing the amount of the dollar change between years by the amount for the base year. This is illustrated in the following tabulation, using data from the comparative income statement shown above:

**LO 1**

Explain the uses of dollar and percentage changes, trend percentages, component percentages, and ratios.

| | In Thousands | | | Increase or (Decrease) | | | |
|---|---|---|---|---|---|---|---|
| | | | | 2002 over 2001 | | 2001 over 2000 | |
| | Year 2002 | Year 2001 | Year 2000 | Amount | % | Amount | % |
| Net sales . . . . . . . . . . . . . . | $600 | $500 | $400 | $100 | 20% | $100 | 25% |
| Net income . . . . . . . . . . . . | 36 | 40 | 50 | (4) | (10) | (10) | (20) |

*Dollar and percentage changes*

Although net sales increased $100,000 in both 2001 and 2002, the percentage change differs because of the change in the base from 2000 to 2001. These calculations present no problems when the figures for the base year are positive amounts. If a negative amount or a zero amount appears in the base year, however, a percentage change cannot be computed. Thus if Benson Corporation had incurred a net loss in 2001, the percentage change in net income from 2001 to 2002 could not have been calculated.

**Evaluating Percentage Changes in Sales and Earnings**   Computing the percentage changes in sales, gross profit, and net income from one year to the next gives insight into a company's rate of growth. If a company is experiencing growth in its economic activities, sales and earnings should increase at *more than the rate of inflation*. Assume, for example, that a company's sales increase by 6% while the general price level rises by 10%. The entire increase in the dollar amount of sales may be explained by inflation, rather than by an increase in sales volume (the number of units sold). In fact, the company may well have sold *fewer* goods than in the preceding year.

In measuring the dollar or percentage change in *quarterly* sales or earnings, it is customary to compare the results of the current quarter with those of the *same quarter in the preceding year*. Use of the same quarter of the preceding year as the base period prevents our analysis from being distorted by seasonal fluctuations in business activity.

**Percentages Become Misleading When the Base Is Small**   Percentage changes may create a misleading impression when the dollar amount used as a base is unusually small. Occasionally we hear a television newscaster say that a company's profits have increased by a very large percentage, such as 900%. The initial impression created by such a statement is that the company's profits must now be excessively large. But assume, for example, that a company had net income of $100,000 in its first year, that in the second year net income drops to $10,000, and that in the third year net income returns to the $100,000 level. In this third year, net income has increased by $90,000, representing a 900% increase over the profits of the second year. What needs to be added is that this 900% increase in profits in the third year follows a very small profit in the second year and *exactly offsets* the 90% decline in profits in the second year.

## Trend Percentages

The changes in financial statement items from a base year to following years are often expressed as *trend percentages* to show the extent and direction of change. Two steps are necessary to compute trend percentages. First, a base year is selected and each item in the financial statements for the base year is given a weight of 100%. The second step is to express each item in the financial statements for following years as a percentage of its base-year amount. This computation consists of dividing an item such as sales in the years after the base year by the amount of sales in the base year.

For example, assume that 1997 is selected as the base year and that sales in the base year amounted to $300,000 as shown below. The trend percentages for sales are computed by dividing the sales amount of each following year by $300,000. Also shown in the illustration are the yearly amounts of net income. The trend percentages for net income are computed by dividing the net income amount for each following year by the base-year amount of $15,000.

|  | 2002 | 2001 | 2000 | 1999 | 1998 | 1997 |
|---|---|---|---|---|---|---|
| Sales . . . . . . . . . . . | $450,000 | $360,000 | $330,000 | $321,000 | $312,000 | $300,000 |
| Net income . . . . . . . | 22,950 | 14,550 | 21,450 | 19,200 | 15,600 | 15,000 |

When the computations described above have been made, the trend percentages will appear as follows:

| | 2002 | 2001 | 2000 | 1999 | 1998 | 1997 |
|---|---|---|---|---|---|---|
| Sales .......................... | 150% | 120% | 110% | 107% | 104% | 100% |
| Net income ...................... | 153 | 97 | 143 | 128 | 104 | 100 |

These trend percentages indicate a very modest growth in sales in the early years and accelerated growth in 2001 and 2002. Net income also shows an increasing growth trend with the exception of the year 2001, when net income declined despite a solid increase in sales. The problem was overcome in 2002 with a sharp rise in net income. Overall the trend percentages give a picture of a profitable, growing enterprise.

During the first six months of 1999, **Fruit of the Loom, Inc.,** reported operating income of $28.1 million, compared to $160.7 million reported for the first six months of 1998. These figures represent an 83% decline in operating performance, computed as follows:

| | |
|---|---|
| Decline in operating income ($160.7 − $28.1) ....................... | $132.6 |
| Base period operating income (first 6 months of 1998) ............... | $160.7 |
| Percentage decrease ($132.6 ÷ $160.7) ........................... | 83% |

How much of an increase in operating income would be required in the first six months of 2000 to return to the 1998 level? Many people erroneously guess 96%. However, the correct answer is an astounding 472%, computed as follows:

| | |
|---|---|
| Required increase to reach 2000 operating level (from $28.1 to $160.7) ..... | $132.6 |
| Base period operating income (first 6 months of 1999) ................ | $ 28.1 |
| Required percentage increase ($132.6 ÷ $28.1) ..................... | 472% |

Unfortunately, **Fruit of the Loom, Inc.**, did not increase its operating income anywhere near the required 472% during the first six months of 2000.

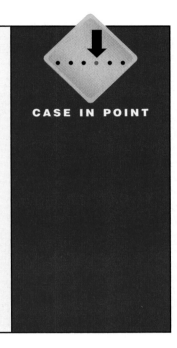

**CASE IN POINT**

## Component Percentages

Component percentages indicate the *relative size* of each item included in a total. For example, each item in a balance sheet could be expressed as a percentage of total assets. This shows quickly the relative importance of each type of asset as well as the relative amount of financing obtained from current creditors, long-term creditors, and stockholders. By computing component percentages for several successive balance sheets, we can see which items are increasing in importance and which are becoming less significant.

Another application of component percentages is to express all items in an income statement as a percentage of net sales. Such a statement is called a *common size income statement*. A condensed income statement in dollars and in common size form follows:

| **Income Statement** | | | | |
|---|---|---|---|---|
| | **Dollars** | | **Component Percentages** | |
| | 2002 | 2001 | 2002 | 2001 |
| Net sales ......................... | $1,000,000 | $600,000 | 100.0% | 100.0% |
| Cost of goods sold .................. | 700,000 | 360,000 | 70.0 | 60.0 |
| Expenses (including income taxes) ......................... | 250,000 | 180,000 | 25.0 | 30.0 |
| Net income ....................... | $ 50,000 | $ 60,000 | 5.0% | 10.0% |

*Are the year-to-date changes favorable?*

Looking only at the component percentages, we see that the increase in cost of goods sold (60% to 70%) was only partially offset by the decrease in expenses as a percentage of net sales, causing net income to decrease from 10% to 5% of net sales.

## Ratios

A ratio is a simple mathematical expression of the relationship of one item to another. Every percentage may be viewed as a ratio—that is, one number expressed as a percentage of another.

Ratios may be stated in several ways. To illustrate, let us consider the current ratio, which expresses the relationship between a company's most liquid assets (current) and its liabilities that require payment soon (current). If current assets are $100,000 and current liabilities are $50,000, we may say either that the current ratio is 2 to 1 (which is written as 2:1) or that current assets are 200% of current liabilities. Either statement correctly summarizes the relationship—that is, that current assets are twice as large as current liabilities.

Ratios are particularly important in understanding financial statements because they permit us to compare information from one financial statement with information from another financial statement. For example, we might compare net income (taken from the income statement) with total assets (taken from the balance sheet) to see how effectively management is using available resources to earn a profit. For a ratio to be useful, however, the two amounts being compared must be logically related. In subsequent sections of this chapter, we will make extensive use of ratios to better demonstrate important dimensions of an enterprise's financial activities.

## Standards of Comparison

In using dollar and percentage changes, trend percentages, component percentages, and ratios, financial analysts constantly search for some standard of comparison against which to judge whether the relationships they have found are favorable or unfavorable. Two such standards are (1) the past performance of the company and (2) the performance of other companies in the same industry. For internal management purposes, another important comparison is with expected or budgeted numbers.

**Past Performance of the Company**  Comparing financial information for a current period with similar information for prior years affords some basis for judging whether the condition of the business is improving or worsening. This comparison of data over time is sometimes called *horizontal* analysis, to express the idea of reviewing data for a number of consecutive periods. It is distinguished from *vertical,* or *static,* analysis, which refers to the review of the financial information within a single accounting period.

In addition to determining whether the situation is improving or becoming worse, horizontal analysis may aid in making estimates of future prospects. Because changes may reverse their direction at any time, however, projecting past trends into the future always involves risk.

A weakness of horizontal analysis is that comparison with the past does not afford any basis for evaluation in absolute terms. The fact that net income was 2% of sales last year and is 3% of sales this year indicates improvement, but if there is evidence that net income *should be* 7% of sales, the record for both years is unfavorable.

**Industry Standards**  The limitations of horizontal analysis may be overcome to some extent by finding appropriate benchmarks against which to measure a particular company's performance. The benchmarks used by most analysts are the performance of comparable companies and the average performance of several companies in the same industry.[1]

---

[1] Industry data are available from a number of sources. For example, Robert Morris Associates publishes *Annual Statement Studies,* which includes data from many thousands of annual reports, grouped into several hundred industry classifications. Industry classifications are subdivided further by company size. Dun & Bradstreet, Inc., annually publishes *Key Business Ratios* for more than 800 lines of business.

Assume, for example, that the revenue of Alpha Airlines drops by 5% during the current year. If the revenue for the airlines industry had dropped an average of 15% during this year, Alpha's 5% decline might be viewed as a *favorable* performance. As another example, assume that Omega Co. earns a net income equal to 3% of net sales. This would be substandard if Omega were a manufacturer of commercial aircraft, but it would be satisfactory performance if it were a retail grocery chain because of the difference in earnings expected in the two industries.

When we compare a given company with its competitors or with industry averages, our conclusions are valid only if the companies in question are reasonably comparable. Because of the large number of diversified companies formed in recent years, the term *industry* is difficult to define, and even companies that fall roughly within the same industry may not be comparable in many respects. For example, one company may engage only in the marketing of oil products; another may be a fully integrated producer from the well to the gas pump; yet both are said to be in the oil industry.

 The tremendous growth in international capital issuance and trading and the large increase in global merger and acquisition activity have fueled the need of investors, equity research analysts, and other financial statement users to read and analyze non-domestic financial statements and make cross-border financial comparisons. In particular, two issues confront those doing accounting analysis of international companies. First, there is high variation in accounting measurement, disclosure, and audit quality across countries. Second, obtaining the information necessary to conduct cross-border accounting analyses is frequently difficult and sometimes not possible. Financial reporting in China is a case in point. Until recently China did not have financial reporting and external auditing in forms familiar to Westerners.

**CASE IN POINT**

## Quality of Earnings

Profits are the lifeblood of a business entity. No entity can survive for long and accomplish its other goals unless it is profitable. Continuous losses drain assets from the business, consume owners' equity, and leave the company at the mercy of creditors. In assessing the prospects of a company, we are interested not only in the total *amount* of earnings but also in the *rate* of earnings on sales, on total assets, and on owners' equity. In addition, we must look at the *stability* and *source* of earnings. An erratic earnings performance over a period of years, for example, is less desirable than a steady level of earnings. A history of increasing earnings is preferable to a flat earnings record.

A breakdown of sales and earnings by *major product lines* may be useful in evaluating the future performance of a company. Publicly owned companies include with their financial statements supplementary schedules showing sales and profits by product line and by geographical area. These schedules assist financial analysts in forecasting the effect on the company of changes in consumer demand for particular types of products.

Financial analysts often express the opinion that the earnings of one company are of higher quality than earnings of other similar companies. This concept of *quality of earnings* arises because each company's management can choose from a variety of accounting principles and methods, all of which are considered generally acceptable. A company's management often is under heavy pressure to report rising earnings, and accounting policies may be tailored toward this objective. We have already pointed out the impact on current reported earnings of the choice between the LIFO and FIFO methods of inventory valuation and the choice of depreciation policies. In judging the quality of earnings, the financial analyst should consider whether the accounting principles and methods selected by management lead to a conservative measurement of earnings (high quality) or tend to inflate reported earnings (low quality).

**LO 2**

Discuss the quality of a company's earnings, assets, and working capital.

YOUR TURN

### You as CFO of a Publicly Traded Company

Assume you are the chief financial officer of a company traded on the New York Stock Exchange. Your company is followed by several investment analysts who provide information and advice to their clients about which stocks to buy and sell. As part of the information provided to investors, these financial analysts also project annual earnings per share for each company they follow. Assume it is November and your stock prices have recently been depressed and your chance of achieving the analysts' projected earnings per share numbers is low. The CEO and president of the company believes his job is in jeopardy if the financial results are not equal to or better than the analysts' projected earnings-per-share number. He has been putting pressure on you to use accounting techniques that will increase earnings. What should you do?

*Our comments appear on page 652.

### Quality of Assets and the Relative Amount of Debt

Although a satisfactory level of earnings may be a good indication of the company's long-run ability to pay its debts and dividends, we must also look at the composition of assets, their condition and liquidity, the timing of repayment of liabilities, and the total amount of debt outstanding. A company may be profitable and yet be unable to pay its liabilities on time; sales and earnings may appear satisfactory, but plant and equipment may be deteriorating because of poor maintenance policies; valuable patents may be expiring; substantial losses may be imminent due to slow-moving inventories and past-due receivables. Companies with large amounts of debt often are vulnerable to increases in interest rates and to even temporary reductions in cash inflows.

### Impact of Inflation

During a period of significant inflation, financial statements prepared in terms of historical costs do not reflect fully the economic resources or the real income (in purchasing power) of a business enterprise. The FASB recommends that companies include in their annual reports supplementary schedules showing the effects of inflation on their financial statements. Inclusion of these supplementary disclosures is voluntary, not mandatory. Most companies do *not* include these supplementary schedules because of the high cost of developing this information, as well as the fact that users of financial statements do not generally find the information to be particularly useful.

## MEASURES OF LIQUIDITY AND CREDIT RISK

*Liquidity* refers to a company's ability to meet its continuing obligations as they arise. For example, a company may have borrowed money and must make quarterly interest and principal payments to a financial institution. A company may purchase its inventory and other necessities on credit and pay the seller within 30 days of the purchase date.

We have emphasized throughout this text the importance to investors, creditors, and other users of financial statements of information that permits them to assess the amount, timing, and uncertainty of future cash flows from the enterprise to them. As a result, analyzing an enterprise's liquidity and its credit risk is very important and is a natural place for us to start our study of analyzing financial statements.

In this section we learn about ways to assess liquidity, starting with the classified balance sheet and then looking at a number of ratios commonly used to glean information about liquidity from the financial statements.

## A Classified Balance Sheet

In a classified balance sheet, assets usually are presented in three groups: (1) current assets, (2) plant and equipment, and (3) other assets. Liabilities are classified into two categories: (1) current liabilities and (2) long-term debt. A classified balance sheet for Computer Barn appears on page 600.

The classifications *current assets* and *current liabilities* are especially useful in evaluating the short-term liquidity—or solvency—of the business entity.

**LO 3**

Explain the nature and purpose of classifications in financial statements.

**Current Assets**   **Current assets** are relatively liquid resources. This category includes cash, investments in marketable securities, receivables, inventories, and prepaid expenses. To qualify as a current asset, an asset must already be cash or must be capable of *being converted into cash* or used up within a relatively short period of time, without interfering with normal business operations.

Current assets are tied to an enterprise's **operating cycle**. Most companies have several operating cycles within a year. This means that they take cash and purchase inventory, sell the inventory, and collect the receivable in cash several times within a year. For these companies, the time period used to identify current assets is one year, so any asset that is expected to be converted into cash within one year is classified as a current asset in the enterprise's balance sheet. Some enterprises, however, have relatively long operating cycles. For example, a company that constructs very large items (for example, airplanes or ships) may have a production period that extends well beyond one year. In these cases, the length of the company's operating cycle is used to define those assets that are classified as current. While most current assets are expected to be converted into cash, we also include as current assets those that will be used up or consumed during the year or operating cycle, if longer. For example, prepaid expenses are classified as current assets on the basis that their having been paid in advance preserves cash that otherwise would have to be paid in the current period. Combining these ideas, **current assets** can be defined as assets that are already cash, or are expected to be converted into cash or used up within the next year or operating cycle, whichever is longer.

In a balance sheet, current assets are listed in order of liquidity. (The closer an asset is to becoming cash, the greater its liquidity.) Thus cash always is listed first among the current assets, usually followed by investments in marketable securities, receivables, inventory, and prepaid expenses, in that order.

**Current Liabilities**   **Current liabilities** are *existing debts* that are expected to be satisfied by using the enterprise's current assets. Among the most common current liabilities are notes payable (due within one year), accounts payable, unearned revenue, and accrued expenses, such as income taxes payable, salaries payable, or interest payable. In the balance sheet, notes payable usually are listed first, followed by accounts payable; other types of current liabilities may be listed in any sequence.

The *relationship* between current assets and current liabilities is as important as the total dollar amount in either category. Current liabilities must be paid in the near future, and the cash to pay these liabilities is expected to come from current assets. Thus decision makers evaluating the *short-term* liquidity of a business often compare the relative amounts of current assets and current liabilities, whereas an evaluation of *long-term* credit risk requires a comparison of total assets to total liabilities.

We will now use Computer Barn's classified balance sheet to examine some widely applied measures of short-term liquidity and long-term credit risk.

*A classified balance sheet*

**LO 4**

Prepare a classified balance sheet and compute widely used measures of liquidity and credit risk.

| COMPUTER BARN | | | |
|---|---|---|---|
| **Balance Sheet** | | | |
| **December 31, 2002** | | | |

**Assets**

**Current assets:**

| | | | |
|---|---|---|---|
| Cash | | | $ 30,000 |
| Marketable Securities | | | 11,000 |
| Notes Receivable | | | 5,000 |
| Accounts Receivable | | | 60,000 |
| Inventory | | | 70,000 |
| Prepaid Expenses | | | 4,000 |
| Total current assets | | | $180,000 |

**Plant and equipment:**

| | | | |
|---|---|---|---|
| Land | | $151,000 | |
| Building | $120,000 | | |
| Less: Accumulated Depreciation | 9,000 | 111,000 | |
| Sales Fixtures and Equipment | $ 45,000 | | |
| Less: Accumulated Depreciation | 27,000 | 18,000 | |
| Total plant and equipment | | | 280,000 |

**Other assets:**

| | | | |
|---|---|---|---|
| Land Held as a Future Building Site | | | 170,000 |
| Total assets | | | $630,000 |

**Liabilities & Stockholders' Equity**

**Current liabilities:**

| | | | |
|---|---|---|---|
| Notes Payable (due in 6 months) | | | $ 10,000 |
| Accounts Payable | | | 62,000 |
| Income Taxes Payable | | | 13,000 |
| Sales Taxes Payable | | | 3,000 |
| Accrued Expenses Payable | | | 8,000 |
| Unearned Revenue and Customer Deposits | | | 4,000 |
| Total current liabilities | | | $100,000 |

**Long-term liabilities:**

| | | | |
|---|---|---|---|
| Mortgage Payable (due in 10 years) | | | 110,000 |
| Total liabilities | | | $210,000 |

**Stockholders' equity:**

| | | | |
|---|---|---|---|
| Capital Stock (15,000 shares issued and outstanding) | | $150,000 | |
| Retained Earnings | | 270,000 | |
| Total stockholders' equity | | | 420,000 |
| Total liabilities & stockholders' equity | | | $630,000 |

## Working Capital

Working capital is a measurement often used to express the relationship between current assets and current liabilities. **Working capital** is the *excess* of current assets over current liabilities. Computer Barn's working capital amounts to *$80,000,* computed as follows:

| Current assets | $180,000 |
|---|---|
| Less: Current liabilities | 100,000 |
| Working capital | $ 80,000 |

*Working capital varies by industry and company size*

Recall that current assets are expected to convert into cash within a relatively short period of time, and that current liabilities usually require a prompt cash payment. Thus working capital measures a company's potential excess *sources* of cash over its upcoming *uses* of cash.

The amount of working capital that a company needs to remain solvent varies with the size of the organization and the nature of its business activities.[2] An analyst familiar with the nature of a company's operations usually can determine from the amount of working capital whether the company is in a sound financial position or is heading for financial difficulties.

## Current Ratio

A widely used measure of short-term debt-paying ability is the **current ratio**. This ratio is computed by *dividing* total current assets by total current liabilities.

In the illustrated balance sheet of Computer Barn, current assets amount to $180,000 and current liabilities total $100,000. Therefore, Computer Barn's current ratio is *1.8 to 1,* computed as follows:

| Current assets | $180,000 |
|---|---|
| Current liabilities | $100,000 |
| Current ratio ($180,000 ÷ $100,000) | 1.8 to 1 |

*A widely used measure of liquidity*

A current ratio of 1.8 to 1 means that the company's current assets are 1.8 times as large as its current liabilities.

The *higher* the current ratio, the more liquid the company appears to be. Historically, some bankers and other short-term creditors have believed that a company should have a current ratio of 2 to 1 or higher to qualify as a good credit risk. Such rules of thumb must be used carefully, however, because many successful businesses have current ratios of less than 2 to 1 because their receivables and inventory convert into cash quickly relative to the amount and timing of their payables. Likewise, it is possible for financially weak businesses to have high current ratios as a result of slow turnover in receivables and inventory. In other words, care must be taken in interpreting all ratios, including the current ratio, to ensure that inappropriate conclusions are not reached as a result of superficial analysis. Confirming the information communicated via one ratio by looking at other financial measures is often a good way to help ensure a valid interpretation.

## Quick Ratio

Inventory and prepaid expenses are the *least liquid* of the current assets. In a business with a long operating cycle, it may take several months to convert inventory into cash. Therefore, some short-term creditors prefer the **quick ratio** (sometimes called the acid-test ratio) to the current ratio as a measure of short-term solvency.

---

[2] A company with current liabilities in excess of its current assets has a *negative* amount of working capital. Negative working capital does not necessarily mean that a company is insolvent. As explained in the Case in Point on the next page, telephone companies may fall into this category.

The quick ratio compares only the *most liquid* current assets—called **quick assets**—with current liabilities. Quick assets include cash, marketable securities, and receivables—the current assets that can be converted most quickly into cash. Computer Barn's quick ratio is *1.06 to 1,* computed as follows:

| | |
|---|---|
| Quick assets (cash, marketable securities, and receivables) . . . . . . . . . . . . . . . . . | $106,000 |
| Current liabilities . . . . . . . . . . . . . . . . . . . . . . . . . . . . . . . . . . . . . . . . . . . . . . . . . . | $100,000 |
| Quick ratio ($106,000 ÷ $100,000) . . . . . . . . . . . . . . . . . . . . . . . . . . . . . . . . . . . . | 1.06 to 1 |

*A more demanding measure of liquidity*

Quick ratios are especially useful in evaluating the liquidity of companies that have inventories of slow-moving merchandise (such as real estate), or inventories that have become excessive in size.

## Debt Ratio

If a business fails and must be liquidated, the claims of creditors take priority over those of the owners. But if the business has a great deal of debt, there may not be enough assets even to make full payment to all creditors.

A basic measure of the safety of creditors' claims is the **debt ratio**, which states total liabilities as a *percentage* of total assets. A company's debt ratio is computed by dividing total liabilities by total assets, as shown below for Computer Barn:

| | |
|---|---|
| Total liabilities . . . . . . . . . . . . . . . . . . . . . . . . . . . . . . . . . . . . . . . . . . . . . . . . . . . . | $210,000 |
| Total assets . . . . . . . . . . . . . . . . . . . . . . . . . . . . . . . . . . . . . . . . . . . . . . . . . . . . . . . | $630,000 |
| Debt ratio ($210,000 ÷ $630,000) . . . . . . . . . . . . . . . . . . . . . . . . . . . . . . . . . . . . . | 33⅓% |

The debt ratio is not a measure of short-term liquidity. Rather, it is a measure of creditors' *long-term* risk. The smaller the portion of total assets financed by creditors, the smaller the risk that the business may become unable to pay its debts. From the creditors' point of view, the *lower* the debt ratio, the *safer* their position.

Many financially sound American companies traditionally have maintained debt ratios under 50%. But again, the financial analyst must be familiar with industry characteristics. Banks, for example, have very high debt ratios—often over 90%.

## Evaluating Financial Ratios

We caution users of financial statements *against* placing much confidence in rules of thumb, such as *a current ratio should be at least 2 to 1, a quick ratio should be at least 1 to 1,* or *a debt ratio should be under 50%.* To interpret any financial ratio properly, the decision maker must first understand the characteristics of the company and the industry in which it operates.

Retailers, for example, tend to have higher current ratios than do wholesalers or manufacturing companies. Service-type businesses—which have no inventory—generally have lower current ratios than merchandising or manufacturing companies. Large businesses with good credit ratings and reliable sources of cash receipts are able to operate with lower current ratios than are small companies whose continuous inflow of cash may be less predictable.

**CASE IN POINT**

Large telephone companies are regarded within the business community as pillars of financial strength. Yet these companies do not have high current ratios. Such financially sound companies as **Bell Atlantic, BellSouth NYNEX**, and **Pacific Telesis** often operate with current ratios of less than 1 to 1.

Although a high current ratio is one indication of strong debt-paying ability, an extremely high ratio—say, 4 or 5 to 1—may indicate that *too much* of the company's resources are tied up in current assets. In maintaining such a highly liquid position, the company may be using its financial resources inefficiently and not earning the return that could be earned if the assets were invested in an alternative way.

**Standards for Comparison**   Financial analysts generally use two criteria in evaluating the reasonableness of a financial ratio. One criterion is the *trend* in the ratio over a period of years. By reviewing this trend, analysts are able to determine whether a company's performance or financial position is improving or deteriorating. Second, analysts often compare a company's financial ratios with those of *similar companies* and with *industry wide averages*. These comparisons assist analysts in evaluating a particular ratio in light of the company's current business environment.

**Annual Reports**   Publicly owned corporations issue **annual reports** that provide a great deal of information about the company. For example, annual reports include comparative financial statements that have been audited by a firm of independent public accountants. They also include five- or ten-year *summaries* of key financial data, and **management's discussion and analysis** of the company's operating results, liquidity, and financial position. This is where management identifies and discusses favorable and unfavorable trends and events that may affect the company in the future. (For example, in Appendix A, find the management discussion in the **Tootsie Roll Industries, Inc.**, annual report.)

Annual reports are mailed directly to all stockholders of the corporation. They are also available to the public either through the Internet, in libraries, or by writing or calling the stockholder relations department of the corporation.

**Industry Information**   Financial information about *entire industries* is available through financial publications (such as Dun & Bradstreet, Inc.), and through on-line databases (such as Media General Financial Services). Such information allows investors and creditors to compare the financial health of an individual company with the industry in which that company operates.

**CASE IN POINT**

**Media General Financial Services** continuously updates financial ratios for individual companies and provides norms for entire industries. As an example of industry norm data, the average current ratios of several industry groupings are shown below for a recent year:

| Industry Group | Average Current Ratio |
| --- | --- |
| Air transportation (major carriers) | .9 to 1 |
| Retail (general merchandise) | 1.9 to 1 |
| Retail (apparel) | 2.3 to 1 |
| Wholesale (grocery) | 1.2 to 1 |
| Manufacturing (computers) | 1.6 to 1 |
| Telephone (regional) | .8 to 1 |

**Usefulness and Limitations of Financial Ratios**   A financial ratio expresses the relationship of one amount to another. Most users of financial statements find that certain ratios assist them in quickly evaluating the financial position, profitability, and future prospects of a business. A comparison of key ratios for several successive years usually indicates whether the business is becoming stronger or weaker. Ratios also provide a way to compare quickly the financial strength and profitability of different companies.

Users of financial statements should recognize, however, that ratios have several limitations. For example, management may enter into year-end transactions that temporarily improve key ratios—a process called **window dressing**.

To illustrate, the balance sheet of Computer Barn (page 600) includes current assets of $180,000 and current liabilities of $100,000, indicating a current ratio of *1.8 to 1*. What would happen if shortly before year-end, management used $20,000 of the company's cash to pay accounts payable that are not due until January of 2003? This transaction would reduce current assets to $160,000 ($180,000 − $20,000) and current liabilities to $80,000 ($100,000 − $20,000), resulting in an increase in the current ratio to a more impressive 2 to 1 ($160,000 ÷ $80,000). Is the company really better off as a result of having simply paid $20,000 of liabilities early? The answer is probably no, although looking only at the current ratio one might think it is stronger after paying the $20,000 than before. Such steps to window dress the financial statements are common and, within reason, are a natural part of financial reporting. The astute reader of financial statements needs to be aware of this and should look for instances where there is evidence that extreme steps have been taken to artificially improve a company's appearance. Usually this can be done by looking at multiple financial measures rather than focusing on a single financial measure.

Financial statement ratios contain the same limitations as do the dollar amounts used in financial statements. For example, many assets are reported at historical cost rather than current market value. Also, financial statement ratios express only *financial* relationships. They give no indication of a company's progress in achieving nonfinancial goals, such as improving customer satisfaction or worker productivity. A thorough analysis of investment opportunities involves more than merely computing and comparing financial ratios.

**No Ratio Ever Tells the Whole Story**  Each financial ratio focuses on only *one aspect* of a company's total financial picture. A high current ratio, for example, does not guarantee solvency, nor does a low current ratio signal that bankruptcy is near. There are numerous factors of greater importance to a company's future performance than one or more financial ratios.

In summary, ratios are useful tools, but they can be interpreted properly only by individuals who understand the characteristics of the company and its environment.

YOUR TURN

### You as a Potential Investor

Assume that you have several thousand dollars to invest in the stock market. Given that "people will always have to eat," you have decided to explore the possibility of investing in **Wendy's** and **McDonald's**. Your analysis of each company's financial statements reveals that both have negative working capital and both have current and quick ratios of less than 1 to 1.

Based on your findings, should you be concerned about the short-term liquidity (solvency) of these two companies? Explain.

*Our comments appear on page 653.

## Concluding Comment — Solvency, Credit Risk, and the Law

Accountants view a business entity as separate from the other economic activities of its owners, regardless of how the business is organized. The law, however, draws an important distinction between *corporations* and *unincorporated* business organizations. Users of financial statements should understand this legal distinction, as it may affect both creditors and owners.

Under the law, the owners of unincorporated businesses (sole proprietorships and partnerships) are *personally liable* for any and all debts of the business organization. Therefore, creditors of unincorporated businesses often base their lending decisions on the solvency of the *owners,* rather than the financial strength of the business entity.[3]

If a business is organized as a corporation, however, the owners (stockholders) are *not* personally responsible for the debts of the business. Creditors may look *only to the business entity* in seeking payment of their claims. Therefore, the solvency of the business entity becomes much more important if the business is organized as a corporation.

**Small Corporations and Loan Guarantees**   Small corporations often do not have sufficient financial resources to qualify for the credit they need. In such cases, creditors may require that one or more of the company's stockholders personally guarantee (or cosign) specific debts of the business entity. By cosigning debts of the corporation, the individual stockholders *do* become personally liable for the debt if the corporation fails to make payment.

Two brothers, Bob and Jack, each decided to form small businesses. Bob started a small appliance store that was organized as a sole proprietorship. Jack started a car wash that was organized as a corporation, with himself as the primary stockholder. As the businesses grew, each needed additional capital for expansion purposes. The bank was willing to loan additional funds to Bob's appliance store because Bob had considerable personal assets, and the bank knew that if necessary, it could access those assets for repayment. Jack's business, on the other hand, had a more difficult time getting the additional funding it required because of the limited liability feature of his corporation. Jack, too, had significant personal resources, and he agreed to cosign a note with the company so that he could obtain the required bank financing. While the two businesses were initially organized as different legal forms, they became similar when Jack committed his personal assets to the company to obtain the bank financing.

CASE IN POINT

## MEASURES OF PROFITABILITY

Measures of a company's *profitability* are of interest to equity investors and management, and are drawn primarily from the income statement. The measures that we discuss in this chapter include percentage changes in key measurements, gross profit rates, operating income, net income as a percentage of sales, earnings per share, return on assets, and return on equity.

Public opinion polls show that many people believe that most businesses earn a profit equal to 30% or more of the sales price of their merchandise. Actually, this is far from true. Most successful companies earn a net income of between 5% and, perhaps, 15% of sales revenue.

In a recent **Kmart** income statement, revenues were $33,674 million and net income was $518 million. While both numbers are large in absolute terms, net income was only 1.5% of sales ($518 ÷ $33,674). Of every dollar of sales revenue, the company's costs exceeded 98 cents. While this does not sound like a particularly strong level of performance, it actually represented an improvement over its prior two years of operations.

CASE IN POINT

### Classifications in the Income Statement

An income statement may be prepared in either the *multiple-step* or the *single-step* format. The multiple-step income statement is more useful in illustrating accounting

---

[3] In a *limited* partnership, only the *general partners* are personally responsible for the debts of the business. Every limited partnership must have one or more general partners.

concepts because it provides more detailed information than the single-step format. A multiple-step income statement for Computer Barn is shown on page 607.

A knowledge of accounting does not enable you to say what the level of corporate earnings *should be;* however, it does enable you to read audited financial statements that show what corporate earnings *actually are.* Moreover, you are aware that the information in published financial statements of corporations has been audited by CPA firms and has been reviewed in detail by government agencies, such as the Securities and Exchange Commission (SEC). Consequently, you know that the profits reported in these published financial statements are reasonably reliable; they have been determined in accordance with generally accepted accounting principles and verified by independent experts.

## Some Specific Examples of Corporate Earnings and Losses

Not all leading corporations earn a profit every year. For the ten years from 1981 through 1990, **Pan American Airways** reported a net loss each year. Late in 1991, Pan Am—at one time America's "flagship" airline—ceased operations. Many American corporations had some bad years in the early 1990s. Each of America's Big Three automakers reported huge losses. So did most of the nation's major airlines. Even **IBM** sustained a net loss—the first in the company's 80-year history.

The oil companies have been particularly subject to criticism for so-called excessive profits, so let us briefly look at the profits of **ExxonMobil**, the world's largest oil company. A recent annual report (audited by **PricewaterhouseCoopers LLP**) shows that 1999 profits amounted to a little over $7.9 billion. Standing alone, that figure seems enormous—but we need to look a little farther. The total revenue was over $185 billion, so net income amounted to slightly more than 4% of sales. On the other hand, income taxes, excise taxes, and other taxes and duties levied on **Exxon** amounted to more than $56 billion, or about 7 times as much as the company's profit. Thus taxation represents a far greater portion of the cost of a gallon of gasoline than does the oil company's profit.

## Multiple-Step Income Statements

**LO 5**

Prepare a multiple-step and a single-step income statement and compute widely used measures of profitability.

A multiple-step income statement draws its name from the *series of steps* in which costs and expenses are deducted from revenue. As a first step, the cost of goods sold is deducted from net sales to determine the subtotal *gross profit.* As a second step, operating expenses are deducted to obtain a subtotal called **operating income** (or income from operations). As a final step, income taxes expense and other nonoperating items are taken into consideration to arrive at *net income.*

Notice that the income statement is divided into four major sections: (1) revenue, (2) cost of goods sold, (3) operating expenses, and (4) nonoperating items. Multiple-step income statements are noted for their numerous sections and the development of significant subtotals.

**The Revenue Section**   In a merchandising company, the revenue section of the income statement usually contains only one line, entitled *net sales.* (Other types of revenue, if any, appear in the final section of the statement.)

Investors and managers are vitally interested in the *trend* in net sales. As one means of evaluating this trend, they often compute the percentage change in net sales from year to year. A **percentage change** is the dollar amount of the *change* in a financial measurement, expressed as a percentage. It is computed by dividing the dollar amount of increase or decrease by the dollar amount of the measurement *before* the change occurred. (Dollar changes *cannot* be expressed as percentages if the financial statement amount in the earlier period is zero or has changed from a negative amount to a positive amount.)

In our economy, most prices increase over time. The average increase in prices during the year is called the *rate of inflation.* Because of inflation, a company's net sales may increase slightly from year to year even if the company is not selling greater amounts of merchandise. If a company's physical sales volume is increasing, net sales usually will grow faster than the rate of inflation.

If a company's sales grow faster than the *industry average,* the company increases its **market share**—that is, its share of total industry sales.

Publicly owned corporations include in their annual reports schedules summarizing operating data—such as net sales—for a period of 5 or 10 years. This information is also readily available through several on-line databases.

**The Cost of Goods Sold Section**   The second section of a merchandising company's income statement shows cost of goods sold for the period. Cost of goods sold usually appears as a single dollar amount, which includes such incidental items as freight costs and normal shrinkage losses.

**Gross Profit: A Key Subtotal**   In a multiple-step income statement, gross profit appears as a subtotal. This makes it easy for users of the income statement to compute the company's *gross profit rate* (or profit margin).

| COMPUTER BARN<br>Income Statement<br>For the Year Ended December 31, 2002 | | | |
|---|---|---|---|
| Net sales | | | $900,000 |
| Less: Cost of goods sold (including transportation-in) | | | 540,000 |
| Gross profit | | | $360,000 |
| Less: Operating expenses: | | | |
| Selling expenses: | | | |
| Sales Salaries and Commissions | $64,800 | | |
| Advertising | 42,000 | | |
| Delivery Service | 14,200 | | |
| Depreciation: Store Equipment | 9,000 | | |
| Other Selling Expenses | 6,000 | | |
| Total selling expenses | | $136,000 | |
| General and Administrative Expenses: | | | |
| Administrative and Office Salaries | $93,000 | | |
| Utilities | 3,100 | | |
| Depreciation: Building | 3,000 | | |
| Other General and Administrative Expenses | 4,900 | | |
| Total general and administrative expenses | | 104,000 | |
| Total operating expenses | | | 240,000 |
| Operating income | | | $120,000 |
| Less (add): Nonoperating items: | | | |
| Interest Expense | $12,000 | | |
| Purchase Discounts Lost | 1,200 | | |
| Interest Revenue | (3,200) | | 10,000 |
| Income before income taxes | | | $110,000 |
| Income Taxes Expense | | | 38,000 |
| Net income | | | $ 72,000 |
| Earnings per share | | | $4.80 |

*Income statement in multiple-step format*

**CASE IN POINT**

**Procter & Gamble** is a major consumer products company that manufactures and sells a wide variety of well-known brands, including Folgers coffee, Cover Girl beauty care, Bounty paper towels, and Pampers diapers. Sales (in millions) for the five-year period ending in 1999 were as follows:

|  | 1999 | 1998 | 1997 | 1996 | 1995 |
|---|---|---|---|---|---|
| Sales | $38,125 | $37,154 | $35,764 | $35,284 | $33,482 |
| Percentage increase | 2.6% | 3.9% | 1.4% | 5.4% | — |

Sales consistently grew during the five-year period, with the rate of growth ranging from 5.4% in 1996 to 1.4% in 1997. Each year's percentage is computed by taking the difference from the previous year and dividing that amount by the previous year's total. For example, the rate of growth in sales for 1999 over 1998 is computed as follows: [($38,125 − $37,154)/$37,154 = 2.6%]. The following interpretation of the 1999 growth percentage is presented in the company's 1999 annual report: "Net sales grew to a record $38.1 billion, up 3% versus last year. While this growth rate was below our expectations, we are encouraged by the increased percentage of sales in products that leverage our technology advantages."

The gross profit rate is gross profit expressed as a *percentage of net sales*. In 2002, Computer Barn earned an average gross profit rate of *40%*, computed as follows:

| | |
|---|---|
| Dollar amount of gross profit . . . . . . . . . . . . . . . . . . . . . . . . . . . . . . . . . . . . . . . . . | $360,000 |
| Net sales . . . . . . . . . . . . . . . . . . . . . . . . . . . . . . . . . . . . . . . . . . . . . . . . . . . . . . . . | $900,000 |
| Gross profit rate ($360,000 ÷ $900,000) . . . . . . . . . . . . . . . . . . . . . . . . . . . . . . . . . | 40% |

In evaluating the gross profit rate of a particular company, the analyst should consider the rates earned in prior periods, as well as the rates earned by *other companies* in the same industry. For most merchandising companies, gross profit rates usually lie between 20% and 50%, depending on the types of products they sell. These rates usually are lowest on fast-moving merchandise, such as groceries, and highest on specialty and novelty products.

Under normal circumstances, a company's gross profit rate tends to remain *reasonably stable* from one period to the next. Significant changes in this rate may provide investors with an early indication of changing consumer demand for the company's products.

**CASE IN POINT**

The gross profit percentage of most companies remains relatively constant over time. For example, the following are the gross profit rates of four major U.S. corporations for the years 1997, 1998, and 1999:

|  | 1999 | 1998 | 1997 |
|---|---|---|---|
| Sony . . . . . . . . . . . . . . . . . . . . . . . . . . . . . . . . . . . . . . . . . . . . . . . . . . . . | 32% | 32% | 31% |
| Microsoft . . . . . . . . . . . . . . . . . . . . . . . . . . . . . . . . . . . . . . . . . . . . . . . . | 86 | 84 | 82 |
| Walgreens . . . . . . . . . . . . . . . . . . . . . . . . . . . . . . . . . . . . . . . . . . . . . . . | 27 | 27 | 28 |
| Litton Industries . . . . . . . . . . . . . . . . . . . . . . . . . . . . . . . . . . . . . . . . . | 22 | 23 | 22 |

While the percentages vary considerably from one industry to another, for each company the rates are relatively constant for all three years.

**The Operating Expense Section**   Operating expenses are incurred for the purpose of *producing revenue*. These expenses often are subdivided into the classifications of *selling expenses* and *general and administrative expenses*. Subdividing operating expenses into functional classifications aids management and other users of the statements in separately evaluating different aspects of the company's operations. For example, selling expenses often rise and fall in concert with changes in net sales. Administrative expenses, on the other hand, usually remain more constant from one period to the next.

**Operating Income: Another Key Subtotal**   Some of the revenues and expenses of a business result from activities other than the company's basic business operations. Common examples include interest earned on investments and income taxes expense.

*Operating income* (or income from operations) shows the relationship between revenue earned from customers and expenses incurred in producing this revenue. In effect, operating income measures the profitability of a company's *basic or core business operations* and leaves out other types of revenue and expenses.

**Nonoperating Items**   Revenue and expenses that are not directly related to the company's primary business activities are listed in a final section of the income statement following operating income.

Two significant nonoperating items are interest expense and income taxes expense. Interest expense results from the manner in which assets are *financed,* not the manner in which these assets are used in business operations. Income taxes expense is not included among the operating expenses because paying income taxes *does not help to produce revenue.* Nonoperating revenues, such as interest and dividends earned on investments, also are listed in this final section of the income statement.

**Net Income**   Many equity investors consider net income (or net loss) to be the most important figure in the income statement. This amount represents the overall increase (or decrease) in owners' equity resulting from all profit-directed activities during the period.

Financial analysts often compute net income as a *percentage of net sales* (net income divided by net sales). This measurement provides an indication of management's *ability to control expenses* and to retain a reasonable portion of its revenue as profit.

The normal ratio of net income to net sales varies greatly by industry. In some industries, companies may be successful by earning a net income equal to only 2% or 3% of net sales. In other industries, net income may be much higher. In 2002, Computer Barn's net income amounts to 8% of net sales, which is very good for a computer retailer.

| | |
|---|---|
| Net income . . . . . . . . . . . . . . . . . . . . . . . . . . . . . . . . . . . . . . . . . . . . . . . . . . . . . . | $ 72,000 |
| Net sales . . . . . . . . . . . . . . . . . . . . . . . . . . . . . . . . . . . . . . . . . . . . . . . . . . . . . . . . . . . . | $900,000 |
| Net income as a percentage of net sales ($72,000 ÷ $900,000) . . . . . . . . . . . . . . . | 8% |

**LO 6**

Put a company's net income into perspective by relating it to sales, assets, and stockholders' equity.

## Earnings per Share

Ownership of a corporation is evidenced by *shares* of capital stock. What does the net income of a corporation mean to someone who owns, say, 100 shares of a corporation's capital stock? To assist individual stockholders in relating the corporation's net income to *their ownership shares*, large corporations compute **earnings per share** and show these amounts at the bottom of their income statements.[4]

---

[4] Only publicly held corporations are *required* to report earnings on a per share basis. For small businesses such as Computer Barn, the reporting of earnings per share is optional.

In the simplest case, earnings per share is net income, expressed on a per-share basis. For example, the balance sheet on page 600 indicates that Computer Barn has 15,000 shares of capital stock outstanding.[5] Assuming these shares had been outstanding all year, earnings per share amounts to *$4.80:*

| | |
|---|---:|
| Net income . . . . . . . . . . . . . . . . . . . . . . . . . . . . . . . . . . . . . . . . . . . . . . . . . . . . . . . . . . . . . . . . . . | $72,000 |
| Shares of capital stock outstanding . . . . . . . . . . . . . . . . . . . . . . . . . . . . . . . . . . . . . . . . . . . . . | 15,000 |
| Earnings per share ($72,000 ÷ 15,000 shares) . . . . . . . . . . . . . . . . . . . . . . . . . . . . . . . . | $4.80 |

Earnings per share is perhaps the most widely used of all accounting ratios. The *trend* in earnings per share—and the expected earnings in future periods—are *major factors* affecting the market value of a company's shares.

## Price-Earnings Ratio

**LO 7**

Compute the ratios widely used in financial statement analysis and explain the significance of each.

Financial analysts express the relationship between the market price of a company's stock and the underlying earnings per share as a **price-earnings (p/e) ratio**. This ratio is computed by dividing the current market price per share of the company's stock by annual earnings per share. (A p/e ratio cannot be computed for a period in which the company incurs a net loss.)

To illustrate, assume that at the end of 2002, Computer Barn's capital stock is trading among investors at a market price of *$96* per share. The p/e ratio of the company's stock is computed as follows:

| | |
|---|---:|
| Current market price per share of stock . . . . . . . . . . . . . . . . . . . . . . . . . . . . . . . . . . . . . . . . | $96 |
| Earnings per share (for the last 12 months) . . . . . . . . . . . . . . . . . . . . . . . . . . . . . . . . . . . . . | $4.80 |
| Price-earnings ratio ($96 ÷ $4.80) . . . . . . . . . . . . . . . . . . . . . . . . . . . . . . . . . . . . . . . . . . . . | 20 |

Technically, this ratio is 20 to 1. But it is common practice to omit the "to 1" and merely to describe a p/e ratio by the first number. The p/e ratios of many publicly owned corporations are quoted daily in the financial pages of many newspapers.

The p/e ratio reflects *investors' expectations* concerning the company's *future performance.* The more optimistic these expectations, the higher the p/e ratio is likely to be. Traditionally, stocks of financially sound companies with stable earnings usually sell at between 12 and 15 times earnings. If investors anticipate rapid earnings growth, p/e ratios rise into the twenties, thirties, or even higher.

A p/e ratio of 10 or less often indicates that investors expect earnings to *decline* from the current level. It could also mean, however, that the stock is *undervalued.* Likewise, a stock with a p/e ratio of 30 or more usually means that investors expect earnings to *increase* from the current level. However, it may also signal that the stock is *overvalued.*

One word of caution. If earnings decline to *very low levels,* the price of the stock usually does not follow the earnings all the way down. Therefore, a company with *very low earnings* is likely to have a *high p/e ratio* even if investors are not optimistic about future earnings.

---

[5] Assume that all 15,000 shares have been outstanding throughout the year. Computation of earnings per share in more complex situations is addressed in Chapter 12.

*Income statement in the single-step format*

| COMPUTER BARN<br>Income Statement<br>For the Year Ended December 31, 2002 | | |
|---|---:|---:|
| **Revenue:** | | |
| Net sales | | $900,000 |
| Interest earned | | 3,200 |
| Total revenue | | $903,200 |
| **Less: Costs and expenses:** | | |
| Cost of goods sold | $540,000 | |
| Selling expenses | 136,000 | |
| General and administrative expenses | 104,000 | |
| Interest expense | 12,000 | |
| Purchase discounts lost | 1,200 | |
| Income taxes expense | 38,000 | |
| Total costs and expenses | | 831,200 |
| Net income | | $ 72,000 |
| Earnings per share | | $4.80 |

## Single-Step Income Statements

In their annual reports, many publicly owned corporations present their financial statements in a highly condensed format. For this reason, the *single-step* income statement is widely used in annual reports. The 2002 income statement of Computer Barn appears above in single-step format.

The single-step form of income statement takes its name from the fact that all costs and expenses are deducted from total revenue in a single step. No subtotals are shown for gross profit or for operating income, although the statement provides investors with enough information to compute these subtotals on their own.

## Evaluating the Adequacy of Net Income

How much net income must a business earn to be considered successful? Obviously, the dollar amount of net income that investors consider adequate depends on the *size of the business*. An annual net income of $1 million might seem impressive for an automobile dealership but would represent very poor performance for a company the size of **General Motors**, **Ford**, or **DaimlerChrysler**.

Investors usually consider two factors in evaluating a company's profitability: (1) the trend in earnings and (2) the amount of current earnings in relation to the amount of the resources needed to produce the earnings.

Most investors regard the *trend* in earnings from year to year as more important than the amount of net income in the current period. Equity investors stand to benefit from the company's performance over the long run. Years of steadily increasing earnings may increase the value of the stockholders' investment manyfold.

In evaluating the current level of earnings, many investors use *return on investment* analysis.

## Return on Investment (ROI)

Throughout this text, we have emphasized that a basic purpose of accounting is to assist decision makers in efficiently allocating and using economic resources. In deciding where to invest their money, equity investors want to know how efficiently companies utilize resources. The most common method of evaluating the efficiency with which financial resources are employed is to compute the rate of return earned on these resources. This rate of return is called the *return on investment,* or *ROI.*

Mathematically, computing the return on investment is a simple concept: the annual return (or profit) generated by the investment is stated as a *percentage* of the average amount invested throughout the year. The basic idea is illustrated by the following formula:

*ROI general formula*

$$\text{Return on Investment (ROI)} = \frac{\text{Return}}{\text{Average Amount Invested}}$$

The return is earned throughout the period. Therefore, it is logical to express this return as a percentage of the *average* amount invested during the period, rather than the investment at year-end. The average amount invested usually is computed by adding the amounts invested as of the beginning and end of the year, and dividing this total by 2.

The concept of ROI is applied in many different situations, such as evaluating the profitability of a business, a branch location, or a specific investment opportunity. As a result, a number of variations in the basic ROI ratio have been developed, each suited to a particular type of analysis. These ratios differ in the manner in which return and average amount invested are defined. We will discuss two common applications of the ROI concept: *return on assets* and *return on equity*.

## Return on Assets (ROA)

This ratio is used in evaluating whether management has earned a reasonable return with the assets under its control. In this computation, return usually is defined as *operating income,* since interest expense and income taxes are determined by factors other than the manner in which assets are used. The **return on assets** is computed as follows:

*The return on total assets is operating income*

$$\text{Return on Assets (ROA)} = \frac{\text{Operating Income}}{\text{Average Total Assets}}$$

Let us now determine the return on assets earned by the management of Computer Barn in 2002. Operating income, as shown in the income statement on page 607, amounts to *$120,000.* Assume that Computer Barn's assets at the beginning of 2002 totaled $570,000. The illustrated balance sheet on page 600 shows total assets of $630,000 at year-end. Therefore, the company's *average* total assets during the year amounted to *$600,000* [($570,000 + $630,000) ÷ 2]. The return on assets in 2002 is *20%,* determined as follows:

$$\frac{\text{Operating Income}}{\text{Average Total Assets}} = \frac{\$120,000}{\$600,000} = 20\%$$

Most successful businesses earn a return on average total assets of, perhaps, 15% or more. At this writing, businesses must pay interest rates of between 6% and 12% to borrow money. If a business is well managed and has good future prospects, management should be able to earn a return on assets that is higher than the company's cost of borrowing.

## Return on Equity (ROE)

The return on assets measures the efficiency with which management has utilized the assets under its control, regardless of whether these assets were financed with debt or equity capital. The **return on equity** ratio, in contrast, looks only at the return earned by management on the stockholders' investment—that is, on *owners' equity.*

The return to stockholders is *net income,* which represents the return from all sources, both operating and nonoperating. Thus return on equity is computed as follows:

*The return on equity is net income*

$$\text{Return on Equity (ROE)} = \frac{\text{Net Income}}{\text{Average Total Stockholders' Equity}}$$

To illustrate, let us again turn to the 2002 financial statements of Computer Barn. The company earned net income of *$72,000.* The year-end balance sheet (page 600) shows total stockholders' equity of $420,000. To enable us to complete our computation, we will assume that the stockholders' equity at the *beginning* of the year amounted to $380,000.

Therefore, the *average* stockholders' equity for the year amounts to *$400,000* [($380,000 + $420,000) ÷ 2]. The return on stockholders' equity in 2002 is *18%*, computed as follows:

$$\frac{\textbf{Net Income}}{\textbf{Average Total Stockholders' Equity}} = \frac{\$72,000}{\$400,000} = 18\%$$

Traditionally, stockholders have expected to earn an average annual return of 12% or more from equity investments in large, financially strong companies. Annual returns on equity of 30% or more are not uncommon, especially in rapidly growing companies with new or highly successful products.

The return on equity may be higher or lower than the overall return on assets, depending on how the company has financed its assets and on the amounts of its nonoperating revenue and expenses. A company that suffers a net loss provides its stockholders with a *negative* return on stockholders' equity.

The returns on assets and on equity earned by a few well-known corporations in 1999 are shown below:

| | Return on Assets | Return on Equity |
|---|---|---|
| Microsoft | 35% | 47% |
| Procter & Gamble | 12% | 31% |
| Parker Hannifin | 8% | 17% |
| ConAgra | 3% | 10% |

Many companies earn approximately the same rates of return year after year. In others, the annual rates of return fluctuate greatly, particularly when net income significantly changes.

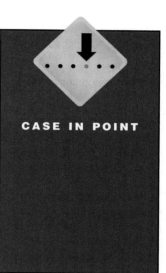

CASE IN POINT

## COMPREHENSIVE ILLUSTRATION: SEACLIFF COMPANY

Now that we have presented techniques that are useful in better understanding an enterprise's financial statements, we will show the comprehensive analysis of a company. This illustration draws from material presented in this chapter as well as from information presented earlier in the text. We take a comprehensive look at the analysis of financial statements from the perspectives of three important groups: common stockholders, long-term creditors, and short-term creditors.

The basic information for our analysis is contained in a set of condensed two-year comparative financial statements for Seacliff Company shown below and on the following pages. Summarized statement data, together with computations of dollar increases and decreases, and component percentages where applicable, have been compiled. For convenience in this illustration, relatively small dollar amounts have been used in the Seacliff Company financial statements.

**SEACLIFF COMPANY**
**Comparative Income Statement**
**For the Years Ended December 31, 2002, and December 31, 2001**

| | 2002 | 2001 | Increase or (Decrease) Dollars | Increase or (Decrease) % | Percentage of Net Sales 2002 | Percentage of Net Sales 2001 |
|---|---|---|---|---|---|---|
| Net sales | $900,000 | $750,000 | $150,000 | 20.0 | 100.0 | 100.0 |
| Cost of goods sold | 530,000 | 420,000 | 110,000 | 26.2 | 58.9 | 56.0 |
| Gross profit on sales | $370,000 | $330,000 | $ 40,000 | 12.1 | 41.1 | 44.0 |
| Operating expenses: | | | | | | |
| Selling expenses | $117,000 | $ 75,000 | $ 42,000 | 56.0 | 13.0 | 10.0 |
| General and administrative expenses | 126,000 | 95,000 | 31,000 | 32.6 | 14.0 | 12.7 |
| Total operating expenses | $243,000 | $170,000 | $ 73,000 | 42.9 | 27.0 | 22.7 |
| Operating income | $127,000 | $160,000 | $ (33,000) | (20.6) | 14.1 | 21.3 |
| Interest expense | 24,000 | 30,000 | (6,000) | (20.0) | 2.7 | 4.0 |
| Income before income taxes | $103,000 | $130,000 | $ (27,000) | (20.8) | 11.4 | 17.3 |
| Income taxes | 28,000 | 40,000 | (12,000) | (30.0) | 3.1 | 5.3 |
| Net income | $ 75,000 | $ 90,000 | $ (15,000) | (16.7) | 8.3 | 12.0 |
| Earnings per share of common stock | $ 13.20 | $ 20.25 | $ (7.05) | (34.8) | | |

**SEACLIFF COMPANY**
**Statement of Retained Earnings**
**For the Years Ended December 31, 2002, and December 31, 2001**

| | 2002 | 2001 | Increase or (Decrease) Dollars | Increase or (Decrease) % |
|---|---|---|---|---|
| Retained earnings, beginning of year | $176,000 | $115,000 | $ 61,000 | 53.0 |
| Net income | 75,000 | 90,000 | (15,000) | (16.7) |
| | $251,000 | $205,000 | $ 46,000 | 22.4 |
| Less: Dividends on common stock ($5.00 per share in 2001, $4.80 per share in 2002) | $ 24,000 | $ 20,000 | $ 4,000 | 20.0 |
| Dividends on preferred stock ($9 per share) | 9,000 | 9,000 | | |
| | $ 33,000 | $ 29,000 | $ 4,000 | 13.8 |
| Retained earnings, end of year | $218,000 | $176,000 | $ 42,000 | 23.9 |

## SEACLIFF COMPANY
### Condensed Comparative Balance Sheet*
### December 31, 2002, and December 31, 2001

| Assets | 2002 | 2001 | Increase or (Decrease) Dollars | % | Percentage of Total Assets 2002 | 2001 |
|---|---|---|---|---|---|---|
| Current assets | $390,000 | $288,000 | $102,000 | 35.4 | 41.1 | 33.5 |
| Plant and equipment (net) | 500,000 | 467,000 | 33,000 | 7.1 | 52.6 | 54.3 |
| Other assets (loans to officers) | 60,000 | 105,000 | (45,000) | (42.9) | 6.3 | 12.2 |
| Total assets | $950,000 | $860,000 | $ 90,000 | 10.5 | 100.0 | 100.0 |
| **Liabilities & Stockholders' Equity** | | | | | | |
| Liabilities: | | | | | | |
| Current liabilities | $112,000 | $ 94,000 | $ 18,000 | 19.1 | 11.8 | 10.9 |
| 12% long-term note payable (due in 7 years) | 200,000 | 250,000 | (50,000) | (20.0) | 21.1 | 29.1 |
| Total liabilities | $312,000 | $344,000 | $(32,000) | (9.3) | 32.9 | 40.0 |
| Stockholders' equity: | | | | | | |
| 9% preferred stock, $100 par, callable at 105 | $100,000 | $100,000 | — | — | 10.5 | 11.6 |
| Common stock, $50 par | 250,000 | 200,000 | $ 50,000 | 25.0 | 26.3 | 23.2 |
| Additional paid-in capital | 70,000 | 40,000 | 30,000 | 75.0 | 7.4 | 4.7 |
| Retained earnings | 218,000 | 176,000 | 42,000 | 23.9 | 22.9 | 20.5 |
| Total stockholders' equity | $638,000 | $516,000 | $122,000 | 23.6 | 67.1 | 60.0 |
| Total liabilities & stockholders' equity | $950,000 | $860,000 | $ 90,000 | 10.5 | 100.0 | 100.0 |

*In order to focus attention on important subtotals, this statement is highly condensed and does not show individual asset and liability items. These details will be introduced as needed in the next discussion. For example, a list of Seacliff Company's current assets and current liabilities appears on page 623.

## SEACLIFF COMPANY
### Condensed Comparative Statement of Cash Flows
### For the Years Ended December 31, 2002, and December 31, 2001

| | 2002 | 2001 | Increase or (Decrease) Dollars | % |
|---|---|---|---|---|
| Cash flows from operating activities: | | | | |
| Net cash flows from operating activities | $ 19,000 | $ 95,000 | $(76,000) | (80.0) |
| Cash flows from investing activities: | | | | |
| Purchases of plant assets | (63,000) | (28,000) | (35,000) | 125.0 |
| Collections of loans from officers | 45,000 | (35,000) | 80,000 | N/A* |
| Net cash used by investing activities | $(18,000) | $(63,000) | $ 45,000 | (71.4) |
| Cash flows from financing activities: | | | | |
| Dividends paid | $(33,000) | $(29,000) | $ (4,000) | 13.7 |
| Repayment of long-term debt | (50,000) | –0– | (50,000) | N/A* |
| Proceeds from issuing capital stock | 80,000 | –0– | 80,000 | N/A* |
| Net cash used by financing activities | $ (3,000) | $(29,000) | $ 26,000 | (89.7) |
| Net increase (decrease) in cash and cash equivalents | $ (2,000) | $ 3,000 | $ (5,000) | N/A* |
| Cash and cash equivalents, beginning of the year | 40,000 | 37,000 | 3,000 | 8.1 |
| Cash and cash equivalents, end of the year | $ 38,000 | $ 40,000 | $ (2,000) | (5.0) |

*N/A indicates that computation of the percentage change is not appropriate. Percentage changes cannot be determined if the base year is zero or if a negative amount (cash outflow) changes to a positive amount (cash inflow).

---

**SEACLIFF COMPANY**
**Notes to Financial Statements**
**For the Years Ended December 31, 2002, and December 31, 2001**

**Note 1—Accounting Policies**

*Inventories*   Inventories are determined by the LIFO method.

*Depreciation*   Depreciation is computed by the straight-line method. Buildings are depreciated over 40 years, and equipment and fixtures over periods of 5 or 10 years.

**Note 2—Unused Lines of Credit**

The company has a confirmed line of credit in the amount of $35,000. None was in use at December 31, 2002.

**Note 3—Contingencies and Commitments**

As of December 31, 2002, the company has no material commitments or noncancellable obligations. There currently are no loss contingencies known to management.

**Note 4—Current Values of Financial Instruments**

All financial instruments appear in the financial statements at dollar amounts that closely approximate their current values.

**Note 5—Concentrations of Credit Risk**

The company engages in retail sales to the general public from a single location in Seattle, Washington. No individual customer accounts for more than 2% of the company's total sales or accounts receivable. Accounts receivable are unsecured.

---

**LO 8**

Analyze financial statements from the viewpoints of common stockholders, creditors, and others.

## Analysis by Common Stockholders

Common stockholders and potential investors in common stock look first at a company's earnings record. Their investment is in shares of stock, so *earnings per share* and *dividends per share* are of particular interest.

**Earnings per Share of Common Stock**   As indicated in Chapter 12, earnings per share of common stock are computed by dividing the income applicable to the common stock by the weighted-average number of shares of common stock outstanding during the year. Any preferred dividend requirements must be subtracted from net income to determine income applicable to common stock, as shown in the following computations for Seacliff Company:

*Earnings related to number of common shares outstanding*

| **Earnings per Share of Common Stock** | | 2002 | 2001 |
|---|---|---|---|
| Net income | | $75,000 | $90,000 |
| Less: Preferred dividend requirements | | 9,000 | 9,000 |
| Income applicable to common stock | (a) | $66,000 | $81,000 |
| Shares of common stock outstanding, during the year | (b) | 5,000 | 4,000 |
| Earnings per share of common stock (a ÷ b) | | $ 13.20 | $ 20.25 |

Notice that earnings per share have decreased by *$7.05* in 2002, representing a decline of nearly *35%* from their level in 2001 ($7.05 ÷ $20.25 = 34.8%). Common stockholders consider a decline in earnings per share to be an unfavorable development. A decline in earnings per share generally represents a decline in the profitability of the company and creates uncertainty as to the company's prospects for future growth.

With such a significant decline in earnings per share, we should expect to see a decline in the market value of Seacliff's common stock during 2002. [For purposes of our illustration, we assume the common stock had a market value of *$160* at December

31, 2001, and of *$132* at the end of 2002. This drop of $28 per share represents a *17½%* decline in the market value of every common stockholder's investment ($28 decline ÷ $160 = 17.5%).]

**Price-Earnings Ratio**  As we mentioned earlier in this chapter, the relationship between the market price of common stock and earnings per share is widely recognized and is expressed as a ratio, called the *price-earnings ratio* (or *p/e ratio*). The p/e ratio is determined by dividing the market price per share by the annual earnings per share.

The average p/e ratio of the 30 stocks included in the Dow Jones Industrial Average has varied widely in recent years, ranging from a low of about 10 to a high of about 18. The outlook for future earnings is the major factor influencing a company's p/e ratio. Companies with track records of rapid growth may sell at p/e ratios of perhaps 20 to 1, or even higher. Companies with "flat" earnings or earnings expected to decline in future years often sell at price-earnings ratios below, say, 10 to 1.

At the end of 2001, Seacliff's p/e ratio was approximately *8 to 1* ($160 ÷ $20.25 = 7.9), suggesting that investors *were expecting* earnings to decline in 2002. At December 31, 2002, the price-earnings ratio was *10 to 1* ($132 ÷ $13.20 = 10.0). A p/e ratio in this range suggests that investors expect future earnings to stabilize around the current level.

**Dividend Yield**  Dividends are of prime importance to some stockholders, but a secondary factor to others. Some stockholders invest primarily to receive regular cash income, while others invest in stocks principally with the expectation of rising market prices. If a corporation is profitable and retains its earnings for expansion of the business, the expanded operations should produce an increase in the net income of the company and thus tend to make each share of stock more valuable.

In comparing the merits of alternative investment opportunities, we should relate earnings and dividends per share to the *market value* of the stock. Dividends per share divided by market price per share determine the *yield* rate of a company's stock. Dividend yield is especially important to those investors whose objective is to maximize the dividend revenue from their investments. For Seacliff, the dividend yield on its common stock was 3.1% in 2001 ($5/$160) and 3.6% in 2002 ($4.80/$132).

**Summary of Earnings and Dividend Data for Seacliff**  The relationships of Seacliff's per-share earnings and dividends to its year-end stock prices are summarized below:

| | Market Value per Share | Earnings per Share | Price-Earnings Ratio | Dividends per Share | Dividend Yield, % |
|---|---|---|---|---|---|
| Date | | | | | |
| Dec. 31, 2001 . . . . . . . . . . . | $160 | $20.25 | 8 | $5.00 | 3.1 |
| Dec. 31, 2002 . . . . . . . . . . . | 132 | 13.20 | 10 | 4.80 | 3.6 |

*Earnings and dividends related to market price of common stock*

The decline in market value during 2002 presumably reflects the decreases in both earnings and dividends per share. Investors appraising this stock at December 31, 2002, should consider whether a price-earnings ratio of 10 and a dividend yield of 3.6% meet their expectations in light of alternative investment opportunities. These investors will also place considerable weight on estimates of the company's prospective future earnings and the probable effect of such estimated earnings on the market price of the stock and on dividend payments.

**Revenue and Expense Analysis**  The trend of earnings of Seacliff Company is unfavorable, and stockholders will want to know the reasons for the decline in net income. The comparative income statement on page 614 shows that despite a 20% increase in net sales, net income fell from $90,000 in 2001 to $75,000 in 2002, a decline of 16.7%.

As a percentage of net sales, net income fell from 12% to only 8.3%. The primary causes of this decline were the increases in selling expenses (56.0%), in general and administrative expenses (32.6%), and in the cost of goods sold (26.2%), all of which exceeded the 20% increase in net sales.

Let us assume that further investigation reveals Seacliff Company decided in 2002 to reduce its sales prices in an effort to generate greater sales volume. This would explain the decrease in gross profit rate from 44% to 41.1% of net sales. Since the dollar amount of gross profit increased $40,000 in 2002, the strategy of reducing sales prices to increase volume would have been successful if there had been little or no increase in operating expenses. However, operating expenses rose by $73,000, resulting in a $33,000 decrease in operating income.

The next step is to find which expenses increased and why. An investor may be limited here, because detailed operating expenses are not usually shown in published financial statements. Some conclusions, however, can be reached on the basis of even the condensed information available in the comparative income statement for Seacliff Company shown on page 614.

The substantial increase in selling expenses presumably reflects greater selling effort during 2002 in an attempt to improve sales volume. However, the fact that selling expenses increased $42,000 while gross profit increased only $40,000 indicates that the cost of this increased sales effort was not justified in terms of results. Even more bothersome is the increase in general and administrative expenses. Some growth in administrative expenses might be expected to accompany increased sales volume, but because some of the expenses are fixed, the growth generally should be *less than proportional* to any increase in sales. The increase in general and administrative expenses from 12.7% to 14% of sales would be of concern to informed investors.

Management generally has greater control over operating expenses than over revenue. The *operating expense ratio* is often used as a measure of management's ability to control its operating expenses. The unfavorable trend in this ratio for Seacliff Company is shown as follows:

*Does a higher operating expense ratio indicate higher net income?*

| **Operating Expense Ratio** | | |
| --- | --- | --- |
| | **2002** | **2001** |
| Operating expenses . . . . . . . . . . . . . . . . . . . . . . . . . . . . . . . . . . . . . . | (a) $243,000 | $170,000 |
| Net sales . . . . . . . . . . . . . . . . . . . . . . . . . . . . . . . . . . . . . . . . . . . . . | (b) $900,000 | $750,000 |
| Operating expense ratio (a ÷ b) . . . . . . . . . . . . . . . . . . . . . . . . . . | 27.0% | 22.7% |

If management were able to increase the sales volume while at the same time increasing the gross profit rate and decreasing the operating expense ratio, the effect on net income could be dramatic. For example, if in the year 2003 Seacliff Company can increase its sales by 11% to $1,000,000, increase its gross profit rate from 41.1 to 44%, and reduce the operating expense ratio from 27 to 24%, its operating income will increase from $127,000 to $200,000 ($1,000,000 − $560,000 − $240,000), an increase of over 57%.

## Return on Investment (ROI)

The rate of return on investment (often called ROI) is a measure of management's efficiency in using available resources. Regardless of the size of the organization, capital is a scarce resource and must be used efficiently. In judging the performance of branch managers or of companywide management, it is reasonable to raise the question: What rate of return have you earned on the resources under your control?

**Return on Assets**    An important test of management's ability to earn a return on funds supplied from all sources is the rate of return on total assets.

As noted previously, the income figure used in computing this ratio should be *operating income,* since interest expense and income taxes are determined by factors other than the efficient use of resources. Operating income is earned throughout the year and therefore should be related to the *average* investment in assets during the year. The computation of this ratio of Seacliff Company is shown as follows, assuming total assets at the beginning of 2001 were $820,000:

| Percentage Return on Assets | | |
|---|---|---|
| | 2002 | 2001 |
| Operating income . . . . . . . . . . . . . . . . . . . . . . . . . . . . . . . . . . . . . . . . (a) $127,000 | | $160,000 |
| Total assets, beginning of year . . . . . . . . . . . . . . . . . . . . . . . . . . . (b) $860,000 | | $820,000 |
| Total assets, end of year . . . . . . . . . . . . . . . . . . . . . . . . . . . . . . . . (c) $950,000 | | $860,000 |
| Average investment in assets [(b + c) ÷ 2] . . . . . . . . . . . . . . . . (d) $905,000 | | $840,000 |
| Return on assets (a ÷ d) . . . . . . . . . . . . . . . . . . . . . . . . . . . . . . 14% | | 19% |

*Earnings related to investment in assets*

This ratio shows that the rate of return earned on the company's assets fall in 2002. Before drawing conclusions as to the effectiveness of Seacliff's management, however, we should consider the trend in the return on assets earned by other companies of similar kind and size.

**Return on Common Stockholders' Equity**   We introduced the concept of return on equity using a company that had only one class of capital stock. Therefore, the return on equity was simply net income divided by average stockholders' equity. But Seacliff has issued both preferred stock *and* common stock. The preferred stock does not participate fully in the company's earnings; rather, the return to preferred stockholders is limited to their dividend. Thus, we must adjust the return on equity computation to reflect the return on *common* stockholders' equity.

The return to common stockholders is equal to net income *less* any preferred dividends. Thus the return on common stockholders' equity is computed as follows, assuming common stockholders' equity at the beginning of 2001 was $355,000:

| Return on Common Stockholders' Equity | | |
|---|---|---|
| | 2002 | 2001 |
| Net income . . . . . . . . . . . . . . . . . . . . . . . . . . . . . . . . . . . . . . . . . | $ 75,000 | $ 90,000 |
| Less: Preferred dividend requirements . . . . . . . . . . . . . . . . . . . . . . | 9,000 | 9,000 |
| Net income applicable to common stock . . . . . . . . . . . . . . . . . . . . (a) | $ 66,000 | $ 81,000 |
| Common stockholders' equity, beginning of year . . . . . . . . . . . . . . (b) | $416,000 | $355,000 |
| Common stockholders' equity, end of year . . . . . . . . . . . . . . . . . . (c) | $538,000 | $416,000 |
| Average common stockholders' equity [(b + c) ÷ 2] . . . . . . . . . . . . (d) | $477,000 | $385,500 |
| Return on common stockholders' equity (a ÷ d) . . . . . . . . . . . . . . | 13.8% | 21.0% |

*Does the use of leverage benefit common stockholders?*

In both years, the rate of return on common stockholders' equity was higher than the 12% rate of interest paid to long-term creditors or the 9% dividend rate paid to preferred stockholders. This result was achieved through the favorable use of leverage.

## Leverage

Applying leverage means using borrowed money to earn a return *greater* than the cost of borrowing, increasing net income and the return on common stockholders' equity. In other words, if you can borrow money at 12% and use it to earn 20%, you will benefit by doing so. However, leverage can act as a double-edged sword; the effects may be favorable or unfavorable to the holders of common stock.

If the rate of return on total assets should fall *below* the average rate of interest on borrowed capital, leverage will *reduce* the return on common stockholders' equity. In this situation, paying off the loans that carry high interest rates would appear to be a logical move. However, many companies do not have enough cash to retire long-term debt on short notice. Therefore, the common stockholders may become locked in to the unfavorable effects of leverage.

In deciding how much leverage is appropriate, the common stockholders should consider the *stability* of the company's return on assets as well as the relationship of this return to the average cost of borrowed capital. If a business incurs so much debt that it becomes unable to meet the required interest and principal payments, the creditors may force liquidation or reorganization of the business.

**MANAGEMENT STRATEGY**

Management determines the financial structure of the company. The financial (or capital) structure is the proportion of debt and equity capital and the particular forms of debt (e.g., long versus short) and equity (e.g., common versus preferred) chosen to finance the assets of the firm. Management maximizes the firm's value by minimizing the firm's cost of financing its assets.

When determining the financial structure, management must consider the impact of changes in the structure of its financial reports because creditors frequently use financial ratios in debt agreements with firms. These agreements (called debt covenants) frequently require the firm to repay the debt if the firm's financial ratios fall outside of predetermined ranges identified in the agreement. Thus managers must be aware of these pre-existing agreements and the associated accounting ratios when considering a change to their capital structure via additional borrowing or issuing of additional equity.

**Debt Ratio**   One indicator of the amount of leverage used by a business is the debt ratio. This ratio measures the proportion of the total assets financed by creditors, as distinguished from stockholders. It is computed by dividing total liabilities by total assets. A *high* debt ratio indicates an extensive use of leverage, that is, a large proportion of financing provided by creditors. A low debt ratio, on the other hand, indicates that the business is making little use of leverage.

The debt ratio at year-end for Seacliff is determined as follows:

*Proportion of assets financed by creditors*

| Debt Ratio | | |
| --- | --- | --- |
| | **2002** | **2001** |
| Total liabilities ................................................ | (a) $312,000 | $344,000 |
| Total assets (or total liabilities & stockholders' equity) ............ | (b) $950,000 | $860,000 |
| Debt ratio (a ÷ b)............................................ | 32.8% | 40.0% |

Seacliff Company has a lower debt ratio in 2002 than in 2001. Is this favorable or unfavorable?

From the viewpoint of the common stockholder, a high debt ratio will produce maximum benefits if management is able to earn a rate of return on assets greater than the rate of interest paid to creditors. However, a high debt ratio can be *unfavorable* if the return on assets falls *below* the rate of interest paid to creditors. Since the return on total assets earned by Seacliff Company has declined from 19% in 2001 to a relatively low 14% in 2002, the common stockholders probably would *not* want to risk a high debt ratio. The action by management in 2002 of retiring $50,000 in long-term liabilities will help to protect the common stockholders from the unfavorable effects of leverage if the rate of return on assets continues to decline.

## Analysis by Long-Term Creditors

Bondholders and other long-term creditors are primarily interested in three factors: (1) the rate of return on their investment, (2) the firm's ability to meet its interest requirements, and (3) the firm's ability to repay the principal of the debt when it falls due.

**Yield Rate on Bonds**   The yield rate on bonds or other long-term indebtedness cannot be computed in the same manner as the yield rate on shares of stock, because bonds, unlike stocks, have a definite maturity date and amount. The ownership of a 12%, 10-year, $1,000 bond represents the right to receive $120 each year for 10 years plus the right to receive $1,000 at the end of 10 years. If the market price of this bond is $950, the yield rate on an investment in the bond is the rate of interest that will make the *present value* of these two contractual rights equal to the $950 market price.

When bonds sell at maturity value, the yield rate is equal to the bond interest rate. *The yield rate varies inversely with changes in the market price of the bond.* If interest rates rise, the market price of existing bonds will fall; if interest rates decline, the price of bonds will rise. If the price of a bond is above maturity value, the yield rate is less than the bond interest rate; if the price of a bond is below maturity value, the yield rate is higher than the bond interest rate.

**Interest Coverage Ratio**   Bondholders feel that their investments are relatively safe if the issuing company earns enough income to cover its annual interest obligations by a comfortable margin.

A common measure of creditors' safety is the ratio of operating income available for the payment of interest to the annual interest expense, called the *interest coverage ratio* or *times interest earned*. This computation for Seacliff Company would be as follows:

| Interest Coverage Ratio | | |
|---|---|---|
| | **2002** | **2001** |
| Operating income (before interest and income taxes) . . . . . . . . . . . . . | (a) $127,000 | $160,000 |
| Annual interest expense . . . . . . . . . . . . . . . . . . . . . . . . . . . . . . . | (b) $ 24,000 | $ 30,000 |
| Interest coverage (a ÷ b) . . . . . . . . . . . . . . . . . . . . . . . . . . . . . . | 5.3 times | 5.3 times |

*Long-term creditors watch this ratio*

The ratio remained unchanged at a satisfactory level during 2002. A ratio of 5.3 times interest earned would be considered strong in many industries. In the electric utilities industry, for example, the interest coverage ratio for the leading companies presently averages about 3, with the ratios of individual companies varying from 2 to 6.

**Debt Ratio**   Long-term creditors are interested in the percentage of total assets financed by debt, as distinguished from the percentage financed by stockholders. The percentage of total assets financed by debt is measured by the debt ratio, which was computed on the preceding page.

From a creditor's viewpoint, the lower the debt ratio the better, since this means that stockholders have contributed a higher percentage of the funds to the business, and therefore the margin of protection to creditors against a shrinkage of the assets is high.

| Debt Ratio | | |
|---|---|---|
| | **2002** | **2001** |
| Total liabilities . . . . . . . . . . . . . . . . . . . . . . . . . . . . . . . . . . . . | (a) $312,000 | $344,000 |
| Total assets . . . . . . . . . . . . . . . . . . . . . . . . . . . . . . . . . . . . . . | (b) $950,000 | $860,000 |
| Debt ratio (a ÷ b) . . . . . . . . . . . . . . . . . . . . . . . . . . . . . . . . . . | 32.8% | 40% |

The debt ratio, or the percentage of assets financed by debt, decreased from 2001 to 2002 from 40% to 32.8%. This would generally be considered by long-term creditors to be a favorable change because the debt burden, including required interest payments, is less in 2002 than in 2001, thereby making the claim of each creditor more secure.

**Secured Claims**   Sometimes the claims of long-term creditors are secured with specific collateral, such as the land and buildings owned by the borrower. In these situations, the secured creditors may look primarily to the *value of the collateral* in assessing the safety of their claims.

Assets pledged as collateral to secure specific liabilities are disclosed in notes to the financial statements. As Seacliff makes no such disclosures, we may assume that none of its assets has been pledged as collateral to secure specific liabilities.

## Analysis by Short-Term Creditors

Bankers and other short-term creditors share the interest of stockholders and bondholders in the profitability and long-run stability of a business. Their primary interest, however, is in the current position of the company—its ability to generate sufficient funds (working capital) to meet current operating needs and to pay current debts promptly. Thus the analysis of financial statements by a banker considering a short-term loan, or by a trade creditor investigating the credit status of a customer, is likely to center on the working capital position of the prospective debtor.

**Amount of Working Capital**   Working capital is the excess of current assets over current liabilities. It represents the cash and near-cash assets that provide a "cushion" of liquidity over the amount expected to be needed in the near future to satisfy maturing obligations. The details of the working capital of Seacliff Company are shown on the following page.

This schedule shows that current assets increased $102,000, while current liabilities rose by only $18,000, with the result that working capital increased $84,000.

**Quality of Working Capital**   In evaluating the debt-paying ability of a business, short-term creditors should consider the quality of working capital as well as the total dollar amount. The principal factors affecting the quality of working capital are (1) the nature of the current assets and (2) the length of time required to convert these assets into cash.

The schedule on page 623 shows an unfavorable shift in the composition of Seacliff Company's working capital during 2002: cash decreased from 13.9% to 9.7% of current assets, while inventory rose from 41.6% to 46.2%. Inventory is a less liquid resource than cash. Therefore, the quality of working capital is not as liquid as in 2001. *Turnover rates* (or *ratios*) may be used to assist short-term creditors in estimating the time required to turn assets such as receivables and inventory into cash.

**Accounts Receivable Turnover Rate**   As explained in Chapter 7, the accounts receivable turnover rate indicates how quickly a company converts its accounts receivable into cash. The accounts receivable turnover *rate* is determined by dividing net sales by the average balance of accounts receivable.[6] The number of *days* required (on average) to collect accounts receivable then may be determined by dividing the number of days in a year (365) by the turnover rate. These computations follow using the data in our Seacliff example, assuming accounts receivable at the beginning of 2001 were $80,000:

---

[6] Ideally, the accounts receivable turnover is computed by dividing net *credit* sales by the *monthly* average of receivables. Such detailed information, however, generally is not provided in annual financial statements.

| Accounts Receivable Turnover | | |
|---|---|---|
| | **2002** | **2001** |
| Net sales .............................................. | (a) $900,000 | $750,000 |
| Receivables, beginning of year ............................. | $ 86,000 | $ 80,000 |
| Receivables, end of year ................................... | $117,000 | $ 86,000 |
| Average receivables ...................................... | (b) $101,500 | $ 83,000 |
| Receivable turnover per year (a ÷ b) ....................... | 8.9 times | 9.0 times |
| Average number of days to collect receivables (divide 365 days by receivable turnover) ........................ | 41 days | 41 days |

*Are customers paying promptly?*

**SEACLIFF COMPANY**
**Comparative Schedule of Working Capital**
**As of December 31, 2002, and December 31, 2001**

| | 2002 | 2001 | Increase or (Decrease) | | Percentage of Total Current Items | |
|---|---|---|---|---|---|---|
| | | | Dollars | % | 2002 | 2001 |
| Current assets: | | | | | | |
| Cash ................................................ | $ 38,000 | $ 40,000 | $ (2,000) | (5.0) | 9.7 | 13.9 |
| Receivables (net) ........................... | 117,000 | 86,000 | 31,000 | 36.0 | 30.0 | 29.9 |
| Inventories ...................................... | 180,000 | 120,000 | 60,000 | 50.0 | 46.2 | 41.6* |
| Prepaid expenses ........................... | 55,000 | 42,000 | 13,000 | 31.0 | 14.1 | 14.6 |
| Total current assets ................................... | $390,000 | $288,000 | $102,000 | 35.4 | 100.0 | 100.0 |
| Current liabilities: | | | | | | |
| Notes payable to creditors ................................... | $ 14,600 | $ 10,000 | $ 4,600 | 46.0 | 13.1* | 10.7* |
| Accounts payable ............................. | 66,000 | 30,000 | 36,000 | 120.0 | 58.9 | 31.9 |
| Accrued liabilities .............................. | 31,400 | 54,000 | (22,600) | (41.9) | 28.0 | 57.4 |
| Total current liabilities ..................................... | $112,000 | $ 94,000 | $ 18,000 | 19.1 | 100.0 | 100.0 |
| Working capital ................................... | $278,000 | $194,000 | $ 84,000 | 43.3 | | |

*Amounts adjusted so that totals equal 100.0.

There has been no significant change in the average time required to collect receivables. The interpretation of the average age of receivables depends upon the company's credit terms and the seasonal activity immediately before year-end. For example, if the company grants 30-day credit terms to its customers, the above analysis indicates that accounts receivable collections are lagging. If the terms are for 60 days, however, collections are being made ahead of schedule.

**Inventory Turnover Rate** The inventory turnover rate indicates how many times during the year the company is able to sell a quantity of goods equal to its average inventory. Mechanically, this rate is determined by dividing the cost of goods sold for the year by the average amount of inventory on hand during the year. The number of days required to sell this amount of inventory may be determined by dividing 365 days by the turnover rate. These computations were explained in Chapter 8 and are demonstrated as follows using the data of Seacliff Company, assuming inventory at the beginning of 2001 was $100,000:

| Inventory Turnover | | 2002 | 2001 |
|---|---|---|---|
| Cost of goods sold | (a) | $530,000 | $420,000 |
| Inventory, beginning of year | | $120,000 | $100,000 |
| Inventory, end of year | | $180,000 | $120,000 |
| Average inventory | (b) | $150,000 | $110,000 |
| Average inventory turnover per year (a ÷ b) | | 3.5 times | 3.8 times |
| Average number of days to sell inventory (divide 365 days by inventory turnover) | | 104 days | 96 days |

The trend indicated by this analysis is unfavorable, since the length of time required for Seacliff to turn over (sell) its inventory is increasing.

Companies that have low gross profit rates often need high inventory turnover rates in order to operate profitably. This is merely another way of saying that if the gross profit rate is low, a high volume of transactions is necessary to produce a satisfactory amount of profits. Companies that sell high markup items, such as jewelry stores and art galleries, can operate successfully with much lower inventory turnover rates.

**Operating Cycle**   The inventory turnover rate indicates how quickly inventory *sells,* but not how quickly this asset converts into *cash.* Short-term creditors, of course, are interested primarily in the company's ability to generate cash.

The period of time required for a merchandising company to convert its inventory into cash is called the *operating cycle.* The next illustration appeared in Chapter 6 but is repeated below for your convenience.

*The operating cycle repeats continuously*

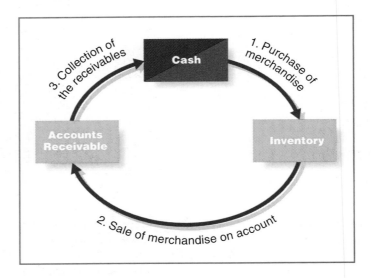

Seacliff's operating cycle in 2002 was approximately 145 days, computed by adding the 104 days required to turn over inventory and the average 41 days required to collect receivables. This compares to an operating cycle of only 137 days in 2001, computed as 96 days to dispose of the inventory plus 41 days to collect the resulting receivables. From the viewpoint of short-term creditors, the *shorter* the operating cycle, the *higher the quality* of the borrower's working capital. Therefore, these creditors would regard the lengthening of Seacliff Company's operating cycle as an unfavorable trend.

**Current Ratio**   The current ratio expresses the relationship between current assets and current liabilities. A strong current ratio provides considerable evidence that a company will be able to meet its obligations coming due in the near future. The current ratio for Seacliff Company is computed as follows:

| Current Ratio | | |
| --- | --- | --- |
| | **2002** | **2001** |
| Total current assets | (a) $390,000 | $288,000 |
| Total current liabilities | (b) $112,000 | $ 94,000 |
| Current ratio (a ÷ b) | 3.5 | 3.1 |

*Does this indicate satisfactory debt-paying ability?*

**Quick Ratio**   Because inventories and prepaid expenses are further removed from conversion into cash than other current assets, the *quick ratio* is sometimes computed as a supplement to the current ratio. The quick ratio compares the most liquid current assets (cash, marketable securities, and receivables) with current liabilities. Seacliff Company has no marketable securities; its quick ratio is computed as follows:

| Quick Ratio | | |
| --- | --- | --- |
| | **2002** | **2001** |
| Quick assets (cash and receivables) | (a) $155,000 | $126,000 |
| Current liabilities | (b) $112,000 | $ 94,000 |
| Quick ratio (a ÷ b) | 1.4 | 1.3 |

*A measure of liquidity*

Here again the analysis reveals a favorable trend and a strong position. If the credit periods extended to customers and granted by creditors are roughly equal, a quick ratio of 1.0 or better is considered satisfactory.

**Unused Lines of Credit**   From the viewpoint of a short-term creditor, a company's unused lines of credit represent a resource almost as liquid as cash. An unused line of credit means that a bank has agreed in advance to lend the company any amount, up to the specified limit. As long as this line of credit remains available, creditors know that the business can borrow cash quickly and easily for any purpose, including payments of creditors' claims.

Existing unused lines of credit are *disclosed* in notes accompanying the financial statements. Short-term creditors would view Seacliff's $35,000 line of credit (Note 2 to the financial statements) as enhancing the company's liquidity.

## Cash Flow Analysis

We often have stressed the importance of a company being able to generate sufficient cash flows from its operations. In 2001, Seacliff generated net cash flows of $95,000 from its operating activities—a relatively "normal" amount, considering that net income for the year was $90,000. This $95,000 remained *after* payment of interest to creditors and amounted to more than three times the dividends paid to stockholders. Thus in 2001 the net cash flows from operating activities appeared quite sufficient to ensure that Seacliff could pay its interest obligations and also pay dividends.

In 2002, however, net cash flows from operating activities declined to $19,000, an amount far below the company's $75,000 net income and only approximately 58% of the amount of dividends paid. Stockholders and creditors alike would view this dramatic decline in cash flows as a negative and potentially dangerous development.

A reconciliation of Seacliff's net income in 2002 with its net cash flows from operating activities is shown at the top of the following page.

*Why was the cash flow from operations so low?*

| | | |
|---|---:|---:|
| Net income | | $ 75,000 |
| Add: | | |
| Depreciation expense | $30,000 | |
| Increase in notes payable to suppliers | 4,600 | |
| Increase in accounts payable | 36,000 | 70,600 |
| | | $145,600 |
| | | |
| Less: | | |
| Increase in accounts receivable | $31,000 | |
| Increase in inventories | 60,000 | |
| Increase in prepaid expenses | 13,000 | |
| Decrease in accrued liabilities | 22,600 | 126,600 |
| Net cash flows from operating activities | | $ 19,000 |

(As explained in Chapter 13, the FASB requires companies to provide this type of reconciliation either in the statement of cash flows or in a supplemental schedule.)

The primary reasons for Seacliff's low net operating cash flows appear to be the growth in uncollected accounts receivable and inventories, combined with the substantial reduction in accrued liabilities. Given the significant increase in sales during 2002, the increase in accounts receivable is to be expected. The large reduction in accrued liabilities may be a one-time event that will not necessarily recur next year. The large increase in inventory, however, may have reduced Seacliff's liquidity unnecessarily.

Seacliff's financial position, particularly its short-term liquidity, would appear considerably stronger if its increased sales volume were supported by a higher *inventory turnover rate,* instead of a larger inventory.

**Cash Flows from Operations to Current Liabilities**   An additional measure of liquidity that is sometimes computed, based in part on information from the statement of cash flows, is the ratio of cash flows from operations to current liabilities. This measure provides evidence of the company's ability to cover its currently maturing liabilities from normal operations. For 2001 and 2002, the ratio is computed for Seacliff Corporation as follows:

| Cash Flows from Operations to Current Liabilities | | |
|---|---:|---:|
| | **2002** | **2001** |
| Cash flows from operations | (a) $ 19,000 | $95,000 |
| Current liabilities | (b) $112,000 | $94,000 |
| Cash flows from operations to current liabilities (a ÷ b) | .17 | 1.01 |

As you can see from this measure, Seacliff was much stronger in 2001 than in 2002. In 2001, operating cash flows were slightly more than current liabilities at year-end, indicating an ability to cover current obligations from normal operations without regard to the amount of existing current assets. In 2002, however, operations provided only 17% as much cash as is needed to meet current obligations, implying a need to rely more heavily on existing current assets than in 2001.

## Usefulness of Notes to Financial Statements

A set of financial statements normally is accompanied by several *notes,* disclosing information useful in *interpreting* the statements. Users should view these notes as an *integral part* of the financial statements.

In preceding chapters we have identified many items that are disclosed in notes accompanying the financial statements. Among the most useful are the following:

- Accounting policies and methods.
- Unused lines of credit.
- Significant commitments and loss contingencies.
- Current values of financial instruments (if different from the carrying values shown in the statements).
- Dividends in arrears.
- Concentrations of credit risk.
- Assets pledged to secure specific liabilities.

The notes accompanying Seacliff's financial statements are quite clean—that is, they contain no surprises or cause for concern. Of course, the unused line of credit disclosed in Note 2 would be of interest to anyone evaluating the company's short-term debt-paying ability.

**You as a Financial Analyst**

Assume that you are a financial analyst and that two of your clients are requesting your advice on certain companies as potential investments. Both clients are interested in purchasing common stock. One is primarily interested in the dividends to be received from the investment. The second is primarily interested in the growth of the market value of the stock. What information would you advise your clients to focus on in their respective analyses?

*Our comments appear on page 653.

**YOUR TURN**

## SOME CONCLUDING COMMENTS

### Sources of Financial Information

For the most part, our discussion in this chapter has been limited to the kinds of analysis that can be performed by external users who do not have access to the company's accounting records. Investors and creditors must rely to a considerable extent on the financial statements published in annual and quarterly reports. In the case of publicly owned corporations, additional information is filed with the Securities and Exchange Commission (SEC) and is available to the public in hard copy, as well as on the Internet. In fact, the Internet is the fastest growing source of *free* information available to decision makers in this information age.

Many financial analysts who evaluate the financial statements and future prospects of publicly owned companies sell their conclusions and investment recommendations for a fee. For example, detailed financial analyses of most large companies are available from **Standard & Poor's**, **Moody's Investors Service**, and **The Value Line Investment Survey**. Anyone may subscribe to these investment services.

Bankers and major creditors usually are able to obtain detailed financial information from borrowers simply by requesting it as a condition for granting a loan. Suppliers and other trade creditors may obtain some financial information about almost any business from credit-rating agencies, such as **Dun & Bradstreet**.

### Financial Analysis and Stock Price

Assume that a company has rapidly increasing net sales and earnings, and also earns high returns on assets and stockholders' equity. Is its stock a "good buy" at the present price?

Stock prices, like p/e ratios, are a *measure of investors' expectations*. A company may be highly profitable and growing fast. But if investors had expected even better performance, the market price of its stock may decline. Similarly, if a troubled company's losses are smaller than expected, the price of its stock may rise.

In financial circles, evaluating stock price by looking at the underlying profitability of the company is termed **fundamental analysis**. This approach to investing works better in the long run than in the short run. In the short run, stock prices can be significantly affected by many factors, including short-term interest rates, current events, political events, fads, and rumors. But in the long run, good companies increase in value.

In summary, successful investing requires more than an understanding of accounting concepts. It requires experience, judgment, patience, and the ability to absorb some losses. But a knowledge of accounting concepts is invaluable to the long-term investor—and it reduces the risk of "getting burned."

## Summary of Analytical Measurements

The financial ratios and other measurements introduced throughout this textbook, including this chapter—and their significance—are summarized below.

| Ratios or Other Measurements | Method of Computation | Significance |
|---|---|---|
| **Measures of short-term liquidity** | | |
| Current ratio | $\dfrac{\text{Current Assets}}{\text{Current Liabilities}}$ | A measure of short-term debt-paying ability |
| Quick ratio | $\dfrac{\text{Quick Assets}}{\text{Current Liabilities}}$ | A measure of short-term debt-paying ability |
| Working capital | Current Assets − Current Liabilities | A measure of short-term debt-paying ability |
| Net cash provided by operating activities | Appears in the statement of cash flows | Indicates the cash generated by operations after allowing for cash payment of expenses and operating liabilities |
| Cash flow from operations to current liabilities | $\dfrac{\text{Cash Flows from Operating Activities}}{\text{Current Liabilities}}$ | Indicates ability to cover currently maturing obligations from recurring operations |
| Receivables turnover rate | $\dfrac{\text{Net Sales}}{\text{Average Accounts Receivable}}$ | Indicates how quickly receivables are collected |
| Days to collect average accounts receivable | $\dfrac{\text{365 days}}{\text{Receivables Turnover Rate}}$ | Indicates in days how quickly receivables are collected |
| Inventory turnover rate | $\dfrac{\text{Cost of Goods Sold}}{\text{Average Inventory}}$ | Indicates how quickly inventory sells |
| Days to sell the average inventory | $\dfrac{\text{365 days}}{\text{Inventory Turnover Rate}}$ | Indicates in days how quickly inventory sells |
| Operating cycle | Days to Sell Inventory + Days to Collect Receivables | Indicates in days how quickly cash invested in inventory converts back into cash |
| Free cash flow | Net Cash from Operating Activities − Cash Used for Investing Activities and Dividends | Excess of operating cash flow over basic needs |
| **Measures of long-term credit risk** | | |
| Debt ratio | $\dfrac{\text{Total Liabilities}}{\text{Total Assets}}$ | Percentage of assets financed by creditors; indicates relative size of the equity position |
| Trend in net cash provided by operating activities | Appears in comparative statements of cash flows | Indicator of a company's ability to generate the cash necessary to meet its obligations |
| Interest coverage ratio | $\dfrac{\text{Operating Income}}{\text{Annual Interest Expense}}$ | Indicator of a company's ability to meet its interest payment obligations |
| **Measures of profitability** | | |
| Percentage changes; that is, in net sales and net income | $\dfrac{\text{Dollar Amount of Change}}{\text{Financial Statement Amount in the Earlier Year}}$ | The rate at which a key measure is increasing or decreasing; the "growth rate" |

(Continued on next page)

| Ratios or Other Measurements | Method of Computation | Significance |
|---|---|---|
| Gross profit rate | $\dfrac{\text{Gross Profit}}{\text{Net Sales}}$ | A measure of the profitability of the company's products |
| Operating expense ratio | $\dfrac{\text{Operating Expenses}}{\text{Net Sales}}$ | A measure of management's ability to control expenses |
| Operating income | Gross Profit − Operating Expenses | The profitability of a company's basic business activities |
| Net income as a percentage of net sales | $\dfrac{\text{Net Income}}{\text{Net Sales}}$ | An indicator of management's ability to control costs |
| Earnings per share | $\dfrac{\text{Net Income − Preferred Dividends}}{\text{Average Number of Common Shares Outstanding}}$ | Net income applicable to each share of common stock |
| Return on assets | $\dfrac{\text{Operating Income}}{\text{Average Total Assets}}$ | A measure of the productivity of assets, regardless of how the assets are financed |
| Return on equity | $\dfrac{\text{Net Income}}{\text{Average Total Equity}}$ | The rate of return earned on the stockholders' equity in the business |
| Return on common stockholders' equity | $\dfrac{\text{Net Income − Preferred Dividends}}{\text{Average Common Stockholders' Equity}}$ | The rate of return earned on the common stockholders' equity appropriate when company has both common and preferred stock |
| **Measures for evaluating the current market price of common stock** | | |
| Market value of financial instruments | Quoted in financial press or disclosed in financial statements | Reflects both investors' expectations and current market conditions |
| Price-earnings ratio | $\dfrac{\text{Current Stock Price}}{\text{Earnings per Share}}$ | A measure of investors' expectations about the company's future prospects |
| Dividend yield | $\dfrac{\text{Annual Dividend}}{\text{Current Stock Price}}$ | Dividends expressed as a rate of return on the market price of the stock |
| Book value per share | $\dfrac{\text{Common Stockholders' Equity}}{\text{Shares of Common Stock Outstanding}}$ | The recorded value of net assets underlying each share of common stock |

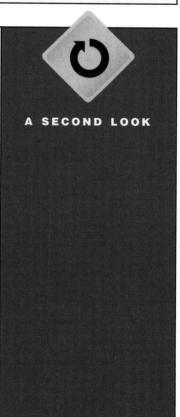

**A SECOND LOOK**

## Johnson & Johnson

As we opened Chapter 14, we took a quick look at some key ratios from **Johnson & Johnson**'s financial statements, including the current ratio (1.77 in 1999) and the return on assets (14%). We raised the issue of needing comparative information for these ratios to be meaningful, including information about **Johnson & Johnson** over several time periods and industry information that would allow comparisons with other similar companies.

Many companies, including **Johnson & Johnson**, include in their annual reports multiyear summaries of key financial statement information. For example, in the 1999 **Johnson & Johnson** annual report, a "Summary of Operations and Statistical Data 1989–1999 is a rich source of information over 11 years. While this summary does not include everything that could be found in the individual financial statements of each year, it does include many key items that provide a picture of the company's experience over a relatively long period of time. For example, the summary shows that the return on stockholders' equity ranged from a low of $16.1 million in 1992 to $29.4 million in 1994, with 1999 (the most current year) being $27.5 million. Similarly, basic earnings per share ranged from a low of $.67 in 1992 to $3.00 in 1999. The summary from which this information is drawn actually includes 41 pieces of information for each of the 11 years included in the summary, although each information item is not applicable in every year.

Companies have a great deal of latitude in preparing the multiyear summaries included in their annual reports. Some companies, such as **Johnson & Johnson**, present more dollar amounts and relatively few ratios. Others emphasize ratios that have been computed based on information in the financial statements in a manner similar to that illustrated in this chapter. A multiyear summary, combined with the more detailed information presented in the full financial statements that typically include the three most recent years can be very helpful in gaining a long-term understanding of the financial success (or failure) of a company.

# END-OF-CHAPTER REVIEW

## SUMMARY OF LEARNING OBJECTIVES

### LO 1

**Explain the uses of dollar and percentage changes, trend percentages, component percentages, and ratios.**

An important aspect of financial statement analysis is determining relevant relationships among specific items of information. Companies typically present financial information for more than one time period, which permits users of the information to make comparisons that help them understand changes over time. Dollar and percentage changes and trend percentages are tools for comparing information from successive time periods. Component percentages and ratios, on the other hand, are tools for establishing relationships and making comparisons within an accounting period. Both types of comparisons are important in understanding an enterprise's financial position, results of operations, and cash flows.

### LO 2

**Discuss the quality of a company's earnings, assets, and working capital.**

Assessing the quality of information is an important aspect of financial statement analysis. Enterprises have significant latitude in the selection of financial reporting methods within generally accepted accounting principles. Assessing the quality of a company's earnings, assets, and working capital is done by evaluating the accounting methods selected for use in preparing financial statements. Management's choice of accounting principles and methods that are in the best long-term interests of the company, even though they may currently result in lower net income or lower total assets or working capital, leads to a conclusion of high quality in reported accounting information.

### LO 3

**Explain the nature and purpose of classifications in financial statements.**

In classified financial statements, items with certain common characteristics are placed together in a group, or classification. The purpose of these classifications is to develop subtotals that will assist users in analyzing the financial statements.

### LO 4

**Prepare a classified balance sheet and compute widely used measures of liquidity and credit risk.**

In a classified balance sheet, assets are subdivided into the categories of current assets, plant and equipment, and other assets. Liabilities are classified either as current or long-term.

The liquidity measures derived from the balance sheet are as follows:

**Working capital.** Current assets minus current liabilities.

**Current ratio.** Current assets divided by current liabilities.

**Quick ratio.** Quick assets divided by current liabilities.

A measure of long-term credit risk is the debt ratio, which is total liabilities expressed as a percentage of (divided by) total assets.

### LO 5

**Prepare a multiple-step and a single-step income statement and compute widely used measures of profitability.**

In a multiple-step income statement, the cost of goods sold is deducted from net sales to provide the subtotal, gross profit. Operating expenses then are deducted to arrive at income from operations. As a final step, nonoperating items are added together and subtracted from income from operations to arrive at net income. In a single-step income statement, all revenue items are listed first, and then all expenses are combined and deducted from total revenue.

The profitability measures discussed in this chapter are as follows:

**Percentage change.** The dollar amount of change in a financial statement item from one period to the next, expressed as a percentage of (divided by) the item value in the earlier of the two periods being compared.

**Gross profit rate.** Dollar amount of gross profit divided by net sales. A measure of the profitability of a company's products.

**Net income as a percentage of sales.** Net income divided by net sales. A measure of management's ability to control expenses.

**Earnings per share.** In the simplest case, net income divided by shares of capital stock outstanding. Indicates the earnings applicable to each share of stock.

**Price-earnings ratio.** Market price of the stock, divided by earnings per share. A measure of investors' expectations regarding future profitability.

**Return on assets.** Operating income divided by average total assets. Measures the return generated by assets, regardless of how the assets are financed.

**Return on equity.** Net income divided by average total equity. Indicates the rate of return earned on owners' equity.

### LO 6

**Put a company's net income into perspective by relating it to sales, assets, and stockholders' equity.**

Financial accounting information is most useful if viewed in comparison with other relevant information. Net income is an important measure of the financial success of an enterprise. To make the amount of net income even more useful than if it were viewed simply in isolation, it is often compared with the sales from which net income results, the assets used to generate the income, and the amount of stockholders' equity invested by owners to earn the net income.

## LO 7

**Compute the ratios widely used in financial statement analysis and explain the significance of each.**

Ratios are mathematical calculations that compare one financial statement item with another financial statement item. The two items may come from the same financial statement, such as the current ratio, which compares the amount of current assets with the amount of current liabilities, both of which appear in the statement of financial position (balance sheet). On the other hand, the items may come from two different financial statements, such as the return on stockholders' equity, which compares net income from the income statement with the amount of stockholders' equity from the statement of financial position (balance sheet). Accountants and financial analysts have developed many ratios that place information from a company's financial statements in a context to permit better understanding to support decision making.

## LO 8

**Analyze financial statements from the viewpoints of common stockholders, creditors, and others.**

Different groups of users of financial statements are interested in different aspects of a company's financial activities. Short-term creditors are interested primarily in the company's ability to make cash payments in the short term; they focus their attention on operating cash flows and current assets and liabilities. Long-term creditors, on the other hand, are more interested in the company's long-term ability to pay interest and principal and would not limit their analysis to the company's ability to make cash payments in the immediate future. The focus of common stockholders can vary from one investor to another, but generally stockholders are interested in the company's ability to pay dividends and increase the market value of the stock of the company. Each group may focus on different information in the financial statements to meet its unique objectives.

Up to this point in this text, we have focused primarily on the preparation and use of financial information as done in the United States. As you know, however, the financial barriers between countries are rapidly disappearing, and extensive business activities are now carried out across borders. For that reason, in Chapter 15 we introduce the subject of international business and accounting. The globalization of business is one of the most dramatic changes that has ever occurred in business, and it promises to continue to have a significant impact on business activity for many years to come.

## KEY TERMS INTRODUCED OR EMPHASIZED IN CHAPTER 14

**annual report** (p. 603) A document issued annually by publicly owned companies to their stockholders. Includes audited comparative financial statements, management's discussion and analysis of performance and liquidity, and other information about the company.

**classified financial statements** (p. 592) Financial statements in which similar items are arranged in groups, and subtotals are shown to assist users in analyzing the statements.

**comparative financial statements** (p. 592) Financial statements of one company for two or more years presented in a side-by-side format to facilitate comparison.

**consolidated financial statements** (p. 592) Financial statements that show the combined activities of a parent company and its subsidiaries.

**current assets** (p. 599) Cash and other assets that can be converted into cash or used up within one year or the operating cycle (whichever is longer) without interfering with normal business operations.

**current liabilities** (p. 599) Existing liabilities that are expected to be satisfied by using the enterprise's current assets.

**current ratio** (p. 601) Current assets divided by current liabilities. A measure of short-term debt-paying ability.

**debt ratio** (p. 602) Total liabilities divided by total assets. Represents the portion of total assets financed by debt, rather than by equity capital.

**earnings per share** (p. 609) Net income expressed on a per-share basis.

**fundamental analysis** (p. 628) Evaluating the reasonableness of a company's stock price by evaluating the performance and financial strength of the company.

**management's discussion and analysis** (p. 603) A discussion by management of the company's performance during the current year and its financial position at year-end. These discussions are included in the annual reports of publicly owned companies.

**market share** (p. 607) A company's percentage share of total dollar sales within its industry.

**operating cycle** (p. 599) The time required to invest cash in inventory, sell the inventory, and collect the receivable, resulting in an increase in cash.

**operating income** (p. 606) A subtotal in a multiple-step income statement representing the income resulting from the company's principal business activities.

**parent company** (p. 592) A corporation that does portions of its business through other companies that it owns (termed *subsidiaries*).

**percentage change** (p. 606) The change in a dollar amount between two accounting periods, expressed as a percentage of the amount in an earlier period. Used in evaluating rates of growth (or decline).

**price-earnings (p/e) ratio** (p. 610) The current market price of a company's capital stock, expressed as a multiple of earnings per share. Reflects investors' expectations regarding future earnings.

**quick assets** (p. 602) The most liquid current assets. Include only cash, marketable securities, and receivables.

**quick ratio** (p. 601) Quick assets (cash, marketable securities, and receivables) divided by current liabilities. A measure of short-term debt-paying ability. (Sometimes referred to as the acid-test ratio.)

**return on assets** (p. 612) Operating income expressed as a percentage of average total assets. A measure of the efficiency with which management utilizes the assets of a business.

**return on equity** (p. 612) Net income expressed as a percentage of average total stockholders' equity. A measure of the rate of return earned on the stockholders' equity in the business.

**subsidiary** (p. 592) A company that is owned and operated by a parent company. In essence, the subsidiary is a part of the parent organization.

**window dressing** (p. 604) Measures taken by management to make a business look as strong as possible at the balance sheet date.

**working capital** (p. 600) Current assets less current liabilities. A measure of short-term debt-paying ability.

## DEMONSTRATION PROBLEM

The following data are adapted from a recent annual report of **Walgreen Drug Stores**, (dollar amounts are stated in millions):

|  | 1999 | 1998 |
|---|---|---|
| **Balance sheet data:** | | |
| Quick assets . . . . . . . . . . . . . . . . . . . . . . . . . . . . . . . . . . . . . . . . | $  628.3 | $  517.6 |
| Current assets . . . . . . . . . . . . . . . . . . . . . . . . . . . . . . . . . . . . . . | 3,221.7 | 2,623.1 |
| Current liabilities . . . . . . . . . . . . . . . . . . . . . . . . . . . . . . . . . . . | 1,923.8 | 1,580.1 |
| Stockholders' equity . . . . . . . . . . . . . . . . . . . . . . . . . . . . . . . . . | 3,484.3 | 2,848.9 |
| Total assets . . . . . . . . . . . . . . . . . . . . . . . . . . . . . . . . . . . . . . . . | 5,906.7 | 4,901.6 |
| **Income statement data:** | | |
| Net sales . . . . . . . . . . . . . . . . . . . . . . . . . . . . . . . . . . . . . . . . . . | $17,838.8 | $15,306.6 |
| Gross profit . . . . . . . . . . . . . . . . . . . . . . . . . . . . . . . . . . . . . . . | 4,860.2 | 4,167.2 |
| Operating income . . . . . . . . . . . . . . . . . . . . . . . . . . . . . . . . . . | 1,015.4 | 835.2 |
| Net income . . . . . . . . . . . . . . . . . . . . . . . . . . . . . . . . . . . . . . . . | 624.1 | 510.8 |

During 1999, the company used a significant amount of its cash reserves to finance the expansion of property, plant, and equipment.

### Instructions
**a.** Compute the following for 1999 and 1998. (Round to one decimal place.)

　**1.** Working capital

　**2.** Current ratio

　**3.** Quick ratio

**b.** Comment on the trends in the liquidity measures and state whether **Walgreens** appears to be solvent at the end of 1999.

**c.** Compute the percentage changes for 1999 in the amounts of net sales and net income. (Round to one-tenth of 1%.)

**d.** Compute the following for 1999 and 1998. (Round to one-tenth of 1%. For items **3** and **4,** use the year-end amounts stated above as substitutes for average assets and average stockholders' equity.)

　**1.** Gross profit rate

　**2.** Net income as a percentage of sales

　**3.** Return on assets

　**4.** Return on stockholders' equity

**e.** Comment on the trends in the profitability measures computed in parts **c** and **d.**

## Solution to the Demonstration Problem

**a.**

|  | 1999 | 1998 |
|---|---|---|
| **1.** **Working capital:** | | |
| $3,221.7 − 1,923.8 ................................. | $1,297.9 | |
| $2,623.1 − 1,580.1 ................................. | | $1,043 |
| **2.** **Current ratio:** | | |
| $3,221.7 ÷ 1,923.8 ................................. | 1.67 to 1 | |
| $2,623.1 ÷ 1,580.1 ................................. | | 1.66 to 1 |
| **3.** **Quick ratio:** | | |
| $628.3 ÷ 1,923.8 ................................. | .33 to 1 | |
| $517.6 ÷ 1,580.1 ................................. | | .33 to 1 |

**b.** Working capital at the end of 1999 has increased relative to 1998, whereas the current and quick ratios have both stayed essentially the same. The relatively low quick ratio may be of some concern in terms of the company's ability to satisfy its future obligations.

**c.** Percentage change from 1998:

|  | 1999 |
|---|---|
| Net sales: [($17,838.8 − $15,306.6) ÷ $15,306.6] ........................... | +16.5% |
| Net income: [($624.1 − $510.8) ÷ 510.8] ................................. | +22.2% |

**d.**

|  | 1999 | 1998 |
|---|---|---|
| **1.** **Gross profit rate:** | | |
| $4,860.2 ÷ $17,838.8 ................................. | 27.2% | |
| $4,167.2 ÷ $15,306.6 ................................. | | 27.2% |
| **2.** **Net income as a percentage of sales:** | | |
| $624.1 ÷ $17,838.8 ................................. | 3.5% | |
| $510.8 ÷ $15,306.6 ................................. | | 3.3% |
| **3.** **Return on assets:** | | |
| $1,015.4 ÷ $5,906.7 ................................. | 17.2% | |
| $835.2 ÷ $4,901.6 ................................. | | 17.0% |
| **4.** **Return on equity:** | | |
| $624.1 ÷ $3,484.3 ................................. | 17.9% | |
| $510.8 ÷ $2,848.9 ................................. | | 17.9% |

**e.** The trends in the profitability measures are positive. Net sales are increasing faster than the rate of inflation (which was about 4% in 1999 and 1998). Note the rise in both net income as a percentage of sales and return on assets. These trends indicate that costs and expenses are not increasing as quickly as revenue (signs of efficient management). Finally, the return on equity is higher than the return on assets. This suggests that management has financed assets in a manner advantageous to stockholders.

## SELF-TEST QUESTIONS

*Answers to these questions appear on page 653.*

**1.** Which of the following usually is *least* important as a measure of short-term liquidity?

   **a.** Quick ratio.

   **b.** Current ratio.

    **c.** Debt ratio.

    **d.** Cash flows from operating activities.

2. In each of the past five years, the net sales of Delta Co. have increased at about half the rate of inflation, but net income has increased at approximately *twice* the rate of inflation. During this period, the company's total assets, liabilities, and equity have remained almost unchanged; dividends are approximately equal to net income. These relationships suggest (indicate all correct answers):

    **a.** Management is successfully controlling costs and expenses.

    **b.** The company is selling more merchandise every year.

    **c.** The annual return on assets has been increasing.

    **d.** Financing activities are likely to result in a net use of cash.

3. From the viewpoint of a stockholder, which of the following relationships do you consider of *least* significance?

    **a.** The return on assets consistently is higher than the industry average.

    **b.** The return on equity has increased in each of the past five years.

    **c.** Net income is greater than the amount of working capital.

    **d.** The return on assets is greater than the rate of interest being paid to creditors.

4. The following data are available from the annual report of Newport Marine:

| | | | |
|---|---|---|---|
| Current assets . . . . . . . . . . . . | $ 480,000 | Current liabilities . . . . . . . . . . | $300,000 |
| Average total assets . . . . . . . . | 2,000,000 | Operating income . . . . . . . . . | 240,000 |
| Average total equity . . . . . . . . | 800,000 | Net income . . . . . . . . . . . . . | 80,000 |

Which of the following statements are correct? (More than one statement may be correct.)

    **a.** The return on equity exceeds the return on assets.

    **b.** The current ratio is .625 to 1.

    **c.** Working capital is $1,200,000.

    **d.** None of the above answers is correct.

5. Hunter Corporation's net income was $400,000 in 2001 and $160,000 in 2002. What percentage increase in net income must Hunter achieve in 2003 to offset the decline in profits in 2002?

    **a.** 60%.     **b.** 150%.     **c.** 600%.     **d.** 67%.

6. If a company's current ratio declined in a year during which its quick ratio improved, which of the following is the most likely explanation?

    **a.** Inventory is increasing.

    **b.** Inventory is declining.

    **c.** Receivables are being collected more rapidly than in the past.

    **d.** Receivables are being collected more slowly than in the past.

7. In financial statement analysis, the most difficult of the following items to predict is whether:

    **a.** The company's market share is increasing or declining.

    **b.** The company will be solvent in six months.

    **c.** Profits will increase in the coming year.

    **d.** The market price of capital stock will rise or fall over the next two months.

# ASSIGNMENT MATERIAL

## DISCUSSION QUESTIONS

1. In financial statement analysis, what is the basic objective of observing trends in data and ratios? Suggest some other standards of comparison.

2. In financial statement analysis, what information is produced by computing a ratio that is not available in a simple observation of the underlying data?

3. Distinguish between *trend percentages* and *component percentages*. Which would be better suited for analyzing the change in sales over a term of several years?

4. Differentiate between *horizontal* and *vertical* analysis.

5. Assume that Chemco Corporation is engaged in the manufacture and distribution of a variety of chemicals. In analyzing the financial statements of this corporation, why would you want to refer to the ratios and other measurements of companies in the chemical industry? In comparing the financial results of Chemco Corporation with another chemical company, why would you be interested in the accounting principles used by the two companies?

6. Explain how the following accounting practices tend to raise or lower the quality of a company's earnings. (Assume the continuance of inflation.)

   **a.** Adoption of an accelerated depreciation method rather than straight-line depreciation.

   **b.** Adoption of FIFO rather than LIFO for the valuation of inventories.

   **c.** Adoption of a 7-year life rather than a 10-year life for the depreciation of equipment.

7. What is the basic purpose of *classifications* in financial statements? Identify the classifications widely used in a balance sheet, a multiple-step income statement, and a statement of cash flows.

8. Distinguish between the terms *classified, comparative,* and *consolidated* as they apply to financial statements. May a given set of financial statements have more than one of these characteristics?

9. Identify three liquidity measures. Explain briefly how each is computed.

10. What is the characteristic common to all *current assets?* Many retail stores regularly sell merchandise on installment plans, calling for payments over a period of 24 or 36 months. Do such receivables qualify as current assets? Explain.

11. What is the *quick ratio?* Under what circumstances are short-term creditors most likely to regard a company's quick ratio as more meaningful than its current ratio?

12. The current assets of Foxall Corporation are cash, $80,000; accounts receivable, $340,000; and inventory, $120,000. Current liabilities amount to $320,000. Compute the current ratio, quick ratio, and the amount of working capital.

13. How is the debt ratio computed? Is this ratio a measure of short-term liquidity, or something else?

14. Distinguish between a multiple-step and a single-step income statement. Which format results in the higher amount of net income?

15. Identify four ratios or other analytical tools used to evaluate profitability. Explain briefly how each is computed.

16. Assume that the net sales of a large department store have grown annually at a rate of 5% over each of the past several years. Do you think that the store is selling 5% more merchandise each year? Explain.

17. How does income taxes expense differ from normal operating expenses such as advertising and salaries? How is income taxes expense presented in a multiple-step income statement?

18. Distinguish between *operating income* and *net income*.

19. Net sales of the Walland General Store have been increasing at a reasonable rate, but net income has been declining steadily as a percentage of these sales. What appears to be the problem?

20. Why might earnings per share be more significant to a stockholder in a large corporation than the total amount of net income?

21. Assume that Congress announces its intention to limit the prices and profits of pharmaceutical companies as part of an effort to control health care costs. What effect would you expect this announcement to have on the p/e ratios and stock prices of pharmaceutical companies such as **Merck** and **Bristol-Myers/Squibb**? Explain.

22. Under what circumstances might a company have a high p/e ratio even when investors are *not* optimistic about the company's future prospects?

23. Farmer Company earned a 16% return on its total assets. Current liabilities are 10% of total assets. Long-term bonds carrying an 11% coupon rate are equal to 30% of total assets. There is no preferred stock. Is this application of leverage favorable or unfavorable from the viewpoint of Farmer Company's stockholders?

24. Ahi Co. has a current ratio of 3 to 1. Ono Corp. has a current ratio of 2 to 1. Does this mean that Ahi's operating cycle is longer than Ono's? Why?

25. An investor states, "I bought this stock for $50 several years ago and it now sells for $100. It paid $5 per share in dividends last year so I'm earning 10% on my investment." Evaluate this statement.

**26.** Alpine Products experiences a considerable seasonal variation in its business. The high point in the year's activity comes in November, the low point in July. During which month would you expect the company's current ratio to be higher? If the company were choosing a fiscal year for accounting purposes, what advice would you give?

**27.** Under what circumstances would you consider a corporate net income of $1 million for the year as being unreasonably low? Under what circumstances would you consider a corporate profit of $1 million as being unreasonably high?

## EXERCISES

### EXERCISE 14.1

Percentage Changes

**LO 1**

Selected information taken from financial statements of Lopez Company for two successive years follows. You are to compute the percentage change from 2001 to 2002 whenever possible.

|  | 2002 | 2001 |
|---|---|---|
| a. Accounts receivable | $126,000 | $150,000 |
| b. Marketable securities | –0– | 250,000 |
| c. Retained earnings | 80,000 | (80,000) |
| d. Notes receivable | 120,000 | –0– |
| e. Notes payable | 860,000 | 800,000 |
| f. Cash | 84,000 | 80,000 |
| g. Sales | 990,000 | 900,000 |

### EXERCISE 14.2

Trend Percentages

**LO 1**

Compute *trend percentages* for the following items taken from the financial statements of Waterman Plumbing Fixtures over a five-year period. Treat 1998 as the base year. State whether the trends are favorable or unfavorable. (Dollar amounts are stated in thousands.)

|  | 2002 | 2001 | 2000 | 1999 | 1998 |
|---|---|---|---|---|---|
| Sales | $81,400 | $74,000 | $61,500 | $59,000 | $50,000 |
| Cost of goods sold | 58,500 | 48,000 | 40,500 | 37,000 | 30,000 |

### EXERCISE 14.3

Common Size Income Statements

**LO 1**

Prepare *common size* income statements for Prosser Company, a sole proprietorship, for the two years shown below by converting the dollar amounts into percentages. For each year, sales will appear as 100% and other items will be expressed as a percentage of sales. (Income taxes are not involved as the business is not incorporated.) Comment on whether the changes from 2001 to 2002 are favorable or unfavorable.

|  | 2002 | 2001 |
|---|---|---|
| Sales | $500,000 | $400,000 |
| Cost of goods sold | 330,000 | 268,000 |
| Gross profit | $170,000 | $132,000 |
| Operating expenses | 140,000 | 116,000 |
| Net income | $ 30,000 | $ 16,000 |

### EXERCISE 14.4

Accounting Terminology

**LO 1–7**

The following are 12 technical accounting terms introduced or emphasized in this chapter:

| | | |
|---|---|---|
| P/e ratio | Market share | Current ratio |
| Debt ratio | Earnings per share | Operating income |
| Quick ratio | Operating activities | Return on equity |
| Subsidiary | Comparative financial statements | Parent company |

Each of the following statements may (or may not) describe one of these technical terms. For each statement, indicate the term described, or answer "None" if the statement does not correctly describe any of the terms.

**a.** A ratio that relates the total net income of a corporation to the holdings of individual stockholders.

**b.** The classification in a statement of cash flows from which it is most important to generate positive cash flows.

**c.** A measure of the long-term safety of creditors' positions.

**d.** A measure of investors' expectations of the future profitability of a business.

**e.** An ROI measure of the effectiveness with which management utilizes a company's resources, regardless of how those resources are financed.

**f.** A company that does business through other companies that it owns.

**g.** A measure of the profitability of a company's *primary* business activities.

**h.** The most widely used measure of short-term debt-paying ability.

**i.** A form of business organization in which the owners are *personally* liable for the debts of the business organization.

**j.** Financial statements in which similar items are grouped in a manner that develops useful subtotals.

**Tyco Toys** is a manufacturer of toys and children's products. The following are selected items appearing in a recent balance sheet (dollar amounts are in millions):

**EXERCISE 14.5**

Measures of Liquidity

**LO 3, 4**

| | |
|---|---:|
| Cash and short-term investments | $ 47.3 |
| Receivables | 159.7 |
| Inventories | 72.3 |
| Prepaid expenses and other current assets | 32.0 |
| Total current liabilities | 130.1 |
| Total liabilities | 279.4 |
| Total stockholders' equity | 344.0 |

**a.** Using the information above, compute the amounts of Tyco's (1) quick assets and (2) total current assets.

**b.** Compute the company's (1) quick ratio, (2) current ratio, and (3) working capital. (Round ratios to one decimal place.)

**c.** Discuss whether the company appears solvent from the viewpoint of a short-term creditor.

**EXERCISE 14.6**

Multiple-Step Income Statements

**LO 5**

**SALTER, INC.**
**Statement of Earnings**
**For the Year Ended December 31, 2002**

| | |
|---|---:|
| Net sales | $ 4,395,253 |
| Costs and expenses: | |
| Cost of goods sold | (2,821,455) |
| Operating expenses | (1,004,396) |
| Interest revenue | 15,797 |
| Earnings before income taxes | $ 585,199 |
| Income taxes | (231,160) |
| Net earnings | $ 354,039 |
| Earnings per share | $1.58 |

Comparative balance sheets report average total assets for the year of *$2,443,068* and average total equity of *$1,740,437* (dollar amounts in thousands, except earnings per share).

**a.** Prepare an income statement for the year in a multiple-step format.

**b.** Compute the (1) gross profit rate, (2) net income as a percentage of net sales, (3) return on assets, and (4) return on equity for the year. (Round computations to the nearest one-tenth of 1%.)

**c.** Explain why interest revenue is not included in the company's gross profit computation.

**EXERCISE 14.7**

Comparative Analysis

**LO 6**

**Parker Hannifin Corporation** reported the following basic earnings per share figures for the 11 years ending in 2000:

| | | | | | | | |
|---|---|---|---|---|---|---|---|
| 1990 | $1.00 | 1993 | .60 | 1996 | 2.15 | 1999 | 2.85 |
| 1991 | .54 | 1994 | .48 | 1997 | 2.46 | 2000 | 3.34 |
| 1992 | .58 | 1995 | 1.97 | 1998 | 2.91 | | |

Throughout this period, the average number of shares of common stock outstanding remained relatively constant, ranging from a low of 108,632,000 in 1991 to a high of 110,331,000 in 2000. Diluted earnings per share averaged between $.01 and $.02 per share lower than basic earnings per share throughout the 1990–2000 period.

**a.** Compute the percentage change in basic earnings per share for each year from 1991 through 2000. What conclusions can you reach about the pattern of basic earning per share over this period of time?

**b.** What does the information provided above about the average number of outstanding shares of common stock and basic earnings per share allow you to conclude about the company's net income over this period of time?

**c.** Should the risk of conversion of other securities into common stock be of particular risk to the common stockholders of **Parker Hannifin Corporation**?

**EXERCISE 14.8**

ROI

**LO 6**

Shown below are selected data from a recent annual report of **Sprint Corporation**, a large telecommunications provider. (Dollar amounts are in millions.)

| | Beginning of the Year | End of the Year |
|---|---|---|
| Total assets . . . . . . . . . . . . . . . . . . . . . . . . . . . . . . . . . . . | $14,548 | $15,196 |
| Total stockholders' equity . . . . . . . . . . . . . . . . . . . . . . . . . | 4,562 | 4,674 |
| Operating income . . . . . . . . . . . . . . . . . . . . . . . . . . . . . . . | | 2,422 |
| Net income . . . . . . . . . . . . . . . . . . . . . . . . . . . . . . . . . . . . | | 349 |

**a.** Compute for the year **Sprint**'s return on average total assets. (Round computations to the nearest one-tenth of 1%.)

**b.** Compute for the year **Sprint**'s return on average total stockholders' equity. (Round computations to the nearest one-tenth of 1%.)

**c.** Could the increase in **Sprint**'s total stockholders' equity for the year be the result of an increase in *market value* of the company's stock? Explain.

**EXERCISE 14.9**

Computing and Interpreting Rates of Change

Selected information from the financial statements of Jose's Hardware includes the following:

| | 2002 | 2001 |
|---|---|---|
| Net sales . . . . . . . . . . . . . . . . . . . . . . . . . . . . . . . . . . . . . . | $2,200,000 | $2,000,000 |
| Total expenses . . . . . . . . . . . . . . . . . . . . . . . . . . . . . . . . . | 1,998,000 | 1,800,000 |

**a.** Compute the percentage change in 2002 for the amounts of (1) net sales and (2) total expenses.

**b.** Using the information developed in part **a,** express your opinion as to whether the company's *net income* for 2002:

1. Increased at a greater or lower percentage rate than did net sales.
2. Represented a larger or smaller percentage of net sales revenue than in 2001. For each answer, explain your reasoning *without* making any computations or references to dollar amounts.

Obtain from your library (or other source) the most recent annual report of a publicly owned company.

a. Using the annual report data, compute the basic measures of liquidity, long-term credit risk, and profitability summarized in the table on pages 628–629. Compare these measures to the appropriate industry norms available in your library. Briefly comment on your findings.

b. Using the financial pages of a daily newspaper (such as *The Wall Street Journal*), determine (1) the current market price of your company's common stock, (2) its 52-week high and low market prices, and (3) its p/e ratio. Briefly comment on your findings.

c. Based on your analysis in parts **a** and **b,** make a recommendation as to whether investors should buy shares of the stock, hold the shares they currently own, or sell the shares they currently own. Defend your position.

**EXERCISE 14.10**

Research Problem

**LO 6**

The annual report of a publicly owned corporation includes *management's discussion and analysis* of the company's operations, financial condition, and liquidity. The annual report of **Tootsie Roll Industries, Inc.,** including the discussion and analysis by management, appears in Appendix A at the end of this textbook.

Read management's discussion and analysis. Identify at least five items that should be of interest to investors, but which investors would *not* be able to determine for themselves from the financial statements. Briefly discuss the *usefulness* of each disclosure to investors. Be prepared to explain your findings in class, including references to the appropriate pages and paragraphs in the illustrated discussion.

**EXERCISE 14.11**

Tootsie Roll Industries, Inc., Management Discussion and Analysis

**LO 3, 4, 6**

Assume that you will soon graduate from college and that you have job offers with two pharmaceutical firms. The first offer is with Alpha Research, a relatively new and aggressive company. The second is with Omega Scientific, a very well-established and conservative company.

Financial information pertaining to each firm, and to the pharmaceutical industry as a whole, is as follows:

**EXERCISE 14.12**

Evaluating Employment Opportunities

**LO 4, 6**

| Financial Measure | Alpha | Omega | Industry Average |
|---|---|---|---|
| Current ratio | 2.2 to 1 | 4.5 to 1 | 2.5 to 1 |
| Quick ratio | 1.2 to 1 | 2.8 to 1 | 1.5 to 1 |
| Return on assets | 17% | 8% | 10% |
| Return on equity | 28% | 14% | 16% |
| P/e ratio | 20 to 1 | 10 to 1 | 12 to 1 |

The Omega offer is for $36,000 per year. The Alpha offer is for $32,000. However, unlike Omega, Alpha awards its employees a stock option bonus based on profitability for the year. Each option enables the employee to purchase shares of Alpha's common stock at a significantly reduced price. The more profitable this company is, the more stock each employee can buy at a discount.

Show how the above information may help you justify accepting the Alpha Research offer, even though the starting salary is $4,000 lower than the Omega Scientific offer.

Selected financial data for Fowler's, a retail store, appear as follows:

**EXERCISE 14.13**

Ratios for a Retail Store

|  | 2002 | 2001 |
|---|---|---|
| Sales (all on account) | $750,000 | $610,000 |
| Cost of goods sold | 495,000 | 408,000 |
| Average inventory during the year | 110,000 | 102,000 |
| Average receivables during the year | 150,000 | 100,000 |

a. Compute the following for both years:

1. Gross profit percentage
2. Inventory turnover
3. Accounts receivable turnover

b. Comment on favorable and unfavorable trends.

**EXERCISE 14.14**

Computing Ratios

**LO 7**

A condensed balance sheet for Hattaway Corporation prepared at the end of the year appears as follows:

| Assets | | Liabilities & Stockholders' Equity | |
|---|---|---|---|
| Cash . . . . . . . . . . . . . . . . . . . | $ 65,000 | Notes payable (due in 6 | |
| Accounts receivable . . . . . . . . | 155,000 | months) . . . . . . . . . . . . . . . | $ 40,000 |
| Inventory . . . . . . . . . . . . . . . . | 270,000 | Accounts payable . . . . . . . . . . . | 110,000 |
| Prepaid expenses . . . . . . . . . . | 60,000 | Long-term liabilities . . . . . . . . . | 330,000 |
| Plant & equipment (net) . . . . . . | 570,000 | Capital stock, $5 par . . . . . . . . . | 300,000 |
| Other assets . . . . . . . . . . . . . . | 90,000 | Retained earnings . . . . . . . . . . | 430,000 |
| Total . . . . . . . . . . . . . . . . . . . | $1,210,000 | Total . . . . . . . . . . . . . . . . . . . | $1,210,000 |

During the year the company earned a gross profit of $1,116,000 on sales of $2,790,000. Accounts receivable, inventory, and plant assets remained almost constant in amount throughout the year.

Compute the following:

a. Current ratio

b. Quick ratio

c. Working capital

d. Debt ratio

e. Accounts receivable turnover (all sales were on credit)

f. Inventory turnover

g. Book value per share of capital stock

**EXERCISE 14.15**

Current Ratio, Debt Ratio, and Earnings per Share

**LO 7**

Selected items from successive annual reports of Tipper, Inc., appear as follows:

| | 2002 | 2001 |
|---|---|---|
| Total assets (40% of which are current) . . . . . . . . . . . . . . . . . . . . . . . . | $400,000 | $325,000 |
| Current liabilities . . . . . . . . . . . . . . . . . . . . . . . . . . . . . . . . . . . . . . | $ 80,000 | $100,000 |
| Bonds payable, 12% . . . . . . . . . . . . . . . . . . . . . . . . . . . . . . . . . . . | 100,000 | 50,000 |
| Capital stock, $5 par value . . . . . . . . . . . . . . . . . . . . . . . . . . . . . . . | 100,000 | 100,000 |
| Retained earnings . . . . . . . . . . . . . . . . . . . . . . . . . . . . . . . . . . . . . | 120,000 | 75,000 |
| Total liabilities & stockholders' equity . . . . . . . . . . . . . . . . . . . . . . . . | $400,000 | $325,000 |

Dividends of $26,000 were declared and paid in 2002.

Compute the following:

a. Current ratio for 2002 and 2001

b. Debt ratio for 2002 and 2001

c. Earnings per share for 2002

Selected data from the financial statements of Italian Marble Co. and Spanish Stone Products for the year just ended follow. Assume that for both companies dividends declared were equal in amount to net earnings during the year and therefore stockholders' equity did not change. The two companies are in the same line of business.

| | Italian Marble Co. | Spanish Stone Products |
|---|---|---|
| Total liabilities . . . . . . . . . . . . . . . . . . . . . . . . . . . . . . . . . . . | $ 200,000 | $ 100,000 |
| Total assets . . . . . . . . . . . . . . . . . . . . . . . . . . . . . . . . . . . . | 800,000 | 400,000 |
| Sales (all on credit) . . . . . . . . . . . . . . . . . . . . . . . . . . . . . . | 1,800,000 | 1,200,000 |
| Average inventory . . . . . . . . . . . . . . . . . . . . . . . . . . . . . . . | 240,000 | 140,000 |
| Average receivables . . . . . . . . . . . . . . . . . . . . . . . . . . . . . | 200,000 | 100,000 |
| Gross profit as a percentage of sales . . . . . . . . . . . . . . . . . . | 40% | 30% |
| Operating expenses as a percentage of sales . . . . . . . . . . . . | 36% | 25% |
| Net income as a percentage of sales . . . . . . . . . . . . . . . . . . | 3% | 5% |

Compute the following for each company:

**a.** Net income

**b.** Net income as a percentage of stockholders' equity

**c.** Accounts receivable turnover

**d.** Inventory turnover

## PROBLEMS

Outdoors, Inc., manufactures camping equipment. Shown below for the current year are the income statement for the company and a common size summary for the industry in which the company operates. (Notice that the percentages in the right-hand column are *not* for Outdoors, Inc., but are average percentages for the industry.)

| | Outdoors, Inc. | Industry Average |
|---|---|---|
| Sales (net) . . . . . . . . . . . . . . . . . . . . . . . . . . . . . . . . . . . . . . . . | $20,000,000 | 100% |
| Cost of goods sold . . . . . . . . . . . . . . . . . . . . . . . . . . . . . . . . . . | 9,800,000 | 57 |
| Gross profit on sales . . . . . . . . . . . . . . . . . . . . . . . . . . . . . . . . . | $10,200,000 | 43% |
| Operating expenses: | | |
| Selling . . . . . . . . . . . . . . . . . . . . . . . . . . . . . . . . . . . . . . . . | $ 4,200,000 | 16% |
| General and administrative . . . . . . . . . . . . . . . . . . . . . . . . . . | 3,400,000 | 20 |
| Total operating expenses . . . . . . . . . . . . . . . . . . . . . . . . . . . . . | $ 7,600,000 | 36% |
| Operating income . . . . . . . . . . . . . . . . . . . . . . . . . . . . . . . . . . . | $ 2,600,000 | 7% |
| Income taxes . . . . . . . . . . . . . . . . . . . . . . . . . . . . . . . . . . . . . . | 1,200,000 | 3 |
| Net income . . . . . . . . . . . . . . . . . . . . . . . . . . . . . . . . . . . . . . . | $ 1,400,000 | 4% |
| Return on assets . . . . . . . . . . . . . . . . . . . . . . . . . . . . . . . . . . . | 23% | 14% |

## Instructions

**a.** Prepare a two-column common size income statement. The first column should show for Outdoors, Inc., all items expressed as a percentage of net sales. The second column should show the equivalent industry average for the data given in the problem. The purpose of this common size statement is to compare the operating results of Outdoors, Inc., with the average for the industry.

b. Comment specifically on differences between Outdoors, Inc., and the industry average with respect to gross profit on sales, selling expenses, general and administrative expenses, operating income, net income, and return on assets. Suggest possible reasons for the more important disparities.

**PROBLEM 14.2**

Analysis to Identify Favorable and Unfavorable Trends

**LO 3, 5**

The following information was developed from the financial statements of Custom Logos, Inc. At the beginning of 2002, the company's former supplier went bankrupt, and the company began buying merchandise from another supplier.

|  | 2002 | 2001 |
|---|---|---|
| Gross profit on sales | $1,008,000 | $1,134,000 |
| Income before income taxes | 230,400 | 252,000 |
| Net income | 172,800 | 189,000 |
| Net income as a percentage of net sales | 6.0% | 7.5% |

**Instructions**

a. Compute the net sales for each year.

b. Compute the cost of goods sold in dollars and as a percentage of net sales for each year.

c. Compute operating expenses in dollars and as a percentage of net sales for each year. (Income taxes expense is not an operating expense.)

d. Prepare a condensed comparative income statement for 2001 and 2002. Include the following items: net sales, cost of goods sold, gross profit, operating expenses, income before income taxes, income taxes expense, and net income. Omit earnings per share statistics.

e. Identify the significant favorable and unfavorable trends in the performance of Custom Logos, Inc. Comment on any unusual changes.

**PROBLEM 14.3**

Measures of Liquidity

**LO 3, 4**

Some of the accounts appearing in the year-end financial statements of Zero Degree Frozen Dinners appear below. This list includes all of the company's current assets and current liabilities.

| | |
|---|---|
| Sales | $1,980,000 |
| Accumulated depreciation: equipment | 370,000 |
| Notes payable (due in 90 days) | 70,000 |
| Retained earnings | 241,320 |
| Cash | 67,600 |
| Capital stock | 150,000 |
| Marketable securities | 175,040 |
| Accounts payable | 125,430 |
| Mortgage payable (due in 15 years) | 320,000 |
| Salaries payable | 7,570 |
| Dividends | 25,000 |
| Income taxes payable | 14,600 |
| Accounts receivable | 230,540 |
| Inventory | 179,600 |
| Unearned revenue | 10,000 |
| Unexpired insurance | 4,500 |

**Instructions**

a. Prepare a schedule of the company's current assets and current liabilities. Select the appropriate items from the above list.

b. Compute the current ratio and the amount of working capital. Explain how each of these measurements is computed. State, with reasons, whether you consider the company to be in a strong or weak current position.

**Safeway, Inc.,** is one of the world's largest supermarket chains. Shown below are selected items adapted from a recent **Safeway** balance sheet. (Dollar amounts are in millions.)

| | |
|---|---|
| Cash | $   74.8 |
| Receivables | 152.7 |
| Merchandise inventories | 1,191.8 |
| Prepaid expenses | 95.5 |
| Fixtures and equipment | 2,592.9 |
| Retained earnings | 284.4 |
| Total current liabilities | 1,939.0 |

**Instructions**

**a.** Using the information above, compute the amounts of **Safeway**'s total current assets and total quick assets.

**b.** Compute the company's (1) current ratio, (2) quick ratio, and (3) working capital. (Round to one decimal place.)

**c.** From these computations, are you able to conclude whether **Safeway** is a good credit risk for short-term creditors or on the brink of bankruptcy? Explain.

**d.** Is there anything unusual about the operating cycle of supermarkets that would make you think that they normally would have lower current ratios than, say, large department stores?

**e.** What *other types of information* could you utilize in performing a more complete analysis of **Safeway**'s solvency?

A recent balance sheet of Sweet As Sugar, Inc., included the following items, among others. (Dollar amounts are stated in thousands.)

| | |
|---|---|
| Cash | $ 47,524 |
| Marketable securities (short-term) | 55,926 |
| Accounts receivable | 23,553 |
| Inventories | 32,210 |
| Prepaid expenses | 5,736 |
| Retained earnings | 121,477 |
| Notes payable to banks (due within one year) | 20,000 |
| Accounts payable | 5,912 |
| Dividends payable | 1,424 |
| Accrued liabilities (short-term) | 21,532 |
| Income taxes payable | 6,438 |

The company also reported total assets of $353,816 thousand, total liabilities of $81,630 thousand, and a return on total assets of *18.1%*.

**Instructions**

**a.** Compute Sweet As Sugar's (1) quick assets, (2) current assets, and (3) current liabilities.

**b.** Compute Sweet As Sugar's (1) quick ratio, (2) current ratio, (3) working capital, and (4) debt ratio. (Round to one decimal place.)

**c.** Discuss the company's liquidity from the viewpoints of (1) short-term creditors, (2) long-term creditors, and (3) stockholders.

**PROBLEM 14.6**

Financial Statement Analysis

LO 4, 5

Shown below are selected data from the financial statements of Hamilton Trade, a retail furniture store.

| | |
|---|---:|
| **From the balance sheet:** | |
| Cash | $ 30,000 |
| Accounts receivable | 150,000 |
| Inventory | 200,000 |
| Plant assets (net of accumulated depreciation) | 500,000 |
| Current liabilities | 150,000 |
| Total stockholders' equity | 300,000 |
| Total assets | 1,000,000 |
| **From the income statement:** | |
| Net sales | $1,500,000 |
| Cost of goods sold | 1,080,000 |
| Operating expenses | 315,000 |
| Interest expense | 84,000 |
| Income taxes expense | 6,000 |
| Net income | 15,000 |
| **From the statement of cash flows:** | |
| Net cash provided by operating activities (including interest paid of $79,000) | $ 40,000 |
| Net cash used in investing activities | (46,000) |
| Financing activities: | |
|   Amounts borrowed    $50,000 | |
|   Repayment of amounts borrowed    (14,000) | |
|   Dividends paid    (20,000) | |
|     Net cash provided by financing activities | 16,000 |
| Net increase in cash during the year | $ 10,000 |

## Instructions

**a.** Explain how the interest expense shown in the income statement could be $84,000, when the interest payment appearing in the statement of cash flows is only $79,000.

**b.** Compute the following (round to one decimal place):

  **1.** Current ratio

  **2.** Quick ratio

  **3.** Working capital

  **4.** Debt ratio

**c.** Comment on these measurements and evaluate Hamilton Trade's short-term debt-paying ability.

**d.** Compute the following ratios (assume that the year-end amounts of total assets and total stockholders' equity also represent the average amounts throughout the year):

  **1.** Return on assets

  **2.** Return on equity

**e.** Comment on the company's performance under these measurements. Explain *why* the return on assets and return on equity are so different.

**f.** Discuss (1) the apparent safety of long-term creditors' claims and (2) the prospects for Hamilton Trade continuing its dividend payments at the present level.

Listed below is the working capital information for Jimenez Products, Inc., at the beginning of the year.

**PROBLEM 14.7**

Evaluating Short-Term
Debt-Paying Ability

**LO 4, 7**

| | |
|---|---:|
| Cash | $405,000 |
| Temporary investments in marketable securities | 216,000 |
| Notes receivable—current | 324,000 |
| Accounts receivable | 540,000 |
| Allowance for doubtful accounts | 27,000 |
| Inventory | 432,000 |
| Prepaid expenses | 54,000 |
| Notes payable within one year | 162,000 |
| Accounts payable | 445,500 |
| Accrued liabilities | 40,500 |

The following transactions are completed during the year:

**0.** Sold on account inventory costing $72,000 at a "reduced for quick sale" price of $65,000.

**1.** Issued additional shares of capital stock for cash, $800,000.

**2.** Sold temporary investments costing $60,000 for $54,000 cash.

**3.** Acquired temporary investments, $105,000. Paid cash.

**4.** Wrote off uncollectible accounts, $18,000.

**5.** Sold on account inventory costing $75,000 for $90,000.

**6.** Acquired plant and equipment for cash, $480,000.

**7.** Declared a cash dividend, $240,000.

**8.** Declared a 10% stock dividend.

**9.** Paid accounts payable, $120,000.

**10.** Purchased goods on account, $90,000.

**11.** Collected cash on accounts receivable, $180,000.

**12.** Borrowed cash from a bank by issuing a short-term note, $250,000.

### Instructions

**a.** Compute the amount of quick assets, current assets, and current liabilities at the beginning of the year as shown by the above account balances.

**b.** Use the data compiled in part **a** to compute: (1) current ratio, (2) quick ratio, and (3) working capital.

**c.** Indicate the effect (Increase, Decrease, or No Effect) of each independent transaction listed above on the current ratio, quick ratio, working capital, and net cash flows from operating activities. Use the following format (item **0** is given as an example):

| | Effect on | | | |
|---|:---:|:---:|:---:|:---:|
| Item | Current Ratio | Quick Ratio | Working Capital | Net Cash Flows from Operating Activities |
| 0 | D | I | D | NE |

Barker Department Store has advertised for an accounting student to work in its accounting department during the summer, and you have applied for the job. To determine whether you are familiar with the content of classified financial statements, use the following data provided by the controller of Barker. The data are derived from the store's operations in the year ended December 31, 2001.

Available information (dollar amounts in thousands):

**PROBLEM 14.8**

Classified Financial
Statements; Ratio Analysis

**LO 4, 5, 7**

| | |
|---|---:|
| Net sales . . . . . . . . . . . . . . . . . . . . . . . . . . . . . . . . . . . . . . . . . . . . | $10,000 |
| Net income . . . . . . . . . . . . . . . . . . . . . . . . . . . . . . . . . . . . . . . . . . | ? |
| Current liabilities . . . . . . . . . . . . . . . . . . . . . . . . . . . . . . . . . . . . | 2,000 |
| Selling expenses . . . . . . . . . . . . . . . . . . . . . . . . . . . . . . . . . . . . | 1,000 |
| Long-term liabilities . . . . . . . . . . . . . . . . . . . . . . . . . . . . . . . . . | 1,600 |
| Total assets (and total liabilities & stockholders' equity) . . . . . . . . . . . . . . . . . . . . . . | 6,800 |
| Stockholders' equity . . . . . . . . . . . . . . . . . . . . . . . . . . . . . . . . . | ? |
| Gross profit . . . . . . . . . . . . . . . . . . . . . . . . . . . . . . . . . . . . . . . . | ? |
| Cost of goods sold . . . . . . . . . . . . . . . . . . . . . . . . . . . . . . . . . . | 7,000 |
| Current assets . . . . . . . . . . . . . . . . . . . . . . . . . . . . . . . . . . . . . | 4,000 |
| Income taxes expense and other nonoperating items . . . . . . . . . . . . . . . . . . . | 220 |
| Operating income . . . . . . . . . . . . . . . . . . . . . . . . . . . . . . . . . . . | ? |
| General and administrative expenses . . . . . . . . . . . . . . . . . . . . . . . | 980 |
| Plant and equipment . . . . . . . . . . . . . . . . . . . . . . . . . . . . . . . . . | 2,600 |
| Other assets . . . . . . . . . . . . . . . . . . . . . . . . . . . . . . . . . . . . . . . | ? |

## Instructions

**a.** Using the supplied data, prepare for Barker Department Store a condensed:

   **1.** Classified balance sheet at December 31, 2001.

   **2.** Multiple-step income statement for the year ended December 31, 2001. Show supporting computations used in determining any missing amounts. (*Note:* Your financial statements should include only as much detail as these captions permit. For example, the first asset listed in your balance sheet will be "Current assets . . . $4,000.")

**b.** Compute at year-end the company's:

   **1.** Current ratio.

   **2.** Working capital.

**c.** Compute the company's 2001:

   **1.** Gross profit rate.

   **2.** Return on total assets. (Round to the nearest percent.)

   **3.** Return on total stockholders' equity.

*Note:* In the last two computations, use the amounts of total assets and stockholders' equity from your classified balance sheet as a substitute for the average amounts during the year.)

**d.** Assume that you get the summer job with Barker Department Store. Your first project is to compute the store's working capital and current ratio as of June 1, 2002. You notice that both measures differ significantly from the December 31, 2001, amounts computed in part **b.** Explain why these measures may have changed so dramatically in just five months.

**PROBLEM 14.9**

Basic Ratio Analysis

**LO 4, 5, 7**

**Blockbuster Entertainment Corporation** operates under the name **Blockbuster Video** and is engaged primarily in the business of renting videotapes. Shown below are selected data from a recent annual report. (Dollar amounts are stated in thousands.)

| | Beginning of the Year | End of the Year |
|---|---:|---:|
| Total current assets . . . . . . . . . . . . . . . . . . . . . . . . . . . . . . . | $ 54,130 | $ 92,592 |
| Total current liabilities . . . . . . . . . . . . . . . . . . . . . . . . . . . . | 63,481 | 83,357 |
| Total assets . . . . . . . . . . . . . . . . . . . . . . . . . . . . . . . . . . . . . | 234,698 | 417,413 |
| Total stockholders' equity . . . . . . . . . . . . . . . . . . . . . . . . . | 124,058 | 208,189 |
| Operating income . . . . . . . . . . . . . . . . . . . . . . . . . . . . . . . . | | 76,141 |
| Net income . . . . . . . . . . . . . . . . . . . . . . . . . . . . . . . . . . . . . | | 44,152 |

The company has long-term liabilities that bear interest at annual rates ranging from 11% to 16%.

**Instructions**

**a.** Compute the company's current ratio at (1) the *beginning* of the year and (2) the *end* of the year. (Carry to two decimal places.)

**b.** Compute the company's working capital at (1) the beginning of the year and (2) the end of the year. (Express dollar amounts in thousands.)

**c.** Is the company's short-term debt-paying ability improving or deteriorating? As a short-term creditor, would you consider the company to be as good a credit risk as, say, **BellSouth**—a regional telephone company with a current ratio of *.9 to 1?* Explain.

**d.** Compute the company's (1) return on average total assets and (2) return on average stockholders' equity. (Round average assets and average equity to the nearest dollar and final computations to the nearest 1%.)

**e.** As an equity investor, do you think that Blockbuster's management is utilizing the company's resources in a reasonably efficient manner? Explain.

At the end of the year, the following information was obtained from the accounting records of Wexler Products:

**PROBLEM 14.10**

Ratios; Consider Advisability of Incurring Long-Term Debt

**LO 5, 7**

| | |
|---|---|
| Sales (all on credit) | $2,750,000 |
| Cost of goods sold | 1,755,000 |
| Average inventory | 351,000 |
| Average accounts receivable | 300,000 |
| Interest expense | 45,000 |
| Income taxes | 84,000 |
| Net income | 159,000 |
| Average investment in assets | 1,800,000 |
| Average stockholders' equity | 795,000 |

**Instructions**

**a.** From the information given, compute the following:

  **1.** Inventory turnover

  **2.** Accounts receivable turnover

  **3.** Total operating expenses

  **4.** Gross profit percentage

  **5.** Return on average stockholders' equity

  **6.** Return on average assets

**b.** Wexler has an opportunity to obtain a long-term loan at an annual interest rate of 12% and could use this additional capital at the same rate of profitability as indicated by the given data. Would obtaining the loan be desirable from the viewpoint of the stockholders? Explain.

Shown below are selected financial data for Another World and Imports, Inc., at the end of the current year:

**PROBLEM 14.11**

Ratios: Evaluation of Two Companies

**LO 5, 7, 8**

| | Another World | Imports, Inc. |
|---|---|---|
| Net credit sales | $675,000 | $560,000 |
| Cost of goods sold | 504,000 | 480,000 |
| Cash | 51,000 | 20,000 |
| Accounts receivable (net) | 75,000 | 70,000 |
| Inventory | 84,000 | 160,000 |
| Current liabilities | 105,000 | 100,000 |

Assume that the year-end balances shown for accounts receivable and for inventory approximate the average balances of these items throughout the year.

### Instructions

**a.** For each of the two companies, compute the following:

1. Working capital
2. Current ratio
3. Quick ratio
4. Number of times inventory turned over during the year and the average number of days required to turn over inventory (round computation to the nearest day)
5. Number of times accounts receivable turned over during the year and the average number of days required to collect accounts receivable (round computation to the nearest day)
6. Operating cycle

**b.** From the viewpoint of a short-term creditor, comment on the *quality* of each company's working capital. To which company would you prefer to sell $20,000 in merchandise on a 30-day open account?

**PROBLEM 14.12**

Ratios; Goodyear versus B.F. Goodrich

**LO 4, 5, 7**

**Goodyear Tire and Rubber** and **B.F. Goodrich** are two of the world's largest publicly owned manufacturers of tire products. Shown below are data from the companies' recent annual reports. (Dollar amounts are stated in thousands.)

| | Goodyear | Goodrich |
|---|---|---|
| Total current assets . . . . . . . . . . . . . . . . . . . . . . . . . . . . . . . . | $3,841,600 | $ 950,000 |
| Total current liabilities . . . . . . . . . . . . . . . . . . . . . . . . . . . . . | 2,736,300 | 600,700 |
| Total quick assets . . . . . . . . . . . . . . . . . . . . . . . . . . . . . . . . . | 1,883,300 | 459,300 |
| Average total assets . . . . . . . . . . . . . . . . . . . . . . . . . . . . . . . | 9,789,600 | 2,489,600 |
| Average stockholders' equity . . . . . . . . . . . . . . . . . . . . . . . . | 3,281,700 | 1,000,800 |
| Operating income . . . . . . . . . . . . . . . . . . . . . . . . . . . . . . . . . | 1,135,400 | 242,900 |
| Net income . . . . . . . . . . . . . . . . . . . . . . . . . . . . . . . . . . . . . . | 611,000 | 118,000 |

### Instructions

**a.** Compute the following for each company (round computations to one decimal place):

1. Current ratio
2. Quick ratio
3. Working capital
4. Return on average total assets
5. Return on average total stockholders' equity

**b.** From the viewpoint of a short-term creditor, which of these companies appears to have the greater short-term debt-paying ability? Explain.

**c.** In which company does management appear to be using the resources under its control most efficiently? Explain the reasons for your answer.

**PROBLEM 14.13**

Effects of Transactions on Various Ratios

**LO 7**

Listed in the left-hand column is a series of 12 business transactions and events relating to the activities of Remler Industries. Opposite each transaction is listed a particular ratio used in financial analysis.

| Transaction | Ratio |
|---|---|
| (1) Purchased inventory on open account | Quick ratio |
| (2) A larger physical volume of goods was sold at smaller unit prices | Gross profit percentage |
| (3) Corporation declared a cash dividend | Current ratio (assume ratio is greater than 1:1) |
| (4) An uncollectible account receivable was written off against the allowance account | Current ratio (assume ratio is greater than 1:1) |
| (5) Issued additional shares of common stock and used proceeds to retire long-term debt | Debt ratio |
| (6) Paid stock dividend on common stock, in common stock | Earnings per share |
| (7) Conversion of a portion of bonds payable into common stock (ignore income taxes) | Interest coverage ratio |
| (8) Appropriated retained earnings | Rate of return on stockholders' equity |
| (9) During period of rising prices, company changed from FIFO to LIFO method of inventory pricing | Inventory turnover |
| (10) Paid a previously declared cash dividend | Debt ratio |
| (11) Purchased factory supplies on open account | Current ratio (assume ratio is greater than 1:1) |
| (12) Issued shares of capital stock in exchange for patents | Debt ratio |

**Instructions**

What effect would each transaction or event have on the ratio listed opposite to it? That is, as a result of this event would the ratio increase, decrease, or remain unchanged? Your answer for each of the 12 transactions should include a brief explanation.

## CASES AND UNSTRUCTURED PROBLEMS

Holiday Greeting Cards is a local company organized late in July of 2001. The company's net income for each of its first six calendar quarters of operations is summarized below. (Amounts are stated in thousands of dollars.)

**CASE 14.1**

Season's Greetings

**LO 1**

|  | 2002 | 2001 |
|---|---|---|
| First quarter (Jan. through Mar.) | $ 253 | –0– |
| Second quarter (Apr. through June) | 308 | –0– |
| Third quarter (July through Sept.) | 100 | $ 50 |
| Fourth quarter (Oct. through Dec.) | 450 | 500 |
| Total for the calendar year | $1,111 | $550 |

Glen Wallace reports the business and economic news for a local radio station. On the day that Holiday Greeting Cards released the above financial information, you heard Wallace make the following statement during his broadcast: "Holiday Greeting Cards enjoyed a 350% increase in its profits for the fourth quarter, and profits for the entire year were up by over 100%."

## Instructions

**a.** Show the computations that Wallace probably made in arriving at his statistics. (Hint: Wallace did not make his computations in the manner recommended in this chapter. His figures, however, can be developed from the financial data above.)

**b.** Do you believe that Wallace's percentage changes present a realistic impression of Holiday Greeting Cards' rate of growth in 2002? Explain.

**c.** What figure would you use to express the percentage change in Holiday's fourth-quarter profits in 2002? Explain why you would compute the change in this manner.

**CASE 14.2**

Evaluating Debt-Paying Ability

**LO 3, 4, 5**

You are a loan officer with First Kansas Bank. Dan Scott owns two successful restaurants, each of which has applied to your bank for a $250,000 one-year loan for the purpose of opening a second location. Condensed balance sheets for the two business entities are shown below.

**KANSAS STEAK RANCH**
**Balance Sheet**
**December 31, 2002**

| Assets | | Liabilities & Stockholders' Equity | |
|---|---|---|---|
| Current assets . . . . . . . . . . . . | $ 75,000 | Current liabilities . . . . . . . . . . . . | $ 30,000 |
| Plant and equipment . . . . . . . . | 300,000 | Long-term liabilities . . . . . . . . . . | 200,000 |
| | | Capital stock . . . . . . . . . . . . . . | 100,000 |
| | | Retained earnings . . . . . . . . . . | 45,000 |
| | | Total liabilities & | |
| Total assets . . . . . . . . . . . . . | $375,000 | stockholders' equity . . . . . . . . | $375,000 |

**THE STOCKYARDS**
**Balance Sheet**
**December 31, 2002**

| Assets | | Liabilities & Owners' Equity | |
|---|---|---|---|
| Current assets . . . . . . . . . . . . . | $ 24,000 | Current liabilities . . . . . . . . . . . | $ 30,000 |
| Plant and equipment . . . . . . . . . | 301,000 | Long-term liabilities . . . . . . . . . | 200,000 |
| | | Capital, Dan Scott . . . . . . . . . | 95,000 |
| | | Total liabilities & | |
| Total assets . . . . . . . . . . . . . . | $325,000 | owners' equity . . . . . . . . . . . | $325,000 |

Both restaurants are popular and have been successful over the past several years. Kansas Steak Ranch has been slightly more profitable, but the operating results for the two businesses have been quite similar. You think that either restaurant's second location should be successful. On the other hand, you know that restaurants are a very "faddish" type of business and that their popularity and profitability can change very quickly.

Dan Scott is one of the wealthiest people in Kansas. He made a fortune—estimated at more than $2 billion—as the founder of Micro Time, a highly successful manufacturer of computer software. Scott now is retired and spends most of his time at Second Life, his 50,000-acre cattle ranch. Both of his restaurants are run by experienced professional managers.

## Instructions

**a.** Compute the current ratio and working capital of each business entity.

**b.** Based on the information provided in this case, which of these businesses do you consider to be the better credit risk? Explain fully.

**c.** What simple measure might you insist upon that would make the other business as good a credit risk as the one you identified in part **b**? Explain.

Home Improvement Centers owns a chain of nine retail stores that sell building materials, hardware, and garden supplies. In early October, the company's current ratio is 1.7 to 1. This is about normal for the company, but it is lower than the current ratios of several large competitors. Management feels that to qualify for the best credit terms from its suppliers, the company's year-end balance sheet should indicate a current ratio of at least 2 to 1.

**CASE 14.3**

Strategies to Improve the Current Ratio

 **LO 4**

### Instructions

**a.** Indicate whether taking each of the following actions would increase or decrease the company's current ratio. Explain your reasoning.

1. Pay some of the company's current liabilities
2. Purchase large amounts of inventory on account
3. Offer credit customers a special discount if they pay their account balance prior to year-end

**b.** Propose several other ethical steps that management might take to increase the company's current ratio prior to year-end.

During each of the past 10 years, Palmer Corporation has increased the common stock dividend per share by about 10%. Total dividends now amount to $9 million per year, consisting of $2 million paid to preferred stockholders and $7 million paid to common stockholders. The preferred stock is cumulative but not convertible. Annual net income had been rising steadily until two years ago, when it peaked at $44 million. Last year, increased competition caused net income to decline to $37 million. Management expects income to stabilize around this level for several years. This year, Palmer Corporation issued bonds payable. The contract with bondholders requires the company to limit total dividends to not more than 25% of net income.

**CASE 14.4**

Limit on Dividends

 **LO 8**

### Instructions

Evaluate this situation from the perspective of:

**a.** Common stockholders.

**b.** Preferred stockholders.

MicroLabs develops and manufactures pharmaceutical products. The company has been growing rapidly during the past 10 years, due primarily to having discovered, patented, and successfully marketed dozens of new products. Profits have increased annually by 30% or more. The company pays no dividend but has a very high price-earnings ratio. Due to its rapid growth and large expenditures for research and development, the company has experienced occasional cash shortages. To solve this problem, MicroLabs has decided to improve its cash position by (1) requiring customers to pay for products purchased on account from the company in 30 days instead of 60 days and (2) reducing expenditures for research and development by 25%.

**CASE 14.5**

Improving Cash Flow

 **LO 8**

### Instructions

Evaluate this situation from the perspective of:

**a.** Short-term creditors.

**b.** Common stockholders.

Metro Utilities has outstanding 16 issues of bonds payable, with interest rates ranging from $5\frac{1}{2}\%$ to 14%. These bonds were sold over several years during which interest rates varied dramatically. The company's rate of return on assets consistently averages 12%. Almost every year, the company issues additional bonds to finance growth, to pay maturing bonds, or to call outstanding bonds when advantageous. During the current year, long-term interest rates have fallen dramatically. At the beginning of the year, these rates were between 12% and 13%; now, however, they are down to between 8% and 9%. Management currently is planning a large 8% bond issue.

**CASE 14.6**

Declining Interest Rate

 **LO 8**

### Instructions

Evaluate this situation from the perspective of:

**a.** Holders of $5\frac{1}{2}\%$ bonds, maturing in 11 years but callable now at 103.

**b.** Holders of 14% bonds, maturing in 23 years but callable now at 103.

**c.** Common stockholders.

## INTERNET ASSIGNMENT

**INTERNET 14.1**

Evaluating Liquidity and Profitability

**LO 7, 8**

Locate the **Stockmaster** website at the following address:

**www.stockmaster.com**

Find the category "Top Stocks" and select one of the listed companies.

### Instructions

**a.** Click on the "Profile" category (one of the options at the top of the screen) and read the description of the company's type of business. Why is understanding the industry and type of business an important starting point for effective financial analysis?

**b.** Go back one screen and then click on the "Financials" category. Find the summary table of ratios in this chapter on pages 628–629. Calculate three of the listed ratios under each of the following categories: "Measures of short-term liquidity" and "Measures of profitability." Show your work in calculating these ratios. Write a brief statement describing what you have learned about your company's liquidity and profitability.

**c.** Why do you think the Internet has become such a widely used source of financial information by investors and creditors?

*Internet sites are time and date sensitive. It is the purpose of these exercises to have you explore the Internet. You may need to use the Yahoo! search engine http://www.yahoo.com (or other favorite search engine) to look for a company's current site.*

## BUSINESS WEEK ASSIGNMENT

**CASE 14.7**

**LO 5, 6**

A March 6, 2000 *Business Week* article titled "For Online Pet Stores, It's Dog-Eat-Dog" discusses slim margins and a crowded market that point toward a brutal shakeout, concluding that "FIDO should have chewed up a few of these online pet store business plans." Arlene Weintraub and Robert D. Hof go on to conclude that pet supplies have never been a lucrative business. For example, operating margins are a razor-thin 2% at **Petsmart** and 4.5% for its competitor, **Petco**. Competitors are willing to lose millions of dollars to grab market share, a fact that concerns investors.

To illustrate this point, consider the following scenario: **Pets.com**'s financial statements show that it paid $13.4 million for the goods it sold for just $5.8 million. For every dollar that **Pets.com** pays suppliers such as **Ralston Purina Co.** for dog food and **United Parcel Service Inc.** for shipping, it collects 43 cents from its customers. That means it's losing 57 cents on every dollar of sales—even before the really big expenses like advertising and overhead. **Petsmart** isn't doing much better. For every dollar that it pays suppliers, it's collecting 62 cents.

### Instructions

If you were a current investor in one of the companies referred to above, what would you ask the management and board of directors of the company at the annual stockholders' meeting? What information would you use to prepare for that meeting?

## OUR COMMENTS ON THE "YOUR TURN" CASES

**As CFO of a Publicly Traded Company (p. 598)** Accounting techniques that increase earnings and are in compliance with Generally Accepted Accounting Principles can be used to legally improve the financial picture of the company. However, using these techniques to the point that investors or creditors cannot assess the quality of earnings can be an ethical problem. The Code of Ethics for Professional Accountants published by the International Federation of Accountants discusses the conflict between professional accountants' duty to society versus their immediate self-interest or their duty of loyalty to their employers. For example, the Code of Ethics states:

A distinguishing mark of a profession is acceptance of its responsibility to the public. The accounting profession's public consists of clients, credit grantors, governments, employers, employees, investors, the business and financial community, and others who rely on the objectivity and integrity of professional accountants to maintain the orderly functioning of commerce.

**As a Potential Investor (p. 604)** It is common for fast-food restaurants (such as **Wendy's** and **McDonald's**) to report seemingly low measures of short-term liquidity. This does not mean, however, that these companies will have difficulty paying their current liabilities as they become due. In fact, both **Wendy's** and **McDonald's** are extremely *liquid* companies. The reason the financial measures of their liquidity appear insufficient is that (1) all their sales are cash sales and, therefore, they have no accounts receivable, and (2) their inventory converts into cash at a faster rate than their current liabilities come due.

**As a Financial Analyst (p. 627)** For your client who is primarily interested in the dividends that will be received, you might advise him or her to evaluate much as a short-term creditor would. This would focus attention on liquidity—the current and quick ratios and the extent to which operating activities are generating positive cash flows. Also, you should suggest that he or she look at the company's dividend policy and the consistency with which dividends have been paid in the past. For the investor that is more interested in the market value of the stock, you should suggest that he or she look at a broader set of information that focuses on the long-term potential for successful operations of the companies being considered—net income, growth over time in sales, and return on assets and stockholders' equity. You should also suggest that he or she look at the pattern of changes in the value of the stock of the companies. For both investors, information in management's discussion and analysis may be helpful in identifying companies that are consistent with the specific investment objectives of each client.

## ANSWERS TO SELF-TEST QUESTIONS

**1.** c    **2.** a, c, d    **3.** c    **4.** d (see below)    **5.** b (see below)    **6.** a    **7.** d

Why answers a, b, and c in question **4** are incorrect:

**a.** The return on assets, 12% ($240,000 ÷ $2,000,000), exceeds the return on equity, which is 10% ($80,000 ÷ $800,000).

**b.** The current ratio is 1.6 to 1 ($480,000 ÷ $300,000).

**c.** Working capital amounts to $180,000 ($480,000 − $300,000).

Increase in net income required in question **5**: ($400,000 − $160,000) ÷ $160,000 = 150%

# COMPREHENSIVE PROBLEM 3

## Tootsie Roll Industries, Inc.

### ANALYSIS OF THE FINANCIAL STATEMENTS OF A PUBLICLY OWNED CORPORATION

The purpose of this Comprehensive Problem is to acquaint you with the content of an annual report. It is based upon the 1999 annual report of **Tootsie Roll Industries, Inc.**, reproduced in Appendix A of this textbook. The problem contains three major parts, which are independent of one another. *Part I* is designed to familiarize you with the content of an annual report; *Part II* involves analysis of the company's liquidity; and *Part III* analyzes the trend in its profitability.

*If you work this problem as a group assignment, each group member should be prepared to discuss the group's findings and conclusions in class.*

A good starting point for understanding the financial statements of a company such as **Tootsie Roll Industries, Inc.**, is to understand the accounting policies used in preparing those statements. The first note accompanying the financial statements provides a brief description of the major accounting policies the company used. Most of the areas discussed in this note have been covered in this text.

### Part I

Annual reports include not only comparative financial statements but also the following sources of information:

* Multiyear summary of financial highlights, a summary of key statistics for the past five or ten years.
* A letter from management addressed *To Our Stockholders*.
* A discussion by management of the results of operations and the company's financial condition.
* Several pages of *Notes* that accompany the financial statements.
* Reports by management and by the independent auditors in which they express their respective responsibilities for the financial statements.

#### Instructions
Answer each of the following questions and briefly explain *where* in the statements, notes, or other sections of the annual report you located the information used in your answer.
**a.** How many years are covered in each of the primary comparative financial statements? Were all of these statements audited? Name the auditors. What were the auditors' conclusions concerning these statements?
**b.** **Tootsie Roll Industries, Inc.**, combines its statement of retained earnings with another financial statement. Where are details about changes in the amount of retained earnings found?
**c.** Over the three years presented, have the company's annual net cash flows been positive or negative from (1) operating activities, (2) investing activities, and (3) financing activities? Has the company's cash balance increased or decreased during each of these three years?
**d.** What was the amount of net sales during the *fourth quarter* of the fiscal year ended December 31, 1999? What was the percentage change in this fourth quarter's net sales relative to sales in the fourth quarter of the prior year? Comment on the pattern of quarterly sales *within* the year, and offer your own explanation for this pattern.
**e.** What does management conclude about the company's general financial conditions? What are the primary indicators of the company's financial strength in the eyes of management?
**f.** In what foreign countries did the company operate during 1999? How important were international activities to the company's 1999 success?

### Part II

Assume that you are the credit manager of a medium-size supplier of ingredients used to manufacture candy. **Tootsie Roll Industries** wants to make credit purchases from your company, with payment due in 60 days.

## Instructions

**a.** As general background, read the section *Management's Discussion and Analysis of Financial Condition and Results of Operations.* Next compute the following for the fiscal years ending December 31, 1999, and December 31, 1998 (round percentages to the nearest tenth of one percent, and other computations to one decimal place):

   **1.** Current ratio.

   **2.** Quick ratio.

   **3.** Amount of working capital.

   **4.** Percentage change in working capital from the prior year.

   **5.** Percentage change in cash and cash equivalents from the prior year.

**b.** Based upon your analysis in part **a**, does the company's liquidity appear to have *increased* or *decreased* during the most recent fiscal year? Explain.

**c.** Comment on the company's liquidity.

**d.** Other than the ability of **Tootsie Roll** to pay for its purchases, do you see any major considerations that should enter into your company's decision? Explain.

**e.** Your company assigns each customer one of the four credit ratings listed below. Assign a credit rating to **Tootsie Roll Industries** and write a memorandum explaining your decision. (In your memorandum, you may refer to any of your computations or observations in parts **a** through **c**, and to any information contained in the annual report.)

## Possible Credit Ratings

**A Outstanding**   Little or no risk of inability to pay. For customers in this category, we fill any reasonable order without imposing a credit limit. The customer's credit is reevaluated annually.

**B Good**   Customer has good debt-paying ability but is assigned a credit limit that is reviewed every 90 days. Orders above the credit limit are accepted only on a cash basis.

**C Marginal**   Customer appears sound, but credit should be extended only on a 30-day basis and with a relatively low credit limit. Creditworthiness and credit limit are reevaluated every 90 days.

**D Unacceptable**   Customer does not qualify for credit.

## Part III

As general background, read the *Five-Year Summary of Earnings and Financial Highlights,* the letter addressed *To Our Stockholders,* and *Management's Discussion and Analysis of Financial Condition and Results of Operations.*

## Instructions

**a.** Compute the following for the fiscal years ending December 31, 1999, and December 31, 1998 (round percentages to the nearest tenth of one percent):

   **1.** Percentage change in net sales (relative to the prior year).

   **2.** Percentage change in net earnings.

   **3.** Gross profit rate.

   **4.** Net income as a percentage of sales.

   **5.** Return on average total assets.

   **6.** Return on average total equity.

**b.** Write a statement that describes your conclusion(s) concerning trends in **Tootsie Roll's** profitability during the period covered in your analysis in part **a** above. Justify your conclusion(s).

# GLOBAL BUSINESS AND ACCOUNTING

## Learning Objectives

*After studying this chapter, you should be able to:*

1. Define four mechanisms companies use to globalize their business activities.

2. Identify how global environmental forces—(a) political and legal systems, (b) economic systems, (c) culture, and (d) technology and infrastructure—affect a company's ability to compete globally.

3. Demonstrate how to convert an amount of money from one currency to another.

4. Compute gains or losses on receivables or payables that are stated in a foreign currency when exchange rates fluctuate.

5. Describe several techniques for "hedging" against losses from fluctuations in exchange rates.

6. Understand how global sourcing increases product cost complexity.

7. Explain the importance of the Foreign Corrupt Practices Act.

© Bob Krist/Picturesque/PictureQuest

For 8,000 years, beer has been brewed in the Middle East and North Africa. In Denmark, there is evidence that beer has been part of daily life for 6,000 years. The **Carlsberg Group** of Denmark (**www.carlsberg.com**) is one of the world's major international brewing groups. The Group has a workforce of approximately 22,000 employees and sells its products, including the Carlsberg and Tuborg beer brands, in about 150 markets worldwide. The parent company, **Carlsberg A/S**, is publicly traded and quoted on the Copenhagen Stock Exchange; however, **Carlsberg** is not listed on U.S. stock exchanges. Many companies claim that the cost of preparing accounting reports that are required for listing on U.S. exchanges is prohibitive.

In the March 6, 2000, issue of *Business Week,* Mike McNamee's article, "Commentary: Can the SEC Make Foreign Companies Play by Its Rules?", discussed a battle between the U.S. Securities and Exchange Commision (SEC) and international companies that want access to the world's richest capital market. The SEC's mission is to protect investors and maintain the integrity of U.S. security markets. The SEC is considering allowing non-U.S. companies to use international accounting standards rather than forcing them to comply with the standards passed by the Financial Accounting Standards Board (FASB). The forces pushing for acceptance of international accounting rules are formidable; U.S. stock exchanges are leading the charge.

● ● ●

In this chapter you will be introduced to the international forces that impact accounting procedures, rules, and regulations. These forces create significant business challenges that all companies encounter to an increasing degree as they become more global.

Accounting rules, procedures, and standards in almost any chosen country are different from those in the United States and different from those in other countries. Although some developing countries are adopting the international accounting standards discussed in the opening story, developed countries such as the United Kingdom, Japan, and Germany have established their own accounting rules, procedures, and standards. The goal of the International Accounting Standards Committee is to identify a set of accounting standards that will be acceptable to all governments and their related securities markets. This is a very ambitious goal because accounting rules, procedures, and standards are affected by the political, legal, economic, and cultural systems in which they are embedded. Thus, the variations in these systems from country to country have a significant impact on how investors and creditors understand and use financial statement information.

The objective of this chapter is to introduce you to the complexity of global business and to explore some of the accounting issues associated with global business. This is only a brief introduction. As your business education progresses, additional details will be added to the ideas introduced here.

## GLOBALIZATION

**Globalization** is the process of managers assessing the impact of international activities on the future of their company. Globalization is a continuous process; at the most basic level, a purely domestic company's ability to compete is influenced by changes in foreign exchange rates, technological advances, cultural diversity, and international political and economic issues. An example of a higher level of globalization is a multinational enterprise whose production and sales locations span multiple foreign locations from raw materials extraction to final product assembly and sales. **The Gillette Company**, a global Fortune 500 company, is a good example of a multinational with an explicit global mission. The exhibit below shows the global reach of **Gillette**, which produces products in 20 countries that are sold in more than 200 countries around the world.

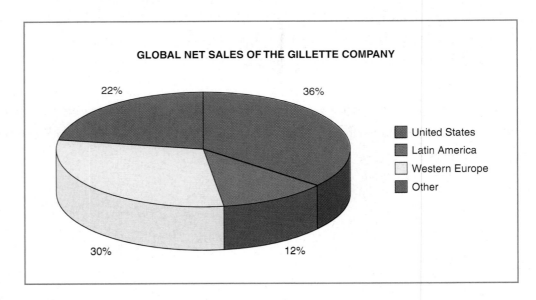

**GLOBAL NET SALES OF THE GILLETTE COMPANY**

- 36% — United States
- 12% — Latin America
- 30% — Western Europe
- 22% — Other

**LO 1**
Define four mechanisms companies use to globalize their business activities.

Globalization typically progresses through a series of stages that include exporting, licensing, joint ventures, wholly owned subsidiaries, and, finally, global sourcing. **Exporting** is, at the simplest level, selling a good or service to a foreign customer. While *exporting* maintains control over product creation, *licensing* gives up some control for a monetary return. **International licensing** is a contractual agreement between a company and a foreign party allowing the use of trademarks, patents, technology, designs, processes, intellectual property, or other proprietary advantage. Most major multinational food manufacturing companies are involved in some form of international product licensing. An **international joint venture** is a company owned by two or more companies from different countries. A **wholly owned international subsidiary** is created when a company uses its own funds to construct or purchase 100% equity control of a foreign subsidiary. Finally, **global sourcing** is the close coordination of R&D, manufacturing, and marketing across national boundaries and typically includes all of the four stages, resulting in a very high level of globalization.

As shown in the exhibit below, companies typically engage in globalization through an outward growth path. Those companies wishing to globalize typically progress through the following stages: (1) exporting domestically produced products, (2) establishing licensing and joint venture arrangements, (3) creating wholly owned subsidiaries, and (4) full-scale global sourcing. In practice, there are many subcategories that are not shown in the exhibit, and companies may pursue multiple globalization processes simultaneously.

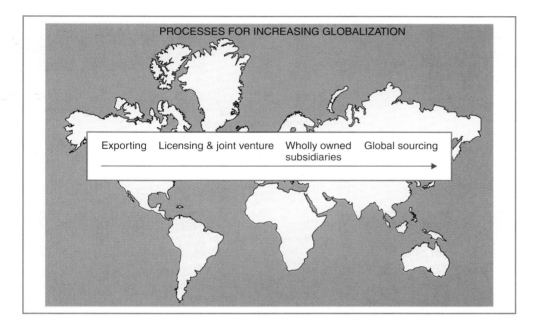

PROCESSES FOR INCREASING GLOBALIZATION

Exporting    Licensing & joint venture    Wholly owned subsidiaries    Global sourcing

The strategic direction of planned globalization has implications for the type of accounting information gathered, created, and reported. For example, the type of accounting information gathered and reported for a joint venture operation will be more detailed and control oriented than information gathered and reported to monitor a licensing agreement. In a wholly owned subsidiary, information is needed to help maintain control over resources; that same information would be unnecessary for a licensing arrangement. If the wholly owned subsidiary is part of the outward growth path and located in a foreign location, the company will also monitor information about that foreign location. As companies become more global, many additional environmental variables must be tracked as part of normal business processes.

 **General Mills** provides an excellent example of the globalization process. Exporting of flour began shortly after the creation of the company in 1928. Today, **General Mills** exports 650 items to 100 markets. Its first international business, **General Mills Canada**, was started in 1954. Joint ventures and licensing agreements with Nestlé in Europe (1989), Maizena in Latin America (1994), and, most recently, Want Want Holdings Ltd. in China (1998) have made **General Mills** a multinational company.

CASE IN POINT

# ENVIRONMENTAL FORCES SHAPING GLOBALIZATION

**LO 2**

Identify how global
environmental forces—
(a) political and legal systems,
(b) economic systems,
(c) culture, and (d) technology and infrastructure
affect a company's ability
to compete globally.

Companies expanding internationally as a means of fulfilling strategic objectives need to understand how international environmental forces affect the accounting information measured, reported, and created. We consider these environmental forces in four categories: (1) political and legal systems, (2) economic systems, (3) culture, and (4) technology and infrastructure.

You should not think of these categories as independent. A country's economy and culture have an influence on its political and legal structures. Culture affects and is affected by economics. As illustrated below, the technological position of a country is dependent on political, demographic, and cultural issues.

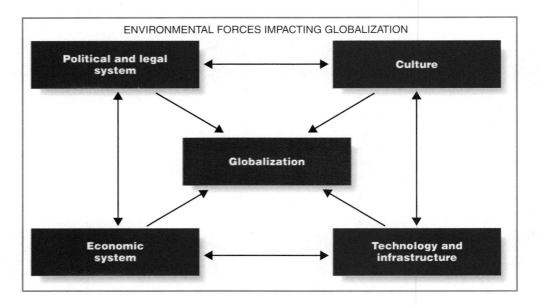

## Political and Legal Systems

**LO 2a**

Identify how political and legal
systems affect a company's
ability to compete globally.

Managers operating in or planning operations in foreign settings must track and attempt to manage political risks associated with the country of operation. Political risk occurs when governments shift asset ownership from the company to the government or when the company relinquishes command over operations due to government intervention. For example, when Iran nationalized its oil industry in the late 1970s, many companies lost ownership of the assets they had invested in oil exploration, drilling, and oil delivery.

Laws enacted by foreign governments often have an impact on the net profits earned from international activities. Taxes, tariffs, and licensing fees vary substantially from country to country. Laws restricting the flow of currency can affect the amounts of foreign-earned profits that can be transferred out and used elsewhere. Ownership requirements are a common form of governmental control. For example, governments in China and India have made creating wholly owned subsidiaries in their countries very difficult. Joint ventures in China typically result in Chinese companies (or citizens) owning at least 51% of the joint venture company.

Other types of political intervention include content or value-added requirements and sourcing requirements. Trade agreements often specify the source of raw materials or labor content to allow preferential treatment in tariffs and customs for products or services that are produced in the regions covered by the agreement. For example, NAFTA (the North American Free Trade Agreement) specifies **regional value content** conditions to qualify for favorable tariff and customs duty treatment. Regional value content requirements come into play when a good is manufactured partially in countries that are members of the free trade agreement and partially in countries that are not. These rules can be very complex and dictate the amount of total cost or the percentage of the sales price that must be added in those countries that have signed the free trade agreement.

Governments create tariffs, duties, and special trade zones that affect the cost associated with producing and selling goods and services in global markets. Because countries wish to encourage or discourage particular types of importing or exporting activities, they use their political powers to regulate cross-border commerce. For example, the U.S. government has identified several **foreign trade zones** within the United States. Goods imported into these zones are duty-free until they leave the zone. Companies that import raw materials frequently set up their factories in these trade zones. These companies are not required to pay duty on the imported raw materials until the finished product is shipped out of the zone. A delay in paying the duty enlarges the company's working capital as discussed in Chapter 14.

 Mexico has created special laws for a **maquiladora**, which is a joint venture manufacturing plant located typically in northern Mexico. These companies enjoy exemptions from Mexican laws governing foreign companies. In addition, the United States grants exemptions from, or reductions in, customs duties on re-exported goods (that is, raw materials sent from the United States to Mexico for assembly and exported back into the United States for insertion into the finished product). Companies that create maquiladoras benefit from high-quality labor at low wages.

**CASE IN POINT**

The costs added by the governments where a company is operating or planning to operate must be considered when resource allocation decisions are made. A manager practicing global sourcing will need information on taxes, tariffs, local content laws, and so on to make effective, competitive resource decisions.

*Legal reporting* requirements vary significantly from country to country. Differences in accounting practices reflect the influences that shape business activity in the country, the legal environment in which the business operates, and the primary providers of capital for the business. For example, in the United Kingdom and the United States, reporting requirements are based primarily on the need to provide useful information for investors and creditors. This need results from those countries having many companies that raise capital by selling their securities in well-developed capital markets. In Europe and Japan, on the other hand, banks provide much of the capital for business. In those countries, accounting requirements are more legalistic and are intended to satisfy governmental reporting requirements, including income tax reporting. In South America, financial reporting is oriented toward the needs of governmental planning and follows practices dictated by the government.

These differences in accounting practices create problems in trying to analyze and compare accounting information. For example, financial reporting in the United States is based primarily on the principle of historical cost without adjustment for changes in general price levels. Some South American countries, on the other hand, have experienced such high rates of inflation that inflation-adjusted information is required. Similarly, differences exist in the financial reporting requirements in the United States and Mexico in such important areas as earnings per share, consolidation of financial statements, and reporting for retiree medical and insurance benefits. These differences cause the financial statements of a U.S. company and those of a Mexican company to be different and difficult to compare.

As long as an enterprise operates solely within its own borders, differences in financial reporting practices between countries are not as significant a problem as they are if business activity extends across borders. When a company buys or sells products in another country, the lack of comparability of accounting information becomes a greater problem. Similarly, **cross-border financing**, in which a company sells its securities in the capital markets of another country, has become increasingly popular. Business activities that cross borders create the need for more comparable information between companies that reside in different countries. This, in turn, has led to an interest in the **harmonization of accounting standards**, a phrase used to describe the standardization of accounting methods and principles used in different countries throughout the world. The **International Accounting Standards Committee** (IASC), mentioned in the opening *Business Week* excerpt, is particularly interested in harmonization and is charged with the responsibility of establishing and gaining acceptance of international accounting standards. The IASC represents 110 professional organizations and over 1 million accounting professionals worldwide. While the IASC has no regulatory authority in any country, it uses its influence to move the reporting standards of all countries closer together in hopes of better harmonizing those standards. For countries that do not have well-developed capital markets, IASC standards provide a model that often has a significant influence on their early attempts to develop standardized accounting practices.

As countries change and grow, governments try to manage that growth through political and legal means. For example, in addition to creating legal reporting requirements for companies wishing to raise capital in equity markets, governments also use tax incentives for individuals that encourage or discourage ownership of stocks. Employment and governmental policies also affect the level of individual savings, which has an impact on the availability of capital in a specific country. Educational policies impact the literacy rate, extent of formal education and training, and level of management development. The political and legal structures of each country provide the framework for their economic structures. Although the political, legal, and economic structures are discussed here as separate ideas, you should think of these structures as highly related. These structures evolve and change over time, affecting the flow of capital and goods across borders.

**CASE IN POINT**

In 1993 the IASC and the International Organization of Securities Commissions (IOSCO) reached a very significant agreement on a comprehensive list of forty core standards. The agreement asserts that on completion of the core standards acceptable to IOSCO, it will endorse the international accounting standards and recommend them for cross-border capital raising and listing purposes in all global markets. The U.S. Securities and Exchange Commission (SEC) is a member of IOSCO.

In May 1999 after IASC completed work on the key components of the forty standards, the Technical Committee of IOSCO assessed the IASC's core standards. They decided to recommend that IOSCO members permit foreign issuers to use IASC standards in addition to national standards for cross-border offering and listing purposes. For current information on this process see: www.IASC.org.uk.

## Economic Systems

**LO 2b**

Identify how economic systems affect a company's ability to compete globally.

The economic systems under which businesses operate significantly affect the form and availability of accounting information. In a **planned economy**, the government uses central planning to allocate resources and determine output among various segments of the economy. Land and production facilities are government owned and controlled. The former Soviet Union and Soviet Eastern Bloc countries used central planning and had planned economies. China continues to use central planning extensively. In **market economies**, ownership of land and the means of production are private, and markets dictate the allocation of resources and the output among segments of the economy.

Companies formerly operating in a planned economy can encounter significant difficulties when attempting to operate in a market economy. The reverse can also be true. Many companies from market economies have been unsuccessful when attempting to do business in foreign locations that are primarily planned economies.

In 2000, **Amoco Corporation** abandoned a joint venture in Russia because of bureaucratic and technological difficulties. The number of failed and abandoned joint ventures in Russia is a reminder that expertise in one economic system may not transfer to other locations.

**CASE IN POINT**

Obtaining capital and creating international business partnerships require an understanding of international differences in how capital is acquired and how businesses are organized. Although the United States has a strong capital market where companies can acquire capital by issuing equity shares in the company, many other countries have either no capital market or a very restricted, low-volume market. In those countries, banks or governments are the dominant providers of capital. Islamic governments (Iran and Sudan) do not allow banks to make interest payments to depositors. Instead, individual depositors share in the bank's profits. Commercial borrowers pay the bank and its depositors a share of their profits instead of interest. Government restrictions on the availability of capital significantly influence how accounting information is created and reported.

In some countries businesses arrange themselves into **industrial organizations** as one method of raising capital. In South Korea and Japan, companies group themselves into conglomerates representing different industries. South Korean conglomerates, called *chaebol,* and Japanese conglomerates, called *keiretsu,* consist of companies that are grouped as customers and suppliers, and they usually contain a bank. Within these cartels of companies, suppliers receive loans, investment capital, technology, and long-term supply agreements from customers higher up on the pyramid. Suppliers integrate their operations with other suppliers and with their customers. Transactions between suppliers and customers are not arm's-length as in most U.S. transactions. In the United States, antitrust and price-fixing laws preclude the type of organized business groups found in Japan and South Korea.

## Culture

Think of culture as the mental mindset that affects the way individuals in a society act and perceive each other's actions.[1] U.S. cultural practices have significant effects on the way foreign companies conduct business in the United States. Likewise, certain forms of advertising, methods of acquiring business, and hierarchical organizational structures, which are common practices in the United States, would not be acceptable in some international settings. Cultural differences mandate that companies wishing to do business in diverse cultural settings invest in training for their current employees, hire new employees with cultural expertise, or, more often, both. Ignoring cultural variables can create significant business problems.

**LO 2c**

Identify how culture affects a company's ability to compete globally.

Experts on culture have identified several significant variables that differ among international locations. Those that have significant implications for accounting production and use include the following:

- *Individualism versus collectivism.* The degree of interdependence that a society maintains among individuals, where high interdependence connotes collectivism. Citizens of Asian countries typically score higher on collectivism than those in the United States.
- *Uncertainty avoidance.* The extent to which members of a society feel uncomfortable or threatened by unknown or uncertain situations. Citizens of South American countries score high on uncertainty avoidance.

[1] For a more detailed discussion of the information in this section, see G. Hofstede, *Cultures and Organizations: Software of the Mind* (Berkshire, England: McGraw-Hill, 1991).

- *Short- versus long-term orientation.* With a long-term orientation, perseverance, thriftiness, maintaining order, and lasting relationships are highly valued. A short-term orientation focuses on the past and the present, ignores the future, and values personal stability.
- *Large versus small power distance.* Large power distance cultures accept unequally distributed power within and across institutions and organizations. The idea that everyone is created equal or should have an equal voice is more highly valued in small power distance societies.

The table below provides a rough measure of the relative differences between selected countries.

| Country | Individualism | Uncertainty Avoidance | Long-Term Orientation | High Power Distance |
|---|---|---|---|---|
| Japan | L | H | H | M |
| South Korea | L | H | H | H |
| Brazil | L | H | M | H |
| Italy | M | H | * | M |
| Germany | M | M | L | L |
| United States | H | M | L | M |
| Great Britain | H | L | L | L |
| Sweden | M | L | L | L |

H = High, M = Medium, L = Low.
*Not available.

We can use the above table to understand how cultural variables can affect both the type of accounting information that is produced and how that information is used. For example, compare the rankings for Asian and South American countries (Japan, South Korea, and Brazil) with European and North American countries (Germany, Great Britain, and United States). The Asian and South American countries have generally higher rankings on long-term orientation, uncertainty avoidance, and power distance, but lower rankings on individualism.

Studies have shown that in South Korea and Japan, where collectivism is high, less emphasis is placed on the transparency of financial statements for investors and the professionalism of accountants is low. The needs of creditors are given preference over the needs of investors, and the government—in particular the tax authority—has significant influence over financial reporting requirements. Thus, because financing for companies comes primarily from a bank in the keiretsu or chaebol, most financial accounting information is kept within the collectivist group. In addition, because of the strict government control of accounting regulations, the accounting profession in Asian countries has been slow to develop. The relative number of independent accountants is small, but increasing in many Asian countries.

Cultural differences pose significant problems regarding the design and administration of accounting systems. A budgeting system that is effective for a British subsidiary may be inappropriate and demotivating for an Asian subsidiary. Even within countries, there are highly diverse groups in terms of religion, ethnic groups, language, and income level. These differences have implications for effective business management. For example, the name *Coca-Cola* in China was first rendered as *Ke-kou-ke-la*. After thousands of signs had been printed, the **Coca-Cola Company** discovered the phrase means "Bite the wax tadpole" or "Female horse stuffed with wax," depending on the dialect!

The Japanese government is creating amendments to the Japanese securities law that will radically change the way companies in Japan report financial statement information. Business leaders in Japan are calling it Japan's accounting "Big Bang." As the Japanese Finance Ministry phases in these tougher accounting standards over the next several years, managers of several Japanese companies will be changing their business strategies.

For example, until recently, parent companies in Japan only counted operations as subsidiaries if they had more than 50% ownership. However, because of keiretsu structures, big companies often control their smaller suppliers and sometimes shift unwanted losses from the parent's books to these affiliates. Thus, investors have difficulty figuring out the profitability of the big company. Under the Big Bang rules, if the parent exercises de facto control by financing the affiliate's debt or picking its board, the parent must consolidate the affiliate as a 100% owned subsidiary. It is expected that under the new rules, Japan's **Mazda Motor Corp.** must consolidate 88 more dealers and parts suppliers (many of them unprofitable) into its financial statements. Under the new rules of the Big Bang, Japanese companies will re-examine the strategies that link them to their affiliates.

**MANAGEMENT STRATEGY**

## Technology and Infrastructure

Training and educational differences further complicate global business through variation in the infrastructure, educational level, and ability to transfer information and knowledge between and among various geographic locations and peoples. These differences can create significant barriers to successful international operations. Thus companies that create joint ventures or start wholly owned operations in some foreign locations find few employees with the education and technical training available in the U.S. workforce.

**LO 2d**

Identify how technology and infrastructure affect a company's ability to compete globally.

 Western-style management training is a very recent development in many countries. Budapest has one of the oldest graduate management programs in Eastern Europe, and it was founded in 1988.

**CASE IN POINT**

More specifically, because companies in formerly planned economies used centrally determined accounts and procedures, accounting as a profession did not exist in Eastern Europe prior to 1988. Thus companies establishing business operations in Eastern European locations have difficulty locating trained accounting personnel and, as a result, prior business records are unreliable. Prior to the early 1990s, there were no independent auditors, public accountants, or management accountants in most Eastern European countries.

Differences in internal accounting systems can also create problems in international business dealings, particularly when one organization acquires or creates a joint venture with another. Internal accounting information is critical for understanding how a business operates, and how to value that business, which is one of the main functions of accountants. Cultural, educational, language, and software differences hinder the free flow of information. Potential benefits from acquired international operations are sometimes lost because of the inability to transfer valuable information within and between international companies.

Most Europeans and Japanese know that the Internet is entering a new wireless phase. More than 9 million Japanese and Europeans exchange E-mail and surf websites on their wireless phones. The new mobile E-commerce that will arise from the wireless Web will be all about speed and location. In contrast, the established architecture of the PC universe (big disk drives, large monitors, and miles of optical fibers) presents technological and infrastructure inpediments to wireless E-commerce.

**Infrastructure** impediments also pose problems for globalization. Poor access to communication equipment (for example, telephones, faxes, and computers), necessary R&D facilities (for example, specialized laboratory equipment, computer-aided design or manufacturing), and fluctuating or unreliable power sources create significant hurdles to establishing international business in some locations. For example, plants in many developing countries are not heated or cooled, which can create adverse operating environments for equipment that relies on lubricants and coolants. Inadequate transportation systems can slow the transfer of goods in and out of an international location. Accountants, who estimate costs for inventory balance sheet items or cost of goods sold, need to incorporate these unexpected costs into their computations to properly compute the cost of exported products.

**Automatic Feed Co.**, an Ohio company that makes and installs sophisticated coil processing equipment, experienced significant technological problems when it exported its product to an **Isuzu** joint venture plant in Chong Qing, China. When transporting the product to its destination, 20 out of 26 shipping containers were temporarily lost and mislaid; and during installation, unexpected power spikes destroyed three computers.

## FOREIGN CURRENCIES AND EXCHANGE RATES

In addition to the environmental characteristics just discussed, companies with international business dealings encounter problems from multiple currencies. Consider, for example, a Japanese company that sells merchandise to a U.S. corporation. The Japanese company will want to be paid in Japanese currency—yen—but the U.S. company's bank account contains U.S. dollars. Thus one currency must be converted into another.

Most banks participate in an international currency exchange that enables them to buy foreign currencies at the prevailing *exchange rate*. Thus a U.S. corporation can pay a liability to a Japanese company through the international banking system. The U.S. company will pay its bank in dollars. The bank will then use these dollars to purchase the required amount of yen on the international currency exchange and will arrange for delivery of the yen to the Japanese company's bank.[2]

---

[2] Alternatively, the U.S. company may send the Japanese company a check (or a bank draft) stated in dollars. The Japanese company can then arrange to have the dollars converted into yen through its bank in Japan.

## Exchange Rates

A currency **exchange rate** is the amount it costs to purchase one unit of currency with another currency. Thus the exchange rate may be viewed as the "price" of buying one unit of a foreign currency, stated in terms of the domestic currency (which for our purpose is U.S. dollars). Exchange rates fluctuate daily, based on the worldwide supply and demand for particular currencies. The current exchange rate between the dollar and most major currencies is published daily in the financial press. For example, a few of the exchange rates recently listed in *The Wall Street Journal* are shown below.

| Country | Currency | Exchange Rate (in Dollars) |
|---------|----------|----------------------------|
| Britain | Pound (£) | $1.6295 |
| France | French franc (FF) | 0.1576 |
| Japan | Yen (¥) | 0.0106 |
| Mexico | Peso ($) | 0.1058 |
| Germany | Deutsche mark (DM) | 0.5283 |

*U.S. dollar equivalents for five foreign currencies*

Exchange rates may be used to determine how much of one currency is equivalent to a given amount of another currency. Assume that a U.S. company owes a Japanese company 1 million yen (expressed ¥1,000,000). How many dollars are needed to settle this obligation, assuming that the current exchange rate is $0.0106 per yen? To restate an amount of foreign currency in terms of the equivalent amount of U.S. dollars, we multiply the foreign currency amount by the exchange rate, as follows:[3]

**LO 3**

Demonstrate how to convert an amount of money from one currency to another.

| Amount Stated in Foreign Currency | × Exchange Rate (in Dollars) | = Equivalent Number of U.S. Dollars |
|-----------------------------------|------------------------------|-------------------------------------|
| ¥1,000,000 | × $0.0106 per yen | = $10,600 |

This process of restating an amount of foreign currency in terms of the equivalent number of dollars is called *translating* the foreign currency.

**Exchange Rate Jargon** In the financial press, currencies are often described as "strong" or "weak," or as rising or falling against one another. For example, an evening newscaster might say, "A strong dollar rose sharply against the weakening British pound, but fell slightly against the Japanese yen and the Swiss franc." What does this tell us about exchange rates?

To understand such terminology, we must remember that an exchange rate is simply the price of one currency *stated in terms of another currency*. Throughout this chapter, we refer to the prices of various foreign currencies stated in terms of *U.S. dollars*. In other countries, however, the U.S. dollar is a foreign currency, and its price is stated in terms of the local (domestic) currency.

To illustrate, consider our table from *The Wall Street Journal*, which shows the exchange rate for the Japanese yen to be $0.0106. At this exchange rate, $1 is equivalent to ¥94 (¥94 × $0.0106 per yen = $1). Thus, while we would say that the exchange rate for the Japanese yen is *$0.0106*, the Japanese would say that the exchange rate for the U.S. dollar is *¥94*.

---

[3] To convert an amount of dollars into the equivalent amount of a foreign currency, we would *divide* the dollar amount by the exchange rate. For example, $10,600 ÷ $0.0106 per yen = ¥1,000,000.

Now let us assume that the exchange rate for the yen (stated in dollars) rises to $0.0109. At this exchange rate, $1 is equivalent to only ¥92 (¥92 × $0.0109 = $1). In the United States, we would say that the exchange rate for the yen has *risen* from $0.0106 to $0.0109. In Japan, however, they would say that the exchange rate for the dollar has *fallen* from ¥94 to ¥92. In the financial press, it might be said that "the yen has risen against the dollar" or that "the dollar has fallen against the yen." The two statements mean the same thing—that the yen has become more valuable relative to the dollar.

Now let us return to our original phrase, "A strong dollar rose sharply against the weakening British pound, but fell slightly against the Japanese yen and the Swiss franc." When exchange rates are stated in terms of U.S. dollars, this statement means that the price (exchange rate) of the British pound fell sharply, but the prices of the Japanese yen and the Swiss franc rose slightly. A currency is described as "strong" when its exchange rate is rising relative to most other currencies and as "weak" when its exchange rate is falling. Exchange rates fluctuate because of changes in the environmental forces discussed earlier in this chapter.

## Accounting for Transactions with Foreign Companies

**LO 4**

Compute gains or losses on receivables or payables that are stated in a foreign currency when exchange rates fluctuate.

When a U.S. company buys or sells merchandise in a transaction with a foreign company, the transaction price may be stipulated either in U.S. dollars or in units of the foreign currency. If the price is stated in *dollars,* the U.S. company encounters no special accounting problems. The transaction may be recorded in the same manner as are similar transactions with domestic suppliers or customers.

If the transaction price is stated in terms of the *foreign currency,* the company encounters two accounting problems. First, as the U.S. company's accounting records are maintained in dollars, the transaction price must be *translated* into dollars before the transaction can be recorded. The second problem arises when (1) the purchase or sale is made *on account* and (2) the exchange rate *changes* between the date of the transaction and the date that the account is paid. This fluctuation in the exchange rate will cause the U.S. company to experience either a *gain* or a *loss* in the settlement of the transaction.

**Credit Purchases with Prices Stated in a Foreign Currency** Assume that on August 1 a U.S. company buys merchandise from a British company at a price of 10,000 British pounds (£10,000), with payment due in 60 days. The exchange rate on August 1 is *$1.63* per British pound. The entry on August 1 to record this purchase (assuming use of a perpetual inventory system) would be:

*The amount of a foreign currency credit purchase is determined by using the exchange rate on the date it is journalized*

| | | |
|---|---:|---:|
| Inventory | 16,300 | |
|    Accounts Payable | | 16,300 |
| To record the purchase of merchandise from a British company | | |
|   for £10,000 when the exchange rate is $1.63 per pound | | |
|   (£10,000 × $1.63 = $16,300). | | |

Let us now assume that by September 30, when the £10,000 account payable must be paid, the exchange rate has fallen to *$1.61* per British pound. If the U.S. company had paid for the merchandise on August 1, the cost would have been $16,300. On September 30, however, only *$16,100* is needed to pay the £10,000 liability (£10,000 × $1.61 = $16,100). Thus *the decline in the exchange rate has saved the company $200.* This savings is recorded in the accounting records as a *Gain on Fluctuations in Foreign Exchange Rates.* The entry on September 30 to record payment of the liability and recognition of this gain would be:

*The foreign exchange rate gain for the credit purchase is determined by using the exchange rate on the payment date*

| | | |
|---|---:|---:|
| Accounts Payable | 16,300 | |
|    Cash | | 16,100 |
|    Gain on Fluctuations in Foreign Exchange Rates | | 200 |

To record payment of £10,000 liability to British company and to
  recognize gain from decline in exchange rate:

| | |
|---|---|
| Original liability (£10,000 × $1.63) . . . . . . . . . . . . . . . . . . . . | $16,300 |
| Amount paid (£10,000 × $1.61) . . . . . . . . . . . . . . . . . . . . . | 16,100 |
| Gain from decline in exchange rate . . . . . . . . . . . . . . . . . . | $  200 |

Now let us assume that instead of declining, the exchange rate had *increased* from $1.63 on August 1 to *$1.66* on September 30. Under this assumption, the U.S. company would have to pay *$16,600* in order to pay off the £10,000 liability on September 30. Thus the company would be paying *$300 more* than if the liability had been paid on August 1. This additional $300 cost was caused by the increase in the exchange rate and should be recorded as a loss. The entry on September 30 would be:

| | | |
|---|---|---|
| Accounts Payable  . . . . . . . . . . . . . . . . . . . . . . . . . . . . . . . . . . . . | 16,300 | |
| Loss on Fluctuations in Foreign Exchange Rates  . . . . . . . . . . . . . . . . . . . | 300 | |
| Cash . . . . . . . . . . . . . . . . . . . . . . . . . . . . . . . . . . . . . . . . . . . . . . . . | | 16,600 |

To record payment of £10,000 liability to British company and
  to recognize loss from increase in exchange rate:

| | |
|---|---|
| Original liability (£10,000 × $1.63) . . . . . . . . . . . . . . . . . . . . | $16,300 |
| Amount paid (£10,000 × $1.66) . . . . . . . . . . . . . . . . . . . . . | 16,600 |
| Loss from increase in exchange rate . . . . . . . . . . . . . . . . . | $  300 |

*A foreign exchange rate loss occurs if the exchange rate increases between the credit purchase date and the payment date*

In summary, having a liability that is fixed in terms of a foreign currency results in a gain for the debtor if the exchange rate declines between the date of the transaction and the date of payment. The gain results because fewer dollars will be needed to repay the debt than had originally been owed. An increase in the exchange rate, on the other hand, causes the debtor to incur a loss. In this case, the debtor will have to spend more dollars than had originally been owed in order to purchase the foreign currency needed to pay the debt.

**Credit Sales with Prices Stated in a Foreign Currency**   A company that makes credit *sales* at prices stated in a foreign currency also will experience gains or losses from fluctuations in the exchange rate. To illustrate, let us change our preceding example to assume that the U.S. company *sells* merchandise on August 1 to the British company at a price of £10,000. We shall again assume that the exchange rate on August 1 is $1.63 per British pound and that payment is due in 60 days. The entry on August 1 to record this sale would be:

| | | |
|---|---|---|
| Accounts Receivable  . . . . . . . . . . . . . . . . . . . . . . . . . . . . . . . . . . | 16,300 | |
| Sales . . . . . . . . . . . . . . . . . . . . . . . . . . . . . . . . . . . . . . . . . . . . . . . | | 16,300 |

To record sale to British company with sales price set at £10,000
  (£10,000 × $1.63) = $16,300. To be collected in 60 days.

In 60 days (September 30), the U.S. company will collect from the British company the U.S. dollar equivalent of £10,000. If the exchange rate on September 30 has fallen to $1.61 per pound, the U.S. company will collect only $16,100 (£10,000 × $1.61 = $16,100) in full settlement of its account receivable. Since the receivable had originally been equivalent to $16,300, the decline in the exchange rate has caused a loss of $200 to the U.S. company. The entry to be made on September 30 would be:

| | | |
|---|---|---|
| Cash  . . . . . . . . . . . . . . . . . . . . . . . . . . . . . . . . . . . . . . . . . . . . . . | 16,100 | |
| Loss on Fluctuations in Foreign Exchange Rates  . . . . . . . . . . . . . . . . . . . | 200 | |
| Accounts Receivable  . . . . . . . . . . . . . . . . . . . . . . . . . . . . . . . . . . | | 16,300 |

To record collection of £10,000 receivable from British
  company and to recognize loss from fall in exchange
  rate since date of sale:

| | |
|---|---|
| Original sales price (£10,000 × $1.63) . . . . . . . . . . . . . . . . | $16,300 |
| Amount received (£10,000 × $1.61) . . . . . . . . . . . . . . . . . . | 16,100 |
| Loss from decline in exchange rate . . . . . . . . . . . . . . . . . . | $  200 |

*A foreign exchange rate loss occurs when the exchange rate decreases between the credit sales date and the payment date*

Now consider the alternative case, in which the exchange rate rises from $1.63 at August 1 to $1.66 at September 30. In this case, the British company's payment of £10,000 will convert into $16,600, creating a gain for the U.S. company. The entry on September 30 would then be:

| | | |
|---|---|---|
| Cash | 16,600 | |
|     Accounts Receivable | | 16,300 |
|     Gain on Fluctuations in Foreign Exchange Rates | | 300 |
| To record collection of £10,000 receivable from British | | |
|   company and to recognize gain from increase in | | |
|   exchange rate: | | |
|     Original sales price (£10,000 × $1.63) | $16,300 | |
|     Amount received (£10,000 × $1.66) | 16,600 | |
|     Gain from incease in exchange rate | $ 300 | |

### Adjustment of Foreign Receivables and Payables at the Balance Sheet Date

We have seen that fluctuations in exchange rates may cause gains or losses for companies with accounts payable or receivable in foreign currencies. Exchange rates fluctuate on a daily basis. For convenience, however, the company usually waits until the account is paid or collected before recording the related gain or loss. An exception to this convenient practice occurs at the end of the accounting period. An *adjusting entry* is made to recognize any gains or losses that have accumulated on any foreign payables or receivables through the balance sheet date.

To illustrate, assume that on November 10 a U.S. company buys equipment from a Japanese company at a price of 10 million yen (¥10,000,000), payable on January 10 of the following year. If the exchange rate is $0.0100 per yen on November 10, the entry to record the purchase would be:

*Assets purchased on account must be recorded in dollars using the exchange rate on the date of purchase*

| | | |
|---|---|---|
| Equipment | 100,000 | |
|     Accounts Payable | | 100,000 |
| To record purchase of equipment from Japanese company at | | |
|   a price of ¥10,000,000, payable January 10 (¥10,000,000 × | | |
|   $0.0100 = $100,000). | | |

Now assume that on December 31, the exchange rate has fallen to $0.0097 per yen. At this exchange rate, the U.S. company's account payable is equivalent to only $97,000 (¥10,000,000 × $0.0097). Gains and losses from changes in exchange rates are recognized in the period *in which the change occurs*. Therefore, the American company should make an adjusting entry to restate its liability at the current dollar-equivalent and to recognize any related gain or loss. This entry, dated December 31, would be:

*The foreign exchange rate gain on accounts payable is included in year-end statements*

| | | |
|---|---|---|
| Accounts Payable | 3,000 | |
|     Gain on Fluctuations in Foreign Exchange Rates | | 3,000 |
| To adjust balance of ¥10,000,000 account payable to amount | | |
|   indicated by year-end exchange rate: | | |
|     Original account balance | $100,000 | |
|     Adjusted balance (¥10,000,000 × $0.0097) | 97,000 | |
|     Required adjustment | $ 3,000 | |

Similar adjustments should be made for any other accounts payable or receivable at year-end that are fixed in terms of a foreign currency.

If the exchange rate changes again between the date of this adjusting entry and the date that the U.S. company pays the liability, an additional gain or loss must be recognized. Assume, for example, that on January 10 the exchange rate has risen to $0.0099 per yen. The U.S. company must now spend $99,000 to buy the ¥10,000,000 needed to pay its liability to the Japanese company. Thus, the rise in the exchange rate has caused the U.S. company a $2,000 loss since year-end. The entry to record payment of the account on January 10 would be:

| Accounts Payable . . . . . . . . . . . . . . . . . . . . . . . . . . . . . . . . . . . . . . . . . . . | 97,000 | |
| Loss on Fluctuations in Foreign Exchange Rates . . . . . . . . . . . . . . . . . . . . | 2,000 | |
|    Cash . . . . . . . . . . . . . . . . . . . . . . . . . . . . . . . . . . . . . . . . . . . . . . . . . . | | 99,000 |

To record payment of ¥10,000,000 payable to Japanese company and to recognize loss from rise in exchange rate since year-end:

| Account payable, December 31 . . . . . . . . . . . . . . . . . . . . . . . . . . . . . | $97,000 |
| Amount paid, January 10 . . . . . . . . . . . . . . . . . . . . . . . . . . . . . . . . . | 99,000 |
| Loss from increase in exchange rate . . . . . . . . . . . . . . . . . . . . . . . . | $ 2,000 |

Notice the *overall effect* of entering into this credit transaction stated in yen was a $1,000 gain due to fluctuations in the exchange rate for the yen between November 10 and the date of payment (January 10). The U.S. company recognized a $3,000 gain on fluctuations in the exchange rate from November 10 through the balance sheet date (December 31). This was partially offset in the next fiscal year by a $2,000 loss on fluctuations in the exchange rate between December 31 and January 10. The overall effect can be computed directly by multiplying the amount of the foreign currency times the *change* in exchange rates between the transaction date and the payment date (¥10,000,000 × [$0.0100 − $0.0099] = $1,000 gain).

---

Notice that the cash effects from foreign exchange rate fluctuations for associated transactions do not occur until the transaction is completed and the payment is made. That is, foreign exchange rate gains or losses recorded for receivables or payables do not involve cash flows (excluding tax effects). As we have demonstrated, the cash flow effect of the exchange rate fluctuation associated with the credit transaction for the purchase of equipment occurs on the date of payment, January 10 (expected cash outflow = $100,000; actual cash outflow = $99,000). The $3,000 gain recorded at the balance sheet date and the $2,000 loss recorded at the date of payment have no associated cash flow effects.

**CASH EFFECTS**

---

Gains and losses from fluctuations in exchange rates on transactions carried out in a foreign currency should be included in the income statement. They typically follow income from operations and are presented in a manner much like interest expense and gains and losses on the sale of plant assets.

## Currency Fluctuations—Who Wins and Who Loses?

Gains and losses from fluctuations in exchange rates are sustained by companies (or individuals) that have either payables or receivables that are *fixed in terms of a foreign currency.* United States companies that import foreign products usually have large foreign liabilities. Companies that export U.S. products to other countries are likely to have large receivables stated in foreign currencies.

As foreign exchange rates (stated in dollars) *fall,* U.S.-based importers will gain and exporters will lose. When a foreign exchange rate falls, the foreign currency becomes *less expensive.* Therefore, importers will have to spend fewer dollars to pay their foreign liabilities. Exporters, on the other hand, will have to watch their foreign receivables become worth fewer and fewer dollars.

When foreign exchange rates *rise,* this situation reverses. Importers will lose, because more dollars are required to pay the foreign debts. Exporters will gain, because their foreign receivables become equivalent to an increasing number of dollars.

**Strategies to Avoid Losses from Rate Fluctuations**  There are two basic approaches to avoiding losses from fluctuations in foreign exchange rates. One approach is to insist that receivables and payables be settled at specified amounts of domestic currency. The other approach is called *hedging* and can be accomplished in a number of ways.

To illustrate the first approach, assume that a U.S. company makes large credit sales to companies in Mexico, but anticipates that the exchange rate for the Mexican peso will gradually decline. The U.S. company can avoid losses by setting its *sales prices in dollars*. Then, if the exchange rate does decline, the Mexican companies will have to spend more pesos to pay for their purchases, but the U.S. company will not receive fewer dollars. On the other hand, the U.S. company will benefit from making credit *purchases* from Mexican companies at *prices stated in pesos,* because a decline in the exchange rate will reduce the number of dollars needed to pay for these purchases.

The interests of the Mexican companies, however, are exactly the opposite of those of the U.S. company. If the Mexican companies anticipate an increase in the exchange rate for the U.S. dollar, they will want to buy at prices stated in pesos and sell at prices stated in dollars. Ultimately, the manner in which the transactions will be priced simply depends on which company is in the better bargaining position.

**LO 5**

Describe several techniques for "hedging" against losses from fluctuations in exchange rates.

**Hedging**   **Hedging** refers to the strategy of "sitting on both sides of the fence"—that is, of taking offsetting positions so that your gains and losses tend to offset one another. To illustrate the concept, assume that you make a large bet on a football game. Later you have second thoughts about the bet, and you want to eliminate your risk of incurring a loss. You could "hedge" your original bet by making a similar bet on the other team. In this way, you will lose one bet, but you will win the other—your loss will be offset by a corresponding gain.

A company that has similar amounts of accounts receivable and accounts payable in the same foreign currency automatically has a hedged position. A decrease in the foreign exchange rate will cause losses on the foreign receivables and gains on the foreign payables. If the exchange rate rises, the gains on the foreign receivables will be offset by losses on the foreign payables.

Most companies, of course, do *not* have similar amounts of receivables and payables in the same foreign currency. However, they may create this situation by buying or selling foreign currency **future contracts**. These contracts, commonly called *futures,* are the right to receive a specified quantity of foreign currency at a future date. In short, they are accounts receivable in foreign currency. Thus a company that has only foreign accounts payable may hedge its position by purchasing a similar dollar amount of foreign currency future contracts. Then, if the exchange rate rises, any losses on the foreign payables will be offset by a gain in the value of the future contracts.

A company with only foreign receivables may hedge its position by *selling* future contracts, thus receiving dollars today and *creating a liability* payable in foreign currency.

**Exchange Rates and Competitive Prices**   Up to this point, we have discussed only the gains and losses incurred by companies that have receivables or payables stated in a foreign currency. However, fluctuations in exchange rates change the *relative prices* of goods produced in different countries. Exchange rate fluctuations may make the prices of a country's products more or less competitive both at home and to customers throughout the world. Even a small store with no foreign accounts receivable or payable may find its business operations greatly affected by fluctuations in foreign exchange rates.

Consider, for example, a small store in Kansas that sells a U.S.-made brand of television sets. If foreign exchange rates fall, which happens when the dollar is strong, the price of foreign-made television sets will decline. Thus, the store selling U.S.-made television sets may have to compete with stores selling imported television sets at lower prices. Also, a strong dollar makes U.S. goods *more expensive to customers in foreign countries*. Thus a U.S. television manufacturer will find it more difficult to sell its products abroad.

The situation reverses when the dollar is weak—that is, when foreign exchange rates are relatively high. A weak dollar makes foreign imports more expensive to U.S. consumers. Also, a weak dollar makes U.S. products less expensive to customers in foreign countries.

**You as a Consumer**

Assume you are in the market for a new racing bicycle. You are considering buying an Italian, British, or U.S. racing bicycle. You have recently heard news that the dollar is strengthening against the Italian lira and is falling against the British pound. These trends are expected to continue for another month. How would this news affect your assessment of choices among racing bicycles?

*Our comments appear on page 690.

**YOUR TURN**

In summary, we may say that a strong U.S. dollar *helps companies that sell foreign-made goods in the U.S. market.* A weak dollar, on the other hand, *gives a competitive advantage to companies that sell U.S. products both at home and abroad.*

## Consolidated Financial Statements That Include Foreign Subsidiaries

In Chapter 14, we discussed the concept of *consolidated* financial statements. These statements view the operations of the parent company and its subsidiaries as if the affiliated companies were a single business entity. Several special accounting problems arise in preparing consolidated financial statements when subsidiaries operate in foreign countries. First, the accounting records of the foreign subsidiaries must be translated into U.S. dollars. Second, the accounting principles in use in the foreign countries may differ significantly from U.S. generally accepted accounting principles.

These problems pose interesting challenges to professional accountants and will be addressed in later accounting courses. Readers of the financial statements of U.S.-based corporations, however, should know that the consolidated financial statements of these companies are expressed in U.S. dollars and conform to U.S. generally accepted accounting principles.

## GLOBAL SOURCING

Differences in exchange rates can create significant complexities for firms practicing global sourcing. An article in the *Los Angeles Times* illustrated the additional problems associated with determining the cost of producing a doll using inputs from several countries. The exhibit on page 674 traces the multicountry path of a Barbie™ doll from its raw materials source in a Saudi Arabian oil field to U.S. toy stores. After the oil is refined to produce ethylene, Taiwan uses the ethylene to produce vinyl pellets that are shipped to Dongguan in China's Guangdong province. At the Chinese joint-venture factory, 5,500 workers, paid between $30 and $40 per month, make the plastic doll and her clothes. However, most of the machinery and tools, including the plastic mold injection machines, are imported from the United States, Europe, and Japan. The molds themselves come directly from the United States. Japan contributes Barbie™'s nylon hair. Hong Kong manages the entire process, arranging banking and insurance, supervising exporting and importing, and overseeing transportation back to the United States. Finally, U.S. domestic packaging, trucking, advertising, and other functions that employ thousands of U.S. workers result in a $10.00 Barbie™ at your local toy store. **Mattel Inc.** has indicated that the typical profit from the sale of a Barbie™ is about $1.00.

**LO 6**

Understand how global sourcing increases product cost complexity.

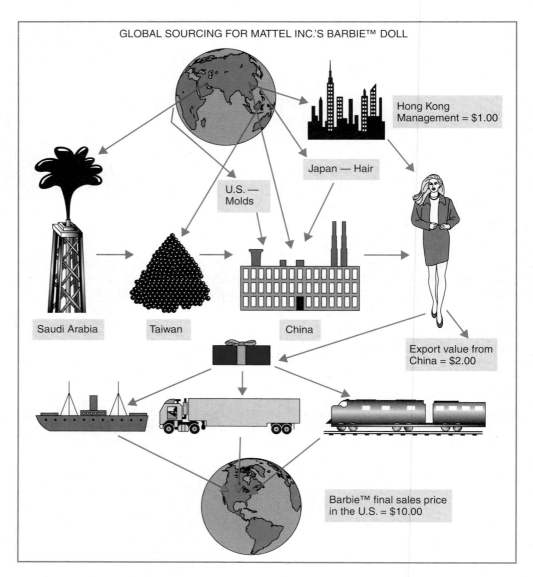

The table below illustrates the costs and exchange rate issues involved in the production of a Barbie™ doll. Panel A below provides the currency exchange rates for the countries involved in global sourcing for the Barbie™ doll. Panel B includes estimated product export costs for the **Mattel Inc.** Barbie™ made at the Meitai factory in Dongguan, China. The estimated costs in the exhibit are based on a single day's reported exchange rates (January 10, 2000). Companies must choose a representative exchange rate to compute the cost buildup in their domestic currency.

| Estimated Product Cost for Barbie™* | | |
| --- | --- | --- |
| **Panel A: Exchange Rates†** | | |
| **Country** | **Currency** | **U.S. $ Equivalent** |
| Saudi Arabia | Riyal | .2667 |
| Taiwan | Taiwanese dollar | .0326 |
| Hong Kong | Hong Kong dollar | .1286 |
| Japan | Yen | .0095 |
| China | Renminbi | .1225 |
| †Based on exchange rates from www.xe.net/ucc/, January 10, 2000. | | |

| Estimated Product Cost for Barbie™* (continued) | | |
|---|---|---|
| **Panel B: Estimated Product Cost Buildup** | | |
| **Input** | **Foreign Currency Value** | **U.S. $ Equivalent** |
| Raw materials: | | |
| Saudi Arabia | 0.6374 riyal | $0.17 |
| Taiwan | 4.908 Taiwanese dollars | 0.16 |
| Japan | 22.11 yen | 0.21 |
| China | 0.898 renminbi | 0.11 |
| Direct labor: | | |
| China | 2.857 renminbi | 0.35 |
| Overhead: | | |
| Hong Kong | 7.776 Hong Kong dollars | 1.00 |
| Total export cost | | $2.00 |

*Estimates based on information provided in R. Tempest, "Barbie and the World Economy," *Los Angeles Times,* September 22, 1996, p. 1.

The information in the exhibit and associated table do not provide details about customs duties, import and export fees, multicountry tax laws, and tax treaties. These are also costs of doing business in a global environment. Many companies underestimate the cost of globalizing their business operations because they are not familiar with the environmental characteristics discussed at the beginning of this chapter. Making accurate estimates of costs for global sourcing is a challenge for companies wishing to become more global.

## Foreign Corrupt Practices Act

In many countries, product costs also include expenses incurred to expedite official paperwork. Kenyan business executives refer to *kitu kidogo* ("something small"), the Chinese pay *huilu,* Russians shell out *vzyatka,* and Middle Easterners pay *baksheesh.* In dozens of countries around the world, bribery is part of doing business. In many countries, this officially sanctioned corruption is not viewed as wrong or unethical. However, U.S.-based businesses are prohibited from influence peddling. The **Foreign Corrupt Practices Act** (FCPA), passed in 1977 and amended in 1986 by the U.S. Congress, prescribes fines and jail time for American managers violating its rules. Over the past 20 years, some U.S. companies have complained about the advantage experienced by international competitors who are not bound by the FCPA.

Experiences in the past 5 to 10 years have changed international attitudes about the impact of corrupt practices on economic viability. In particular, the 1997–1998 Asian crisis was blamed partly on graft and influence peddling. According to some estimates, corruption associated with doing business in China can add 5 percent to operating costs. Corruption can be so rampant that companies refuse to operate in some foreign locations, causing countries to lose valuable direct foreign investment.

The International Monetary Fund and the World Bank instituted policies in the late 1990s to cut off funding to countries ignoring corrupt practices. In 1997, $292 million in loans to Kenya were suspended until policies and procedures to prevent corruption were instituted. Many of the recommended policies and procedures are modeled after the FCPA. The scope of the FCPA is very broad. Under FCPA rules, it is illegal for all U.S. companies, their affiliates, and their agents to bribe a government official. Criminal and civil prosecution can lead to fines of up to $2 million for the company and $100,000 for executives involved, with prison terms of up to five years.

**YOUR TURN**

### You as Head of International Acquisitions

Assume you are the head of international acquisitions for a large multinational toy company traded on the New York Stock Exchange. You have been involved for several months in a deal to acquire a large facility in a midsize city in central China that will be remodeled by your company to produce a range of toy products for the Chinese market. For a variety of reasons, progress has been extremely slow on completing the acquisition. In particular, city administrators have continually delayed issuing the necessary paperwork. You decide to fly to China to meet with the city's top three officials. During your meeting it becomes clear that the three city officials would guarantee processing the associated paperwork much faster if your company would provide a significant payment to each of them to help expedite the necessary work. These administrators pointed out that a German company that acquired a facility in the city the previous year was willing to pay extra to expedite paperwork.

Your CEO has made it clear to you that the China project is very important and expediting it is critical for its long-run success. What should you do?

*Our comments appear on p. 690.

**LO 7**

Explain the importance of the Foreign Corrupt Practices Act.

The FCPA has implications for accounting in two specific areas: record keeping and internal control procedures. The act requires that all payments, including improper payments, be recorded and disclosed. Further, the act requires an adequate system of internal controls that maintains the integrity of the company's assets, allowing only authorized personnel to have access to them. The 1986 amendment to the FCPA distinguished between *influence peddling,* to motivate the awarding of business that would not otherwise have been awarded, and *facilitating payments,* to motivate officials to undertake actions more rapidly than they might otherwise. A facilitating payment might be given to a customs official to expedite imported merchandise through customs. This latter type of payment is not illegal under the act. Companies engaging in globalization must ensure that their cross-border employees comply with the FCPA.

**A SECOND LOOK**

### The Carlsberg Group

**Carlsberg** sells its product in 150 markets worldwide and has 73 local brewing production facilities in more than 40 countries. Some of these production facilities involve licensing arrangements, some are joint ventures, and others are wholly owned subsidiaries. They are a truly global public company, but their shares are not quoted on any U.S. stock exchanges. The financial reporting requirements for U.S. exchanges are more stringent than other exchanges and these requirements sometimes discourage companies from trying to list their shares on U.S. exchanges.

Production facilities in multiple countries create issues, including exchange rate fluctuations, that complicate **Carlsberg**'s ability to manage. Accounting information is a very important component of the information used by **Carlsberg** to help them operate in their global environment. Both financial and managerial accounting information are critical for making operating decisions and understanding the results of those decisions.

In the next chapter, you will learn how management accounting systems help companies like **Carlsberg** to manage their global operations. You will see how these systems (1) provide a means of assigning decision-making authority, (2) present information useful to decision-makers, and (3) help evaluate the decisions made by managers.

## SUMMARY OF LEARNING OBJECTIVES

### LO 1

**Define four mechanisms companies use to globalize their business activities.**

Companies globalize their business activities through exporting, licensing, joint ventures, and wholly owned subsidiaries. Multinational companies use a global sourcing approach.

### LO 2

**Identify how global environmental forces—(a) political and legal systems, (b) economic systems, (c) culture, and (d) technology and infrastructure—affect a company's ability to compete globally.**

Countries use their political and legal systems to transfer and control business assets. Market versus centrally planned economic systems create different demands on business enterprises. Culture influences business relationships through beliefs and expectations of customers and business associates. The technology and infrastructure of each global location will affect the type and costs of business activities.

### LO 3

**Demonstrate how to convert an amount of money from one currency to another.**

To convert a foreign currency to an equivalent dollar amount, multiply the foreign currency by the foreign exchange rate. To convert a dollar amount into an equivalent amount of foreign currency, divide the dollar amount by the exchange rate.

### LO 4

**Compute gains or losses on receivables or payables that are stated in a foreign currency when exchange rates fluctuate.**

The receivable or payable is recorded on the date the transaction is agreed to using the prevailing exchange rate. When exchanging cash completes the transaction, the exchange rate at the completion date is used to record the cash flow; the difference between the cash exchanged and the receivable or payable is recorded as a foreign exchange gain or loss.

### LO 5

**Describe several techniques for "hedging" against losses from fluctuations in exchange rates.**

Hedging is offsetting the potential for losses from foreign exchange rate fluctuations. It can be accomplished by having offsetting receivables and payables in the foreign currency or by buying or selling foreign currency future contracts.

### LO 6

**Understand how global sourcing increases product cost complexity.**

When some of the activities of designing, developing, producing, marketing, and servicing a product or service occur in more than one country, then global considerations affect product costs. These considerations include foreign exchange gains and losses, taxes, import and export duties, trade agreements, foreign trade zones, and limitations on currency flows.

### LO 7

**Explain the importance of the Foreign Corrupt Practices Act.**

The FCPA prohibits influence peddling through bribery in international locations. The act requires companies engaged in global business activities to maintain good record keeping and adequate internal controls to safeguard company assets.

In this chapter, we introduced basic international business terminology and ideas. We discussed the variety of global business environments companies face when creating international business opportunities. The variety of environments causes differences in externally reported accounting information and internal accounting information use and demand. Keep in mind the international dimensions discussed here and question their impact on the ideas presented earlier in this book.

## KEY TERMS INTRODUCED OR EMPHASIZED IN CHAPTER 15

**cross-border financing** (p. 661) Occurs when a company sells its securities in the capital markets of another country.

**exchange rate** (p. 667) The amount it costs to purchase one unit of currency with another currency.

**exporting** (p. 658) Selling a good or service to a foreign customer in a foreign country.

**Foreign Corrupt Practices Act** (p. 675) Passed in 1977 and amended in 1986 by the U.S. Congress, prescribes fines and jail time for American managers violating its rules. It distinguishes between illegal influence peddling to motivate awarding of business that would not otherwise have been awarded and legal facilitating payments made to motivate officials to undertake actions more rapidly than they might otherwise.

**foreign trade zones** (p. 661) Goods imported into these designated U.S. areas are duty free until they leave the zone.

**future contracts** (p. 672) A contract giving the right to receive a specified quantity of foreign currency at a future date.

**globalization** (p. 658) The process of managers becoming aware of the impact of international activities on the future of their company.

**global sourcing** (p. 659) The close coordination of R&D, manufacturing, and marketing across national boundaries.

**harmonization of accounting standards** (p. 662) The standardization of accounting methods and principles used in different countries throughout the world.

**hedging** (p. 672) The practice of minimizing or eliminating risk of loss associated with foreign currency fluctuations.

**industrial organizations** (p. 663) Exist when companies group themselves into conglomerates representing different industries. South Korean conglomerates, called *chaebol,* and Japanese conglomerates, called *keiretsu,* consist of companies that are grouped as customers and suppliers and usually contain a bank.

**infrastructure** (p. 666) Access to communication, transportation, and utilities provided to businesses in each global location.

**International Accounting Standards Committee** (p. 662) Established in 1973 and charged with the responsibility of creating and promulgating international standards.

**international joint venture** (p. 659) A company owned by two or more companies from different countries.

**international licensing** (p. 658) A contractual agreement between a company and a foreign party allowing the use of trade-marks, patents, technology, designs, processes, intellectual property, or other proprietary advantage.

**maquiladora** (p. 661) A joint venture manufacturing plant located in Mexico that enjoys exceptions from Mexican laws governing foreign companies. The United States allows exemptions from, or reductions in, customs duties on re-exported goods from maquiladoras.

**market economics** (p. 662) Exist when ownership of land and the means of production are private and markets dictate the allocation of resources and the output among segments of the economy.

**planned economy** (p. 662) Exists when the government uses central planning to allocate resources and determine output among various segments of the economy. Government ownership of land and the means of production characterize planned economies.

**regional value content** (p. 660) Rules that dictate the amount of total cost that must be added in those countries that have signed a free trade agreement. Products that satisfy these rules receive favorable tariffs and custom duty.

**wholly owned international subsidiary** (p. 659) Created through a company's foreign direct investment; using domestically generated funds in another country to purchase 100% equity control of a foreign subsidiary.

# DEMONSTRATION PROBLEM

IronMan, Inc., is a U.S. company that manufactures exercise machines and distributes several lines of imported bicycles. Selected transactions of the company are as follows:

**Oct. 4**    Purchased manufacturing equipment from Rhine Mfg. Co., a German company. The purchase price was DM400,000, due in 60 days. Current exchange rate, $0.7020 per deutsche mark. (Debit the Equipment account.)

**Oct. 18**    Purchased 2,500 racing bicycles from Ninja Cycles, a Japanese company, at a price of ¥60,000,000. Payment is due in 90 days; the current exchange rate is $0.0110 per yen. (IronMan uses the perpetual inventory system.)

**Nov. 15**    Purchased 1,000 touring bicycles from Royal Lion Ltd., a British corporation. The purchase price was £192,500, payable in 30 days. Current exchange rate, $1.65 per British pound.

**Dec. 3**    Issued a check to First Bank for the U.S. dollar-equivalent of DM400,000 in payment of the account payable to Rhine Mfg. Co. Current exchange rate, $0.7110 per deutsche mark.

**Dec. 15**    Issued a check to First Bank for dollar-equivalent of £192,500 in payment of the account payable to Royal Lion Ltd. Current exchange rate, $1.60 per British pound.

## Instructions

**a.** Prepare entries in general journal form to record the preceding transactions.

**b.** Prepare the December 31 adjusting entry relating to the account payable to Ninja Cycles. The year-end exchange rate is $0.0113 per Japanese yen.

**c.** Identify some methods that IronMan, Inc., could use to decrease its exposure to foreign exchange rate fluctuations.

**d.** Discuss environmental characteristics of Japan, Germany, and the United Kingdom that influence their exchange rate fluctuations.

## Solution to the Demonstration Problem

**a.** The general journal entries to record the transactions are as follows:

| **GENERAL JOURNAL** | | | |
|---|---|---|---|
| **Date** | **Account Titles and Explanation** | **Debit** | **Credit** |
| Oct. 4 | Equipment . . . . . . . . . . . . . . . . . . . . . . . . . . . . . . . . . . . | 280,800 | |
| | Accounts Payable (Rhine Mfg. Co.) . . . . . . . . . . . . . . . | | 280,800 |
| | To record purchase of equipment from Rhine Mfg. Co. for DM400,000, exchange rate $0.7020 per deutsche mark (DM400,000 × $0.7020 = $280,800). | | |
| Oct. 18 | Inventory . . . . . . . . . . . . . . . . . . . . . . . . . . . . . . . . . . . | 660,000 | |
| | Accounts Payable (Ninja Cycles) . . . . . . . . . . . . . . . . | | 660,000 |
| | Purchase 2,500 bicycles from Ninja Cycles for ¥60,000,000, exchange rate $0.0110 (¥60,000,000 × $0.0110 = $660,000). | | |
| Nov. 15 | Inventory . . . . . . . . . . . . . . . . . . . . . . . . . . . . . . . . . . . | 317,625 | |
| | Accounts Payable (Royal Lion Ltd.) . . . . . . . . . . . . . . . | | 317,625 |
| | Purchased 1,000 bicycles from Royal Lion Ltd. for £192,500, due in 30 days. Exchange rate $1.65 per pound (£192,500 × $1.65 = $317,625). | | |
| Dec. 3 | Accounts Payable (Rhine Mfg. Co.) . . . . . . . . . . . . . . . . . | 280,800 | |
| | Loss on Fluctuations of Foreign Exchange Rates . . . . . . . . | 3,600 | |
| | Cash . . . . . . . . . . . . . . . . . . . . . . . . . . . . . . . . . . . . . | | 284,400 |
| | Paid DM400,000 liability to Rhine Mfg. Co. (Original balance less amount paid equals loss: $280,800 − (DM400,000 × $0.7110) = −$3,600). | | |
| Dec. 15 | Accounts Payable (Royal Lion Ltd.) . . . . . . . . . . . . . . . . . | 317,625 | |
| | Gain on Fluctuations of Foreign Exchange Rates . . . . . . | | 9,625 |
| | Cash . . . . . . . . . . . . . . . . . . . . . . . . . . . . . . . . . . . . . | | 308,000 |
| | Paid £192,500 liability to Royal Lion Ltd. (Original balance less amount paid equals gain: $317,625 − (£192,500 × $1.60) = $9,625). | | |

**b.** The December 31 adjusting entry for the account payable to Ninja Cycles:

| **GENERAL JOURNAL** | | | |
|---|---|---|---|
| **Date** | **Account Titles and Explanation** | **Debit** | **Credit** |
| Dec. 31 | Loss on Fluctuations in Foreign Exchange Rates . . . . . . . . . . | 18,000 | |
| | Accounts Payable (Ninja Cycles) . . . . . . . . . . . . . . . . . . . | | 18,000 |
| | To adjust balance of ¥60,000,000 liability to amount indicated by year-end exchange rate: (Original balance less adjusted balance equals loss: $660,000 − (¥60,000,000 × $0.0113) = − $18,000). | | |

**c.** IronMan could use offsetting payables and receivables to control potential foreign exchange rate losses. For example, if IronMan could export its exercise equipment to Japan, then it would have a receivable to offset its payable. IronMan could also purchase future contracts maturing at the same time the liabilities were due. Gains and losses on the future contracts would offset gains and losses resulting from foreign currency fluctuations.

**d.** Germany has a lower volume and smaller capitalized equities market. Banks are the major providers of capital to businesses in Germany. Japan has *keiretsu* organizations for many of its industrial groups. These organizations include manufacturers, distributors, wholesalers, retailers, and suppliers who work together and share resources. The accounting profession is much weaker in both Germany and Japan than in the United States. The United Kingdom is most like the United States with active equity markets, a strong accounting profession, and similar accounting rules.

## SELF-TEST QUESTIONS

*Answers to these questions appear on page 690.*

1. Which of the following statements are *true* about globalization methods? (Identify all correct answers.)
   a. International licensing involves the creation of a new company that is owned by two or more firms from different countries.
   b. Exporting involves contracts that allow a foreign company to use a domestic company's trademarks, patents, processes, or technology.
   c. Global sourcing involves the close coordination of research and development, purchasing, marketing, and manufacturing across national boundaries.
   d. A wholly owned international subsidiary is created when a foreign government owns 100% of the equity in a U.S.-based firm.

2. Which of the following environmental factors can affect the cost of doing business in a foreign country?
   a. The educational level of the workforce.
   b. Laws regulating the transfer of profits out of a country.
   c. Tax and tariff regulations.
   d. Restricted access to communication and transportation networks.

3. A country whose citizens are highly group oriented and who accept unequal power distributions between and within organizations would be considered:
   a. Individualistic and low power distance.
   b. Collectivist and high power distance.
   c. Individualistic and high power distance.
   d. Collectivist and low power distance.

4. On March 1, Laton Products (a U.S. firm) purchased manufacturing inputs from a Mexican supplier for 20,000 pesos, payable on June 1. The exchange rate for pesos on March 1 was $0.17. If the exchange rate increases to $0.19 on June 1, what amount of gain or loss would be reported by Laton related to the currency exchange?
   a. $400 gain.
   b. $200 loss.
   c. $400 loss.
   d. $200 gain.

5. On January 1, a German company purchased merchandise from a U.S. firm for $50,000, payable on March 1. The exchange rate for deutsche marks on January 1 was $0.70. If the exchange rate increases to $0.72 on March 1, what amount of gain or loss would the U.S. firm report related to currency fluctuations?
   a. $1,000 gain.
   b. $1,000 loss.
   c. $500 gain.
   d. No gain or loss would be reported.

## ASSIGNMENT MATERIAL

## DISCUSSION QUESTIONS

1. In general terms, identify several factors that prompt different countries to develop different accounting principles.

2. What is the International Accounting Standards Committee? Why has the committee been unable to obtain global application of its standards?

3. Translate the following amounts of foreign currency into an equivalent number of U.S. dollars using the exchange rates in the table on page 667.

   **a.** £800,000

   **b.** ¥350,000

   **c.** DM50,000

4. Assume that a U.S. company makes a purchase from a German company and agrees to pay a price of 2 million deutsche marks.

   **a.** How will the U.S. company determine the cost of this purchase for the purpose of recording it in the accounting records?

   **b.** Briefly explain how a U.S. company can arrange the payment of deutsche marks to a German company.

5. A recent newspaper shows the exchange rate for the British pound at $1.63 and for the yen at $0.0106. Does this indicate that the pound is a stronger currency than the yen? Explain.

6. Explain how an increase in a foreign exchange rate will affect a U.S. company that makes:

   **a.** Credit sales to a foreign company at prices stated in the foreign currency.

   **b.** Credit purchases from a foreign company at prices stated in the foreign currency.

   **c.** Credit sales to a foreign company at prices stated in U.S. dollars.

7. You are the purchasing agent for a U.S. business that purchases merchandise on account from companies in Mexico. The exchange rate for the Mexican peso has been falling against the dollar and the trend is expected to continue for at least several months. Would you prefer that the prices for purchases from the Mexican companies be specified in U.S. dollars or in Mexican pesos? Explain.

8. CompuTech is a U.S.-based multinational corporation. Foreign sales are made at prices set in U.S. dollars, but foreign purchases are often made at prices stated in foreign currencies. If the exchange rate for the U.S. dollar has risen against most foreign currencies throughout the year, would CompuTech have recognized primarily gains or losses as a result of exchange rate fluctuations? Explain.

9. Explain two ways in which a company that makes purchases on account from foreign companies can protect itself against the losses that would arise from a sudden increase in the foreign exchange rate.

10. What does the *globalization* of business mean? Think of two companies with which you are familiar. How would you describe their level of globalization?

11. Why is it important for a company and its management accountants to understand its level of globalization?

12. You've just read in *The Wall Street Journal* that the U.S. dollar has weakened relative to the Italian lira. All else equal, what would you expect to happen to the quantity of Italian leather jackets sold in the United States? Why?

13. A U.S. company purchased a shipment of fabrics from Bahrain for 3,500,000 dinars. At current exchange rates, what is the value of this contract in U.S. dollars?

14. What is the difference between an international licensing agreement and an international joint venture?

15. If a company seeks to increase its level of globalization through an outward growth path, what types of activities is it likely to engage in?

16. To maintain a high level of control over production operations and final product quality, what types of globalization activities could a company engage in?

17. How might the organization of a production process differ between countries that are individualistic and collectivist?

18. What do the phrases *high power distance* and *low power distance* mean? How would the organizational structures of companies operating in high and low power distance countries differ?

19. A French furniture maker agrees to purchase wood stain from a U.S. paint manufacturer. If all payments are to be made in U.S. dollars, which company bears the risk of exchange rate gains and losses?

20. In the United States, what is a foreign trade zone? What is the advantage of operating in one?

21. What is meant by the phrase *natural hedging against exchange rate risk?*

# EXERCISES

**EXERCISE 15.1**

Global Business Terminology

**LO 1–7**

The following are nine global business terms used in this chapter:

| | | |
|---|---|---|
| Hedging | Foreign exchange risk | International Accounting |
| Foreign Corrupt | Planned economy | Standards Committee |
| Practices Act | International licensing | Harmonization |
| Globalization | | Exporting |

Each of the following statements may describe one of these terms. For each statement, indicate the global business term described, or answer "None" if the statement does not correctly describe any of the terms.

a. The amount it costs to purchase one unit of currency with another currency.

b. Selling a good or service to a foreign customer.

c. A cross-border contractual agreement allowing one company to use trademarks, patents, or technology of another company.

d. Distinguishes between illegal influence peddling and legal facilitating payments.

e. The practice of minimizing or eliminating risk of loss associated with foreign currency fluctuations.

f. Markets dictate the allocation of resources and output among segments of the economy.

g. The group charged with the responsibility of creating and encouraging the use of international accounting standards.

**EXERCISE 15.2**

External Financial Reports and Globalization

**LO 1, 2**

With a group of two or three students, choose a publicly traded global company that you think you might want to invest in some time in the future. Use the Internet or annual report data to answer the following questions.

a. In which geographical regions does the company operate?

b. What is the proportion of total sales represented by foreign sales? How has this changed over the past 5 to 10 years?

c. What efforts has the company recently undertaken to increase/decrease globalization (for example, joint ventures, licensing agreements, etc.)?

d. What are the company's hedging practices/policies?

e. Have any overseas activities been unsuccessful, discontinued, or resulted in asset losses? If so, what happened?

f. Overall, how aggressively do you feel this company is pursuing globalization?

**EXERCISE 15.3**

NAFTA and Regional Value Content

**LO 2, 6**

To qualify for favorable tariff and customs duty treatment under NAFTA, a product or service must meet regional value content requirements. The regional value content is defined as the final selling price of the good or service less costs incurred outside the United States, Canada, or Mexico. The regional value content must be (1) greater than or equal to 60% of the selling price of the finished good or (2) greater than or equal to 50% of the cost of the finished good.

Larron Products manufactures an electronic sensor that it markets and sells in the United States. Components from Germany and Japan are shipped to Mexico, where they are assembled into the final product and shipped to the United States. The current sales price per unit is $1,600 and

10,000 units are expected to be sold during the coming year. Per-unit costs of producing the sensor are as follows:

| | |
|---|---|
| German components | $100 |
| Japanese components | 500 |
| Mexican labor and materials | 400 |

Perform the computations to determine if this sensor qualifies for favorable treatment under either of the NAFTA content requirements (60% of the selling price or 50% of the cost).

The Central Intelligence Agency (CIA) of the U.S. government maintains an Internet site containing information on various countries (www.odci.gov/cia/publications/factbook/index.html/). The site is a database known as the "World Fact Book." Use the CIA data or other publicly available data (for example, the State Department's website: (www.state.gov/www/issues/economic/trade_reports) to answer the following questions about Indonesia.

**a.** What are the country's main exports and imports?

**b.** What is the educational and job classification composition of the labor force?

**c.** How would you describe the infrastructure and technology base of the country?

**d.** What are the political and legal risks of doing business there?

**e.** If you were advising a U.S. company that wanted to locate a wholly owned subsidiary in Indonesia, what aspects of the country would you stress that management take into account when deciding whether to invest there and how to organize the subsidiary's manufacturing process?

**EXERCISE 15.4**

Locating International Business Information

**LO 2, 6, 7**

Indicate whether each of the companies or individuals in the following independent cases would benefit more from a strong U.S. dollar (relatively low foreign exchange rates) or a weak U.S. dollar (relatively high foreign exchange rates). Provide a brief explanation of your reasoning.

**a. Boeing** (a U.S. aircraft manufacturer that sells many planes to foreign customers)

**b.** A **Nikon** camera store in Beverly Hills, California (Nikon cameras are made in Japan.)

**c. Toyota** (made by the Japanese auto manufacturer in Japan)

**d.** The Mexico City dealer for **Caterpillar** tractors (made in the United States)

**e.** A U.S. tourist visiting England

**f.** A small store that sells U.S.-made video recorders in Toledo, Ohio. (The store has no foreign accounts receivable or payable.)

**EXERCISE 15.5**

Currency Fluctuations: Who Wins and Who Loses?

**LO 2, 4**

The following table summarizes the facts of five independent cases (labeled **a** through **e**) of U.S. companies engaging in credit transactions with foreign corporations while the foreign exchange rate is fluctuating:

**EXERCISE 15.6**

Foreign Currency Transactions

**LO 3, 4**

| | Column | | | |
|---|---|---|---|---|
| Case | Type of Credit Transaction 1 | Currency Used in Contract 2 | Exchange Rate Direction 3 | Effect on Income 4 |
| a | Sales | Foreign currency | Falling | _____ |
| b | Purchases | U.S. dollars | Rising | _____ |
| c | _____ | Foreign currency | Rising | Loss |
| d | Sales | _____ | Falling | No effect |
| e | Purchases | Foreign currency | _____ | Gain |

You are to fill in each blank space after evaluating the information about the case provided in the other three columns. The content of each column and the word or words that you should enter in the blank spaces are described as follows:

*Column 1* indicates the type of credit transaction in which the U.S. company engaged with the foreign corporations. The answer entered in this column should be either *Sales* or *Purchases*.

*Column 2* indicates the currency in which the invoice price is stated. The answer may be either *U.S. dollars* or *Foreign currency*.

*Column 3* indicates the direction in which the foreign currency exchange rate has moved between the date of the credit transaction and the date of settlement. The answer entered in this column may be either *Rising* or *Falling*.

*Column 4* indicates the effect of the exchange rate fluctuation on the income of the American company. The answers entered in this column are to be selected from the following: *Gain, Loss,* or *No effect.*

**EXERCISE 15.7**

Foreign Corrupt Practices Act

Company A, a U.S. company, has a subsidiary located in Country Z, where various forms of bribery are accepted and expected. To oversee the operations of the subsidiary, A sent one of its top U.S. managers to Country Z. Manager M engaged in the following activities while in Country Z during recent months of operation:

**a.** Paid the equivalent of $200 to a government inspector to reschedule the inspection date of a new manufacturing facility from April 15 to February 15.

**b.** Paid an average of $50 each to four local police officers who are in charge of patrolling the area around the new manufacturing facility. The officers have agreed to increase the number of times they check the area.

**c.** Company N, a domestic company, is in competition with Company A for a government contract. Company A has learned that N has given approximately $5,000 to the official who will make the final contract decision. To remain in the running, Manager M authorized Company A to pay an equal amount to the official.

**d.** The electric utilities are government owned and operated. Due to the frequency of severe storms, there are often power outages due to downed lines. Manager M has paid the official in charge of coordinating repair crews $200 to ensure that the manufacturing plant's power is one of the first restored.

Under the Foreign Corrupt Practices Act, as amended, which of the above activities do you think would be considered illegal? From an operations standpoint, which of the above activities would be considered bad management practice? Are there solutions other than bribery?

# ▌ PROBLEMS

**PROBLEM 15.1**

Exchange Rates and Export Decision

The Cramer Cookie Company is located in Denmark. It is a relatively new company and so far has sold its products only in its home country. In December, Cramer determined that it had excess capacity to produce more of its special Christmas cookies. It is trying to decide whether to use that capacity to ship a batch of cookies overseas. The marketing department has determined that the United States and Great Britain are the two most viable markets. Cramer has enough excess capacity to produce only one batch, which can be shipped to either country. The materials and labor cost to produce the batch amount to 8,500 kroner. The marketing department, which located a shipping company that could deliver to either location, also provided the following information:

| | **United States** | **Great Britain** |
|---|---|---|
| Shipping cost | 3,000 U.S. dollars | 2,000 U.S. dollars |
| Duties/customs charges and miscellaneous selling expenses | 400 U.S. dollars | 480 British pounds |
| Total sales revenue | 5,200 U.S. dollars | 2,800 British pounds |
| Exchange rate data | 1 krone = 0.147 U.S. dollars | 1 krone = 0.088 British pounds |

## Instructions

**a.** If Cramer exports the batch to the United States, what is its estimated profit/loss in Danish kroner?

**b.** If Cramer exports the batch to Great Britain, what is its estimated profit/loss in Danish kroner?

**c.** If the British pound has exhibited rather large fluctuations relative to the Danish kroner recently, how might this impact Cramer's decision on which country to ship to?

Europa-West is a U.S. corporation that purchases automobiles from European manufacturers for distribution in the United States. A recent purchase involved the following events:

**Nov. 12** Purchased automobiles from West Berlin Motors for DM2,000,000, payable in 60 days. Current exchange rate, $0.7025 per deutsche mark. (Europa-West uses the perpetual inventory system.)

**Dec. 31** Made year-end adjusting entry relating to the DM2,000,000 account payable to West Berlin Motors. Current exchange rate, $0.7147 per deutsche mark.

**Jan. 11** Issued a check to World Bank for $1,421,400 in full payment of the account payable to West Berlin Motors.

**PROBLEM 15.2**

Gains and Losses from Exchange Rate Fluctuations

**LO 1, 3–5**

## Instructions

**a.** Prepare in general journal form the entries necessary to record the preceding events.

**b.** Compute the exchange rate (price) of the deutsche mark in U.S. dollars on January 11.

**c.** Explain a hedging technique that Europa-West might have used to protect itself from the possibility of losses resulting from a significant increase in the exchange rate for the deutsche mark.

Wallerton, Inc., is a U.S. company that conducts some business in Canada. The pro forma income statement for next year is shown below. Wallerton wants to know the impact of three possible exchange rate scenarios for the Canadian dollar on its pro forma income statement: Assume one Canadian dollar is equivalent to either $.75, $.80, or $.85 in U.S. dollars. Note that Wallerton's sales in the United States are higher when the Canadian dollar is stronger because Canadian competitors are priced out of the U.S. market.

**PROBLEM 15.3**

Exchange Rates and Income Effects

**LO 3–6**

| WALLERTON, INC.<br>Pro Forma Income Statement<br>For the Period Ending December 31, 2002 | | |
|---|---|---|
| | **U.S. Business** | **Canadian Business** |
| Sales | $304.00 | C$    4 |
| Cost of Goods Sold | 50.00 | 200 |
| **Gross Profit** | **$254.00** | **C$(196)** |
| Operating Expenses: | | |
|   Fixed | 30.00 | –0– |
|   Variable | 30.72 | –0– |
| Total | $ 60.72 | –0– |
| Operating Earnings | $193.28 | C$(196) |
| Interest Expenses | 3.00 | 10 |
| **Earnings before Tax** | **$190.28** | **C$(206)** |

## Additional information

| Possible Exchange Rate | Projected U.S. Sales |
|---|---|
| $.75 | $300 |
| .80 | 304 |
| .85 | 307 |

### Instructions

**a.** Complete the chart in the working papers related to the following pro forma income statements in U.S. dollars:

|  | C$ = $.75 | C$ = $.80 | C$ = $.85 |
|---|---|---|---|
| Sales: |  |  |  |
| (1) U.S. |  |  |  |
| (2) Canadian |  |  |  |
| (3) Total |  |  |  |
|  |  |  |  |
| Cost of Goods Sold |  |  |  |
| (4) U.S. |  |  |  |
| (5) Canadian |  |  |  |
| (6) Total |  |  |  |
|  |  |  |  |
| **(7) Gross Profit** |  | $97.20 |  |
|  |  |  |  |
| Operating Expenses: |  |  |  |
| (8) U.S. Fixed |  |  |  |
| (9) U.S. Variable |  |  |  |
| 10% of Sales |  |  |  |
| (10) Total |  |  |  |
| **Operating Earnings** |  |  | $29.36 |
|  |  |  |  |
| Interest Expenses: |  |  |  |
| (12) U.S. |  |  |  |
| (13) Canadian |  |  |  |
| (14) Total |  |  |  |
| **Earnings Before Tax** | $32.20 |  |  |

**b.** Explain the impact of a stronger Canadian dollar on Earnings Before Tax.

**PROBLEM 15.4**

Exchange Rates and
Production Decisions

**LO 3, 4**

The Ulsa Company has manufacturing subsidiaries in Malaysia and Malta. It is considering shipping the subcomponents of Product Y to one or the other of these countries for final assembly. The final product will be sold in the country where it is assembled. Other information is as follows:

|  | Malaysia | Malta |
|---|---|---|
| Average exchange rate | $1 = 4.30 ringgit | $1 = 0.40 lira |
| Import duty | 5% | 15% |
| Income tax rate | 20% | 10% |
| Unit selling price of Product Y | 645 ringgit | 70 lira |
| Price of subcomponent | 215 ringgit | 20 lira |
| Final assembly costs | 200 ringgit | 25 lira |
| Number of units to be sold | 12,000 units | 8,000 units |

In both countries, the import duties are based on the value of the incoming goods in the receiving country's currency.

## Instructions

**a.** For each country, prepare an income statement on a per-unit basis denominated in that country's currency.

**b.** In which country would the highest profit per unit (in dollars) be earned?

**c.** In which country would the highest total profit (in dollars) be earned?

Form a group of students and research a trade agreement (other than NAFTA) involving a group of countries. (Examples include the World Trade Agreement [WAT] and Mercosur's Common External Tariff [CET]—Latin America.) How do the requirements for the researched trade agreement differ from or remain the same as those listed for NAFTA?

**PROBLEM 15.5**

Global Trade Agreements

**LO 2, 6**

Wolfe Computer is a U.S. company that manufactures portable personal computers. Many of the components for the computer are purchased abroad, and the finished product is sold in foreign countries as well as in the United States. Among the recent transactions of Wolfe are the following:

**PROBLEM 15.6**

A Comprehensive Problem on Exchange Rate Fluctuations

**LO 1, 3–5**

**Oct. 28** Purchased from Mitsutonka, a Japanese company, 20,000 disk drives. The purchase price was ¥180,000,000, payable in 30 days. Current exchange rate, $0.0105 per yen. (Wolfe uses the perpetual inventory method; debit the Inventory of Raw Materials account.)

**Nov. 9** Sold 700 personal computers to the Bank of England for £604,500 due in 30 days. The cost of the computers, to be debited to the Cost of Goods Sold account, was $518,000. Current exchange rate, $1.65 per British pound. (Use one compound journal entry to record the sale and the cost of goods sold. In recording the cost of goods sold, credit Inventory of Finished Goods.)

**Nov. 27** Issued a check to Inland Bank for $1,836,000 in *full payment* of account payable to Mitsutonka.

**Dec. 2** Purchased 10,000 gray-scale monitors from German Optical for DM1,200,000, payable in 60 days. Current exchange rate, $0.7030 per deutsche mark. (Debit Inventory of Raw Materials.)

**Dec. 9** Collected dollar-equivalent of £604,500 from the Bank of England. Current exchange rate, $1.63 per British pound.

**Dec. 11** Sold 10,000 personal computers to Computique, a French retail chain, for FF75,000,000, due in 30 days. Current exchange rate, $0.1900 per French franc. The cost of the computers, to be debited to Cost of Goods Sold and credited to Inventory of Finished Goods, is $7,400,000.

## Instructions

**a.** Prepare in general journal form the entries necessary to record the preceding transactions.

**b.** Prepare the adjusting entries needed at December 31 for the DM1,200,000 account payable to German Optical and the FF75,000,000 account receivable from Computique. Year-end exchange rates, $0.7000 per deutsche mark and $0.1894 per French franc. (Use a separate journal entry to adjust each account balance.)

**c.** Compute (to the nearest dollar) the unit sales price of computers in U.S. dollars in either the November 9 or December 11 sales transaction. (The sales price is the same in each transaction.)

**d.** Compute the exchange rate for the yen, stated in U.S. dollars, on November 27.

**e.** Explain how Wolfe Computer could have hedged its position to reduce the risk of loss from exchange rate fluctuations on (1) its foreign payables and (2) its foreign receivables.

Consider the annual report of **Tootsie Roll Industries, Inc.,** that appears in Appendix A at the end of this textbook. Use this report to assess the globalization of **Tootsie Roll** by answering the following questions:

**PROBLEM 15.7**

**Tootsie Roll**'s Globalization

**LO 1, 2, 5, 6**

**a.** What are the locations of **Tootsie Roll**'s international subsidiaries? What other global operations does **Tootsie Roll** undertake?

**b.** Refer to note 11. What percentages of net assets, sales revenue, and earnings were obtained from international operations in 1999? in 1998?

c. What explanation does management provide in their operating report for the trend in international sales and earnings between 1998 and 1999?

d. Refer to the income statement. How did foreign currency translation adjustments impact earnings? Is there any evidence that management undertakes any formal hedging to attempt to reduce the impact of currency exchange risk on earnings?

e. Refer to note 3: What percentage of current taxes was paid to foreign countries?

f. Do you believe **Tootsie Roll Industries, Inc.**, is a multinational company? Why or why not?

# CASES AND UNSTRUCTURED PROBLEMS

**CASE 15.1**

Decisions to Globalize Are Complex

 **LO 1, 2**

Bristow Inc. is interested in establishing a presence in Country Y. Bristow is expecting demand for several of its products to increase in that country because a major customer, Kale Enterprises, is building a large manufacturing plant in Y. Bristow has been supplying Kale's other foreign manufacturing operations mainly through exporting. However, shipping costs and long delivery times have been somewhat troublesome to both companies in the past. Bristow has also identified several other companies native to Country Y as potential customers.

Bristow currently has operations only in the United States. Kale Enterprises is a successful global company with operations in over 20 countries. Bristow's managers have identified the following possible options:

a. Simply export to Country Y.

b. A company in Y has expressed an interest in licensing Bristow's technology and has the capability and capacity to produce the products used by Kale.

c. A joint venture with Kale may be possible, but managers for Kale would be willing to enter into an agreement only if substantial control for Bristow's operations is given to Kale managers.

d. Bristow's managers have located a company that could be purchased and operated as a subsidiary. The company currently produces products similar to Bristow, but it is using outdated technology.

**Instructions**

Discuss what factors should be considered when choosing among the above options. Develop a list of additional information you believe would be useful in making the decision.

**CASE 15.2**

Disclosure Requirements

**LO 2, 4**

The International Organization of Securities Commissions (IOSCO) is a group of top securities administrators from about 50 countries. The Securities and Exchange Commission (SEC) is a member of IOSCO. IOSCO is a primary supporter of the internationalization of accounting standards through the International Accounting Standards Committee (IASC). At a recent meeting a discussion of the pros and cons of internationalizing accounting standards included the following arguments:

**Pro:**

Having the same accounting standards for external reporting for all securities markets will reduce misunderstandings and create comparable information. For example, investors will be able to compare the financial reports of similar companies located in, say, the United States with those located in China and decide where best to allocate their investments. One set of accounting standards will also save corporations money because they will not need multiple sets of books to track their international operations.

**Con:**

Requiring companies that list on all global securities exchanges to use the same external reporting requirements will mislead investors. For example, in countries where the majority of investment funds come from banks in the form of long-term borrowing, debt to equity ratios will look very different than those of comparable U.S. firms. Accounting information must reflect its environment. Besides, as all business becomes global, reporting requirements will naturally evolve to what investors demand.

## Instructions

Write a one-page summary reflecting your opinion about the value of harmonizing accounting standards for global equity markets. Support your opinions by referencing comparable cross-country companies you have located on the Internet.

## BUSINESS WEEK ASSIGNMENT

Inside **Motorola Inc.**, the device was code-named Dragon Ball—a secret weapon to crack open China's wireless Internet market. Renamed Accompli and now on sale in Beijing and Shanghai, the product is a nifty combination of mobile phone, handheld computer, and wireless Internet device. To tailor it to local tastes and win over China's protectionist officials, **Motorola** developed the $600 handset and sourced everything from chipsets to software in China.

**CASE 15.3**

Environment of Business

**LO 2, 6, 7**

## Instructions

**a.** Identify two other students to form a group (or your instructor will identify these students). With your group members visit the website of the World Bank www.worldbank.int. Prepare a two-page typed paper identifying as many political, legal, economic, cultural, and technological/infrastructure issues as you can that you think **Motorola** likely considered in choosing to develop Dragon Ball.

**b.** Discuss with your group members the meaning of the last two sentences in the above quotation from the May 22, 2000, issue of *Business Week* (B. Einhorn and A. Webb, "Wireless in Cyberspace: China Surfing"). In particular, be prepared to discuss in class whether you think **Motorola**'s decision to "win over China's protectionist officials" is unethical or a violation of the Foreign Corrupt Practices Act.

## INTERNET ASSIGNMENT

The National Association of Foreign Trade Zones (FTZs) maintains an Internet site containing information on U.S. foreign trade zones. Locate the site by searching under "foreign trade zone," or go to:

**INTERNET 15.1**

U.S. Foreign Trade Zones

**LO 1, 2, 6**

### www.naftz.org

## Instructions

**a.** How many general-purpose foreign trade zones are there in the United States?

**b.** What is the difference between a zone and a subzone?

**c.** In your state, how many foreign trade zones are there and where are they located? What types of businesses use them?

**d.** Other information is available at the site. Use that information to answer the following:

   **1.** How are FTZs created?

   **2.** What businesses utilize FTZs?

   **3.** What benefits can firms obtain from operating in FTZs?

*Internet sites are time and date sensitive. It is the purpose of these exercises to have you explore the Internet. You may need to use the Yahoo! search engine http://www.yahoo.com (or other favorite search engine) to look for a company's current web address.*

## OUR COMMENTS ON THE "YOUR TURN" CASES

**You as a Consumer (p. 673)** If the U.S. dollar strengthens against the Italian lira over the coming month, then goods imported from Italy should cost U.S. customers less. Goods imported from the United Kingdom should cost more as the dollar weakens against the pound. As the dollar strengthens, you can purchase more lira with each dollar; therefore, you should investigate the prices of racing bicycles imported from Italy. If you believe the dollar will continue to strengthen over the coming month, you should delay your shopping to get the highest benefit from the exchange rate fluctuations toward the end of the month.

**You as Head of International Acquisitions (p. 676)** It is true that in many countries there are no laws that prohibit businesses from paying government officials from other countries a bribe. In Germany businesses that make bribery payments to government officials *inside* of Germany are engaging in unethical and illegal activities. But these same activities are considered ethical and legal for business dealings with government officials *outside* of Germany. In the United States, these bribery payments are illegal; it is considered unethical to make payments to government officials within the United States or in other countries.

Unless the payments suggested by the three city officials are small enough and meet the guidelines of facilitating payments, the payments would be illegal under the Foreign Corrupt Practices Act. However, before directly telling the Chinese officials that you are unwilling to make payments to expedite the paperwork, other alternatives could be considered. Given the nature of the products made by the company (toys) and the plan to sell the product to Chinese customers, a potential solution is to make a charitable donation to the city to create a park or play area for Chinese children. By taking this approach, instead of the direct payment to the city officials, the company gets the benefit of avoiding the illegal bribe and creating some goodwill with the citizens of the city. In addition, the city officials can take credit for the negotiation that created the new park.

## ANSWERS TO SELF-TEST QUESTIONS

**1.** c **2.** a, b, c, d **3.** b **4.** c (.17 − .19) × 20,000 **5.** d (the transaction was denominated in dollars)

# 16

# MANAGEMENT ACCOUNTING:

## A Business Partner

## Learning Objectives

*After studying this chapter, you should be able to:*

1. Explain the three principles guiding the design of management accounting systems.

2. Describe the three basic types of manufacturing costs.

3. Distinguish between product costs and period costs.

4. Describe how manufacturing costs flow through perpetual inventory accounts.

5. Distinguish between direct and indirect manufacturing costs.

6. Explain the purpose of overhead application rates and the importance of basing these rates on significant cost drivers.

7. Prepare a schedule of the cost of finished goods manufactured.

Photograph by Carleton Bailie © The Boeing Company

# The Boeing Company

The **Boeing Company** is the world's largest aerospace company (total revenues for 1999 were $58 billion). It makes the largest number of commercial jetliners and military aircraft in the world. In addition, it is the nation's largest NASA contractor. Despite its size, in the late 1990s, **Boeing** had some operating difficulties within its commercial airline division.

The CFO for **Boeing** helped turn the problems around by analyzing the amount of value each product was providing to the company's bottom line. This analysis ultimately determined which programs were making or losing money for **Boeing**. Based on the outcome of the analysis, key operational metrics were established and reported on a regular basis in a value scorecard. Designed to track various performance metrics, the scorecard details the company's progress toward reducing inventory, reducing costs, streamlining operations, and maximizing total shareholder returns.

● ● ●

Because accounting information is critical for assessing an organization's output, performance measurement and reporting are key activities frequently coordinated through accounting. In this chapter you will learn how management accounting becomes an important business partner. Management accounting information links decision-making authority with the information necessary to make decisions. It also provides a means to assess decision performance. This chapter introduces the foundations of management accounting.

# MANAGEMENT ACCOUNTING: BASIC FRAMEWORK

As illustrated in the opening story describing the CFO's duties at **Boeing Company**, **management accounting** is the design and use of accounting information systems inside the company to achieve the company's objectives. Three principles govern how management accounting systems are designed. First, management accounting systems help to decide who has decision-making authority over company assets. Second, accounting information produced by or created from the management accounting system supports planning and decision making. Finally, management accounting reports provide a means of monitoring, evaluating, and rewarding performance.

## Management Accounting's Role in Assigning Decision-Making Authority

**LO 1**

Explain the three principles guiding the design of management accounting systems.

To achieve organizational goals, managers are assigned decision-making authority for some of the firm's assets. For example, plant managers typically are responsible for decisions about equipment in the plant, employees at the plant, the physical plant layout, and sources of raw materials, among other things. Within the plant, the materials inventory manager may be delegated decision-making responsibility for reordering materials, and the production supervisor may be delegated decision-making responsibility for assigning employees to jobs on the production line. The point is that all members of an organization have some decision-making authority.

Employees within a corporation know their decision-making responsibilities because they are outlined in a variety of ways, such as in job descriptions, verbal instructions from their supervisors, and management accounting system documents and reports. Just as you have received a course syllabus that outlines your instructor's standards for you to follow to earn an A or B in this course, managers receive management accounting reports that outline expected outcomes to help achieve the organization's goals. Just as you have decision-making responsibility over the "assets" necessary to achieve an A or B (the time you allocate to studying), managers have decision-making responsibility over the assets included in their management accounting reports.

## Management Accounting's Role in Decision Making

Managers need reliable and timely information on which to base their decisions. For example, the plant manager needs information to help assess if equipment is inefficient or if certain work arrangements and plant layouts are more productive than others. Thus managers need both historical information (for example, the current equipment's cost and productivity) and projected information (for example, the productivity and cost of other available equipment). They need information oriented both toward their specific operations and toward other parts of the organization's value chain. A **value chain** is the linked set of activities and resources necessary to create and deliver the product or service to the customer. Therefore, plant managers will require information from other parts of the value chain such as engineering or sales. They need information from both internal operations and externally oriented benchmark sources.

More and more organizations are sharing information. It is very common for organizations to participate in and undertake **benchmark studies**. Independent consulting companies often create benchmark reports by collecting information from companies in the same industry. These studies show an organization how their costs and processes compare to others in their industry. Organizations also share information with customers and suppliers in their value chain. For example, in order for shipments from suppliers to arrive at the exact time they are needed for use in production (just-in-time inventory systems), buyers and suppliers share their production information. Customers often require or are voluntarily provided quality information. Thus the management accounting system provides a variety of past- and future-oriented information for users both inside and outside of the firm.

## Management Accounting's Role in Performance Evaluation and Rewards

The assets over which managers have decision-making authority do not belong to these managers. The corporation owns these assets, and the returns from these assets belong to the corporation. To make sure the assets are earning a good return, the corporation monitors the outcomes of the decisions made by the managers. When the corporation is owned by shareholders, the external financial statements discussed in previous chapters serve this monitoring role for the corporation as a whole. Parallel monitoring systems

### THE ACCOUNTING SYSTEM

| **Financial Accounting** | **Management Accounting** |
|---|---|
| Purpose | Purpose |
| *To provide investors, creditors, and other external parties with useful information about the financial position, financial performance, and cash flow prospects of an enterprise.* | *To provide managers with information useful for planning, evaluating and rewarding performance, and sharing with other outside parties. To apportion decision-making authority over firm resources.* |
| Types of Reports | Types of Reports |
| *Primarily financial statements (statement of financial position or balance sheet, income statement, statement of cash flows) and related notes and supplemental disclosures that provide investors, creditors, and other users information to support external decision-making processes.* | *Many different types of reports, depending on the nature of the business and the specific information needs of management. Examples include budgets, financial projections, benchmark studies, activity-based cost reports, and cost-of-quality assessments.* |
| Standards for Presentation | Standards for Presentation |
| *Generally accepted accounting principles, including those formally established in the authoritative accounting literature and standard industry practice.* | *Rules are set within each organization to produce information most relevant to the needs of management. Management needs include reporting to both external constituents and internal users.* |
| Reporting Entity | Reporting Entity |
| *Usually the company viewed as a whole.* | *A component of the company's value chain, such as a business segment, supplier, customer, product line, department, or product.* |
| Time Periods Covered | Time Periods Covered |
| *Usually a year, quarter, or month. Most reports focus on completed periods. Emphasis is placed on the current (latest) period, with prior periods often shown for comparison.* | *Any period—year, quarter, month, week, day, even a work shift. Some reports are historical in nature; others focus on estimates of results expected in future periods.* |

| Users of Information | Users of Information |
|---|---|
| *Outsiders as well as managers. For financial statements, these outsiders include stockholders, creditors, prospective investors, regulatory authorities, and the general public.* | *Management (different reports to different managers), customers, auditors, suppliers, and others involved in an organization's value chain.* |

are designed to serve similar functions inside corporations. For example, many companies prepare plant-level income statements. Headquarters' executives compare these plant-level financial statements with budgets to monitor the decisions made by plant managers. Frequently, managerial rewards and bonuses are related to the outcomes of these internally prepared financial statements.

Notice that the accounting system must be designed to fulfill all of the three roles just described simultaneously. The system must clearly allocate decision-making authority, provide information for decision making, and furnish information for evaluating and rewarding performance. The accounting system must be constantly monitored and adjusted to make sure all three roles are achieved.

## Accounting Systems: A Business Partner

Creating accounting information systems that can satisfy the demands of both external users (shareholders, creditors, IRS, SEC) and internal users (plant managers, marketing managers, human resource personnel, CFO, CEO) is very challenging. The exhibit on page 659 outlines the demands placed on accounting information systems. Users want accounting information for different, sometimes conflicting, reasons. Information necessary for planning and decision making is likely to be future oriented, and information for monitoring is likely to be historical. Shareholders, creditors, and the IRS do not expect information that is as timely, or at the same level of detail, as the information needed by a plant manager. Yet the same accounting information system usually serves multiple sets of users. Employees use it across a multitude of organizational levels and job responsibilities, and it spreads over numerous geographic areas with different cultures, languages, currencies, and economic environments. Companies such as the **Boeing Company** are much better than they were 10 years ago at designing cost-efficient accounting information systems to serve multiple users. One of the primary reasons for better accounting information systems is the advance in systems' technological capabilities.

Due to rapidly evolving changes in technology and information needs, business managers study management accounting throughout their professional careers. In fact, many companies require employees to complete training in a variety of accounting techniques. Professional certification is available to individuals who plan to make their career in management accounting. The Institute of Certified Management Accountants sponsors two certification exams, the Certified Management Accountant (CMA) exam and the Certified in Financial Management (CFM) exam. To become either a CMA or a CFM, an individual must meet educational and experience requirements as well as pass a rigorous examination.

**CASE IN POINT**

**John Deere and Company**, headquartered in Moline, Illinois, uses self-directed production work teams.[1] These teams are given *decision-making authority* over their equipment scheduling and work assignments. To help these teams make decisions that help the corporation achieve its goals, team members attend training sessions about activity-based costing, a management accounting technique. The team members can then use the activity-based cost information provided by the firm's accounting system for *decision making*. One work team reengineered its assembly-line methods by bringing together and consolidating 12 manufacturing steps at a single site. The team cut assembly costs by over 10% and earned a *reward* that was tied to the team's improved *performance*.

[1]Kevin Kelly, "The New Soul of John Deere," *Business Week*, January 31, 1994, pp. 64–66.

As you progress through the remaining chapters, keep in mind the three principles of management accounting systems: assigning decision-making authority, making and supporting decisions, and evaluating and rewarding performance. Most of the procedures and techniques discussed in the remaining chapters are aimed at one of these principles. In addition, you will encounter many familiar terms and concepts because of the overlap of management and financial accounting. After all, a single accounting system serves both sets of users. It is common for managers to use information about revenues, expenses, and assets in their daily decision making. Managers alter the accounting information (for example, by product line or customer) as needed to make decisions.

## ACCOUNTING FOR MANUFACTURING OPERATIONS

A merchandising company buys its inventory in a ready-to-sell condition. Therefore, its cost of goods is mostly composed of the purchase price of the products it sells. A *manufacturing* company, however, *produces* the goods that it sells. As a consequence, its cost of goods sold consists of various **manufacturing costs**, including the cost of materials, wages earned by production workers, and a variety of other costs relating to the operation of a production facility.[2]

Manufacturing operations are an excellent example of how managerial and financial accounting overlap because manufacturing costs are of vital importance to both financial and managerial accountants. Financial accountants use manufacturing costs to determine the cost of goods sold and inventory values reported in financial statements. Management accountants also rely on prompt and reliable information about manufacturing costs to help answer such questions as:

- What sales price must we charge for our products to earn a reasonable profit?
- Is it possible to lower the cost of producing a particular product line in order to be more price competitive?
- Is it less expensive to buy certain parts used in our products than to manufacture these parts ourselves?
- Should we automate our production process with a robotic assembly line?

### Classifications of Manufacturing Costs

A typical manufacturing company purchases raw materials and converts these materials into finished goods through the process of production. The conversion from raw materials to finished goods results from utilizing a combination of labor and machinery. Thus manufacturing costs are often divided into three broad categories:

1. **Direct materials**—the raw materials and component parts used in production whose costs are directly traceable to the products manufactured.

2. **Direct labor**—wages and other payroll costs of employees whose efforts are directly traceable to the products they manufacture, either by hand or with machinery.

3. **Manufacturing overhead**—a catch-all classification, which includes all manufacturing costs *other than* the costs of direct materials and direct labor. Examples include factory utilities, supervisor salaries, equipment repairs, and depreciation on machinery.

**LO 2**

Describe the three basic types of manufacturing costs.

---

[2]Manufacturing costs are the cost of producing inventory, which is an asset. Therefore, these expenditures are termed *costs* rather than *expenses*. Unexpired costs are assets; expired costs are expenses.

Note that manufacturing costs are *not* immediately recorded as current period expenses. Rather, they are costs of *creating inventory*, and they remain on the balance sheet until the inventory is sold. For this reason, manufacturing costs are often called *product costs* (or inventoriable costs).

## Product Costs versus Period Costs

**LO 3**

Distinguish between product costs and period costs.

The terms *product costs* and *period costs* are helpful in explaining the difference between manufacturing costs and operating expenses. In a manufacturing environment, **product costs** are those costs incurred to manufacture inventory. Thus, until the related goods are sold, product costs *represent inventory*. As such, they are reported on the balance sheet as an asset. When the goods are ultimately sold, product costs are transferred from the balance sheet to the income statement, where they are deducted from revenue as the cost of goods sold.

Operating expenses that are associated with *time periods*, rather than with the production of inventory, are referred to as **period costs**. Period costs are charged directly to expense accounts on the assumption that their benefit is recognized entirely in the period when the cost is incurred. Period costs include all selling expense, general and administrative expenses, interest expense, and income tax expense. In short, period costs are classified on the income statement separately from cost of goods sold, as deductions from a company's gross profit.

The flow of product costs and period costs through the financial statements is shown in the diagram below.

To further illustrate the distinction between product and period costs, consider two costs that, on the surface, appear quite similar: the depreciation of a warehouse used to store raw materials versus depreciation of a warehouse used to store finished goods. Depreciation of the raw materials warehouse is considered a *product cost* (a component of manufacturing overhead) because the building is part of the manufacturing process. Once the manufacturing process is complete and the finished goods are available for sale, all costs associated with their storage are considered selling expenses. Thus the depreciation of the finished goods warehouse is a *period cost*.

## Product Costs and the Matching Principle

Underlying the distinction between product costs and period costs is a familiar accounting concept—the *matching principle*. In short, product costs should be reported on the income statement only when they can be matched against product revenue. To illustrate,

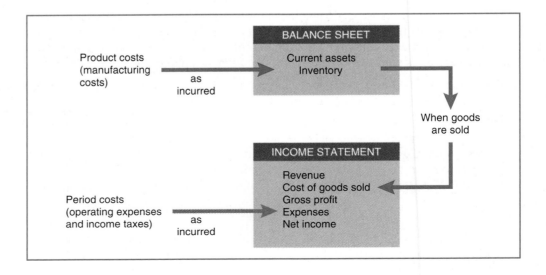

consider a real estate developer who starts a tract of 10 homes in May of the current year. During the year, the developer incurs material, labor, and overhead costs amounting to $1 million (assume $100,000 per house). By the end of December, none of the houses has been sold. How much of the $1 million in construction costs should appear on the developer's income statement for the current year?

The answer is *none*. These costs are not related to any revenue earned by the developer during the current year. Instead, they are related to future revenues the developer will earn when the houses are eventually sold. Therefore, at the end of the current year, the $1 million of product costs should appear in the developer's balance sheet as *inventory*. As each house is sold, $100,000 will be deducted from sales revenue as cost of goods sold. This way, the developer's income statements in future periods will properly match sales revenue with the cost of each sale.

---

Classifying costs as period or product costs can have significant cash effects when the classification determines in what period the cost appears on the income statement as an expense. Using the real estate developer example above, assume the $1 million in construction cost was classified as a period expense rather than a product expense. The current period's net income would be substantially reduced by the additional $1 million in expenses, and the cash flow associated with the current year's income taxes would be significantly reduced.

**CASH EFFECTS**

---

## Inventories of a Manufacturing Business

In the preceding example, assume all 10 houses were completed by the end of the year. In this case the developer's inventory consists only of finished goods. Most manufacturing companies, however, typically account for *three types* of inventory:

1. **Materials inventory**—raw materials on hand and available for use in the manufacturing process.
2. **Work in process inventory**—partially completed goods on which production activities have been started but not yet completed.
3. **Finished goods inventory**—unsold finished products available for sale to customers.

*Not all of a manufacturer's inventory is in a "ready to sell" condition*

All three of these inventories are classified on the balance sheet as current assets. The cost of the materials inventory is based on its purchase price. The work in process and finished goods inventories are based on the costs of direct material, direct labor, and manufacturing overhead assigned to them.

---

 In many countries such as Argentina and Greece, inventory valuation does not conform to the lower of cost or market value rules used in the United States. In addition, many countries, including Brazil, Korea, Mexico, Nigeria, Poland, and Taiwan allow upward revaluation of property and equipment. These differences in accounting methods make comparing inventory values of companies from different parts of the world very difficult.

**CASE IN POINT**

---

Manufacturing companies may use either a perpetual or a periodic inventory system. Perpetual systems have many advantages, however, such as providing managers with up-to-date information about the amounts of inventory on hand and the per-unit costs of manufacturing products. For these reasons, virtually all large manufacturing companies use *perpetual inventory systems*. Also, the flow of manufacturing costs through the inventory accounts and into the cost of goods sold is most easily illustrated in a perpetual inventory system. Therefore, we will assume the use of a perpetual inventory system in our discussion of manufacturing activities.

## The Flow of Costs Parallels the Flow of Physical Goods

**LO 4**

Describe how manufacturing costs flow through perpetual inventory accounts.

When a perpetual inventory system is in use, the flow of manufacturing costs through the company's general ledger accounts closely parallels the physical flow of goods through the production process. This relationship is illustrated below. The boxes in the bottom portion of the diagram represent six *general ledger accounts* used by manufacturing companies to account for their production activities: (1) Materials Inventory, (2) Direct Labor, (3) Manufacturing Overhead, (4) Work in Process Inventory, (5) Finished Goods Inventory, and (6) Cost of Goods Sold.

## Accounting for Manufacturing Costs: An Illustration

To illustrate accounting for manufacturing costs, we will assume that Conquest, Inc., manufactures high-quality mountain bikes in Bend, Oregon. The company relies on cost information to monitor its production efficiency, set prices, and maintain control over its inventories.

Conquest carefully tracks the flow of manufacturing costs through its general ledger accounts as illustrated on the facing page. The figures shown represent all of Conquest's manufacturing costs for 2002. The debit and credit entries summarize the numerous transactions recorded by the company throughout the year.

Our use of several colors in this illustration will help you follow the flow of manufacturing costs through these accounts. The beginning balances in the three inventory accounts are shown in black. Manufacturing costs, and the arrows showing the transfer of these costs from one account to another, are shown in red. Account balances at year-end, which will appear in the company's financial statements, are shown in blue.

Let us now look more closely at exactly how the company's manufacturing costs flow through these general ledger accounts.

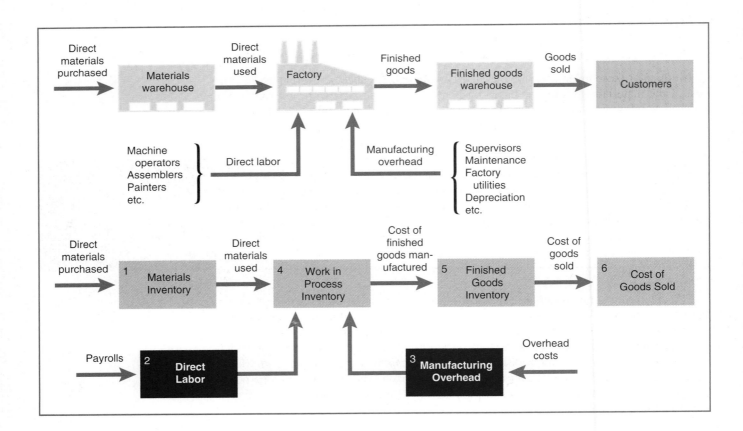

CONQUEST, INC.
Summary of Manufacturing Costs
For the Year Ended December 31, 2002

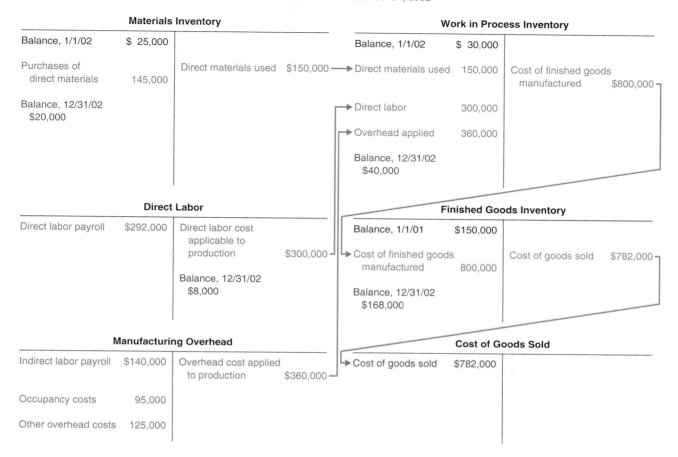

## Direct Materials

*Direct materials* are the raw materials and component parts that become an integral part of finished products and can be traced directly and conveniently to products manufactured. Conquest's direct materials include lightweight alloy tubing for cycle frames, brakes, shifting levers, pedals, sprockets, tires, and so on. The mountain bikes assembled from these components are Conquest's *finished goods*.

The terms *direct materials* and *finished goods* are defined from the viewpoint of individual manufacturing companies. For example, Conquest views brake components as a direct material. However, the **Shimano Company** (a brake manufacturer) views the brake components it sells to Conquest as finished goods.

Conquest uses a perpetual inventory system. Accordingly, the costs of direct materials purchased are debited directly to the Materials Inventory account. As these materials are placed into production, their costs are transferred from the Materials Inventory account to the Work in Process Inventory account by debiting Work in Process Inventory and crediting Materials Inventory. The balance remaining in the Materials Inventory account at year-end represents the cost of direct materials on hand and ready for use.

Some materials used in the production process cannot be traced conveniently or directly to the finished goods manufactured. For Conquest, examples include bearing grease, welding materials, and material used in factory maintenance such as cleaning compounds. These items are referred to as **indirect materials** and are classified as part of manufacturing overhead.

## Direct Labor

The Direct Labor account is used to record the payroll cost of direct workers and assign this cost to the goods they help manufacture.[3] Direct workers are those employees who work directly on the goods being manufactured, either by hand or with machines.

Conquest employs five classifications of direct laborers. Each classification and its corresponding job description are as follows:

| Classification | Job Description |
| --- | --- |
| Cutters | Cut alloy tubing into appropriate lengths. |
| Welders | Transform the cut pieces of alloy tubing into bicycle frames. |
| Painters | Prime and paint each frame. |
| Assemblers | Partially assemble each bicycle in preparation for packing. |
| Packers | Pack the partially assembled bicycles in boxes. |

There are two separate and distinct aspects of accounting for direct labor costs. The first involves the *payment* of cash made to the direct workers at the end of each pay period. At each payroll date, the Direct Labor account is debited for the total direct labor payroll, and an offsetting credit is made to Cash. The second aspect involves the *application* of direct labor costs to the goods being produced. As direct labor employees contribute to the production process during the period, the cost of their labor is *applied* to production by debiting the Work in Process Inventory account and crediting the Direct Labor account.

In our T accounts on the preceding page, the flow of direct labor costs looks similar to the flow of direct materials costs. There is, however, one significant difference. Materials are purchased *before* they are used; therefore, the Materials Inventory account has a *debit* balance equal to the cost of unused materials on hand. The services of employees, however, are used before the employees are paid. Thus the credits to the Direct Labor account are recorded *throughout* the payroll period, but the debits are not recorded until the *end* of the payroll period. If the balance sheet date falls between payroll dates and before adjusting entries are made, the Direct Labor account will have a *credit* balance representing the amount owed to employees for work already performed. This credit balance should be listed in the balance sheet as *wages payable*, a current liability.

Many employees in a manufacturing plant do not work directly on the goods being manufactured. Examples at Conquest include factory supervisors, maintenance personnel, forklift drivers, and security guards. These **indirect labor** costs, which are handled in a fashion similar to that used for indirect materials costs, are considered part of Conquest's manufacturing overhead.

---

[3] As explained in Chapter 10, payroll costs include such factors as payroll taxes and "fringe benefits" as well as the wages earned by employees.

Manufacturing costs clearly drive management strategies in some industries. In recent years, large automobile companies have made significant strategic decisions to spin-off subsidiaries that produce auto parts. In particular, both **Ford Motor Company** and **General Motors Corporation (GM)** separated some of their parts manufacturing plants and assigned them to new companies, **Visteon** and **Delphi**, respectively. These new companies continue to supply auto parts to **Ford** and **GM**, but they also compete for other new business. One of the strategic reasons for the spin-offs was that **GM** and **Ford** were having trouble controlling manufacturing costs. In particular, direct labor was a significant factor because United Auto Workers union representatives were very successful negotiators.

**MANAGEMENT STRATEGY**

## Manufacturing Overhead

All manufacturing costs *other than* direct materials and direct labor are classified as *manufacturing overhead*. The Manufacturing Overhead account is used to record all costs classified as "overhead" and assign these costs to products being manufactured.

There are many types of overhead costs. Consequently, Manufacturing Overhead is treated as a *controlling account* for which subsidiary records are typically maintained to keep track of various overhead classifications.

Because of the diverse nature of manufacturing companies, it simply isn't possible to prepare a complete list of all overhead cost types. However, specific examples at Conquest include the following:

1. *Indirect materials costs*
   a. Factory supplies that do not become an integral part of finished goods, such as oil used to lubricate the cutting machines and solvents used to clean the painting machines.
   b. Materials that become an integral part of finished goods but whose cost would require great effort to actually trace to finished goods. These items include grease used in each bike's bearing assembly and the nuts and bolts used to attach shift levers and other component parts.
2. *Indirect labor costs*
   a. Supervisors' salaries.
   b. Salaries of factory maintenance workers, forklift drivers, receiving clerks in the materials warehouse, and factory security personnel.
3. *Plant occupancy costs*
   a. Depreciation of the factory and the materials warehouse.
   b. Insurance and property taxes on land and buildings.
   c. Maintenance and repairs on buildings.
   d. Utilities and telephone costs.
4. *Machinery and equipment costs*
   a. Depreciation of machinery.
   b. Maintenance of machinery.
5. *Cost of regulatory compliance*
   a. Meeting factory safety requirements.
   b. Disposal of waste materials such as empty paint canisters.
   c. Control over factory emissions (meeting clean air standards).

Selling expenses and general and administrative expenses do *not* relate to the manufacturing process and are *not* included in manufacturing overhead. Certain costs, such as insurance, property taxes, and utilities, sometimes apply in part to manufacturing operations and in part to administrative and selling functions. In such cases, these costs are *apportioned* among manufacturing overhead, general and administrative expenses, and selling expenses.

**Recording Overhead Costs**   The Manufacturing Overhead account is debited to record any cost classified as overhead. Examples of costs debited to this account include the payment of indirect labor payrolls, the payment of factory utilities, the recording of depreciation on factory assets, and the purchase of indirect materials.[4] The account credited will vary depending on the nature of the overhead cost. For example, in recording the purchase of indirect materials, the account credited is usually Accounts Payable. In recording depreciation on machinery, however, the account credited is Accumulated Depreciation.

As the items included in total overhead costs are consumed by production activities, the related costs are transferred from the Manufacturing Overhead account into the Work in Process Inventory account (debit Work in Process Inventory, credit Manufacturing Overhead). In the course of the year, all the overhead costs incurred should be assigned to units of product manufactured. Thus, at year-end, the Manufacturing Overhead account should have a zero balance.

**YOUR TURN**

### You as a Shift Supervisor

Assume you are the first shift supervisor of operations on the shop floor of Conquest at its assembly plant in Bend, Oregon. You have decision-making responsibility over assigning personnel so that high quality is maintained on your shift. Thus you assign direct labor to a variety of jobs including equipment operation (cutters, painters, and welders), actual manual assembly (assemblers), and packaging and cleanup. When quality problems occur, the bicycles must be reworked to eliminate the problems. What type of accounting information might be helpful to you in deciding how to assign personnel to rework poor-quality parts?

*Our comments appear on page 729.

### Direct and Indirect Manufacturing Costs

**LO 5**

Distinguish between direct and indirect manufacturing costs.

The costs of direct materials and direct labor may be traced conveniently and directly to specific units of product. At Conquest, for example, it is relatively easy to determine the cost of the metal tubing and the cost of the direct labor that go into making a particular bicycle. For this reason, accountants call these items **direct manufacturing costs**.

Overhead, however, is an **indirect manufacturing cost**. Consider, for example, the types of costs that Conquest classifies as overhead. These costs include property taxes on the factory, depreciation on tools and equipment, supervisors' salaries, and repairs to equipment. How much of these indirect costs should be assigned to each bicycle?

There is no easy answer to this question. By definition, indirect costs *cannot* be traced easily and directly to specific units of production. While these costs are often easier to view *as a whole* than on a per-unit basis, we will see that both financial and management accountants require unit cost information. Therefore, manufacturing companies must develop methods of allocating an appropriate portion of total manufacturing overhead to each product manufactured. The allocation of overhead costs to production is accomplished through the use of **overhead application rates**.

---

[4]Some companies record the purchase of indirect materials in the Materials Inventory account or in a separate inventory account. Our approach is commonly used when the quantity of indirect materials purchased does not differ significantly from the quantity of indirect materials used during each period.

## Overhead Application Rates

There are two reasons manufacturing overhead isn't applied to products by simply dividing the company's annual overhead cost by the number of units produced during the year. First, total overhead costs and total units produced are not known until the end of the period. Second, not all products consume an equal amount of overhead cost.

**LO 6**

Explain the purpose of overhead application rates and the importance of basing these rates on significant cost drivers.

Thus overhead application rates are used to assign manufacturing overhead costs to specific units of production as those units are being produced throughout the accounting period. The rate expresses an expected relationship between manufacturing overhead costs and some *activity base* related to the production process (direct labor hours, machine hours, and so forth). Overhead is then assigned to products *in proportion* to this activity base. For example, a company using direct labor hours as an activity base would allocate the greatest proportion of its overhead costs to those products requiring the most direct labor hours.

The overhead application rate is determined at the *beginning* of the period and is based on *estimated* amounts. The rate is typically computed as follows:

$$\text{Overhead Application Rate} = \frac{\textbf{Estimated Overhead Costs}}{\textbf{Estimated Units in the Activity Base}}$$

The mechanics of computing and using an overhead application rate are quite simple. The challenging problems for accountants are (1) selecting an appropriate activity base and (2) making reliable estimates at the beginning of the accounting period regarding the total of the overhead costs to be incurred and the total units in the activity base that will be required.[5] We will examine the easy topic first—the mechanics underlying the computation and use of overhead application rates.

**Computation and Use of Overhead Application Rates** Assume that at the beginning of 2002, Conquest's management makes the following estimates relating to bicycle manufacturing activity for the upcoming year:

| | |
|---|---|
| Estimated total manufacturing overhead costs for the year . . . . . . . . . . . . . . . | $360,000 |
| Estimated total direct labor hours for the year . . . . . . . . . . . . . . . . . . . . . . . . | 30,000 hours |
| Estimated total machine hours for the year . . . . . . . . . . . . . . . . . . . . . . . . . . . | 10,000 hours |

Using the above estimates, we will illustrate the use of an overhead application rate under two independent assumptions.

**Assumption 1: Conquest Uses Direct Labor Hours as Its Activity Base** If Conquest uses direct labor hours to apply overhead costs, the application rate will be *$12 per direct labor hour* ($360,000 of estimated overhead costs, divided by 30,000 estimated direct labor hours). Throughout the year, manufacturing overhead costs will be assigned in direct proportion to the *actual* direct labor hours required to manufacture the bicycles produced. For example, if a production run of a particular bicycle model uses 200 direct labor hours, $2,400 of manufacturing overhead will be assigned to those units (200 direct labor hours used, multiplied by the $12 application rate). The assignment will be made by debiting the Work in Process Inventory account and crediting the Manufacturing Overhead account for $2,400.

---

[5]Errors in estimating the amount of total overhead costs for the coming period or the number of units in the activity base will cause differences between the actual overhead incurred and the amounts assigned to units manufactured. These differences usually are small and are eliminated by an adjusting entry at the end of the accounting period. We will address this issue in Chapter 17.

**Assumption 2: Conquest Uses Machine Hours as Its Activity Base**    If Conquest chooses to use machine hours to apply overhead costs, its application rate will be *$36 per machine hour* ($360,000 of estimated overhead costs, divided by 10,000 estimated machine hours). Using this approach, manufacturing overhead costs will be assigned to bicycles based on the number of machine hours required to produce them. If 10 machine hours are required for a particular production run, the bicycles in that run will be assigned $360 of overhead costs (10 hours times $36 per hour). Again, the assignment will be made by debiting the Work in Process Inventory account and crediting the Manufacturing Overhead account for $360.

### You as an Equipment Operator

Assume you are the operator of the machinery at Conquest, Inc., and that Conquest is using machine hours as its activity base to apply overhead costs. A co-worker has just approached you suggesting that if you ran the equipment more efficiently and used fewer machine hours, the company would save $36 per machine hour in overhead costs. Thus, if you were able to be 10% more efficient, you could cut overhead costs by $36,000 per year (10% × $360,000) and maybe you could both get a raise. How will you respond to your co-worker?

*Our comments appear on page 729.

## What "Drives" Overhead Costs?

For overhead application rates to provide reliable results, an activity base must be a significant "driver" of overhead costs. To be a **cost driver**, an activity base must be a *causal factor* in the incurrence of overhead costs. In other words, an increase in the number of activity base units (for example, direct labor hours worked) must cause a proportional increase in the actual overhead costs incurred.

Historically, direct labor hours (or direct labor costs) were viewed as the primary driver of overhead costs—and for good reason. Products that required more direct labor often required more indirect labor (supervision), resulted in more wear and tear on machinery (maintenance costs), and consumed a greater amount of factory supplies. Therefore, many manufacturing companies followed the practice of applying all manufacturing overhead costs in proportion to direct labor hours or direct labor costs.

As factories became more highly automated, direct labor became much less of a causal factor in driving many overhead costs. Today, many manufacturing companies find that activity bases such as machine hours, computer time, or the time required to set up a production run result in a better matching of overhead costs and activities.

Historically, the automobile industry was primarily labor intensive. But today, due to the increased use of robotics, it takes only 15 to 20 hours of direct labor to assemble a car. For instance, **Toyota**'s labor costs are about 20% of total revenue, **Chrysler**'s constitute 19%, and **Volvo**'s only 18%.

**The Use of Multiple Overhead Application Rates**    In an attempt to gain a better understanding of what it costs to manufacture different types of products, many companies have begun to implement techniques that rely on the use of *multiple* allocation bases. One such approach, **activity-based costing**, is illustrated in Chapter 17.

In essence, activity-based costing uses multiple allocation bases that represent different types of manufacturing overhead costs. For instance, machine maintenance costs may be allocated using machine hours as an activity base, whereas supervision costs may be allocated using direct labor hours. Different application rates may also be used in each production department and in applying overhead costs to different types of products.

The key point is that each manufactured product should be charged with the overhead costs *generated by* the manufacture of that product. If the activity base used to apply overhead costs is *not* a primary cost driver, the relative production cost of different products may become *significantly distorted*.

Consider, for example, a plant that makes two products; one product is highly labor intensive and the other product is made on a highly automated assembly line. Due to the extremely high maintenance and electricity costs associated with the automation process, the automated assembly line is responsible for 80% of the plant's total overhead cost. If manufacturing overhead is allocated in proportion to direct labor hours, the labor-intensive products will be assigned too much of the total cost. The automated product, responsible for most of these high overhead costs, will be charged with a relatively small share of the total allocation. This, in turn, may lead to many faulty decisions on the part of management.

**The Increasing Importance of Proper Overhead Allocation**   In today's global economy, competition among manufacturing companies is greater than ever before. If a company is to determine whether it can compete effectively in the marketplace, it must first know with some degree of precision its manufacturing costs on a per-unit basis. In highly automated factories, overhead is often the largest of the three basic categories of manufacturing costs. Therefore, the allocation of overhead costs is one of the major challenges facing management accountants.

## Work in Process Inventory, Finished Goods Inventory, and the Cost of Goods Sold

We have devoted much of this chapter to discussing the three types of manufacturing costs—direct materials, direct labor, and manufacturing overhead. We will now shift our attention to the three accounts that provide the structure for the flow of these costs—the Work in Process Inventory account, the Finished Goods Inventory account, and the Cost of Goods Sold account.

The Work in Process Inventory account is used (1) to record the accumulation of manufacturing costs associated with the units of product worked on during the period and (2) to allocate these costs between those units completed during the period and those that are only partially completed.

As direct materials, direct labor, and manufacturing overhead are applied to production, their related costs are debited to the Work in Process Inventory account. The flow of costs into this inventory account (rather than into a corresponding expense account) is consistent with the idea that manufacturing costs are *product costs,* not period costs.

As specific units are completed, the cost of manufacturing them is transferred from the Work in Process Inventory account to the Finished Goods Inventory account. Thus the balance in the Work in Process account represents only the manufacturing costs associated with units still "in process."

It is important to realize that once products are classified as finished goods, *no additional costs are allocated to them.* Therefore, the costs of storing, marketing, or delivering finished goods are regarded as *selling expenses,* not manufacturing costs. When units of finished goods are sold, their related costs must "flow" from the balance sheet through the income statement in compliance with the matching principle. Accordingly, as products are sold, their costs are transferred from the Finished Goods Inventory account to the Cost of Goods Sold account.

**YOUR TURN**

### You as the Chief Financial Officer

Assume that you are CFO of Conquest, Inc., and that you have just received an income statement and balance sheet from plant accountant Jim Sway in Bend, Oregon. In your conversations with Jim you learn that in the recent reporting period, plant manager Darlene Cosky asked that inventory transportation cost, the cost of repairing the plant parking lot, and the newly installed plant landscaping costs all be allocated to cost of production. In addition, when these allocations took place, the plant produced many more bicycles than were sold creating significant increases in the amount of inventory on hand. As a result, most of the costs described by Jim have been assigned to the inventory on hand (included as part of inventory costs on the balance sheet) but have not been assigned to cost of goods sold expenses (included on the income statement). Furthermore, during the recent reporting period both Darlene and Jim earned significant bonuses based on plant profitability. What, if anything, would you do as the CFO?

*Our comments appear on p. 729.

## The Need for Per-Unit Cost Data

Transferring the cost of specific units from one account to another requires knowledge of each unit's *per-unit cost*—that is, the total manufacturing costs assigned to specific units. The determination of unit cost is one of the primary goals of every cost accounting system and will be explained and illustrated more completely in Chapter 17.

Unit costs are of importance to both financial and management accountants. Financial accountants use unit costs in recording the transfer of completed goods from Work in Process to Finished Goods and from Finished Goods to Cost of Goods Sold. Management accountants use the same information to make pricing decisions, evaluate the efficiency of current operations, and plan for future operations.

## Determining the Cost of Finished Goods Manufactured

**LO 7**

Prepare a schedule of the cost of finished goods manufactured.

Most manufacturing companies prepare a **schedule of the cost of finished goods manufactured** to provide managers with an overview of manufacturing activities during the period. Using the information from our illustration on page 701, a schedule of Conquest's cost of finished goods manufactured is shown below.

| CONQUEST, INC. Schedule of the Cost of Finished Goods Manufactured For the Year Ended December 31, 2002 | | |
|---|---:|---:|
| Work in process inventory, beginning of the year | | $ 30,000 |
| Manufacturing cost assigned to production: | | |
| Direct materials used | $150,000 | |
| Direct labor | 300,000 | |
| Manufacturing overhead | 360,000 | |
| Total manufacturing costs | | 810,000 |
| Total cost of all work in process during the year | | $840,000 |
| Less: Work in process inventory, end of the year | | (40,000) |
| Cost of finished goods manufactured | | $800,000 |

Notice that all of the figures in this schedule were obtained from Conquest's Work in Process Inventory account illustrated on page 701. In short, this schedule summarizes the flow of manufacturing costs into and out of the Work in Process Inventory account.

**Purpose of the Schedule**   A schedule of the cost of finished goods manufactured is *not* a formal financial statement and generally does not appear in the company's annual report. Rather, it is intended primarily to assist managers in understanding and evaluating the overall cost of manufacturing products. By comparing these schedules for successive periods, for example, managers can determine whether direct labor or manufacturing overhead is rising or falling as a percentage of total manufacturing costs. In addition, the schedule is helpful in developing information about unit costs.

If a company manufactures only a single product line, its cost per unit simply equals its *cost of finished goods manufactured* divided by the *number of units produced.* For example, if Conquest produces only one line of mountain bike, its average cost per unit would be *$80* had it produced *10,000* finished units during 2002 ($800,000 divided by 10,000 units). If Conquest produced multiple lines of mountain bikes, it would prepare a separate schedule of the cost of finished goods manufactured for each product line.

## Financial Statements of a Manufacturing Company

Let us now illustrate how the information used in our example will be reported in the 2002 income statement and balance sheet of Conquest, Inc.

The company's 2002 income statement is presented below:

| CONQUEST, INC.<br>Income Statement<br>For the Year Ended December 31, 2002 | | |
| --- | --- | --- |
| Sales | | $1,300,000 |
| Cost of Goods Sold | | 782,000 |
| Gross profit on sales | | $ 518,000 |
| Operating expenses: | | |
| Selling Expenses | $135,000 | |
| General and Administrative Expenses | 265,000 | |
| Total operating expenses | | 400,000 |
| Income from operations | | $ 118,000 |
| Less: Interest Expense | | 18,000 |
| Income before income taxes | | $ 100,000 |
| Income Taxes Expenses | | 30,000 |
| Net income | | $ 70,000 |

Notice that no manufacturing costs appear among the company's operating expenses. In fact, manufacturing costs appear in only two places in a manufacturer's financial statements. Costs associated with units *sold* during the period appear in the income statement as the *cost of goods sold.* The $782,000 cost of goods sold figure reported in Conquest's income statement was taken directly from the company's perpetual inventory records. However, this amount may be verified as follows:

| | |
| --- | --- |
| Beginning finished goods inventory (1/1/02) | $150,000 |
| Add: Cost of finished goods manufactured during the year | 800,000 |
| Cost of finished goods available for sale | $950,000 |
| Less: Ending finished goods inventory (12/31/02) | 168,000 |
| Cost of goods sold | $782,000 |

All manufacturing costs associated with goods *still on hand* are classified as *inventory* and appear in the balance sheet. The balance sheet presentation of Conquest's three types of inventory is illustrated on the following page:

*Notice the three types of inventory*

| CONQUEST, INC. | | |
|---|---|---|
| **Partial Balance Sheet** | | |
| **December 31, 2002** | | |
| **Current assets:** | | |
| Cash and Cash Equivalents .................................................. | | $ 60,000 |
| Accounts Receivable (net of allowance for doubtful accounts) ............ | | 190,000 |
| Inventories: | | |
| Materials ........................................... | $ 20,000 | |
| Work in Process ..................................... | 40,000 | |
| Finished Goods ...................................... | 168,000 | |
| Total Inventories ................................................... | | 228,000 |
| Total current assets ............................................... | | $478,000 |

As previously mentioned, Conquest's balance sheet includes a current liability for wages payable equal to the unadjusted $8,000 credit balance in the Direct Labor account.

**A SECOND LOOK**

### Boeing Company

**Boeing Company**'s CFO demonstrated an understanding of the importance of assigning decision-making authority, providing information for decision making, and evaluating and rewarding decision makers. The CFO gave **Boeing Company**'s managerial accounting system a pivotal role in the decision-making process.

Starting with accounting basics, such as which planes and rockets make money, the Boeing CFO created a value scorecard that evaluated and compared the profitability of each unit. These management accounting systems helped improve the efficiency and effectiveness of decision making at **Boeing**.

In the next chapter, you will learn in more detail how management accounting systems are effective for capturing the costs of resources consumed. You will see how companies use these systems to assign the costs of resources consumed to the products and services created. Job order costing systems, activity-based costing systems, and process costing systems are introduced and described to help you understand how accounting systems are designed to fit the processes used to create goods and services.

## SUMMARY OF LEARNING OBJECTIVES

### LO 1

**Explain the three principles guiding the design of management accounting systems.**

First, management accounting systems help to decide who has the decision-making authority over company assets. Second, accounting information produced or created from the management accounting system supports planning and decision making. Finally, management accounting reports provide a means of monitoring, evaluating, and rewarding performance.

### LO 2

**Describe the three basic types of manufacturing costs.**

Direct materials used consist of the parts and materials that become part of the finished products. Direct labor cost consists of the wages paid to factory employees who work directly on the products being manufactured. Manufacturing overhead includes all manufacturing costs other than the cost of materials used and direct labor. Examples of manufacturing overhead include depreciation of machinery and the plant security service.

### LO 3

**Distinguish between product costs and period costs.**

Product costs are the costs of creating inventory. They are treated as assets until the related goods are sold, at which time the product costs are deducted from revenue as the cost of goods sold. Thus goods manufactured this year but not sold until next year are deducted from next year's revenue.

Period costs are charged to expense in the accounting period in which they are incurred. Period costs are not related to production of goods; consequently, they are deducted from revenue on the assumption that the benefits obtained from the expenditures are received in the same period as the costs are incurred. Period costs include general and administrative expense, selling expense, and income taxes expense.

### LO 4

**Describe how manufacturing costs flow through perpetual inventory accounts.**

Manufacturing costs originally are recorded in three controlling accounts: Materials Inventory, Direct Labor, and Manufacturing Overhead. As these costs become applicable to goods placed into production, they are transferred from these manufacturing cost accounts to the Work in Process Inventory account. As units are completed, their cost is transferred from the Work in Process account to Finished Goods Inventory. Then, when units are sold, their costs are transferred from Finished Goods Inventory to the Cost of Goods Sold account.

### LO 5

**Distinguish between direct and indirect manufacturing costs.**

Direct manufacturing costs (direct materials and direct labor) can be identified with specific products. Indirect manufacturing costs are the many elements of manufacturing overhead that apply to factory operations as a whole and cannot be traced to specific products.

### LO 6

**Explain the purpose of overhead application rates and the importance of basing these rates on significant cost drivers.**

An overhead application rate is a device used to assign appropriate amounts of overhead costs to specific units of output (manufactured products). Overhead is an indirect cost, which cannot be directly associated with specific output. However, the overhead application rate expresses the relationship between overhead costs and some activity base that can be traced directly to specific units. The activity base should be the major driver (causal factor) of overhead costs; if the activity base is not the cost driver, the relative production cost of different products may be significantly distorted.

### LO 7

**Prepare a schedule of the cost of finished goods manufactured.**

This schedule summarizes the flow of manufacturing costs into and out of the Work in Process Inventory account. Its purpose is to assist management in understanding and evaluating manufacturing costs incurred in the period.

To prepare this schedule, we start by listing the work in process inventory at the beginning of the year. To this amount we add the materials used, direct labor costs, and overhead for the period. Combining these four items indicates the total cost of all work in process during the period. A final step is deducting the cost of work still in process at the end of the period. This gives us the cost of finished goods manufactured during the period.

The terminology and concepts introduced in this chapter will be used extensively throughout the remaining chapters in this text.

## KEY TERMS INTRODUCED OR EMPHASIZED IN CHAPTER 16

**activity-based costing** (p. 706) A method of allocating manufacturing overhead to products using multiple application rates and a wide variety of cost drivers.

**benchmark study** (p. 694) A study designed to show an organization how its costs and processes compare to others in the industry.

**cost driver** (p. 706) An activity base that can be traced directly to units produced and that serves as a causal factor in the incurrence of overhead costs. Serves as an activity base in an overhead application rate.

**direct labor** (p. 697) Payroll costs for employees who work directly on the products being manufactured, either by hand or with tools.

**direct manufacturing cost** (p. 704) A manufacturing cost that can be traced conveniently and directly into the quantity of finished goods manufactured. Examples include direct materials and direct labor.

**direct materials** (p. 697) Materials and component parts that become an integral part of the manufactured goods and can be traced directly to the finished products.

**finished goods inventory** (p. 699) The completed units that have emerged from the manufacturing process and are on hand available for sale.

**indirect labor** (p. 702) Payroll costs relating to factory employees who do not work directly on the goods being manufactured. Examples are wages of security guards and maintenance personnel. Indirect labor costs are classified as manufacturing overhead.

**indirect manufacturing cost** (p. 704) A manufacturing cost that cannot be conveniently traced into the specific products being manufactured. Examples include property taxes, depreciation on machinery, and other types of manufacturing overhead.

**indirect materials** (p. 702) Materials used in the manufacturing process that cannot be traced conveniently to specific units of production. Examples include lubricating oil, maintenance supplies, and glue. Indirect materials are accounted for as part of manufacturing overhead.

**management accounting** (p. 694) The design and use of accounting information systems inside the firm to achieve the firm's objectives.

**manufacturing costs** (p. 697) The cost of manufacturing goods that will be sold to customers. The basic types of manufacturing costs are direct materials, direct labor, and manufacturing overhead.

**manufacturing overhead** (p. 697) A "catch-all" category including all manufacturing costs other than the costs of direct materials used and direct labor.

**materials inventory** (p. 699) The cost of direct materials on hand and available for use in the manufacturing process.

**overhead application rate** (p. 704) A device used to assign overhead costs to the units being manufactured. Expresses the relationship between estimated overhead costs and some activity base that can be traced directly to manufactured units.

**period costs** (p. 698) Costs that are charged to expense accounts in the period that the costs are incurred. Includes all items classified as "expense."

**product costs** (p. 698) The costs of purchasing or manufacturing inventory. Until the related goods are sold, these product costs represent an asset—inventory. Once the goods are sold, these costs are deducted from revenue as the cost of goods sold.

**schedule of the cost of finished goods manufactured** (p. 708) A schedule summarizing the flow of manufacturing costs into and out of the Work in Process Inventory account. Intended to assist managers in evaluating manufacturing costs.

**value chain** (p. 694) The linked set of activities and resources necessary to create and deliver a product or service to customers.

**work in process inventory** (p. 699) Goods at any stage of the manufacturing process short of completion. As these units are completed, they become finished goods.

## DEMONSTRATION PROBLEM

The following T accounts summarize the flow of manufacturing costs during the current year through the ledger accounts of Marston Manufacturing Company:

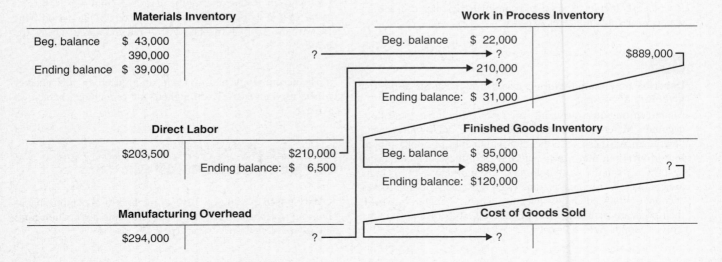

## Instructions

From the data supplied on the previous page, indicate the following amounts. Some amounts already appear in the T accounts; others require short computations.

a. Purchases of direct materials

b. Direct materials used during the year

c. Direct labor costs assigned to production

d. The year-end liability to direct workers for wages payable

e. The overhead costs applied to production during the year, assuming that overhead was applied at a rate equal to 140% of direct labor costs

f. Total manufacturing costs charged to production during the year

g. The cost of finished goods manufactured

h. The cost of goods sold

i. The total costs classified as inventory in the year-end balance sheet

## Solution to the Demonstration Problem

| | |
|---|---:|
| **a.** Purchases of direct materials | $390,000 |
| **b.** Computation of direct materials used: | |
|     Materials inventory, beginning of year | $ 43,000 |
|     Purchases of direct materials | 390,000 |
|     Direct materials available for use | $433,000 |
|     Less: Materials inventory, end of year | 39,000 |
|     Direct materials used | $394,000 |
| **c.** Direct labor costs assigned to production | $210,000 |
| **d.** Year-end liability for direct wages payable | $ 6,500 |
| **e.** Overhead costs applied during the year | |
|     ($210,000 direct labor costs × 140%) | $294,000 |
| **f.** Total manufacturing costs charged to production: | |
|     Direct materials used (part B) | $394,000 |
|     Direct labor costs assigned to production | 210,000 |
|     Manufacturing overhead applied (part E) | 294,000 |
|       Total manufacturing costs charged to production | $898,000 |
| **g.** Cost of finished goods manufactured | $889,000 |
| **h.** Computation of cost of goods sold: | |
|     Beginning inventory of finished goods | $ 95,000 |
|     Cost of finished goods manufactured | 889,000 |
|     Cost of goods available for sale | $984,000 |
|     Less: Ending inventory of finished goods | 120,000 |
|     Cost of goods sold | $864,000 |
| **i.** Total year-end inventory: | |
|     Materials | $ 39,000 |
|     Work in process | 31,000 |
|     Finished goods | 120,000 |
|       Total inventory | $190,000 |

## SELF-TEST QUESTIONS

*Answers to these questions appear on page 729.*

1. Indicate which of the following statements are more descriptive of management accounting than of financial accounting. (More than one answer may be appropriate.)

    a. Recognized standards are used for presentation.

  **b.** Information is tailored to the needs of individual decision makers.

  **c.** Information is more widely distributed.

  **d.** Emphasis is on expected future results.

2. In a manufacturing company, the costs debited to the Work in Process Inventory account represent:

  **a.** Direct materials used, direct labor, and manufacturing overhead.

  **b.** Cost of finished goods manufactured.

  **c.** Period costs and product costs.

  **d.** None of the above; the types of costs debited to this account will depend on the type of products being manufactured.

3. The Work in Process Inventory account had a beginning balance of $4,200 on February 1. During February, the cost of direct materials used was $29,000 and direct labor cost applied to production was $3,000. Overhead is applied at the rate of $20 per direct labor hour. During February, 180 direct labor hours were used in the production process. If the cost of finished goods manufactured was $34,100, compute the balance in the Work in Process Inventory account at the *end* of February.

  **a.** $9,900.    **b.** $1,500.    **c.** $2,100.    **d.** $5,700.

4. The purpose of an overhead application rate is to:

  **a.** Assign a portion of indirect manufacturing costs to each product manufactured.

  **b.** Determine the type and amount of costs to be debited to the Manufacturing Overhead account.

  **c.** Charge the Work in Process Inventory account with the appropriate amount of direct manufacturing costs.

  **d.** Allocate manufacturing overhead to expense in proportion to the number of units manufactured during the period.

5. The accounting records of Newport Mfg. Co. include the following information for the most recent year ended December 31:

|  | Dec. 31 | Jan. 1 |
|---|---|---|
| Inventory of work in process . . . . . . . . . . . . . . . . . . . . . . . . . | $ 20,000 | $10,000 |
| Inventory of finished goods . . . . . . . . . . . . . . . . . . . . . . . . . | 80,000 | 60,000 |
| Direct materials used . . . . . . . . . . . . . . . . . . . . . . . . . . . . . . | 200,000 | |
| Direct labor . . . . . . . . . . . . . . . . . . . . . . . . . . . . . . . . . . . . | 120,000 | |
| Manufacturing overhead (150% of direct labor) . . . . . . . . . . . | 180,000 | |
| Selling expenses . . . . . . . . . . . . . . . . . . . . . . . . . . . . . . . . . | 150,000 | |

Indicate which of the following are correct. (More than one answer may be correct.)

  **a.** Amount debited to the Work in Process Inventory account during the year, $500,000.

  **b.** Cost of finished goods manufactured, $490,000.

  **c.** Cost of goods sold, $470,000.

  **d.** Total manufacturing costs for the year, $650,000.

# ASSIGNMENT MATERIAL

## DISCUSSION QUESTIONS

1. Briefly distinguish between management and financial accounting information in terms of (a) the intended users of the information and (b) the purpose of the information.

2. Briefly explain what is meant by the term *management accounting*.

3. Describe the three principles guiding the design of management accounting systems.

4. Is management accounting information developed in conformity with generally accepted accounting principles or some other set of prescribed standards? Explain.

5. What are the three basic types of manufacturing costs?

6. A manufacturing firm has three inventory controlling accounts. Name each of the accounts, and describe briefly what the balance in each at the end of any accounting period represents.

7. Explain the distinction between *product costs* and *period costs*. Why is this distinction important?

8. Is the cost of disposing of hazardous waste materials resulting from factory operations a product cost or a period cost? Explain.

9. During the current year, Coronado Boat Yard has incurred manufacturing costs of $420,000 in building three large sailboats. At year-end, each boat is about 70% complete. How much of these manufacturing costs should be recognized as expense in Coronado Boat Yard's income statement for the current year? Explain.

10. What amounts are *debited* to the Materials Inventory account? What amounts are *credited* to this account? What type of balance (debit or credit) is this account likely to have at year-end? Explain.

11. During the current year the net cost of direct materials purchased by a manufacturing firm was $340,000, and the direct material inventory increased by $20,000. What was the cost of direct materials *used* during the year?

12. What amounts are debited to the Direct Labor account during the year? What amounts are credited to this account? What type of balance (debit or credit) is this account likely to have at year-end? Explain.

13. The illustration on page 701 includes six ledger accounts. Which of these six accounts often have balances at year-end that appear in the company's formal financial statements? Briefly explain how these balances will be classified in the financial statements.

14. Explain the distinction between a *direct* manufacturing cost and an *indirect* manufacturing cost. Provide two examples of each type of cost.

15. Argo Mfg. Co. uses approximately $1,200 in janitorial supplies to clean the work area and factory equipment each month. Should this $1,200 be included in the cost of direct materials used? Explain.

16. What is meant by the term *overhead application rate?*

17. What is meant by the term *overhead cost driver?* How does the cost driver enter into the computation of an overhead application rate?

18. Identify two possible overhead cost drivers for a company that:

    a. Manufactures handmade furniture using skilled craftspersons and small hand tools.

    b. Manufactures microchips for computers using an assembly line of computer-driven robots.

19. What amounts are *debited* to the Work in Process Inventory account during the year? What amounts are *credited* to this account? What does the year-end balance in this account represent?

20. What amounts are *debited* to the Finished Goods Inventory account during the year? What amounts are *credited* to this account? What type of balance (debit or credit) is this account likely to have at year-end?

21. Briefly describe the computation of the cost of finished goods manufactured as it appears in a schedule of the cost of finished goods manufactured.

22. A schedule of the cost of finished goods manufactured is a helpful tool in determining the per-unit cost of manufactured products. Explain several ways in which information about per-unit manufacturing costs is used by (a) management accountants and (b) financial accountants.

23. Briefly discuss the potential shortcoming of using direct labor hours or direct labor dollars as a primary cost driver in a highly automated company.

# EXERCISES

**EXERCISE 16.1**

Accounting Terminology

**LO 1–6**

Listed below are eight technical accounting terms introduced or emphasized in this chapter:

| | |
|---|---|
| Work in Process Inventory | Cost of finished goods manufactured |
| Overhead application rate | Cost of Goods Sold |
| Period costs | Management accounting |
| Product costs | Manufacturing overhead |

Each of the following statements may (or may not) describe one of these technical terms. For each statement, indicate the accounting term described, or answer "None" if the statement does not correctly describe any of the terms.

**a.** The preparation and use of accounting information designed to assist managers in planning and controlling the operations of a business

**b.** All manufacturing costs other than direct materials used and direct labor

**c.** A means of assigning indirect manufacturing costs to work in process during the period

**d.** A manufacturing cost that can be traced conveniently and directly to manufactured units of product

**e.** The account debited at the time that the Manufacturing Overhead account is credited

**f.** The amount transferred from the Work in Process Inventory account to the Finished Goods Inventory account

**g.** Costs that are debited directly to expense accounts when the costs are incurred

**EXERCISE 16.2**

Basic Types of Manufacturing Costs

**LO 2**

Into which of the three elements of manufacturing cost would each of the following be classified?

**a.** Tubing used in manufacturing bicycles

**b.** Wages paid by an automobile manufacturer to employees who test-drive completed automobiles

**c.** Property taxes on machinery

**d.** Gold bullion used by a jewelry manufacturer

**e.** Wages of assembly-line workers who package frozen food

**f.** Salary of plant superintendent

**g.** Electricity used in factory operations

**h.** Salary of a nurse in a factory first-aid station

**EXERCISE 16.3**

Product Costs and Period Costs

**LO 3, 5**

Indicate whether each of the following should be considered a *product cost* or a *period cost*. If you identify the item as a product cost, also indicate whether it is a *direct* or an *indirect* cost. For example, the answer to item **0** is "indirect product cost." Begin with item **a**.

**0.** Property taxes on factory building

**a.** Cost of disposal of hazardous waste materials to a chemical plant

**b.** Amounts paid by a mobile home manufacturer to a subcontractor who installs plumbing in each mobile home

**c.** Depreciation on sales showroom fixtures

**d.** Salaries of security guards in administrative office building

**e.** Salaries of factory security guards

**f.** Salaries of office workers in the credit department

**g.** Depreciation on raw materials warehouse

**h.** Income taxes on a profitable manufacturing company

The following information was taken from the accounting records of Reliable Tool Corporation:

**EXERCISE 16.4**

Flow of Costs Through
Manufacturing Accounts

**LO 4**

| | |
|---|---:|
| Work in process inventory, beginning of the year | $ 35,000 |
| Cost of direct materials used | 245,000 |
| Direct labor cost applied to production | 120,000 |
| Cost of finished goods manufactured | 675,000 |

Overhead is applied to production at a rate of $30 per machine hour. During the current year, 10,000 machine hours were used in the production process.

Compute the amount of the work in process inventory on hand at year-end.

The production manager of Del Mar Manufacturing Co. has made the following estimates for the coming year:

**EXERCISE 16.5**

Computation and Use of an
Overhead Application Rate

**LO 6**

| | |
|---|---:|
| Estimated manufacturing overhead | $1,200,000 |
| Estimated direct labor cost | $ 500,000 |
| Estimated machine hours | 80,000 hours |

**a.** Compute the overhead application rate based on:
   **1.** Direct labor cost.
   **2.** Machine hours.

**b.** Assume that the manufacture of a particular product requires $2,000 in direct materials, $400 in direct labor, and 62 machine hours. Determine the total cost of manufacturing this product assuming that the overhead application rate is based on:
   **1.** Direct labor cost.
   **2.** Machine hours.

The accounting records of NuTronics, Inc., include the following information for the year ended December 31, 2002.

**EXERCISE 16.6**

Preparing a Schedule of the
Cost of Finished Goods
Manufactured

**LO 7**

| | Dec. 31 | Jan. 1 |
|---|---:|---:|
| Inventory of materials | $ 24,000 | $20,000 |
| Inventory of work in process | 8,000 | 12,000 |
| Inventory of finished goods | 90,000 | 80,000 |
| Direct materials used | 210,000 | |
| Direct labor | 120,000 | |
| Selling expenses | 170,000 | |
| General and administrative expenses | 140,000 | |

Overhead is applied to production at a rate of $24 per direct labor hour. Direct labor workers logged 8,000 hours during the period.

**a.** Prepare a schedule of the cost of finished goods manufactured. (Not all of the data given above are used in this schedule.)

**b.** Assume that the company manufactures a single product and that 20,000 units were completed during the year. What is the average per-unit cost of manufacturing this product?

**EXERCISE 16.7**

Flow of Costs Through
Manufacturing Accounts

**LO 3, 4, 5**

Stone Tools, Inc., had the following estimates available for the upcoming year:

| | |
|---|---|
| Estimated manufacturing overhead ......................................... | $378,000 |
| Estimated direct labor hours ............................................ | 21,000 |

Stone also had the following account balances as of January 1:

| | |
|---|---|
| Direct Materials Inventory ............................................ | $ 8,700 |
| Work in Process Inventory ............................................ | 76,500 |
| Finished Goods Inventory ............................................ | 53,000 |
| Manufacturing Overhead ............................................ | –0– |

During the month of January, all of the following occurred:

1. Direct labor costs were $42,000 or 1,800 hours worked.
2. Direct materials costing $25,750 and indirect materials costing $3,500 were purchased.
3. Sales commissions of $16,500 were earned by the sales force.
4. $26,000 worth of direct materials were used in production.
5. Advertising costs of $6,300 were incurred.
6. Factory supervisors earned salaries of $12,000.
7. Indirect labor costs for the month were $3,000.
8. Monthly depreciation on factory equipment was $4,500.
9. Utilities expense of $7,800 was incurred in the factory.
10. Tools with manufacturing costs of $69,000 were transferred to finished goods.
11. Monthly insurance costs for the factory were $4,200.
12. $3,000 in property taxes on the factory were incurred and paid.
13. Tools with manufacturing costs of $89,000 were sold for $165,000.

   **a.** If Stone applies manufacturing overhead on the basis of direct labor hours, what will be the balances in the Direct Materials, Work in Process, and Finished Goods Inventory accounts at the end of January?

   **b.** As of January 31, what will be the balance in the manufacturing overhead account.

   **c.** What was Stone's operating income for January?

**EXERCISE 16.8**

Overhead Cost Drivers;
Determination and Use
of Unit Cost

**LO 6**

During June, Assembly Department no. 4 of Riverview Electronics produced 12,000 model 201 computer keyboards. Assembly of these units required 1,476 hours of direct labor at a cost of $26,400, direct materials costing $318,960, and 2,880 hours of machine time. Based on an analysis of overhead costs at the beginning of the year, overhead is applied to keyboards using the following formula:

**Overhead = 75% of Direct Labor Cost + $32 per Machine Hour**

**a.** Compute the total amount of overhead cost applied to the 12,000 keyboards.

**b.** Compute the *per-unit cost* of manufacturing these keyboards.

**c.** Briefly explain *why* the department might use *two separate activity bases* in applying overhead costs to one type of product.

**d.** Identify at least two types of overhead costs that might be "driven" by each of the two cost drivers indicated in this situation.

**e.** What appears to be the *primary* driver of overhead costs in the manufacture of keyboards?

**f.** Compute the gross profit that will result from the sale of 2,000 of these keyboards at a sales price of $75 each.

**EXERCISE 16.9**

Manipulating Accounting
Figures

**LO 1**

Joe Felan is the production manager at Utex Corporation. He was recently quoted as saying, "Since management reports aren't subject to generally accepted accounting principles, and they aren't directly used by outside investors and creditors, it's really okay for managers to manipulate the reports as they see fit." Do you agree with Felan's statement? Defend your answer.

# PROBLEMS

Aqua-Marine manufactures fiberglass fishing boats. The manufacturing costs incurred during its first year of operations are shown as follows:

| | |
|---|---|
| Direct materials purchased | $225,000 |
| Direct materials used | 216,000 |
| Direct labor assigned to production | 200,000 |
| Manufacturing overhead | 350,000 |
| Cost of finished goods manufactured (112 boats) | 728,000 |

During the year, 112 completed boats were manufactured, of which 100 were sold. (Assume that the amount of the ending inventory of finished goods and the cost of goods sold are determined using the average per-unit cost of manufacturing a completed boat.)

### Instructions

**a.** Compute each of the following and show all computations:

   **1.** The average per-unit cost of manufacturing a completed boat during the current year

   **2.** The year-end balances of the inventories of materials, work in process, and finished goods

   **3.** The cost of goods sold during the year

**b.** For the current year, the costs of direct materials purchased, direct labor assigned to production, and actual manufacturing overhead total $775,000. Is this the amount of manufacturing costs deducted from revenue in the current year? Explain fully.

Road Ranger Corporation began operations early in the current year, building luxury motor homes. During the year, the company started and completed 50 motor homes at a cost of $60,000 per unit. Of these, 48 were sold for $95,000 each and two remain in finished goods inventory. In addition, the company had six partially completed units in its factory at year-end. Total costs for the year (summarized alphabetically) were as follows:

| | |
|---|---|
| Direct materials used | $ 750,000 |
| Direct labor applied to production | 900,000 |
| Income taxes expense | 100,000 |
| General and administrative expenses | 500,000 |
| Manufacturing overhead | 1,800,000 |
| Selling expenses | 500,000 |

### Instructions

Compute the following for the current year:

**a.** Total manufacturing costs charged to work in process during the period

**b.** Cost of finished goods manufactured

**c.** Cost of goods sold

**d.** Gross profit on sales

**e.** Ending inventories of (1) work in process and (2) finished goods

The flow of manufacturing costs through the ledger accounts of Superior Locks, Inc., in the current year is illustrated on the next page in summarized form.

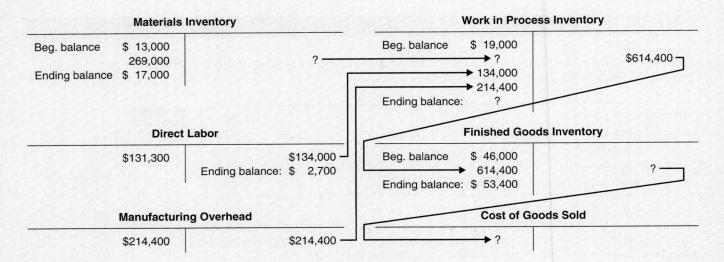

**Materials Inventory**

| | |
|---|---|
| Beg. balance | $ 13,000 |
| | 269,000 |
| Ending balance | $ 17,000 |

**Work in Process Inventory**

| | |
|---|---|
| Beg. balance | $ 19,000 |
| | ? |
| | 134,000 |
| | 214,400 |
| Ending balance: | ? |

$614,400

**Direct Labor**

| | |
|---|---|
| $131,300 | $134,000 |
| | Ending balance: $ 2,700 |

**Finished Goods Inventory**

| | |
|---|---|
| Beg. balance | $ 46,000 |
| | 614,400 |
| Ending balance: $ 53,400 | ? |

**Manufacturing Overhead**

| | |
|---|---|
| $214,400 | $214,400 |

**Cost of Goods Sold**

?

**Instructions**

Indicate the amounts requested below. Some amounts are shown in the T accounts above; others require short computations. (Show all computations.)

a. Purchases of direct materials

b. The cost of direct materials used

c. Direct labor costs assigned to production

d. The year-end liability for direct wages payable

e. The overhead application rate in use throughout the year, assuming that overhead is applied as a percentage of direct labor costs

f. Total manufacturing costs charged to the Work in Process Inventory account during the current year

g. The cost of finished goods manufactured

h. The year-end balance in the Work in Process Inventory account

i. The cost of goods sold

j. The total amount of inventory listed in the year-end balance sheet

**PROBLEM 16.4**

The Flow of Manufacturing
Costs Through Perpetual
Inventory Records

The following T accounts summarize the flow of manufacturing costs during the current year through the ledger accounts of Gronback Corporation:

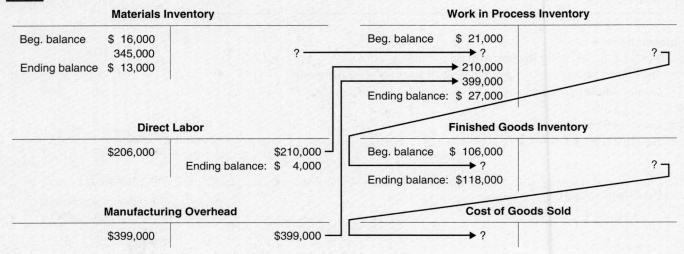

**Materials Inventory**

| | |
|---|---|
| Beg. balance | $ 16,000 |
| | 345,000 |
| Ending balance | $ 13,000 |

**Work in Process Inventory**

| | |
|---|---|
| Beg. balance | $ 21,000 |
| | ? |
| | 210,000 |
| | 399,000 |
| Ending balance: $ 27,000 | |

?

**Direct Labor**

| | |
|---|---|
| $206,000 | $210,000 |
| | Ending balance: $ 4,000 |

**Finished Goods Inventory**

| | |
|---|---|
| Beg. balance | $ 106,000 |
| | ? |
| Ending balance: $118,000 | ? |

**Manufacturing Overhead**

| | |
|---|---|
| $399,000 | $399,000 |

**Cost of Goods Sold**

?

## Instructions

From the data supplied on the previous page, indicate the following amounts. Some amounts are shown in the T accounts; others require short computations. (Show all computations.)

a. Purchases during the year of direct materials

b. The cost of direct materials used

c. Direct labor payrolls paid during the year

d. Direct labor costs assigned to production

e. The overhead application rate in use during the year, assuming that overhead is applied as a percentage of direct labor costs

f. Total manufacturing costs charged to the Work in Process Inventory account during the year

g. The cost of finished goods manufactured

h. The cost of goods sold

i. The total costs to be classified as inventory in the year-end balance sheet

The balances in the perpetual inventory accounts of Hillsdale Manufacturing Corporation at the beginning and end of the current year are as follows:

**PROBLEM 16.5**

The Flow of Manufacturing Costs: A Comprehensive Problem

**LO 3, 4, 7**

| | End of Year | Beginning of Year |
|---|---|---|
| Inventory accounts: | | |
| Materials | $26,000 | $22,000 |
| Work in Process | 9,000 | 5,000 |
| Finished Goods Inventory | 25,000 | 38,000 |

The total dollar amounts debited and credited during the year to the accounts used in recording manufacturing activities are as follows:

| | Debit Entries | Credit Entries |
|---|---|---|
| Account: | | |
| Materials Inventory | $410,000 | $    ? |
| Direct Labor | 189,000 | 192,000 |
| Manufacturing Overhead | 393,600 | 393,600 |
| Work in Process Inventory | ? | ? |
| Finished Goods Inventory | ? | ? |

## Instructions

a. Using these data, state or compute for the year the following amounts:

1. Direct materials purchased

2. Direct materials used

3. Payments of direct labor payrolls

4. Direct labor cost assigned to production

5. The overhead application rate used during the year, assuming that overhead was applied as a percentage of direct labor costs

6. Total manufacturing costs charged to the Work in Process Inventory account during the year

7. The cost of finished goods manufactured

8. Cost of goods sold

9. The total amount to be classified as inventory in the year-end balance sheet

b. Prepare a schedule of the cost of finished goods manufactured.

**PROBLEM 16.6**

Determining and Reporting
Product Cost Information

**LO 4, 7**

The following are 2002 data regarding Baby Buddy, one of the major products manufactured by the Toledo Toy Company:

| | |
|---|---|
| Purchases of direct materials | $332,000 |
| Direct materials used | 333,600 |
| Direct labor payrolls (paid during the year) | 176,700 |
| Direct labor costs assigned to production | 180,000 |
| Manufacturing overhead (incurred and applied) | 288,000 |

During the year 60,000 units of this product were manufactured and 62,100 units were sold. Selected information concerning inventories during the year follows:

| | Dec. 31 | Jan. 1 |
|---|---|---|
| Materials | $  ? | $12,800 |
| Work in Process | 4,700 | 4,100 |
| Finished Goods, Jan. 1 (3,000 units @ $13) | ? | 39,000 |

**Instructions**

a. Prepare a schedule of the cost of finished goods manufactured for the Baby Buddy product in 2002.

b. Compute the average cost of Baby Buddy completed in 2002.

c. Compute the cost of goods sold associated with the sale of Baby Buddy in 2002. Assume that there is a first-in, first-out (FIFO) flow through the Finished Goods Inventory account and that all units completed in 2002 are assigned the per-unit costs determined in part **b**.

d. Compute the amount of inventory relating to Baby Buddy that will be listed in the company's balance sheet at December 31, 2002. Show supporting computations for the year-end amounts of materials inventory and finished goods inventory.

e. Explain where the $180,000 in direct labor costs assigned to production in 2002 affect the company's 2002 income statement and balance sheet.

**PROBLEM 16.7**

Determining and Reporting
Product Cost Information

**LO 4, 7**

The following are the beginning and ending balances in the inventory accounts of Nevis Tools for 2002:

| | End of Year | Beginning of Year |
|---|---|---|
| Inventory accounts: | | |
| Materials | $62,400 | $ 56,400 |
| Work in Process | 28,800 | 31,200 |
| Finished Goods Inventory | ? | 117,600 |

The amounts debited and credited during the year to the accounts used in recording manufacturing costs are as follows:

| | Debit Entries | Credit Entries |
|---|---|---|
| Account: | | |
| Materials Inventory | $ 828,000 | $    ? |
| Direct Labor | 474,000 | 480,000 |
| Manufacturing Overhead | 1,056,000 | 1,056,000 |
| Cost of Goods Sold | 2,370,000 | –0– |
| Work in Process Inventory | ? | ? |
| Finished Goods Inventory | ? | ? |

## Instructions

**a.** Using the given information, state (or compute) for 2002 the following amounts:

1. Direct materials purchased
2. Direct materials used
3. Direct labor payrolls paid during the year
4. Direct labor costs assigned to units being manufactured
5. The year-end liability for direct wages payable
6. The overhead application rate, assuming that overhead costs are applied to units being manufactured using 24,000 direct labor hours as an estimated activity base
7. Total manufacturing costs debited to the Work in Process Inventory account
8. Cost of finished goods manufactured
9. Ending inventory of finished goods

**b.** Prepare a schedule of the cost of finished goods manufactured for the year.

The accounting records of the Idaho Paper Company include the following information relating to the current year:

|  | Dec. 31 | Jan. 1 |
|---|---|---|
| Materials inventory ........................................ | $ 20,000 | $ 25,000 |
| Work in process inventory ................................ | 37,500 | 40,000 |
| Finished goods inventory, Jan. 1 (10,000 units @ $21 per unit) ........ | ? | 210,000 |
| Purchases of direct materials during year ..................... | 330,000 | |
| Direct labor costs assigned to production ..................... | 375,000 | |
| Manufacturing overhead applied to production ................. | 637,500 | |

**PROBLEM 16.8**

Determining Unit Costs Using the Cost of Finished Goods Manufactured

**LO 4, 7**

The company manufactures a single product; during the current year, *45,000* units were manufactured and *40,000* units were sold.

## Instructions

**a.** Prepare a schedule of the cost of finished goods manufactured for the current year. (Show a supporting computation of the cost of direct materials *used* during the year.)

**b.** Compute the average per-unit cost of production during the current year.

**c.** Compute the cost of goods sold during the year, assuming that the FIFO (first-in, first-out) method of inventory costing is used.

**d.** Compute the cost of the inventory of finished goods at December 31 of the current year, assuming that the FIFO (first-in, first-out) method of inventory costing is used.

Mayville Company, a sole proprietorship, reports the following information pertaining to its 2002 operating activities:

|  | 12/31/02 Balance | 1/1/02 Balance |
|---|---|---|
| Materials Inventory ....................................... | $20,000 | $40,000 |
| Work in Process Inventory ................................ | 29,000 | 60,000 |
| Finished Goods Inventory ................................ | 52,000 | 42,000 |

**PROBLEM 16.9**

Preparing an Income Statement Using the Cost of Finished Goods Manufactured

**LO 4, 7**

During the year, the company purchased $30,000 of direct materials and incurred $21,000 of direct labor costs. Total manufacturing overhead costs for the year amounted to $18,000. Selling and administrative expenses amounted to $60,000, and the company's annual sales amounted to $200,000.

**Instructions**

**a.** Prepare Mayville's schedule of the cost of finished goods manufactured for 2002.

**b.** Prepare Mayville's 2002 income statement (ignore income taxes).

**PROBLEM 16.10**

Preparing an Income Statement Using the Cost of Finished Goods Manufactured

**LO 4, 7**

Ridgeway Company reports the following information pertaining to its 2002 operating activities:

| | 12/31/02 Balance | 1/1/02 Balance |
|---|---|---|
| Materials Inventory | $70,000 | $60,000 |
| Work in Process Inventory | 41,000 | 29,000 |
| Finished Goods Inventory | 16,000 | 21,000 |

During the year, the company purchased $35,000 of direct materials and incurred $22,000 of direct labor costs. Total manufacturing overhead costs for the year amounted to $19,000. Selling and administrative expenses amounted to $30,000, and the company's annual sales amounted to $80,000.

**Instructions**

**a.** Prepare Ridgeway's schedule of the cost of finished goods manufactured for 2002.

**b.** Prepare Ridgeway's 2002 income statement (ignore income taxes).

**PROBLEM 16.11**

Measuring Unit Cost

**LO 3, 4, 7**

Early in the year, John Raymond founded Raymond Engineering Co. for the purpose of manufacturing a special flow control valve that he had designed. Shortly after year-end, the company's accountant was injured in a skiing accident, and no year-end financial statements have been prepared. However, the accountant had correctly determined the year-end inventories at the following amounts:

| | |
|---|---|
| Materials | $46,000 |
| Work in process | 31,500 |
| Finished goods (3,000 units) | 88,500 |

As this was the first year of operations, there were no beginning inventories.

While the accountant was in the hospital, Raymond improperly prepared the following income statement from the company's accounting records:

| | | |
|---|---|---|
| Net sales | | $610,600 |
| Cost of goods sold: | | |
| Purchases of direct materials | $181,000 | |
| Direct labor costs assigned to production | 110,000 | |
| Manufacturing overhead applied to production | 170,000 | |
| Selling expenses | 70,600 | |
| Administrative expenses | 132,000 | |
| Total costs | | 663,600 |
| Net loss for year | | $ (53,000) |

Raymond was very disappointed in these operating results. He states, "Not only did we lose more than $50,000 this year, but look at our unit production costs. We sold 10,000 units this year at a cost of $663,600; that amounts to a cost of $66.36 per unit. I know some of our competitors are able to manufacture similar valves for about $35 per unit. I don't need an accountant to know that this business is a failure."

## Instructions

**a.** Prepare a schedule of the cost of finished goods manufactured for the year. (As there were no beginning inventories, your schedule will start with "Manufacturing costs assigned to production:.") Show a supporting computation for the cost of direct materials used during the year.

**b.** Compute the average cost per unit manufactured.

**c.** Prepare a corrected income statement for the year, using the multiple-step format. If the company has earned any operating income, assume an income tax rate of 30%. (Omit earnings per share figures.)

**d.** Explain whether you agree or disagree with Raymond's remarks that the business is unprofitable and that its unit cost of production ($66.36, according to Raymond) is much higher than that of competitors (around $35). If you disagree with Raymond, explain any errors or shortcomings in his analysis.

William Nelson, the chief accountant of West Texas Guitar Company, was injured in an automobile accident shortly before the end of the company's first year of operations. At year-end, a clerk with a very limited understanding of accounting prepared the following income statement, which is unsatisfactory in several respects:

**PROBLEM 16.12**

Effect on Income Statement of Errors in Handling Manufacturing Costs

**LO 3, 4, 7**

| WEST TEXAS GUITAR COMPANY<br>Income Statement<br>For the Year Ended December 31, 20__ | | |
|---|---|---|
| Net sales | | $ 1,300,000 |
| Cost of goods sold: | | |
| Purchases of direct materials | $460,000 | |
| Direct labor | 225,000 | |
| Indirect labor | 90,000 | |
| Depreciation on machinery—factory | 50,000 | |
| Rent | 144,000 | |
| Insurance | 16,000 | |
| Utilities | 28,000 | |
| Miscellaneous manufacturing overhead | 34,600 | |
| Other operating expenses | 273,800 | |
| Dividends declared on capital stock | 46,000 | |
| Cost of goods sold | | $(1,367,400) |
| Loss for year | | $    (67,400) |

You are asked to help management prepare a corrected income statement for the first year of operations. Management informs you that 60% of the rent, insurance, and utilities applies to factory operations, and that the remaining 40% should be classified as period expense. Also, the correct ending inventories are as follows:

| Material | $ 38,000 |
|---|---|
| Work in process | 10,000 |
| Finished goods | 110,400 |

As this is the first year of operations, there were no beginning inventories.

## Instructions

**a.** Identify the shortcomings and errors in the above income statement. Based on the shortcomings you have identified, explain whether you would expect the company's actual net income for the first year of operations to be higher or lower than the amount shown.

**b.** Prepare schedules to determine:

**1.** The cost of direct materials used.

2. Total manufacturing overhead.

c. Prepare a schedule of cost of finished goods manufactured during the year. (Use the amounts computed in part **b** as the costs of direct materials used and manufacturing overhead.)

d. Prepare a corrected income statement for the year, using a multiple-step format. Assume that income taxes expense amounts to 30% of income before income taxes.

# CASES AND UNSTRUCTURED PROBLEMS

**CASE 16.1**

Poor Drivers Are
Cost Drivers

**LO 6**

Ye Olde Bump & Grind, Inc., is an automobile body and fender repair shop. Repair work is done by hand and with the use of small tools. Customers are billed based on time (direct labor hours) and materials used in each repair job.

The shop's overhead costs consist primarily of indirect materials (welding materials, metal putty, and sandpaper), rent, indirect labor, and utilities. Rent is equal to a percentage of the shop's gross revenue for each month. The indirect labor relates primarily to ordering parts and processing insurance claims. The amount of indirect labor, therefore, tends to vary with the size of each job.

Henry Lee, manager of the business, is considering using either direct labor hours or number of repair jobs as the basis for allocating overhead costs. He has estimated the following amounts for the coming year:

| | |
|---|---:|
| Estimated total overhead .................................... | $123,000 |
| Estimated direct labor hours ................................ | 10,000 |
| Estimated number of repair jobs ............................. | 300 |

## Instructions

a. Compute the overhead application rate based on (1) direct labor hours and (2) number of repair jobs.

b. Shown below is information for two repair jobs:

**Job 1** Repair a dented fender. Direct material used, $25; direct labor hours, 5; direct labor cost, $75.

**Job 2** Repair an automobile involved in a serious collision. Direct materials used, $3,800; direct labor hours, 200; direct labor cost, $3,000.

Determine the *total cost* of each repair job, assuming that overhead costs are applied to each job based on:

1. Direct labor hours.

2. Number of repair jobs.

c. Discuss the results obtained in part **b**. Which overhead application method appears to provide the more realistic results? Explain the reasoning behind your answer, addressing the issue of what "drives" overhead costs in this business.

**CASE 16.2**

The Meadowbrooke Miracle

**LO 2, 3, 4, 7**

Prescott Manufacturing operates several plants, each of which produces a different product. Early in the current year, John Walker was hired as the new manager of the Meadowbrooke Plant. At year-end, all the plant managers are asked to summarize the operations of their plants at a meeting of the company's board of directors. John Walker displayed the following information on a chart as he made his presentation:

| | Current Year | Last Year |
|---|---:|---:|
| Inventories of finished goods: | | |
| Beginning of the year (30,000 units in the current year and 10,000 units last year) ............................ | $255,000 | $ 85,000 |
| End of the year (20,000 units in the current year and 30,000 units last year) ................................ | 202,000 | 255,000 |
| Cost of finished goods manufactured ........................ | 909,000 | 1,020,000 |

Walker made the following statements to the board: "As you know, sales volume has remained constant for the Meadowbrooke Plant. Both this year and last, our sales amounted to 100,000 units. We have made real gains, however, in controlling our manufacturing costs. Through efficient plant operations, we have reduced our cost of finished goods manufactured by over $100,000. These economies are reflected in a reduction of the manufacturing cost per unit sold from $10.20 last year ($1,020,000 ÷ 100,000 units) to $9.09 in the current year ($909,000 ÷ 100,000 units)."

Father Alan Carter is president of St. Mary's University and is a member of Prescott Manufacturing's board of directors. However, Father Carter has little background in the accounting practices of manufacturing companies, and he asks you for assistance in evaluating Walker's statements.

### Instructions

**a.** As a preliminary step to your analysis, compute the following for the Meadowbrooke Plant in each of the two years:

   **1.** Cost of goods sold

   **2.** Number of finished units manufactured

   **3.** Average cost per unit manufactured

   **4.** Average cost per unit sold

**b.** Evaluate the statements made by Walker. Comment specifically on Walker's computation of the manufacturing cost of units sold and on whether it appears that the reduction in the cost of finished goods sold was achieved through more efficient operations.

Classic Cabinets has one factory in which it produces two product lines. Walter manages the Wood Division, which produces wood cabinets, and Mary manages the Metal Division, which produces metal cabinets. Estimated unit production costs for the two types of cabinets are as follows:

**CASE 16.3**

Effect of Overhead Application on Performance Evaluation

**LO 1, 5, 6**

|  | Wood | Metal |
|---|---|---|
| Direct materials | $50.00 | $35.00 |
| Direct labor cost | 20.00 | 30.00 |
| Manufacturing overhead | 16.30 | 24.45 |
| Total production cost per unit | $86.30 | $89.45 |
| | | |
| Selling price per unit | $ 180 | $ 160 |
| Direct labor hours required per unit | 2 | 3 |
| Direct labor cost per hour | $ 10 | $ 10 |

At the end of the year, total overhead costs are allocated to each division based on direct labor hours used. A breakdown of estimated yearly overhead costs is as follows:

| Salaries: | |
|---|---|
| Walter | $ 50,000 |
| Mary | 50,000 |
| Maintenance | 20,000 |
| Utilities | 16,000 |
| Property taxes | 10,000 |
| Annual straight-line depreciation: | |
| Equipment, Wood Division | 80,000 |
| Equipment, Metal Division | 120,000 |
| Total overhead | $346,000 |

Demand for cabinets over the past several years has been steady and is not expected to change. The Marketing Department estimates that approximately 10,000 wood cabinets and 7,500 metal cabinets will be sold each year for the foreseeable future. Each manager's performance evaluation is based on the total production cost per unit for his or her product line. The manager that succeeds in reducing unit costs by the greatest amount from those estimated on the previous page will earn a bonus.

Mary is considering purchasing a new machine for $500,000 that will last approximately 10 years and have no salvage value. If the machine is purchased, the direct labor hours required to produce a metal cabinet will be reduced to 2.5 hours.

### Instructions

**a.** If the machine is purchased, what will be the total unit costs of production for each type of cabinet assuming all other cost and production estimates are correct?

**b.** From Mary's point of view, should the machine be purchased? Discuss whether Mary and Walter should be given sole authority over which equipment to purchase for their respective divisions.

**c.** What information do you think is necessary to decide whether to purchase the machine?

**d.** If the machine is purchased, do you think the performance evaluation of Walter and Mary will be accurate and fair under the current system?

## *BUSINESS WEEK* ASSIGNMENT                           BusinessWeek

**CASE 16.4**

E-Commerce Costs

**LO 3**

In an April 3, 2000, article in *Business Week* titled "Commentary: Earth to Dot-Com Accountants," author Catherine Yang describes some aggresive accounting methods used by dot-com companies. In particular, she states, "Amazon.com Inc. is one of a number of companies which assigns some costs to sales and marketing expenses rather than to the cost of goods sold. That's an advantage because investors view dot-com companies marketing expenditures as a necessary ramp-up cost, while cost of goods sold eats into gross margins." Classifying these costs as marketing expenses indentifies them as period costs rather than product costs.

A July 10, 2000, *Business Week* cover story entitled "Can Amazon Make It?" also analyzed **Amazon.com**'s financial health. R. Hoff, D. Sparks, E. Neuborne, and W. Zellner reported that **Amazon** built a "vast network of distribution centers . . . over the past couple of years. While largely empty and unused, the centers gave **Amazon** a leg up on online and traditional rivals last Christmas."

### Instructions

**a.** Prepare a printed, one-page, double-spaced report. In the report, identify what type of costs **Amazon** and other dot-coms might be including in marketing expenses rather than in cost of goods sold as suggested above.

**b.** If your last name begins with A through K assume you are an accountant working for Amazon and write a short paragraph defending **Amazon.com Inc.**'s decision to classify the costs identified in part **a** as marketing expenses. If your last name begins with L through Z assume you are part of the SEC's accounting enforcement division and write a short paragraph explaining why these costs should not be classified as marketing expenses.

## INTERNET ASSIGNMENT

**INTERNET 16.1**

Calculating Cost of
Goods Manufactured

**LO 4, 7**

**Pfizer, Inc.**, develops and manufactures various pharmaceutical products. Visit its home page at the following address:

**www.pfizer.com**

From the home page, access the most recent annual report.

### Instructions

**a.** What categories of inventory does Pfizer show on its balance sheet?

**b.** Using the income statement and inventory information from the balance sheet, calculate the cost of finished goods manufactured for the most recent year.

**c.** What elements of manufacturing overhead can you identify using the annual report?

*Internet sites are time and date sensitive. It is the purpose of these exercises to have you explore the Internet. You may need to use the Yahoo! search engine* http://www.yahoo.com *(or other favorite search engine) to look for a company's current web address.*

## OUR COMMENTS ON THE "YOUR TURN" CASES

**As a Shift Supervisor (p. 704)**   When choosing personnel for rework, several considerations are necessary. If you must choose among the existing set of direct labor, you would want to consider the cost associated with idle equipment. If a cutter, welder, or painter is assigned to do rework and, as a result, equipment is idle, the company will lose not only the productivity of the direct labor time but also the productivity of the equipment. In addition to the cost of idle equipment, the labor cost associated with each category of labor would be useful information. Finally, in considering who should be involved in rework, a consideration of the source of the quality problem is critical. Frequently, processes can be redesigned or better raw materials can be obtained to eliminate quality problems and the associated rework. Employees typically do not deliberately create poor-quality products. When the source of the problem is the employee, frequently, training will eliminate the problem.

**As an Equipment Operator (p. 706)**   You should point out to your co-worker that the composition of the overhead for Conquest includes many costs that are not related to the number of machine hours. For example, indirect labor costs for forklift drivers, shop floor supervisor, and factory security will not decline if you reduce the machine hours by 10%. Reducing the number of machine hours will not affect the amount of cost incurred for indirect labor, and only machine-related overhead costs might be reduced (for example, depreciation, equipment repair, some indirect supplies—oil or cleaning fluids). In fact, if the expected number of machine hours were 9,000 rather than the 10,000 hours discussed in the chapter, the overhead application rate probably would be $40 per hour ($360,000 ÷ 9,000 hours) rather than the $36 per hour discussed in the chapter.

**As a Chief Financial Officer (p. 708)**   According to financial reporting standards and the matching principle, the costs described by Jim that were charged to cost of production should be charged as period expenses and should have appeared on the income statement as administrative expenses. You should talk with the plant manager, Darlene Cosky, and ask why the allocations described by Jim Sway were made to cost of production. Ms. Cosky may have been confused and may have believed that the costs described by Jim were appropriate to be allocated to cost of production. However, if Jim Sway had adequate training as an accountant, he should have known that these costs were period expenses and should not be assigned to cost of production. The ethical issue for the CFO to resolve is whether Darlene and/or Jim made these allocations with the intent of manipulating plant income for their own gain.

An additional issue is that determining and communicating guidelines about costs that are appropriately allocated to cost of production typically falls to the CFO, internal auditor, or controller. External auditors will want to see that these guidelines exist and are followed. If these guidelines do not exist, then the CFO bears some responsibility.

## ANSWERS TO SELF-TEST QUESTIONS

**1.** b, d   **2.** a   **3.** d   **4.** a   **5.** a, b, c

# ACCOUNTING SYSTEMS FOR MEASURING COSTS

## Learning Objectives

*After studying this chapter, you should be able to:*

1. Explain the purposes of cost accounting systems.

2. Distinguish between the processes for creating goods and services that are suited to job order costing, process costing, and activity-based costing.

3. Describe the purpose and the content of a job cost sheet.

4. Account for the flow of costs when using job order costing.

5. Account for the flow of costs when using process costing.

6. Demonstrate how equivalent units are computed.

7. Demonstrate how costs are assigned to equivalent units using process costing.

8. Define *activity cost pools* and provide several examples.

9. Demonstrate how activity bases are used to assign cost pools to units produced.

© Tony Arruza/Corbis

## Harley-Davidson, Inc.

In 1901 William Harley, 21, and Arthur Davidson, 20, began experiments designed to take the work out of bicycling. In 1903 they produced exactly three motorcycles in Milwaukee.

**Harley-Davidson** erected its first building on Juneau Avenue in 1906 and incorporated in 1907. That year they produced 150 motorcycles. By 1913 the original 28-by-80-foot factory had grown to 297,110 square feet. As production rose to 12,904, their motorcycles began to dominate racing events. **Harley-Davidson** motorcycles proved their military value in Mexican border skirmishes with Pancho Villa. When the United States entered World War I, some 20,000 cycles were used before the war's end. By 1920 **Harley-Davidson** was the largest motorcycle manufacturer in the world.

● ● ●

Over the remaining years **Harley-Davidson**'s production of motorcycles ranged from a low of 3,700 during the Depression to 90,000 produced for the military in World War II. Current yearly production is more than 100,000 motorcycles. When production fluctuates as it has for **Harley-Davidson**, it is critical for business planning purposes to have a clear understanding of the cost associated with production. Companies such as **Harley-Davidson** (**www.harley-davidson.com**) track their production costs by using cost accounting systems described in this chapter.

# COST ACCOUNTING SYSTEMS

An organization's accounting system must provide a good "map" that links the costs and the processes used to create goods and/or services. Employees need this information to assess how well they use the company's resources. Determining the least costly combination of direct labor, direct materials, and overhead to create a product or service is critical for an organization to remain competitive. A good cost accounting system will provide a map to match the processes that consume resources with associated costs so that managers can decide how to best provide products or services to customers.

Processes used to create goods and services vary widely. In the case of motorcycle manufacturers, the process used to create large numbers of identical motorcycles is significantly different than the process used to construct a specially ordered racing motorcycle. Tracking and measuring resources consumed by different types of manufacturing processes is the focus of this chapter. We will consider three widely used cost accounting procedures in this chapter: job order costing, process costing, and activity-based costing. These methods differ because the underlying production processes that are being tracked and measured differ.

**CASE IN POINT**

The city of Indianapolis, Indiana, implemented activity-based costing to help city employees understand and manage resources consumed by city activities. The new system helped the city to choose government activities that were appropriate to privatize and helped to improve the efficiency of those city activities that were not privatized. Over a three-year period, city planners identified $80 million in cost savings. Equally impressive were the improvements in service output that accompanied the cost savings.

**LO 1**

Explain the purposes of cost accounting systems.

**Cost accounting systems** are the methods and techniques used by enterprises to track resources consumed in creating and delivering products and services to customers. Employees use the information provided by cost accounting systems to help them manage the activities that consume resources. Management uses the information produced by cost accounting systems to evaluate and reward employee performance. In addition, the information produced by cost accounting systems is used for external reporting requirements. Inventories, cost of goods sold, and period costs are tracked by cost accounting systems and are reported on the balance sheet and income statement of the annual report.

In a manufacturing company, cost accounting systems help attain two important management objectives: (1) to determine unit manufacturing costs and (2) to provide managers with useful information for planning and cost control functions. As we saw in Chapter 16, *unit costs* are determined by tracing direct materials, direct labor, and manufacturing overhead to specific units of production.

A unit of product is defined differently in different industries. It is easy to think of units as individual products, such as automobiles or television sets. In some industries, however, units of production may be stated in tons, gallons, kilowatt hours, board-feet, or any other appropriate unit of output.[1] Regardless of how they are stated, unit costs provide a basis for inventory valuation and determination of the cost of goods sold. They also provide managers with information for setting prices, deciding what products to manufacture, evaluating the efficiency of operations, and controlling costs.

---

[1]Some service industries also express their operating costs on a per-unit basis. The units of product used in the airline industry, for example, are *passenger miles flown*.

*Cost control* refers to keeping costs at reasonable levels. When cost accounting systems provide timely information about unit costs, managers can react quickly should costs begin to rise to unacceptable levels. By comparing current unit costs with budgeted costs and other target measures, managers are able to identify those areas in which corrective actions are most needed.

## Basic Cost Accounting Methods

Cost accounting systems are typically designed to accommodate the specific needs of individual companies. In this chapter, we demonstrate three accounting systems for measuring and tracking resource consumption: job order costing, process costing, and activity-based costing. Job order and process costing are methods for tracking resource consumption directly to individual services and products. Activity-based costing tracks resource consumption by the activities that are undertaken to create products and services. Overhead items are often the focus of activity-based costing.

**Job order costing** is typically used by companies that tailor their goods or services to the specific needs of individual customers. In job order costing, the costs of direct materials, direct labor, and manufacturing overhead are accumulated separately for each job. A "job" represents the goods manufactured or services provided to fill a particular order, or production of a batch of a particular product. If a job contains multiple units of a product, unit costs are determined by dividing the total cost charged to the job by the number of units manufactured.

Construction companies use job order cost systems because each construction project has unique characteristics that affect its costs. Job order cost systems are also used by shipbuilders, motion picture studios, defense contractors, print shops, and custom furniture makers. In addition, these systems are widely used in service organizations, such as automotive repair shops, accounting firms, law firms, doctors' offices, and hospitals.

**Process costing** is most commonly used by companies that produce a "steady stream" of nearly identical products. In process costing, the costs of direct materials, direct labor, and manufacturing overhead are traced to individual *production departments* (or *processes*) responsible for manufacturing products. These costs are then compiled for a given period and are divided by the number of units produced to determine a per-unit cost figure. Companies that use process cost systems include oil refineries, breweries, soft-drink bottlers, flour mills, and most assembly-line or mass-production manufacturing operations.

**Activity-based costing (ABC)** tracks costs to the activities that consume resources. Overhead costs that are not easily traced directly to individual products and services are a primary focus of ABC. For example, the cost of employees who order raw materials for the production process at **Harley-Davidson** is an overhead item not easily traced directly to products. However, the activity of placing and tracking orders can be used as a means of measuring resources consumed.

To summarize, job order costing is appropriate for businesses and companies producing customized jobs that require differing amounts and types of direct labor, direct materials, and overhead. Process costing is used for production processes that produce mass quantities of identical units that use the same amounts and types of direct labor, direct materials, and overhead. Activity-based costing is used to track resources that are not directly traceable to the product or service purchased. Overhead items are typically the focus of ABC methods.

The type of cost accounting system best suited to a particular company *depends on the nature of the company's manufacturing operations.* In fact, a company that is involved in diverse manufacturing activities may use many cost accounting methods concurrently. In the following sections of this chapter, we will illustrate and explain each of these cost accounting systems.

**LO 2**

Distinguish between the processes for creating goods and services that are suited to job order costing, process costing, and activity-based costing.

# ▌ JOB ORDER COSTING

The distinguishing characteristic of job order costing is that manufacturing costs are accumulated *separately for each job*. As explained in Chapter 16, all manufacturing costs are charged (debited) to the Work in Process Inventory account as incurred. In job costing, Work in Process Inventory is a controlling (or summary) account, supported by **job cost sheets** for each job. Collectively, the job cost sheets serve as a subsidiary ledger showing the manufacturing costs charged to each job.

If a company is using an accounting software package, job cost information is recorded in computer-based files. However, the form and content of most job cost records are basically the same, regardless of whether they are maintained manually or by computer.

## The Job Cost Sheet

**LO 3**

Describe the purpose and the content of a job cost sheet.

Job cost sheets are the heart of job order costing. A separate job cost sheet is prepared for each job and is used to accumulate a record of all manufacturing costs charged to the job. Once the job is finished, the job cost sheet indicates the cost of the finished goods manufactured and provides the information necessary to compute the unit costs of production.

Direct manufacturing costs (direct materials used and direct labor) are recorded on the job cost sheet as quickly as these costs can be traced to the job. Once the job is complete, overhead costs are applied using an overhead application rate. Shown below is a completed job cost sheet of the Oak & Glass Furniture Co. This job involved the manufacture of 100 dining tables of a particular style.

---

**OAK & GLASS FURNITURE CO.**

**JOB COST SHEET**  831

Product __French Court dining tables__   Date started __4/03/02__

Number of units manufactured __100__   Date completed __4/21/02__

### COSTS CHARGED TO THIS JOB

| MANUFACTURING DEPARTMENT | DIRECT MATERIALS | DIRECT LABOR | | MANUFACTURING OVERHEAD | |
|---|---|---|---|---|---|
| | | HOURS | COST | RATE | COST APPLIED |
| Milling & Carving | $10,000 | 70 | $14,000 | 150% | $21,000 |
| Finishing | 15,000 | 300 | 6,000 | 150% | 9,000 |

### COST SUMMARY AND UNIT COSTS

| | Total Costs | Unit Costs |
|---|---|---|
| Direct materials used | $25,000 | $250 |
| Direct labor | 20,000 | 200 |
| Manufacturing overhead applied | 30,000 | 300 |
| Cost of finished goods manufactured __(100 tables)__ | $75,000 | $750 |

Throughout the production process, manufacturing costs traceable to the job are accumulated in the "Costs charged to this job" section of the job cost sheet. The "Cost summary" section is filled in when the job is completed.

The total cost of completing job no. 831 is *$75,000*. Upon completion of the job, this amount should be transferred from the Work in Process Inventory account to the Finished Goods Inventory account. The unit cost figures shown in the job cost sheet are determined by dividing the total manufacturing costs by the 100 units manufactured.

## Flow of Costs in Job Costing: An Illustration

Pages 738 and 739 illustrate the flow of costs for Oak & Glass Furniture Co. This flowchart summarizes the company's manufacturing operations during the month of January. Notice that each of the inventory controlling accounts (Materials, Work in Process, and Finished Goods) is supported by a subsidiary ledger.

In our flowchart, all subsidiary ledger accounts are shown in T account form to conserve space. In practice, the individual job cost sheets serve as the subsidiary ledger for the Work in Process Inventory controlling account. Also, the subsidiary ledger accounts for direct materials and finished goods would have additional columns providing detailed information as to quantities on hand and unit costs.

We will now use Oak & Glass Furniture Co. to explain the flow of manufacturing costs when using job order costing.

**LO 4**

Account for the flow of costs when using job order costing.

## Accounting for Direct Materials

In a perpetual inventory system, purchases of direct materials are posted from the purchases journal to the accounts in the materials subsidiary ledger. The entries in the subsidiary ledger indicate the type, quantity, and cost of the material purchased. At the end of each month, a summary entry is made debiting the Materials Inventory controlling account for the total cost of direct materials purchased during the period. (The offsetting credit normally is to Accounts Payable.)

To obtain materials for use in the production process, the production department must issue a *materials requisition* form to the materials warehouse. This requisition shows the quantity of materials needed and the job on which these materials will be used.

Copies of these requisitions are sent to the accounting department, where the cost of the materials placed into production is determined from the materials subsidiary ledger. The cost of the requisitioned materials is entered on the requisition form and in the subsidiary ledger accounts. In the subsidiary ledgers, usage of direct materials is recorded by (1) entering the cost of the materials used on the appropriate job cost sheet and (2) crediting the materials subsidiary ledger.

Multinational companies frequently source their direct materials from many countries. Because suppliers of direct materials are located in different countries, the costs of those materials are affected by international differences that do not affect direct materials sourced from domestic suppliers. Such factors as import duties, exchange rate fluctuations, and foreign taxes have an impact on the cost of direct materials making the purchasing function more complex for companies sourcing internationally.

**CASE IN POINT**

At month-end, all the materials requisitions issued during the month are totaled, and the following summary entry is made in the controlling accounts:

| | | |
|---|---|---|
| Work in Process Inventory .................................... | 50,000 | |
|     Materials Inventory ....................................... | | 50,000 |
| To record the cost of all direct materials placed into production during Jan. | | |

*Recording materials used during the month*

## Accounting for Direct Labor Costs

Debits to the Direct Labor account arise from making payments to direct factory workers; the offsetting credit is to the Cash account.[2] Payments to *indirect* factory workers (such as supervisors and security guards) are debited to Manufacturing Overhead, not to the Direct Labor account.

The Direct Labor account is credited as direct labor is *used*—that is, as employees work on specific jobs. A number of mechanical and computerized means have been developed for determining the direct labor cost applicable to each job. One common method is to prepare *time cards* for each employee, showing the number of hours worked on each job, the employee's rate of pay, and the direct labor cost chargeable to each job. These time cards become the basis for preparing factory payrolls and for posting direct labor costs to the work in process subsidiary ledger accounts (job cost sheets).

At the end of each month, a summary entry is made debiting Work in Process Inventory and crediting the Direct Labor account for all direct labor costs assigned to jobs during the month. For Oak & Glass, this entry is as follows:

*Recording direct labor costs*

| | | |
|---|---|---|
| Work in Process Inventory . . . . . . . . . . . . . . . . . . . . . . . . . . . . . . . . . . . . | 60,000 | |
|     Direct Labor . . . . . . . . . . . . . . . . . . . . . . . . . . . . . . . . . . . . . . . . . . . . | | 60,000 |
| To record in the general ledger all direct labor costs charged to | | |
|   jobs during Jan. | | |

Notice that the Direct Labor account is debited when employees are *paid,* but it is credited for the cost of work *performed* on jobs. Work is performed on a daily basis, but employees are paid only at periodic intervals, such as every two weeks. Thus the direct labor cost charged to jobs does not necessarily equal the amount paid to employees during the month. In our example, $60,000 of direct labor was assigned to the three jobs in process, but payments to employees totaled only $52,000. Thus the unadjusted $8,000 credit balance of the Direct Labor account at month-end represents a *liability for accrued wages payable.*

## Accounting for Overhead Costs

Manufacturing overhead includes all manufacturing costs *other than* the costs of direct materials and direct labor. Manufacturing Overhead is a controlling account; the details of the many different types of overhead costs are kept in a subsidiary ledger.

The Manufacturing Overhead account is debited for the *actual* amount of overhead costs incurred during the period. In our illustration, actual overhead costs in January total $93,000. These costs are posted to the overhead account from several sources. Indirect labor costs, for example, come from payroll records; purchases of indirect materials and payments of utility bills are posted from the voucher register or from special journals; and depreciation of plant assets comes from end-of-period adjusting entries in the general journal.

**Application of Overhead Costs to Jobs** As explained in Chapter 16, overhead is an *indirect* cost and cannot be traced conveniently to specific jobs or units. Therefore, a predetermined **overhead application rate** often is used to assign appropriate amounts of overhead costs to work in process. Oak & Glass uses an overhead application rate equal to *150% of direct labor cost.* Therefore, each job cost sheet is charged with overhead costs equal to 150% of the direct labor cost relating to the job.

The entry to apply overhead costs to the job cost sheet usually is made when the job is completed. However, overhead costs also should be applied to any jobs that are still

---

[2]To the extent that amounts are withheld from employees' pay for such purposes as income taxes and Social Security taxes, the offsetting credits are to various current liability accounts. Accounting for payrolls was discussed in Chapter 10.

in process at the end of the accounting period. At the end of each month, a summary entry is made in the general ledger to record all overhead costs applied to jobs during the period, as follows:

| | | |
|---|---|---|
| Work in Process Inventory . . . . . . . . . . . . . . . . . . . . . . . . . . . . . . . . . . . . . | 90,000 | |
|     Manufacturing Overhead . . . . . . . . . . . . . . . . . . . . . . . . . . . . . . . . . . . | | 90,000 |

*Entry to apply overhead costs to production*

To charge the Work in Process controlling account with
overhead costs applied to jobs during the month (150% of
direct labor costs for the month; $60,000 × 150% = $90,000).

**Over- or Underapplied Overhead**   In our example, actual overhead costs incurred during January amounted to $93,000, while the overhead applied to jobs using the overhead application rate totaled only $90,000. We should not expect that applied overhead will exactly equal actual overhead because the predetermined overhead application rate is based on *estimates*.

A debit balance in the Manufacturing Overhead account at month-end indicates that overhead applied to jobs was *less* than the actual overhead costs incurred during the month. Therefore, a debit balance remaining in the Manufacturing Overhead account is called **underapplied overhead**. A credit balance remaining in the account indicates that overhead applied to jobs *exceeded* actual overhead costs; thus a credit balance is termed **overapplied overhead**.

The month-end balances remaining in the Manufacturing Overhead account normally are allowed to accumulate throughout the year. These amounts tend to balance out from month to month, and the amount of overapplied or underapplied overhead at year-end usually *is not material* in dollar amount. In this case, the year-end balance in the Manufacturing Overhead account may be closed *directly to the Cost of Goods Sold,* on the grounds that most of the error is applicable to goods sold during the year. If the year-end balance in the overhead account *is material* in dollar amount, it should be apportioned among the Work in Process Inventory, Finished Goods Inventory, and Cost of Goods Sold accounts.

### You as a Treasurer

Assume you are the treasurer of ABI, Inc., a manufacturer of industrial lasers. Among your many responsibilities is supervising preparation of the company's tax returns. The assistant treasurer has pointed out to you that the controller is allocating the material amount of the underapplied overhead from last period among the Work-in-Progress Inventory, Finished Goods Inventory, and Cost of Goods Sold accounts. The assistant suggests that assigning the entire amount of underapplied overhead to cost of goods sold would have advantageous tax consequences. She says the result would be a higher cost of goods sold expense on the income statement and resulting lower profits. Lower profits would, in turn, reduce taxes. How should you respond?

*Our comments appear on page 775.

**YOUR TURN**

## Accounting for Completed Jobs

We have now explained how manufacturing costs are charged (debited) to the Work in Process Inventory account and how the costs of specific jobs are separately accumulated on job cost sheets.

As each job is completed, the job cost sheet is removed from the work in process subsidiary ledger and the manufacturing costs on the sheet are totaled to determine the cost of finished goods manufactured. This cost then is transferred from the Work in Process Inventory account to the Finished Goods Inventory account.

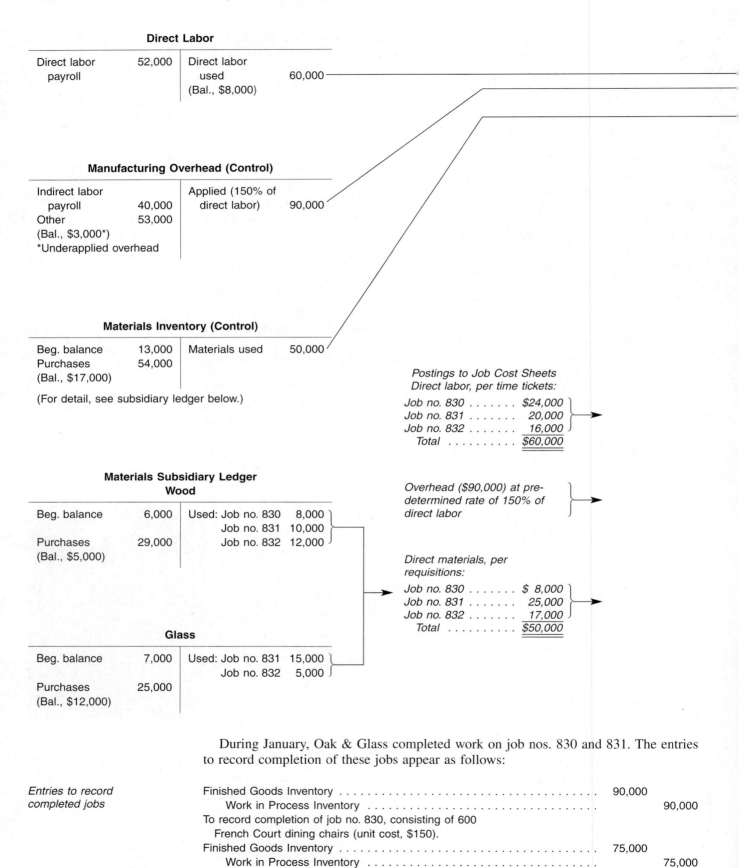

**Direct Labor**

| | | | |
|---|---|---|---|
| Direct labor payroll | 52,000 | Direct labor used (Bal., $8,000) | 60,000 |

**Manufacturing Overhead (Control)**

| | | | |
|---|---|---|---|
| Indirect labor payroll | 40,000 | Applied (150% of direct labor) | 90,000 |
| Other | 53,000 | | |
| (Bal., $3,000*) | | | |
| *Underapplied overhead | | | |

**Materials Inventory (Control)**

| | | | |
|---|---|---|---|
| Beg. balance | 13,000 | Materials used | 50,000 |
| Purchases | 54,000 | | |
| (Bal., $17,000) | | | |

(For detail, see subsidiary ledger below.)

Postings to Job Cost Sheets
Direct labor, per time tickets:

Job no. 830 . . . . . . . $24,000
Job no. 831 . . . . . . . 20,000
Job no. 832 . . . . . . . 16,000
Total . . . . . . . . . $60,000

**Materials Subsidiary Ledger**
**Wood**

| | | | | |
|---|---|---|---|---|
| Beg. balance | 6,000 | Used: Job no. 830 | 8,000 |
| | | Job no. 831 | 10,000 |
| Purchases | 29,000 | Job no. 832 | 12,000 |
| (Bal., $5,000) | | | |

Overhead ($90,000) at pre-determined rate of 150% of direct labor

Direct materials, per requisitions:

Job no. 830 . . . . . . . $ 8,000
Job no. 831 . . . . . . . 25,000
Job no. 832 . . . . . . . 17,000
Total . . . . . . . . . $50,000

**Glass**

| | | | | |
|---|---|---|---|---|
| Beg. balance | 7,000 | Used: Job no. 831 | 15,000 |
| | | Job no. 832 | 5,000 |
| Purchases | 25,000 | | |
| (Bal., $12,000) | | | |

During January, Oak & Glass completed work on job nos. 830 and 831. The entries to record completion of these jobs appear as follows:

*Entries to record completed jobs*

| | | |
|---|---|---|
| Finished Goods Inventory . . . . . . . . . . . . . . . . . . . . . . . . . . . . . . . . . . . . . . . . | 90,000 | |
| Work in Process Inventory . . . . . . . . . . . . . . . . . . . . . . . . . . . . . . . . . | | 90,000 |

To record completion of job no. 830, consisting of 600 French Court dining chairs (unit cost, $150).

| | | |
|---|---|---|
| Finished Goods Inventory . . . . . . . . . . . . . . . . . . . . . . . . . . . . . . . . . . . . . . . . | 75,000 | |
| Work in Process Inventory . . . . . . . . . . . . . . . . . . . . . . . . . . . . . . . . . | | 75,000 |

To record completion of job no. 831, consisting of 100 French Court dining tables (unit cost, $750).

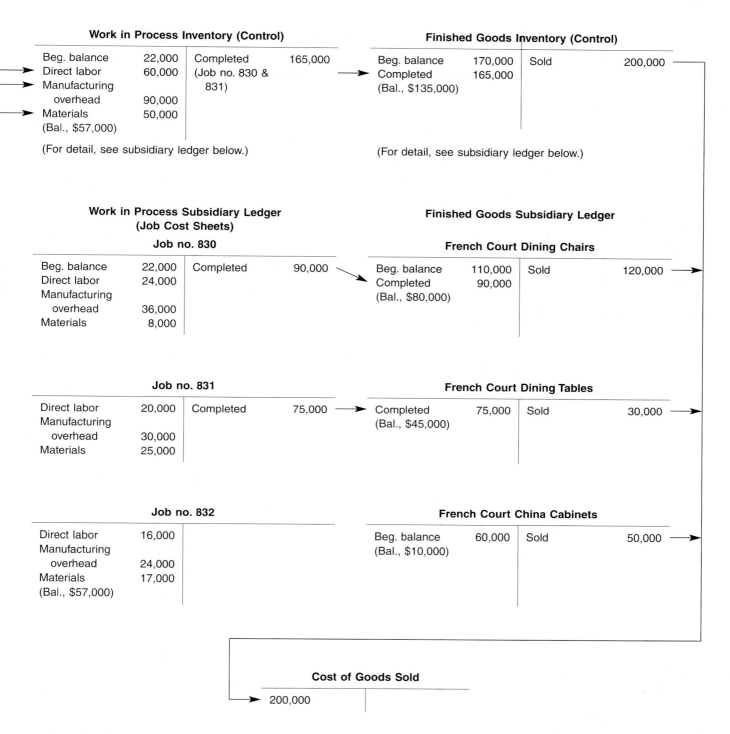

### Work in Process Inventory (Control)

| | | | |
|---|---|---|---|
| Beg. balance | 22,000 | Completed | 165,000 |
| Direct labor | 60,000 | (Job no. 830 & | |
| Manufacturing | | 831) | |
| overhead | 90,000 | | |
| Materials | 50,000 | | |
| (Bal., $57,000) | | | |

(For detail, see subsidiary ledger below.)

### Finished Goods Inventory (Control)

| | | | |
|---|---|---|---|
| Beg. balance | 170,000 | Sold | 200,000 |
| Completed | 165,000 | | |
| (Bal., $135,000) | | | |

(For detail, see subsidiary ledger below.)

### Work in Process Subsidiary Ledger
### (Job Cost Sheets)
#### Job no. 830

| | | | |
|---|---|---|---|
| Beg. balance | 22,000 | Completed | 90,000 |
| Direct labor | 24,000 | | |
| Manufacturing | | | |
| overhead | 36,000 | | |
| Materials | 8,000 | | |

### Finished Goods Subsidiary Ledger
#### French Court Dining Chairs

| | | | |
|---|---|---|---|
| Beg. balance | 110,000 | Sold | 120,000 |
| Completed | 90,000 | | |
| (Bal., $80,000) | | | |

#### Job no. 831

| | | | |
|---|---|---|---|
| Direct labor | 20,000 | Completed | 75,000 |
| Manufacturing | | | |
| overhead | 30,000 | | |
| Materials | 25,000 | | |

#### French Court Dining Tables

| | | | |
|---|---|---|---|
| Completed | 75,000 | Sold | 30,000 |
| (Bal., $45,000) | | | |

#### Job no. 832

| | | |
|---|---|---|
| Direct labor | 16,000 | |
| Manufacturing | | |
| overhead | 24,000 | |
| Materials | 17,000 | |
| (Bal., $57,000) | | |

#### French Court China Cabinets

| | | | |
|---|---|---|---|
| Beg. balance | 60,000 | Sold | 50,000 |
| (Bal., $10,000) | | | |

### Cost of Goods Sold

| | | |
|---|---|---|
| 200,000 | | |

As sales of the finished units occur, the unit cost figure will be used in determining the cost of goods sold. For example, the sale of 40 of the French Court dining tables at a total sales price of $48,000 is recorded as follows:

| | | |
|---|---|---|
| Accounts Receivable (Anthony's Fine Furniture) | 48,000 | |
| Sales | | 48,000 |
| Sold 40 French Court dining tables on account, terms 2/10, n/30. | | |
| Cost of Goods Sold | 30,000 | |
| Finished Goods Inventory | | 30,000 |
| To record the cost of the 40 French Court dining tables sold to Anthony's Fine Furniture (40 × $750 cost per unit = $30,000). | | |

### Job Order Costing in Service Industries

In the preceding discussion, we have emphasized the use of job order costing in manufacturing companies. However, many service industries also use this method to accumulate the costs of servicing a particular customer.

In a hospital, for example, each patient represents a separate "job," and the costs of caring for the patient are accumulated on a job cost sheet. Costs of such items as medicine, blood transfusions, and x-rays represent the usage of direct materials; services rendered by doctors are direct labor. The costs of nursing, meals, linen service, and depreciation of the hospital building and equipment all are part of the hospital's overhead. In a hospital, overhead often is applied to each patient's account at a predetermined daily rate.

**CASE IN POINT**

Congress passed legislation requiring hospitals that receive reimbursements from Medicare and Medicaid to measure and report the average unit costs of their "products." The products are defined as specific types of medical procedures, such as heart transplants, tonsillectomies, and deliveries (births). Thus hospitals must develop cost accounting systems capable of determining the average cost of providing each of these types of services.

## PROCESS COSTING

As emphasized in the preceding section, job order costing is appropriate when each unit of product, or "batch" of production, is manufactured to different specifications. Many companies, however, produce a *continuous stream of identical units*, such as bottles of beer, gallons of gasoline, or kilowatt hours of electricity. When identical products are produced in a continuous stream, there are no distinct "jobs." Therefore, companies engaging in mass production often use *process costing* rather than job order costing.

Mass production usually involves a series of specific steps, or manufacturing *processes*. Process costing measures separately the cost of performing *each process* and then allocates these costs to the units processed during the month.

Process costing serves two related purposes. First, it measures the cost of goods manufactured on both a total and per-unit basis. This information is used in valuing inventories and in recording the cost of goods sold. But process costing also provides management with information about the *per-unit cost of performing each step* in the production process. This information is useful in evaluating the *efficiency* of production departments and often draws attention to potential cost savings.

**CASE IN POINT**

Large bottles of Heinz ketchup used to have two labels—one in front and one on the back. Through a careful analysis of manufacturing costs, production managers found that **Heinz** could save several hundred thousand dollars per year by applying only one label.

### Work in Process Accounts—The Key to Process Costing

Process costing uses a separate Work in Process Inventory account to measure the costs incurred in *each production process*. Costs flow through these accounts *in sequence*, just as the units on an assembly line move from one production process to the next. Only when the units complete the *final* production process are their costs transferred to the Finished Goods Inventory account. An illustration for a company with three manufacturing processes appears on the following page.

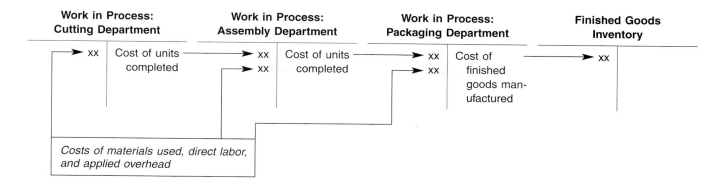

**Accounting for Material, Labor, and Applied Overhead**   Each Work in Process account is charged (debited) for the materials used, direct labor, and overhead that relate to *that specific process*. For example, only those materials that require cutting are charged to the Cutting Department. Component parts sent directly to the Assembly Department are charged to the Assembly Department's Work in Process account. Direct labor and overhead costs also are applied separately to each Work in Process account.

**LO 5**

Account for the flow of costs when using process costing.

**Costs Flow from One Process to the Next**   Units in production pass from one process to the next. Process costing parallels this physical flow of units by transferring their *cost* from one Work in Process account to the next.

Assume that during the current month, $200,000 in manufacturing costs were charged to the Cutting Department. Assume also that this department cut enough material to manufacture 10,000 units of product, and that the cut materials were transferred to the Assembly Department. At month-end, the following journal entry would be made to summarize the transfer of cut materials during the month:

| | | |
|---|---|---|
| Work in Process: Assembly Department . . . . . . . . . . . . . . . . . . . . . . . . . | 200,000 | |
|     Work in Process: Cutting Department . . . . . . . . . . . . . . . . . . . . . . | | 200,000 |

To transfer cost of completely processed units from the Cutting
Department to the Assembly Department. Cutting cost per unit, $20
($200,000 ÷ 10,000 units).

*Transferring work from one department to the next*

In essence, the output of the Cutting Department is a form of "direct material" charged to the Assembly Department.

Notice that we transferred *all $200,000* of the Cutting Department's production costs to the Assembly Department. In effect, we assumed that all of the Cutting Department's costs are applicable to the *units completed and transferred during the month.*

## Process Costing and Equivalent Units

Companies that have significant ending work in process inventories in their departments must assign product costs to unfinished units. Consider the Assembly Department in the previous example. Suppose that in addition to the cut materials transferred by the Cutting Department, the Assembly Department added direct labor, additional direct materials, and overhead. Assume the cut materials transferred from the Cutting Department are machined and polished over the first one-third of the assembly production process. In the second third of the assembly process, additional trim materials are added to the polished cut materials. Finally, the cut, polished, and trimmed assembled units are dipped in a chemical bath to finish the units. The following page shows an illustration of the production process in the Assembly Department.

If, at the end of the reporting period, the Assembly Department has units that are two-thirds finished (that is, they have not yet had the chemical finishing bath), some cost should be assigned to those units. To be consistent with the matching principle, any significant costs incurred in creating work in process should be assigned to work in process inventories.

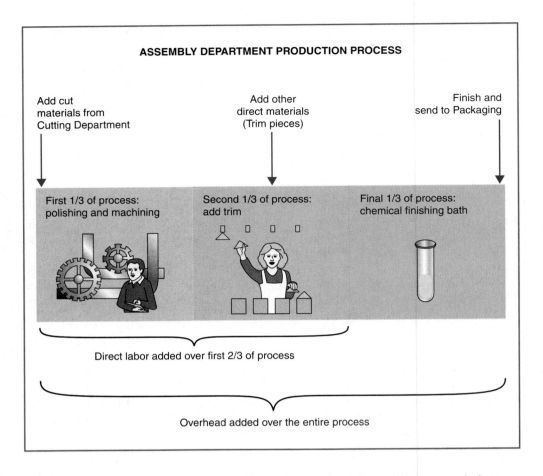

**ASSEMBLY DEPARTMENT PRODUCTION PROCESS**

Add cut materials from Cutting Department

Add other direct materials (Trim pieces)

Finish and send to Packaging

First 1/3 of process: polishing and machining

Second 1/3 of process: add trim

Final 1/3 of process: chemical finishing bath

Direct labor added over first 2/3 of process

Overhead added over the entire process

To recognize partially completed work in process units, companies use a technique referred to as **equivalent units**. An equivalent unit is a measure that represents the percentage of a completed unit's cost that is present in a partially finished unit. Thus the Assembly Department's work in process that is two-thirds complete would be considered 100% complete with respect to cutting materials, trim materials, and direct labor. However, the work in process units are only two-thirds complete (66.6667%) with respect to overhead.

Companies compute the equivalent units associated with completed units and with work in process as a way to assign costs to inventories. It is important to remember that *equivalent unit amounts are computed separately for each significant input added in the production process*. In the Assembly Department, these resources include the cut material transferred from the Cutting Department, the trim materials, the direct labor, and the overhead.

To illustrate the process more fully, consider a typical month for the Assembly Department. During the month of March, 10,000 units of cut materials were transferred from the Cutting Department. At the beginning of the month, 1,000 units that were one-third finished were in the Assembly Department's beginning work in process. At the end of March, 3,000 units were in ending work in process and they were two-thirds finished. The following costs were recorded in March:

| | |
|---|---:|
| Beginning work in process | $ 25,000 |
| Direct labor for March | 105,000 |
| Cut materials | 200,000 |
| Trim materials | 44,000 |
| Overhead | $174,000 |
| Total | $548,000 |

The following equivalent unit computations are for the Assembly Department for March:

| Work Done in March | Equivalent Units of Resource Inputs Consumed in March | | | |
| | Cut Materials | Trim Materials | Direct Labor | Overhead |
|---|---|---|---|---|
| Beginning work in process | –0– | 1,000 | 500 | 666⅔ |
| Started and completed | 7,000 | 7,000 | 7,000 | 7,000 |
| Ending work in process | 3,000 | 3,000 | 3,000 | 2,000 |
| Total equivalent units | 10,000 | 11,000 | 10,500 | 9,666⅔ |

**LO 6**

Demonstrate how equivalent units are computed.

The equivalent unit computation shows that for the 1,000 *beginning work in process* units no cut materials were added in March. The cut materials for the units in beginning work in process were added in February. However, because those beginning work in process units were only one-third finished at the beginning of March, the trim materials had not yet been added. Thus, for those 1,000 units, 100% of the trim materials were added in March. For direct labor, which is added over the first two-thirds of the process, 50% of the direct labor was added in February and the remaining 50% was added in March. Thus 500 equivalent units (50% × 1,000 units) of direct labor were added to the beginning work in process units in March. Finally, 66⅔% of the overhead was added in March, resulting in 666⅔ equivalent units of overhead (1,000 units × 66⅔%).

The *started and completed* units are those units from the 10,000 units started in March that are also transferred to the Packaging Department in March. However, total finished units transferred to Packaging include both the units in beginning work in process and those that are started and completed in March. In computing started and completed units, always assume a first-in, first-out (FIFO) inventory flow. It is calculated as follows:

**Started and Completed = Started − Ending Work in Process**

or

**Started and Completed = Transferred Out − Beginning Work in Process**

For the Assembly Department, started and completed equals 7,000 units (10,000 − 3,000, *or* 8,000 − 1,000). For these 7,000 units, 100% of each resource was added during the month of March. Total *finished units transferred* to Packaging equal the 7,000 started and completed in March plus the 1,000 units from beginning work in process, or a total of 8,000 units.

The *ending work in process* required 100% of cut and trim materials and 100% of direct labor to be added in March. However, because the 3,000 units left in ending work in process were only two-thirds complete at the end of March, not all relevant overhead, particularly the chemical bath, has been added. The equivalent units of overhead for those 3,000 units are 2,000 equivalent units (66⅔% × 3,000).

## Cost per Equivalent Unit

To determine the amount of cost to assign to the three types of inventories—beginning work in process, ending work in process, and started and completed—managers compute the cost per equivalent unit. This simple averaging technique divides the cost

Demonstrate how costs are assigned to equivalent units using process costing.

accumulated for each resource in a given time frame by the associated total equivalent units for each resource. For example, divide the total direct labor cost for March, $105,000, by the total equivalent units for direct labor, 10,500, to get $10 of direct labor cost per equivalent unit.

| | Cut Materials | Trim Materials | Direct Labor | Overhead |
|---|---|---|---|---|
| Total equivalent units | 10,000 | 11,000 | 10,500 | 9,666⅔ |
| Total cost of resource for March | $200,000 | $44,000 | $105,000 | $174,000 |
| Cost per equivalent unit | $20 | $4 | $10 | $18 |

The total per-unit cost of the started and completed units in March is $52 ($20 + $4 + $10 + $18). The costs of the resource inputs and the associated units transferred in March for the Assembly Department are shown in the work in process T account below.

**Details for the Assembly Department
Work in Process Inventory for March**

| | | | |
|---|---|---|---|
| Beg. balance (1,000 units) | $ 25,000 | Cost transferred to Packaging: (8,000 units) | |
| | | (1) from beg. work in process: | |
| Direct labor | 105,000 | Beg. balance | $ 25,000 |
| | | Work in March | |
| Direct materials: | | Trim (1,000 × $4) | 4,000 |
| Cutting | 200,000 | Direct labor | |
| Trim | 44,000 | (500 × $10) | 5,000 |
| | | Overhead | |
| | | (666⅔ × $18) | 12,000 |
| Overhead | 174,000 | (2) Started and completed | |
| | | (7,000 × $52) | 364,000 |
| Total to account for: | $548,000 | | |
| | | Total transferred out (8,000 units) | $410,000 |
| Ending balance: | | | |
| Direct materials: | | | |
| Cut (3,000 equivalent units × $20) | $ 60,000 | | |
| Trim (3,000 equivalent units × $4) | 12,000 | | |
| Direct labor (3,000 equivalent units × $10) | 30,000 | | |
| Overhead (2,000 equivalent units × $18) | 36,000 | | |
| Total ending work in process (3,000 units) | $138,000 | | |

The 3,000 units in ending work in process are assigned $138,000, which will be the April beginning Work in Process balance. During the month of March, $410,000 of costs are transferred from Assembly to Packaging. The following journal entry would be made to summarize the transfer of costs from Assembly to Packaging:

Work in Process: Packaging . . . . . . . . . . . . . . . . . . . . . . . . . . . . . . . . . . . . . 410,000
    Work in Process: Assembly . . . . . . . . . . . . . . . . . . . . . . . . . . . . . . . . .         410,000
To transfer cost of completely processed units from the
Assembly Department to the Packaging Department.

*Transfer costs of units
completed from one
department to the next*

Notice that the $200,000 transferred from Cutting to Assembly is now being passed on
to the Packaging Department as the goods flow through the production process.

In some automated manufacturing environments, units pass through production processes
very quickly—often within several minutes or less. Thus, the number of units "in process" at
any one time can be insignificant in relation to the number of units processed during the month.
For this reason, some companies simply ignore beginning and ending Work in Process and
assign all production costs to those units completed and transferred during the month. By
choosing a strategy of assigning all costs to units completed and transferred, companies greatly
simplify process costing. In these cases, accountants need only make a series of month-end
entries transferring the total costs of each Work in Process account to the next (or from the
final Work in Process account to Finished Goods Inventory).*

*These cost-transfer entries must be made in *sequence,* beginning with the first Work in Process
account, because each entry *increases* the costs charged to the next department.

**MANAGEMENT
STRATEGY**

### You as a Production Manager

You are the production manager of the Assembly Department described in this chapter. One of
your responsibilities is to determine if costs are remaining relatively stable from month to month.
Assume the $25,000 that is associated with the 1,000 units in beginning work in process for
March is composed of $5,050 of direct labor, $15,450 of direct materials, and $4,500 for Over-
head. Determine the cost per equivalent unit for the work done in February on the beginning
work in process units. Were direct labor, direct materials, and overhead costs higher or lower in
February or March? Speculate about why these costs might differ from one month to the next.

*Our comments appear on page 775.

**YOUR TURN**

## Flow of Costs in Process Costing: An Illustration

Assume that RainTree Cola produces a bottled soft drink. The company has two production departments: the Syrup Department, which mixes the cola syrup; and the Bottling Department, which bottles a mixture of this cola syrup and carbonated water.

    In the current month, the Syrup Department produced *75,000 gallons* of syrup, which
was used by the Bottling Department in producing *10 million bottles* of RainTree Cola.
The flow of manufacturing costs through RainTree's Work in Process accounts is illustrated on the following page.

    The entries in *red* represent the costs of materials, direct labor, and overhead charged
to production during the month. These entries to record materials used and direct labor
were made *throughout the period,* based on materials requisitions and employees' time
cards. Overhead was applied at month-end, using a separate overhead application rate
for each department. The entries shown in *green* and in *blue* are the entries made at
month-end to transfer the cost of units processed during the period from one department
to the next.

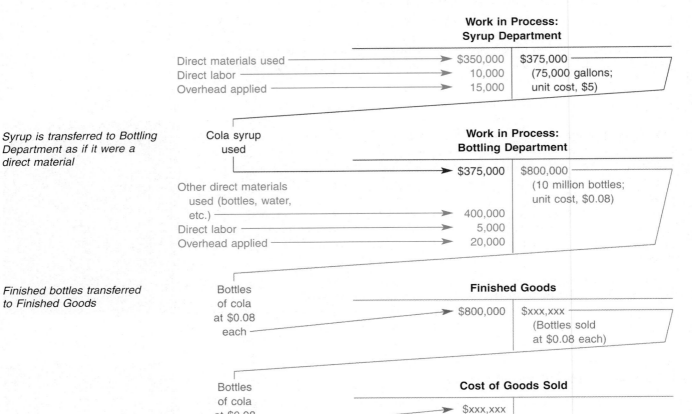

**Flow of Costs in Process Costing**
**(All costs applied to completed units)**

*Syrup is transferred to Bottling Department as if it were a direct material*

*Finished bottles transferred to Finished Goods*

## Computing and Using Unit Costs

Per-unit processing costs are easily computed using process costing methods—not just for the finished products but also for the output of each department. For example, the cost of finished goods emerging from the Bottling Department this month was *$0.08 per bottle* ($800,000 ÷ 10 million bottles produced); the cost of syrup produced in the Syrup Department was *$5 per gallon* ($375,000 ÷ 75,000 gallons).[4]

RainTree's management will use the unit cost data provided by process costing for many purposes, including the following:

- Setting sales prices
- Evaluating the efficiency of manufacturing departments
- Forecasting future manufacturing costs
- Valuing inventories and measuring the cost of goods sold, in both financial statements and income tax returns

---

[4]Notice that in each of our two departments, "units" of output are defined differently. In the Syrup Department, units are expressed in *gallons of syrup*, whereas in the Bottling Department, units are defined as *bottles of cola.*

**You as a Product-Line Manager**

Assume you are the manager of the RainTree Cola product line. As one of your responsibilities, you must motivate, evaluate, and reward the performance of the managers of the Syrup Department and the Bottling Department. How could you use the process costing information to help with these management responsibilities?

*Our comments appear on page 775.

**YOUR TURN**

## Evaluating Departmental Efficiency

In evaluating the efficiency of a department, management should consider only those costs incurred as a result of *that department's activities*. Costs transferred in from other processing departments should not be allowed to "cloud the picture."

To illustrate, consider the Bottling Department in our example. As shown on page 746, a total of $800,000 was charged to the Bottling Department during the current month. But $375,000 of this cost was transferred in from the Syrup Department. This $375,000 represents the cost of *making syrup,* not the cost of bottling cola.

Manufacturing costs resulting from *bottling activities* include only the direct materials, direct labor, and overhead charged to the Bottling Department. For RainTree's Bottling Department, these costs total *$425,000,* or *$0.0425 per unit* ($425,000 ÷ 10 million bottles produced).

In summary, total unit costs *accumulate* as the product passes from one processing department to the next. These total unit costs are used in valuing inventory, measuring the cost of goods sold, and evaluating the overall efficiency of manufacturing operations. But in evaluating the efficiency of a particular processing department, management should look primarily at the costs incurred *within that department*.

Of course, managers can also compute the per-unit costs of the materials, direct labor, and overhead incurred within each department. This detailed cost information should assist them in quickly identifying the *cause of any change* in a product's total unit cost.

## ACTIVITY-BASED COSTING (ABC)

In Chapter 16, we illustrated how manufacturing overhead costs may be applied to production using an overhead application rate based on a single cost driver (such as direct labor hours). This approach works well for many companies, especially if all products are manufactured in a similar manner.

But now consider a company that uses *very different processes* in manufacturing different products. The factors that drive overhead costs may vary greatly among different product lines. Such companies may benefit from *activity-based costing* (called ABC).

In ABC, *many different* activity bases (or cost drivers) are used in applying overhead costs to products. Thus ABC recognizes the special overhead considerations of each product line. As a result, overhead allocations tend to be more useful. In addition, ABC provides management with information about the cost of performing various overhead activities.

**Ford Motor Company** used ABC techniques to cut costs by 20% in its accounts payable department. The process was so successful that it led to a wholesale reworking of **Ford**'s procurement system. Previously, when a supplier shipped an ordered part, a clerk attempted to reconcile three documents—the purchase order, the receiving document, and the vendor's invoice. When all three agreed, payment was issued. Now orders are entered into a database. When the part arrives, the receiving department checks the database for agreement and approves payment. The payment is automatically issued to the supplier upon approval.

**CASE IN POINT**

Define *activity cost pools* and provide several examples.

**How ABC Works**   The first step in ABC is to subdivide overhead costs into a number of **activity cost pools**. Each cost pool represents a type of overhead *activity,* such as building maintenance, purchasing materials, heating the factory, and machinery repairs. The overhead costs in each pool then are applied to production *separately.* In short, ABC separately identifies and makes use of the *most appropriate cost driver* for applying each category of overhead costs.

**The Benefits of ABC**   Measurement of unit costs may assist managers in several ways. For example, it helps them in setting sales prices and in evaluating the profitability of each product line. ABC also helps managers to better understand what activities drive overhead costs. This understanding may inspire them to develop new operating procedures that may reduce overhead costs.

### ABC versus a Single Application Rate: A Comparison

Assume that Master File, Inc., makes two lines of file cabinets: (1) metal file cabinets, sold through office supply outlets for commercial use, and (2) wooden file cabinets, sold through fine furniture stores for home use.

In a typical year, the company produces and sells approximately 42,000 metal cabinets and 9,000 wooden cabinets. Total manufacturing overhead at this level of production averages *$249,600 per year* and is currently allocated to products at a rate of *$1.60 per direct labor hour (DLH)*, as computed below.

***Step 1: Compute total direct labor hours at normal levels of production.***

*Overhead applied using direct labor hours*

| | |
|---|---|
| Metal cabinets (42,000 units per year × 2 DLH per unit) . . . . . . . . . . . . . . . . . . | 84,000 DLH |
| Wooden cabinets (9,000 units per year × 8 DLH per unit) . . . . . . . . . . . . . . . . | 72,000 DLH |
| Total DLH at normal production levels . . . . . . . . . . . . . . . . . . . . . . . . . . . . . . | 156,000 DLH |

***Step 2: Compute the overhead application rate per DLH.***

| | |
|---|---|
| Overhead application rate ($249,600 ÷ 156,000 DLH) . . . . . . . . . . . . . . . . . . . | $1.60 per DLH |

Using direct labor hours as a single activity base, the company's total manufacturing costs per unit average *$38.20* for metal cabinets and *$117.80* for wooden cabinets, as shown below.

*Total unit cost*

| | Metal Cabinets | Wooden Cabinets |
|---|---|---|
| Direct materials . . . . . . . . . . . . . . . . . . . . . . . . . . . . . . . . . . . . . . . . | $15.00 | $ 25.00 |
| Direct labor (at $10.00 per hour) . . . . . . . . . . . . . . . . . . . . . . . . . . . . | 20.00 | 80.00 |
| Manufacturing overhead (at $1.60 per DLH) . . . . . . . . . . . . . . . . . . . . | 3.20 | 12.80 |
| Total manufacturing costs per unit . . . . . . . . . . . . . . . . . . . . . . . . . . . | $38.20 | $117.80 |

Master File sets its selling prices at *160%* of total manufacturing costs. Thus the company sells its metal cabinets for *$61.12* (total unit cost of $38.20 × 160%) and its wooden cabinets for *$188.48* (total unit cost of $117.80 × 160%). At these prices, the metal cabinets sell for about *$3 less* per unit than comparable cabinets sold by Master File's competitors. However, the price of wooden cabinets averages *$10 more* per unit than comparable products available on the market.

Glen Brown, Master File's marketing director, believes that sales of the wooden cabinets have suffered as a result of the company's pricing policy. He recently hired a consultant, Lisa Scott, to evaluate how prices are set. Scott drafted the following memo summarizing her findings:

---

MEMO

DATE: January 16

TO: Glen Brown, Marketing Director, Master File, Inc.

FROM: Lisa Scott, Consultant, Scott & Associates

Having carefully examined Master File's pricing policy, I find it consistent with pricing policies used throughout the office furniture industry. Therefore, I recommend that you continue setting prices at 160% of total manufacturing costs.

I do, however, strongly encourage management to change the method currently used to allocate manufacturing overhead to products. The use of direct labor hours as an activity base is causing an excessive share of total overhead costs to be allocated to the wooden cabinet line. Let me explain what is happening.

The wooden product line is very labor intensive in comparison to the metal cabinet line (that is, it takes an average of eight direct labor hours to manufacture a wooden cabinet, compared to an average of two direct labor hours to manufacture a metal cabinet). Because manufacturing overhead is allocated on the basis of direct labor hours, each wooden cabinet receives a far greater cost allocation than each metal cabinet. This would be appropriate if direct labor hours were the primary overhead *cost driver*. The fact is, however, that direct labor hours are not a significant driver of your overhead costs.

My analysis of manufacturing overhead at Master File, Inc., reveals that the most significant cost drivers are activities most closely associated with the metal cabinet line. Thus it would make sense if your company selected activity bases that allocate more overhead costs to the metal cabinets. This would indicate a lower cost for the wooden cabinets and provide justification for lowering their selling prices, making them more in line with the competition.

I suggest that we make an appointment to discuss using *activity-based costing* at Master File, Inc.

---

Assume that Master File decides to implement ABC as suggested by the consultant. Remember that the company's *total overhead costs* at normal levels of production average *$249,600 per year*. Let us assume that these overhead costs fall into two broad categories: (1) Maintenance Department costs and (2) utilities costs. The diagram on the following page illustrates how these costs may be allocated to Master File's product lines using ABC.

**Maintenance Department Costs** The Maintenance Department incurs approximately *$180,000* of Master File's total overhead costs. The department has five full-time employees. Three employees are responsible for repair work, such as fixing the large cutting and bending machines used to manufacture metal file cabinets. The other two employees are responsible for set-up activities, such as adjusting machinery prior to each production run.

Using ABC, Master File identifies repair activities and set-up activities as separate *activity cost pools*. Thus each pool is assigned a portion of the department's $180,000 in total costs. Management believes that the *number of employees* engaged in each activity is the most significant *cost driver* of the Maintenance Department's total costs.

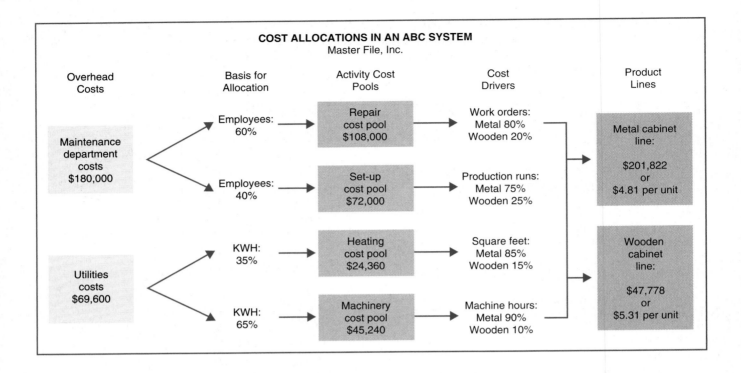

**COST ALLOCATIONS IN AN ABC SYSTEM**
Master File, Inc.

Using the number of employees as an *activity base, $108,000* is assigned to the *repair cost pool*, and *$72,000* is assigned to the *set-up cost pool*, as computed below.

**Assigning Maintenance Department Costs to Activity Pools**

**Step 1: Establish the percentage of total Maintenance Department costs to be assigned to each activity cost pool using the number of employees as an activity base.**

|  |  | % of total |
|---|---|---|
| Employees engaged in repair activities | 3 | 60% |
| Employees engaged in set-up activities | 2 | 40% |
| Employees in the Maintenance Department | 5 | 100% |

**Step 2: Assign total Maintenance Department costs of $180,000 to each activity cost pool based on the percentages computed in step 1.**

*Maintenance costs assigned to cost pools*

| | |
|---|---|
| Costs assigned to the repair cost pool ($180,000 × 60%) | $108,000 |
| Costs assigned to the set-up cost pool ($180,000 × 40%) | 72,000 |
| Total Maintenance Department costs assigned | $180,000 |

The costs assigned to each cost pool must now be allocated to Master File's two product lines. Management has determined that the *number of work orders* is the most appropriate activity base for allocating the *repair cost pool* to each product line. The Maintenance Department receives approximately *250* repair work orders each year. Of these, about *200* are related to the metal cabinet line, and *50* are related to the wooden cabinet line. In a typical year, the metal cabinets are allocated approximately *$86,400* from the repair costs pool, whereas wooden cabinets are allocated approximately *$21,600*, as computed below.

### Allocation of Repair Cost Pool to Each Product Line

*Step 1: Establish the percentage of repair cost pool to be allocated to each product line using the number of work orders as an activity base.*

|  |  | % of total |
| --- | --- | --- |
| Work orders related to metal cabinet line per year . . . . . . . . . . . . . . . . . . | 200 | 80% |
| Work orders related to wooden cabinet line per year . . . . . . . . . . . . . . . . | 50 | 20% |
| Total work orders per year . . . . . . . . . . . . . . . . . . . . . . . . . . . . . . . . . . | 250 | 100% |

*Step 2: Allocate $108,000 from the repair cost pool to each product line based on the percentages computed in step 1.*

| | |
| --- | --- |
| Costs allocated to the metal cabinet line ($108,000 × 80%) . . . . . . . . . . . . . . . . . | $ 86,400 |
| Costs allocated to the wooden cabinet line ($108,000 × 20%) . . . . . . . . . . . . . . . . | 21,600 |
| Total repair costs allocated to both product lines . . . . . . . . . . . . . . . . . . . . . . . . | $108,000 |

*Repair cost pool allocated to each product line*

The *number of production runs* is determined to be the most significant driver of set-up costs. Thus production runs will serve as the activity base for allocating the *set-up cost pool* to each product line. Master File schedules approximately *200* production runs each year. Of these, about *150* are for metal cabinets, and *50* are for wooden cabinets. Thus, in a typical year, the metal cabinets are allocated approximately *$54,000* from the set-up cost pool, whereas wooden cabinets are allocated about *$18,000*, computed below.

### Allocation of Set-up Cost Pool to Each Product Line

*Step 1: Establish the percentage of set-up cost pool to be allocated to each product line using the number of production runs as an activity base.*

|  |  | % of total |
| --- | --- | --- |
| Production runs of metal cabinets per year . . . . . . . . . . . . . . . . . . . . . . . | 150 | 75% |
| Production runs of wooden cabinets per year . . . . . . . . . . . . . . . . . . . . . | 50 | 25% |
| Total production runs per year . . . . . . . . . . . . . . . . . . . . . . . . . . . . . . . | 200 | 100% |

*Step 2: Allocate $72,000 from the set-up cost pool to each product line based on the percentages computed in step 1.*

| | |
| --- | --- |
| Costs allocated to the metal cabinet line ($72,000 × 75%) . . . . . . . . . . . . . . . . . . | $54,000 |
| Costs allocated to the wooden cabinet line ($72,000 × 25%) . . . . . . . . . . . . . . . . . | 18,000 |
| Total set-up costs allocated to both product lines . . . . . . . . . . . . . . . . . . . . . . . . | $72,000 |

*Set-up cost pool allocated to each product line*

In summary, the Maintenance Department averages $108,000 in repair-related costs and $72,000 in set-up costs each year (or total costs of $180,000). Thus, at normal levels of production, ABC allocates $86,400 in repair costs to the metal cabinet line and $21,600 in repair costs to the wooden cabinet line. In addition, ABC allocates $54,000 in set-up costs to the metal cabinet line and $18,000 in set-up costs to the wooden cabinet line.

**Utilities Costs**    Utilities costs account for nearly *$69,600* of Master File's total manufacturing overhead costs. A large portion of this amount is incurred to heat the factory and supply power to the large machines used in manufacturing the metal cabinet line.

Thus, using ABC, Master File identifies heating demands and machinery power demands as separate *activity cost pools*. As such, each of these pools is assigned a portion of the $69,600 utilities costs. Management believes that the *number of kilowatt hours (KWH)* required for each activity is the most significant driver of utilities costs. Using KWH as an *activity base*, *$24,360* is assigned to the *heating cost pool*, whereas *$45,240* is assigned to the *machinery cost pool*, as computed below.

### Assigning Utilities Costs to Activity Pools

*Step 1: Establish the percentage of total utilities costs to be assigned to each activity cost pool using the number of KWH as an activity base.*

|  |  | % of total |
|---|---|---|
| KWH per year for heating requirements | 175,000 | 35% |
| KWH per year for machinery requirements | 325,000 | 65% |
| KWH required per year | 500,000 | 100% |

*Step 2: Assign total utilities costs of $69,600 to each activity cost pool based on the percentages computed in step 1.*

*Utilities costs assigned to cost pools*

| | |
|---|---|
| Costs assigned to the heating cost pool ($69,600 × 35%) | $24,360 |
| Costs assigned to the machinery cost pool ($69,600 × 65%) | 45,240 |
| Total utilities costs assigned | $69,600 |

The costs assigned to each of these cost pools must now be allocated to the metal and wooden product lines. Management believes that *square feet* of production space occupied by each product line is the most appropriate activity base for allocating the *heating cost pool*. Of the company's 40,000 square feet of production space, about *34,000* is dedicated to the metal cabinet line, and *6,000* is dedicated to the wooden cabinet line. Thus, in a typical year, the metal cabinets are allocated *$20,706* of heating pool costs, whereas wooden cabinets are allocated only *$3,654,* computed below and on the following page.

### Allocation of Heating Cost Pool to Each Product Line

*Step 1: Establish the percentage of heating cost pool to be allocated to each product line using square feet of production space as an activity base.*

|  |  | % of total |
|---|---|---|
| Square feet occupied by the metal cabinet line | 34,000 | 85% |
| Square feet occupied by the wooden cabinet line | 6,000 | 15% |
| Square feet of total production space occupied | 40,000 | 100% |

***Step 2: Allocate $24,360 in heating cost pool to each product line based on the per-centages computed in step 1.***

| | |
|---|---|
| Costs allocated to the metal cabinet line ($24,360 × 85%) . . . . . . . . . . . . . . . . . . . . | $20,706 |
| Costs allocated to the wooden cabinet line ($24,360 × 15%) . . . . . . . . . . . . . . . . . . | 3,654 |
| Total heating costs allocated to both product lines . . . . . . . . . . . . . . . . . . . . . . . . | $24,360 |

*Heating cost pool allocated to each product line*

The *number of machine hours* is determined to be the most significant driver of machinery power costs. Thus machine hours will serve as the activity base for allocating the *machinery cost pool* to each product line. The company utilizes approximately *50,000* machine hours each year. Of these, about *45,000* pertain to machinery used to manufacture metal cabinets, and *5,000* pertain to machines used for making wooden cabinets. Thus, in a typical year, the metal cabinets are allocated approximately *$40,716* of machinery pool costs, whereas wooden cabinets are allocated approximately *$4,524*, as shown below.

### Allocation of Machinery Cost Pool to Each Product Line

***Step 1: Establish the percentage of machinery cost pool to be allocated to each product line using the number of machine hours as an activity base.***

| | | % of total |
|---|---|---|
| Machine hours used for metal cabinets per year . . . . . . . . . . . . . . . . . . | 45,000 | 90% |
| Machine hours used for wooden cabinets per year . . . . . . . . . . . . . . . | 5,000 | 10% |
| Total machine hours per year . . . . . . . . . . . . . . . . . . . . . . . . . . . . | 50,000 | 100% |

***Step 2: Allocate $45,240 in machinery cost pool to each product line based on the per-centages computed in step 1.***

| | |
|---|---|
| Costs allocated to the metal cabinet line ($45,240 × 90%) . . . . . . . . . . . . . . . . . . . . | $40,716 |
| Costs allocated to the wooden cabinet line ($45,240 × 10%) . . . . . . . . . . . . . . . . . . . | 4,524 |
| Total machinery costs allocated to both product lines . . . . . . . . . . . . . . . . . . . . . . . | $45,240 |

*Machinery costs allocated to each product line*

In summary, annual utilities costs average $24,360 for heating and $45,240 for powering machinery (for a total of $69,600). At normal levels of production, ABC allocated approximately $20,706 of heating costs to the metal cabinet line and $3,654 of heating costs to the wooden cabinet line. In addition, it allocates $40,716 of machinery power costs to the metal cabinet line and $4,524 to the wooden cabinet line.

## You as a Plant Accountant

Assume you are the plant accountant for Master File, Inc. Before implementing the ABC procedures just described, what additional concerns would you raise?

*Our comments appear on page 775.

**YOUR TURN**

## Determining Unit Costs Using ABC

**LO 9**

Demonstrate how activity bases are used to assign cost pools to units produced.

We may now compute Master File's overhead costs on a *per-unit* basis. At normal levels of activity, the company produces and sells 42,000 metal file cabinets and 9,000 wooden file cabinets per year. Thus the unit manufacturing overhead cost of each metal cabinet is *$4.81*, compared to *$5.31* for each wooden cabinet. These unit costs are computed below.

*Unit costs using ABC*

|  | Metal Cabinets | Wooden Cabinets |
|---|---|---|
| Maintenance Department costs: |  |  |
| Allocated from the repair cost pool | $ 86,400 | $21,600 |
| Allocated from the set-up cost pool | 54,000 | 18,000 |
| Utilities costs: |  |  |
| Allocated from the heating cost pool | 20,706 | 3,654 |
| Allocated from the machinery cost pool | 40,716 | 4,524 |
| Total manufacturing costs allocated to each line | $201,822 | $47,778 |
| Total units produced and sold per year | 42,000 | 9,000 |
| Manufacturing overhead costs per unit | $ 4.81 | $ 5.31 |

Two observations should be made regarding these figures. First, at normal levels of activity, Master File's ABC process allocates the entire $249,600 in annual overhead costs to each product line ($201,822 to the metal cabinet line and $47,778 to the wooden cabinet line). Second, the amount of manufacturing overhead allocated to each product is significantly *different* than what was allocated using a single activity base, as shown below.

*Comparing methods*

|  | Metal Cabinets | Wooden Cabinets |
|---|---|---|
| Manufacturing overhead allocated using ABC | $4.81 | $5.31 |
| Manufacturing overhead applied using direct labor hours (DLH): |  |  |
| Metal cabinets (2 DLH × $1.60 per DLH) | 3.20 |  |
| Wooden cabinets (8 DLH × $1.60 per DLH) |  | 12.80 |
| Differences in overhead application per unit | $1.61 | $(7.49) |

As indicated, manufacturing overhead applied to the metal file cabinets using ABC is *$1.61 more* than it was when a single activity base of direct labor hours was used. However, the amount applied to the wooden cabinets using ABC is *$7.49 less* than it was previously. As a consequence, Master File is likely to *raise* the selling price of its metal file cabinets and *lower* the selling price of its wooden file cabinets, as shown below.

*Change in selling price using ABC*

|  | Metal Cabinets | Wooden Cabinets |
|---|---|---|
| Direct materials | $15.00 | $ 25.00 |
| Direct labor (at $10.00 per hour) | 20.00 | 80.00 |
| Manufacturing overhead (using the ABC system) | 4.81 | 5.31 |
| Total manufacturing costs per unit | $39.81 | $110.31 |
| Sales price as a percentage of total manufacturing cost | 160% | 160% |
| Selling prices indicated by the ABC system | $63.70 | $176.50 |
| Selling prices indicated by the single activity base system | 61.12 | 188.48 |
| Price increase (reduction) indicated by the ABC system | $ 2.58 | $ (11.98) |

If Master File maintains its current pricing policy, it will raise the price of metal file cabinets by *$2.58* per unit and lower the price of its wooden file cabinets by *$11.98* per unit.[3]

You will recall that Master File currently is selling its metal filing cabinets for about *$3 less* than competitive products. Therefore, the metal cabinet prices will remain competitive even if their sales price is raised by $2.58 per unit. However, the company's wooden file cabinets have been priced at *$10.00 more* than competitive products. Thus, by lowering the unit selling price by $11.98, Master File's wooden cabinets can now be priced competitively *without sacrificing product quality*.

---

Reallocating overhead costs to products based on ABC procedures has no cash flow effects unless managers change some of their decisions as a result of the new cost numbers. In the example just provided, managers are considering changing the selling prices of filing cabinets. The managers hope these selling price changes will increase sales revenue and thus increase cash inflow. If managers can use the ABC information to manage more effectively and efficiently the activities that consume resources, then cash outflows associated with those activities will decline. The important point is that adopting ABC procedures will not change cash flows unless the information provided by ABC systems affects management decision making.

**CASH EFFECTS**

---

## THE TREND TOWARD MORE INFORMATIVE COST ACCOUNTING SYSTEMS

Today's global economy is fiercely competitive. To a large extent, competitive means cost-efficient. If you cannot produce quality products efficiently, you may lose out to the Japanese, the Germans, the Koreans, or a company down the street.

Up to this point, we have discussed job order, process, and activity-based costing methods. Job order costing has two advantages: (1) it measures the costs of products produced in "batches," and (2) unit costs are determined as soon as the job is complete. Process costing, however, has the advantage of providing detailed information about the cost of performing each step in the manufacturing process. In an ABC system, the allocation of manufacturing overhead is based on the specific activities that drive overhead costs. Thus ABC should provide a more useful measure of each product's cost.

To provide their managers with more types of useful information, many companies today have "hybrid" cost systems, designed to realize the advantages of job order, process, and activity-based costing.

---

Most automakers mass-produce cars in large "production runs." After a run, they may reconfigure their assembly line to produce a different model. These companies combine the principles of job order and process costing. Each production run is viewed as a "job." But within that job, the costs of each manufacturing process are measured separately. These cost systems provide management with timely unit cost information about each production process in the manufacture of each model car and truck.

Such systems sound complicated—and they are. But if you want to compete in a worldwide multibillion-dollar market, your managers need unit cost information at their fingertips.

For example, until recently, major automakers all manufactured the seats for their cars. But today, every American car maker purchases its seats from an independent supplier. They all recognized that supplier prices were less than it cost them to manufacture the seats themselves.

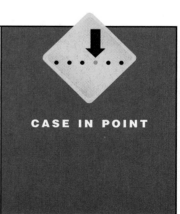

**CASE IN POINT**

---

[3]To keep our illustration short, we assumed that maintenance and utilities costs were Master File's *only* manufacturing overhead costs. Consequently, overhead costs are relatively low in comparison to the cost of direct materials and direct labor. In many companies, overhead represents a much larger component of total manufacturing costs. Thus cost distortions often are significantly greater than those shown here.

As companies become increasingly cost-conscious, we will see more sophisticated, more detailed, and more accurate cost accounting methods. But these methods will continue to employ the basic concepts introduced in this chapter.

**A SECOND LOOK**

### Harley-Davidson, Inc.

Even before the 2000 Olympic Games in Sydney, Australia, **Harley-Davidson** had been providing its world-class motorcycles to escort Olympic torchbearers. During the Torch Relay, members of the Australian police force escorted 10,000 torchbearers on four specially designed **Harley-Davidson** Road King police motorcycles. The relay lasted 100 days and covered more than 16,000 kilometers (almost 10,000 miles) of Australia's rugged terrain.

The motorcycles created for the 2000 Olympics are examples of the specially designed products that benefit from the use of job order costing. In addition, the opening story about **Harley-Davidson**'s production levels describes producing large numbers of a model where all units are alike, a type of production that benefits from process costing techniques. Finally, activity-based costing approaches are effective for tracking and controlling the variety of overhead costs incurred by a company such as **Harley-Davidson** in its production processes. **Harley-Davidson** is likely to use some aspects of all the cost systems introduced in this chapter. The next chapter introduces the idea of a company's value chain and explains how cost systems can help companies manage their businesses across that value chain.

## SUMMARY OF LEARNING OBJECTIVES

### LO 1

**Explain the purposes of cost accounting systems.**

Cost accounting systems provide information useful for managing the activities that consume resources. Managers use the information to evaluate and reward employee performance. In addition, the cost information is reported on external financial statements as, for example, inventories, cost of goods sold, and period expenses.

### LO 2

**Distinguish between the processes for creating goods and services that are suited to job order costing, process costing, and activity-based costing.**

Job order costing methods are appropriate for businesses and companies producing customized jobs that require differing amounts and types of direct labor, direct materials, and overhead. Process costing is used for production processes that produce mass quantities of identical units that use the same amounts and types of direct labor, direct materials, and overhead. Activity-based costing is used to track resources that are not directly traceable to the product or service produced. Overhead items are typically the focus of ABC methods. It is not uncommon to find all of these costing methods being used by the same company for different purposes and costs.

### LO 3

**Describe the purpose and the content of a job cost sheet.**

The purpose of a job cost sheet is to keep track of all manufacturing costs relating to a particular job. Each job cost sheet shows the cost of all the materials, direct labor, and factory overhead charged to the job. The job cost sheets of all jobs in process serve as a subsidiary ledger supporting the balance of the Work in Process Inventory controlling account.

### LO 4

**Account for the flow of costs when using job order costing.**

Costs flow from the Direct Labor account, the Direct Materials Inventory account, and the Manufacturing Overhead account into the Work in Process Inventory account. As jobs are completed, the accumulated costs are transferred to the Finished Goods Inventory account. As units are sold, their costs flow from the Finished Goods Inventory account to the Cost of Goods Sold account.

### LO 5

**Account for the flow of costs when using process costing.**

Costs in process costing flow in basically the same manner as costs in a job order cost system. Throughout the period, the costs of direct labor, direct materials, and manufacturing overhead are charged to the appropriate Work in Process accounts. At the end of each period, costs in each Work in Process account are transferred to the next Work in Process (or Finished Goods) account, representing the cost of units on which processing has been completed.

### LO 6

**Demonstrate how equivalent units are computed.**

Equivalent units are measures of productive activity that include work performed on partially completed units. The basic idea is that performing, say, 50% of the processing on 500 units is equivalent to performing all of the processing on 250 units.

### LO 7

**Demonstrate how costs are assigned to equivalent units using process costing.**

Costs associated with beginning work in process from the previous period and costs added to work in process for the current period are pooled for each significant input. Dividing total costs by total equivalent units provides cost per equivalent unit for each input. The equivalent units associated with the units transferred out are multiplied by the cost per equivalent unit to determine the amount of cost to transfer out.

### LO 8

**Define activity cost pools and provide several examples.**

Activity cost pools are the costs of resources consumed by an activity that is necessary to produce a good or service. Types of overhead activity cost pools include building maintenance, utilities, purchasing activities, and machinery repairs, among others.

### LO 9

**Demonstrate how activity bases are used to assign cost pools to units produced.**

Activity bases are the measures of the activity that consumes the associated resource cost pool. Thus, for the purchasing activities cost pool, the activity base is the number of purchase orders processed. Dividing the activity cost pool by the activity base provides the cost per unit of activity. Activity costs are assigned to the product by tracking the activity base associated with the product and multiplying it by the appropriate cost per unit of activity.

In this chapter we have emphasized the measurement of unit costs. In upcoming chapters, we will see how managers control these costs and utilize cost information in planning and decision making.

## KEY TERMS INTRODUCED OR EMPHASIZED IN CHAPTER 17

**activity-based costing** (p. 733) Cost accounting method that tracks indirect costs to the activities that consume resources.

**activity cost pools** (p. 748) Overhead categories that represent the costs associated with an activity that consumes overhead resources.

**cost accounting systems** (p. 732) The methods and techniques used by enterprises to track resources consumed in creating and delivering products and services to customers.

**equivalent units** (p. 742) A measure of the work done during an accounting period. Includes work done on beginning and ending inventories of work in process as well as work on units completely processed during the period.

**job cost sheet** (p. 734) A record used in job order costing to summarize the manufacturing costs (materials, labor, and overhead) applicable to each job or batch of production. Job cost sheets may be viewed as a subsidiary ledger supporting the balance of the Work in Process Inventory control account.

**job order costing** (p. 733) A cost accounting method under which the focal point of costing is a quantity of product known as a *job* or *lot*. Costs of direct materials, direct labor, and manufacturing overhead applicable to each job are compiled to arrive at average unit cost.

**overhead application rate** (p. 736) A device used to apply a normal amount of overhead costs to work in process. The rate is predetermined at the beginning of the year and expresses the percentage relationship between estimated total overhead for the year and the estimated total of some cost driver, such as direct labor hours, direct labor costs, or machine hours. Use of the overhead application rate causes overhead to be charged to work in process in proportion to the amount of "cost driver" traceable to those units.

**over- or underapplied overhead** (p. 737) The difference between the actual manufacturing overhead incurred during the period and the amount applied to work in process by use of a predetermined overhead application rate.

**process costing** (p. 733) A cost accounting method used mostly in industries characterized by continuous mass production. Costs are assigned to a manufacturing process or department before being averaged over units produced.

## DEMONSTRATION PROBLEM

1. Oceanview Enterprises is a print shop that uses job order costing. Overhead is applied to individual jobs at a predetermined rate based on direct labor costs. The job cost sheet for job no. 21 appears below.

---

### JOB COST SHEET

JOB NUMBER: __21__          DATE STARTED: __Feb. 1__

PRODUCT: __Income Tax Handbook__          DATE COMPLETED: __Feb. 6__

UNITS COMPLETED: __2,500__

| | |
|---|---:|
| Direct materials used . . . . . . . . . . . . . . . . . . . . . . . . . . . . . . . . . . . . . | $3,200 |
| Direct labor . . . . . . . . . . . . . . . . . . . . . . . . . . . . . . . . . . . . . . . . . . . . . | 400 |
| Manufacturing overhead applied . . . . . . . . . . . . . . . . . . . . . . . . . . . . . | 1,200 |
| Total cost of job no. 21 . . . . . . . . . . . . . . . . . . . . . . . . . . . . . . . . . . . | $4,800 |
| Unit cost ($4,800 ÷ 2,500 units) . . . . . . . . . . . . . . . . . . . . . . . . . . . . | $ 1.92 |

---

### Instructions

Prepare general journal entries to:

**a.** Summarize the manufacturing costs charged to job no. 21. (Use one compound entry.)

**b.** Record the completion of job no. 21.

**c.** Record the credit sale of 2,000 units from job no. 21 at a unit sales price of $4. Record in a separate entry the related cost of goods sold.

## Solution to Demonstration Problem 1

| GENERAL JOURNAL | | |
|---|---|---|
| a. Work in Process Inventory ................................ | 4,800 | |
|     Materials Inventory ..................................... | | 3,200 |
|     Direct Labor ......................................... | | 400 |
|     Manufacturing Overhead .................................. | | 1,200 |
|   Manufacturing costs incurred on job no. 21. | | |
| b. Finished Goods Inventory .............................. | 4,800 | |
|     Work in Process Inventory ............................. | | 4,800 |
|   To record completion of job no. 21. | | |
| c. Accounts Receivable ................................... | 8,000 | |
|     Sales ............................................. | | 8,000 |
|   To record credit sale of 2,000 units from job no. 21 @ $4 per unit. | | |
|   Cost of Goods Sold .................................... | 3,840 | |
|     Finished Goods Inventory .............................. | | 3,840 |
|   To record cost of sales for 2,000 units from job no. 21 (2,000 × $1.92 per unit). | | |

2. Magna Bin, Inc., manufactures large metal waste containers that are purchased by local sanitation departments. Containers are produced in two processing departments, Fabricating and Painting. In the Fabricating Department, all of the direct materials are added at the beginning of the process, overhead is applied evenly throughout the entire process, and labor is added evenly only during the last 50% of the process. In the Painting Department, materials and labor are added evenly throughout the first half of the process, while overhead is applied evenly throughout the entire process. Magna Bin uses process costing and had the following cost and production information available for the month of January:

| | Fabricating Department | Painting Department |
|---|---|---|
| Direct materials costs ............................... | $ 7,740 | $13,752 |
| Direct labor costs .................................. | 18,060 | 8,022 |
| Manufacturing overhead applied ..................... | 27,090 | 12,033 |
| Units in beginning work in process .................. | 0 | 0 |
| Units started during Jan. ........................... | 750 | 600 |
| Units completed and transferred out ................ | 600 | 510 |

At the end of January, units remaining in work in process in the Fabricating Department were 30% complete, while units in ending work in process in the Painting Department were 70% complete. During the month, 450 containers were sold at an average selling price of $180 each.

### Instructions

**a.** Calculate the number of equivalent units produced for each cost category in each of the two departments during January.

**b.** Based on equivalent units, what were the fabricating cost, painting cost, and total cost of producing a container in January?

**c.** Prepare the journal entries summarizing the manufacturing costs charged to the Fabricating Department and the Painting Department.

**d.** Prepare the month-end journal entries to transfer the costs of containers moved from the Fabricating Department to the Painting Department and from the Painting Department to Finished Goods Inventory.

**e.** Prepare the entries to record the sales made in January and the corresponding reduction of Finished Goods Inventory.

**f.** Using T accounts, calculate the ending balances in the Work in Process accounts and Finished Goods Inventory.

## Solution to Demonstration Problem 2

### a. Equivalent Units of Production — Fabricating Department

|  | Direct Materials | Labor | Overhead |
|---|---|---|---|
| Beginning work in process . . . . . . . . . . . . . . . | 0 | 0 | 0 |
| Started and completed . . . . . . . . . . . . . . . . . . | 600 | 600 | 600 |
| Ending work in process . . . . . . . . . . . . . . . . . | 150 | 0 | 45 (150 × 0.3) |
| Total equivalent units . . . . . . . . . . . . . . . . . . . | 750 | 600 | 645 |

*Note:* Since the units in ending work in process are 30% complete, all direct materials have been added, no direct labor has been used, and 30% of the overhead has been applied.

### Equivalent Units of Production — Painting Department

|  | Direct Materials | Labor | Overhead |
|---|---|---|---|
| Beginning work in process . . . . . . . . . . . . . . . | 0 | 0 | 0 |
| Started and completed . . . . . . . . . . . . . . . . . . | 510 | 510 | 510 |
| Ending work in process . . . . . . . . . . . . . . . . . | 90 | 90 | 63 (90 × 0.7) |
| Total equivalent units . . . . . . . . . . . . . . . . . . . | 600 | 600 | 573 |

*Note:* Since the units in ending work in process are 70% complete, all direct materials and labor have been added, while only 70% of the overhead has been applied.

**b.** Fabricating costs per container produced during January:

| | |
|---|---|
| Direct materials costs ($7,740 ÷ 750 equivalent units) . . . . . . . . . . . . . . . . . . . . . . . . . | $10.32 |
| Direct labor costs ($18,060 ÷ 600 equivalent units) . . . . . . . . . . . . . . . . . . . . . . . . . . | 30.10 |
| Manufacturing overhead ($27,090 ÷ 645 equivalent units) . . . . . . . . . . . . . . . . . . . . . . | 42.00 |
| Fabricating costs per container . . . . . . . . . . . . . . . . . . . . . . . . . . . . . . . . . . . . . . . | $82.42 |

Painting costs per container produced during January:

| | |
|---|---|
| Direct materials costs ($13,752 ÷ 600 equivalent units) . . . . . . . . . . . . . . . . . . . . . . . . | $ 22.92 |
| Direct labor costs ($8,022 ÷ 600 equivalent units) . . . . . . . . . . . . . . . . . . . . . . . . . . . | 13.37 |
| Manufacturing overhead ($12,033 ÷ 573 equivalent units) . . . . . . . . . . . . . . . . . . . . . . | 21.00 |
| Painting costs per container . . . . . . . . . . . . . . . . . . . . . . . . . . . . . . . . . . . . . . . . | $ 57.29 |
| Total cost per container ($82.42 + $57.29) . . . . . . . . . . . . . . . . . . . . . . . . . . . . . . . . | $139.71 |

**c.** Work in Process—Fabricating . . . . . . . . . . . . . . . . . . . . . . . . . . . .    52,890.00
    Direct Materials Inventory . . . . . . . . . . . . . . . . . . . . . . . . . . . . . .        7,740.00
    Direct Labor . . . . . . . . . . . . . . . . . . . . . . . . . . . . . . . . . . . . . . .      18,060.00
    Manufacturing Overhead Applied . . . . . . . . . . . . . . . . . . . . . . . .      27,090.00

   Summary of costs incurred during January by the Fabricating Department.

Work in Process—Painting . . . . . . . . . . . . . . . . . . . . . . . . . 33,807.00
    Direct Materials Inventory . . . . . . . . . . . . . . . . . . . . . . . .           13,752.00
    Direct Labor . . . . . . . . . . . . . . . . . . . . . . . . . . . . . . . .            8,022.00
    Manufacturing Overhead Applied . . . . . . . . . . . . . . . . . . . .           12,033.00

Summary of costs incurred during January by the Painting
Department.

**d.** Work in Process—Painting . . . . . . . . . . . . . . . . . . . . . . . . . 49,452.00
(600 units transferred × $82.42 cost/unit)
    Work in Process—Fabricating . . . . . . . . . . . . . . . . . . . . . .           49,452.00

To transfer the cost of completely processed units from the
  Fabricating Department to the Painting Department.

Finished Goods Inventory . . . . . . . . . . . . . . . . . . . . . . . . . . 71,252.10
(510 units transferred × $139.71 cost/unit)
    Work in Process—Painting . . . . . . . . . . . . . . . . . . . . . . . .           71,252.10
To transfer the cost of completely processed units from the Painting
  Department to Finished Goods Inventory.

**e.** Sales Revenue . . . . . . . . . . . . . . . . . . . . . . . . . . . . . . . . . 81,000.00
(450 units sold × $180/unit)
    Cash, Accounts Receivable . . . . . . . . . . . . . . . . . . . . . . . .           81,000.00
To record sales made during Jan.
Cost of Goods Sold . . . . . . . . . . . . . . . . . . . . . . . . . . . . . . 62,869.50
(450 units sold × $139.71 cost/unit)
    Finished Goods Inventory . . . . . . . . . . . . . . . . . . . . . . . . .           62,869.50
To record the cost of goods sold during Jan.

**f.**

| Work in Process—Fabricating | | | |
|---|---|---|---|
| Direct materials | 7,740.00 | | |
| Direct labor | 18,060.00 | | |
| Manufacturing overhead applied | 27,090.00 | 49,452.00 | Transferred to Painting |
| Ending balance | 3,438.00 | | |

| Work in Process—Painting | | | |
|---|---|---|---|
| From Fabricating | 49,452.00 | | |
| Direct materials | 13,752.00 | | |
| Direct labor | 8,022.00 | | |
| Manufacturing overhead applied | 12,033.00 | 71,252.10 | Transferred to Finished Goods Inventory |
| Ending balance | 12,006.90 | | |

| Finished Goods Inventory | | | |
|---|---|---|---|
| From Painting | 71,252.10 | | |
| | | 62,869.50 | Costs of Goods Sold |
| Ending balance | 8,382.60 | | |

# SELF-TEST QUESTIONS

*Answers to these questions appear on page 775.*

**1.** If CustomCraft uses *job order* costing, each of the following is true, *except:*

    **a.** Individual job cost sheets accumulate all manufacturing costs applicable to each job and together constitute a subsidiary ledger for the Work in Process Inventory account.

    **b.** Direct labor cost applicable to individual jobs is recorded when paid by a debit to Work in Process Inventory and a credit to Cash, as well as by entering the amount on the job cost sheets.

    **c.** The amount of direct materials used in individual jobs is recorded by debiting the Work in Process Inventory account and crediting the Materials Inventory account, as well as by entering the amount used on job cost sheets.

    **d.** The manufacturing overhead applied to each job is transferred from the Manufacturing Overhead account to the Work in Process Inventory account, as well as entered on the individual job cost sheets.

2. When job costing is in use, *underapplied* overhead:

    **a.** Represents the cost of manufacturing overhead that relates to unfinished jobs.

    **b.** Is indicated by a credit balance remaining at year-end in the Manufacturing Overhead account.

    **c.** Is closed out at year-end into the Cost of Goods Sold account if the amount is not material.

    **d.** Results when actual overhead costs incurred during a year are less than the amounts applied to individual jobs.

3. Which of the following businesses would most likely use *job* costing?

    **a.** A print shop that specializes in wedding invitations.

    **b.** A company that makes frozen pizzas.

    **c.** A brewery.

    **d.** An oil refinery.

4. Which of the following businesses would most likely use *process* costing?

    **a.** A law firm.

    **b.** A maker of frozen orange juice.

    **c.** A hospital.

    **d.** An auto repair shop.

5. Nut House manufactures and sells jars of peanut butter. All of the company's output passes through five production processes, which are performed in sequential order. Identify all correct answers, assuming that process costing is in use.

    **a.** The processing departments may define "units of output" differently.

    **b.** Costs transferred from one processing department are charged to the next processing department (or to finished goods).

    **c.** The cost accounting system separately measures the per-unit cost of each manufacturing process.

    **d.** Some portion of total manufacturing overhead should be charged to each processing department.

6. Indicate which of the following phrases correctly completes this sentence: "Equivalent units of production. . . ." (Indicate all correct answers.)

    **a.** Are a measure of productive activity.

    **b.** Represent work done on units still in process, as well as those completed during the period.

    **c.** Are used as the basis for computing per-unit costs in most process cost accounting systems.

    **d.** Are computed separately for each significant input consumed in the production process.

7. Which of the following are *true* regarding activity-based costing?

    **a.** A primary goal of using ABC is a more useful allocation of manufacturing overhead to product lines.

    **b.** Under ABC, direct labor hours are never used to allocate overhead costs to activity pools or product lines.

    **c.** The use of ABC is indicated when it is suspected that each of a firm's product lines consumes approximately the same amount of overhead resources but the current allocation scheme assigns each line a substantially different amount.

    **d.** ABC can be used in conjunction with process costing.

8. Which of the following would be the most appropriate basis for allocating the costs of plant insurance that covers equipment theft and damage?

    **a.** Direct labor hours.

    **b.** Value of equipment.

    **c.** Machine hours.

    **d.** Square feet of plant space.

9. Using ABC to allocate manufacturing overhead can help managers to:
   a. Identify what activities drive overhead costs.
   b. Set product prices.
   c. Locate inefficiencies in the production process.
   d. Do all of the above.

## ASSIGNMENT MATERIAL

### DISCUSSION QUESTIONS

1. What is a cost accounting system?
2. What are the major objectives of a cost accounting system in a manufacturing company?
3. What factors should be taken into account in deciding whether to use job order costing or process costing in any given manufacturing situation?
4. Northwest Power produces electricity. Would you expect the company to use job order or process costing? Explain.
5. Rodeo Drive Jewelers makes custom jewelry for celebrities. Would you expect the company to use job order or process costing? Explain.
6. Describe the three kinds of charges on a job cost sheet. For what general ledger controlling account do job cost sheets constitute supporting detail?
7. What documents serve as the basis for charging the costs of direct materials used in production to the Work in Process Inventory account?
8. What documents serve as the basis for charging direct labor costs to specific jobs or production departments?
9. What is meant by underapplied overhead? By overapplied overhead?
10. Gerox Company applies manufacturing overhead on the basis of machine-hours, using a predetermined overhead rate. At the end of the current year, the Manufacturing Overhead account has a credit balance. What are the possible explanations for this? What disposition should be made of this balance?
11. Taylor & Malone is a law firm. Would the concepts of job order or process costing be more appropriate for this type of service business? Explain.
12. Briefly explain the operation of process costing, including the manner in which the unit costs of finished goods are determined.
13. Some companies that use process costing simply assign the entire cost of production to those units completed and transferred during the month, even if some units remain in process at the end of the period. Is this practice reasonable?
14. Melrose Company uses process costing with three work in process departments. It recently transferred $100,000 from the second work in process account to the third. Briefly describe the costs included in the $100,000 transferred.
15. Discuss how managers use information they obtain from process costing.
16. Explain the term *equivalent units*. In a fast-moving, assembly-line operation, are the equivalent units likely to differ significantly from the number of units completed during a month? Explain.
17. Define the term *activity base*.
18. Define the term *cost driver*.
19. Why is the use of a single activity base inappropriate for some companies?
20. Describe how activity-based costing can improve overhead cost allocations in companies that produce a diverse line of products.
21. What is an *activity cost pool*?
22. Why is the use of direct labor hours as an activity base likely to be inappropriate in a highly mechanized production facility?
23. Describe the steps in implementing activity-based costing.
24. Discuss the potential benefits associated with using activity-based costing.

## EXERCISES

**EXERCISE 17.1**

Accounting Terminology

**LO 1, 2, 3, 6, 8**

Listed below are seven technical accounting terms introduced or emphasized in this chapter.

Job order costing
Process costing
Overapplied overhead
Activity-based costing

Equivalent units
Cost of finished goods manufactured
Job cost sheet

Each of the following statements may (or may not) describe these technical terms. For each statement, indicate the term described, or answer "None" if the statement does not correctly describe any of the terms.

**a.** The type of cost accounting method likely to be used in a **Coca-Cola** bottling plant.

**b.** The total of all direct labor, direct materials, and manufacturing overhead transferred from work in process to finished goods.

**c.** A measure of the *quantity* of production work done during a time period, including work on partially completed units.

**d.** A debit balance remaining in the Manufacturing Overhead account at the end of the period.

**e.** The type of cost accounting method likely to be used by a construction company.

**f.** The type of cost accounting method likely to be used for overhead costs.

**EXERCISE 17.2**

Flow of Costs in a Cost Accounting System

**LO 4, 5**

For each of the four accounts listed below, prepare an example of a journal entry that would cause the account to be (1) debited and (2) credited. Assume perpetual inventory records are maintained. Include written explanations with your journal entries and use "XXX" in place of dollar amounts.

**a.** Materials Inventory
**b.** Direct Labor

**c.** Manufacturing Overhead
**d.** Finished Goods Inventory

**EXERCISE 17.3**

Flow of Costs in Job Order Costing

**LO 1–4**

The information below was taken from the job cost sheets of Bates Company.

| Job Number | Manufacturing Costs as of June 30 | Manufacturing Costs in July |
|---|---|---|
| 101 | $4,200 | |
| 102 | 3,240 | |
| 103 | 900 | $2,000 |
| 104 | 2,250 | 4,000 |
| 105 | | 6,000 |
| 106 | | 3,700 |

During July, jobs no. 103 and 104 were completed, and jobs no. 101, 102, and 104 were delivered to customers. Jobs no. 105 and 106 are still in process at July 31. From this information, compute the following:

**a.** The work in process inventory at June 30

**b.** The finished goods inventory at June 30

**c.** The cost of goods sold during July

**d.** The work in process inventory at July 31

**e.** The finished goods inventory at July 31

**EXERCISE 17.4**

Journal Entries in Job Order Costing

**LO 1–4**

Riverside Engineering is a machine shop that uses job order costing. Overhead is applied to individual jobs at a predetermined rate based on direct labor costs. The job cost sheet for job no. 321 appears at the top of the following page.

```
                            JOB COST SHEET

  JOB NUMBER: _321_           DATE STARTED:     May 10
  PRODUCT: _2." Brass Check Valves_   DATE COMPLETED: May 21
  UNITS COMPLETED: _4,000_


  Direct materials used  . . . . . . . . . . . . . . . . . . . . . . . . . . . . . . . .   $ 7,720
  Direct labor  . . . . . . . . . . . . . . . . . . . . . . . . . . . . . . . . . . . . . . .    1,400
  Manufacturing overhead applied  . . . . . . . . . . . . . . . . . . . . . . . .    3,080
  Total cost of job no. 321  . . . . . . . . . . . . . . . . . . . . . . . . . . . . .   $12,200
  Unit cost ($12,200 ÷ 4,000 units)  . . . . . . . . . . . . . . . . . . . . .    $3.05
```

Prepare general journal entries to:

**a.** Summarize the manufacturing costs charged to job no. 321. (Use one compound entry.)

**b.** Record the completion of job no. 321.

**c.** Record the credit sale of 2,100 units from job no. 321 at a unit sales price of $5. Record in a separate entry the related cost of goods sold.

Indicate whether job order, process, or activity-based costing is appropriate for each of the following businesses. Explain why.

**a.** Old Home Bakery, Inc. (a commercial bakery that produces standardized products)

**b.** Baxter, Claxter, and Stone, CPAs

**c.** Thompson Construction Company

**d.** Satin Wall Paints, Inc.

**e.** Apache Oil and Gas Refinery

**f.** Dr. Carr's Auto Body Shoppe

**g.** Health-Rite Vitamins

**h.** Shampoo Products International

**EXERCISE 17.5**

Appropriate Types of Cost Accounting Systems

**LO 2**

Starr Scopes, Inc., produces telescopes for use by high school students. All direct materials used in the production of telescopes are added at the beginning of the manufacturing process. Labor and overhead are added evenly thereafter, as each unit is assembled, adjusted, and tested. Starr Scopes uses process costing and had the following unit production information available for the months of January and February:

**EXERCISE 17.6**

Calculating Equivalent Units

**LO 6**

| | Jan. | Feb. |
|---|---|---|
| Number of units in beginning work in process inventory . . . . . . . . . . . . . . . . . . . . | 0 | 50 |
| Number of units started during the month . . . . . . . . . . . . . . . . . . . . . . . . . . . . . . | 200 | 300 |
| Total number of units transferred to finished goods . . . . . . . . . . . . . . . . . . . . . . | 150 | 250 |

The units remaining in work in process at the end of January were approximately 40% complete. During the month of February, all of the beginning work in process units were completed and the units remaining in work in process at the end of the month were approximately 75% complete.

**a.** For the month of January, calculate the equivalent units produced for each of the two cost categories—direct materials *and* labor and overhead.

**b.** For the month of February, calculate the equivalent units produced for each of the two cost categories—direct materials *and* labor and overhead.

**EXERCISE 17.7**

Calculating Equivalent Units

Superior Lighting, Inc., mass produces reading lamps. Materials used in constructing the body of the lamp are added at the start of the process, while the materials used in wiring the lamps are added at the halfway point. All labor and overhead are added evenly throughout the manufacturing process. Superior uses process costing and had the following unit production information available for the months of June and July:

|  | June | July |
| --- | --- | --- |
| Number of lamps in beginning work in process .......................... | 850 | 1,200 |
| Lamps transferred to finished goods ..................................... | 3,500 | 3,300 |
| Number of lamps in ending work in process .......................... | 1,200 | 900 |

In June, the lamps in beginning work in process were approximately 80% complete, while those in ending work in process were only 30% complete. In July, the units remaining in ending work in process were 60% complete. All lamps in ending work in process are finished during the next month.

**a.** For the month of June, calculate the equivalent units produced for the three major cost categories—body materials, wiring materials, and labor and overhead.

**b.** For the month of July, calculate the equivalent units produced for the three major cost categories—body materials, wiring materials, and labor and overhead.

**EXERCISE 17.8**

Process Costing

**LO 5**

Shamrock Industries uses process costing. All of the company's manufacturing activities take place in a single processing department. The following production report was prepared for the month of June:

| | |
| --- | --- |
| Direct materials ............................................ | $ 89,750 |
| Direct labor ................................................. | 28,975 |
| Manufacturing overhead applied ........................... | 40,275 |
| Total costs to account for in June ......................... | $159,000 |

The amounts of work in process at the beginning and end of the month were immaterial and assigned no dollar value. During June, 13,250 units were completed, of which 10,000 were sold on account at $25 per unit.

**a.** Prepare a journal entry to summarize the total manufacturing costs applied to production in June.

**b.** Prepare the journal entry to transfer completed units from work in process to the finished goods warehouse in June.

**c.** Prepare the journal entries to record the sale of 10,000 units manufactured during the period and the related cost of goods sold.

**EXERCISE 17.9**

Computing Costs per Equivalent Unit

**LO 6, 7**

Old Victrola, Inc., produces top-quality stereos and uses process costing. The manufacture of stereos is such that direct materials, labor, and overhead are all added evenly throughout the production process. Due to the smooth production process, only one cost category—manufacturing costs—is used for equivalent unit calculations. Old Victrola had the following cost and production information available for the months of March and April:

| | March | April |
| --- | --- | --- |
| Direct materials costs ................................... | $ 978,460 | $1,168,310 |
| Direct labor costs ....................................... | 2,562,260 | 3,041,940 |
| Manufacturing overhead applied ....................... | 3,438,640 | 3,571,030 |
| Total manufacturing costs ............................ | $6,979,360 | $7,781,280 |
| Units in beginning work in process ..................... | 7,000 | 4,800 |
| Units transferred to finished goods .................... | 18,500 | 23,000 |
| Units in ending work in process ....................... | 4,800 | 6,400 |

Beginning work in process was 30% complete in March and 60% complete in April. Ending work in process was 60% complete in March and 35% complete in April.

a. For each of the two months, calculate the equivalent units of production.

b. Based on equivalent units produced, did total manufacturing costs per unit increase or decrease between March and April?

c. Did the direct materials cost per equivalent unit increase or decrease between March and April?

One of Sun Appliance's products is a dishwasher. Two processing departments are involved in the dishwasher's manufacture. The tub is assembled in one department, and a second department assembles and installs the motor. There is no beginning or ending work in process in either department. During March, the company incurred the following costs in the manufacture of 4,000 dishwashers.

**EXERCISE 17.10**

Computing and Using Unit Costs

**LO 1, 5, 7**

|  | Tub Department | Motor Department |
|---|---|---|
| Direct materials | $150,000 | $96,000 |
| Direct labor | 12,000 | 18,000 |
| Manufacturing overhead | 18,000 | 6,000 |

a. Compute the following *per-unit* costs for the month of March:

1. Tub assemblies transferred to the Motor Department
2. Assembling a motor and installing it
3. Completed dishwashers
4. Materials used in assembling the tub
5. Direct labor cost of assembling and installing a motor

b. Which of these unit costs would be most useful to management in evaluating the overall monthly efficiency of the Motor Department? Explain your reasoning.

Listed below are the eight activity cost pools used by the Charvez Corporation.

**EXERCISE 17.11**

Selecting Activity Bases

**LO 8**

| | |
|---|---|
| Production set-up costs | Maintenance costs |
| Heating costs | Design and engineering costs |
| Machinery power costs | Materials warehouse costs |
| Purchasing department costs | Product inspection costs |

Suggest an appropriate activity base for allocating each of the above activity cost pools to products. (Consider each cost pool independently.)

Costume Kings has two product lines: machine-made costumes and hand-made costumes. The company assigns $80,000 in manufacturing overhead costs to two cost pools: power costs and inspection costs. Of this amount, the power cost pool has been assigned $32,000 and the inspection cost pool has been assigned $48,000. Additional information about each product line is shown below.

**EXERCISE 17.12**

Allocating Activity Cost Pools

**LO 8, 9**

|  | Machine-Made | Hand-Made |
|---|---|---|
| Sales revenue | $240,000 | $160,000 |
| Direct labor and materials costs | $120,000 | $ 96,000 |
| Units produced and sold | 48,000 | 16,000 |
| Machine hours | 96,000 | 4,000 |
| Square feet of production space | 1,200 | 800 |
| Material orders received | 150 | 100 |
| Quality control inspection hours | 2,000 | 500 |

a. Allocate the manufacturing overhead from the activity cost pools to each product line. Use what you believe are the most significant cost drivers from the information provided.

**b.** Compute the cost per unit of machine-made costumes and hand-made costumes.

**c.** On a per-unit basis, which product line appears to be the most profitable? Explain.

# PROBLEMS

**PROBLEM 17.1**

Job Order Costing:
Computations and Journal
Entries

**LO 1–4**

Chesapeake Sailmakers uses job order costing. Manufacturing overhead is charged to individual jobs through the use of a predetermined overhead rate based on direct labor costs. The following information appears in the company's Work in Process Inventory controlling account for the month of June:

| | |
|---|---|
| Debits to account: | |
| Balance, June 1 . . . . . . . . . . . . . . . . . . . . . . . . . . . . . . . . . . . . . . . . . . . . . . | $ 7,200 |
| Direct materials . . . . . . . . . . . . . . . . . . . . . . . . . . . . . . . . . . . . . . . . . . . . . | 12,000 |
| Direct labor . . . . . . . . . . . . . . . . . . . . . . . . . . . . . . . . . . . . . . . . . . . . . . . | 9,000 |
| Manufacturing overhead (applied to jobs as 150% of direct labor cost) . . . . . . . . . . | 13,500 |
| Total debits to account . . . . . . . . . . . . . . . . . . . . . . . . . . . . . . . . . . . . . | $41,700 |
| Credits to account: | |
| Transferred to Finished Goods Inventory account . . . . . . . . . . . . . . . . . . . . . . . . . | 33,200 |
| Balance, June 30 . . . . . . . . . . . . . . . . . . . . . . . . . . . . . . . . . . . . . . . . . . . . | $ 8,500 |

## Instructions

**a.** Assuming that the direct labor charged to the jobs still in process at June 30 amounts to $2,100, compute the amount of manufacturing overhead and the amount of direct materials that have been charged to these jobs as of June 30.

**b.** Prepare general journal entries to summarize:

   **1.** The manufacturing costs (direct materials, direct labor, and overhead) charged to production during June.

   **2.** The transfer of production completed during June to the Finished Goods Inventory account.

   **3.** The cash sale of 90% of the merchandise completed during June at a total sales price of $46,500. Show the related cost of goods sold in a separate journal entry.

**PROBLEM 17.2**

Job Order Costing: Journal
Entries and Cost Flows

**LO 1–4**

The following information relates to the manufacturing operations of O'Shaughnessy Mfg. Co. during the month of March. The company uses job order costing.

**a.** Purchases of direct materials during the month amount to $59,700. (All purchases were made on account.)

**b.** Materials requisitions issued by the Production Department during the month total $56,200.

**c.** Time cards of direct workers show 2,000 hours worked on various jobs during the month, for a total direct labor cost of $30,000.

**d.** Direct workers were paid $26,300 in March.

**e.** Actual overhead costs for the month amount to $34,900 (for simplicity, you may credit Accounts Payable).

**f.** Overhead is applied to jobs at a rate of $18 per direct labor hour.

**g.** Jobs with total accumulated costs of $116,000 were completed during the month.

**h.** During March, units costing $128,000 were sold for $210,000. (All sales were made on account.)

## Instructions

Prepare general journal entries to summarize each of these transactions in the company's general ledger accounts.

Georgia Woods, Inc., manufactures furniture to customers' specifications and uses job order costing. A predetermined overhead rate is used in applying manufacturing overhead to individual jobs. In Department One, overhead is applied on the basis of machine-hours, and in Department Two, on the basis of direct labor hours. At the beginning of the current year, management made the following budget estimates to assist in determining the overhead application rate:

**PROBLEM 17.3**

Job Order Costing: A Comprehensive Problem

**LO 1–4**

|  | Department One | Department Two |
|---|---|---|
| Direct labor cost | $300,000 | $225,000 |
| Direct labor hours | 20,000 | 15,000 |
| Manufacturing overhead | $420,000 | $337,500 |
| Machine-hours | 12,000 | 7,500 |

Production of a batch of custom furniture ordered by City Furniture (job no. 58) was started early in the year and completed three weeks later on January 29. The records for this job show the following cost information:

|  | Department One | Department Two |
|---|---|---|
| Job order for City Furniture (job no. 58): |  |  |
| Direct materials cost | $10,100 | $ 7,600 |
| Direct labor cost | $16,500 | $11,100 |
| Direct labor hours | 1,100 | 740 |
| Machine-hours | 750 | 500 |

Selected additional information for January is as follows:

|  | Department One | Department Two |
|---|---|---|
| Direct labor hours—month of January | 1,600 | 1,200 |
| Machine-hours—month of January | 1,100 | 600 |
| Manufacturing overhead incurred in January. | $39,010 | $26,540 |

### Instructions

a. Compute the predetermined overhead rate for each department.

b. What is the total cost of the furniture produced for City Furniture?

c. Prepare the entries required to record the sale (on account) of the furniture to City Furniture. The sales price of the order was $147,000.

d. Determine the over- or underapplied overhead for each department at the end of January.

Precision Instruments, Inc., uses job order costing and applies manufacturing overhead to individual jobs by using predetermined overhead rates. In Department A, overhead is applied on the basis of machine hours, and in Department B, on the basis of direct labor hours. At the beginning of the current year, management made the following budget estimates as a step toward determining the overhead application rates:

**PROBLEM 17.4**

Job Order Costing: A Comprehensive Problem

**LO 1–4**

|  | Department A | Department B |
|---|---|---|
| Direct labor | $420,000 | $300,000 |
| Manufacturing overhead | $540,000 | $412,500 |
| Machine-hours | 18,000 | 1,900 |
| Direct labor hours | 28,000 | 25,000 |

Production of 4,000 tachometers (job no. 399) was started in the middle of January and completed two weeks later. The cost records for this job show the following information:

|  | Department A | Department B |
|---|---|---|
| Job no. 399 (4,000 units of product): | | |
| Cost of materials used on job . . . . . . . . . . . . . . . . . . . . | $6,800 | $4,500 |
| Direct labor cost . . . . . . . . . . . . . . . . . . . . . . . . . . . . . | $8,100 | $7,200 |
| Direct labor hours . . . . . . . . . . . . . . . . . . . . . . . . . . . . | 540 | 600 |
| Machine-hours . . . . . . . . . . . . . . . . . . . . . . . . . . . . . . . | 250 | 100 |

### Instructions

**a.** Determine the overhead rate that should be used for each department in applying overhead costs to job no. 399.

**b.** What is the total cost of job no. 399, and what is the unit cost of the product manufactured on this production order?

**c.** Prepare the journal entries required to record the sale (on account) of 1,000 of the tachometers to SkiCraft Boats. The total sales price was $19,500.

**d.** Assume that actual overhead costs for the year were $517,000 in Department A and $424,400 in Department B. Actual machine-hours in Department A were 17,000, and actual direct labor hours in Department B were 26,000 during the year. On the basis of this information, determine the over- or underapplied overhead in each department for the year.

**PROBLEM 17.5**

Process Costing

**LO 5, 6, 7**

The Great Oak Furniture Company produces rocking chairs in two departments, Assembly and Finishing. In the Assembly Department, all direct materials (wood) are entered into production at the start of the process. Various machines cut the raw wood into appropriate pieces and workers assemble the pieces into chairs. Thus, in the Assembly Department, all direct labor and overhead is incurred evenly throughout the process. The Finishing Department then takes the chairs, applies numerous coats of stain and varnish, and finally buffs and packages the completed chairs. Thus, in the Finishing Department, direct materials are added evenly throughout the first half of the process, while direct labor is added evenly throughout the last half. Overhead is incurred evenly over the entire finishing process. Great Oak uses process costing and had the following cost and production information available for January, its first month of operation:

|  | Assembly Department | Finishing Department |
|---|---|---|
| Direct materials cost . . . . . . . . . . . . . . . . . . . . . . . . . . | $29,025 | $ 7,760 |
| Direct labor cost . . . . . . . . . . . . . . . . . . . . . . . . . . . . . | 11,610 | 15,580 |
| Manufacturing overhead applied . . . . . . . . . . . . . . . . . . | 14,190 | 6,228 |
| Total manufacturing costs . . . . . . . . . . . . . . . . . . . . . . | $54,825 | $29,568 |
| Units in beginning work in process . . . . . . . . . . . . . . . . | 0 | 0 |
| Units started . . . . . . . . . . . . . . . . . . . . . . . . . . . . . . . | 750 | 575 |
| Units completed and transferred out . . . . . . . . . . . . . . . | 575 | 435 |
| Units in ending work in process . . . . . . . . . . . . . . . . . . | 175 | 140 |
| Percentage complete—ending work in process . . . . . . . . . . . . . | 40% | 60% |

During the month of January, 400 rocking chairs were sold and shipped to customers at a retail price of $220 each.

### Instructions

**a.** For January, calculate the equivalent units produced by the Assembly Department and the Finishing Department for the three cost categories—direct materials, direct labor, and manufacturing overhead.

**b.** Calculate the assembly, finishing, and total cost of producing a rocking chair during January.

**c.** For the month of January, prepare the journal entries summarizing the manufacturing costs charged to the Assembly Department and the Finishing Department.

**d.** For January, prepare the month-end journal entries to transfer the costs of chairs moved from the Assembly Department to the Finishing Department and from the Finishing Department to Finished Goods Inventory.

**e.** Prepare the entries to record the sales made in January and the corresponding reduction of Finished Goods Inventory.

**f.** Using T accounts, calculate the ending balances in the Work in Process accounts and Finished Goods Inventory.

Toll House makes chocolate chip cookies. The cookies pass through three production processes: mixing the cookie dough, baking, and packaging. Toll House uses process costing.

The following are data concerning the costs incurred in each process during May, along with the number of units processed:

**PROBLEM 17.6**

Process Costing

**LO 5, 7**

|  | Mixing | Baking | Packaging |
|---|---|---|---|
| Direct materials | $3,600 | $ 0 | $1,020 |
| Direct labor | 3,000 | 1,800 | 2,100 |
| Manufacturing overhead | 6,000 | 12,000 | 1,200 |
| Output | 14,000 lbs. | 4,000 gross* | 48,000 boxes |

*A gross is 12 dozen.

To ensure freshness, cookies are baked and packaged on the same day that the dough is mixed. Thus the company has no inventory still in process at the end of a business day.

**Instructions**

**a.** Prepare a separate journal entry summarizing the costs incurred by the Mixing Department in preparing 14,000 pounds of cookie dough in May. In the explanation of your entry, indicate the department's unit cost.

**b.** Prepare the month-end entry recording the transfer of cookie dough to the Baking Department during May.

**c.** Prepare a journal entry summarizing the costs incurred by the Baking Department in May (excluding the costs transferred from the Mixing Department). In the explanation, indicate the *cost per gross* of the baking process.

**d.** Prepare the month-end entry recording the transfer of cookies from the Baking Department to the Packaging Department in May.

**e.** Prepare a journal entry summarizing the costs incurred by the Packaging Department in May. In the explanation, indicate the packaging cost per box.

**f.** Prepare the month-end entry to record the transfers in May of cases of cookies from the Packaging Department to the finished goods warehouse. In the explanation, indicate the total cost per box transferred.

**g.** Briefly explain how management will use the unit cost information appearing in entries **a, c, e,** and **f.**

Norton Chemical Company produces two products: Amithol and Bitrite. The company uses activity-based costing (ABC) to allocate manufacturing overhead to these products. The costs incurred by Norton's Purchasing Department average $80,000 per year and constitute a major portion of the company's total manufacturing overhead.

Purchasing Department costs are assigned to two activity cost pools: (1) the order cost pool and (2) the inspection cost pool. Costs are assigned to the pools based on the number of employees engaged in each activity. Of the department's five full-time employees, one is responsible for ordering raw materials, and four are responsible for inspecting incoming shipments of materials.

**PROBLEM 17.7**

Applying Overhead Costs Using ABC

**LO 8, 9**

Costs assigned to the order pool are allocated to products based on the total number of purchase orders generated by each product line. Costs assigned to the inspection pool are allocated to products based on the number of inspections related to each product line.

For the upcoming year, Norton estimates the following activity levels:

|  | Total | Amithol | Bitrite |
|---|---|---|---|
| Purchase orders generated .......................... | 10,000 | 2,000 | 8,000 |
| Inspections conducted ............................... | 2,400 | 1,800 | 600 |

In a normal year, the company conducts 2,400 inspections to sample the quality of raw materials. The large number of Amithol-related inspections is due to quality problems experienced in the past. The quality of Bitrite materials has been consistently good.

### Instructions

**a.** Assign the Purchasing Department's costs to the individual cost pools.

**b.** Allocate the order cost pool to the individual product lines.

**c.** Allocate the inspection cost pool to the individual product lines.

**d.** Suggest how Norton might reduce manufacturing costs incurred by the Purchasing Department.

**PROBLEM 17.8**

ABC versus Use of a Single
Activity Base

Dixon Robotics manufactures three robot models: the A3B4, the BC11, and the C3PO. Dixon allocates manufacturing overhead to each model based on machine hours. A large portion of the company's manufacturing overhead costs is incurred by the Maintenance Department. This year, the department anticipates that it will incur $100,000 in total costs. The following estimates pertain to the upcoming year:

| Model | Estimated Machine Hours | Estimated Units of Production |
|---|---|---|
| A3B4 | 20,000 | 6,250 |
| BC11 | 15,000 | 5,000 |
| C3PO | 5,000 | 2,500 |

Ed Smith, Dixon's cost accountant, suspects that unit costs are being distorted by using a single activity base to allocate Maintenance Department costs to products. Thus he is considering the implementation of activity-based costing (ABC).

Under the proposed ABC method, the costs of the Maintenance Department would be allocated to the following activity cost pools using the number of work orders as an activity base: (1) the repairs pool and (2) the janitorial pool. Of the 2,000 work orders filed with the Maintenance Department each year, approximately 400 relate to repair activities, and 1,600 relate to janitorial activities.

Machinery repairs correlate with the number of production runs of each robot model. Thus the repairs pool would be allocated to robots based on each model's corresponding number of production runs. Janitorial services correlate with square feet of production space. Thus the janitorial pool would be allocated to products based on the square feet of production space devoted to each robot model. The following table provides a summary of annual production run activity and square footage requirements:

| Model | Estimated Number of Production Runs | Estimated Square Feet of Production Space Used |
|---|---|---|
| A3B4 | 50 | 5,000 |
| BC11 | 150 | 10,000 |
| C3PO | 200 | 25,000 |

### Instructions

**a.** Calculate the amount of Maintenance Department costs that would be allocated to each robot model (on a per-unit basis) using machine hours as an activity base.

**b.** Calculate the amount of Maintenance Department costs that would be allocated to each robot model (on a per-unit basis) using the proposed ABC method.

**c.** Are cost allocations distorted using machine hours as a single activity base? Explain your answer.

# CASES AND UNSTRUCTURED PROBLEMS

The Kendahl Plastics Corporation contracts with NASA to manufacture component parts used in communications satellites. NASA reimburses Kendahl on the basis of the actual manufacturing costs it incurs, plus a fixed percentage. Prior to being awarded a contract, Kendahl must submit a bid that details the estimated costs associated with each project. An examination of Kendahl's job cost sheets reveals that actual costs consistently exceed cost estimates quoted during the bidding process. As a consequence, NASA ends up paying considerably more than the bids Kendahl submits.

A Kendahl representative was recently quoted as saying, "We really aren't overcharging NASA for the work that we do. The actual costs shown on our job cost sheets seem high only because we are forced to understate our bid estimates in order to be awarded contracts. It's a common practice, and everybody does it. The truth of the matter is, companies that quote realistic bid prices are not awarded contracts."

**CASE 17.1**

The Bidding Wars

**LO 1, 2, 3**

### Instructions
Let us assume that it is common practice to purposely underestimate bids in order to win NASA contracts. Is it wrong for Kendahl to take part in this activity as long as it does not overstate the actual costs it incurs?

Viking Beer is a microbrewery that produces one type of beer. The production level is 18,000 gallons per month, which is bottled in 192,000 twelve-ounce bottles. The beer is brewed in batches of 3,600 gallons, which is the capacity of the fermenting tanks. Each batch requires six days of processing, during which it passes through six separate production processes.

Viking uses process costing. All manufacturing costs incurred during the month are assigned to the 192,000 bottles produced; no valuation is assigned to the 3,600 gallons currently sitting in the fermenting tanks.

Viking has hired Matt Brown, a recent college graduate, as a cost analyst. After learning about the company's cost accounting system, Brown sent the following memo to Viking's controller:

**CASE 17.2**

Evaluation of a Cost System: Does It Meet the Company's Needs?

**LO 1, 2, 4, 5, 7**

> I have two suggestions as to how we might improve our cost accounting system. First, our beer is processed in identifiable batches; so we could use *job order,* rather than process costing. This would enable us to determine separately the cost of each batch.
>
> Second, we always have 3,600 gallons of beer in the fermenting tanks. But our cost accounting system assigns all manufacturing costs during the period to the finished goods produced. Some of these costs should be assigned to the beer in the fermenting tanks and identified as "work in process inventory." This can be done by computing the *equivalent units* that these 3,600 gallons represent.

### Instructions
As Viking's controller, draft a memo responding to Brown's suggestions.

Dave Miller is the controller of the Mica Corporation. Mica produces five industrial cleaning products. Miller recently decided to implement activity-based costing at Mica. In designing the system, he decided to identify heating costs as a separate cost pool. These costs will be allocated to products using the square feet of production space as a cost driver. Thus the more square footage a particular product line requires, the greater its allocation of heating costs will be.

Miller has asked each production manager to submit an estimate of the production space occupied by their respective product lines. The figures he receives will be used to allocate the heating cost pool. The five production managers at Mica are paid an annual bonus based on their ability to control production costs traceable to their respective product lines.

**CASE 17.3**

Implementing ABC

**LO 8, 9**

### Instructions

**a.** What ethical concern do you have regarding the method used to gather information about space utilization at Mica?

**b.** What suggestions do you have regarding how this information should be gathered?

## BUSINESS WEEK ASSIGNMENT                          BusinessWeek

**CASE 17.4**

Cost Systems and Efficiency

**LO 1, 2, 4, 8**

### Custom-Made Doors

Only about four years ago, **Weyerhaeuser Company**'s Wisconsin door factory was on the verge of being closed. The factory was operating at half of its capacity but costs were running at the same level as a full-capacity plant. What a change a few years have made.

In "How an Intranet Opened Up the Door to Profits" (*Business Week,* July 26, 1999), Marcia Stepanek reported that

> Today, the plant—which cuts, glues, drills, and shapes customized doors according to each buyer's desire—is profitable again. . . . Experts give much credit to **Weyerhaeuser**'s installation of a state-of-the-art, in-house communications network that uses the Internet to compare prices in a heartbeat, boost on-time deliveries, and track orders as they move through the plant. . . . Thanks to more precise information about costs and lead times, doors are now priced according to what each option actually adds to the total cost of manufacture. Executives who once prided themselves on their pricing prowess discovered that some of their generations-old calculations were faulty.

In one case, a distributor that company executives thought was one of their best customers was actually costing them money.

### Instructions

Choose one of the following cost systems and write a one-page report explaining how **Weyerhaeuser Company**'s Wisconsin door manufacturing plant could use that costing system in conjunction with its in-house communication network and the Internet to improve pricing and reduce costs.

- Process Costing System
- Activity-Based Costing System
- Job Order Costing System

## INTERNET ASSIGNMENT

**INTERNET 17.1**

Manufacturing
Processes

**LO 2, 8**

The **Wrigley Company** manufactures chewing gum. Visit its home page at the following address:

**www.wrigley.com**

From the home page, click on the choices labeled "The Story of Chewing Gum" and "How Wrigley's Gum Is Made."

### Instructions

**a.** Prepare a simple flowchart that illustrates the major steps in the manufacture of chewing gum.

**b.** If Wrigley uses process costing, how many separate processing departments might be used and what would you label them?

**c.** What do you think are the major types of manufacturing overhead at **Wrigley**? What activity bases could be used to assign each type of overhead to the processing departments you listed in part **b**?

*Internet sites are time and date sensitive. It is the purpose of these exercises to have you explore the Internet. You may need to use the Yahoo! search engine* http://www.yahoo.com *(or other favorite search engine) to look for a company's current web address.*

# OUR COMMENTS ON THE "YOUR TURN" CASES

**As a Treasurer (p. 737)**  In most cases, U.S. Internal Revenue regulations require that inventory costs be accumulated for tax purposes in a manner consistent with that used for financial reporting purposes. Therefore, since FASB reporting requirements state that material amounts of over/under applied overhead must be apportioned among the Work in Process and Finished Goods inventory accounts and the Cost of Goods Sold expense account, you should tell the assistant treasurer that it would be improper to allocate the entire amount of underapplied overhead to Cost of Goods Sold as a means to reduce ABI's company tax burden.

**As a Production Manager (p. 745)**  To determine if resource usage costs for February were higher than resource usage costs in March, compute February's costs per equivalent unit as follows:

| | |
|---|---|
| Direct labor ($5,050 ÷ 500 equivalent units) . . . . . . . . . . . . . . . . . . . . . . . . . . . . . . | $10.10 |
| Direct materials (cut materials only) ($15,450 ÷ 1,000 equivalent units) . . . . . . . . . . . . . | 15.45 |
| Overhead ($4,500 ÷ 333⅓ equivalent units) . . . . . . . . . . . . . . . . . . . . . . . . . . . . . . . | 13.50 |

As production manager of the Assembly Department, you have little control over the cost of the cutting materials that are transferred from the Cutting Department. For reasons beyond your control, those costs were significantly lower in February ($15.45) than in March ($20.00). However, direct labor and overhead are directly under your control. Although direct labor decreased in March ($10.00) as compared to February ($10.10), overhead is much higher in March at $18.00 per equivalent unit as compared to February's $13.50 per equivalent unit. An investigation into the reason for this significant increase in overhead costs during March should be undertaken.

**As a Product-Line Manager (p. 747)**  To document the performance of the managers of the Bottling and Syrup Departments, you may consider developing a budget system to compare actual and budgeted costs. Require the managers of each department to prepare an annual budget for monthly (or weekly) resource usage. Then track the actual monthly (or weekly) equivalent unit cost of each significant resource input in each department and compare it to the budgeted amounts. Rewards or bonuses could be provided based on meeting or exceeding budgeted targets.

**As a Plant Accountant (p. 753)**  When considering implementing new costing procedures such as ABC, you should consider the additional costs associated with tracking and measuring multiple activity bases. At Master File, changing to the proposed ABC methods would require tracking work orders, number of production runs, kilowatt hours for heating versus machining, square feet occupied, and machine hours used. Thus ABC requires tracking five drivers, compared to the single-driver approach, which requires only one driver—direct labor hours. In addition to the costs associated with the physical data collection, you should consider the possibility of information overload costs on the ABC information user. There are no benefits from adopting ABC methods if users cannot use the information for decision making. Providing too much information with too much detail can result in information overload, making the information useless or, at worst, causing poor decision-making outcomes.

# ANSWERS TO SELF-TEST QUESTIONS

**1.** b   **2.** c   **3.** a   **4.** b   **5.** a, b, c, d   **6.** a, b, c   **7.** a, c, d   **8.** b   **9.** d

# 18

# COSTING AND THE VALUE CHAIN

## Learning Objectives

*After studying this chapter, you should be able to:*

1. Define the value chain and describe its basic components.

2. Distinguish between non-value-added and value-added activities.

3. Explain how activity-based management is related to activity-based costing (ABC).

4. Describe the target costing process and list its components.

5. Identify the relationship between target costing and the value chain.

6. Explain the nature and goals of a just-in-time (JIT) manufacturing system.

7. Identify the components of the cost of quality.

8. Describe the characteristics of quality measures.

Dell

**Dell Computer Corporation**, headquartered in Round Rock, Texas, is the world's leading direct sales company selling computer systems. The company ranks number one in market share in the United States according to Q200 IDC data. With computer sales of $50 million over the Internet each day, **Dell** has become a master of analyzing and evaluating all components of its value chain to eliminate non-value-added activities.

For example, **Dell** doesn't start assembling a computer until the order is booked. A just-in-time philosophy applies to **Dell**'s entire value chain including suppliers, assemblers, and distributors. Most of **Dell**'s suppliers warehouse components just minutes from **Dell**'s factories. A computer ordered at 9 A.M. on Monday can be loaded on a delivery truck 15 hours later.

● ● ●

This chapter describes how to manage value chain costs. In addition, we introduce and explain the distinctions between value-added and non-value-added activities in the value chain, the components of the cost of quality across the value chain, and the relationship between activity-based management, target costing, and the value chain.

## THE VALUE CHAIN

**LO 1**

Define the value chain and describe its basic components.

To focus on core operations, management begins by identifying components of the organization's value chain. In Chapter 16, we defined the **value chain** as the set of activities and resources necessary to create and deliver the product or service valued by customers. The typical components of a simple value chain are shown below.

Obviously, the details of each organization's value chain will look different. Further, the value chain for each particular product or service within an organization can be very different. Consider **Dell Computer Corporation**, the company discussed in the opening story. On its home page, **Dell** lists some of its products and services: desktop PCs, notebook PCs, software and servers. These categories represent different markets with different types of suppliers and customers. For example, product characteristics that are valued by a typical notebook PC customer will differ significantly from those valued by a desktop PC customer. In addition, the suppliers for PCs and software differ significantly. Creating a value chain to satisfy diverse customer needs is a major challenge for most businesses.

For each of a company's products and services, the following components of the value chain are active:

- *Research and development (R&D) and design activities* include the creation of ideas and the development of prototype products, processes, and services.
- *Suppliers and production-related activities* include the procurement of raw materials and supplies and the activities needed to convert them into finished goods and services.
- *Marketing and distribution activities* are designed to provide information to potential customers and make the products and services accessible to customers.
- *Customer service activities* are those resources consumed by supporting the product or service after it is sold to the customer.

### Value- and Non-Value-Added Activities

**LO 2**

Distinguish between non-value-added and value-added activities.

Organizations attempt to identify and eliminate the **non-value-added activities** in their value chains. **Value-added activities** add to the product's or service's desirability in the eyes of the consumer. Non-value-added activities do not add to the product's desirability. Thus, when an organization consumes non-value-added resources, it can decrease its costs if the activity that consumes that resource can be eliminated without changing the product's desirability. An example of a non-value-added activity is having large amounts

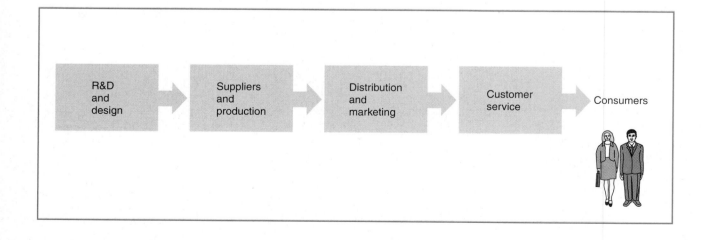

of raw materials, work in process, or finished goods inventory. **Dell**'s management recognizes the cost associated with inventories because part of the crux of their operating plan is a focus on tight inventory control. Just-in-time inventory management processes, discussed later in this chapter, have been developed to reduce the consumption of non-value-added resources associated with large amounts of inventories.

### You as a Raw Materials Inventory Manager

Assume you are the manager of raw materials for a lumber mill. What types of resources are being consumed when a large amount of redwood logs sits idle, waiting to be put through the mill?

*Our comments appear on page 807.

**YOUR TURN**

In the previous two chapters, we concentrated our cost analysis only on the production phase of the value chain. However, resources are consumed across the value chain. Organizations attempt to minimize resource consumption at all points on the value chain while simultaneously providing the products and services desired by consumers at competitive prices. In this chapter, we will consider other cost accounting procedures and techniques that have been developed to assess resource use and costs in all parts of the value chain. These procedures include *activity-based management,* which is effective over the entire value chain; *target costing,* designed for the R&D and design phase of the value chain; *just-in-time inventory procedures;* and, finally, *total quality management,* which is also relevant over the entire value chain.

## ACTIVITY-BASED MANAGEMENT

In Chapter 17, we introduced activity-based costing (ABC) and provided an ABC example focused on production overhead. The basic procedures related to ABC include the following:

1. Identify the *activity.*
2. Create an associated *activity cost pool.*
3. Identify an *activity measure.*
4. Create the *cost per unit of activity.*

Let's return to the Master File, Inc., example used in Chapter 17 and the activity associated with equipment repair. You may recall that the Maintenance Department for Master File has five full-time employees that are responsible for repair and set-up work on the machinery used to cut and bend metal to form file cabinets. The Maintenance Department's total cost pool is $180,000, which is divided between $108,000 and $72,000—the cost pools associated with repair activity and set-up activity, respectively. For the repair activity cost pool, we used the number of work orders issued for repairs (250 per year) as the activity measure. Thus the cost per work order is determined by dividing $108,000 by the total number of work orders issued per year, or $432 ($108,000 ÷ 250) per work order. Two hundred of the 250 repair work orders experienced each year are related to the normal production of 42,000 metal file cabinets. The resulting per metal file cabinet expense for repairs is determined as follows:

**200 work orders × $432 per work order = $86,400 ÷ 42,000 metal file cabinets**
**= $2.057 per metal file cabinet**

Chapter 17's focus was on assigning cost to units of the product—in the above case, metal file cabinets. However, activity-based cost information is also important in management decision making. Remember that management is trying to eliminate non-value-added activities from the value chain. If the activity of equipment repair can be eliminated from the value chain *without increasing the cost associated with the total value chain,* then it is a non-value-added activity. The process of using activity-based costs to help reduce and eliminate non-value-added activities is **activity-based management**. Master File, Inc., may be able to redesign its equipment layout, acquire higher-quality metal materials as inputs, buy new equipment, outsource repair work for less than $432 per work order, or use some combination of these management decisions to reduce or eliminate the repair activity and associated resources.

**CASE IN POINT**

The **United States Postal Service (USPS)** used activity-based costing information prepared by consultants to help manage its costs. The consultant's study estimated the costs associated with processing the **USPS** cash and check transactions each year to exceed $1 billion. Activity-based management led **USPS** to reduce the costs associated with revenue transactions from postal customers by implementing credit and debit card processing. The use of credit and debit cards made funds available faster, reduced bad debt collection costs, and reduced the risk of cash losses from employee fraud. The consultant's study estimated the cost associated with processing to be $0.048 per cash dollar collected versus $0.027 per credit card dollar processed.[1]

## Activity-Based Management Across the Value Chain

While activity-based cost information is very important in the production portion of the value chain, it is also very useful for assessing activities associated with period expenses such as R&D, distribution, administration, finance, marketing, and customer service. In many organizations, period expenses are more significant contributors to profitability than product costs.

**Managing Activities: An Illustration**    ABC information helps managers compare their organization's cost per activity to externally competitive costs. To illustrate, consider Boards and More, Inc., a company that provides lumber and packaging products. The chief financial officer (CFO) has decided to undertake a study of the finance-related activities provided by the Accounting and Finance (A&F) Department. The activities performed by the A&F Department are identified and divided into four main categories: (1) transaction-related activities, (2) external financial reporting, (3) annual planning and budgeting, and (4) specially requested analyses. The table on the following page outlines those activities and the related percentage of resources consumed for each.

The ABC analysis in the table provides information to help the CFO manage the activities of the A&F Department. Boards and More's A&F Department has a total pool of 30 employees, representing a yearly cost pool of $1,415,600. First examine the transaction-related activities. These activities are undertaken to ensure basic journal entries are properly recorded and monitored throughout the firm. Account clerks complete much of the detail work. However, internal auditors are concerned that safeguards are in place to eliminate error and fraud in recording transactions. Budget and financial analysts are also involved in comparing transactions to budgeted numbers, undertaking analyses for external reporting purposes and other special business analyses. The CFO estimates $397,150 as the cost pool associated with transaction-related activities.

---

[1]Coopers & Lybrand, *Cash/Check/Credit/Debit Card Productivity Study,* 1994.

| Boards and More, Inc. Accounting and Finance Department | | | | |
|---|---|---|---|---|
| **Labor Category** | **Activity Category** | | | **Total Labor Resources** |
| | **Transaction-Related** | **Financial Reporting** | **Planning and Budgeting** | **Special Analyses** | |

| **Labor Category** | **Transaction-Related** | **Financial Reporting** | **Planning and Budgeting** | **Special Analyses** | **Total Labor Resources** |
|---|---|---|---|---|---|
| Clerks | 2/3 (66.67%) | 1/6 (16.67%) | 1/6 (16.66%) | 0 | 22,080 hours = (12 clerks, 46 weeks @ 40 hr per week @ $20/hr) = $441,600 |
| | $294,400 | $73,600 | $73,600 | $0 | |
| Finance analysts | 1/6 (16.67%) | 1/3 (33.33%) | 1/6 (16.67%) | 1/3 (33.33%) | 5 salaried analysts @ $45,000 each = $225,000 |
| | $37,500 | $75,000 | $37,500 | $75,000 | |
| Budget analysts | 1/6 (16.67%) | 1/6 (16.67%) | 1/3 (33.33%) | 1/3 (33.33%) | 6 salaried analysts @ $39,000 = $234,000 |
| | $39,000 | $39,000 | $78,000 | $78,000 | |
| Internal auditors | 1/4 (25%) | 1/2 (50%) | 1/4 (25%) | 0 | 3 salaried auditors @ $35,000 each = $105,000 |
| | $26,250 | $52,500 | $26,250 | $0 | |
| Senior analysts and CFO | 0 | 1/4 (25%) | 1/4 (25%) | 1/2 (50%) | 3 senior analysts @ $75,000 each and 1 CFO @ $185,000 = $410,000 |
| | $0 | $102,500 | $102,500 | $205,000 | |
| **Total Activity Resources** | $397,150 | $342,600 | $317,850 | $358,000 | **$1,415,600** |

A software vendor has presented the CFO with data showing that employee time associated with transaction activities could be cut in half with its popular software package, "Transaction Reduction." The software vendor quotes a price of $450,000 for the fully installed package including employee training. If the CFO purchases the software and the vendor's analysis is correct, the software will recover its initial cost after 2.27 years, computed as follows:

$$\text{Transaction Activities Cost Pool} = \$397,150 \times 50\% \text{ savings per year}$$
$$= \$198,575 \text{ per year}$$

$$\text{"Transaction Reduction" Costs} = \$450,000 \div \$198,575 \text{ per year}$$
$$= 2.266 \text{ years to recover}$$

However, if the software vendor's data analysis applies only to the resources associated with clerks and not to other employee resources, the time before recovery of the software cost extends to 3.06 years ($294,400 × 50% = $147,200; $450,000 ÷ $147,200 = 3.06 years). The CFO may be concerned that a longer time to recover the initial investment would be undesirable given rapid change in software technology. In order to determine the exact resources (clerks versus analysts) that might be affected by the new software, a more detailed analysis than that just displayed must be undertaken.

**CASE IN POINT**

**Johnson & Johnson** did away with monthly closing of its books and all related transactions. Now closings occur quarterly. **Johnson & Johnson** also speeded up processes in its finance function. What used to take 26 days on average now takes 7. All told, **Johnson & Johnson** cut its worldwide finance budget by $84 million, and many of the cost savings came from reductions in transaction-related processing costs.

### ABC: A Subset of Activity-Based Management

ABC information must be created before management of the activity can occur. To see this, consider the ABC data from Boards and More, Inc. Suppose the external auditors for Boards and More proposed to the CFO that the external auditors could perform the internal audit function for $90,000. At the simplest level, this might be considered a cost reduction because the three internal auditors consume $105,000 in resources and the proposed outsourcing consumes $90,000 in resources. Closer inspection of the external auditor's proposal reveals that the activities under consideration are restricted to those in the financial reporting area. The ABC data, however, tells the CFO that these activities comprise only half of the total internal audit activities. Thus the true resource cost savings from the external auditor's proposal would be $52,500, rather than $105,000, and the CFO should reject the proposal.

Managing the internal audit activity at Boards and More requires a clear understanding of the activities that consume resources *and* the costs associated with these resources. In addition, having benchmark information about competitive practices can help the company identify non-value-added activities. This benchmark information can be in the form of industry studies, competitive outside bids, or internal prototyping. Thus ABC is a critical component of activity-based management, but managing the activities also requires benchmark information. The illustration below captures the details of activity-based management.

**LO 3**

Explain how activity-based management is related to activity-based costing (ABC).

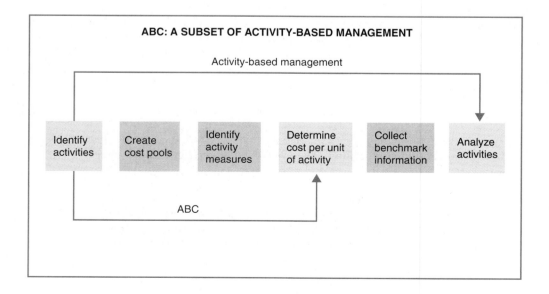

**ABC: A SUBSET OF ACTIVITY-BASED MANAGEMENT**

Activity-based management

Identify activities → Create cost pools → Identify activity measures → Determine cost per unit of activity → Collect benchmark information → Analyze activities

ABC

Choosing to adopt an activity-based management system is a strategic decision by management that ultimately affects product pricing, outsourcing, customer relations, and organizational structure decisions among others. Furthermore, thanks to the falling price of computing power, even small companies can now implement activity-based management. For example, activity-based cost information frequently reveals that customers assumed to be marginal in profit contribution are big profit generators and vice versa. Companies using ABC software do a better job of tracking costs related to quality, packing, and shipping. Often they begin to make smarter strategic production decisions about which lines of business they should be in and which assets should be sold.

**MANAGEMENT STRATEGY**

## THE TARGET COSTING PROCESS

The previous example based on Boards and More, Inc., is aimed at considering activities of existing, established processes. **Target costing** is a business process aimed at the earliest stages of new product and service development, before creation and design of production methods. It is a process driven by the customer, focused on design, and encompassing the entire life of the product. The objective is to create for the organization a production process that provides adequate profits. By focusing simultaneously on profit and cost planning over the entire value chain, organizations are able to tap synergies among the various value chain parts. Consideration of the entire value chain at the product development phase is critical because research demonstrates that 80% of production-related expenses are committed once the production process begins. These committed resources cannot be changed later without great cost to the company.

The target costing process begins with the customer. Customer desires about functionality, quality, and, most important, price drive the analysis. As acknowledged in the chapter opener, having a clear understanding of customer needs is critical. There are likely to be functional requirements that must be present to meet customer needs. Further, the customer may be unwilling to trade off functional requirements for lower price or lower quality. Knowing customer requirements also means understanding competitor offerings. Consumers do not operate in a vacuum. They demand product characteristics based on what is available in the marketplace. If a competitor offers a higher-quality product with a similar functionality at a lower price, then companies attempt to reengineer their processes to meet that competition.

**LO 4**
Describe the target costing process and list its components.

**General Electric Co.**'s jet engine business was in trouble in the early 1990s. Demand for new engines plummeted and profits declined precipitously. In 1993, **GE** decided to adopt target costing processes. **GE** first approached its airline customers to find out how to redesign its engines and reduce costs. **GE** found that its engines for the Boeing 747 and Boeing 767 could be made without a manifold, a $10,000 part, because customers believed the manifold's cost outweighed its benefits.

**CASE IN POINT**

### Components of the Target Costing Process

At the most basic level, the *desired* target cost is the cost of resources that should be consumed to create a product that can be sold at a target price. The target price is determined through interaction with consumers. However, management must determine an acceptable profit margin for the product to compute the desired target cost. That profit margin, although not considered in detail here, is a function of the type of business and the demands of the marketplace. The basic target cost formula is as follows:

**Target Cost = Target Price − Profit Margin**

Target costing can be understood by considering its four components. First, significant resources are consumed in *planning and market analysis.* During planning, the customer niche is identified and thoroughly documented. The second component, *development,* is focused on product feasibility studies. Development involves a cycle of testing and reformulating the product to understand customer requirements. These first two components lead to an expected target price. The third phase, *production design,* follows the establishment of the product concept in the development phase. Engineering and experienced production personnel use **value engineering** to determine the least costly combination of resources to create a product desired by the customer. Finally, *production* begins and a continuous improvement process is used to attain the target cost. These latter two stages are where the achievement of the target cost occurs. The diagram below illustrates the components of the target costing process.

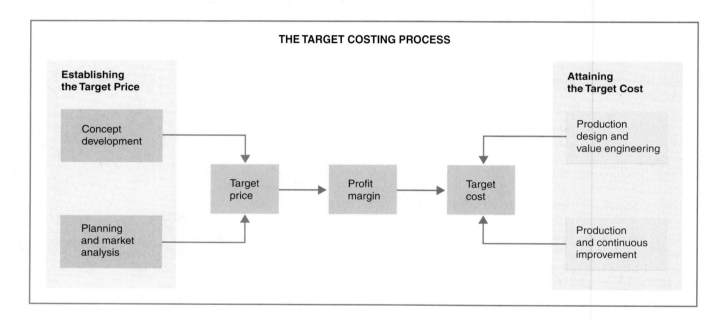

### Target Costing: An Illustration

To illustrate the target costing process, we will use Boards and More, Inc., the company previously discussed. One of Boards and More's product lines is paper packaging products. The company bids on packaging jobs for such products as laundry soap, cereal boxes, and pancake mix. The typical value chain for the cardboard boxes is shown on the facing page. The value chain for these packaging materials includes the research and development objective of creating cardboard with superior quality and strength at the lowest possible weight. Boards and More produces the cardboard in large rolls that are shipped to suppliers for printing and box formation before the boxes are shipped to the soap manufacturer.

In a recent survey of the soap box market by Boards and More's Marketing and Planning Department, customers expressed dissatisfaction with currently available packaging. Further analysis revealed soap manufacturers believe the packaging is too heavy, increasing their shipping costs. Soap consumers are also unhappy with the ink used because when the boxes get wet, the printing bleeds or rubs off.

A cross-functional, cross-organizational team is assembled to create a product to satisfy customer needs. Notice that two sets of customers, both in the value chain, are important: the soap manufacturer and the soap consumer. The product creation team consists of marketing, design engineering, accounting, and production engineering personnel from Boards and More and similar personnel from the printing firm and the soap com-

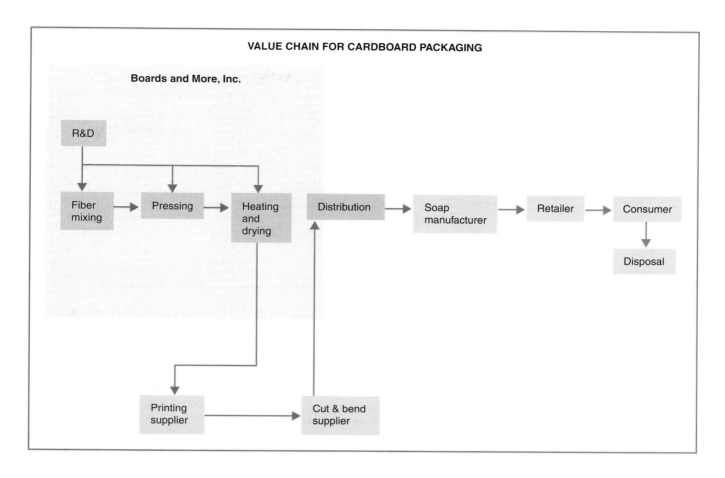

VALUE CHAIN FOR CARDBOARD PACKAGING

pany. The charge to the team is to create new paperboard for the cardboard soap boxes that satisfies customers' needs.

## You as a Team Leader

Assume you are the leader of the Boards and More product creation team for the new soap box design. At the initial meeting of the cross-organizational team, a serious reservation is raised by the team members from the printing firm about the confidentiality and intellectual properties of any new designs created by the overall team. The printing firm has a policy of keeping all printing formulas and processes secret to protect its competitive advantage in the marketplace. The printing firm team members point out that five years ago, Boards and More engineers used an idea that they got while talking with the engineers from the printing firm. The printing firm representatives are creating reservations so serious that the viability of the soap box design project is threatened. What should you do?

*Our comments appear on page 807.

**YOUR TURN**

Observe that although Boards and More leads the new product team, all members of the value chain should participate in new product creation. If the new cardboard created by Boards and More is of a lighter weight but cannot properly absorb ink, then the solution is not viable. Similarly, if the cardboard is lightweight but its strength does not allow proper filling by the machinery at the soap manufacturer, then the solution is not feasible. Finally, in addition to the design changes that Boards and More considers undertaking, other team members from the printing or soap companies may want to modify or change their processes to satisfy the ultimate customer, the soap consumer.

The marketing team members provide information about the customer requirements and the design engineers link those requirements to the functions of the paperboard. A small sample of relevant requirements and functions is listed below. The "high" or "low" indicates the importance of the function in satisfying the requirement and the "+" or "−" indicates if the function and requirement are positively or negatively associated.

| | | Cardboard Functions | |
| | Requirements | Ability to Bend and Cut | Absorption Rate |
|---|---|---|---|
| Soap Consumer Requirements | Box is easy to pour. | High (+) | Low |
| | Pink does not bleed when wet. | Low | High (+) |
| Soap Manufacturer Requirements | Box is lightweight for shipping. | High (+) | High (+) |
| | Box is strong for filling. | High (−) | Low |

The requirements/functions table helps the design engineers to focus on product functions that can best meet the needs of the customers. In this case, the ability to bend and cut the cardboard is very important for how easy the box is to pour, its weight, and its strength. Unfortunately, the current technology in paperboard implies that although lightweight cardboard is easier to bend and cut and is easier for the consumer to pour, it is not strong enough to meet the soap manufacturer's requirements. It seems clear from the table that if the box could be made stronger while simultaneously maintaining light weight and high absorption, several consumer requirements could be met. Of course, the problem of the additional cost associated with the lighter weight paperboard must be considered.

The marketing members of the team must determine the target price consumers are willing to pay to gain the desired requirements. After market surveys, it becomes clear that soap consumers are unwilling to pay more than the current price of $4.50 per box for the desired requirements. The soap manufacturer is thus unwilling to increase the amount it pays to Boards and More, $2.30, for the printed soap boxes.

Additional investigation reveals competitors are about to release new packaging designed to solve some of these problems—plastic bottles. The plastic bottles are lightweight and strong and have labels that eliminate the printing problems. Although this new packaging approach does not require a price increase, the head marketing and engineering managers at Boards and More are skeptical of its acceptance by soap consumers because of pouring problems. The narrow neck of the plastic jug causes the powdered soap to clump together as it pours, creating problems for the consumer. It is clear, however, that competitors are working to solve these problems.

The design engineers, working with the accountants who have gathered ABC information, have come up with a potential solution to meet customer requirements as illustrated below.

| | Cardboard—Cost per Box | | |
| Solutions | Current ABC-Based Cost | Initial Target Cost | Value Engineered Target Cost |
|---|---|---|---|
| Fiber mix | $0.52 | $0.55 | $0.55 |
| Pressing requirements | 0.08 | 0.05 | 0.05 |
| Drying time | 0.04 | 0.06 | 0.05 |
| Bend and cut—outsourced | 0.33 | 0.33 | 0.30 |
| Printing—outsourced | 0.75 | 0.78 | 0.77 |
| **Total** | **$1.72** | **$1.77** | **$1.72** |

The design engineers propose an initial target cost of $1.77. Lowering the wood fiber content of the paperboard and using microscopic plastic fibers that reduce weight and increase strength generates this initial target cost. The new mixture would require fewer pounds of pressure when being rolled but would require longer drying time and higher heat during drying. The paperboard would then be ready for printing. However, the printing company determines the new paperboard would require new printing technology because of absorption problems created by the plastic fibers. The new paperboard would increase printing costs by $0.03 and the total cost by $0.05 per box ($1.72 to $1.77).

Because the initial target cost of $1.77 is too high to maintain previous margins, value engineering becomes critical. Cost must be driven out of the value chain or the proposed solution will not be acceptable. One piece of the value chain not yet considered is the bending and cutting used to create the box. Boards and More approaches the supplier that bends and cuts the boxes before they are shipped to the soap manufacturer. Boards and More asks for a price cut of $0.03 from the current price because the bending and cutting process should be easier and less costly, and the supplier agrees. Then Boards and More suggests splitting the remaining $0.02 of the total cost increase with the printer to achieve the target of $1.72, the price the soap producer is willing to pay. The printer agrees to the $0.01 reduction and Boards and More finds a way to cut $0.01 out of its heating and drying costs. Through value engineering across the value chain, suppliers and producers are able to arrive at the desired target cost.

One aspect of target costing not yet discussed is consideration of product costs over the life of the product. **Life-cycle costing** is the consideration of all potential resources consumed by the product over its entire life. These costs stretch from product development and R&D costs through warranty and disposal costs. In the Boards and More case, if the new paperboard mix for the soap boxes creates additional disposal costs for the soap consumer, these costs must be considered. For example, Boards and More needs to understand the impact of the new paperboard mix that contains plastic fibers on the ability of consumers to recycle the soap boxes and on their own potential environmental costs. These additional product life-cycle considerations are a formal part of the target costing process.

---

**CASH EFFECTS**

Team members involved in the target costing process must consider current and future cash flow effects associated with new product development. For example, if the proposed solution at Boards and More requires new equipment to accommodate the heating and drying of the new paperboard mix, the impact of the equipment purchase and of associated changes in future depreciation expenses on cash flows should be considered. Assume the new heating equipment has a purchase price of $500,000 and is expected to increase the annual depreciation expense from $100,000 to $150,000 per year. Cash flow consequences will include (1) the immediate purchase price cash outflow (net of any inflow from disposing of the old equipment) and (2) the annual tax savings cash inflows that result from $50,000 higher depreciation expense and consequently lower operating income. It is not clear, however, that cash inflows from higher revenues will occur. The decision to purchase the equipment is a capital budgeting decision. We discuss capital budgeting in more detail in Chapter 25.

---

## Characteristics of the Target Costing Process

**LO 5**

Identify the relationship between target costing and the value chain.

Notice several characteristics in our illustration of the target costing process. First, the entire value chain is involved in driving cost out while satisfying customer needs. Second, process understanding is the cornerstone of target costing. A clear understanding of the connection between the key components of the process and the associated costs is critical for focusing value engineering efforts. Third, target costing requires an emphasis on the product's functional characteristics and their importance to the customer. Fourth, a primary objective of the target costing process is to reduce development time.

The cross-functional, cross-organizational team approach allows for simultaneous, rather than sequential, consideration of possible solutions, speeding up new product development time. Finally, ABC information is very useful in determining which process changes will drive costs out of the activities necessary to achieve the target cost.

## JUST-IN-TIME INVENTORY PROCEDURES

One approach used to drive cost out of the production process is a **just-in-time (JIT) manufacturing system**. The phrase "just in time" refers to acquiring materials and manufacturing goods only as needed to fill customer orders. JIT systems are sometimes described as *demand pull* manufacturing because production is totally driven by customer demand. This contrasts with more traditional *supply push* systems in which manufacturers simply produce as many goods as possible.

A JIT system is characterized by extremely small or nonexistent inventories of materials, work in process, and finished goods. Materials are scheduled to arrive only as needed, and products flow quickly from one production process to the next without having to move into temporary storage facilities. Finished goods in excess of existing customer orders are not produced.

Storing large amounts of inventory can be costly and lead to liquidity problems when cash is tied up in inventory. Should inventory items spoil or become obsolete, the company's investment is never recovered. One goal of a JIT system is to reduce or eliminate costs associated with storing inventory, most of which *do not add value* to the product.[2]

JIT is much more than an approach to inventory management. It is a philosophy of *eliminating non-value-added activities* and *increasing product quality* throughout the manufacturing process. As discussed previously, the term *non-value-added activities* refers to those functions that *do not* directly increase the worth of a product to a customer. Examples of non-value-added activities include storing direct materials, setting up machinery, and time during which machinery or employees stand idle. Cost savings achieved through the reduction or elimination of non-value-added activities usually *do not influence customer satisfaction.*

*Value-added activities,* in contrast, *do* increase the value of the product to the customer. Examples include product design, all manufacturing processes, manufacturing to customer specifications, and convenient channels of distribution.

### JIT, Supplier Relationships, and Product Quality

**LO 6**

Explain the nature and goals of a just-in-time (JIT) manufacturing system.

Perhaps the most important goal of a successful JIT system is to control product costs without sacrificing product quality. This goal is achieved, in part, by cultivating strong and lasting relationships with a limited number of select suppliers.

It is important to understand that reliable vendor relationships are essential for achieving long-term quality, even if the prices charged are not the lowest available. A product's quality is only as good as its weakest component. Thus, if quality is a goal, the cost of raw materials should not be the determining factor in selecting a supplier. In fact, slightly higher prices may actually result in *quality improvement and cost savings* in the long run. For instance, once reliable suppliers have demonstrated their ability to consistently deliver quality materials, a JIT manufacturer may reduce the time devoted to inspecting and testing materials received.

---

[2]Factors considered in determining the optimal size of inventories were discussed in Chapter 8.

Since the North American Free Trade Agreement (NAFTA) went into effect in 1994, Mexico's worldwide exports have more than doubled. Mexico has achieved this increased productivity, in part, by focusing on quality. The demand for quality from foreign customers is a key impetus for change. One example is IMSA, part of a Monterrey, Nuevo Leon, conglomerate that supplies metal to the auto, construction, and appliance industries. IMSA used the Internet and business operations software to cut its response time, improve on-time delivery, and cut work in process inventories by 30%.

CASE IN POINT

Implementing a successful JIT system involves much more than reliable vendor relationships. To achieve a goal of *zero defects,* quality must be designed-in and manufactured-in, rather than achieved by inspecting out defective products at the *end* of the manufacturing process. Therefore, in a JIT system, products must be designed in a manner that simplifies the manufacturing process and reduces the risk of defects.

In addition to product design requirements, the workers in a JIT system must be extremely versatile. Since products are produced only as needed, workers must be able to shift quickly from the production of one product to another. To do so, they must learn to perform various tasks and operate different machines. Many companies have found that this concept of *flexible manufacturing* improves employee morale, skill, and productivity.

In order to accommodate the demands of flexible manufacturing within a JIT system, an efficient plant layout is critical. Machines used in sequential order must be close to each other to achieve a smooth and rapid flow of work in process. Since machinery downtime can interrupt the entire production process, *equipment reliability* is also a vital concern. To help ensure reliability, workers in JIT systems are often trained to perform *preventive maintenance* on the machinery they use and make many routine repairs themselves.

## Measures of Efficiency in a JIT System

Timing is of critical importance in a JIT system. Therefore, time measurements are essential for scheduling production activities in a manner that avoids bottlenecks and ensures that jobs are completed "just in time."

The length of time required for a product to pass completely through a manufacturing process is called the **cycle time**. The cycle time is often viewed as containing four separate elements: (1) processing time, (2) storage and waiting time, (3) movement time, and (4) inspection time. *Only during processing time, however, is value added to the product.* Ideally, the other elements of a product's cycle time should be reduced as much as possible.

A widely used measure of efficiency in a JIT system is the **manufacturing efficiency ratio** (or throughput ratio). This measure expresses the time spent in value-added activities (processing activities) as a percentage of total cycle time. The ratio is calculated as follows:

$$\text{Manufacturing Efficiency Ratio} = \frac{\text{Value-Added Time}}{\text{Cycle Time}}$$

The primary purpose of the manufacturing efficiency ratio is to highlight the percentage of time spent in non-value-added activities. The optimal efficiency ratio is *100%,* which indicates that *no* time is being spent on non-value-added activities. In practice, however, this ratio is always considerably less than 100%. But in many cases, this ratio should provide managers with a wake-up call. Companies that have not made concerted efforts to improve efficiency sometimes have manufacturing efficiency ratios *less than 10%.* Improvements in efficiency often translate directly into cost savings for a company.

**Measuring Quality**    Accounting systems in JIT companies measure *quality,* as well as costs and cycle times. One widely used measure of production quality is *defects per million* units produced. In some companies, defect rates have been reduced to less than one defective part per million units of production. Other measures of quality include merchandise returns, number of warranty claims, customer complaints, and the results of customer satisfaction surveys.

A JIT system does not, in itself, ensure quality. Rather, it establishes *striving for quality* as a basic goal of the organization.

### A Concluding Comment

The principles of JIT manufacturing offer many benefits to manufacturing companies. Among the most significant are the following:

1. A reduction in unit cost through increased efficiency and the reduction or elimination of non-value-added activities
2. Constant improvement in product quality
3. Greater challenge, variety, and responsibility for production workers
4. Reduction in the risk that not all output can be sold

The most commonly cited characteristic of JIT systems—maintenance of inventories at near-zero levels—is *not appropriate for all companies.* If a company does not have access to highly reliable sources of supply, it should maintain reasonable inventories of materials. If the company has a lengthy cycle time, or if it cannot achieve a nearly zero-defects level of production, it should consider maintaining an adequate inventory of finished goods to ensure prompt deliveries to customers. *All* companies, however, can benefit from the basic *philosophy* of the JIT approach, which is *striving to eliminate inefficiency and to improve product quality.*

## TOTAL QUALITY MANAGEMENT AND THE VALUE CHAIN

The adoption of JIT techniques demonstrates that current global competitive market conditions require firms to compete on quality and costs. As evidence of the importance of quality, the International Organization for Standardization has developed quality standards referred to as **ISO 9000**. These standards identify quality guidelines for design development, production, inspection, installation, and servicing of products and services. Many purchasers of goods and services require the supplier to be "ISO 9000 certified." Certification requires a third-party detailed audit and documentation of the processes and procedures of the supplier for quality conformance. U.S. auto manufacturers have developed their own similar set of standards, *QSO 9000,* and require their suppliers to have this quality certification.

Thus the cost of ignoring quality is very high, most notably from lost sales. Companies that are able to compete globally on quality and cost inevitably have well-developed **total quality management (TQM)** processes. Total quality management includes assigning responsibility for managing quality, providing good quality measures for decision making, and evaluating and rewarding quality performance. Accountants participate in this measurement and reporting process by designing systems that can track quality and assign cost to quality failures.

### Components of the Cost of Quality

Four components of quality are typically considered when designing a measurement system to track quality costs:

- *Prevention costs* are the cost of resources consumed in activities that prevent defects from occurring. Examples include employee training, quality process audits, quality concern issues embedded in target costing processes for new products, and supplier quality evaluations (ISO 9000).

- *Appraisal costs* are incurred to ensure that products conform to quality standards. Examples include inspection of raw materials, in-process inventories, and finished goods; inspection and monitoring of production processes; and equipment inspection and maintenance programs to ensure quality.

- *Internal failure costs* include additional production-related costs incurred to correct low-quality output. Examples include rework, downtime, engineering change orders, scrap, retesting, and reinspection.

- *External failure costs* are the largest and most difficult to measure. These costs are incurred because quality failures are allowed to enter the market. They include lost sales, costs due to returns and allowances, warranty costs, product liability costs, and lost goodwill.

**LO 7**
Identify the components of the cost of quality.

These four types of quality costs are not independent. Obviously, if more time and effort are spent ensuring that defective goods do not leave the firm, lower external failure costs are likely. In fact, quality cost tradeoffs have been identified and can be represented by the following graph:

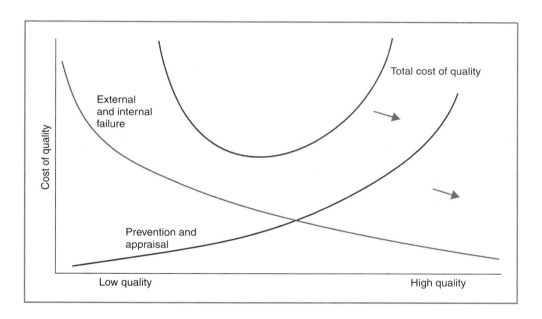

The graph demonstrates that as more resources are consumed in the prevention and appraisal categories, the costs associated with external and internal failures will decline. Designing processes to produce high-quality units through prevention of failures pays off in lower rework, higher customer satisfaction, more repeat business, and lower warranty costs, among other benefits. A focus on prevention occurs during the target costing process described earlier. But prevention also includes identifying high-quality suppliers, as discussed in the section about just-in-time inventory procedures.

The arrows have been included in the graph above to show a phenomenon that has been occurring over the past 20 years. Prior to computerized equipment becoming commonplace in manufacturing plants and offices, quality had to be inspected into the product through the consumption of labor resources. Using labor to inspect all incoming raw materials, work in process on the shop floor, and finished goods is very expensive and not as reliable as might be desired. The use of computerized technology to perform quality inspections has reduced appraisal costs and improved appraisal reliability. The reduction in appraisal and prevention costs has shifted the cost curves, making high quality a less costly option.

A second, important development leading to the prominence of TQM is the recognition of the interconnectedness of the value chain. If quality is low in one part of the value chain, quality costs can increase for all components in that chain. A supplier providing low-quality inputs can cause the buyer to incur rework and warranty expenses. A retailer that provides low-quality access for the consumer will hurt sales and affect the entire value chain. Therefore, the entire value chain must participate in a total quality management approach.

**CASE IN POINT**

**Texas Instruments'** Materials and Control Group tracked its cost of quality categories over a six-year period. It discovered that after the initial adoption of TQM practices, prevention and appraisal costs increased and remained fairly constant over the six-year period. However, as the six-year period wore on, failure costs declined, causing the total cost of quality to decrease. Many of these prevention-related costs were associated with ensuring high-quality inputs through managing supplier relations.

## Measuring the Cost of Quality

**LO 8**

Describe the characteristics of quality measures.

Quality is a multidimensional concept. Multiple measures are necessary to capture the varied aspects of quality. Most firms begin by creating a cost of quality report based on the four components of quality discussed previously. The following table is an example of such a quarterly report for Boards and More, Inc.:

| BOARDS AND MORE, INC. Quality Cost Report For Quarter Ended September 30, 2001 | | | |
|---|---|---|---|
| | Cost | TQM Category Cost | Percentage of Sales |
| Prevention costs: | | | |
| Training | $12,000 | | |
| Maintenance | 10,000 | | |
| Quality planning | 8,000 | $30,000 | 3.2% |
| Appraisal costs: | | | |
| Inspections—Materials | 6,000 | | |
| Inspections—Equipment | 2,000 | | |
| Supplier relations | 4,000 | | |
| Testing | 5,000 | 17,000 | 1.8 |
| Internal failure costs: | | | |
| Rework | 5,000 | | |
| Downtime | 7,000 | | |
| Scrap | 8,000 | 20,000 | 2.1 |
| External failure costs: | | | |
| Warranty | 4,500 | | |
| Lost sales | 20,000 | | |
| Repairs | 6,500 | 31,000 | 3.3 |
| Totals | | $98,000 | 10.4% |

Simply reporting quality costs does not help companies manage the associated activities. Twenty thousand dollars in lost sales is a significant non-value-added cost that Boards and More would like to eliminate. In order to eliminate these costs, management must understand and track the activities that created them. In other words, management must determine the cost drivers of lost sales, rework, warranty costs, and so on. Measuring and managing quality requires multiple measures of these cost drivers. Thus customer satisfaction surveys, vendor rating systems, measures of manufacturing defect rates, downtime, on-time deliveries, and so on are tracked and measured by companies using total quality management approaches.

### You as an Equipment Repair Manager

Assume that it is your responsibility to maintain equipment at Boards and More and that you have just received the quarterly quality report shown on the previous page. The manager of the production line suggests that scrap and rework are high because the equipment has not been properly maintained. What types of tradeoffs are involved in scheduling equipment for routine maintenance? What other cost drivers could explain high scrap and rework costs?

*Our comments appear on page 807.

**YOUR TURN**

One frequently used quality measure is the defect rate. Some companies require their suppliers to provide evidence of inspection quality and defect rates before they are added to preferred supplier lists. A defect rate is commonly measured in parts per million. An item can be classified as defective if it does not meet prespecified standards or tolerance limits. These rates are typically tracked at inspection points.

## Productivity and Quality

Measuring quality without simultaneous concern for productivity can be a recipe for bankruptcy. Quality and productivity are ultimately linked, and managers prefer to undertake activities that reduce the costs associated with low quality *and* increase productivity. Fortunately, this is often possible. Managers frequently find that activities that reduce scrap and rework also increase productivity.

Productivity is usually measured by comparing inputs and outputs. Quality improvements are evident when the amount of input is reduced for a given, fixed level of output. In the quality cost report, the column labeled "Percentage of Sales" is a productivity measure. The outputs are sales dollars and the inputs are the resources consumed by quality-related activities. Increases in quality for Boards and More are signaled by a decrease in the total quality cost as a percentage of sales dollars. Earlier in this chapter, we discussed another productivity measure—the JIT manufacturing efficiency ratio. It compares the input, value-added time, and the output, cycle time, to obtain a measure of productivity throughput.

## MANAGING ACROSS THE VALUE CHAIN

We have identified four techniques commonly used by organizations to manage costs over their value chain. The underlying objective of these four techniques—activity-based management, the target costing process, just-in-time procedures, and total quality management—is to eliminate non-value-added activities from the value chain. This objective is achieved by assigning employees the responsibility for managing these non-value-added activities, providing information about the cost of these activities, and rewarding managers who eliminate these activities. The customer ultimately defines non-value-added activities. It is true that in determining the shape and structure of the value chain, the customer is king.

## Dell Computer Corporation

**Dell**'s computers are manufactured one at a time and to order in their facilities in Austin, Texas; Nashville, Tennessee; Eldorado do Sul, Brazil; Limerick, Ireland; Penang, Malaysia; and Xaimen, China. Despite the complications of international value chains, **Dell** has the industry's most efficient value chain processes—procurement, manufacturing, and distribution. Companies create these types of efficiencies based on the principles introduced and discussed in this chapter. For example, eliminating non-value-added activities by using activity-based management, target costing, just-in-time, and total quality management principles and practices are key methods for improving value chain efficiency and effectiveness.

Managers also need to understand the basic relationships between cost, volume, and profit to help manage the value chain. Cost-volume-profit relationship ideas are described and demonstrated in the following chapter.

## SUMMARY OF LEARNING OBJECTIVES

**LO 1**

**Define the value chain and describe its basic components.**
We define the value chain as the set of activities and resources necessary to create and deliver the product or service valued by customers. Its basic components include research and development, production and supplier relations, marketing and distribution, and customer service activities.

**LO 2**

**Distinguish between non-value-added and value-added activities.**
Value-added activities add to the product's or service's desirability in the eyes of the consumer. Non-value-added activities do not add to the product's desirability.

**LO 3**

**Explain how activity-based management is related to activity-based costing (ABC).**
Activity-based management requires an understanding of the link between activities that consume resources and the costs associated with those resources. The objective of ABC is to create the cost per unit of measured cost driver. The objective of activity-based management is to manage the activities that drive those costs.

**LO 4**

**Describe the target costing process and list its components.**
Target costing is a business process aimed at the earliest stages of new product and service development. The components of target costing consist of concept development through planning and market analysis; product development using value engineering; and production with continuous improvement goals.

**LO 5**

**Identify the relationship between target costing and the value chain.**
The entire value chain is involved in the target costing process to identify activities that drive cost out while satisfying customer needs. A primary objective of the target costing process is to reduce development time. The cross-functional, cross-organizational value chain approach allows for simultaneous, rather than sequential, consideration of possible solutions, speeding up new product development time.

**LO 6**

**Explain the nature and goals of a just-in-time (JIT) manufacturing system.**
In a JIT system, materials are acquired and goods are produced just in time to meet sales requirements. Thus production is pulled by customer demand, rather than pushed by an effort to produce inventory. The goals of a JIT system are to eliminate (minimize) non-value-added activities and to increase the focus on product quality throughout the production process.

**LO 7**

**Identify the components of the cost of quality.**
Quality costs are classified into four groups: (1) costs associated with preventing poor quality from occurring, (2) costs of appraising and inspecting quality into the product, (3) internal failure costs that are incurred to correct quality problems before the customer receives the good or service, and (4) external failure costs that happen when an unsatisfactory good or service is delivered to a customer.

**LO 8**

**Describe the characteristics of quality measures.**
Quality measures must be customer focused because quality failures can be identified only by customers. These measures should be multidimensional, including both financial and nonfinancial components to help management focus on activities that drive quality costs.

Accounting methods and techniques that help decision makers manage the value chain were the focus of this chapter. We discussed how managing the value chain's core operations by driving costs out, and as a result creating customer satisfaction, improves company value. Using target costing, activity-based management, just-in-time inventory methods, and total quality management, managers can identify and reduce or eliminate non-value-added activities. In the remaining chapters we discuss other management accounting methods that help to identify decision-making authority, provide information to aid decision making, and evaluate decision-making performance.

## KEY TERMS INTRODUCED OR EMPHASIZED IN CHAPTER 18

**activity-based management** (p. 780) The process of using activity-based costs to help reduce and eliminate non-value-added activities.

**cycle time** (p. 789) The length of time for a product to pass completely through a specific manufacturing process or the manufacturing process viewed as a whole. Used as a measure of efficiency in JIT systems.

**ISO 9000** (p. 790) Standards disseminated by the International Organization for Standardization that provide quality guidelines for design development, production, inspection, installation, and servicing of products and services.

**just-in-time (JIT) manufacturing system** (p. 788) An approach to manufacturing that reduces or eliminates non-value-added activities, such as maintenance of inventories. Focuses on both efficiency and product quality.

**life-cycle costing** (p. 787)  The consideration of all potential resources consumed by the product over its entire life. It is an important part of the target costing process where target costing teams estimate all potential costs to the consumer over the product's life.

**manufacturing efficiency ratio** (p. 789)  Processing time stated as a percentage of cycle time. Used as a measure of efficiency in JIT systems.

**non-value-added activity** (p. 778)  An activity within the value chain that does not make the product or service more valuable to the customer.

**target costing** (p. 783)  A business process aimed at the earliest stages of new product and service development, before creation and design of production methods. It is a process driven by the customer, focused on design, and encompassing the entire life of the product.

**total quality management** (p. 790)  An approach to eliminating wasteful activities and improving quality throughout the value chain by assigning quality management responsibility, monitoring quality costs, and rewarding low-cost, high-quality results.

**value-added activity** (p. 778)  An activity within the value chain that makes the product or service more valuable to the customer.

**value chain** (p. 778)  The set of activities necessary to create and distribute a desirable product or service to a customer.

**value engineering** (p. 784)  The methods used by engineers and production personnel to determine the least costly combination of resources to create a product desired by the customer.

## DEMONSTRATION PROBLEM

At the beginning of 2002, Suskin, Inc., initiated a quality improvement program. Considerable effort was expended to reduce the number of defective units produced. By the end of the year, reports from the production manager revealed that scrap and rework had both decreased. The CFO was pleased to hear of the success but wanted some assessment of the financial impact of the improvements. To make this assessment, the following financial data were collected for the current and preceding two years:

|  | 2000 | 2001 | 2002 |
|---|---|---|---|
| Sales | $10,000,000 | $10,000,000 | $10,000,000 |
| Scrap | 450,000 | 400,000 | 300,000 |
| Rework | 625,000 | 600,000 | 400,000 |
| Product inspection | 100,000 | 120,000 | 125,000 |
| Product warranty | 875,000 | 800,000 | 600,000 |
| Quality training | 20,000 | 40,000 | 80,000 |
| Materials inspection | 80,000 | 40,000 | 40,000 |

### Instructions

a. Classify the costs as prevention, appraisal, internal failure, and external failure.

b. Compute total quality cost as a percentage of sales for each of the two years. By how much has profit increased because of quality improvements between 2000, 2001, and 2002?

c. Graph the prevention and appraisal costs versus the internal and external failure costs for 2000, 2001, and 2002. Extrapolate the curves to show the optimal quality point.

d. Consider the quality costs as non-value-added activities. Describe how these activities might be eliminated.

## Solution to the Demonstration Problem

**a.**

| | Prevention | Appraisal | Internal Failure | External Failure | |
|---|---|---|---|---|---|
| | Quality Training | Product and Materials Inspection | Scrap and Rework | Product Warranty | **Totals** |
| 2000 | $20,000 | $180,000 | $1,075,000 | $875,000 | $2,150,000 |
| 2001 | 40,000 | 160,000 | 1,000,000 | 800,000 | 2,000,000 |
| 2002 | 80,000 | 165,000 | 700,000 | 600,000 | 1,545,000 |
| Change in cost 2000–2001 | +20,000 | −20,000 | −75,000 | −75,000 | −150,000 |
| Change in cost 2001–2002 | +40,000 | +5,000 | −300,000 | −200,000 | −455,000 |

**b.**

| Year | Total Quality Cost ÷ Sales | Profit Increase = Cost Decrease |
|---|---|---|
| 2000 | $2,150,000 ÷ $10,000,000 = 21.5% | |
| 2001 | $2,000,000 ÷ $10,000,000 = 20.00% | $2,150,000 − 2,000,000 = $150,000 |
| 2002 | $1,545,000 ÷ $10,000,000 = 15.45% | $2,000,000 − 1,545,000 = $455,000 |

**c.**

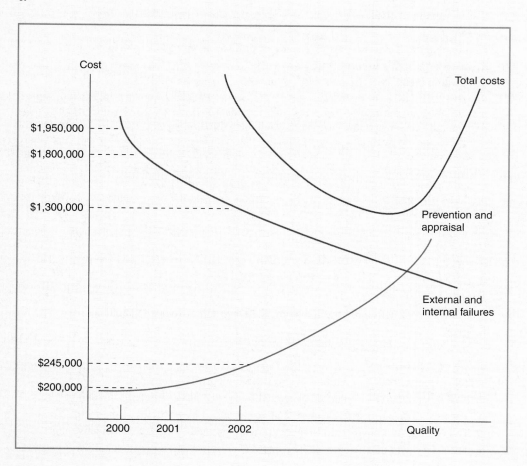

d. Non-value-added activities are those that can be eliminated without reducing the value (that is, increasing the cost or lowering the quality) of the product to the customer. The following example solutions assume that costs to the customer will not increase and quality will be maintained. Many other activities may drive these costs, and other solutions are viable.

| Quality Category | Activity | Example Solution |
|---|---|---|
| Scrap | Machine problem | New equipment/better maintenance |
| | Labor problem | Quality training and/or incentives |
| Rework | Too many parts | Value engineering |
| | Employee carelessness | Quality training and/or incentives |
| Product inspection | Poor-quality raw materials | Supplier quality certification programs |
| | Poor equipment maintenance | New equipment maintenance program |
| Product warranty | Inspection failures | Buy equipment that will be more reliable |
| | Too many parts | Value engineering |
| Materials inspections | Transportation-in problem | Quality certification for shippers |
| | Supplier ships poor-quality goods | Quality certification for suppliers |

# SELF-TEST QUESTIONS

*Answers to these questions appear on page 807.*

1. Which of the following would be considered non-value-added activities by a bakery's bread customers?
   a. The mixing of flour, eggs, milk, and other ingredients into bread dough.
   b. Baking the bread.
   c. Shipping the loaves to a warehouse to await distribution to local stores.
   d. Delivering loaves to local stores.
   e. Rotating bread stock in the stores so that older loaves are sold first.

2. Premo Pens, Inc., is in the process of developing a new pen to replace its existing top-of-the-line Executive Model. Market research has identified the critical features the pen must have, and it is estimated that customers would be willing to pay $30 for a pen with these features. Premo's production manager estimates that with existing equipment it will cost $26 to produce the proposed model. The current Executive Model sells for $24 and has a total production cost of $20. A competitor sells a pen similar to the proposed model, but without Premo's patented easy retract feature, for $28. It is estimated to cost the competitor $25 to produce. If Premo seeks to earn a 20% return on sales on the new model, which of the following represents the target cost for the new pen?
   a. $26.00.
   b. $22.40.
   c. $24.00.
   d. $19.80.

3. JIT inventory systems strive to:
   a. Cultivate long-term relationships with a select group of reliable suppliers.
   b. Keep inventories at minimal levels.
   c. Improve overall product quality.
   d. All of the above.

4. Which of the following would *not* be considered a cost of quality?
   a. Lost sales due to bad publicity generated by a large product liability lawsuit.
   b. The cost of repairing merchandise that was dropped by a forklift in the factory.
   c. The amount of a bonus paid to the work team producing the fewest defective units.
   d. The salary paid to an employee who answers customer questions about a firm's products.

5. Which of the following would *not* be classified as an external failure cost?
   a. Extra shipping charges incurred to rush a customer an order that was delayed for rework.
   b. Costs incurred for a product recall.
   c. The cost of product liability insurance.
   d. The cost of maintaining a customer complaint hotline.

## ASSIGNMENT MATERIAL

## DISCUSSION QUESTIONS

1. What are three important criteria for successful business process management?
2. Describe the main components of a typical value chain.
3. Suppose you are interested in opening up a new restaurant in your area. What specific activities would you undertake in the research and development and design stage of the value chain for the restaurant?
4. What activities would make up the marketing and distribution component of the value chain of a local fire department?
5. Distinguish between value-added and non-value-added activities and provide an example of each.
6. Assume you are the manager of the finished goods warehouse of a stereo manufacturer. What costs are being incurred as stereos are stored while awaiting shipment to retail stores?
7. What is the objective of target costing?
8. Why is target costing most effectively applied at the research and development and production process design stage of the value chain?
9. What is the objective of activity-based management and how does it differ from activity-based costing?
10. Briefly explain the nature and goals of a JIT manufacturing system.
11. Why is the output of a JIT system likely to contain fewer defective units than the output of a traditional manufacturing system?
12. Why is JIT often described as a "philosophy," rather than as an inventory management technique?
13. List and describe the four components of the cost of quality and provide examples of each.
14. What is life-cycle costing and why should it be used in the target costing process?
15. What is required for a firm to become "ISO 9000 certified"?

## EXERCISES

The following are eight technical accounting terms introduced or emphasized in this chapter:

| | |
|---|---|
| Activity-based management | Total quality management |
| Just-in-time manufacturing system | Target costing |
| Life-cycle costing | Value-added activity |
| Non-value-added activity | Value engineering |

**EXERCISE 18.1**

Accounting Terminology

**LO 2, 3, 6**

Each of the following statements may (or may not) describe one of these terms. For each statement, indicate the accounting term described, or answer "none" if the statement does not correctly describe any of these terms.

a. Can be eliminated without changing a product's desirability in the eyes of consumers.
b. The focus of this costing method is to assign manufacturing costs to final products.
c. The process of determining the least costly combination of resources needed to create a product desired by customers.
d. This method considers all costs borne by the consumer from purchase to disposal of a product.
e. If eliminated, the product's desirability to consumers is decreased.

**f.** The process of using activity-based costs to help reduce and eliminate non-value-added activities.

**g.** A method in which a product's selling price is determined by adding a fixed amount to the product's current production cost.

**h.** An approach that explicitly monitors quality costs and rewards quality-enhancing behavior.

**i.** An important aspect of this method is the reduction of unnecessary inventories.

**EXERCISE 18.2**

Value Chain Activities

**LO 1**

Assume you have just been hired as the management accountant in charge of providing your firm's managers with product cost information. Identify the activities you might undertake for the following four value chain components:

**a.** Research and development

**b.** Production

**c.** Marketing

**d.** Customer service

**EXERCISE 18.3**

Value-Added versus
Non-Value-Added Activities

**LO 2, 3**

Dainty Diners, Inc., produces various types of bird feeders. The following is a detailed description of the steps involved in the production of wooden bird feeders:

1. Raw materials, such as wood, nails, and clear plastic are purchased.
2. The raw materials are unloaded from the delivery truck into a raw materials storage area.
3. The purchase order is checked for accuracy by an employee doing a visual count of the items.
4. The materials are inspected for defects such as rotting, excessive knots, and scratches.
5. The Cutting Department orders raw materials by sending a requisition form to the raw materials storage area.
6. When a requisition is received, raw materials are moved from the storage area to the Cutting Department.
7. The wood and plastic are cut into properly sized pieces.
8. The cut pieces are stacked and moved to a work in process warehouse.
9. The Assembly Department orders cut pieces when they are needed by sending a requisition form to the work in process warehouse.
10. When a requisition is received, cut pieces are moved from the work in process warehouse to the Assembly Department.
11. The cut pieces are assembled into a bird feeder.
    **a.** For each of the above steps, indicate whether it is a value-added or non-value-added activity.
    **b.** For each of the non-value-added activities, determine whether it can be eliminated; if it cannot be eliminated, suggest ways in which the costs could be minimized or productive efficiency increased.

**EXERCISE 18.4**

Activity-Based Management

**LO 3**

Blake Furniture, Inc., maintains an Accounts Receivable Department that currently employs eight people. Blake is interested in doing an activity analysis because an outside firm has offered to take over a portion of the activities currently handled by the Accounts Receivable Department. The four main activities handled by the department are (1) billing and recording payments, (2) customer service activities, (3) financial reporting and analysis, and (4) collecting delinquent accounts.

The salaries paid to the department's employees are as follows:

| | |
|---|---|
| Manager, 1 @ $60,000 per year | $ 60,000 |
| Clerks, 5 @ $30,000 per year | 150,000 |
| Account specialists, 2 @ $40,000 per year | 80,000 |
| Total | $290,000 |

It is estimated that the manager of the Accounts Receivable Department spends an equal amount of her time supervising the four main activities. The clerks spend approximately half of their time on billing and recording payments. Their remaining time is divided equally between reporting activities and customer service. The two account specialists spend half of their time on delinquent account activities, and the rest of their time is split equally between financial analysis activities and customer service activities that the clerks are not qualified to perform.

Paypro, Inc., has proposed that it can perform all the activities related to collecting delinquent accounts for a fee of $50,000 per year. The manager of Paypro argues that Blake can save $30,000 because the $80,000 in salaries paid to the specialists who currently handle all delinquent accounts can be eliminated. If the contract is accepted, it is estimated that the manager of the Accounts Receivable Department would need to devote a quarter of her time dealing with Paypro employees.

**a.** Using the information given, prepare an activity table such as that on page 781 to calculate the personnel devoted to each of the four main activities of the Accounts Receivable Department.

**b.** Should Blake accept Paypro's offer to take over its delinquent account activities?

On Point, Inc., is interested in producing and selling a deluxe electric pencil sharpener. Market research indicates that customers are willing to pay $40 for such a sharpener and that 20,000 units could be sold each year at this price. The cost to produce the sharpener is currently estimated to be $34.

**EXERCISE 18.5**

Target Costing

**LO 4, 5**

**a.** If On Point requires a 20% return on sales to undertake production of a product, what is the target cost for the new pencil sharpener?

**b.** If a competitor sells basically the same sharpener for $36, what would On Point's target cost be to maintain a 20% return on sales?

**c.** At a price of $36, On Point estimates that it can sell 21,000 sharpeners per year. Assuming target costs are reached, would On Point earn more or less profit per year at the $36 selling price compared to the original estimated selling price of $40?

The Nanner Corporation is trying to determine how long it takes for one product to pass through the production process. The following information was gathered regarding how many days the product spent in various production activities:

**EXERCISE 18.6**

Just-in-Time Manufacturing

**LO 6**

| Activity | Number of Days |
|---|---|
| Inspection | 5 |
| Storage | 6 |
| Assembly | 3 |
| Handling | 2 |
| Painting | 3 |
| Packaging | 1 |

**a.** Which of the above activities are value-added?

**b.** What is Nanner's total cycle time?

**c.** Determine Nanner's manufacturing efficiency ratio.

**d.** If Nanner implements a total quality management program and a just-in-time inventory system, which of the above activities could be eliminated? What would be the change in Nanner's manufacturing efficiency ratio?

Chris Hines is the manager of Lumble Manufacturing and is interested in doing a cost of quality analysis. The following cost and revenue data are available for the most recent year ended December 31:

**EXERCISE 18.7**

Cost of Quality

**LO 7**

| | |
|---|---:|
| Sales revenue . . . . . . . . . . . . . . . . . . . . . . . . . . . . . . . . . . . . . . . . . . . | $250,000 |
| Cost of goods sold . . . . . . . . . . . . . . . . . . . . . . . . . . . . . . . | 140,000 |
| Warranty expense . . . . . . . . . . . . . . . . . . . . . . . . . . . . . . . . | 22,000 |
| Inspection costs . . . . . . . . . . . . . . . . . . . . . . . . . . . . . . . . | 12,000 |
| Scrap and rework . . . . . . . . . . . . . . . . . . . . . . . . . . . . . . . . | 8,000 |
| Product returns due to defects . . . . . . . . . . . . . . . . . . . . . . . . | 6,000 |
| Depreciation expense . . . . . . . . . . . . . . . . . . . . . . . . . . . . . . | 10,000 |
| Machine maintenance expense . . . . . . . . . . . . . . . . . . . . . . . . | 2,000 |
| Wage expense . . . . . . . . . . . . . . . . . . . . . . . . . . . . . . . . . . | 35,000 |
| Machine breakdown costs . . . . . . . . . . . . . . . . . . . . . . . . . . | 4,000 |
| Estimated lost sales due to poor quality . . . . . . . . . . . . . . . . . . . | 5,000 |

**a.** Classify each of the above costs into the four quality cost categories and prepare a cost of quality report for Lumble.

**b.** What percentage of sales revenue is being spent on prevention and appraisal activities?

**c.** What percentage of sales revenue is being spent on internal and external failure costs?

# ▮ PROBLEMS

**PROBLEM 18.1**

Identifying Value-Added and
Non-Value-Added Activities

**LO 2, 6**

Castner Corporation is considering implementation of a JIT inventory system. The company's industrial engineer recently conducted a study to determine the average number of days spent in
each activity of the production process. The following table summarizes her findings:

| Production Activity | Number of Days |
|---|---:|
| Inspecting materials . . . . . . . . . . . . . . . . . . . . . . . . . . . . . . . . | 3 |
| Storing materials . . . . . . . . . . . . . . . . . . . . . . . . . . . . . . . . . | 17 |
| Moving materials into production . . . . . . . . . . . . . . . . . . . . . . | 3 |
| Setting up production equipment . . . . . . . . . . . . . . . . . . . . . . | 2 |
| Cutting materials . . . . . . . . . . . . . . . . . . . . . . . . . . . . . . . . . | 6 |
| Bending materials . . . . . . . . . . . . . . . . . . . . . . . . . . . . . . . . | 5 |
| Assembling finished products . . . . . . . . . . . . . . . . . . . . . . . . . | 9 |
| Painting finished products . . . . . . . . . . . . . . . . . . . . . . . . . . . | 5 |

**Instructions**

**a.** Identify Castner's value-added production activities.

**b.** Identify Castner's non-value-added production activities.

**c.** Calculate Castner's total cycle time.

**d.** Determine Castner's manufacturing efficiency ratio.

**e.** Which of the above activities might be reduced or eliminated if Castner implemented a JIT
system?

**f.** What ethical issues might be related to eliminating some of the non-value-added activities?

**PROBLEM 18.2**

Activity-Based Management
and Target Costing

**LO 2–4**

The Kallapur Company manufactures two products: KAP1, which sells for $120; and QUIN,
which sells for $220. Estimated cost and production data for the current year are as follows:

| | KAP1 | QUIN |
|---|---:|---:|
| Direct materials cost . . . . . . . . . . . . . . . . . . . . . . . . . . . . . . . . | $30 | $45 |
| Direct labor cost (@ $12/hr) . . . . . . . . . . . . . . . . . . . . . . . . . . | $24 | $60 |
| Estimated production (units) . . . . . . . . . . . . . . . . . . . . . . . . . . | 25,000 | 15,000 |

In addition, fixed manufacturing overhead is estimated to be $2,000,000 and variable overhead is estimated to equal $3 per direct labor hour. Kallapur desires a 15% return on sales for all of its products.

## Instructions

**a.** Calculate the target cost for both KAP1 and QUIN.

**b.** Estimate the total manufacturing cost per unit of each product if fixed overhead costs are assigned to products on the basis of estimated production in units. Which of the products is earning the desired return?

**c.** Recalculate the total manufacturing cost per unit if fixed overhead costs are assigned to products on the basis of direct labor hours. Which of the products is earning the desired return?

**d.** Based on the confusing results of parts **b** and **c**, Kallapur's manager decides to perform an activity analysis of fixed overhead. The results of the analysis are as follows:

| Activity | Costs | Driver | Demands KAP1 | Demands QUIN |
|---|---|---|---|---|
| Machine setups | $ 400,000 | # of setups | 100 | 400 |
| Purchase orders | 600,000 | # of orders | 200 | 100 |
| Machining | 500,000 | # of machine-hours | 2,000 | 6,000 |
| Inspection | 200,000 | # of batches | 50 | 30 |
| Shipping to customers | 300,000 | # of shipments | 300 | 200 |
| Total fixed overhead | $2,000,000 | | | |

Estimate the total manufacturing cost per unit of each product if activity-based costing is used for assigning fixed overhead costs. Under this method, which product is earning the desired return?

**e.** What proportion of fixed overhead is value-added? In attempting to reach the target cost for QUIN, which activity would you look to improving first and why?

**f.** Kallapur's production manager believes that design changes would reduce the number of setups required for QUIN to 25. Fixed overhead costs for setups would remain unchanged. What will be the impact of the design changes on the manufacturing costs of both products? Which of the products will earn the desired return?

**g.** An alternative to the design change is to purchase a new machine that will reduce the number of setups for KAP1 to 20 and the number of setups for QUIN to 80. The machine will also reduce fixed setup costs to $200,000. Calculate the manufacturing costs for each product if the machine is purchased. Should QUIN be redesigned or should the machine be purchased? Why?

Meiger Mining, Inc., has just discovered two new mining sites for iron ore. Geologists and engineers have come up with the following estimates regarding costs and ore yields if the mines are opened:

**PROBLEM 18.3**

Target Costing

**LO 4**

| | Site A | Site B |
|---|---|---|
| Variable extraction costs per ton | $3.80 | $4.00 |
| Fixed costs over the life of the mine: | | |
| Blasting | $150,000 | $185,000 |
| Construction | 225,000 | 240,000 |
| Maintenance | 25,000 | 20,000 |
| Restoration costs | 40,000 | 35,000 |
| Total fixed costs | $440,000 | $480,000 |
| Total tons of ore that can be extracted over the life of the mine: | 200,000 | 160,000 |

Meiger's owners currently demand a return of 20% of the market price of iron ore.

## Instructions

**a.** If the current market price of iron ore is $8 per ton, what is Meiger's target cost per ton?

**b.** Given the $8 market price, should either of the mines be opened?

**c.** The engineer working on Site B believes that if a custom conveyor system is installed, the variable extraction cost could be reduced to $3 per ton. The purchase price of the system is $25,000, but the costs to restore the site will increase to $45,000 if it is installed. Given the current $8 market price, should Meiger install the conveyor and open Site B?

**PROBLEM 18.4**

Cost of Quality

**LO 7**

Arusetta, Inc., produces a popular brand of air conditioners that is backed by a five-year warranty. In the year 2001, Arusetta began implementing a total quality management program that has resulted in significant changes in its cost of quality. Listed below is Arusetta's financial information relating to sales and quality for the past two years.

|  | 2001 | 2002 |
|---|---|---|
| Sales revenue | $500,000 | $500,000 |
| Warranty expense | 22,000 | 18,500 |
| Product design | 5,000 | 15,000 |
| Scrap | 2,000 | 1,200 |
| Process reengineering | 8,000 | 12,000 |
| Raw materials inspections | 4,800 | 2,300 |
| Product liability claims | 5,000 | 8,500 |
| Rework | 3,100 | 2,800 |
| Returns resulting from defects | 7,000 | 4,500 |
| Supplier certification costs | 500 | 2,500 |
| Preventive maintenance on equipment | 1,300 | 2,600 |
| Final inspection costs | 10,000 | 7,000 |
| Employee quality training | 1,200 | 4,000 |
| Equipment breakdown repair costs | 8,500 | 3,000 |
| Estimate of lost sales due to quality problems | 10,000 | 10,000 |

## Instructions

**a.** Prepare a cost of quality report for Arusetta covering the years 2001 and 2002. Your report should divide the above costs into the four categories of quality costs and include total dollar amounts for each category.

**b.** How have the total amounts of prevention and external failure costs changed over the two years? What are some possible explanations for these changes?

**c.** At Arusetta, preventive maintenance has a direct effect on the repair costs associated with equipment breakdowns. Did the decrease in repair costs justify the increase in maintenance costs?

**d.** Why might Arusetta's estimate of lost sales remain the same despite the adoption of the total quality management program?

# CASES AND UNSTRUCTURED PROBLEMS

**CASE 18.1**

Activity-Based Management and Target Costing

**LO 2–4**

Dana Martin, president of Mays Electronics, is concerned about the end of the year marketing report. According to Mary O'Brien, marketing manager, a price decrease for the coming year was again needed to maintain the company's market share of integrated circuit boards (CBs). The current selling price of $18 per unit was producing a $2 per-unit profit—half the customary $4 per-unit profit. Foreign competitors keep reducing their prices, and to match their latest reduction, the price must drop from $18 to $14. This price drop would put Mays' price below the cost to produce and sell a CB. How could other firms sell for such a low price?

Determined to find out if there are problems with the company's operations, Dana decided to hire a consultant to evaluate the way in which the CBs were produced and sold. After two weeks, the consultant had identified the following activities and costs associated with producing 120,000 CBs:

| Activity | Cost |
| --- | --- |
| Setups | $ 125,000 |
| Materials handling | 180,000 |
| Inspection | 122,000 |
| Customer support | 120,000 |
| Customer complaints | 100,000 |
| Warranty expense | 170,000 |
| Storage | 80,000 |
| Rework | 75,000 |
| Direct materials | 500,000 |
| Utilities | 48,000 |
| Manual insertion labor* | 250,000 |
| Other direct labor | 150,000 |
| Total costs | $1,920,000 |

*Diodes, resistors, and integrated circuits are inserted manually into the circuit board.

The consultant indicated that some preliminary activity analysis shows that per-unit costs can be reduced by at least $7. The marketing manager indicates that the market share for the CBs could be increased by 50% if the price could be reduced to $12.

## Instructions

**a.** For each activity, determine whether it is value-added or non-value-added.

**b.** If all the non-value-added activities could be eliminated, by how much would the cost per CB decrease? Was the consultant correct in her preliminary cost reduction assessment?

**c.** Compute the target cost required to maintain Mays' current market share while earning the usual profit of $4 per unit. Also compute the target cost required to expand sales by 50%. By how much would the cost per unit need to be reduced to achieve each target?

**d.** The consultant also revealed the following: switching to automated insertion would save $90,000 of direct labor, $20,000 in rework, and $40,000 in warranty costs. The yearly cost of the necessary machinery would be $50,000. With this additional information, what is the potential cost reduction per unit available? Can Mays achieve the target cost to maintain its current market share?

**e.** In an effort to reach the target cost, Mays solicited suggestions from customers, suppliers, employees, and other consultants. The following were found to be feasible:

- Mays' production manager believes that the factory can be redesigned so that material handling costs can be reduced by $100,000—which would in turn result in a $10,000 savings in rework costs. The cost to redesign the factory would be $20,000.

- A supplier suggests leasing a machine that would reduce setup costs by $80,000. The yearly cost to lease the machine is $15,000.

- A customer, KD, Inc., proposes setting up a just-in-time delivery system between Mays, KD, and Mays' largest raw materials supplier. This would reduce Mays' storage costs by $45,000, while increasing shipping costs by only $5,000.

- An employee suggests that Mays train all its employees in quality control measures and then offer a bonus for meeting quality targets. An outside consultant estimates that the cost of the training and bonus would be $35,000. In return, inspections could be eliminated and rework, customer complaint costs, and warranty work could be reduced by $120,000.

If all of the above suggestions are implemented, including the automation of the insertion process, would Mays reach the target cost needed to maintain current market share?

**CASE 18.2**

Just-in-Time Frozen Dinners

**LO 1, 2, 6**

Healthy Times produces four types of frozen TV dinners that it sells to supermarkets and independent grocery stores. The company operates from two locations: a manufacturing plant and a refrigerated warehouse located a few blocks away. (Administrative offices are located in the manufacturing plant.)

The types of dinners to be produced each week are scheduled a week in advance, based on customer orders. The *number* of dinners produced, however, is always the same. The company runs its production facilities at full capacity—20,000 units per day—to minimize fixed manufacturing costs per unit.

Every Friday, local suppliers deliver to Healthy Times' factory the fresh vegetables, chicken, fish, and other ingredients required for the following week's production. (Materials are abundant in the region.) These ingredients then are cut into meal-sized portions, "fresh frozen" using special equipment, and transported by truck to the refrigerated warehouse. The company maintains an inventory of frozen ingredients equal to approximately two weeks' production.

Every day, ingredients for 20,000 dinners are brought by truck from the warehouse to the factory. All dinners produced in a given production run must be of the same type. However, production workers can make the machinery "setup" changes necessary to produce a different type of frozen dinner in about 10 minutes.

Monday through Thursday, Healthy Times produces one type of dinner each day. On Friday, it manufactures whatever types of dinners are needed to balance its inventories. Completed frozen dinners are transported back to the refrigerated warehouse on a daily basis.

Frozen dinners are shipped daily from the warehouse to customers. All shipments are sent by independent carriers. Healthy Times usually maintains about a 10-day inventory of frozen dinners in the warehouse. Recently, however, daily sales have been averaging about 2,000 units less than the level of production, and the finished goods inventory has swelled to a 25-day supply.

Marsha Osaka, the controller of Healthy Times, recently read about the JIT inventory system used by Toyota in its Japanese production facilities. She is wondering whether a JIT system might benefit Healthy Times.

**Instructions**

**a.** In *general terms,* describe a JIT manufacturing system. Identify the basic goals of a JIT manufacturing system and any basic conditions that must exist for the system to operate efficiently.

**b.** Identify any non-value-added activities in Healthy Times' operations that might be reduced or eliminated in a JIT system. Also identify specific types of costs that might be reduced or eliminated.

**c.** Assume that Healthy Times *does* adopt a JIT manufacturing system. Prepare a description of the company's operations under such a system. (Your description should be consistent with the details provided above.)

**d.** Explain whether or not you think that a JIT system would work for Healthy Times. Provide specific reasons supporting your conclusion.

---

## *BUSINESS WEEK* ASSIGNMENT                    BusinessWeek

**CASE 18.3**

Value Chain Costs

**LO 6, 7, 8**

Sometimes emphasizing one management practice without considering the overall impact across the firm can be problematic. Consider the following quote, from Peter Galuszka and Stephanie Forest-Anderson's article, "Just-in-Time Manufacturing Is Working Overtime," in *Business Week,* November 8, 1999.

> When manufacturers were pummeled in the 1980s by foreign competition . . . workforces were cut, just-in-time inventory methods were added and extra controls were taken on to track production. . . . Now lean operations have come back to haunt them. . . . **Manco Inc.**, a unit of **Henkel Group**, for instance, has been running machinery to make duct tape 23 hours a day. The Avon (Ohio) company is delaying preventive maintenance until January and in the meantime is absorbing the extra overtime costs.

**Instructions**

**a.** With a partner either assigned by your instructor or one that you choose, list the additional costs that **Manco** is experiencing by using just-in-time processes.

**b.** With your partner write a one-paragraph argument comparing the costs and benefits of the following processes for **Manco**:

- Just-in-time management processes.
- Total quality management processes.

## INTERNET ASSIGNMENT

**3M Corporation** has implemented several programs to encourage its employees to innovate and initiate new ideas. Access its home page at the following address:

**INTERNET 18.1**

**LO 1, 4, 5**

**www.3m.com**

At the home page, choose the option labeled "**3M** Innovations."

### Instructions
Choose a **3M** innovation from the list and answer the following questions:

**a.** What part of the value chain is targeted by the innovation?

**b.** Was a team involved in the innovation? Who were the team members?

**c.** Do you believe target costing would be an effective and useful tool for the innovation? Why?

*Internet sites are time and date sensitive. It is the purpose of these exercises to have you explore the Internet. You may need to use the Yahoo! search engine* http://www.yahoo.com *(or other favorite search engine) to find a company's current web address.*

## OUR COMMENTS ON THE "YOUR TURN" CASES

**As a Raw Materials Inventory Manager (p. 779)**  When redwood logs sit idle, waiting to be put through the mill, the company forgoes customer sales. Also forgone is the opportunity to use working capital tied up in the cost of cutting and transporting logs to the staging area.

**As a Team Leader (p. 785)**  Corporate espionage is a very serious issue for most firms. So the reservations raised by the printing firm representatives are significant. You can begin by pointing out that if a patent, copyright, or trademark application has been filed, intellectual property rights are typically protected. However, an idea generated at a meeting of engineers, as described by printing firm representatives, would not involve violations of intellectual property rights unless the specific idea had been patented or copyrighted. Because you do not wish to stifle creative discussion on the team, you could propose that the team consider confidentiality agreements or some form of work segregation or both.

Some companies require cross-functional design teams to sign confidentiality agreements that require team members not to discuss (outside of the team) design considerations offered by team members from other firms. In addition, many firms deliberately segregate their engineers into work groups that are not allowed to work with or interact with two or more firms that might be competitors. The ethical issues surrounding intellectual property rights in cross-organizational design teams involve difficult legal issues. Most companies involve their legal counsel in the resolution of these issues.

**As an Equipment Repair Manager (p. 793)**  As the equipment repair manager, you understand that equipment that is not properly maintained will result not only in more scrap and rework but also in significant downtime for major repairs. Equipment downtime creates bottlenecks for production processes that can ripple throughout the value chain.

Cost drivers other than equipment failures could explain scrap and rework. For example, poor quality raw materials that do not meet incoming quality specifications can create scrap and rework. Also, transporting work in process between workstations can create quality problems. Finally, the workers may be the source of quality failures.

## ANSWERS TO SELF-TEST QUESTIONS

**1.** c, e   **2.** c [$30 − (.2 × $30)]   **3.** d   **4.** d   **5.** a

# 19

# COST-VOLUME-PROFIT ANALYSIS

## Learning Objectives

*After studying this chapter, you should be able to:*

1. Explain how fixed, variable, and semivariable costs respond to changes in the volume of business activity.

2. Explain how economies of scale can reduce unit costs.

3. Prepare a cost-volume-profit graph.

4. Compute contribution margin and explain its usefulness.

5. Determine the sales volume required to earn a desired level of operating income.

6. Use the contribution margin ratio to estimate the change in operating income caused by a change in sales volume.

7. Use CVP relationships to evaluate a new marketing strategy.

© 2000 Ford Motor Company and Wieck Photo DataBase, Inc.

Recently, **Ford Motor Company** managed to earn more than any automaker in history. In "The Power of Smart Pricing" (*Business Week,* April 10, 2000), Peter Coy described how **Ford** achieved this feat by using a new pricing strategy that helped change the mix of vehicles it sells. Amazingly, during the same time period that it achieved record earnings, **Ford**'s U.S. market share fell. Ordinarily a falling U.S. market share would be serious cause for alarm. But what really happened at **Ford** was a decrease in sales of low-margin vehicles, such as Escorts and Aspires, and an increase in sales of high-margin vehicles, such as Crown Victorias and Explorers. **Ford** cut prices on its most profitable vehicles just enough to spur demand but not so much that they ceased to have attractive margins.

● ● ●

**Ford** was able to get a clear picture of how the fixed and variable costs of producing their different product lines respond to volume changes. That is, **Ford** clearly understands the relationship between their costs, volumes, and profits. By using cost-volume-profit analysis, companies such as **Ford** are able to increase their overall profitability. This chapter will help you understand cost-volume-profit relationships and how they can be useful for business decisions such as product pricing.

One of the most important analytical tools used by many managers is cost-volume-profit analysis (or *CVP analysis*). CVP analysis is a means of learning how costs and profits behave in response to changes in the level of business activity. An understanding of these relationships is essential in developing plans and budgets for future business operations.

Cost-volume-profit analysis may be used by managers to answer questions such as the following:

- What level of sales must be reached to cover all expenses, that is, to break even?
- How many units of a product must be sold to earn a specific operating income?
- What will happen to our profitability if we expand capacity?
- What will be the effect of changing salespeople's compensation from fixed monthly salaries to a commission of 10% on sales?
- If we increase our spending on advertising to $100,000 per month, what increase in sales volume will be required to maintain our current level of income from operations?

The concepts of cost-volume-profit analysis may be applied to the business as a whole; to individual segments of the business such as a division, a branch, or a department; or to a particular product line.

## COST-VOLUME RELATIONSHIPS

To illustrate the relationships between costs and activity levels, we examine the operation of McKinley Airlines, a small charter service based in Fairbanks, Alaska. Assume that the *average* monthly cost of operating the airline is $66,000. Obviously, in any given month, it would be mere coincidence if the company's *actual* total cost exactly equaled $66,000. Indeed, many factors may cause its actual expenses to be more or less than the average. Throughout this chapter, we will discover the importance of determining which factors drive costs and how managers can use this information to improve their planning and control activities.

Managers using CVP analysis begin by identifying the activities that cause costs to vary. For each activity the manager seeks some measurable base that allows increases or decreases in that activity to be matched with increases or decreases in costs. For example, one activity that causes costs to vary is the use of machines. Machine-hours is a measurable base that can be used to match the wear and tear on the machine and the electricity consumed by the machine with costs associated with the machine, like depreciation and utilities expense.

An activity base may be expressed in a variety of ways, depending on the nature of the company's operations. For example, in retail environments, an activity base may be defined in terms of *output,* such as units sold or dollars of sales revenue. In manufacturing operations, it is sometimes more appropriate to select key elements of production *input* as an activity base, such as direct labor hours or machine-hours. Airlines often consider *passenger miles flown* to be their most significant cost driver. Accordingly, we will use this measurement for studying the behavior of costs at McKinley Airlines.

Having identified passenger miles as an appropriate activity base, we will next classify each of the airline's operating costs into one of three broad categories: fixed costs, variable costs, and semivariable costs.

**LO 1**

Explain how fixed, variable, and semivariable costs respond to changes in the volume of business activity.

**Fixed Costs (and Fixed Expenses)**     **Fixed costs** are those costs and expenses that *do not change* significantly in response to changes in an activity base. McKinley's depreciation expense is an example of a fixed cost, as the monthly depreciation expense does not vary with the number of passenger miles flown. Depending on the nature of a particular business, fixed costs can also include administrative and executive salaries, property taxes, rents and leases, and many types of insurance protection.

**Variable Costs (and Variable Expenses)**   A **variable cost** is one whose total rises or falls in approximate proportion to changes in an activity base. McKinley's fuel expense is an example of a variable cost, as it changes in approximate proportion to the number of passenger miles flown. For instance, if total passenger miles increase by 10% in a given month, we would expect to see a similar increase in fuel expense.

**Semivariable Costs (and Semivariable Expenses)**   **Semivariable costs** are sometimes called *mixed costs* because they contain both a *fixed* and *variable* component. The monthly fee McKinley pays to the Fairbanks airport is a good example of a semivariable cost, since it contains both a fixed base rate and an added charge for each passenger mile flown. The fixed portion pertains to the rental of hangar space for McKinley's aircraft, which remains constant regardless of its flight activity. The variable portion pertains to the airline's use of the passenger terminal. The more passenger miles McKinley flies during a given month, the higher the terminal usage fee charged by the airport.

The concept of semivariable costs often applies when a variety of different costs are combined in one broad category. In manufacturing, for example, overhead includes a variety of fixed and variable costs. The fixed costs may include property taxes, supervisor salaries, and depreciation expense. The variable costs may include supplies, electricity, and machinery repairs.

 Identifying and separating fixed and variable costs is not easy. This task is significantly more complicated when products are manufactured in and transferred between international locations. For example, in Jordan, because of cultural and legal differences, some costs that might be classified as fixed costs in the United States are classified as variable costs or vice versa in Jordanian accounts. Examples of the costs impacted are product warranty, freight expenses, interest expenses, and wages. Culturally acceptable methods for delaying payments, bargaining for lower sales prices, and bureaucratic delays may transform a cost thought of as variable in the United States, into a fixed recurring expense in an international location. In Jordan, for instance, the government bureaucracy is difficult and laws change unexpectedly. Clearing items through customs takes inordinate numbers of repeat visits to airports or seaports and is frequently mentioned as an additional cost of doing business in Jordan.

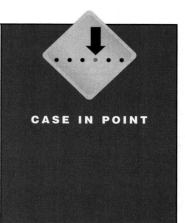

**CASE IN POINT**

## Cost-Volume Relationships: A Graphic Analysis

To illustrate cost-volume behavior, we shall examine the following somewhat simplified data pertaining to McKinley's fixed, variable, and semivariable costs:

| Type of Cost | Amount |
|---|---|
| Fixed costs | |
| Insurance . . . . . . . . . . . . . . . . . . . . . . . . . . . . . . . . . . . . . . . . | $11,000 per month |
| Depreciation . . . . . . . . . . . . . . . . . . . . . . . . . . . . . . . . . . . . . | $ 8,000 per month |
| Salaries . . . . . . . . . . . . . . . . . . . . . . . . . . . . . . . . . . . . . . . . | $20,000 per month |
| Variable costs | |
| Fuel and maintenance . . . . . . . . . . . . . . . . . . . . . . . . . . . . . . . | 8 cents per mile |
| Semivariable costs | |
| Airport usage fees . . . . . . . . . . . . . . . . . . . . . . . . . . . . . . . . . | $3,000 per month + 2 cents per passenger mile |

We have expressed these cost-volume relationships graphically in the diagrams on the following page (for each cost type and in total). Carefully note the relationship between volume (monthly passenger miles flown) and cost in each diagram.

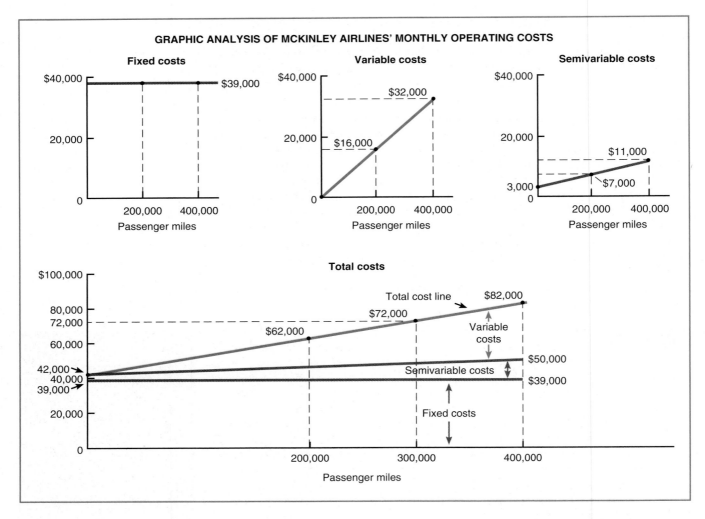

**GRAPHIC ANALYSIS OF MCKINLEY AIRLINES' MONTHLY OPERATING COSTS**

We can read from the total cost graph the estimated monthly cost for any assumed volume of passenger miles. As shown, if McKinley anticipates a volume of 300,000 passenger miles in any given month, its estimated total cost is $72,000, or 24 cents per passenger mile. By separating all fixed and variable cost elements, we can generalize McKinley's cost-volume relationship and simply state that the monthly cost of operating the airline, for any given number of passenger miles, is approximately *$42,000 plus 10 cents for each passenger mile flown.*

The effect of volume on McKinley's *total unit cost* (its cost per passenger mile) can be observed by converting its total cost figures to average cost figures as shown below. Note that the average total cost per passenger mile decreases as passenger miles increase.

*Note decrease in cost per passenger mile as volume increases*

| McKinley Airlines' Cost per Passenger Mile | | | |
|---|---|---|---|
| Total passenger miles . . . . . . . . . . . . . . . . . . . . . . . . . . | 200,000 | 300,000 | 400,000 |
| Costs | | | |
| Variable (8 cents per passenger mile) . . . . . . . . . . . . . . . | $16,000 | $24,000 | $32,000 |
| Fixed ($11,000 + $8,000 + $20,000) . . . . . . . . . . . . . . . . | 39,000 | 39,000 | 39,000 |
| Semivariable: | | | |
| Variable portion (2 cents per passenger mile) . . . . . . . . . . | 4,000 | 6,000 | 8,000 |
| Fixed portion . . . . . . . . . . . . . . . . . . . . . . . . . | 3,000 | 3,000 | 3,000 |
| Total operating costs . . . . . . . . . . . . . . . . . . . . . . . . . . | $62,000 | $72,000 | $82,000 |
| Cost per passenger mile . . . . . . . . . . . . . . . . . . . . . . . . | $0.31 | $0.24 | $0.205 |

McKinley's unit cost behavior is presented graphically below for both total cost and fixed cost. You can see that the distance between the two cost curves (representing variable costs of 10 cents per passenger mile) *remains constant* across a range of activity base volumes.

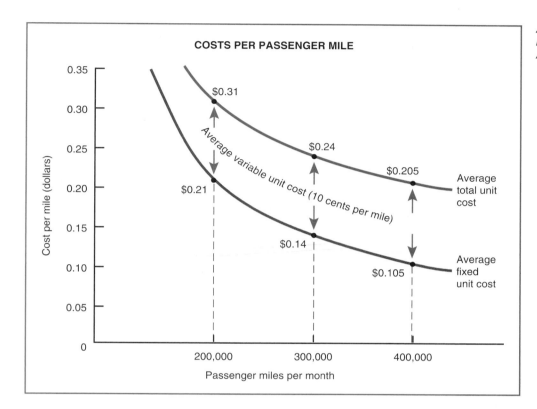

*Average cost per passenger mile of operating McKinley Airlines*

## The Behavior of Per-Unit Costs

In our example, note that the *variable cost per passenger mile* remains constant at 10 cents, regardless of the number of passenger miles flown. However, on a *per-passenger mile basis,* the fixed cost component gets smaller as passenger miles increase and larger as passenger miles decrease. This is because total fixed costs do not vary with changes in the activity base. As illustrated on the previous page, fixed costs decrease from 21 cents per passenger mile to 10.5 cents per passenger mile as monthly activity increases from 200,000 passenger miles to 400,000 passenger miles.

---

### You as a Manager

Assume that you are the manager of ground operations for **Northwest Airlines** at the Detroit Metro Airport. You have just been informed that the plane size between Philadelphia and Detroit will be increased from a Boeing 737 to a 727 and is expected to generate 50 additional passengers per flight. What ground operations costs do you think will increase because of the additional 50 passengers per flight? What ground operations costs will not be affected?

*Our comments appear on page 843.

**YOUR TURN**

---

## Economies of Scale

The decrease in McKinley's fixed cost per unit at higher levels of activity represents a more efficient use of the company's productive assets—its aircraft. In general, *most*

**LO 2**

Explain how economies of
scale can reduce unit costs.

*businesses can reduce unit costs by using their facilities more intensively.*[1] These savings are called **economies of scale**.

To illustrate, assume that an automobile plant incurs fixed costs of $8.4 million per month and has the capacity to produce 7,000 automobiles per month. The fixed cost per unit manufactured is shown below at three different levels of production.

| Fixed Costs per Month | Level of Production | Fixed Cost per Unit |
|---|---|---|
| $8,400,000 | 4,000 cars | $2,100 |
| 8,400,000 | 6,000 cars | 1,400 |
| 8,400,000 | 7,000 cars | 1,200 |

Notice that by producing 7,000 cars per month, the automaker's manufacturing costs are *$900 less* per automobile than if the automaker produces only 4,000 cars each month ($2,100 − $1,200 = $900). This cost advantage results from fully utilizing the company's production facilities and, therefore, spreading the company's fixed costs over as many units as possible.

Economies of scale are most apparent in businesses with *high fixed costs,* such as airlines, oil refineries, steel mills, and utility companies. Most large companies automatically realize some economies of scale. This is one of the reasons why it is difficult for a small company to compete with a much larger one. But smaller companies also can realize their own economies of scale by *using their facilities as intensively as possible.*

**CASE IN POINT**

Many airlines, including some of the nation's largest, have been losing money in recent years. But relatively small **Southwest Airlines** has been doing very well. Why? Because **Southwest** operates *at or near full capacity*—that is, with a paying passenger in almost every seat.

As a result, **Southwest** incurs lower fixed costs per passenger mile than its competitors. This enables **Southwest** to earn a higher profit margin than most airlines and to offer very competitive fares—which keep those seats full.

### Additional Cost Behavior Patterns

Cost relationships are seldom as simple as those in our example involving the operation of McKinley Airlines. However, the operating costs of all businesses exhibit variable, semivariable, and fixed characteristics.

In addition to the cost behaviors we have described thus far, some business costs increase in lump-sum steps as shown in graph **(a)** at the top of the facing page. For example, when production reaches a point where another supervisor and crew must be added, a lump-sum addition to labor costs occurs. Other costs may vary along a curve rather than a straight line, as shown in graph **(b)**. For example, when a production schedule requires employees to work overtime, labor cost per unit may rise more rapidly than volume because of the overtime premium.

Taking all the possible variations of cost behavior into account would add greatly to the complexity of cost-volume analysis. How far from reality are the assumed straight-

---

[1]Increasing the level of activity can increase certain per-unit costs, such as direct labor—especially if overtime rates must be paid. Seldom, however, do such cost increases fully offset the economies achieved from a higher level of output.

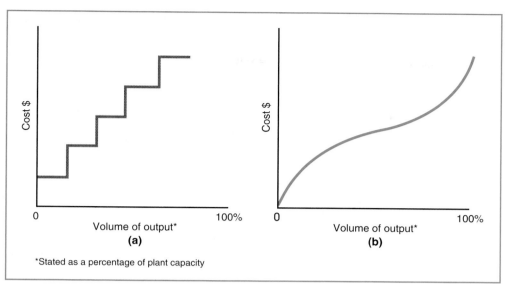

line relationships shown on page 812? Fortunately, there are two factors that make straight-line approximations of cost behavior useful for analytical purposes.

First, unusual patterns of cost behavior tend to offset one another. If we were to plot actual total costs incurred by a business over a time period in which volume changes occurred, the result might appear as in the cost-volume graph **(a)** at the bottom of this page. Notice that the cost pattern approximates a straight line, even though the actual points do not fall on the line itself.

Second, unusual patterns of cost behavior are most likely to occur at extremely high or extremely low levels of volume. For example, if output were increased to near 100% of plant capacity, variable costs would curve sharply upward because of payments for overtime. An extreme decline in volume, on the other hand, might require shutting down plants and extensive layoffs, thereby reducing some expenditures that are usually considered fixed costs. Most businesses, however, operate somewhere between perhaps 45% and 80% of capacity and try to avoid large fluctuations in volume. For a given business, the probability that volume will vary outside of a fairly narrow range is usually remote. The range over which output may be expected to vary is called the **relevant range**, as shown in graph **(b)** below. Within this relevant range, the assumption that total costs vary in straight-line relation to changes in volume is reasonably realistic for most companies.

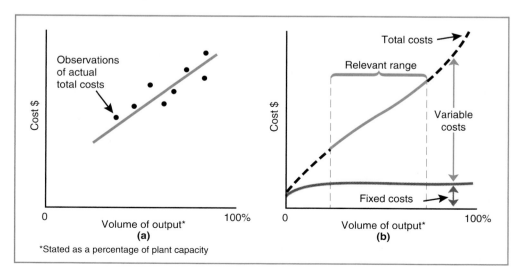

# COST BEHAVIOR AND OPERATING INCOME

Having gained an understanding of various cost behaviors, we can now expand our discussion to include the relationships among costs (both manufacturing costs *and* operating expenses), revenue, and operating income as follows:

Revenue − Variable Costs − Fixed Costs = Operating Income

This basic relationship sets the stage for introducing cost-volume-profit analysis, a widely used management planning tool. Cost-volume-profit analysis is often called *break-even analysis,* in reference to the point at which total revenue exactly equals total cost. The **break-even point** may be defined as the level of activity at which operating income is equal to *zero.* Its computation often serves as a starting point in decisions involving cost-volume-profit relationships.

Before we proceed with an illustration, one last point must be emphasized. The term *profit* in cost-volume-profit analysis refers to *operating income, not net income.* This is because income taxes and nonoperating gains and losses do not possess the characteristics of variable costs or fixed costs.

---

**CASH EFFECTS**    Cost-volume-profit analysis tells managers very little about cash flow effects. Revenue, for example, could be either cash sales or accounts receivable sales. However, cash flow information can be important in CVP analysis when an activity that causes cash to vary significantly is a cost driver. Consider a company selling two products. Product A is primarily cash-based sales and product B results in long-term holdings of outstanding accounts receivable balances. Managers may decide to include a cost in product B's CVP analysis representing the lost opportunity to earn a return on the cash tied up in the accounts receivable balance.

---

## Cost-Volume-Profit Analysis: An Illustration

Assume that ProGlide Skate Company manufactures high-quality, in-line skates. The company currently sells its product to wholesale distributors in California, Washington, and Oregon. Because of the rapid growth in the popularity of in-line skates, the company is considering distributing to several East Coast wholesalers as well. Although wholesale prices vary depending on the quantity of skates purchased by a distributor, revenue consistently *averages* $90 per pair of skates sold. ProGlide's monthly operating statistics are shown below.

*Note variable and fixed cost elements*

| | Dollars | Percentage of Sales Price |
|---|---|---|
| Average selling price per pair | $90.00 | 100% |
| Variable expenses per pair | | |
|    Direct labor cost | 2.25 | 2.5% |
|    Direct materials cost | 28.25 | 31.4% |
|    Variable manufacturing overhead | 3.10 | 3.4% |
|    Variable administrative expenses | 2.40 | 2.7% |
| Total variable cost per pair | 36.00 | 40.0% |
| Unit contribution margin and contribution margin ratio | | |
|    (discussed on pages 818–819) | $54.00 | 60.0% |
| Fixed costs | | |
|    Administrative salaries | $23,000 | |
|    Insurance | 1,300 | |
|    Depreciation | 5,000 | |
|    Advertising | 8,500 | |
| Total fixed cost per month | $37,800 | |

Notice that income taxes are not included among the monthly operating expenses. Income taxes are neither fixed nor variable because they depend on the amount of taxable income, rather than sales volume.

CVP analysis may be performed either by stating the cost-volume-profit relationships in the form of mathematical formulas or by illustrating them visually in a graph. Let us begin with a graph.

## Preparing and Using a Cost-Volume-Profit Graph

The *cost-volume-profit* (or *break-even*) graph below is based on ProGlide's cost and revenue statistics. The graph shows the reader, at a glance, the break-even point in units and in dollars.

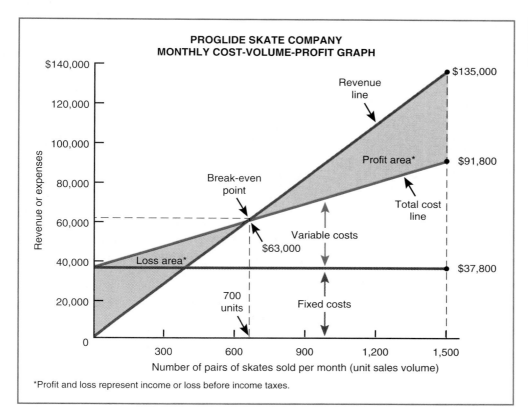

**LO 3**
Prepare a cost-volume-profit graph.

The horizontal axis represents the activity base, which for ProGlide is pairs of skates sold per month. Since the company is not equipped to manufacture more than 1,500 units per month, this is assumed to be the upper limit of the relevant range. The vertical axis of the graph represents dollars of revenue and costs corresponding to various levels of unit sales activity. The steps in drawing this graph are as follows:

1. Draw the total revenue line. This line runs from $0 to $135,000 in total revenue, which is the maximum revenue that the company can currently generate, given its monthly production capacity of 1,500 units. Note that the slope of the total revenue line equals the average selling price per unit of $90.

2. Draw the fixed cost line. This is a horizontal line representing a constant $37,800 monthly fixed cost at all volumes within the company's relevant range of activity.

3. Draw the total cost line. Starting where the fixed cost line intercepts the vertical axis at $37,800, the total cost line will rise by $54,000 to a total cost of $91,800. This is the total cost the company expects to incur, given its monthly production capacity of 1,500 units. Note that, for any level of activity, the distance from the fixed cost line to the total cost line represents the company's *total variable cost* and that the slope

of the total cost line equals the company's *variable cost per unit* of $36. Thus, for each additional pair of skates that the company sells, its total cost will increase by $36.

4. Label the point at which the revenue line intersects the total cost line as the *break-even point*. Note that ProGlide's break-even point is at 700 units, which corresponds to $63,000 in total revenue.

The operating profit or loss expected at any sales volume equals the distance between the total revenue line and the total cost line. Since this distance is zero at the break-even point, operating income at the break-even point must be zero, verified as follows:

*Computation verifying the break-even point in our graph*

| | | |
|---|---:|---:|
| Revenue (700 pairs of skates × $90 per pair) ..................... | | $63,000 |
| Costs and expenses: | | |
| Fixed ........................................... | $37,800 | |
| Variable (700 pairs of skates × $36 per pair) ..................... | 25,200 | 63,000 |
| Operating income .................................... | | $ –0– |

If ProGlide is able to operate at its monthly capacity of 1,500 units, its monthly operating income will amount to $43,200 ($135,000 in revenue, less $91,800 in total costs).

## Contribution Margin: A Key Relationship

**LO 4**

Compute the contribution margin and explain its usefulness.

We have shown that variable costs change in direct proportion to revenue. Thus the generation of an additional dollar of revenue will result in an additional amount of variable cost. The operating data for ProGlide (page 816) indicate that variable costs account for 40% of every sales dollar. In other words, for every $1 in revenue that the company earns, it can expect to incur 40 cents in variable costs. The remaining 60 cents is called the **contribution margin**.

The contribution margin is simply the *amount by which revenue exceeds variable costs.* Prior to reaching the break-even point, every $1 of ProGlide's revenue generates 60 cents in contribution margin to help cover *fixed costs.* Once sales pass the break-even point, every $1 in additional revenue contributes 60 cents toward *operating income.* The allocation of every revenue dollar between ProGlide's variable costs and contribution margin is illustrated below.

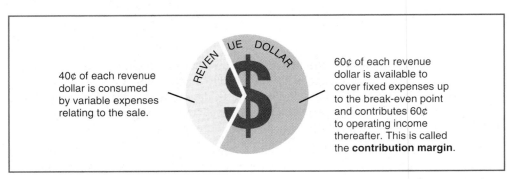

Contribution margin may be expressed as a percentage of revenue, as a total dollar amount for the period (total revenue less total variable expenses), or as the **contribution margin per unit** (unit sales price less the variable cost per unit). For example, the average contribution margin *per pair of skates* sold by ProGlide is *$54,* computed as follows:

**Unit Contribution Margin = Unit Selling Price − Variable Cost per Unit**

$$= \quad \$90 \quad - \quad \$36$$

$$= \$54$$

**Contribution Margin Ratio**   When contribution margin is expressed as a *percentage of revenue,* it is termed **contribution margin ratio**. This ratio may be computed either by dividing the total contribution margin for the period by total revenue, or on a per-unit basis as follows:

$$\text{Contribution Margin Ratio} = \frac{\text{Contribution Margin per Unit}}{\text{Unit Sales Price}}$$

Using ProGlide's per-unit data on page 816, we can compute the contribution margin ratio as follows:

$$\text{Contribution Margin Ratio} = \frac{\$54}{\$90} = 60\%$$

Once again, prior to breaking even, a contribution margin ratio of 60% means that 60 cents of every sales dollar helps to cover fixed costs. Once the break-even point is reached, every additional sales dollar provides a 60-cent increase in operating profit.

We will now examine how the important concept of contribution margin can be used to answer some fundamental questions about a company's operations.

## How Many Units Must We Sell?

The concept of contribution margin provides a quick means of determining the *unit sales volume* required for a business to break even or earn any desired level of operating income. Knowing the break-even sales volume can be of vital importance, especially to companies deciding whether to introduce a new product line, build a new plant, or in some cases, remain in business.

To illustrate the relationship between sales volume and contribution margin, assume that we want to compute how many pairs of skates ProGlide must sell in a month to break even. From the cost-volume-profit graph on page 817, we can see that the answer is 700 units. We will now prove that this is so. At the break-even point, the company must generate a total contribution exactly equal to its fixed costs. The data on page 816 show that monthly fixed costs amount to *$37,800.* Given a contribution margin of *$54* from each pair of skates, the company must sell 700 pairs per month to break even, as follows:

**LO 5**
Determine the sales volume required to earn a desired level of operating income.

$$\text{Sales Volume (in units)} = \frac{\$37,800}{\$54} = 700 \text{ units per month}$$

This reasoning can be taken one step further to find not only the unit sales volume needed to break even but also the unit sales volume needed to achieve *any desired level of operating income.* The following formula enables us to do this:

$$\text{Sales Volume (in units)} = \frac{\text{Fixed Costs} + \text{Target Operating Income}}{\text{Contribution Margin per Unit}}$$

For example, how many pairs of skates must ProGlide sell to earn a monthly operating income of *$5,400?*

$$\text{Sales Volume (in units)} = \frac{\$37,800 + \$5,400}{\$54} = 800 \text{ units per month}$$

## How Many Dollars in Sales Must We Generate?

To find the *dollar sales volume* a company must generate for a given target of operating income, we could first compute the required sales volume in units and then multiply our answer by the average selling price per unit. Thus ProGlide would have to generate approximately *$72,000* in revenue (800 pairs of skates × $90) to earn a monthly operating income of $5,400.

Taking a more direct approach to compute the required sales volume, we can simply substitute the *contribution margin ratio* for the contribution margin per unit in our CVP formula, as follows:

$$\text{Sales Volume (in dollars)} = \frac{\text{Fixed Costs} + \text{Target Operating Income}}{\text{Contribution Margin Ratio}}$$

To illustrate, let us again compute the sales volume required for ProGlide to earn a monthly operating income of $5,400:

$$\text{Sales Volume (in dollars)} = \frac{\$37,800 + \$5,400}{60\%} = \$72,000 \text{ per month}$$

## What Is Our Margin of Safety?

The dollar amount by which actual sales volume *exceeds* the break-even sales volume is called the **margin of safety**. It also represents the dollar amount by which sales can *decline* before an operating loss is incurred. In today's volatile economy, it is important for managers to understand the extent to which their companies can endure a downturn in sales. ProGlide's monthly sales volume required to break even is:

$$\text{Sales Volume (in dollars)} = \frac{\$37,800}{60\%} = \$63,000 \text{ per month}$$

Thus, if monthly sales total *$73,000,* the margin of safety for that month is *$10,000* ($73,000 − $63,000).

The margin of safety can provide a quick means of estimating operating income at any projected sales level. This relationship is summarized as follows:

**Operating Income = Margin of Safety × Contribution Margin Ratio**

The rationale for this formula stems from the fact that the margin of safety represents sales dollars *in excess of* the break-even point. Therefore, if fixed costs have already been covered, the *entire contribution margin of these sales increases operating income.*

To illustrate, let us assume that we estimate ProGlide's sales to be $72,000 next month. Given that its break-even sales volume is $63,000, its estimated margin of safety is $9,000. Thus the projected operating income is *$5,400* ($9,000 × 60%).

**MANAGEMENT
STRATEGY**

Management must carefully consider the implications of using contribution margin ratios for strategic decisions. An underlying assumption of the contribution margin ratio is that the relationship identified between variable costs per unit, total fixed costs, and volume is static *within the relevant volume range.* If an outcome of the strategic decision is to move out of the relevant volume range, then management must reconsider the cost-volume relationship. For example, the contribution margin ratio of 60% for ProGlide is based on a static sales price per unit of $90, a static variable cost per unit of $36, and a static total fixed cost of $37,800. If management decides that, for strategic reasons, it needs to increase volume to 1,900 units, it must consider these impacts on

1. **Variable costs:** Would overtime be required to increase volumes to this level?
2. **Fixed costs:** Is current factory space adequate to produce 1,900 units?
3. **Sales price:** Is there sufficient demand at $90 to sell 1,900 units?

Using cost-volume-profit relationships in strategic decision making must be tempered by the restrictive assumptions of the methods discussed here.

## What Change in Operating Income Do We Anticipate?

As stated, the contribution margin ratio in our example is 60%. Thus, once break-even is reached, every additional dollar of sales increases ProGlide's operating income by 60 cents. Conversely, a $1 sales decline lowers profitability by 60 cents. This relationship may be summarized as follows:

$$\text{Change in Operating Income} = \text{Change in Sales Volume} \times \text{Contribution Margin Ratio}$$

Therefore, if ProGlide estimates a $5,000 increase in monthly sales, it would anticipate a corresponding increase in operating income of $3,000 ($5,000 × 60%).

**LO 6**

Use the contribution margin ratio to estimate the change in operating income caused by a change in sales volume.

## Business Applications of CVP

The use of cost-volume-profit analysis is not limited to accountants. On the contrary, it provides valuable information to many individuals throughout an organization. Cost-volume-profit relationships are widely used during the budget process to set sales targets, estimate costs, and provide information for a variety of decisions.

To illustrate, let us consider several ways in which cost-volume-profit relationships might be used by the management of ProGlide Skate Company. As previously mentioned, the popularity of roller blading has prompted ProGlide to consider distribution to East Coast wholesalers. Different managers within the company will naturally have different, yet interrelated, planning concerns regarding the implementation of this new market strategy.

We now will examine the concerns of three ProGlide executives.

**Director of Advertising**   Assume that ProGlide is currently selling approximately *900 pairs* of skates each month. In response to the new market strategy, the company's director of advertising is asking for an increase of $1,500 in her monthly budget. She plans to use these funds to advertise in several East Coast trade publications. From her experience, she is confident that the advertisements will result in monthly orders from East Coast distributors for 500 pairs of skates. She wishes to emphasize the impact of her request on the company's *operating income.*

**LO 7**

Use CVP relationships to evaluate a new marketing strategy.

**Analysis**   We begin by calculating the company's current monthly income based on current sales of 900 units. We will then compute estimated monthly income based on 1,400 units, taking into account the additional advertising costs of $1,500 (an increase in total fixed costs from $37,800 to $39,300 per month). This will enable us to estimate the impact of the proposed advertising expenditures on monthly operating income.

Using the company's operating statistics shown on page 816, its current operating income is computed as follows:

| | |
|---|---|
| Sales (900 units @ $90) . . . . . . . . . . . . . . . . . . . . . . . . . . . . . . . . . . . . . | $81,000 |
| Variable costs (40% of sales) . . . . . . . . . . . . . . . . . . . . . . . . . . . . . . . . . | (32,400) |
| Contribution margin (60% of sales) . . . . . . . . . . . . . . . . . . . . . . . . . . . . . | 48,600 |
| Current monthly fixed costs . . . . . . . . . . . . . . . . . . . . . . . . . . . . . . . . . . . | (37,800) |
| Current monthly operating income . . . . . . . . . . . . . . . . . . . . . . . . . . . . . . | $10,800 |

As the proposed advertising is viewed as a fixed cost, this expenditure does not affect ProGlide's contribution margin ratio of *60%*. Based on projected monthly sales of *$126,000* (1,400 units × $90), the projected monthly operating income can be determined as follows:

$$\text{Projected Sales} = \frac{\text{Fixed Costs} + \text{Projected Operating Income}}{\text{Contribution Margin Ratio}}$$

$$\$126,000 = \frac{\$39,300 + \text{Projected Operating Income}}{60\%}$$

$$\text{Projected Operating Income} = 60\% \, (\$126,000) - \$39,300$$
$$= \$36,300 \text{ per month}$$

The target income figure is $25,500 higher than the present monthly figure of $10,800 ($36,300 − $10,800 = $25,500). Thus the director of advertising believes that her request for an additional $1,500 is well justified.

**Plant Manager**  ProGlide's plant manager does not completely agree with the advertising director's projections. He believes that the increased demand for the company's product will initially put pressure on the plant's production capabilities. To cope with the pressure, he asserts that many factory workers will be required to work excessive overtime hours, causing an increase in direct labor costs of approximately *$1.80 per unit*. Assuming that he is correct, he wants to know the *sales volume in units* required to achieve the advertising director's projected monthly income figure of $36,300.

**Analysis**  Holding the selling price at $90 per unit, the $1.80 overtime premium will reduce ProGlide's current contribution margin from $54 per unit to $52.20 per unit as follows:

$$\text{Unit Contribution Margin} = \text{Selling Price} - \text{Unit Variable Cost}$$
$$= \$90.00 - (\$36.00 + \$1.80)$$
$$= \$52.20$$

If the director of advertising receives a monthly increase of $1,500 in her budget, and if a $36,300 income target is established, the number of units that must be sold is computed as follows:

$$\text{Projected Unit Sales} = \frac{\text{Fixed Costs} + \text{Target Operating Income}}{\text{Unit Contribution Margin}}$$
$$= \frac{\$39,300 + \$36,300}{\$52.20}$$
$$= 1,448 \text{ units per month}$$

Given that 1,448 units is approaching the upper limit of ProGlide's 1,500 unit production capacity, the plant manager remains cautiously optimistic regarding the company's ability to market its product through East Coast distributors. Accordingly, he recommends that the company begin planning to increase plant capacity as soon as possible.

**YOUR TURN**

### You as a Plant Accountant

Assume you are the plant accountant and that you have a budgeted fixed overhead of $20,800 per month for a production level at normal capacity of 1,000 units per month. Thus your overhead application rate has been set at $20,800/1,000 units or $20.80 per unit. You realize that a production increase to 1,500 units per month will result in overapplying fixed overhead to the tune of $10,400 per month (500 units × $20.80). You are hesitant to bring up the problem of the overhead application rate with the plant manager because both of you receive a yearly bonus based on plant profitability. If overhead is being overapplied because production is at 1,500 units, the application rate is too high ($20.80 versus $20,800/ 1,500 = $13.87 per unit) and the projected sales volume of 1,500 units does not occur, significant fixed overhead costs will be assigned to the unsold inventories. As a result, plant income will be larger and your bonus as well as the plant manager's will be larger. What should you do?

*Our comments appear on page 843.

**Vice President of Sales**   The vice president of sales isn't convinced that an increase in the monthly advertising budget of $1,500 will yield sales of 500 units per month in the East Coast region. Her estimate is more conservative, at 350 units per month (for total monthly sales of *1,250 units*). Assume that the monthly advertising budget is increased by $1,500, and that direct labor costs actually do increase by $1.80 per unit because of the overtime premium required to meet increased production demands. If the vice president of sales is correct regarding her 1,250 unit projection, she wants to know the extent to which the company would have to *raise its selling prices* (above the current price of $90 per unit) to achieve a target monthly income figure of $36,300.

**Analysis**   If 1,250 units are sold each month instead of 1,400 units, the contribution margin per unit must increase in order for the company to achieve the same target income (taking the increases in advertising and direct labor costs into consideration). Once again, we use the following formula:

$$\text{Projected Unit Sales} = \frac{\text{Fixed Costs} + \text{Target Operating Income}}{\text{Contribution Margin per Unit}}$$

$$1{,}250 \text{ units} = \frac{\$39{,}300 + \$36{,}300}{\text{Contribution Margin per Unit}}$$

$$\text{Contribution Margin per Unit} = \frac{\$39{,}300 + \$36{,}300}{1{,}250 \text{ units}}$$

$$= \$60.48$$

Recall that the unit contribution margin is computed as follows:

$$\textbf{Unit Contribution Margin} = \textbf{Unit Selling Price} - \textbf{Unit Variable Cost}$$

Thus, given a required unit contribution margin of $60.48 and a variable cost per unit of $37.80, we can easily solve for the required unit selling price as follows:

$$\$60.48 = \text{Unit Selling Price} - \$37.80$$
$$\text{Unit Selling Price} = \$60.48 + \$37.80$$
$$= \$98.28$$

Faced with an extremely competitive wholesale sporting goods market, the vice president of sales is worried that a 9.2% price increase (from $90.00 per unit to $98.28 per unit) is likely to have an adverse effect on the company's total sales. Therefore, she recommends that the price remain at $90 per unit and that the company's target monthly income figure be lowered accordingly.

---

**You as a Product-Line Manager**

Assume that you are the product-line manager for ProGlide Skate Company and the decision about the East Coast sales initiative is your responsibility. What additional information would you want before making your decision? What would you recommend and why?

*Our comments appear on page 843.

**YOUR TURN**

## Additional Considerations in CVP

In practice, the application of cost-volume-profit analysis is often complicated by various operating factors, including (1) different products with different contribution margins,

(2) determining semivariable cost elements, and (3) complying with the assumptions of cost-volume-profit analysis. Let us address such considerations.

## CVP Analysis When a Company Sells Many Products

ProGlide sells only a single product. Most companies however, sell a mix of many different products. In fact, the term **sales mix** often is used to describe the relative percentages of total sales provided by different products.

Different products usually have different contribution margin ratios. In many cases, decisions are based on the contribution margin of a particular product. But often managers apply cost-volume relationships to the business *viewed as a whole.* For this purpose, they use the *average* contribution margin ratio, reflecting the company's current sales mix.

The average contribution margin ratio may be computed by *weighting* the contribution margin ratios of each product line by the *percentage of total sales* which that product represents.

To illustrate, assume that in addition to skates, ProGlide sells helmets. Contribution margin ratios for the two product lines are skates, 60% and helmets, 80%. Skates account for 90% of total sales, and helmets, the other 10%. The *average* contribution margin ratio for ProGlide's sales "mix" is computed as follows:

|  | Product CM Ratio | | Percentage of sales | |
|---|---|---|---|---|
| Skates . . . . . . . . . . . . . . . . . . . . . . . . . . . . . . . | 60% | × | 90% | = 54% |
| Helmets . . . . . . . . . . . . . . . . . . . . . . . . . . . . . . | 80% | × | 10% | = 8% |
| Average contribution margin ratio . . . . . . . . . . . . . . | | | | 62% |

**Improving the "Quality" of the Sales Mix** Notice that helmets have a higher contribution margin ratio than skates. A business can improve its average contribution ratio, and its overall profitability, by shifting its sales mix to include more products with *high contribution margin ratios.* This is the strategy used by **Ford** and described in the chapter opener.

Sales of products with the high contribution margins often are described as *quality sales* because they contribute so greatly to the company's profitability. At ProGlide, management should be thinking of ways to *sell more helmets.* Almost every business encourages its salespeople to aggressively market the high-margin products.

**CASE IN POINT**

If you buy a new car, you will find the dealer anxious to sell you many "options": fancy sound systems, custom trim packages, special paint, a larger engine—the list goes on and on. Almost every car in the showroom will be fully equipped. This is because the basic economy models have very low contribution margin ratios—perhaps 12% or less. But those with "options"? That's a different story.

## Determining Semivariable Cost Elements: The High-Low Method

As previously discussed, semivariable costs have both a fixed portion and a variable portion. Throughout this chapter we have simplified the handling of semivariable costs by providing the fixed and variable components for you. In practice, one must estimate the fixed and variable elements of semivariable costs. Several mathematical techniques may be used to accomplish this task. We will focus on one approach called the **high-low method**.[2]

To illustrate the high-low method, assume that some portion of ProGlide's total administrative cost is fixed and that some portion varies with the level of production. Information pertaining to production and administrative costs for the first six months of the year is shown below:

|  | Total Units Produced | Total Administrative Costs |
|---|---|---|
| Jan. | 900 | $25,060 |
| Feb. | 850 | 25,040 |
| Mar. | 925 | 25,183 |
| Apr. | 950 | 25,280 |
| May | 875 | 25,140 |
| June | 910 | 25,194 |

To find the *variable portion* of total administrative costs, we relate the change in cost to the change in the activity base between the highest and the lowest months of production activity:

|  | Total Units Produced | Total Administrative Costs |
|---|---|---|
| Apr. (highest) | 950 | $25,280 |
| Feb. (lowest) | 850 | 25,040 |
| Changes | 100 | $ 240 |

Notice that a 100-unit increase in production results in a $240 increase in administrative costs. Therefore, the variable element of this cost may be estimated at $240 per 100 units, or *$2.40 per unit.*

To determine the fixed portion of the monthly administrative cost, we take the *total monthly cost* at either the high point or the low point, and deduct the *variable* administrative cost from that amount. The following computation uses the highest level of activity to determine the fixed cost portion:

$$\textbf{Fixed Cost} = \textbf{Total Cost} - \textbf{Variable Cost}$$
$$= \textbf{\$25,280} - (\textbf{\$2.40 per unit} \times \textbf{950 units})$$
$$= \textbf{\$25,280} - \textbf{\$2,280}$$
$$= \textbf{\$23,000 per month}$$

Note that the variable and fixed administrative costs correspond to those reported in ProGlide's monthly summary of average operating statistics on page 816.

We have now developed a **cost formula** for monthly administrative costs: *$23,000 + $2.40 per unit.* In addition to helping the company evaluate the reasonableness of administrative costs incurred in a given month, this formula is also valuable in forecasting administrative costs likely to be incurred in the future. For example,

---

[2]Other approaches to determining the fixed and variable elements of semivariable costs include the least squares method and regression analysis. These techniques are typically discussed in a cost accounting course.

what amount of administrative cost should ProGlide expect in a month in which it has scheduled 930 units of production? The answer is approximately *$25,232*, determined as follows:

| | |
|---|---|
| Monthly fixed administrative cost | $23,000 |
| Variable costs ($2.40 × 930 units) | 2,232 |
| Total estimated administrative cost | $25,232 |

## Assumptions Underlying Cost-Volume-Profit Analysis

Throughout the chapter we have relied on certain assumptions that have simplified the application of cost-volume-profit analysis. In practice, however, some of these assumptions may not always hold true. These assumptions include:

1. Sales price per unit is assumed to remain constant.
2. If more than one product is sold, the proportion of the various products sold (the sales mix) is assumed to remain constant.
3. Fixed costs (expenses) are assumed to remain constant at all levels of sales within a relevant range of activity.
4. Variable costs (expenses) are assumed to remain constant as a percentage of sales revenue.
5. For manufacturing companies, the number of units produced is assumed to equal the number of units sold each period.

Even if some of these assumptions are violated, cost-volume-profit analysis can still be a useful planning tool for management. As changes take place in selling prices, sales mix, expenses, and production levels, management should update and revise its analysis.

## Summary of Basic Cost-Volume-Profit Relationships

In this chapter, we have demonstrated a number of ratios and mathematical relationships that are useful in cost-volume-profit analysis. For your convenience, these relationships are summarized below.

| Measurement | Method of Computation |
|---|---|
| Contribution Margin | Sales Revenue − Total Variable Costs |
| Unit Contribution Margin | Unit Sales Price − Variable Costs per Unit |
| Contribution Margin Ratio | $\frac{\text{Unit Sales Price} - \text{Variable Costs per Unit}}{\text{Unit Sales Price}}$ or $\frac{\text{Sales} - \text{Total Variable Costs}}{\text{Sales}}$ |
| Sales Volume (in units) | $\frac{\text{Fixed Costs} + \text{Target Operating Income}}{\text{Unit Contribution Margin}}$ |
| Sales Volume (in dollars) | $\frac{\text{Fixed Costs} + \text{Target Operating Income}}{\text{Contribution Margin Ratio}}$ |
| Margin of Safety | Actual Sales Volume − Break-even Sales Volume |
| Operating Income | Margin of Safety × Contribution Margin Ratio |
| Change in Operating Income | Change in Sales Volume × Contribution Margin Ratio |

## Ford Motor Company

**A SECOND LOOK**

Many companies have gotten serious about cutting costs. **Ford Motor Company**, however, is one of the few companies that also understands the importance of product pricing strategies. By gathering information about market demand and combining it with their understanding of their production costs and capabilities, **Ford** management has learned to control the routine over- and underpricing that exists in many companies.

A key to good pricing is a clear understanding of the basic ideas introduced in this chapter. Knowing the impact of economies of scale, how volume fluctuations impact fixed and variable costs, the importance of contribution margins and break-even analysis, and the demand for the products and services produced are critical for making profitable business decisions.

Other factors are important for pricing strategies. For example, an awareness of the distinctions between opportunity costs, sunk costs, and out-of-pocket costs as they relate to particular business decisions is essential. Recognizing constraints and bottlenecks and their impact on contribution margins and identifying nonfinancial factors that affect business decisions are also significant. **Ford** executives consider these additional issues in their pricing strategies. The next chapter introduces these additional topics and other concepts that are important for business decisions.

# END-OF-CHAPTER REVIEW

## SUMMARY OF LEARNING OBJECTIVES

### LO1

**Explain how fixed, variable, and semivariable costs respond to changes in the volume of business activity.**

Fixed costs (fixed expenses) remain unchanged despite changes in sales volume, while variable costs (or expenses) change in direct proportion to changes in sales volume. With a semivariable cost, part of the cost is fixed and part is variable. Semivariable costs change in response to a change in the level of activity, but they change by less than a proportionate amount.

### LO 2

**Explain how economies of scale can reduce unit costs.**

Economies of scale are reductions in unit cost that can be achieved through a higher volume of activity. One economy of scale is fixed costs that are spread over a larger number of units, thus reducing unit cost.

### LO 3

**Prepare a cost-volume-profit graph.**

The vertical axis on a break-even graph is dollars of revenue or costs, and the horizontal axis is unit sales. Lines are plotted on the graph showing revenue and total costs at different sales volumes. The vertical distance between these lines represents the amount of operating income (or loss). The lines intersect at the break-even point.

### LO 4

**Compute contribution margin and explain its usefulness.**

Contribution margin is the excess of revenue over variable costs. Thus it represents the amount of revenue available to cover fixed costs and to provide an operating profit. Contribution margin is useful in estimating the sales volume needed to achieve earnings targets, or the income likely to result from a given sales volume.

### LO 5

**Determine the sales volume required to earn a desired level of operating income.**

The sales volume (in units) required to earn a target profit is equal to the sum of the fixed costs plus the target profit, divided by the unit contribution margin. To determine the sales volume in dollars, the sum of the fixed costs plus the target profit is divided by the contribution margin ratio.

### LO 6

**Use the contribution margin ratio to estimate the change in operating income caused by a change in sales volume.**

Multiplying the expected dollar change in sales volume by the contribution margin ratio indicates the expected change in operating income.

### LO 7

**Use CVP relationships to evaluate a new marketing strategy.**

An understanding of CVP relationships assists managers in estimating the changes in revenue and in costs which are likely to accompany a change in sales volume. Thus they are able to estimate the likely effects of marketing strategies on overall profitability.

An understanding of cost behavior—the manner in which costs normally respond to changes in the level of activity—is required in each remaining chapter of this textbook. In these chapters, we will explore the use of accounting information in evaluating the performance of managers and departments, in planning future business operations, and in making numerous types of management decisions. The concepts and terminology introduced in Chapter 19 will be used extensively in these discussions.

## KEY TERMS INTRODUCED OR EMPHASIZED IN CHAPTER 19

**break-even point** (p. 816) The level of sales at which a company neither earns an operating profit nor incurs a loss. Revenue exactly covers costs and expenses.

**contribution margin** (p. 818) Sales minus variable costs. The portion of sales revenue that is not consumed by variable costs and, therefore, is available to cover fixed costs and contribute to operating income.

**contribution margin per unit** (p. 818) The excess of unit sales price over variable cost per unit; the dollar amount contributed by the sale of each unit toward covering fixed costs and generating operating income.

**contribution margin ratio** (p. 819) The contribution margin expressed as a percentage of sales price. Represents the percentage of each revenue dollar that is available to cover fixed costs or to provide an operating profit.

**cost formula** (p. 825) A mathematical statement expressing the expected amount of a cost in terms of the fixed element of the cost and/or the portion of the cost that varies in response to changes in some activity base. For example, the cost formula for a semivariable cost might be $2,500 per month, plus 5% of net sales.

**economies of scale** (p. 814) A reduction in unit cost achieved through a higher volume of output.

**fixed costs** (p. 810) Costs and expenses that remain unchanged despite changes in the level of the activity base.

**high-low method** (p. 825) A method of dividing a semivariable (or mixed) cost into its fixed and variable elements by relating the change in the cost to the change in the activity base between the highest and lowest levels of observed activity.

**margin of safety** (p. 820) Amount by which actual sales exceed the break-even point.

**relevant range** (p. 815) The span or range of output over which output is likely to vary and assumptions about cost behavior are generally valid. Excludes extreme volume variations.

**sales mix** (p. 824) The relative percentages of total sales generated by each type of product that a business sells.

**semivariable costs** (p. 811) Costs and expenses that respond to changes in the level of the activity base by less than a proportionate amount.

**variable costs** (p. 811) Costs and expenses that vary directly and proportionately with changes in the level of the activity base.

## ■ DEMONSTRATION PROBLEM

The management of the Fresno Processing Company has engaged you to assist in the development of information to be used for management decisions.

The company has the capacity to process 20,000 tons of cottonseed per year. This processing results in several salable products, including oil, meal, hulls, and lint.

A marketing study indicates that the company can sell its output for the coming year at $200 per ton processed.

You have determined the company's cost structure to be as follows:

| | |
|---|---|
| Cost of cottonseed | $80 per ton |
| Processing costs: | |
|    Variable | $26 per ton |
|    Fixed | $340,000 per year |
| Marketing costs | All variable, $44 per ton |
| Administrative costs | All fixed, $300,000 per year |

### Instructions

**a.** Compute (1) the contribution margin and (2) the contribution margin ratio per ton of cottonseed processed.

**b.** Compute the break-even sales volume in (1) dollars and (2) tons of cottonseed.

**c.** Assume that the company's budget calls for an operating income of $240,000. Compute the sales volume required to reach this profit objective, stated (1) in dollars and (2) in tons of cottonseed.

**d.** Compute the maximum amount that the company can afford to pay per ton of raw cottonseed and still break even by processing and selling 16,000 tons during the current year.

### Solution to the Demonstration Problem

**a.** (1) Total revenue per ton of cottonseed ............................ $200

     Less: Variable costs:

        Cottonseed ........................................ $80

        Processing ........................................ 26

        Marketing ........................................ 44    150

     Unit contribution margin ($200 − $150) ......................... $ 50

  (2) Contribution margin ratio ($50 ÷ $200) ......................... 25%

**b.** (1) Break-even dollar sales volume:

| | |
|---|---:|
| Fixed costs ($340,000 + $300,000) | $ 640,000 |
| Contribution margin ratio (part **a**) | 25% |
| Break-even dollar sales volume ($640,000 ÷ 0.25) | $2,560,000 |

(2) Break-even unit sales volume (in tons):

| | |
|---|---:|
| Fixed costs (per previous) | $ 640,000 |
| Unit contribution margin (part **a**) | $ 50 |
| Break-even unit sales volume, stated in tons of cottonseed products ($640,000 ÷ $50) | 12,800 |

(Alternative computation: break-even dollar sales volume, $2,560,000, divided by unit sales price, $200, equals 12,800 tons.)

**c.** (1) Required dollar sales volume:

| | |
|---|---:|
| Fixed expenses | $ 640,000 |
| Add: Target operating income | 240,000 |
| Required contribution margin | $ 880,000 |
| Contribution margin ratio (part **a**) | 25% |
| Required dollar sales volume ($880,000 ÷ 0.25) | $3,520,000 |

(2) Required unit sales volume:

| | |
|---|---:|
| Required dollar sales volume [from (**1**)] | $3,520,000 |
| Unit sales price | $ 200 |
| Required unit sales volume, in tons ($3,520,000 ÷ $200) | 17,600 |

(Alternative computation: required contribution margin to cover fixed expenses and target operating income, $880,000, [part **c**(1)], divided by unit contribution margin, $50 per ton, equals 17,600 tons.)

**d.**

| | | |
|---|---:|---:|
| Total revenue (16,000 tons × $200) | | $3,200,000 |
| Less: Costs other than cottonseed: | | |
| Processing (16,000 tons × $26) | $416,000 | |
| Marketing (16,000 tons × $44) | 704,000 | |
| Fixed costs | 640,000 | 1,760,000 |
| Maximum amount that can be paid for 16,000 tons of cottonseed, while allowing company to break even | | $1,440,000 |
| Maximum amount that can be paid per ton of cottonseed, while allowing company to break even ($1,440,000 ÷ 16,000 tons) | | $90 |

## SELF-TEST QUESTIONS

*Answers to these questions appear on page 843.*

1. During the current year, the net sales of Ridgeway, Inc., were 10% below last year's level. You should expect Ridgeway's semivariable costs to:

   **a.** Decrease in total, but increase as a percentage of net sales.

   **b.** Increase in total and increase as a percentage of net sales.

   **c.** Decrease in total and decrease as a percentage of net sales.

   **d.** Increase in total, but decrease as a percentage of net sales.

2. Marston Company sells a single product at a sales price of $50 per unit. Fixed costs total $15,000 per month, and variable costs amount to $20 per unit. If management reduces the

sales price of this product by $5 per unit, the sales volume needed for the company to break even will:

- **a.** Increase by $5,000.
- **c.** Increase by $2,000.
- **b.** Increase by $4,500.
- **d.** Remain unchanged.

3. Olsen Auto Supply typically earns a contribution margin ratio of 40%. The store manager estimates that by spending an additional $5,000 per month for radio advertising, the store will be able to increase its operating income by $3,000 per month. The manager is expecting the radio advertising to increase monthly dollar sales volume by:

- **a.** $12,500.
- **b.** $8,000.
- **c.** $7,500.
- **d.** Some other amount.

4. Shown below are the monthly high and low levels of direct labor hours and of total manufacturing overhead for Apex Mfg. Co.

|  | Direct Labor Hours | Total Manufacturing Overhead |
|---|---|---|
| Highest observed level | 6,000 | $17,000 |
| Lowest observed level | 4,000 | 14,000 |

In a month in which 5,000 direct labor hours are used, the *fixed element* of total manufacturing overhead costs should be approximately:

- **a.** $15,500.
- **b.** $8,000.
- **c.** $7,500.
- **d.** $8,000 plus $1.50 per unit.

5. Driver Company manufactures two products. Data concerning these products are shown below:

|  | Product A | Product B |
|---|---|---|
| Total monthly demand (in units) | 1,000 | 200 |
| Sales price per unit | $400 | $500 |
| Contribution margin ratio | 30% | 40% |
| Relative sales mix | 80% | 20% |

If fixed costs are equal to $320,000, what amount of total sales revenue is needed to break even?

- **a.** $914,286.
- **b.** $457,143.
- **c.** $320,000.
- **d.** $1,000,000.

# ASSIGNMENT MATERIAL

## DISCUSSION QUESTIONS

1. Why is it important for management to understand cost-volume-profit relationships?
2. What is an *activity base* and why is it important in analyzing cost behavior?
3. What is the effect of an increase in activity on the following items?
   - **a.** Total variable costs
   - **b.** Variable costs per unit of activity
4. What is the effect of an increase in activity on the following items?
   - **a.** Total fixed costs
   - **b.** Fixed costs per unit of activity
5. The simplifying assumption that costs and volume vary in straight-line relationships makes the analysis of cost behavior much easier. What factors make this a reasonable and useful assumption in many cases?
6. Define the *relevant range* of activity.

7. Explain how the high-low method determines:

   **a.** The variable portion of a semivariable cost.

   **b.** The fixed portion of a semivariable cost.

8. Define (a) *contribution margin,* (b) *contribution margin ratio,* and (c) *average contribution margin ratio.*

9. What important relationships are shown on a cost-volume-profit (break-even) graph?

10. Klein Company has a contribution margin ratio of 35%. What dollar sales volume per month is necessary to produce a monthly operating income of $30,000, if fixed costs are $145,000 per month?

11. Explain how the unit contribution margin can be used to determine the unit sales required to break even.

12. Hurst Company has variable costs of $26 per unit and a contribution margin ratio of 35%. Compute the selling price per unit.

13. Define *margin of safety.*

14. Explain the probable effect on operating income of a $19,000 increase in sales volume by a company with variable costs of $75 per unit and a contribution margin ratio of 40%.

15. An executive of a large American steel company put the blame for lower net income for a recent fiscal period on the "shift in product mix to a higher proportion of export sales." Sales for the period increased slightly while net income declined by 28%. Explain how a change in product (sales) mix to a higher proportion in export sales could result in a lower level of net income.

16. Explain why businesses normally can reduce unit costs by utilizing their facilities more intensively.

17. A company's relevant range of production output is 1,000 units to 5,000 units per month. It currently operates at an average output of 3,500 units. Management is considering raising this figure to 4,500 units. To do so, an additional forklift would have to be rented at $1,000 per month. What cost-volume-profit assumption is being violated? How can management compensate for this violation?

## EXERCISES

**EXERCISE 19.1**

Accounting Terminology

**LO 1, 2, 4**

Listed below are nine technical accounting terms introduced in this chapter:

| | | |
|---|---|---|
| Variable costs | Relevant range | Contribution margin |
| Break-even point | Fixed costs | Semivariable costs |
| Economies of scale | Sales mix | Unit contribution margin |

Each of the following statements may (or may not) describe one of these technical terms. For each statement, indicate the accounting term described, or answer "None" if the statement does not correctly describe any of the terms.

**a.** The level of sales at which revenue exactly equals costs and expenses

**b.** Costs that remain unchanged despite changes in sales volume

**c.** The span over which output is likely to vary and assumptions about cost behavior generally remain valid

**d.** Sales revenue less variable costs and expenses

**e.** Unit sales price minus variable costs per unit

**f.** The reduction in unit cost achieved from a higher level of output

**g.** Costs that respond to changes in sales volume by less than a proportionate amount

**h.** Operating income less variable costs

**EXERCISE 19.2**

Patterns of Cost Behavior

**LO 1**

Explain the effects of an increase in the volume of activity on the following costs. (Assume volume remains within the relevant range.)

**a.** Total variable costs

**b.** Variable costs per unit

c. Total fixed costs

d. Fixed costs per unit

e. Total semivariable costs

f. Semivariable costs per unit

Explain whether you regard each of the following costs or categories of costs as fixed, variable, or semivariable with respect to net sales. Briefly explain your reasoning. If you do not believe that a cost fits into any of these classifications, explain.

a. The cost of goods sold

b. Salaries to salespeople (These salaries include a monthly minimum amount, plus a commission on all sales.)

c. Income taxes expense

d. Property taxes expense

e. Depreciation expense on a sales showroom, based on the straight-line method of depreciation

f. Depreciation expense on a sales showroom, based on the double-declining-balance method of depreciation

**EXERCISE 19.3**

Classification of Various Costs

The following information is available regarding the total manufacturing overhead of Bursa Mfg. Co. for a recent four-month period:

**EXERCISE 19.4**

High-Low Method of Cost Analysis

|  | Machine Hours | Manufacturing Overhead |
|---|---|---|
| Jan. | 5,500 | $311,500 |
| Feb. | 3,200 | 224,000 |
| Mar. | 4,900 | 263,800 |
| Apr. | 2,800 | 184,600 |

a. Use the high-low method to determine:

1. The variable element of manufacturing overhead costs per machine-hour.

2. The fixed element of monthly overhead cost.

b. Bursa expects machine-hours in May to equal 5,300. Use the cost relationships determined in part **a** to forecast May's manufacturing overhead costs.

c. Suppose Bursa had used the cost relationships determined in part **a** to estimate the total manufacturing overhead expected for the months of February and March. By what amounts would Bursa have over- or underestimated these costs?

City Ambulance Service estimates the monthly cost of responding to emergency calls to be $19,500 plus $110 per call.

a. In a month in which the company responds to 125 emergency calls, determine the estimated:

1. Total cost of responding to emergency calls.

2. Average cost of responding to emergency calls.

b. Assume that in a given month, the number of emergency calls was unusually low. Would you expect the average cost of responding to emergency calls during this month to be higher or lower than in other months? Explain.

**EXERCISE 19.5**

Using a Cost Formula

Through using the high-low method, Regency Hotels estimates the total costs of providing room service meals to amount to $5,950 per month, plus 30% of room service revenue.

a. What is the contribution margin ratio of providing room service meals?

b. What is the break-even point for room service operations in terms of total room service revenue?

c. What would you expect to be the total cost of providing room service in a month in which room service revenue amounts to $15,000?

**EXERCISE 19.6**

Using a Cost Formula

**LO 4, 5**

**EXERCISE 19.7**

Computing Required Sales Volume

The following is information concerning a product manufactured by Ames Brothers:

| | |
|---|---:|
| Sales price per unit . . . . . . . . . . . . . . . . . . . . . . . . . . . . . . . . . . . . . . . . . . . . | $   70 |
| Variable cost per unit . . . . . . . . . . . . . . . . . . . . . . . . . . . . . . . . . . . . . . . . . | 43 |
| Total fixed manufacturing and operating costs (per month) . . . . . . . . . . . . . . . . . . . | 405,000 |

Determine the following:

a. The unit contribution margin

b. The number of units that must be sold each month to break even

c. The unit sales level that must be reached to earn an operating income of $270,000 per month

**EXERCISE 19.8**

Computing Sales Volume

**LO 4–6**

Porter Corporation has fixed costs of $660,000, variable costs of $24 per unit, and a contribution margin ratio of 40%.

Compute the following:

a. Unit sales price and unit contribution margin for the above product

b. The sales volume in units required for Porter Corporation to earn an operating income of $300,000

c. The dollar sales volume required for Porter Corporation to earn an operating income of $300,000

**EXERCISE 19.9**

Computing Contribution Margin Ratio and Margin of Safety

**LO 4, 5**

The following information relates to the only product sold by Harper Company:

| | |
|---|---:|
| Sales price per unit . . . . . . . . . . . . . . . . . . . . . . . . . . . . . . . . . . . . . . . . . . . . | $   24 |
| Variable cost per unit . . . . . . . . . . . . . . . . . . . . . . . . . . . . . . . . . . . . . . . . . . | 18 |
| Fixed costs per year . . . . . . . . . . . . . . . . . . . . . . . . . . . . . . . . . . . . . . . . . . . | 240,000 |

a. Compute the contribution margin ratio and the dollar sales volume required to break even.

b. Assuming that the company sells 75,000 units during the current year, compute the margin of safety sales volume (dollars).

**EXERCISE 19.10**

Computing Sales Volume

**LO 4–6**

The Jackson Company recently calculated its break-even sales revenue to be $15,000. For each dollar of sales revenue, $0.70 goes to cover variable costs.

Compute the following:

a. The contribution margin ratio

b. Total fixed costs

c. The sales revenue that would have to be generated to earn an operating income of $9,000

**EXERCISE 19.11**

Relating Contribution Margin Ratio to Sales Price

**LO 1, 4, 5, 6**

Firebird Mfg. Co. has a contribution margin ratio of 45% and must sell 25,000 units at a price of $80 each in order to break even. Compute:

a. Total fixed costs.

b. Variable costs per unit.

**EXERCISE 19.12**

Computing the Break-Even Point

**LO 4, 5, 6**

Malibu Corporation has monthly fixed costs of $63,000. It sells two products for which it has provided the following information:

| | Sales Price | Contribution Margin |
|---|---:|---:|
| Product 1 . . . . . . . . . . . . . . . . . . . . . . . . . . . . . . . . . . . | $10 | $6 |
| Product 2 . . . . . . . . . . . . . . . . . . . . . . . . . . . . . . . . . . . | 10 | 3 |

**a.** What total monthly sales revenue is required to break even if the relative sales mix is 40% for Product 1 and 60% for Product 2?

**b.** What total monthly sales revenue is required to earn a monthly operating income of $12,000 if the relative sales mix is 25% for Product 1 and 75% for Product 2?

For each of the six independent situations below, compute the missing amounts.

**a.** Using contribution margin per unit

|  | Sales | Variable Costs | Contribution Margin per Unit | Fixed Costs | Operating Income | Units Sold |
|---|---|---|---|---|---|---|
| (1) | $_____ | $120,000 | $20 | $_____ | $25,000 | 4,000 |
| (2) | 180,000 | _____ | ___ | 45,000 | 30,000 | 5,000 |
| (3) | 600,000 | _____ | 30 | 150,000 | 90,000 | _____ |

**b.** Using the contribution margin ratio

|  | Sales | Variable Costs | Contribution Margin Ratio | Fixed Costs | Operating Income |
|---|---|---|---|---|---|
| (1) | $900,000 | $720,000 | ___% | $_____ | $95,000 |
| (2) | 600,000 | _____ | 40% | _____ | 75,000 |
| (3) | _____ | _____ | 30% | 90,000 | 60,000 |

Chaps & Saddles, a retailer of tack and western apparel, earns an average contribution margin of 45% on its sales volume. Recently, the advertising manager of a local "country" radio station offered to run numerous radio advertisements for Chaps & Saddles at a monthly cost of $1,800.

Compute the amount by which the proposed radio advertising campaign must increase Chaps & Saddles' monthly sales volume to:

**a.** Pay for itself.

**b.** Increase operating income by $1,000 per month. (Round computations to the nearest dollar.)

You have been hired as a consultant to assist the following companies with cost-volume-profit analysis:

Freeman's Retail Floral Shop

Susquehanna Trails Bus Service

Wilson Pump Manufacturers

McCauley & Pratt, Attorneys at Law

Suggest an appropriate activity base for each of these clients.

Tom Klem is the controller of Watson Manufacturing, Inc. He estimates that the company's break-even point in sales dollars is $2 million. However, he recently told all of the regional sales managers that sales of $3 million were needed to break even. He also told them that if the company failed to break even, the sales force would be reduced in size by 40%. Klem believes that his tactics will motivate the sales force to generate record profits for the upcoming year.

Is his approach to motivating employees ethical? What other approaches might he use?

# PROBLEMS

**PROBLEM 19.1**

Using Cost-Volume-Profit Formulas

**LO 4, 5, 6**

MURDER TO GO! writes and manufactures murder mystery parlor games that it sells to retail stores. The following is per-unit information relating to the manufacture and sale of this product:

| | |
|---|---|
| Unit sales price . . . . . . . . . . . . . . . . . . . . . . . . . . . . . . . . . . . . . . . . . . . . . . . . . . | $   28 |
| Variable cost per unit . . . . . . . . . . . . . . . . . . . . . . . . . . . . . . . . . . . . . . . . . . . . . | 7 |
| Fixed costs per year . . . . . . . . . . . . . . . . . . . . . . . . . . . . . . . . . . . . . . . . . . . . . | 240,000 |

### Instructions

Determine the following, showing as part of your answer the formula that you used in your computation. For example, the formula used to determine the contribution margin ratio (part **a**) is:

$$\text{Contribution Margin Ratio} = \frac{\text{Unit Sales Price} - \text{Variable Costs per Unit}}{\text{Unit Sales Price}}$$

**a.** Contribution margin ratio

**b.** Sales volume (in dollars) required to break even

**c.** Sales volume (in dollars) required to earn an annual operating income of $450,000

**d.** The margin of safety sales volume if annual sales total 40,000 units

**e.** Operating income if annual sales total 40,000 units

**PROBLEM 19.2**

Using Cost-Volume-Profit Formulas

**LO 4–6**

Arrow Products typically earns a contribution margin ratio of 25% and has current fixed costs of $80,000. Arrow's general manager is considering spending an additional $20,000 to do one of the following:

**1.** Start a new ad campaign that is expected to increase sales revenue by 5%.

**2.** License a new computerized ordering system that is expected to increase Arrow's contribution margin ratio to 30%.

Sales revenue for the coming year was initially forecast to equal $1,200,000 (that is, without implementing either of the above options).

### Instructions

**a.** For each option, how much will projected operating income increase or decrease relative to initial predictions?

**b.** By what percentage would sales revenue need to increase to make the ad campaign as attractive as the ordering system?

**PROBLEM 19.3**

Setting Sales Price and Computing the Break-Even Point

**LO 4–7**

Thermal Tent, Inc., is a newly organized manufacturing business that plans to manufacture and sell 50,000 units per year of a new product. The following estimates have been made of the company's costs and expenses (other than income taxes):

| | Fixed | Variable per Unit |
|---|---|---|
| Manufacturing costs: | | |
|    Direct materials . . . . . . . . . . . . . . . . . . . . . . . . . . . . . . . . . . . . . . . . . | | $47 |
|    Direct labor . . . . . . . . . . . . . . . . . . . . . . . . . . . . . . . . . . . . . . . . . . . . . | | 32 |
|    Manufacturing overhead . . . . . . . . . . . . . . . . . . . . . . . . . . . . . . . . . . . | $340,000 | 4 |
| Period expenses: | | |
|    Selling expenses . . . . . . . . . . . . . . . . . . . . . . . . . . . . . . . . . . . . . . . . . | | 1 |
|    Administrative expenses . . . . . . . . . . . . . . . . . . . . . . . . . . . . . . . . . . . | 200,000 | |
| Totals . . . . . . . . . . . . . . . . . . . . . . . . . . . . . . . . . . . . . . . . . . . . . . . . . . . | $540,000 | $84 |

## Instructions

**a.** What should the company establish as the sales price per unit if it sets a target of earning an operating income of $260,000 by producing and selling 50,000 units during the first year of operations? (*Hint:* First compute the required contribution margin per unit.)

**b.** At the unit sales price computed in part **a**, how many units must the company produce and sell to break even? (Assume all units produced are sold.)

**c.** What will be the margin of safety (in dollars) if the company produces and sells 50,000 units at the sales price computed in part **a**? Using the margin of safety, compute operating income at 50,000 units.

**d.** Assume that the marketing manager thinks that the price of this product must be no higher than $94 to ensure market penetration. Will setting the sales price at $94 enable Thermal Tent to break even, given the plans to manufacture and sell 50,000 units? Explain your answer.

Blaster Corporation manufactures hiking boots. For the coming year, the company has budgeted the following costs for the production and sale of 30,000 pairs of boots:

**PROBLEM 19.4**

Estimating Costs and Profits

**LO 1, 4, 5**

|  | Budgeted Costs | Budgeted Costs per Pair | Percentage of Costs Considered Variable |
|---|---|---|---|
| Direct materials ......................... | $ 630,000 | 21 | 100% |
| Direct labor ............................. | 300,000 | 10 | 100 |
| Manufacturing overhead (fixed and variable) ....... | 720,000 | 24 | 25 |
| Selling and administrative expenses ............. | 600,000 | 20 | 20 |
| Totals ................................ | $2,250,000 | $75 | |

## Instructions

**a.** Compute the sales price per unit that would result in a budgeted operating income of $900,000, assuming that the company produces and sells 30,000 pairs. (*Hint:* First compute the budgeted sales revenue needed to produce this operating income.)

**b.** Assuming that the company decides to sell the boots at a unit price of $121 per pair, compute the following:

**1.** Total fixed costs budgeted for the year

**2.** Variable costs per unit

**3.** The unit contribution margin

**4.** The number of pairs that must be produced and sold annually to break even at a sales price of $121 per pair

Stop-n-Shop operates a downtown parking lot containing 800 parking spaces. The lot is open 2,500 hours per year. The parking charge per car is 50 cents per hour; the average customer parks two hours. Stop-n-Shop rents the lot for $7,250 per month. The lot supervisor is paid $24,000 per year. Five employees who handle the parking of cars are paid $300 per week for 50 weeks, plus $600 each for the two-week vacation period. Employees rotate vacations during the slow months when four employees can handle the reduced load of traffic. Lot maintenance, payroll taxes, and other costs of operating the parking lot include fixed costs of $3,000 per month and variable costs of 5 cents per parking-space hour.

**PROBLEM 19.5**

Preparing a "Break-Even" Graph

**LO 3–6**

## Instructions

**a.** Draw a cost-volume-profit graph for Stop-n-Shop on an annual basis. Use thousands of parking-space hours as the measure of volume of activity. [Stop-n-Shop has an annual capacity of 2 million parking-space hours (800 spaces × 2,500 hours per year).]

**b.** What is the contribution margin ratio? What is the annual break-even point in dollars of parking revenue?

c. Suppose that the five employees were taken off the hourly wage basis and paid 30 cents per car parked, with the same vacation pay as before. (1) How would this change the contribution margin ratio and total fixed costs? (Hint: The variable costs per parking-space hour will now include 15 cents, or one-half of the 30 cents paid to employees per car parked, because the average customer parks for two hours.) (2) What annual sales revenue would be necessary to produce operating income of $300,000 under these circumstances?

**PROBLEM 19.6**

Drawing a Cost-Volume-Profit Graph

**LO 3, 4, 6**

Rainbow Paints operates a chain of retail paint stores. Although the paint is sold under the Rainbow label, it is purchased from an independent paint manufacturer. Guy Walker, president of Rainbow Paints, is studying the advisability of opening another store. His estimates of monthly costs for the proposed location are:

| | |
|---|---|
| Fixed costs: | |
|    Occupancy costs . . . . . . . . . . . . . . . . . . . . . . . . . . . . . . . . . . . . . . . . . . . . . . . . . | $3,160 |
|    Salaries . . . . . . . . . . . . . . . . . . . . . . . . . . . . . . . . . . . . . . . . . . . . . . . . . . . . . . . . . | 3,640 |
|    Other . . . . . . . . . . . . . . . . . . . . . . . . . . . . . . . . . . . . . . . . . . . . . . . . . . . . . . . . . . . | 1,200 |
| Variable costs (including cost of paint) . . . . . . . . . . . . . . . . . . . . . . . . . . . . . . . . . . | $6 per gallon |

Although Rainbow stores sell several different types of paint, monthly sales revenue consistently averages $10 per gallon sold.

**Instructions**

a. Compute the contribution margin ratio and the break-even point in dollar sales and in gallons sold for the proposed store.

b. Draw a monthly cost-volume-profit graph for the proposed store, assuming 3,000 gallons per month as the maximum sales potential.

c. Walker thinks that the proposed store will sell between 2,200 and 2,600 gallons of paint per month. Compute the amount of operating income that would be earned per month at each of these sales volumes.

**PROBLEM 19.7**

Understanding Break-Even Relationships

**LO 1, 2, 4, 5, 6**

EasyWriter manufactures an erasable ballpoint pen, which sells for $1.75 per unit. Management recently finished analyzing the results of the company's operations for the current month. At a break-even point of 40,000 units, the company's total variable costs are $50,000 and its total fixed costs amount to $20,000.

**Instructions**

a. Calculate the contribution margin per unit.

b. Calculate the company's margin of safety if monthly sales total 45,000 units.

c. Estimate the company's monthly operating loss if it sells only 38,000 units.

d. Compute the total cost per unit at a production level of (1) 40,000 pens per month and (2) 50,000 pens per month. Explain the reason for the change in unit costs.

**PROBLEM 19.8**

Cost-Volume-Profit Analysis; Preparing a Graph

**LO 3–7**

Simon Teguh is considering investing in a vending machine operation involving 20 vending machines located in various plants around the city. The machine manufacturer reports that similar vending machine routes have produced a sales volume ranging from 800 to 1,000 units per machine per month. The following information is made available to Teguh in evaluating the possible profitability of the operation.

1. An investment of $45,000 will be required, $9,000 for merchandise and $36,000 for the 20 machines.

2. The machines have a service life of five years and no salvage value at the end of that period. Depreciation will be computed on the straight-line basis.

3. The merchandise (candy and soft drinks) retails for an average of 75 cents per unit and will cost Teguh an average of 25 cents per unit.

4. Owners of the buildings in which the machines are located are paid a commission of 5 cents per unit of candy and soft drinks sold.

5. One person will be hired to service the machines. The salary will be $1,500 per month.

6. Other expenses are estimated at $600 per month. These expenses do not vary with the number of units sold.

## Instructions

**a.** Determine the unit contribution margin and the break-even volume in units and in dollars per month.

**b.** Draw a monthly cost-volume-profit graph for sales volume up to 1,000 units per machine per month.

**c.** What sales volume in units and in dollars per month will be necessary to produce an operating income equal to a 30% annual return on Teguh's $45,000 investment? (Round to the nearest unit.)

**d.** Teguh is considering offering the building owners a flat rental of $30 per machine per month in lieu of the commission of 5 cents per unit sold. What effect would this change in commission arrangement have on his *monthly* break-even volume in terms of units?

Precision Systems manufactures tape decks and currently sells 18,500 units annually to producers of sound reproduction systems. Jay Wilson, president of the company, anticipates a 15% increase in the cost per unit of direct labor on January 1 of next year. He expects all other costs and expenses to remain unchanged. Wilson has asked you to assist him in developing the information he needs to formulate a reasonable product strategy for next year.

You are satisfied that volume is the primary factor affecting costs and expenses and have separated the semivariable costs into their fixed and variable segments. Beginning and ending inventories remain at a level of 1,000 units.

Below are the current-year data assembled for your analysis:

**PROBLEM 19.9**

Analyzing the Effects of Changes in Costs

**LO 4, 5, 6**

| | | |
|---|---:|---:|
| Sales price per unit | | $100 |
| Variable costs per unit: | | |
| Direct materials | $10 | |
| Direct labor | 20 | |
| Manufacturing overhead and selling and administrative expenses | 30 | 60 |
| Contribution margin per unit (40%) | | $ 40 |
| Fixed costs | | $390,000 |

## Instructions

**a.** What increase in the selling price is necessary to cover the 15% increase in direct labor cost and still maintain the current contribution margin ratio of 40%?

**b.** How many tape decks must be sold to maintain the current operating income of *$350,000* if the sales price remains at $100 and the 15% wage increase goes into effect? (*Hint:* First compute the unit contribution margin.)

**c.** Wilson believes that an additional $700,000 of machinery (to be depreciated at 20% annually) will increase present capacity (20,000 units) by 25%. If all tape decks produced can be sold at the present price of $100 per unit and the wage increase goes into effect, how would the estimated operating income before capacity is increased compare with the estimated operating income after capacity is increased? Prepare schedules of estimated operating income at full capacity *before* and *after* the expansion.

**Intel, Inc.**, produces two versions of its popular Pentium processors. For the coming year, fixed manufacturing costs are projected to equal $150,000. Information regarding forecast unit selling prices, variable costs, and demand for each processor is as follows:

**PROBLEM 19.10**

Analyzing the Effects of Changes in Costs and Volume

**LO 4, 6, 7**

| | Unit Selling Price | Unit Variable Manufacturing Costs | Units Demanded |
|---|:---:|:---:|:---:|
| Pentium | $100 | $ 40 | 5,000 |
| Pentium II | 530 | 110 | 1,000 |

## Instructions

Suppose **Intel** must choose only one of the processors to manufacture. Analyze the following scenarios.

**a.** Based on the above prices, costs, and demand, which processor will result in the highest operating income?

**b. Intel**'s marketing managers project that if the selling price of the Pentium processor is reduced by 25%, demand will double. Likewise, if the selling price of the Pentium II is reduced by 60%, demand will triple. Will adopting either of these alternative pricing strategies result in greater operating income than that found in part **a** (assuming no changes in manufacturing costs)?

**c. Intel** has an opportunity to adopt a new manufacturing process that will increase its fixed costs to $250,000. The new process will reduce the variable manufacturing costs of the Pentium to $20 per unit and of the Pentium II to $75 per unit. Assuming the process is adopted, which processor should be manufactured and at which of the two suggested prices should it be sold to earn the highest operating income? Should the process be adopted?

**d.** What overall strategy combination (that is, original versus new process, Pentium versus Pentium II, original versus alternative selling price) should be chosen to maximize expected operating income? If your answer is different than in part **a**, explain why it results in a greater level of operating income.

**PROBLEM 19.11**

Analyzing the Effects of Changes in Costs and Volume

**LO 4, 6**

Percula Farms raises marine fish for sale in the aquarium trade. Each year, Percula obtains a batch of approximately 1 million eggs from a local supplier. Percula's manager is trying to decide whether to use the farm's facilities to raise Maroon Clownfish or Queen Angelfish. Clownfish eggs cost $5,500 per batch, while angelfish eggs cost $9,500 per batch. Due to differences in needs, only one species may be raised at a time and only one batch of fish can be raised in any 52-week period.

With current facilities, approximately 10% of clownfish eggs and 5% of angelfish eggs can be successfully raised to maturity. Clownfish take approximately 35 weeks to grow to a salable size, while angelfish take 50 weeks. Angelfish also require more care than clownfish. Each week, angelfish need two complete water changes and 20 feedings, while clownfish need only one water change and 15 feedings. Each feeding costs $150 and each water change costs $1,000. Heating and lighting costs equal $400 per week of rearing, regardless of which fish are being raised. Fixed overhead costs for the year amount to $80,000. Percula can sell clownfish for $4 each and angelfish for $10 each.

**Instructions**

**a.** Which species should Percula raise to earn the highest operating income for the year?

**b.** Other than fixed costs, which factors or categories of costs seem to have the greatest influence on operating income?

**c.** Percula's manager is considering the following improvements, each of which will cost an additional $8,000 for the year. Due to resource limitations, only one can be implemented.

1. Purchasing a higher quality filter material that will significantly improve water conditions in the rearing tanks. The higher water quality will increase the survival rates to 12% for clownfish and 6% for angelfish. The need for water changes will also be reduced to one each week for both species of fish. Due to the higher yields, feeding costs will increase to $160 each.

2. Installing newer, more efficient equipment that will reduce heating and lighting costs to $300 per week of rearing. The new equipment will promote more stable conditions, increasing the survival rates of clownfish to 10.5% and of angelfish to 5.5%. The slight change in survival rates is not expected to increase feeding costs.

Using your answers to part **b** above (with no calculations), which options do you think will be more beneficial?

**d.** Perform the necessary calculations to check if your answer to part **c** was correct. Should either of the investments be undertaken, and if so, which fish species should be raised?

**PROBLEM 19.12**

CVP with Multiple Products

**LO 4, 5, 6**

Lifefit Products sells running shoes and shorts. The following is selected per-unit information for these two products:

|  | Shoes | Shorts |
|---|---|---|
| Sales price | $50 | $5 |
| Variable costs and expenses | 35 | 1 |
| Contribution margin | $15 | $4 |

Fixed costs and expenses amount to *$378,000* per month.

Lifefit has total sales of $1 million per month, of which 80% results from the sale of running shoes and the other 20% from sales of shorts.

## Instructions

**a.** Compute separately the contribution margin ratio for each line of products.

**b.** Assuming the current sales mix, compute:

1. Average contribution margin ratio of total monthly sales.
2. Monthly operating income.
3. The monthly break-even sales volume (stated in dollars).

**c.** Assume that through aggressive marketing, Lifefit is able to *shift its sales mix* toward more sales of shorts. Total sales remain $1 million per month, but now 30% of this revenue stems from sales of shorts. Using this new sales mix, compute:

1. Average contribution margin ratio of total monthly sales.
2. Monthly operating income.
3. The monthly break-even sales volume (stated in dollars).

**d.** Explain *why* the company's financial picture changes so significantly with the new sales mix.

Assume that you are preparing a seminar on cost-volume-profit analysis for nonaccountants. Sev-

# CASES AND UNSTRUCTURED PROBLEMS

eral potential attendees have approached you and have asked why they should be interested in learning about your topic. The individuals include:

1. A factory worker who serves as her company's labor union representative in charge of contract negotiations.
2. A purchasing agent in charge of ordering raw materials for a large manufacturing company.
3. A vice president of sales for a large automobile company.
4. A director of research and development for a pharmaceutical company.

## Instructions

What unique reasons would you give each of these individuals to motivate them in coming to your seminar?

Purple Cow operates a chain of drive-ins selling primarily ice cream products. The following information is taken from the records of a typical drive-in now operated by the company:

**CASE 19.1**

CVP from Different Points of View

**CASE 19.2**

Evaluating Marketing Strategies

**LO 1, 4, 5, 6, 7**

| | | |
|---|---|---|
| Average selling price of ice cream per gallon | | $ 14.80 |
| Number of gallons sold per month | | 3,000 |
| Variable costs per gallon: | | |
| Ice cream | $4.60 | |
| Supplies (cups, cones, toppings, etc.) | 2.20 | |
| Total variable expenses per gallon | | $ 6.80 |
| Fixed costs per month: | | |
| Rent on building | | $ 2,200.00 |
| Utilities and upkeep | | 760.00 |
| Wages, including payroll taxes | | 4,840.00 |
| Manager's salary, including payroll taxes but | | |
| excluding any bonus | | 2,500.00 |
| Other fixed expenses | | 1,700.00 |
| Total fixed costs per month | | $12,000.00 |

Based on these data, the monthly break-even sales volume is determined as follows:

$$\frac{\$12{,}000 \text{ (fixed costs)}}{\$8.00 \text{ (contribution margin per unit)}} = 1{,}500 \text{ gallons (or \$22,200)}$$

### Instructions

a. Currently, all store managers have contracts calling for a bonus of 20 cents per gallon for each gallon sold *beyond* the break-even point. Compute the number of gallons of ice cream that must be sold per month in order to earn a monthly operating income of $10,000 (round to the nearest gallon).

b. To increase operating income, the company is considering the following two alternatives:

1. Reduce the selling price by an average of $2.00 per gallon. This action is expected to increase the number of gallons sold by 20%. (Under this plan, the manager would be paid a salary of $2,500 per month without a bonus.)

2. Spend $3,000 per month on advertising without any change in selling price. This action is expected to increase the number of gallons sold by 10%. (Under this plan, the manager would be paid a salary of $2,500 per month without a bonus.)

Which of these two alternatives would result in the higher monthly operating income? How many gallons must be sold per month under each alternative for a typical outlet to break even? Provide schedules in support of your answers.

c. Draft a memo to management indicating your recommendations with respect to these alternative marketing strategies.

---

## BUSINESS WEEK ASSIGNMENT
BusinessWeek

**CASE 19.3**

Variable and Fixed Costs in E-Commerce

**LO 1, 4, 6**

According to a *Business Week* article by David Rocks titled "UPS: Will This IPO Deliver" (November 15, 1999)

The explosion of e-commerce should also give **UPS** a boost, as shoppers buy on the Web and have purchases shipped home or to the office. . . . Still it's not likely that **UPS** can get the same kind of explosive bottom-line growth that a pure e-commerce play can achieve. After all, to move all those packages, it must add trucks and drivers; Web retailers, on the other hand, incur relatively few additional fixed costs to accommodate higher volumes.

### Instructions

For this assignment, if your last name begins with M through Z, focus on **Amazon.com**. However, if your last name begins with A through L, focus on **UPS**.

a. Identify types of variable and fixed product costs that would be specific to your assigned company and not likely to be costs encountered by the other company. For each cost, explain why they would not likely be incurred by the other company. (For additional help, visit the investor relations portion of www.amazon.com or www.ups.com.)

b. Explain which company, **Amazon.com** or **UPS**, would have a higher contribution margin ratio and why.

---

## INTERNET ASSIGNMENT

**INTERNET 19.1**

Gross Margin Versus Contribution Margin

**LO 4**

Visit the home page of the **Ford Motor Company** at the following address:

**www.ford.com**

Locate "Investor Information" and access the most recent annual report. Locate the note entitled "10-year Vehicle Factory Sales Summary."

## Instructions

**a.** For the most recent year, how many total vehicles (cars and trucks) were sold by **Ford** worldwide?

**b.** Using the "Automotive" section of the income statement, calculate the average manufacturing cost per vehicle sold. Calculate the average sales revenue per vehicle sold. What is the average gross profit earned per vehicle sold?

**c.** Conceptually, what is the difference between the contribution margin per vehicle and the gross profit per vehicle you calculated in part **b**?

**d.** Can you use the financial statements to calculate contribution margin per vehicle?

*Internet sites are time and date sensitive. It is the purpose of these exercises to have you explore the Internet. You may need to use the Yahoo! search engine* http://www.yahoo.com *(or other favorite search engine) to find a company's current web address.*

## OUR COMMENTS ON THE "YOUR TURN" CASES

**As a Manager (p. 813)**   An increase of 50 passengers per flight will cause an increase in any ground operations cost that is related to an activity that varies with number of passengers on each plane. For example, baggage handlers, ticket agents, the plane's cabin maintenance crew, and so on will all have more work per flight. If the total number of flights remains unchanged, then additional personnel may be necessary in each of these categories. Ground operations costs that may not be affected are costs that vary by the number of flights—for example, landing and takeoff fees, gate charges, external plane maintenance, de-icing, and so on.

**As a Plant Accountant (p. 822)**   You should inform the plant manager that the overhead application rate must be adjusted if the monthly production increases to 1,500 units. The Institute of Management Accountants has adopted a code of ethical conduct that includes the following description of integrity for management accountants:

> Management accountants have a responsibility to avoid actual or apparent conflicts of interest and advise all appropriate parties of any potential conflict.[1]

This directive implies that you have an obligation to avoid the apparent conflict the arises because of the connection between the overhead application rate and the possible bonus. It also suggests that all appropriate parties to any conflict of interest be informed and that would be your immediate supervisor, the plant manager.

**As a Product-Line Manager (p. 823)**   In order to make the decision about the additional advertising expenditure and the amount of incremental East Coast sales it is likely to generate, you as the product-line manager should seek the following additional information:

1. Competitors' likely reaction to your expansion
2. Additional value chain costs such as distribution, logistics, and so on
3. The possibility of creating additional capacity through acquisitions
4. The probability of changes in raw materials costs due to increased demand
5. Other markets for expansion that might be more profitable (for example, nice weather locations)

## ANSWERS TO SELF-TEST QUESTIONS

**1.** a     **2.** c (from $25,000 to $27,000)     **3.** d ($20,000)     **4.** b     **5.** d

---

[1]Source: www.imanet.org/content/About_IMA/EthicsCenter/Code_of_Ethics/Ethical_Standards.htm

# INCREMENTAL ANALYSIS

## Learning Objectives

*After studying this chapter, you should be able to:*

1. Explain what makes information relevant to a particular business decision.

2. Discuss the relevance of opportunity costs, sunk costs, and out-of-pocket costs in making business decisions.

3. Use incremental analysis in common business decisions.

4. Discuss how contribution margin can be maximized when one factor limits productive capacity.

5. Identify nonfinancial considerations and creatively search for better courses of action.

Office Depot, Inc.

# Office Depot, Inc.

As the Internet matures, some old brick-and-mortar retailers such as **Office Depot, Inc.** are having the last laugh according to David Rocks in his *Business Week* article, "Why Office Depot Loves the Net" (September 27, 1999). **Office Depot** has leveraged its solid brand name, extensive local distribution, and hefty purchasing power to match and undercut discount-minded cyber-rivals.

By focusing primarily on business-to-business, **Office Depot** created customized Web pages for its corporate clients. Customers also can use the Net to check inventory at the nearest store or warehouse. Thus **Office Depot** has used the Net to leverage their bricks and mortar. Because **Office Depot** was able to create its Net business on an existing network of warehouses, 2,000 delivery trucks, and phone-order sales to its existing customer base, the overall incremental investment to become a Web-based company was near zero.

● ● ●

In making the decision to launch their Web-based business, **Office Depot** needed to assess the relevant costs and revenues associated with the Internet venture. This decision-making approach is called incremental analysis and it helps companies such as **Office Depot** use their existing assets more efficiently. This chapter explains incremental analysis and shows you how to apply it to a variety of business decisions.

## THE CHALLENGE OF CHANGING MARKETS

Short-run business decisions are inherently different from future-oriented, long-run strategic plans. Short-run decisions are made with a fixed set of resources and must meet the demands of the current marketplace. There is no time to create demand or acquire a significantly different resource base. However, all organizations engage in long-run strategic planning and short-run decision making simultaneously.

This chapter focuses on short-run decisions sometimes referred to as *incremental decision making*. We focus on common concepts used for short-run decisions such as sunk costs, opportunity costs, out-of-pocket costs, and incremental costs and revenues. These concepts are important in several universal business decision settings and are illustrated here for these specific decisions: special order decisions, product mix decisions, make or buy decisions, and joint product decisions. We begin with a very simple but familiar decision setting to allow you to become familiar with the ideas and terminology.

## THE CONCEPT OF RELEVANT COST INFORMATION

Kevin Anderson is a sophomore at the University of Minnesota in Minneapolis. Following the most brutal winter ever recorded in the state's history, Anderson is faced with an extremely important decision: Should he drive to Miami for spring break, or should he fly?

If he drives, he will leave on Saturday, stay in a roadside motel Saturday night, and arrive in Miami late Sunday evening. This option will allow him to enjoy five full days in Miami (Monday through Friday). However, he would have to leave the following Saturday, and spend another Saturday night in a motel, to arrive back in Minneapolis late Sunday evening.

If he flies, he will simply leave on Saturday morning and arrive in Miami late that night. This option will allow him to relax on the beach for seven full days before having to fly back to Minnesota the following Sunday.

To help make his decision as objective as possible, Kevin has compiled a list of what he believes are the most relevant factors affecting his decision:

- Cost per night to stay in a motel is $80.
- Cost to have someone watch Rex (Kevin's dog) is $5 per day.
- Eating out costs approximately $20 per day.
- In February, Kevin paid $600 for six months' car insurance.
- Cost of gasoline to drive to Miami and back is about $200.
- An airline ticket and taxi service cost $500.

Let's help Kevin analyze this information and make a decision regarding his vacation plans.

If he decides to drive to Florida, he must stay a total of eight nights in a motel (two nights on the interstate and six nights in Miami). If he decides to fly, he must also stay eight nights in a motel (from Saturday through Saturday in Miami). Thus, if we assume that the cost of a room in Miami does not differ significantly from the cost of a room along the interstate, motel charges are not relevant in deciding between driving or flying.

The same logic applies to the cost of caring for Rex and the cost of Kevin's meals. Regardless of how Kevin gets to Miami, he will be away from Minneapolis a total of nine days and eight nights. Thus Rex will require the same amount of care, and Kevin's total food costs will be about the same, whether he drives or flies.

How about the $600 Kevin spent in February for car insurance? This cost has already been incurred and will not be affected by whether Kevin drives or flies. Such past costs, which cannot be affected by future decisions, are termed **sunk costs**. Sunk costs are *not relevant* to making decisions about the future.

In financial terms, Kevin's decision can be made by comparing the $200 he would spend for gasoline if he drives to the $500 he would spend for an airline ticket and taxi if he flies. Thus we may be tempted to tell him to drive and save $300.

However, there are other nonfinancial factors Kevin may wish to consider. For instance, how much does he value the two extra days he can spend on the beach if he flies? What physical condition will he be in if he decides to drive? How much "wear-and-tear" must his car endure if he drives? Might his car break down and spoil his plans? Which mode of transportation is the safest?

In the remainder of this chapter we will learn how to identify and use information relevant to specific types of business decisions. Although our discussion will take place in a business context, many of the fundamental concepts involved are similar to those faced by Kevin Anderson.

## Relevant Information in Business Decisions

Identifying all of the information relevant to a particular business decision is a challenging task, because relevance is a broad concept. The process requires an understanding of quantitative and *qualitative* information, a grasp of legal issues, sensitivity to ethical concerns, and an ability to discern fact from opinion. In short, identifying the information relevant to a decision requires *judgment*—and more careful thought than first meets the eye. To simplify matters, our discussion will focus primarily on relevant *financial information*—namely, costs and revenues.

**LO 1**

Explain what makes information relevant to a particular business decision.

Virtually all business decisions involve choosing among alternative courses of action. The only information relevant to a decision is that *which varies among the possible courses of action being considered.* Costs, revenues, and other factors that *do not vary* among possible courses of action *are not relevant* to the decision.

To illustrate the concept of relevant information, assume that the Redstar Ketchup Company is closed for a labor strike. During the strike, Redstar is incurring costs of approximately $15,000 per week for utilities, interest, and salaries of nonstriking employees. A major film company has offered to rent the ketchup factory for a week at a price of $10,000 to shoot several scenes of a new Robo Cop movie. If the factory is rented, Redstar's management estimates that its cleanup costs will amount to nearly $2,000. Based solely on this information, would it be profitable to rent the ketchup factory to the film company?

If the factory is rented, Redstar's profitability for the week may be measured as follows:

| | | |
|---|---:|---:|
| Revenue | | $10,000 |
| Costs and expenses: | | |
| Weekly factory expenses | $15,000 | |
| Cleanup costs | 2,000 | 17,000 |
| Operating income (loss) | | $(7,000) |

Does an anticipated operating loss of $7,000 mean that Redstar should refuse the film company's offer? A closer examination reveals that not all of the information in this income statement is *relevant* to the decision at hand. Indeed, the $15,000 in weekly factory expenses will continue *whether or not* the factory is rented to the film company.

Thus the relevant factors in this decision are the *differences* in the costs incurred and the revenue earned under the alternative courses of action (renting or not renting). These differences are referred to often as **incremental (or differential) costs** and **revenues**. The following analysis focuses upon these incremental revenues and costs:

| | Reject Offer | Accept Offer | Incremental Analysis |
|---|---|---|---|
| Revenue . . . . . . . . . . . . . . . . . . . . . . . . . . . . . . . . . . | $     0 | $10,000 | $10,000 |
| Costs and expenses: | | | |
| Weekly factory expenses . . . . . . . . . . . . . . . . . . . . | (15,000) | (15,000) | 0 |
| Estimated cleanup costs . . . . . . . . . . . . . . . . . . . . | 0 | (2,000) | (2,000) |
| Operating income (loss) . . . . . . . . . . . . . . . . . . . . . . | $(15,000) | $ (7,000) | $ 8,000 |

Our analysis shows that accepting the film company's offer will result in $10,000 of incremental revenue but only $2,000 in incremental costs. Thus renting the ketchup factory to the film company will benefit Redstar by reducing its operating loss for the week by $8,000.

Before we begin to examine relevant information related to specific types of business decisions, it is appropriate to introduce three important cost concepts: (1) opportunity costs, (2) sunk costs, and (3) out-of-pocket costs.

## Opportunity Costs

**LO 2**

Discuss the relevance of opportunity costs, sunk costs, and out-of-pocket costs in making business decisions.

An **opportunity cost** is the benefit that *could have been obtained* by pursuing an alternative course of action. For example, assume that you pass up a summer job that pays $4,000 to attend summer school. The $4,000 may be viewed as an opportunity cost of attending summer school.

Although opportunity costs are *not recorded* in a company's accounting records, they are important factors to consider in many business decisions. Unfortunately, they sometimes are *not known* at the time a decision is made. To illustrate, consider the previous example involving the Redstar Ketchup Company.

We concluded that Redstar could reduce its operating loss by $8,000 by renting its factory to the film company. Assume, however, that the labor strike ends *just before filming begins*. As a consequence, Redstar must forgo any profit that the factory could have earned during the week that filming is in process. Thus, if operating profit for the week could have totaled $25,000, the *opportunity cost* of renting to the film company is the $25,000 forgone.

## Sunk Costs Versus Out-of-Pocket Costs

As mentioned earlier, a *sunk cost* is one that has *already been incurred* and cannot be changed by future actions. For example, Redstar's investment in its ketchup factory is a sunk cost. This cost will not change regardless of whether Redstar rents the factory, resumes operations, or lets the building stand vacant.

The only costs *relevant* to a decision are those that *vary* among the courses of action being considered. Sunk costs are *not relevant* because they *cannot be changed*, regardless of what decision is made.

In contrast to sunk costs, the term **out-of-pocket cost** is often used to describe costs that have *not yet* been incurred and that *may vary* among the possible courses of action. For example, Redstar's estimated cleanup expenditures are considered out-of-pocket costs. Out-of-pocket costs are normally identified as relevant in most business decisions.

Airlines and hotels have recognized the sunk cost of unused capacity and created strategies over the years to segment their customers by their willingness to pay. Airlines, for example, have offered super low fares with restrictions for travelers on tight budgets and created business-class seating for those willing to pay more. Now prices for seats on the same flight can be as unique as snowflakes.

Its not clear if these same management strategies can be applied to other industries. The sunk cost of unused capacity in the car and steel industries also results in the opportunity cost of lost revenues. So it makes sense to cut prices to fill capacity, but only if other customers are willing to pay more. However, this requires segmenting the market so that full-price customers can't see the bargains that others are getting. As auto companies move to made-to-order sales over the Internet, they may use such management strategies to help them create similar market segments.

**MANAGEMENT STRATEGY**

Cash effects differ among the concepts of opportunity costs, sunk costs, and out-of-pocket costs. Sunk costs represent cash outflows that have already occurred. No cash flow effects are associated with opportunity costs. They do not represent cash outflows or inflows. Out-of-pocket costs usually refer to planned cash outflows. Considering the cash effects of short-run business decisions is critical in an ongoing enterprise. More small businesses fail because of poor short-run cash planning than for any other reason.

**CASH EFFECTS**

# INCREMENTAL ANALYSIS IN COMMON BUSINESS DECISIONS

Let us now see how incremental analysis can be used in a variety of business decisions.

## Special Order Decisions

Companies sometimes receive large special orders to provide merchandise at less than the regular price. Typically, these orders are not from a company's regular customers.

To illustrate, assume that Par Four manufactures golf balls that it distributes exclusively through professional golf shops in the United States. Although the company has the capacity to manufacture 2 million balls per month, its current sales volume requires that only 800,000 units be produced. At this level of output, monthly manufacturing costs average approximately $480,000, or *$0.60* per ball as follows:

**LO 3**

Use incremental analysis in common business decisions.

| Manufacturing costs: | |
|---|---|
| Variable ($0.20 per ball × 800,000 balls) | $160,000 |
| Fixed | 320,000 |
| Total cost of manufacturing 800,000 balls per month | $480,000 |
| Average manufacturing cost per ball ($480,000 ÷ 800,000 balls) | $  0.60 |

*Average cost per ball*

Assume that Par Four receives a special order from NGC, a company that sells golf products in Japan, for 500,000 "special label" golf balls per month. The balls would be imprinted with the NGC name and logo and would not in any way be identified with Par Four.

To avoid direct competition with Par Four's regular customers, NGC has agreed not to sell these balls outside of Japan. However, it is willing to pay Par Four only *$250,000* per month for the special order, which amounts to *$0.50* per ball. Would it be profitable for Par Four to accept this order?

At first glance, the order appears to be unprofitable. Not only is NGC's offer of $0.50 per ball much less than the regular sales price of $1.25, it is even less than Par Four's *$0.60* per-unit manufacturing cost. However, before we decide to reject NGC's order, let us first perform an incremental analysis of the costs and revenue relevant to this decision:

| | Production Level | | |
| --- | --- | --- | --- |
| | Without Special Order (800,000 balls) | With Special Order (1,300,000 balls) | Incremental Analysis |
| Sales: | | | |
| Regular sales @ $1.25 . . . . . . . . . . | $1,000,000 | $1,000,000 | $ –0– |
| Special order @ $0.50 . . . . . . . . . . . | –0– | 250,000 | 250,000 |
| Manufacturing costs: | | | |
| Variable @ $0.20 per ball . . . . . . . . | (160,000) | (260,000) | (100,000) |
| Fixed manufacturing costs | | | |
| per month . . . . . . . . . . . . . . . . . | (320,000) | (320,000) | –0– |
| Gross profit on sales . . . . . . . . . . . . | $ 520,000 | $ 670,000 | $ 150,000 |

Our analysis indicates that accepting NGC's special order would generate incremental revenue of $250,000 and incremental costs of $100,000. Therefore, the order would *increase* Par Four's monthly gross profit on sales by *$150,000*.

The relevant factors in this type of decision are the incremental (additional) revenues that will be earned and the incremental costs that will be incurred by accepting the order. Only the additional variable costs of $0.20 per unit are relevant to this decision, because the fixed costs remain $320,000 regardless of whether the order is accepted or not. Thus the $0.60 average manufacturing cost, which includes fixed costs per unit, is *not relevant* to this decision.[1]

We can reach the same conclusion regarding this special order by returning to the concept of *contribution margin* discussed in Chapter 19. Recall that a product's contribution margin per unit is its selling price per unit less its unit variable cost. In our example, the unit selling price of the special order is $0.50, and the unit variable cost is $0.20. Thus the contribution margin associated with the special order is *$0.30 per unit*. In other words, each golf ball sold to NGC *contributes $0.30 to Par Four's operating profit. Thus the special order should increase operating income by $150,000 per month* (500,000 balls × $0.30 per unit).

In evaluating the merits of a special order such as the one received by Par Four, managers should consider the effect that filling the order might have on the company's regular sales volume and selling prices. Obviously, it would not be wise for Par Four to sell golf balls at $0.50 apiece to a domestic company, which might then try to sell the balls to Par Four's regular customers for less than Par Four's normal selling price of $1.25 per ball. Par Four's management should also consider how the company's regular cus-

---

[1] In our discussion, we evaluate only the *profitability* of accepting this order. Some countries have "antidumping" laws that legally prohibit a foreign company from selling its products in that country at a price below the average full manufacturing cost per unit. Par Four should, of course, consider the legal as well as the economic implications of accepting this special order.

tomers might react if word gets out about the special order. These customers may also demand a $0.50-per-ball selling price!

### You as a Sales Representative

Assume that you are a sales representative for Par Four. One of your best customers, Clubs & Caddies, a chain of retail golf shops, heard about the special order shipment to NGC in Japan. Clubs & Caddies has been paying $0.80 per ball and would like the same special order price given to NGC. In fact the purchasing manager at Clubs & Caddies said it would be unethical if you do not sell at the same price per ball that you charge NGC. How should you respond?

*Our comments appear on page 869.

YOUR TURN

In summary, incremental analysis is a useful tool for evaluating the effects of expected short-term changes in revenues and costs. Managers should always be alert, however, to the long-run implications of their actions.

## Production Constraint Decisions

In the previous example, we demonstrated how a contribution margin approach can be used in incremental analyses. The contribution margin approach often applies when the availability of a particular production input (such as a raw material, skilled labor, floor space, etc.) is limited. An understanding of contribution margin concepts enables managers to decide what products to manufacture (or purchase for resale) and what products to eliminate in order to *maximize the contribution margin per unit of the limited input.*

Assume that you are offered two equally satisfactory jobs, one paying $8 per hour and one paying $12 per hour. If you are able to work only 40 hours per week and you wish to maximize the amount you earn per hour of your time, you would naturally choose the job paying $12 per hour. For the same reason, if a company's output is limited by a particular resource, such as labor or machine-hours, management should use this resource in a way that maximizes total contribution margin.

To illustrate this concept, assume that Fran's Studio creates three products: (1) watercolor paintings, (2) oil paintings, and (3) custom frames. Total output, however, is limited to what can be produced in 6,000 hours of direct labor. The average contribution margin per direct labor hour required to complete each of the studio's products is as follows:

**LO 4**

Discuss how contribution margin can be maximized when one factor limits productive capacity.

| Product | Unit Selling Price | − Unit Variable Costs | = Unit Contribution Margin | ÷ Direct Labor Hours Required per Unit | = Contribution Margin per Hour |
|---|---|---|---|---|---|
| Watercolor paintings . . . . . . . . | $ 90 | $30 | $ 60 | 2 | $30 |
| Oil paintings . . . . . . . | 160 | 60 | 100 | 4 | 25 |
| Custom frames . . . . . | 35 | 15 | 20 | 1 | 20 |

Notice that oil paintings generate the highest contribution margin on a per-unit basis ($100). However, watercolors are the studio's most profitable product in terms of their *contribution margin per direct-labor hour.*

In general, when capacity is constrained by the limited availability of a particular input, a company should attempt to maximize its contribution margin per unit *of that input.* The following table shows the total contribution margin Fran's Studio would earn if it used all 6,000 of its annual labor hours to create a single product line:

| | Total Capacity × (Hours) | Contribution Margin per Hour of Direct Labor | Total Contribution = Margin If Only One Product Is Created |
|---|---|---|---|
| Watercolors . . . . . . . . . . . . . . . . . | 6,000 | $30 | $180,000 |
| Oil paintings . . . . . . . . . . . . . . . | 6,000 | 25 | 150,000 |
| Custom frames . . . . . . . . . . . . . | 6,000 | 20 | 120,000 |

This schedule shows that the studio can maximize its total contribution margin and, therefore, its operating income, by creating only *watercolor paintings*.

In most cases, however, a company cannot simply manufacture the single product that is most profitable. For example, the demand for watercolors may not be sufficient to allow Fran's Studio to sell all of the watercolor paintings it is capable of producing. In this case, operating income would be maximized by creating oil paintings once the demand for watercolors is satisfied. If the demand for oil paintings is also met, any remaining direct labor hours would be devoted to producing custom frames.

Another important consideration is that some of the studio's labor hours may have to be used to produce custom frames that *support the sale of paintings*. Even though frames contribute less to the studio's operating income than paintings do, many customers may wish to have the studio frame the paintings they purchase. Thus, in addition to understanding the contribution margins of its products, a company must also attempt to understand the complementary nature of its products. That is, does the sale of one product contribute to the sale of another? Products for which sales of one contribute to the sales of another are called **complementary products**.

**YOUR TURN**

### You as a Store Manager

Assume that you are the store manager of Fran's Studio. Fran would like you to expand the store by selling posters and prints in addition to the watercolors and oil paintings currently produced by the studio. Do you think the posters and prints are complementary with the other products sold at Fran's Studio? Explain why or why not.

*Our comments appear on page 869.

## Make or Buy Decisions

In many manufacturing operations, a company must decide whether to produce a certain part required in the assembly of its finished products or to buy the part from outside suppliers. If the company is currently producing a part that could be purchased at a lower cost from outsiders, profits *may* be increased by a decision to buy the part and utilize the company's own manufacturing resources for other purposes.

For example, if a company can buy for $5 per unit a part that costs the company $6 per unit to produce, the choice seems to be clearly in favor of buying. But the astute reader will quickly raise the question "What is included in the cost of $6 per unit?" Assume that the $6 unit cost of producing a normal required volume of 10,000 units per month was determined as follows:

| Manufacturing costs: | |
|---|---|
| Direct materials . . . . . . . . . . . . . . . . . . . . . . . . . . . . . . . . . . . . . . . . . . . . . . . . . . | $ 8,000 |
| Direct labor . . . . . . . . . . . . . . . . . . . . . . . . . . . . . . . . . . . . . . . . . . . . . . . . . . . . . . | 12,500 |
| Variable overhead . . . . . . . . . . . . . . . . . . . . . . . . . . . . . . . . . . . . . . . . . . . . . . . . | 10,000 |
| Fixed overhead per month . . . . . . . . . . . . . . . . . . . . . . . . . . . . . . . . . . . . . . . . . . | 29,500 |
| Total cost of manufacturing 10,000 units per month . . . . . . . . . . . . . . . . . . . . . | $60,000 |
| Average manufacturing cost per unit ($60,000 ÷ 10,000 units) . . . . . . . . . . . . . . | $6 |

Assume that a review of operations indicates that if the production of this part were discontinued, all the cost of direct materials and direct labor plus $9,000 of variable overhead would be eliminated. In addition, $2,500 of the fixed overhead would be eliminated. These, then, are the *relevant costs* in producing the 10,000 units of the component part, and we can summarize them as follows:

| | Make the Part | Buy the Part | Incremental Analysis |
|---|---|---|---|
| Manufacturing costs for 10,000 units: | | | |
| Direct materials | $ 8,000 | | $ 8,000 |
| Direct labor | 12,500 | | 12,500 |
| Variable overhead | 10,000 | $ 1,000 | 9,000 |
| Fixed overhead | 29,500 | 27,000 | 2,500 |
| Purchase price of part, $5 per unit | | 50,000 | (50,000) |
| Total cost to acquire part | $60,000 | $78,000 | $(18,000) |

*Is it cheaper to make or to buy?*

Our analysis shows that making the part will cost $60,000 per month, while buying the part will cost $78,000. Thus the company will save $18,000 per month by continuing to make the part.

In our example, we assumed that only $9,000 of the variable overhead incurred in producing the part would be eliminated if the part were purchased. We also assumed that $2,500 of the fixed overhead could be eliminated if the part were purchased. The purpose of these assumptions was to show that not all variable costs are incremental and that some fixed costs may be incremental in a given situation.

What if the company could have used its production facilities to manufacture a new product line that would increase overall profitability by $25,000 per month? If this were the case, the $25,000 profit would be viewed as the *opportunity cost* of using the company's production facilities to manufacture a component part. Obviously, the company should not forego a $25,000 profit to save $18,000. Thus, when the opportunity cost is considered, it becomes evident that the company should buy the part and use its production facilities to manufacture the new product.

In addition to evaluating the opportunity costs associated with a make or buy decision, managers must evaluate other important concerns. For instance, does the decision to make or buy involve issues of product quality? Are there questions regarding the decision's impact on production scheduling and flexibility? Have certain long-term implications been considered such as product availability and maintaining reliable supplier relationships? Ignoring important questions such as these is a common source of error in incremental analyses.

 Make or buy decisions can have significant long-run strategic implications particularly in international settings. In the past, companies in Japan preferred not to source from suppliers outside of Japan. This policy can create significant problems if the company exports its finished product. For example, until relatively recently many automobile companies in Japan produced their autos in Japan and exported them to markets in the United States and Asia. In the late 1980s and early 1990s, foreign exchange fluctuations between the U.S. dollar and the Japanese yen made it difficult for Japan to sell products in the United States at a profit. In the 1990s Japanese auto companies changed their strategies and began building assembly plants in the countries where they sold their products. With this strategy the Japanese auto companies pay for the cost of production using the same currency that they receive from customers when they sell their product. This strategy allows a company to avoid foreign exchange fluctuation risk.

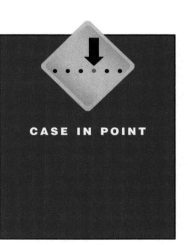

**CASE IN POINT**

## Sell, Scrap, or Rebuild Decisions

Another problem companies face is what to do with obsolete or defective products. Management must decide whether to devote the resources to rebuild these units, sell them at a reduced price, or simply scrap them.

To illustrate, assume that Computex, Inc., has in its inventory 500 computers that cost $325,000 to produce. Unfortunately, their processors now are considered technologically obsolete. Thus management must decide what to do with these machines. It is considering the following options:

1. Sell the computers "as is" to Television Shopping Network (TSN) for $250,000.
2. Sell them for $235,000 to surrounding school districts for use in their computer labs.
3. Scrap the existing processor in each machine and replace it with a faster, state-of-the-art chip at a total cost of $190,000. If this option is selected, the rebuilt computers could be sold for $450,000.

Regardless of which option Computex chooses, the $325,000 originally incurred to manufacture these computers is a *sunk cost* and is therefore *irrelevant* to the decision at hand. The only relevant costs and revenues are those that *vary* among the alternatives under consideration. An incremental analysis of the three options appears as follows:

|  | Sell to TSN | Sell to Schools | Rebuild |
|---|---|---|---|
| Incremental revenue | $250,000 | $235,000 | $450,000 |
| Incremental costs | 0 | 0 | 190,000 |
| Incremental income | $250,000 | $235,000 | $260,000 |

Notice that no matter which option Computex selects, it will *not be able* to fully recover the $325,000 that it already has invested in these computers.

Rebuilding the computers with the faster chip appears to be the company's most profitable course of action. However, management may wish to consider several other factors. For example, does Computex have *sufficient plant capacity* to rebuild these computers without reducing its production of other products?

If rebuilding these computers interferes with the production of other products, the "rebuild" option involves an *opportunity cost*—the profit foregone on the products that could have been manufactured instead. If this opportunity cost exceeds *$10,000*, Computex would maximize its income by selling these computers to TSN and using its production facilities to manufacture other products.

Next, there may be a long-term advantage in selling the computers to schools, even though this appears to be the *least* profitable alternative. Relative to selling the computers to TSN, selling to the schools involves a $15,000 opportunity cost. But management may consider this opportunity cost to be *cost-effective advertising*. The students who use these computers—and their parents—may become customers for other Computex products.

Incremental analysis provides an excellent starting point for many business decisions. Seldom, however, does this analysis tell the whole story.

**CASE IN POINT**

In 1994, **Adolph Coors Co.** launched a product called Zima, a clear malt concoction, designed to attract young consumers. **Coors** chose to expend significant out-of-pocket costs on Zima. However, despite lavishing 38% of **Coors'** entire 1994 advertising budget ($38 million) and much more on packaging, merchandising, and product development, Zima never sustained its expected market share. Analysts suggested that the loss suffered by **Coors** was not the out-of-pocket costs but the opportunity costs of diverting the time, money, and attention to an unsuccessful product.[2]

---

[2]Richard A. Melcher, "Why Zima Faded So Fast," *Business Week*, March 10, 1997.

## Joint Product Decisions

Many companies produce multiple products from common raw materials and a shared production process. Examples include oil refineries, lumber and steel mills, and meat processing companies. Products resulting from a shared manufacturing process are termed **joint products**, and the manufacturing costs that relate to these products as a group are called **joint costs**.

In such manufacturing processes, two business issues arise. One is how to allocate joint costs among the various types of products manufactured. The second incremental type of decision is whether some types of products should be *processed further* to create an even more valuable finished good.

**Joint Costs**   Let us first address the issue of joint costs. Assume that CharCore mixes together wood chips and pine oil. After joint manufacturing costs of *$2,000* have been incurred, this mixture separates into two salable products: granulated charcoal and methyl alcohol. How should the $2,000 in joint costs be allocated between these products?

There is no "right" way to allocate joint costs, but the most common method is in proportion to the *relative sales value* of the products produced. Assume that the quantity of charcoal produced by CharCore's $2,000 in joint manufacturing costs has a sales value of *$5,000* and that the alcohol has a sales value of *$9,000*. Thus the batch of products collectively has a sales value of *$14,000*.

The $2,000 in joint costs could be allocated between these products as follows:

| | |
|---|---:|
| Charcoal [$2,000 in joint costs × ($5,000/$14,000)] ......................... | $   714 |
| Alcohol [$2,000 in joint costs × ($9,000/$14,000)] ......................... | 1,286 |

**Decisions After the Split-Off Point**   Once joint products can be separated, they have reached what is called the **split-off point**. At this point, each product may be sold *independently of the other,* or it may be processed further.

Again consider CharCore. The company may sell its charcoal and alcohol after the split-off point without further processing, or it may continue processing either of these products. CharCore can use the granulated charcoal to manufacture air filters, and the methyl alcohol to make cleaning solvent. The following diagram illustrates CharCore's options and reflects current sales prices and manufacturing costs:

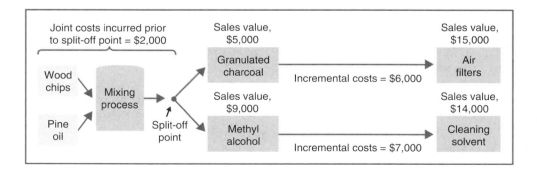

The decision of whether to sell the charcoal and alcohol or to continue processing is based on the incremental costs and revenues expected *after* the split-off point. An analysis of these costs and revenues appears as follows:

| | |
|---|---:|
| Revenue if charcoal is used to make air filters | $15,000 |
| Less: Revenue if charcoal is sold at split-off point | 5,000 |
|   Incremental revenue from air filters | 10,000 |
|   Less: Incremental cost to produce air filters | 6,000 |
| Net increase (decrease) in operating income from air filters | $ 4,000 |
| Revenue if alcohol is used to make cleaning solvent | $14,000 |
| Less: Revenue if alcohol is sold at split-off point | 9,000 |
|   Incremental revenue from solvent | 5,000 |
|   Less: Incremental cost to produce cleaning solvent | 7,000 |
| Net increase (decrease) in operating income from solvent | $ (2,000) |

Based on this analysis, CharCore currently should use its charcoal to produce air filters, but it should sell its alcohol at the split-off point. The optimal course of action may change, however, with fluctuations in the prices of these products or in incremental manufacturing costs.

## Concluding Comments

We have merely scratched the surface in discussing the possible kinds of analyses that might be prepared in making business decisions. Our coverage in this chapter, however, has been sufficient to establish the basic principles that lie behind such analyses. The profitability of a course of action depends on the *incremental* revenue and expenses. However, *opportunity costs* may play a major role in the decision.

**LO 5**

Identify nonfinancial considerations and creatively search for better courses of action.

We also have stressed that, in addition to quantitative information, many *nonfinancial* factors must be taken into consideration. It would be irresponsible and short-sighted for managers to seek solutions and base decisions entirely on revenue and cost figures. Indeed, most business decisions also require an examination of legal issues, a sensitivity to ethical implications, and an ability to distinguish fact from opinion. Thus, while incremental analysis is an excellent tool for evaluating alternative courses of action, managers should not automatically follow the first course of action that holds a promise of increased profitability. Rather, they should always be alert to the possibility that a more satisfactory, and perhaps more creative, solution exists.

**A SECOND LOOK**

### Office Depot, Inc.

Incremental analysis helps companies such as **Office Depot, Inc.** to make their existing assets more profitable. By recognizing that the incremental revenues significantly exceeded the incremental costs of using the World Wide Web to sell their products to corporate customers such as **Procter and Gamble Co.** and **MCI World Com Inc.**, **Office Depot** increased overall profitability without significantly altering their fixed asset base. The key was recognizing that the incremental cost of an electronic sale made over the Internet was much less than the incremental cost of sales made in stores or through catalog sales.

    When organizing the decision processes described in this chapter, companies typically use responsibility accounting procedures and techniques to assign the decision-making authority. Chapter 21 explains the different types of decision-making centers used by firms and shows how they are interrelated through a company's management accounting system.

# END-OF-CHAPTER REVIEW

## SUMMARY OF LEARNING OBJECTIVES

**LO 1**

**Explain what makes information relevant to a particular business decision.**

Only information that varies among the alternative courses of action being considered is relevant to the decision. Costs or revenues that do not vary among the alternative courses of action are not relevant to the decision.

**LO 2**

**Discuss the relevance of opportunity costs, sunk costs, and out-of-pocket costs in making business decisions.**

An opportunity cost is the benefit that could have been obtained by pursuing another course of action. Opportunity costs often are subjective, but they are important considerations in any business decision. Sunk costs, on the other hand, have already been incurred as a result of past actions. These costs cannot be changed regardless of the action taken and are not relevant to the decision at hand. Out-of-pocket costs will be incurred in the future and are relevant if they will vary among the possible courses of action.

**LO 3**

**Use incremental analysis in common business decisions.**

Incremental analysis is the technique of comparing one course of action to another by determining the differences expected to arise in revenue and in costs.

**LO 4**

**Discuss how contribution margin can be maximized when one factor limits productive capacity.**

Identify the production input factor that limits the amount of output. Then determine the output mix that maximizes the contribution margin per unit of the limiting factor.

**LO 5**

**Identify nonfinancial considerations and creatively search for better courses of action.**

Examples of relevant nonfinancial information include legal and ethical considerations and the long-run effects of decisions on company image, employee morale, and the environment. Also, managers should search creatively for alternative courses of action. Unless a company selects the best possible course of action, it incurs an opportunity cost. Opportunity costs are not recorded in the accounting records, but they may determine the success or failure of a business enterprise.

Throughout this chapter we have explored how managers identify and use relevant information to make business decisions. The decisions in our illustrations had mostly short-run consequences; that is, their impact affected only a single reporting period. In Chapters 21 through 23 we will learn how budgets are developed and used to assist managers in short-run planning. Chapter 24 shows how companies evaluate and reward managers' decision-making performance. In Chapter 25, we will examine how managers approach decisions having long-run consequences. We will discover that, unlike short-run decisions, long-run decisions are difficult, if not impossible, to reverse.

## KEY TERMS INTRODUCED OR EMPHASIZED IN CHAPTER 20

**complementary products** (p. 852) Those products for which sales of one may contribute to the sales of another.

**incremental (or differential) cost** (p. 847) The increase or decrease in total costs incurred by selecting one course of action over another.

**incremental (or differential) revenue** (p. 848) The increase or decrease in total revenue earned by selecting one course of action over another.

**joint costs** (p. 855) Costs incurred in manufacturing processes that produce several different products. Joint costs cannot be traced directly to the individual types of products manufactured and, therefore, must be allocated in a more or less arbitrary manner.

**joint products** (p. 855) Products that share, in part, common materials and production processes.

**opportunity cost** (p. 848) The benefit foregone by not pursuing an alternative course of action. Opportunity costs are not recorded in the accounting records but are important in making many types of business decisions.

**out-of-pocket costs** (p. 848) Costs that have not yet been incurred and that may vary among alternative courses of action.

**split-off point** (p. 855) The point at which separate and distinct joint products emerge from common materials and a shared production process.

**sunk cost** (p. 847) A cost that has been incurred as a result of past actions. Sunk costs are irrelevant to decisions involving future actions.

# DEMONSTRATION PROBLEM

Calkist Mfg. is a multiple product manufacturer. One product line consists of motors for lawn-mowers, and the company produces three different models. Calkist is currently considering a proposal from a supplier who wants to sell the company blades for the lawnmower motor line.

The company currently produces all the blades it requires. In order to meet customers' needs, Calkist currently produces three different blades for each motor model (nine different blades). The supplier is offering to provide five varieties of blades for each model. A total of fifteen blades would considerably expand the variety of cutting ability for the motors available to customers. The supplier would charge Calkist $25 per blade, regardless of blade type.

For the coming year Calkist has projected the costs of its own blade production as follows (based on projected volume of 10,000 units):

| | |
|---|---:|
| Direct materials . . . . . . . . . . . . . . . . . . . . . . . . . . . . . . . . . . . . . . . . . . . . . . . . . . . . | $ 75,000 |
| Direct labor . . . . . . . . . . . . . . . . . . . . . . . . . . . . . . . . . . . . . . . . . . . . . . . . . . . . . . . . | 65,000 |
| Variable overhead . . . . . . . . . . . . . . . . . . . . . . . . . . . . . . . . . . . . . . . . . . . . . . . . . . | 55,000 |
| Fixed overhead | |
|    Depreciation . . . . . . . . . . . . . . . . . . . . . . . . . . . . . . . . . . . . . . . . . . . . . . . . . . . | 50,000 |
|    Property taxes . . . . . . . . . . . . . . . . . . . . . . . . . . . . . . . . . . . . . . . . . . . . . . . . . | 15,000 |
|    Factory supervision . . . . . . . . . . . . . . . . . . . . . . . . . . . . . . . . . . . . . . . . . . . . | 35,000 |
| Total production costs . . . . . . . . . . . . . . . . . . . . . . . . . . . . . . . . . . . . . . . . . . . . . . | $295,000 |

Assume (1) the equipment utilized to produce the blades has no alternative use and no market value, (2) the space occupied by blade production will remain idle if the company purchases rather than makes the blades, and (3) factory supervision costs reflect the salary of a production supervisor who would be dismissed from the firm if blade production ceased.

### Instructions

**a.** Determine the net monetary advantage or disadvantage of purchasing (rather than manufacturing) the blades required for motor production in the coming year.

**b.** Determine the level of motor production where Calkist would be indifferent between buying and producing the blades. If the future volume level is predicted to decrease, would that influence Calkist's decision?

**c.** For this part only, assume that the space presently occupied by blade production could be leased to another firm for $45,000 per year. How would this affect the make or buy decision?

**d.** Name at least four other factors Calkist should take into account in making the decision.

## Solution to the Demonstration Problem

**a.** This is a make or buy decision, so compare the incremental cost to make with the incremental cost to buy.

| Incremental Costs Per Unit | Make the Blades |
|---|---:|
| Direct materials . . . . . . . . . . . . . . . . . . . . . . . . . . . . . . . . . . . . . . . . . . . . | $ 7.50 |
| ($75,000 ÷ 10,000 units) | |
| Direct labor . . . . . . . . . . . . . . . . . . . . . . . . . . . . . . . . . . . . . . . . . . . . . . | 6.50 |
| ($65,000 ÷ 10,000 units) | |
| Variable overhead . . . . . . . . . . . . . . . . . . . . . . . . . . . . . . . . . . . . . . . . | 5.50 |
| ($55,000 ÷ 10,000 units) | |
| Supervision . . . . . . . . . . . . . . . . . . . . . . . . . . . . . . . . . . . . . . . . . . . . . | 3.50 |
| ($35,000 ÷ 10,000 units) | |
|    Total cost . . . . . . . . . . . . . . . . . . . . . . . . . . . . . . . . . . . . . . . . . . . . | $23.00 |

Compare the cost to make the blades for 10,000 motors, $23.00, with the cost to buy, $25.00. There is a net $2.00 disadvantage if Calkist chose to buy the blades.

**b.** Calkist will be indifferent between buying and making the blades when the total costs are equal. Total costs for making and buying will be equal at the volume level where the variable costs per unit times the volume plus the fixed avoidable costs are equal to the supplier's offered cost of $25.00 per unit times the volume.

(Direct materials + Direct labor + Variable overhead) $\times$ Volume + Supervision = Cost to buy $\times$ Volume. Let volume in units = V

($7.50 + $6.50 + $5.50) $\times$ V + $35,000 = $25.00 $\times$ V

$19.50 $\times$ V + $35,000 = $25.00 $\times$ V

$35,000 = $25.00 $\times$ V − $19.50 $\times$ V

$35,000 = $5.50 $\times$ V

V = 6364 units of blades.

As volume of production decreases, Calkist's average per-unit cost of in-house production increases. If the volume falls below 6,364 motors, then Calkist will want to buy the blades from the supplier.

**c.** If the space presently occupied by blade production could be leased to another firm for $45,000 per year, Calkist would face an opportunity cost associated with in-house blade production for the 10,000 units of $4.50 per unit. Add that to the original cost:

$$\$23.00 + \$4.50 = \$27.50 = \text{New cost to make}$$

Now Calkist should buy because the cost to make, $27.50, is higher than the cost to buy, $25.00.

**d.** Other factors that Calkist should consider before choosing to buy from the outside supplier include the following:

- The quality of the supplier's products.
- The shipping reliability of the supplier.
- Alternative uses of production capacity.
- The impact on the current workforce if employees are laid off.
- The long-term financial stability of the supplier.
- Other suppliers' ability to provide the blades.
- The ability to generate new sales from the increased variety of blades.

## SELF-TEST QUESTIONS

*Answers to these questions appear on page 869.*

*The following data relate to questions 1 and 2.*

One of Phoenix Computer's products is WizardCard. The company currently produces and sells 30,000 WizardCards per month, although it has the plant capacity to produce 50,000 units per month. At the 30,000 unit-per-month level of production, the average per-unit cost of manufacturing WizardCards is $45, consisting of $15 in variable costs and $30 in fixed costs. Phoenix sells WizardCards to retail stores for $90 each. Computer Marketing Corp. has offered to purchase 10,000 WizardCards per month at a reduced price. Phoenix can manufacture these additional units with no change in fixed manufacturing costs.

**1.** In deciding whether to accept this special order from Computer Marketing Corp., Phoenix should be *least* concerned with:

**a.** What Computer Marketing Corp. intends to do with the WizardCards.

**b.** The $45 average cost of manufacturing WizardCards.

**c.** The opportunity cost of not accepting the order.

**d.** The incremental cost of manufacturing an additional 10,000 WizardCards per month.

2. Assume that Phoenix decides to accept the special order at a unit sales price that will add $400,000 per month to its operating income. The unit price of the special order will be:

   a. $85.

   b. $70.

   c. $55.

   d. Some other amount.

3. When faced with a limited availability of machine-hours, management should consider producing those products that:

   a. Have the highest contribution margin per unit.

   b. Have the highest contribution margin ratios.

   c. Require the fewest machine-hours to produce.

   d. Contribute the highest contribution margin per machine-hour.

4. Consultant Frank Alvarez recently commented that the most common error made by his clients is ignoring opportunity costs associated with business decisions. The costs Alvarez was referring to are:

   a. Benefits foregone by selecting one course of action over another.

   b. The out-of-pocket costs of implementing a particular business decision.

   c. Costs that make future opportunities possible.

   d. Costs that have made past opportunities possible.

5. Which of the following questions would *not* be relevant to a make or buy decision?

   a. Will the supplier make a product that is equal in quality to our own?

   b. Will the supplier meet our specified delivery dates?

   c. For how long will the supplier be committed to the quoted price?

   d. All of the above questions are relevant.

# ASSIGNMENT MATERIAL

## DISCUSSION QUESTIONS

1. Discuss what makes information "relevant."

2. A company regularly sells 100,000 washing machines at an average price of $250. The average cost of producing these machines is $180. Under what circumstances might the company accept an order for 20,000 washing machines at $175 per machine?

3. The Wilson Corporation produces a large number of fishing products. The costs per unit of a particular fishing reel are as follows:

| | |
|---|---:|
| Direct materials and direct labor | $7.00 |
| Variable factory overhead | 4.00 |
| Fixed factory overhead | 2.00 |

   The company recently decided to buy 10,000 fishing reels from another manufacturer for $12.50 per unit because "it was cheaper than our cost of $13.00 per unit." Evaluate the decision only on the basis of the cost data given.

4. Define *opportunity costs* and explain why they represent a common source of error in making cost analyses.

5. What is the difference between a *sunk cost* and an *out-of-pocket cost?*

6. What nonfinancial considerations should be taken into account when deciding whether to accept a special order?

7. Harvey Corporation produces several joint products from common materials and shared production processes. Why are costs incurred up to the split-off point not relevant in deciding which products Harvey sells at the split-off point and which products it processes further?

8. The **Gillette Corporation** sells blade razors near or below their manufacturing cost. It also sells razor blades that have a relatively high contribution margin. Explain why **Gillette** does not eliminate its unprofitable razor line and sell only blades.

9. Suggest an approach for maximizing profit when faced with scarce resources.

## EXERCISES

Listed below are seven technical accounting terms introduced or emphasized in this chapter.

| | |
|---|---|
| Opportunity cost | Sunk cost |
| Out-of-pocket cost | Split-off point |
| Joint products | Relevant information |
| Incremental analysis | |

**EXERCISE 20.1**

Accounting Terminology

**LO 1–5**

Each of the following statements may (or may not) describe one of these terms. For each statement, indicate the accounting term or terms described, or answer "none" if the statement does not correctly describe any of these terms.

a. Examination of differences between costs to be incurred and revenues to be earned under different courses of action.

b. A cost incurred in the past that cannot be changed as a result of future actions.

c. Costs and revenues that are expected to vary, depending on the course of action decided on.

d. The benefit foregone by not pursuing an alternative course of action.

e. Products made from common raw materials and shared production processes.

f. A cost yet to be incurred that will require future payment and may vary among alternative courses of action.

g. The point at which manufacturing costs are split equally between ending inventory and cost of goods sold.

Sutherland manufactures and sells 110,000 laser printers each month. A principal component part in each printer is its paper feed drive. Sutherland's plant currently has the monthly capacity to produce 150,000 drives. The unit costs of manufacturing these drives (up to 150,000 per month) are as follows:

**EXERCISE 20.2**

Incremental Analysis: Accepting a Special Order

**LO 1–3**

| | |
|---|---|
| Variable costs per unit: | |
|   Direct materials . . . . . . . . . . . . . . . . . . . . . . . . . . . . . . . . . . . . . . . . . . . . . . . | $45 |
|   Direct labor . . . . . . . . . . . . . . . . . . . . . . . . . . . . . . . . . . . . . . . . . . . . . . . | 25 |
|   Variable manufacturing overhead . . . . . . . . . . . . . . . . . . . . . . . . . . . . . . . . . . | 5 |
| Fixed costs per month: | |
|   Fixed manufacturing overhead . . . . . . . . . . . . . . . . . . . . . . . . . . . . . . . . . . | $1,430,000 |

Desk-Mate Printers has offered to buy 20,000 paper feed drives from Sutherland to be used in its own printers. Compute the following:

a. The average unit cost of manufacturing each paper feed drive assuming that Sutherland manufactures only enough drives for its own laser printers.

b. The incremental unit cost of producing an additional paper feed drive.

c. The per-unit sales price that Sutherland should charge Desk-Mate to earn $500,000 in monthly pretax profit on the sale of drives to Desk-Mate.

The cost to Swank Company of manufacturing 20,000 units of a particular part is $255,000, of which $100,000 is fixed and $155,000 is variable. The company can buy the part from an outside supplier for $8 per unit. Fixed costs will remain the same regardless of Swank's decision. Should the company buy the part or continue to manufacture it? Prepare a comparative schedule in the format illustrated on page 853.

**EXERCISE 20.3**

Incremental Analysis: Make or Buy Decision

**LO 1–3**

**EXERCISE 20.4**

Sunk Costs: Scrap or Rework Decision

**LO 1–3**

Road Master Shocks has 20,000 units of a defective product on hand that cost $123,500 to manufacture. The company can either sell this product as scrap for $4.18 per unit or it can sell the product for $10 per unit by reworking the units and correcting the defects at a cost of $119,200. What should the company do? Prepare a schedule in support of your recommendation.

**EXERCISE 20.5**

Scarce Resources

**LO 1–4**

The Gunst Company produces three video games: Android, Bio-Mutant, and Cyclops. Cost and revenue data pertaining to each product are as follows:

|  | Android | Bio-Mutant | Cyclops |
| --- | --- | --- | --- |
| Selling price | $100 | $60 | $125 |
| Direct labor | 48 | 24 | 60 |
| Direct materials | 9 | 8 | 16 |
| Variable overhead | 7 | 4 | 9 |

At the present time, demand for each of the company's products far exceeds its capacity to produce them. Thus management is trying to determine which of its games to concentrate on next week in filling its backlog of orders. Gunst's direct labor rate is $12 per hour and only 1,000 hours of direct labor are available each week. Determine the maximum total contribution margin the company can make by its best use of the 1,000 available hours.

**EXERCISE 20.6**

Joint Products

**LO 1–3**

Treadwell Pharmaceuticals produces two medications in a joint process: Amoxiphore and Benidrate. With each production run, Treadwell incurs $4,000 in common costs up to the split-off point.

Amoxiphore can be sold for $2,700 at the split-off point or be processed further at a cost of $1,600, at which time it can be sold for $4,200. However, if Amoxiphore is sold at the split-off point, its side effects include nausea and headaches. If it is processed further, these side effects are diminished. Demand for Amoxiphore far exceeds Treadwell's production capacity.

Benidrate can be sold for $2,400 at the split-off point or be processed further at a cost of $3,700, at which time it can be sold for $6,000.

**a.** Determine which product is more profitable to process beyond the split-off point.

**b.** What nonfinancial issues should the company consider regarding its processing decisions?

**EXERCISE 20.7**

Pricing a Special Order

**LO 1–3**

Mazeppa Corporation sells relays at a selling price of $28 per unit. The company's cost per unit, based on full capacity of 160,000 units, is as follows:

| | |
| --- | --- |
| Direct materials | $6 |
| Direct labor | 4 |
| Overhead (⅔ of which is variable) | 9 |

Mazeppa has been approached by a distributor in Montana who has offered to buy a special order consisting of 30,000 relays. Mazeppa has the capacity to fill the order. However, it will incur an additional shipping cost of $2 for each relay it sells to the distributor.

**a.** Assume that Mazeppa is currently operating at a level of 100,000 units. What unit price should it charge the distributor if it wishes to increase operating income by $2 for each unit included in the special order?

**b.** Assume that Mazeppa is currently operating at full capacity. To fill the special order, regular customers will have to be turned away. Now what unit price should it charge the distributor if it wishes to increase total operating income by $60,000 more than it would be without accepting the special order?

## PROBLEMS

**PROBLEM 20.1**

Evaluating a Special Order

**LO 1–3, 5**

D. Lawrance designs and manufactures fashionable men's clothing. For the coming year, the company has scheduled production of 40,000 suede jackets. Budgeted costs for this product are as follows:

| | Unit Costs (40,000 Units) | Total |
|---|---|---|
| Variable manufacturing costs | $50 | $2,000,000 |
| Variable selling expenses | 20 | 800,000 |
| Fixed manufacturing costs | 10 | 400,000 |
| Fixed operating expenses | 5 | 200,000 |
| Total costs and expenses | $85 | $3,400,000 |

The management of D. Lawrance is considering a special order from Discount Apparel for an additional 10,000 jackets. These jackets would carry the Discount Apparel label, rather than the D. Lawrance label. In all other respects, they would be identical to the regular D. Lawrance jackets.

Although D. Lawrance regularly sells its jackets to retail stores at a price of $150 each, Discount Apparel has offered to pay only $80 per jacket. However, because no sales commissions would be involved with this special order, D. Lawrance will incur variable selling expenses of only $5 per unit on these sales, rather than the $20 it normally incurs. Accepting the order would cause no change in the company's fixed manufacturing costs or fixed operating costs. D. Lawrance has enough plant capacity to produce 55,000 jackets per year.

## Instructions

**a.** Using incremental revenue and incremental costs, compute the expected effect of accepting this special order on D. Lawrance's operating income.

**b.** Briefly discuss any other factors that you believe D. Lawrance's management should consider in deciding whether to accept the special order. Include nonfinancial as well as financial considerations.

Visionary Game Company sells 600,000 units per year of a particular video game cartridge at $12 each. The current unit cost of the game is broken down as follows:

**PROBLEM 20.2**

Evaluating a Special Order

**LO 1–3**

| | |
|---|---|
| Direct materials | $3.00 |
| Direct labor | 1.00 |
| Variable factory overhead | 3.50 |
| Fixed factory overhead | 1.50 |
| Total | $9.00 |

At the beginning of the current year, Visionary received a special order for 10,000 of these game cartridges per month, *for one year only,* at a sales price of $8 per unit. To fill the order, Visionary will have to rent additional assembly space at a cost of $12,000 ($1,000 per month).

## Instructions

Compute the estimated increase or decrease in annual operating income that will result from accepting this special order.

Crafty Tools manufactures an electric motor that it uses in several of its products. Management is considering whether to continue manufacturing the motors or to buy them from an outside source. The following information is available:

**PROBLEM 20.3**

Make or Buy Decision

**LO 1–3**

**1.** The company needs 10,000 motors per year. The motors can be purchased from an outside supplier at a cost of $20 per unit.

**2.** The unit cost of manufacturing the motors is $42, computed as follows:

| | |
|---|---:|
| Direct materials . . . . . . . . . . . . . . . . . . . . . . . . . . . . . . . . . . . . . . . . . . . . . . . . . . . . . . . | $ 96,000 |
| Direct labor . . . . . . . . . . . . . . . . . . . . . . . . . . . . . . . . . . . . . . . . . . . . . . . . . . . . . . . . . | 120,000 |
| Factory overhead: | |
| Variable . . . . . . . . . . . . . . . . . . . . . . . . . . . . . . . . . . . . . . . . . . . . . . . . . . . . . . . . . | 90,000 |
| Fixed . . . . . . . . . . . . . . . . . . . . . . . . . . . . . . . . . . . . . . . . . . . . . . . . . . . . . . . . . . . | 114,000 |
| Total manufacturing costs . . . . . . . . . . . . . . . . . . . . . . . . . . . . . . . . . . . . . . . . . . . . . | $420,000 |
| Cost per unit ($420,000 ÷ 10,000 units) . . . . . . . . . . . . . . . . . . . . . . . . . . . . . . . . . . . | $42 |

3. Discontinuing the manufacture of motors will eliminate all the raw materials and direct labor costs but will eliminate only 75% of the variable factory overhead costs.

4. If the motors are purchased from an outside source, machinery used in the production of motors will be sold at its book value. Accordingly, no gain or loss will be recognized. The sale of this machinery would also eliminate $4,000 in fixed costs associated with depreciation and taxes. No other reductions in fixed factory overhead will result from discontinuing the production of motors.

### Instructions

a. Prepare a schedule in the format illustrated on page 853 to determine the incremental cost or benefit of buying the motors from the outside supplier. Based on this schedule, would you recommend that the company manufacture the motors or buy them from the outside source?

b. Assume that if the motors are purchased from the outside source, the factory space previously used to produce motors can be used to manufacture an additional 7,000 power trimmers per year. Power trimmers have an estimated contribution margin of $10 per unit. The manufacture of the additional power trimmers would have no effect on fixed factory overhead. Would this new assumption change your recommendation as to whether to make or buy the motors? In support of your conclusion, prepare a schedule showing the incremental cost or benefit of buying the motors from the outside source and using the factory space to produce additional power trimmers.

**PROBLEM 20.4**

Make or Buy Decision

Parsons Plumbing & Heating manufactures thermostats that it uses in several of its products. Management is considering whether to continue manufacturing the thermostats or to buy them from an outside source. The following information is available:

1. The company needs 80,000 thermostats per year. Thermostats can be purchased from an outside supplier at a cost of $6 per unit.

2. The cost of manufacturing thermostats is $7.50 per unit, computed as follows:

| | |
|---|---:|
| Direct materials . . . . . . . . . . . . . . . . . . . . . . . . . . . . . . . . . . . . . . . . . . . . . . . . . . . . . . . | $156,000 |
| Direct labor . . . . . . . . . . . . . . . . . . . . . . . . . . . . . . . . . . . . . . . . . . . . . . . . . . . . . . . . . | 132,000 |
| Manufacturing overhead: | |
| Variable . . . . . . . . . . . . . . . . . . . . . . . . . . . . . . . . . . . . . . . . . . . . . . . . . . . . . . . . . | 168,000 |
| Fixed . . . . . . . . . . . . . . . . . . . . . . . . . . . . . . . . . . . . . . . . . . . . . . . . . . . . . . . . . . . | 144,000 |
| Total manufacturing costs . . . . . . . . . . . . . . . . . . . . . . . . . . . . . . . . . . . . . . . . . . . . . | $600,000 |
| Cost per unit ($600,000 ÷ 80,000 units) . . . . . . . . . . . . . . . . . . . . . . . . . . . . . . . . . . . | $7.50 |

3. Discontinuing the manufacture of the thermostats will eliminate all of the direct materials and direct labor costs but will eliminate only 60% of the variable overhead costs.

4. If the thermostats are purchased from an outside source, certain machinery used in the production process would no longer have to be leased. Accordingly, $9,200 of fixed overhead costs could be avoided. No other reductions will result from discontinuing production of the thermostats.

## Instructions

**a.** Prepare a schedule to determine the incremental cost or benefit of buying thermostats from the outside supplier. Based on this schedule, would you recommend that the company manufacture thermostats or buy them from the outside source?

**b.** Assume that if thermostats are purchased from the outside source, the factory space previously used to produce thermostats can be used to manufacture an additional 6,000 heat-flow regulators per year. These regulators have an estimated contribution margin of $18 per unit. The manufacture of the additional heat-flow regulators would have no effect on fixed overhead.

   Would this new assumption change your recommendation as to whether to make or buy thermostats? In support of your conclusion, prepare a schedule showing the incremental cost or benefit of buying thermostats from the outside source and using the factory space to produce additional heat-flow regulators.

Optical Instruments produces two models of binoculars. Information for each model is as follows:

**PROBLEM 20.5**

Determining the Most Profitable Product Given Scarce Resources

**LO 1–4**

|  | Model 100 | Model 101 |
|---|---|---|
| Sales price per unit | $200 | $135 |
| Costs and expenses per unit: | | |
| Direct materials | $51 | $38 |
| Direct labor | 33 | 30 |
| Manufacturing overhead (applied at the rate of $18 per machine-hour, ⅓ of which is fixed and ⅔ variable) | 36 | 18 |
| Variable selling expenses | 30 | 15 |
| Total costs and expenses per unit | 150 | 101 |
| Profit per unit | $ 50 | $ 34 |
| Machine-hours required to produce one unit | 2 | 1 |

Total manufacturing overhead amounts to $180,000 per month, one-third of which is fixed. The demand for either product is sufficient to keep the plant operating at full capacity of 10,000 machine-hours per month. Assume that *only one product is to be produced in the future.*

## Instructions

**a.** Prepare a schedule showing the contribution margin per machine-hour for each product.

**b.** Explain your recommendation as to which of the two products should be discontinued.

Gulf Breeze Corporation produces three products for water skiing enthusiasts: life vests, tow ropes, and water skis. Information relating to each product line is as follows:

**PROBLEM 20.6**

Scarce Resources

**LO 1–5**

|  | Life Vests | Tow Ropes | Water Skis |
|---|---|---|---|
| Selling price | $58 | $25 | $175 |
| Direct materials | 12 | 3 | 75 |
| Direct labor | 20 | 10 | 80 |
| Variable overhead | 6 | 2 | 4 |

Gulf Breeze pays its direct labor workers an average of $10 per hour. At full capacity, 65,000 direct labor hours are available per year. The marketing department has just released the following sales estimates for the upcoming year: life vests (25,000 units), tow ropes (15,000 units), water skis (5,000 units). Based on these figures, demand for the current year is expected to exceed the company's direct labor capacity.

**Instructions**

a. What products should Gulf Breeze produce to maximize its operating income?

b. The company's marketing manager believes that the production of the least profitable product is needed to "support" the demand for the most profitable products. How may this influence management's decision regarding the company's production schedule?

**PROBLEM 20.7**

Sell or Rebuild Deficient Units

**LO 1–3, 5**

BestView manufactures computer monitors. The company's color monitors are very popular, but it has an inventory of 1,000 large-screen, black-and-white monitors for which there is little demand. BestView is considering the following options for disposing of these monitors:

1. Sell them to a discount mail-order company at a total price of $150,000. The mail-order firm would then sell these monitors at a unit price of $399.

2. Convert them to color monitors at a remanufacturing cost of $700 per unit. These monitors then could be sold to computer stores for $1,200 each.

The black-and-white monitors had been manufactured at a cost of $450 per unit. The cost of manufacturing color monitors of the same size, however, normally amounts to $800 per unit.

**Instructions**

a. Perform an incremental analysis of the revenue, costs, and gross profit resulting from converting the black-and-white monitors to color as compared with selling them to the mail-order firm.

b. Identify any sunk costs, out-of-pocket costs, and possible opportunity costs.

c. Indicate which of these options you would select and explain your reasoning, assuming that BestView currently:

1. Has substantial excess capacity.

2. Is operating at full capacity manufacturing color monitors.

**PROBLEM 20.8**

Sell or Rebuild

**LO 1–3, 5**

Silent Sentry manufacturers gas leak detectors that are sold to homeowners throughout the United States at $25 a piece. Each detector is equipped with a sensory cell that is guaranteed to last two full years before needing to be replaced. The company currently has 50,000 gas leak detectors in its inventory that contain sensory cells that had been purchased from a discount vendor. Silent Sentry engineers estimate that these sensory cells will last only 18 months before needing to be replaced. The company has incurred the following unit costs related to the 50,000 detectors:

| | |
|---|---|
| Direct materials . . . . . . . . . . . . . . . . . . . . . . . . . . . . . . . . . . . . . . . . . . | $10 |
| Direct labor . . . . . . . . . . . . . . . . . . . . . . . . . . . . . . . . . . . . . . . . . . . . . . | 2 |
| Variable overhead . . . . . . . . . . . . . . . . . . . . . . . . . . . . . . . . . . . . . . . . . . | 3 |
| Fixed overhead . . . . . . . . . . . . . . . . . . . . . . . . . . . . . . . . . . . . . . . . . . | 1 |
| Total . . . . . . . . . . . . . . . . . . . . . . . . . . . . . . . . . . . . . . . . . . . . . . . | $16 |

Silent Sentry is currently evaluating three options regarding the 50,000 detectors:

1. Scrap the inferior sensory cell in each unit and replace it with a new one at a cost of $8 each. The units could then be sold at their full unit price of $25.

2. Sell the units with the inferior sensory cells at a discounted unit price of $24. This option would also involve changing the packaging of each unit to inform the buyer that the estimated life of the sensory cell is 18 months. The estimated out-of-pocket cost associated with the packaging changes is $3 per unit.

3. Sell each unit "as is" with its current packaging to a discount buyer in a foreign country. The buyer has offered to pay Silent Sentry a unit price of $22.

**Instructions**

a. Perform an incremental analysis of these options. Based on the analysis, which option should Silent Sentry choose?

b. What nonfinancial concerns should the company take into consideration?

Kelp Company produces three joint products from seaweed. At the split-off point, three basic products emerge: Sea Tea, Sea Paste, and Sea Powder. Each of these products can either be sold at the split-off point or be processed further. If they are processed further, the resulting products can be sold as delicacies to health food stores. Cost and revenue information is as follows:

**PROBLEM 20.9**

Joint Products

| Product | Pounds Produced | Sales Value and Additional Costs If Processed Further | | |
| | | Sales Value at Split-Off | Final Sales Value | Additional Cost |
| --- | --- | --- | --- | --- |
| Sea Tea .................... | 9,000 | $60,000 | $ 90,000 | $35,000 |
| Sea Paste .................. | 4,000 | 80,000 | 160,000 | 50,000 |
| Sea Powder ................ | 2,000 | 70,000 | 85,000 | 14,000 |

**Instructions**

**a.** Which products should Kelp process beyond the split-off point?

**b.** At what price per pound would it be advantageous for Kelp Company to sell Sea Paste at the split-off point rather than process it further?

## CASES AND UNSTRUCTURED PROBLEMS

We have made the point that managers often attempt to maximize the contribution margin per unit of a particular resource that limits output capacity. The following are five familiar types of businesses:

**1.** Small medical or dental practice

**2.** Restaurant

**3.** Supermarket

**4.** Builder of residential housing

**5.** Auto dealer's service department

**CASE 20.1**

Factors That Limit Capacity

**Instructions**

**a.** For each type of business, identify the factor that you believe is most likely to limit potential output capacity.

**b.** Suggest several ways (other than raising prices) the business can maximize the contribution margin per unit of this limiting resource. (*Hint:* These businesses often *do* implement the types of strategies you are likely to suggest. Thus your solution to this case may explain basic characteristics of businesses that you personally have observed.)

McFriendly Software recently developed new spreadsheet software, Easy-Calc, which it intends to market by mail through ads in computer magazines. Just prior to introducing Easy-Calc, McFriendly receives an unexpected offer from Jupiter Computer to buy all rights to the software for $10 million cash.

**CASE 20.2**

Relevant Information and Opportunity Costs

**Instructions**

**a.** Is the $10 million offer "relevant" financial information?

**b.** Describe McFriendly's opportunity cost if it (1) accepts Jupiter's offer and (2) turns down the offer and markets Easy-Calc itself. Would these opportunity costs be recorded in McFriendly's accounting records? If so, explain the journal entry to record these costs.

**c.** Briefly describe the extent to which the dollar amounts of the two opportunity costs described in part **b** are known to management at the time of the decision of whether to accept Jupiter's offer.

**d.** Might there be any other opportunity costs to consider at the time of making this decision? If so, explain briefly.

McKay Chemical Company is based in the town of Swampton. The company is Swampton's "economic lifeblood," generating annual income of $100 million and employing nearly 75% of its workforce. McKay produces many hazardous wastes as byproducts of its manufacturing processes. Proper disposal of these byproducts in compliance with environmental regulations would cost McKay in excess of $10 million per year. Rather than comply, McKay has chosen for two decades to dump its hazardous wastes in a field at the outskirts of Swampton's city limits. For doing so, it pays a fine of $100,000 per year. The following information also pertains to McKay Chemical Company and the town of Swampton:

1. A reporter has threatened to expose McKay Chemical Company on a 60-minute, prime-time television news program. The story could result in a national boycott of the company's products and fines of up to $50 million. A boycott could reduce the company's income by as much as $25 million per year. However, the reporter has agreed not to air the story if McKay pays her a consulting fee of $1 million per year.

2. The townspeople are becoming increasingly concerned that the illegal dumping may eventually pollute the groundwater and present a serious health hazard. However, most are equally concerned that if the company's practices are exposed, Swampton and its inhabitants would face financial ruin.

3. The judge who hands down the $100,000 fine each year is also a major shareholder of McKay Chemical Company and serves on its board of directors. He invests the annual fine in a scholarship fund available on the basis of need to children of McKay's employees. Over the years, many of the scholarship recipients have gone on to become successful doctors, teachers, scientists, and other productive members of society.

Assume that you have just been appointed as the new chief executive officer of McKay Chemical. You have been presented with the facts described in this case, along with the following incremental analysis performed by an assistant:

| | Pay the Consulting Fee | Risk Public Exposure | Incremental Analysis |
|---|---|---|---|
| Consulting fee | $(1,000,000) | | $ 1,000,000 |
| Potential fines | 0 | $(50,000,000) | (50,000,000) |
| Reduction in current fines | 0 | 100,000 | 100,000 |
| Additional disposal costs | 0 | (10,000,000) | (10,000,000) |
| Potential cost of boycott | 0 | (25,000,000) | (25,000,000) |
| Net cost of options | $(1,000,000) | $(84,900,000) | $(83,900,000) |

**Instructions**
a. Identify any shortcomings in the preceding incremental analysis.
b. Draft a memorandum to the board of directors summarizing what you intend to do about this situation.

## *BUSINESS WEEK* ASSIGNMENT    BusinessWeek

The chairman and CEO of **Gateway Inc.**, Theodore Waitt, has guided San Diego-based **Gateway** toward a new business strategy. This strategy was described by Steven Brull in a July 19, 1999, *Business Week* article titled "A Net Gain for **Gateway**?" He wrote

At the core of Waitt's strategy is a simple idea: grab customers early on and keep them generating incremental revenue through a variety of services. The relationship starts with the purchase of a PC. . . . Then **Gateway** wants to lock in those customers through financing, Internet access, and a personalized portal that will steer them to **Gateway**'s E-commerce sites. That way, the cost of acquiring ISP, portal, or website customers is slashed because the work is being done by the PC sale . . . the cost of selling to a repeat customer is 7 to 10 times lower than acquiring a new buyer.

## Instructions

**a.** Write a paragraph that identifies the sunk costs, opportunity costs, and incremental costs associated with the **Gateway** strategy described in the quote.

**b.** Identify nonfinancial considerations that **Gateway** should consider when thinking about this new strategy.

## INTERNET ASSIGNMENT

The **Dow Corporation** produces a wide variety of products ranging from raw chemicals that are used as inputs by other firms to final goods that are sold to consumers. Access **Dow**'s home page at the following address:

**INTERNET 20.1**

**LO 3, 4, 5**

### www.dow.com

## Instructions

**a.** Choose two or three product areas to explore on the website. Based on your investigations, what types of incremental decisions are most likely to be made for each of the product areas?

**b.** What do you think **Dow**'s limiting resources might be?

**c.** In addition to profit considerations, what other qualitative factors might be considered in **Dow**'s incremental decision making?

*Internet sites are time and date sensitive. It is the purpose of these exercises to have you explore the Internet. You may need to use the Yahoo! search engine* http://www.yahoo.com *(or other favorite search engine) to find a company's current web address.*

## OUR COMMENTS ON THE "YOUR TURN" CASES

**You as a Sales Representative (p. 851)** You should inform the purchasing manager at Clubs & Caddies about the Robinson-Patman Act that prohibits price discrimination under some conditions. Price discrimination results when a supplier charges different *competing* purchasers different prices. The Robinson-Patman Act prohibits price discrimination when purchasers compete with one another in the sale of their products. Exceptions occur when:

1. The discriminatory lower price is in response to changing conditions in the market for, or marketability of, the commodities involved (such as the sale of discontinued products).
2. The discriminatory lower price is made to meet an equally low price of a competitor.
3. The discriminatory lower price makes only due allowance for specific cost differences such as those resulting from long production runs and bulk shipments.

Unless Clubs & Caddies can (1) order a shipment large enough so that Par Four obtains cost reductions from long production runs and/or bulk shipments or (2) demonstrate a lower-price offer from a competitor, then under the Robinson-Patman Act, the lower price would be illegal. The price to the Japanese company, NGC, does not fall under the Robinson-Patman Act because NGC does not compete on sales of its products with Clubs & Caddies.

**You as a Store Manager (p. 852)** The prints and posters are complementary with frames but may be substitutes for the oil paintings and watercolors. A *substitute* is a product purchased instead of another product. If posters and prints are purchased instead of oil paintings and watercolors and if their contribution margins are lower, then Fran's Studio will lose money. If the contribution margin for a poster is $5, you will need to make 20 poster sales (20 × $5 each = $100 total contribution margin) to generate the same contribution margin as one oil painting ($100 contribution margin per unit). Understanding whether products are complements or substitutes is critical when assessing future profitability.

## ANSWERS TO SELF-TEST QUESTIONS

**1.** b  **2.** c [$15 + ($400,000 ÷ 10,000 cards)]  **3.** d  **4.** a  **5.** d

# The Gilster Company

The Gilster Company, a machine tooling firm, has several plants. One plant, located in St. Falls, Minnesota, uses a job order costing system for its batch production processes. The St. Falls plant has two departments through which most jobs pass. Plantwide overhead, which includes the plant manager's salary, accounting personnel, cafeteria, and human resources, is budgeted at $200,000. During the past year, actual plantwide overhead was $190,000. Each department's overhead consists primarily of depreciation and other machine-related expenses. Selected budgeted and actual data from the St. Falls plant for the past year are as follows:

|  | Department A | Department B |
|---|---|---|
| Budgeted department overhead | | |
| (excludes plantwide overhead) | $100,000 | $500,000 |
| Actual department overhead | 110,000 | 520,000 |
| Expected activity: | | |
| Direct labor hours | 50,000 | 10,000 |
| Machine-hours | 10,000 | 50,000 |
| Actual activity: | | |
| Direct labor hours | 51,000 | 9,000 |
| Machine-hours | 10,500 | 52,000 |

For the coming year, the accountants at St. Falls are in the process of helping the sales force create bids for several jobs. Projected data pertaining to job no. 110 are as follows:

| | |
|---|---|
| Direct materials | $20,000 |
| Direct labor cost: | |
| Department A (2,000 hr) | 30,000 |
| Department B (500 hr) | 6,000 |
| Machine-hours projected: | |
| Department A | 100 |
| Department B | 1,200 |
| Units produced | 10,000 |

## Instructions

**a.** Assume the St. Falls plant uses a single plantwide overhead rate to assign *all* overhead (plantwide and department) costs to jobs. Use expected direct labor hours to compute the overhead rate. Find the overhead rate and determine the projected amount of total manufacturing costs per unit for the units in job no. 110.

**b.** Recalculate the projected manufacturing costs for job no. 110 using three separate rates: one rate for plantwide overhead and two separate department overhead rates, all based on machine-hours.

**c.** The sales policy at St. Falls dictates that job bids be calculated by adding 30% to total manufacturing costs. What would be the bid for job no. 110 using (1) the overhead rate from part **a** and (2) the overhead rate from part **b**? Explain why the bids differ. Which of the overhead allocation methods would you recommend and why?

**d.** Using the allocation rates in part **b**, compute the under- or overapplied overhead for the St. Falls plant for the year. Explain the impact on net income of assigning the under- or overapplied overhead to cost of goods sold rather than prorating the amount between inventories and cost of goods sold.

**e.** A St. Falls subcontractor has offered to produce the parts for job no. 110 for a price of $8 per unit. Assume the St. Falls sales force has already committed to the bid price based on the calculations in part **b**. Should St. Falls buy the $8 per unit part from the subcontractor or continue to make the parts for job no. 110 itself?

**f.** Would your response to part **e** change if the St. Falls plant could use the facilities necessary to produce parts for job no. 110 for another job that could earn an incremental profit of $15,000?

**g.** If the subcontractor mentioned in part **e** is located in Mexico, what additional international environmental issues, other than price, will Gilster and St. Falls management need to evaluate?

**h.** If Gilster Company management decides to undertake a target costing approach to pricing its jobs, what types of changes will it need to make for such an approach to be successful?

# RESPONSIBILITY ACCOUNTING AND TRANSFER PRICING

## Learning Objectives

*After studying this chapter, you should be able to:*

1. **Distinguish among cost centers, profit centers, and investment centers.**

2. **Explain the need for responsibility center information and describe a responsibility accounting system.**

3. **Prepare an income statement showing contribution margin and responsibility margin.**

4. **Distinguish between *traceable* and *common* fixed costs.**

5. **Explain the usefulness of the contribution margin and responsibility margin in making short-term and long-term decisions.**

6. **Describe three transfer pricing methods and explain when each is useful.**

*7. **Explain the differences between full costing and variable costing.**

*8. **Use a variable costing income statement in CVP analysis.**

American Airlines

---

*Supplemental Topic,* "Variable Costing."

It is possible that you have already enrolled in a frequent flier program and have accumulated some miles. If not, the likelihood that you will or could is high because miles are awarded for many activities besides flying. Miles are awarded for using a credit card, renting a car, staying at hotels and motels, buying groceries, or even using your telephone. What you may not know is that when **American Airlines** started its frequent flier program in the early 1980s, investors and regulators were concerned that as the miles built up, airlines would build up huge future liabilities for those miles.

In the 1990s, however, **American Airlines** successfully converted its frequent flier program from a cost generator into a revenue generator. They achieved this transformation by changing the organizational responsibility structure for frequent flier programs. These programs were changed from being responsible for only costs (a *cost center*) to being responsible for both costs and revenues (a *profit center*).

● ● ●

As a result, airline employees created the idea that miles can be thought of as a marketing tool. They sold other companies on the marketing idea. Now when you buy groceries, stay in a hotel, or use a credit card or your telephone you can earn frequent flier miles. Credit card companies such as **VISA** and supermarkets such as **Safeway Inc.** have partnered with **American Airlines**. According to Wendy Zellner in "You've Got Miles!" (*Business Week*, March 6, 2000) these marketers pay the airline about 2 cents a mile resulting in revenues of hundreds of millions of dollars each year. This chapter explains the purpose of responsibility centers and demonstrates the accounting impact of identifying different types of responsibility centers.

The opening story about **American Airlines**, demonstrates that every organization must assign responsibility for decision making. An organization's employees need guidelines that determine their responsibilities for organizational resources. These guidelines are in the form of job descriptions, work rules, union agreements, and organizational hierarchies. By creating profit centers and business units, companies are designing an organizational hierarchy of responsibility centers that determines decision-making authority. Profit center managers are responsible for decisions to create short-run profits. Business unit managers have more significant responsibilities for strategic business decisions.

Once the authority for decision making has been assigned, organizations must evaluate and reward decision outcomes. Giving profit-related, decision-making authority to profit center managers also requires merit-based pay and performance reviews for those managers. Performance evaluation mechanisms are necessary to make sure decision outcomes are consistent with an organization's long-term strategic goals and objectives.

In this chapter we identify common organizational responsibility structures and their related accounting implications for performance evaluation and rewards. We show how decision-making authority over organizational resources must be linked, through a responsibility accounting system, to performance evaluation and rewards. Understanding how businesses organize decision-making responsibility will help you clarify your own responsibilities within organizations you currently work for or will work for in the future.

## RESPONSIBILITY CENTERS

Most businesses are organized into a number of different subunits that perform different functions. For example, a manufacturing company typically has departments specializing in purchasing, production, sales, shipping, accounting, finance, and personnel. Production departments and sales departments often are further subdivided along different product lines or geographical areas. Organizing a business in this manner enables managers and employees to specialize in specific types of business activity. This type of organization also helps to establish clear lines of management responsibility.

Companies use many different names to describe their internal operating units, including divisions, departments, branches, product lines, and sales territories. In our discussion, we generally will use the term **responsibility center** to describe a subunit within a business organization. A designated manager is responsible for directing the activities of each such center.

In most business organizations, large responsibility centers are further subdivided into smaller ones. Consider, for example, a retail store within a chain such as **Sears** or **Wal-Mart**. Each store is a responsibility center under the control of a store manager. Each store is further divided into many separate sales departments, such as appliances, automotive products, and sporting goods. Each sales department also is a responsibility center, under the control of a department manager. These department managers report to, and are supervised by, the store manager.

### The Need for Information About Responsibility Center Performance

An income statement measures the overall profit performance of a business entity. However, managers also need accounting information measuring the performance of *each center* within the business organization. This information assists managers in the following tasks:

1. *Planning and allocating resources.* Management needs to know how well various sections of the business are performing to set future performance goals and to allocate resources to those responsibility centers offering the greatest profit potential. If one

product line is more profitable than another, for example, the company's overall profitability may increase by allocating more production capacity to the more profitable product.

2. *Controlling operations.* One use of responsibility center data is to identify those portions of the business that are performing inefficiently or below expectations. When revenue lags, or costs become excessive, center information helps to focus management's attention on those areas responsible for the poor performance. If a part of the business is unprofitable, perhaps it should be discontinued.

3. *Evaluating the performance of center managers.* As each center is an area of management responsibility, the performance of the center provides one basis for evaluating the skills of the center manager.

Thus measuring the performance of each center in the business organization is an important function of any accounting system designed to meet the needs of management.

## Cost Centers, Profit Centers, and Investment Centers

Business responsibility centers are usually classified as cost centers, profit centers, or investment centers. To illustrate, assume that Healthcorp owns and manages a 700-bed hospital and seven clinics located throughout the greater Chicago area. Each clinic is equipped with its own medical lab and x-ray facilities.

**LO 1**

Distinguish among cost centers, profit centers, and investment centers.

**Cost Centers**  A **cost center** is a business section that incurs costs (or expenses) but does not directly generate revenue.[1] Healthcorp views its administrative departments—accounting, finance, data processing, and legal services—as cost centers. In addition, it also views laundry, maintenance, and janitorial functions as cost centers. Each cost center provides services to other Healthcorp centers. However, none sells goods or services directly to Healthcorp's patients.

The decision-making responsibility assigned to cost center managers includes decisions about input resources. For a janitorial cost center manager at Healthcorp, input-related decisions would include hiring of personnel, assignment of personnel, obtaining the right equipment, and monitoring the use of janitorial resources. However, the janitorial cost center manager would not try to sell the department's services to other customers. Therefore, output-related decisions—such as pricing, type of service to offer, and choice of target markets—are not typically the responsibility of cost center managers.

### You as a Responsibility Center Manager

Assume you are the manager of janitorial services at Healthcorp. Your decision-making authority includes hiring personnel, buying supplies, assigning personnel to clean the clinics and the hospital, and inspecting clinics and hospitals for the quality of services provided. What information would be useful to upper management in evaluating your performance?

*Our comments appear on page 912.

YOUR TURN

Cost centers are evaluated primarily on (1) their ability to control costs and (2) the *quantity* and the *quality* of the services that they provide. Because cost centers do not directly generate revenue, income statements are not prepared for them. However, accounting systems must accumulate separately the costs incurred by each cost center.

---

[1]Cost centers sometimes generate insignificant amounts of revenue, but the direct generation of revenue is incidental to the basic purpose of the center.

In some cases, costs serve as an objective basis for evaluating the performance of a cost center. For example, Healthcorp's laundry service can be evaluated primarily on the basis of its cost per patient-day. In evaluating the performance of its maintenance department, the focus is less on costs and more on a subjective assessment of whether medical equipment is properly maintained.

Evaluating the performance of Healthcorp's accounting department is even more subjective. Here, management must compare the department's costs with the "value" of services provided to the organization. Such services include meeting the financial and income tax reporting requirements, as well as providing managers with information necessary to run the business.

**Profit Centers**     A **profit center** is a part of a business that generates *both revenue and costs*.[2] At Healthcorp, the hospital and each of its seven clinics are primary profit centers. Within the hospital, the pharmacy, radiology, emergency room, and food services also are viewed as profit centers.[3] Likewise, in each clinic the medical lab and x-ray department are considered profit centers. Examples of profit centers in other types of organizations might include product lines, sales territories, retail outlets, and specific sales departments within each retail outlet.

In a profit center, managers have decision-making responsibility over both input- and output-related resources. They are responsible for using the center's resources in the least costly method possible to generate the highest revenue for an ongoing business. At Healthcorp, the manager of the x-ray department must compete for business with other x-ray departments at other health-related facilities. The x-ray manager may choose to expend resources on advertising the x-ray department's services to local physicians as a means of generating more revenue. However, profit center managers do not have authority or responsibility for major capital acquisitions. If the manager of the x-ray department wanted new, very expensive x-ray equipment, responsibility to make such a large capital expenditure would be made by the hospital's CEO or the clinic's top manager.

Profit centers are evaluated primarily on their profitability. Thus Healthcorp prepares *responsibility income statements* that show separately the revenue and expenses of each profit center within the company. These results are compared with budgeted amounts, prior period performance, and, most important, the profitability of other profit centers.

Assume, for example, each of the labs in Healthcorp's seven clinics is profitable. On a square-foot basis, however, the x-ray departments are far *more profitable*. In this case, management might consider closing some labs and using the space for additional x-ray facilities. (If labs are closed, lab work could be provided by independent medical laboratories.)

**CASE IN POINT**

A **revenue center** is a business unit that focuses primarily on the accumulation of sales. A revenue center manager is evaluated on the generation of sales revenue and has responsibility for pricing and market choice decisions. Although there are some instances of revenue centers in the United States (primarily marketing departments), revenue centers are more frequent in other parts of the world. In particular, Japanese companies have historically had a strong strategic emphasis on gaining market share. Surveys show that Japanese companies are more likely to emphasize revenue growth by using return on sales as their primary performance measure.

---

[2]In this chapter, we continue the convenient practice of using the term *costs* to describe both unexpired costs (such as finished goods inventory) and expired costs (such as the cost of goods sold).

[3]Food services is considered a profit center in our example because it is assumed that hospital patients are billed separately for meals. If meals were not an itemized patient charge, food services would be considered a cost center.

**Investment Centers**   Some profit centers also qualify as investment centers. An **investment center** is a profit center for which management has been given decision-making responsibility for making significant capital investments related to the center's business activities. At Healthcorp, the hospital and its seven clinics are considered investment centers as well as profit centers because the managers of each clinic and the hospital are responsible for making profit center *and* related capital investment choices. Thus the hospital CEO and clinic managers could make major investment-related decisions, such as repaving the parking areas or purchasing new x-ray equipment. However, large strategic capital investments usually are reserved for the board of directors. Deciding to build an eighth clinic or considering a merger with another hospital are decisions reserved for collaboration between top management and the board.

Corporate boards of directors are also evaluated by shareholders of their companies. The directors must be elected and can be rejected if shareholders do not think they are performing satisfactorily. *Business Week* publishes an annual evaluation of the worst and best corporate boards based on feedback from shareholders and the governance rules and procedures used by the boards.

**CASE IN POINT**

To evaluate the performance of an investment center, it is necessary to measure objectively the cost of assets used in the center's operations. The performance of each investment center is evaluated using return on investment measurements. These return on investment performance measures are discussed in Chapter 24.

Not all profit centers can be evaluated as investment centers. For example, if a profit center shares common facilities with other parts of the business, it may be difficult to determine the precise "amount of assets invested" in the profit center. Thus, while profit centers that share common facilities can be evaluated with respect to their *profitability*, they usually are not evaluated in terms of their *return on investment*.

As previously mentioned, Healthcorp's hospital has several profit centers—pharmacy, radiology, emergency room, and food services. These centers share many common facilities, such as the hospital's parking lot, central heating, and mainframe computer support. The allocation of these shared assets to each profit center would be highly arbitrary. Thus we cannot objectively evaluate these segments as investment centers. Similarly, even though each clinic's lab and x-ray department are separate profit centers, they are not considered investment centers because they also share many common facilities.

**You as a Clinic Manager**

You are a clinic manager at Healthcorp. You report directly to the board of directors, and the Compensation Committee of the board evaluates your performance and decides on your raises and bonuses. The Compensation Committee has gathered performance information for each of the clinics. The committee plans to divide a bonus pool among the clinic managers based on these performance numbers. Given that your clinic is only two years old and the other clinics are all at least seven years old, and on average 10 years old, how do you feel about the committee's plan? What other information should the board consider?

*Our comments appear on page 912.

**YOUR TURN**

# RESPONSIBILITY ACCOUNTING SYSTEMS

**LO 2**

Explain the need for responsibility center information and describe a responsibility accounting system.

An accounting system designed to measure the performance of each center within a business is referred to as a **responsibility accounting system**. Measuring performance along the lines of management responsibility is an important function. A responsibility accounting system holds individual managers accountable for the performance of the business centers under their control. In addition, such systems provide top management with information useful in identifying strengths and weaknesses among units throughout the organization.

The operation of a responsibility accounting system involves three basic steps. First, *budgets* are prepared for each responsibility center. Budgets serve as performance targets for each subunit in an organization. Second, the accounting system *measures the performance* of each responsibility center. Third, timely *performance reports* are prepared that compare the actual performance of each center with the amounts budgeted. Frequent performance reports help center managers keep their performance "on target." They also assist top management in evaluating the performance of each manager.

In this chapter, we emphasize the second step in the operation of a responsibility accounting system—measuring the performance of each responsibility center. (The use of budgets and of performance reports is discussed in more depth in the following three chapters.)

## Responsibility Accounting: An Illustration

**LO 3**

Prepare an income statement showing contribution margin and responsibility margin.

The key to a responsibility accounting system is the ability to measure separately the operating results of each *responsibility center* within the organization. These results can then be summarized in a series of *responsibility income statements*.

A **responsibility income statement** shows not only the operating results of a particular part of a business but also the revenue and expenses *of each profit center* within that part. Such income statements enable managers to review quickly the performance of the various profit centers under their control.

To illustrate, assume that NuTech Electronics has two divisions: Retail and Mail-Order. The Retail Division consists of two retail stores; each retail store, in turn, has two profit centers: a Sales Department and a Repairs Department. A partial diagram of responsibility income statements for NuTech appears on the following page.[4]

As you read down the NuTech illustration, you are looking at smaller and smaller parts of the company. The recording of revenue and costs must begin at the *bottom* of the illustration—that is, for the *smallest* areas of management responsibility. If income statements are to be prepared for each profit center in the 42nd Street store, for example, NuTech's chart of accounts must be sufficiently detailed to measure separately the revenue and costs of these departments. The income statements for larger responsibility centers then may be prepared primarily by combining the amounts appearing in the income statements of the smaller subunits. Notice, for example, that the total sales of the 42nd Street store ($200,000) are equal to the sum of the sales reported by the two profit centers within the store ($180,000 and $20,000).

## Assigning Revenue and Costs to Responsibility Centers

In responsibility income statements, revenue is assigned first to the profit center responsible for earning that revenue. Assigning revenue to the proper department is relatively easy. Electronic cash registers, for example, automatically classify sales revenue by the department of origin.

---

[4]NuTech also prepares responsibility income statements showing the profit centers in the Mail-Order Division and in the Baker Street store. To conserve space, these statements are not included in our illustration.

In assigning costs to parts of a business, two concepts generally are applied:

---

### Illustration of a Responsibility Accounting System for NuTech Electronics

**Investment Centers Defined as Divisions**

| | | Investment Centers | |
| --- | --- | --- | --- |
| | Entire Company | Retail Division | Mail-Order Division |
| Sales | $900,000 | $500,000 | $400,000 |
| Variable costs | 400,000 | 240,000 | 160,000 |
| Contribution margins | $500,000 | $260,000 | $240,000 |
| Fixed costs traceable to divisions | 360,000 | 170,000 | 190,000 |
| Division responsibility margins | $140,000 | $ 90,000 | $ 50,000 |
| Common fixed costs | 40,000 | | |
| Operating income | $100,000 | | |
| Income taxes expense | 35,000 | | |
| Net income | $ 65,000 | | |

**Profit Centers Defined as Stores in the Retail Division**

| | | Profit Centers | |
| --- | --- | --- | --- |
| | Retail Division | 42nd Street Store | Baker Street Store |
| Sales | $500,000 | $200,000 | $300,000 |
| Variable costs | 240,000 | 98,000 | 142,000 |
| Contribution margins | $260,000 | $102,000 | $158,000 |
| Fixed costs traceable to stores | 140,000 | 60,000 | 80,000 |
| Store responsibility margins | $120,000 | $ 42,000 | $ 78,000 |
| Common fixed costs | 30,000 | | |
| Responsibility margin for division | $ 90,000 | | |

**Profit Centers Defined as Departments in the 42nd Street Store**

| | | Profit Centers | |
| --- | --- | --- | --- |
| | 42nd Street Store | Sales Department | Repairs Department |
| Sales | $200,000 | $180,000 | $ 20,000 |
| Variable costs | 98,000 | 90,000 | 8,000 |
| Contribution margins | $102,000 | $ 90,000 | $ 12,000 |
| Fixed costs traceable to departments | 32,000 | 18,000 | 14,000 |
| Departmental responsibility margins | $ 70,000 | $ 72,000 | $ (2,000) |
| Common fixed costs | 28,000 | | |
| Responsibility margin for store | $ 42,000 | | |

---

1. *Costs are classified into the categories of variable costs and fixed costs.*[5] When costs are classified in this manner, a subtotal may be developed in the income statement showing the *contribution margin* of the business center. Arranging an income statement in

---

[5]In Chapter 19, we discussed techniques such as the "high-low method" for separating semivariable costs into their variable and fixed elements.

this manner is termed the *contribution margin approach* and is widely used in preparing reports for use by managers.

2. *Each center is charged with only those costs that are "directly traceable" to that center.* A cost is directly traceable to a particular center if that center is *solely responsible* for the cost being incurred. Thus traceable costs should *disappear if the center is discontinued.*

The question of whether a cost is traceable to a particular center is not always clear-cut. In assigning costs to centers, accountants must often exercise professional judgment.

**YOUR TURN**

### You as a Department Manager

Assume that the Mail-Order Division of NuTech consists of two departments, Sales and Packaging. Also, assume that you are the manager of the Sales Department. To meet the profit goals and expectations of your division head, you have been promising customers that their orders will be expedited. The manager of the Packaging Department came to your office and was very angry. She said that expedited orders are causing her budget overruns because of labor overtime and special packaging requirements. She said that the Packaging Department would no longer be able to guarantee expedited sales orders. She also suggested that it was unethical for you to meet your budgeted goals by causing the Packaging Department to be unable to meet its budgeted goals. How would you respond?

*Our response is on page 913.

In the following discussion, we examine the various elements of NuTech's performance report that were prepared using the contribution margin approach.

## Variable Costs

In responsibility income statements, variable costs are those costs that change in approximate proportion to changes in the center's sales volume. For NuTech, variable costs include the cost of goods sold, sales commissions paid to salespeople for each system they sell, parts and labor costs incurred by each store's Repairs Department, and numerous other operating expenses that vary with sales volume.

Because variable costs are related to specific revenue dollars, they are usually traced directly to the profit center responsible for generating those revenues. For instance, the cost of a home stereo system sold at NuTech's 42nd Street store is directly traceable to the Sales Department of that store. In a similar fashion, parts and labor costs incurred in repairs are directly traceable to the Repairs Department. If a particular profit center were eliminated, all of its variable costs normally would disappear.

## Contribution Margin

**Contribution margin** (revenue minus variable costs) is an important tool for cost-volume-profit analysis. For example, the effect of a change in sales volume on operating income may be estimated by either (1) multiplying the change in unit sales by the contribution margin per unit or (2) multiplying the dollar change in sales volume by the contribution margin ratio. (To assist in this type of analysis, responsibility income statements often include percentages as well as dollar amounts. A responsibility income statement with percentage columns is illustrated on page 883.)

Contribution margin expresses the relationship between revenue and variable costs but ignores fixed costs. Thus contribution margin is primarily a *short-run* planning tool. It is useful primarily in decisions relating to price changes, short-run promotional campaigns, or changes in the level of output that will not significantly affect fixed costs. As we discussed in Chapter 20, for longer-term decisions, such as whether to build a new plant or close a particular profit center, managers must consider *fixed costs* as well as contribution margin.

## Fixed Costs

For a business to be profitable, total contribution margin must exceed total fixed costs. However, many fixed costs cannot be easily traced to specific parts of a business. Thus a distinction is often drawn in responsibility income statements between *traceable fixed costs* and *common fixed costs*.

## Traceable Fixed Costs

**Traceable fixed costs** are those that are easily traced to a specific business center. In short, traceable fixed costs arise because of a center's existence and *could be eliminated* if the related center were closed. Examples of traceable fixed costs include salaries of the center's employees and depreciation of buildings and equipment used exclusively by that center.

**LO 4**

Distinguish between *traceable* and *common* fixed costs.

In determining the extent to which a specific center adds to the profitability of the business, traceable fixed costs are typically subtracted from the contribution margin. In a responsibility income statement, the contribution margin less traceable fixed costs is termed the **responsibility margin**. For example, on page 882 we see that NuTech's margins for its 42nd Street store and its Baker Street store are $42,000 and $78,000, respectively.

---

Activity-based costing (ABC) management techniques, described in Chapters 17 and 18, have greatly increased the portion of a company's total costs that are traceable to specific business segments. The resulting strategic implications are sometimes startling. For example, after **Safety-Kleen** adopted ABC it pruned product lines, reorganized operations, and expanded into new markets based on ABC information.

    **Chrysler Corporation** estimated that its ABC implementation generated hundreds of millions of dollars in benefits through simplifying product designs and eliminating unproductive, inefficient, or redundant activities.

**MANAGEMENT STRATEGY**

---

## Common Fixed Costs

**Common fixed costs** (or indirect fixed costs) *jointly benefit several parts of the business.* The level of these fixed costs usually would not change significantly even if one of the centers deriving benefits from these costs were discontinued.

Consider, for example, a large department store, such as a **Broadway** or a **Nordstrom**. Every department in the store derives some benefit from the store building. However, such costs as depreciation and property taxes on the store will continue at current levels even if one or more of the departments within the store is discontinued. Thus, from the viewpoint of the centers within the store, depreciation on the building is a common fixed cost.

Common fixed costs cannot be assigned to specific subunits except by arbitrary means, such as in proportion to relative sales volume or square feet of space occupied. In an attempt to measure the "overall profitability" of each profit center, some businesses allocate common fixed costs to subunits along with traceable costs. A common approach, however, is to charge each profit center only with those costs *directly traceable* to that part of the business. In this text, we follow this latter approach.

### Common Fixed Costs Include Costs Traceable to Service Departments   In a responsibility income statement, the category of traceable fixed costs usually includes only those fixed costs *traceable to profit centers*. Costs traceable to *service departments*,

such as the accounting department, benefit many parts of the business. Thus the costs of operating service departments are classified in a responsibility income statement as common fixed costs. For example, the $28,000 in common fixed costs shown in the income statement of NuTech's 42nd Street store includes the costs of operating the store's accounting, security, and maintenance departments, as well as other storewide costs such as depreciation, utilities expense, and the store manager's salary.

Most service departments are evaluated as cost centers. Therefore, the responsibility accounting system should accumulate separately the costs traceable to each service department.

**Common Fixed Costs Are Traceable to Larger Responsibility Centers**    All costs are traceable to *some level* of the organization. To illustrate this concept, a portion of the responsibility accounting system of NuTech Electronics is repeated below, with emphasis on the fixed costs in the 42nd Street store.

**Profit Centers Defined as Stores in the Retail Division**

|  | Retail Division | Profit Centers | |
| --- | --- | --- | --- |
|  |  | 42nd Street Store | Baker Street Store |
| Sales | $500,000 | $200,000 | $300,000 |
| Variable costs | 240,000 | 98,000 | 142,000 |
| Contribution margins | $260,000 | $102,000 | $158,000 |
| Fixed costs traceable to stores | 140,000 | ➤ 60,000 | 80,000 |
| Store responsibility margins | $120,000 | $ 42,000 | $ 78,000 |
| Common fixed costs | 30,000 |  |  |
| Responsibility margin for division | $ 90,000 |  |  |

**Profit Centers Defined as (Departments) in the 42nd Street Store**

|  | 42nd Street Store | Profit Centers | |
| --- | --- | --- | --- |
|  |  | Sales Department | Repairs Department |
| Sales | $200,000 | $180,000 | $ 20,000 |
| Variable costs | 98,000 | 90,000 | 8,000 |
| Contribution margins | $102,000 | $ 90,000 | $ 12,000 |
| Fixed costs traceable to departments | 32,000 | 18,000 | 14,000 |
| Departmental responsibility margins | $ 70,000 | $ 72,000 | $ (2,000) |
| Common fixed costs | 28,000 |  |  |
| Responsibility margin for store | $ 42,000 |  |  |

We have made the point that certain storewide costs, such as the operation of the maintenance department and the store manager's salary, are not traceable to the specific profit centers within the store. These costs are, however, easily traceable to the 42nd Street store. Therefore, whether these costs are classified as traceable or "common" depends on whether we define the centers as stores or as departments within the stores.

As we move up a responsibility reporting system to broader and broader areas of responsibility, common costs at the lower levels of management responsibility *become traceable costs* as they fall under the control of the managers of larger responsibility centers.

## Responsibility Margin

We have mentioned that contribution margin provides an excellent tool for evaluating the effects of short-run decisions on profitability. Such decisions typically do not involve changes in a company's fixed costs. Unlike short-run decisions, long-run decisions often have fixed cost implications. Thus the *responsibility margin* is considered a more useful *longer-run* measure of profitability than the contribution margin because it takes into consideration changes in fixed costs traceable to a particular business center. Examples of such long-run decisions include whether to expand current capacity, to add a new profit center, or to eliminate a profit center that is performing poorly.

**LO 5**

Explain the usefulness of the contribution margin and responsibility margin in making short-term and long-term decisions.

To illustrate how the responsibility margin of a profit center can be used to measure performance, we will examine NuTech's Retail and Mail-Order divisions. The company's income statement for these two divisions is shown below. (The format is identical to that shown on the top of page 879, except for the inclusion of *component percentages* which accompany the dollar amounts.)

| | Entire Company | | Business Centers | | | |
| | | | Retail Division | | Mail-Order Division | |
| | Dollars | % | Dollars | % | Dollars | % |
|---|---|---|---|---|---|---|
| Sales | $900,000 | 100.0% | $500,000 | 100.0% | $400,000 | 100.0% |
| Variable costs | 400,000 | 44.4 | 240,000 | 48.0 | 160,000 | 40.0 |
| Contribution margins | $500,000 | 55.6% | $260,000 | 52.0% | $240,000 | 60.0% |
| Fixed costs traceable to divisions | 360,000 | 40.0 | 170,000 | 34.0 | 190,000 | 47.5 |
| Division responsibility margin | $140,000 | 15.6% | $ 90,000 | 18.0% | $ 50,000 | 12.5% |
| Common fixed costs | 40,000 | 4.4 | | | | |
| Operating income | $100,000 | 11.1%* | | | | |
| Income taxes expense | 35,000 | 3.9 | | | | |
| Net income | $ 65,000 | 7.2% | | | | |

*Small errors may appear in adding or subtracting percentage amounts due to rounding.

Which of NuTech's two divisions is most profitable? The answer depends on whether you are making short-run decisions, in which fixed costs do not change, or long-run decisions, in which changes to fixed costs become important factors.

First, let us consider a short-run decision. Assume that NuTech's management has recently budgeted $5,000 for a radio advertising campaign. However, it is not certain whether to use the $5,000 to promote its Retail Division or its Mail-Order Division.

Assume that management believes that the $5,000 in radio advertising will result in approximately $20,000 in additional sales for whichever division is advertised. In this case, management should spend its advertising dollars promoting the *Mail-Order Division*, because this division has the higher contribution margin ratio. An additional $20,000 in mail-order sales generates *$12,000* in contribution margin ($20,000 × 60%), whereas $20,000 in retail sales generates contribution margin of only *$10,400* ($20,000 × 52%).[6]

---

[6]Notice that the additional contribution margin generated in *either* division is expected to exceed the cost of the advertising. This suggests that management should aggressively advertise *both* of NuTech's divisions. Creative decision making should not "come to an end" with the identification of the best of the proposed alternatives.

Now let us take a longer-run view. Assume that NuTech has decided to downsize and continue operating only one of its divisions. Given that current revenue and cost relationships are expected to remain relatively stable over time, which division would you recommend that NuTech continue to operate? The answer is the *Retail Division*.

After considering fixed costs, we see that the Retail Division contributes *$90,000* to NuTech's net income, but the Mail-Order Division contributes only *$50,000*. Stated another way, if the Mail-Order Division is discontinued, all of the revenue, variable costs, and traceable fixed costs relating to it should disappear. In short, the company would lose the $50,000 monthly *responsibility margin* now produced by this division. This, of course, is preferable to losing the $90,000 monthly margin currently provided by the Retail Division.

In summary, when making short-run decisions that do not affect fixed costs, managers should attempt to generate the greatest *contribution margin* for the additional costs incurred. This usually means emphasizing those centers with the highest contribution margin ratios. When making long-run decisions, however, managers must consider fixed cost implications. This requires a shift in focus to *responsibility margins* and *responsibility margin ratios*.

## When Is a Responsibility Center "Unprofitable"?

In deciding whether a specific profit center is "unprofitable," numerous factors must be considered. Responsibility margin, however, is a good starting point. As we've seen, this margin indicates the extent to which a profit center earns an adequate contribution margin to cover its traceable fixed costs.

To illustrate, consider the following income statement prepared by NuTech's 42nd Street store:

| | 42nd Street Store | Profit Centers | |
| --- | --- | --- | --- |
| | | Sales Department | Repairs Department |
| Sales . . . . . . . . . . . . . . . . . . . . . . . . . . . . . . . | $200,000 | $180,000 | $ 20,000 |
| Variable costs . . . . . . . . . . . . . . . . . . . . . . . . | 98,000 | 90,000 | 8,000 |
| Contribution margins . . . . . . . . . . . . . . . . . . . | $102,000 | $ 90,000 | $ 12,000 |
| Fixed costs traceable to departments . . . . . . . . | 32,000 | 18,000 | 14,000 |
| Departmental responsibility margins . . . . . . . . . | $ 70,000 | $ 72,000 | $ (2,000) |
| Common fixed costs . . . . . . . . . . . . . . . . . . . . | 28,000 | | |
| Responsibility margin for store . . . . . . . . . . . . | $ 42,000 | | |

According to these data, discontinuing the Repairs Department would eliminate $20,000 in revenue and $22,000 in costs ($8,000 in variable costs and $14,000 in traceable fixed costs). Thus closing this department might well increase the profitability of the store by *$2,000*—its negative margin.

However, as we learned in Chapter 20, NuTech's management should take into consideration many other factors. For example, is the Repairs Department consistently unprofitable, or was this an unusual month? Does the existence of the Repairs Department contribute to the store's ability to sell merchandise? What alternative use could be made of the space now used by the Repairs Department? Thus, even though the Repairs Department is unprofitable, there may be other factors to consider before deciding that this department should be closed.

## Evaluating Responsibility Center Managers

Some fixed costs traceable to a center are simply beyond the manager's immediate control. If a center is saddled with high costs that are beyond the manager's control, the center's reported performance may not be indicative of its manager's individual performance.

This can be an extremely sensitive issue, especially when a manager's compensation or bonus is affected.

To illustrate, assume that NuTech's 42nd Street store has been open since 1956, whereas its Baker Street store has been in operation for only three years. Consequently, the depreciation and property taxes applicable to the Baker Street store far exceed those incurred at the 42nd Street store. If the bonus paid to the manager of the Baker Street store is based solely on the store's responsibility margin, this manager will be unjustly penalized for serving at the newer location.

In response to this type of problem, some companies subdivide traceable fixed costs as *controllable fixed costs* or *committed fixed costs*. **Controllable fixed costs** are those under the manager's immediate control, such as salaries and advertising. **Committed fixed costs** are those that the manager cannot readily change, such as depreciation and property taxes. In the responsibility income statement, controllable fixed costs can be deducted from the contribution margin to arrive at a subtotal called **performance margin**. Committed fixed costs then can be deducted from the performance margin to determine the *responsibility margin*.

Subdividing traceable costs in this manner draws a distinction between the performance of a center manager and the profitability of a center as a long-term investment. The performance margin includes only the revenue and costs *under the manager's direct control*, making it useful in evaluating the manager's ability to control costs. The responsibility margin, however, is used for measuring and evaluating the long-term profitability of the *center* viewed as a whole.

In the late 1990s **Siemens AG**, reorganized using profit centers with the explicit objective of eliminating layers of bureaucracy left over from the centralized decision-making practices used earlier. The profit center format gives managers in local markets authority to cut costs and bid for projects. In return, they were rewarded with merit-based pay and bonuses for meeting corporate profitability goals.

**CASE IN POINT**

## Arguments Against Allocating Common Fixed Costs to Business Centers

We have mentioned that some companies follow a policy of allocating common fixed costs among the business centers benefiting from those costs. The bases used for allocating common costs are necessarily arbitrary, such as relative sales volume or square feet of floor space occupied by the center. In a responsibility income statement, responsibility margin less common fixed costs is called "operating income."

We do *not* recommend this practice, for several reasons:

1. *Common fixed costs often would not change even if a business center were eliminated.* Therefore, an allocation of these costs only distorts the amount contributed by each center to the income of the company.

   To illustrate this point, assume that $10,000 in common costs are allocated to a center that has a responsibility margin of only $4,000. Also assume that total common costs would not change even if the center were eliminated. The allocation of common costs makes the center *appear* to be unprofitable, showing an operating loss of $6,000 ($4,000 responsibility margin, less $10,000 in allocated common fixed costs). However, closing the center would actually *reduce* the company's income by *$4,000*, as the center's $4,000 margin would be lost, but common fixed costs would not change.

2. *Common fixed costs are not under the direct control of the center's managers.* Therefore, allocating these costs to the center does not assist in evaluating the performance of managers.

3. *Allocation of common fixed costs may imply changes in profitability that are unrelated to the center's performance.* To illustrate this point, assume that $50,000 in monthly common fixed costs are allocated equally to each of five profit centers. Thus each profit center is charged with *$10,000* of these costs. Now assume that one of the profit centers is discontinued but that the monthly level of common fixed costs does not change. Each of the four remaining profit centers will now be charged with *$12,500* in common fixed costs ($50,000 ÷ 4). Thus the continuing profit centers are made to appear less profitable because of an event (closure of the fifth profit center) that is *unrelated* to their activities.

## Transfer Prices

All of NuTech's profit centers sell products or services to customers *outside* of the organization. But many profit centers supply some of their output to other parts of the business.

**CASE IN POINT**

Before **PepsiCo** spun off its restaurant divisions, the Pepsi Cola Division, which manufactures the famous soft drink, supplied Pepsi to Taco Bell, KFC, and Pizza Hut. These restaurant divisions were charged a transfer price, which was an interdivision charge, by the Pepsi Cola Division.

When products (either goods or services) are transferred from one department to another, *transfer prices* may play an important role in the evaluation of departmental performance. A **transfer price** is the dollar amount used in recording this interdepartmental transfer.

We have already seen examples of transfer prices. In our study of process cost accounting systems (Chapter 17), we saw that manufacturing costs are transferred from one Work in Process account to the next. In essence, these manufacturing costs are the *transfer prices* of the goods transferred from one processing department to another.

Cost should be used as a transfer price only if the department *producing* the product is evaluated as a *cost center*. (Production departments normally are cost centers.) But cost is *not* a satisfactory transfer price for the output of a *profit center*.

**Transfer Prices for Profit Centers**   Profit centers normally *sell* their output. But some profit centers, such as the Pepsi Cola Division in our Case in Point, also provide a portion of their output to other business units within the business organization.

If cost were used as a transfer price, the profit center would be using some of its resources in a manner that *produces no profit*. Supplying more product to internal parts of the business at cost, rather than to outside customers at a profit, would *reduce* the department's contribution margin, responsibility margin, and other measures of departmental performance.

On the other hand, the department receiving the transferred goods at cost would be getting a bargain. Presumably, this operating cost would be well below market, thus making that department look unusually profitable. In short, using cost as a transfer price would *shift margin* from the department that *produced* the product to the departments that eventually sell that product to outside customers.

For this reason, many companies now use *market value* as the transfer price of products produced in profit centers. In this way, the departmental profit winds up in the profit center that *produced* the product, rather than in the center to which the product was transferred.

**Transfer Prices When Market Prices Don't Exist** Unfortunately, well-defined markets for transferred products do not usually exist. When market prices do not exist for the good or service being transferred, companies use other types of transfer prices. We discuss two types of transfer prices, a negotiated transfer price and a cost-plus transfer price.

Many companies ask their division managers to negotiate an acceptable transfer price, generally referred to as a **negotiated transfer price**. During the negotiation process, the supplying and buying divisions agree on a transfer price. That negotiated transfer price allocates the profits associated with the transferred product between the two divisions.

As an example, assume Division A supplies a component that Division B includes in an assembled finished product sold by B. The total per-unit cost of creating the component in Division A is $42.00. Division B adds other components to the product transferred by A and builds them into the finished product that sells for $150.00. Assume the total costs added by Division B equal $78.00 per unit. Profit on the finished product is computed as follows:

**Finished Product Profits = Sales Price −(Costs in Division A + Costs in Division B)**

| $30 | = | $150 | −( | $42 | + | $78 | ) |

Divisions A and B divide the total profits for the finished product by agreeing on a transfer price. For example, if they agree on a negotiated transfer price of $53, then the profits for Division A will be $11 = $53 − $42 and the profits for Division B will be $19 = $150 − ($53 + $78). With this profit allocation, Division A earns 20.75% on each sales dollar ($11/$53) and Division B earns 12.67% on each sales dollar ($19/$150).

A second approach to determining a transfer price when no market price exists is to add a predetermined markup to the total cost of the product transferred. This second type of transfer price is called a **cost-plus transfer price**. For example, some companies may want responsibility managers to transfer products internally, but they may not want to use negotiation. By requiring a 15% or 20% markup over cost, companies automatically allocate some profit to the supplying division. In this example, with a 20% markup, Division A would transfer the component to Division B at $50.40 = $42 + .2 ($42). Profits for Division A would be $8.40 and profits for Division B would be $30 − $8.40 = $21.60. With this allocation, Division A earns 16.7% profit on each sales dollar ($8.40/$50.40) and Division B earns 14.4% of profit on each sales dollar ($21.60/$150).

**LO 6**

Describe three transfer pricing methods and explain when each is useful.

**Two Types of Transfer Prices When No Market Price Exists**

| | Division A | | Division B | | |
| | Negotiated | Cost-plus | Negotiated | Cost-plus | Total Firm |
|---|---|---|---|---|---|
| Revenues | $53.00 | $50.40 | $150.00 | $150.00 | $150.00 |
| Component costs | 42.00 | 42.00 | — | — | 42.00 |
| Costs from A | — | | 53.00 | 50.40 | |
| Other costs | — | | 78.00 | 78.00 | 78.00 |
| Gross profits | $11.00 | $ 8.40 | $ 19.00 | $ 21.60 | $ 30.00 |
| Return on sales | 20.75% | 16.67% | 12.67% | 14.4% | 20% |

The above table suggests that the manager of Division A would prefer the negotiated transfer price and the manager of Division B would prefer the cost-plus transfer price. Because the transfer price allocates profits between the two divisions and because significant portions of these managers' evaluations are based on their division profits, determining a fair transfer price can be very controversial. Frequently, central administration must step in and provide guidance to resolve transfer pricing issues.

**Transfer Prices for Multinational Companies**    Setting appropriate transfer prices becomes much more complicated if parts of a business are located in different countries. If goods are shipped across international borders, the transfer price may be affected by taxes, duties and tariffs, and international trade agreements. In addition, the market value of the goods may be quite different in the country in which they are manufactured and in the country to which they are shipped.

---

**CASH EFFECTS**     Intercompany transfer price entries are eliminated when cash flow statements are constructed. Transfer prices are not revenue for a firm and they do not generate cash flows. However, international transfer prices between a firm's subsidiaries in two countries with different tax rates can have cash flow impacts for the overall firm.

As a simple example, consider the ABC Company where two divisions, A and B, are necessary to make widgets that Division B sells to the public for $10. The production costs are $3 in Division A and $4 in Division B. Thus the profit per widget is $3 [$10 − ($3 + $4)]. If the transfer price between A and B is set at $4.50, then the $3 profit per widget is divided equally ($1.50 each) between the two divisions. This transfer price has no cash flow effects if the divisions are subject to the same tax and tariff structures. However, if Division B is located in a high-tax country (50%) and Division A is located in a low-tax country (10%), then ABC will experience cash flow tax effects. The $4.50 transfer price will cause Division B to record taxable profits of $1.50 per unit and be taxed at a rate of 50%, or $0.75 per unit. Profits for Division A will be taxed at 10%, or $0.15 per unit. The ABC Company could save taxes and increase cash flows by using a $6 transfer price where all profits are allocated to Division A and the low-tax country.

This simple example illustrates the potential cash flow effects of international transfers. The actual laws and regulations governing international transfer pricing are complex and vary from country to country.

---

**Some Concluding Comments on Transfer Prices**    Transfer prices usually are not paid in cash; they are only *entries made in the accounting records* to record the "flow" of goods and services among departments within the business.[7]

In essence, the transfer price may be viewed as revenue earned by the segment supplying the products and as a cost (or expense) to the segments receiving them. As these departmental revenues and costs are of equal amount, transfer prices have no direct effect on the company's *overall* net income.

## Nonfinancial Objectives and Information

Thus far, we have emphasized measuring only the *financial* performance of responsibility centers within a business organization. In addition to financial criteria, many firms specify *nonfinancial* objectives that they consider important to their basic goals. A responsibility accounting system can be designed to gather both financial and nonfinancial information about each of its centers. Shown on the following page are some common nonfinancial measures that managers often evaluate. These concepts are discussed more fully in Chapter 24.

---

[7]If the transfer of products is between subsidiary corporations, the transfer prices may, in fact, be paid in cash.

| Nonfinancial Performance Measures | |
| --- | --- |
| **Product Quality** | **Personnel** |
| Number of defective parts | Number of sick days taken |
| Number of customer returns | Employee turnover |
| Number of customer complaints | Number of grievances filed |
| **Marketing** | **Efficiency and Capacity** |
| Number of new customers | Cycle time (manufacturing businesses) |
| Number of sales calls initiated | Occupancy rates (hotels and motels) |
| Market share | Passenger miles flown (airline industry) |
| Number of product stockouts | Patient-days (hospitals) |
| | Transactions processed (banking) |

Among the factors used by **McDonald's Corporation** to evaluate a restaurant manager is the manager's performance on the company's QSC standards. "QSC" stands for "quality, service, and cleanliness." Each restaurant manager periodically is rated on these standards by a member of **McDonald's** supervisory staff. Among the many items listed on **McDonald's** QSC rating forms are:

*Quality:* Temperature, appearance, quantity, and taste of food servings.

*Service:* Appearance and general conduct of employees; use of proper procedures in greeting customers.

*Cleanliness:* Cleanliness in all areas in the kitchen, front counter, tables, and restrooms. Appearance of building exterior and parking lot.

**CASE IN POINT**

## RESPONSIBILITY CENTER REPORTING IN FINANCIAL STATEMENTS

In this chapter, we have focused on responsibility centers from the *perspective of management*. From this perspective, centers are defined along areas of management responsibility, beginning with the very smallest units of the business, such as departments or each salesperson's "territory."

A large corporation may have literally thousands of centers for which information is developed. This information is intended to assist management in planning and controlling *every aspect* of business operations.

The Financial Accounting Standards Board (FASB) requires large corporations to disclose certain "segment information" in notes to their financial statements. This disclosure includes the net sales, operating income, and identifiable assets of the major industries and geographic regions in which the company operates.

The segment information appearing in financial statements is *far less detailed* than the responsibility center information developed for management. But of course it serves a very different purpose. The users of an annual report are evaluating the overall profitability and future prospects of the company *viewed as a whole*, not evaluating the efficiency of every department, store, and production process. For financial reporting purposes, some publicly owned corporations subdivide their operations into only two "segments"; few (if any) show more than 10.

**A SECOND LOOK**

### American Airlines

The use of cost, profit, and investment responsibility centers helps companies such as **American Airlines** achieve their objectives. **American** has numerous lines of business (credit cards, incentive miles programs, group travel services, travel programs for seniors, etc.) that benefit from the use of responsibility accounting systems. Companies that combine the use of responsibility centers to assign decision-making authority to managers with the responsibility center financial statements described in this chapter can evaluate the performance of each center and its manager.

Chapter 22 explains how responsibility centers are linked to each other through the organization's operational budget. You will also learn how these budgets can be used as a means of assessing progress toward achieving organizational goals and objectives.

---

## SUPPLEMENTAL TOPIC

### VARIABLE COSTING

Our preceding examples involving NuTech Electronics illustrated the activities of a typical *merchandising company*. In a merchandising company, the entire cost of goods sold represents a *variable cost*. In the financial statements of a manufacturing company, however, the cost of goods sold is based on what it costs to *manufacture* the inventory that was sold. As we learned in earlier chapters, some of these manufacturing costs are variable, while others are fixed. The conventional practice of including both variable and fixed manufacturing costs in the valuation of inventories and costs of goods sold is called **full costing**. Full costing is the method *required* by generally accepted accounting principles and by income tax regulations.

We have seen that for the purposes of making management decisions, it is often more useful to have an income statement in which variable and fixed costs are reported separately and the contribution margin is clearly indicated. Arranging the income statement of a manufacturing company in this format involves a technique called *variable costing*.

Under **variable costing**, the cost of goods sold includes only *variable manufacturing costs*. Fixed manufacturing costs are viewed as *period costs* and are deducted separately in the income statement after the determination of the contribution margin. Before discussing variable costing further, let us briefly review some of the basic concepts of accounting for manufacturing costs.

**LO 7**

Explain the differences between full costing and variable costing.

### Full Costing: The Traditional View of Product Costs

In Chapter 16, we made the distinction between *product costs* and *period costs*. **Product costs** are the costs of manufacturing inventory and are debited to the Work in Process Inventory account. From this account, product costs flow into the Finished Goods Inventory account, from which they eventually flow into the Cost of Goods Sold account. Thus product costs are offset against revenue in the period in which the related goods are *sold*. **Period costs**, on the other hand, are charged directly to expense accounts and are deducted from revenue in the period in which they are *incurred*.

*Under full costing, all manufacturing costs are treated as product costs*, regardless of whether these costs are variable or fixed. Since all manufacturing costs are absorbed by the products, full costing often is called **absorption costing**.

## Variable Costing: A Different View of Product Costs

Some manufacturing costs are variable costs and some manufacturing costs are fixed. The costs of direct materials and direct labor are examples of variable costs. Examples of fixed manufacturing costs include overhead items such as depreciation on plant assets, factory insurance premiums, and supervisor salaries. Recall that under full costing, these fixed overhead costs were *applied* to products using an activity base such as direct labor hours.

However, under variable costing, *only variable manufacturing costs* are applied to products. *All fixed manufacturing costs are treated as period costs.* Thus, instead of being classified as an asset until inventory is sold, fixed overhead costs are classified immediately as expenses of the current period. The diagrams on the next page compare the flow of costs under full costing versus variable costing.

In reports intended for use by managers, variable costing has two distinct advantages over full costing:

1. The format of the variable costing income statement easily lends itself to cost-volume-profit analysis.
2. Responsibility margin (or income from operations) is *not affected* by short-run fluctuations in the level of production.

## An Illustration of Variable Costing

The differences between variable costing and full costing may be illustrated by comparing partial income statements prepared under each method. Assume, for example, that on June 1, Hamilton Manufacturing Company opened a new plant in Nashville. Data for the plant's first month of operations are as follows:

| | Full Costing | Variable Costing |
|---|---|---|
| **Units manufactured and units sold:** | | |
| Number of units manufactured (all completed by June 30) | | 11,000 |
| Number of units sold | | 10,000 |
| Units in inventory of finished goods at June 30 | | 1,000 |
| **Sales revenue and selling and administrative expenses:** | | |
| Net sales (10,000 units sold @ $20) | | $200,000 |
| Selling and administrative expenses: | | |
| Variable ($2 per unit sold) | | 20,000 |
| Fixed | | 30,000 |
| **Manufacturing costs (per unit manufactured):** | | |
| Direct materials | $ 4 | $ 4 |
| Direct labor | 3 | 3 |
| Manufacturing overhead: | | |
| Fixed ($55,000 ÷ 11,000 units manufactured) | 5 | –0– |
| Variable | 1 | 1 |
| Total cost per unit manufactured | $13 | $ 8 |

Notice the difference in *total cost per unit manufactured* under the two costing methods. When full costing is applied, the $55,000 in fixed manufacturing overhead is allocated to the 11,000 units produced. Thus the cost assigned to each finished unit includes

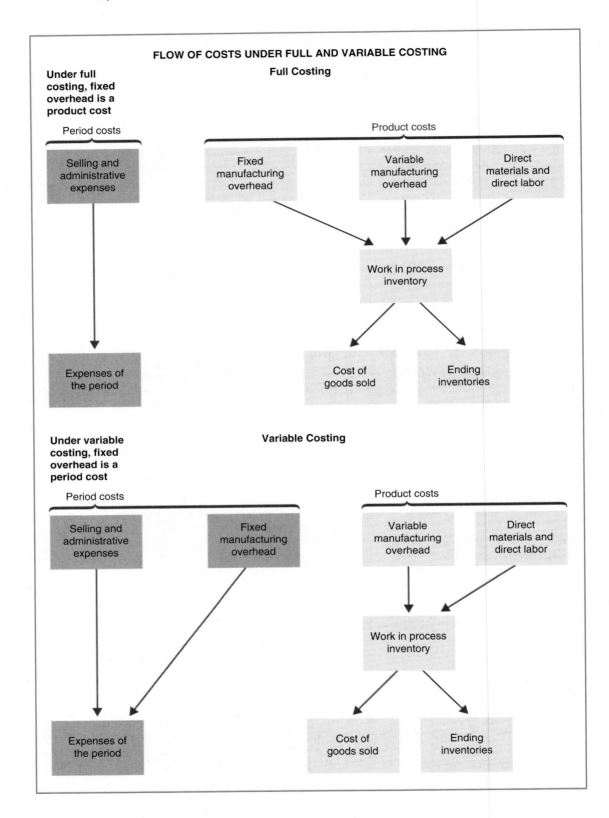

$5 of fixed manufacturing overhead. Under variable costing, however, only *variable man-ufacturing costs* are included in unit cost.[1]

The treatment of these fixed manufacturing costs creates an important difference between full costing and variable costing. Under full costing, we will use the *$13* unit cost to determine the cost of goods sold and ending inventory. Under variable costing, these amounts will be determined using the *$8* unit cost.

Partial income statements and ending inventory figures for the Nashville Plant prepared under full and variable costing are illustrated below.

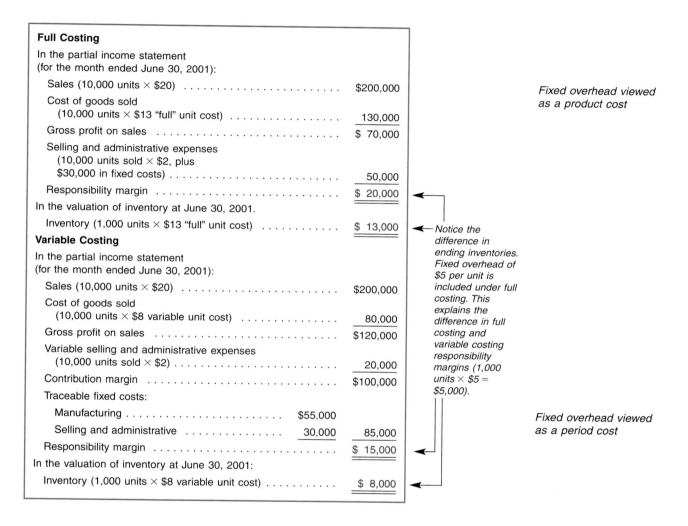

**Full Costing**

In the partial income statement
(for the month ended June 30, 2001):

| | |
|---|---:|
| Sales (10,000 units × $20) . . . . . . . . . . . . . . . . . . . . . . . | $200,000 |
| Cost of goods sold (10,000 units × $13 "full" unit cost) . . . . . . . . . . . . . . . . | 130,000 |
| Gross profit on sales . . . . . . . . . . . . . . . . . . . . . . . . . . | $ 70,000 |
| Selling and administrative expenses (10,000 units sold × $2, plus $30,000 in fixed costs) . . . . . . . . . . . . . . . . . . . . . . . | 50,000 |
| Responsibility margin . . . . . . . . . . . . . . . . . . . . . . . . . | $ 20,000 |

In the valuation of inventory at June 30, 2001.

| | |
|---|---:|
| Inventory (1,000 units × $13 "full" unit cost) . . . . . . . . . . . | $ 13,000 |

*Fixed overhead viewed as a product cost*

**Variable Costing**

In the partial income statement
(for the month ended June 30, 2001):

| | | |
|---|---:|---:|
| Sales (10,000 units × $20) . . . . . . . . . . . . . . . . . . . . . . . | | $200,000 |
| Cost of goods sold (10,000 units × $8 variable unit cost) . . . . . . . . . . . . . . | | 80,000 |
| Gross profit on sales . . . . . . . . . . . . . . . . . . . . . . . . . . | | $120,000 |
| Variable selling and administrative expenses (10,000 units sold × $2) . . . . . . . . . . . . . . . . . . . . . . . | | 20,000 |
| Contribution margin . . . . . . . . . . . . . . . . . . . . . . . . . . | | $100,000 |
| Traceable fixed costs: | | |
| Manufacturing . . . . . . . . . . . . . . . . . . . . . . . | $55,000 | |
| Selling and administrative . . . . . . . . . . . . . . | 30,000 | 85,000 |
| Responsibility margin . . . . . . . . . . . . . . . . . . . . . . . | | $ 15,000 |

In the valuation of inventory at June 30, 2001:

| | |
|---|---:|
| Inventory (1,000 units × $8 variable unit cost) . . . . . . . . . . | $ 8,000 |

*Notice the difference in ending inventories. Fixed overhead of $5 per unit is included under full costing. This explains the difference in full costing and variable costing responsibility margins (1,000 units × $5 = $5,000).*

*Fixed overhead viewed as a period cost*

**Treatment of Fixed Manufacturing Costs**   We have stressed the point that under full costing, fixed manufacturing costs are viewed as *product costs*, whereas under variable costing, they are viewed as *period costs*. Let us now illustrate what that means in terms of the valuation of inventories and the amount of profit (responsibility margin) reported under each method.

In our illustration, Hamilton's fixed manufacturing costs total $55,000, or $5 per unit manufactured. If we view these costs as *product costs*—under the full costing method—they will be assigned to those units sold during the period and be deducted from revenue as part of cost of goods sold. During June, the Nashville plant produced 11,000

---

[1]Under both methods, fixed and variable selling and administrative costs are treated as *period costs*. Accordingly, these costs are *never* allocated to the units manufactured during the period.

units, of which 10,000 were sold. Notice that the cost of goods sold in the full costing income statement is *$130,000* (10,000 units sold × $13), and ending inventory is valued at *$13,000* (1,000 units in inventory × $13). Thus, of the period's *$55,000* of fixed manufacturing costs, *$50,000* is *included in the cost of goods sold* (10,000 units sold × $5 per unit), and *$5,000* is *included in finished goods inventory* (1,000 units in inventory × $5 per unit).

Under variable costing, the entire fixed manufacturing cost is treated as a *period cost*. Notice that *the entire $55,000 is deducted from revenue* and that none is assigned to ending inventory. Thus, under variable costing, ending inventory is valued at only the variable manufacturing cost of *$8* per unit.

Observe how the full costing method affects the amount of responsibility margin reported by Hamilton's Nashville plant. Under full costing, fixed manufacturing costs are *deferred to future periods*. Instead of being deducted from revenue immediately, a portion of these costs is *carried forward* as part of the cost of inventory. These costs are *released* from inventory and included as part of costs of goods sold in the period in which the inventory to which they have been assigned is *sold*. In our illustration, $5,000 in fixed manufacturing cost was carried forward in inventory under the full costing method. This explains why the corresponding ending inventory figure and responsibility margin are $5,000 higher under full costing.

In summary, full costing results in a *higher* responsibility margin than does variable costing *when more units are produced than are sold* (that is, when finished goods inventory increases during the period). In periods *when more units are sold than are produced* (that is, when finished goods inventory decreases for the period), full costing results in *lower* responsibility margins because previously deferred fixed costs are included in the cost of goods sold.

**Using a Variable Costing Income Statement**   The *variable costing* income statement readily lends itself to cost-volume-profit analysis. To illustrate, let us use the variable costing income statement to determine the dollar sales volume needed for Hamilton's Nashville plant to earn a monthly responsibility margin of $50,000. As a first step, we may compute the plant's contribution margin ratio directly from the income statement as follows: $100,000 contribution margin ÷ $200,000 net sales = *50%*. We may then compute the required sales volume using the following cost-volume-profit relationships:

$$\text{Sales Volume} = \frac{\text{Fixed Costs} + \text{Target Responsibility Margin}}{\text{Contribution Margin Ratio}}$$

$$= \frac{\$85,000 + \$50,000}{.50} = \$270,000$$

## Fluctuation in the Level of Production

Two accounting measurements widely used in evaluating the performance of a manufacturing center of a business are the unit cost of manufactured products and responsibility margin. A significant shortcoming in the full costing approach is that both of these performance measurements are affected by short-term fluctuation in the level of production. This complicates the process of evaluating the performance of a center. The manager performing the evaluation must determine whether changes in unit cost and in responsibility margin represent important changes in performance or merely the effects of a temporary change in the number of units produced.

This problem arises because under full costing, fixed manufacturing costs are included in the cost of finished goods manufactured. If the level of production temporarily rises, fixed costs per unit will decline. If production temporarily declines, fixed costs per unit will increase. In either case, the changes in fixed costs per unit will also affect total unit manufacturing cost.

**LO 8**

Use a variable costing income statement in CVP analysis.

In addition to causing changes in unit cost, fluctuations in the level of production may cause some fixed costs to be deferred into inventory, or released from inventory. For example, if production rises *above* the level of current sales, some of the fixed costs of the period are *deferred* into inventory, rather than being offset against the revenue of the current period. If production temporarily falls *below* the level of sales, the fixed costs of prior periods are *released* from inventory and charged against the revenue of the current period.

Most accountants agree that short-term fluctuations in the level of production, by themselves, do *not* represent changes in the profitability of a responsibility center. Profits result from sales, not merely from production. An advantage of variable costing is that unit cost, contribution margin, and responsibility margin—all important measurements of segment performance—are *not affected* by short-run fluctuations in the level of production.

To illustrate, we will take two years of operations at the Jogman Stereo Division of Yato Manufacturing. We will assume that sales, variable costs per unit, and total fixed costs remain *unchanged* in both years. The only change is a temporary fluctuation in the division's annual level of production. Specifically, it produced *60,000* units in Year 1 and only *40,000* units in Year 2.[2] Operating data for the two years are shown below.

| Operating Data for the Jogman Stereo Division | | |
|---|---|---|
| | | **Years 1 and 2** |
| Annual unit sales ............................................ | | 50,000 |
| Unit sales price ............................................. | | $ 18 |
| Annual net sales (50,000 × $18) ............................. | | 900,000 |
| Annual fixed costs: | | |
| Manufacturing ........................................... | | 240,000 |
| Selling and administrative ............................... | | 130,000 |
| | **Year 1** | **Year 2** |
| Number of units manufactured .............................. | 60,000 | 40,000 |
| Cost per unit manufactured (full costing): | | |
| Variable manufacturing costs ............................. | $ 7 | $ 7 |
| Fixed manufacturing costs ($240,000 divided by number of units manufactured during the year) ........... | 4 | 6 |
| Total unit cost of finished goods manufactured (full costing) ........................................... | $11 | $13 |

From these operating data, the responsibility income statements on the next page were prepared under the variable and full costing approaches.

**Analysis of Illustration**   Remember, we have assumed that nothing has changed at the Jogman Stereo Division from Year 1 to Year 2 *except for the level of production.* Notice that in the *variable costing* income statements, the division reports the *same amounts* of contribution margin and responsibility margin in both years. The $7 unit cost of finished goods manufactured also remains unchanged. Thus the key measurements of segment performance are *not affected* by the change in the level of production. Under variable costing, contribution margin and responsibility margin change only when there is a

---

[2]To simplify this illustration, we assume that there is no beginning inventory and that all selling and administrative expenses are fixed costs.

## Income Statements for the Jogman Division

### Full Costing

| | Year 1 | | Year 2 | |
|---|---|---|---|---|
| Sales (50,000 units) | | $900,000 | | $900,000 |
| Cost of goods sold: | | | | |
| Beginning inventory | $ –0– | | $110,000 | |
| Cost of finished goods manufactured | 660,000[a] | | 520,000[c] | |
| Cost of goods available for sale | $660,000 | | $630,000 | |
| Less: Ending inventory | 110,000[b] | | –0– | |
| Cost of goods sold | | 550,000 | | 630,000 |
| Gross profit | | $350,000 | | $270,000 |
| Selling and administrative expenses | | 130,000 | | 130,000 |
| Responsibility margin | | $220,000 | | $140,000 |

### Variable Costing

| | Year 1 | | Year 2 | |
|---|---|---|---|---|
| Sales (50,000 units) | | $900,000 | | $900,000 |
| Variable cost of goods sold (50,000 units @ $7) | | 350,000 | | 350,000 |
| Contribution margin | | $550,000 | | $550,000 |
| Traceable fixed costs: | | | | |
| Manufacturing | $240,000 | | $240,000 | |
| Selling and administrative | 130,000 | 370,000 | 130,000 | 370,000 |
| Responsibility margin | | $180,000 | | $180,000 |

[a]60,000 units @ $11 per unit.
[b]10,000 units @ $11 per unit.
[c]40,000 units @ $13 per unit.

change in (1) sales revenue, (2) variable costs per unit, or (3) fixed costs incurred during the period.

Under *full costing,* however, changes in the level of production *can* cause significant changes in key measurements of performance. These changes result from both the change in traceable fixed costs per unit and fixed costs carried forward in inventory or released from inventory. Let us now look at the reasons behind the fluctuation in the amounts of responsibility margin reported by the Jogman Stereo Division under the full costing approach.

**Year 1: More Units Produced Than Sold**   Notice that under full costing in Year 1, fixed manufacturing costs amounted to *$4 per unit* ($240,000 ÷ 60,000 units manufactured). During Year 1, the division manufactured 10,000 more units than it sold. Thus, under full costing, *$40,000* in fixed manufacturing costs were deferred (or carried forward) in ending inventory. This deferral explains why the responsibility margin reported in Year 1 is $40,000 *higher* than the responsibility margin shown under variable costing for the same period.

**Year 2: Fewer Units Are Produced Than Sold**   Now consider the results reported under full costing in Year 2. In the second year, unit sales exceeded production by 10,000 units. Thus, to fill all of its orders, the division *sold all of the units it produced in Year 2 and all of the units it carried forward from Year 1.* As the company sold the inventory carried forward from Year 1, the $40,000 in fixed manufacturing costs associated with it became part of the cost of goods sold in Year 2. Thus the responsibility margin reported in Year 2 under full costing is $40,000 *lower* than that shown under variable costing.

**Summary**    Because the full costing method associates fixed manufacturing costs with units of production, the amount of fixed manufacturing cost offset against revenue varies with the relationship between the number of units produced and the number sold. If production temporarily exceeds unit sales, some fixed manufacturing costs are deferred to future periods, and responsibility margin will be higher than would be reported under variable costing. If fewer units are produced during the period than are sold, fixed costs deferred in prior periods are offset against current revenue as inventory is drawn down. Thus, responsibility margin reported for the current period will be lower than would result from variable costing.

Under variable costing, the level of production has *no effect* on responsibility margin, because all fixed manufacturing costs are offset against revenue as they are incurred, *regardless* of the level of production.

In the long run, the total amounts of responsibility margin reported under full costing and variable costing should be very similar. Over the long run, the number of units produced tends to equal the number of units sold. In the short run, however, variable costing provides managers with more reliable measurement of the performance of the subunits engaged in manufacturing activities.

## Why Is Variable Costing Unacceptable for Use in Financial Statements and Income Tax Returns?

We have shown that in several respects variable costing may be more useful than full costing as a basis for many management decisions. Why then is variable costing not also used in financial statements and income tax returns? The answer to this question is that variable costing omits fixed manufacturing costs from the valuation of the ending inventory. Financial accountants and income tax authorities argue that variable costing significantly understates the "full" cost of manufacturing this asset. As a result of understating ending inventories, variable costing may understate net income, especially for a growing business with steadily increasing inventories.

# END-OF-CHAPTER REVIEW

## SUMMARY OF LEARNING OBJECTIVES

### LO 1

**Distinguish among cost centers, profit centers, and investment centers.**

A cost center is a responsibility center that incurs costs (or expenses) but does not directly generate revenue. A profit center is a business center that generates both revenue and costs. Some profit centers are also considered investment centers. An investment center is a profit center for which management is able to measure objectively the cost of assets used in the center's operations.

### LO 2

**Explain the need for responsibility center information and describe a responsibility accounting system.**

Responsibility center information presents separately the operating results of each business center within an organization. A responsibility accounting system shows the performance of the center under each manager's control.

### LO 3

**Prepare an income statement showing contribution margin and responsibility margin.**

In responsibility income statements, revenue is assigned to the profit center responsible for generating that revenue. Two concepts are used in assigning and classifying expenses. First, each center is charged only with those costs directly traceable to the center. Second, costs charged to the center are subdivided between the categories of variable costs and fixed costs. Subtracting variable costs from revenue indicates the center's contribution margin; subtracting traceable fixed costs indicates the responsibility margin.

### LO 4

**Distinguish between *traceable* and *common* fixed costs.**

A cost is traceable to a particular center if that center is solely responsible for the cost being incurred. Traceable costs should disappear if the center is discontinued. Common costs are not traceable to a particular center. Thus common costs will not disappear if the center is discontinued.

### LO 5

**Explain the usefulness of the contribution margin and responsibility margin in making short-term and long-term decisions.**

Fixed costs generally cannot be changed in the short run. Therefore, the effects of short-run strategies on operating income are equal to the change in contribution margin (revenue less variable costs). In the long run, however, strategies may affect changes in the fixed costs traceable to a business center. Therefore, the profitability of long-run strategies may be evaluated in terms of changes in responsibility margin (revenue less variable costs and less traceable fixed costs).

### LO 6

**Describe three transfer pricing methods and explain when each is useful.**

Transfer prices are the dollar amounts used by the supplying and buying divisions within a company to record the exchange of a good or service. When an external market exists for the product or service, then most companies use the market price as the transfer price. When no external market exists, then companies use either negotiated transfer prices or cost-plus transfer prices. Negotiated transfer prices are used when the buying and supplying divisions can agree on a transfer price. Where negotiation is too costly or not possible many companies add a predetermined mark-up to the supplying division's total cost to determine the transfer price.

### *LO 7

**Explain the differences between full costing and variable costing.**

Under full costing, fixed manufacturing costs are viewed as product costs and are included in the cost of finished goods manufactured. Under variable costing, fixed manufacturing costs are treated as period expenses. An income statement prepared on a variable costing basis is useful for cost-volume-profit analysis; however, variable costing is not acceptable for use in published financial statements or income tax returns.

### *LO 8

**Use a variable costing income statement in CVP analysis.**

In a variable costing income statement, costs are subdivided into the classifications of variable costs and fixed costs. This classification permits arranging an income statement in a manner showing subtotals for contribution margin and total fixed costs—two key amounts in cost-volume-profit analysis.

One purpose of this chapter is to "tie together" many of the concepts introduced in the preceding management accounting chapters. Notice, for example, how such concepts as the distinction between variable costs and fixed costs, cost-volume-profit relationships, the nature of period costs and product costs, and the flow of manufacturing costs through an accounting system have played major roles in our evaluation of a responsibil-

---

*Supplemental Topic*, "Variable Costing."

ity center's performance. In the next chapter, we introduce the topic of budgeting. The budget provides one of the major standards with which current performance is compared.

## KEY TERMS INTRODUCED OR EMPHASIZED IN CHAPTER 21

**absorption costing** (p. 890) See *full costing*.

**committed fixed costs** (p. 885) Fixed costs that are traceable to a responsibility center but that, in the short run, cannot readily be changed by the center's manager.

**common fixed costs** (p. 881) Fixed costs that are of joint benefit to several responsibility centers. These common costs cannot be traced to the centers deriving the benefit, except by arbitrary means.

**contribution margin** (p. 880) Revenue less variable costs; also, the amount of revenue available to contribute toward fixed costs and operating income (or responsibility margin). The key statistic for most types of cost-volume-profit analysis.

**controllable fixed costs** (p. 885) Fixed costs that are under the direct control of the center's manager.

**cost center** (p. 875) The part of a business that incurs costs but that does not directly generate revenue.

**cost-plus transfer price** (p. 887) The transfer price that results from adding a predetermined markup to the total cost of the product transferred.

**full costing** (p. 890) The traditional method of product costing in which both fixed and variable manufacturing costs are treated as product costs and charged to inventories. Also called *absorption costing*.

**investment center** (p. 877) A profit center for which management has been given decision-making responsibility for making significant capital investments related to the center's business activities.

**negotiated transfer price** (p. 887) The transfer price that results when the supplying and buying divisions negotiate and agree on a transfer price.

**performance margin** (p. 885) A subtotal in a responsibility income statement designed to assist in evaluating the performance of a manager based solely on revenues and expenses under the manager's control. Consists of contribution margin less the controllable fixed costs traceable to the department.

**period costs** (p. 890) Costs that are deducted as expense in the period in which they are incurred, rather than being classified as assets.

**product costs** (p. 890) Costs that become part of the inventory value of work in process and finished goods. These costs are deducted from revenue in the period that the related goods are sold.

**profit center** (p. 876) The part of a business that directly generates revenue as well as incurs costs.

**responsibility accounting system** (p. 878) An accounting system that separately measures the performance of each responsibility center in the organization.

**responsibility center** (p. 874) The part of a business a particular manager is in charge of and held responsible for.

**responsibility income statement** (p. 878) An income statement that subdivides the operating results of a business segment among the profit centers comprising that segment.

**responsibility margin** (p. 881) Revenue less variable costs and traceable fixed costs. A long-run measure of the profitability of a profit center. Consists of the revenue and costs likely to disappear if the responsibility center were eliminated.

**revenue center** (p. 876) A business unit that focuses on the accumulation of sales revenue.

**traceable fixed costs** (p. 881) Fixed costs that are directly traceable to a specific center. These costs usually would be eliminated if the center were discontinued.

**transfer price** (p. 886) The dollar amount used in recording products (either goods or services) supplied to one part of a business by another.

**variable costing** (p. 890) The technique of product costing in which only the variable manufacturing costs are regarded as product costs. Fixed manufacturing costs are treated as period costs. Useful for management purposes, but not acceptable for use in financial statements or income tax returns. Also called *direct costing*.

## ▌ DEMONSTRATION PROBLEM

Reed Mfg. Co. operates two plants that produce and sell floor tile. Shown below are the operating results of both plants during 2001, the company's first quarter of operations:

|  | St. Louis Plant | Springville Plant |
| --- | --- | --- |
| Sales | $2,000,000 | $2,000,000 |
| Variable costs | 720,000 | 880,000 |
| Traceable fixed costs | 750,000 | 550,000 |

During the quarter, common fixed costs relating to both plants amounted to $500,000.

**Instructions**

**a.** Prepare a partial income statement for Reed with responsibility by plant. Conclude with the company's income from operations.

**b.** At which plant would a $200,000 increase in sales contribute the most to Reed's operating income?

**c.** What types of costs and expenses might be included in the company's $500,000 common fixed costs?

## Solution to the Demonstration Problem

**a.** Responsibility income statement:

| | Profit Centers | | |
| --- | --- | --- | --- |
| | Reed Mfg. Co. | St. Louis Plant | Springville Plant |
| Sales | $4,000,000 | $2,000,000 | $2,000,000 |
| Variable costs | 1,600,000 | 720,000 | 880,000 |
| Contribution margin | $2,400,000 | $1,280,000 | $1,120,000 |
| Traceable fixed costs | 1,300,000 | 750,000 | 550,000 |
| Responsibility margin | $1,100,000 | $ 530,000 | $ 570,000 |
| Common fixed costs | 500,000 | | |
| Income from operations | $ 600,000 | | |

**b.** The St. Louis plant has a contribution margin ratio of 64% ($1,280,000 ÷ $2,000,000). Thus, should its sales increase by $200,000, the company's operating income would increase by $128,000 ($200,000 × 64%). The Springville plant has a contribution margin ratio of 56% ($1,120,000 ÷ $2,000,000). Should its sales increase by $200,000, the company's operating income would increase by only $112,000 ($200,000 × 56%).

**c.** The $500,000 would include fixed costs not directly traceable to either plant. Such items might include charges related to legal fees, corporate accounting and personnel departments, centralized computer facilities, and the salaries of corporate officers.

# SELF-TEST QUESTIONS

*Answers to these questions appear on page 913.*

**1.** Which of the following is a common fixed cost to the sales departments in a department store?

**a.** Salaries of store security personnel.

**b.** Salaries of sales department managers.

**c.** Cost of goods sold.

**d.** Depreciation on fixtures used exclusively in a specific sales department.

**2.** In preparing an income statement that measures contribution margin and responsibility margin, two concepts are applied in classifying costs. One is whether the costs are variable or fixed. The other is whether the costs are:

**a.** Product costs or period costs.

**b.** Traceable to the responsibility center.

**c.** Under the control of the manager.

**d.** Transfer prices.

**3.** A subtotal used in evaluating the performance of a responsibility center manager, as distinct from the performance of the center, is:

**a.** Contribution margin, less traceable fixed costs.

**b.** Sales, less committed costs.

**c.** Contribution margin, plus fixed costs deferred into inventory.

**d.** Contribution margin, less controllable fixed costs.

**4.** The Knuckles and Brackets Division transfers a component product to the Assembly Division. Both divisions are part of Automakers Inc. and are organized as profit centers. Automakers has a general policy of using a 10% mark-up for cost-based transfer prices. Knuckles and Brackets also can sell the component product in the open market to other automobile companies for $75. The cost to make the component is $55. By transferring the component internally, the Knuckles and Brackets Division saves $5 in sales expenses and transportation costs. The manager of the Knuckles and Brackets Division wants the transfer price to be $75 and the manager of the Assembly Division wants the transfer price to be $70. Which of the following are **not** true:

**a.** If the transfer price is $75 then the divisions are using a market-based transfer price.

**b.** If the transfer price is $40 then the divisions are using a cost-based transfer price.

**c.** If the transfer price is $70 then the divisions are using a negotiated transfer price.

**d.** If the transfer price is $70 then both divisions are sharing the profits.

**e.** If the transfer price is $55 then the Knuckles and Brackets Division is keeping all the profits.

*****5.** During its first year of operations, Marco Mfg. Co. manufactured 5 million units, of which 4 million were sold. Manufacturing costs for the year were as follows:

| | |
|---|---|
| Fixed manufacturing costs | $10,000,000 |
| Variable manufacturing costs | $3 per unit |

Which of the following answers is correct? (In all cases, assume that unit sales for the year remain at 4 million; more than one answer may be correct.)

**a.** Under variable costing, income from operations will be $2,000,000 less than full costing.

**b.** Under full costing, the cost of goods sold would have been $2 million greater if Marco had manufactured only 4 million units during the year.

**c.** Under variable costing, the amount of manufacturing costs deducted from revenue during the year will be $22 million, regardless of the number of units manufactured.

**d.** Under full costing, Marco's net income would have been higher for the first year of operations if more units had been manufactured.

## ASSIGNMENT MATERIAL

## DISCUSSION QUESTIONS

**1.** What are some of the uses that management may make of accounting information about individual responsibility centers of the business?

**2.** Explain how a responsibility accounting system can assist managers in controlling the costs of a large business organization.

**3.** Distinguish among a *cost center*, a *profit center*, and an *investment center*, and give an example of each.

**4.** Marshall's Grocery Store has a small bakery that sells coffee and baked goods at very low prices. (For example, coffee and one doughnut cost 25 cents.) The basic purpose of the bakery is to attract customers to the store and to make the store "smell like a bakery." In each period, costs traceable to the bakery exceed revenue. Would you evaluate the bakery as a cost center or as a profit center? Explain.

---

*Supplemental Topic*, "Variable Costing."

5. Explain why setting transfer prices can be controversial when a product is being transferred between two profit centers.

6. What is a *responsibility accounting system?*

7. The operation of a responsibility accounting system involves three basic steps. In this chapter, we emphasize the second step: measuring the performance of each responsibility center. List all three steps in the logical sequence of occurrence.

8. In a responsibility accounting system, should the recording of revenue and costs begin at the largest areas of responsibility or the smallest? Explain.

9. In the responsibility income statements illustrated in this chapter, two concepts are used in classifying costs. What are these concepts?

10. Distinguish between *traceable* and *common* fixed costs. Give an example of each type of fixed cost for an auto dealership with a sales department and a service department.

11. How do the costs of operating *service departments* (organized as cost centers) appear in a responsibility income statement?

12. DeskTop, Inc., operates a national sales organization. The income statements prepared for each sales territory are created by product line. In these income statements, the sales territory manager's salary is treated as a common fixed cost. Will this salary be viewed as a common fixed cost at all levels of the organization? Explain.

13. Assume that Department A has a higher contribution margin ratio, but a lower responsibility margin ratio, than Department B. If $10,000 in advertising is expected to increase the sales of either department by $50,000, in which department can the advertising dollars be spent to the best advantage?

14. Criticize the following statement: "In our business, we maximize profits by closing any department that does not show a responsibility margin ratio of at least 15%."

15. What is the relationship between contribution margin and responsibility margin? Explain how each of these measurements is useful in making management decisions.

16. What does a consistently negative responsibility margin imply will happen to the operating income of the business if the center is closed? Why? Identify several other factors that should be considered in deciding whether or not to close the center.

17. Briefly explain the distinction between *controllable* fixed costs and *committed* fixed costs. Also explain the nature and purpose of performance margin in a responsibility income statement.

18. The controller of Fifties, a chain of drive-in restaurants, is considering modifying the monthly income statements by charging all costs relating to operations of the corporate headquarters to the individual restaurants in proportion to each restaurant's gross revenue. Do you think that this would increase the usefulness of the responsibility income statement in evaluating the performance of the restaurants or the restaurant managers? Explain.

19. Explain why using cost as a transfer price is *inappropriate* when the center producing the product is evaluated as a *profit center*.

*20. Distinguish between *variable costing* and *full costing*. Which method is used in financial statements? Which method is used in income tax returns?

*21. Explain why a variable costing income statement provides a better basis for cost-volume-profit analysis than does a full costing income statement.

*22. Rose Speakers, a division of Innovative Sound, temporarily increases production to exceed unit sales, thereby causing its inventory of finished goods to increase. Explain the effect of this action on the responsibility margin reported by Rose under (a) full costing and (b) variable costing.

---

*Supplemental Topic*, "Variable Costing."

## EXERCISES

The following are nine technical accounting terms introduced or emphasized in this chapter:

Responsibility margin   Transfer price   Common fixed costs

Contribution margin   Cost-plus transfer price   Traceable fixed costs

Performance margin   Product costs   Committed fixed costs

**EXERCISE 21.1**

Accounting Terminology

**LO 1, 4, 6**

Each of the following statements may (or may not) describe one of these technical terms. For each statement, indicate the accounting term described, or answer "None" if the statement does not correctly describe any of the terms.

**a.** The costs deducted from contribution margin to determine responsibility margin

**b.** Cost to produce plus a predetermined markup

**c.** Fixed costs that are readily controllable by the manager

**d.** A subtotal in a responsibility income statement, equal to responsibility margin plus committed fixed costs

**e.** The subtotal in a responsibility income statement that is most useful in evaluating the short-run effect of various marketing strategies on the income of the business

**f.** The subtotal in a responsibility income statement that comes closest to indicating the change in income from operations that would result from closing a particular part of the business

**g.** The amount used in recording products or services supplied by one business unit to another

Video World owns and operates a national chain of video game arcades. Indicate whether Video World would evaluate each of the following as an investment center, a profit center (other than an investment center), or a cost center. Briefly explain the reasons for your answer.

**a.** An individual video arcade within a chain of video arcades

**b.** A snack bar within one of the company's arcades

**c.** A particular video game within one of the company's arcades

**d.** The security officers at each arcade location

**EXERCISE 21.2**

Types of Responsibility Centers

**LO 1**

The controller of Maxwell Department Store is preparing an income statement, divided by sales departments and including subtotals for contribution margin, performance margin, and responsibility margin. Indicate the appropriate classification of the seven items (**a** through **g**) listed below. Select from the following cost classifications:

**EXERCISE 21.3**

Classification of Costs in an Income Statement

**LO 4, 5**

Variable costs

Traceable fixed costs—controllable

Traceable fixed costs—committed

Common fixed costs

None of the above

**a.** Cost of operating the store's accounting department

**b.** Cost of advertising specific product lines (classify as a fixed cost)

**c.** Sales taxes on merchandise sold

**d.** Depreciation on the hydraulic lifts used in the Automotive Service Department

**e.** Salaries of departmental sales personnel

**f.** Salary of the store manager

**g.** Cost of merchandise sold in the Sportswear Department

Look at footnote 11 in **Tootsie Roll Industries'** annual report in Appendix A. The footnote details segments of **Tootsie Roll's** business. Answer the following questions based on the information in footnote 11:

**a.** What are the segments presented by **Tootsie Roll**? Are these segments likely to be cost, profit, or investment centers? Explain your answers.

**EXERCISE 21.4**

**Tootsie Roll Industries'** Units

**LO 1, 4, 6**

**b.** What is the dollar amount of sales that are transferred between the segments in 1999? Are transfers increasing or decreasing between 1998 and 1999? Speculate about why the transfers between segments might increase or decrease.

**EXERCISE 21.5**

Preparing a Responsibility Income Statement

Gemini Technologies has two product lines: lasers and integrated circuits. During the current month, the two product lines reported the following results:

| | Lasers | Circuits |
|---|---|---|
| Sales | $500,000 | $800,000 |
| Variable costs (as a percentage of sales) | 40% | 60% |
| Traceable fixed costs | 200,000 | 250,000 |

In addition, fixed costs common to both product lines amounted to $80,000.

Prepare an income statement showing percentages as well as dollar amounts. Conclude your statement with income from operations for the business and with the responsibility margin for each product line.

**Exercises 21.6, 21.7, and 21.8 are based on the following data:**

Shown below is a segmented income statement for Drexel-Hall during the current month:

| | Drexel-Hall | | Store 1 | | Store 2 | | Store 3 | |
|---|---|---|---|---|---|---|---|---|
| | Dollars | % | Dollars | % | Dollars | % | Dollars | % |
| Sales | $1,800,000 | 100% | $600,000 | 100% | $600,000 | 100% | $600,000 | 100% |
| Variable costs | 1,080,000 | 60 | 372,000 | 62 | 378,000 | 63 | 330,000 | 55 |
| Contribution margin | $ 720,000 | 40% | $228,000 | 38% | $222,000 | 37% | $270,000 | 45% |
| Traceable fixed costs: controllable | 432,000 | 24 | 120,000 | 20 | 102,000 | 17 | 210,000 | 35 |
| Performance margin | $ 288,000 | 16% | $108,000 | 18% | $120,000 | 20% | $ 60,000 | 10% |
| Traceable fixed costs: committed | 180,000 | 10 | 48,000 | 8 | 66,000 | 11 | 66,000 | 11 |
| Store responsibility margins | $ 108,000 | 6% | $ 60,000 | 10% | $ 54,000 | 9% | $ (6,000) | (1)% |
| Common fixed costs | 36,000 | 2 | | | | | | |
| Income from operations | $ 72,000 | 4% | | | | | | |

All stores are similar in size, carry similar products, and operate in similar neighborhoods. *Store 1* was established first and was built at a lower cost than were Stores 2 and 3. This lower cost results in less depreciation expense for Store 1. *Store 2* follows a policy of minimizing both costs and sales prices. *Store 3* follows a policy of providing extensive customer service and charges slightly higher prices than the other two stores.

**EXERCISE 21.6**

Evaluation of Responsibility Centers and Center Managers

Use the data presented above for Drexel-Hall to answer the following questions:

**a.** Assume that by spending an additional $15,000 per month in advertising a particular store, Drexel-Hall can increase the sales of that store by 10%. Which store should the company advertise to receive the maximum benefit from this additional advertising expenditure? Explain.

**b.** From the viewpoint of top management, which is the most profitable of the three stores? Why?

**c.** Which store manager seems to be pursuing the most effective strategy in managing his or her store? Why?

**EXERCISE 21.7**

Closing an Unprofitable Business Unit

Top management of Drexel-Hall is considering closing Store 3. The three stores are close enough together that management estimates closing Store 3 would cause sales at Store 1 to increase by $60,000, and sales at Store 2 to increase by $120,000. Closing Store 3 is not expected to cause any change in common fixed costs.

Compute the increase or decrease that closing Store 3 should cause in:

**a.** Total monthly sales for Drexel-Hall Stores.

**b.** The monthly responsibility margins of Stores 1 and 2.

**c.** The company's monthly income from operations.

The marketing manager of Drexel-Hall is considering two alternative advertising strategies, each of which would cost $15,000 per month. One strategy is to advertise the name Drexel-Hall, which is expected to increase the monthly sales at all stores by 5%. The other strategy is to emphasize the low prices available at Store 2, which is expected to increase monthly sales at Store 2 by $150,000, but to reduce sales by $30,000 per month at Stores 1 and 3.

Determine the expected effect of each strategy on the company's overall income from operations.

**EXERCISE 21.8**

Cost-Volume-Profit Analysis

**LO 1–4**

Delmar Foods has two divisions: (1) a Processed Meat Division and (2) a Frozen Pizza Division. Delmar's frozen pizzas use processed meat as a topping. The company's Processed Meat Division supplies the Frozen Pizza Division with all of its meat toppings. Delmar managers are paid bonuses based on their division's profitability.

The manager of the Processed Meat Division argues for a transfer price based on a market value approach. The manager of Frozen Pizza Division favors a transfer price based on a cost approach. Explain how Delmar's bonus system may influence each manager's opinion regarding which approach to use in establishing a transfer price.

**EXERCISE 21.9**

Transfer Pricing

**LO 1, 2, 6**

The following are the manufacturing costs of Hensley Products for its first year of operations:

**\*EXERCISE 21.10**

Comparison of Full Costing and Variable Costing

**LO 7, 8**

| Variable manufacturing costs per unit: | | |
|---|---:|---:|
| Direct materials used | $ | 15 |
| Direct labor | | 12 |
| Variable manufacturing overhead | | 3 |
| Fixed manufacturing overhead | | 3,400,000 |

**a.** Compute the cost of goods sold using full costing and assuming that the company:

  **1.** Manufactured and sold 200,000 units.

  **2.** Manufactured 340,000 units and sold 200,000 units.

**b.** Compute the cost of goods sold using the variable costing approach under each of the two assumptions given in part **a**.

**c.** Explain why full costing resulted in different cost of goods sold amounts than those computed using variable costing under each assumption given in part **a**.

The following are cost and sales data for Aluminum Products, Inc., at the end of its first year of operations:

**\*EXERCISE 21.11**

Full Costing versus Variable Costing

**LO 7, 8**

| Sales (100,000 units @ $50) | $5,000,000 |
|---|---:|
| Manufacturing costs (125,000 units): | |
| Variable | 1,750,000 |
| Fixed | 2,125,000 |
| Selling and administrative expenses (all fixed) | 750,000 |

**a.** Compute the per-unit manufacturing cost that will be used in the valuation of inventory and in the determination of the cost of goods sold under (1) full costing and (2) variable costing.

---

*\*Supplemental Topic*, "Variable Costing."

**b.** Compute the income from operations for the year, assuming the use of (1) full costing and (2) variable costing.

**c.** Explain the cause of the different amounts of income from operations under the full costing and variable costing approaches.

## PROBLEMS

**PROBLEM 21.1**

Types of Responsibility Centers and Basis for Evaluation

**LO 1**

Listed below are parts of various well-known businesses:

1. The Women's Sportswear Department in a **Sears** store
2. The Marriott Marquis, the Manhattan Island hotel of **Marriott Corporation**
3. The Central Accounting Department of **Daimler Chrysler Corporation**
4. The Subscriptions Billing Department of *The Wall Street Journal*
5. The Emporium on Main Street, a gift souvenir shop at **Disneyland**
6. The Milton, Pennsylvania, plant of **American Home Foods Corporation**

### Instructions

**a.** Indicate whether each part represents an investment center, a profit center (other than an investment center), or a cost center.

**b.** Briefly explain the criteria that are used in evaluating (1) investment centers, (2) profit centers, and (3) cost centers.

**PROBLEM 21.2**

Preparing and Using Responsibility Income Statements

**LO 3–5**

Regal Flair Enterprises has two product lines: jewelry and women's apparel. Cost and revenue data for each product line for the current month are as follows:

|  | Product Lines | |
| --- | --- | --- |
|  | Jewelry | Apparel |
| Sales . . . . . . . . . . . . . . . . . . . . . . . . . . . . . . . . . . . . . . . . . . . . . | $800,000 | $450,000 |
| Variable costs as a percentage of sales . . . . . . . . . . . . . . . . . . . . . . . | 55% | 28% |
| Fixed costs traceable to product lines . . . . . . . . . . . . . . . . . . . . . . . . | $200,000 | $250,000 |

In addition to the costs shown above, the company incurs monthly fixed costs of $100,000 common to both product lines.

### Instructions

**a.** Prepare Regal Flair Enterprises' responsibility income statement for the current month. Report the responsibility margin for each product line and income from operations for the company as a whole. Also include columns showing all dollar amounts as percentages of sales.

**b.** Assume that a marketing survey shows that a $75,000 monthly advertising campaign focused on either product line should increase that product line's monthly sales by approximately $150,000. Do you recommend this additional advertising for either or both product lines? Show computations to support your conclusions.

**c.** Management is considering expanding one of the company's two product lines. An investment of a given dollar amount is expected to increase the sales of the expanded product line by $300,000. It is also expected to increase the traceable fixed costs of the expanded product line by 75%. Based on this information, which product line do you recommend expanding? Explain the basis for your conclusion.

**PROBLEM 21.3**

Preparing and Using a Responsibility Income Statement

**LO 3–5**

The Giant Chef Equipment Company is organized into two divisions: Commercial Sales and Home Products. During June, sales for the Commercial Sales Division totaled $1,500,000, and its contribution margin ratio averaged 34%. Sales generated by the Home Products Division totaled $900,000, and its contribution margin ratio averaged 50%. Monthly fixed costs traceable to each division total $180,000. Common fixed costs for the month amount to $120,000.

## Instructions

**a.** Prepare Giant Chef Equipment's responsibility income statement for the current month. Be certain to report responsibility margin for each division and income from operations for the company as a whole. Also include columns showing all dollar amounts as percentages of sales.

**b.** Compute the dollar sales volume required for the Home Products Division to earn a monthly responsibility margin of *$500,000*.

**c.** A marketing study indicates that sales in the Home Products Division would increase by *5%* if advertising expenditures for the division were increased by *$15,000* per month. Would you recommend this increase in advertising? Show computations to support your decision.

Health Tech, Inc., sells home exercise equipment. The company has two sales territories, Eastern and Western. Two products are sold in each territory: FasTrak (a Nordic ski simulator) and Row-Master (a stationary rowing machine).

During January, the following data are reported for the Eastern territory:

**PROBLEM 21.4**

Preparing Responsibility Income Statements in a Responsibility Accounting System

|  | FasTrak | RowMaster |
|---|---|---|
| Sales . . . . . . . . . . . . . . . . . . . . . . . . . . . . . . . . . . . . . . . . . . . . . . . | $400,000 | $750,000 |
| Contribution margin ratios . . . . . . . . . . . . . . . . . . . . . . . . . . . . . . . | 60% | 40% |
| Traceable fixed costs . . . . . . . . . . . . . . . . . . . . . . . . . . . . . . . . . . . | 80,000 | 150,000 |

Common fixed costs in the Eastern territory amounted to $120,000 during the month.

During January, the Western territory reported total sales of $600,000, variable costs of $270,000, and a responsibility margin of $200,000. Health Tech also incurred $180,000 of common fixed costs that were not traceable to either sales territory.

In addition to being profit centers, each territory is also evaluated as an investment center. Average assets utilized by the Eastern and Western territories amount to $15,000,000 and $10,000,000, respectively.

## Instructions

**a.** Prepare the January income statement for the Eastern territory by product line. Include columns showing percentages as well as dollar amounts.

**b.** Prepare the January income statement for the company showing profits by sales territories. Conclude your statement with income from operations for the company and with responsibility margins for the two territories. Show percentages as well as dollar amounts.

**c.** Compute the rate of return on average assets earned in each sales territory during the month of January.

**d.** In part **a**, your income statement for the Eastern territory included $120,000 in common fixed costs. What happened to these common fixed costs in the responsibility income statement shown in part **b**?

**e.** The manager of the Eastern territory is authorized to spend an additional $50,000 per month in advertising one of the products. Based on past experience, the manager estimates that additional advertising would increase the sales of either product by $120,000. On which product should the manager focus this advertising campaign? Explain.

**f.** Top management is considering investing several million dollars to expand operations in one of its two sales territories. The expansion would increase traceable fixed costs to expanded territory in proportion to its increase in sales. Which territory would be the best candidate for this investment? Explain.

Shown on the following page are responsibility income statements for Butterfield, Inc., for the month of March.

**PROBLEM 21.5**

Analysis of Responsibility Income Statements

## Instructions

**a.** The company plans to initiate an advertising campaign for one of the two products in Division 1. The campaign would cost $10,000 per month and is expected to increase the sales of whichever product is advertised by $30,000 per month. Compute the expected increase in the responsibility margin of Division 1 assuming that (1) product A is advertised and (2) product B is advertised.

**b.** Assume that the sales of both products by Division 1 are equal to total manufacturing capacity. To increase sales of either product, the company must increase manufacturing facilities, which means an increase in traceable fixed costs in approximate proportion to the expected increase in sales. In this case, which product line would you recommend expanding? Explain.

| | Investment Centers | | | | | |
| | Butterfield, Inc. | | Division 1 | | Division 2 | |
| | Dollars | % | Dollars | % | Dollars | % |
| --- | --- | --- | --- | --- | --- | --- |
| Sales . . . . . . . . . . . . . . . . | $450,000 | 100% | $300,000 | 100% | $150,000 | 100% |
| Variable costs . . . . . . . . . . . | 225,000 | 50 | 180,000 | 60 | 45,000 | 30 |
| Contribution margin . . . . . . . | $225,000 | 50% | $120,000 | 40% | $105,000 | 70% |
| Fixed costs traceable to divisions . . . . . . . . . . . . | 135,000 | 30 | 63,000 | 21 | 72,000 | 48 |
| Division responsibility margins . . . . . . . . . . . . . | $ 90,000 | 20% | $ 57,000 | 19% | $ 33,000 | 22% |
| Common fixed costs . . . . . . | 45,000 | 10 | | | | |
| Income from operations . . . . | $ 45,000 | 10% | | | | |

| | Profit Centers | | | | | |
| | Division 1 | | Product A | | Product B | |
| | Dollars | % | Dollars | % | Dollars | % |
| --- | --- | --- | --- | --- | --- | --- |
| Sales . . . . . . . . . . . . . . . . | $300,000 | 100% | $100,000 | 100% | $200,000 | 100% |
| Variable costs . . . . . . . . . . . | 180,000 | 60 | 52,000 | 52 | 128,000 | 64 |
| Contribution margin . . . . . . . | $120,000 | 40% | $ 48,000 | 48% | $ 72,000 | 36% |
| Fixed costs traceable to products . . . . . . . . . . . . | 42,000 | 14 | 26,000 | 26 | 16,000 | 8 |
| Product responsibility margins . . . . . . . . . . . . . | $ 78,000 | 26% | $ 22,000 | 22% | $ 56,000 | 28% |
| Common fixed costs . . . . . . | 21,000 | 7 | | | | |
| Responsibility margin for division . . . . . . . . . . . . . | $ 57,000 | 19% | | | | |

**c.** The income statement for Division 1 includes $21,000 in common fixed costs. What happens to these fixed costs in the income statements for Butterfield, Inc.?

**d.** Assume that in April the monthly sales in Division 2 increase to $200,000. Compute the expected effect of this change on the operating income of the company (assume no other changes in revenue or cost behavior).

**e.** Prepare an income statement for Butterfield, Inc., by division, under the assumption stated in part **d**. Organize this income statement in the format illustrated above, including columns for percentages.

**PROBLEM 21.6**

Evaluating an Unprofitable Business Center

**LO 3–5**

FlyWiz, Inc., is a small manufacturer of professional fishing equipment. The company has two divisions: the Rod Division and the Reel Division. Data for the month of January are as follows:

| | Entire Company | Profit Centers Rod Division | Profit Centers Reel Division |
|---|---|---|---|
| Sales | $64,000 | $26,000 | $38,000 |
| Variable costs | 29,000 | 13,000 | 16,000 |
| Contribution margins | $35,000 | $13,000 | $22,000 |
| Traceable fixed costs | 27,000 | 17,000 | 10,000 |
| Division responsibility margins | $ 8,000 | $ (4,000) | $12,000 |
| Common fixed costs | 3,000 | | |
| Monthly operating income | $ 5,000 | | |

Nick Fulbright, the company's chief financial officer since January 1 of the current year, wants to close the unprofitable Rod Division. He believes that doing so will benefit FlyWiz and bene-fit him, given that his end-of-year bonus is to be based on the company's overall operating in-come. In a recent interview, Nick summarized his business philosophy as follows: "A company is only as strong as its least profitable segment. As long as I'm at the financial helm, only the strongest shall survive at FlyWiz."

### Instructions
**a.** Had the Rod Division been closed on *January 1*, what would the company's operating income for the month have been?

**b.** After learning about Nick's business philosophy, the Rod Division's director of marketing made the following statement: "Nick Fulbright may understand numbers, but he doesn't understand the complementary relationship between rods and reels, nor the seasonal nature of our busi-ness." What did the director of marketing mean by this statement? How might such informa-tion influence Nick's assessment of the company's Rod Division?

**c.** By how much would the Rod Division's monthly sales have to increase for it to generate a positive responsibility margin of $4,000 in any given month? Show all of your computations.

Westfall Corporation has two divisions: the Motor Division and the Pump Division. The Motor Division supplies the motors used by the Pump Division. The Pump Division produces approxi-mately 10,000 pumps annually. Thus it receives 10,000 motors from the Motor Division each year. The market price of these motors is $350. Their total variable cost is $185 per unit. The market price of the pumps is $500. The unit variable cost of each pump, excluding the cost of the motor, is $75.

The Motor Division is currently operating at full capacity, producing 20,000 motors per year (10,000 of which are transferred to the Pump Division). The demand for the motors is so great that all 20,000 units could be sold to outside customers if the Pump Division acquired its motors elsewhere. The Motor Division uses the full market price of $350 as the transfer price charged to the Pump Division.

The manager of the Pump Division asserts that the Motor Division benefits from the inter-company transfers because of reduced advertising costs. Thus he wants to negotiate a lower trans-fer price of $320 per unit.

**PROBLEM 21.7**

Transfer Pricing Decisions

**LO 1, 2, 3, 6**

### Instructions
**a.** Compute the contribution margin earned annually by each division and by the company as a whole using the current transfer price.

**b.** Compute the contribution margin that would be earned annually by each division and by the company as a whole if the discounted transfer price were used.

**c.** What issues and concerns should be considered in setting a transfer price for intercompany transfers of motors?

**\*PROBLEM 21.8**

Variable Costing

**LO 7, 8**

Lathrop Corporation manufactures and sells a single product. The following costs were incurred during 2002, the company's first year of operations:

| | |
|---|---|
| Variable costs per unit: | |
|   Direct materials used | $18 |
|   Direct labor | 9 |
|   Variable manufacturing overhead | 3 |
|   Variable selling and administrative expenses | 7 |
| Fixed costs for the year: | |
|   Manufacturing overhead | $900,000 |
|   Selling and administrative expenses | 250,000 |

During the year, the company manufactured 90,000 units, of which 75,000 were sold at a price of $60 per unit. The 15,000 units in inventory at year-end were all finished goods.

### Instructions

**a.** Assuming that the company uses full costing:

  **1.** Determine the per-unit cost of each finished good manufactured during 2002.

  **2.** Prepare a partial income statement for the year, ending with income from operations.

**b.** Assuming that the company uses variable costing:

  **1.** Determine the per-unit cost of each finished good manufactured during 2002.

  **2.** Prepare a partial income statement for the year, ending with income from operations.

**c.** Explain why your income statements in parts **a** and **b** result in different amounts of income from operations. Indicate which costing approach is used in published financial statements, and briefly explain the usefulness of the other approach.

**d.** Using the data contained in the variable costing income statement, compute (1) the contribution margin per unit sold and (2) the unit sales volume that must be manufactured and sold annually for Lathrop Corporation to break even.

# CASES AND UNSTRUCTURED PROBLEMS

**CASE 21.1**

Allocating Fixed Costs to Responsibility Centers

**LO 1, 2, 4**

You have just been hired as the controller of Land's End Hotel. The hotel prepares monthly responsibility income statements in which all fixed costs are allocated among the various profit centers in the hotel, based on the relative amounts of revenue generated by each profit center.

Robert Chamberlain, manager of the hotel dining room, argues that this approach understates the profitability of his department. "Through developing a reputation as a fine restaurant, the dining room has significantly increased its revenue. Yet the more revenue we earn, the larger the percentage of the hotel's operating costs that are charged against our department. Also, whenever vacancies go up, rental revenue goes down, and the dining room is charged with a still greater percentage of overall operating costs. Our strong performance is concealed by poor performance in departments responsible for keeping occupancy rates up." Chamberlain suggests that fixed costs relating to the hotel should be allocated among the profit centers based on the number of square feet occupied by each department.

Debra Mettenburg, manager of the Sunset Lounge, objects to Chamberlain's proposal. She points out that the lounge is very big, because it is designed for hotel guests to read, relax, and watch the sunset. Although the lounge does serve drinks, the revenue earned in the lounge is small in relation to its square footage. Many guests just come to the lounge for the free hors d'oeuvres and don't even order a drink. Chamberlain's proposal would cause the lounge to appear unprofitable; yet a hotel must have some "open space" for its guests to sit and relax.

---

*\*Supplemental Topic*, "Variable Costing."

**Instructions**

**a.** Separately evaluate the points raised by each of the two managers.

**b.** Suggest your own approach to allocating the hotel's fixed costs among the various profit centers.

Osborn Diversified Products, Inc., is a billion-dollar manufacturing company with headquarters in Dayton, Ohio. The company has 15 divisions, two of which are the Battery Division and the Golf Cart Division. The company's Battery Division supplies the Golf Cart Division with batteries used to power electric carts.

Jim Peterson, age 45, is the general manager of the Battery Division. Jim has been with the company for 18 years and has done a remarkable job managing his operations. Unfortunately, due to health reasons, his physician has ordered that he take early retirement effective immediately. Jim is the single parent of a daughter who is currently a sophomore at a private university in Boston.

Sara Morrison, age 65, is the general manager of the Golf Cart Division. She has been with the company for 40 years and has been subjected to intense ridicule regarding her performance. In a fit of rage, the company's CEO recently told Sara that he "regrets the day he ever promoted a woman to division manager." Sara and her husband Rob are independently wealthy with a net worth in excess of $20 million. She will happily retire from the company with a full pension in several months.

Both Jim and Sara receive bonuses based on the responsibility margins earned by their respective divisions. However, Jim's contract specifies that his bonus is to be calculated *net of any intercompany transactions*. Thus his bonus is based on the Battery Division's segment margin *less* that portion earned from selling batteries to the Golf Cart Division.

Due to an undetected computer error, Jim's recent bonus was *not* calculated net of intercompany transactions. As such, the bonus was approximately $40,000 *more* than it should have been. Jim is the only division manager affected by the error. No one else in the company is aware that the error occurred. In view of Jim's personal situation, his attorney has advised him—off the record—to keep the money because the probability of the mistake being detected is *extremely remote*. Due to the design of the company's responsibility accounting system, the only person likely to ever detect the error is Sara, and the chance that she will do so prior to her retirement is slim.

**Instructions**

**a.** Will this billion-dollar company be significantly damaged by the error in computing Jim's bonus? If you were in Jim's situation, what would you do? Defend your answer.

**b.** Assume that Sara becomes aware of the error one week prior to her retirement. She remains bitter over the criticism and sexist remarks she has received from the company's CEO, yet she is basically an honest person. What would you do if you were Sara?

**c.** Is it ethical for Jim's attorney to suggest—albeit off the record—that Jim keep the money? What would you do if you were Jim's attorney?

**d.** Assume that you are Jim's daughter, who attends a private Boston university. You have learned that the only chance your father has of keeping you enrolled at this prestigious institution is to subsidize your tuition with the excess $40,000 he received from his company. However, if you were to transfer back to Ohio and live at home, there would be sufficient funds to pay for your education. What would you do in her situation? Defend your answer.

**CASE 21.2**

An Ethical Dilemma

**LO 1, 3, 6**

---

**BUSINESS WEEK ASSIGNMENT**

BusinessWeek

In a March 29, 1999, *Business Week* article titled "The Doctor Is for Sale," author Mark Hyman describes a new trend in sports franchises as follows:

> Giants fans will be able to leave their seats not only for a hot dog or brew but also for an x-ray or a throat culture . . . Catholic Healthcare West is paying the [San Francisco] Giants a cool $15 million over 12 years for the stadium space and other marketing goodies.
>
> For the franchises, health-care agreements are simply smart business. The right deal can turn what had been a team expense—medical care for players—into a profit center . . . some

**CASE 21.3**

Baseball and Profit Centers

**LO 1, 2, 4, 5**

in the medical community say the marriage of sports teams and health-care groups can be troubling. . . . "It's not an appropriate use of our funds as a nonprofit, research-oriented hospital," says Toby Gordon. . . . Questions also arise about the criteria teams use to select their physicians. Are they seeking out the finest medical minds or the highest bidders?

### Instructions

a. Choose a partner, or your instructor may assign you a partner. One of you should take the perspective of the sports franchise and the other health-care provider's perspective. Identify short-run revenues and expenses associated with the profit center described above using your chosen perspective.

b. With your partner, debate the ethical issues raised in the above quote. Do these ethical issues also involve short- and long-run profit issues?

## INTERNET ASSIGNMENT

**INTERNET 21.1**

**LO 1–3**

**General Mills** produces and sells a variety of food products in numerous countries. Access its home page at the following address:

**www.generalmills.com**

The **Kirby Company** manufactures and sells one product line—vacuum cleaners and their accessories. Access its home page at the following address:

**www.kirby.com**

### Instructions

a. Based on information from the website, how would you divide **General Mills** into responsibility centers based on product lines? Give examples of possible investment centers, profit centers, and cost centers.

b. Based on information from the website, how would you divide **Kirby** into responsibility centers? Give examples of possible investment centers, profit centers, and cost centers.

c. What organizational factors might account for the differences between the two firms' responsibility center systems?

*Internet sites are time and date sensitive. It is the purpose of these exercises to have you explore the Internet. You may need to use the Yahoo! search engine* http://www.yahoo.com *(or other favorite search engine) to find a company's current web address.*

## OUR COMMENTS ON THE "YOUR TURN" CASES

**As a Responsibility Center Manager (p. 875)**   To evaluate the effectiveness of decisions about janitorial services, management should make comparisons between the cost and quality of internally versus externally provided janitorial services. Janitorial services could be evaluated by creating information from internal and external benchmarks. A comparison of the seven clinics, assuming they have similar cleaning needs, can be used to create the internal benchmarks. External benchmark information can be generated from inquiries to cleaning service businesses and by talking to other health care companies that outsource their cleaning services. Efficiency of input use at the highest level of quality output should be the focus of performance evaluation information. Using the smallest amount of resources to achieve the highest quality of cleaning should be the goal.

**As a Clinic Manager (p. 877)**   If the measure of assets is historically based book value, then your assets will have a much higher value because your asset base is much newer than the other clinics. Thus your numbers will be affected and you will need to generate a higher profit than other clinics to have a comparable profitability. The board could adjust the assets of each clinic to reflect market values in order to make the numbers more comparable. The board also could consider other variables. Robert S. Kaplan, a Harvard Business School professor, recommends that evaluations be based on a "balanced score card" approach, where financial outcomes are only one of four categories firms use to evaluate performance. The other categories are customer satisfaction, contribution to firm learning and innovation, and internal productivity. The balanced scorecard is discussed in Chapter 24.

**You as a Department Manager (p. 880)**   To begin, it is unethical to *knowingly* increase the overall inefficiency and cost of the company to meet your budget goals. However, you should point out to the manager of the Packaging Department that the Sales Department's responsibility report does not provide the cost associated with an expedited order. As a result, you were not aware that the decisions you were making to meet your budget goals were causing cost overruns in the Packaging Department. A method to resolve this problem is to discuss with the division manager or corporate controller the shared responsibility for the costs of expediting. The company's controller can modify the responsibility accounting system to charge the Sales Department with the extra labor and shipping costs of processing rush orders. After this change is made, the Sales Department will be motivated to make a greater effort to give the Packaging Department adequate notice of all sales orders.

## ANSWERS TO SELF-TEST QUESTIONS

**1.** a    **2.** b    **3.** d    **4.** b, e    **5.** a, b, c, d

# 22

# OPERATIONAL BUDGETING

## Learning Objectives

*After studying this chapter, you should be able to:*

1. Explain how a company can be "profit rich, yet cash poor."

2. Discuss the benefits that a company may derive from a formal budgeting process.

3. Explain two philosophies that may be used in setting budgeted amounts.

4. Describe the elements of a master budget.

5. Prepare the budgets and supporting schedules included in a master budget.

6. Prepare a flexible budget and explain its uses.

© Dwayne E. Newton/Photo Edit

# Nike, Inc.

Bill Bowerman, head of the track team at University of Oregon, created a better running shoe by pouring rubber into his waffle iron in 1971. This "rubber waffle" was the first step in the creation of the sole of the modern running shoe. Bowerman met Phil Knight at the University of Oregon and they became partners in a company that was a precursor to **Nike, Inc.**, named after the Greek goddess of victory. **Nike** now earns more than $6.5 billion in revenues per year.

Lately, fashions have changed and sales of athletic shoes have gone south. **Nike**, along with other athletic shoe makers, experienced flat revenues and lagging profits from the late 1990s into early 2000. In an attempt to reverse this trend, **Nike** has tried to reinvent itself. According to Louise Lee's article, "Can Nike Still Do It?" in the February 21, 2000, *Business Week*, one of the important financial tools **Nike** is using to improve profitability is its operating budget.

For the first time in years, **Nike** executives are taking a hard look at costs. Years of breakneck growth encouraged free spending. In the past, managers had plenty of big-picture goals but no hard budget numbers to rein them in. Now, managers have to hold expense increases to about 3% below revenue increases. **Nike** has spent much of the past two years increasing financial accountability around the company to make employees more conscious of sales performance and expenses.

●  ●  ●

This chapter outlines the basics of operational budgeting, a tool that helps management make the organization accountable for sales and expenses.

Companies such as **Nike Inc.** use the budget (1) to assign decision-making authority over the company's resources, (2) to coordinate and implement plans, and (3) to hold employees accountable for the results of their decision making.

In this chapter, we will show you how to *construct* responsibility budgets and *use* those budgets to assign decision-making authority and hold employees accountable for their decisions. The master budget and its many components are detailed. Using the master budget as a means to implement planning and control through flexible budgeting is explained. By the time you finish studying this chapter, you should appreciate the role of budgeting as a cornerstone of successful business activity.

## PROFIT RICH, YET CASH POOR

**LO 1**

Explain how a company can be "profit rich, yet cash poor."

In January of 2001, Nancy Conrad founded Network Technologies, Inc. (NTI). NTI manufactures a screening device designed to safeguard personal computers against viruses transmitted through networks. Unlike disinfectant programs that remove viruses from infected hard drives, the NTI product actually screens all incoming network transmissions. If a virus is detected, it is destroyed *before* it can infect a computer's hard drive and cause damage to files.

Operating from a small manufacturing facility in Baltimore, NTI struggled through its first nine months of operations. However, the company experienced a very strong fourth quarter and managed to finish the year with total sales of $900,000 and a net income of $144,000.

The following profitability measures were taken from NTI's financial report for the year ended December 31, 2001:

*Note strong profitability*

| Selected Profitability Measures | NTI | Industry Average |
|---|---|---|
| Gross profit percentage (gross profit ÷ sales) | 60% | 45% |
| Net income percentage (net income ÷ sales) | 16% | 12% |
| Return on equity (net income ÷ average shareholders' equity) | 29% | 18% |
| Return on assets (net income ÷ average total assets) | 15% | 14% |

Even though NTI appears to be *profitable* relative to industry averages, it is plagued by severe *cash flow problems.* In fact, for the year ending December 31, 2001, NTI reported a *$250,000 negative cash flow from operations.* Unable to obtain additional bank credit, Conrad loaned her company $36,000 on January 1, 2002, so that payroll checks would clear.

The liquidity measures presented below were also taken from NTI's December 31, 2001, financial report. Unlike the profitability measures, these measures are all well *below* industry averages.

*Note weak liquidity*

| Selected Liquidity Measures | NTI | Industry Average |
|---|---|---|
| Current ratio (current assets ÷ current liabilities) | 1.4 | 2.4 |
| Quick ratio (quick assets ÷ current liabilities) | 0.6 | 1.5 |
| Inventory turnover (cost of goods sold ÷ average inventory) | 2.2 | 7.3 |
| Accounts receivable turnover (net sales ÷ average receivables) | 4.5 | 8.0 |

What we see happening at NTI is a dilemma common to many businesses. In short, the company is *profit rich, yet cash poor.* How can a profitable business experience cash flow problems? Surprisingly, we will see that this condition often stems from *rapid growth.*

## Operating Cash Flows: The Lifeblood of Survival

In response to a surge in demand experienced in the fourth quarter of 2001, NTI disbursed large sums of cash to manufacture goods available for sale. NTI's cash was literally *tied up* in direct materials, work in process, and finished goods inventories as units were produced. Furthermore, as these goods were sold, cash remained tied up in accounts receivable. The following diagram of NTI's **operating cycle** illustrates the cause and severity of its cash flow problems:[1]

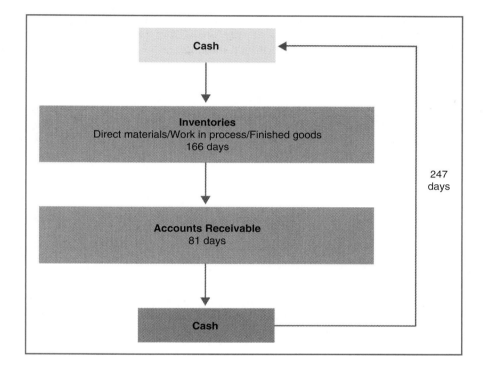

*Note long operating cycle*

As shown, NTI's operating cycle during 2001 averaged 247 days.[2] In other words, *cash was tied up in inventory and receivables for 247 days before converting back into cash.* Throughout its operating cycle, however, payrolls, materials purchases, debt service, and overhead costs all required disbursements of cash on a timely basis (for example, 30 days). No wonder NTI's 2001 statement of cash flows reported a $250,000 negative cash flow from operations!

Fortunately, if NTI develops a comprehensive plan to control its operating activities, it may be possible to correct these cash flow problems. Such a plan is referred to as a *master budget.* In the sections that follow, we will introduce and discuss the budgeting process in detail. Then, later in the chapter, we will return to the NTI illustration and develop a master budget for its first two quarters of operations in 2002.

---

[1]The *operating cycle* of a manufacturing firm is the average time period between the purchase of direct materials and the conversion of these materials back into cash.

[2]NTI's operating cycle of 247 days is equal to the number of days required to turn over inventory (365 days ÷ 2.2 inventory turnover = 166 days) plus the number of days required to turn over accounts receivable (365 days ÷ 4.5 accounts receivable turnover = 81 days).

## BUDGETING: THE BASIS FOR PLANNING AND CONTROL

A **budget** is a comprehensive *financial plan* setting forth the expected route for achieving the financial and operational goals of an organization. Budgeting is an essential step in effective financial planning. Even the smallest business will benefit from preparing a formal written plan for its future operations, including the expected levels of sales, expenses, net income, cash receipts, and cash outlays.

The use of a budget is a key element of financial planning and it assists managers in controlling costs. Managers compare actual costs with the budgeted amounts and take corrective action as necessary. Thus controlling costs means keeping actual costs in line with the financial plan.

Virtually all economic entities—businesses, governmental agencies, universities, churches, and individuals—engage in some form of budgeting. For example, a college student with limited financial resources may prepare a list of expected monthly cash payments to see that they do not exceed expected monthly cash receipts. This list is a simple form of a cash budget.

**CASE IN POINT**

The federal government also prepares an operating budget each year. In 2001, the budget is $2.02 trillion. Primary revenue sources are from corporate taxes (10%), individual taxes (48%), and social insurance and payroll taxes (34%).

While all businesses engage in some degree of planning, the extent to which plans are formalized in written budgets varies from one business to another. Large, well-managed companies generally have carefully developed budgets for every aspect of their operations. Inadequate or sloppy budgeting is a characteristic of companies with weak or inexperienced management.

### Benefits Derived from Budgeting

A budget is a forecast of future events. In fact, the process of budgeting is often called *financial forecasting*. Careful planning and preparation of a formal budget benefit a company in many ways, including the following:

1. *Enhanced management responsibility*. On a day-to-day basis, most managers focus their attention on the routine problems of running the business. In preparing a budget, however, managers are forced to consider all aspects of a company's internal activities and to make estimates of future economic conditions, including costs, interest rates, demand for the company's products, and the level of competition. Thus budgeting increases management's awareness of the company's external economic environment.

2. *Assignment of decision-making responsibilities*. Because the budget shows the expected results of future operations, management is forewarned of and responsible for financial problems. If, for example, the budget shows that the company will run short of cash during the summer months, the responsible manager has advance warning to hold down expenditures or obtain additional financing.

3. *Coordination of activities.* Preparation of a budget provides management with an opportunity to coordinate the activities of the various departments within the business. For example, the production department should be budgeted to produce approximately the same quantity of goods the sales department is budgeted to sell. A written budget shows department managers in quantitative terms exactly what is expected of their departments during the upcoming period.

4. *Performance evaluation.* Budgets show the expected costs and expenses for each department as well as the expected output, such as revenue to be earned or units to be produced. Thus the budgets provide a yardstick with which each department's actual performance may be measured.

## Establishing Budgeted Amounts

Comparisons of actual performance with budgeted amounts are widely used in evaluating the performance of departments and of department managers. Two basic philosophies prevail today that dictate the levels at which budgeted amounts should be set. We will identify these philosophies as (1) the *behavioral* approach and (2) the *total quality management* approach. We will first discuss the behavioral approach, which currently is the more widely used budgeting philosophy.

**The Behavioral Approach**   The assumption underlying the behavioral approach is that managers will be most highly motivated if they view the budget as a *fair* basis for evaluating a responsibilty center's performance. Therefore, budgeted amounts are set at *reasonable and achievable levels;* that is, at levels that *can be achieved* through reasonably efficient operations. A department that operates in a highly efficient manner should be able to *exceed* the budgeted level of performance. Failure to stay within the budget, in contrast, is viewed as an unacceptable level of performance.

**The Total Quality Management Approach**   A basic premise of total quality management is that every individual and segment of the organization constantly should strive for improvement. The entire organization is committed to the goal of *completely eliminating* inefficiency and non-value-added activities. In short, the organization strives to achieve *perfection* across its entire value chain.

As a step toward achieving this goal, budgeted amounts may be set at levels representing *absolute efficiency.* Departments generally will fall somewhat short of achieving this level of performance. However, even small failures to achieve the budgeted performance serve to direct management's attention toward those areas in which there is room for improvement.

**Selecting and Using a Budgeting Approach**   The approach used in setting budget amounts reflects the philosophy and goals of top management. Under either approach, however, managers should *participate actively* in the budgeting process. Department managers generally are the best source of information as to the levels of performance that can be achieved within their departments. These managers also should understand both the intended purpose of the budget and the philosophy underlying the development of budgeted amounts.

In comparing actual performance with budgeted amounts, top management should consider the philosophy used in developing the budgeted amounts. If a behavioral approach is employed, a highly efficient unit may *exceed* the budgeted level of performance. If a total quality management approach is used, a highly efficient unit should fall *slightly short* of the budget standards.

In the remainder of this chapter and in our assignment material, we will assume that budgeted amounts are set at *reasonable and achievable levels* (that is, the behavioral approach). Using this approach will enable us to illustrate and discuss actual levels of performance both above and below budgeted levels.

**LO 2**
Discuss the benefits that a company may derive from a formal budgeting process.

**LO 3**
Explain two philosophies that may be used in setting budgeted amounts.

**CASE IN POINT**

Operational budgeting for multinational companies can be very complex. For example, **Nike Inc.** has global operations in 140 countries. International sales account for more than one-third of their revenues. Because it collects revenues and pays expenses in foreign currencies, **Nike** experiences foreign exchange rate fluctuation risks. Managers try to forecast exchange rates during the budgeting period and undertake measures that dampen the impact of the exchange rate changes on the revenues, assets, liabilities, and expenses incurred in these foreign operations.

## The Budget Period

As a general rule, the period covered by a budget should be long enough to show the effect of management policies but short enough so that estimates can be made with reasonable accuracy. This suggests that different types of budgets should be made for different time spans.

*Capital expenditures budgets*, which summarize plans for major investments in plant and equipment, might be prepared to cover plans for as long as 5 to 10 years. Projects such as building a new factory or an oil refinery require many years of planning and expenditures before the new facilities are ready for use.

Most operating budgets and financial budgets cover a period of one fiscal year. Companies often divide these annual budgets into four quarters, with budgeted figures for each quarter. The first quarter is then subdivided into budget targets for each month, while only quarterly figures are shown for the next three quarters. As the end of each quarter nears, the budget for the next quarter is reviewed, revised for any changes in economic conditions, and divided into monthly budget targets. This process assures that the budget is reviewed at least several times each year and that the budgeted figures for the months just ahead are based on current conditions and estimates. In addition, budgeted figures for relatively short periods of time enable managers to compare actual performance to the budget without waiting until year-end.

**MANAGEMENT STRATEGY**

### Continuous Budgeting

An increasing number of companies follow a policy of **continuous budgeting,** whereby a new month is added to the end of the budget as the current month draws to a close. Thus the budget always covers the upcoming 12 months. One advantage of continuous budgeting is that it stabilizes the planning horizon at one year ahead. Under the fiscal year approach, the planning period becomes shorter as the year progresses. Also, continuous budgeting forces managers into a continuous review and reassessment of the budget estimates and the company's current progress.

## The Master Budget: A Package of Related Budgets

The "budget" is not a single document. Rather, the **master budget** consists of a number of interrelated budgets that collectively summarize all the planned activities of the business. The elements of a master budget vary depending on the size and nature of the business. A typical master budget for a manufacturing company would include the following:

**LO 4**

Describe the elements of a master budget.

1. Operating budgets
   a. Sales forecast
   b. Production schedule (stated in *units* to be produced)
   c. Manufacturing cost budget
   d. Cost of goods sold budget and ending inventory budgets
   e. Operating expense budget

2. Capital expenditures budget
3. Budgeted financial statements
   a. Budgeted income statement
   b. Cash budget
   c. Budgeted balance sheet

Some elements of the master budget are *organized by responsibility center*. The budgeted income statement, for example, indicates the budgeted revenue and expenses of each profit center. The cash budget shows the budgeted cash flows for each cost center as well as each revenue center. The production schedule and manufacturing cost budget indicate the unit production and manufacturing costs budgeted for each production process. The portion of the budget relating to an individual responsibility center is called a **responsibility budget**. As explained in Chapter 21, responsibility budgets are an important element of a responsibility accounting system.

The manager for the in-house travel responsibility center at the German global conglomerate **Siemens** used his decision-making responsibility to cut the travel budget by 10%, while simultaneously increasing the number of trips taken. Hundreds of **Siemens** employees are in the air each day, giving the in-house travel manager leverage to bargain with airlines. Also, everyone except the top executives must fly economy class in Europe.

**CASE IN POINT**

The many budgets and schedules making up the master budget are closely interrelated. Some of these relationships are illustrated in the diagram below.

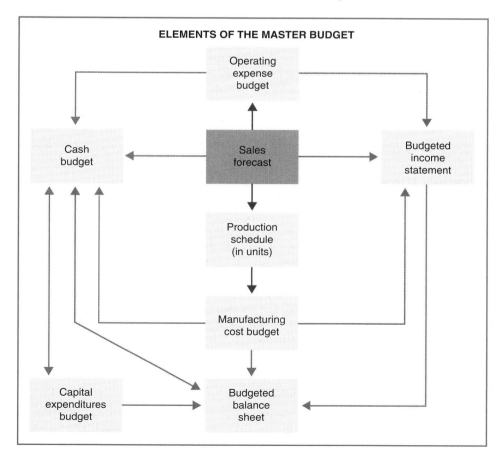

**ELEMENTS OF THE MASTER BUDGET**

## Steps in Preparing a Master Budget

Some parts of the master budget should not be prepared until other parts have been completed. For example, the budgeted financial statements are not prepared until the sales, manufacturing, and operating expense budgets are available. This is the logical sequence of steps for preparing the annual elements of the master budget:

1. *Prepare a sales forecast.* The sales forecast is the starting point in the preparation of a master budget. This forecast is based on past experience, estimates of general business and economic conditions, and expected levels of competition. A forecast of the expected level of sales is a prerequisite to scheduling production and to budgeting revenue and variable costs. The arrows in our budget diagram indicate that information flows from this forecast into several other budgets.

2. *Prepare budgets for production, manufacturing costs, and operating expenses.* Once the level of sales has been forecast, production may be scheduled and estimates made of the expected manufacturing costs and operating expenses for the year. These elements of the master budget depend on both the level of sales and cost-volume relationships.

3. *Prepare a budgeted income statement.* The budgeted income statement is based on the sales forecast, the manufacturing costs comprising the cost of goods sold, and the budgeted operating expenses.

4. *Prepare a cash budget.* The cash budget is a forecast of the cash receipts and cash payments for the budget period. The cash budget is affected by many of the other budget estimates.

    The budgeted level of cash receipts depends on the sales forecast, credit terms offered by the company, and the company's experience in collecting accounts receivable from customers. Budgeted cash payments depend on the forecasts of manufacturing costs, operating expenses, and capital expenditures, as well as the credit terms offered by suppliers. Anticipated borrowing, debt repayment, cash dividends, and issuance of capital stock also are reflected in the cash budget.

5. *Prepare a budgeted balance sheet.* A projected balance sheet cannot be prepared until the effects of cash transactions on various asset, liability, and owners' equity accounts have been determined. In addition, the balance sheet is affected by budgeted capital expenditures and budgeted net income.

The capital expenditures budget covers a span of many years. This budget is continuously reviewed and updated, but usually it is not prepared anew on an annual basis.

## Preparing the Master Budget: An Illustration

Let us now return to the NTI illustration introduced at the beginning of the chapter. Even though the company's first year of operations was profitable, it experienced significant cash flow problems due to rapid sales growth in the fourth quarter of 2001.

We will now develop NTI's master budget for the first two quarters of 2002. A primary objective of this process is to help NTI avoid the cash flow problems experienced during 2001. Shown on the following page is the company's balance sheet, dated January 1, 2002.

Sales of NTI's product are expected to increase throughout 2002. However, the company will drastically cut back production during the first quarter to liquidate some of the finished goods inventory currently on hand. As of January 1, there is no work in process inventory. No capital expenditures are planned for 2002.

## Operating Budget Estimates

The first step in preparing NTI's master budget is to develop each of its operating budgets for the first two quarters of 2002. Information from these budgets will be used to prepare budgeted quarterly income statements. All of the information needed to estimate

**LO 5**

Prepare the budgets and supporting schedules included in a master budget.

budgeted *income from operations* comes from the operating budget estimates. For easy reference to these budgets throughout the remainder of the chapter, we refer to them as *Schedule A1* through *Schedule A7*.

## NTI
## Balance Sheet
## January 1, 2002

### Assets

Current assets:

| | | |
|---|---|---|
| Cash | | $ 10,000 |
| Receivables | | 225,000 |
| Inventories (FIFO method) | | |
|   Direct Materials | $ 60,000 | |
|   Finished Goods | 240,000 | 300,000 |
| Prepayments | | 5,000 |
|   Total current assets | | $540,000 |
| Plant and equipment: | | |
|   Buildings and Equipment | $420,000 | |
|   Less: Accumulated Depreciation | 20,000 | |
|     Total plant and equipment | | 400,000 |
| Total assets | | $940,000 |

### Liabilities & Stockholders' Equity

Current liabilities:

| | | |
|---|---|---|
| Notes Payable, to officer (12 months @ 12%) | | $ 36,000 |
| Notes Payable, to bank (3 months @ 14%) | | 246,000 |
| Other Current Payables | | 50,000 |
| Income Taxes Payable | | 64,000 |
|   Total current liabilities | | $396,000 |
| Stockholders' equity: | | |
|   Capital Stock, no par, 10,000 shares outstanding | $400,000 | |
|   Retained Earnings | 144,000 | 544,000 |
| Total liabilities & stockholders' equity | | $940,000 |

**The Sales Forecast (Schedule A1)**   Bob Poole, NTI's marketing director, is optimistic that demand for the company's product will continue to grow in 2002. He estimates that sales will reach 8,000 units in the first quarter and 10,000 units in the second quarter. Sales estimates for the third and fourth quarters are 30,000 units and 40,000 units, respectively. To keep its product affordable to a wide range of users, NTI is committed to holding its selling price per unit at $75 throughout the year. On the basis of this information, the following sales forecast is prepared:

**Schedule A1**

| Sales Forecast | 1st Quarter | 2nd Quarter |
|---|---|---|
| Budgeted sales (in units) | 8,000 | 10,000 |
| Selling price per unit | $    75 | $    75 |
| Budgeted sales (in dollars) | $600,000 | $750,000 |

**Production Schedule (Schedule A2)**   Upon examining performance reports for 2001, Joe Reco, NTI's production manager, concluded that he had overreacted to the rapid sales growth experienced in the fourth quarter. As a consequence, the company was carrying an excessive inventory of finished goods at the start of 2002. He immediately adopted a new policy for 2002 to increase inventory turnover and improve operating cash flows. The number of units in the finished goods inventory will now be held to *10%* of the unit sales volume anticipated in the following quarter.

Given a sales forecast of 10,000 units for the second quarter, the desired finished goods inventory at the end of the first quarter is 1,000 units. Likewise, given a sales forecast of 30,000 units for the third quarter, the desired finished goods inventory at the end of the second quarter is 3,000 units. Based on these projections, the following production schedule is prepared:

| Schedule A2 | | |
| --- | --- | --- |
| **Production Schedule (in Units)** | **1st Quarter** | **2nd Quarter** |
| Budgeted unit sales (Schedule A1) . . . . . . . . . . . . . . . . . . . . . . . . . | 8,000 | 10,000 |
| Add: Desired ending inventory of finished goods . . . . . . . . . . . . . . . | 1,000 | 3,000 |
| Units budgeted to be available for sale . . . . . . . . . . . . . . . . . . . . . | 9,000 | 13,000 |
| Less: Beginning inventory of finished goods . . . . . . . . . . . . . . . . . . | 8,000 | 1,000 |
| Planned production of finished goods . . . . . . . . . . . . . . . . . . . . . . | 1,000 | 12,000 |

**YOUR TURN**

## You as a Production Manager

You are a production manager at NTI. If the manager of the Sales Department informs you that revised third-quarter sales will be 15,000 units and not the 30,000 originally estimated, whom would you need to contact for coordination and planning purposes?

*Our comments appear on page 952.

**Manufacturing Cost Estimates (Schedule A3)**   Lisa Scott, NTI's cost accountant, has thoroughly analyzed the company's variable and fixed manufacturing costs. She is confident that variable manufacturing costs per unit will not increase during the first half of 2002. She also believes that fixed manufacturing overhead will hold steady at approximately $15,000 per quarter. Based on her analysis, she compiled the following manufacturing cost estimates:

| Schedule A3 | |
| --- | --- |
| **Manufacturing Cost Estimates** | **1st and 2nd Quarters** |
| Variable costs per unit manufactured: | |
| Direct materials . . . . . . . . . . . . . . . . . . . . . . . . . . . . . . . . . . . . . . | $   15 |
| Direct labor . . . . . . . . . . . . . . . . . . . . . . . . . . . . . . . . . . . . . . . . . | 5 |
| Variable manufacturing overhead . . . . . . . . . . . . . . . . . . . . . . . . . . | 7 |
| Fixed manufacturing overhead (per quarter) . . . . . . . . . . . . . . . . . . . . | $15,000 |

**Manufacturing Cost Budget (Schedule A4)**   Combining the production schedule estimates in *Schedule A2* with the manufacturing cost figures in *Schedule A3*, the following manufacturing cost budget is developed:

**Schedule A4**

| Manufacturing Cost Budget | 1st Quarter |
| --- | --- |
| Variable manufacturing costs: | |
| Direct materials used (1,000 units @ $15) | $15,000 |
| Direct labor (1,000 units @ $5) | 5,000 |
| Variable manufacturing overhead (1,000 units @ $7) | 7,000 |
| Fixed manufacturing overhead per quarter | 15,000 |
| Total cost of finished goods manufactured | $42,000 |
| Manufacturing costs per unit ($42,000 ÷ 1,000 units) | $42.00 |
| | **2nd Quarter** |
| Variable manufacturing costs: | |
| Direct materials used (12,000 units @ $15) | $180,000 |
| Direct labor (12,000 units @ $5) | 60,000 |
| Variable manufacturing overhead (12,000 units @ $7) | 84,000 |
| Fixed manufacturing overhead per quarter | 15,000 |
| Total cost of finished goods manufactured | $339,000 |
| Manufacturing costs per unit ($339,000 ÷ 12,000 units) | $28.25 |

Note that the budgeted manufacturing costs in the first quarter total *$42.00 per unit*, compared to *$28.25 per unit* in the second quarter. These amounts differ due to a *decrease in fixed manufacturing costs per unit* anticipated in the second quarter. During the first quarter, $15,000 in fixed manufacturing costs is allocated to 1,000 units produced (or *$15.00 per unit*). During the second quarter, however, $15,000 is allocated to 12,000 units produced (or *$1.25 per unit*).

### You as a Cost Accountant

You are a cost accountant for NTI. The product line manager for the screening device, Betty Barlow, has come to you in a very agitated state. She manages a profit center for the screening device product and is evaluated on the profitability of the number of units sold each quarter. She wants you to explain why the units that are produced in the first quarter will add a $33 per unit contribution to profit ($75 − $42), but the units from the second quarter's production will add $46.75 per unit ($75 − $28.25). Can you explain why this is happening? Can you think of a method to eliminate this problem?

*Our comments appear on page 952.

YOUR TURN

**Ending Finished Goods Inventory (Schedule A5)**  As mentioned, NTI recently adopted a policy stating that the number of units in finished goods inventory at the end of each quarter should amount to *10%* of the unit sales volume anticipated in the following quarter.

Thus, applying this policy in conjunction with the unit cost figures shown in *Schedule A4*, ending inventory estimates are determined as follows:

| Schedule A5 | | |
| --- | --- | --- |
| **Ending Finished Goods Inventory** | **1st Quarter** | **2nd Quarter** |
| 1,000 units (Schedule A2) @ $42.00 (Schedule A4) . . . . . . . . . . . . . . . . | $42,000 | |
| 3,000 units (Schedule A2) @ $28.25 (Schedule A4) . . . . . . . . . . . . . . . . . . . . . | | $84,750 |

**Cost of Goods Sold Budget (Schedule A6)**   A manufacturing company's cost of goods sold is equal to its beginning finished goods inventory, plus the cost of goods manufactured during the period, less its ending finished goods inventory.

Thus the budget estimates for cost of goods sold in *Schedule A6* are computed using the beginning finished goods inventory figure from the balance sheet on page 923 and information from *Schedules A4* and *A5.*

| Schedule A6 | | |
| --- | --- | --- |
| **Cost of Goods Sold Budget** | **1st Quarter** | **2nd Quarter** |
| Finished goods, beginning inventory (per balance sheet) . . . . . . . . . . . . . | $240,000 | $ 42,000 |
| Add: Cost of finished goods manufactured (Schedule A4) . . . . . . . . . . . . | 42,000 | 339,000 |
| Cost of goods available for sale . . . . . . . . . . . . . . . . . . . . . . . . . . . . . | $282,000 | $381,000 |
| Less: Finished goods, ending inventory (Schedule A5) . . . . . . . . . . . . . . | 42,000 | 84,750 |
| Cost of goods sold . . . . . . . . . . . . . . . . . . . . . . . . . . . . . . . . . . . . . . . | $240,000 | $296,250 |

**Operating Expense Budget (Schedule A7)**   NTI's variable operating expenses amount to $7.50 per unit. Most of this cost applies to sales commissions. The company's fixed operating expenses of $175,000 pertain primarily to the salaries of its officers. Based on this information, the following operating expense budget is prepared:

| Schedule A7 | | |
| --- | --- | --- |
| **Operating Expense Budget** | **1st Quarter** | **2nd Quarter** |
| Variable operating expenses ($7.50 per unit sold) . . . . . . . . . . . . . . . . . | $ 60,000 | $ 75,000 |
| Fixed operating expenses (per quarter) . . . . . . . . . . . . . . . . . . . . . . . . . | 175,000 | 175,000 |
| Total selling and administrative expenses . . . . . . . . . . . . . . . . . . . . . | $235,000 | $250,000 |

## Budgeted Income Statement

NTI's budgeted income statements are based on estimates from *Schedules A1* through *A7.* In addition, they include budgeted amounts for interest expense and income tax expense. Interest expense and income taxes are also reported on *Schedules B5* and *B6* discussed later in the chapter. The following discussion explains how these figures were determined.

The $36,000 note payable reported in the January 1, 2002, balance sheet is the loan from NTI's president, Nancy Conrad. The note is payable in four quarterly installments of $9,000, *plus* accrued interest on the outstanding balance at the end of each quarter. The note's interest rate is 12% (or 3% quarterly). Thus interest due at the end of the first quarter is $1,080 ($36,000 × 3%), whereas interest due at the end of the second quarter is only $810 ($27,000 × 3%).

The $246,000 note payable is the remaining principal owed on a loan that originated early in 2001. The note's interest rate is 14% (or 3.5% quarterly). The entire $246,000, plus $8,610 in accrued interest ($246,000 × 3.5%), is due at the end of the first quarter of 2002. Thus total interest expense budgeted on notes payable for the first quarter is $9,690 ($1,080 plus $8,610).

Income tax expense is budgeted at 40% of income before income taxes.

Based on this information, we prepared the following budgeted income statements:

| NTI Budgeted Income Statements For the First Two Quarters of 2002 | 1st Quarter | 2nd Quarter |
|---|---|---|
| Sales (Schedule A1) | $600,000 | $750,000 |
| Cost of goods sold (Schedule A6) | 240,000 | 296,250 |
| Gross profit on sales | $360,000 | $453,750 |
| Operating expenses: | | |
| Selling and administrative expenses (Schedule A7) | $235,000 | $250,000 |
| Interest expense (Schedule B6) | 9,690 | 810 |
| Total operating expenses | $244,690 | $250,810 |
| Income before income taxes | $115,310 | $202,940 |
| Income taxes, 40% average rate (Schedule B7) | 46,124 | 81,176 |
| Net income | $ 69,186 | $121,764 |

The budgeted income statement shows the effects that budgeted activities are expected to have on NTI's revenue, expenses, and net income. However, it is not indicative of the company's cash flow expectations for the first two quarters of 2002. *Recall that during 2001 the company was profit rich, yet it remained cash poor.*

Thus we must now prepare *financial budget estimates* to formulate NTI's quarterly cash flow expectations. These estimates will also help us to prepare the company's budgeted balance sheets each quarter.

## Financial Budget Estimates

The estimates and data necessary to prepare the cash budget and budgeted balance sheets are called *financial budget estimates*. To avoid confusing these figures with the *operating budget estimates* used to prepare the budgeted income statement, we will refer to them as *Schedule B1* through *Schedule B8*. The amounts to be used in the preparation of NTI's cash budget are highlighted in *red*.

**Budgeted Direct Materials Purchases and Inventory (Schedule B1)** In *Schedule A4*, we estimated that $15,000 of direct materials would be *used* during the first quarter. However, in the preparation of a cash budget, we are concerned about the cost of direct materials to be *purchased* each quarter. To estimate the purchase of direct materials we must consider both the expected use of materials and the desired direct materials inventory at the end of each quarter.

Let us assume that the production manager feels that the direct materials inventory of $60,000 reported on NTI's January 1 balance sheet is too high. Thus he recommends that it be reduced to $50,000 by the end of the first quarter. However, in anticipation of a strong third quarter, he estimates that the direct materials inventory will need to be increased to $80,000 by the end of the second quarter. Based on these estimates, the purchase of direct materials can be determined as follows:

| Schedule B1 Direct Materials Purchases and Inventory | 1st Quarter | 2nd Quarter |
|---|---|---|
| Direct materials used (Schedule A4) ........................... | $15,000 | $180,000 |
| Desired ending direct materials inventory ....................... | 50,000 | 80,000 |
| Direct materials available for use .............................. | $65,000 | $260,000 |
| Less: Inventory at the beginning of the quarter ................... | 60,000 | 50,000 |
| Budgeted direct materials purchases ......................... | $ 5,000 | $210,000 |

**Means of Financing Costs and Expenses (Schedule B2)** The next step in preparing a cash budget is to estimate the portion of budgeted costs and expenses that will require *cash payment in the near future*.

**CASH EFFECTS** Certain expenses will *not* require an outlay of cash. These include (1) expenses that result from the expiration of prepaid items (such as insurance policies) and (2) the depreciation of plant assets. Thus *only* those costs and expenses financed by *current payables* (which include immediate *cash* payments as well as accounts payable and accrued expenses) will require cash payments.

*Schedule B2* separates the costs and expenses financed by NTI's current payables from those related to the expiration of prepayments and depreciation. The column headed "Current Payables" indicates the portion of current costs and expenses that requires cash disbursements in the near future. Examples of these items include purchases of direct materials (whether for cash or on account), factory payrolls, and various overhead costs. The amounts shown under the columns headed "Expired Prepayments" and "Depreciation" are reported as *expenses* in the company's budgeted income statement. However, these amounts do not call for future disbursements of cash. We may assume that the expired prepayment estimates were made based on an evaluation of the company's insurance policies.

| Schedule B2 Means of Financing Costs and Expenses Other Than Interest and Taxes | Total | Current Payables | Expired Prepayments | Depreciation |
|---|---|---|---|---|
| 1st quarter: | | | | |
| Direct materials purchases (Schedule B1) ...................... | $ 5,000 | $ 5,000 | | |
| Direct labor (Schedule A4) ............... | 5,000 | 5,000 | | |
| Manufacturing overhead— variable and fixed (Schedule A4) ......... | 22,000 | 15,500 | $3,000 | $3,500 |
| Selling and administrative expenses (Schedule A7) ..................... | 235,000 | 232,500 | 1,000 | 1,500 |
| Total ..................................... | $267,000 | $258,000 | $4,000 | $5,000 |

**Schedule B2**

| Means of Financing Costs and Expenses Other Than Interest and Taxes | Total | Current Payables | Expired Prepayments | Depreciation |
|---|---|---|---|---|
| 2nd quarter: | | | | |
| Direct materials purchases (Schedule B1) ...................... | $210,000 | $210,000 | | |
| Direct labor (Schedule A4) ............... | 60,000 | 60,000 | | |
| Manufacturing overhead— variable and fixed (Schedule A4) ......... | 99,000 | 91,400 | $4,100 | $3,500 |
| Selling and administrative expenses (Schedule A7) ...................... | 250,000 | 247,100 | 1,400 | 1,500 |
| Total ............................... | $619,000 | $608,500 | $5,500 | $5,000 |

**Payments on Current Payables (Schedule B3)** The purpose of the following schedule is to estimate the cash payments required each quarter for the costs and expenses classified as current payables in *Schedule B2:*

**Schedule B3**

| Payments on Current Payables | 1st Quarter | 2nd Quarter |
|---|---|---|
| Balance at beginning of quarter .................................. | $ 50,000 | $ 75,000 |
| Increase in payables during the quarter (Schedule B2) .............. | 258,000 | 608,500 |
| Total payables during quarter .............................. | $308,000 | $683,500 |
| Less: Estimated balance at the end of quarter .................... | 75,000 | 100,000 |
| Payments on current payables during quarter ...................... | $233,000 | $583,500 |

The starting point in *Schedule B3* is the $50,000 beginning payables balance appearing in NTI's January 1, 2002, balance sheet (page 923). To this amount, we add the total payables budgeted in *Schedule B2*. The balance of current payables at the end of the first quarter was estimated by Paul Foss, NTI's treasurer, after making a thorough analysis of suppliers' credit terms. Note the beginning balance of current payables for the second quarter is simply the ending balance from the first quarter.

**Prepayments Budget (Schedule B4)** This schedule budgets the expected cash payments for prepayments made during the period. For NTI, these payments involve its insurance policies. Thus preparation of the schedule called for an analysis of all policies reported on the January 1, 2002, balance sheet and their anticipated expiration of prepayments shown in *Schedule B2*. Based on this analysis, the following prepayments budget was prepared:

**Schedule B4**

| Prepayments Budget | 1st Quarter | 2nd Quarter |
|---|---|---|
| Balance at beginning of quarter ............................... | $ 5,000 | $ 7,000 |
| Estimated cash expenditure during quarter ....................... | 6,000 | 6,500 |
| Total prepayments ..................................... | $11,000 | $13,500 |
| Less: Expiration of prepayments (Schedule B2) .................... | 4,000 | 5,500 |
| Prepayments at end of quarter ................................ | $ 7,000 | $ 8,000 |

**Debt Service Budget (Schedule B5)**    The purpose of this schedule is to summarize the cash payments (both principal and interest) required to service NTI's debt each quarter. NTI has two notes payable outstanding on January 1, 2002.

The 12%, $36,000 note payable is the loan from Nancy Conrad, NTI's president. The loan agreement calls for quarterly payments of $9,000 plus interest accrued on the outstanding balance at a quarterly rate of 3%. Thus the debt service on this note in the first quarter equals $9,000 in principal plus interest of $1,080 ($36,000 × 3%), or a cash outlay of *$10,080*. The note's debt service in the second quarter equals $9,000 in principal plus interest of $810 ($27,000 × 3%), or a cash outlay of *$9,810*.

The 14%, $246,000 note payable is to NTI's bank. The loan agreement calls for payment of the entire $246,000 at the end of the first quarter of 2002, plus interest accrued at a quarterly rate of 3.5%. Thus the debt service on this note in the first quarter equals $246,000 plus interest of $8,610 ($246,000 × 3.5%), or a cash outlay of *$254,610*. There is no debt service cost associated with this note in the second quarter.

As shown below, the total debt service budget is *$264,690* in the first quarter and *$9,810* in the second quarter.

| Schedule B5 | | |
|---|---|---|
| **Debt Service Budget** | **1st Quarter** | **2nd Quarter** |
| Notes payable at the beginning of the quarter | $282,000 | $27,000 |
| Interest expense for the quarter | 9,690 | 810 |
|    Total principal plus accrued interest | $291,690 | $27,810 |
| Less: Cash payments (principal and interest) | 264,690 | 9,810 |
| Notes payable at the end of the quarter | $ 27,000 | $18,000 |

**Budgeted Income Taxes (Schedule B6)**    The budgeted cash payments for income tax expense are summarized on the following page. Each quarter, NTI makes income tax payments equal to its income tax liability at the beginning of that quarter. NTI's $64,000 liability at the beginning of the first quarter was taken from its January 1, 2002, balance sheet. The $46,124 liability at the beginning of the second quarter is simply the income tax liability at the end of the first quarter.

| Schedule B6 | | |
|---|---|---|
| **Budgeted Income Taxes** | **1st Quarter** | **2nd Quarter** |
| Income tax liability at beginning of quarter | $ 64,000 | $ 46,124 |
| Estimated income taxes for the quarter (per budgeted income statement) | 46,124 | 81,176 |
|    Total accrued income tax liability | $110,124 | $127,300 |
| Cash payment of amount owed at beginning of quarter | 64,000 | 46,124 |
| Income tax liability at end of quarter | $ 46,124 | $ 81,176 |

**Estimated Cash Receipts from Customers (Schedule B7)**    All of NTI's sales are made on account. As such, the sole source of cash receipts is the collection of accounts receivable. As shown in the table on page 917, NTI turned over its accounts receivable 4.5 times during 2001. Thus the average account was outstanding for *81 days* (365 days ÷ 4.5 = 81).

In an attempt to improve cash flow performance in 2002, NTI's credit manager, Richard Baker, set the following goals for his department: (1) to collect the entire $225,000 of accounts receivable reported on the January 1, 2002, balance sheet by the end of the first quarter, and (2) to collect 75% of quarterly sales during the quarter in which they are made, and collect the remaining 25% in the subsequent quarter. If successful, Baker estimates that NTI's average collection period will be reduced from 81 days to 30 days.

The following schedule shows the budgeted cash collections under the new collection policy. Losses for uncollectible accounts are ignored in our example.

---

**Schedule B7**

| Estimated Cash Receipts from Customers | 1st Quarter | 2nd Quarter |
|---|---|---|
| Balance of receivables at beginning of year ..................... | $225,000 | |
| Collections on first quarter sales of $600,000— 75% in first quarter and 25% in second quarter ................. | 450,000 | $150,000 |
| Collections on second quarter sales of $750,000— 75% in second quarter and 25% in third quarter ................. | | 562,500 |
| Cash receipts from customers ............................. | $675,000 | $712,500 |

---

**Budgeted Accounts Receivable (Schedule B8)**  As shown below, the beginning accounts receivable balance, plus credit sales and minus collections on account, equals the estimated ending balance of accounts receivable.

---

**Schedule B8**

| Budgeted Accounts Receivable | 1st Quarter | 2nd Quarter |
|---|---|---|
| Balance at beginning of quarter ............................ | $225,000 | $150,000 |
| Sales on account during quarter (Schedule A1) .................. | 600,000 | 750,000 |
| Total accounts receivable ............................... | $825,000 | $900,000 |
| Less: Estimated collections on accounts receivable (Schedule B7) ...................................... | 675,000 | 712,500 |
| Estimated accounts receivable at end of quarter ................ | $150,000 | $187,500 |

---

## The Cash Budget

Using NTI's financial budget estimates from *Schedules B1* through *B8,* the cash budget that follows is developed for the first two quarters of 2002:

| NTI Cash Budget For the First Two Quarters of 2002 | | |
|---|---|---|
| | **1st Quarter** | **2nd Quarter** |
| Cash balance at beginning of quarter . . . . . . . . . . . . . . . | $ 10,000 | $117,310 |
| Cash receipts: | | |
| Cash received from customers | | |
| (Schedule B7) . . . . . . . . . . . . . . . . . . . . . . . . . | 675,000 | 712,500 |
| Total cash available . . . . . . . . . . . . . . . . . . . . . . . | $685,000 | $829,810 |
| Cash payments: | | |
| Payment of current payables | | |
| (Schedule B3) . . . . . . . . . . . . . . . . . . . . . . . . . | $233,000 | $583,500 |
| Prepayments (Schedule B4) . . . . . . . . . . . . . . . . . . . | 6,000 | 6,500 |
| Debt service, including interest | | |
| (Schedule B5) . . . . . . . . . . . . . . . . . . . . . . . . . | 264,690 | 9,810 |
| Income tax payments (Schedule B6) . . . . . . . . . . . . . . | 64,000 | 46,124 |
| Total disbursements . . . . . . . . . . . . . . . . . . . . . . | $567,690 | $645,934 |
| Cash balance at end of the quarter . . . . . . . . . . . . . . . | $117,310 | $183,876 |

NTI's budgeted cash position for the first two quarters of 2002 is a vast improvement over its actual cash position at the end of 2001. We have discussed two primary reasons for the anticipated turnaround. First, a new policy was developed to improve control of inventory management and production scheduling. Second, ambitious goals were established to tighten credit policies. Keep in mind that these cash figures are based completely on budget *estimates*. Thus only if management's estimates and expectations are *realistic* will the company's cash flow problems be resolved.

**YOUR TURN**

### You as Manager of the Credit Department

Assume you are the manager of NTI's credit department. Nancy Conrad, the founder of NTI has asked you to manage receivables and payables by leading and lagging. Leading receivables implies collecting cash from customers more quickly than previously. Lagging payables means delaying payment to creditors. You are concerned that what Conrad is suggesting is unethical. What should you do?

*Our comments appear on page 952.

## Budgeted Balance Sheets

We now have the necessary information to forecast NTI's financial position at the end of each of the next two quarters. The company's budgeted balance sheets are shown on the following page. The budget schedules used to derive various figures are indicated parenthetically.

## Using Budgets Effectively

In preparing a budget, managers are forced to consider carefully all aspects of the company's activities. This study and analysis should, in itself, enable managers to do a better job of managing.

The primary benefits of budgeting, however, stem from the uses made of budgeted information. Among these benefits are (1) advance warning of and assignment of responsibility for conditions that require corrective action, (2) coordination of activities among all departments within the organization, and (3) the creation of standards for evaluating performance. Let us consider how NTI's master budget serves these functions.

## NTI
## Budgeted Balance Sheets
## As of the End of the First Two Quarters of 2002

|  | 1st Quarter | 2nd Quarter |
|---|---|---|
| **Current assets:** |  |  |
| Cash (per cash budget) | $117,310 | $183,876 |
| Receivables (Schedule B8) | 150,000 | 187,500 |
| Inventories (FIFO method) |  |  |
| Direct materials (Schedule B1) | 50,000 | 80,000 |
| Finished goods (Schedule A5) | 42,000 | 84,750 |
| Prepayments (Schedule B4) | 7,000 | 8,000 |
| Total current assets | $366,310 | $544,126 |
| **Plant and equipment:** |  |  |
| Buildings and equipment | $420,000 | $420,000 |
| Less: Accumulated depreciation | (25,000) | (30,000) |
| Total plant and equipment | $395,000 | $390,000 |
| Total assets | $761,310 | $934,126 |
| **Current liabilities:** |  |  |
| Notes payable, to officer, 12% (Schedule B5) | $ 27,000 | $ 18,000 |
| Other current payables (Schedule B3) | 75,000 | 100,000 |
| Income taxes payable (Schedule B6) | 46,124 | 81,176 |
| Total current liabilities | $148,124 | $199,176 |
| **Stockholders' equity:** |  |  |
| Capital stock, no par, 10,000 shares outstanding | $400,000 | $400,000 |
| Retained earnings, beginning of quarter | 144,000 | 213,186 |
| Quarterly income (per budgeted income statements) | 69,186 | 121,764 |
| Total stockholders' equity | $613,186 | $734,950 |
| Total liabilities & stockholders' equity | $761,310 | $934,126 |

**Advance Warning of and Responsibility for Decision Making**   Earlier in this chapter, we described NTI's financial condition as *profit rich, yet cash poor*. We attributed this condition to the rapid sales growth experienced in the fourth quarter of 2001. In short, a sudden surge in demand for NTI's product caused excessive amounts of cash to become *tied up* in inventories and receivables. As a result, one of management's major responsibilities at the start of 2002 is generating enough cash flow from operations to meet obligations as they become due. Had a master budget been prepared in 2001, management would have been *forewarned* of this condition, thereby making the severity of the current situation less threatening to the company's survival.

The Canadian auto-parts giant **Magna International, Inc.**, found that as the company grew, the lack of a strong budget system created some significant problems in the early 1990s. Debt grew too fast and **Magna** violated some debt covenants. The CEO, Frank Stronach, turned **Magna** around by imposing discipline and planning through the budget process.[3]

**CASE IN POINT**

---

[3]William C. Symonds, "Frank Stronach's Secret? Call It Empower Steering," *Business Week*, May 1, 1995, pp. 63–65.

**Coordination of the Activities of Departments** The budget provides a comprehensive plan enabling all of the departments to work together in a coordinated manner. For example, the Production Department knows the quantity of goods to produce to meet the expected needs of the Sales Department. The Purchasing Department, in turn, is informed of the quantities of direct materials that must be ordered to meet the requirements of the Production Department. The budgeting process requires that managers of departments and other segments of the organization *communicate with each other*.

**A Yardstick for Evaluating Management Performance** The comparison of actual results with budgeted amounts is a common means of evaluating performance in organizations. As discussed in Chapter 21, we learned that the evaluation of performance should be based only on those revenues and costs that are *under the control* of the person being evaluated. Therefore, for the purposes of evaluation, budgeted fixed costs should be subdivided into the categories of *controllable costs* and *committed costs*.

## Flexible Budgeting

Performance may become difficult to evaluate if the actual level of activity (either sales or production) differs substantially from the level originally budgeted. A **flexible budget** is one that can be adjusted easily to show budgeted revenue, costs, and cash flows at *different levels* of activity. Thus, if a change in volume lessens the usefulness of the original budget, a new budget may be prepared quickly to reflect the actual level of activity for the period.

To illustrate the usefulness of a flexible budget, assume that on March 31, 2002, Joe Reco (NTI's production manager) is presented with the **performance report** shown below. The report compares the manufacturing costs originally budgeted for the quarter (*Schedule A4*, page 925) with his department's actual performance for the period.

At first glance, it appears that Reco's performance is quite poor, as all production costs exceed the amounts budgeted. However, we have deliberately omitted one piece of information from this performance report. To meet a higher-than-expected customer demand for NTI's product, the production department produced *1,500 units* instead of the *1,000 units* originally budgeted for the first quarter.

Under these circumstances, we should reevaluate our conclusions concerning Reco's ability to control manufacturing costs. At this higher level of production, variable manufacturing costs should naturally exceed the amounts originally budgeted. In order to evaluate his performance, the budget must be adjusted to indicate the levels of cost that *should be incurred* in manufacturing 1,500 units.

**LO 6**

Prepare a flexible budget and explain its uses.

| NTI | | | |
|---|---|---|---|
| **Performance Report of the Production Department** | | | |
| **For the 1st Quarter Ended March 31, 2002** | | | |
| | Amount Budgeted | Actual | Over or (Under) Budget |
| Manufacturing costs: | | | |
| Direct materials used | $15,000 | $21,000 | $ 6,000 |
| Direct labor | 5,000 | 7,000 | 2,000 |
| Variable manufacturing overhead | 7,000 | 9,500 | 2,500 |
| Fixed manufacturing overhead | 15,000 | 15,750 | 750 |
| Total manufacturing costs— first quarter | $42,000 | $53,250 | $11,250 |

Flexible budgeting may be viewed as combining the concepts of budgeting and cost-volume-profit analysis. Using the variable and fixed cost estimates from *Schedule A3* (page 924), the manufacturing cost budget for NTI can be revised to reflect any level of production. For example, in the following schedule, these relationships are used to forecast quarterly manufacturing costs at three different levels of production:

|  | Level of Production (in Units) | | |
| --- | --- | --- | --- |
|  | **500** | **1,000** | **1,500** |
| Manufacturing Cost Estimates from Schedule A3 | | | |
| Variable costs: | | | |
| Direct materials ($15 per unit) ..................... | $ 7,500 | $15,000 | $22,500 |
| Direct labor ($5 per unit) .......................... | 2,500 | 5,000 | 7,500 |
| Variable manufacturing overhead ($7 per unit) ........... | 3,500 | 7,000 | 10,500 |
| Fixed costs: | | | |
| Manufacturing overhead ($15,000 per quarter) ........... | 15,000 | 15,000 | 15,000 |
| Total manufacturing costs—First Quarter ............... | $28,500 | $42,000 | $55,500 |

Notice that budgeted *variable* manufacturing costs change with the level of production, whereas budgeted *fixed* costs remain the same.

We can now modify the performance report for NTI's production department to reflect the actual *1,500* unit level of production achieved during the first quarter of 2002. The modified report is presented below.

This comparison paints quite a different picture from the report presented above. Considering the actual level of production, the production manager has kept all manufacturing costs below budgeted amounts, with the exception of fixed overhead (most of which may be committed costs).

The techniques of flexible budgeting may also be applied to profit centers by applying cost-volume-profit relationships to the actual level of *sales* achieved.

**Computers and Flexible Budgeting**   Adjusting the entire budget to reflect a different level of sales or production would be a sizable task in a manual system. In a computer-based system, however, it can be done quickly and easily. Once the

| NTI — Performance Report of the Production Department — For the 1st Quarter Ended March 31, 2002 | | | | |
| --- | --- | --- | --- | --- |
|  | Level of Production (In Units) | | | Actual Costs Over or (Under) Flexible Budget |
|  | Originally Budgeted 1,000 | Flexible Budget 1,500 | Actual Cost 1,500 | |
| Manufacturing costs: | | | | |
| Direct materials used .......... | $15,000 | $22,500 | $21,000 | $(1,500) |
| Direct labor ................ | 5,000 | 7,500 | 7,000 | (500) |
| Variable overhead ........... | 7,000 | 10,500 | 9,500 | (1,000) |
| Fixed overhead ............. | 15,000 | 15,000 | 15,750 | 750 |
| Total manufacturing costs ..................... | $42,000 | $55,500 | $53,250 | $(2,250) |

cost-volume-profit relationships have been entered into a budgeting program, the computer almost instantly performs the computations necessary to generate a complete master budget for any level of business activity. There are numerous budgeting software programs available on the market. However, many managers choose to develop their own budgeting programs using spreadsheet packages.

Managers often use their budgeting software to generate complete budgets under many different assumptions. These managers use a standard cost system to provide the costs of resources consumed. We will discuss standard cost systems in the next chapter. For managers using standard costs, software becomes a valuable planning tool with which to assess the expected impact of changes in sales, production, and other key variables on all aspects of their operations.

## CASE IN POINT

The widespread use of computers in budgeting is not limited to business applications. Many individuals now rely on budgeting programs to pay monthly bills, balance their checkbooks, keep track of mortgages, and simplify the filing of income tax forms. Many personal budgeting software packages cost less than $30 and are easy to learn and to use.

## A SECOND LOOK

### Nike, Inc.

As the size of the athletic shoe market contracts, companies such as **Nike**, **Reebok**, and **Converse** are adjusting their strategies to both capture more revenues and reduce costs. To increase revenues, these shoe makers are becoming substantially more customer focused. Customer focused efforts include using specialized technologies for shoes for specific sports such as soccer and sophisticated high-tech devices that measure individual feet with the objective of providing shoes customized to the individual shopper's feet.

In addition to creating strategies that increase revenues, the chapter opener demonstrates that cost control is a significant focus for **Nike**. Identifying areas for cost reduction, clarifying how the reductions will be implemented, and pinpointing who is responsible for implementing the reductions are activities that are carried out in the budgeting process. Another accounting tool that helps companies control their costs is a standard costing system. Standard costing systems are explained in the following chapter.

## SUMMARY OF LEARNING OBJECTIVES

### LO 1

**Explain how a company can be "profit rich, yet cash poor."**
Companies must often tie up large sums of cash in direct materials, work in process, and finished goods inventories. As finished goods are sold, cash continues to remain tied up in accounts receivable. Thus, a company may be reporting record profits, yet still experience cash flow problems.

### LO 2

**Discuss the benefits that a company may derive from a formal budgeting process.**
The benefits of budgeting are the benefits that come from thinking ahead. Budgeting helps to coordinate the activities of the different departments, provides a basis for evaluating department performance, and provides managers with responsibility for future decision making. In addition, budgeting forces management to estimate future economic conditions, including costs of materials, demand for the company's products, and interest rates.

### LO 3

**Explain two philosophies that may be used in setting budgeted amounts.**
The most widely used approach is to set budgeted amounts at levels that are reasonably achievable under normal operating conditions. The goal in this case is to make the budget a fair and reasonable basis for evaluating performance.

An alternative is to budget an ideal level of performance. Under this approach, departments normally fall somewhat short of budgeted performance, but the variations may identify areas in which improvement is possible.

### LO 4

**Describe the elements of a master budget.**
A "master budget" is a group of related budgets and forecasts that together summarize all the planned activities of the business. A master budget usually includes a sales forecast, production schedule, manufacturing costs budget, operating expense budget, cash budget, capital expenditures budget, and projected financial statements. The number and type of individual budgets and schedules that make up the master budget depend on the size and nature of the business.

### LO 5

**Prepare the budgets and supporting schedules included in a master budget.**
A logical sequence of steps in preparing a master budget is discussed on page 922. The operating budget estimates are used primarily in preparing a budgeted income statement, whereas the financial estimates are used in preparing the cash budget and budgeted balance sheets.

### LO 6

**Prepare a flexible budget and explain its uses.**
A flexible budget shows budgeted revenue, costs, and profits for different levels of business activity. Thus a flexible budget can be used to evaluate the efficiency of departments throughout the business even if the actual level of business activity differs from management's original estimates. The amounts included in a flexible budget at any given level of activity are based on cost-volume-profit relationships.

Chapter 22 serves as something of a link between the preceding several chapters and the next chapters. The preparation of a master budget closely relates to the use of standard costs, covered in the next chapter, and draws heavily on concepts regarding cost flows, product costing, cost-volume-profit analysis, and responsibility accounting. In our next chapters, we will see how managers select and utilize budget information for controlling operations and when making decisions pertaining to investments in long-term assets.

## KEY TERMS INTRODUCED OR EMPHASIZED IN CHAPTER 22

**budget** (p. 918) A plan or forecast for a future period expressed in quantitative terms. Establishes objectives and aids in evaluating subsequent performance.

**continuous budgeting** (p. 920) A technique of extending the budget period by one month as each month passes. Therefore, the budget always covers the upcoming 12 months.

**flexible budget** (p. 934) A budget that can readily be revised to reflect budgeted amounts given the actual levels of activity (sales and production) achieved during the period. Makes use of cost-volume-profit relationships to restate the master budget for the achieved level of activity.

**master budget** (p. 920) An overall financial and operating plan, including budgets for all aspects of business operations and for all responsibility centers.

**operating cycle** (p. 917) The average time required for the cash invested in inventories to be converted into the cash ultimately collected on sales made to customers.

**performance report** (p. 934) A schedule comparing the actual and budgeted performance of a particular responsibility center.

**responsibility budget** (p. 921) A portion of the master budget showing the budgeted performance of a particular responsibility center within the organization.

# DEMONSTRATION PROBLEM

Gertz Corporation is completing its master budget for the first two quarters of the current year. The following financial budget estimates (labeled *E1* through *E5*) have been prepared:

### Payments on Current Payables (E1)

|  | 1st Quarter | 2nd Quarter |
| --- | --- | --- |
| Balance at beginning of quarter | $244,000 | $ 80,000 |
| Budgeted increase in payables during the quarter | 300,000 | 320,000 |
| Total payables during quarter | $544,000 | $400,000 |
| Less: Estimated balance at end of quarter | 80,000 | 90,000 |
| Payments on current payables during quarter | $464,000 | $310,000 |

### Prepayments Budget (E2)

|  | 1st Quarter | 2nd Quarter |
| --- | --- | --- |
| Balance at beginning of quarter | $ 5,000 | $ 7,000 |
| Estimated cash expenditure during quarter | 8,000 | 9,000 |
| Total prepayments | $ 13,000 | $ 16,000 |
| Less: Expiration of prepayments | 6,000 | 8,000 |
| Prepayments at end of quarter | $ 7,000 | $ 8,000 |

### Debt Service Budget (E3)

|  | 1st Quarter | 2nd Quarter |
| --- | --- | --- |
| Notes payable at the beginning of the quarter | $ 50,000 | $ 49,000 |
| Interest expense for the quarter | 1,500 | 1,470 |
| Total principal plus accrued interest | $ 51,500 | $ 50,470 |
| Less: Cash payments (principal and interest) | 2,500 | 2,500 |
| Notes payable at the end of the quarter | $ 49,000 | $ 47,970 |

### Budgeted Income Taxes (E4)

|  | 1st Quarter | 2nd Quarter |
| --- | --- | --- |
| Income tax liability at beginning of quarter | $ 25,000 | $ 30,000 |
| Estimated income taxes for the quarter (per budgeted income statement) | 30,000 | 40,000 |
| Total accrued income tax liability | $ 55,000 | $ 70,000 |
| Cash payment of amount owed at beginning of quarter | 25,000 | 30,000 |
| Income tax liability at end of quarter | $ 30,000 | $ 40,000 |

| Estimated Receipts from Customers (E5) | 1st Quarter | 2nd Quarter |
|---|---|---|
| Balance of receivables at beginning of year ..................... | $150,000 | |
| Collections on first quarter sales of $500,000— 60% in first quarter and 40% in the second quarter .............. | 300,000 | $200,000 |
| Collections on second quarter sales of $600,000— 60% in the second quarter and 40% in the third quarter ........... | | 360,000 |
| Cash receipts from customers ............................... | $450,000 | $560,000 |

## Instructions

**a.** Prepare a cash budget for Gertz Corporation for the first two quarters of the current year. Assume that the company's cash balance at the beginning of the first quarter is $50,000.

**b.** Discuss any cash flow problems revealed by your budget.

## Solution to the Demonstration Problem

**a.** The following cash budget can be prepared using the financial budget estimates provided:

| GERTZ CORPORATION Cash Budget First Two Quarters of Current Year | 1st Quarter | 2nd Quarter |
|---|---|---|
| Cash balance at beginning of quarter ..................... | $ 50,000 | $    500 |
| Cash receipts: | | |
| Cash received from customers (E5) ..................... | 450,000 | 560,000 |
| Total cash available ..................................... | $500,000 | $560,500 |
| Cash payments: | | |
| Payment of current payables (E1) ..................... | $464,000 | $310,000 |
| Prepayments (E2) .................................... | 8,000 | 9,000 |
| Debt service, including interest (E3) ................... | 2,500 | 2,500 |
| Income tax payments (E4) ............................ | 25,000 | 30,000 |
| Total disbursements .................................... | $499,500 | $351,500 |
| Cash balance at end of the quarter ...................... | $    500 | $209,000 |

**b.** The cash budget reveals that Gertz expects to disburse more cash than it will collect during the first quarter. As a result, a cash balance of only $500 is budgeted for the end of that quarter. Because these figures are estimates, it is possible that its cash balance may actually be less than the amount budgeted. Thus Gertz should arrange for a line of credit now, in the event that a short-term loan becomes necessary. It does not appear that the company will have any cash flow problems during the second quarter.

## SELF-TEST QUESTIONS

*Answers to these questions appear on page 952.*

**1.** Which of the following statements correctly describes relationships within the master budget? (More than one answer may be correct.)

    **a.** The manufacturing budget is based in large part on the sales forecast.

   **b.** In many elements of the master budget, the amounts budgeted for the upcoming quarter are reviewed and subdivided into monthly budget figures.

   **c.** The manufacturing cost budget affects the budgeted income statement, the cash budget, and the budgeted balance sheet.

   **d.** The capital expenditures budget has a greater effect on the budgeted income statement than it does on the budgeted balance sheet.

2. During the first quarter of its operations, Morris Mfg. Co. expects to sell 50,000 units and create an ending inventory of 20,000 units. Variable manufacturing costs are budgeted at $10 per unit, and fixed manufacturing costs at $100,000 per quarter. The company's treasurer expects that 80% of the variable manufacturing costs will require cash payment during the quarter and that 20% will be financed through accounts payable and accrued liabilities. Only 50% of the fixed manufacturing costs are expected to require cash payments during the quarter.

   In the cash budget, payments for manufacturing costs during the quarter will total:

   **a.** $800,000.     **b.** $610,000.     **c.** $600,000.     **d.** $450,000.

3. Rodgers Mfg. Co. prepares a flexible budget. The original budget forecasts sales of 100,000 units @ $20 and operating expenses of $300,000 fixed, plus $2 per unit. Production was budgeted at 100,000 units. Actual sales and production for the period totaled 110,000 units. When the budget is adjusted to reflect these new activity levels, which of the following budgeted amounts will increase, but by *less than* 10%?

   **a.** Sales revenue.

   **b.** Variable manufacturing costs.

   **c.** Fixed manufacturing costs.

   **d.** Total operating expenses.

4. Lamberton Manufacturing Company has just completed its master budget. The budget indicates that the company's operating cycle needs to be shortened. Thus the company will likely attempt:

   **a.** Stocking larger inventories.

   **b.** Reducing cash discounts for prompt payment.

   **c.** Tightening credit policies.

   **d.** None of the above selections is correct.

5. Which of the following is *not* an element of the master budget?

   **a.** The capital expenditures budget.

   **b.** The production schedule.

   **c.** The operating expense budget.

   **d.** All of the above are elements of the master budget.

6. Which of the following is *not* a potential benefit of using budgets?

   **a.** Enhanced coordination of firm activities.

   **b.** More motivated managers.

   **c.** More accurate external financial statements.

   **d.** Improved interdepartmental communication.

# ASSIGNMENT MATERIAL

## DISCUSSION QUESTIONS

1. Explain the relationship between the management functions of *planning* and *controlling costs*.

2. Briefly explain at least three ways in which a business may expect to benefit from preparing a formal budget.

3. Criticize the following quotation:

   "At our company, budgeted revenue is set so high and budgeted expenses so low that no department can ever meet the budget. This way, department managers can never relax; they are motivated to keep working harder no matter how well they are already doing."

4. Identify at least five budgets or schedules that are often included in the master budget of a manufacturing business.

5. List in a logical sequence the major steps in the preparation of a master budget.

6. Why is the preparation of a sales forecast one of the earliest steps in preparing a master budget?

7. What are *responsibility budgets*? What responsibility centers would serve as the basis for preparing responsibility sales budgets in a large retail store, such as **Sears** or **Nordstrom**?

8. What is a *flexible budget*? Explain how a flexible budget increases the usefulness of budgeting as a means of evaluating performance.

9. An article in *Business Week* stated that approximately one-third of the total federal budget is considered "controllable." What is meant by a budgeted expenditure being controllable? Give two examples of government expenditures that may be considered "noncontrollable."

10. Explain why companies that undergo periods of rapid growth often experience cash flow problems.

## EXERCISES

The following information is from the manufacturing budget and the budgeted financial statements of Wexler Fabrication:

| | |
|---|---:|
| Direct materials inventory, Jan. 1 | $ 65,000 |
| Direct materials inventory, Dec. 31 | 80,000 |
| Direct materials budgeted for use during the year | 250,000 |
| Accounts payable to suppliers of materials, Jan. 1 | 50,000 |
| Accounts payable to suppliers of materials, Dec. 31 | 75,000 |

Compute the budgeted amounts for:

**a.** Purchases of direct materials during the year.

**b.** Cash payments during the year to suppliers of materials.

**EXERCISE 22.1**

Budgeting Purchases and Cash Payments

**LO 4, 5**

On January 1, Salter Corporation determined that its direct materials inventory needs to contain 6,500 pounds of materials by March 31. To achieve this goal, Salter will have to use 10 pounds of direct material for every pound that it purchases during the upcoming quarter. Based on the company's budgeted sales volume, management estimates that 10,000 pounds of direct materials need to be purchased by March 31.

Determine how many pounds are in Salter's beginning direct materials inventory on January 1.

**EXERCISE 22.2**

Estimating Direct Materials Inventory

**LO 4, 5**

The Mercury Bag Company produces plastic grocery bags. The managers at Mercury are trying to develop budgets for the upcoming quarter. The following data have been gathered:

| | |
|---|---|
| Projected sales in units | 1,200 cases |
| Selling price per case | $240 |
| Inventory at the beginning of the quarter | 150 cases |
| Target inventory at the end of the quarter | 100 cases |
| Direct labor hours needed to produce one case | 2 hours |
| Direct labor wages | $10 per hour |
| Direct materials cost per case | $8 |
| Variable manufacturing overhead cost per case | $6 |
| Fixed overhead costs for the upcoming quarter | $220,000 |

**EXERCISE 22.3**

Production Budgets

**LO 4, 5**

**a.** Using the above information, develop Mercury's sales forecast in dollars and production schedule in units.

**b.** What is Mercury's budgeted variable manufacturing cost per case?

**c.** Prepare Mercury's manufacturing cost budget.

**d.** What is the projected ending value of the Inventory account?

**EXERCISE 22.4**

Production and Direct
Materials Budget

**LO 4, 5**

Safe 'n' Bright, Inc., produces outside doors for installation on homes. The following information was gathered to prepare budgets for the upcoming year beginning January 1:

| | |
|---|---|
| Sales forecast in units . . . . . . . . . . . . . . . . . . . . . . . . . . . . . . . . . . . . . . . . . . . . . . . . | 5,500 doors |
| Finished goods inventory, Jan. 1 . . . . . . . . . . . . . . . . . . . . . . . . . . . . . . . . . . . . . . . . | 620 doors |
| Target finished goods inventory, Dec. 31 . . . . . . . . . . . . . . . . . . . . . . . . . . . . . . | 480 doors |
| Raw materials inventory—steel, Jan. 1 . . . . . . . . . . . . . . . . . . . . . . . . . . . . . . . | 40,000 pounds |
| Target inventory—steel, Dec. 31 . . . . . . . . . . . . . . . . . . . . . . . . . . . . . . . . . . . . . | 80,000 pounds |
| Raw materials inventory—glass, Jan. 1 . . . . . . . . . . . . . . . . . . . . . . . . . . . . . . . | 6,000 square feet |
| Target inventory—glass, Dec. 31 . . . . . . . . . . . . . . . . . . . . . . . . . . . . . . . . . . . . | 4,000 square feet |
| Budgeted purchase price—steel . . . . . . . . . . . . . . . . . . . . . . . . . . . . . . . . . . . | $4 per pound |
| Budgeted purchase price—glass . . . . . . . . . . . . . . . . . . . . . . . . . . . . . . . . . . . | $2 per square foot |

The manufacture of each door requires 20 pounds of steel and 6 square feet of glass.

**a.** Prepare the production schedule in units for Safe 'n' Bright.

**b.** Using the production schedule, develop the direct materials purchases budgets for steel and glass.

**c.** Why might Safe 'n' Bright's target level of steel inventory be higher than last year's ending balance and the target level of glass inventory be lower than last year's ending balance?

**EXERCISE 22.5**

Budgeting for Prepayments

**LO 4, 5**

Springfield Company's master budget includes estimated costs and expenses of $325,000 for its third quarter of operations. Of this amount, $300,000 is expected to be financed with current payables. Depreciation expense for the quarter is budgeted at $20,000. Springfield's prepayments balance at the end of the third quarter is expected to be twice that of its prepayments balance at the beginning of the quarter. The company estimates it will prepay expenses totaling $8,000 in the third quarter. What is Springfield's budgeted prepayments balance at the end of the third quarter?

**EXERCISE 22.6**

Budgeting for Interest Expense

**LO 4, 5**

On February 1, 2002, Willmar Corporation borrowed $100,000 from its bank by signing a 12%, 15-year note payable. The note calls for 180 monthly payments of $1,200. Each payment includes an interest and a principal component.

**a.** Compute the interest expense in February.

**b.** Compute the portion of Willmar's March 31, 2002, $1,200 payment that will be applied to the principal of the note.

**c.** Compute the carrying value of the note on April 30, 2002 (round to the nearest dollar).

**EXERCISE 22.7**

Operating Expense Budget

**LO 4, 5**

Last month, Widner Corporation generated sales of $800,000 and incurred selling and administrative expenses of $320,000, half of which were variable. This month, the company estimates that it will generate sales of $900,000. Management does not anticipate any changes in unit variable costs. However, it does expect fixed selling and administrative costs to increase by $5,000.

Compute Widner's total selling and administrative expense budget for the upcoming month.

**EXERCISE 22.8**

Budgeting Cash Receipts

**LO 4, 5**

Sales on account for the first two months of the current year are budgeted as follows:

| | |
|---|---|
| Jan. . . . . . . . . . . . . . . . . . . . . . . . . . . . . . . . . . . . . . . . . . . . . . . . . . . . . . . . . . . . . | $600,000 |
| Feb. . . . . . . . . . . . . . . . . . . . . . . . . . . . . . . . . . . . . . . . . . . . . . . . . . . . . . . . . . . . | 800,000 |

All sales are made on terms of 2/10, n/30; collections on accounts receivable are typically made as follows:

| | |
|---|---:|
| Collections within the month of sale: | |
| Within discount period | 60% |
| After discount period | 15% |
| Collections within the month following sale: | |
| Within discount period | 15% |
| After discount period | 7% |
| Returns, allowances, and uncollectibles | 3% |
| Total | 100% |

Compute the estimated cash collections on accounts receivable for the month of *February*.

On March 1 of the current year, Spicer Corporation has compiled information to prepare a cash budget for March, April, and May. All of the company's sales are made on account. The following information has been provided by Spicer's management:

**EXERCISE 22.9**

Budgeting an Ending Cash Balance

**LO 4, 5**

| Month | Credit Sales |
|---|---|
| Jan. | $300,000 (actual) |
| Feb. | 400,000 (actual) |
| Mar. | 600,000 (estimated) |
| Apr. | 700,000 (estimated) |
| May | 800,000 (estimated) |

The company's collection activity on credit sales historically has been as follows:

| | |
|---|---:|
| Collections in the month of the sale | 50% |
| Collections one month after the sale | 30 |
| Collections two months after the sale | 15 |
| Uncollectible accounts | 5 |

Spicer's total cash expenditures for March, April, and May have been estimated at $1,200,000 (an average of $400,000 per month). Its cash balance on March 1 of the current year is $500,000. No financing or investing activities are anticipated during the second quarter.

Compute Spicer's budgeted cash balance at the ends of March, April, and May.

The flexible budget at the 70,000-unit and the 80,000-unit levels of activity is shown below.

**EXERCISE 22.10**

Preparing a Flexible Budget

**LO 6**

| | 70,000 Units | 80,000 Units | 90,000 Units |
|---|---|---|---|
| Sales | $1,400,000 | $1,600,000 | $ |
| Cost of goods sold | 840,000 | 960,000 | |
| Gross profit on sales | $ 560,000 | $ 640,000 | $ |
| Operating expenses ($90,000 fixed) | 370,000 | 410,000 | |
| Operating income | $ 190,000 | $ 230,000 | $ |
| Income taxes (30% of operating income) | 57,000 | 69,000 | |
| Net income | $ 133,000 | $ 161,000 | $ |

Complete the flexible budget at the 90,000-unit level of activity. Assume that the cost of goods sold and variable operating expenses vary directly with sales and that income taxes remain at 30% of operating income.

## EXERCISE 22.11

More on Flexible Budgeting

 **LO 6**

The cost accountant for Amalfi Leather Goods prepared the following monthly performance report relating to the Finishing Department:

| | Budgeted Production (10,000 Units) | Actual Production (11,000 Units) | Variances Favorable | Variances Unfavorable |
|---|---|---|---|---|
| Direct materials used ...... | $300,000 | $320,000 | | $20,000 |
| Direct labor ............. | 100,000 | 115,000 | | 15,000 |
| Variable manufacturing overhead ............. | 20,000 | 21,500 | | 1,500 |
| Fixed manufacturing overhead ............. | 150,000 | 149,200 | $800 | |

Prepare a revised performance report in which the variances are computed by comparing the actual costs incurred with estimated costs *using a flexible budget* for 11,000 units of production.

## EXERCISE 22.12

Budget Estimates

 **LO 2, 3**

William George is the marketing manager at the Crunchy Cookie Company. Each quarter, he is responsible for submitting a sales forecast to be used in the formulation of the company's master budget. George consistently understates the sales forecast because, as he puts it, "I am reprimanded if actual sales are less than I've projected, and I look like a hero if actual sales exceed my projections."

a. What would you do if you were the marketing manager at the Crunchy Cookie Company? Would you also understate sales projections? Defend your answer.

b. What measures might be taken by the company to discourage the manipulation of sales forecasts?

# PROBLEMS

## PROBLEM 22.1

Budgeting Manufacturing Overhead

 **LO 4, 5**

Fargo Enterprises manufactures a component that is processed successively by Department A and Department B. Manufacturing overhead is applied to units produced at the following budgeted costs:

| | Manufacturing Overhead per Unit Fixed | Variable | Total |
|---|---|---|---|
| Department A ....................................... | $12 | $6 | $18 |
| Department B ....................................... | 10 | 4 | 14 |

These budgeted overhead costs per unit are based on a normal volume of production of 6,000 units per month. In January, variable manufacturing overhead in Department B is expected to be 25% above budget because of major scheduled repairs to equipment. The company plans to produce 5,000 units during January.

### Instructions

Prepare a budget for manufacturing overhead costs in January. Use three column headings: Total, Department A, and Department B.

## PROBLEM 22.2

Budgeting Labor Costs

**LO 4, 5**

Sun Mountain Foods manufactures a product that is first dry roasted and then packed for shipment to customers. The product's direct labor cost per pound is budgeted using the following information:

|                      | Direct Labor Hours per Pound | Budgeted Direct Labor Cost per Hour |
|----------------------|:---------------------------:|:----------------------------------:|
| Process:             |                             |                                    |
| Dry roasting ....................... | .025                        | $8.40                              |
| Packing ........................ | .012                        | 7.50                               |

The budget for November calls for the production of 200,000 pounds of product. November's direct labor costs for dry roasting are expected to be 6% above budget due to anticipated scheduling inefficiencies. However, direct labor costs in the packing room are expected to be 4% below budget because of changes in equipment layout.

**Instructions**

Prepare a budget for direct labor costs in November. Use three column headings: Total, Dry Roasting, and Packing.

Renfrow International manufactures and sells a single product. In preparing its master budget for the current quarter, the company's controller has assembled the following information:

**PROBLEM 22.3**

Budgeting Production, Inventories, and Cost of Sales

|                      | Units    | Dollars      |
|----------------------|---------:|-------------:|
| Sales (budgeted) ...................................... | 150,000  | $7,500,000   |
| Finished goods inventory, beginning of quarter ................... | 38,000   | 975,000      |
| Finished goods inventory, end of quarter ...................... | 28,000   | ?            |
| Cost of finished goods manufactured (assume a budgeted manufacturing cost of $28 per unit) ................. | ?        | ?            |

Renfrow International used the average cost method of pricing its inventory of finished goods.

**Instructions**

Compute the following budgeted quantities or dollar amounts:

**a.** Planned production of finished goods (in units)

**b.** Cost of finished goods manufactured

**c.** Ending finished goods inventory (Remember that in using the average cost method, you must first compute the average cost of units available for sale.)

**d.** Cost of goods sold

Harmony Corporation manufactures and sells a single product. In preparing the budget for the first quarter, the company's cost accountant has assembled the following information:

**PROBLEM 22.4**

Short Budgeting Problem

LO 4, 5

|                      | Units    | Dollars       |
|----------------------|---------:|--------------:|
| Sales (budgeted) ..................................... | 150,000  | $12,150,000   |
| Finished goods inventory, Jan. 1 (actual) ...................... | 30,000   | 1,080,000     |
| Finished goods inventory, Mar. 31 (budgeted) .................. | 20,000   | ?             |
| Cost of finished goods manufactured (budgeted manufacturing cost is $39 per unit) ...................... | ?        | ?             |

The company uses the first-in, first-out method of pricing its inventory of finished goods.

**Instructions**

Compute the following budgeted quantities or dollar amounts:

**a.** Planned production of finished goods (in units)

**b.** Cost of finished goods manufactured

**c.** Finished goods inventory, March 31 (Remember to use the first-in, first-out method in pricing the inventory.)

**d.** Cost of goods sold

**PROBLEM 22.5**

Budgeting for Cash

**LO 4, 5**

Barnum Distributors wants a projection of cash receipts and cash payments for the month of November. On November 28, a note will be payable in the amount of $98,500, including interest. The cash balance on November 1 is $29,600. Accounts payable to merchandise creditors at the end of October were $217,000.

The company's experience indicates that 70% of sales will be collected during the month of sale, 20% in the month following the sale, and 7% in the second month following the sale; 3% will be uncollectible. The company sells various products at an average price of $11 per unit. Selected sales figures are as follows:

|  | Units |
|---|---|
| Sept.—actual | 40,000 |
| Oct.—actual | 60,000 |
| Nov.—estimated | 80,000 |
| Dec.—estimated | 50,000 |
| Total estimated for the current year | 800,000 |

Because purchases are payable within 15 days, approximately 50% of the purchases in a given month are paid in the following month. The average cost of units purchased is $7 per unit. Inventories at the end of each month are maintained at a level of 2,000 units plus 10% of the number of units that will be sold in the following month. The inventory on October 1 amounted to 8,000 units.

Budgeted operating expenses for November are $220,000. Of this amount, $90,000 is considered fixed (including depreciation of $35,000). All operating expenses, other than depreciation, are paid in the month in which they are incurred.

The company expects to sell fully depreciated equipment in November for $8,400 cash.

**Instructions**

Prepare a cash budget for the month of November, supported by schedules of cash collections on accounts receivable and cash payments for purchases of merchandise.

**PROBLEM 22.6**

Estimating Borrowing
Requirements

**LO 1, 2, 4, 5**

Potter Corporation sells office supplies to government agencies. At the beginning of the current quarter, the company reports the following selected account balances:

| | |
|---|---|
| Cash | $ 10,000 |
| Accounts receivable | 200,000 |
| Current payables | 85,000 |

Potter's management has made the following budget estimates regarding operations for the current quarter:

| | |
|---|---|
| Sales (estimated) | $500,000 |
| Total costs and expenses (estimated) | 400,000 |
| Debt service payment (estimated) | 145,000 |
| Tax liability payment (estimated) | 45,000 |

Of Potter's total costs and expenses, $30,000 is quarterly depreciation expense, and $20,000 represents the expiration of prepayments. The remaining $350,000 is to be financed with current payables. The company's ending prepayments balance is expected to be the same as its beginning prepayments balance. Its ending current payables balance is expected to be $20,000 more than its beginning balance.

All of Potter's sales are on account. Approximately 65% of its sales are collected in the quarter in which they are made. The remaining 35% is collected in the following quarter. Because all of the company's sales are made to government agencies, it experiences virtually no uncollectible accounts.

Potter's minimum cash balance requirement is $10,000. Should the balance fall below this amount, management negotiates a short-term loan with a local bank. The company's debt ratio (liabilities ÷ assets) is currently 80%.

## Instructions

**a.** Compute Potter's budgeted cash receipts for the quarter.

**b.** Compute Potter's payments of current payables budgeted for the quarter.

**c.** Compute Potter's cash prepayments budgeted for the quarter.

**d.** Prepare Potter's cash budget for the quarter.

**e.** Estimate Potter's short-term borrowing requirements for the quarter.

**f.** Discuss problems Potter might encounter in obtaining short-term financing.

Rizzo's has been in business since January of the current year. The company buys frozen pizza crusts and resells them to large supermarket chains in five states. The following information pertains to Rizzo's first four months of operations:

**PROBLEM 22.7**

Budgeted Income Statement and Cash Budget

**LO 1, 2, 4, 5**

| | Purchases | Sales |
|---|---|---|
| Jan. . . . . . . . . . . . . . . . . . . . . . . . . . . . . . . . . . . . . . . . . . . . . . . . . | $40,000 | $62,000 |
| Feb. . . . . . . . . . . . . . . . . . . . . . . . . . . . . . . . . . . . . . . . . . . . . . . | 32,000 | 49,000 |
| Mar. . . . . . . . . . . . . . . . . . . . . . . . . . . . . . . . . . . . . . . . . . . . . . . | 44,000 | 65,000 |
| Apr. . . . . . . . . . . . . . . . . . . . . . . . . . . . . . . . . . . . . . . . . . . . . . . | 24,000 | 42,000 |

Rizzo's expects to open several new sales territories in May. In anticipation of increased volume, management forecasts May sales at $72,000. To meet this demand, purchases in May are budgeted at $42,000. The company maintains a gross profit margin of approximately 40%.

All of Rizzo's sales are on account. Due to strict credit policies, the company has no bad debt expense. The following collection performance is anticipated for the remainder of the year:

| | |
|---|---|
| Percent collected in month of sale . . . . . . . . . . . . . . . . . . . . . . . . . . . . . . . . . . . . | 30% |
| Percent collected in month following sale . . . . . . . . . . . . . . . . . . . . . . . . . . . . . . | 60% |
| Percent collected in the second month following sale . . . . . . . . . . . . . . . . . . . . . . . | 10% |

Rizzo's normally pays for 80% of its purchases in the month that the purchases are made. The remaining amount is paid in the following month. The company's fixed selling and administrative expenses average $12,000 per month. Of this amount, $4,000 is depreciation expense. Variable selling and administrative expenses are budgeted at 5% of sales. The company pays all of its selling and administrative expenses in the month that they are incurred.

Rizzo's debt service is $5,000 per month. Of this amount, approximately $4,500 represents interest expense, and $500 is payment on the principal. The company's tax rate is approximately 35%. Quarterly tax payments are made at the end of March, June, September, and December.

## Instructions

**a.** Prepare Rizzo's budgeted income statement for May.

**b.** Prepare Rizzo's cash budget for May. Assume that the company's cash balance on May 1 is $25,000.

**c.** Explain why Rizzo's budgeted cash flow in May differs from its budgeted net income.

Jake Marley, owner of Marley Wholesale, is negotiating with the bank for a $200,000, 90-day, 12% loan effective July 1 of the current year. If the bank grants the loan, the proceeds will be $194,000, which Marley intends to use on July 1 as follows: pay accounts payable, $150,000; purchase equipment, $16,000; add to bank balance, $28,000.

The current working capital position of Marley Wholesale, according to financial statements as of June 30, is as follows:

**PROBLEM 22.8**

Preparing a Cash Budget

**LO 1, 2, 4, 5**

| | |
|---|---:|
| Cash in bank . . . . . . . . . . . . . . . . . . . . . . . . . . . . . . . . . . . . . . . . . . . . . . . . . . . . . | $ 20,000 |
| Receivables (net of allowance for doubtful accounts) . . . . . . . . . . . . . . . . . . . . . . | 160,000 |
| Merchandise inventory . . . . . . . . . . . . . . . . . . . . . . . . . . . . . . . . . . . . . . . . . . . . . | 90,000 |
| Total current assets . . . . . . . . . . . . . . . . . . . . . . . . . . . . . . . . . . . . . . . . . . . . . . . | $270,000 |
| Accounts payable (including accrued operating expenses) . . . . . . . . . . . . . . . . . . . | 150,000 |
| Working capital . . . . . . . . . . . . . . . . . . . . . . . . . . . . . . . . . . . . . . . . . . . . . . . . . . | $120,000 |

The bank loan officer asks Marley to prepare a forecast of his cash receipts and cash payments for the next three months to demonstrate that the loan can be repaid at the end of September.

Marley has made the following estimates, which are to be used in preparing a three-month cash budget: Sales (all on account) for July, $300,000; August, $360,000; September, $270,000; and October, $200,000. Past experience indicates that 80% of the receivables generated in any month will be collected in the month following the sale, 19% will be collected in the second month following the sale, and 1% will prove uncollectible. Marley expects to collect $120,000 of the June 30 receivables in July and the remaining $40,000 in August.

Cost of goods sold consistently has averaged about 65% of sales. Operating expenses are budgeted at $36,000 per month plus 8% of sales. With the exception of $4,400 per month depreciation expense, all operating expenses and purchases are on account and are paid in the month following their incurrence.

Merchandise inventory at the end of each month should be sufficient to cover the following month's sales.

### Instructions

a. Prepare a monthly cash budget showing estimated cash receipts and cash payments for July, August, and September, and the cash balance at the end of each month. Supporting schedules should be prepared for estimated collections on receivables, estimated merchandise purchases, and estimated payments for operating expenses and of accounts payable for merchandise purchases.

b. On the basis of this cash forecast, write a brief report to Marley explaining whether he will be able to repay the $200,000 bank loan at the end of September.

**PROBLEM 22.9**

Preparing and Using a
Flexible Budget

**LO 2, 4–6**

Four Flags is a retail department store. The following cost-volume relationships were used in developing a flexible budget for the company for the current year:

| | Yearly Fixed Expenses | Variable Expenses per Sales Dollar |
|---|---:|---:|
| Cost of merchandise sold . . . . . . . . . . . . . . . . . . . . . . . . . . . | | $0.600 |
| Selling and promotion expense . . . . . . . . . . . . . . . . . . . . . . . | $ 210,000 | 0.082 |
| Building occupancy expense . . . . . . . . . . . . . . . . . . . . . . . . . | 186,000 | 0.022 |
| Buying expense . . . . . . . . . . . . . . . . . . . . . . . . . . . . . . . . . . . | 150,000 | 0.040 |
| Delivery expense . . . . . . . . . . . . . . . . . . . . . . . . . . . . . . . . . . | 111,000 | 0.010 |
| Credit and collection expense . . . . . . . . . . . . . . . . . . . . . . . . | 72,000 | 0.002 |
| Administrative expense . . . . . . . . . . . . . . . . . . . . . . . . . . . . . | 531,000 | 0.003 |
| Totals . . . . . . . . . . . . . . . . . . . . . . . . . . . . . . . . . . . . . . . . . . | $1,260,000 | $0.759 |

Management expected to attain a sales level of $12 million during the current year. At the end of the year, the actual results achieved by the company were as follows:

| Net sales | $10,500,000 |
|---|---|
| Cost of goods sold | 6,180,000 |
| Selling and promotion expense | 1,020,000 |
| Building occupancy expense | 420,000 |
| Buying expense | 594,000 |
| Delivery expense | 183,000 |
| Credit and collection expense | 90,000 |
| Administrative expense | 564,000 |

## Instructions

**a.** Prepare a schedule comparing the actual results with flexible budget amounts developed for the actual sales volume of $10,500,000. Organize your schedule as a partial multiple-step income statement, ending with operating income. Include separate columns for (1) flexible budget amounts, (2) actual amounts, and (3) any amount over or (under) budget. Use the cost-volume relationships given in the problem to compute the flexible budget amounts.

**b.** Write a statement evaluating the company's performance in relation to the plan reflected in the flexible budget.

Braemar Saddlery uses department budgets and performance reports in planning and controlling its manufacturing operations. The following annual performance report for the custom saddle production department was presented to the president of the company:

**PROBLEM 22.10**

Flexible Budgeting

**LO 2, 4–6**

| | Budgeted Costs for 5,000 Units | | Actual Costs Incurred | Over or (Under) Budget |
|---|---|---|---|---|
| | Per Unit | Total | | |
| Variable manufacturing costs: | | | | |
| Direct materials | $ 30.00 | $150,000 | $171,000 | $21,000 |
| Direct labor | 48.00 | 240,000 | 261,500 | 21,500 |
| Indirect labor | 15.00 | 75,000 | 95,500 | 20,500 |
| Indirect materials, supplies, etc. | 9.00 | 45,000 | 48,400 | 3,400 |
| Total variable manufacturing costs | $102.00 | $510,000 | $576,400 | $66,400 |
| Fixed manufacturing costs: | | | | |
| Lease rental | $ 9.00 | $ 45,000 | $ 45,000 | –0– |
| Salaries of foremen | 24.00 | 120,000 | 125,000 | $ 5,000 |
| Depreciation and other | 15.00 | 75,000 | 78,600 | 3,600 |
| Total fixed manufacturing costs | $ 48.00 | $240,000 | $248,600 | $ 8,600 |
| Total manufacturing costs | $150.00 | $750,000 | $825,000 | $75,000 |

Although a production volume of 5,000 saddles was originally budgeted for the year, the actual volume of production achieved for the year was *6,000* saddles. Direct materials and direct labor are charged to production at actual cost. Factory overhead is applied to production at the predetermined rate of 150% of the actual direct labor cost.

After a quick glance at the performance report showing an unfavorable manufacturing cost variance of $75,000, the president said to the accountant: "Fix this thing so it makes sense. It looks as though our production people really blew the budget. Remember that we exceeded our budgeted production schedule by a significant margin. I want this performance report to show a better picture of our ability to control costs."

## Instructions

**a.** Prepare a revised performance report for the year on a flexible budget basis. Use the same format as the production report above, but revise the budgeted cost figures to reflect the actual production level of *6,000* saddles.

**b.** Briefly comment on Braemar's ability to control its variable manufacturing costs.

**c.** What is the amount of over- or underapplied manufacturing overhead for the year? (Note that a standard cost system is not used.)

# CASES AND UNSTRUCTURED PROBLEMS

**CASE 22.1**

Budgeting in a Nutshell

**LO 2, 5**

The purpose of this problem is to demonstrate some of the interrelationships in the budgeting process. Shown below is a very simple balance sheet at January 1, along with a simple budgeted income statement for the month. (Assume dollar amounts are stated in thousands; you also may state dollar amounts in this manner.)

| NUTSHELL Balance Sheet January 1 | | | | NUTSHELL Budgeted Income Statement for January | |
|---|---|---|---|---|---|
| **Assets** | | **Liabilities & Equity** | | Sales . . . . . . . . . . . | $100 |
| Cash . . . . . . . . . . | $ 40 | Accounts | | Cost of goods | |
| Accounts | | payable . . . . . . . | $ 30 | sold . . . . . . . . . . | 60 |
| receivable . . . . . | 120 | Owners' | | Gross profit . . . . . . | $ 40 |
| Inventory . . . . . . . | 50 | equity . . . . . . . . | 180 | Expenses . . . . . . . . | 25 |
| Total . . . . . . . . . . | $210 | Total . . . . . . . . . . | $210 | Net income . . . . . . . | $ 15 |

As Nutshell has no plant assets, there is no depreciation expense. Prepare a cash budget for January and a budgeted balance sheet as of January 31.

These budgets are to reflect *your own assumptions* as to the amounts of cash and credit sales, collections of receivables, purchases of inventory, and payments to suppliers. We require only that the cash balance be *$50* at January 31, that receivables and inventory *change* from the January 1 levels, and that the company engage in *no* "financing" or "investing" activities (as these terms are used in a statement of cash flows).

Clearly state your assumptions as part of your solution, and be prepared to explain in class how they result in the amounts shown in your budgets.

**CASE 22.2**

An Ethical Dilemma

**LO 1–3**

Beta Computers is experiencing financial difficulties attributed to declining sales of its mainframe computer systems. Several years ago, the company obtained a large loan from the Midland State Bank. The covenants of the loan agreement strictly state that if Beta is unable to maintain a current ratio of 3:1, a quick ratio of 1:1, and a return on assets of 12%, the bank will exercise its right to liquidate the company's assets in settlement of the loan. To monitor Beta's performance, the bank demands quarterly financial statements that have been reviewed by an independent CPA.

Nick Price, Beta's CEO, has just reviewed the company's master budget projections for the first two quarters of the current year. What he has learned is disturbing. If sales trends continue, it appears that Beta will be in violation of its loan covenants by the end of the second quarter. If these projections are correct, the bank might foreclose on the company's assets. As a consequence, Beta's 750 employees will join the ranks of the unemployed.

In February of the current year, Rembrant International contacted Beta to inquire about purchasing a custom-configured mainframe computer system. Not only would the sale generate over a million dollars in revenue, it would put Beta back in compliance with its loan covenants. Unfortunately, Rembrant International is an extremely bad credit risk, and the likelihood of collecting on the sale is slim. Nonetheless, Nick Price approved the sale on February 1, which resulted in the recording of a $1.4 million receivable.

On March 31, Edgar Gamm, CPA, arrived at Beta's headquarters. In Gamm's opinion, the $1.4 million receivable from Rembrant International should immediately be written off as uncollectible. Of course, if the account is written off, Beta will be in violation of its loan covenants and the bank will soon foreclose. Gamm told Price that it is his professional duty to prevent any material misstatement of the company's assets.

Price reminded Gamm that if the account is written off, 750 employees will be out of work, and that Gamm's accounting firm probably could not collect their fee for this engagement. Price then showed Gamm Beta's master budget for the third and fourth quarters of the current year. The budget indicated a complete turnaround for the company. Gamm suspected, however, that most of the budget's estimates were overly optimistic.

**Instructions**

a. Should Gamm insist that the Rembrant International account be classified as uncollectible? Should the optimistic third and fourth quarter master budget projections influence his decision? What would you do if you were in his position? Defend your actions.

b. If you were the president of the Midland State Bank, what would you do if you discovered that the Rembrant International account constituted a large portion of Beta's reported liquid assets and sales activity for the quarter? How would you react if Edgar Gamm's accounting firm had permitted Beta to classify the account as collectible?

## ◼ *BUSINESS WEEK* ASSIGNMENT | BusinessWeek

**CASE 22.3**

College Tuition and Budgeting

**LO 2, 6**

The following quote is from "Commentary: What Can K.O. Inequality? College" by Aaron Bernstein in a May 31, 1999, *Business Week* article:

Bachchi Nguyen, 20, probably wouldn't make it through college without grants and loans. It's not that she's a slacker. The University of California at Riverside junior juggles an 18-unit course load in business administration and works 15 hours a week as a bank teller. Nguyen's parents, who immigrated from Vietnam in 1992, can't help with the $13,000-a-year tuition. Her father, a construction worker, and her mother have 10 children, two still at home. "The grants and loans take some pressure off my shoulders," says Nguyen, who has gotten $3,000 a year in federal Pell grants plus $10,000 in loans so far.

**Instructions**

a. Identify the benefits Bachchi Nguyen would get by preparing an annual budget.

b. Could Ms. Nguyen benefit from a flexible budget—how?

## ◼ INTERNET ASSIGNMENT

**INTERNET 22.1**

**LO 3–5**

Access the Web page for the U.S. government's annual operating budget created by the Office of Management and Budget at the following address:

**www.access.gpo.gov/su_docs/budget**

Access "A Citizen's Guide to the Federal Budget" and go to the section labeled "How Does the Government Create a Budget?"

**Instructions**

a. In general, how do the steps that the U.S. government takes to create a budget differ from the steps described in this chapter for a manufacturing firm?

b. What is the U.S. government's equivalent to a sales forecast?

c. What is the difference between "Budget Authority" and "Budget Outlay"? What types of activities might these two terms be applied to in a manufacturing firm?

*Internet sites are time and date sensitive. It is the purpose of these exercises to have you explore the Internet. You may need to use the Yahoo! search engine http://www.yahoo.com (or other favorite search engine) to find a company's current web address.*

## OUR COMMENTS ON THE "YOUR TURN" CASES

**As a Production Manager (p. 924)**   Such a significant change in the forecast would require coordination both inside and outside of the firm. The entire value chain would be involved in revising and coordinating plans. Suppliers would need to be notified, employees might expect less work, retail outlets would need to adjust shelf space, and logistics modifications would be required. Half of the number of previously planned shipments would be made.

**As a Cost Accountant (p. 925)**   The projected profitability per unit varies from $33 in the first quarter to $46.75 in the second quarter because the projected fixed costs of $15,000 are distributed over 1,000 units to be produced in the first quarter and 12,000 units to be produced in the second quarter. To avoid this problem, most manufacturers use projected normal production activity as the base for assigning fixed costs. Thus, over the two quarters, expected activity is 13,000 units of production (1,000 from the first quarter and 12,000 from the second quarter), and expected fixed expenses are $30,000 ($15,000 × 2 quarters). Thus the projected fixed cost per unit is $2.31 per unit ($30,000 ÷ 13,000 units). This approach simplifies record keeping (ending inventories will be costed at $15 for direct materials, $5 for direct labor, $7 for variable overhead, and $2.31 for fixed overhead—a total of $29.31 per unit). This method also smooths profitability over cyclical production.

**As Credit Department Manager (p. 932)**   Leading and lagging receivables and payables is not unethical and is widely used as a means for managing working capital. In particular, managing to collect receivables as quickly as possible and delaying payment of payables as long as legally possible can be good financial management. However, these financial management techniques must be balanced against the costs of losing customers or annoying creditors. Creating business practices that result in poor business relations with customers and creditors can be bad for future relationships. For example, many companies do not aggressively manage receivables because they do not want to create business practices that encourage customers to move their business to a competitor.

## ANSWERS TO SELF-TEST QUESTIONS

**1.** a, b, c   **2.** b   (70,000 units × $10 per unit × 80%) + ($100,000 × 50%) = $610,000
**3.** d   **4.** c   **5.** d   **6.** c

## Learning Objectives

*After studying this chapter, you should be able to:*

1. Explain how standard costs assist managers in controlling costs.

2. Explain the difference between setting ideal standards and setting reasonably achievable standards.

3. Compute variable cost variances and explain the meaning of each.

4. Compute fixed cost variances and explain the meaning of each.

5. Discuss the causes of specific cost variances.

PhotoEdit

Creating **Wrigley Company** chewing gum is a complex process that begins with grinding, melting, and purifying base materials using high-speed centrifuges and filter machines. Then, the gum base is mixed and combined with sweeteners; flavors are added at just the right moment and in just the right amounts. The sweetened gum is sent through a series of rollers to form a thin, wide ribbon. A light coating of finely powdered sugar or sugar substitute is added to enhance flavor and to keep the gum from sticking. The continuous ribbon is then scored in a pattern of single sticks. The sticks are conditioned by controlling the temperature and humidity while the gum cools to make sure the finished gum will stay fresh on store shelves. The final stage is packaging. In one continuous process, a machine receives and wraps the sticks, applies the outer wrapper and seals the ends of each package. Finally these packages are shipped to a store near you. See www.wrigley.com for a more complete description of this process.

**Wrigley Company** can monitor the costs associated with creating its chewing gum by using a standard costing system. Creating expected standard amounts of inputs such as material, labor, and machine hours can help **Wrigley** manage its costs. These standard input amounts can be matched with standard input costs to create an expected standard cost for a package of **Wrigley's™** gum. The actual costs for the gum created during a period can be compared to the standard expected costs to gauge where there are cost overruns.

• • •

This chapter introduces and explains standard costing procedures used by many companies such as **Wrigley**.

Hundreds of companies discovered the importance of cost control as a means of survival in fiercely competitive markets of the late 1990s. By implementing an organized, companywide process for controlling costs, a firm can reverse its sinking earnings trend and recover its market position. One important tool companies use to control ongoing operating costs is a standard cost system.

In preceding chapters, we demonstrated how accounting systems are used to assign decision-making authority by creation of responsibility centers and the use of operational budgets. Standard costs, responsibility centers, and operational budgets combine to create an effective system for maintaining cost control. The managers who have decision-making authority over company resources compare their actual results with the standard costs embedded in the budgets. When the actual results and the standard costs are significantly different, managers take corrective action to control the costs that have strayed from the standard.

## STANDARD COST SYSTEMS

A cost accounting system becomes more useful when it includes the *budgeted* or *expected* amounts of manufacturing costs to serve as standards for comparison with the costs actually incurred. These budgeted amounts are called *standard costs* (or *cost standards*). An accounting system that accumulates product, service, or process costs using standard input prices and quantities is a **standard cost system**. Standard costs are used with both job order and process cost systems.

A **standard cost** is the per-unit cost *expected* to be incurred under normal (but efficient) operating conditions. Standard costs are estimated separately for the materials, direct labor, and overhead relating to each type of product that the company manufactures. Comparison of the actual costs with these cost standards quickly directs management's attention to situations in which actual costs differ from expected levels.

Differences between actual and standard input prices or quantities are called **variances**. A variance is said to be *favorable* when actual input costs or quantities are *less* than standard. When actual input costs or quantities *exceed* the standard, the variance is said to be *unfavorable*.

A standard cost system makes use of *both* actual and standard costs. The actual costs are recorded in the Materials, Direct Labor, and Overhead accounts in the manner described in prior chapters. However, the amounts charged to the work in process accounts are the *standard costs* for the number of units produced. Any differences between the actual costs incurred and the standard costs charged to the work in process accounts are recorded in special *cost variance accounts*.

A separate cost variance account is maintained for each type of cost variance. Thus the cost accounting system provides managers with detailed information as to the *nature and amount* of the differences between actual and expected (standard) manufacturing costs.

How do standard costs and variance accounts assist management in controlling costs? By quickly bringing differences in actual and expected costs to management's attention. Otherwise, these cost differences might flow unnoticed into the Finished Goods Inventory and Cost of Goods Sold accounts.

**LO 1**

Explain how standard costs assist managers in controlling costs.

### Establishing and Revising Standard Costs

Standard costs are established and revised each period during the budgeting process. Standard costs are continually reviewed and periodically revised if significant changes occur in production methods or in the prices paid for material, labor, and overhead.

**LO 2**

Explain the difference between setting ideal standards and setting reasonably achievable standards.

What should the expectations of management be as they establish standard cost targets? This is an important question. Under *ideal* conditions, management would leave no room for any inefficiencies in the production process—there would be no waste, spoilage, fatigue, breakdowns, cost overruns, etc. However, ideal expectations are unrealistic and would result in cost standards impossible to achieve. Hence, management's level of expectation must be something *less than ideal*.

## You as a Production Manager

Assume you supervise the production line for a product called Wingdits. Over several previous years, the average demand for Wingdits has required about 80% of production capacity, but recently the manager has required the production line to be run at 100% capacity.

Your production line has been designated as a responsibility cost center and you have the authority to make input-related decisions such as ordering raw materials, hiring employees to work on the production line, and maintaining the equipment used to produce Wingdits. For the past several months, the plant manager has been questioning your management ability because the actual costs of producing Wingdits are significantly higher than the expected standard costs. What could explain the significant difference between actual and standard costs of the recently produced Wingdits? What related ethical issues should you raise with the plant manager?

*Our comments appear on page 986.

**YOUR TURN**

The level of production output plays an important role in determining cost standards. For instance, grossly underutilized production facilities often experience varying degrees of cost inefficiency. Conversely, the stress and demands imposed on production facilities operating at full capacity can cause cost overruns. Thus, as previously stated, standards should correspond to what costs should be under *normal* operating conditions for a particular company.

Establishing realistic cost standards requires input from many different sources—often including people from outside of the business organization.

To encourage an overall strategy of continuous improvement within their organizations, many companies create programs that require continuous improvement (reductions) in standard costs. Japanese companies have implemented the continuous improvement idea through cost reduction programs called *kaizen* costing. For example, **Nissan Motor Company, Ltd.**, and **Isuzu Motors, Ltd.**, use kaizen costing to manage their costs. These continuous improvement strategies motivate employees to find creative and innovative approaches to reducing costs.

**MANAGEMENT STRATEGY**

## Direct Material Standards

The first step in establishing standard costs for direct materials is identifying the specific materials required to produce each product. The setting of direct material standards involves both the *cost* and the *quantity* of each material used. For example, assume that the standard cost of mozzarella cheese used in the production of frozen pizzas is $2.40 per pound. If the standard quantity of cheese allowed per pizza is one-quarter of a pound, the standard cost of cheese per pizza is $0.60 ($2.40 per pound times ¼ pound).

The setting of direct material standards also involves assessing relationships among cost, quality, and selling prices. High-quality materials generally cost more than low-quality materials. However, the use of high-quality materials often results in less waste, less spoilage, and fewer product defects. In Chapter 18 we pointed out that the cost and quality of materials used in production are key factors in determining selling prices, which, in turn, significantly influence customer demand.

Issues relating to storage, availability, waste disposal, and shipping costs also should be taken into consideration.

### Direct Labor Standards

Establishing standard costs for direct labor is similar to the process of establishing direct material standards. First, the specific direct labor requirements to produce each product must be identified. Once this has been accomplished, the setting of direct labor standards involves both the *wage rate* and the amount of *time allowed* to produce each product. For example, assume that the standard wage rate of a production worker in a furniture manufacturing company is $15 per hour. If the standard number of direct labor hours (DLH) allowed to produce a particular table is 3 hours, the standard direct labor cost per table is $45 ($15 per DLH times 3 DLH).

The setting of reasonable direct labor standards often requires input from personnel managers, industrial engineers, union representatives, supervisors, cost accountants, and factory employees.

### Manufacturing Overhead Standards

Standard overhead cost per unit is based on an estimate of total overhead at the *normal* level of production. Various cost drivers and, perhaps, activity-based costing may be used in developing the standard overhead cost per unit. Once this standard has been established, however, overhead is applied to production at the standard cost per unit.

**CASE IN POINT**

Some companies are allowing workers to set their own standards by using time and motion techniques formerly used by industrial engineers. When standards are set by industrial engineers rather than by the workers themselves, workers pay scant attention to them. At the **Toyota–General Motors** joint-venture plant in Fremont, California, work teams standardize each task so that every member of the team will perform the task in the same way. Teams compare their actual results to standards and to the actual results and standards created by other teams on other shifts. Team members periodically update standards when they find more efficient methods for achieving their tasks.

### Standard Costs and Variance Analysis: An Illustration

To illustrate the use of standard costs and the computation of variances, we will examine the operations of Brice Mills in Moscow, Idaho. Among the company's major products are laminated wooden beams used in the construction industry. The production process involves two steps. First, 2-inch by 12-inch boards of varying lengths are cut from rough white pine lumber supplied by wholesalers from throughout the Pacific Northwest. These boards are then glued together, like a sandwich, to form a laminated beam. The more 2-inch by 12-inch boards used in the lamination, the stronger the beam. One of the most common beams that Brice manufactures on a regular basis is 20 feet long and requires six layers of pine boards. At normal capacity, the company produces *700* of these beams each month.

When finished, each beam contains 240 board-feet of lumber. However, because of waste caused by knots, warps, cracks, and blade cuts, Brice allows *264 board-feet* as the standard quantity for each 20-foot beam manufactured. The company's standard cost of rough white pine is $0.25 per board-foot. Therefore, the standard cost of direct materials is $66 per beam (264 board-feet × $0.25 per foot).

Converting rough lumber into boards suitable for finished beams requires a variety of direct labor tasks. For instance, boards must be cut and planed, glued together, pressed, and coated with a protective sealant. Brice has established a standard of 1.5 direct labor hours for each beam it produces. Its standard labor rate is $12 per hour, resulting in a standard direct labor cost of $18 per beam.

Let us now consider the standard *overhead* cost per beam. Manufacturing overhead includes both *fixed* and *variable* costs. **Fixed manufacturing costs** are those that *are not affected* by short-term changes in the level of production. Examples include supervisors' salaries, depreciation on machinery, and property taxes on the factory. **Variable manufacturing costs**, on the other hand, rise and fall in *approximate proportion* to changes in production volume. The best examples of variable production costs are direct materials and direct labor. However, certain overhead costs also are variable, including machinery repairs and the amounts of electricity and indirect materials (such as glue) used in production.

Brice budgets total fixed overhead relating to the production of beams at $5,600 per month. At the normal production level of 700 beams per month, this amounts to *$8 per beam* ($5,600 ÷ 700 beams). In addition, Brice expects to incur *$6 per beam* in variable overhead. Thus the company's standard cost for overhead is estimated at *$14 per unit*.

The following table summarizes the standard costs Brice expects to incur in the manufacture of its 20-foot beams. (Throughout this illustration, we show standard costs in *red*, actual costs in *blue*, and cost variances in *black*.)

| | | |
|---|---:|---:|
| Direct materials (264 board-feet at $0.25 per board-foot) | | $66 |
| Direct labor (1.5 DLH at $12 per DLH) | | 18 |
| Manufacturing overhead: | | |
|   Fixed ($5,600 per month ÷ 700 units) | $8 | |
|   Variable ($4 per DLH × 1.5 DLH allowed per unit) | 6 | 14 |
| Standard cost per unit | | $98 |

During March, Brice experienced several production delays. As a result of these delays, only 600 beams were produced (or 100 fewer than "normal" monthly output). There were no units in process either at the beginning or at the end of March. *Total* manufacturing costs *actually incurred* to produce 600 beams during the month were as follows:

| | | |
|---|---:|---:|
| Direct materials (180,000 board-feet at $0.20 per board-foot) | | $36,000 |
| Direct labor (1,080 DLH at $13 per DLH) | | 14,040 |
| Manufacturing overhead: | | |
|   Fixed | $5,000 | |
|   Variable | 3,680 | 8,680 |
| Actual total cost of finished goods manufactured | | $58,720 |

By comparing the actual costs incurred in March to the standard costs allowed to actually produce 600 beams, we can determine the *total cost variance* for the month as follows:

| | |
|---|---:|
| Actual total costs for March (from above) | $58,720 |
| Standard costs allowed for producing 600 units (600 units × $98) | 58,800 |
| Total favorable cost variance (actual costs are less than standard) | $ 80 |

As shown above, total costs incurred to manufacture 600 20-foot beams during the month *were actually $80 less than* the standard cost allowed. Thus the *total variance* from standard is said to be *favorable*. Because it is favorable, one might jump to the conclusion that operating efficiency is slightly better than expected and that no corrective actions are necessary. We will see, however, that the $80 total variance from standard does not provide enough detailed information to adequately assess manufacturing efficiency. Only by comparing actual costs of direct materials, direct labor, and overhead to their related standard costs can we begin to understand the dynamics of the numerous interrelationships involved. Let us begin by determining the portion of the company's total variance attributable to the price and quantity of direct materials used in March.

**LO 3**

Compute variable cost variances and explain the meaning of each.

## Materials Price and Quantity Variances

In establishing the standard material cost for each unit of product, two factors are considered: (1) the *quantity* of materials required and (2) the *prices* that should be paid to acquire these materials. Therefore, a total cost variance for materials can result from differences in the quantities used, in the prices paid to suppliers, or a combination of these factors.

Let us compute the total materials variance incurred by Brice in the production of *600* laminated beams in March. As we have stated, a cost variance is the *difference* between the actual cost and the standard cost of the unit produced. Thus Brice had a $3,600 favorable materials variance for the 600 beams produced in March:

| | |
|---|---:|
| Standard quantity at standard price: | |
| 158,400 board-feet × $0.25 per board-foot ........................... | $39,600 |
| Actual quantity at actual price: | |
| 180,000 board-feet × $0.20 per board-foot ........................... | 36,000 |
| Total materials cost variance (favorable) ........................... | $ 3,600 |

This cost variance is *favorable* because the actual costs were *less* than standard.

We will now see, however, that this $3,600 favorable variance has two distinct components: (1) a $9,000 favorable *materials price variance* and (2) a $5,400 unfavorable *materials quantity variance*.

The favorable **materials price variance** resulted from the purchasing agent acquiring lumber for *5 cents less* than the standard cost of $0.25 per square foot. The formula for computing the materials price variance is as follows:

**Materials Price Variance = Actual Quantity Used × (Standard Price − Actual Price)**
$$= \textbf{180,000 board-feet} \times (\$0.25 - \$0.20)$$
$$= \textbf{\$9,000 (Favorable)}$$

(*Note:* The formulas for computing all of the cost variances discussed in this chapter are summarized on page 968.)

The unfavorable **materials quantity variance** resulted from the production department using more lumber than the cost standard allows. The production department actually used 180,000 board-feet of pine in producing 600 beams. But the standard cost allows only 264 board-feet per beam, or *158,400* for the production of 600 beams. Therefore, the production department has used *21,600 more board-feet of lumber* than the materials cost standard allows. The computation of the materials quantity variance is as follows:

**Materials Quantity Variance = Standard Price × (Standard Quantity −**
**Actual Quantity)**
$$= \textbf{\$0.25} \times (\textbf{158,400 board-feet} - \textbf{180,000 board-feet})$$
$$= \textbf{−\$5,400 (or \$5,400 Unfavorable)}$$

(*Note:* All of our variance formulas result in a *negative number* when the variance is *unfavorable* and in a *positive number* when the variance is *favorable*.)

The following diagram illustrates how the two materials cost variances explain the *difference* between the standard materials cost for producing 600 beams and the actual costs incurred by Brice:

| **Actual Quantity at Actual Price** 180,000 Board-Feet × $0.20 $36,000 | **Actual Quantity at Standard Price** 180,000 Board-Feet × $0.25 $45,000 | **Standard Quantity Allowed at Standard Price** 158,400 Board-Feet × $0.25 $39,600 |
|---|---|---|

**Materials Price Variance** $9,000 Favorable     **Materials Quantity Variance** $5,400 Unfavorable

**Total Materials Variance, $3,600 Favorable**

The following journal entry is made to record the cost of materials used during March and the related cost variances:

| | | |
|---|---|---|
| Work in Process Inventory (at standard cost) | 39,600 | |
| Materials Quantity Variance (unfavorable) | 5,400 | |
|    Materials Price Variance (favorable) | | 9,000 |
|    Direct Materials Inventory (at actual cost) | | 36,000 |
| To record the cost of direct materials used in March. | | |

*Record material costs and related variances*

Notice that the Work in Process Inventory account is debited for the *standard cost* of materials used, and the Direct Materials Inventory account is credited for the *actual cost* of materials used. The difference between the standard and actual total cost is recorded in the two *cost variance accounts.*[1] Unfavorable variances are recorded by debit entries because they represent costs in excess of the budgeted standards. Favorable variances, however, are recorded by credit entries because they represent cost savings relative to standard amounts.

---

Variances do represent actual costs (savings) to companies as compared to what was expected based on standard costs. However, cash flows do not occur when the variances are recognized. Cash flows occur when accounts payable (for raw materials or overhead) or wages payable (for labor) are actually paid.

**CASH EFFECTS**

---

## Labor Rate and Efficiency Variances

Brice incurred actual direct labor costs of $14,040 in March. The standard labor cost allowed for manufacturing 600 beams is only $10,800 (600 units × 1.5 hours per unit × $12 per hour). Thus the company is faced with an unfavorable labor variance of *$3,240* ($10,800 − $14,040). We can gain additional insight regarding the reasons for this overrun by separating the total variance amount into two elements—a *labor rate variance* and a *labor efficiency variance*.

Actual labor costs are a function of: (1) the wage rate paid to direct labor workers and (2) the number of direct labor hours worked. A **labor rate variance** shows the extent to which hourly wage *rates* contributed to deviations from standard costs. The **labor efficiency variance** indicates the extent to which the number of *labor hours* worked during the period contributed to deviations from standard costs.

---

[1] An alternative is to record the materials price variance at the time the materials are purchased. Such alternatives are discussed in cost accounting courses.

The labor rate variance is equal to the actual number of hours worked multiplied by the difference between the standard wage rate and the actual wage rate. Time cards show that 1,080 direct labor hours were used in March. The average wage rate for the month was $13 per hour. Thus the labor rate variance for Brice is computed as follows:

**Labor Rate Variance = Actual Labor Hours × (Standard Rate − Actual Rate)**
= 1,080 hours × ($12 − $13)
= −$1,080 (or $1,080 Unfavorable)

An *unfavorable* labor rate variance can result from using highly paid employees to perform lower-payscale jobs, poor scheduling, or incurring excessive overtime costs.[2] Since the production manager is usually responsible for assigning employees to production activities, he or she normally is responsible for labor rate variances. (But, as we will see in our example, this is not always the case.)

The *labor efficiency variance* (also called the *labor usage variance*) is a measure of worker productivity. This variance is favorable when workers are able to complete the scheduled production in fewer hours than allowed by the standard. It is unfavorable when wasted time or low productivity causes actual hours to exceed the standard. The labor efficiency variance is computed by multiplying the standard hourly wage rate by the difference between the standard hours allowed and actual hours used. Brice allows *900* direct labor hours to produce 600 beams (600 units × 1.5 hours per unit). Given that *1,080* hours were actually required, the company's *unfavorable* labor efficiency variance for March is computed as follows:

**Labor Efficiency Variance = Standard Hourly Rate × (Standard Hours − Actual Hours)**
= $12 per hour × (900 hours − 1,080 hours)
= −$2,160 (or $2,160 Unfavorable)

The *unfavorable* labor efficiency variance indicates that direct labor workers were unable to manufacture the 600 beams in the standard time allowed. Once again, the production manager is responsible for worker productivity and usually is held accountable for the labor variance.

The labor efficiency variance and the labor rate variance are closely related. For instance, excessive direct labor hours may cause both the labor efficiency variance and the labor rate variance to be unfavorable if, due to the excess hours, workers must be paid at overtime rates.

The two labor cost variances may be summarized as follows:

| Actual Hours at Actual Rate | Actual Hours at Standard Rate | Standard Hours at Standard Rate |
|---|---|---|
| 1,080 DLH × $13 | 1,080 DLH × $12 | 900 DLH × $12 |
| $14,040 | $12,960 | $10,800 |

Labor Rate Variance $1,080 Unfavorable — Labor Efficiency Variance $2,160 Unfavorable

Total Materials Variance, $3,240 Unfavorable

The following journal entry is made to record the cost of direct labor charged to production during March:

---

[2]If the standard level of production requires overtime even with efficient scheduling, the overtime wage rate should be reflected in the standard cost.

| | | |
|---|---|---|
| Work in Process Inventory (at standard cost) . . . . . . . . . . . . . . . . . . . . . . . | 10,800 | |
| Labor Rate Variance (unfavorable) . . . . . . . . . . . . . . . . . . . . . . . . . . . . . . | 1,080 | |
| Labor Efficiency Variance (unfavorable) . . . . . . . . . . . . . . . . . . . . . . . . . . | 2,160 | |
|     Direct Labor (at actual cost) . . . . . . . . . . . . . . . . . . . . . . . . . . . . . . . | | 14,040 |
| To record the cost of direct labor charged to production in March. | | |

*Record labor costs and related variances*

In similar fashion to the way direct material costs were charged to production, the Work in Process Inventory account is debited for the *standard labor cost* allowed, and the Direct Labor account is credited for the *actual labor cost* incurred. The unfavorable labor rate and efficiency variances are recorded by debit entries, because they both represent costs in excess of the budgeted standards.

Creating low standard costs for direct labor sometimes involves a trade-off between wage rates and time allowed. For example, many competitive high-tech companies such as **Cisco Systems Inc.** and **Compaq Computers** do not assemble their own products. U.S. companies are attracted to central European countries such as Hungary and the Czech Republic because they have low labor costs. However, frequently this labor is less efficient than more skilled labor available in the United States. Even so, the lower labor costs more than offset the loss of efficiency and result in low standard labor costs.

**CASE IN POINT**

## Manufacturing Overhead Variances

The difference between actual manufacturing overhead costs incurred and the standard overhead costs charged to production is called the *overhead variance.* Whereas direct materials and direct labor are *variable costs,* manufacturing overhead is comprised of both variable and fixed cost components. Therefore, the analysis of the overhead cost variance differs somewhat from the analysis of materials and labor variances. We will now examine two elements of the overhead cost variance—the *spending variance* and the *volume variance.*[3]

**The Overhead Spending Variance**   The most important element of the overhead cost variance is the **spending variance**. This variance is the difference between the *standard overhead allowed* for a given level of output and the actual overhead costs incurred during the period. The overhead spending variance for Brice Mills in March may be computed as follows:

| | | |
|---|---|---|
| Standard overhead costs allowed at 600 units of production: | | |
|   Fixed overhead costs . . . . . . . . . . . . . . . . . . . . . . . . . . . . . . . . . . . . . | $5,600 | |
|   Variable overhead ($6 per beam × 600 beams) . . . . . . . . . . . . . . . . . . . | 3,600 | $9,200 |
| Actual overhead costs incurred in March: | | |
|   Fixed overhead costs . . . . . . . . . . . . . . . . . . . . . . . . . . . . . . . . . . . . . | $5,000 | |
|   Variable overhead . . . . . . . . . . . . . . . . . . . . . . . . . . . . . . . . . . . . . . . | 3,680 | 8,680 |
| Overhead spending variance (favorable) . . . . . . . . . . . . . . . . . . . . . . . . . | | $ 520 |

The spending variance is typically the responsibility of the production manager. In many cases, much of the spending variance involves *controllable* overhead costs. For

---

[3]"Three-way" and "four-way" analysis of the overhead variances are covered in more advanced cost accounting courses.

this reason, it sometimes is called the *controllable* variance. At Brice, the production manager has kept variable overhead costs very close to standard and has kept fixed costs well below the $5,600 amount budgeted.

**The Overhead Volume Variance** The **volume variance** represents the difference between the overhead *applied to work in process* (at standard cost) and the overhead expected at the actual level of production. We will see that the volume variance is caused simply by the difference between the *normal volume* of output (*700 units* per month) and the *actual volume* of output (*600 units* in March).

In a standard cost system, overhead is charged to work in process using standard unit costs. On page 959, we determined that Brice's standard manufacturing overhead cost was $14 per unit. Thus its Work in Process Inventory account was debited with $14 in overhead costs for each unit produced during the month. The more units produced during the month, the more overhead costs are charged to production.

In essence, a standard cost system treats all overhead as a *variable cost.* In reality, however, manufacturing overhead includes many fixed costs. Treating manufacturing overhead as a variable cost *automatically* causes a cost variance whenever the level of production varies from the norm.

To illustrate the variances that result from applying overhead to production in a standard cost system, let us compare the overhead costs that Brice would apply to production at three different levels of monthly output of its 20-foot beams:

**LO 4**

Compute fixed cost variances and explain the meaning of each.

*Illustration of the volume variance at different levels of output*

|  | Actual production (in units) | | |
|---|---|---|---|
|  | **600** | **700** | **800** |
| Overhead applied to work in process using a $14 standard rate | $8,400 | $9,800 | $11,200 |
| Budgeted overhead: | | | |
| Fixed | $5,600 | $5,600 | $ 5,600 |
| Variable ($6 per unit) | 3,600 | 4,200 | 4,800 |
| Total | $9,200 | $9,800 | $10,400 |
| Volume variances—favorable (unfavorable) | $ (800) | $ –0– | $ 800 |

Notice that at an actual level of production of 700 beams per month, the normal level of output, there is no volume variance. This is because our $14 standard cost figure *assumes* that 700 units will actually be produced each month. As shown on page 959, the $14 unit cost *includes $8 per unit in fixed costs* ($5,600 of budgeted fixed overhead ÷ 700 units). Whenever actual production is less than 700 units, less than $5,600 in fixed overhead costs will be applied to production. In March, for example, only *600 beams* were actually produced. Thus use of a standard cost that includes *$8 in fixed costs* applies only *$4,800 in fixed overhead costs* to production. The remaining *$800* in fixed overhead is recorded as an *unfavorable* volume variance. It is viewed as an unfavorable variance because fixed overhead has been *underapplied,* which means that additional overhead costs must be charged to the units produced.

The situation reverses whenever actual production *exceeds* the normal level. Had Brice's actual output in March been *800* units, the application of overhead using a standard rate of $14 per unit would have applied *more than* $5,600 in fixed overhead costs to production ($8 of fixed cost per unit × 800 units = $6,400). Here, the $800 volume variance is viewed as *favorable*. It is favorable because the cost standard has charged production with *too much* fixed overhead, making the actual costs look low by comparison.

The key point is that volume variances *occur automatically* whenever actual output differs from the level of output assumed in computing the standard overhead cost per unit. Over time, average production levels should equal the normal level used in developing the standard cost. Thus the favorable and unfavorable volume variances should balance out during the year.

As long as the production department is producing the desired number of units, volume variances do *not* indicate either efficient or inefficient performance. Volume variances are simply the natural result of fluctuations in the level of production from month to month. These fluctuations often occur because of seasonal sales demand, efforts to increase or decrease inventory levels, or holidays and vacations. Thus, unless the production department fails to produce a scheduled number of units, no manager should be considered responsible for a volume variance.

Prior to 1983, Medicare reimbursed hospitals for patient care on a cost-plus basis. That is, the hospitals submitted the cost of a procedure, such as a tonsillectomy, and Medicare paid them that cost plus a markup for profit. After 1983, Medicare instituted a reimbursement policy based on a standard cost for each procedure. These standards, called *DRGs* (diagnosis-related groups), are applied universally to all hospitals requesting reimbursements for inpatient hospital care. Thus the DRG for a tonsillectomy is the same for a hospital in Vermont as for one in Florida. The effect of using DRGs was dramatic. Insurance companies began to reimburse based on the DRGs and hospitals became much more cost-conscious. Imposing standard reimbursements dramatically slowed the rising cost of health care.

**CASE IN POINT**

**Summary of the Overhead Cost Variances**  The overhead spending and volume variances experienced by Brice Mills in March may be summarized as follows:

| Actual Overhead | | Budgeted Overhead @ 600 Units | | Overhead Applied at Standard Cost |
|---|---|---|---|---|
| Fixed | $5,000 | Fixed | $5,600 | 600 × $14 per unit |
| Variable | 3,680 | Variable | 3,600 | |
| Total | $8,680 | Total | $9,200 | $8,400 |

Spending Variance
$520 Favorable

Volume Variance
$800 Unfavorable

Total Overhead Variance, $280 Unfavorable

As shown, the $8,680 in overhead costs that Brice actually incurred is *$520 less* than the budgeted overhead at the 600 units level of production. Thus, its overhead spending variance is favorable. Its $800 volume variance is a direct result of actual output being *100 units less* than normal.

The following journal entry is made to apply overhead costs to production during March:

| | | |
|---|---|---|
| Work in Process Inventory (at standard cost) | 8,400 | |
| Overhead Volume Variance (unfavorable) | 800 | |
| Overhead Spending Variance (favorable) | | 520 |
| Manufacturing Overhead (at actual cost) | | 8,680 |
| To apply overhead to production in March. | | |

*Record overhead costs and related variances*

## Valuation of Finished Goods

We have seen that in a standard cost system, costs are charged to the Work in Process Inventory account at standard. Thus finished goods also are valued at standard as their costs are transferred to the Finished Goods Inventory account and to the Cost of Goods Sold account. The entry made at the end of March to record the completion of 600 beams is:

*Transfer costs to finished goods*

| | | |
|---|---|---|
| Finished Goods Inventory: 20-Foot Beams | 58,800 | |
|     Work in Process Inventory: 20-Foot Beams | | 58,800 |
| To record completion during March of 600 20-foot beams at standard cost (600 units × $98 per unit = $58,800). | | |

Notice that the inventory of finished goods is valued at *standard cost*. As beams are sold, their standard cost ($98 per beam) will be transferred into the Cost of Goods Sold account.

**What About the Cost Variance Accounts?**  The balances in the variance accounts represent *differences* between actual manufacturing costs and the standard costs used to value the finished goods inventory and cost of goods sold. These balances are typically allowed to accumulate in the variance accounts from month to month.

Often, the favorable and the unfavorable variances will balance out during the year, leaving only a small amount in each variance account at year-end. In this case, the variance accounts are simply closed into the Cost of Goods Sold account. However, if the balances in the variance accounts at the end of the year represent *a material dollar amount*, the amount should be apportioned among the Work in Process Inventory, Finished Goods Inventory, and the Cost of Goods Sold accounts.

## Evaluating Cost Variances from Different Perspectives

**LO 5**

Discuss the causes of specific cost variances.

Early in April, Brice's cost accountant prepared cost variance summary reports on each of the company's product lines for distribution at the monthly staff meeting. Among those attending the meeting were (1) the director of purchasing, (2) the production manager, (3) the quality control inspector, (4) the employee grievance representative, and (5) the sales manager. The report they were given pertaining to the production of 20-foot beams is shown below.

**BRICE MILLS**
**Cost Variance Summary Report**
**for 20-Foot Laminated Beams**
**March 2001**

| Total Variance to Be Explained | | |
|---|---|---|
| Standard manufacturing costs allowed (600 units × $98) | | $58,800 |
| Actual manufacturing costs incurred in March | | 58,720 |
| Total manufacturing cost variance—favorable | | $    80 |
| Breakdown of Individual Variances | | |
| Material price variance—favorable | $ 9,000 | |
| Material quantity variance—unfavorable | (5,400) | |
|   Total material variance—favorable | | $ 3,600 |
| Labor rate variance—unfavorable | $(1,080) | |
| Labor efficiency variance—unfavorable | (2,160) | |
|   Total labor variance—unfavorable | | (3,240) |
| Overhead spending variance—favorable | $  520 | |
| Overhead volume variance—unfavorable | (800) | |
|   Total overhead variance—unfavorable | | (280) |
| Total manufacturing cost variance—favorable | | $    80 |

Let us now consider these cost variances from the perspectives of various department managers.

**Accounting**   The cost accountant opened the meeting announcing that she had a combination of "good news" and "bad news." On the bright side, she was encouraged that the company's total manufacturing cost variance for 20-foot beams was favorable for the first time in many months (albeit only $80). She was especially pleased about the successful effort to control manufacturing overhead costs associated with this product, as revealed by the $520 favorable overhead spending variance. However, she immediately expressed concern regarding several unfavorable variances experienced across all product lines during the month. In particular, she was troubled by a consistent pattern of unfavorable labor rate, labor efficiency, and material quantity variances. The remainder of her presentation was spent stressing the severity of these unfavorable variances.

**Purchasing**   The first person to respond to the cost accountant's comments was the purchasing agent. Taking a defensive posture, he stressed that none of the unfavorable variances experienced during the month was under his control. In fact, he bragged that *favorable price variances* across all product lines, including the $9,000 favorable price variance for 20-foot beams, "saved the company from financial disaster in March." He pounded the table, exclaiming that he had "shopped for price" in three different states, getting what he believed to be the best bargain possible for rough, white pine lumber.

**Production**   The production manager stood up and confronted the purchasing agent. He verbally attacked the purchasing department, accusing it of acquiring materials of "grossly inferior quality." He told the group that the lumber he and his crew had been issued was green and full of knots, warps, and cracks. In his opinion, these defects were the direct cause of the unfavorable material usage variances experienced across all product lines. He also believed that numerous production bottlenecks resulting from poor quality materials had caused production output in March to be significantly less than normal.

**Quality Control**   The quality control inspector concurred with the production manager's assessment. She noted that many of the company's product lines, especially its 20-foot beams, either failed to pass inspection or did so only marginally. Never in recent history had there been a month in which she rejected so many beams.

**Factory Workers**   The employee grievance representative is a member of the production crew elected to communicate grievances to management. His comments provided a unique perspective to what had become an emotionally heated meeting. He conveyed to the group that factory morale in March had hit an all-time low. He admitted that every member of the production crew knew productivity was way down (as reflected by the unfavorable labor efficiency variances), yet added that everyone thought the inferior materials were the cause of the problem. He concluded by saying that the only good thing about inferior materials is "the overtime pay we earn working extra hours." (The $1,080 unfavorable labor rate variance for laminated beams resulted primarily from the overtime pay rates.)

**Marketing**   The sales manager argued that even with overtime and extra shifts, demand during March still exceeded output. He told the company's cost accountant that this was one of those occasions when an unfavorable volume variance had severe implications. To illustrate his point, he noted that the unfavorable volume variance associated with the production of 20-foot beams (caused by producing 600 units instead of the normal 700 units) translated directly into $16,000 of lost sales in March. He also worried that the beams that were sold may not have been of the quality customers had come to expect. His remarks raised questions regarding the company's legal liability should a beam fail because of structural defects.

### You as a Plant Manager

You are the plant manager for Brice. You have recently implemented a bonus system for your employees that provides a 10% bonus for favorable variances. What are the potential benefits and costs of such a bonus system?

*Our comments appear on page 986.

**YOUR TURN**

## In Conclusion . . .

We have illustrated that cost information is not just for cost accountants. Indeed, it affects virtually every aspect of business operations. At Brice, the savings from purchasing inexpensive materials made the purchasing department look good but created cost overruns and other problems throughout the organization.

While a cost accounting system does not solve such problems, it can bring the many dimensions of the problem *promptly to management's attention.*

**Summary of Cost Variances**    For your convenience, the six cost variances discussed in this chapter are summarized below.

| Variance | Computation | Manager Responsible |
|---|---|---|
| **Materials:** | | |
| Price variance | Actual Quantity × (Standard Price − Actual Price) | Purchasing agent |
| Quantity variance | Standard Price × (Standard Quantity − Actual Quantity) | Production manager |
| **Labor:** | | |
| Rate variance | Actual Hours × (Standard Hourly Rate − Actual Hourly Rate) | Production manager |
| Efficiency variance | Standard Hourly Rate × (Standard Hours − Actual Hours) | Production manager |
| **Overhead:** | | |
| Spending variance | Budgeted Overhead (at Actual Production Level) − Actual Overhead | Production manager (to extent variance relates to controllable costs) |
| Volume variance | Applied Overhead (at Standard Rate) − Budgeted Overhead (at Actual Production Level) | None—this variance results from scheduling production at any level other than "normal" |

## A Final Note: JIT Systems and Variance Analysis

A JIT approach, as discussed in Chapter 18, can reduce or eliminate many unfavorable cost variances. For instance, long-term pricing agreements with a select group of suppliers can virtually eliminate materials price variances. Material usage variances caused by defective materials also may be minimized. Should a batch of inferior materials be encountered, the production process is halted and the supplier is contacted to resolve the problem immediately. Thus, rather than discovering quality control problems after the fact, a JIT system makes it possible to detect and correct quality problems *as they occur*.

Workers in a JIT system must be able to shift production quickly from one product to another. Adherence to carefully planned production schedules reduces idle time and eliminates non-value-added activities. As a consequence, labor efficiency variances often are improved under a JIT approach.

Well-trained employees, *working smarter and more efficiently*, can minimize the need for overtime hours. Thus JIT systems may reduce or eliminate unfavorable labor rate variances. Finally, by cutting overhead costs associated with non-value-added activities, JIT systems also help management avoid unfavorable overhead spending variances.

**A SECOND LOOK**

### Wrigley Company

**Wrigley Company** has posted respectable growth for decades by expanding into international markets and controlling costs with cost systems, such as the standard costing systems described in this chapter. However, in the last few years the market for **Wrigley**'s traditional sugar-based chewing gum has declined. **Wrigley** is responding to that decline by creating new product lines designed to appeal to younger consumers.

Introduction of new products to new markets requires careful planning and the expenditure of additional capital. To motivate managers to think strategically about existing and new products and processes, companies carefully design their performance evaluation systems to hold managers accountable for making and carrying out strategic plans. The next chapter describes and demonstrates performance evaluation systems that companies such as **Wrigley** use to motivate their managers.

# END-OF-CHAPTER REVIEW

## SUMMARY OF LEARNING OBJECTIVES

### LO 1

**Explain how standard costs assist managers in controlling costs.**
Standard costs are the expected (or budgeted) costs per unit. When standard costs are used in a cost accounting system, differences between actual costs and standard costs promptly are brought to management's attention.

### LO 2

**Explain the difference between setting ideal standards and setting reasonably achievable standards.**
The most widely used approach is to set budgeted amounts at levels that are reasonably achievable under normal operating conditions. The goal in this case is to make the cost standard a fair and reasonable basis for evaluating performance.

An alternative is to budget an ideal level of performance. Under this approach, departments normally fall somewhat short of budgeted performance, but the variations may identify areas in which improvement is possible.

### LO 3

**Compute variable cost variances and explain the meaning of each.**
Cost variances are computed by comparing actual costs to standard costs and explaining the reasons for any differences. Differences in the cost of materials used may be caused either by variations in the price paid to purchase materials or in the quantity of materials used. Differences in the cost of direct labor may be caused by variations in wage rates or in the number of hours worked. Variances from budgeted levels of variable overhead may be caused by differences in outlays for controllable overhead expenditures or in the actual and budgeted levels of production.

### LO 4

**Compute fixed cost variances and explain the meaning of each.**
To compute fixed overhead cost variances, compare the actual fixed overhead to the budgeted fixed overhead and compare the budgeted fixed overhead to the applied fixed overhead. Fixed cost variances can result from spending more than budgeted in fixed cost categories or from a difference between the projected volume used to create the overhead application rate and the actual production used to apply overhead.

### LO 5

**Discuss the causes of specific cost variances.**
Materials variances may be caused by the quality and price of materials purchased and by the efficiency with which these materials are used. Labor variances stem from workers' productivity, pay scales of workers placed on the job, and the quality of the materials with which they work. Overhead variances result both from actual spending and from differences between actual and normal levels of production.

## KEY TERMS INTRODUCED OR EMPHASIZED IN CHAPTER 23

**fixed manufacturing cost** (p. 959) A manufacturing cost that, in the short run, does not vary in response to changes in the level of production.

**labor efficiency variance** (p. 961) The portion of the total labor variance caused by a difference between the standard and actual number of labor hours to complete the task. Computed as Standard Hourly Rate × (Standard Hours − Actual Hours). Also called labor usage variance.

**labor rate variance** (p. 961) The portion of the total labor variance caused by a difference between the standard hourly wage rate and the rate actually paid to workers. Usually stems from overtime or using workers at a different pay scale than assumed in developing the standard cost. Computed as Actual Hours × (Standard Hourly Rate − Actual Hourly Rate).

**materials price variance** (p. 960) The portion of the total materials variance caused by paying a different price to purchase materials than was assumed in the standard cost. Computed as Actual Quantity × (Standard Unit Price − Actual Unit Price).

**materials quantity variance** (p. 960) The portion of the total materials variance caused by using more or less material in the production process than is called for in the standards. Computed as Standard Unit Price × (Standard Quantity − Actual Quantity).

**spending variance** (p. 963) The portion of the total overhead variance caused by incurring more overhead costs than are allowed for the actual level of activity achieved.

**standard cost** (p. 956) The budgeted cost that should be incurred under normal, efficient conditions.

**standard cost system** (p. 956) A system that accumulates product, service, or process costs using standard input prices and quantities.

**variable manufacturing cost** (p. 959) A manufacturing cost that varies in approximate proportion to the number of units produced.

**variance** (p. 956) A difference between the actual level of cost incurred and the standard (budgeted) level for the cost. The total cost variance may be subdivided into separate cost variances indicating the amount of variance attributable to specific causal factors.

**volume variance** (p. 964) The portion of the total overhead variance that results from a difference between the actual level of production and the "normal" level assumed in computing the standard unit cost. In effect, the volume variance is a misallocation of fixed overhead costs and often is not relevant in evaluating performance.

## DEMONSTRATION PROBLEM

Krueger Corporation recently implemented a standard cost system. The company's cost accountant has gathered the following information needed to perform a variance analysis at the end of the month:

| Standard Cost Information | |
|---|---|
| Direct materials . . . . . . . . . . . . . . . . . . . . . . . . . . . . . . . . . . . . . . . . . | $5 per pound |
| Quantity allowed per unit . . . . . . . . . . . . . . . . . . . . . . . . . . . . . . . . . . . | 100 pounds per unit |
| Direct labor rate . . . . . . . . . . . . . . . . . . . . . . . . . . . . . . . . . . . . . . . . . | $20.00 per hour |
| Hours allowed per unit . . . . . . . . . . . . . . . . . . . . . . . . . . . . . . . . . . . . . | 2 hours per unit |
| Fixed overhead budgeted . . . . . . . . . . . . . . . . . . . . . . . . . . . . . . . . . . | $12,000 per month |
| Normal level of production . . . . . . . . . . . . . . . . . . . . . . . . . . . . . . . . . . | 1,200 units |
| *Variable overhead* application rate . . . . . . . . . . . . . . . . . . . . . . . . . . . | $ 2.00 per unit |
| *Fixed overhead* application rate ($12,000 ÷ 1,200 units) . . . . . . . . . . . | 10.00 per unit |
| *Total overhead* application rate . . . . . . . . . . . . . . . . . . . . . . . . . . . . . . | $12.00 per unit |
| **Actual Cost Information** | |
| Cost of materials purchased and used . . . . . . . . . . . . . . . . . . . . . . . . | $468,000 |
| Pounds of materials purchased and used . . . . . . . . . . . . . . . . . . . . . . | 104,000 pounds |
| Cost of direct labor . . . . . . . . . . . . . . . . . . . . . . . . . . . . . . . . . . . . . . . | $ 46,480 |
| Hours of direct labor . . . . . . . . . . . . . . . . . . . . . . . . . . . . . . . . . . . . . . | 2,240 hours |
| Cost of variable overhead . . . . . . . . . . . . . . . . . . . . . . . . . . . . . . . . . . | $ 2,352 |
| Cost of fixed overhead . . . . . . . . . . . . . . . . . . . . . . . . . . . . . . . . . . . . | $ 12,850 |
| Volume of production . . . . . . . . . . . . . . . . . . . . . . . . . . . . . . . . . . . . . . | 1,000 units |

## Instructions

**a.** Compute the direct materials price variance, given an actual price of $4.50 per pound ($468,000 ÷ 104,000 pounds).

**b.** Compute the materials quantity variance, given a standard quantity of 100,000 pounds allowed to produce 1,000 units (1,000 units × 100 pounds per unit).

**c.** Prepare a journal entry summarizing the cost of direct materials charged to production.

**d.** Compute the labor rate variance, given an actual labor rate of $20.75 per hour ($46,480 ÷ 2,240 hours).

**e.** Compute the labor efficiency variance.

**f.** Prepare a journal entry summarizing the cost of direct labor charged to production.

**g.** Compute the overhead spending variance.

**h.** Compute the overhead volume variance.

**i.** Prepare a journal entry summarizing the application of overhead costs to production.

## Solution to the Demonstration Problem

**a.** Materials Price Variance = Actual Quantity Used × (Standard Price − Actual Price)

$$= 104,000 \text{ pounds} × (\$5.00 − \$4.50)$$
$$= \$52,000 \text{ Favorable}$$

**b.** Materials Quantity Variance = Standard Price × (Standard Quantity − Actual Quantity)

= $5.00 per pound × (100,000 − 104,000)

= −$20,000 (or $20,000 Unfavorable)

**c.** 

| | | |
|---|---|---|
| Work in Process Inventory (at standard cost) . . . . . . . . . . . . . . . . . . . | 500,000* | |
| Materials Quantity Variance (unfavorable) . . . . . . . . . . . . . . . . . . . . . | 20,000 | |
|    Direct Materials Inventory (at actual cost) . . . . . . . . . . . . . . . . . | | 468,000 |
|    Materials Price Variance (favorable) . . . . . . . . . . . . . . . . . . . . . . | | 52,000 |

To record the cost of direct materials charged to production.

*1,000 actual units × 100 pounds allowed per unit × $5 per pound = $500,000

**d.** Labor Rate Variance = Actual Labor Hours × (Standard Rate − Actual Rate)

= 2,240 hours × ($20.00 − $20.75)

= −$1,680 (or $1,680 Unfavorable)

**e.** Labor Efficiency Variance = Standard Rate × (Standard Hours − Actual Hours)

= $20 × (2,000 hours* − 2,240 hours)

= −$4,800 (or $4,800 Unfavorable)

*1,000 units × 2 hours per unit.

**f.** 

| | | |
|---|---|---|
| Work in Process Inventory (at standard cost) . . . . . . . . . . . . . . . . . | 40,000* | |
| Labor Rate Variance (unfavorable) . . . . . . . . . . . . . . . . . . . . . . . . . | 1,680 | |
| Labor Efficiency Variance (unfavorable) . . . . . . . . . . . . . . . . . . . . . | 4,800 | |
|    Direct Labor (at actual cost) . . . . . . . . . . . . . . . . . . . . . . . . . . . | | 46,480 |

To record the cost of direct labor charged to production

*1,000 actual units × 2 hours allowed per unit × $20.00 per hour = $40,000

**g.** 

| | | |
|---|---|---|
| Standard overhead costs allowed at 1,000 units of production: | | |
|    Fixed overhead costs . . . . . . . . . . . . . . . . . . . . . . . . . . . . . . . . . | $12,000 | |
|    Variable overhead ($2 per unit × 1,000 units) . . . . . . . . . . . . . . | 2,000 | $14,000 |
| Actual overhead costs incurred in March: | | |
|    Fixed overhead costs . . . . . . . . . . . . . . . . . . . . . . . . . . . . . . . . . | $12,850 | |
|    Variable overhead . . . . . . . . . . . . . . . . . . . . . . . . . . . . . . . . . . . . | 2,352 | 15,202 |
| Overhead spending variance (unfavorable) . . . . . . . . . . . . . . . . . . | | $ (1,202) |

**h.** 

| | | |
|---|---|---|
| Overhead *applied* to work in process (1,000 units × $12) . . . . . . . | | $12,000 |
| Standard overhead *allowed* (at 1,000 units): | | |
|    Fixed . . . . . . . . . . . . . . . . . . . . . . . . . . . . . . . . . . . . . . . . . . . . . | $12,000 | |
|    Variable ($2 per unit) . . . . . . . . . . . . . . . . . . . . . . . . . . . . . . . . . | 2,000 | |
|    Total overhead *allowed* at standard . . . . . . . . . . . . . . . . . . . . . | | 14,000 |
| Overhead volume variance (unfavorable) . . . . . . . . . . . . . . . . . . . . | | $(2,000) |

**i.** 

| | | |
|---|---|---|
| Work in Process Inventory (at standard cost) . . . . . . . . . . . . . . . . . . | 12,000 | |
| Overhead Spending Variance (unfavorable) . . . . . . . . . . . . . . . . . . . | 1,202 | |
| Overhead Volume Variance (unfavorable) . . . . . . . . . . . . . . . . . . . . | 2,000 | |
|    Manufacturing Overhead (at actual cost) . . . . . . . . . . . . . . . . . . | | 15,202 |

To apply overhead to production.

## SELF-TEST QUESTIONS

*Answers to these questions appear on page 986.*

**1.** The labor rate variance is determined by multiplying the difference between the actual labor rate and the standard labor rate by:

  **a.** The standard labor hours allowed for a given level of output.

  **b.** The standard labor rate.

  **c.** The actual hours worked during the period.

  **d.** The actual labor rate.

**2.** Which of the following is *not* a possible cause of an unfavorable direct labor efficiency variance?

    **a.** Lack of motivation.

    **b.** Low-quality materials.

    **c.** Poor supervision.

    **d.** All of the above could be considered possible causes of an unfavorable labor efficiency variance.

**3.** An unfavorable overhead volume variance indicates that:

    **a.** Total fixed overhead exceeds the standard amount budgeted.

    **b.** Variable overhead per unit exceeds the standard amount budgeted.

    **c.** Actual production was less than the normal volume of output.

    **d.** Actual production was more than the normal volume of output.

**4.** A favorable overhead spending variance means that:

    **a.** Overhead has been overapplied.

    **b.** Overhead has been underapplied.

    **c.** Actual production was less than the normal volume of output.

    **d.** None of the above.

**5.** Modern Art, Inc., produces hand-painted foam mouse pads. The following budgeted and actual results are for a recent month in which actual production was equal to budgeted production.

|  | **Budgeted Amount** | **Actual Result** |
|---|---|---|
| Direct materials: Foam | | |
|   Usage | 1.5 square feet per pad | 1.3 square feet per pad |
|   Price | $0.15 per square foot | $0.18 per square foot |
| Direct labor: | | |
|   Usage | .25 hours per pad | .30 hours per pad |
|   Rate | $15 per hour | $13 per hour |

Which of the following are *true?*

    **a.** The materials price variance is favorable.

    **b.** The direct labor rate variance is favorable.

    **c.** The materials quantity variance is unfavorable.

    **d.** The direct labor efficiency variance is unfavorable.

## ASSIGNMENT MATERIAL

## DISCUSSION QUESTIONS

**1.** Define *standard costs* and briefly indicate how they may be used by management in planning and control.

**2.** What is wrong with the following statement: "There are three basic kinds of cost accounting systems: job order, process, and standard"?

**3.** Once standard costs are established, what conditions would require that standards be revised?

**4.** List the variances from standard cost that are generally computed for direct materials, direct labor, and manufacturing overhead.

**5.** Would a production manager be equally responsible for an unfavorable materials price variance and an unfavorable materials quantity variance? Explain.

**6.** What is meant by a favorable labor efficiency variance? How is the labor efficiency variance computed?

7. Explain the cause of an unfavorable and of a favorable overhead *volume variance.*

8. Why is an unfavorable overhead volume variance not usually considered in evaluating the performance of the production department manager?

# EXERCISES

**EXERCISE 23.1**

Accounting Terminology

**LO 1–5**

The following are seven technical terms introduced in this chapter:

| | | |
|---|---|---|
| Spending variance | Materials price variance | Standard costs |
| Labor rate variance | Materials quantity variance | Volume variance |
| Labor efficiency variance | | |

Each of the following statements may (or may not) describe one of these technical terms. For each statement, indicate the accounting term discussed, or answer "None" if the statement does not correctly describe any of the terms.

a. The budgeted costs of producing a product under normal conditions.

b. The dollar amount associated with the difference between the actual direct labor hours required and the standard number of direct labor hours allowed for a given level of production under normal conditions.

c. A variance that is always favorable when actual production levels exceed normal levels.

d. The portion of the total materials variance caused by using more or less material than allowed for at a given level of output.

e. The portion of the total overhead variance caused by incurring more overhead costs than allowed for at a given level of production.

f. The portion of the total materials variance for which a company's purchasing agent is often responsible.

g. The portion of the total labor variance that is related to the differences between the actual hourly wages paid and the budgeted standard wage.

**EXERCISE 23.2**

Relationships Among Standard Costs, Actual Costs, and Cost Variances

**LO 3**

The standard costs and variances for direct materials, direct labor, and factory overhead for the month of May are as follows:

| | | Variances | |
|---|---|---|---|
| | Standard Cost | Unfavorable | Favorable |
| Direct materials .................... | $ 90,000 | | |
| Price variance .................... | | $4,500 | |
| Quantity variance .................... | | | $2,700 |
| Direct labor ........................ | 180,000 | | |
| Rate variance ....................... | | | 1,800 |
| Efficiency variance ................. | | 5,400 | |
| Manufacturing overhead ............... | 270,000 | | |
| Spending variance ................... | | | 3,600 |
| Volume variance .................... | | | 2,400 |

Determine the *actual costs* incurred during the month of May for direct materials, direct labor, and manufacturing overhead.

**EXERCISE 23.3**

Computing Materials Cost Variances

**LO 3**

One of the products of Hearts & Flowers is a one-pound box of chocolate candy, packaged in a box bearing the customer's logo. (Minimum order, 100 boxes.) The standard cost of the chocolate candy used is $2 per pound. During November, 20,000 of these one-pound boxes were produced, requiring 20,800 pounds of chocolate candy at a total direct materials cost of $42,640.

Determine the materials price variance and quantity variance with respect to the candy used producing this product.

Gumchara Corporation reported the following information with respect to the material required to manufacture amalgam florostats during the current month:

| | |
|---|---|
| Standard price per gram of material | $1.25 |
| Standard quantity of material per amalgam florostat | 4 grams |
| Actual materials purchased and used in production | 2,800 grams |
| Actual amalgam florostats produced during the month | 520 units |
| Actual cost of materials purchased | $3,920 |
| Normal monthly output | 550 units |

a. Determine Gumchara's materials price variance.
b. Determine Gumchara's materials quantity variance.
c. Will Gumchara's overhead volume variance be favorable or unfavorable? Why?

One of the most popular products of Loring Glassworks is a hand-decorated vase. The company's standard cost system calls for .75 hours of direct labor per vase, at a standard wage rate of $8.25. During September, Loring produced 4,000 vases at an actual direct labor cost of $24,464 for 2,780 direct labor hours.

a. What was the average hourly pay rate of the direct workers producing the vases in September?
b. Compute the labor rate and efficiency variances for the month.
c. Was using workers on the payscale indicated in part a an effective strategy? Explain.

Marlo Enterprises produces radon mitigation pumps. Information pertaining to the company's monthly direct labor usage is provided below:

| | |
|---|---|
| Standard labor rate per hour | $16 |
| Standard hours allowed per radon mitigation pump | 0.5 hours |
| Actual pumps produced during the current month | 9,000 |
| Actual labor hours worked during the current month | 3,600 |
| Actual labor cost for the current month | $64,800 |

a. Compute the company's labor rate variance.
b. Compute the company's labor efficiency variance.
c. An extremely large order of radon mitigation pumps was filled during the month for exportation to Saudi Arabia. Filling this order resulted in extended hours for many of the company's workers. Which labor variance reflects the extra hours worked by Marlo's employees? Was their time well utilized? Explain.

The following computation of the materials variances of Weitzen Foods is incomplete. The missing data are labeled **(a)** through **(d)**.

| | |
|---|---|
| Materials price variance = 3,640 pounds × | |
| [(a) standard price − $9.00 actual price] | $910 Unfavorable |
| Materials quantity variance = (b) × | |
| [3,800 pounds − (c) actual quantity] | $ (d) |

Supply the missing data for items **(a)** through **(d)**. Prepare a caption describing the item, as well as indicating the dollar amount and physical quantity. Briefly explain each answer, including how you determined the amount.

**EXERCISE 23.8**
Interpreting Variances

**LO 5**

The manager of a manufacturing firm received the following information related to the last period's direct materials and direct labor variances:

| | |
|---|---|
| Direct materials price variance: | Favorable |
| Direct materials quantity variance: | Favorable |
| Direct labor rate variance: | Unfavorable |
| Direct labor efficiency variance: | Favorable |

a. Ignoring all other variances, what are possible reasons for a favorable direct materials price variance?
b. Given that the quality of direct materials purchased was exactly as expected, how would you explain the above combination of the four variances?

**EXERCISE 23.9**
Understanding Overhead
Cost Variances

**LO 3, 4**

Ringo Corporation applied $7,200 of manufacturing overhead to production during the month. Its actual overhead costs for the month were $8,000. The cost accountant reports that Ringo's unfavorable spending variance for the month totals $1,500.
    Did Ringo produce more or less than its normal output for the month? Defend your answer.

**EXERCISE 23.10**
Computing Overhead
Cost Variances

**LO 3, 4**

From the following information for Alfred Industries, compute the overhead spending variance and the volume variance.

| | | |
|---|---|---|
| Standard manufacturing overhead based on normal monthly volume: | | |
| Fixed ($300,000 ÷ 20,000 units) | $15.00 | |
| Variable ($100,000 ÷ 20,000 units) | 5.00 | $20.00 |
| Units actually produced in current month | | 18,000 units |
| Actual overhead costs incurred (including $300,000 fixed) | | $383,800 |

**EXERCISE 23.11**
Overhead Cost Variances

**LO 3–5**

Zeta, Inc., produces handwoven rugs. Budgeted production is 5,000 rugs per month and the standard direct labor required to make each rug is 2 hours. All overhead is allocated based on direct labor hours. Zeta's manager is interested in what caused the recent month's $3,000 unfavorable overhead variance. The following information was available to aid in the analysis:

| | Budgeted Amounts | Actual Results |
|---|---|---|
| Production in units | 5,000 | 4,500 |
| Total labor hours | 10,000 | 9,000 |
| Total variable overhead | $ 60,000 | $55,000 |
| Total fixed overhead | 40,000 | 38,000 |
| Total overhead | $100,000 | $93,000 |

a. What was the overhead spending variance for the month?
b. What was the overhead volume variance?
c. What corrective actions should Zeta's manager undertake related to the unfavorable overhead variance?

**EXERCISE 23.12**
Understanding Overhead
Variances

**LO 3, 4**

McGill's overhead spending variance is unfavorable by $600. The company's accountant credited the Cost of Goods Sold account for $4,200 to close out any over- or underapplied overhead at the end of the current period.
    Compute McGill's overhead volume variance.

Nolan Mills uses a standard cost system. During May, Nolan manufactured 15,000 pillowcases, using 27,000 yards of fabric costing $3.05 per yard and incurring direct labor costs of $19,140 for 3,300 hours of direct labor. The standard cost per pillowcase assumes 1.75 yards of fabric at $3.10 per yard, and .2 hours of direct labor at $5.95 per hour.

**a.** Compute both the price variance and quantity variance relating to direct materials used in the manufacture of pillowcases in May.

**b.** Compute both the rate variance and efficiency variance for direct labor costs incurred in manufacturing pillowcases in May.

**EXERCISE 23.13**
Computing Materials and Labor Variances
**LO 3**

For each of the following variances, briefly explain at least one probable cause and indicate the department manager (if any) responsible for the variance.

**a.** A favorable materials price variance

**b.** An unfavorable labor rate variance

**c.** A favorable volume variance

**d.** An unfavorable materials quantity variance

**EXERCISE 23.14**
Causes of Cost Variances
**LO 1, 3, 5**

# PROBLEMS

The cost accountant for Brown Pharmaceuticals has informed you that the company's materials quantity variance for the drug Zantig was exactly equal to its materials price variance for the year. The company's normal level of production is 45 batches of Zantig per year. However, due to uncertainties regarding government funding, it produced only 40 batches during the current year. Other cost information regarding Zantig's direct materials is as follows:

**PROBLEM 23.1**
Understanding Materials Cost Variances
**LO 1, 3, 5**

| | |
|---|---|
| Standard price per gram of material | $50 |
| Actual kilograms purchased and used during the year | 100 kg |
| Actual cost of material purchased during the period | $5,000,000 |
| Number of grams per kilogram | 1,000 grams |

## Instructions

**a.** Compute Brown's materials price variance.

**b.** Compute the standard quantity of material allowed per batch of Zantig produced.

**c.** Why would you not expect Brown to have a large materials quantity variance?

Wilson's materials quantity variance for the current month was exactly one-half of its materials price variance. Both variances were unfavorable. The company's cost accountant has supplied us with the following standard cost information:

**PROBLEM 23.2**
Understanding Materials Cost Variances
**LO 1, 3**

| | |
|---|---|
| Standard price per pound of material | $15 |
| Actual pounds purchased and used during the month | 600 pounds |
| Actual cost per pound of material purchased and used | $16 |
| Actual units manufactured during the month | 500 units |
| Normal productive output per month | 550 units |

## Instructions

**a.** Compute Wilson's materials price variance.

**b.** Compute the standard quantity of material allowed for producing 550 units of product.

**c.** Record the journal entry to charge work in process for the cost of materials used during the month.

**d.** Compute Wilson's overhead volume variance if it is twice the amount of its materials quantity variance. Is the volume variance favorable or unfavorable? How do you know?

**PROBLEM 23.3**

Computing and Journalizing
Cost Variances

**LO 1, 3, 4**

AgriChem Industries manufactures fertilizer concentrate and uses cost standards. The fertilizer is produced in 500-pound batches; the normal level of production is 250 batches of fertilizer per month. The standard costs per batch are as follows:

|  |  | Standard Costs per Batch |
|---|---|---|
| Direct materials: | | |
| Various chemicals (500 pounds per batch at $0.60/pound) . . . . . . . . . . | | $300 |
| Direct labor: | | |
| Preparation and blending (25 hours per batch at $7.00/hour) . . . . . . . . . . | | 175 |
| Manufacturing overhead: | | |
| Fixed ($50,000 per month ÷ 250 batches) . . . . . . . . . . . . . . . . . . . . . . | $200 | |
| Variable (per batch) . . . . . . . . . . . . . . . . . . . . . . . . . . . . . . . . . . . | 25 | 225 |
| Total standard cost per batch of fertilizer . . . . . . . . . . . . . . . . . . . . . . . . . | | $700 |

During January, the company temporarily reduced the level of production to 200 batches of fertilizer. Actual costs incurred in January were as follows:

| | |
|---|---|
| Direct materials (102,500 pounds at $0.57/pound) . . . . . . . . . . . . . . . . . . . . . . . | $ 58,425 |
| Direct labor (4,750 hours at $6.80/hour) . . . . . . . . . . . . . . . . . . . . . . . . . . . . . | 32,300 |
| Manufacturing overhead . . . . . . . . . . . . . . . . . . . . . . . . . . . . . . . . . . . . . . . | 54,525 |
| Total actual costs (200 batches) . . . . . . . . . . . . . . . . . . . . . . . . . . . . . . . . . . | $145,250 |
| Standard cost of 200 batches (200 batches × $700 per batch) . . . . . . . . . . . . . . | 140,000 |
| Net unfavorable cost variance . . . . . . . . . . . . . . . . . . . . . . . . . . . . . . . . . . . . | $ 5,250 |

**Instructions**

You have been engaged to explain in detail the elements of the $5,250 net unfavorable cost variance, and to record the manufacturing costs for January in the company's standard cost accounting system.

**a.** As a first step, compute the materials price and quantity variances, the labor rate and efficiency variances, and the overhead spending and volume variances for the month.

**b.** Prepare journal entries to record the flow of manufacturing costs through the standard cost system and the related cost variances. Make separate entries to record the costs of direct materials used, direct labor, and manufacturing overhead. Work in Process Inventory is to be debited only with standard costs.

**PROBLEM 23.4**

Computing and Journalizing
Cost Variances

**LO 1, 3, 4**

American Hardwood Products uses standard costs in a process cost system. At the end of the current month, the following information is prepared by the company's cost accountant:

| | Direct Materials | Direct Labor | Manufacturing Overhead |
|---|---|---|---|
| Actual costs incurred . . . . . . . . . . . . . . . . . . . . . . | $96,000 | $82,500 | $123,240 |
| Standard costs . . . . . . . . . . . . . . . . . . . . . . . | 90,000 | 84,000 | 115,500 |
| Materials price variance (favorable) . . . . . . . . . . . . . | 2,400 | | |
| Materials quantity variance (unfavorable) . . . . . . . . . | 8,400 | | |
| Labor rate variance (favorable) . . . . . . . . . . . . . . . | | 3,000 | |
| Labor efficiency variance (unfavorable) . . . . . . . . . . | | 1,500 | |
| Overhead spending variance (unfavorable) . . . . . . . . | | | 3,240 |
| Overhead volume variance (unfavorable) . . . . . . . . . | | | 4,500 |

The total standard cost per unit of finished product is $30. During the current month, 9,000 units were completed and transferred to the finished goods inventory and 8,800 units were sold. The inventory of work in process at the end of the month consists of 1,000 units that are 65% completed. There was no inventory in process at the beginning of the month.

## Instructions

**a.** Prepare journal entries to record all variances and the costs incurred (at standard) in the Work in Process account. Prepare separate compound entries for (1) direct materials, (2) direct labor, and (3) manufacturing overhead.

**b.** Prepare journal entries to record (1) the transfer of units finished to the Finished Goods Inventory account and (2) the cost of goods sold (at standard) for the month.

**c.** Assuming that the company operated at 90% of its normal capacity during the current month, what is the amount of the budgeted fixed manufacturing overhead per month?

Sven Enterprises is a large producer of gourmet pet food. During April, it produced 147 batches of puppy meal. Each batch weighs 1,000 pounds. To produce this quantity of output, the company purchased and used 148,450 pounds of direct material at a cost of $593,800. It also incurred direct labor costs of $17,600 for the 2,200 hours worked by employees on the puppy meal crew. Manufacturing overhead incurred at the puppy meal plant during April totaled $3,625, of which $2,450 was considered fixed. Sven's standard cost information for 1,000-pound batches of puppy meal is as follows:

**PROBLEM 23.5**

Computing and Journalizing Cost Variances

**LO 1, 3, 4**

| | |
|---|---:|
| Direct materials standard price . . . . . . . . . . . . . . . . . . . . . . . . . . . . . . . . | $4.20 per pound |
| Standard quantity allowed per batch . . . . . . . . . . . . . . . . . . . . . . . . . . | 1,020 pounds |
| Direct labor standard rate . . . . . . . . . . . . . . . . . . . . . . . . . . . . . . . . . . . | $8.50 per hour |
| Standard hours allowed per batch . . . . . . . . . . . . . . . . . . . . . . . . . . . . | 14 direct labor hours |
| Fixed overhead budgeted . . . . . . . . . . . . . . . . . . . . . . . . . . . . . . . . . . . | $2,800 per month |
| Normal level of production . . . . . . . . . . . . . . . . . . . . . . . . . . . . . . . . . . | 140 batches per month |
| Variable overhead application rate . . . . . . . . . . . . . . . . . . . . . . . . . . . . | $ 9.00 per batch |
| Fixed overhead application rate<br>  ($2,800 ÷ 140 batches) . . . . . . . . . . . . . . . . . . . . . . . . . . . . . . . . . . | 20.00 per batch |
| Total overhead application rate . . . . . . . . . . . . . . . . . . . . . . . . . . . . . . | $29.00 per batch |

## Instructions

**a.** Compute the materials price and quantity variances.

**b.** Compute the labor rate and efficiency variances.

**c.** Compute the manufacturing overhead spending and volume variances.

**d.** Record the journal entry to charge materials (at standard) to work in process.

**e.** Record the journal entry to charge direct labor (at standard) to work in process.

**f.** Record the journal entry to charge manufacturing overhead (at standard) to work in process.

**g.** Record the journal entry to transfer the 147 batches of puppy meal produced in April to finished goods.

**h.** Record the journal entry to close any over- or underapplied overhead to cost of goods sold.

Slick Corporation is a small producer of synthetic motor oil. During May, the company produced 5,000 cases of lubricant. Each case contains twelve quarts of synthetic oil. To achieve this level of production, Slick purchased and used 16,500 gallons of direct material at a cost of $20,625. It also incurred average direct labor costs of $15 per hour for the 4,200 hours worked in May by its production personnel. Manufacturing overhead for the month totaled $9,950, of which $2,200 was considered fixed. Slick's standard cost information for each case of synthetic motor oil is as follows:

**PROBLEM 23.6**

Computing and Journalizing Cost Variances

**LO 1, 3, 4**

| | |
|---|---:|
| Direct material standard price . . . . . . . . . . . . . . . . . . . . . . . . . . . . . . . . . . . . . | $1.30 per gallon |
| Standard quantity allowed per case . . . . . . . . . . . . . . . . . . . . . . . . . . . . . | 3.25 gallons |
| Direct labor standard rate . . . . . . . . . . . . . . . . . . . . . . . . . . . . . . . . . . . . . | $16 per hour |
| Standard hours allowed per case . . . . . . . . . . . . . . . . . . . . . . . . . . . . . . | 0.75 direct labor hours |
| Fixed overhead budgeted . . . . . . . . . . . . . . . . . . . . . . . . . . . . . . . . . . . . . | $2,600 per month |
| Normal level of production . . . . . . . . . . . . . . . . . . . . . . . . . . . . . . . . . . . . | 5,200 cases per month |
| Variable overhead application rate . . . . . . . . . . . . . . . . . . . . . . . . . . . . . . | $1.50 per case |
| Fixed overhead application rate<br>  ($2,600 ÷ 5,200 cases) . . . . . . . . . . . . . . . . . . . . . . . . . . . . . . . . . . . . . | 0.50 per case |
| Total overhead application rate . . . . . . . . . . . . . . . . . . . . . . . . . . . . . . . . | $2.00 per case |

### Instructions

**a.** Compute the materials price and quantity variances.

**b.** Compute the labor rate and efficiency variances.

**c.** Compute the manufacturing overhead spending and volume variances.

**d.** Prepare the journal entries to:

  **1.** Charge materials (at standard) to work in process.

  **2.** Charge direct labor (at standard) to work in process.

  **3.** Charge manufacturing overhead (at standard) to work in process.

  **4.** Transfer the cost of the 5,000 cases of synthetic motor oil produced in May to finished goods.

  **5.** Close any over- or underapplied overhead into the cost of goods sold.

**PROBLEM 23.7**

Computing and Journalizing
Cost Variances

**LO 1, 3, 4**

The accountants for Polyglaze, Inc., have developed the following information regarding the standard cost and the actual cost of a product manufactured in June:

| | Standard<br>Cost | Actual<br>Cost |
|---|---:|---:|
| Direct materials: | | |
|   Standard: 10 ounces at $0.15 per ounce . . . . . . . . . . . . . . . . . . . . . . | $1.50 | |
|   Actual: 11 ounces at $0.16 per ounce . . . . . . . . . . . . . . . . . . . . . . . . | | $1.76 |
| Direct labor: | | |
|   Standard: .50 hours at $10.00 per hour . . . . . . . . . . . . . . . . . . . . . . | 5.00 | |
|   Actual: .45 hours at $10.40 per hour . . . . . . . . . . . . . . . . . . . . . . . . | | 4.68 |
| Manufacturing overhead: | | |
|   Standard: $5,000 fixed cost and $5,000 variable cost for<br>    10,000 units normal monthly volume . . . . . . . . . . . . . . . . . . . . . . | 1.00 | |
|   Actual: $5,000 fixed cost and $4,600 variable cost for 8,000<br>    units actually produced in June . . . . . . . . . . . . . . . . . . . . . . . . . | | 1.20 |
| Total unit cost . . . . . . . . . . . . . . . . . . . . . . . . . . . . . . . . . . . . . . . . . . . . . | $7.50 | $7.64 |

### Instructions

**a.** Compute the materials price variance and the materials quantity variance, indicating whether each is favorable or unfavorable. Prepare the journal entry to record the cost of direct materials used during June in the Work in Process account (at standard).

**b.** Compute the labor rate variance and the labor efficiency variance, indicating whether each is favorable or unfavorable. Prepare the journal entry to record the cost of direct labor used during June in the Work in Process account (at standard).

**c.** Compute the overhead spending variance and the overhead volume variance, indicating whether each is favorable or unfavorable. Prepare the journal entry to assign overhead cost to production in June.

Heritage Furniture Co. uses a standard cost system. One of the company's most popular products is an oak entertainment center that looks like an old ice box but houses a television, stereo, or other electronic components. The per-unit standard costs of the entertainment center, assuming a "normal" volume of 1,000 units per month, are as follows:

| | | |
|---|---|---|
| Direct materials, 100 board-feet of wood at $1.30 per foot | | $130.00 |
| Direct labor, 5 hours at $8.00 per hour | | 40.00 |
| Manufacturing overhead (applied at $22 per unit) | | |
|   Fixed ($15,000 ÷ 1,000 units of normal production) | $15.00 | |
|   Variable | 7.00 | 22.00 |
|     Total standard unit cost | | $192.00 |

During July, 800 entertainment centers were scheduled and produced at the following actual unit costs:

| | |
|---|---|
| Direct materials, 110 feet at $1.20 per foot | $132.00 |
| Direct labor, 5½ hours at $7.80 per hour | 42.90 |
| Manufacturing overhead, $18,480 ÷ 800 units | 23.10 |
|   Total actual unit cost | $198.00 |

**Instructions**

**a.** Compute the following cost variances for the month of July:
1. Materials price variance
2. Materials quantity variance
3. Labor rate variance
4. Labor efficiency variance
5. Overhead spending variance
6. Volume variance

**b.** Prepare journal entries to assign manufacturing costs to the Work in Process Inventory account and to record cost variances for July. Use separate entries for (1) direct materials, (2) direct labor, and (3) overhead costs.

**c.** Comment on any significant problems or areas of cost savings revealed by your computation of cost variances. Also comment on any possible causal relationships between significant favorable and unfavorable cost variances.

PuzzCo Corporation has supplied us with the following information:

| | |
|---|---|
| Standard production costs allowed | |
|   for actual level of output achieved | $400,000 |
| Variances: | |
|   Total materials variance (favorable) | $ 6,000 |
|   Total direct labor variance (favorable) | 1,100 |
|   Total overhead variances (unfavorable) | 3,000 |
| Other Information: | |
| Actual units produced | 22,000 units |
| Normal or expected production | 22,000 units |
| Actual cost per pound of materials | $2/pound |

Direct labor averaged .85 hours per unit produced, which was .05 hours above the standard time allowed per unit produced. Actual total direct labor cost was $280,500.

The materials price variance equals the overhead volume variance. The actual quantity of materials used during the period was 90% of the standard quantity allowed.

**Instructions**

Compute the following for PuzzCo:

a. Materials quantity variance

b. Standard quantity of materials allowed to produce 22,000 units

c. Actual quantity of materials used to produce 22,000 units

d. Actual direct labor rate per hour

e. Standard direct labor rate per hour

f. Labor rate variance

g. Labor efficiency variance

h. Overhead spending variance

**PROBLEM 23.10**

Understanding Cost Variances: Solving for Missing Data

**LO 1, 3, 4**

The Ripley Corporation has supplied us with the following information obtained from its standard cost system in June:

| | |
|---|---|
| Standard price of direct materials | $6 per pound |
| Actual price of direct materials | $5 per pound |
| Standard direct labor rate | $9 per hour |
| Actual direct labor hours in June | 5,000 hours |

The following journal entries were made during June with respect to Ripley's standard cost system:

| | | |
|---|---|---|
| Work in Process Inventory (at standard cost) | 50,000 | |
| Materials Quantity Variance | 1,200 | |
|     Direct Materials Inventory (at actual cost) | | 49,200 |
|     Materials Price Variance | | 2,000 |
| To record the cost of direct materials used in June. | | |

| | | |
|---|---|---|
| Work in Process Inventory (at standard cost) | 80,000 | |
| Labor Rate Variance | 10,000 | |
| Labor Efficiency Variance | 4,500 | |
|     Direct Labor (at actual cost) | | 94,500 |
| To record the cost of direct labor charged to production in June. | | |

| | | |
|---|---|---|
| Work in Process Inventory (at standard cost) | 25,000 | |
| Overhead Spending Variance | 2,000 | |
|     Overhead Volume Variance | | 5,000 |
|     Manufacturing Overhead (at actual cost) | | 22,000 |
| To apply overhead to production in June. | | |

**Instructions**

a. Determine the actual quantity of materials purchased and used in production during June.

b. Determine the standard quantity of materials allowed for the productive output achieved during June.

c. Determine the actual average direct labor rate in June.

d. Determine the standard direct labor hours allowed for the production output achieved during June.

e. Determine the total overhead costs allowed for the production output achieved during June.

f. Prepare a journal entry to record the transfer of all work in process to finished goods at the end of June.

**g.** Close all cost variances directly to the Cost of Goods Sold account at the end of June.

**h.** Was Ripley's production output in June more or less than its normal level of output? How can you tell?

The Anton Company manufactures wooden magazine stands. An accountant for Anton just finished completing the variance report for the current month. After printing the report, his computer's hard disk crashed, effectively destroying most of the actual results for the month. All that the accountant remembers is that actual production was 220 stands and that all materials purchased were used in production. The following information is also available:

**PROBLEM 23.11**

Understanding Variance Calculations

**LO 3, 4**

---

**Current Month: Budgeted Amounts**

Budgeted production: 200 magazine stands

Direct materials: Wood

| | |
|---|---|
| Usage | 3 square feet per stand |
| Price | $0.25 per square foot |

Direct labor:

| | |
|---|---|
| Usage | .5 hours per stand |
| Rate | $10 per hour |

Variable overhead (allocated based on direct labor hours)

| | |
|---|---|
| Rate per labor hour | $4 |
| Rate per stand | $2 |

Fixed overhead (allocated based on direct labor hours)

| | |
|---|---|
| Rate per labor hour | $6 |
| Rate per stand | $3 |

**Current Month: Variances**

| | | |
|---|---|---|
| Direct materials price variance | $33 | Unfavorable |
| Direct materials quantity variance | –0– | |
| Direct labor rate variance | 231 | Favorable |
| Direct labor efficiency variance | 550 | Unfavorable |
| Overhead volume variance | 60 | Favorable |
| Overhead spending variance | 210 | Unfavorable |

---

**Instructions**

Using the budget for the current month and the variance report, construct the items below.

**a.** What was the actual purchase price per square foot of wood?

**b.** How many labor hours did it actually take to produce each stand?

**c.** What was the actual wage rate paid per hour?

**d.** What was actual total overhead for the month?

## CASES AND UNSTRUCTURED PROBLEMS

Cabinets, Inc., is a large manufacturer of modular kitchen cabinets, sold primarily to builders and developers. The company uses a standard cost system. Standard production costs have been developed for each type of cabinet; these costs, and any cost variances, are charged to the production department. A budget also has been developed for the sales department. The sales department is credited with the gross profit on sales (measured at standard costs) and is charged with selling expenses and any variations between budgeted and actual selling expenses.

**CASE 23.1**

It's Not My Fault

**LO 1, 3–5**

In early April, the manager of the sales department asked the production department to fill a rush order of kitchen cabinets for a tract of 120 homes. The sales manager stated that the entire order must be completed by May 31. The manager of the production department argued that an order of this size would take 12 weeks to produce. The sales manager answered, "The customer needs it on May 31, or we don't get the business. Do you want to be responsible for our losing a customer who makes orders of this size?"

Of course, the production manager did not want to take that responsibility. Therefore, he gave in and processed the rush order by having production personnel work overtime through April and May. As a result of the overtime, the performance reports for the production department in those months showed large, unfavorable labor rate variances. The production manager, who in the past had prided himself on coming in under budget, now has very ill feelings toward the sales manager. He also has stated that the production department will never again accept a rush order.

### Instructions

**a.** Identify any problem that you see in the company's standard cost system or in the manner in which cost variances are assigned to the responsible managers.

**b.** Make recommendations for changing the cost accounting system to reduce or eliminate any problems that you have identified.

**CASE 23.2**

Determination and Use of Standard Costs

Armstrong Chemical began operations in January. The company manufactures an acrylic car wax called Tough-Coat. The following standard cost estimates were developed several months before the company began operations, based on an estimated production of 1,000,000 units (pints):

| | |
|---|---|
| Material X-1 (1 ounce) | $1.00 |
| Material X-2 (1 pound) | 0.50 |
| Direct labor | 0.80 |
| Manufacturing overhead ($1,400,000 ÷ 1,000,000 units) | 1.40 |
| Total estimated standard cost per pint | $3.70 |

During the year, 1,000,000 pints of Tough-Coat were actually produced, of which 900,000 were sold. Actual costs incurred during the year were:

| | |
|---|---|
| Material X-1 purchased, 1,200,000 ounces @ $0.70 | $ 840,000 |
| Material X-2 purchased, 1,150,000 pounds @ $0.50 | 575,000 |
| Direct labor | 880,000 |
| Manufacturing overhead | 1,400,000 |
| Total production cost incurred during the year | $3,695,000 |

The company's inventories at the end of the year consisted of the following, with the Finished Goods inventory stated at standard cost:

| | | |
|---|---|---|
| Direct materials: | | |
| Material X-1, 200,000 ounces @ $0.70 | $140,000 | |
| Material X-2, 100,000 pounds @ $0.50 | 50,000 | $190,000 |
| Finished Goods: | | |
| Tough-Coat, 100,000 pints @ $3.70 standard cost | | 370,000 |
| Total inventory at December 31 | | $560,000 |

The independent Certified Public Accountant who has been engaged to audit the company's financial statements wants to adjust the valuation of Finished Goods inventory to "a revised standard cost" that would take into account the favorable price variance on material X-1 ($0.30 per ounce) and the 10% wage increase early in the year. (An unfavorable quantity variance on material X-2 was caused by spoilage in production; the CPA feels no adjustment to the standard should be made for this type of item.)

The president of the company objects on the following grounds: "Such a revision is not necessary because the cost of material X-1 already shows signs of going up and the wage increase was not warranted because the productivity of workers did not increase one bit. Furthermore, if we revise our inventory figure of $560,000, our operating income will be reduced from the current level of $50,000." You are called in by the president to help resolve the controversy.

## Instructions

**a.** Do you agree with the president that revision of the $3.70 standard cost figure is not necessary?

**b.** Assume that you conclude that the standards for this first year of operations should be revised. Compute a "revised standard cost per unit" and determine the value to be assigned to the ending inventory of finished units using this revised standard cost.

**c.** What effect would this revaluation of Finished Goods inventory have on the company's operating income?

**d.** Using the *original* standards, compute the following:

1. Materials price variance and quantity variance for material X-1
2. Materials price variance and quantity variance for material X-2
3. Total direct labor variance (do not separate into rate variance and usage variance)
4. Total manufacturing overhead variance

## BUSINESS WEEK ASSIGNMENT

BusinessWeek

The following quote is from "Management by Web" by John Byrnes is an August 28, 2000, *Business Week* article:

Digitization means removing human minds and hands from an organization's routine tasks and replacing them with computers and networks . . . think of it this way: a typical bank transaction costs $1.25 when handled by a teller, 54 cents when done by phone, or 24 cents at an ATM. But the same transaction processed over the Internet, without the hefty capital and real estate costs of ATMs, costs a mere 2 cents. The productivity improvement isn't incremental. Its revolutionary—on the order of more than 60 times.

**CASE 23.3**

Technology and Changing Standards

**LO 2, 5**

## Instructions

**a.** With a partner, identify the types of costs that are reduced by changing from a teller to the phone; from the phone to the ATM; and from the ATM to the Internet for processing a bank transaction.

**b.** Discuss how determining standard costs can be impacted by productivity changes occurring because of digitization.

## INTERNET ASSIGNMENT

Each year, a large clothing store in New York City sends its top five salespersons to a five-day retreat in Orlando, Florida. The retreat begins on the first Monday in February and ends the following Friday afternoon. The company must purchase five coach class airline tickets from New York City to Orlando, Florida. The budgeted airfare for the trip is $1,000 per person.

As the assistant in charge of purchasing the tickets, visit the Web sites of Delta and Continental Airlines at the following addresses:

**INTERNET 23.1**

Standards for Travel Costs

**LO 4, 5**

**www.delta-air.com**

**www.flycontinental.com**

Find the lowest fare among the two airlines for a round-trip flight leaving the first Monday morning in February and returning Friday evening.

### Instructions

a. Based on the lowest fare, calculate the total spending variance related to the ticket purchase. Is it favorable or unfavorable?

b. Does the standard seem reasonable given current ticket prices? What factors might determine whether the price variance is favorable or unfavorable?

*Internet sites are time and date sensitive. It is the purpose of these exercises to have you explore the Internet. You may need to use the Yahoo! search engine* http://www.yahoo.com *(or other favorite search engine) to find a company's current web address.*

## OUR COMMENTS ON THE "YOUR TURN" CASES

**As a Production Manager (p. 957)**   A production line that has been operating at 100% capacity for several months is likely to have multiple problems. Maintenance of equipment becomes difficult when it is continually operating. Without maintenance, equipment failures become more common. It may be necessary to hire additional workers who are less experienced than the current employees. They require training and learning time to become as productive as the standard allows. Suppliers may have had difficulty providing enough raw materials to meet the demand, and they may have raised the price of their materials. Finally, general congestion-related costs will also increase. For example, more frequent movement of materials and inventory and more factory cleaning and associated general supplies will likely be needed. All of these types of costs were not incorporated in the initial standards because they were based on the plant operating at 80% capacity. Therefore, actual costs at 100% capacity will be much higher than the standard costs based on 80% capacity.

In addition, ethical issues arise related to equipment and employees. Failing to properly maintain equipment because it is operating at 100% capacity can eventually destroy the equipment. Also, demanding that employees work overtime or work harder can create stress and safety hazards as well as increase employee turnover. An ethical trade-off between meeting short-run demand and maintaining the long-run health of the company can create difficult issues for managers.

**As a Plant Manager (p. 968)**   The bonus is intended to motivate managers to make decisions that result in actual resource use and costs that are lower than the standard input quantities and costs. However, evaluating and motivating *individual* behaviors based on standard cost variances can discourage cooperation. The purchasing manager may fail to cooperate with the production manager in purchasing high-quality materials. The production manager may employ less skilled workers to save on input wages at the expense of low productivity and quality. Because production from a plant is a team-oriented activity (workers are dependent on each other to produce high-quality output), individual competitive rewards may be very costly. Companies try to avoid these costs by measuring and rewarding employees for multiple variances at multiple levels in the company. Many companies use profit sharing at either the plant or firm level to encourage cooperation among workers.

## ANSWERS TO SELF-TEST QUESTIONS

1. c    2. d    3. c    4. d    5. b and d

# REWARDING BUSINESS PERFORMANCE

## Learning Objectives

*After studying this chapter, you should be able to:*

1. Explain the importance of incentive systems for motivating performance.

2. Use the DuPont system to evaluate business performance.

3. Identify and explain the criticisms of using return on investment (ROI) as the only performance measure.

4. Calculate and explain residual income (RI) and economic value added (EVA).

5. Use the balanced scorecard to identify, evaluate, and reward business performance.

6. Identify and explain the components of management compensation and the trade-offs that compensation designers make.

Herman Miller Inc. and Hedrich-blessing Merick, nick.

# Herman Miller, Inc.

Located in Zeeland, Michigan since 1923, **Herman Miller, Inc.** is a leader in designing, manufacturing, and installing office furniture. In the 1960s **Herman Miller** introduced the first open plan office furniture system; that is, the cubicle. The cubicle has been widely adopted and has generated many office jokes including numerous Dilbert cartoon strips. At the same time, the company's products have won numerous awards and—complemented by primary furniture-management services—generated nearly $2 billion in revenue during fiscal 2000.[1] **Herman Miller** is widely recognized for both its innovative products and business practices.

One of the interesting things about **Herman Miller** is that every employee with more than one year of service owns stock in the company. As a result, employee-owners know that one of their primary goals is to create value for the company's shareholders. To help achieve that objective, **Herman Miller** uses a performance measurement and compensation system called "Economic Value Added" (EVA) which is linked to each employee's incentive compensation.[2] Their EVA plan shifts focus from the budget performance to the short- and long-term continuous improvements that create economic value.

● ● ●

This chapter discusses the links between performance measurement systems, actual performance, and incentive compensation. We also discuss such concepts as EVA, budget-based performance measurement, and employee stock options.

---

[1] See the Herman Miller, Inc., website at www.hermanmiller.com for more information on these awards
[2] EVA® is a registered trademark of Stern Stewart & Co., New York, NY.

# MOTIVATION AND ALIGNING GOALS AND OBJECTIVES

Your goals and objectives for this course might be to get a high grade and learn important accounting tools that will help you in the future. Alternatively, you or other students might view this as a required course and you may not be interested in accounting. In such a case, a goal might be to simply pass the course with the least amount of effort. Your instructor also has goals and objectives for this course. The instructor's goals for you and the other students are that you master the subject matter and understand its importance for business. This goal may or may not be consistent with any individual student's goals. Thus, students' goals are sometimes not consistent with the instructor's goals.

Even when your goals are consistent with your instructor's goals, it can be difficult for you to determine how to achieve the goals. For example, students face many demands that compete for their time, such as working at a job, reading a good novel, bowling, other course work, or snowboarding. You and your fellow students must determine how to allocate your resources (time and effort in this instance) among the competing activities to achieve your goals.

## Communicating Goals and Objectives

An instructor's goals are communicated to students by the course syllabus and through assignments, class discussions, and periodic examinations. The course syllabus directs your attention to the topics that the instructor decides are important. Periodic feedback also provides a mechanism that helps align students' goals with those of the instructor. For example, to measure progress toward the instructor's goals, you receive periodic grades for exercises, class participation, and/or examinations. This feedback is both an attempt to steer you toward the goals that the instructor has for the course and an indication if you are making progress in achieving those goals.

This periodic feedback is an attention-getting device that helps students allocate their valuable resources—time and effort. If the feedback suggests you are not allocating enough time and effort to accounting to learn the material and/or earn the grade that is one of your goals for the course, you will be likely to allocate more time and effort to studying accounting.

## Accounting Information and Feedback about Goal Achievement

**LO 1**

Explain the importance of incentive systems for motivating performance.

Just as you have objectives and goals you are trying to achieve by studying accounting, most organizations have objectives and goals they are trying to achieve in their operations. Just as you make choices about what to do with the resources under your control, an organization's employees must make choices about the resources for which they are responsible. Accounting information can align employees' goals with the organization's and provide feedback and incentives that guide employees in using the resources under their control to achieve the organization's goals.

Consider, for example, that your course syllabus is similar to an organization's annual budget (see Chapter 22) because both provide guidance about important goals. Such goals could include which chapters to study for your course and production quota figures for employees in an organization. Further, similar to the grading feedback that helps direct your attention and resources, periodically comparing accounting information resulting from the actual outcomes against the budgeted accounting information shows employees how well they have allocated their resources and suggests how to reallocate resources in the future.

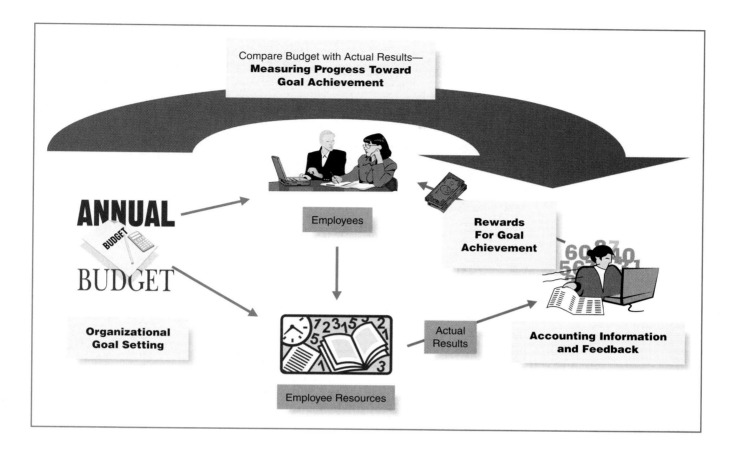

Compare Budget with Actual Results—
**Measuring Progress Toward Goal Achievement**

ANNUAL
BUDGET

BUDGET

Employees

**Rewards For Goal Achievement**

**Organizational Goal Setting**

Employee Resources

Actual Results

**Accounting Information and Feedback**

## Rewarding Goal Achievement

This chapter focuses on motivating business employees, customers, suppliers, and others in and outside of the company to help the organization achieve its goals and objectives. The following illustration shows how accounting information plays an important role in aligning employee and organizational goals and in motivating employees to achieve those goals. Generating motivation requires three undertakings: First, the accounting system helps *create and set goals* and objectives through planning information such as budgeting. Second, the accounting system *measures progress* toward the goals and provides *feedback* about that progress. And third, accounting-based information is instrumental in allocating *rewards* for progress toward goal achievement. The illustration shows the role of the accounting system in motivating employees to achieve the organizations' goals. Accounting systems are an important management tool for generating motivation.

## THE DUPONT SYSTEM

One of the first systems to focus on business performance measurement was created during the early 1900s by managers at the **Du Pont de Nemours Powder Company**. Managers at **DuPont** wanted a method to help them set goals and measure progress toward achieving objectives. These managers began by experimenting with a performance evaluation system that still has many advocates around the world. Because **DuPont**'s owners received significant bank loans for their business, the managers needed a system to control and evaluate their operations that would ensure repayment of the loans.

## Return on Investment

After tracing the costs and revenues associated with their products, **DuPont**'s managers soon realized that product line profits were an incomplete performance measure. The profit computations included no measure of the amount of invested capital for each product line. Two product lines could be returning the same profit, for example $250,000, but one product line might require twice as many assets (say $4 million versus $2 million) to produce the same profit. Thus, the **DuPont** managers created the idea of **return on investment** or **ROI.** ROI was introduced in Chapter 14 and defined as profit divided by average investment. Although ROI is usually discussed as a percent, it basically tells managers the amount of earnings expected for the average invested dollar. In the example above, the ROI of the two product lines would be:

**Product line 1 ROI = 6.25% = $250,000 ÷ $4,000,000**

**Product line 2 ROI = 12.5% = $250,000 ÷ $2,000,000**

Thus for the first product line, managers earned $.0625 on the average invested dollar. For the second product line, however, they earned $.125 per average invested dollar. If a company financed its assets with bank loans carrying an interest rate of 8%, then the first product line would not provide a large enough return on invested capital to repay the loans.

The **DuPont** managers wanted to assess ROI for different segments of their business as well as for different product lines. This broader use of ROI requires careful measures of the invested capital for each segment and/or product line. Tracking plant, properties, and inventories to each segment and product line is challenging work.

Not satisfied with knowing only the ROI, the **DuPont** managers developed a system to help them understand the component parts of ROI so that they could determine what causes ROI to change. The exhibit on the next page shows the **DuPont** managers' definition of the component parts of ROI as the product of capital turnover (sales ÷ total investment) and return on sales (earnings ÷ sales).

**CASE IN POINT**

A survey by H. Wijewardena and A. De Zoysa reported in volume 34, number 1 of the 1999 *International Journal of Accounting* compared Australian and Japanese companies' use of divisional performance measures. The survey shows that 37% of Japanese companies use ROI compared to 59% of Australian companies. In contrast, 82% of Japanese companies use return on sales (ROS) compared to 40% of Australian companies. The Japanese emphasis on ROS is characteristic of a strong focus on growing market share. The Australian emphasis on ROI is more consistent with a focus on pleasing stockholders.

## The Components of Return on Investment

**LO 2**

Use the DuPont System to evaluate business performance.

The component parts of ROI, capital turnover and return on sales, give managers a way to compare product line ROIs and a way to evaluate changes in ROI over time. **Capital turnover** tells managers about how the invested capital is generating (or "turning over") sales dollars, that is, the amount of monetary sales that can be expected from a dollar of invested capital. **Return on sales** indicates the operating earnings or profitability that can be expected from one dollar of sales. Operating earnings rather than net income is used to compute return on sales because operating earnings better reflect the resources that managers can control. Thus, the **DuPont system of performance measurement** analyzes business performance by considering both the earnings per sales dollar and the investment used to generate those sales dollars.

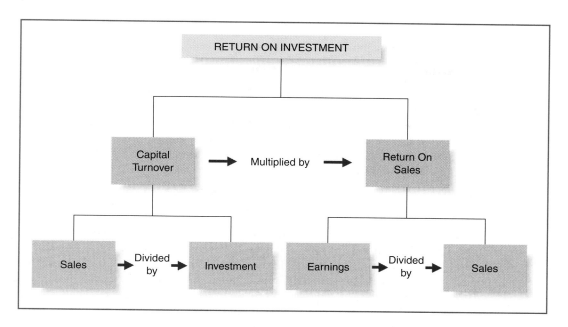

To better understand how the components of ROI can help evaluate and assess business processes, consider the following information for two product lines of the Bastille Company, a producer of fine French dining products.

Although the ROI is significantly higher for the Cookware product line, additional analysis will clarify the role of the components of ROI. To explain their roles, we analyze the ROI component information computed in the exhibit below for the Bastille Company.

| | Year 1 | |
|---|---|---|
| | **Fine China** | **Cookware** |
| Sales | $1,500,000 | $ 400,000 |
| Cost of goods sold | 750,000 | 100,000 |
| Operating expenses | 300,000 | 90,000 |
| Operating earnings | 450,000 | 210,000 |
| Average invested capital | $6,000,000 | $1,400,000 |
| ROI | ( 450,000 ÷ 6,000,000) = 7.5% | (210,000 ÷ 1,400,000) = 15% |
| Return on sales | ( 450,000 ÷ 1,500,000) = 30% | (210,000 ÷ 400,000) = 52.5% |
| Capital turnover | (1,500,000 ÷ 6,000,000) = 25% | (400,000 ÷ 1,400,000) = 28.57% |

| | Year 2 | |
|---|---|---|
| | **Fine China** | **Cookware** |
| Sales | $1,700,000 | $ 400,000 |
| Cost of goods sold | 840,000 | 102,500 |
| Operating expenses | 330,000 | 91,500 |
| Operating earnings | 530,000 | 206,000 |
| Average invested capital | $6,200,000 | $1,300,000 |
| ROI | ( 530,000 ÷ 6,200,000) = 8.55% | (206,000 ÷ 1,300,000) = 15.85% |
| Return on sales | ( 530,000 ÷ 1,700,000) = 31.18% | (206,000 ÷ 400,000) = 51.5% |
| Capital turnover | (1,700,000 ÷ 6,200,000) = 27.42% | (400,000 ÷ 1,300,000) = 30.77% |

## Return on Sales

For the Fine China Division in Year 1, the return on sales show that each sales dollar generates $.30 of earnings. For the Cookware Division, however, each sales dollar generates $.525 of earnings. To have an impact on return on sales, a division manager could *reduce* cost of goods sold or operating expenses without any impact on revenues or *increase* revenues without a proportional impact on expenses.

In Year 2, the manager of the Fine China Division increased revenues from $1,500,000 to $1,700,000 without a proportional increase in cost of goods sold. Although cost of goods sold did increase, the percentage increase was smaller than the percentage increase in revenues as shown below.

**Revenue increase**            $= 13.3\% = [\$1,700,000 - \$1,500,000] \div \$1,500,000$
**Cost of goods sold increase** $= 12\% = [\$840,000 - \$750,000] \div \$750,000$

In addition, the manager of the Fine China Division kept the percentage increase in other operating expenses below the 13.3% increase in revenues ([$330,000 − $300,000] ÷ $300,000 = 10%). The return on sales increase of 1% from Year 1 to Year 2 shows that the combination of efforts to increase revenue and have a smaller increase in cost resulted in increased earnings of more than $.01 for each dollar of sales revenue.

The Cookware Division manager did not fare as well with return on sales between Years 1 and 2 as the manager of the Fine China Division. By comparing return on sales in Year 1 and Year 2, you can see that the Cookware Division showed a drop of $.01 of earnings (52.5% − 51.5% = 1%) for each sales dollar. Using our DuPont method to analyze the Cookware Division shows that revenues remained constant while cost of goods sold and operating expenses increased.

**Constant revenue**              $= 0\% = (\$400,000 - \$400,000).$
**Cost of goods sold increase**   $= 2.5\% = ([\$100,000 - \$102,500] \div \$100,000).$
**Operating expenses increase**   $= 1.7\% = ([\$90,000 - \$91,500] \div \$90,000).$

### You as Cookware Division Manager

Assume you are the manager of the Cookware Division. Your boss has criticized your division's performance in Year 2 specifically targeting the return on sales. When planning your operating budget for year 3, what strategies might you consider that could improve your division's return on sales?

*Our responses appear on page 1015.

**YOUR TURN**

## Capital Turnover

The capital turnover ratio for the Cookware Division in Year 1 shows $.286 of sales for each dollar of invested capital. The Cookware Division's capital turnover increased in Year 2 to $.308 of sales per dollar of capital. How was the Cookware manager able to increase capital turnover despite total sales revenue that remained flat from Year 1 to Year 2? The manager reduced the amount of invested capital by $100,000 ($1,400,000 − $1,300,000). Generating constant sales using a smaller amount of invested capital is one method that managers can use to improve capital turnover.

The turnover ratio for Fine China tells us that this division is creating $.25 of sales for each dollar of invested capital. The turnover ratio improved significantly in Year 2 to $.274 per dollar of invested capital. How was the manager of Fine China able to achieve this increase? By increasing sales without a proportional increase in invested capital as shown below. Evidently the additional capital expenditures made by the manager of the Fine China Division significantly improved sales revenue.

$$\text{Sales increase} = 13.3\% = ([\$1,700,000 - \$1,500,000] \div \$1,500,000)$$
$$\text{Capital increase} = 3.3\% = ([\$6,200,000 - \$6,000,000] \div \$6,000,000)$$

## CRITICISMS OF ROI

The primary reason for using any performance measurement criteria such as ROI is to motivate employees to make decisions consistent with the goals and objectives of the organization. ROI motivates managers to earn the highest possible profits while using the minimum amount of average invested capital. Thus, managers who are measured and rewarded only on their divisions' ROI may decide to increase profits and decrease capital in their divisions in ways inconsistent with the best interests of the whole company. There are three primary criticisms of using ROI and the DuPont system as the only business performance measurement.

**LO 3**

Identify and explain the criticisms of using return on investment (ROI) as the only performance measure.

### The Short Horizon Problem

The first criticism is the short horizon problem that occurs because managers frequently move from one job to another. As a result, many people believe ROI encourages a short-term orientation to the detriment of longer-term planning. For example, the Cookware Division manager in the example discussed above, might know that he will soon be transferred to another job assignment. By selling assets to reduce the average invested capital, he can improve his ROI now. Even though those assets may be critical for the long-run success of the division, because he will not be managing the division in the long run, he is not concerned about long-run issues.

Alternatively, the same manager might reduce cost of goods sold expenses by purchasing inferior-quality merchandise from suppliers at a lower price. The reduction in cost of goods sold expense increases the annual operating earnings for this period. However, the long-run impact of the poor-quality inputs could be reflected in the firm's overall reputation. Poor-quality cookware could have serious reputation repercussions for the entire Bastille Company including the Fine China Division.

### Failing to Undertake Profitable Investments

A second problem with using ROI as the only business performance measure is that, under some circumstances, it presents an incentive for a manager to reject a good project that would increase the ROI for the firm as a whole. The project rejection occurs when investing in the project would reduce the division's ROI. Reconsider the information for the Bastille Company in Year 1. Notice that the average ROI for Bastille Company is 8.9%, as shown below:

| Division—Year 1 | Operating Earnings | Average Capital | ROI |
|---|---|---|---|
| Fine China . . . . . . . . . . . . . . . . . . . . . . | $450,000 | $6,000,000 | 7.5% |
| Cookware . . . . . . . . . . . . . . . . . . . . . . . | 210,000 | 1,400,000 | 15% |
| Bastille Company—Total . . . . . . . . . . . . . | $660,000 | $7,400,000 | 8.9% |

If an opportunity arose in Year 2 for the Cookware Division to undertake an investment of $500,000 with expected annual operating earnings of $55,000 (an ROI of 11% for the project), the division manager would likely choose not to undertake the investment. As shown below, the proposed investment would lower the Cookware Division's ROI to 13.95%, but it would improve the Bastille Company's average ROI to 9.05%.

**Cookware ROI** $\quad 13.95\% = (\$210,000 + \$55,000) \div (\$1,400,000 + \$500,000)$
**Bastille Company ROI** $\quad 9.05\% = (\$660,000 + \$55,000) \div (\$500,000 + \$7,400,000)$

Because it would lower the division's ROI even though it would improve the company's ROI, a division manager evaluated on the division's ROI would not undertake the project.

### Measurement Problems

A third criticism of ROI is the inherent difficulty in measuring both the average invested capital and the actual operating earnings associated with that capital. Many units within an organization share invested capital and often the allocation of capital between those units is arbitrary. For example, if both the Cookware and Fine China Divisions share costs associated with a research and development facility and administrative headquarters, how will the invested capital of those activities be allocated between the two divisions? Managers frequently complain that those allocations are arbitrary and should not be included in the evaluation of their business units. Yet if these units were stand-alone businesses, they would have some invested capital in administration and research and development. Organizations constantly struggle with how to make capital allocations in their attempt to evaluate business performance.

**CASE IN POINT**

When Hector de Jesus Ruiz was growing up in the 1950s in the Mexican border town of Piedras Negras, just across the Rio Grande from Eagle Pass, Texas, his ambitions were as modest as his upbringing. Now he is the head of **Advanced Micro Devices Inc. (AMD)**, a perennial rival to chip giant **Intel Corporation**. He must be able to assess the return on investment needed to remain competitive with **Intel**. One reason **Intel** is being challenged is **AMD**'s Athlon microprocessor, which is faster and cheaper than **Intel**'s flagship Pentium III and has won **AMD** dozens of corporate customers, including 9 of the top 10 PC makers. Allocating assets to determine the ROI of new chip designs presents a challenging task for Ruiz.

## RESIDUAL INCOME AND ECONOMIC VALUE ADDED

**LO 4**

Calculate and explain residual income (RI) and economic value added (EVA).

In response to the criticisms leveled at ROI, other financially based business performance measures have been created. Two of these measures, residual income (RI) and economic value added (EVA) are described here. These measures also help managers evaluate the profitability of particular parts of the business related to a specific investment base. But these measures do not suffer from some of the horizon and underinvestment criticisms leveled at ROI.

### Residual Income

The amount by which operating earnings exceed a minimum acceptable return on average invested capital is referred to as **residual income**. It is calculated as follows:

$$\text{Residual Income} = \text{Operating Earnings} - \text{Minimum Acceptable Return} \times \left( \text{Invested Capital} \right).$$

To understand how residual income avoids some of the criticisms associated with ROI, consider the previous example where the manager of the Cookware Division had the opportunity to undertake a new project. The expected operating earnings for the project were $55,000 on invested capital of $500,000 (project ROI = 11%). If the minimum acceptable return for the Cookware Division is set at 10% and residual income is the performance measure, then the division manager would be motivated to undertake the investment opportunity. Consider the following computation:

> ### Residual Income for Cookware Division
>
> Without the project $= (\$210{,}000) - .10\ (\$1{,}400{,}000) = \underline{\$70{,}000}$
>
> With the project $= (\$210{,}000 + \$55{,}000) - .10\ (\$1{,}400{,}000 + \$500{,}000) = \underline{\$75{,}000}$

Although the concept of residual income was developed by **General Motors Corporation** in the 1920s and later refined by **General Electric Company** in the 1950s, generally it has been unused in performance measurement plans. Recently, however, consultants have repackaged the residual income concept into economic value added.

## Economic Value Added

Referred to in the popular press as EVA, **economic value added** is a refinement of the residual income measure. EVA has gained significant popularity as a component of compensation plans. Companies such as **Quaker Oats**, **Herman Miller** (see opening story), **Eli Lilly**, and **Coca-Cola** have used EVA to measure business performance. Like residual income, EVA does not motivate managers to turn down investments that are expected to earn a return below their current ROI but above the minimum acceptable return to the firm. EVA is computed as follows:

$$\text{EVA} = \begin{matrix}\text{After-Tax} \\ \text{Operating} \\ \text{Income}\end{matrix} - \left\{\begin{matrix}\text{Division's Total} \\ \text{Assets}\end{matrix} - \begin{matrix}\text{Division's Current} \\ \text{Liabilities}\end{matrix}\right\} \times \begin{matrix}\text{Weighted-Average} \\ \text{Cost of Capital}\end{matrix}$$

This formula can apply to a division or a total company. The weighted-average cost of capital is a more refined measure of the acceptable minimum return discussed above. It encompasses the average after-tax cost of long-term borrowing and the cost of equity. It is typically measured by the treasurer of the firm. Modifying the EVA computations to fit specific divisions and companies is an art. One consulting firm that measures EVA has more than 150 possible adjustments to reported accounting measures that it uses in determining EVA. Using EVA and residual income concepts in incentive plans motivates managers to eliminate assets that earn less than the minimum required return and invest in those projects that earn more than that required return.

**Stern Stewart & Co.**, the consulting firm that has a trademark on **economic value added** is concerned that EVA undervalues a company such as **Amazon.com Inc.** that's losing money now because it's spending tons of money creating options for the future. Therefore, **Stern Stewart** is tweaking its EVA measures to incorporate forward-looking measures such as options. **Stern Stewart** believes that the generic EVA rankings, which have been published by *Fortune* magazine, are "relatively simplistic" because they ignore the value of companies' options.

**CASE IN POINT**

## THE BALANCED SCORECARD

A major criticism of ROI, RI, and EVA as performance evaluation tools is that they focus on only one component of the business, financial outcomes.

**CASH EFFECTS** Beyond just focusing on financial outcomes, none of the business performance measures discussed to this point consider cash flow performance. ROI, EVA, and RI use accrual-based accounting information. In organizations where cash flow management is a critical success factor, performance evaluation and rewards should be based on cash flow measures. Some examples of such measures include the accounts receivable turnover ratio or the length of the operating cycle.

Focusing on financial numbers rather than on supplier quality might motivate the manager of the Cookware Division to change to a poor-quality supplier. As discussed in Chapter 18, total quality management includes careful consideration of quality across the entire **value chain**. Below is the value chain for the Cookware Division's product line. For the Bastille Company's cookware line to be successful, all parts of the value chain must add value. Thus, performance measurement systems that ignore the links in the value chain run the risk of a failure somewhere on the chain. That failure could result in the failure of the cookware product. Recently, a new approach for setting strategic goals and measuring progress toward those goals across the entire value chain has been developed. This new approach is referred to as the balanced scorecard.

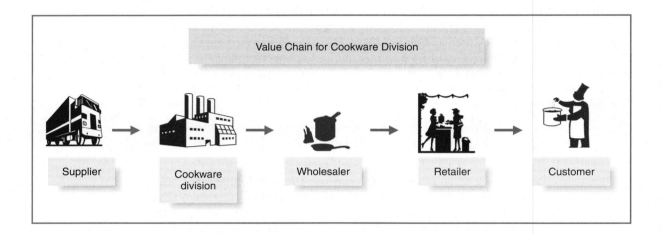

Value Chain for Cookware Division

Supplier → Cookware division → Wholesaler → Retailer → Customer

**LO 5**

Use the balanced scorecard to identify, evaluate, and reward business performance.

Developed in the early 1990s by two Harvard Business School professors, the **balanced scorecard** is a system for performance measurement that links a company's strategy to specific goals and objectives, provides measures for assessing progress toward those goals, and indicates specific initiatives to achieve those goals. It is a systematic attempt to create a business performance measurement process that integrates objectives across the span of the value chain. The main objective of the balanced scorecard is achieving the organization's strategic goals.

Unlike the DuPont system that focuses on the financial measure of ROI, the balanced scorecard looks at firm performance through four lenses, only one of which focuses on financial performance. As identified in the exhibit on the facing page, the four lenses include (1) the traditional financial perspective discussed previously in this chapter; (2) a customer perspective; (3) a business process perspective; and (4) the learning and growth perspective. Below we describe each of these lenses, including their associated performance measures.

## The Financial Perspective

Managers use the **financial perspective** lens of the balanced scorecard to view the company through the eyes of creditors and shareholders. This lens helps employees consider the impact of strategic decisions on the traditional financial measures by which shareholders and creditors evaluate business performance. The balance sheet, income statement, and statement of cash flows are the underlying financial measures associated with the financial perspective. Return on investment, return on sales, sales turnover, residual income, and economic value added are performance measures described earlier in this chapter that are used with the financial perspective.

Most companies use the domestic parent's currency to evaluate the financial performance of their international subsidiaries. Using the domestic currency for financial performance evaluation creates a question about which exchange rate to use when translating the budget and the actual results. Many companies use two separate exchange rates. They use the actual rate at the budget date to translate the budget and the actual rate at the end of the reporting period to translate the actual results of operations. When these two separate rates are used for performance evaluation, the manager of the international operation is expected to make strategic decisions to manage operations in response to exchange rate fluctuation.

**MANAGEMENT STRATEGY**

## The Customer Perspective

The customer perspective lens of the balanced scorecard provides a means for employees to consider their customers' needs and the markets in which their products sell. Through the **customer perspective** lens employees examine how the organization's strategies, products, and services add value for the customer. Customer retention, customer satisfaction, customer quality perceptions, market share growth, and customer profitability are business performance measures relevant to the customer perspective.

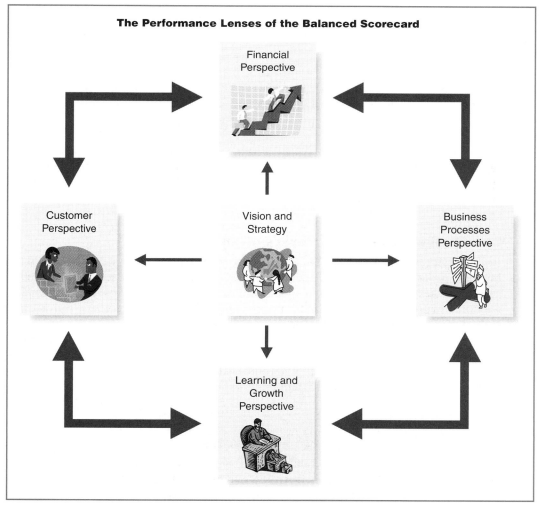

**The Performance Lenses of the Balanced Scorecard**

Financial Perspective

Customer Perspective

Vision and Strategy

Business Processes Perspective

Learning and Growth Perspective

Source: R. S. Kaplan and D. Norton, *The Balanced Scorecard: Translating Study into Action.* Boston: HBS Press, 1997.

| Balanced Scorecard Lens | Strategies | Measures |
|---|---|---|
| **Financial Perspective** | 1. Improve shareholder perceptions | • Net income<br>• ROI<br>• EVA<br>• Residual income |
| | 2. Improve credit rating—reduce risk | • Bond ratings |
| **Customer Perspective** | 1. Improve customer relations—wholesalers and retailers | • Customer retention<br>  —Wholesale<br>  —Retail<br>• Number of returns |
| | 2. Increase orders from profitable customers | • Market share<br>• Customer profitability |
| **Business Process Perspective** | 1. Improve supplier relations | • Number quality certified<br>• Number of vendors<br>• % of on-time deliveries |
| | 2. Improve quality of manufacturing processes | • % machine downtime<br>• Velocity/cycle time<br>• % of orders filled<br>• Scrap as a % of raw materials |
| | 3. Improve delivery | • Number of on-time deliveries |
| **Learning and Growth Perspective** | 1. Improve retention of employees | • Turnover<br>• Employee satisfaction |
| | 2. Improve employee productivity | • Number and cost savings from process improvements<br>• Hours of employee training |
| | 3. Increase new product development | • Number of new patents<br>• % of sales from new products |

## The Business Process Perspective

Both just-in-time inventory and the total quality management ideas are embodied in the **business process perspective** lens. This balanced scorecard lens focuses on internal business processes and external business relations with suppliers and distributors. Quality measures such as amounts of scrap, downtime, number of defects, costs of rework, and the number of warranty claims enable assessment of the quality of internal processes. Other internal processes are monitored with measures such as manufacturing cycle time, percent of on-time deliveries, and percent of orders filled. Finally, relations with suppliers and distributors are assessed with both quality measures (on-time delivery, parts defects per million from suppliers) and profitability measures (profitability per distributor arrangement).

## The Learning and Growth Perspective

The balanced scorecard also recognizes the importance of intangibles to the strategic goals of organizations by using the **learning and growth perspective** lens. This lens focuses on the people, information systems, and organizational procedures in place for organizational learning and growth. Employee satisfaction, retention, skill, development, and training undertaken are measures focused on people. This lens also measures the reliability, accuracy, and consistency of the information provided by the organizations' information systems. Without reliability and accuracy, measuring progress toward organizational goal achievement becomes dubious. The number of patents awarded, amount of training programs offered, and money spent on training and development reflect organizational procedures that enhance learning and growth.

## Difficulties with the Balanced Scorecard

Companies using the balanced scorecard have identified several difficulties in using the four lenses described above. First, organizations have difficulty assessing the importance or weights attached to the various perspectives that are part of the scorecard. Second, measuring, quantifying, and evaluating some of the qualitative components that are part of the balanced scorecard present significant technical hurdles. A third difficulty arises frequently due to a lack of clarity and sense of direction resulting from the large number of measures suggested by the four perspectives. Finally, scorecard users suggest that the time and expense required to maintain and operate a fully designed and functioning balanced scorecard system can be significant.

Organizations can avoid some of these difficulties by limiting the number of measures used in each of the perspectives to critical business issues. In particular, when management chooses the measures to be used with the balanced scorecard, they should use those measures that present the best evidence for cause and effect linkages and significant impacts on the organization's strategy. At any point in time trade-offs are likely to exist between the various strategic goals in the balanced scorecard.

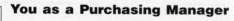
### You as a Purchasing Manager

Assume that as the manager of purchasing for the BCD Company you have been asked to participate in the design of a balanced scorecard. In particular you have been asked to suggest measures that could be used to evaluate purchasing activities. Having seen the consultants' report, you realize that the measures you suggest will be tied to your bonus each year. Your department has been collecting benchmark information about the suppliers used by other purchasing departments in similar companies. You are aware that your department has been choosing higher-priced suppliers because you believe that the quality of materials provided by these suppliers is superior. Which measures should you suggest?

*Our comments appear on page 1016.

## MANAGEMENT COMPENSATION

Early recognition of the importance of incentive systems for employee motivation occurred when **General Motors Corporation** started their bonus plan in 1918. Its specific objectives were to align the manager's goals and objectives with the goals of the corporation. Because **General Motors** decentralized their operating decisions they had to create a method to let the operating managers know whether their decisions were consistent with those of the overall corporation. Since that time, incentive compensation design has become an art. Multiple consulting companies now provide boards of directors and management with information about how to create and operate incentive compensation plans. We discuss the major compensation design features next.

**LO 6**

Identify and explain the components of management compensation and the trade-offs that compensation designers make.

## Components of Management Compensation

**Fixed Salary**     Nearly all companies pay fixed salaries to employees. Sometimes union contracts guarantee a minimum fixed salary with an opportunity to earn more through overtime. In addition many employees are paid a fixed hourly pay rate for a fixed number of hours per week or per month. Most managers receive a fixed salary component as part of their compensation. Guaranteeing a fixed level of compensation that will not be affected by uncontrollable forces reduces employee risk.

**Bonuses**     Corporations use bonus systems for managers across the organization, not just at the highest levels. At lower levels these bonus schemes are designed to let all employees share in company profits during a good year. Many automobile companies give employees bonuses based on profit-sharing results.

Profit center managers receive bonuses typically ranging from 25% to 50% of their base salaries. These bonus plans take on many forms with different characteristics: Some rely heavily on awards of company stock and others use cash. Some compensation systems provide the bonus in the current period and some provide a bonus that is harvested in future periods. For example, many companies use stock options as part of the bonus compensation. **Stock options** give an employee the right to purchase a prespecified number of shares at a prespecified price within a certain future time period; they provide incentives for managers to increase stock prices.

The awarding of most bonuses is based on accounting information. The objective of this chapter is to help you to understand the role accounting plays in performance evaluation and employee motivation. To be able to understand this role, you must become familiar with the many design choices that are available when constructing incentive and business performance evaluation systems.

**CASE IN POINT**

Stock options have been used more widely in recent years to reward business performance. They have become something employees negotiate along with salaries and raises. Option packages can include protection from takeovers, termination, or a falling stock price. An option plan's vesting timetable is important. Only vested employees can use their options to purchase stock at the prespecified price. Thus, employees also negotiate the vesting time. Stock options can create significant tax issues and a tax adviser is usually consulted before exercising options.

## Design Choices for Management Compensation

Several important design choices must be made when creating incentive compensation systems for managers. Managerial jobs involve multiple tasks and varying degrees of risk. Boards of directors try to design compensation schemes that both reward performance across multiple dimensions and reduce the impact on compensation of the various risks that managers face. Compensation designers can choose from a variety of design criteria to develop individual compensation schemes for managers. We present a few of the more common design choices here.

**Choice of Time Horizon**     The *horizon* choice denotes the emphasis management should place on current performance versus future performance. An important consideration is how to reward managers for doing a good job now while also encouraging them to think about future performance. For an example of this type of choice, consider the contrast between a current cash bonus versus a current bonus of restricted stock options. Both of these bonuses can be based on current performance, but the cash bonus does not encourage a future orientation. The restricted stock option typically is structured so that employees can obtain cash for the options in the future only if they stay with the company and the company's stock price increases. In this case, managers are less likely to trade off increasing current performance at the expense of future performance.

**Choice of Fixed versus Variable Bonus**　Another important concern for compensation designers is to create a fixed or variable bonus computation approach. In choosing how to award a bonus, many companies choose either a fixed bonus formula or a variable or more subjective approach. Some firms award a fixed dollar bonus for each percent of ROI above the minimum. This means managers know that if their ROI increases above the minimum, they will earn a fixed dollar amount for each 1%. However, sometimes unexpected and uncontrollable events occur and fixed bonus schemes are not flexible. In addition, fixed schemes do not usually accommodate a complex system like a balanced scorecard.

**Choice of Stock- versus Accounting-Based Performance Evaluation**　Compensation designers also choose to base performance evaluation on accounting information and/or on stock market information. By using stock price information, the managers' incentives are aligned with those of the shareholders. However, one argument against an overemphasis on stock-based compensation is that this approach creates too much risk for managers. Because managers' jobs are tied into the same company as the stock, managers could be more risk averse in their decision making than shareholders would want them to be. Thus, most companies tie incentives not only to stock market information but also to accounting information.

**Choice of Rewarding Local versus Companywide Performance**　The choice of how much emphasis to put on rewarding local performance over rewarding companywide performance is especially controversial. Some companies want their divisions to operate as independent businesses. Other companies want the divisions to cooperate and integrate to maximize total companywide profitability. Under some incentive compensation schemes, employees could be motivated to make decisions that improve the performance of their department or division, but might not help the company achieve its overall objectives and goals. Balancing employees' attention on both local goals and companywide goals is a challenging task. Many companies attempt to achieve this balance by combining fixed salary for local performance and bonuses for companywide performance. This is the approach that Herman Miller used by providing employees with stock bonuses in addition to their regular salaries.

**Choice of Cooperative versus Competitive Incentive Schemes**　Incentive plans can be designed to allow teams of employees to share equally in performance outcomes or to reward individual performance. A cooperative incentive motivates employees to work together to achieve the best result as a group. These types of incentives are designed to reward everyone for a good outcome regardless of each individual's actual contribution to that outcome. Examples of cooperative incentives include the Herman Miller example just mentioned where employees are given stock as part of their compensation. When the company as a whole performs well, the employees' stock price increases and they benefit from the group's efforts.

A competitive incentive, on the other hand, motivates employees to do better jobs than their co-workers. You are probably familiar with competitive incentives because grades in your classes frequently are curved and only a fixed percentage of As are awarded. Other examples of competitive incentives include promotions. Although many employees may want to be promoted to a better position, when only one position exists only one employee can receive the reward.

## Goals and Rewards in Life

As you can see, setting goals, measuring progress toward goal achievement, and designing reward plans that recognize goal achievement are some of the most difficult tasks faced by managers. All of us struggle when determining our goals, both current and future. In deciding on these goals, we keep in mind the rewards we are likely to get as we progress toward goal achievement. Some of these rewards are monetary and are current. Other rewards will occur in the future. Measuring and rewarding goal achievement helps motivate all of us in our daily pursuits.

**A SECOND LOOK**

### Herman Miller Inc.

An April 3, 2000, *Business Week* article by David Rocks reported that **Herman Miller Inc.** has reduced the time it takes to build and deliver a furniture order by more than a week and boosted on-time shipments from about 75% (five years ago) to nearly 98% in 2000. They have inventory turns of 27 per year; furniture selection and layout can be processed at a client's office in two hours rather than the weeks other furniture makers require. Finally, order entry errors have been slashed to almost nothing from more than 20% resulting in a large drop in faulty shipments. Measuring business performance on the multiple dimensions described above for **Herman Miller** is consistent with the balanced scorecard approach illustrated in this chapter.

One of the reasons **Herman Miller** was able to achieve these significant improvements is that the firm chose to increase its investment in information systems. The company's $500 million investment in technology allows customers, dealers, salespeople, logistics personnel, and workers on the shop floor to communicate about orders. However, the decision to undertake the needed extensive capital investment in new technology was a challenging undertaking. Analyzing and choosing capital investments are some of the most important decisions made by management. The tools described in the next chapter are useful for assessing proposed capital investments.

## SUMMARY OF LEARNING OBJECTIVES

**LO 1**

**Explain the importance of incentive systems for motivating performance.**

Employees may have goals and objectives that differ from those of the organization. Incentive systems provide a tool that helps align employee goals with those of the organization by drawing attention to the organization's goals, by choosing to measure particular components of performance, and by rewarding employees for the actual outcomes associated with those components of performance being measured.

**LO 2**

**Use the DuPont system to evaluate business performance.**

The DuPont system measures return on investment (ROI) by dividing the operating earnings of a product line or division by the average invested capital used in that product line or division. ROI can be broken into two components, return on sales and capital turnover. Return on sales is computed by dividing the operating income by the total sales for the particular business segment or product line. It tells managers the amount of earnings generated from one dollar of sales. Capital turnover is a measure created by dividing sales by the average invested capital to generate those sales. Capital turnover tells managers the amount of sales generated by a dollar of invested capital.

**LO 3**

**Identify and explain the criticisms of using return on investment (ROI) as the only performance measure.**

Return on investment provides a systematic method for evaluating a product line or business segment. It is a percent that can be used to compare financial performance across products and/or business segments. ROI can be broken into its component parts to further analyze business performance. Criticisms of ROI include that it motivates short-term decision making, that managers choose to underinvest in projects with acceptable ROIs from the firm's perspective, that it is difficult to match invested capital with sales and operating earnings, and that ROI focuses only on financial measures and ignores other important components of the value chain.

**LO 4**

**Calculate and explain residual income (RI) and economic value added (EVA).**

Residual income is the amount by which operating earnings exceed a minimum acceptable return on the average invested capital. Economic value added is a refinement of the residual in-

come measure that makes many adjustments for items such as taxes, interest, and amortization. Like RI, EVA does not motivate managers to turn down investments expected to earn a return below their current ROI, but above the minimum acceptable return to the firm.

**LO 5**

**Use the balanced scorecard to identify, evaluate, and reward business performance.**

The balanced scorecard uses four lenses to consider business performance. These lenses provide financial, business process, customer, and learning and growth perspectives. Each of these perspectives helps to identify goals, strategies to achieve the goals, and measures to assess goal achievement.

**LO 6**

**Identify and explain the components of management compensation and the trade-offs that compensation designers make.**

In creating management compensation plans designers consider multiple characteristics such as fixed salary versus bonuses and the types of bonuses (cash, stock, or stock options). In addition, there are numerous design trade-offs that include choosing the time horizon over which compensation is available, choosing to emphasize local versus global performance, or choosing a cooperative or a competitive incentive scheme.

The focus of this chapter is rewarding business performance using incentive compensation systems to motivate decision makers to align their goals and objectives with the organization's. We discussed how the DuPont ROI system measures financial performance and why some critics think ROI is flawed. We saw how RI and EVA can correct some of the criticisms of ROI. The balanced scorecard is a broader means for directing, measuring and rewarding business performance. Finally, we described the components of and design choices for management compensation. In the remaining chapter we discuss capital budgeting tools. These are financial tools that managers use to decide which major investments to undertake.

## KEY TERMS INTRODUCED OR EMPHASIZED IN CHAPTER 24

**balanced scorecard** (p. 998) A system for performance measurement that links a company's strategy to specific goals, measures that assess progress toward those goals, and specific initiatives to achieve those goals. This systematic business performance measurement process integrates objectives across four business lenses to achieve the organization's strategic goals.

**business process perspective** (p. 1000) The balanced scorecard lens through which internal business processes, supplier relations, and distributor relations are strategically analyzed and evaluated.

**capital turnover** (p. 992) A measure created by dividing sales by the average invested capital to generate those sales. Capital turnover tells managers the amount of sales generated by a dollar of invested capital.

**customer perspective** (p. 999) The balanced scorecard lens through which organizations analyze and measure their customers' needs, expectations, and outcomes that will lead to business success.

**DuPont system of performance measurement** (p. 992) A method that analyzes business performance by considering both the earnings per sales dollar and the investment used to generate those sales dollars.

**economic value added (EVA)** (p. 997) A specific type of residual income that is computed by multiplying the after-tax weighted average cost of capital by total assets minus current liabilities and subtracting that product from the after-tax operating income.

**financial perspective** (p. 998) The balanced scorecard lens that managers and shareholders (or other financial stakeholders) use to view the organization's business performance.

**learning and growth perspective** (p. 1000) The balanced scorecard lens that focuses on the people, information systems, and organizational procedures in place for organizational learning and growth.

**residual income (RI)** (p. 996) The amount by which operating earnings exceed a minimum acceptable return on the average invested capital. The minimum rate of return represents the opportunity cost of using the invested capital.

**return on investment (ROI)** (p. 992) The operating income divided by the average invested capital associated with the generation of that income.

**return on sales (ROS)** (p. 992) Computed by dividing the operating income by the total sales for the particular business segment or product line. It tells managers the amount of earnings generated from one dollar of sales.

**stock options** (p. 1002) An employee receives the right to purchase a prespecified number of shares at a prespecified price within a certain future time period. Options provide incentives for managers to increase stock prices.

**value chain** (p. 998) The set of activities necessary to create and distribute a desirable product or service to a customer.

## DEMONSTRATION PROBLEM

The Bergly Automart is a full-service auto dealer with three divisions: the New Car, Used Car, and Service divisions. Budget information for the coming year for these three divisions is shown below. Each division manager's annual evaluation and bonus is based on divisional ROI.

The manager of the New Car Division complains that one reason the sales and resulting earnings for the New Car Division are not higher is because of the reputation of the Service Division. Because the Service Division does not have the most recent equipment (e.g., a new hydraulic lift) customers buy their new cars from a competitor on the other side of town that has a service department with new equipment, including new lifts that make their service quicker and better. The manager of the New Car Division has requested that other evaluation techniques be considered such as residual income or a balanced scorecard approach that might resolve this problem.

| Bergly Automart | | | |
| --- | --- | --- | --- |
| | New Car | Used Car | Service |
| Average investment | $ 5,000,000 | $1,000,000 | $500,000 |
| Sales revenue | 10,000,000 | 5,000,000 | 600,000 |
| Cost of goods sold | 8,750,000 | 4,000,000 | 300,000 |
| Operating expenses | 750,000 | 800,000 | 175,000 |
| Operating earnings | 500,000 | 200,000 | 125,000 |

### Instructions

**a.** Compute the ROI for each of the divisions and the entire company. Use the DuPont method to analyze their return on sales and capital turnover.

**b.** Assume the Service Division is considering installing a new hydraulic lift. Upon investigating, the manager of the division finds that the lift would add $100,000 to the division's average invested capital and that the Service Division's operating earnings would increase by $20,000 per year.

1. What is the ROI of the investment in the new hydraulic lift?
2. What impact does the investment in the hydraulic lift have on the Service Division's ROI?
3. What is the impact on Bergly Automart's overall ROI?
4. Would the manager of the Service Division be motivated to undertake such an investment?

c. Compute the residual income for each division if the minimum required rate of return for Bergly Automart is 15%. Would the Service Division purchase the hydraulic lift if the performance evaluation were based on the division's residual income and a 10% bonus of residual income were awarded? Show calculations to support your answer.

d. What measures might be appropriate for Bergly Automart to use for its divisions it uses if a balanced scorecard to evaluate and reward the division managers?

## Solution to the Demonstration Problem

a.

| | Bergly Automart | | |
|---|---|---|---|
| Divisions | ROI | Return on Sales | Capital Turnover |
| New Car ......... | $500,000 ÷ $5,000,000 = 10% | $500,000 ÷ $10,000,000 = 5% | $10,000,000 ÷ $5,000,000 = 200% |
| Used Car ........ | $200,000 ÷ $1,000,000 = 20% | $200,000 ÷ $ 5,000,000 = 4% | $ 5,000,000 ÷ $1,000,000 = 500% |
| Service .......... | $125,000 ÷ $ 500,000 = 25% | $125,000 ÷ $ 600,000 = 20.8% | $ 600,000 ÷ $ 500,000 = 120% |
| Bergly ........... | $825,000 ÷ $6,500,000 = 12.7% | $825,000 ÷ $15,600,000 = 5.3% | $15,600,000 ÷ $6,500,000 = 240% |

Return on sales is much lower for the New Car and Used Car divisions than for the Service Division reflecting the small markups typical for new and used car sales. To offset the lower return on sales, the capital turnover for both new and used cars is higher.

b. 1. ROI of the hydraulic lift = $20,000 ÷ $100,000 = 20%
2. Impact of the lift on the Service Division's ROI: ($125,000 + $20,000) ÷ ($500,000 + $100,000) = 24%
3. Impact on the Bergly Automart ROI:
($500,000 + $200,000 + $125,000 + $20,000) ÷
($5,000,000 + $1,000,000 + $500,000 + $100,000) = 12.8%
4. Because adding the new lift will lower the Service Division's ROI and presumably lower the bonus received by the Service Division manager, the division manager will not purchase the new lift even though it improves the Bergly Automart's ROI.

c.

| Divisions | Residual Income without Lift | Bonus |
|---|---|---|
| New Car ..................... | $500,000 − .15 × ($5,000,000) = ($250,000) | −0− |
| Used Car ................... | $200,000 − .15 × ($1,000,000) = $ 50,000 | $5,000 |
| Service .................... | $125,000 − .15 × ($ 500,000) = $ 50,000 | $5,000 |

Service Division residual income after purchasing the lift:

$$\$145,000 - .15 \times (\$600,000) = \$55,000.$$

The Service Division manager's bonus would increase to $5,500 and thus the manager would purchase the lift.

d. Many answers are possible, for example:

| Division | Financial | Business Process | Customer | Learning and Growth |
|---|---|---|---|---|
| **New Car** | Residual income of both division and company. | • Number of customers processed. | • Customer satisfaction. <br>• Number of retained customers. | • Sales seminars attended. <br>• Accessibility and use of knowledge of new car models. |
| **Used Car** | Residual income of both division and company. | • Number of used cars acquired. <br>• Number of customers processed. | • Customer satisfaction. <br>• Number of retained customers. | • Sales seminars attended. <br>• Information on used car market gathered. |
| **Service** | Residual income of both division and company. | • Efficiency of services performed. <br>• Number of cars to be serviced in process. <br>• Number of reworks. | • Number of complaints. <br>• Customer satisfaction. <br>• Lost customers. | • Service training time. |

# SELF-TEST QUESTIONS

*Answers to these questions appear on page 1016.*

1. Which of the following are not part of the components of the DuPont system for measuring and evaluating business performance?
   a. Return on sales.
   b. Residual income.
   c. Return on investment.
   d. Capital turnover.
   e. Number of patents.

2. Premo Pens is a division of InCommunicato, Inc. Premo generates annual revenue of $162,000, operating earnings of $55,000, and average assets of $400,000. InComunicato expects its divisions to earn a minimum required return of 12%. Which of the following does not represent either return on sales, residual income, or return on investment for Premo Pens?
   a. 13.75%.
   b. $7,000.
   c. 34%.
   d. 40.5%.
   e. $9,000.

3. Criticisms of return on investment as the only performance measure include:
   a. ROI focuses on short-term decisions.
   b. ROI is focused on only one component of the value chain.
   c. Managers evaluated based only on ROI are sometimes motivated not to make an investment that is in the best interest of the organization as a whole.
   d. All of the above.

4. Which of the following is not represented in the balanced scorecard?
   a. A learning and growth perspective.
   b. The internal business processes perspective.

    **c.** The government's perspective.

    **d.** The customers' perspective.

    **e.** The financial perspective.

5. Which of the following is not likely to be included in the typical components of management compensation?

    **a.** Company stock options.

    **b.** Cash bonuses.

    **c.** Free meals.

    **d.** Fixed salary.

    **e.** Company stock.

## ASSIGNMENT MATERIAL

## DISCUSSION QUESTIONS

1. Identify three ways that accounting systems help align the goals of employees and the goals of the organization.

2. Describe the main components of return on investment (ROI).

3. Suppose you are interested in opening a new restaurant in your area. What specific activities would you identify as goals for your restaurant?

4. What activities would make up the learning and growth component of the balanced scorecard for a large public accounting firm?

5. Distinguish between the four lenses of the balanced scorecard and provide an example of a business measure for each category for a family-owned grocery store.

6. Assume you are the manager of the finished goods warehouse of a computer manufacturer. Which business measures might help the company achieve its balanced scorecard goals?

7. What is the objective of calculating residual income?

8. What are some problems that companies have encountered in using the balanced scorecard?

9. How does the calculation of EVA differ from ROI?

10. Briefly explain the main components of management compensation.

11. Why is residual income suggested as an improvement over ROI for business measurement?

12. In designing a compensation plan for the manager of the international operations of **Tootsie Roll Industries**, what trade-offs should the company board of directors consider?

13. How would you expect the components of return on investment to be different for a mostly Internet-based retailer compared to a more traditional brick-and-mortar retailer (e.g., **Amazon.com** versus **Barnes & Noble**)?

14. Under which circumstances is a fixed salary preferable to a pure bonus compensation system?

15. Marsha's pet store employs six employees. Their duties are to sell pets, replenish the stock, keep the pets' cages clean, feed the pets, and maintain good records. Marsha pays a fixed hourly rate and a commission on sales of pets. Lately Marsha has been finding that the records have not been maintained and the stock has not been replenished. However, pet sales are good and the pets' cages are clean. How might Marsha's reward structure motivate the employees to pay more attention to the pets than to other duties?

## EXERCISES

Listed below are eight terms introduced or emphasized in this chapter:

| | |
|---|---|
| Residual income | Balanced scorecard |
| Management compensation | Return on investment |
| Return on sales | Stock options |
| Business process lens | Capital turnover |

**EXERCISE 24.1**

Accounting Terminology

**LO 2–6**

Each of the following statements may (or may not) describe one of these terms. For each statement, indicate the term described, or answer "none" if the statement does not correctly describe any of these terms.

**a.** Tells managers the incremental operating earnings for each additional sales dollar.

**b.** The focus of this business performance measurement is the sales dollars earned from each invested dollar.

**c.** A tool used by managers and owners of organizations to align manager's goals with the organization's goals.

**d.** This method considers all costs borne by the consumer from purchase to disposal of a product.

**e.** A business performance measurement that takes into account the minimum required return on the assets employed.

**f.** Measures for this category of business performance are associated with eliminating non-value-added costs from the value chain.

**g.** A method in which a product's selling price is determined by adding a fixed amount to the product's current production cost.

**h.** This performance evaluation method is criticized for motivating managers, in some instances, to ignore investments that are in the best interest of the company as a whole.

**i.** An important aspect of this method is the consideration of the many perspectives of the multiple stakeholders in an organization.

**EXERCISE 24.2**

Balanced Scorecard Activities

Assume you have just been hired as the management accountant in charge of providing your firm's managers with product information. What activities might you undertake if you were participating in the design of a balanced scorecard?

**EXERCISE 24.3**

Employee Motivation

A recent *Wall Street Journal* Quiz was about the impact of technology at the office.[3] Quiz respondents were requested to say whether a specific activity was unethical. Forty-nine percent of respondents said that using office technology for playing games at work is unethical and 54% said that shopping on the Internet at work is unethical. Which performance evaluation and incentive systems would encourage or discourage these behaviors?

**EXERCISE 24.4**

ROI versus EVA measures

**LO 2–4**

The Sapsora Company uses ROI to measure the performance of its operating divisions and to reward division managers. A summary of the annual reports from two divisions is shown below. The company's weighted average cost of capital is 15%.

| | Division A | Division B |
| --- | --- | --- |
| Total assets . . . . . . . . . . . . . . . . . . . . . . . . . . . . . . . . . . . . . | $5,600,000 | $9,200,000 |
| Current liabilities . . . . . . . . . . . . . . . . . . . . . . . . . . . . . . . . . . . | 800,000 | 1,200,000 |
| After-tax operating income . . . . . . . . . . . . . . . . . . . . . . . . . . . . | 960,000 | 1,440,000 |
| ROI . . . . . . . . . . . . . . . . . . . . . . . . . . . . . . . . . . . . . . . . . . . . | 20% | 18% |

**a.** Which division is more profitable?

**b.** Would EVA more clearly show the relative contribution of the two divisions to the company as a whole? Show the computations.

**c.** Suppose the manager of Division A was offered a one-year project that would increase his investment base by $100,000 and show a profit of $17,000. Would the manager choose to invest in the new project?

---

[3]Source: *The Wall Street Journal*, October 21, 1999, page B1.

An investment center in the Shellforth Corporation was asked to identify three proposals for its capital budget. Details of those proposals are:

**EXERCISE 24.5**

Performance and ROI versus Residual Income

**LO 2–4**

|  | Capital Budget Proposals | | |
|---|---|---|---|
|  | **A** | **B** | **C** |
| Capital required ................................... | $95,000 | $40,000 | $75,000 |
| Annual operating return .............................. | 23,000 | 10,000 | 10,500 |

Shellforth uses residual income to evaluate all capital budgeting projects. Its minimum required return is 15%.

**a.** Assume you are the investment center manager. Which project do you prefer? Why?

**b.** Assume your investment center's current ROI is 20% and that the president of Shellforth is thinking about using ROI for investment center evaluation. Would your preferences for the projects listed above change? Why?

Jennifer Baskiter is president and CEO of Plants&More.com, an Internet company that sells plants and flowers. The success of her start-up Internet company has motivated her to expand and create two divisions. One division focuses on sales to the general public and the other focuses on business-to-business sales to hotels, restaurants, and other firms that want plants and flowers for their businesses. She is considering using return on investment as a means of evaluating her divisions and their managers. She has hired you as a compensation consultant. What issues or concerns would you raise regarding the use of ROI for evaluating the divisions and their managers?

**EXERCISE 24.6**

Concerns about ROI

**LO 2, 3**

You are the manager of the Midwest Region, a 27-restaurant division that is part of the chain "Bites and Bits." The restaurants offer casual dining and compete with such chains in your region as **Olive Garden** and **Chi Chi's**. You receive an annual cash bonus of 5% of sales when residual income in your region exceeds the required minimum return on invested capital of 15%. You are using a similar performance evaluation scheme to reward each of the managers in your 27 restaurants.

You are concerned that important performance variables are being overlooked. For example, you have heard complaints from other regions and in your own region that the quality of the food is bad, it is difficult to retain serving staff in the restaurants, and finding a good chef is very difficult. At an upcoming planning meeting for all regional directors, the agenda includes considering the business performance evaluation and compensation plan. What could you say about the current compensation plan and what would you propose to remedy the problems?

**EXERCISE 24.7**

Compensation Choices

**LO 1, 5, 6**

# PROBLEMS

The Empire Hotel is a full-service hotel in a large city. Empire is organized into three departments that are treated as investment centers. Budget information for the coming year for these three departments is shown below. The managers of each of the departments are evaluated and bonuses are awarded each year based on ROI.

**PROBLEM 24.1**

Empire Hotel

**LO 2–4**

| Empire Hotel | | | |
|---|---|---|---|
|  | **Hotel Rooms** | **Restaurants** | **Health Club–Spa** |
| Average investment ................ | $ 8,000,000 | $5,000,000 | $1,000,000 |
| Sales revenue .................... | 10,000,000 | 2,000,000 | 600,000 |
| Operating expenses .............. | 8,500,000 | 1,250,000 | 450,000 |
| Operating earnings .............. | 1,500,000 | 750,000 | 150,000 |

### Instructions

**a.** Compute the ROI for each department. Use the DuPont method to analyze the return on sales and capital turnover.

**b.** Assume the Health Club–Spa is considering installing new exercise equipment. Upon investigating, the manager of the division finds that the equipment would cost $50,000 and that sales revenue would increase by $8,000 per year as a result of the new equipment. What is the ROI of the investment in the new exercise equipment? What impact does the investment in the exercise equipment have on the Health Club–Spa's ROI? Would the manager of the Health Club–Spa be motivated to undertake such an investment?

**c.** Compute the residual income for each department if the minimum required return for the Empire Hotel is 17%. What would be the impact of the investment in (b) on the Health Club–Spa's residual income?

---

**PROBLEM 24.2**

Empire Hotel and Balanced Scorecard

Consider the Empire Hotel discussed in Problem 24.1. The manager of the Restaurants Department complains that sales and resulting earnings for the restaurants are not higher due to the poor reputation of the Hotel Rooms Department. Because the Hotel Rooms Department does not have the best housekeeping staff, the overall reputation of the hotel is slipping. The manager of the Hotel Rooms Department counters that to keep operating expenses under control and improve ROI, wages for housekeeping have been cut. The manager of the Restaurant Department has requested that other evaluation techniques be considered such as residual income or a balanced scorecard approach that might resolve this problem.

### Instructions

Consider which balanced scorecard measures might be useful to the Empire Hotel in evaluating the Hotel Rooms Department. In doing so, identify:

**a.** The organizational goal that the measure is designed to support.

**b.** The employee resources and efforts that will be affected by the measurement.

**c.** How the employees should receive feedback and be rewarded for progress toward achieving the goals.

---

**PROBLEM 24.3**

Evaluating Business Unit Performance

The manager of Watson Cosmetic's Perfume Division is evaluated on her division's return on investment and residual income. The company requires that all divisions generate a minimum return on invested assets of 8%. Consistent failure to achieve this minimum target is grounds for the dismissal of a division manager. The annual bonus paid to division managers is 1% of residual income in excess of $100,000. The Perfume Division's operating margin for the year was $9 million, during which time its average invested capital was $60 million.

### Instructions

**a.** Compute the Perfume Division's return on investment and residual income.

**b.** Will the manager of the Perfume Division receive a bonus for her performance? If so, how much will it be?

**c.** In reporting her investment center's performance for the past 10 years, the manager of the Perfume Division accounted for the depreciation of her division's assets by using an accelerated depreciation method allowed for tax purposes. As a result, virtually all of the assets under her control are fully depreciated. Given that the company's other division managers use straight-line depreciation, is her use of an accelerated method ethical? Defend your answer.

---

**PROBLEM 24.4**

**Tootsie Roll Industries'**
Segment Performance Evaluation

Use the **Tootsie Roll Industries, Inc.** Annual Report in Appendix A at the end of this textbook to compute the following business segment performance measures.

### Instructions

**a.** Use note 11, "Geographic Area and Sales Information," to compute the ROI of the two major business segments of **Tootsie Roll Industries, Inc.** Use net earnings and net assets to compute ROI. Compare the performance of the two segments.

**b.** Analyze the ROI computations in part **a** by using the DuPont method to calculate return on sales and capital turnover. Compare your results to part **a**'s ROI results. What conclusions can you draw?

**c.** Read the "To Our Shareholders" part of the annual report. Consider the headings used for the different sections. Classify those headings using the four lenses of the balanced scorecard.

Bob Banker is the manager of one location of the Fastwhere Inc. chain, which is a delivery service. Banker's location is currently earning an ROI of 14% on existing average capital of $750,000. The minimum required return for Fastwhere Inc. is 12%. Banker is considering several additional investment projects, which are independent of existing operations and are independent of each other. The following table lists the projects:

| Project | Required Capital | ROI |
|---|---|---|
| A–1 | $150,000 | 14.1% |
| A–2 | 300,000 | 20 |
| A–3 | 250,000 | 13.5 |
| A–4 | 400,000 | 12.5 |
| A–5 | 500,000 | 9.8 |

**PROBLEM 24.5**
ROI and Residual Income at Fastwhere Inc.
**LO 2–4**

### Instructions

**a.** Which of the above projects would Banker choose for investment if his objective is to maximize his location's ROI?

**b.** Which projects increase the value of Fastwhere Inc.?

**c.** Which projects have a negative residual income?

**d.** Create two rankings for the projects in the order of acceptability if Banker is evaluated (1) on ROI and then (2) on residual income.

**e.** Based on the projects in the list explain why underinvestment is a problem when using ROI for evaluation purposes.

Joyce Biginskor, manages the Assembly Department at Valance Autoparts, a part supplier to large auto companies. Valance has recently adopted a balanced scorecard for the entire company. As a result, the plant manager for each production facility has a set of strategic goals, measurements, and rewards designed to motivate employees to achieve the company's overall goals.

The plant manager has implemented the balanced scorecard throughout each department. The balanced scorecard measures that specifically apply to the Assembly Department are primarily related to business process measures and learning and growth measures. In particular, the assembly line and related employees supervised by Biginskor are evaluated on efficiency measures and learning and growth measures. The learning and growth measures are employee absenteeism, retention, and satisfaction. Operating efficiencies are measured by cycle time, amount of work-in-process inventory, hours of machine downtime, number of defects, cost of rework, and productivity per employee. Biginskor obtains a monthly cash bonus if she can increase the learning and growth measures and reduce inefficiencies in the operations.

During the first year that the balanced scorecard was used at Valance, Biginskor did not earn a bonus. She has been particularly frustrated because whenever she reduces the work in process inventory on the shop floor, cycle time increases. When she reduces the hours of machine downtime, the defects increase and employee satisfaction decreases.

The plant manager decides to hire your consulting firm, Consultants Incorporated, to help evaluate the new balanced scorecard performance measurement and compensation scheme.

**PROBLEM 24.6**
Balanced Scorecard in the Assembly Department
**LO 5, 6**

### Instructions

Choose a partner to round out your consulting team and write a memo to the plant manager that explains the problems the manager is encountering in the Assembly Department. In the report identify with bullet points the problems that she is having with the balanced scorecard system and provide suggestions to the plant manager to help remedy the problems.

## CASES AND UNSTRUCTURED PROBLEMS

**CASE 24.1**

Business Performance and
Transfer Prices

**LO 2, 3, 4, 6**

Wolfe Computer manufactures computers and peripheral equipment. The following data relate to Wolfe's Printer Division for the year just ended:

| | |
|---|---:|
| Contribution margin | $11,000,000 |
| Operating margin | 6,000,000 |
| Average total assets | 50,000,000 |

The Printer Division is evaluated as an investment center. Wolfe expects all of its investment centers to earn a minimum annual return of 10% on average invested capital. Division managers receive a bonus equal to 1% of their division's residual income.

The Printer Division's most popular product is a color printer called the XLC. The division has the capacity to manufacture 30,000 XLCs per year, at a manufacturing cost of $100 per unit. Last year it produced XLCs at full capacity; 25,000 of these printers were sold to independent computer stores for $250 per unit, and the other 5,000 were transferred to Wolfe's Mail-Order Division, which sells them for $300 per unit. Transfers of inventory among units of Wolfe computer are recorded in the company's accounting records at cost.

As Wolfe's new controller, you are attending a planning meeting of division managers. Kay Green, manager of the Mail-Order Division, has asked for 15,000 XLCs in the coming year. She states, "Net income will increase if the Mail-Order Division sells more XLCs. After all, we get the highest sales price."

David Lee, manager of the Printer Division replies, "Sorry Kay, we can't do that. Just look at last year—if we'd supplied you with 15,000 XLCs, we wouldn't have made minimum ROI."

### Instructions

**a.** Compute the Printer Division's ROI and residual income based on last year's data.

**b.** Evaluate the statements made by Green and Lee. (Show how supplying 15,000 XLCs to Mail-Order would have affected the Printer Division's ROI for last year.)

**c.** Offer suggestions to resolve this situation. Show how your suggestions would have affected the Printer Division's results last year if they had been in effect then.

**d.** Do you think that your comments in part **c** might raise an ethical dilemma to be resolved by Wolfe's top management? If so, explain the nature of this potential problem and your personal recommendations about how to resolve it. (*Hint:* Expect to hear from Lee before the day is over.)

## *BUSINESS WEEK* ASSIGNMENT                                    BusinessWeek

**CASE 24.2**

Technology and ROI

**LO 1, 2, 5**

In the article, "Return to Spender," in the January 31, 2000, *Business Week,* Dennis Berman advises using ROI as a means of evaluating technology. He says

> To get the most out of the ROI numbers, you may want to try an incremental tech-spending approach: paying piecemeal for small, self-contained units that are part of a bigger project. Monitoring the ROI on each piece gives you more control over budgets that threaten to spin out of control.

To demonstrate how to use ROI for technology, Berman provided the following example:

> You're contemplating spending $105,000 over the next three years on a local-area network upgrade for 30 employees. How do you know you'll get your money's worth? One way is to calculate a return-on-investment ratio. [The following] figures reflect expenses and benefits over a three-year period:

**Investment:**

$24,000 **Hardware acquisition**—New network routers, servers, wiring

14,000 **Software acquisition**—Software licenses, antivirus protection

8,000 **Installation**—Four-day project, including removal of old network

3,000 **Training**—Week of on-site training, computer tutorials

35,000 **Support**—Three-year maintenance contract, cost of downtime, and data loss

21,000 **Maintenance**—Cost of network transition, hardware/software updates, disaster recovery costs

20,000 **Futz factor**—Time wasted surfing Internet over new network connections

**Total: $125,000**

**Return:**

$ 60,000 **Labor**—Savings from cutting secretarial help by one-third total hours

15,000 **Materials**—Reduced costs of paper and photocopies

108,000 **Efficiency**—Eliminating time wasted by inefficient document sharing (5 hrs. per mo. per employee @ $20/hr. average wage)

72,000 **Increased Output**—Net profits based on using saved time for additional projects

**Total: $255,000**

**Net return on investment: 104%**

## Instructions

**a.** From the preceding list, identify which investments and returns you think would be difficult to measure. Explain why they would be difficult to measure.

**b.** If you were using a balanced scorecard, what other information would you collect to decide whether to purchase the technology upgrade?

## INTERNET ASSIGNMENT

To obtain a better understanding of economic value added, visit the website that outlines the EVA philosophy of **Stern Stewart & Company** at:

**INTERNET 24.1**

Stern Stewart's EVA

**LO 1, 4, 5**

**www.eva.com**

List the four Ms necessary to become an EVA company and define each one.

Search the Internet using the phrase "return on investment." Visit at least three sites that are generated by your search activities. Describe three business activities that are linked to ROI in the websites. Identify problems that might arise from evaluating these business activities.

**INTERNET 24.2**

Return on Investment

**LO 1–3**

*Internet sites are time and date sensitive. It is the purpose of these exercises to have you explore the Internet. You may need to use the Yahoo! search engine* http://www.yahoo.com *(or other favorite search engine) to find a company's current web address.*

## OUR COMMENTS ON THE "YOUR TURN" CASES

**As Cookware Division Manager (p. 994)** One way to increase return on sales is to increase operating earnings without decreasing sales revenue. Under these circumstances reducing cost of goods sold and/or operating expenses increases operating earnings. Cost of goods sold expenses are expenses related to producing the cookware. Direct labor, direct materials, and overhead items are included. Reducing the per unit cost of these inputs to the production process and maintaining the same level of sales will improve operating earnings.

In addition, decreasing operating expenses also increases operating earnings. Operating expenses include selling and administrative expenses. Finally, increasing sales revenue without impacting expenses will improve operating earnings. Charging a higher price for the cookware without reducing the volume of sales will improve the return on sales measure in Year 3.

**As Purchasing Department Manager (p. 1001)** The measures you suggest should be related to the vision and mission of the overall company. For example, if the company's strategy is to be the low-cost producer, then it is likely that the suppliers' prices will be an important measure. However, if the company's emphasis is on the quality of the products they produce then perhaps quality-related measures are most important. The important point is not to let the incentive system drive the choice of measures. The chosen measures must be consistent with the mission and vision of the company.

## ANSWERS TO SELF-TEST QUESTIONS

**1.** b, e     **2.** d, e     **3.** d     **4.** c     **5.** c

# Utease Corporation

The Utease Corporation has many production plants across the midwestern United States. A newly opened plant, the Bellingham plant, produces and sells one product. The plant is treated, for responsibility accounting purposes, as a profit center. The unit standard costs for a production unit, with overhead applied based on direct labor hours, are as follows:

| Manufacturing costs (per unit based on expected activity of 24,000 units or 36,000 direct labor hours): | |
| --- | --- |
| Direct materials (2 pounds at $20) ..................................... | $ 40.00 |
| Direct labor (1.5 hours at $90) ........................................ | 135.00 |
| Variable overhead (1.5 hours at $20) .................................. | 30.00 |
| Fixed overhead (1.5 hours at $30) ..................................... | 45.00 |
| Standard cost per unit ............................................... | $250.00 |
| | |
| Budgeted selling and administrative costs: | |
| Variable ............................................................ | $5 per unit |
| Fixed .............................................................. | $1,800,000 |
| | |
| Expected sales activity: 20,000 units at $425.00 per unit | |
| Desired ending inventories: 10% of sales | |

Assume this is the first year of operation for the Bellingham plant. During the year, the company had the following activity:

| | |
| --- | --- |
| Units produced ........................................... | 23,000 |
| Units sold ................................................ | 21,500 |
| Unit selling price ........................................ | $420 |
| Direct labor hours worked ............................... | 34,000 |
| Direct labor costs ....................................... | $3,094,000 |
| Direct materials purchased ............................... | 50,000 pounds |
| Direct materials costs ................................... | $1,000,000 |
| Direct materials used .................................... | 50,000 pounds |
| Actual fixed overhead .................................... | $1,080,000 |
| Actual variable overhead ................................. | $620,000 |
| Actual selling and administrative costs .................. | $2,000,000 |

In addition, all over- or underapplied overhead and all product cost variances are adjusted to cost of goods sold.

## Instructions
**a.** Prepare a production budget for the coming year based on the available standards, expected sales, and desired ending inventories.
**b.** Prepare a budgeted responsibility income statement for the Bellingham plant for the coming year.
**c.** Find the direct labor variances. Indicate if they are favorable or unfavorable and why they would be considered as such.

**d.** Find the direct materials variances (materials price variance and quantity variance).

**e.** Find the total over- or underapplied (both fixed and variable) overhead. Would cost of goods sold be a larger or smaller expense item after the adjustment for over- or underapplied overhead?

**f.** Calculate the actual plant operating profit for the year.

**g.** Explain the difference between the budgeted operating profit and the actual operating profit for the Bellingham plant for its first year of operation. What part of the difference do you believe is the plant manager's responsibility?

**h.** Assume Utease Corporation is planning to change its evaluation of business operations in all plants from the profit center format to the investment center format. If the average invested capital at the Bellingham plant is $8,950,000, compute the return on investment (ROI) for the first year of operation. Use the DuPont method of evaluation to compute the return on sales (ROS) and capital turnover for the plant.

**i.** Assume that under the investment center evaluation plan the plant manager will be awarded a bonus based on ROI. If the manager has the opportunity in the coming year to invest in new equipment for $500,000 that will generate incremental earnings of $75,000 per year, would the manager undertake the project? Why or why not? What other evaluation tools could Utease use for their plants that might be better?

**j.** The chief financial officer of Utease Corporation wants to include a charge in each investment center's income statement for corporatewide administrative expenses. Should the Bellingham plant manager's annual bonus be based on plant ROI after deducting the corporatewide administrative fee? Why or why not?

# CHAPTER

# 25

# CAPITAL BUDGETING

## Learning Objectives

*After studying this chapter, you should be able to:*

1. Explain the nature of capital investment decisions.

2. Identify nonfinancial factors in capital investment decisions.

3. Evaluate capital investment proposals using
   (a) payback period,
   (b) return on investment, and
   (c) discounted cash flows.

4. Discuss the relationship between net present value and an investor's required rate of return.

5. Explain the behavioral issues involved in capital budgeting and identify how companies try to control the capital budgeting process.

Permission granted by Caterpillar Inc.

In the 1890s Benjamin Holt and Daniel Best were experimenting with various forms of steam tractors that resulted in track-type tractors with the gasoline-powered engines of modern heavy-duty equipment. In 1925 the two separate companies founded by Holt and Best merged to form **Caterpillar Tractor Company** headquartered in Peoria, Illinois. **Caterpillar Inc.** is the world's largest manufacturer of construction and mining equipment, diesel and natural gas engines, and industrial gas turbines. **Caterpillar** sells products in 200 countries around the globe.

**Caterpillar** products and components are manufactured in 41 plants in the United States and 49 plants throughout the world (Australia, Belgium, Brazil, Canada, England, France, Germany, Hungary, India, Indonesia, Italy, Japan, Mexico, The Netherlands, Northern Ireland, People's Republic of China, Poland, Russia, South Africa, and Sweden). During the last five years **Caterpillar** introduced approximately 300 new or improved products such as the new skid steer loader pictured here.

● ● ●

The processes that companies use to make decisions about which new products to produce and where to locate new plants are complex. These processes include a careful evaluation of accounting-related financial information. **Caterpillar** uses a financial tool called capital budgeting to help decide which products to make and where to build a new plant. This chapter introduces the basic concepts of capital budgeting and gives you a sense of how management uses this financial tool to make operating decisions.

**Caterpillar Inc.** made large, irreversible capital investments in flexible manufacturing equipment in the early 1990s. The payoff for this capital investment did not begin to occur until the late 1990s. Significant risk was associated with its investment plans. In economic downturns, companies can reduce the number of employees. When the economy improves, they can hire more. However, disposing of or acquiring specially designed plant assets to accommodate economic changes is much more difficult and cannot be quickly accomplished.

## CAPITAL INVESTMENT DECISIONS

**LO 1**

Explain the nature of capital investment decisions.

One of the greatest challenges managers face is making capital investment decisions. The term **capital investment** refers broadly to large expenditures made to purchase plant assets, develop new product lines, or acquire subsidiary companies. Such decisions commit financial resources for large periods of time and are difficult, if not impossible, to reverse once the funds are invested. Thus companies stand to benefit from good capital investments (or suffer from poor ones) for many years.

The process of evaluating and prioritizing capital investment opportunities is called **capital budgeting**. Capital budgeting relies heavily on *estimates of future operating results*. These estimates often involve a considerable degree of uncertainty and should be evaluated accordingly. In addition, many *nonfinancial* factors are taken into consideration.

### Financial and Nonfinancial Considerations

Perhaps the most important financial consideration in capital budgeting is the expected effects on *future cash flows* and *future profitability*. But in some cases, nonfinancial considerations are the deciding factor.

**CASE IN POINT**

Many companies make environmental capital investments that are not measured against the financial requirements established for acceptable capital investments. For example, **Novartis**, a Swiss-based diversified company, produces a chemical additive used to increase the shelf life of a wide range of products. Several compounds used in producing this chemical have significant environmental, health, and safety implications, and **Novartis** makes significant capital expenditures to reduce related environmental exposure. **Novartis**'s accounting system is not able to capture the environmental cost associated with the manufacture of the chemical additive because those costs are disbursed throughout the reporting system. Thus a complete financial evaluation of associated environmental capital investments is not possible.

The following table provides a few more examples of capital investment proposals in which *nonfinancial* factors may be the primary consideration:

**LO 2**

Identify nonfinancial factors in capital investment decisions.

| Investment Proposal | Nonfinancial Considerations |
|---|---|
| Pollution control system | Environmental concerns |
| | Corporate image |
| New factory lighting | Better working conditions |
| | Product quality |
| Employee health club | Employee morale |
| | Healthier employees |
| Employee child care facility | Accommodate working parents |
| | Enhance scheduling flexibility |

We will now address three widely used methods of evaluating the *financial* aspects of capital investment proposals: payback period, return on average investment, and discounting future cash flows.

## Evaluating Capital Investment Proposals: An Illustration

To illustrate the application of capital budgeting techniques, we will evaluate two investments being considered by the Maine LobStars (commonly referred to as the Stars), a minor league baseball team from Portland, Maine. The first involves the purchase of 10 vending machines for the team's Portland stadium. The second involves the purchase of a new bus to replace the one currently in use.

The Stars' stadium currently has no concession stand for preparing and selling food during games. Steve Wilson, the team's owner, has received several bids for constructing a concession stand under the stadium bleachers. The low bid of $150,000 includes a 1,000-square-foot cement block building, equipped with cash registers, deep fryers, a grill, soda machines, and a walk-in freezer and cooler. Unfortunately, the most that the struggling organization is willing to invest for this purpose is $75,000.

Wilson recently received an alternative proposal from VendiCorp International. VendiCorp sells vending machines that dispense hot and cold sandwiches and drinks. The company has offered to sell 10 vending machines to the Stars for $75,000 ($7,500 each). While the machines are in use, VendiCorp is responsible for keeping them stocked with sandwiches and drinks. At the end of a five-year estimated life, VendiCorp will repurchase the machines for $5,000 ($500 each). VendiCorp will also provide the Stars with an insurance and maintenance contract costing $3,000 per year.

Estimates provided by VendiCorp indicate that the 10 machines will take in $1,875 per ball game. The Stars play 45 home games each season. Thus, the machines have the potential to generate annual revenue of $84,375 ($1,875 per game × 45 games). Of this amount, VendiCorp is to receive $50,625, representing the cost of goods sold (60% of sales). The Stars are required to reimburse VendiCorp only for those items that sell. The machines are expected to increase the Stars' net income by $10,000 per year, computed as follows:

**LO 3**

Evaluate capital investment proposals using (a) payback period, (b) return on investment, and (c) discounted cash flows.

| **Estimated Increases in Annual Revenue and Expenses from Vending Machines** | | |
|---|---|---|
| Increase in annual revenue from investment | | $84,375 |
| Less: Cost of goods sold (60% of sales paid to VendiCorp) | | 50,625 |
| Increase in annual gross profit (40% of sales) | | $33,750 |
| Less: Cost of maintenance & insurance contract | $ 3,000 | |
| Depreciation [($75,000 − $5,000) ÷ 5 years] | 14,000 | |
| Increase in utilities & miscellaneous costs | 350 | (17,350) |
| Increase in annual pretax income from investment | | $16,400 |
| Less: Additional income taxes (approximately 39%) | | 6,400 |
| Increase in annual net income from investment | | $10,000 |

*Calculating increase to income*

Most capital budgeting techniques involve analysis of the *annual net cash flows* pertaining to an investment. Annual net cash flows refer to the excess of cash receipts over cash disbursements in a given year. We may assume in our example that all of the vending machine revenue is received in cash, and that all expenses (other than depreciation) are immediately paid in cash. In other words, the *only difference* between net income and net cash flows relates to depreciation expense.

---

**CASH EFFECTS**    The annual net cash flows expected to be generated by the vending machines are $24,000, determined as follows:

| | |
|---|---:|
| Increase in annual net income from investment | $10,000 |
| Annual depreciation expense | 14,000 |
| Annual net cash flows from investment | $24,000 |

This computation reflects the fact that depreciation is a *noncash expense*. Thus the recognition of depreciation expense causes the annual net income from an investment to be *less* than the amount of the net annual cash flows.

---

In our example, the vending machines are expected to increase *both* net income and net cash flows. But the real question is whether these increases *are adequate to justify the required investment*. We will attempt to answer this question using three different capital budgeting techniques.

## Payback Period

The **payback period** is the length of time necessary to recover the entire cost of an investment from the resulting annual net cash flows. In our example, the payback period is computed as follows:

*Payback calculation*

$$\frac{\textbf{Amount to Be Invested}}{\textbf{Estimated Annual Net Cash Flows}} = \frac{\$75,000}{\$24,000} = 3.125 \textbf{ years}$$

In selecting among alternative investment opportunities, a short payback period is considered desirable because the more quickly an investment's cost is recovered, the sooner the funds may be put to other use. A short payback period also reduces the risk that changes in economic conditions will prevent full recovery of an investment.

However, the payback period should never be the only factor considered in a major capital budgeting decision because it ignores two important issues. First, it ignores the total profitability and cash flows anticipated over the *entire life* of an investment (in this case, five years). Second, it ignores the *timing* of the future cash flows. We will address this issue in greater depth later in the chapter.

## Return on Average Investment

The **return on average investment (ROI)** is the average annual net income from an investment expressed as a percentage of the *average* amount invested. The Stars will initially have to invest $75,000 to purchase 10 new vending machines. However, each year depreciation expense will reduce the carrying value of these machines by a total of $14,000. Because the annual net cash flow is expected to exceed net income by this amount, we may view depreciation expense as providing for the *recovery* of the amount originally invested. Thus the amount that the Stars will have invested in the equipment at any given time is represented by the carrying value of the vending machines (their cost less accumulated depreciation).

When straight-line depreciation is used, the carrying value of an asset decreases uniformly over the asset's life. Thus the average carrying value over the life of an asset is equal to the amount halfway between its original cost and its salvage value. If the salvage value is zero, the average carrying value (or average investment) is simply one-half of the asset's original cost.

Mathematically, the average amount invested over the life of an asset may be determined as follows:

$$\text{Average Investment} = \frac{\text{Original Cost} + \text{Salvage Value}}{2}$$

*Average investment calculation*

Thus, over the life of the 10 new vending machines, the Stars will have an average investment of ($75,000 + $5,000) ÷ 2, or *$40,000.* We may compute the expected return on average investment as follows:

$$\frac{\text{Average Estimated Net Income}}{\text{Average Investment}} = \frac{\$10,000}{\$40,000} = 25\%$$

*Return on average investment calculation*

In deciding whether 25% is a satisfactory rate of return, Wilson should consider such factors as the reliability of VendiCorp's forecasts of income and cash flows, the return available from other investment opportunities, and the Stars' cost of capital.[1] In comparing alternative investment opportunities, managers prefer the one with the *lowest risk,* the *highest rate of return,* and the *shortest payback period.*

The concept of return on investment shares a common weakness with the payback method. It fails to consider that the **present value** of an investment depends on the *timing* of its future cash flows. Cash flows received late in the life of an investment, for example, are of *less value* to an investor today than cash flows of equal amount received early in the life of an investment. The return on investment computation simply ignores the question of whether cash receipts will occur early or late in the life of an investment. It also fails to consider whether the purchase price of the investment must be paid in advance or in installments stretching over a period of years. *Discounting* future cash flows is a technique that does take into account cash flow timing issues.

---

At **Fields Devereaux Architects & Engineers**, the decision to provide their 55 employees with the ability to access the Internet could be made with the payback criterion. The decision to hook up to the Internet was easy to make because the yearly expected savings from reducing other forms of more costly communication—such as faxes, phone calls, messenger services, and overnight deliveries—was much higher than the initial hook-up costs. Thus payback was an adequate criterion because the time value of money was not a relevant issue.

**CASE IN POINT**

## Discounting Future Cash Flows

As explained in earlier chapters, the present value of a future cash flow is the amount that a knowledgeable investor would pay today for the right to receive that future amount. Arriving at a present value figure depends on (1) the amount of the future cash flow, (2) the length of time that the investor must wait to receive the cash flow, and (3) the rate of return required by the investor. *Discounting* is the process by which the present value of cash flows (the **discounted cash flows**) is determined.

The use of present value tables to discount future cash flows is demonstrated in Appendix B (at the end of this text). Those who are not familiar with the concept of present value or with present value tables should read the appendix before continuing with this chapter.

For your convenience, the two present value tables presented in the appendix are repeated on the following page. *Table 1* shows the present value of a *single lump-sum payment* of $1 to be received in *n* periods (years) in the future. *Table 2* shows the present value of a $1 *annuity*—that is, $1 to be received *each year* for *n* consecutive years. For illustrative purposes, both tables have been kept short. They include only selected discount rates and only extend for a limited number of periods. However, they contain the appropriate rates and periods for all of the problem material in this chapter.

---

[1] A firm's cost of capital refers to the cost of financing investments. In situations where an investment is entirely financed with debt, the cost of capital is the interest rate paid by the firm on borrowed funds. For investments that are financed all or in part with equity, the computation is more complex. Approaches for determining a firm's cost of capital are addressed in a corporate finance course.

## Table 1
### Present Values of $1 Due in *n* Periods*

| Number of Periods (*n*) | Discount Rate | | | | | | | | |
|---|---|---|---|---|---|---|---|---|---|
| | 1% | 1½% | 5% | 6% | 8% | 10% | 12% | 15% | 20% |
| 1 | .990 | .985 | .952 | .943 | .926 | .909 | .893 | .870 | .833 |
| 2 | .980 | .971 | .907 | .890 | .857 | .826 | .797 | .756 | .694 |
| 3 | .971 | .956 | .864 | .840 | .794 | .751 | .712 | .658 | .579 |
| 4 | .961 | .942 | .823 | .792 | .735 | .683 | .636 | .572 | .482 |
| 5 | .951 | .928 | .784 | .747 | .681 | .621 | .567 | .497 | .402 |
| 6 | .942 | .915 | .746 | .705 | .630 | .564 | .507 | .432 | .335 |
| 7 | .933 | .901 | .711 | .665 | .583 | .513 | .452 | .376 | .279 |
| 8 | .923 | .888 | .677 | .627 | .540 | .467 | .404 | .327 | .233 |
| 9 | .914 | .875 | .645 | .592 | .500 | .424 | .361 | .284 | .194 |
| 10 | .905 | .862 | .614 | .558 | .463 | .386 | .322 | .247 | .162 |
| 20 | .820 | .742 | .377 | .312 | .215 | .149 | .104 | .061 | .026 |
| 24 | .788 | .700 | .310 | .247 | .158 | .102 | .066 | .035 | .013 |
| 36 | .699 | .585 | .173 | .123 | .063 | .032 | .017 | .007 | .001 |

*The present value of $1 is computed by the formula $p = 1/(1 + i)^n$, where $p$ is the present value of $1, $i$ is the discount rate, and $n$ is the number of periods until the future cash flow will occur. Amounts in this table have been rounded to three decimal places and are shown for a limited number of periods and discount rates. Many calculators are programmed to use this formula and can compute present values when the future amount is entered along with values for $i$ and $n$.

## Table 2
### Present Values of $1 to Be Received Periodically for *n* Periods

| Number of Periods (*n*) | Discount Rate | | | | | | | | |
|---|---|---|---|---|---|---|---|---|---|
| | 1% | 1½% | 5% | 6% | 8% | 10% | 12% | 15% | 20% |
| 1 | 0.990 | 0.985 | 0.952 | 0.943 | 0.926 | 0.909 | 0.893 | 0.870 | 0.833 |
| 2 | 1.970 | 1.956 | 1.859 | 1.833 | 1.783 | 1.736 | 1.690 | 1.626 | 1.528 |
| 3 | 2.941 | 2.912 | 2.723 | 2.673 | 2.577 | 2.487 | 2.402 | 2.283 | 2.106 |
| 4 | 3.902 | 3.854 | 3.546 | 3.465 | 3.312 | 3.170 | 3.037 | 2.855 | 2.589 |
| 5 | 4.853 | 4.783 | 4.329 | 4.212 | 3.993 | 3.791 | 3.605 | 3.352 | 2.991 |
| 6 | 5.795 | 5.697 | 5.076 | 4.917 | 4.623 | 4.355 | 4.111 | 3.784 | 3.326 |
| 7 | 6.728 | 6.598 | 5.786 | 5.582 | 5.206 | 4.868 | 4.564 | 4.160 | 3.605 |
| 8 | 7.652 | 7.486 | 6.463 | 6.210 | 5.747 | 5.335 | 4.968 | 4.487 | 3.837 |
| 9 | 8.566 | 8.361 | 7.108 | 6.802 | 6.247 | 5.759 | 5.328 | 4.772 | 4.031 |
| 10 | 9.471 | 9.222 | 7.722 | 7.360 | 6.710 | 6.145 | 5.650 | 5.019 | 4.192 |
| 20 | 18.046 | 17.169 | 12.462 | 11.470 | 9.818 | 8.514 | 7.469 | 6.259 | 4.870 |
| 24 | 21.243 | 20.030 | 13.799 | 12.550 | 10.529 | 8.985 | 7.784 | 6.434 | 4.937 |
| 36 | 30.108 | 27.661 | 16.547 | 14.621 | 11.717 | 9.677 | 8.192 | 6.623 | 4.993 |

The **discount rate** may be viewed as an investor's *required rate of return*. The present value of an investment's future cash flows is the maximum amount that an investor should be willing to pay for the investment and still expect to earn the required rate of return. Therefore, an investment is considered desirable when its cost is less than the present value of its future cash flows. In such cases, the expected rate of return *exceeds* the rate of return required by the investor. Conversely, when the cost of an investment exceeds the present value of its future cash flows, its expected return is *less* than that required by the investor.

The higher the discount rate being used, the lower the resulting present value figure will be. Thus the *higher the required rate of return* for a particular investment, the *less* an investor will be willing to pay for the investment. The appropriate discount rate (or required rate of return) for determining the present value of a specific investment depends on the nature of the investment, the alternative investment opportunities available, and the investor's cost of capital.

The required rate of return is adjusted in many companies for a variety of strategic reasons. For example, management may allow a lower required rate of return when there is a strategic necessity to penetrate a new market or to acquire new technology. Also, for certain capital expenditures, such as new technology, estimating the cash flows and the timing of those cash flows can be extremely difficult. Managers know that establishing a high required rate of return will place projects with higher cash flows occurring in the more distant future at a disadvantage. With a high discount rate, projects with high net cash flows received several years in the future will have low net present values.

**MANAGEMENT STRATEGY**

Let us now apply the concept of discounting cash flows to our example. We shall assume that the Stars require a *15%* annual rate of return on all capital investments. The 10 vending machines are expected to generate annual net cash flows of $24,000 for five years. *Table 2* shows that the present value of $1 to be received annually for five years, discounted at 15%, is *3.352*. Therefore, the present value of $24,000 received annually for five years is $24,000 × 3.352, or *$80,448*.

In addition to these annual cash flows, Wilson expects that VendiCorp will repurchase the machines from the Stars at the end of five years for $5,000 (their salvage value). Referring to *Table 1*, we see that the present value of $1 to be received in five years, discounted at 15%, is *.497*. Thus the present value of $5,000 to be received at the end of five years is $5,000 × .497, or *$2,485*. We may now analyze the proposal to invest in the 10 vending machines in the following manner:

| | |
|---|---:|
| Present value of expected annual cash flows ($24,000 × 3.352) . . . . . . . . . . . . . . . . | $80,448 |
| Present value of proceeds from disposal ($5,000 × .497) . . . . . . . . . . . . . . . . . . . . | 2,485 |
| Total present value of investment's future cash flows . . . . . . . . . . . . . . . . . . . . . | $82,933 |
| Cost of investment (payable in advance) . . . . . . . . . . . . . . . . . . . . . . . . . . . . . | 75,000 |
| Net present value of proposed investment . . . . . . . . . . . . . . . . . . . . . . . . . . . . | $ 7,933 |

*Investment's net present value*

This analysis indicates that the present value of the vending machines' future cash flows, discounted at a rate of 15%, amounts to *$82,933*. This is the *maximum amount* that the Stars could invest in these machines and still expect to earn the required annual return of 15%. As the actual cost of the investment is only $75,000, the machines have the potential to earn a rate of return *in excess* of 15%.

The **net present value** of VendiCorp's proposal is the difference between the total present value of the net cash flows and the cost of the investment. If the net present value is equal to zero, the rate of return is equal to the discount rate. A *positive* net present value means that the investment is expected to provide a rate of return *greater* than the discount rate, whereas a *negative* net present value means that the investment is likely to yield a return *less* than the discount rate. In financial terms, proposals with a positive net present value are considered acceptable and those with a negative net present value are viewed as unacceptable. These relationships may be summarized as follows:

**LO 4**

Discuss the relationship between net present value and an investor's required rate of return.

| Net Present Value (NPV) | Interpretation |
|---|---|
| NPV > Zero | Return exceeds the discount rate. |
| NPV = Zero | Return is equal to the discount rate. |
| NPV < Zero | Return is less than the discount rate. |

Based on our cash flow analysis, purchase of the vending machines appears to be an acceptable proposal. However, there are numerous nonfinancial issues that might be considered before making a decision based *purely on the numbers.*

For instance, all of the revenue and expense estimates used in determining these financial measures were supplied by VendiCorp. It is entirely possible that these estimates may be overly optimistic. Furthermore, Wilson knows nothing about VendiCorp's business reputation. What assurances does he have that VendiCorp will honor its agreement to stock the machines with fresh merchandise before each game, maintain the machines when they break down, and repurchase the machines for $5,000 at the end of five years? Has Wilson obtained bids from other suppliers of vending machines? Or has he considered an arrangement with an outside catering service to provide concessions at the Stars' home ball games? Finally, perhaps there are unrelated investment opportunities to consider, such as investing in a new pitching machine, team uniforms, or new stadium seats.

**YOUR TURN**

**You as a Chief Financial Officer**

You are attending your first meeting with the management team for the Maine LobStars. Your job is to discuss planned capital budgeting projects to get management's approval. Management, including the owner, Steve Wilson, is accustomed to looking at payback period and return on average assets. However, you have also prepared net present value information for management's review. Steve Wilson complains that the net present value information is redundant and unnecessary. How will you respond?

*Our comments appear on page 1047.

## Replacing Assets

Many capital investment decisions involve the possible replacement of existing assets. Such decisions involve several decision-making techniques, including identifying *relevant information, incremental analysis,* and *discounting future cash flows.* Careful consideration also should be given to the *income tax effects* of the decision and to *nonfinancial factors.*

**Data for an Illustration**   To illustrate, assume the Maine LobStars own an old bus that transports the team from game to game. This old bus guzzles gas, frequently needs repair, has no air conditioning, and is cramped and uncomfortable. An opportunity arises to purchase another bus that, although used, is larger, in better condition, has air conditioning, and is more fuel efficient.

The following financial data relate to this capital investment proposal:

| | |
|---|---|
| Cost of new bus . . . . . . . . . . . . . . . . . . . . . . . . . . . . . . . . . . . . . . . . . . . . . . . | $65,000 |
| Book value of existing bus . . . . . . . . . . . . . . . . . . . . . . . . . . . . . . . . . . . . . . . . | 25,000 |
| Current sales value of existing bus . . . . . . . . . . . . . . . . . . . . . . . . . . . . . . . . . . | 10,000 |
| Estimated annual operating costs (gas, repairs, insurance): | |
| New bus . . . . . . . . . . . . . . . . . . . . . . . . . . . . . . . . . . . . . . . . . . . . . . . . . . . . . . . | 18,000 |
| Existing bus . . . . . . . . . . . . . . . . . . . . . . . . . . . . . . . . . . . . . . . . . . . . . . . . . . . . | 30,000 |

We will make a simplifying assumption that both buses have a remaining useful life of five years, with no salvage value.

Notice that the old bus has a book value of $25,000, but a current sales value of only $10,000. At first glance, the resulting *$15,000 loss* upon disposal appears to be an argument against replacing the old bus. But the cost of the old bus is a **sunk cost** and therefore is *not relevant* to the decision.

The current book value of the old bus is merely what remains of this sunk cost. If the old bus is sold, its book value is offset against the sales proceeds. But if the old bus is kept, its book value will be recognized as depreciation expense over the next five years. Thus the Stars *cannot avoid* recognizing this cost as expense (or loss) *regardless of which decision is made*. From a present-value standpoint, there actually is some *benefit* to recognizing this sunk cost as a loss in the current period because the related *income tax deduction* will occur now, rather than over the remaining life of the bus.

In deciding whether to replace the old bus, the Stars should determine the present value of the *incremental net cash flows* resulting from this action. This present value may be compared with the cost of the new bus to determine whether the proposal will provide the required rate of return.

**Determining the Present Value of Incremental Cash Flows**  To compute the incremental annual cash flows from acquiring the new bus, we must consider both the annual savings in operating costs and the difference in *annual income taxes*. The Stars' annual income taxes expense will be affected by purchasing the new bus because of the difference in annual operating expenses and in the annual deductions for depreciation. (To simplify our computations, we will assume the Stars use straight-line depreciation for tax purposes.)

The data on page 1028 show that the new bus is expected to produce a $12,000 annual savings in operating costs. However, annual depreciation on the new bus will be $13,000 ($65,000 ÷ 5 years), whereas annual depreciation on the old bus is only $5,000 ($25,000 ÷ 5 years). This $8,000 increase in depreciation expense means that purchasing the new bus will *increase taxable income* by $4,000 per year ($12,000 annual cost savings, less $8,000 in additional depreciation). Assuming a tax rate of 40%, purchase of the new bus will *increase annual income tax expense* by *$1,600* ($4,000 × 40%). Thus the incremental annual net cash flows from purchasing the new bus amount to *$10,400* ($12,000 savings in operating costs, less $1,600 in additional income taxes).

The Stars require a 15% return on capital investments. Referring to the annuity table on page 1026, we see that the present value of $1 received annually for five years is *3.352*. Therefore, the $10,400 received annually for five years, discounted at 15%, has a present value of *$34,861* ($10,400 × 3.352). In addition to the present value of the *annual* cash flows, however, we should consider two other factors: the $10,000 sales proceeds from the old bus, and the tax savings resulting from the loss on disposal.

The $10,000 proceeds from the sale will be received immediately and, therefore, have a present value of *$10,000.* The $15,000 loss on disposal results in a $6,000 tax savings at the end of the first year ($15,000 × 40%). The present value of $6,000 one year hence, discounted at 15%, is *$5,220* ($6,000 × .870), as determined from Table 1.

**Summary of Financial Considerations**  We now can determine the net present value of this proposal as follows:

| | |
|---|---:|
| Present value of incremental annual cash flows . . . . . . . . . . . . . . . . . . . . . . . . . . . . . | $ 34,861 |
| Present value of proceeds from sale of old bus . . . . . . . . . . . . . . . . . . . . . . . . . . . . | 10,000 |
| Present value of tax savings from loss on disposal . . . . . . . . . . . . . . . . . . . . . . . . | 5,220 |
| Total present value . . . . . . . . . . . . . . . . . . . . . . . . . . . . . . . . . . . . . . . . . . . | $ 50,081 |
| Less: Cost of new bus . . . . . . . . . . . . . . . . . . . . . . . . . . . . . . . . . . . . . . . . . . | 65,000 |
| Net present value . . . . . . . . . . . . . . . . . . . . . . . . . . . . . . . . . . . . . . . . . . . . . | $(14,919) |

Thus this proposal fails to provide the Stars with its required minimum return on capital investments of 15%. (***Question:*** What is the most that the Stars could pay for the new bus and earn a 15% return? ***Answer:*** $50,081, the present value of the cash flows, discounted at 15%.)

**YOUR TURN**

### You as a Transportation Manager

Assume you manage transportation for the LobStars. You have just seen the proposal for acquiring the new bus with its accompanying financial figures. You know that the operating costs for the new bus will not be $18,000 per year but will more likely be $8,000, $12,000, $20,000, $24,000, and $26,000 for years 1 through 5, respectively. Do you have an ethical responsibility to mention this fact, given that operating costs average $18,000 over five years [($8,000 + $12,000 + $20,000 + $24,000 + $26,000) ÷ 5 = $18,000]?

*Our comments appear on page 1047.

**Nonfinancial Considerations**   Just because a capital investment proposal fails to provide the desired rate of return does not necessarily mean that it should be rejected. On page 1022 of this chapter, we identified several types of capital investments likely to provide little or no financial return, but which management may consider worthwhile for other reasons.

Should the Stars buy the new bus? Probably so. Yes, they have to pay about $15,000 more than a price that provides the desired 15% return. But on the other hand, the team will travel in greater comfort and with *greater reliability* for a period of *five years*. (What would be the *opportunity cost* of missing a ball game because the old bus breaks down?) Actually, $15,000 seems a small price to pay for the nonfinancial benefits that the new bus is likely to provide.

Finally, has the team considered all of the available options? Surely, this isn't the only used bus for sale. And what would be the cost of chartering bus service, rather than owning their own bus?

**CASE IN POINT**

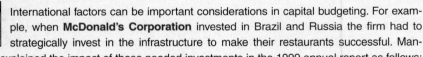

International factors can be important considerations in capital budgeting. For example, when **McDonald's Corporation** invested in Brazil and Russia the firm had to strategically invest in the infrastructure to make their restaurants successful. Management explained the impact of these needed investments in the 1999 annual report as follows: "It is also not surprising that the returns in emerging markets are lower than in established markets due to the substantial infrastructure investment required to support rapid restaurant growth."

## Behavioral Considerations in Capital Budgeting

**LO 5**

Explain the behavioral issues involved in capital budgeting and identify how companies try to control the capital budgeting process.

The accuracy of capital budgets is critically dependent on cash flows and project life-span estimates. However, the estimates created by employees involved in capital budgeting need careful consideration for two reasons. First, because the results of the capital budgeting process have serious implications for employees, their estimates may be overly pessimistic or optimistic. Second, capital budgeting involves estimates from many sources within and outside of the company; thus there are many opportunities for errors to creep into the process.

Pessimistic or optimistic estimates arise because employees are frequently evaluated on outcomes that clearly depend on the amount and type of capital investments the company chooses. For example, the manager of a profit center is likely to be paid a bonus based on the center's profits each quarter. Assume the profit center's profitability depends on the efficiency of currently operating equipment. In providing data for a capital investment proposal for new equipment, that profit center manager may be overly optimistic about the efficiency of the new equipment and overly pessimistic about the projected efficiency of the current equipment in order to persuade management to acquire new equipment.

Because choices among capital budgeting proposals determine future directions of the firm, careful evaluation and aggregation of data are critical. Most capital budgeting proposals require input from a variety of different individuals. For example, in the case of the LobStars bus decision, estimates of the sales prices of the new and old buses, the operating expenses of the new and old buses, and the lifespans of the new and old buses are likely to come from numerous sources within and outside of the organization. Operating expense information may come from the accountant, sales prices for old and new buses may be gathered from outside of the organization, and the lifespan estimates may come from the bus mechanic. The reliability of these estimates can be a critical factor in the final choices made among capital budget proposals.

Companies establish internal controls for the capital budgeting process to help guard against overly optimistic or pessimistic estimates and aggregation errors. Many companies use routing forms that require all upper-level managers to sign off on large capital budgeting proposals. Many companies use a finance department's expertise to review and complete analyses about the accuracy of estimates. The largest strategic capital investments ordinarily require approval by the board of directors.

In addition, many companies track capital budget projects as they are implemented. Managers compare the projected expenditures with the actual installation and operating costs to identify weaknesses in their planning processes. Capital budget planners, who know that a **capital budget audit** will be undertaken, will be less likely to be overly optimistic or pessimistic about their estimates. Just as you are careful about planning your expenditures from your checking account because you know the bank audits your balance, capital budget planners are more careful when they know an audit of their proposed investment expenditures will be undertaken.

## IN SUMMARY . . .

We now have discussed three methods of evaluating the *financial* aspects of capital investment opportunities. The financial consequences of capital investments are relevant—even if the business has little choice but to make the expenditure.

You probably noticed how much income taxes complicated our analysis of decisions about replacing assets. Income taxes *do* complicate business decisions—and in many situations, it is tax considerations that dictate the appropriate course of action. We urge *all* financial decision makers *always to consider the tax consequences* of their actions.

Don't forget that *nonfinancial* considerations drive many business decisions. Businesses must operate in a *socially responsible* manner, which often involves a sacrifice of profitability—especially in the short term. Remember also the concept of *opportunity costs*. There often is a better alternative awaiting discovery by those who are perceptive, innovative, and persistent.

Various agencies and departments of the federal government track capital investment activity very closely. For example, the Commerce Department's Bureau of Economic Analysis tracks business investment by category <www.bea.doc.gov>. The Federal Reserve Board tracks the change in output of business equipment.

**CASE IN POINT**

**A SECOND LOOK**

**Caterpillar Inc.**

As the world's largest provider of construction and mining equipment, **Caterpillar** makes extensive capital investments worldwide. To help manage the $26 billion in assets, **Caterpillar** managers use the net present value tools described in this chapter to help make capital budgeting decisions.

    **Caterpillar** is a company that exemplifies most of the accounting-related tools and techniques described in this textbook. It is publicly listed on the New York Stock Exchange and must comply with the financial reporting requirements discussed in Chapters 1 through 14. **Caterpillar** also uses most of the management accounting techniques discussed in Chapters 16 through 25. Chapter 15 describing global business and accounting is particularly relevant to **Caterpillar**. The opening vignette illustrates that **Caterpillar** is truly a global company.

## A CONCLUDING COMMENT FROM THE AUTHORS

We appreciate having the opportunity of addressing you through this text. It is indeed a privilege to share our views of accounting and business with so many students.

    The writing of this text has taught us much. All of us have had to challenge, research, verify, and rethink much of what we thought we already knew. We hope the experience of this course proves as rewarding to you.

## SUMMARY OF LEARNING OBJECTIVES

### LO 1

**Explain the nature of capital investment decisions.**
Capital investment decisions generally refer to projects or proposals that require the purchase of plant assets. These decisions are crucial to the long-run financial health of a business enterprise. Not only do they require that resources be committed for long periods of time, they are also difficult or impossible to reverse once funds have been invested and a project has begun.

### LO 2

**Identify nonfinancial factors in capital investment decisions.**
Nonfinancial factors may dictate the appropriate course of action. Such factors may include, for example, compliance with laws, corporate image, employee morale, and various aspects of social responsibility. Management must remain alert to such considerations.

### LO 3

**Evaluate capital investment proposals using (a) payback period, (b) return on investment, and (c) discounted cash flows.**
The payback period is the length of time needed to recover the cost of an investment from the resulting net cash flows. However, this type of investment analysis fails to consider the total life and overall profitability of the investment.

Return on average investment expresses the average estimated net income from the investment as a percentage of the average investment. This percentage represents the rate of return earned on the investment. A shortcoming is that average estimated net income ignores the timing of future cash flows. Therefore, no consideration is given to the time value of money.

Discounting future cash flows determines the net present value of an investment proposal. Proposals with a positive net present value usually are considered acceptable, while proposals with a negative net present value are considered unacceptable. This technique considers both the life of the investment and the timing of future cash flows.

### LO 4

**Discuss the relationship between net present value and an investor's required rate of return.**
The discount rate used in determining an investment's net present value may be viewed as the investor's minimum required return for that investment. Thus, when an investment's net present value is positive, its expected rate of return exceeds the minimum return required by the investor. Conversely, a negative net present value suggests that an investment's return potential is less than the minimum return required by the investor.

### LO 5

**Explain the behavioral issues involved in capital budgeting and identify how companies try to control the capital budgeting process.**
Employees may be optimistic or pessimistic in their capital budgeting cash flow estimates because their futures are affected by the selected capital budgeting proposals. Firms audit capital budgeting projects to attempt to control for overly optimistic or pessimistic estimates.

This book has introduced you to the basic concepts of financial accounting, management accounting, and, to a lesser extent, income taxes. We are confident that you will find this background useful throughout your career. However, we also recommend that you continue your study of accounting with additional courses. We particularly recommend a course in cost accounting and an introductory course in taxation.

## KEY TERMS INTRODUCED OR EMPHASIZED IN CHAPTER 25

**capital budget audit** (p. 1031) The process where managers compare the projected expenditures with the actual installation and operating costs of a capital budgeting project to identify weaknesses in their planning processes.

**capital budgeting** (p. 1022) The process of planning and evaluating proposals for investments in plant assets.

**capital investments** (p. 1022) Large capital expenditures that typically involve the purchase of plant assets.

**discount rate** (p. 1026) The minimum required rate of return used by an investor to discount future cash flows to their present value.

**discounted cash flows** (p. 1025) The present value of future cash flows.

**net present value** (p. 1027) The excess of the present value of the net cash flows expected from an investment over the amount to be invested. Net present value is one method of ranking alternative investment proposals.

**payback period** (p. 1024) The length of time necessary to recover the cost of an investment through the cash flows generated by that investment. Payback period is one criterion used in making capital budgeting decisions.

**present value** (p. 1025) The amount of money today that is considered equivalent to a cash inflow or outflow expected to take place in the future. The present value of money is always less than its future amount, since money on hand today can be invested to become the equivalent of a larger amount in the future.

**return on average investment (ROI)** (p. 1024) The average annual net income from an investment expressed as a percentage of the average amount invested. Return on average invest-

ment is one method of ranking alternative investment proposals according to their profitability.

**sunk cost** (p. 1029) A cost that has been incurred irrevocably by past actions. Sunk costs are irrelevant to decisions regarding future actions.

## DEMONSTRATION PROBLEM

Grover Contracting, Inc., is considering the purchase of a new cement truck costing $150,000. Grover intends to keep the truck for five years before trading it in on a new one. The truck's estimated salvage value at the end of the five-year period is approximately $25,000. The truck is expected to increase annual income and cash flows by the following amounts:

| Year | Increase in Income | Increase in Net Cash Flows |
|------|-------------------:|---------------------------:|
| 1 .......................................................... | $10,000 | $ 37,500 |
| 2 .......................................................... | 12,000 | 37,500 |
| 3 .......................................................... | 14,000 | 37,500 |
| 4 .......................................................... | 16,000 | 37,500 |
| 5 .......................................................... | 18,000 | 37,500 |
| | $70,000 | $187,500 |

### Instructions

**a.** Compute the payback period associated with this investment.

**b.** Compute the return on average investment of this proposal.

**c.** Compute the net present value of this investment if Grover requires a minimum return of 12%.

**d.** Comment on your findings.

### Solution to the Demonstration Problem

**a.** The payback period of the investment is computed as follows:

$$\frac{\text{Amount to Be Invested}}{\text{Estimated Annual Net Cash Flow}} = \frac{\$150,000}{\$37,500} = \underline{\underline{4 \text{ years}}}$$

**b.** The return on average investment may be determined in three steps:

*Step 1: Compute average investment.*

$$\frac{\text{Original Cost} + \text{Salvage Value}}{2} = \frac{\$150,000 + \$25,000}{2} = \underline{\underline{\$87,500}}$$

*Step 2: Compute average estimated net income.*

$$\frac{\text{Total Income}}{\text{Estimated Useful Life}} = \frac{\$70,000}{5 \text{ years}} = \underline{\underline{\$14,000}}$$

*Step 3: Compute average return on investment.*

$$\frac{\text{Average Estimated Net Income}}{\text{Average Investment}} = \frac{\$14,000}{\$87,500} = \underline{\underline{16\%}}$$

**c.** The net present value of the investment is computed as follows:

| Table 1 | |
|---|---|
| Present value of salvage value discounted at 12% for 5 years ($25,000 × .567) . . . . . . . . . . . . . . . . . . . . . . . . . . . . | $ 14,175 |
| **Table 2** | |
| Present value of net cash flows discounted at 12% for 5 years ($37,500 × 3.605) . . . . . . . . . . . . . . . . . . . . . . . . . | 135,188 |
| Total present value of future cash flows . . . . . . . . . . . . . . . . . . . . . . . . . | $149,363 |
| Amount to be invested (payable in advance) . . . . . . . . . . . . . . . . . . . . . . . . | 150,000 |
| Net present value of proposed investment . . . . . . . . . . . . . . . . . . . . . . . . . | $ (637) |

**d.** Two of the three measures regarding the cement truck investment are encouraging. First, the payback period of four years is less than the truck's estimated life of five years. Second, the return on average investment of 16% is greater than Grover's minimum required return of 12%. However, a negative net present value of $637 reveals that the truck's return, in present value terms, is actually less than 12%. Had the company's minimum required return been 10% instead of 12%, the net present value of the investment would be positive by $7,688, computed as follows:

| Table 1 | |
|---|---|
| Present value of salvage value discounted at 10% for 5 years ($25,000 × .621) . . . . . . . . . . . . . . . . . . . . . . . . . . . . | $ 15,525 |
| **Table 2** | |
| Present value of net cash flows discounted at 10% for 5 years ($37,500 × 3.791) . . . . . . . . . . . . . . . . . . . . . . . . . | 142,163 |
| Total present value of future cash flows . . . . . . . . . . . . . . . . . . . . . . . . . | $157,688 |
| Amount to be invested (payable in advance) . . . . . . . . . . . . . . . . . . . . . . . . | 150,000 |
| Net present value of proposed investment . . . . . . . . . . . . . . . . . . . . . . . . . | $ 7,688 |

Because the net present value of the truck is negative when a discount rate of 12% is used and positive when a discount rate of 10% is used, we know that the truck's expected return is between 10% and 12%.

## SELF-TEST QUESTIONS

*Answers to these questions appear on page 1047.*

**1.** Which of the following capital budgeting measures requires the discounting of an investment's future cash flows?

  **a.** Payback period.

  **b.** Net present value.

  **c.** Return on average investment.

  **d.** All of the above require the discounting of an investment's future cash flows.

**2.** Which of the following is of least importance in determining whether to replace an old piece of equipment?

  **a.** The incremental costs and revenue associated with the new piece of equipment.

  **b.** The estimated cost of the new piece of equipment.

  **c.** The historical cost of the old piece of equipment.

  **d.** The estimated salvage value of the new piece of equipment.

**3.** If the net present value of an investment proposal is positive, what conclusions can be drawn? (Identify all correct answers.)

    **a.** The discount rate used is less than the investment's estimated return.

    **b.** The investment's estimated return exceeds the minimum return required by the investor.

    **c.** The discount rate used equals the minimum return required by the investor.

    **d.** The investment generates cash flows with a present value in excess of its cost.

4. Western Mfg. Co. is considering two capital budgeting proposals, each with a 10-year life, and each requiring an initial cash outlay of $50,000. Proposal A shows a higher return on average investment than Proposal B, but Proposal B shows the higher net present value. The most probable explanation is that:

    **a.** Expected cash inflows tend to occur earlier in Proposal B.

    **b.** Total expected cash inflows are greater in Proposal B.

    **c.** The payback period is shorter in Proposal A.

    **d.** The discounted future cash flows approach makes no provision for recovery of the original $50,000 investment.

5. Copy Center is considering replacing its old copying machine, which has a $3,200 book value, with a new one. Discounted cash flow analysis of the proposal to acquire the new machine shows an estimated net present value of $2,800. If the new machine is acquired, the old machine will have no resale value and will be given away. The loss on disposal of the old machine:

    **a.** Is an opportunity cost of purchasing the new machine.

    **b.** Exceeds the net present value of the new machine, indicating that the new machine should not be acquired.

    **c.** Has already been deducted in arriving at the $2,800 net present value of the new machine.

    **d.** Is a sunk cost and is not relevant to the decision at hand, except as it affects the timing of income tax payments.

## ASSIGNMENT MATERIAL

## DISCUSSION QUESTIONS

1. What is *capital budgeting?* Why are capital budgeting decisions crucial to the long-run financial health of a business enterprise?

2. A company invests $100,000 in plant assets with an estimated 20-year service life and no salvage value. These assets contribute $10,000 to annual net income when depreciation is computed on a straight-line basis. Compute the payback period and explain your computation.

3. What is the major shortcoming of using the payback period as the only criterion in making capital budgeting decisions?

4. What factors should an investor consider in appraising the adequacy of the rate of return from a specific investment proposal?

5. Discounting a future cash flow at 15% results in a lower present value than does discounting the same cash flow at 10%. Explain why.

6. What factors determine the present value of a future cash flow?

7. Discounting cash flows takes into consideration one characteristic of the earnings stream that is ignored in the computation of return on average investment. What is this characteristic and why is it important?

8. What nonfinancial considerations should be taken into account regarding a proposal to install a fire sprinkler system in a finished goods warehouse?

9. A particular investment proposal has a positive net present value of $20 when a discount rate of 8% is used. The same proposal has a negative net present value of $2,000 when a discount rate of 10% is used. What conclusions can be drawn about the estimated return of this proposal?

10. What factors might a company consider in establishing a minimum required return on an investment proposal?

11. A particular investment proposal has a payback period that exceeds the investment's expected life. The investment has no salvage value. Will this proposal's net present value be positive or negative? Explain your answer.

12. Is an investment's average estimated net income used to compute its return on average investment the same thing as the incremental annual cash flows used to compute its net present value? Explain your answer.

13. What can be said about an investment proposal that has a net present value of zero?

14. Depreciation expense does not require payment in cash. However, it is an important consideration in the discounting of an investment's future cash flows. Explain why.

15. What steps can a firm take to ensure that employee estimates of the costs, revenues, and cash flows from a proposed capital investment are not overly optimistic or pessimistic?

## EXERCISES

The following are 10 technical accounting terms introduced or emphasized in this chapter:

**EXERCISE 25.1**

Accounting Terminology

**LO 1–5**

| | | |
|---|---|---|
| Net present value | Capital budgeting | Incremental analysis |
| Discount rate | Payback period | Present value |
| Sunk cost | Salvage value | Return on average investment |
| Capital budget audit | | |

Each of the following statements may (or may not) describe one of these technical terms. For each statement, indicate the accounting term described, or answer "None" if the statement does not correctly describe any of the terms.

a. The examination of differences among revenue, costs, and cash flows under alternative courses of action.

b. A cost incurred in the past that cannot be changed as a result of future actions.

c. The process of planning and evaluating proposals for investments in plant assets.

d. The average annual net income from an investment expressed as a percentage of the average amount invested.

e. The length of time necessary to recover the entire cost of an investment from resulting annual net cash flows.

f. The present value of an investment's expected future cash flows.

g. The amount of money today that is considered equivalent to the cash flows expected to take place in the future.

h. The required rate of return used by an investor to discount future cash flows to their present value.

i. Often an investment's final cash flows to be considered in discounted cash flow analysis.

The Heartland Paper Company is considering the purchase of a new high-speed cutting machine. Two cutting machine manufacturers have approached Heartland with proposals: (1) Toledo Tools and (2) Akron Industries. Regardless of which vendor Heartland chooses, the following incremental cash flows are expected to be realized:

**EXERCISE 25.2**

Payback Period

**LO 1–3**

| Year | Incremental Cash Inflows | Incremental Cash Outflows |
|---|---|---|
| 1 | $26,000 | $20,000 |
| 2 | 27,000 | 21,000 |
| 3 | 32,000 | 26,000 |
| 4 | 35,000 | 29,000 |
| 5 | 34,000 | 28,000 |
| 6 | 33,000 | 27,000 |

a. If the machine manufactured by Toledo Tools costs $27,000, what is its expected payback period?

**b.** If the machine manufactured by Akron Industries has a payback period of 66 months, what is its cost?

**c.** Which of the machines is most attractive based on its respective payback period? Should Heartland base its decision entirely on this criterion? Explain your answer.

**EXERCISE 25.3**

Understanding Return on Average Investment Relationships

**LO 1, 3**

Foz Co. is considering four investment proposals (A, B, C, and D). The following table provides data concerning each of these investments:

|  | A | B | C | D |
|---|---|---|---|---|
| Investment cost | $40,000 | $45,000 | $25,000 | $ ? |
| Estimated salvage value | 8,000 | 5,000 | ? | 4,000 |
| Average estimated net income | 6,000 | ? | 3,400 | 3,000 |
| Return on average investment | ? | 32% | 20% | 15% |

Solve for the missing information pertaining to each investment proposal.

**EXERCISE 25.4**

Discounting Cash Flows

**LO 3**

Using the tables on page 1026, determine the present value of the following cash flows, discounted at an annual rate of 15%:

**a.** $10,000 to be received 20 years from today

**b.** $15,000 to be received annually for 10 years

**c.** $10,000 to be received annually for five years, with an additional $12,000 salvage value expected at the end of the fifth year

**d.** $30,000 to be received annually for the first three years, followed by $20,000 received annually for the next two years (total of five years in which cash is received)

**EXERCISE 25.5**

Understanding Net Present Value Relationships

**LO 1, 3, 4**

The following information relates to three independent investment decisions, each with a 10-year life and no salvage value:

|  | A | B | C |
|---|---|---|---|
| Investment cost | $ ? | $141,250 | $88,320 |
| Incremental annual cash inflows | 16,000 | 35,000 | 19,000 |
| Incremental annual cash outflows | 6,000 | ? | 7,000 |
| Discount rate yielding a net present value of zero | 10% | 12% | ? |

Using the present value tables on page 1026, solve for the missing information pertaining to each investment proposal.

**EXERCISE 25.6**

Analyzing a Capital Investment Proposal

**LO 1, 3**

Bowman Corporation is considering an investment in special-purpose equipment to enable the company to obtain a four-year government contract for the manufacture of a special item. The equipment costs $300,000 and would have no salvage value when the contract expires at the end of the four years. Estimated annual operating results of the project are as follows:

| | | |
|---|---|---|
| Revenue from contract sales | | $325,000 |
| Expenses other than depreciation | $225,000 | |
| Depreciation (straight-line basis) | 75,000 | 300,000 |
| Increase in net income from contract work | | $ 25,000 |

All revenue and all expenses other than depreciation will be received or paid in cash in the same period as recognized for accounting purposes. Compute the following for Bowman's proposal to undertake the contract work:

a. Payback period

b. Return on average investment

c. Net present value of the proposal to undertake contract work, discounted at an annual rate of 12% (Refer to annuity table on page 1026.)

Northwest Records is considering the purchase of Seattle Sound, Inc., a small company that promotes and manages "grunge" bands. The terms of the agreement require that Northwest pay the current owners of Seattle Sound $530,000 to purchase the company. Northwest executives estimate that the investment will generate annual net cash flows of $200,000. They do not feel, however, that demand for grunge music will extend beyond four years. Therefore, they plan to liquidate the entire investment in Seattle Sound at its projected book value of $50,000 at the end of the fourth year. Due to the high risk associated with this venture, Northwest requires a minimum rate of return of 20%.

a. Compute the payback period for Northwest's proposed investment in Seattle Sound.

b. Compute the net present value of the Seattle Sound proposal, using the tables on page 1026.

c. What nonfinancial factors would you recommend that Northwest executives take into consideration regarding this proposal?

**EXERCISE 25.7**

Analyzing Capital Investment Proposal

**LO 1–4**

Pack & Carry is debating whether to invest in new equipment to manufacture a line of high quality luggage. The new equipment would cost $900,000, with an estimated four-year life and no salvage value. The estimated annual operating results with the new equipment are as follows:

**EXERCISE 25.8**

Analyzing Capital Investment Proposal

**LO 1, 3**

| | | |
|---|---:|---:|
| Revenue from sales of new luggage | | $975,000 |
| Expenses other than depreciation | $675,000 | |
| Depreciation (straight-line basis) | 225,000 | (900,000) |
| Increase in net income from the new line | | $ 75,000 |

All revenue from the new luggage line and all expenses (except depreciation) will be received or paid in cash in the same period as recognized for accounting purposes. You are to compute the following for the investment in the new equipment to produce the new luggage line:

a. Annual cash flows

b. Payback period

c. Return on average investment

d. *Total* present value of the expected future annual cash inflows, discounted at an annual rate of 12%

e. *Net* present value of the proposed investment discounted at 12%

The division managers of the Chester Construction Corporation submit capital investment proposals each year for evaluation at the corporate level. Typically, the total dollar amount requested by the divisional managers far exceeds the company's capital investment budget. Thus each proposal is first ranked by its estimated net present value as a primary screening criterion.

Jeff Hensel, the manager of Chester's commercial construction division, often overstates the projected cash flows associated with his proposals, and thereby inflates their net present values. He does so because, in his words, "Everybody else is doing it."

a. Assume that all the division managers do overstate cash flow projections in their proposals. What would you do if you were recently promoted to division manager and had to compete for funding under these circumstances?

b. What controls might be implemented to discourage the overstatement of capital budgeting estimates by the division managers?

**EXERCISE 25.9**

Competing Investment Proposals

**LO 1, 2, 5**

# PROBLEMS

### PROBLEM 25.1

Capital Budgeting and
Determination of Annual Net
Cash Flows

**LO 1–4**

Toying With Nature wants to take advantage of children's current fascination with dinosaurs by adding several scale-model dinosaurs to its existing product line. Annual sales of the dinosaurs are estimated at 80,000 units at a price of $6 per unit. Variable manufacturing costs are estimated at $2.50 per unit, incremental fixed manufacturing costs (excluding depreciation) at $45,000 annually, and additional selling and general expenses related to the dinosaurs at $55,000 annually.

To manufacture the dinosaurs, the company must invest $350,000 in design molds and special equipment. Since toy fads wane in popularity rather quickly, Toying With Nature anticipates the special equipment will have a three-year service life with only a $20,000 salvage value. Depreciation will be computed on a straight-line basis. All revenue and expenses other than depreciation will be received or paid in cash. The company's combined federal and state income tax rate is 40%.

#### Instructions

**a.** Prepare a schedule showing the estimated increase in annual net income from the planned manufacture and sale of dinosaur toys.

**b.** Compute the annual net cash flows expected from this project.

**c.** Compute for this project the (1) payback period, (2) return on average investment, and (3) net present value, discounted at an annual rate of 15%. Round the payback period to the nearest tenth of a year and the return on average investment to the nearest tenth of a percent.

### PROBLEM 25.2

Analyzing Capital Investment
Proposals

**LO 1–4**

Micro Technology is considering two alternative proposals for modernizing its production facilities. To provide a basis for selection, the cost accounting department has developed the following data regarding the expected annual operating results for the two proposals:

|  | Proposal 1 | Proposal 2 |
| --- | --- | --- |
| Required investment in equipment | $360,000 | $350,000 |
| Estimated service life of equipment | 8 years | 7 years |
| Estimated salvage value | $ –0– | $ 14,000 |
| Estimated annual cost savings (net cash flow) | 75,000 | 76,000 |
| Depreciation on equipment (straight-line basis) | 45,000 | 48,000 |
| Estimated increase in annual net income | 30,000 | 28,000 |

#### Instructions

**a.** For each proposal, compute the (1) payback period, (2) return on average investment, and (3) net present value, discounted at an annual rate of 12%. (Round the payback period to the nearest tenth of a year and the return on investment to the nearest tenth of a percent.)

**b.** Based on your analysis in part **a**, state which proposal you would recommend and explain the reasons for your choice.

### PROBLEM 25.3

Analyzing Capital Investment
Proposals

**LO 1–4**

Banner Equipment Co. is evaluating two alternative investment opportunities. The controller of the company has prepared the following analysis of the two investment proposals:

|  | Proposal A | Proposal B |
| --- | --- | --- |
| Required investment in equipment | $220,000 | $240,000 |
| Estimated service life of equipment | 5 years | 6 years |
| Estimated salvage value | $ 10,000 | $ –0– |
| Estimated annual net cash flow | 60,000 | 60,000 |
| Depreciation on equipment (straight-line basis) | 42,000 | 40,000 |
| Estimated annual net income | 18,000 | 20,000 |

## Instructions

**a.** For each proposed investment, compute the (1) payback period, (2) return on average investment, and (3) net present value, discounted at an annual rate of 12%. (Round the payback period to the nearest tenth of a year and the return on investment to the nearest tenth of a percent.)

**b.** Based on your computations in part **a,** which proposal do you consider to be the better investment? Explain.

Marengo is a popular restaurant located in the Chilton Resort. Management feels that enlarging the facility to incorporate a large outdoor seating area will enable Marengo to continue to attract existing customers as well as handle large banquet parties that now must be turned away. Two proposals are currently under consideration. Proposal A involves a temporary walled structure and umbrellas used for sun protection; Proposal B entails a more permanent structure with a full awning cover for use even in inclement weather. Although the useful life of each alternative is estimated to be 10 years, Proposal B results in higher salvage value due to the awning protection. The accounting department of Chilton Resort and the manager of Marengo have assembled the following data regarding the two proposals:

**PROBLEM 25.4**

Capital Budgeting Using Multiple Models

**LO 1–4**

| | Proposal A | Proposal B |
|---|---|---|
| Required investment | $400,000 | $500,000 |
| Estimated life of fixtures | 10 years | 10 years |
| Estimated salvage value | $ 20,000 | $ 50,000 |
| Estimated annual net cash flow | 80,000 | 95,000 |
| Depreciation (straight-line basis) | 38,000 | 45,000 |
| Estimated annual net income | ? | ? |

## Instructions

**a.** For each proposal, compute the (1) payback period, (2) return on average investment, and (3) net present value discounted at management's required rate of return of 15%. (Round the payback period to the nearest tenth of a year and the return on investment to the nearest tenth of a percent.)

**b.** Based on your analysis in part **a,** state which proposal you would recommend and explain the reasons for your choice.

V. S. Yogurt is considering two possible expansion plans. Proposal A involves opening 10 stores in northern California at a total cost of $3,150,000. Under another strategy, Proposal B, V. S. Yogurt would focus on southern California and open six stores for a total cost of $2,500,000. Selected data regarding the two proposals have been assembled by the controller of V. S. Yogurt as follows:

**PROBLEM 25.5**

Capital Budgeting Using Multiple Models

**LO 1–4**

| | Proposal A | Proposal B |
|---|---|---|
| Required investment | $3,150,000 | $2,500,000 |
| Estimated life of store locations | 7 years | 7 years |
| Estimated salvage value | $ –0– | $ 400,000 |
| Estimated annual net cash flow | 750,000 | 570,000 |
| Depreciation on equipment (straight-line basis) | 450,000 | 300,000 |
| Estimated annual net income | ? | ? |

## Instructions

**a.** For each proposal, compute the (1) payback period, (2) return on average investment, and (3) net present value, discounted at management's required rate of return of 15%. (Round the payback period to the nearest tenth of a year and the return on investment to the nearest tenth of a percent.)

**b.** Based on your analysis in part **a**, state which proposal you would recommend and explain the reasoning behind your choice.

**PROBLEM 25.6**

Analyzing Capital Investment Proposal

**LO 1–4**

Rothmore Appliance Company is planning to introduce a built-in blender to its line of small home appliances. Annual sales of the blender are estimated at 10,000 units at a price of $35 per unit. Variable manufacturing costs are estimated at $15 per unit, incremental fixed manufacturing costs (other than depreciation) at $40,000 annually, and incremental selling and general expenses relating to the blenders at $50,000 annually.

To build the blenders, the company must invest $240,000 in molds, patterns, and special equipment. Since the company expects to change the design of the blender every four years, this equipment will have a four-year service life with no salvage value. Depreciation will be computed on a straight-line basis. All revenue and expenses other than depreciation will be received or paid in cash. The company's combined state and federal tax rate is 40%.

**Instructions**

**a.** Prepare a schedule showing the estimated annual net income from the proposal to manufacture and sell the blenders.

**b.** Compute the annual net cash flows expected from the proposal.

**c.** Compute for this proposal the (1) payback period (round to the nearest tenth of a year), (2) return on average investment (round to the nearest tenth of a percent), and (3) net present value, discounted at an annual rate of 15%.

**PROBLEM 25.7**

Considering Financial and Nonfinancial Factors

**LO 1–4**

Doctors Hanson, Dominick, and Borchard are radiologists living in Fargo, North Dakota. They realize that many of the state's small, rural hospitals cannot afford to purchase their own magnetic resonance imaging devices (MRIs). Thus the doctors are considering whether it would be feasible for them to form a corporation and invest in their own mobile MRI unit. The unit would be transported on a scheduled basis to more than 100 rural hospitals using an 18-wheel tractor-trailer. The cost of a tractor-trailer equipped with MRI equipment is approximately $1,250,000. The estimated life of the investment is eight years, after which time its salvage value is expected to be no more than $100,000.

The doctors anticipate that the investment will generate incremental revenue of $800,000 per year. Incremental expenses (which include depreciation, insurance, fuel, maintenance, their salaries, and income taxes) will average $700,000 per year. Net incremental cash flows will be reinvested back into the corporation. The only difference between incremental cash flows and incremental income is attributable to depreciation expense. The doctors require a minimum return on their investment of 12%.

**Instructions**

**a.** Compute the payback period of the mobile MRI proposal.

**b.** Compute the return on average investment of the proposal.

**c.** Compute the net present value of the proposal using the tables on page 1026.

**d.** What nonfinancial factors should the doctors consider in making their decisions?

**PROBLEM 25.8**

Analyzing Competing Capital Investment Proposals

**LO 1–4**

Jefferson Mountain is a small ski resort located in central Pennsylvania. In recent years, the resort has experienced two major problems: (1) unusually low annual snowfalls and (2) long lift lines. To remedy these problems, management is considering two investment proposals. The first involves a $125,000 investment in equipment used to make artificial snow. The second involves the $180,000 purchase of a new high-speed chairlift.

The most that the resort can afford to invest at this time is $200,000. Thus it cannot afford to fund both proposals. Choosing one proposal over the other is somewhat problematic. If the resort funds the snow-making equipment, business will increase, and lift lines will become even longer than they are currently. If it funds the chairlift, lines will be shortened, but there may not be enough natural snow to attract skiers to the mountain.

The following estimates pertain to each of these investment proposals:

|  | Snow-Making Equipment | Chair Lift |
|---|---|---|
| Estimated life of investment .............................. | 20 years | 36 years |
| Estimated incremental annual revenue of investment .......... | $40,000 | $54,000 |
| Estimated incremental annual expense of investment (including taxes) ................................. | 15,000 | 19,000 |

Neither investment is expected to have any salvage value. Furthermore, the only difference between incremental cash flow and incremental income is attributable to depreciation. Due to inherent risks associated with the ski industry and the resort's high cost of capital, a minimum return on investment of 20% is required.

**Instructions**

**a.** Compute the payback period of each proposal.

**b.** Compute the return on average investment of each proposal.

**c.** Compute the net present value of each proposal using the tables on page 1026.

**d.** What nonfinancial factors should be considered?

**e.** Which proposal, if either, do you recommend as a capital investment?

Sonic, Inc., sells business software. Currently, all of its programs come on 3.5-inch floppy disks. Due to their complexity, some of these applications occupy as many as seven disks. Not only are 3.5-inch disks cumbersome for customers to load, they are relatively expensive for Sonic to purchase. The company does not intend to discontinue using 3.5-inch disks altogether. However, it does want to reduce its reliance on the floppy disk medium.

Two proposals are being considered. The first is to provide software on laser disks. Doing so requires a $300,000 investment in duplicating equipment. The second is to make software available through a computerized "modem bank." In essence, programs would be downloaded directly from Sonic using telecommunication technology. Customers would gain access to Sonic's mainframe using a modem, specify the program they wish to order, and provide their name, address, and credit card information. The software would then be transferred directly to the customer's hard drive, and copies of the users' manual and registration material would be mailed the same day. This proposal requires an initial investment of $240,000.

The following information pertains to these proposals. Due to rapidly changing technology, neither proposal is expected to have any salvage value or an estimated life exceeding six years.

**PROBLEM 25.9**

Analyzing Competing Capital Investment Proposals

|  | Laser Disk Equipment | Modem Bank Installation |
|---|---|---|
| Estimated incremental annual revenue of investment ......... | $300,000 | $160,000 |
| Estimated incremental annual expense of investment (including taxes) ................................. | 250,000 | 130,000 |

The only difference between Sonic's incremental cash flows and its incremental income is attributable to depreciation. A minimum return on investment of 15% is required.

**Instructions**

**a.** Compute the payback period of each proposal.

**b.** Compute the return on average investment of each proposal.

**c.** Compute the net present value of each proposal using the tables on page 1026.

**d.** What nonfinancial factors should be considered?

**e.** Which of Sonic's employees would most likely underestimate the benefits of investing in the modem bank? Why?

**f.** Which proposal, if either, do you recommend Sonic choose?

**PROBLEM 25.10**

Replacing Existing Equipment

**LO 1–3, 5**

EnterTech has noticed a significant decrease in the profitability of its line of portable CD players. The production manager believes that the source of the trouble is old, inefficient equipment used to manufacture the product. The issue raised, therefore, is whether EnterTech should (1) buy new equipment at a cost of $120,000 or (2) continue using its present equipment.

It is unlikely that demand for these portable CD players will extend beyond a five-year time horizon. Thus EnterTech estimates that both the new equipment and the present equipment will have a remaining useful life of five years and no salvage value.

The new equipment is expected to produce annual cash savings in manufacturing costs of $34,000, before taking into consideration depreciation and taxes. However, management does not believe that the use of new equipment will have any effect on sales volume. Thus their decision rests entirely on the magnitude of the potential cost savings.

The old equipment has a book value of $100,000. However, it can be sold for only $20,000 if it is replaced. EnterTech has an average tax rate of 40% and uses straight-line depreciation for tax purposes. The company requires a minimum return of 12% on all investments in plant assets.

**Instructions**

**a.** Compute the net present value of the new machine using the tables on page 1026.

**b.** What nonfinancial factors should EnterTech consider?

**c.** If the manager of EnterTech is uncertain about the accuracy of the cost savings estimate, what actions could be taken to double-check the estimate?

# CASES AND UNSTRUCTURED PROBLEMS

**CASE 25.1**

How Much Is That Laser in the Window?

**LO 2, 3, 4**

The management of Metro Printers is considering a proposal to replace some existing equipment with a new highly efficient laser printer. The existing equipment has a current book value of $2,200,000 and a remaining life (if not replaced) of 10 years. The laser printer has a cost of $1,300,000 and an expected useful life of 10 years. The laser printer would increase the company's annual cash flows by reducing operating costs and by increasing the company's ability to generate revenue. Susan Mills, controller of Metro Printers, has prepared the following estimates of the laser printer's effect on annual earnings and cash flow:

| | | |
|---|---:|---:|
| Estimated increase in annual cash flows (before taxes): | | |
|    Incremental revenue | $140,000 | |
|    Cost savings (other than depreciation) | 110,000 | $250,000 |
| Reduction in annual depreciation expense: | | |
|    Depreciation on existing equipment | $220,000 | |
|    Depreciation on laser printer | 130,000 | 90,000 |
| Estimated increase in income before income taxes | | $340,000 |
| Increase in annual income taxes (40%) | | 136,000 |
| Estimated increase in annual net income | | $204,000 |
| Estimated increase in annual net cash flows | | |
|    ($250,000 − $136,000) | | $114,000 |

Don Adams, a director of Metro Printers, makes the following observation: "These estimates look fine, but won't we take a huge loss in the current year on the sale of our existing equipment? After the invention of the laser printer, I doubt that our old equipment can be sold for much at all." In response, Mills provides the following information about the expected loss on the sale of the existing equipment:

| | |
|---|---:|
| Book value of existing printing equipment . . . . . . . . . . . . . . . . . . . . . . . . . . . . . . . | $2,200,000 |
| Estimated current sales price, net of removal costs . . . . . . . . . . . . . . . . . . . . . . . | 200,000 |
| Estimated loss on sale, before income taxes . . . . . . . . . . . . . . . . . . . . . . . . . . . . | $2,000,000 |
| Reduction in current year's income taxes as a result of loss (40%) . . . . . . . . . . . | 800,000 |
| Loss on sale of existing equipment, net of tax savings . . . . . . . . . . . . . . . . . . . . . | $1,200,000 |

Adams replies, "Good grief, our loss would be almost as great as the cost of the laser itself. Add this $1,200,000 loss to the $1,300,000 cost of the laser, and we're into this new equipment for $2,500,000. I'd go along with a cost of $1,300,000, but $2,500,000 is out of the question."

### Instructions

**a.** Compute the net present value of the proposal to sell the existing equipment and buy the laser printer, discounted at an annual rate of 15%. In your computation, make the following assumptions regarding the timing of cash flows:

**1.** The purchase price of the laser printer will be paid in cash immediately.

**2.** The $200,000 sales price of the existing equipment will be received in cash immediately.

**3.** The income tax benefit from selling the equipment will be realized one year from today.

**4.** Metro uses straight-line depreciation in both its income tax returns and its financial statements.

**5.** The annual net cash flows may be regarded as received at year-end for each of the next 10 years.

**b.** Is the cost to Metro Printers of acquiring the laser printer $2,500,000, as Adams suggests? Explain fully.

Grizzly Community Hospital in central Wyoming provides healthcare services to families living within a 200-mile radius. The hospital is extremely well equipped for a relatively small, community facility. However, it does not have renal dialysis equipment for kidney patients. Those patients requiring dialysis must travel as far as 300 miles to receive care.

**CASE 25.2**

Dollars and Cents versus a Sense of Ethics

**LO 1–5**

Several of the staff physicians have proposed that the hospital invest in a renal dialysis center. The minimum cost required for this expansion is $4.5 million. The physicians estimate that the center will generate revenue of $1.15 million per year for approximately 20 years. Incremental costs, including the salaries of professional staff, will average $850,000 annually. Grizzly is exempt from paying any income taxes. The only difference between annual net income and net cash flows is caused by depreciation expense. The center is not expected to have any salvage value at the end of 20 years.

The administrators of the hospital strongly oppose the proposal for several reasons: (1) they do not believe that it would generate the hospital's minimum required return of 12% on capital investments, (2) they do not believe that kidney patients would use the facility even if they could avoid traveling several hundred miles to receive treatment elsewhere, (3) they do not feel that the hospital has enough depth in its professional staff to operate a dialysis center, and (4) they are certain that $4.5 million could be put to better use, such as expanding the hospital's emergency services to include air transport by helicopter.

The issue has resulted in several heated debates between the physicians and the hospital administrators. One physician has even threatened to move out of the area if the dialysis center is not built. Another physician was quoted as saying, "All the administrators are concerned about is the almighty dollar. We are a hospital, not a profit-hungry corporation. It is our ethical responsibility to serve the healthcare needs of central Wyoming's citizens."

### Instructions

Form small groups of four or five persons. Within each group, designate who will play the role of the hospital's physicians and who will play the role of the hospital's administrators. Then engage in a debate from each party's point of view. Be certain to address the following:

a. Financial factors and measures

b. Nonfinancial factors such as (1) ethical responsibility, (2) quality of care issues, (3) opportunity costs associated with alternative uses of $4.5 million, (4) physician morale, and (5) whether a community hospital should be run like a business

c. Measures that could be taken to check for overly optimistic or pessimistic estimates

## BUSINESS WEEK ASSIGNMENT     BusinessWeek

**CASE 25.3**

Net Present Value and Your Education

**LO 1, 2, 3, 5**

In an April 3, 2000, *Business Week* article titled "The B-School on Your Desk," author Larry Armstrong describes a new method for learning net present value techniques:

> You need some training in corporate finance to get you ready for your next move up the ladder. But rather than travel to a business school's executive program for several weeks, you sit down at your computer and log on to Unext.com, an online management education center.

> In a trice you're transported to a role-playing game: Asset Valuation. You're a new employee at Panhandle Energy, and your boss has asked you to figure out which of four different oil fields the company should invest in. He thinks you should use the net present value method to estimate profit potential.

### Instructions

a. Consider taking the class described in the *Business Week* article above. How would you go about determining the net present value of taking an online course in corporate finance versus enrolling in a traditional college or university course? Which cash flows and time horizons would you consider relevant to this decision?

b. List nonfinancial factors that would be important to you when choosing between investing in an online course and a traditional college or university course.

## INTERNET ASSIGNMENT

**INTERNET 25.1**

Capital Investment History

**LO 1, 2, 5**

The **Sears Roebuck Company**, founded in the late 1800s, has made many significant capital investment decisions throughout its history. Access the **Sears'** website at the following address:

**www.sears.com**

Locate the historical section by clicking on the "About Sears," "For the Public," and "Sears History" icons in that order.

### Instructions

a. Identify what you would consider to be major strategic capital investment decisions undertaken by **Sears** since 1886.

b. For one such decision, discuss the nonfinancial issues that likely would have been considered.

c. A common capital investment decision undertaken by retailers is whether to invest funds in a store that is earning less than the desired level of profit (in the hopes that the investment will generate higher profits) or close the location altogether. In evaluating both options, which employee groups would you expect to overstate the benefits of additional investment? Which groups would understate the benefits of additional investment?

*Internet sites are time and date sensitive. It is the purpose of these exercises to have you explore the Internet. You may need to use the Yahoo! search engine* http://www.yahoo.com *(or other favorite search engine) to find a company's current web address.*

## OUR COMMENTS ON THE "YOUR TURN" CASES

**As a Chief Financial Officer (p. 1028)**   Explain to Steve Wilson the value added by computing the net present value of the capital investment projects. Make it clear by a demonstration that the payback method or the average rate of return on invested assets will sometimes give the wrong signal about a capital investment project. The payback period method values all cash flows as if they occurred simultaneously. We know that if we received all cash inflows on the first day of a capital project's life, we could invest that cash in a bank account and earn a basic return over the rest of the life of the project. However, if we don't receive cash inflows until the end of the second year in a capital project's life, we forego the two-year basic return we could earn from the bank. So in this latter case, we forego the interest we could earn and incur an opportunity cost. Both the payback and the average rate of return on assets methods ignore opportunity costs associated with the time value of money.

**As a Transportation Manager (p. 1030)**   One of the standards of ethical conduct for management accountants is to disclose information that could be expected to influence the user. The timing and amounts of cash flows can make a difference in present value computations. Consider the present value computations of the operating cash flows for the new bus that you have identified: $8,000 + $12,000 + $20,000 + $24,000 + $26,000. Assume in the following table that the operating cash outflows occur at the end of each of the five years and that the discount factor is 15%.

| Year | Cash Outflows | × | Discount Factor | = | Present Value |
|---|---|---|---|---|---|
| 1 | $ 8,000 | | .870 | | $ 6,960 |
| 2 | 12,000 | | .756 | | 9,072 |
| 3 | 20,000 | | .658 | | 13,160 |
| 4 | 24,000 | | .572 | | 13,728 |
| 5 | 26,000 | | .497 | | 12,922 |
| Total present value of operating outflows | | | | | $55,842 |

Compare the result in the previous table with the present value of the average estimate of $18,000 paid out annually for five years. Referring to the annuity table, we see that the present value of $1 paid out annually for five years is 3.352. Therefore, the present value of the $18,000 average annual cash outflows for five years is *$60,336* ($18,000 × 3.352). Because your more knowledgeable estimates of the operating expenses show lower expenses in early years and higher expenses in later years, the estimated net present value of the operating cash outflows is lower by $4,494 ($60,336 − $55,842). Thus, it is your ethical responsibility to provide the more accurate cash flow estimates.

## ANSWERS TO SELF-TEST QUESTIONS

**1.** b     **2.** c     **3.** a, b, d     **4.** a     **5.** d

# A NEW GENERATION

Tootsie Roll Annual Report

Tootsie Roll
Industries, Inc.

Annual Report 1999

## *Corporate Profile*

Tootsie Roll Industries, Inc. has been engaged in the manufacture and sale of candy for 103 years. Our products are primarily sold under the familiar brand names, Tootsie Roll, Tootsie Roll Pops, Caramel Apple Pops, Child's Play, Charms, Blow Pop, Blue Razz, Cella's, Mason Dots, Mason Crows, Junior Mints, Charleston Chew, Sugar Daddy and Sugar Babies.

## *Corporate Principles*

We believe that the differences among companies are attributable to the caliber of their people, and therefore we strive to attract and retain superior people for each job.

We believe that an open family atmosphere at work combined with professional management fosters cooperation and enables each individual to maximize his or her contribution to the company and realize the corresponding rewards.

We do not jeopardize long-term growth for immediate, short-term results.

We maintain a conservative financial posture in the deployment and management of our assets.

We run a trim operation and continually strive to eliminate waste, minimize cost and implement performance improvements.

We invest in the latest and most productive equipment to deliver the best quality product to our customers at the lowest cost.

We seek to outsource functions where appropriate and to vertically integrate operations where it is financially advantageous to do so.

We view our well known brands as prized assets to be aggressively advertised and promoted to each new generation of consumers.

*Melvin J. Gordon, Chairman and Chief Executive Officer and Ellen R. Gordon, President and Chief Operating Officer.*

# To Our Shareholders

We are pleased to report that 1999 was another year of record performance for Tootsie Roll Industries. Sales for the year were $397 million, an increase of $8 million or 2% over the prior year. Net earnings were $71 million, an increase of $4 million or 6% over the prior year. Earnings per share were up by an even greater 7% due to the lower number of average shares outstanding this year than last year.

This year represented the twenty-third consecutive year in which the company posted record sales and the eighteenth consecutive year in which record earnings were achieved. Milestones such as these reflect both the enduring strength of our many fine brands and the company's continuing commitment to bottom line performance.

Other notable events during 1999 were:

- The quarterly cash dividend rate increased by 23%.

- 756,700 of the company's common shares were repurchased on the open market.

- Capital expenditures were accelerated to support the current and future needs of the company.

Despite the considerable financial resources committed to these activities, the company's balance sheet strengthened further during 1999. We remain ready to respond quickly to future growth opportunities as they arise.

## Sales and Marketing

Our strategy for sales growth is threefold: first, we look for ways to expand the sales of existing products; second, we try to introduce new products and product line extensions; and, third, we seek to acquire brands that will integrate well with our business. We reviewed several possible acquisitions during 1999, increased our distribution and added both new products and product line extensions to our well-known brands.

Gains experienced in our core brands were the result of another strong Halloween sales period and continued implementation of targeted promotional programs such as shippers, combo packs and bonus packages throughout the year.

One such promotion that was particularly successful in the Tootsie Roll line during 1999 was our "Family Learning Fun Pack" computer software offer. This on-pack, self-liquidating promotion featured a customized CD-ROM consisting of three of today's most highly rated educational software programs-a $60 retail value for $4.99. This promotion was carried on over 60 million specially marked packages of our most popular products and reinforced the attributes of "family fun at a good value" that these brands convey to consumers. The promotion also helped to increase the shelf turns that make our products perennial favorites in the retail trade.

Another successful promotion was our "Y2K compliant" Tootsie Roll Milennium Bank, a whimsical twist on our popular line of fun banks. Filled with chewy Tootsie Roll Midgees, this special Y2K bank came in three assorted designs, each featuring upscale gold foil graphics along with a unique millennium message, and made a perfect gift to commemorate the new millennium.

# Financial Highlights

|  | December 31, | |
|---|---|---|
|  | 1999 | 1998 |
|  | (in thousands except per share data) | |
| Net Sales | $396,750 | $388,659 |
| Net Earnings | 71,310 | 67,526 |
| Working Capital | 168,423 | 175,155 |
| Net Property, Plant and Equipment | 95,897 | 83,024 |
| Shareholders' Equity | 430,646 | 396,457 |
| Average Shares Outstanding* | 48,974 | 49,482 |
| Per Share Items* |  |  |
| Net Earnings | $1.46 | $1.36 |
| Shareholders' Equity | 8.88 | 8.05 |
| Cash Dividends Paid | .24 | .19 |

*Based on average shares outstanding adjusted for stock dividends and 2-for-1 stock split.

As is customary for the company, the third quarter was our highest selling period in 1999 due to Halloween shipments. Our bagged goods, including variety packs containing popular assortments of the company's offerings, helped increase Halloween sales, particularly among the mass merchandise, drug and warehouse club classes of trade.

Other seasonal sales gains came from our Valentine's Day, Easter and Christmas bagged goods. During 1999, we redesigned the packaging graphics throughout these lines to give them a fresh and appealing look on store shelves. Positive sales trends indicate that these changes were rewarded with increased popularity among consumers.

The Charms line benefited from continued growth of the Super Blow Pop, a 1.35 ounce version of our popular gum-filled confection. The introduction of Way 2 Sour Blow Pops added to growth in the Charms division. This new pop delivers three intense taste sensations that appeal to today's kids: a super sour outer candy shell, followed by a sweet inner candy shell, and, finally, a super sour bubble gum center. Distinguished by high impact neon colored graphics and blended into an assortment of five popular flavors, this product is available as count goods, in bags and in both the regular and the "super" 1.35 ounce size, and has been an instant success.

Another new item in the Charms line that was introduced in 1999 is S'Moresels. Reminiscent of the popular treat long-enjoyed at campfires, S'Moresels combine a chewy marshmallow nougat center, crunchy bits of graham cracker and chocolatey goodness into a convenient and promising new confection.

During 1999, we also updated the Charms flat pop line by modifying the product mix to keep up with today's taste preferences and by rejuvenating the packaging graphics to incorporate more contemporary design elements.

These marketing efforts are typical of our focus of maintaining the identity and vitality of our core brands while searching for evolutionary ways to update and extend these franchises to new items and new distribution opportunities.

## Advertising and Public Relations

As we have done for many years, we again employed television as the chief medium to convey our advertising messages. Children and adults in selected spot and cable markets were targeted with the famous "How Many Licks?" and "That's a Blow Pop!" themes during the peak sales season. At other times during the year, adults watching talk, game and adventure shows were encouraged to enjoy our popular Caramel Apple Pops, or to satisfy their children's urges for a chocolatey candy treat with Tootsie Rolls and Tootsie Pops, two of our delicious, low fat confections.

Our website, "tootsie.com," was enhanced by the addition of an interactive children's game. The site also serves as a vehicle from which Tootsie fans can obtain not only historical and product information, but also current information about our financial performance and other developments through the periodic posting of press releases.

Junior Mints celebrated its 50th anniversary during 1999. Named after the popular 1949 Broadway production "Junior Miss," this unique mint with the creamy center has endured as one of America's favorite confections. This occasion was commemorated by another in our series of collectable tins, this one featuring a 50th anniversary banner in a festive Christmas motif, and by extensive press coverage and a series of radio interviews on top rated morning programs.

## Manufacturing and Distribution

Capital investments of $20 million were made during the year to increase productive capacity, improve product quality or reduce cost. For many years we have viewed such investments as being vital to maintaining our stature as one of the industry's most efficient competitors. We believe that the wisdom of this strategy is evident in the 18% after-tax profit margin the company delivered in 1999.

In addition, our new distribution facility in Covington, Tennessee, was brought on line in time for our peak storage and shipping period. This facility features the leading edge inventory tracking and control technology that we have deployed throughout our operations.

## Purchasing

Prices for certain of our major raw materials increased somewhat, while packaging and minor ingredient costs remained stable in 1999. Costs reflected generally moderate inflationary pressure domestically and reasonable worldwide demand. We continue to utilize hedging strategies, where we deem it appropriate to do so, as a means of insulating the company from unpredictable spot market fluctuations and to lock in prices for major commodities when they are at attractive levels.

All purchases, such as corrugated and film, are competitively bid. This policy enables us to leverage the high volumes of those items that we buy annually and further control our costs.

## Information Technology

During 1999, we continued to deploy leading edge data processing technology. Whether in transaction processing, production control or electronic communications, data management has been another long standing priority of the company.

During 1999, we installed a current version of the enterprise resource planning (ERP) software we use, and completed our extensive preparations for the transition to the Year 2000. As a result of these initiatives, we can happily report that the company did not experience any business disruptions from Year 2000 issues.

## International

1999 was also a good year for the international dimension of the company. In Mexico, stabilizing local economic conditions and aggressive new marketing programs resulted in sales increases. The absence of currency devaluations experienced during 1998, along with the new production efficiences from the capital investments we have made in recent years, increased the profitability of this operation. In this regard, we completed another phase of the modernization program in our Mexican plant during 1999.

Sales growth in Canada came from general distribution gains, further growth in the Charms line, including the introduction of Way 2 Sour Blow Pops, and another strong Halloween. Our distribution in the mass merchandise, drug and warehouse club trade classes continues to grow in this market.

Positive sales trends developed in several other international markets where strong local distribution relationships have been formed.

## Dividends

We distributed our thirty-fifth consecutive 3% stock dividend in April and increased the quarterly cash dividend rate by 23% in July. Also, 1999 was the fifty-seventh consecutive year in which the company has paid cash dividends.

After considering the payment of dividends, the construction of a new distribution center and cash invested in other fixed asset additions, our balance sheet strengthened further during the year. With considerable financial reserves, we remain watchful for appropriate strategic acquisitions and other growth opportunities.

## In Conclusion....

Record results were achieved in 1999 in spite of several unprecedented events in the industry. Consolidation in the sales brokerage community and several significant business combinations in the retail industry required us to forge new relationships and to adapt our offerings to meet changing retail philosophies.

Achieving records such as those Tootsie Roll established during 1999 required contributions from many constituencies. In this regard, we extend our sincere appreciation to our customers and consumers, along with our many loyal employees, suppliers, sales brokers and shareholders, for making 1999 another record year.

*Melvin J Gordon*

Melvin J Gordon
Chairman of the Board and
Chief Executive Officer

*Ellen R Gordon*

Ellen R. Gordon
President and
Chief Operating Officer

# Management's Discussion and Analysis of Financial Condition and Results of Operations

(in thousands except per share, percentage and ratio figures)

NET SALES
Millions of dollars

| 95 | 96 | 97 | 98 | 99 |
|----|----|----|----|----|
| $313 | $341 | $376 | $389 | $397 |

NET EARNINGS
Millions of dollars

| 95 | 96 | 97 | 98 | 99 |
|----|----|----|----|----|
| $40.4 | $47.2 | $60.7 | $67.5 | $71.3 |

## FINANCIAL REVIEW

This financial review discusses the company's financial condition, results of operations, liquidity and capital resources. It should be read in conjunction with the Consolidated Financial Statements and related footnotes that follow this discussion.

## FINANCIAL CONDITION

Our financial condition was further strengthened by the record operating results we achieved in 1999. Net earnings for the year increased 5.6% to $71,310 and shareholders' equity grew by 8.6% to $430,646. Cash and investments in marketable securities increased by $23,501 during the year.

Cash generated from operating activities was used to fund share repurchases of $26,869, capital expenditures of $20,283 and cash dividends of $11,313. Adjusting for stock dividends, the quarterly cash dividend rate was increased by 22.6% in 1999, which marked the fifty-seventh consecutive year in which cash dividends have been paid.

A 3% stock dividend was also distributed to shareholders during the year. This was the thirty-fifth consecutive year that a stock dividend has been distributed.

Our financial position in 1999 compared to 1998, measured by commonly used financial ratios, is as follows: the current ratio fell from 4.3:1 to 4.0:1. This reflects an increase in the investments in marketable securities that are classified as non-current due to their maturity dates. For the same reason, working capital also declined by $6,732 to $168,423.

Current liabilities to net worth remained comparable at 13.0% versus 13.5% in the prior year, as did debt to equity at 1.7% versus 1.9%. The company continues to finance its operations with funds generated from operations rather than with borrowed funds.

Our history of successful operations, coupled with our conservative financial posture, has left us well positioned to respond quickly to future growth opportunities that may arise. In this regard, the company is aggressively seeking acquisitions to complement our existing operations.

## RESULTS OF OPERATIONS

1999 vs. 1998

1999 was our twenty-third consecutive year of record sales achievement. Sales of $396,750 were up 2.1% over 1998 sales of $388,659. The third quarter, driven by Halloween sales, continued to be our largest selling period and surpassed levels attained in previous years. Also in 1999, the timing of certain Halloween shipments had a favorable effect on the third quarter and a corresponding unfavorable impact on the fourth quarter as compared to the prior year.

Throughout the year, sales were favorably impacted by successful promotional programs as we continued to broaden distribution in mass merchandisers and other select trade classes with our core product offerings. Line extensions, new products and seasonal packs all contributed to added sales.

Sales growth occurred in our two most significant foreign operations as well. In Mexico, stabilizing local conditions and aggressive new marketing and promotional programs complemented the already strong business we have developed for the Christmas holiday season in that market.

Sales growth in our Canadian operation is attributable to another strong Halloween season coupled with further distribution gains in the mass merchandiser and grocery trade classes. Also, the new Way 2 Sour Blow Pop was successfully introduced in this market.

GROSS MARGIN
*Millions of dollars*

| | | | $201 | $204 |
| $146 | $162 | $187 | | |
| 95 | 96 | 97 | 98 | 99 |

SHAREHOLDERS'
EQUITY
*Millions of dollars*

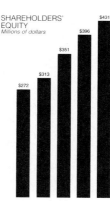

| | | | | $431 |
| | | | $396 | |
| | | $351 | | |
| | $313 | | | |
| $272 | | | | |
| 95 | 96 | 97 | 98 | 99 |

Cost of goods sold, as a percentage of sales, remained steady at 48.5% versus 48.3%. This reflects generally stable cost levels for packaging and minor ingredients, although certain of our raw material costs did increase somewhat. These increases were largely offset by higher production efficiencies associated with increased volumes in relation to fixed costs. The company continues to focus on cost control throughout all levels of its operations.

Gross margin dollars grew by 1.6% to $204,189, and remained steady as a percent of sales at 51.5% versus 51.7% in 1998, due to the factors cited above. Gross margins as a percent of sales in the third and fourth quarters continue to be somewhat lower due to the seasonal nature of our business and to the product mix sold in those quarters.

Operating expenses, comprised of marketing, selling, advertising, physical distribution, general and administrative expenses and goodwill amortization, as a percentage of sales, declined slightly from 25.7% to 25.1%. This improvement is due to effective expense control programs aimed at holding down costs. Earnings from operations increased by 3.2% to $104,519, or 26.3% of sales, as a result of favorable gross margins and operating expenses.

Other income increased by $2,130 to $6,928, primarily reflecting significantly lower foreign exchange losses in Mexico where local economic conditions have improved. Also, interest expense was lower and interest income was higher due to lower average borrowings and increased investments in marketable securities during 1999. Interest income was also higher in 1999 due to higher interest rates. As a majority of our interest income is not subject to federal income tax, the effective tax rate declined from 36.3% to 36.0%.

Consolidated net earnings rose 5.6% to a new company record of $71,310. Earnings per share increased by 7.4% to $1.46 from the previous record of $1.36 reached in 1998. Earnings per share increased by a greater percent than net earnings due to lower average shares outstanding during 1999 as a result of share repurchases made during the year.

Our net earnings as a percent of sales increased to 18.0% from 17.4%. 1999 was the eighteenth consecutive year of record earnings achievement for the company.

"Comprehensive earnings" is a way to look at earnings whereby traditionally reported net earnings must be adjusted by items that are normally recorded directly to the equity accounts. By this

measure, our earnings are $72,893 or 6.5% higher than in 1998.

1998 vs. 1997

1998 represented the twenty-second consecutive year of record sales. Sales reached $388,659, an increase of 3.5% over 1997 sales of $375,594. Increases were seen in each quarter, and the third quarter, which was driven by another successful Halloween season, continued to be our largest selling period.

Sales throughout the year were favorably impacted by successful promotional programs. Increases were seen in all major trade classes and in all major domestic brands. Line extensions, new products and seasonal packs also contributed to sales gains.

Domestic sales growth was partially offset by declines in the sales of our Mexican subsidiary due to currency devaluations and difficult local market conditions. Sales in our Canadian operation increased due to distribution gains, seasonal sales growth at Halloween and a new product introduction. These increases were also partially offset by adverse currency translation.

Cost of goods sold, as a percentage of sales, decreased from 50.1% to 48.3%. This reflected favorable ingredient

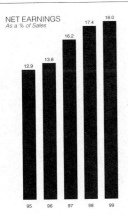

NET EARNINGS
*As a % of Sales*

12.9  13.8  16.2  17.4  18.0
95    96    97    98    99

NET EARNINGS
*Per Share*

$.81  $.95  $1.22  $1.36  $1.46
95    96    97     98     99

costs and increased operating efficiencies associated with higher production volumes coupled with stable packaging and labor costs. Consequently, gross margin, which was $201,042 or 7.3% higher than in 1997, improved as a percentage of sales from 49.9% to 51.7%.

Gross margins as a percent of sales have historically been lower in the third and fourth quarters of the year due to the seasonal nature of our business and the product mix sold at that time of year. This occurred again in 1998.

Operating expenses as a percent of sales were 25.7% in 1998, a decrease of .2% versus 1997. This improvement is due to effective expense control programs aimed at keeping costs in check. Earnings from operations were $101,265 or 26.1% of sales versus 24.0% in 1997, reflecting the combined effects of an increased gross margin percentage and lower operating costs as a percent of sales.

Other income decreased to $4,798, due to exchange losses from Mexico, partially offset by higher investment income.

Earnings per share rose 11.5% to a new company record of $1.36 or $67,526 from the previous record of $1.22 or $60,682 in 1997. This represents an improvement in earnings as a percent of sales to 17.4% and the

seventeenth consecutive year of record earnings for the company.

Comprehensive earnings were $68,472 or 13.7% higher than in 1997.

## LIQUIDITY AND CAPITAL RESOURCES

Cash flows from operating activities were $72,935, $77,735 and $68,176 in 1999, 1998 and 1997, respectively. The decrease in 1999 was principally attributable to an increase in prepaid expenses and other assets, partially offset by higher net earnings and increases in income taxes payable and deferred. Also, depreciation expense was lower in 1999 because some equipment became fully depreciated during 1998, and due to foreign currency translation.

The increase in 1998 was attributable to higher net earnings than in 1997, augmented by other receivables, inventory, deferred compensation and other liabilities and income taxes payable and deferred. This was partially offset by accounts receivable and accounts payable and accrued liabilities.

Cash flows from investing activities reflect net increases in marketable securities of $6,710, $19,951 and $23,087 as well as capital expenditures of $20,283, $14,878 and $8,611 in 1999, 1998 and 1997, respectively.

Cash flows from financing activities reflect share repurchases of $26,869, $13,445 and $14,401 in 1999, 1998 and 1997, respectively. In 1998 there was a short term borrowing which was subsequently repaid during that same year. Cash dividends of $11,313 were paid in 1999, the fifty-seventh consecutive year in which we have paid cash dividends.

### Year 2000 Conversion

During 1998 and 1999 the company undertook an extensive program to ensure that its operations would not be adversely impacted by software failures arising from calculations using the year 2000 date. This program entailed a thorough evaluation of the risks and costs associated with this problem, a plan to remediate "Y2K" problems that were identified, and the development of contingency plans.

Since the majority of systems used throughout the company were found to be year 2000 compliant, this program was precautionary in nature and did not have a material impact on the company or its operations, and the company did not experience any significant business disruptions on January 1, 2000.

The results of our operations and our financial condition are expressed in the following financial statements.

CONSOLIDATED STATEMENT OF

# *Earnings, Comprehensive Earnings and Retained Earnings*

TOOTSIE ROLL INDUSTRIES, INC. AND SUBSIDIARIES                                          (in thousands except per share data)

|  | For the year ended December 31, | | |
|---|---|---|---|
|  | **1999** | 1998 | 1997 |
| Net sales | $396,750 | $388,659 | $375,594 |
| Cost of goods sold | 192,561 | 187,617 | 188,313 |
| Gross margin | 204,189 | 201,042 | 187,281 |
| Selling, marketing and administrative expenses | 96,964 | 97,071 | 94,488 |
| Amortization of intangible assets | 2,706 | 2,706 | 2,706 |
| Earnings from operations | 104,519 | 101,265 | 90,087 |
| Other income, net | 6,928 | 4,798 | 5,274 |
| Earnings before income taxes | 111,447 | 106,063 | 95,361 |
| Provision for income taxes | 40,137 | 38,537 | 34,679 |
| Net earnings | $ 71,310 | $ 67,526 | $ 60,682 |
|  |  |  |  |
| Net earnings | $ 71,310 | $ 67,526 | $ 60,682 |
| Other comprehensive earnings (loss), net of tax |  |  |  |
| Unrealized gains (losses) on securities | 930 | 976 | (417) |
| Foreign currency translation adjustments | 653 | (30) | (17) |
| Other comprehensive earnings (loss) | 1,583 | 946 | (434) |
| Comprehensive earnings | $ 72,893 | $ 68,472 | $ 60,248 |
|  |  |  |  |
| Retained earnings at beginning of year | $164,652 | $159,124 | $136,352 |
| Net earnings | 71,310 | 67,526 | 60,682 |
| Cash dividends ($.24, $.19 and $.15 per share) | (11,654) | (9,484) | (7,472) |
| Stock dividends | (65,689) | (52,514) | (30,438) |
| Retained earnings at end of year | $158,619 | $164,652 | $159,124 |
| Earnings per share | $ 1.46 | $ 1.36 | $ 1.22 |
| Average common and class B common shares outstanding | 48,974 | 49,482 | 49,725 |

(The accompanying notes are an integral part of these statements.)

CONSOLIDATED STATEMENT OF
# Financial Position
TOOTSIE ROLL INDUSTRIES, INC. AND SUBSIDIARIES

(in thousands)

## Assets

December 31,

| | 1999 | 1998 |
|---|---|---|
| CURRENT ASSETS: | | |
| Cash and cash equivalents | $ 88,504 | $ 80,744 |
| Investments | 71,002 | 83,176 |
| Accounts receivable trade, less allowances of $2,032 and $2,184 | 19,032 | 19,110 |
| Other receivables | 5,716 | 3,324 |
| Inventories: | | |
| Finished goods and work-in-process | 20,689 | 21,395 |
| Raw materials and supplies | 14,396 | 15,125 |
| Prepaid expenses | 3,124 | 3,081 |
| Deferred income taxes | 2,069 | 2,584 |
| Total current assets | 224,532 | 228,539 |
| PROPERTY, PLANT AND EQUIPMENT, at cost: | | |
| Land | 7,981 | 7,774 |
| Buildings | 30,330 | 22,226 |
| Machinery and equipment | 145,789 | 133,601 |
| | 184,100 | 163,601 |
| Less—Accumulated depreciation | 88,203 | 80,577 |
| | 95,897 | 83,024 |
| OTHER ASSETS: | | |
| Intangible assets, net of accumulated amortization of $23,497 and $20,791 | 85,137 | 87,843 |
| Investments | 87,167 | 59,252 |
| Cash surrender value of life insurance and other assets | 36,683 | 28,765 |
| | 208,987 | 175,860 |
| | $529,416 | $487,423 |

(The accompanying notes are an integral part of these statements.)

(in thousands except per share data)

# *Liabilities and Shareholders' Equity*

December 31,

| | 1999 | 1998 |
|---|---|---|
| CURRENT LIABILITIES: | | |
| Accounts payable | $ 12,845 | $ 12,450 |
| Dividends payable | 3,035 | 2,514 |
| Accrued liabilities | 31,945 | 31,297 |
| Income taxes payable | 8,284 | 7,123 |
| Total current liabilities | 56,109 | 53,384 |
| NONCURRENT LIABILITIES: | | |
| Deferred income taxes | 9,520 | 9,014 |
| Postretirement health care and life insurance benefits | 6,557 | 6,145 |
| Industrial development bonds | 7,500 | 7,500 |
| Deferred compensation and other liabilities | 19,084 | 14,923 |
| Total noncurrent liabilities | 42,661 | 37,582 |
| SHAREHOLDERS' EQUITY: | | |
| Common stock, $.69-4/9 par value— | | |
| 120,000 and 50,000 shares authorized— | | |
| 32,854 and 32,439, respectively, issued | 22,815 | 22,527 |
| Class B common stock, $.69-4/9 par value— | | |
| 40,000 and 20,000 shares authorized— | | |
| 15,707 and 15,422, respectively, issued | 10,908 | 10,710 |
| Capital in excess of par value | 249,236 | 210,064 |
| Retained earnings, per accompanying statement | 158,619 | 164,652 |
| Accumulated other comprehensive earnings | (8,940) | (10,523) |
| Treasury stock (at cost)— | | |
| 50 shares and 25 shares, respectively | (1,992) | (973) |
| | 430,646 | 396,457 |
| | $529,416 | $487,423 |

CONSOLIDATED STATEMENT OF

# Cash Flows

TOOTSIE ROLL INDUSTRIES, INC. AND SUBSIDIARIES                                        (in thousands)

|  | For the year ended December 31, | | |
|---|---|---|---|
|  | 1999 | 1998 | 1997 |
| **CASH FLOWS FROM OPERATING ACTIVITIES:** | | | |
| Net earnings | $71,310 | $67,526 | $60,682 |
| Adjustments to reconcile net earnings to net cash provided by operating activities: | | | |
| Depreciation and amortization | 9,979 | 12,807˙ | 12,819 |
| (Gain) loss on retirement of fixed assets | (43) | 118 | 26 |
| Changes in operating assets and liabilities: | | | |
| Accounts receivable | 400 | (915) | 199 |
| Other receivables | (2,392) | 1,358 | (2,526) |
| Inventories | 1,592 | (106) | (6,463) |
| Prepaid expenses and other assets | (15,672) | (7,723) | (6,622) |
| Accounts payable and accrued liabilities | 968 | (596) | 9,624 |
| Income taxes payable and deferred | 2,232 | (625) | (2,049) |
| Postretirement health care and life insurance benefits | 412 | 241 | 269 |
| Deferred compensation and other liabilities | 4,162 | 5,004 | 1,932 |
| Other | (13) | 646 | 285 |
| Net cash provided by operating activities | 72,935 | 77,735 | 68,176 |
| **CASH FLOWS FROM INVESTING ACTIVITIES:** | | | |
| Capital expenditures | (20,283) | (14,878) | (8,611) |
| Purchase of held to maturity securities | (238,949) | (259,112) | (68,982) |
| Maturity of held to maturity securities | 235,973 | 240,195 | 27,473 |
| Purchase of available for sale and trading securities | (117,694) | (217,799) | (304,910) |
| Sale and maturity of available for sale and trading securities | 113,960 | 216,765 | 323,332 |
| Net cash used in investing activities | (26,993) | (34,829) | (31,698) |
| **CASH FLOWS FROM FINANCING ACTIVITIES:** | | | |
| Issuance of notes payable | — | 7,000 | — |
| Repayments of notes payable | — | (7,000) | — |
| Treasury stock purchases | (1,019) | (973) | — |
| Shares repurchased and retired | (25,850) | (12,472) | (14,401) |
| Dividends paid in cash | (11,313) | (9,150) | (7,303) |
| Net cash used in financing activities | (38,182) | (22,595) | (21,704) |
| Increase in cash and cash equivalents | 7,760 | 20,311 | 14,774 |
| Cash and cash equivalents at beginning of year | 80,744 | 60,433 | 45,659 |
| Cash and cash equivalents at end of year | $88,504 | $80,744 | $60,433 |
| Supplemental cash flow information: | | | |
| Income taxes paid | $38,827 | $40,000 | $36,716 |
| Interest paid | $   453 | $   803 | $   389 |

(The accompanying notes are an integral part of these statements.)

# *Notes to Consolidated Financial Statements* ($ in thousands except per share data)

TOOTSIE ROLL INDUSTRIES, INC. AND SUBSIDIARIES

## NOTE 1—SIGNIFICANT ACCOUNTING POLICIES:

### Basis of consolidation:

The consolidated financial statements include the accounts of Tootsie Roll Industries, Inc. and its wholly-owned subsidiaries (the company), which are primarily engaged in the manufacture and sale of candy products. All significant intercompany transactions have been eliminated.

The preparation of financial statements in conformity with generally accepted accounting principles requires management to make estimates and assumptions that affect the reported amounts of assets and liabilities and disclosure of contingent assets and liabilities at the date of the financial statements and the reported amounts of revenues and expenses during the reporting period. Actual results could differ from those estimates.

### Revenue recognition:

Revenues are recognized when products are shipped. Accounts receivable are unsecured.

### Cash and cash equivalents:

The company considers temporary cash investments with an original maturity of three months or less to be cash equivalents.

### Investments:

Investments consist of various marketable securities with maturities of generally less than one year. In accordance with Statement of Financial Accounting Standards (SFAS) No. 115, "Accounting For Certain Investments in Debt and Equity Securities," the company's debt and equity securities are considered as either held to maturity, available for sale or trading. Held to maturity securities represent those securities that the company has both the positive intent and ability to hold to maturity and are carried at amortized cost. Available for sale securities represent those securities that do not meet the classification of held to maturity, are not actively traded and are carried at fair value. Unrealized gains and losses on these securities are excluded from earnings and are reported as a separate component of shareholders' equity, net of applicable taxes, until realized. Trading securities relate to deferred compensation arrangements and are carried at fair value.

### Inventories:

Inventories are stated at cost, not in excess of market. The cost of domestic inventories ($29,111 and $31,307 at December 31, 1999 and 1998, respectively) has been determined by the last-in, first-out (LIFO) method. The excess of current cost over LIFO cost of inventories approximates $5,008 and $5,016 at December 31, 1999 and 1998, respectively. The cost of foreign inventories ($5,974 and $5,213 at December 31, 1999 and 1998, respectively) has been determined by the first-in, first-out (FIFO) method.

From time to time, the company enters into commodity futures and option contracts in order to fix the future price of certain key ingredients which may be subject to price volatility (primarily sugar and corn syrup). Gains or losses, if any, resulting from these contracts are considered as a component of the cost of the ingredients being hedged. At December 31, 1999 the company had open contracts to purchase most of its expected 2000 sugar usage.

### Property, plant and equipment:

Depreciation is computed for financial reporting purposes by use of both the straight-line and accelerated methods based on useful lives of 20 to 35 years for buildings and 12 to 20 years for machinery and equipment. For income tax purposes the company uses accelerated methods on all properties. Depreciation expense was $7,663, $10,101 and $9,947 in 1999, 1998 and 1997, respectively.

### Carrying value of long-lived assets:

In the event that facts and circumstances indicate that the company's long-lived assets may be impaired, an evaluation of recoverability would be performed. Such an evaluation entails comparing the estimated future undiscounted cash flows associated with the asset to the asset's carrying amount to determine if a write down to market value or discounted cash flow value is required. The company considers that no circumstances exist that would require such an evaluation.

### Postretirement health care and life insurance benefits:

The company provides certain postretirement health care and life insurance benefits. The cost of these postretirement benefits is accrued during employees' working careers.

### Income taxes:

The company uses the liability method of computing deferred income taxes.

### Intangible assets:

Intangible assets represent the excess of cost over the acquired net tangible assets of operating companies and is amortized on a straight-line basis over a 40 year period. The company assesses the recoverability of its intangible assets using undiscounted future cash flows.

### Foreign currency translation:

During 1997, management determined that the Mexican economy was hyper-inflationary. Accordingly, the US dollar was used as the functional currency for the company's Mexican operations, and translation gains and losses were included in the determination of 1997 and 1998 earnings. Effective January 1, 1999, management determined that the Mexican economy was no longer hyper-inflationary and designated the local currency as the functional currency. Accordingly, the net effect of translating the Mexican operations' financial statements was reported in a separate component of shareholders' equity during 1999.

### Comprehensive earnings:

Comprehensive earnings includes net earnings, foreign currency translation adjustments and unrealized gains/losses on marketable securities.

### Earnings per share:

A dual presentation of basic and diluted earnings per share is not required due to the lack of potentially dilutive securities under the company's simple capital structure. Therefore, all earnings per share amounts represent basic earnings per share.

## NOTE 2—ACCRUED LIABILITIES:

Accrued liabilities are comprised of the following:

| | December 31, | |
|---|---|---|
| | 1999 | 1998 |
| Compensation | $ 8,993 | $ 8,433 |
| Other employee benefits | 4,067 | 4,143 |
| Taxes, other than income | 2,248 | 2,460 |
| Advertising and promotions | 8,508 | 8,451 |
| Other | 8,129 | 7,810 |
| | $31,945 | $31,297 |

## NOTE 3—INCOME TAXES:

The domestic and foreign components of pretax income are as follows:

| | 1999 | 1998 | 1997 |
|---|---|---|---|
| Domestic | $110,052 | $106,667 | $93,318 |
| Foreign | 1,395 | (604) | 2,043 |
| | $111,447 | $106,063 | $95,361 |

The provision for income taxes is comprised of the following:

| | 1999 | 1998 | 1997 |
|---|---|---|---|
| Current: | | | |
| Federal | $34,290 | $34,373 | $29,764 |
| Foreign | 783 | 618 | 626 |
| State | 4,294 | 4,286 | 3,836 |
| | 39,367 | 39,277 | 34,226 |
| Deferred: | | | |
| Federal | 1,039 | (250) | 738 |
| Foreign | (388) | (479) | (368) |
| State | 119 | (11) | 83 |
| | 770 | (740) | 453 |
| | $40,137 | $38,537 | $34,679 |

Deferred income taxes are comprised of the following:

| | December 31, | |
|---|---|---|
| | 1999 | 1998 |
| Workers' compensation | $ 396 | $ 413 |
| Reserve for uncollectible accounts | 467 | 547 |
| Other accrued expenses | 1,214 | 1,137 |
| VEBA funding | (347) | (478) |
| Other, net | 339 | 965 |
| Net current deferred income tax asset | $ 2,069 | $ 2,584 |

| | December 31, | |
|---|---|---|
| | 1999 | 1998 |
| Depreciation | $10,563 | $9,371 |
| Postretirement benefits | (2,220) | (2,132) |
| Deductible goodwill | 5,647 | 5,176 |
| Deferred compensation | (4,947) | (4,244) |
| Accrued commissions | 2,011 | 1,729 |
| Foreign subsidiary tax loss carryforward | (1,898) | (1,428) |
| Other, net | 364 | 542 |
| Net long-term deferred income tax liability | $ 9,520 | $9,014 |

At December 31, 1999, gross deferred tax assets and gross deferred tax liabilities are $14,897 and $22,348, respectively.

The effective income tax rate differs from the statutory rate as follows:

| | 1999 | 1998 | 1997 |
|---|---|---|---|
| U.S. statutory rate | 35.0% | 35.0% | 35.0% |
| State income taxes, net | 2.6 | 2.6 | 2.7 |
| Amortization of intangible assets | 0.4 | 0.4 | 0.5 |
| Other, net | (2.0) | (1.7) | (1.8) |
| Effective income tax rate | 36.0% | 36.3% | 36.4% |

The company has not provided for U.S. federal or foreign withholding taxes on $4,303 of foreign subsidiaries' undistributed earnings as of December 31, 1999 because such earnings are considered to be permanently reinvested. When excess cash has accumulated in the company's foreign subsidiaries and it is advantageous for tax or foreign exchange reasons, subsidiary earnings may be remitted, and income taxes will be provided on such amounts. It is not practicable to determine the amount of income taxes that would be payable upon remittance of the undistributed earnings.

## NOTE 4—SHARE CAPITAL AND CAPITAL IN EXCESS OF PAR VALUE:

| | Common Stock | | Class B Common Stock | | Treasury Stock | | Capital in excess of par value |
|---|---|---|---|---|---|---|---|
| | Shares | Amount | Shares | Amount | Shares | Amount | |
| | (000's) | | (000's) | | (000's) | | |
| Balance at January 1, 1997 | 15,617 | $10,845 | 7,387 | $ 5,130 | — | $ — | $171,589 |
| Issuance of 3% stock dividend | 465 | 323 | 221 | 153 | — | — | 29,868 |
| Conversion of Class B common shares to common shares | 61 | 42 | (61) | (42) | — | — | — |
| Purchase and retirement of common shares | (292) | (202) | — | — | — | — | (14,198) |
| Balance at December 31, 1997 | 15,851 | 11,008 | 7,547 | 5,241 | — | — | 187,259 |
| Issuance of 3% stock dividend | 473 | 329 | 225 | 156 | — | — | 51,780 |
| Purchase of shares for the treasury | — | — | — | — | (20) | (973) | — |
| Issuance of 2-for-1 stock split | 16,305 | 11,323 | 7,748 | 5,381 | (5) | — | (16,704) |
| Conversion of Class B common shares to common shares | 98 | 68 | (98) | (68) | — | — | — |
| Purchase and retirement of common shares | (288) | (201) | — | — | — | — | (12,271) |
| Balance at December 31, 1998 | 32,439 | 22,527 | 15,422 | 10,710 | (25) | (973) | 210,064 |
| Issuance of 3% stock dividend | 971 | 674 | 461 | 320 | (1) | — | 64,514 |
| Purchase of shares for the treasury | — | — | — | — | (24) | (1,019) | — |
| Conversion of Class B common shares to common shares | 176 | 122 | (176) | (122) | — | — | — |
| Purchase and retirement of common shares | (732) | (508) | — | — | — | — | (25,342) |
| Balance at December 31, 1999 | 32,854 | $22,815 | 15,707 | $10,908 | (50) | $(1,992) | $249,236 |

The Class B Common Stock has essentially the same rights as Common Stock, except that each share of Class B Common Stock has ten votes per share (compared to one vote per share of Common Stock), is not traded on any exchange, is restricted as to transfer and is convertible on a share-for-share basis, at any time and at no cost to the holders, into shares of Common Stock which are traded on the New York Stock Exchange.

Average shares outstanding and all per share amounts included in the financial statements and notes thereto have been adjusted retroactively to reflect annual three percent stock dividends and the two-for-one stock split distributed in 1998.

## NOTE 5—NOTES PAYABLE AND INDUSTRIAL DEVELOPMENT BONDS:

During 1992, the company entered into an industrial development bond agreement with the City of Covington, Tennessee. The bond proceeds of $7.5 million were used to finance the expansion of the company's existing facilities. Interest is payable at various times during the year based upon the interest calculation option (fixed, variable or floating) selected by the company. As of December 31, 1999 and 1998, interest was calculated under the floating option (4.7% and 3.7%, respectively) which requires monthly payments of interest. Principal on the bonds is due in its entirety in the year 2027.

In connection with the issuance of the bonds, the company entered into a letter of credit agreement with a bank for the amount of principal outstanding plus 48 days' accrued interest. The letter of credit, which expires in January 2001, carries an annual fee of 32 1/2 basis points on the outstanding principal amount of the bonds.

## NOTE 6—EMPLOYEE BENEFIT PLANS:

### Pension plans:

The company sponsors defined contribution pension plans covering certain nonunion employees with over one year of credited service. The company's policy is to fund pension costs accrued based on compensation levels. Total pension expense for 1999, 1998 and 1997 approximated $2,062, $1,951 and $2,153, respectively. The company also maintains certain profit sharing and savings-investment plans. Company contributions in 1999, 1998 and 1997 to these plans were $616, $582 and $540, respectively.

The company also contributes to multi-employer defined benefit pension plans for its union employees. Such contributions aggregated $713, $680 and $609 in 1999, 1998 and 1997, respectively. The relative position of each employer associated with the multi-employer plans with respect to the actuarial present value of benefits and net plan assets is not determinable by the company.

### Postretirement health care and life insurance benefit plans:

The company provides certain postretirement health care and life insurance benefits for corporate office and management employees. Employees become eligible for these benefits if they meet minimum age and service requirements and if they agree to contribute a portion of the cost. The company has the right to modify or terminate these benefits. The company does not fund postretirement health care and life insurance benefits in advance of payments for benefit claims.

The changes in the accumulated postretirement benefit obligation at December 31, 1999 and 1998 consist of the following:

| | December 31, | |
| --- | --- | --- |
| | 1999 | 1998 |
| Benefit obligation, beginning of year | $6,163 | $5,904 |
| Net periodic postretirement benefit cost | 531 | 438 |
| Benefits paid | (137) | (197) |
| Benefit obligation, end of year | $6,557 | $6,145 |

Net periodic postretirement benefit cost included the following components:

| | 1999 | 1998 | 1997 |
| --- | --- | --- | --- |
| Service cost—benefits attributed to service during the period | $306 | $258 | $251 |
| Interest cost on the accumulated postretirement benefit obligation | 302 | 279 | 285 |
| Amortization of unrecognized net gain | (77) | (99) | (101) |
| Net periodic postretirement benefit cost | $531 | $438 | $435 |

For measurement purposes, an 8.0% annual rate of increase in the per capita cost of covered health care benefits was assumed for 1999; the rate was assumed to decrease gradually to 5.5% for 2004 and remain at that level thereafter. The health care cost trend rate assumption has a significant effect on the amounts reported. The weighted-average discount rate used in determining the accumulated postretirement benefit obligation was 7.25% and 6.25% at December 31, 1999 and 1998, respectively.

Increasing or decreasing the health care trend rates by one percentage point in each year would have the following effect:

| | 1% Increase | 1% Decrease |
| --- | --- | --- |
| Effect on postretirement benefit obligation | $646 | $(530) |
| Effect on total of service and interest cost components | $117 | $ (92) |

## NOTE 7—OTHER INCOME, NET:

Other income (expense) is comprised of the following:

| | 1999 | 1998 | 1997 |
| --- | --- | --- | --- |
| Interest income | $7,449 | $6,934 | $5,764 |
| Interest expense | (453) | (756) | (483) |
| Dividend income | 611 | 822 | 999 |
| Foreign exchange losses | (126) | (2,140) | (447) |
| Royalty income | 263 | 155 | 312 |
| Miscellaneous, net | (816) | (217) | (871) |
| | $6,928 | $4,798 | $5,274 |

## NOTE 8—COMMITMENTS:

Rental expense aggregated $457, $432 and $477 in 1999, 1998 and 1997, respectively.

Future operating lease commitments are not significant.

## NOTE 9—COMPREHENSIVE INCOME:

Components of accumulated other comprehensive earnings (loss) are shown as follows:

| | Foreign Currency Items | Unrealized Gains (Losses) on Securities | Accumulated Other Comprehensive Earnings/(Loss) |
| --- | --- | --- | --- |
| Balance at January 1, 1997 | $(11,035) | $ — | $(11,035) |
| Change during period | (17) | (417) | (434) |
| Balance at December 31, 1997 | (11,052) | (417) | (11,469) |
| Change during period | (30) | 976 | 946 |
| Balance at December 31, 1998 | (11,082) | 559 | (10,523) |
| Change during period | 653 | 930 | 1,583 |
| Balance at December 31, 1999 | $(10,429) | $ 1,489 | $ (8,940) |

The individual tax effects of each component of other comprehensive earnings for the year ended December 31, 1999 are shown as follows:

| | Before Tax Amount | Tax Expense | Net-of-Tax Tax Amount |
| --- | --- | --- | --- |
| Foreign currency translation adjustment | $ 653 | $ — | $ 653 |
| Unrealized gains (losses) on securities: | | | |
| Unrealized holding gains (losses) arising during 1999 | 1,504 | (556) | 948 |
| Less: reclassification adjustment for gains (losses) realized in earnings | 28 | (10) | 18 |
| Net unrealized gains | 1,476 | (546) | 930 |
| Other comprehensive earnings | $2,129 | $(546) | $1,583 |

## NOTE 10—DISCLOSURES ABOUT THE FAIR VALUE OF FINANCIAL INSTRUMENTS:

### Carrying amount and fair value:

The carrying amount approximates fair value of cash and cash equivalents because of the short maturity of those instruments. The fair values of investments are estimated based on quoted market prices. The fair value of the company's industrial development bonds approximates their carrying value because they have a floating interest rate. The carrying amount and estimated fair values of the company's financial instruments are as follows:

| | 1999 | | 1998 | |
| --- | --- | --- | --- | --- |
| | Carrying Amount | Fair Value | Carrying Amount | Fair Value |
| Cash and cash equivalents | $ 88,504 | $ 88,504 | $80,744 | $80,744 |
| Investments held to maturity | 110,245 | 111,151 | 106,415 | 109,182 |
| Investments available for sale | 37,390 | 37,390 | 28,214 | 28,214 |
| Investments in trading securities | 10,534 | 10,534 | 7,799 | 7,799 |
| Industrial development bonds | 7,500 | 7,500 | 7,500 | 7,500 |

A summary of the aggregate fair value, gross unrealized gains, gross unrealized losses and amortized cost basis of the company's investment portfolio by major security type is as follows:

| | December 31, 1999 | | | | December 31, 1998 | | | |
| --- | --- | --- | --- | --- | --- | --- | --- | --- |
| | Amortized Cost | Fair Value | Unrealized Gains | Unrealized Losses | Amortized Cost | Fair Value | Unrealized Gains | Unrealized Losses |
| **Held to Maturity:** | | | | | | | | |
| Unit investment trusts of preferred stocks | $ 2,592 | $ 4,618 | $ 2,026 | $ — | $ 3,626 | $ 5,978 | $ 2,352 | $ — |
| Tax-free commercial paper | — | — | — | — | 8,250 | 8,250 | — | — |
| Municipal bonds | 109,256 | 108,160 | — | (1,096) | 96,828 | 97,266 | 438 | — |
| Unit investment trusts of municipal bonds | 959 | 935 | — | (24) | 979 | 956 | — | (23) |
| Private export funding securities | 4,933 | 4,933 | — | — | 4,982 | 4,982 | — | — |
| | $ 117,740 | $ 118,646 | $ 2,026 | $ (1,120) | $ 114,665 | $ 117,432 | $ 2,790 | $ (23) |
| **Available for Sale:** | | | | | | | | |
| Municipal bonds | $ 40,930 | $ 40,603 | $ — | $ (327) | $ 39,397 | $ 39,264 | $ — | $ (133) |
| Mutual funds | 3,007 | 5,698 | 2,691 | — | 3,007 | 4,028 | 1,021 | — |
| | $ 43,937 | $ 46,301 | $ 2,691 | $ (327) | $ 42,404 | $ 43,292 | $ 1,021 | $ (133) |

Held to maturity securities of $7,495 and $8,250 and available for sale securities of $8,911 and $15,078 were included in cash and cash equivalents at December 31, 1999 and 1998, respectively. There were no securities with maturities greater than three years and gross realized gains and losses on the sale of available for sale securities in 1999 and 1998 were not significant.

### NOTE 11—GEOGRAPHIC AREA AND SALES INFORMATION:
Summary of sales, net earnings and assets by geographic area

| | 1999 | | | 1998 | | | 1997 | | |
| --- | --- | --- | --- | --- | --- | --- | --- | --- | --- |
| | United States | Mexico and Canada | Consolidated | United States | Mexico and Canada | Consolidated | United States | Mexico and Canada | Consolidated |
| Sales to unaffiliated customers | $365,975 | $30,775 | $396,750 | $363,569 | $25,090 | $388,659 | $346,487 | $29,107 | $375,594 |
| Sales between geographic areas | 3,787 | 1,794 | | 2,805 | 4,374 | | 1,694 | 3,314 | |
| | $369,762 | $32,569 | | $366,374 | $29,464 | | $348,181 | $32,421 | |
| Net earnings | $ 69,917 | $ 1,393 | $ 71,310 | $ 68,521 | $ (995) | $ 67,526 | $ 58,898 | $ 1,784 | $ 60,682 |
| Total assets | $505,152 | $24,264 | $529,416 | $467,265 | $20,158 | $487,423 | $414,629 | $22,113 | $436,742 |
| Net assets | $409,160 | $21,486 | $430,646 | $378,892 | $17,565 | $396,457 | $332,410 | $18,753 | $351,163 |

Total assets are those assets associated with or used directly in the respective geographic area, excluding intercompany advances and investments.

**Major customer**

Revenues from a major customer aggregated approximately 17.9%, 17.2% and 15.9% of total net sales during the years ended December 31, 1999, 1998 and 1997, respectively.

# Report of Independent Accountants

To the Board of Directors and Shareholders of Tootsie Roll Industries, Inc.

In our opinion, the accompanying consolidated statement of financial position and the related consolidated statements of earnings, comprehensive earnings and retained earnings and of cash flows present fairly, in all material respects, the financial position of Tootsie Roll Industries, Inc. and its subsidiaries at December 31, 1999 and 1998, and the results of their operations and their cash flows for each of the three years in the period ended December 31, 1999, in conformity with accounting principles generally accepted in the United States. These financial statements are the responsibility of the Company's management; our responsibility is to express an opinion on these financial statements based on our audits. We conducted our audits of these statements in accordance with auditing standards generally accepted in the United States, which require that we plan and perform the audit to obtain reasonable assurance about whether the financial statements are free of material misstatement. An audit includes examining, on a test basis, evidence supporting the amounts and disclosures in the financial statements, assessing the accounting principles used and significant estimates made by management, and evaluating the overall financial statement presentation. We believe that our audits provide a reasonable basis for the opinion expressed above.

*PricewaterhouseCoopers LLP*

Chicago, Illinois
February 11, 2000

# *Quarterly Financial Data*

TOOTSIE ROLL INDUSTRIES, INC. AND SUBSIDIARIES

(Thousands of dollars except per share data)

| 1999 | First | Second | Third | Fourth | Total |
|---|---|---|---|---|---|
| Net sales | $74,200 | $88,265 | $152,667 | $81,618 | $396,750 |
| Gross margin | 38,815 | 45,902 | 77,651 | 41,821 | 204,189 |
| Net earnings | 12,325 | 14,751 | 29,283 | 14,951 | 71,310 |
| Net earnings per share | .25 | .30 | .60 | .31 | 1.46 |
| **1998** | | | | | |
| Net sales | $69,701 | $85,931 | $144,230 | $88,797 | $388,659 |
| Gross margin | 36,966 | 45,133 | 73,251 | 45,692 | 201,042 |
| Net earnings | 11,217 | 13,910 | 27,216 | 15,183 | 67,526 |
| Net earnings per share | .22 | .28 | .55 | .31 | 1.36 |
| **1997** | | | | | |
| Net sales | $66,258 | $82,287 | $140,645 | $86,404 | $375,594 |
| Gross margin | 33,323 | 41,382 | 69,746 | 42,830 | 187,281 |
| Net earnings | 9,751 | 12,507 | 24,695 | 13,729 | 60,682 |
| Net earnings per share | .20 | .25 | .50 | .27 | 1.22 |

Net earnings per share is based upon average outstanding shares as adjusted for 3% stock dividends issued during the second quarter of each year and the 2-for-1 stock split effective July 13, 1998.

---

1999-1998 QUARTERLY SUMMARY OF TOOTSIE ROLL INDUSTRIES, INC. STOCK PRICE AND DIVIDENDS PER SHARE

STOCK PRICES*

| | 1999 | | 1998 | |
|---|---|---|---|---|
| | High | Low | High | Low |
| 1st Qtr . . . | 46-15/16 | 39-3/4 | 38-13/32 | 29-27/32 |
| 2nd Qtr . . | 46-3/4 | 38-1/8 | 40-3/4 | 34-31/32 |
| 3rd Qtr . . . | 39-7/16 | 30 | 47-1/4 | 33-3/4 |
| 4th Qtr . . . | 33-7/16 | 29-13/16 | 42-7/8 | 34-1/8 |

*NYSE — Composite Quotations adjusted for the 2-for-1 stock split effective July 13, 1998

Estimated Number of shareholders at 12/31/99 . . . . . . . . . . . 9,500

DIVIDENDS**

| | 1999 | 1998 |
|---|---|---|
| 1st Qtr . . . . . . | $.0510 | $.0389 |
| 2nd Qtr . . . . . | $.0625 | $.0510 |
| 3rd Qtr . . . . . | $.0625 | $.0510 |
| 4th Qtr . . . . . . | $.0625 | $.0510 |

NOTE: In addition to the above cash dividends, a 3% stock dividend was issued on 4/21/99 and 4/22/98.

**Cash dividends are restated to reflect 3% stock dividends and the 2-for-1 stock split.

# *Five Year Summary of Earnings and Financial Highlights*

TOOTSIE ROLL INDUSTRIES, INC. AND SUBSIDIARIES

(Thousands of dollars except per share, percentage and ratio figures)

| (See Management's Comments starting on page 5) | 1999 | 1998 | 1997 | 1996 | 1995 |
|---|---|---|---|---|---|
| **Sales and Earnings Data** | | | | | |
| Net sales | $396,750 | $ 388,659 | $ 375,594 | $ 340,909 | $ 312,660 |
| Gross margin | 204,189 | 201,042 | 187,281 | 162,420 | 145,922 |
| Interest expense | 453 | 756 | 483 | 1,498 | 1,515 |
| Provision for income taxes | 40,137 | 38,537 | 34,679 | 27,891 | 23,670 |
| Net earnings | 71,310 | 67,526 | 60,682 | 47,207 | 40,368 |
| % of sales | 18.0% | 17.4% | 16.2% | 13.8% | 12.9% |
| % of shareholders' equity | 16.6% | 17.0% | 17.3% | 15.1% | 14.8% |
| **Per Common Share Data (1)** | | | | | |
| Net sales | $ 8.10 | $ 7.85 | $ 7.55 | $ 6.84 | $ 6.27 |
| Net earnings | 1.46 | 1.36 | 1.22 | .95 | .81 |
| Shareholders' equity | 8.88 | 8.05 | 7.08 | 6.27 | 5.46 |
| Cash dividends declared | .24 | .19 | .15 | .13 | .11 |
| Stock dividends | 3% | 3% | 3% | 3% | 3% |
| **Additional Financial Data** | | | | | |
| Working capital | $168,423 | $ 175,155 | $ 153,355 | $ 153,329 | $ 109,643 |
| Net cash provided by operating activities | 72,935 | 77,735 | 68,176 | 76,710 | 50,851 |
| Net cash used in (provided by) investing activities | 26,993 | 34,829 | 31,698 | 52,364 | 14,544 |
| Net cash used in financing activities | 38,182 | 22,595 | 21,704 | 26,211 | 5,292 |
| Property, plant & equipment additions | 20,283 | 14,878 | 8,611 | 9,791 | 4,640 |
| Net property, plant & equipment | 95,897 | 83,024 | 78,364 | 81,687 | 81,999 |
| Total assets | 529,416 | 487,423 | 436,742 | 391,456 | 353,816 |
| Long term debt | 7,500 | 7,500 | 7,500 | 7,500 | 7,500 |
| Shareholders' equity | 430,646 | 396,457 | 351,163 | 312,881 | 272,186 |
| Average shares outstanding (1) | 48,974 | 49,482 | 49,725 | 49,873 | 49,873 |

(1)  Adjusted for annual 3% stock dividends and the 2-for-1 stock splits effective July 13, 1998 and July 11, 1995.

# Board of Directors

Melvin J. Gordon[1]       Chairman of the Board and
                         Chief Executive Officer

Ellen R. Gordon[1]       President and Chief Operating Officer

Charles W. Seibert[2][3]  Retired Banker

Lana Jane Lewis-Brent[2][3]  President, Paul Brent Designer, Inc.

[1]Member of the Executive Committee
[2]Member of the Audit Committee
[3]Member of the Compensation Committee

# Officers

Melvin J. Gordon        Chairman of the Board and
                        Chief Executive Officer

Ellen R. Gordon         President and Chief Operating Officer

G. Howard Ember, Jr.    Vice President, Finance & Asst. Secy.

John W. Newlin, Jr.     Vice President, Manufacturing

Thomas E. Corr          Vice President, Marketing & Sales

James M. Hunt           Vice President, Physical Distribution

Barry P. Bowen          Treasurer & Asst. Secy.

Daniel P. Drechney      Controller

# Offices, Plants

Executive Offices       7401 S. Cicero Ave.
                        Chicago, Illinois 60629
                        www.tootsie.com

Plants                  Chicago, Illinois
                        Covington, Tennessee
                        Cambridge, Massachusetts
                        New York, New York
                        Mexico City, Mexico

Foreign Sales Offices   Mexico City, Mexico
                        Mississauga, Ontario

# Subsidiaries

C.C. L.P., Inc.
C.G.C. Corporation
C.G.P., Inc.
Cambridge Brands, Inc.
Cambridge Brands Mfg., Inc.
Cambridge Brands Services, Inc.
Cella's Confections, Inc.
Charms Company
Charms L.P.
Charms Marketing Company
Henry Eisen Advertising Agency, Inc.
J.T. Company, Inc.
Tootsie Roll of Canada Ltd.
Tootsie Roll Central Europe Ltd.

The Tootsie Roll Company, Inc.
Tootsie Roll Management, Inc.
Tootsie Roll Mfg., Inc.
Tootsie Rolls—Latin America, Inc.
Tootsie Roll Worldwide Ltd.
The Sweets Mix Company, Inc.
TRI de Latino America S.A. de C.V.
TRI Finance, Inc.
TRI International Co.
TRI-Mass., Inc.
TRI Sales Co.
Tutsi S.A. de C.V.
World Trade & Marketing Ltd.

# Other Information

Stock Exchange          New York Stock Exchange, Inc.
                        (Since 1922)

Stock Identification    Ticker Symbol: TR
                        CUSIP No. 890516 10-7

Stock Transfer Agent    ChaseMellon Shareholder Services, L.L.C.
and Stock Registrar     Overpeck Centre
                        85 Challenger Road
                        Ridgefield Park, NJ 07660
                        1-800-851-9677
                        www.chasemellon.com

Independent             PricewaterhouseCoopers LLP
Accountants             200 East Randolph Drive
                        Chicago, IL 60601

General Counsel         Becker Ross Stone DeStefano & Klein
                        317 Madison Avenue
                        New York, NY 10017

Annual Meeting          May 1, 2000
                        Mutual Building, Room 1200
                        909 East Main Street
                        Richmond, VA 23219

Printed on recycled paper.

# THE TIME VALUE OF MONEY: FUTURE AMOUNTS AND PRESENT VALUES

## THE CONCEPT

One of the most basic—and important—concepts of investing is the *time value* of *money*. This concept is based on the idea that an amount of money available today can be safely invested to accumulate to a larger amount in the future. As a result, an amount of money available today is considered to be equivalent in value to a *larger sum* available at a future date.

In our discussions, we will refer to an amount of money available today as a *present value*. In contrast, an amount receivable or payable at a future date will be described as a *future amount*.

To illustrate, assume that you place $500 in a savings account that earns interest at the rate of 8% per year. The balance of your account at the end of each of the next four years is illustrated on the following page.

These balances represent different time values of your $500 investment. When you first open the account, your investment has a *present value* of only $500. As time passes, the value of your investment increases to the *future amounts* illustrated in the graph. (Throughout this Appendix, present values will be illustrated in **red**, and future amounts will be shown in **blue**.)

### Relationships between Present Values and Future Amounts

The difference between a present value and any future amount is the *interest* that is included in the future amount. We have seen that interest accrues over time. Therefore, the difference between the present value and a future amount depends on *two factors:* (1) the *rate of interest* at which the present value increases and (2) the *length of time* over which interest accumulates. (Notice in our graph, the farther away the future date, the larger the future amount.)

**Learning Objectives**

*After studying this appendix, you should be able to:*

1. **Explain what is meant by the *time value of money*.**

2. **Describe the relationships between *present values* and *future amounts*.**

3. **Explain three basic ways in which decision makers apply the time value of money.**

4. **Compute future amounts and the investments necessary to accumulate future amounts.**

5. **Compute the present values of future cash flows.**

6. **Discuss accounting applications of the concept of present value.**

**LO 1**

Explain what is meant by the *time value* of money.

**LO 2**

Describe the relationships between *present values* and *future amounts*.

*Future values are bigger, but are they worth more? This is the real issue.*

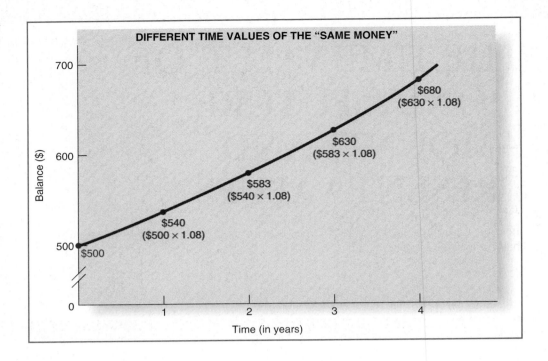

**Present Values Change over Time**   The present value of an investment gradually increases toward the future amount. In fact, when a future date *arrives,* what once was a future amount becomes the present value of the investment. For example, at the end of the first year, $540 will no longer be a future amount—it will be the present value of your savings account.

**The Basic Concept (Stated Several Different Ways)**   Notice that the present value of our savings account is *always less than its future amounts.* This is the basic idea underlying the time value of money. But this idea often is expressed in different ways, including the following:

- A present value is always *less than* a future amount.
- A future amount is always *greater than* a present value.
- A dollar available today is always worth *more* than a dollar that does not become available until a future date.
- A dollar available at a future date is always worth *less* than a dollar that is available today.

Read these statements carefully. All four reflect the idea that a present value is the "equivalent" of a larger number of dollars at a future date. This is what is meant by the time value of money.

## Compound Interest

The relationships between present values and future amounts assume that the interest earned on the investment is *reinvested,* rather than withdrawn. This concept often is called *compounding the interest.* Compounding has an interesting effect. Reinvesting the interest causes the amount invested to increase each period. This, in turn, causes more interest to be earned in each successive period. Over a long period of time, an investment in which interest is compounded continuously will increase to surprisingly large amounts.

In 1626, Peter Minuit is said to have purchased Manhattan Island from a group of Indians for $24 worth of "beads, cloth, and trinkets." This episode often is portrayed as an incredible bargain—even a "steal." But if the Indians had invested this $24 to earn interest at a compound interest rate of, say, 8%, they would have more than enough money today to buy the island back—along with everything on it.

**CASE IN POINT**

## Applications of the Time Value of Money Concept

**LO 3**
Explain three basic ways in which decision makers apply the time value of money.

Investors, accountants, and other decision makers apply the time value of money in three basic ways. These applications are summarized below, along with a typical example.

1. The amount to which an investment will accumulate over time. *Example:* If we invest $5,000 each year and earn an annual rate of return of 10%, how much will be accumulated after 10 years?
2. The amount that must be invested every period to accumulate a required future amount. *Example:* We must accumulate a $200 million bond sinking fund over the next 20 years. How much must we deposit into this fund each year, assuming that the fund's assets will be invested to earn an annual rate of return of 8%?
3. The present value of cash flows expected to occur in the future. *Example:* Assuming that we require a 15% return on our investments, how much can we afford to pay for new machinery that is expected to reduce production costs by $20,000 per year for the next 10 years?

We will now introduce a framework for answering such questions.

## FUTURE AMOUNTS

A future amount is simply the dollar amount to which a present value *will accumulate* over time. As we have stated, the difference between a present value and a related future amount depends on (1) the interest rate and (2) the period of time over which the present value accumulates.

Starting with the present value, we may compute future amounts through a series of multiplications, as illustrated in our graph on page 1070. But there are faster and easier ways. For example, many financial calculators are programmed to compute future amounts; you merely enter the present value, the interest rate, and the number of periods. Or you may use a *table of future amounts,* such as **Table FA–1** illustrated on the following page.

### The Tables Approach

**LO 4**
Compute future amounts and the investments necessary to accumulate future amounts.

A table of future amounts shows the future amount to which *$1* will accumulate over a given number of periods, assuming that it has been invested to earn any of the illustrated interest rates. We will refer to the amounts shown in the body of this table as *factors,* rather than as dollar amounts.

To find the future amount of a present value *greater* than $1, simply multiply the present value by the factor obtained from the table. The formula for using the table in this manner is:

**Future Amount = Present Value × Factor (from Table FA–1)**

*Approach to computing future amount*

| | | | | | | | | | |
|---|---|---|---|---|---|---|---|---|---|
| **Table FA–1** | | | | | | | | | |
| **Future Value of $1 After n Periods** | | | | | | | | | |
| **Number of Periods (n)** | **Interest Rate** | | | | | | | | |
| | **1%** | **1½%** | **5%** | **6%** | **8%** | **10%** | **12%** | **15%** | **20%** |
| 1 | 1.010 | 1.015 | 1.050 | 1.060 | 1.080 | 1.100 | 1.120 | 1.150 | 1.200 |
| 2 | 1.020 | 1.030 | 1.103 | 1.124 | 1.166 | 1.210 | 1.254 | 1.323 | 1.440 |
| 3 | 1.030 | 1.046 | 1.158 | 1.191 | 1.260 | 1.331 | 1.405 | 1.521 | 1.728 |
| 4 | 1.041 | 1.061 | 1.216 | 1.262 | 1.360 | 1.464 | 1.574 | 1.749 | 2.074 |
| 5 | 1.051 | 1.077 | 1.276 | 1.338 | 1.469 | 1.611 | 1.762 | 2.011 | 2.488 |
| 6 | 1.062 | 1.093 | 1.340 | 1.419 | 1.587 | 1.772 | 1.974 | 2.313 | 2.986 |
| 7 | 1.072 | 1.110 | 1.407 | 1.504 | 1.714 | 1.949 | 2.211 | 2.660 | 3.583 |
| 8 | 1.083 | 1.126 | 1.477 | 1.594 | 1.851 | 2.144 | 2.476 | 3.059 | 4.300 |
| 9 | 1.094 | 1.143 | 1.551 | 1.689 | 1.999 | 2.358 | 2.773 | 3.518 | 5.160 |
| 10 | 1.105 | 1.161 | 1.629 | 1.791 | 2.159 | 2.594 | 3.106 | 4.046 | 6.192 |
| 20 | 1.220 | 1.347 | 2.653 | 3.207 | 4.661 | 6.727 | 9.646 | 16.367 | 38.338 |
| 24 | 1.270 | 1.430 | 3.225 | 4.049 | 6.341 | 9.850 | 15.179 | 28.625 | 79.497 |
| 36 | 1.431 | 1.709 | 5.792 | 8.147 | 15.968 | 30.913 | 59.136 | 153.152 | 708.802 |

Let us demonstrate this approach using the data for our savings account, illustrated on page 1070. The account started with a present value of $500, invested at an annual interest rate of 8%. Thus the future values of the account in each of the next four years can be computed as follows (rounded to the nearest dollar):

*Using the table to compute the amounts in our graph*

| Year | Future Amount | Computation (Using Table FA–1) |
|---|---|---|
| 1 | $540 | $500 × 1.080 = $540 |
| 2 | $583 | $500 × 1.166 = $583 |
| 3 | $630 | $500 × 1.260 = $630 |
| 4 | $680 | $500 × 1.360 = $680 |

Computing a future amount is relatively easy. The more interesting question is: How much must we *invest today* to accumulate a required future amount?

**Computing the Required Investment**    At the end of 2002, Metro Recycling agrees to create a fully funded pension plan for its employees by December 31, 2007 (in five years). It is estimated that $5 million will be required to fully fund the pension plan at December 31, 2007. How much must Metro invest in this plan *today* (December 31, 2002) to accumulate the promised $5 million by the end of 2007, assuming that payments to the fund will be invested to earn an annual return of 8%?

Let us repeat our original formula for computing future amounts using **Table FA–1**:

*Our original formula . . .*

$$\text{Future Amount} = \text{Present Value} \times \text{Factor (from Table FA–1)}$$

In this situation, we *know* the future amount—$5 million. We are looking for the *present value* which, when invested at an interest rate of 8%, will accumulate to $5 million in five years. To determine the *present value,* the formula shown above may be restated as follows:

*restated to find the present value*

$$\text{Present Value} = \frac{\text{Future Amount}}{\text{Factor (from Table FA–1)}}$$

Referring to Table FA–1, we get a factor of *1.469* at the intersection of five periods and 8% interest. Thus, the amount of the required investment at the end of 2002 is $3,403,676 ($5 million ÷ 1.469). Invested at 8%, this amount will accumulate to the required $5 million at the end of five years as illustrated below:

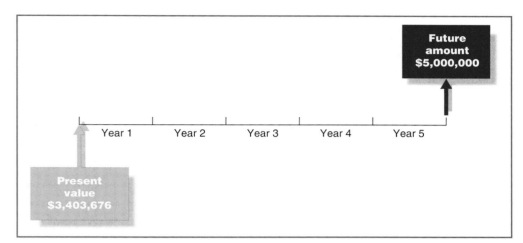

*The future amount of a single investment*

## The Future Amount of an Annuity

In many situations, an investor is to make a *series* of investment payments rather than a single payment. As an example, assume that you plan to invest $500 into your savings account at the end of each of the next five years. If the account pays annual interest of 8%, what will be the balance in your savings account at the end of the fifth year? Tables, such as Table FA–2 on the next page, may be used to answer this question. Table FA–2 presents the future amount of an *ordinary annuity of $1*, which is a series of payments of $1 made at the end of each of a specified number of periods.

To find the future amount of an ordinary annuity of payments greater than $1, we simply multiply the amount of the periodic payment by the factor appearing in the table, as shown below:

$$\frac{\text{Future Amount}}{\text{of an Annuity}} = \text{Periodic Payment} \times \text{Factor (from Table FA–2)}$$

*Approach to computing the future amount of an annuity*

In our example, a factor of 5.867 is obtained from the table at the intersection of five periods and 8% interest. If this factor is multiplied by the periodic payment of $500, we find that your savings account will accumulate to a balance of $2,934 ($500 × 5.867) at the end of five years. Therefore, if you invest $500 at the end of each of the next five years in the savings account, you will accumulate $2,934 at the end of the 5-year period.

While computing the future amount of an investment is sometimes necessary, many business and accounting problems require us to determine the *amount of the periodic payments* that must be made to accumulate the required future amount.

**Computing the Required Periodic Payments**   Assume that Ultra Tech Company is required to accumulate $10 million in a *bond sinking fund* to retire bonds payable five years from now. The *bond indenture* requires Ultra Tech to make equal payments to the fund at the end of each of the next five years. What is the amount of required periodic payment, assuming that the fund will earn 10% annual interest? To answer this question, we simply rearrange the formula shown below for computing the future amount of an annuity:

$$\frac{\text{Future Amount}}{\text{of an Annuity}} = \text{Periodic Payment} \times \text{Factor (from Table FA–2)}$$

*Our original formula . . .*

| Table FA–2 Future Amount of $1 Paid Periodically for *n* Periods | | | | | | | | | |
|---|---|---|---|---|---|---|---|---|---|
| **Number of Periods (n)** | **Interest Rate** | | | | | | | | |
| | **1%** | **1½%** | **5%** | **6%** | **8%** | **10%** | **12%** | **15%** | **20%** |
| 1 | 1.000 | 1.000 | 1.000 | 1.000 | 1.000 | 1.000 | 1.000 | 1.000 | 1.000 |
| 2 | 2.010 | 2.015 | 2.050 | 2.060 | 2.080 | 2.100 | 2.120 | 2.150 | 2.200 |
| 3 | 3.030 | 3.045 | 3.153 | 3.184 | 3.246 | 3.310 | 3.374 | 3.473 | 3.640 |
| 4 | 4.060 | 4.091 | 4.310 | 4.375 | 4.506 | 4.641 | 4.779 | 4.993 | 5.368 |
| 5 | 5.101 | 5.152 | 5.526 | 5.637 | 5.867 | 6.105 | 6.353 | 6.742 | 7.442 |
| 6 | 6.152 | 6.230 | 6.802 | 6.975 | 7.336 | 7.716 | 8.115 | 8.754 | 9.930 |
| 7 | 7.214 | 7.323 | 8.142 | 8.394 | 8.923 | 9.487 | 10.089 | 11.067 | 12.916 |
| 8 | 8.286 | 8.433 | 9.549 | 9.897 | 10.637 | 11.436 | 12.300 | 13.727 | 16.499 |
| 9 | 9.369 | 9.559 | 11.027 | 11.491 | 12.488 | 13.579 | 14.776 | 16.786 | 20.799 |
| 10 | 10.462 | 10.703 | 12.578 | 13.181 | 14.487 | 15.937 | 17.549 | 20.304 | 25.959 |
| 20 | 22.019 | 23.124 | 33.066 | 36.786 | 45.762 | 57.275 | 72.052 | 102.444 | 186.688 |
| 24 | 26.974 | 28.634 | 44.502 | 50.816 | 66.765 | 88.497 | 118.155 | 184.168 | 392.484 |
| 36 | 43.079 | 47.276 | 96.836 | 119.121 | 187.102 | 299.127 | 484.463 | 1014.346 | 3539.009 |

In our example, we know that Ultra Tech is required to accumulate a future amount of $10 million. However, we need to know the amount of the periodic payments that, when invested at 10% annual interest, will accumulate to that future amount. To make this calculation, the formula shown on the previous page may be restated as follows:

*restated to find the amount of the periodic payments*

$$\text{Periodic Payment} = \frac{\text{Future Amount of an Annuity}}{\text{Factor (from Table FA–2)}}$$

The amount of each required payment, therefore, is $1,638,000 ($10 million ÷ **6.105**). If payments of $1,638,000 are made at the end of each of the next five years to a bond sinking fund that earns 10% annual interest, the fund will accumulate to $10 million:

*Future amount of a series of investments*

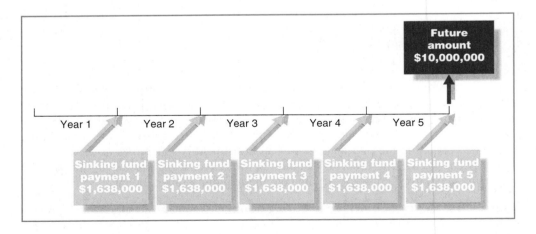

## Interest Periods of Less Than One Year

In our computations of future amounts, we have assumed that interest is paid (compounded) or payments are made annually. Therefore, in using the tables, we used *annual* periods and an *annual* interest rate. Investment payments or interest payments may be made on a more frequent basis, such as monthly, quarterly, or semiannually. **Tables FA–1 and FA–2** may be used with any of these payment periods, *but the rate of interest must represent the interest rate for that period.*

As an example, assume that 24 monthly payments are to be made to an investment fund that pays 12% annual interest rate. To determine the future amount of this investment, we would multiply the amount of the monthly payments by the factor from **Table FA–2** for 24 periods, using a *monthly* interest rate of 1%—the 12% annual rate divided by 12 months.

## PRESENT VALUES

As indicated previously, the present value is *today's* value of funds to be received in the future. While present value has many applications in business and accounting, it is most easily explained in the context of evaluating investment opportunities. In this context, the present value is the amount that a knowledgeable investor would pay *today* for the right to receive an expected future amount of cash. The present value is always *less* than the future amount, because the investor will expect to earn a return on the investment. The amount by which the future cash receipt exceeds its present value represents the investor's profit.

**LO 5**

Compute the present values of future cash flows.

The amount of the profit on a particular investment depends on two factors: (1) the rate of return (called the *discount rate*) required by the investor and (2) the length of time until the future amount will be received. The process of determining the present value of a future cash receipt is called *discounting* the future amount.

To illustrate the computation of present value, assume that an investment is expected to result in a $1,000 cash receipt at the end of one year and that an investor requires a 10% return on this investment. We know from our discussion of present and future values that the difference between a present value and a future amount is the return (interest) on the investment. In our example, the future amount would be equal to 110% of the original investment, because the investor expects 100% of the investment back plus a 10% return on the investment. Thus the investor would be willing to pay *$909* ($1,000 ÷ 1.10) for this investment. This computation may be verified as follows (amounts rounded to the nearest dollar):

| | |
|---|---:|
| Amount to be invested (present value) . . . . . . . . . . . . . . . . . . . . . . . . . . . . . . . . . . . . . . . . | $  909 |
| Required return on investment ($909 × 10%) . . . . . . . . . . . . . . . . . . . . . . . . . . . . . . . . . . | 91 |
| Amount to be received in one year (future value) . . . . . . . . . . . . . . . . . . . . . . . . . . | $1,000 |

If the $1,000 is to be received *two years* in the future, the investor would pay only *$826* for the investment today [($1,000 ÷ 1.10) ÷ 1.10]. This computation may be verified as follows (amounts rounded to the nearest dollar):

| | |
|---|---:|
| Amount to be invested (present value) . . . . . . . . . . . . . . . . . . . . . . . . . . . . . . . . . . . . . . . . | $  826 |
| Required return on investment in first year ($826 × 10%) . . . . . . . . . . . . . . . . . . . . . . | 83 |
| Amount invested after one year . . . . . . . . . . . . . . . . . . . . . . . . . . . . . . . . . . . . . . . . . . . . | $  909 |
| Required return on investment in second year ($909 × 10%) . . . . . . . . . . . . . . . . . . . . | 91 |
| Amount to be received in two years (future value) . . . . . . . . . . . . . . . . . . . . . . . . . . . . | $1,000 |

The amount that our investor would pay today, $826, is the present value of $1,000 to be received two years from now, discounted at an annual rate of 10%. The $174 difference between the $826 present value and the $1,000 future amount is the return (interest revenue) to be earned by the investor over the two-year period.

*Present value of a single future cash flow*

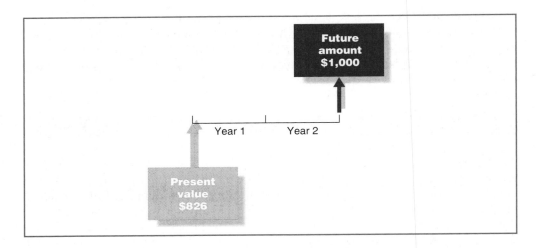

## Using Present Value Tables

Although we can compute the present value of future amounts by a series of divisions, tables are available that simplify the calculations. We can use a table of present values to find the present value of $1 at a specified discount rate and then multiply that value by the future amount as illustrated in the following formula:

*Formula for finding present value*

$$\text{Present Value} = \text{Future Amount} \times \text{Factor (from Table PV-1)}$$

Referring to **Table PV–1** below, we find a factor of **.826** at the intersection of two periods and 10% interest. If we multiply this factor by the expected future cash receipt of $1,000, we get a present value of *$826* ($1,000 × .826), the same amount produced by the series of divisions in our previous illustration.

| **Table PV–1** Present Values of $1 Due in *n* Periods | | | | | | | | | |
|---|---|---|---|---|---|---|---|---|---|
| **Number of Periods (*n*)** | **Discount Rate** | | | | | | | | |
| | **1%** | **1½%** | **5%** | **6%** | **8%** | **10%** | **12%** | **15%** | **20%** |
| 1 | .990 | .985 | .952 | .943 | .926 | .909 | .893 | .870 | .833 |
| 2 | .980 | .971 | .907 | .890 | .857 | .826 | .797 | .756 | .694 |
| 3 | .971 | .956 | .864 | .840 | .794 | .751 | .712 | .658 | .579 |
| 4 | .961 | .942 | .823 | .792 | .735 | .683 | .636 | .572 | .482 |
| 5 | .951 | .928 | .784 | .747 | .681 | .621 | .567 | .497 | .402 |
| 6 | .942 | .915 | .746 | .705 | .630 | .564 | .507 | .432 | .335 |
| 7 | .933 | .901 | .711 | .665 | .583 | .513 | .452 | .376 | .279 |
| 8 | .923 | .888 | .677 | .627 | .540 | .467 | .404 | .327 | .233 |
| 9 | .914 | .875 | .645 | .592 | .500 | .424 | .361 | .284 | .194 |
| 10 | .905 | .862 | .614 | .558 | .463 | .386 | .322 | .247 | .162 |
| 20 | .820 | .742 | .377 | .312 | .215 | .149 | .104 | .061 | .026 |
| 24 | .788 | .700 | .310 | .247 | .158 | .102 | .066 | .035 | .013 |
| 36 | .699 | .585 | .173 | .123 | .063 | .032 | .017 | .007 | .001 |

## What Is the Appropriate Discount Rate?

As explained on the previous page, the *discount rate* may be viewed as the investor's required rate of return. All investments involve some degree of risk that actual future cash flows may turn out to be less than expected. Investors will require a rate of return that justifies taking this risk. In today's market conditions, investors require annual returns of between 5% and 8% on low-risk investments, such as government bonds and certificates of deposit. For relatively high-risk investments, such as the introduction of a new product line, investors may expect to earn an annual return of perhaps 15% or more. When a higher discount rate is used, the present value of the investment will be lower. In other words, as the risk of an investment increases, its value to investors decreases.

## The Present Value of an Annuity

Many investment opportunities are expected to produce annual cash flows for a number of years, instead of one single future cash flow. Let us assume that Camino Company is evaluating an investment that is expected to produce *annual net cash flows of* $10,000 in *each of the next three years.*[1] If Camino Company expects a 12% return on this type of investment, it may compute the present value of these cash flows as follows:

| Year | Expected New Cash Flows | × | Present Value of $1 Discounted at 12% | = | Present Value of Net Cash Flows |
|------|------|---|------|---|------|
| 1 | $10,000 | | .893 | | $ 8,930 |
| 2 | 10,000 | | .797 | | 7,970 |
| 3 | 10,000 | | .712 | | 7,120 |
| Total present value of the investment . . . . . . . . . . . . . . . . . . . . . . . . . . . | | | | | $24,020 |

This analysis indicates that the present value of the expected net cash flows from the investment, discounted at an annual rate of 12%, amounts to $24,020. This is the maximum amount that Camino Company could afford to pay for this investment and still expect to earn the 12% required rate of return, as shown below.

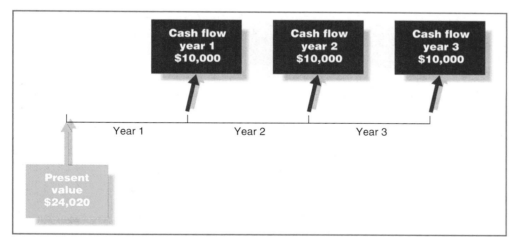

*Present value of a series of cash flows*

In the preceding schedule, we computed the present value of the investment by separately discounting each period's cash flows, using the appropriate factors from **Table PV–1**. Separately discounting each period's cash flows is necessary only when the cash

---

[1] "Annual net cash flows" normally are the net result of a series of cash receipts and cash payments occurring throughout the year. For convenience, we follow the common practice of assuming that the entire net cash flows for each year occur at *year-end.* This assumption causes relatively little distortion and greatly simplifies computations.

flows vary in amount from period to period. Since the annual cash flows in our example are *uniform in amount*, there are easier ways to compute the total present value.

Many financial calculators are programmed to compute the present value of an investment, after the interest rate, the future cash flows, and the number of periods have been entered. Another approach is to refer to a *present value annuity table*, which shows the present value of *$1 to be received each period for a specified number of periods*. An annuity table appears below and is labeled **Table PV–2**.[2]

To illustrate the use of **Table PV-2**, let's return to the example of the investment by Camino Company. That investment was expected to return $10,000 per year for the next three years, and the company's required rate of return was 12% per year. Using **Table PV–2**, we can compute the present value of the investment with the following formula:

*Formula to find the present value of a series of cash flows*

**Present Value of an Annuity = Periodic Cash Flows × Factor (from Table PV–2)**

As illustrated in **Table PV–2**, the present value of $1 to be received at the end of the next three years, discounted at an annual rate of 12%, is **2.402**. If we multiply 2.402 by the expected future annual cash receipt of $10,000, we get a present value of $24,020, which is the same amount produced by the series of calculations made on page 1077.

### Table PV–2
**Present Values of $1 to Be Received Periodically for *n* Periods**

| Number of Periods (*n*) | 1% | 1½% | 5% | 6% | 8% | 10% | 12% | 15% | 20% |
|---|---|---|---|---|---|---|---|---|---|
| 1 | 0.990 | 0.985 | 0.952 | 0.943 | 0.926 | 0.909 | 0.893 | 0.870 | 0.833 |
| 2 | 1.970 | 1.956 | 1.859 | 1.833 | 1.783 | 1.736 | 1.690 | 1.626 | 1.528 |
| 3 | 2.941 | 2.912 | 2.723 | 2.673 | 2.577 | 2.487 | 2.402 | 2.283 | 2.106 |
| 4 | 3.902 | 3.854 | 3.546 | 3.465 | 3.312 | 3.170 | 3.037 | 2.855 | 2.589 |
| 5 | 4.853 | 4.783 | 4.329 | 4.212 | 3.993 | 3.791 | 3.605 | 3.352 | 2.991 |
| 6 | 5.795 | 5.697 | 5.076 | 4.917 | 4.623 | 4.355 | 4.111 | 3.784 | 3.326 |
| 7 | 6.728 | 6.598 | 5.786 | 5.582 | 5.206 | 4.868 | 4.564 | 4.160 | 3.605 |
| 8 | 7.652 | 7.486 | 6.463 | 6.210 | 5.747 | 5.335 | 4.968 | 4.487 | 3.837 |
| 9 | 8.566 | 8.361 | 7.108 | 6.802 | 6.247 | 5.759 | 5.328 | 4.772 | 4.031 |
| 10 | 9.471 | 9.222 | 7.722 | 7.360 | 6.710 | 6.145 | 5.650 | 5.019 | 4.192 |
| 20 | 18.046 | 17.169 | 12.462 | 11.470 | 9.818 | 8.514 | 7.469 | 6.259 | 4.870 |
| 24 | 21.243 | 20.030 | 13.799 | 12.550 | 10.529 | 8.985 | 7.784 | 6.434 | 4.937 |
| 36 | 30.108 | 27.661 | 16.547 | 14.621 | 11.717 | 9.677 | 8.192 | 6.623 | 4.993 |

## Discount Periods of Less Than One Year

The interval between regular periodic cash flows is called the *discount period*. In our preceding examples, we have assumed cash flows once a year. Often cash flows occur on a more frequent basis, such as monthly, quarterly, or semiannually. The present value tables can be used with discount periods of any length, *but the discount rate must be for that length of time.* For example, if we use **Table PV–2** to find the present value of a series of *quarterly* cash payments, the discount rate must be the *quarterly* rate.

There are many applications of the present value concept in accounting. In the next several pages, we will discuss some of the most important of these applications.

---

[2] This table assumes that the periodic cash flows occur at the *end* of each period.

# VALUATION OF FINANCIAL INSTRUMENTS

**LO 6**

Discuss accounting applications of the concept of present value.

Accountants use the phrase *financial instruments* to describe cash, equity investments in another business, and any contracts that call for receipts or payments of cash. (Notice that this phrase applies to all financial assets, as well as most liabilities. In fact, the only common liabilities *not* considered financial instruments are unearned revenue and deferred income taxes.)

Whenever the present value of a financial instrument *differs significantly* from the sum of the expected future cash flows, the instrument is recorded in the accounting records at its *present value*—not at the expected amount of the future cash receipts or payments.

Let us illustrate with a few common examples. Cash appears in the balance sheet at its face amount. This face value *is* a present value—that is, the value of the cash today.

Marketable securities appear in the balance sheet at their *current market values*. These too are present values—representing the amount of cash into which the security can be converted *today*.

Accounts receivable and accounts payable normally appear in the balance sheet at the amounts expected to be collected or paid in the near future. Technically, these are *future amounts,* not present values. But they usually are received or paid within 30 or 60 days. Considering the short periods of time involved, the differences between these future amounts and their present values simply are *not material.*

## Interest-Bearing Receivables and Payables

When a financial instrument calls for the receipt or payment of interest, the difference between present value and the future amounts *does* become material. Thus interest-bearing receivables and payables initially are recorded in accounting records at the *present value* of the future cash flows—also called the "principal amount" of the obligation. This present value often is *substantially less* than the sum of the expected future amounts.

Consider, for example, $100 million in 30-year, 9% bonds payable issued at par. At the issuance date, the present value of this bond issue is $100 million—the amount of cash received. But the future payments to bondholders are expected to total *$370* million, computed as follows:

| | |
|---|---:|
| Future interest payments ($100 million × 9% × 30 years) | $270,000,000 |
| Maturity value of the bonds (due in 30 years) | 100,000,000 |
| Sum of the future cash payments | $370,000,000 |

Thus the $100 million issuance price represents the present value of $370 million in future cash payments to be made over a period of 30 years.

In essence, interest-bearing financial instruments are "automatically" recorded at their present values simply because we do not include future interest charges in the original valuation of the receivable or the liability.

## "Non-Interest-Bearing" Notes

On occasion, companies may issue or accept notes that make no mention of interest, or in which the stated interest rates are unreasonably low. If the difference between the present value of such a note and its face amount is *material,* the note initially is recorded at its present value.

To illustrate, assume that on January 1, 2002, Elron Corporation purchases land from U.S. Development Co. As full payment for this land, Elron issues a $300,000 installment note payable, due in three annual installments of $100,000, beginning on December 31, 2002. This note makes *no mention* of interest charges.

Clearly, three annual installments of $100,000 are not the equivalent of $300,000 available today. Elron should use the *present value* of this note—not the face amount—in determining the cost of the land and reporting its liability.

Assume that a realistic interest rate for financing land over a three-year period currently is 10% per annum. The present value of Elron's installment note, discounted at 10%, is *$248,700* [$100,000, 3-year annuity × **2.487** (from **Table PV–2**)]. Elron should view this $248,700 as the "principal amount" of this installment note payable. The remaining $51,300 ($300,000 − $248,700) represents interest charges included in the installment payments.

Elron should record the purchase of the land and the issuance of this note as follows:[3]

| | | |
|---|---|---|
| Land .......................................................... | 248,700 | |
|    Notes Payable ......................................... | | 248,700 |
| Purchased land, issuing a 3-year installment note payable with a present value of $248,700. | | |

(U.S. Development Co. should make similar computations in determining the sales price of the land and the valuation of its note receivable.)

Elron also should prepare an *amortization table* to allocate the amount of each installment payment between interest expense and reduction in the principal amount of this obligation. This table, based on an original unpaid balance of $248,700, three annual payments of $100,000, and an annual interest rate of 10%, is illustrated below.

| | | | | | |
|---|---|---|---|---|---|
| **AMORTIZATION TABLE**<br>**(3-Year, $300,000 Installment Note Payable,**<br>**Discounted at 10% per Annum)** | | | | | |
| **Interest Period** | **Payment Date** | **Annual Payment** | **Interest Expense (10% of the Last Unpaid Balance)** | **Reduction in Unpaid Balance** | **Unpaid Balance** |
| Issue date | Jan. 1, 2002 | | | | $248,700 |
| 1 | Dec. 31, 2002 | $100,000 | $24,870 | $75,130 | 173,570 |
| 2 | Dec. 31, 2003 | 100,000 | 17,357 | 82,643 | 90,927 |
| 3 | Dec. 31, 2004 | 100,000 | 9,073* | 90,927 | –0– |

*In the last period, interest expense is equal to the amount of the final payment minus the remaining unpaid balance. This compensates for the use of a present value table with factors carried to only three decimal places.

The entry at December 31, 2002, to record the first installment payment will be as follows:

| | | |
|---|---|---|
| Interest Expense ..................................... | 24,870 | |
| Notes Payable ......................................... | 75,130 | |
|    Cash .................................................. | | 100,000 |
| Made annual payment on installment note payable to U.S. Development Co. | | |

---

[3] There is an alternative recording technique that makes use of an account entitled Discount on Notes Payable. This alternative approach produces the same results and will be explained in later accounting courses.

## Market Prices of Bonds

The market price of bonds may be regarded as the *present value* to bondholders of the future principal and interest payments. To illustrate, assume that a corporation issues $1,000,000 face value of 10-year, 9% bonds when the going market rate of interest is 10%. Since bond interest is paid semiannually, we must use 20 *semiannual* periods as the life of the bond issue and a 5% *semiannual* market rate of interest in our present value calculations. The expected issuance price of this bond issue may be computed as follows:

Present value of future principal payments:

$1,000,000 due after 20 semiannual periods, discounted at 5%:

$1,000,000 × .377 (from Table PV–1) . . . . . . . . . . . . . . . . . . . . . . . . .   $377,000

Present value of future interest payments:

$45,000 per period ($1,000,000 × 9% × ½) for 20 semiannual periods,
discounted at 5%: $45,000 × 12.462 (from Table PV–2) . . . . . . . . . . . . . . . . .   560,790

Expected issuance price of bond issue . . . . . . . . . . . . . . . . . . . . . . . . . .   $937,790

## Capital Leases

We briefly discuss capital leases in Chapter 10, but do not illustrate the accounting for these instruments. This appendix gives us an opportunity to explore this topic in greater detail.

A capital lease is regarded as a sale of the leased asset by the lessor to the lessee. At the date of this sale, the lessor recognizes sales revenue equal to the *present value* of the future lease payments receivable, discounted at a realistic rate of interest. The lessee also uses the present value of the future payments to determine the cost of the leased asset and the valuation of the related liability.

To illustrate, assume that on December 1, Pace Tractor uses a *capital lease* to finance the sale of a tractor to Kelly Grading Co. The tractor was carried in Pace Tractor's perpetual inventory records at a cost of $15,000. Terms of the lease call for Kelly Grading Co. to make *24* monthly payments of *$1,000* each, beginning on December 31. These lease payments include an interest charge of *1%* per month. At the end of the 24-month lease, title to the tractor will pass to Kelly Grading Co. at no additional cost.

**Accounting by the Lessor (Pace Tractor)**   Table PV–2 shows that the present value of $1 to be received monthly for 24 months, discounted at 1% per month, is **21.243**. Therefore, the present value of the 24 future lease payments is $1,000 × **21.243**, or *$21,243*. Pace Tractor should record this capital lease as a sale of the tractor at a price equal to the present value of the lease payments, as follows:

Lease Payment Receivable (net) . . . . . . . . . . . . . . . . . . . . . . . . . . . . .   21,243

   Sales . . . . . . . . . . . . . . . . . . . . . . . . . . . . . . . . . . . . . . . . . . .   21,243

Financed sale of a tractor to Kelly Grading Co. using a
  capital lease requiring 24 monthly payments of $1,000.
  Payments include a 1% monthly interest charge.

Cost of Goods Sold . . . . . . . . . . . . . . . . . . . . . . . . . . . . . . . . . . . . .   15,000

   Inventory . . . . . . . . . . . . . . . . . . . . . . . . . . . . . . . . . . . . . . . . .   15,000

To record cost of tractor sold under capital lease.

Notice that the sales price of the tractor is only $21,243, even though the gross amount to be collected from Kelly Grading Co. amounts to $24,000 ($1,000 × 24 payments). The difference between these two amounts, $2,757, will be recognized by Pace Tractor as interest revenue over the term of the lease.

To illustrate the recognition of interest revenue, the entry on December 31 to record collection of the first monthly lease payment (rounded to the nearest dollar) will be:

| | | |
|---|---|---|
| Cash | 1,000 | |
|   Interest Revenue | | 212 |
|   Lease Payments Receivable (net) | | 788 |
| Received first lease payment from Kelly Grading Co.: | | |
|   Lease payment received | $1,000 | |
|   Interest revenue ($21,243 × 1%) | (212) | |
|   Reduction in lease payments receivable | $ 788 | |

After this first monthly payment is collected, the present value of the lease payments receivable is reduced to $20,455 ($21,243 original balance, less $788). Therefore, the interest revenue earned during the *second* month of the lease (rounded to the nearest dollar) will be *$205* ($20,455 × 1%).[4]

**Accounting by the Lessee (Kelly Grading Co.)**   Kelly Grading Co. also should use the present value of the lease payments to determine the cost of the tractor and the amount of the related liability, as follows:

| | | |
|---|---|---|
| Leased Equipment | 21,243 | |
|   Lease Payment Obligation | | 21,243 |
| To record acquisition of a tractor through a capital lease from Pace Tractor. Terms call for 24 monthly payments of $1,000, which include a 1% monthly interest charge. | | |

The entry on December 31 to record the first monthly lease payment (rounded to the nearest dollar) will be:

| | | |
|---|---|---|
| Interest Expense | 212 | |
| Lease Payment Obligation | 788 | |
|   Cash | | 1,000 |
| To record first monthly lease payment to Pace Tractor: | | |
|   Amount of payment | $1,000 | |
|   Interest expense ($21,243 × 1%) | (212) | |
|   Reduction in lease payment obligation | $ 788 | |

## Obligations for Postretirement Benefits

As we explain in Chapter 10, any unfunded obligation for postretirement benefits appears in the balance sheet at the *present value* of the expected future cash outlays to retired employees. The computation of this present value is so complex that it is performed by a professional actuary. But the present value of this obligation normally is far less than the expected future payments, as the cash payments will take place many years in the future.

Each year, the present value of an unfunded obligation for postretirement benefits will increase—as the future payment dates become closer. This steady growth in the present value of the unfunded obligation is recognized annually as part of the company's

---

[4] Both Pace Tractor and Kelly Grading Co. would prepare *amortization tables* showing the allocation of each lease payment between interest and the principal amount due.

current postretirement benefits expense. (One might argue that the growth in this liability actually represents interest expense. Nonetheless, the present value of the liability increases as the payment dates draw closer.)

## Disclosure of Up-to-Date Present Value Information

Financial instruments originally are recorded in accounting records at (or near) their present values. But present values represent future cash flows discounted at *current* interest rates. Thus, as interest rates change, so do the present values of many financial instruments. (For the remainder of this discussion, we refer to present value determined under *current* market conditions as *current value*.)

Cash, investments in marketable securities, and postretirement obligations appear in the financial statements at current values. For most short-term instruments, current values remain quite close to the original carrying values. But for long-term financial instruments, such as bonds payable, current values may differ substantially from the amounts originally recorded.

The FASB requires companies to disclose the current values of financial instruments whenever these values *differ significantly* from the recorded amounts. These disclosures are most likely to affect long-term notes receivable and payable (including bonds payable) and long-term lease obligations.

In computing current value, current interest rates serve as the discount rate. Thus, as interest rates *rise,* current values *fall;* as interest rates *fall,* current values *rise*. The amount of change is greatest on long-term financial instruments for which the future cash flows are fixed—that is, not adjustable to reflect changes in interest rates.

The disclosure of current values can shed light on a company's past investing and financing activities. Assume, for example, that a company's long-term debt has a current value well *below* its carrying value in the company's balance sheet. This means that interest rates have *increased* since the company arranged this debt. Thus the company apparently arranged its long-term financing in a period of low interest rates—a good move.

## Deferred Income Taxes

The only long-term liability *not* shown at the present value of the expected future payments is the obligation for deferred income taxes. Deferred taxes are treated differently because they do not involve a "contract" for future payments. Future payments of deferred taxes, if any, depend on the company's taxable income in future periods and also the corporate income tax laws in future years.

Many accountants believe that deferred income taxes *should* be shown at the estimated present value of the future outlays. This is not likely to happen, however, as the computations would be overwhelmingly complex.

In conclusion, the obligation for deferred income taxes is the only long-term liability that is *not* reported at its present value. Hence, one might argue that these obligations are overstated in terms of an equivalent number of today's dollars.

## CAPITAL BUDGETING: ANOTHER APPLICATION OF PRESENT VALUE

Capital budgeting is the process of planning and evaluating proposals for capital expenditures, such as the acquisition of plant assets or the introduction of a new product line. Perhaps the most widely used approach in the evaluation of proposed capital expenditures is *discounting* the expected future cash flows to their *present value*.

Assume that Globe Mfg. Co. is considering a proposal to purchase new equipment in order to produce a new product. The equipment costs $400,000, has an estimated 10-year service life, and an estimated salvage value of $50,000. Globe estimates that production and sale of the new product will increase the company's annual net cash flows by $100,000 per year for the next 10 years. If Globe requires a 15% annual rate of return on investments of this nature, the present value of these cash flows may be computed as follows:

*Is this project worth a $400,000 investment?*

| | |
|---|---:|
| Present value of expected annual net cash inflows of $100,000 for 10 years, discounted at 15% per year: $100,000 × 5.019 (from **Table PV–2**) | $501,900 |
| Present value of estimated salvage value to be received at the end of the tenth year: $50,000 × .247 (from **Table PV–1**) | 12,350 |
| Present value of estimated future cash inflows | $514,250 |
| Less: Amount to be invested (already a present value) | 400,000 |
| Net present value of proposal | $114,250 |

This analysis indicates that the present value of the expected net cash flows from this investment, discounted at an annual rate of 15%, amounts to $514,250. This is the maximum amount Globe could afford to invest in this project and still expect to earn the required 15% annual rate of return. As the cost of this investment is only $400,000, Globe can expect to earn more than its required 15% return.

The *net present value* of a proposal is the *difference* between the total present value of the future net cash flows and the cost of the investment. When the net present value is equal to zero, the investment provides a rate of return exactly equal to the rate used in discounting the cash flows. A *positive* net present value means that the investment provides a rate of return *greater* than the discount rate; a *negative* net present value means that the investment yields a return of *less* than the discount rate.

Since the discount rate usually is the minimum rate of return required by the investor, proposals with a positive net present value are considered acceptable, and those with a negative net present value are viewed as unacceptable.

# ASSIGNMENT MATERIAL

## DISCUSSION QUESTIONS

1. Explain what is meant by the phrase the *time value of money*.
2. Explain why the present value of a future amount is always *less* than the future amount.
3. Identify the two factors that determine the difference between the present value and the future amount of an investment.
4. Describe three basic investment applications of the concept of the time value of money.
5. Briefly explain the relationships between present value and (a) the length of time until the future cash flow occurs, and (b) the discount rate used in determining present value.
6. Define *financial instruments*. Explain the valuation concept used in initially recording financial instruments in financial statements.
7. Are normal accounts receivable and accounts payable financial instruments? Are these items shown in the balance sheet at their present values? Explain.
8. Identify three financial instruments shown in financial statements at present values that may *differ significantly* from the sum of the expected future payments or receipts.
9. What is the only long-term liability that is *not* recorded at its present value? What are the implications in terms of today's dollars?
10. Assuming no change in the expected amount of future cash flows, what factors may cause the present value of a financial instrument to change? Explain fully.
11. Define *capital budgeting*. Explain briefly how the present value concept relates to capital budgeting decisions.

# PROBLEMS

Use the tables on pages 1072 and 1074 to determine the future amounts of the following investments:

**a.** $20,000 is invested for 10 years, at 6% interest, compounded annually.

**b.** $100,000 is to be received five years from today, at 10% annual interest.

**c.** $10,000 is invested in a fund at the end of each of the next 10 years, at 8% interest, compounded annually.

**d.** $50,000 is invested initially, plus $5,000 is invested annually at the end of each of the next three years, at 12% interest, compounded annually.

**PROBLEM B.1**

Using Future Amount Tables

**LO 1, 2, 4**

Tilman Company is required by a bond indenture to make equal annual payments to a bond sinking fund at the end of each of the next 20 years. The sinking fund will earn 8% interest and must accumulate to a total of $500,000 at the end of the 20-year period.

**PROBLEM B.2**

Bond Sinking Fund

**LO 3, 4**

### Instructions

**a.** Calculate the amount of the annual payments.

**b.** Calculate the total amount of interest that will be earned by the fund over the 20-year period.

**c.** Make the general journal entry to record redemption of the bond issue at the end of the 20-year period, assuming that the sinking fund is recorded on Tilman's accounting records at $500,000 and bonds payable are recorded at the same amount.

**d.** What would be the effect of an increase in the rate of return on the required annual payment? Explain.

Use the tables on pages 1076 and 1078 to determine the present value of the following cash flows:

**a.** $15,000 to be paid annually for 10 years, discounted at an annual rate of 6%. Payments are to occur at the end of each year.

**b.** $9,200 to be received today, assuming that the money will be invested in a 2-year certificate of deposit earning 8% annually.

**c.** $300 to be paid monthly for 36 months, with an additional "balloon payment" of $12,000 due at the end of the thirty-sixth month, discounted at a monthly interest rate of $1\frac{1}{2}\%$. The first payment is to be one month from today.

**d.** $25,000 to be received annually for the first three years, followed by $15,000 to be received annually for the next two years (total of five years in which collections are received), discounted at an annual rate of 8%. Assume collections occur at year-end.

**PROBLEM B.3**

Using Present Value Tables

**LO 1, 2, 5**

On June 30 of the current year, Rural Gas & Electric Co. issued $50,000,000 face value, 9%, 10-year bonds payable, with interest dates of December 31 and June 30. The bonds were issued at a discount, resulting in an effective *semiannual* interest rate of 5%.

**PROBLEM B.4**

Present Value and Bond Prices

**LO 3, 5, 6**

### Instructions

**a.** Compute the issue price for the bond that results in an effective semiannual interest rate of 5%. (*Hint:* Discount both the interest payments and the maturity value over 20 semiannual periods.)

**b.** Prepare a journal entry to record the issuance of the bonds at the sales price you computed in part **a**.

**c.** Explain why the bonds were issued at a discount.

On December 1, Showcase Interiors purchased a shipment of furniture from Colonial House by paying $10,500 cash and issuing an installment note payable in the face amount of $28,800. The note is to be paid in 24 monthly installments of $1,200 each. Although the note makes no mention of an interest charge, the rate of interest usually charged to Showcase Interiors in such transactions is $1\frac{1}{2}\%$ per month.

**PROBLEM B.5**

Valuation of a Note Payable

**LO 3, 5, 6**

**Instructions**

a. Compute the present value of the note payable, using a discount rate of $1\frac{1}{2}\%$ per month.

b. Prepare the journal entries in the accounts of Showcase Interiors on:

1. December 1, to record the purchase of the furniture (debit Inventory).

2. December 31, to record the first $1,200 monthly payment on the note and to recognize interest expense for one month by the effective interest method. (Round interest expense to the nearest dollar.)

c. Show how the liability for this note would appear in the balance sheet at December 31. (Assume that the note is classified as a current liability.)

**PROBLEM B.6**

Capital Leases: A
Comprehensive Problem

**LO 3, 5, 6**

Custom Truck Builders frequently uses long-term lease contracts to finance the sale of its trucks. On November 1, 2002, Custom Truck Builders leased to Interstate Van Lines a truck carried in the perpetual inventory records at $33,520. The terms of the lease call for Interstate Van Lines to make 36 monthly payments of $1,400 each, beginning on November 30, 2002. The present value of these payments, after considering a built-in interest charge of 1% per month, is equal to the regular $42,150 sales price of the truck. At the end of the 36-month lease, title to the truck will transfer to Interstate Van Lines.

**Instructions**

a. Prepare journal entries for 2002 in the accounts of Custom Truck Builders on:

1. November 1, to record the sale financed by the lease and the related cost of goods sold. (Debit Lease Payments Receivable for the $42,150 present value of the future lease payments.)

2. November 30, to record receipt of the first $1,400 monthly payment. (Prepare a compound journal entry that allocates the cash receipt between interest revenue and reduction of Lease Payments Receivable. The portion of each monthly payment recognized as interest revenue is equal to 1% of the balance of the account Lease Payments Receivable, at the beginning of that month. Round all interest computations to the nearest dollar.)

3. December 31, to record receipt of the second monthly payment.

b. Prepare journal entries for 2002 in the accounts of Interstate Van Lines on:

1. November 1, to record acquisition of the leased truck.

2. November 30, to record the first monthly lease payment. (Determine the portion of the payment representing interest expense in a manner parallel to that described in part **a**.)

3. December 31, to record the second monthly lease payment.

4. December 31, to recognize depreciation on the leased truck through year-end. Compute depreciation expense by the straight-line method, using a 10-year service life and an estimated salvage value of $6,150.

c. Compute the net carrying value of the leased truck in the balance sheet of Interstate Van Lines at December 31, 2002.

d. Compute the amount of Interstate Van Lines' lease payment obligation at December 31, 2002.

**PROBLEM B.7**

Valuation of a Note Receivable
with an Unrealistic Interest Rate

**LO 5, 6**

On December 31, Richland Farms sold a tract of land, which had cost $930,000, to Skyline Developers in exchange for $150,000 cash and a five-year, 4% note receivable for $900,000. Interest on the note is payable annually, and the principal amount is due in five years. The accountant for Richland Farms did not notice the unrealistically low interest rate on the note and made the following entry on December 31 to record this sale.

| | | |
|---|---|---|
| Cash | 150,000 | |
| Notes Receivable | 900,000 | |
| Land | | 930,000 |
| Gain on Sale of Land | | 120,000 |
| Sold land to Skyline Developers in exchange for cash and five-year note with interest due annually. | | |

## Instructions

**a.** Compute the present value of the note receivable from Skyline Developers at the date of sale, assuming that a realistic rate of interest for this transaction is 12%. (*Hint:* Consider both the annual interest payments and the maturity value of the note.)

**b.** Prepare the journal entry on December 31 to record the sale of the land correctly. Show supporting computations for the gain or loss on the sale.

**c.** Explain what effects the error made by Richland Farms' accountant will have on (1) the net income in the year of the sale and (2) the combined net income of the next five years. Ignore income taxes.

# FORMS OF BUSINESS ORGANIZATION

## Importance of Business Form

The legal form of a business organization is an important consideration not only when it is first formed but also throughout its operating life. The form of an enterprise affects its ability to raise capital, the relationship between the organization and its owners, and the security of both creditors and owners' claims. Three primary forms of business organization are generally found in the United States—sole proprietorships, partnerships, and corporations.

Corporations carry out the majority of business activity and as a result that form of business organization is the primary focus of this textbook. Sole proprietorships and partnerships are also important, however, because they represent the largest numbers of business organizations in the United States. This appendix supplements the introductory coverage of sole proprietorships and partnerships presented earlier in the text, as well as expands the coverage of corporations as the dominant form of business organization.

## SOLE PROPRIETORSHIPS

A **sole proprietorship** is an unincorporated business owned by one person. Proprietorships are the most common form of business organization because they are so easy to start.

Creating a sole proprietorship requires *no authorization* from any governmental agency. Often the business requires little or no investment of capital. For example, a youngster with a paper route, baby-sitting service, or lawn-mowing business is a sole proprietorship. On a larger scale, sole proprietorships are widely used for farms, service businesses, small retail stores, restaurants, and professional practices, such as medicine, law, and public accounting.

A sole proprietorship provides an excellent model for demonstrating accounting principles because it is the simplest form of business organization. But in the business world, you will seldom encounter financial statements for these organizations.

Most sole proprietorships are relatively small businesses with few—if any—financial reporting obligations. Their needs for accounting information consist primarily of data used in daily business operations—the balance in the company's bank account and the amounts receivable and payable. In fact, many sole proprietorships do not prepare formal financial statements unless some special need arises.

### Learning Objectives

*After studying this appendix, you should be able to:*

1. **Describe the basic characteristics of a sole proprietorship.**

2. **Identify factors to consider in evaluating the profitability and solvency of a sole proprietorship.**

3. **Describe the basic characteristics of a general partnership and of partnerships that limit personal liability.**

4. **Describe the basic characteristics of a corporation.**

5. **Account for corporate income taxes; explain the effects of these taxes on before-tax profits and losses.**

6. **Account for the issuance of capital stock.**

7. **Explain the nature of retained earnings, account for dividends, and prepare a statement of retained earnings.**

8. **Explain why the financial statements of a corporation are interpreted differently from those of an unincorporated business.**

*(continued)*

9. **Discuss the principal factors to consider in selecting a form of business organization.**

*10. **Allocate partnership net income among the partners.**

*Supplemental Topic*, "Partnership Accounting—A Closer Look."

**LO 1**

Describe the basic characteristics of a sole proprietorship.

## The Concept of the Separate Business Entity

For accounting purposes, we treat every business organization—including a sole proprietorship—as an entity separate from the other activities of its owner. This enables us to measure the performance of the business separately from the other financial affairs of its owner.

In the eyes of the law, however, a sole proprietorship is *not* an entity separate from its owner. Under the law, the proprietor is the "entity," and a sole proprietorship merely represents some of this individual's financial activities. The fact that a sole proprietorship and its owner legally are one and the same explains many of the distinctive characteristics of this form of organization.

## Characteristics of a Sole Proprietorship

Among the key characteristics of sole proprietorships are:

- *Ease of formation.* (This explains why these organizations are so common.)

- *Business assets actually belong to the proprietor.* As the business is not a legal entity, it cannot own property. The business assets actually belong to the *proprietor*, not to the business. Therefore, the proprietor may transfer assets in or out of the business *at will.*

- *The business pays no income taxes.* Tax laws do not view a sole proprietorship as separate from the other financial activities of its owner. Therefore, the proprietorship *does not* file an income tax return or pay income taxes. Instead, the *owner* must include the income of the business in his or her *personal* income tax return.

- *The business pays no salary to the owner.* The owner of a sole proprietorship is not working for a salary. Rather, the owner's compensation consists of the entire net income (or net loss) of the business. Hence, any money withdrawn from the business by its owner should be recorded in the owner's *drawing* account, *not* recognized as salaries expense.

- *The owner is personally liable for the debts of the business.* This concept, called **unlimited personal liability**, is too important to be treated as just one item in a list. It deserves special attention.

## Unlimited Personal Liability
### (Subtitle: *The Owner Could Lose EVERYTHING!*)

The owner of a sole proprietorship is *personally responsible* for all of the company's debts. Thus, a business "mishap," such as personal injuries stemming from business operations, may result in enormous personal liability for the business owner.[1]

Unlimited personal liability is *by far* the greatest *disadvantage* to this form of organization. Other forms of business organization provide owners with some means of limiting their personal liability for business debts—but not the sole proprietorship. If business operations entail even a small chance of substantial liability, the owner should consider another form of business organization.

---

[1]Injuries sustained by employees or customers have often resulted in multimillion-dollar liabilities for the business organization. The judgments against a business that result from litigation may exceed available insurance coverage.

**The Gravity Syndicate** is a small business operating in San Diego, California. It offers an un-usual service—bungee jumping from hot air balloons. Although the company is owned by one individual, it is organized as a corporation (wisely, we think).

**CASE IN POINT**

## Accounting Practices of Sole Proprietorships

In the balance sheet of a sole proprietorship, total owner's equity is represented by the balance in the owner's *capital* account. Investments of assets by the owner are recorded by crediting this account. Withdrawals of assets by the owner are recorded by debiting the owner's **drawing account**. At the end of the accounting period, the drawing account and the Income Summary account are closed into the owner's capital account.

The only financial reporting obligation of many sole proprietorships is the information that must be included in the owner's personal income tax return. For this reason, some sole proprietorships base their accounting procedures on *income tax rules,* rather than generally accepted accounting principles.

## Evaluating the Financial Statements of a Proprietorship

**The Adequacy of Net Income**  Sole proprietorships do not recognize any salary ex-pense relating to the owner, nor any interest expense on the capital that the owner has invested in the business. Thus, if the business is to be considered successful, its net in-come should *at least* provide the owner with reasonable compensation for any personal services and equity capital that the owner has provided to the business.

In addition, the net income of a sole proprietorship should be adequate to compen-sate the owner for taking significant *risks.* Many small businesses fail. The owner of a sole proprietorship has *unlimited personal liability* for the debts of the business. There-fore, if a sole proprietorship sustains large losses, the owner can lose *much more* than the amount of his or her equity investment.

In summary, the net income of a sole proprietorship should be sufficient to compen-sate the owner for three factors: (1) personal services rendered to the business, (2) cap-ital invested, and (3) the degree of financial risk that the owner is taking.

**Evaluating Solvency**  For a business organized as a *corporation,* creditors often base their lending decisions on the relationships between assets and liabilities in the corpora-tion's balance sheet. But if the business is organized as a sole proprietorship, the bal-ance sheet is less useful to creditors.

Remember, the assets listed in the balance sheet are owned by the *proprietor,* not by the business. The owner can transfer assets in and out of the business at will. Also, it is the *owner* who is financially responsible for the company's debts. Therefore, the ability of a sole proprietorship to pay its debts depends on the *solvency of the owner,* not on the relationships among the assets and liabilities appearing in the company's balance sheet.

The solvency of a sole proprietor may be affected by many things that *do not appear* in the financial statements of the business. For example, the owner may have great per-sonal wealth—or overwhelming personal debts.

In summary, creditors of a sole proprietorship should look past the balance sheet of the business. The real issue is the debt-paying ability of the *owner.* Creditors of the busi-ness may ask the owner to supply *personal* financial information. They also may inves-tigate the owner's credit history, using such credit-rating agencies as **TRW.**

**LO 2**

Identify factors to consider in evaluating the profitability and solvency of a sole proprietorship.

**A Word of Caution**   In Chapter 1, we discussed several factors that *promote the integrity* of the financial statements of publicly owned companies. Among these safeguards are the structure of internal control, audits by independent accountants, federal securities laws, and the competence and integrity of the professional accountants.

Let us stress that these safeguards apply to the **public information** distributed by publicly owned companies. However, they often *do not* apply to financial information provided by small businesses.

Small businesses may not have the resources—or the need—to establish sophisticated internal control structures. The financial information that they develop usually is *not* audited. Federal securities laws apply only to companies that are publicly owned. And the accounting records of a sole proprietorship often are maintained by the owner, who may have little experience in accounting.

**YOUR TURN**

### You as a Banker

Assume that you are a commercial loan officer at a local bank. Chung Yoo, the owner of a sole proprietorship, has approached you for a $75,000 business loan. Mr. Yoo has provided his tax returns for the past three years, which is the length of time that he has been in business. Because the tax returns were prepared by a CPA, Mr. Yoo is confident that the information in them is all the bank should need to evaluate his company's solvency. Is he correct? Explain.

*Our comments appear on page 1118.

## PARTNERSHIPS

A **partnership** is an unincorporated business owned by two or more *partners*.[2] A partnership often is referred to as a *firm*.

Partnerships are the *least* common form of business organization, but they are widely used for professional practices, such as medicine, law, and public accounting.[3] Partnerships also are used for many small businesses, especially those that are family-owned. Most partnerships are small businesses—but certainly not all.

**CASE IN POINT**

The public accounting firm of **Price Waterhouse**, founded in 1865, began in England as a partnership between Samuel Price and Edwin Waterhouse. As the firm grew, qualified members of its professional staff were "admitted to the partnership." Today, thousands of men and women provide accounting and other professional services worldwide as partners with the merged accounting firms of **Price Waterhouse** and **Coopers & Lybrand**, which together are called **PricewaterhouseCoopers**.

For accounting purposes, we view a partnership as an entity separate from the other activities of its owners. But under the law, the partnership is *not* separate from its owners. Rather, the law regards the partners as personally—*and jointly*—responsible for the activities of the business.

The assets of a partnership do not belong to the business—they belong jointly to all of the partners. Unless special provisions are made, each partner has unlimited personal liability for the debts of the business. The partnership itself pays no income taxes, but the partners include their respective shares of the firm's income in their *personal* income tax returns.

---

[2]A partner may be either an individual or a corporation.

[3]Some state laws prohibit professional practices from incorporating. Therefore, professional practices with more than one owner *must* operate as partnerships.

From a legal standpoint, partnerships have *limited lives*. A partnership ends upon the withdrawal or death of an existing partner. Admission of a new partner terminates the previous partnership and creates a new legal entity. However, this is only a legal distinction. Most partnerships have *continuity of existence* extending beyond the participation of individual partners. Partnership agreements often have provisions that make the retirement of partners and the admission of new partners *routine events* that do not affect the operations of the business.

The term "partnership" actually includes three distinct types of organizations: general partnerships, limited partnerships, and limited liability partnerships. We will begin our discussion with the characteristics of *general partnerships*.

## General Partnerships

In a general partnership, each partner has rights and responsibilities similar to those of a sole proprietor. For example, each **general partner** can withdraw cash and other assets from the business at will.[4] Also, each partner has the full authority of an owner to negotiate contracts binding upon the business. This concept is called **mutual agency**. Every partner also has *unlimited personal liability* for the debts of the firm.

Describe the basic characteristics of a general partnership and of partnerships that limit personal liability.

Combining the characteristics of unlimited personal liability and mutual agency makes a general partnership a potentially dangerous form of business organization. Assume, for example, that you enter into a general partnership with Tom Jones. You agree to split profits and losses "50-50." While you are on vacation, Jones commits the partnership to a contract that it simply does not have the resources to complete. Your firm's failure to complete the contract causes large financial losses to the customer. The customer sues your firm and is awarded a judgment of $5 million by the court.

Jones has few financial resources and declares personal bankruptcy. The holder of the judgment against your firm can hold *you personally liable for the whole $5 million*. The fact that you and Jones agreed to split everything "50-50" does *not* lessen your personal liability to your firm's creditors. You may have a legal claim against Jones for his half of this debt, but so what? Jones is bankrupt.

In summary, general partnerships involve the same unlimited personal liability as sole proprietorships. This risk is intensified, however, because you may be held financially responsible for your partner's actions, as well as for your own.

## Partnerships That Limit Personal Liability

Over the years, state laws have evolved to allow modified forms of partnerships, including limited partnerships and limited liability partnerships. The purpose of these modified forms of partnerships is to *place limits* on the potential liability of individual partners.

**Limited Partnerships**    A **limited partnership** has one or more general partners and one or more limited partners. The general partners are partners in the traditional sense, with unlimited personal liability for the debts of the business and the right to make managerial decisions.

The **limited partners** are basically passive investors. They share in the profits and losses of the business, but they do not participate actively in management and are *not* personally liable for debts of the business. Thus, if the firm has financial troubles, the losses incurred by the limited partners are limited to the amounts they have invested in the business.

The Boston Celtics—the professional basketball team—is organized as a publicly owned limited partnership. This means you can purchase a partnership interest in the team. As one of the limited partners, you participate in all distributions of the team's profits. But you can't make management decisions: You can't hire players, send in plays, or fire the head coach. On the other hand, if the Celtics can't pay their bills, the team's creditors won't come after you.

CASE IN POINT

---

[4]Title to real estate is held in the name of the partnership and, therefore, cannot be sold or withdrawn by any partner at will.

In the past, limited partnerships were widely used for various investment ventures, such as drilling for oil, developing real estate, or making a motion picture. These businesses often lost money—at least in the early years; if they were profitable, the profits came in later years.

For such ventures, the limited partnership concept had great appeal to investors. Limited partners could include their share of any partnership net loss in their personal income tax returns, thus offsetting taxable income from other sources. And as *limited* partners, their financial risk was limited to the amount of their equity investment.

Recent changes in tax laws have greatly restricted the extent to which limited partners may offset partnership losses against other types of income. For this reason, there are fewer limited partnerships today than in the past. But in many cases, investors today can obtain similar tax benefits if the business venture is organized as an *S Corporation*. (S Corporations are discussed later in this chapter.)

**Limited Liability Partnerships**   A **limited liability partnership** is a relatively new form of business organization. States traditionally have required professionals, such as doctors, lawyers, and accountants, to organize their practices either as sole proprietorships or as partnerships. The purpose of this requirement was to ensure that these professionals had unlimited liability for their professional activities.

Over the years, many professional partnerships have grown in size. Several public accounting firms, for example, now have thousands of partners and operate in countries all over the world. Also, lawsuits against professional firms have increased greatly in number and in dollar amount. To prevent these lawsuits from bankrupting innocent partners, the concept of the limited liability partnership has emerged. In this type of partnership, each partner has unlimited personal liability for his or her *own* professional activities, but not for the actions of other partners. Unlike a limited partnership, all of the partners in a limited liability partnership may participate in management of the firm.

## Accounting Practices of Partnerships

In most respects, partnership accounting is similar to that in a sole proprietorship—except there are more owners. As a result, a separate capital account and a separate drawing account are maintained for each partner.

Partnerships, like sole proprietorships, recognize no salaries expense for services provided to the organization by the partners. Amounts paid to partners are recorded in the partner's drawing account.

The statement of owner's equity is replaced by a **statement of partners' equity**, which shows separately the changes in each partner's capital account.[5] A typical statement of partners' equity appears below:

*Changes in capital accounts during the year*

| BLAIR AND CROSS<br>Statement of Partners' Equity<br>For the Year Ended December 31, 2002 | | | |
|---|---|---|---|
| | **Blair** | **Cross** | **Total** |
| Balances, Jan. 1, 2002 . . . . . . . . . . . . . . . . . . . . . . . | $160,000 | $160,000 | $320,000 |
| Add: Additional Investments . . . . . . . . . . . . . . . . . . . | 10,000 | 10,000 | 20,000 |
| Net Income for the Year . . . . . . . . . . . . . . . . . . . . | 30,000 | 30,000 | 60,000 |
| Subtotals . . . . . . . . . . . . . . . . . . . . . . . . . . . . . . | $200,000 | $200,000 | $400,000 |
| Less: Drawings . . . . . . . . . . . . . . . . . . . . . . . . . . | 24,000 | 16,000 | 40,000 |
| Balances, Dec. 31, 2002 . . . . . . . . . . . . . . . . . . . . | $176,000 | $184,000 | $360,000 |

---

[5]In firms with a large number of partners, this statement is condensed to show only the changes in *total* partners' equity.

**Allocating Net Income Among the Partners**   A special feature of a partnership is the need to *allocate* the firm's net income among its partners. Allocating partnership net income means computing each partner's share of total net income (or loss) and crediting (or debiting) this amount to the partner's capital account.

This allocation of partnership income is simply a bookkeeping entry, made as the Income Summary account is closed into the various partners' capital accounts. It *does not* involve any distributions of cash or other assets to the partners.

The amount that an individual partner *withdraws* during the year may *differ substantially* from the amount of partnership net income allocated to that partner. All partners pay personal income taxes on the amount of partnership income *allocated* to them—*not* on the amount of assets withdrawn.

Partners have great freedom in deciding how to allocate the firm's net income among themselves. In the absence of prior agreement, state laws generally provide for an *equal split* among the partners. But this seldom happens. Partners usually agree in advance how the firm's net income will be allocated.

Various features of partnership accounting, including the allocation of net income, are illustrated in the *Supplemental Topic* section of this chapter.

**The Importance of a Partnership Contract**   Every partnership needs a carefully written **partnership contract**, prepared before the firm begins operation. This contract is an *agreement among the partners* as to their rights and responsibilities. It spells out the responsibilities of individual partners, how net income will be allocated, and the amounts of assets that partners are allowed to withdraw.

A partnership contract does not prevent disputes from arising among the partners, but it does provide a contractual foundation for their resolution.

## Evaluating the Financial Statements of a Partnership

**The Adequacy of Net Income**   The net income of a partnership is similar to that of a sole proprietorship. It represents the partners' compensation for (1) personal services, (2) invested capital, and (3) assuming the risks of ownership. Also, the reported net income is a pretax amount because the partnership itself pays no income tax.

The services and capital provided by individual partners may vary, as may the degree of financial risk assumed. Therefore, it is quite difficult to evaluate the income of a partnership. Rather, the individual partners must separately evaluate their *respective shares* of the partnership net income in light of their personal contributions to the firm. Some partners may find the partnership quite rewarding, while others may consider their share of the partnership net income inadequate.

**Evaluating Solvency**   The balance sheet of a partnership is more meaningful than that of a sole proprietorship. This is because there are legal distinctions between partnership assets, which are jointly owned, and the personal assets of individual partners. Another reason is that personal responsibility for business debts may *not* extend to all of the partners.

Creditors should understand the distinctions among the types of partnerships. In a general partnership, all partners have unlimited personal liability for the debts of the business. This situation affords creditors the maximum degree of protection. In a limited partnership, only the *general partners* have personal liability for these obligations. In a limited liability partnership, liability for negligence or malpractice extends only to those partners directly involved.

## CORPORATIONS

Nearly all large businesses—and many small ones—are organized as corporations. There are many more sole proprietorships than corporations; but in dollar volume of business activity, corporations hold an impressive lead. Because of the dominant role of the corporation in our economy, it is important for everyone interested in business, economics, or politics to have an understanding of corporations and their accounting policies.

## What Is a Corporation?

**LO 4**

Describe the basic characteristics of a corporation.

A **corporation** is a *legal entity*, having an existence separate and distinct from that of its owners. The owners of a corporation are called **stockholders** (or shareholders), and their ownership is evidenced by transferable shares of **capital stock**.

A corporation is more difficult and costly to form than other types of organizations. The corporation must obtain a *charter* from the state in which it is formed, and it must receive authorization from that state to issue shares of capital stock. The formation of a corporation usually requires the services of an attorney.

As a separate legal entity, a corporation may own property in its own name. The assets of a corporation belong to the corporation itself, not to the stockholders. A corporation has legal status in court—it may sue and be sued as if it were a person. As a legal entity, a corporation may enter into contracts, is *responsible for its own debts,* and *pays income taxes* on its earnings.

On a daily basis, corporations are run by *salaried professional managers,* not by their stockholders.[6] Thus the stockholders are primarily investors, rather than active participants in the business.

The top level of a corporation's professional management is the **board of directors**. These directors are *elected by the stockholders* and are responsible for hiring the other professional managers. In addition, the directors make major policy decisions, including the extent to which profits of the corporation are distributed to stockholders.

The fact that directors are elected by the stockholders means that a stockholder—or group of stockholders—owning more than 50% of the company's stock effectively controls the corporation. These controlling stockholders have the voting power to elect the directors, who in turn set company policies and appoint managers and corporate officers.

The transferability of corporate ownership, together with professional management, gives corporations a greater *continuity of existence* than other forms of organization. Individual stockholders may sell, give, or bequeath their shares to someone else without disrupting business operations. Thus a corporation may continue its business operations *indefinitely,* without regard to changes in ownership.

The following table contrasts the corporate form of business with a sole proprietorship and a general partnership.

### Characteristics of Forms of Business Organizations

| | Sole Proprietorship | General Partnership | Corporation |
|---|---|---|---|
| 1. Legal status | Not a separate legal entity | Not a separate legal entity | Separate legal entity |
| 2. Liability of owners for business debts | Personal liability for business debts | Personal liability for partnership debts | No personal liability for corporate debts |
| 3. Accounting status | Separate entity | Separate entity | Separate entity |
| 4. Tax status | Income taxable to owner | Income taxable to partners | Files a corporate tax return and pays income taxes on its earnings |
| 5. Persons with managerial authority | Owner | Every partner | Hired professional managers |
| 6. Continuity of the business | Entity ceases with retirement or death of owner | New partnership is formed with a change in partners | Indefinite existence |

---

[6]In many cases, the managers and stockholders are one and the same. That is, managers may own stock, and stockholders may be hired into management roles. Ownership of stock, however, does not *automatically* give the shareholder managerial authority.

## Stockholders' Liability for Debts of a Corporation

The second item in our table—the owners' liability for business debts—deserves special attention. Stockholders in a corporation have *no personal liability* for the debts of the business. If a corporation fails, stockholders' potential losses are limited to the amount of their equity in the business.

To investors in large companies—and to the owners of many small businesses—**limited personal liability** is the *greatest advantage* of the corporate form of business organization.

Creditors, too, should understand that shareholders are not personally liable for the debts of a corporation. Creditors have claims against only the *assets of the corporation*, not the personal assets of the corporation's owners.

## What Types of Businesses Choose the Corporate Form of Organization?

The answer, basically, is *all kinds*.

When we think of corporations, we often think of large, well-known companies such as **IBM**, **General Motors**, and **AT&T**. Indeed, almost all large businesses are organized as corporations. Limited shareholder liability, transferability of ownership, professional management, and continuity of existence make the corporation the best form of organization for pooling the resources of a great many equity investors.

The stocks of these large corporations are traded (bought and sold by investors) on organized securities markets, such as the New York Stock Exchange and the National Association of Securities Dealers Automated Quotations (NASDAQ). Companies whose shares are traded on these exchanges are said to be **publicly owned corporations** because anyone may purchase their stock.

When you purchase stock through an exchange, you normally are acquiring the shares from *another investor* (stockholder), not from the corporation itself. The existence of organized stock exchanges is what makes the stock in publicly owned corporations readily transferable.

Not all corporations, however, are large and publicly owned. Many small businesses are organized as corporations. In fact, many corporations have *only one stockholder*. Corporations that are not publicly owned are said to be **closely held corporations**.

All avid sports fans have seen "The Chicken"—the colorful, comic, and acrobatic entertainer who frequently appears at major sporting events. This big feathered bird is also a successful business venture, known as **The Famous San Diego Chicken**. Ted Giannoulas wears many hats in this closely held corporation: He's the president, board of directors, sole stockholder, and—most important—the man in the chicken suit.

**CASE IN POINT**

Generally accepted accounting principles are basically the same for all types of business organizations. Because of the legal characteristics of corporations, however, there are significant differences in the ways these organizations account for income taxes, salaries paid to owners, owners' equity, and distributions of profits to their owners.

## Accounting for Corporate Income Taxes

One of the principal differences between a corporation and an **unincorporated business** is that the corporation must pay income taxes on its earnings.

Corporate income taxes usually are payable in four quarterly installments. If the company is to properly "match" income taxes with the related revenue, **income taxes**

**LO 5**

Account for corporate income taxes; explain the effects of these taxes on before-tax profits and losses.

**expense** should be recognized in the periods in which the taxable income is *earned*. This is accomplished by making an *adjusting entry* at the end of each accounting period.

Total income taxes expense for the year cannot be accurately determined until the corporation completes its annual income tax return. But the income taxes expense for each accounting period can be *reasonably estimated* by applying the current *tax rate* to the company's *taxable income*. This relationship is summarized below:

$$\begin{array}{c}\textbf{Taxable income}\\\textbf{(determined according}\\\textbf{to tax regulations)}\end{array} \times \begin{array}{c}\textbf{Tax rate}\\\textbf{(set by law)}\end{array} = \begin{array}{c}\textbf{Income taxes}\\\textbf{expense}\end{array}$$

**Taxable income** is computed in conformity with *income tax regulations,* not generally accepted accounting principles. In this introductory discussion, we will assume that taxable income is equal to **income before income taxes**—a subtotal that often appears in a corporate income statement. Income before income taxes is simply total revenue less all expenses *other than* income taxes expense.[7]

Tax rates vary depending on the amount of taxable income. Also, Congress may change these rates from one year to the next. For purposes of illustration, we usually will assume a corporate tax rate of *40%* to include the effects of both federal and state income taxes.

To illustrate the recognition of income taxes expense, assume that in November, Scheiner, Inc., earns income before taxes of $50,000. The month-end adjusting entry to recognize the related income taxes would be:

*Adjusting entry to accrue income taxes for the month*

| | | |
|---|---|---|
| Income Taxes Expense .................................................. | 20,000 | |
| Income Taxes Payable .............................................. | | 20,000 |
| To record estimated income taxes expense on income | | |
| earned in November ($50,000 × 40%). | | |

Income taxes payable is a short-term liability that will appear in Scheiner's balance sheet. The presentation of income taxes expense in the company's November income statement is illustrated below:

*Notice income taxes appear separately from other expenses*

**SCHEINER, INC.**
**Condensed Income Statement**
**For the Month Ended November 30, 2002**

| | |
|---|---|
| Net sales ................................................. | $550,000 |
| Cost of goods sold ........................................ | 350,000 |
| Gross profit ............................................. | $200,000 |
| Expenses (other than income taxes—detail not shown) ........ | 150,000 |
| Income before income taxes ............................... | $ 50,000 |
| Income taxes expense .................................... | 20,000 |
| Net income ............................................. | $ 30,000 |

Income taxes expense differs from other business expenses in that income taxes do not help generate revenue. For this reason, income taxes are often shown separately from other expenses in the income statement—following a subtotal such as Income (or Loss) Before Income Taxes. In an income statement, income taxes expense often is termed *provision for income taxes.*

---

[7]In most cases, *income before taxes* provides a reasonable approximation of *taxable income,* but differences in the determination of income before income taxes and taxable income do exist. We discuss significant differences between these subtotals at various points throughout this textbook, although in-depth discussion of this topic is deferred to more advanced accounting courses.

**Income Taxes in *Unprofitable* Periods**    What happens to income taxes expense when *losses* are incurred? In these situations, the company may recognize a negative amount of income taxes expense. The adjusting entry to record income taxes in an unprofitable accounting period consists of a *debit* to Income Taxes Payable and a *credit* to Income Taxes Expense.

"Negative" income taxes expense means that the company expects to recover from the government some of the income taxes recognized as expense in earlier profitable periods.[8] A negative (credit) balance in the Income Taxes Expense account is offset against the amount of the before-tax loss, as shown below:

| Partial Income Statement—for an *Unprofitable* Period | |
| --- | --- |
| Income (loss) Before Income Taxes | $(100,000) |
| Income tax Benefit (recovery of previously recorded taxes) | 40,000 |
| Net loss | $ (60,000) |

*Income tax benefit reduces a pre-tax loss*

We have seen that income taxes expense *reduces* the amount of before-tax *profits*. Notice now that an income tax *benefit*—representing tax refunds—*reduces the amount of a pretax loss*. Thus income taxes reduce the amounts of *both* profits and losses.

If the Income Taxes Payable account has a *negative (debit) balance* at year-end, it is reclassified in the balance sheet as an *asset,* called "Income Tax Refund Receivable."

## Salaries Paid to Owners

We have made the point that unincorporated businesses record payments to their owners as *drawings,* not as salaries expense. But the owners of a corporation cannot make withdrawals of corporate assets. Also, many of a corporation's employees—perhaps thousands—may also be stockholders. Therefore, corporations make *no distinction* between employees who are stockholders and those who are not. All salaries paid to employees (including employee/stockholders) are recognized by the corporation as *salaries expense*.

## Owners' Equity in a Corporate Balance Sheet

In every form of business organization, there are two basic *sources* of owners' equity: (1) investment by the owners and (2) earnings from profitable operations. State laws require corporations to distinguish in their balance sheets between the amounts of equity arising from each source.

To illustrate, assume the following:

- On January 4, 2000, Mary Foster and several investors started Mary's Cab Co., a closely held corporation, by investing $100,000 cash. In exchange, the corporation issued to these investors 10,000 shares of its capital stock.
- It is now December 31, 2002. Over its three-year life, Mary's Cab Co. has earned total net income of $180,000, of which $60,000 has been distributed to the stockholders as *dividends*.

Shown on the following page is the stockholders' equity section of the company's 2002 balance sheet:

---

[8]Tax refunds are limited to taxes paid in recent years. In this introductory discussion, we assume the company has paid sufficient taxes in prior periods to permit full recovery of any negative tax expense relating to a loss in the current period.

*Owners' equity in a corporate balance sheet*

| Stockholders' equity: | |
| --- | --- |
| Capital stock .................................................. | $100,000 |
| Retained earnings ............................................ | 120,000 |
| Total stockholders' equity ................................. | $220,000 |

The Capital Stock account represents the $100,000 invested in the business by Mary Foster and the other stockholders. This amount often is described as "invested capital," or "paid-in capital."

The $120,000 shown as **retained earnings** represents the *lifetime earnings* of the business, less the amount of cash representing those earnings that has been *distributed to the stockholders as dividends* (that is, $180,000 in net income, less $60,000 in dividends, equals $120,000). Retained earnings often are described as "earned capital."

## The Issuance of Capital Stock

**LO 6**

Account for the issuance of capital stock.

When a corporation receives cash or other assets from its owners, in a sale of capital stock, it records these investment transactions by crediting the Capital Stock account.

For example, the entry made by Mary's Cab Co. to record the issuance of 10,000 shares of capital stock in exchange for $100,000 cash appears below:

*Entry to record issuance of capital stock*

| | | |
| --- | --- | --- |
| Cash ............................................................ | 100,000 | |
| Capital Stock .............................................. | | 100,000 |
| Issued 10,000 shares of capital stock for cash. | | |

## Retained Earnings

**LO 7**

Explain the nature of retained earnings, account for dividends, and prepare a statement of retained earnings.

Retained earnings represent the owners' equity created through profitable operation of the business. Earning net income causes the balance in the Retained Earnings account to increase. However, many corporations follow a policy of *distributing to their stockholders* some of the resources generated by profitable operations. These distributions are termed **dividends**.

Dividends *reduce* both total assets and stockholders' equity (as do drawings in an unincorporated business). The reduction in stockholders' equity is reflected by decreasing the balance in the Retained Earnings account. Retained earnings also are reduced by any *net losses* incurred by the business.

Notice that the balance of the Retained Earnings account does *not* represent the net income or net loss of one specific accounting period. Rather, it represents the *cumulative* net income (or net loss) of the business to date, *less* any amounts that have been distributed to the stockholders as dividends. In short, retained earnings represent the earnings that have been *retained* in the corporation. Some of the largest corporations have become large by consistently retaining in the business most of the resources generated by profitable operations.

**CASE IN POINT**

**Sony's** 2000 annual report shows total stockholders' equity of $20,593 million (2,182,906 yen). Of this total, $13,135 million (1,392,266 yen) or about 64%, represents equity from the original investment of stockholders. The majority of the remainder represents retained earnings that total $11,545 million (1,223,761 yen). This means that over the years, profitable operations have significantly increased the stockholders' investment in the company through the retention rather than the distribution of dividends.

Remember, retained earnings are *an element of owners' equity*. The owners' equity in a business *does not* represent cash or any other asset. The amount of cash owned by a corporation appears in the *asset section* of the balance sheet, *not* in the stockholders' equity section.

## Accounting for Dividends

The owners of a corporation may not withdraw profits from the business at will. Instead, distributions of cash or other assets to the stockholders must be formally authorized— or *declared*—by the company's board of directors. These formal distributions are termed *dividends*. By law, dividends must be distributed to all stockholders *in proportion to the number of shares owned*.

A dividend is officially declared by the board of directors on one date, and then is paid (distributed) in the near future. To illustrate, assume that on December 1, 2002, the directors of Mary's Cab Co. declare a regular quarterly dividend of 50 cents per share on the 10,000 shares of outstanding capital stock. The board's resolution specifies that the dividend will be paid on December 15 to stockholders of record on December 10.

Two entries are required: one on December 1 to record the *declaration* of the dividend, and the other on December 15 to record payment:

| | | | | |
|---|---|---|---|---|
| Dec. | 1 | Dividends | 5,000 | |
| | | Dividends Payable | | 5,000 |
| | | Declared a dividend of 50 cents per share payable | | |
| | | Dec. 15 to stockholders of record on Dec. 10. | | |
| | 15 | Dividends Payable | 5,000 | |
| | | Cash | | 5,000 |
| | | Paid dividend declared on Dec. 1. | | |

*Entry to record the declaration of a dividend . . .*

*. . . and the entry to record its payment*

Notice that at the *declaration date*, December 1, there is no reduction in assets. But the stockholders' right to receive the dividend is recognized as a liability. This liability is discharged on the *payment date*, December 15, when the dividend checks are actually mailed to stockholders. No entry is required on the date of record, December 10.

At the end of the period, the Dividends account is closed into the Retained Earnings account, much as an owner's drawing account is closed into that owner's capital account.[9]

## Closing Entries and the Statement of Retained Earnings

### Updating the Retained Earnings Account for Profits, Losses, and Dividends

To review, the amount of retained earnings is increased by earning net income; it is reduced by incurring net losses and by declaring dividends. In the accounting records, these changes are recorded by *closing* the balances in the Income Summary account and Dividends account into the Retained Earnings account.

To illustrate, assume that at January 1, 2002, Mary's Cab Co. had retained earnings of *$80,000*. During the year, the company earned net income of *$60,000* and paid four quarterly dividends totaling *$20,000*. The entries at December 31 to close the Income Summary and Dividends accounts appear below:

| | | |
|---|---|---|
| Income Summary | 60,000 | |
| Retained Earnings | | 60,000 |
| To close the Income Summary account at the end of a profitable year. | | |

*Net income increases retained earnings . . .*

[9]Instead of using a Dividends account, some corporations follow the procedure of debiting the Retained Earnings account directly at the time that the dividend is declared. This eliminates the need for closing the Dividends account at the end of the period. In this text, we will follow the policy of using—and closing—the separate Dividends account.

<table>
<tr><td>*. . . and dividends reduce retained earnings*</td><td>Retained Earnings .................................................. 20,000</td><td></td></tr>
<tr><td></td><td>   Dividends ................................................</td><td>20,000</td></tr>
</table>

To close the Dividends account, thereby reducing retained
  earnings by the amount of dividends declared during the year.

If the corporation had incurred a *net loss* for the year, the Income Summary account would have had a debit balance. The entry to close the account then would have involved a *debit* to Retained Earnings, which would *reduce* total stockholders' equity, and a credit to the Income Summary account.

**The Statement of Retained Earnings**    Instead of a statement of owner's equity, corporations prepare a **statement of retained earnings**, summarizing the changes in the amount of retained earnings over the year.[10] A statement of retained earnings for Mary's Cab Co. follows:

*Notice the similarity to a statement of owner's equity*

| MARY'S CAB CO.<br>Statement of Retained Earnings<br>For the Year Ended December 31, 2002 | |
|---|---:|
| Retained earnings, Jan. 1, 2002 ....................................... | $ 80,000 |
| Net income for the year ............................................. | 60,000 |
|   Subtotal ...................................................... | $140,000 |
| Less: Dividends ..................................................... | 20,000 |
| Retained earnings, Dec. 31, 2002 .................................... | $120,000 |

The "bottom line" of the statement represents the amount of retained earnings that will appear in the company's year-end balance sheet.

## Evaluating the Financial Statements of a Corporation

**The Adequacy of Net Income**    In some respects, the financial statements of a corporation are *easier* to evaluate than those of an unincorporated business. For example, the income of an *unincorporated* business represents compensation to the owners for three distinct factors:

1. Services rendered to the business.
2. Capital invested in the business.
3. The risks of ownership, which often include unlimited personal liability.

But this is *not the case* with a corporation. If stockholders render services to the business, they are compensated with a salary. The corporation recognizes this salary as an expense in the computation of its net income. Therefore, the net income does *not* serve as compensation to the owners for personal services rendered to the business.

Also, stockholders' financial risk of ownership is limited to the amount of their investment. Thus, the net income of a corporation represents simply the *return on the stockholders' financial investment*. The stockholder need only ask, "Is this net income sufficient to compensate me for risking the amount of my investment?" This makes it relatively easy for stockholders to compare the profitability of various corporations in making investment decisions.

**LO 8**

Explain why the financial statements of a corporation are interpreted differently from those of an unincorporated business.

---

[10]Many corporations instead prepare a *statement of stockholders' equity*, which shows the changes in *all* stockholders' equity accounts over the year. A statement of stockholders' equity is illustrated and discussed in Chapter 12.

Remember also that stockholders *do not* report their respective shares of the corporate net income in their personal income tax returns. However, they must pay personal income taxes on the amount of any dividends received.[11]

**Evaluating Solvency**   When extending credit to an *unincorporated* business, creditors often look to the solvency of the individual *owners,* rather than that of the business entity. This is because the owners often are personally liable for the business debts. But in lending funds to a corporation, creditors generally look only to the *business entity* for repayment. Therefore, the financial strength of the business organization becomes much more important when the business is organized as a corporation.

**Small Corporations and Loan Guarantees**   Small, closely held corporations often do not have sufficient financial resources to qualify for the credit they need. In such cases, creditors may require one or more of the company's stockholders to personally guarantee (or co-sign) specific debts of the business entity. By co-signing debts of the corporation, the individual stockholders *do become personally liable for the debts if the corporation fails to make payment.*

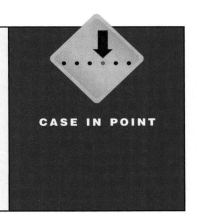

A small family-owned restaurant supply business was organized as a corporation. To operate efficiently, the business needed to purchase merchandise on account. However, the corporation had so few assets that suppliers were unwilling to extend credit. To obtain credit for the business, a major stockholder pledged his vacation home—a condominium on the Hawaiian island of Maui—to secure the company's debt to a particular supplier. With this additional security, the supplier allowed the business to purchase large quantities of merchandise on account.

Unfortunately, the small business became insolvent and was forced into bankruptcy. Not only did the owners' investments in this business become worthless, but one owner also lost his vacation home to the company's creditors.

CASE IN POINT

## The Concept—and the Problem—of "Double Taxation"

*Unincorporated businesses* do not pay income taxes. Instead, each owner pays *personal income taxes* on his or her share of the business net income.

Corporations, in contrast, must pay *corporate income taxes* on their taxable income. In addition, the stockholders must pay personal income taxes on the dividends they receive. Thus corporate earnings may end up being *taxed twice:* once to the corporation as the income is earned and then again to the stockholders when the profits are distributed as dividends.

This concept of taxing a corporation's earnings at two levels is often called **double taxation**. Together, these two levels of taxation can consume as much as *60% to 70%* of a corporation's before-tax income. Few businesses would be able to raise equity capital if investors indeed expected to face such a high overall tax rate. Therefore, careful **tax planning** is *absolutely essential* in any business organized as a corporation.

There are several ways that a corporation legally may avoid the full impact of double taxation. For example, corporations always should pay *salaries* to stockholders who work in the business. These salaries are taxable to the stockholders, but they are expenses of the business, which reduce the corporation's taxable income. Also, the taxation of dividends can be avoided entirely if the corporation *retains* its profits, rather than distributing them as dividends.

---

[11]*S Corporations* are an exception to this rule. See the discussion on page 1104.

**YOUR TURN**

### You as an Investor

Assume that you plan to invest in the stock of a high-tech corporation and that one of your investment goals is to receive dividend income from the stocks that you purchase. You begin your research by examining **Microsoft**, one of the world's most successful software corporations. You discover that, as of 2000, **Microsoft** has never paid a dividend on its common stock. Furthermore, the company's 2000 balance sheet reported holdings of nearly $5 billion in cash and cash equivalents plus approximately $19 billion in other highly liquid investments. With all of these liquid resources available, why do you think **Microsoft** maintains a policy of not paying dividends to its stockholders?

*Our comments appear on page 1119.

### S Corporations

Tax laws allow many small closely held corporations a special tax status under Subchapter S of the tax code.[12] Corporations that qualify for this special tax treatment are called **S Corporations**.

S Corporations *do not* pay corporate income taxes; nor do stockholders pay personal income taxes on the amounts of dividends received. Instead, each stockholder pays *personal* income taxes on his or her share of the corporate net income. Thus the net income of an S Corporation is taxed in the same manner as that of a *partnership*.

S Corporation status is most advantageous in the following situations:

- A profitable corporation plans to distribute most of its earnings as dividends. In this case, organization as an S Corporation avoids the problem of *double taxation*.

- A new corporation is expected to incur *net losses* in its early years of operation. Ordinarily, net losses incurred by a corporation have *no effect* on the stockholders' personal income tax returns. But if the business is organized as an S Corporation, stockholders *may* deduct their share of any net business loss in their personal income tax returns.

From a tax standpoint, S Corporation status may greatly benefit the owners of a closely held corporation. Owners of small businesses should consider this form of organization.

S Corporations are a special case, not the "norm." Unless we specifically state otherwise, you should assume that all corporations used in our examples and assignment materials are regular corporations, not S Corporations.

**LO 9**

Discuss the principal factors to consider in selecting a form of business organization.

## SELECTING AN APPROPRIATE FORM OF BUSINESS ORGANIZATION

Anyone planning to start a business should give careful thought to the form of organization. Among the factors most often considered are:

- The personal liability of the owner(s) for business debts.
- Income tax considerations.
- The need to raise large amounts of equity capital.

---

[12]An S Corporation must have 35 or fewer stockholders, all of whom are individuals and residents of the United States. Thus, while one corporation generally may own stock in another, it may *not* be a stockholder in an S Corporation.

- The owners' need for flexibility in withdrawing assets from the business.
- Whether all owners are to have managerial authority.
- The need for continuity in business operations, despite future changes in ownership.
- The ease and cost of forming the business.

## Incorporating an Established Business

Often a business starts out as a sole proprietorship or partnership, but as it grows larger, it is reorganized as a closely held corporation. Eventually, the business may "go public," meaning that it issues stock to the general public and its shares are traded on an organized stock exchange.

**Benckiser, Inc.**, recently "went public" with a $636 million stock offering. Prior to its public stock offering, Benckiser was organized as a closely held corporation. This once small household products company, best known for its Calgon dishwashing product, now competes internationally with such industry giants as **Procter & Gamble**.

**CASE IN POINT**

When an existing business is reorganized as a corporation, the corporation is a *new business entity*. The valuation of the corporation's assets and liabilities is based on their *current market value* when the new entity is established, not on their values in the accounting records of the previous business entity.

Assume, for example, that Devin Ryan has long owned and operated a sole proprietorship called Ryan Engineering. In January, Ryan decides to *incorporate* his business. He obtains a corporate charter and transfers to the new corporation all of the assets used in his sole proprietorship. The new corporation also assumes responsibility for all of the proprietorship's business debts. In exchange for these net assets (assets less liabilities), Ryan receives 20,000 shares of capital stock in the new corporation.

The following table lists the assets, liabilities, and owner's equity of the sole proprietorship at the date the new business is formed. The left-hand column indicates the amounts of these items in the proprietorship's accounting records. The right-hand column indicates the *current market value* of these items on this date. (In each column, owner's equity is equal to total assets, less total liabilities.)

|  | Amount in Proprietorship's Accounting Records | Current Market Value |
|---|---|---|
| Cash | $ 30,000 | $ 30,000 |
| Accounts Receivable | 75,000 | 60,000 |
| Inventory | 10,000 | 15,000 |
| Land | 40,000 | 100,000 |
| Building | 60,000 | 50,000 |
| Equipment | 70,000 | 80,000 |
| Notes Payable | 55,000 | 55,000 |
| Accounts Payable | 20,000 | 20,000 |
| Owner's Equity | 210,000 | 260,000 |

The entry to establish a new set of records for the business as a corporation, based on the values of the assets received and the liabilities assumed, is as follows:

*The new business records the assets acquired at* current market value

| | | |
|---|---|---|
| Cash | 30,000 | |
| Accounts Receivable | 60,000 | |
| Inventory | 15,000 | |
| Land | 100,000 | |
| Building | 50,000 | |
| Equipment | 80,000 | |
| Notes Payable | | 55,000 |
| Accounts Payable | | 20,000 |
| Capital Stock | | 260,000 |

Acquired assets and assumed liabilities of Ryan Engineering; issued 20,000 shares of capital stock in exchange.

**CASH EFFECTS**

A publicly owned corporation receives cash only when it first sells shares of stock to the investment public (called an "initial public offering," or IPO). Future trading of these securities takes place between individual investors and has no direct impact on the company's cash flows. Yet publicly owned corporations are extremely concerned about growth trends in the market value of their outstanding securities.

Why is this? There are several reasons. First, corporations monitor closely the current market value of their securities because current stock performance directly influences the ability to raise equity capital in the future (through new public offerings). Second, poor stock performance often signals that a company is experiencing financial difficulty. This, in turn, often makes it difficult for the company to obtain credit and may even make potential customers reluctant to buy the goods or services it sells. Finally, a growing number of corporations include stock options in their executive compensation plans. If the market price of the company's stock falls below a certain value, these options become worthless. When this happens, key executives often lose motivation to stay with the company and make the decision to take their "intellectual capital" elsewhere.

## SUPPLEMENTAL TOPIC

### PARTNERSHIP ACCOUNTING—A CLOSER LOOK

There are a number of unique aspects of partnership accounting. In this section, we describe opening the accounts of a new partnership, additional investments and withdrawals by owners, allocating partnership net income among the partners, and closing the accounts at year-end.

### Opening the Accounts of a New Partnership

When a partner contributes assets other than cash, a question always arises as to the value of such assets. The valuations assigned to noncash assets should be their *fair market values* at the date of transfer to the partnership. The valuations assigned must be agreed to by all partners.

To illustrate the opening entries for a newly formed partnership, assume that on January 1, 2002, Joan Blair and Richard Cross, who operate competing retail stores, decide to form a partnership by consolidating their two businesses. A capital account is opened for each partner and credited with the agreed valuation of the *net assets* (total assets less total liabilities) that the partner contributes. The journal entries to open the accounts of the partnership of Blair and Cross are as follows:

| | | |
|---|---:|---:|
| Cash | 40,000 | |
| Accounts Receivable | 60,000 | |
| Inventory | 90,000 | |
|     Accounts Payable | | 30,000 |
|     Joan Blair, Capital | | 160,000 |
| To record the investment by Joan Blair in the partnership of Blair and Cross. | | |

*Entries to record the formation of a partnership*

| | | |
|---|---:|---:|
| Cash | 10,000 | |
| Inventory | 60,000 | |
| Land | 60,000 | |
| Building | 100,000 | |
|     Accounts Payable | | 70,000 |
|     Richard Cross, Capital | | 160,000 |
| To record the investment by Richard Cross in the partnership of Blair and Cross. | | |

Accounting in a partnership is similar to that in a sole proprietorship, except that separate capital accounts are maintained for each partner. These capital accounts show for each partner the amounts invested, the amounts withdrawn, and the appropriate share of partnership net income. In brief, each partner is provided with a history of his or her equity in the firm.

Separate *drawing accounts* also are maintained for each partner. These drawing accounts are debited to record all withdrawals of cash or other assets, including the use of partnership funds to pay a partner's personal debts.

**Additional Investments**   Assume that after six months of operation the firm is in need of more cash, and the partners make additional investments of $10,000 each on July 1. These additional investments are credited to the capital accounts as shown below:

| | | |
|---|---:|---:|
| Cash | 20,000 | |
|     Joan Blair, Capital | | 10,000 |
|     Richard Cross, Capital | | 10,000 |
| To record additional investments. | | |

*Recording an investment of additional capital*

**Closing the Accounts of a Partnership at Year-End**   At the end of the accounting period, the balance in the Income Summary account is closed into the partners' capital accounts. The profits or losses of a partnership may be divided among the partners in *any manner agreed upon* by the partners.

In our illustration, let us assume that Blair and Cross have agreed to share profits equally. (We will discuss other profit-and-loss sharing arrangements later in this section.) Assuming that the partnership earns net income of $60,000 in the first year of operations, the entry to close the Income Summary account is as follows:

| | | |
|---|---:|---:|
| Income Summary | 60,000 | |
|     Joan Blair, Capital | | 30,000 |
|     Richard Cross, Capital | | 30,000 |
| To divide net income for the year in accordance with partnership agreement to share profits equally. | | |

*Closing the income summary: profits shared equally*

The next step in closing the accounts is to transfer the balance of each partner's drawing account to his or her capital account. Assuming that withdrawals during the year amounted to $24,000 for Blair and $16,000 for Cross, the entry at December 31 to close the drawing accounts is as follows:

*Closing the partners' drawing accounts into their capital accounts*

| | | |
|---|---|---|
| Joan Blair, Capital .................................................... | 24,000 | |
| Richard Cross, Capital ............................................... | 16,000 | |
| Joan Blair, Drawing ............................................. | | 24,000 |
| Richard Cross, Drawing ......................................... | | 16,000 |
| To transfer debit balances in partners' drawing accounts to their respective capital accounts. | | |

**Income Statement for a Partnership**    The income statement for a partnership differs from that of a sole proprietorship in only one respect: a final section may be added to show the division of the net income between the partners, as illustrated below for the firm of Blair and Cross. The income statement of a partnership is consistent with that of a sole proprietorship in showing no income taxes expense and no salaries relating to services rendered by partners.

**BLAIR AND CROSS**
**Income Statement**
**For the Year Ended December 31, 2002**

| | | |
|---|---|---|
| Sales ........................................................ | | $600,000 |
| Cost of goods sold ............................................ | | 400,000 |
| Gross profit on sales .......................................... | | $200,000 |
| Operating expenses: | | |
| Selling expenses ............................................ | $100,000 | |
| General & administrative expenses ......................... | 40,000 | 140,000 |
| Net income .................................................. | | $60,000 |
| | | |
| Division of net income: | | |
| To Joan Blair (50%) ......................................... | $ 30,000 | |
| To Richard Cross (50%) ..................................... | 30,000 | $ 60,000 |

**Statement of Partners' Equity**    The partners usually want an explanation of the change in their capital accounts from one year-end to the next. The statement of partners' equity for Blair and Cross appears below (this statement also was illustrated on page 1094):

**BLAIR AND CROSS**
**Statement of Partners' Equity**
**For the Year Ended December 31, 2002**

| | Blair | Cross | Total |
|---|---|---|---|
| Balances, Jan. 1, 2002 ...................... | $160,000 | $160,000 | $320,000 |
| Add: Additional Investments ................... | 10,000 | 10,000 | 20,000 |
| Net Income for the Year .................... | 30,000 | 30,000 | 60,000 |
| Subtotals ................................... | $200,000 | $200,000 | $400,000 |
| Less: Drawings ............................. | 24,000 | 16,000 | 40,000 |
| Balances, Dec. 31, 2002 ..................... | $176,000 | $184,000 | $360,000 |

The balance sheet of Blair and Cross would show the capital balance for each partner, as well as the total equity of $360,000.

## Allocating Partnership Net Income Among the Partners

**LO 10**

Allocate partnership net income among the partners.

Profits earned by partnerships compensate the owners for (1) personal services rendered to the business, (2) capital invested in the business, and (3) assuming the risks of ownership. Recognition of these three factors is helpful in developing an equitable plan for the division of partnership profits.

If one partner devotes full time to the business while another devotes little or no time, the difference in the partners' contributions of time and effort should be reflected in the profit-sharing agreement. If one partner possesses special skills, the profit-sharing agreement should reward this partner's talent. Also, partners may each provide different amounts of capital to the business entity. Again, the differences in the value of the partners' contributions to the business should be reflected in the profit-and-loss sharing agreement.

To recognize the particular contributions of each partner to the business, partnership profit-and-loss sharing agreements often include salary allowances to partners and interest on the balances of partners' capital accounts. These "salaries" and "interest" are *not expenses* of the business; rather, they are *steps in the computation made to divide partnership net income among the partners.*

In the preceding illustrations of the partnership of Blair and Cross, we assumed that the partners invested equal amounts of capital, rendered equal services, and divided net income equally. We are now ready to consider cases in which the partners invest *unequal* amounts of capital and services. Partners can share net income or loss in any manner they choose; however, most profit-sharing agreements fall under one of the following types:

1. A fixed ratio. The fixed ratio method has already been illustrated in the example of the Blair and Cross partnership, in which profits were shared equally, that is, 50% and 50%. Partners may agree upon any fixed ratio such as 60% and 40%, or 70% and 30%.

2. Salary allowances to the partners, with remaining net income or loss divided in a fixed ratio.

3. Interest allowances on partners' capital balances, with remaining net income or loss divided in a fixed ratio.

4. Salary allowances to the partners, interest allowances on partners' capital balances, and remaining net income or loss divided in a fixed ratio.

All these methods of sharing partnership net income are intended to recognize differences in the personal services rendered by partners and in the amounts of capital invested in the firm.

In the illustrations that follow, it is assumed that beginning balances in the partners' capital accounts were Brooke Adams, $160,000, and Ben Barnes, $40,000. At year-end, the Income Summary account showed a credit balance of $96,000, representing the net income for the year.

**Salaries to Partners, with Remainder in a Fixed Ratio**   Because partners often contribute different amounts of personal services, partnership agreements often provide for partners' salaries as a factor in the division of profits.

For example, assume that Adams and Barnes agree to annual salary allowances of $12,000 for Adams and $60,000 for Barnes. These salaries, which total $72,000 per year, are agreed upon by the partners in advance. Of course, the net income of the business is not likely to be exactly $72,000 in a given year. Therefore, the profit-and-loss sharing agreement should also specify a fixed ratio for dividing any profit or loss remaining after giving consideration to the agreed-upon salary allowances. We will assume that Adams and Barnes agree to divide any remaining profit or loss equally.

The division of the $96,000 in partnership net income between Adams and Barnes is illustrated in the schedule shown below. The first step is to allocate to each partner his or her agreed-upon salary allowance. This step allocates $72,000 of the partnership net income. The remaining $24,000 is then divided in the agreed-upon fixed ratio (50-50 in this example).

*Profit sharing: salary allowances and remainder in a fixed ratio*

| Division of Partnership Net Income | | | |
|---|---|---|---|
| | **Adams** | **Barnes** | **Net Income** |
| Net income to be divided . . . . . . . . . . . . . . . . . . . . . . . . | | | $96,000 |
| Salary allowances to partners . . . . . . . . . . . . . . . . . . . | $12,000 | $60,000 | (72,000) |
| Remaining income after salary allowances . . . . . . . . . . . . . . . . . . . . . . . . . . . . . . . . . | | | $24,000 |
| Allocated in a fixed ratio: | | | |
| Adams (50%) . . . . . . . . . . . . . . . . . . . . . . . . . . . . . | 12,000 | | |
| Barnes (50%) . . . . . . . . . . . . . . . . . . . . . . . . . . . . . | | 12,000 | (24,000) |
| Total share to each partner . . . . . . . . . . . . . . . . . . . . | $24,000 | $72,000 | $ –0– |

Under this agreement, Adams's share of the $96,000 profit amounts to $24,000 and Barnes's share amounts to $72,000. The entry to close the Income Summary account would be:

*Notice that the allocation of partnership income is used in this closing entry*

| | | |
|---|---|---|
| Income Summary . . . . . . . . . . . . . . . . . . . . . . . . . . . . . . . . . . . . . . . . . . . . . . | 96,000 | |
| Brooke Adams, Capital . . . . . . . . . . . . . . . . . . . . . . . . . . . . . . . . . . . . . . | | 24,000 |
| Ben Barnes, Capital . . . . . . . . . . . . . . . . . . . . . . . . . . . . . . . . . . . . . . . . | | 72,000 |

To close the Income Summary account by crediting each
  partner with agreed-upon salary allowance and dividing
  the remaining profits equally.

The salary allowances used in dividing partnership net income are sometimes misinterpreted, even by the partners. These salary allowances are merely an agreed-upon device for dividing net income; they are *not expenses* of the business and are *not recorded in any ledger account*. A partner is considered an owner of the business, not an employee. In a partnership, the services that a partner renders to the firm are assumed to be rendered in anticipation of earning a share of the profits, not a salary.

The amount of cash or other assets that a partner withdraws from the partnership may be greater than or less than the partner's salary allowance. Even if a partner decides to withdraw an amount of cash equal to his or her "salary allowance," the withdrawal should be recorded by debiting the partner's drawing account, *not by debiting an expense account*. Let us repeat the main point: *"salary allowances" to partners should not be recorded as expenses of the business.*[1]

### Interest Allowances on Partners' Capital, with Remainder in a Fixed Ratio

Next we shall assume a business situation in which the partners spend very little time in the business and net income depends primarily on the amount of money invested. The profit-sharing plan then might emphasize invested capital as a basis for the first step in allocating income.

For example, assume that Adams and Barnes had agreed that both partners are to be allowed interest at *15%* on their beginning capital balances, with any remaining profit or loss to be divided equally. Net income to be divided is $96,000, and the beginning capital balances are Adams, *$160,000,* and Barnes, *$40,000.*

---

[1]Some exceptions to this general rule will be discussed in more advanced accounting courses.

**Division of Partnership Net Income**

| | Adams | Barnes | Net Income |
|---|---|---|---|
| Net income to be divided . . . . . . . . . . . . . . . . . . . . . . . | | | $96,000 |
| Interest allowances on beginning capital: | | | |
| Adams ($160,000 × 15%) . . . . . . . . . . . . . . . . . . . | $24,000 | | |
| Barnes ($40,000 × 15%) . . . . . . . . . . . . . . . . . . . . | | $ 6,000 | |
| Total allocated as interest allowances. . . . . . . . . . . . | | | (30,000) |
| Remaining income after interest allowances . . . . . . . . . . . . . . . . . . . . . . . . . . . . . . . | | | $66,000 |
| Allocated in a fixed ratio: | | | |
| Adams (50%) . . . . . . . . . . . . . . . . . . . . . . . . . . . . | 33,000 | | |
| Barnes (50%) . . . . . . . . . . . . . . . . . . . . . . . . . . . . | | 33,000 | (66,000) |
| Total share to each partner . . . . . . . . . . . . . . . . . . . | $57,000 | $39,000 | $ –0– |

*Profit sharing: interest on capital and remainder in a fixed ratio*

The entry to close the Income Summary account in this example would be:

| | | |
|---|---|---|
| Income Summary . . . . . . . . . . . . . . . . . . . . . . . . . . . . . . . . . . . . . . . . . | 96,000 | |
| Brooke Adams, Capital . . . . . . . . . . . . . . . . . . . . . . . . . . . . . . . . . . | | 57,000 |
| Ben Barnes, Capital . . . . . . . . . . . . . . . . . . . . . . . . . . . . . . . . . . . | | 39,000 |

To close the Income Summary account by crediting each
partner with interest at 15% on beginning capital and
dividing the remaining profits equally.

*Each partner's capital account is increased by his or her share of partnership net income*

**Salary Allowances, Interest on Capital, and Remainder in a Fixed Ratio**  The preceding example took into consideration the difference in amounts of capital provided by Adams and Barnes but ignored any difference in personal services performed. In the next example, we shall assume that the partners agree to a profit-sharing plan providing for salaries and for interest on beginning capital balances. Salary allowances, as before, are authorized at $12,000 for Adams and $60,000 for Barnes. Beginning capital balances are $160,000 for Adams and $40,000 for Barnes. Partners are to be allowed interest at 10% on their beginning capital balances, and any profit or loss remaining after authorized salary and interest allowances is to be divided equally.

**Division of Partnership Net Income**

| | Adams | Barnes | Net Income |
|---|---|---|---|
| Net income to be divided . . . . . . . . . . . . . . . . . . . . . | | | $96,000 |
| Salary allowances to partners . . . . . . . . . . . . . . . . . . . | $12,000 | $60,000 | (72,000) |
| Income after salary allowances . . . . . . . . . . . . . . . . . . | | | $24,000 |
| Interest allowances on beginning capital: | | | |
| Adams ($160,000 × 10%) . . . . . . . . . . . . . . . . . . . | 16,000 | | |
| Barnes ($40,000 × 10%) . . . . . . . . . . . . . . . . . . . . | | 4,000 | |
| Total allocated as interest allowances . . . . . . . . . . . . | | | (20,000) |
| Remaining income after salary and interest allowances . . . . . . . . . . . . . . . . . . . . . . . . . | | | $4,000 |
| Allocated in a fixed ratio: | | | |
| Adams (50%) . . . . . . . . . . . . . . . . . . . . . . . . . . . . | 2,000 | | |
| Barnes (50%) . . . . . . . . . . . . . . . . . . . . . . . . . . . . | | 2,000 | (4,000) |
| Total share to each partner . . . . . . . . . . . . . . . . . . . | $30,000 | $66,000 | $ –0– |

*Profit sharing: salaries, interest, and remainder in a fixed ratio*

The journal entry to close the Income Summary account in this case will be:

| Income Summary | 96,000 | |
|---|---|---|
| Brooke Adams, Capital | | 30,000 |
| Ben Barnes, Capital | | 66,000 |

To close the Income Summary account by crediting each
partner with authorized salary and interest at 10% on
beginning capital, and dividing the remaining profits equally.

**Authorized Salary and Interest Allowance in Excess of Net Income**   In the
preceding example the total of the authorized salaries and interest was $92,000 and the
net income to be divided was $96,000. Suppose that the net income had been only
$30,000. How should the division have been made?

If the partnership contract provides for salaries and interest on invested capital,
these provisions are to be followed even though the net income for the year is *less*
than the total of the authorized salaries and interest. If the net income of the firm of
Adams and Barnes amounted to only $50,000, this amount would be allocated as
shown below:

*Authorized salary and interest allowances in excess of net income*

| Division of Partnership Net Income | | | |
|---|---|---|---|
| | **Adams** | **Barnes** | **Net Income** |
| Net income to be divided | | | $ 50,000 |
| Salary allowances to partners | $12,000 | $60,000 | (72,000) |
| Residual loss after salary allowances | | | $(22,000) |
| Interest allowances on beginning capital: | | | |
| Adams ($160,000 × 10%) | 16,000 | | |
| Barnes ($40,000 × 10%) | | 4,000 | |
| Total allocated as interest allowances | | | (20,000) |
| Residual loss after salary and interest allowances | | | $(42,000) |
| Allocated in a fixed ratio: | | | |
| Adams (50%) | (21,000) | | |
| Barnes (50%) | | (21,000) | 42,000 |
| Total share to each partner | $ 7,000 | $43,000 | $ –0– |

Unless she is thoroughly familiar with the terms of the partnership contract, Adams
certainly will be surprised at her allocation of net income for this accounting period. The
allocation formula caused Adams to actually be allocated income of only $7,000 for the
period, while Barnes was allocated net income of $43,000. The entry to close the In-
come Summary will be as follows:

*Interesting . . . one partner's "share of the profit" was a loss. Think about it.*

| Income Summary | 50,000 | |
|---|---|---|
| Brooke Adams, Capital | | 7,000 |
| Ben Barnes, Capital | | 43,000 |

To close the Income Summary account by crediting each
partner with authorized salary and interest at 10% on
beginning capital, and dividing the residual loss equally.

Had the net income been even less, say $30,000, Adams would actually have been al-
located a *negative* amount:

| Division of Partnership Net Income | | | |
|---|---|---|---|
| | Adams | Barnes | Net Income |
| Net income to be divided . . . . . . . . . . . . . . . . . . . . . . . | | | $ 30,000 |
| Salary allowances to partners . . . . . . . . . . . . . . . . . . | $12,000 | $60,000 | (72,000) |
| Residual loss after salary allowances . . . . . . . . . . . . . . | | | $(42,000) |
| Interest allowances on beginning capital: | | | |
| Adams ($160,000 × 10%) . . . . . . . . . . . . . . . . . . . | 16,000 | | |
| Barnes ($40,000 × 10%) . . . . . . . . . . . . . . . . . . . | | 4,000 | |
| Total allocated as interest allowances . . . . . . . . . . . | | | (20,000) |
| Residual loss after salary and interest allowances . . . . . . . . . . . . . . . . . . . . . . . . . . . . | | | $(62,000) |
| Allocated in a fixed ratio: | | | |
| Adams (50%) . . . . . . . . . . . . . . . . . . . . . . . . . . . . | (31,000) | | |
| Barnes (50%) . . . . . . . . . . . . . . . . . . . . . . . . . . . . | | (31,000) | 62,000 |
| Total share to each partner . . . . . . . . . . . . . . . . . . . | $ (3,000) | $33,000 | $ –0– |

## ASSIGNMENT MATERIAL

## DISCUSSION QUESTIONS

1. Terry Hanson owns Hanson Sporting Goods, a retail store organized as a sole proprietorship. He also owns a home that he purchased for $200,000 but that is worth $250,000 today. (Hanson has a $140,000 mortgage against this house.) Explain how this house and mortgage should be classified in the financial statements of Hanson Sporting Goods.

2. Jane Miller is the proprietor of a small manufacturing business. She is considering the possibility of joining in partnership with Tom Bracken, whom she considers to be thoroughly competent and congenial. Prepare a brief statement outlining the advantages and disadvantages of the potential partnership to Miller.

3. What is meant by the term *mutual agency?*

4. A real estate development business is managed by two experienced developers and is financed by 50 investors from throughout the state. To allow maximum income tax benefits to the investors, the business is organized as a partnership. Explain why this type of business probably would be a limited partnership rather than a regular partnership.

5. What factors should be considered when comparing the net income figure of a partnership to that of a corporation of similar size?

6. Susan Reed is a partner in Computer Works, a retail store. During the current year, she withdraws $45,000 in cash from this business and takes for her personal use inventory costing $3,200. Her share of the partnership net income for the year amounts to $39,000. What amount must Reed report on her personal income tax return?

7. Distinguish between corporations and partnerships in terms of the following characteristics:
    a. Owners' liability for debts of the business
    b. Transferability of ownership interest
    c. Continuity of existence
    d. Federal taxation on income

8. Explain the meaning of the term *double taxation* as it applies to corporate profits.

*9. What factors should be considered in drawing up an agreement as to the way in which income shall be shared by two or more partners?

---

*Supplemental Topic*, "Partnership Accounting—A Closer Look."

*10. Partner John Young has a choice to make. He has been offered by his partners a choice between no salary allowance and a one-third share in the partnership income or a salary of $16,000 per year and a one-quarter share of residual profits. Write a brief memorandum explaining the factors he should consider in reaching a decision.

# PROBLEMS

**PROBLEM C.1**

Partnership Transactions

**LO 3**

Picture Perfect Company is a partnership among Yolando Gonzales, Willie Todd, and Linda Yeager. The partnership contract states that partnership profits will be split equally among the three partners. During the current year Gonzales withdrew $25,000, Todd withdrew $23,000, and Yeager withdrew $30,000. Net income of Picture Perfect Company amounted to $120,000.

a. Calculate each partner's share of net income for the period.

b. Describe the effects, if any, that partnership operations would have on the individual tax returns of the partners.

c. Prepare a statement of partners' equity for the year. Assume that partners' capital accounts had beginning balances of $50,000, $60,000, and $40,000 for Gonzales, Todd, and Yeager, respectively.

**PROBLEM C.2**

Analysis of Equity

**LO 6, 7**

Shown below are the amounts from the stockholders' equity section of the balance sheets of Lowell Corporation for the years ended December 31, 2001 and 2002:

| | 2002 | 2001 |
|---|---|---|
| Stockholders' equity: | | |
| Capital Stock | $ 50,000 | $ 30,000 |
| Retained Earnings | 200,000 | 180,000 |
| Total stockholders' equity | $250,000 | $210,000 |

a. Calculate the amount of additional investment that the stockholders made during 2002.

b. Assuming that the corporation declared and paid $10,000 in dividends during 2002, calculate the amount of *net income* earned by the corporation during 2002.

c. Explain the significance of the $200,000 balance of retained earnings at December 31, 2002.

**\*PROBLEM C.3**

Division of Partnership Income

**LO 10**

Guenther and Firmin, both of whom are CPAs, form a partnership, with Guenther investing $100,000 and Firmin, $80,000. They agree to share net income as follows:

1. Salary allowances of $80,000 to Guenther and $60,000 to Firmin.

2. Interest allowances at 15% of beginning capital account balances.

3. Any partnership earnings in excess of the amount required to cover the interest and salary allowances to be divided 60% to Guenther and 40% to Firmin.

The partnership net income for the first year of operations amounted to $247,000 before interest and salary allowances. Show how this $247,000 should be divided between the two partners. Use a three-column schedule of the type illustrated on page 1111. List on separate lines the amounts of interest, salaries, and the residual amount divided.

**PROBLEM C.4**

Analysis of Partnership Accounts

**LO 3**

Lucky Burger is a fast-food restaurant that is operated as a partnership of three individuals. The three partners share profit equally. Presented below are selected account balances for the current year before any closing entries are made:

---

*Supplemental Topic, "Partnership Accounting—A Closer Look."*

|  | Debit | Credit |
|---|---|---|
| Glen, Capital | | 55,000 |
| Chow, Capital | | 60,000 |
| West, Capital | | 5,000 |
| Glen, Drawing | 15,000 | |
| Chow, Drawing | 15,000 | |
| West, Drawing | 30,000 | |
| Income Summary | | 75,000 |

## Instructions

On the basis of this information, answer the following questions and show any necessary computations.

**a.** How much must each of the three partners report on his individual income tax return related to this business?

**b.** Prepare a Statement of Partners' Equity for the current year ended December 31. Assume that no partner has made an additional investment during the year.

**c.** Assuming that each of the partners devotes the same amount of time to the business, why might Glen and Chow consider the profit-sharing agreement to be inequitable?

**d.** What factors should the partners consider when evaluating whether the profit from the partnership is adequate?

The Top Hat, Inc., is a chain of magic shops that is organized as a corporation. During the month of June, the stockholders' equity accounts of The Top Hat were affected by the following events:

**PROBLEM C.5**
Stockholders' Equity Transactions

**LO 6, 7**

**June 3**  The corporation sold 1,000 shares of capital stock at $20 per share.

**June 10**  The corporation declared a 25 cents per share dividend on its 20,000 shares of outstanding capital stock, payable on June 23.

**June 23**  The corporation paid the dividend declared on June 10.

**June 30**  The Income Summary account showed a credit balance of $60,000; the corporation's accounts are closed monthly.

## Instructions

**a.** Prepare journal entries for each of the above events in the accounts of The Top Hat. Include the entries necessary to close the Income Summary and Dividends accounts.

**b.** Prepare a statement of retained earnings for June. Assume that the balance of retained earnings on May 31 was $520,000.

William Bost organized Frontier Western Wear, Inc., early in 2001. On January 15, the corporation issued to Bost and other investors 40,000 shares of capital stock at $20 per share.

**PROBLEM C.6**
Stockholders' Equity Transactions—More Challenging

**LO 4, 5, 6, 7**

After the revenue and expense accounts (except Income Taxes Expense) were closed into the Income Summary account at the end of 2001, the account showed a before-tax profit of $120,000. The income tax rate for the corporation is 40%. No dividends were declared during the year.

On March 15, 2002, the board of directors declared a cash dividend of 50 cents per share, payable on April 15.

## Instructions

**a.** Prepare the journal entries for 2001 to (1) record the issuance of the common stock, (2) record the income tax liability at December 31, and (3) close the Income Taxes Expense account.

**b.** Prepare the journal entries in 2002 for the declaration of the dividend on March 15 and payment of the dividend on April 15.

**c.** Operations in 2002 resulted in an $18,000 *net loss*. Prepare the journal entries to close the Income Summary and Dividends accounts at December 31, 2002.

**d.** Prepare the stockholders' equity section of the balance sheet at December 31, 2002. Include a separate supporting schedule showing your determination of retained earnings at that date.

**PROBLEM C.7**
Stockholders' Equity Section

**LO 6, 7**

The two cases described below are independent of each other. Each case provides the information necessary to prepare the stockholders' equity section of a corporate balance sheet.

**a.** Early in 2000, Neal Corporation was formed with the issuance of 50,000 shares of capital stock at $5 per share. The corporation reported a net loss of $32,000 for 2000, and a net loss of $12,000 in 2001. In 2002 the corporation reported net income of $90,000, and declared a dividend of 50 cents per share.

**b.** Willshire Industries was organized early in 1998 with the issuance of 100,000 shares of capital stock at $10 per share. During the first five years of its existence, the corporation earned a total of $800,000 and paid dividends of 25 cents per share each year on the common stock.

**Instructions**

Prepare the stockholders' equity section of the corporate balance sheet for each company for the year ending December 31, 2002.

**PROBLEM C.8**
Comparison of Proprietorship with Corporation

**LO 1, 2, 4, 5, 6, 7, 8**

California Eyeshades is a retail store owned solely by Paul Turner. During the month of November, the equity accounts were affected by the following events:

**Nov. 9**      Turner invested an additional $15,000 in the business.

**Nov. 15**      Turner withdrew $1,500 for his salary for the first two weeks of the month.

**Nov. 30**      Turner withdrew $1,500 for his salary for the second two weeks of the month.

**Nov. 30**      California Eyeshades distributed $1,000 of earnings to Turner.

**Instructions**

**a.** Assuming that the business is organized as a sole proprietorship:

     **1.** Prepare the journal entries to record the above events in the accounts of California Eyeshades.

     **2.** Prepare the closing entries for the month of November. Assume that after closing all of the revenue and expense accounts, the Income Summary account has a balance of $5,000.

**b.** Assuming that the business is organized as a corporation:

     **1.** Prepare the journal entries to record the above events in the accounts of California Eyeshades. Assume that the distribution of earnings on November 30 was payment of a dividend that was declared on November 20.

     **2.** Prepare the closing entries for the month of November. Assume that after closing all of the revenue and expense accounts (except Income Taxes Expense) the Income Summary account has a balance of $2,000. Before preparing the closing entries, prepare the entries to accrue income taxes expense for the month and to close the Income Taxes Expense account to the Income Summary account. Assume that the corporate income tax rate is *30%*.

**c.** Explain the causes of the differences in net income between California Eyeshades as a sole proprietorship and California Eyeshades as a corporation.

**d.** Describe the effects of the business operations on Turner's individual income tax return, assuming that the business is organized as (1) a sole proprietorship and (2) a corporation.

**\*PROBLEM C.9**
Formation of a Partnership

**LO 10**

The partnership of Avery and Kirk was formed on July 1, when George Avery and Dinah Kirk agreed to invest equal amounts and to share profits and losses equally. The investment by Avery consists of $30,000 cash and an inventory of merchandise valued at $56,000.

     Kirk also is to contribute a total of $86,000. However, it is agreed that her contribution will consist of the following assets of her business along with the transfer to the partnership of her business liabilities. The agreed values of the various items as well as their carrying values on Kirk's records are listed below. Kirk also contributes enough cash to bring her capital account to $86,000.

---

*Supplemental Topic*, "Partnership Accounting—A Closer Look."

| | Investment by Kirk | |
|---|---|---|
| | **Balances on Kirk's Records** | **Agreed Value** |
| Accounts Receivable ................................. | $81,680 | $79,600 |
| Inventory ............................................ | 11,400 | 12,800 |
| Office Equipment (net) .............................. | 14,300 | 9,000 |
| Accounts Payable .................................... | 24,800 | 24,800 |

## Instructions

**a.** Draft entries (in general journal form) to record the investments of Avery and Kirk in the new partnership.

**b.** Prepare the beginning balance sheet of the partnership (in report form) at the close of business July 1, reflecting the above transfers to the firm.

**c.** On the following June 30 after one year of operation, the Income Summary account showed a credit balance of $74,000, and the Drawing account for each partner showed a debit balance of $31,000. Prepare journal entries to close the Income Summary account and the drawing accounts at June 30.

A small nightclub called Comedy Tonight was organized as a partnership with Lewis investing $80,000 and Martin investing $120,000. During the first year, net income amounted to $110,000.

**\*PROBLEM C.10**
Sharing Partnership Net Income: Various Methods

**LO 10**

## Instructions

**a.** Determine how the $110,000 net income would be divided under each of the following three independent assumptions as to the agreement for sharing profits and losses. Use schedules of the type illustrated in this chapter to show all steps in the division of net income between the partners.

**1.** Net income is to be divided in a fixed ratio: 40% to Lewis and 60% to Martin.

**2.** Interest at 15% to be allowed on beginning capital investments and balance to be divided equally.

**3.** Salaries of $36,000 to Lewis and $56,000 to Martin; interest at 15% to be allowed on beginning capital investments; balance to be divided equally.

**b.** Prepare the journal entry to close the Income Summary account, using the division of net income developed in part **a(3)**.

Research Consultants has three partners—Axle, Brandt, and Conrad. During the current year their capital balances were: Axle, $180,000; Brandt, $140,000; and Conrad, $80,000. The partnership agreement provides that partners shall receive salary allowances as follows: Axle, $10,000; Brandt, $50,000; Conrad, $28,000. The partners shall also be allowed 12% interest annually on their capital balances. Residual profit or loss is to be divided: Axle, one-half; Brandt, one-third; Conrad, one-sixth.

**\*PROBLEM C.11**
Dividing Partnership Profit and Loss

**LO 10**

## Instructions

Prepare separate schedules showing how income will be divided among the three partners in each of the following cases. The figure given in each case is the annual partnership net income or loss to be allocated among the partners.

**a.** Income of $526,000

**b.** Income of $67,000

**c.** Loss of $32,000

---

*\*Supplemental Topic*, "Partnership Accounting—A Closer Look."

**PROBLEM C.12**
Who Gets the Prime Cut?
Tax Planning and Pitfalls

**LO 1, 4, 5, 9**

Alan Weber originally started Prime Cuts, a small butcher shop, as a sole proprietorship. Then he began advertising in gift catalogs, and his company quickly grew into a large mail-order business. Now Prime Cuts sends meat and seafood all over the world by overnight mail.

At the beginning of the current year, Weber reorganized Prime Cuts as a corporation—with himself as the sole stockholder. This year, the company earned $1 million before income taxes. (For the current year, the corporate income tax rate is *40%*. Weber's *personal* income is taxed at the rate of *45%*.)

With respect to salaries and withdrawals of assets, Weber continued the same policies as when the business had been a sole proprietorship. Although he personally runs the business, he draws no salary. He explains, "Why should I draw a salary? Nowadays, I have plenty of income from other sources. Besides, a salary would just reduce the company's profits—which belong to me."

In recent years, Weber had made monthly transfers from the business bank account to his personal bank account of an amount equal to the company's monthly net income. After Prime Cuts became a corporation, he continued making these transfers by declaring monthly dividends.

### Instructions
**a.** Without regard to income taxes, identify several reasons why it might be *advantageous* for Weber to have incorporated this business.

**b.** Compute the portion of the company's $1 million pretax income that Weber would have retained after income taxes if Prime Cuts *had remained a sole proprietorship*.

**c.** Compute the portion of this $1 million in before-tax income Weber will retain after income taxes, given that Prime Cuts *is now a corporation*.

**d.** Explain the meaning of the term *double taxation*.

**e.** Discuss several ways that Weber legally might have reduced the overall "tax bite" on his company's before-tax earnings.

**PROBLEM C.13**
Developing an Equitable
Plan for Dividing
Partnership Income

**LO 10**

Juan Ramirez and Robert Cole are considering forming a partnership to engage in the business of aerial photography. Ramirez is a licensed pilot, is currently earning $48,000 a year, and has $50,000 to invest in the partnership. Cole is a professional photographer who is currently earning $30,000 a year. He has recently inherited $70,000, which he plans to invest in the partnership.

Both partners will work full-time in the business. After careful study, they have estimated that expenses are likely to exceed revenue by $10,000 during the first year of operations. In the second year, however, they expect the business to become profitable, with revenue exceeding expenses by an estimated $90,000. (Bear in mind that these estimates of expenses do not include any salaries or interest to the partners.) Under present market conditions, a fair rate of return on capital invested in this type of business is 20%.

### Instructions
**a.** On the basis of this information, prepare a brief description of the income-sharing agreement that you would recommend for Ramirez and Cole. Explain the basis for your proposal.

**b.** Prepare a separate schedule for each of the next two years showing how the estimated amounts of net income would be divided between the two partners under your plan. (Assume that the original capital balances for both partners remain unchanged during the two-year period. This simplifying assumption allows you to ignore the changes that would normally occur in capital accounts as a result of divisions of profits, or from drawings or additional investments.)

**c.** Write a brief statement explaining the differences in allocation of income to the two partners and defending the results indicated by your income-sharing proposal.

## ▌ OUR COMMENTS ON THE "YOUR TURN" CASES

**As a Banker (p. 1092)**   There are several reasons why the tax returns of a sole proprietorship do not represent adequately the solvency of the business. First, solvency is best evaluated using information from both a balance sheet and an income statement. The personal income tax returns filed by a sole proprietor reveal income information only. Second, measures of solvency are most reliable when financial reports are prepared in accordance with generally accepted accounting principles (GAAP). Tax returns are based on income tax rules, not GAAP. Finally, the owner of a sole proprietorship can transfer assets in and out of the business at will. Therefore, the ability of a sole proprietorship to pay its debts depends on the solvency of the owner, which is not necessarily reflected in the information reported in the owner's tax return.

**As an Investor (p. 1104)**   One of the reasons that Microsoft has never paid a cash dividend is that Bill Gates, the company's founder, chief executive, and chairman, is also the company's largest stockholder. Gates is not personally in need of cash. So why should Microsoft distribute resources when much of these distributions would be consumed by income taxes (remember, dividend income received by stockholders is taxable)? Wouldn't a better strategy be to retain these resources in the business to finance growth? That's exactly what Gates has done—and it works. Microsoft is among the world's fastest-growing corporations and, as a direct result, Gates is among the world's wealthiest individuals.

# SUBJECT INDEX

## ORGANIZATION/NAME/ TRADEMARK INDEX